Sustainable Water Management—Volume I

Sustainable Water Management—Volume I

Miklas Scholz

MDPI

Basel • Beijing • Wuhan • Barcelona • Belgrade • Novi Sad • Cluj • Manchester

Author
Miklas Scholz
Innovation Management
aconium GmbH
Berlin, Germany

Editorial Office
MDPI
St. Alban-Anlage 66
4052 Basel, Switzerland

This is a reprint of articles published online by the open access publisher MDPI (available at: http://www.mdpi.com). The responsibility for the reprint's title and preface lies with Miklas Scholz, who compiled this reprint.

For citation purposes, cite each article independently as indicated on the article page online and as indicated below:

Lastname, A.A.; Lastname, B.B. Article Title. *Journal Name* **Year**, *Volume Number*, Page Range.

Volume I
ISBN 978-3-03928-609-6 (Hbk)
ISBN 978-3-03928-610-2 (PDF)
doi.org/10.3390/books978-3-03928-610-2

Set
ISBN 978-3-03928-607-2 (Hbk)
ISBN 978-3-03928-608-9 (PDF)

Cover image courtesy of Miklas Scholz

Dedication

I dedicate this book to my extended family and friends, who supported me during my studies and career.

Particular thanks go to my partner Ramilya Galimova; children Philippa Scholz, Jolena Scholz, Felix Hedmark and Jamie Hedmark; twin sister Ricarda Lorey; and mother Gudrun Spieshöfer.

Contents

About the Author

Miklas Scholz

Miklas Scholz (Figure 1), cand. ing., BEng (equiv), PgC, MSc, PhD, DSc, CWEM, CEnv, CSci, CEng, FHEA, FIEMA, FCIWEM, FICE, Fellow of IWA, Fellow of IETI works as a Senior Expert in Water Management for aconium GmbH (previously atene KOM) in Germany, a Wastewater and Microbial Technical Specialist for Nexus by Sweden and a Hydraulic Engineer at Kunststoff-Technik Adams, Germany. Miklas holds the Chair in Civil Engineering as a Professor at The University of Salford, UK. Moreover, he is a Distinguished Professor at Johannesburg University, South Africa, and a Senior Researcher at South Ural State University, The Russian Federation.

Miklas has shown individual excellence, evidenced by world-leading publications, postgraduate supervision and research impact. His main research areas in terms of publication output are the treatment of wetlands, integrated constructed wetlands (ICW), sustainable flood retention basins (SFRB), permeable pavement systems, decision support systems, ponds and capillary suction time. These research areas are evaluated from a multi-disciplinary perspective (Figure 2).

Figure 1: Miklas Scholz.

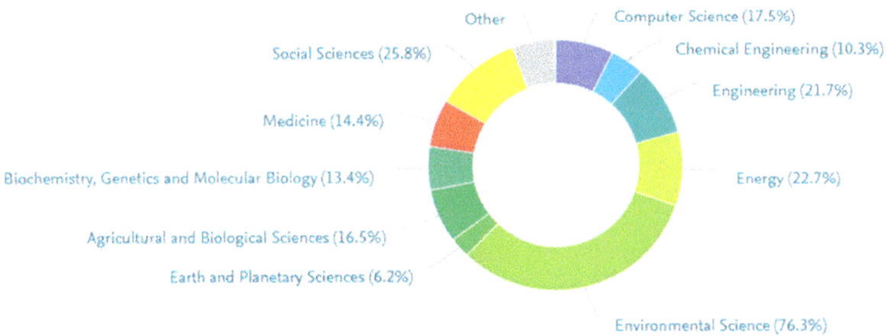

Figure 2: Areas in which Miklas Scholz published up to 2023 according to the research performance assessment solution SciVal.

Prof. Scholz has published 8 books as well as 316 journal articles in 126 different journals. Since 2009, he has been in the top publication ranking of The University of Salford, considering the articles published by all the members of his group. His annual number of publications from 2009 to 2021 are 2009 (13), 2010 (19), 2011 (13), 2012 (21), 2013 (17), 2014 (15), 2015 (17), 2016 (13), 2017 (14), 2018 (14), 2019 (17), 2020 (8), 2021 (38), 2022 (23) and 2023 (9).

Miklas publishes in the following high-impact-factor (≥10) journals: *Water Research; Sustainable Production and Consumption; Sustainable Cities and Society; Global Change Biology; Bioresource Technology; Journal of Retailing and Consumer Services; Desalination and Science of the Total Environment*. His work has attracted a total of 14,288 citations (8424 citations since 2019), resulting in an h-index of 57 and an i10-index of 331. He belongs to the top 2% of academics regarding the highest i10-index in the past 5 years. Prof. Scholz was/is an editor, subeditor and editorial board member (without double counting) of 38, 10 and 111 journals, respectively.

In 2019, Prof. Miklas Scholz was awarded EUR 7 million for the EU Horizon 2020 European Research Executive Agency project "Water Retention and Nutrient Recycling in Soils and Streams for Improved Agricultural Production". Miklas also received EUR 1.52 million for the Joint Programming Initiative Water 2018 project "Research-Based Assessment of Integrated Approaches to Nature-Based Solutions". Prof. Scholz's SFRB concept assesses the multifunctionality of large water bodies with an emphasis on flood- and diffuse pollution-control potential. A novel and unbiased classification system allows all stakeholders to clearly define the purpose of a water body that can be classed as an SFRB. Communication among stakeholders regarding the most appropriate management of an SFRB is greatly enhanced. Moreover, the SFRB concept addresses the need to assess the flood control potential of all European water bodies as part of new legislation.

Miklas Scholz's research activities have contributed to national and international guidelines on wetlands and sustainable drainage systems. His greatest impact on wetland guidelines was performed around ICW in Ireland, Northern Ireland, Scotland and England, where he contributed to the design of guidelines for wetland systems as a research consultant. These guidelines are meant to assist managers regarding all aspects of ICW planning, design, construction, maintenance and management. Moreover, some ICW guidelines were specifically written to aid farmers from Scotland, Northern Ireland and Ireland in facing farmyard runoffs. These guidelines are specifically mentioned in the national legislation.

Additionally, Prof. Scholz's work on guidelines has favored the international acceptance of both SFRB and ICW concepts, as well as the researched hybrid sustainable drainage system. For instance, his work has particularly benefited the British Isles as well as Central and Northern Europe. ICW are currently being constructed in Belgium, Germany, the United States and China.

As the world population rises and faces increasing water scarcity challenges, traditional solutions are no longer an option for addressing water demand. This simple rationale led Scholz to consider the use of non-conventional water resources to match the growing demand for clean, fresh water. For instance, wastewater is often seen as an appropriate alternative for overcoming potential future shortages in water supply. However, increases in environmental and public health problems are expected in the future due to insufficient sanitation and wastewater disposal facilities. For that reason, wastewater treatment and recycling methods have been identified by Scholz and his research groups as fundamental for providing sufficient freshwater in the coming decades. Indeed, water resources are limited mostly because more than 70% of water is consumed for irrigation purposes while wastewater is freely available.

In that sense, Prof. Scholz has identified treated wastewater as a high-potential application for agricultural irrigation, especially if the water treatment methodology is combined with the reuse of nutrients such as nitrogen and phosphorous, which are essential for plant growth. The use of wetlands was selected as one of the most suitable technologies in terms of pollutant removal among the current treatments applied for urban wastewater reuse for irrigation. Their low maintenance costs and energy consumption are among the most attractive advantages. Different research activities carried out in the field have shown that some specific wastewater characteristics determine the wetland design for optimal treatment. The wetland behavior and efficiency concerning wastewater treatment are mainly linked to the macrophyte composition, substrate, hydrology, surface loading rate, influent feeding mode, microorganism availability and temperature.

Prof. Scholz's research showed that constructed wetlands are very effective in removing organics and suspended solids but frequently fail in the sufficient removal of nitrogen, which is relatively low, unless special media with high sorption capacities are used. However, Miklas has shown that nitrogen removal can be improved by using a combination of different types of constructed wetlands.

Foreword

This new textbook has a broad focus and is, therefore, titled "Sustainable Water Management" to attract a wide audience of academics and practitioners. The book covers broad water and environmental engineering aspects relevant to water resources management as well as the treatment of stormwater and wastewater, providing a descriptive overview of complex "black box" systems and the general design issues involved. Fundamental science and engineering principles are explained to address the student and professional markets. Standard and novel design recommendations account for the interests of professional engineers and environmental scientists. The latest research findings in wastewater treatment are discussed to attract academics and senior consultants who could recommend the textbook to final-year and postgraduate students as well as graduate engineers, respectively.

The book deals comprehensively with the design, operation, maintenance as well as water quality monitoring and modeling of traditional and novel wetland systems. It also provides an analysis of asset performance, the modeling of treatment processes and the performance of existing infrastructure in both developed and developing countries, as well as the sustainability and economic issues involved.

The textbook is essential for undergraduate and postgraduate students, lecturers and researchers in the civil and environmental engineering, environmental science, agriculture and ecological fields of sustainable water management. It is a standard reference for the design, operation and management of wetlands by engineers and scientists working for the water industry, local authorities, non-governmental organizations and governmental bodies. Moreover, consulting engineers will be able to apply practical design recommendations and refer to a large variety of practical international case studies, including large-scale field studies.

The explained underlying scientific principles will also be of interest to all concerned with the built environment, including town planners, developers, engineering technicians, agricultural engineers and public health workers. The book has been written for a wide readership, but sufficient hot research topics have been addressed to guarantee a long shelf life of the book. Therefore, case study topics are diverse, and research projects are multidisciplinary, holistic, experimental and modeling-oriented.

The book is predominantly based on experiences gained by the author over the past 12 years. Original material published in 11 MDPI journals has been reprinted. The 40 articles have been grouped in the following sections to improve the readability of the book:

Section 1: Climate Change, Water Resources and Public Health;

Section 2: Agricultural Water Management;

Section 3: Sustainable Flood Retention Basins and Drainage Systems;

Section 4: Water Quality and Technologies;

Section 5: Activated Carbon, Pyrolysis and Graphene; and

Section 6: Water System Modelling.

Each section starts with a summary linking the corresponding articles together. Section 1, comprised of the first five articles, is concerned with the interface between climate change, water resources and public health. Article 1 links surface runoff characteristics to climate change consequences such as draughts. The water-related impacts of climate change on agriculture and, subsequently, on public health are assessed in Article 2. Moreover, this section deals with the climatic impacts on various methods to control mosquito vectors, causing health challenges to humans. Article 4 links climate change to water quality, various water-related challenges and sustainability strategies. Finally, the effects of special weather phenomena on precipitation extremes are evaluated (Article 5).

Agricultural water management is covered in Section 2, comprised of Articles 6 to 17. Article 6 introduces novel water retention and nutrient management technologies and strategies supporting agricultural water management in continental, Pannonian and boreal regions of Europe. Furthermore, experiments with recycled diesel spill-contaminated domestic wastewater treated by reed beds for the irrigation of sweet peppers are evaluated (Article 7). Linked to this contribution are Article 8 on the contamination of soil and two *Capsicum annuum* generations irrigated by reused urban wastewater treated by different reed beds and Article 9 on the assessment of *C. annuum* grown in controlled and semi-controlled environments and irrigated with greywater treated by floating wetland systems. Furthermore, this topic is supported by Article 10, reporting on the response of vegetables to catmium-enriched soil, and Article 11, on the toxicity and bioaccumulation of heavy metals in spinach (*Spinacia oleracea*) grown in a controlled environment.

Another set of articles of Section 2 deals with the water–energy–food nexus: (a) the nexus accessibility and tracking progress towards achieving the sustainable development goals (Article 12); (b) the interplay of the water–energy security and food consumption patterns towards achieving nutrition security (Article 13); and (c) gender and other vulnerabilities to waterenergy accessibility in rural households (Article 14). Furthermore, Article 15 is concerned with mitigating chilling stress by ozone pretreatment and acclimation of sweet pepper grown under unheated plastic greenhouse conditions. Article 16 reports on modifying walkin tunnels through solar energy, fogging and evaporative cooling to mitigate heat stress on tomatoes. Finally, this section is concerned with delineating the cropland dynamics due to extreme environments using Landsat datasets (Article 17).

Sustainable flood retention basins and other drainage systems are analyzed and assessed in the third section (Articles 18 to 23). Article 18 reports on novel methods to assess the risk of dam failure, and Article 19 deals with computing air demand using the Takagi–Sugeno Model for dam outlets. Furthermore, the prediction of multiple functions of sustainable flood retention basins under uncertainty via multi-instance, multi-label learning is covered in Article 20. A strategic framework for the sustainable management of drainage systems has also been proposed (Article 21). Article 22 is more concerned with selecting sustainable drainage structures based on ecosystem service variables estimated by different stakeholder groups. Finally, Article 23 critically reviews the water quality improvement performances of geotextiles within permeable paving systems.

Section 4 deals with water quality challenges and treatment technologies covered by Articles 24 to 30. Article 24 reports on the response of eutrophication to nutrients and hydrological regimes. Article 25 evaluates and predicts groundwater quality for irrigation using integrated water-quality indices, data-driven models and various geographical information system approaches. Furthermore, firewater storage, treatment, recycling and management are covered in Article 26, and Article 27 deals with the assessment of the effluents of a large water treatment plant used for drinking and irrigation water production purposes. This section also introduced, in Article 28, a sustainability ranking method for desalination plants using the Mamdani Fuzzy Logic Inference Systems. Article 29 provides a comprehensive review of the occurrence and removal of non-steroidal anti-inflammatory drugs attained from wastewater observations using electrochemical processes. Section 4 concludes with Article 30, delivering a framework for sustainable planning in and decision-making on resource recovery from wastewater.

The book also deals with activated carbon, pyrolysis and graphene practices in Section 5, covering only three articles. Article 31 addresses the question of how activated carbon can help practitioners. Article 32 highlights opportunities and challenges of high-pressure fast pyrolysis of biomass. In the end, Article 33 covers frictional pressure drop and cost savings for graphene nanoplatelets nanofluids in turbulent flow environments.

Finally, Section 6 covers topical water system-modeling challenges in the remaining six Articles, 34 to 40. Article 34 deals with surface water resources assessment and planning with the mathematical water quality QUAL2KW model. Article 35 reports on a comprehensive assessment of soft computing models in hydrology. Furthermore, the last section is concerned with the quality control and homogeneity analysis of precipitation time series (Article 36). Article 37 deals with climate and geoscience time series parameter forecasting, and Article 38 reports on the assessment of urban green space dynamics influencing surface urban heat stress using advanced geospatial techniques. The final two articles of this book deal with water pipe leakage control, more specifically, optimal pressure management in water distribution systems (Article 39), as well as the appraisal of socio-technical water loss control strategies using cost–benefit analysis (Article 40).

Miklas Scholz
Author

Acknowledgments

I thank all current and previous members of my research groups at The University of Salford, Lund University, University of Johannesburg, South Ural State University and The University of Edinburgh for their research input, as well as all institutions that provided funding for my research. The research work from all co-authors in the reprinted MDPI journal articles is also thankfully acknowledged.

Section 1: Climate Change, Water Resources and Public Health

Section 1, comprised of the first five articles, is concerned with the interface between climate change, water resources and public health. Article 1 links various surface runoff characteristics to climate change consequences such as draughts. A proposed methodology offers a simple, powerful and generic approach for predicting the rate of change in annual runoff under various climate change scenarios. Water-related impacts of climate change on agriculture and, subsequently, on public health are assessed in Article 2. Novel solutions and bioremediation methods have been presented to control environmental pollution and to promote awareness among the scientific community. Moreover, this section deals with climatic impacts on various methods to control mosquito vectors causing serious health challenges to humans (Article 3). The impact of climatic conditions on mosquito-borne diseases, along with conventional and nanotechnology-based approaches used for controlling malaria and dengue fever, have been discussed. Article 4 links climate change to water quality, various water-related challenges and sustainability strategies. Climate change patterns and risks associated with water-related diseases and novel methods for controlling both waterborne and water-related diseases are discussed. Finally, the effects of special weather phenomena on precipitation extremes are evaluated, and policy recommendations for climate change impacts have been made (Article 5).

Keywords: precipitation; public health engineering; reconnaissance drought index; streamflow drought index; surface runoff; sustainability; trend analysis; urbanization; water- and vector-borne disease; water quality

Water **2014**, *6*, 3033-3048; doi:10.3390/w6103033

OPEN ACCESS

water

ISSN 2073-4441

www.mdpi.com/journal/water

Article

Sensitivity of Surface Runoff to Drought and Climate Change: Application for Shared River Basins

Furat A. M. Al-Faraj [1], Miklas Scholz [1,*] and Dimitris Tigkas [2]

[1] School of Computing, Science and Engineering, The University of Salford, Salford, Greater Manchester M5 4WT, UK; E-Mail: F.A.M.Al-Faraj@edu.salford.ac.uk

[2] Laboratory of Reclamation Works and Water Resources Management, School of Rural and Surveying Engineering, National Technical University of Athens, Iroon Polytechniou 9, Athens 15780, Greece; E-Mail: ditigas@mail.ntua.gr

* Author to whom correspondence should be addressed; E-Mail: m.scholz@salford.ac.uk; Tel.: +44-161-295-5921; Fax: +44-161-295-5575.

External Editor: Athanasios Loukas

Received: 5 August 2014; in revised form: 8 September 2014 / Accepted: 30 September 2014 / Published: 13 October 2014

Abstract: This study quantifies the sensitivity of surface runoff to drought and climate change in the Diyala watershed shared between Iraq and Iran. This was achieved through a combined use of a wide range of changes in the amount of precipitation (a decline between 0% and −40%) and in the potential evapotranspiration rate (an increase between 0% and +30%). The Medbasin-monthly rainfall-runoff model (Medbasin-M) was used for runoff simulation. The model was calibrated for twelve hydrologic years (1962−1973), and the simulation results were validated with the observed annual runoff for nine water years (1974−1982). For the calibration period, the correlation coefficient (r), the root mean squared error (RMSE), the mean absolute error (MAE) and the index of agreement (IoA) were 0.893, 2.117, 1.733 and 0.852, respectively. The corresponding values for validation were 0.762, 1.250, 1.093 and 0.863, in this order. The Reconnaissance Drought Index (*RDI*) and the Streamflow Drought Index (*SDI*) were analysed using DrinC software. Three nomographs were introduced to quantify the projected reductions in the annual runoff and the anticipated *RDI* and *SDI* values, respectively. The proposed methodology offers a simple, powerful and generic approach for predicting the rate of change (%) in annual runoff under climate change scenarios.

Keywords: climate alteration; transboundary watershed; river flow; Medbasin model; reconnaissance drought index; streamflow drought index; nomograph; water management; soil storage capacity; runoff curve number

1. Introduction

The sustainable management of water resources in transboundary river basins has become a continuous challenge for riparian states. The differences in policies, development perspectives and priorities make it difficult to achieve a common understanding of the rational use of water. One major point of interest for all shared watercourses is the available volume of runoff, which is an important and crucial factor to meet the water demands of many sectors, such as agriculture, public water supply and fish farms. Drought and climate change are likely to put considerable pressure on water resources management and augment the level of vulnerability, particularly of the downstream countries in transboundary river basins. Climate alteration is anticipated to escalate the recurrence, strength and duration of drought episodes in some regions.

The Intergovernmental Panel on Climate Change (IPCC) reported that the Global Circulation Models have produced a range of likely climate change scenarios according to various simulations [1]. Among others, two main predictions are relevant to droughts: increase in temperature and decrease in precipitation amount in some regions. Drought is a natural phenomenon that can be characterized by three dimensions (variables): severity, duration and spatial extent. Conventionally, droughts are categorized as meteorological, hydrological, agricultural and socio-economic phenomena. Numerous drought indices have been introduced in the literature [2–18]. Among the commonly used indices are the Rainfall Anomaly Index (RAI), Percentage of Normal Precipitation (PNPI), Percent of Normal Index (PNI), Deciles Index (DI), Standardized Precipitation Index (SPI), Standardized Precipitation Evapotranspiration Index (SPEI), Palmer Drought Severity Index (PDSI), Reconnaissance Drought Index (*RDI*), Crop Moisture Index (CMI), Surface Water Supply Index (SWSI), Streamflow Drought Index (*SDI*) and Truncation Threshold Level (TTL; also called Drought Threshold Level (DTL)).

The topic of drought severity has occupied a notable proportion of drought studies, which have been conducted in many countries, such as Iran [4,5], Iraq [6,7], Greece [8,9], Turkey [10], Jordan [11] and Saudi Arabia [12]. Recent articles have pointed out the promising usage of the *RDI* to quantify the severity of drought [4,13–15]. Precipitation (*P*) and potential evapotranspiration (*PET*; directly related to air temperature) are the two key parameters used in *RDI*. In this paper, the severity of drought was judged by means of *RDI*, and the hydrological drought (denoted in this paper as a decline in runoff volume) was characterized by using *SDI* [16–18].

The assessment of the impacts of droughts and of the anticipated climate change on runoff volume is important for providing a common ground for communication between the riparian countries. This study quantifies the impact of possible climate alterations and droughts anticipated in the downstream country Iraq. This was achieved through a mutual usage of a wide array of potential future climate shifts in *P* and *PET* and the Medbasin-M rainfall-runoff model.

The overall aim of the article is to quantify the impact of the anticipated drought and climate change on streamflow available for the lower riparian country, Iraq. The main objectives of this paper are to:

(1) predict the likely proportional change (%) in the annual runoff available for the downstream country; and
(2) anticipate the standardized Reconnaissance Drought Index (RDI_{st}) and *SDI* values due to a wide range of possible future climate change.

This study offers a generic, simple and solid tool to support water managers and decision-makers in shaping better management plans and strategies for water resources that are anticipated to be available in the short to long term.

2. Materials and Methods

2.1. Meteorological Drought Severity (MDS)

Drought severity was assessed through the computation of the *RDI*, more precisely through its standardised form. The initial value (α_k) of *RDI* is calculated for the *i*-th year for a reference period of *k* months according to Equation (1):

$$\alpha_k^{(i)} = \frac{\sum_{j=1}^{k} P_{ij}}{\sum_{j=1}^{k} PET_{ij}}, \quad i = 1(1)N \text{ and } j = 1(1)k \tag{1}$$

where P_{ij} and PET_{ij} are precipitation and potential evapotranspiration of the *j*-th month of the *i*-th year and *N* is the total number of years of the available data. The values of α_k follow satisfactorily both the lognormal and the gamma distributions in a wide range of locations and different reference periods for which they were tested [8,19]. By assuming that the lognormal distribution is applied, Equation (2) can be used for the calculation of the RDI_{st}:

$$RDI_{st}^{(i)} = \frac{y^{(i)} - \bar{y}}{\hat{\sigma}_y} \tag{2}$$

where $y^{(i)}$ is $\ln(\alpha_k^{(i)})$; $\bar{y}$ is its arithmetic mean; and $\hat{\sigma}_y$ is its standard deviation (*SD*). In the case that the gamma distribution is applied, RDI_{st} can be calculated by fitting the gamma probability density function (pdf) to the given frequency distribution of α_k [8,19]. For short reference periods (e.g., monthly or 3-months), which may include zero values for the cumulative precipitation, RDI_{st} can be calculated based on a composite cumulative distribution function, including the probability of zero precipitation, and the gamma cumulative probability. Positive values of RDI_{st} indicate wet periods, while negative values indicate dry periods compared with the normal conditions of the area. The severity of drought events increases when RDI_{st} values are highly negative.

2.2. Streamflow Drought Index

According to [16], if a time series of monthly streamflow volumes Q_{ij} is available, in which *i* denotes the hydrological year and *j* the month within that hydrological year (*j* = 1 for October and *j* = 12 for September), $V_{i,k}$ can be obtained based on Equation (3):

$$V_{i,k} = \sum_{j=1}^{3k} Q_{ij} \quad (3)$$

where $i = 1,2,\ldots,N$, $j = 1,2,\ldots,12$ and $k = 1,2,3,4$. $V_{i,k}$ is the cumulative streamflow volume for the *i*-th hydrological year and the *k*-th reference period, *k* = 1 for October–December, *k* = 2 for October–March, *k* = 3 for October–June and *k* = 4 for October–September. Based on the cumulative streamflow volumes $V_{i,k}$, the Streamflow Drought Index (*SDI*) is defined for each reference period *k* of the *i*-th hydrological year (Equation (4)):

$$SDI_{i,k} = \frac{V_{i,k} - \bar{V}_k}{S_k} \quad (4)$$

where $i = 1,2,\ldots,N$ and $k = 1,2,3,4$. $\bar{V}_k$ and S_k are the mean and *SD*, respectively, of the cumulative streamflow volumes of the reference period *k*, as these are estimated over a long period of time. In this definition, the truncation level is set to $\bar{V}_k$, although other values based on rational criteria could be also used.

Streamflow may follow a skewed probability distribution, which can be approximated well by the family of the gamma distribution functions. The distribution is then transformed to be normal. Using the two-parameter log-normal distribution (for which the normalization is simply reclaiming the natural logarithms of streamflow), the *SDI* index is defined in Equations (5) and (6) are the natural logarithms of cumulative streamflow with mean $\bar{y}_k$ and *SD* $S_{y,k}$, as these statistics are estimated over a long period of time.

$$SDI_{i,k} = \frac{y_{i,k} - \bar{y}_k}{S_{y,k}} \quad (5)$$

where $i = 1,2,\ldots,N$ and $k = 1,2,3,4$ and:

$$y_{i,k} = \ln(V_{i,k}),\ i = 1,2,\ldots,N \text{ and } k = 1,2,3,4 \quad (6)$$

The annual *SDI* index was computed over the period of 30 years between 1962 and 1991. Quantities and descriptive situations of the *SDI* and the RDI_{st} indices, which are provided in the literature [4,17,20–22], were considered in this paper to provide a better representation of drought in spatial distribution mapping (Table 1).

In this study, the calculations were performed using DrinC software [23,24]. DrinC has been recently used in several studies for drought assessment and monitoring [19], predominantly in arid to semi-arid areas, such as Iraq and Iran [25,26]. In this study, the annual RDI_{st} and *SDI* indices were computed over the period of the normal climatic period from 1975 to 1982. The precipitation and runoff data were fitted to the log-normal distribution function in the computation process. The estimation of potential evapotranspiration used in the calculation of *RDI* was obtained through DrinC by using the Blaney–Criddle method [27]. Finally, the RDI_{st} and *SDI* nomographs were developed, which describe the 'departure' from the normal condition based on the "0 scenario". The reference mean annual runoff volume indicating the condition of zero change in both P and PET is referred to as the "0 scenario".

Table 1. Classification of drought conditions based on the standardized Reconnaissance Drought Index (RDI_{st}) and Streamflow Drought Index (SDI) values.

Condition	Range
Extremely wet	(SDI and RDI_{st}) ≥ 2.00
Very wet	$1.5 \leq$ (SDI and RDI_{st}) < 2.00
Moderately wet	$1.00 \leq$ (SDI and RDI_{st}) < 1.50
Near normal	$-1.00 <$ (SDI and RDI_{st}) < 1.00
Moderately dry	$-1.50 <$ (SDI and RDI_{st}) ≤ -1.00
Severely dry	$-2.00 <$ (SDI and RDI_{st}) ≤ -1.50
Extremely dry	(SDI and RDI_{st}) ≤ 2.00

2.3. Rainfall-Runoff Model

The simulation of the river runoff is typically performed through rainfall-runoff models implementing different approaches and various levels of complexity. In this study, the monthly rainfall-runoff model (Medbasin-M) [28,29] was used to simulate the runoff reaction under various climatic conditions on an annual basis. The model uses three calibration parameters. These are the maximum soil storage capacity (S_{max}), the coefficient of the deep percolation (C) and the monthly delay factor (a), which is used to adjust the monthly runoff distribution [30]. The required input data for the model are monthly precipitation and PET data.

A detailed soil and land survey provides the most reliable data, which can be used for estimating the soil storage capacity (S) and obtaining the runoff curve number (CN) as part of the model requirements. However, essential data are not always available and not simply accessible. For this study, the S_{max} was estimated using Equation (7), which has been developed by the Natural Resources Conservation Service (NRCS, formerly known as the Soil Conservation Service), which relates S_{max} to CN [31,32].

$$S_{\max} = 25.4\left(\frac{1{,}000}{CN} - 10\right) \quad (7)$$

The runoff curve number is an empirical parameter, which is mainly a function of the hydrologic soil group, cover type, treatment, hydrologic condition and antecedent runoff condition. References, such as [33], provide detailed guidelines to aid in selecting the appropriate CN values considering the basin characteristics. The CN is an alternative way to estimate the model's parameter S_{max}. However, in this study, there is not sufficient and reliable information, such as land use and soil types, for an accurate calculation of the CN. Therefore, S_{max} was calculated through a model calibration process.

Initial values of CN and C were first assumed. A two-stage process was conducted for the calibration of the model parameters. The first stage involved matching the volumes of observed and simulated hydrographs on an annual basis. In the second stage, the shape of the simulated hydrograph was compared with the shape of the observed hydrograph. A trial and error approach was utilized until the best fit was achieved. The goodness-of-fit indicators, r, RMSE, MAE and index of agreement (IoA), were used for assessing the model performance.

2.4. Methodological Approach

The following steps describe the methodology followed in this paper:

1. The Medbasin-M rainfall-runoff model was calibrated using the monthly *P* and *PET* data for the period of twelve hydrologic years (1962–1973) for which unimpaired streamflow data were observed and used for model calibration. The climatic conditions for the calibration period were mostly near to normal, with some years characterised by moderately wet or moderately dry conditions (Table 1). This allowed the unbiased calibration of the model. About 75% and 92% of the annual precipitations during the calibrated period were between the mean −*SD* and the mean +*SD*, and between mean − 2*SD* and mean + 2*SD*, respectively. The minimum, mean and the maximum annual precipitations were 520 mm, 729 mm and 1,187 mm, respectively. The *SD* was approximately 201 mm. The annual precipitation observed in 1969 was interpreted as an outlier. No other outliers were observed over the calibration time interval. The minimum, mean and maximum *PET* values were 1,215 mm, 1,287 mm and 1,364 mm, respectively. The *SD* was about 58 mm. No outliers were observed.
2. The simulation results were validated using monthly climatic data (*P* and *PET*) and the unregulated observed runoff for a period of nine water years (1974–1982). Some statistical goodness-of-fit tools were employed for calibrating the model and validating the simulation results. These measures are r, RMSE, MAE and IoA ([34,35] for the latter). The following formulas (Equations (8) to (11)) were applied:

$$r = \sqrt{\frac{\sum_{i=1}^{n}[(R_{obs})_i - \bar{R}_{obs}][(R_{obs})_i - \bar{R}_{sim}]}{\{\sum_{i=1}^{n}[(R_{obs})_i - \bar{R}_{obs}]\}^{0.5}\{\sum_{i=1}^{n}[(R_{sim})_i - \bar{R}_{sim}]\}^{0.5}}} \tag{8}$$

$$RMSE = \sqrt{\frac{1}{n}\sum_{i=1}^{n}[(R_{obs})_i - (R_{sim})_i]^2} \tag{9}$$

$$MAE = \frac{1}{n}\sum_{i=1}^{n}|(R_{obs})_i - (R_{sim})_i| \tag{10}$$

$$I_oA = 1 - \frac{\sum_{i=1}^{n}[(R_{obs})_i - (R_{sim})_i]^2}{\sum_{i=1}^{n}[|(R_{obs})_i - \bar{R}_{obs}| + |(R_{sim})_i - \bar{R}_{obs}|]^2} \tag{11}$$

where R_{obs}, R_{sim}, $\bar{R}_{obs}$ and $\bar{R}_{sim}$ are the observed runoff, simulated runoff and the means of the observed and simulated runoffs, respectively. *N* is the number of years and *i* is the time step.
3. The RDI_{st} values were calculated over a time window of 30 years between 1962 and 1991. This was performed to specify which period represents nearly the normal climatic condition (on average) and to assess the constants *a* and *b* of the linear Equations (12) and (13):

$$RDI_{st} = a_1 * Ln(\alpha_{12}) + b_1 \tag{12}$$

$$SDI = a_2 * Ln(runoff) + b_2 \tag{13}$$

where RDI_{st}, α_{12} and *SDI* are the standardized form of the *RDI*, the initial form of the *RDI* and the streamflow drought index, respectively. a_1, a_2, b_1 and b_2 are constants. The period of nearly normal climatic condition expresses the timeframe in which no extreme RDI_{st} values were witnessed and when, on average, the RDI_{st} value is close to zero. The period of eight water years (1975 to 1982), which characterised the normal condition, was used for running the climatic scenarios. Moreover, the period between 1975 and 1982 was devoid of any considerable human construction activities (e.g., hydraulic control structures and large-scale irrigation schemes) in the upstream country, Iran.

4. The Medbasin-M model was used to compute the reference mean annual runoff for the normal climatic condition.
5. The Fifth Assessment Report of the IPCC [1] suggests that the region where the examined basin is located is likely to face a decline in precipitation amount and an increase in mean air temperature as part of climate change. The IPCC [36] highlighted that the annual average river runoff availability is projected to decrease by between 10% and 30% over some dry regions at mid-latitudes by 2050. Some impacted regions presently have water-stressed areas. Furthermore, an increase in drought spells is also projected for mid-latitudes. The IPCC reports also point out with high confidence (defined by IPCC) that climate change has the potential to exacerbate water resource stresses in most regions of Asia. The regional projections of temperature and precipitation in Asia based on a so-identified A2-forced emission scenario using the Atmosphere-Ocean General Circulation Model (AOGCM) simulations show that the rate of decrease in precipitation could reach −40% in winter (between December and February) and −50% in summer (between June and August). The increase in temperature would be in the order of +10% in winter and +6% in summer. It should be noted that these predictions should be considered as valid until the end of the 21st century. The synthetic scenarios for assessing the runoff sensitivity to climate change were formulated through an incremental shift of the historical *P* and *PET* values by a 2% step for a *P* reduction range from 0% to −40% and a *PET* increase from 0% to +30%. Correspondingly, 336 scenarios were developed, representing the mutual impact of deviations in *P* and *PET* values that lie within the aforementioned assortment of scenarios. These scenarios include all possible basin-wide climate change projections, as well as a wide array of drought severity conditions. The Medbasin-M model was repetitively used to simulate the runoff for the 336 scenarios.
6. The anticipated proportional change in the annual runoff (%), corresponding to each scenario, was determined relative to the reference mean annual runoff.
7. A nomograph was used for estimating the projected proportional change (%) in the climate-impacted runoff. The predictable proportional changes in the runoff represent the anticipated runoff reductions (%) relative to the long-term unimpaired mean annual runoff under the normal climatic condition.

2.5. Study Area and Data Availability

The Diyala river basin shared between Iraq and Iran was chosen as an example application basin for this study. The Diyala transboundary river system stretches from its source in the Zagros Mountains of western Iran to Iraq in the east. The river watershed drains a total area of about 32,600 km^2, of which 43% lies in Iraq, and has a total length of 384 km before discharging into the Tigris River south of

Baghdad. The watershed is situated between the latitudes 33.216°N and 35.833°N and the longitudes 44.500°E and 46.833°E (Figure 1). The river basin is located in the arid to semi-arid climate zone. Most runoff is generated during the period of November to May. The yearly average precipitation within the basin is nearly 500 mm. However, the precipitation mainly occurs between November and April, accounting for 90% of the whole water year.

The study is limited to the upper part of the basin with a total area of 17,900 km^2, which is mainly located in the upper riparian state, Iran. In the downstream country Iraq, the examined area is partly controlled by the Derbandikhan dam. In this study, the Derbandikhan hydrometric station (DHS) in Iraq is the control gauging station of the upper portion of the basin. The observed surface runoff at this station was used to calibrate and validate the constructed rainfall-runoff model. The entire basin has been prone to successive episodes of drought, particularly the severe droughts between 1999 and 2001 and the two successive years 2007 and 2008 [25,26]. Moreover, the upper segment of the basin is exceedingly dammed and witnessed the implementation of large-scale water withdrawal schemes at its source in Iran [25,26]. Agriculture represents the main consumer of water among all other sectors.

Figure 1. Diyala watershed (case study example) and the locations of the hydro-meteorological stations.

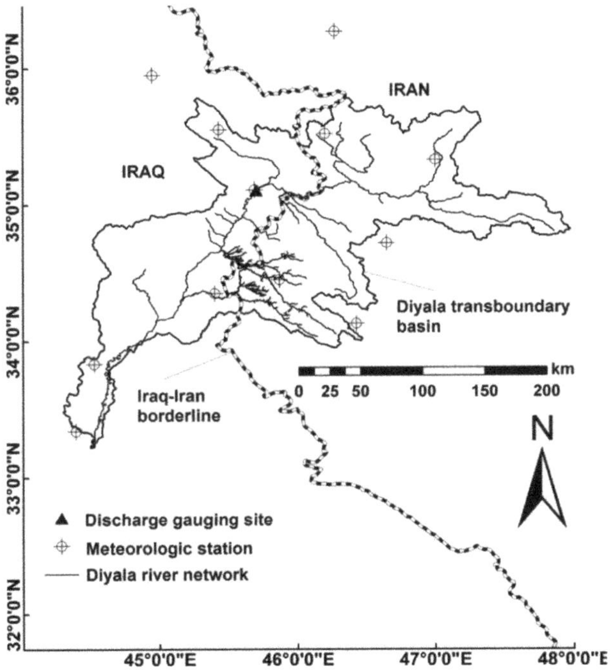

Monthly precipitation and air temperature data from 13 meteorological stations (seven stations in Iran and six stations in Iraq) were available for the period between 1962 and 1991. A long-time series of 30 hydrologic years of daily flow records (1962 to 1991) observed at the DHS (Figure 1) was analysed. Data were obtained from various sources [37–40], such as the Ministry of Agriculture and Water Resources in the Kurdistan region of Iraq and the Iranian Meteorological Organization. Some other meteorological data in Iraq were obtained from the Food and Agricultural Organization of the United Nations [41]. The *PET* time series was computed using the Blaney–Criddle method [27].

3. Results and Discussion

3.1. Model Calibration and Simulation Results after Validation

The statistics, r, RMSE, MAE and IoA, were 0.893, 2.117, 1.733 and 0.852, respectively, during the calibration. After validation, the corresponding statistics were 0.762, 1.250, 1.093 and 0.863, in this order. Results indicate promising model outcomes during the calibration and validation stages. This emphasises that the model can be safely used for further analysis, such as running the synthetic climatic scenarios and determining the proportional change (%) in the mean annual runoff relative to the normal climatic condition. The coefficients associated with Equations (12) and (13) were 4.323, 2.634, 2.204 and −18.554, respectively. The predicted runoff volumes for the calibrated and validated periods against the observed runoff data are illustrated in Figure 2.

Figure 2. Simulated runoff data against the observed runoff records.

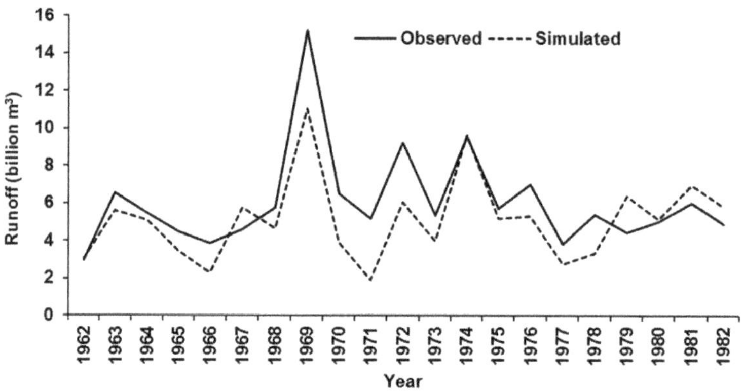

3.2. Anticipated Runoff for Various Climatic Scenarios

Figure 3 illustrates the RDI_{st} over a period of 30 years between 1962 and 1991. The period of eight years of nearly normal climatic conditions (1975 to 1982) was picked for running the climatic scenarios. This period experienced no extreme events, and the average value of RDI_{st} was close to zero. Moreover, findings reveal that the reference mean annual runoff, the initial value of the *RDI* (α_{12}), the RDI_{st} and the *SDI* were as much as 4.87 billion m^3, 0.55, 0.09 and 0.16, respectively. For an extreme climatic condition with a 40% reduction in *P* and a 30% increase in *PET*, the anticipated mean annual runoff, the α_{12}, the RDI_{st} and the *SDI* were about 0.84 billion m^3, 0.26, −3.26 and −3.71, respectively. The projected mean annual runoff for the worst case scenario represents about 17.3% of that referred to as the "0 scenario" (4.87 billion m^3).

Findings suggest a considerable impact that could be caused by climate change on the availability of water resources, particularly for the lower riparian country. Likewise, the study highlights the importance and the urgent need for pro-active plans and actions to cope with the most critical impact of drought and climate change. High-level coordination is required between all relevant parties to reduce the negative impacts and to moderate the economic and environmental losses. Furthermore, successful treatments need to be found to address the consequences that are likely to extend for a longer period after the end of the drought situation.

Figure 3. Selected simulation period for the Reconnaissance Drought Index (*RDI*) applied for different climatic scenarios concerning the Diyala example basin.

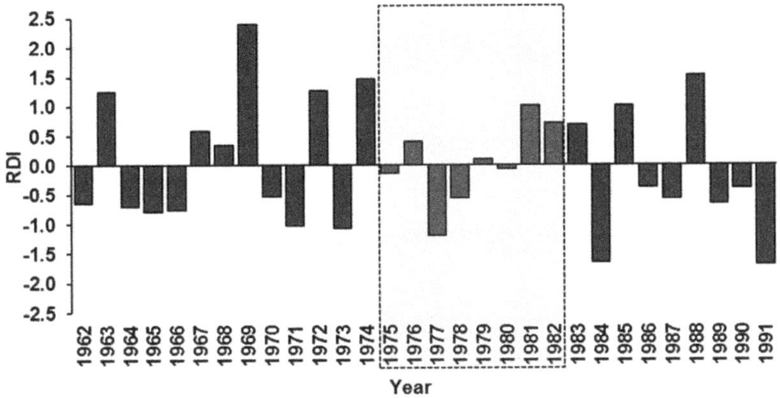

Figure 4 shows the foreseen change (%) in the annual runoff relative to the reference mean annual runoff value referred to as the "0 scenario". It should be stressed that the 0 scenario is based on the climate conditions of 1975–1982; therefore, the percentage of runoff change refers to that period. This figure provides a simple and useful tool that can be used by water managers and decision-makers to obtain the likely reduction (%) of the mean annual runoff according to a wide range of anomalies in *P* and *PET*.

Figure 4. Foreseen runoff changes (%) of the upper Diyala example basin for an array of climatic changes for precipitation (*P*) and potential evapotranspiration (*PET*).

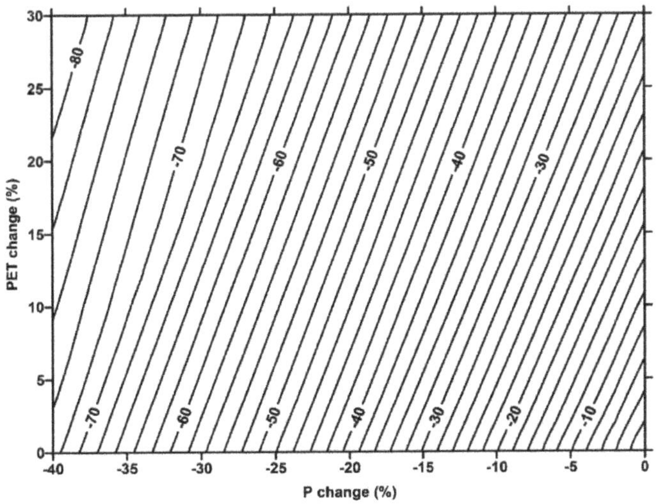

Figures 5 and 6 demonstrate the anticipated RDI_{st} and *SDI* values, respectively, according to possible changes in climatic condition (*P* and *PET*). For water governance decision-making, the problem becomes far more complex, because it deals not only with average anomalies, but also, and more decisively, with extreme events, like severe prolonged drought spells.

Figure 5. Anticipated standardised Reconnaissance Drought Index (RDI_{st}) for the upper Diyala example basin regarding a wide range of climatic scenarios for precipitation (*P*) and potential evapotranspiration (*PET*).

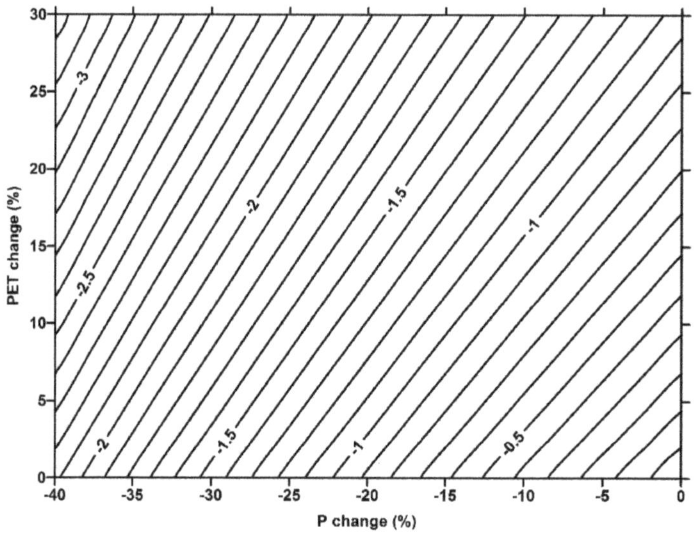

Figure 6. Anticipated Streamflow Drought Index (*SDI*) for the upper Diyala example basin regarding a wide range of climatic scenarios for precipitation (*P*) and potential evapotranspiration (*PET*).

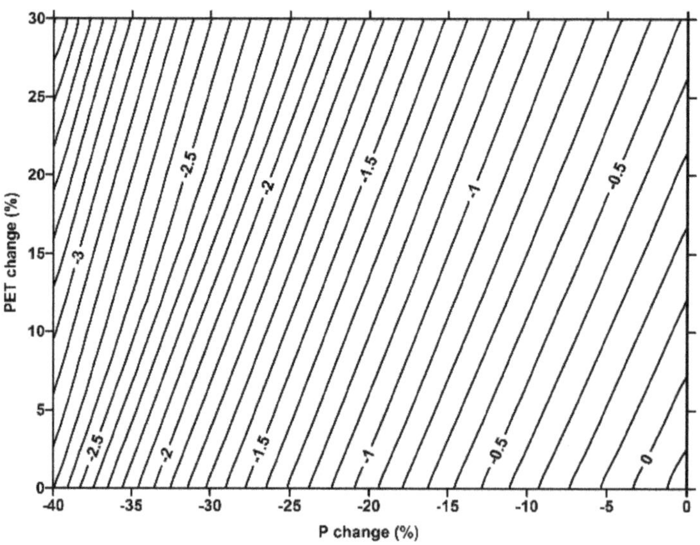

Results reveal a robust relationship between the predicted RDI_{st} and *SDI* values for all examined scenarios (Figure 7). Moreover, both RDI_{st} and *SDI* vary according to drought severity in a similar manner. It is noteworthy to highlight that Figures 4 to 6 collectively represent a solid measure for drought and climate change signatures. The associated methodology should be part of a simple and generic tool that can be used by water managers and decision-makers to estimate the likely projected decline (%) in the mean annual streamflow, which is influenced by climate, and to quantify the drought severity corresponding to a possible decrease in *P* and an increase in *PET*. A pro-active estimation of possible climate change scenarios and their adverse impact on runoff and drought spells would provide the opportunity to improve current decisions concerned with water allocations in time and space. Moreover, the proposed method allows decision-makers to take appropriate actions in advance to avoid the likelihood of adverse impacts of drought and climate change on multi-water users, particularly those in the agricultural sector. This timely tool is of high importance to the lower riparian example country, Iraq, which has become vulnerable to recent frequent drought events and upstream human-induced activities.

The suggested approach is of a generic nature and has merits at national, regional and universal scales. At the national level, it supports water managers and other related stakeholders to take serious steps and actions to handle the anticipated reductions in runoff volume according to various scenarios of climate change and recurrent droughts. At the regional scale, the approach offers a common platform for riparian states for better coordination to reduce possible harmful environmental and socio-economic effects of shared water use in upstream countries on the downstream states. Correspondingly, at the universal level, the approach can be applied to develop similar figures and estimate the possible reductions in annual runoff due to climate alterations and drought episodes.

Figure 7. Relationship between the anticipated standardised Reconnaissance Drought Index (RDI_{st}) and the Streamflow Drought Index (*SDI*) for the upper Diyala example basin.

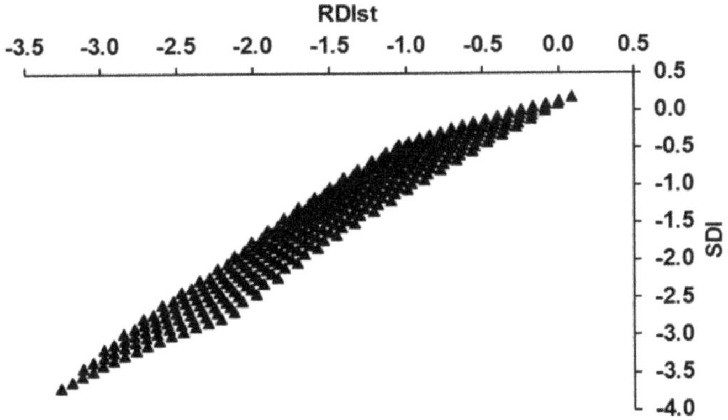

4. Conclusions and Recommendations

A simple, generic, powerful and novel approach was presented for predicting the proportional change (%) in the mean annual runoff under various climate change scenarios and anticipated droughts. The proposed methodology offers a simple and solid tool to support water managers and decision-makers in shaping better management plans and strategies for water resources that are anticipated to be available in the short to long term. Three nomographs were introduced for the anticipated alteration (%) in mean annual runoff, the anticipated RDI_{st} and *SDI*, corresponding to a wide range of potential climate change. A robust relationship was found between the RDI_{st} and *SDI*, indicating that the meteorological and hydrologic drought indices (RDI_{st} and *SDI*) are responding in a similar manner to climate change.

The anticipated anomaly (%) in stream flow can directly be linked to the hydrological and meteorological drought levels through the corresponding nomographs for *SDI* and RDI_{st}. An early assessment of meteorological drought leads to a proactive step that enables decision-makers to predict water availability for the entire water year and plan in advance measures for mitigating drought impacts. Although the nomographs were prepared for annual timescales, the same procedure could be applied for selected shorter periods within the hydrologic year (e.g., three months, six months and nine months). The developed nomographs are supportive tools for formulating strategic alertness plans to combat drought episodes and soften their effects on various water use areas, particularly the agriculture sector.

It is worth mentioning that functional medium- to long-term water management requires dependable data, reliable information and better perception of present and anticipated events in the future. The authors recommend further research work to develop similar nomographs that respond to the relative impact of both basin-wide climate change and upstream human-induced activities (e.g., man-made land use change, river damming and diversion-related hydraulic structures). Moreover, they encourage similar studies for other transboundary basins shared between countries, such as Iraq and Iran, Iraq and Turkey, as well as Mediterranean watersheds.

Acknowledgments

The authors would like to thank the Ministry of Agriculture and Water Resources in the Iraq-Kurdistan Regional Government, particularly the General Directorate for Operation of Dams and Reservoirs and the Directorate for Operation of Derbandikhan Dam for their full support in providing some useful meteorological and hydrological data used in this study.

Author Contributions

Furat Al-Faraj undertook the data analysis and prepared a draft paper. Miklas Scholz wrote the original paper. Dimitris Tigkas provided feedback on the data analysis.

Conflicts of Interest

The authors declare no conflict of interest.

References

1. Intergovernmental Panel on Climate Change. Climate Change 2014: Impacts, Adaptation, and Vulnerability. Available online: http: //www.ipcc.ch/report/ar5/wg2 (accessed on 5 May 2014).
2. Niemeyer, S. New Drought Indices. In Proceedings of the 1st International Conference on Drought Management: Scientific and Technological Innovations (option Méditerranéennes, series A, No. 80), Zaragoza, Spain, 12–14 June 2008.
3. Cloppet, E. Agricultural Drought Indices in France and Europe: Strengths, Weaknesses, and Limitations. In Proceedings of the Expert Meeting, Murcia, Spain, 2–4 June 2010.

4. Zarch, M.A.A.; Malekinezhad, H.; Mobin, M.H.; Dastorani, M.T.; Kousari, M.R. Drought monitoring by reconnaissance drought index (RDI) in Iran. *Water Res. Manag.* **2011**, *25*, 3485–3504.
5. Talaee, P.H.; Tabari, H.; Ardakani, S.S. Hydrological drought in the west of Iran and possible association with large-scale atmospheric circulation patterns. *Hydrol. Proc.* **2012**, *28*, 764–773.
6. Rasheed, A.M.M. Analysis of rainfall drought periods in the North of Iraq using standard precipitation index (SPI). *Al Rafidain Eng. J.* **2010**, *18*, 60–72.
7. United Nations Educational, Scientific and Cultural Organization. *Integrated Drought Risk Management–DRM National Framework for Iraq-Executive Summary*, Technical Report; UNESCO-Iraq office: Baghdad, Iraq, 2013.
8. Tigkas, D. Drought Characterisation and Monitoring in Regions of Greece. *Eur. Water* **2008**, *23–24*, 29–39.
9. Pangalou, D.; Tigkas, D.; Vangelis, H.; Tsakiris, G.; Nanou-Giannarou, A. Drought severity thresholds and drought management in Greece. *Adv. Nat. Technol. Hazards Res.* **2009**, *26*, 243–256.
10. Dogan, S.; Berltay, A.; Singh, V.P. Comparison of multi-monthly rainfall-based drought severity indices, with application to semi-arid Konya closed basin, Turkey. *J. Hydrol.* **2012**, *470–471*, 255–268.
11. Al-Qinna, M.I.; Hammouri, N.A.; Obeidat, M.M.; Ahmad, F.Y. Drought analysis in Jordan under current and future climates. *Clim. Change* **2011**, *106*, 421–440.
12. Tarawneh, Q.Y. Quantification of drought in the Kingdom of Saudi Arabia. *Int. J. Water Res. Arid Environ.* **2013**, *2*, 125–133.
13. Tsakiris, G.; Vangelis, H. Establishing a drought index incorporating evapotranspiration. *Eur. Water* **2005**, *9–10*, 3–11.
14. Khalili, D.; Farnoud, T.; Jamshidi, H.; Kamgar-Haghighi, A.A.; Zand-Parsa, S. Comparability analyses of the SPI and RDI meteorological drought indices in different climatic zones. *Water Res. Manag.* **2011**, *25*, 1737–1757.
15. Elagib, N.A.; Elhag, M.M. Major Climate indicators of ongoing drought in Sudan. *J. Hydrol.* **2011**, *409*, 612–625.
16. Nalbantis, I. Drought and streamflow. *Eur. Water* **2008**, *23–24*, 65–76.
17. Nalbantis, I.; Tsakiris, G. Assessment of hydrological drought revisited. *Water Res. Manag.* **2009**, *23*, 881–897.
18. Allen, P.; Harmel, R.D.; Dunbar, J.A.; Arnold, J.G. Upland contribution of sediment and runoff during extreme drought: A study of the 1947–1956 drought in the Blackland Prairie, Texas. *J. Hydrol.* **2011**, *407*, 1–11.
19. Tsakiris, G.; Nalbantis, I.; Pangalou, D.; Tigkas, D.; Vangelis, H. Drought Meteorological Monitoring Network Design for the Reconnaissance Drought Index (RDI). Available online: http://www.iamz.ciheam.org/medroplan/zaragoza2008/Sequia2008/Session1/D.Tigkas.pdf (accessed on 1 May 2014).
20. Bonsal, B.; Regier, M. Historical comparison of the 2001/2002 drought in the Canadian prairies. *Clim. Res.* **2007**, *33*, 229–242.
21. Tsakiris, G.; Pangalou, D.; Vangelis, H. Regional drought assessment based on the Reconnaissance Drought Index (RDI). *Water Res. Manag.* **2007**, *21*, 821–833.

22. Tigkas, D.; Vangelis, H.; Tsakiris, G. The RDI as a composite climatic index. *Eur. Water* **2013**, *41*, 17–22.
23. Tigkas, D.; Vangelis, H.; Tsakiris, G. The Drought Indices Calculator (DrinC). In Proceedings of the 8th International Conference of EWRA: Water Resources Management in an Interdisciplinary and Changing Context, Porto, Portugal, 26–29 June 2013.
24. Tigkas, D.; Vangelis, H.; Tsakiris, G. DrinC: A software for drought analysis based on drought indices. *Earth Sci. Inform.* **2014**, in press.
25. Al-Faraj, F.A.M.; Scholz, M. Assessment of temporal hydrologic anomalies coupled with drought impact for a transboundary river flow regime. The Diyala watershed case study. *J. Hydrol.* **2014**, *517*, 64–73.
26. Al-Faraj, F.A.M.; Scholz, M. Impact of upstream anthropogenic river regulation on downstream water availability in transboundary river watersheds. *Int. J. Water Res. Dev.* **2014**, in press.
27. Doorenbos, J.; Pruitt, W.O. Guidelines for Predicting Crop Water Requirements. In *Food and Agriculture Organisation (FAO) of the United Nations–Irrigation and Drainage Paper 24*, 2nd ed.; FAO: Rome, Italy, 1977.
28. Tigkas, D.; Tsakiris, G. Medbasin: A Mediterranean rainfall–runoff software package. *Eur. Water* **2004**, *5–6*, 3–11.
29. Tigkas, D.; Vangelis, H.; Tsakiris, G. Drought and climate change impact on streamflow in small watersheds. *Sci. Total Environ.* **2012**, *440*, 33–41.
30. Giakoumakis, S.; Dercas, N.; Karantounias, G. Validation of a Simple Water Balance Model in Pinios River Basin (Peloponnese, Greece). In Proceedings of the 6th International Conference of the European Water Resources Association (EWRA) on Sharing a Common Vision for Our Water Resources, Menton, France, 7–10 September 2005.
31. Soil Conservation Service. *National Engineering Handbook. Section 4 on Hydrology*; Department of Agriculture: Washington, DC, USA, 1972.
32. Gregory, M.A.; Cunningham, B.A.; Schmidt, M.F.; Mack, B.W. Estimating Soil Storage Capacity for Stormwater Modeling Applications. In Proceedings of the 6th Biennial Conference on Stormwater Research and Watershed Management, Southwest Florida, FL, USA, 14–17 September 1999.
33. United States Department of Agriculture. Urban hydrology for small watersheds. In *Technical Release 55 (TR-55)*, 2nd ed.; Natural Resources Conservation Service, Conservation Engineering Division: Washington, DC, USA, 1986.
34. Willmott, C.J. On the validation of models. *Phys. Geogr.* **1981**, *2*, 184–194.
35. Willmott, C.J.; Robesonb, S.M.; Matsuuraa, K. A refined index of model performance. *Int. J. Climatol.* **2012**, *32*, 2088–2094.
36. Intergovernmental Panel on Climate Change (IPCC). *Climate Change 2007: Impacts, Adaptation, and Vulnerability*; Contribution of Working Group II to the Fourth Assessment Report of the IPCC; Cambridge University Press: Cambridge, UK, 2007.
37. Harza Engineering Company and Binnie & Partners. *Hydrological Survey of Iraq*; Discharges for Selected Gauging Stations in Iraq, Report; Harza Engineering Company: Chicago, IL, USA; Binnie & Partners: London, UK, 1958.

38. Harza Engineering Company and Binnie & Partners. *Hydrological Survey of Iraq*; Discharges for Selected Gauging Stations in Iraq, Report; Harza Engineering Company: Chicago, IL, USA; Binnie & Partners: London, UK, 1959.
39. Harza Engineering Company and Binnie & Partners. *Hydrological Survey of Iraq*; Main Report; Harza Engineering Company: Chicago, IL, USA; Binnie & Partners: London, UK, 1963.
40. Ministry of Agriculture and Water Resources-Kurdistan Regional Government (MA and WR-KRG). *Various Official Data Sets, General Directorate of Dams and Reservoirs and Directorate for Operation of Derbandikhan*; MA and WR-KRG: Erbil and Sulaymaniya, Iraq, 2013.
41. Food and Agriculture Organization of the United Nations (FAO). *Hydrogeology of Northern Iraq, Volume 1–Climate, Hydrology, Geomorphology and Geology*; FAO: Rome, Italy, 2004.

International Journal of
Environmental Research and Public Health

MDPI

Review

Water-Related Impacts of Climate Change on Agriculture and Subsequently on Public Health: A Review for Generalists with Particular Reference to Pakistan

Toqeer Ahmed [1], Miklas Scholz [2,3,*], Furat Al-Faraj [2] and Wajeeha Niaz [1]

1 Centre for Climate Research and Development, COMSAS Institute of Information Technology, Islamabad Campus, Park Road, Chak Shahzad, Islamabad 45550, Pakistan; toqeer.ahmed@comsats.edu.pk (T.A.); wajeehaniax@gmail.com (W.N.)

2 Division of Water Resources Engineering, Faculty of Engineering, Lund University, P.O. Box 118, Lund 22100, Sweden; f.a.m.al-faraj@edu.salford.ac.uk

3 Civil Engineering Research Group, School of Computing, Science and Engineering, The University of Salford, The Crescent, Salford M5 4WT, UK

* Correspondence: miklas.scholz@tvrl.lth.se or m.scholz@salford.ac.uk; Tel.: +46-46-222-8920

Academic Editor: Yu-Pin Lin
Received: 30 June 2016; Accepted: 21 October 2016; Published: 27 October 2016

Abstract: Water-related impacts due to change in climatic conditions ranging from water scarcity to intense floods and storms are increasing in developing countries like Pakistan. Water quality and waterborne diseases like hepatitis, cholera, typhoid, malaria and dengue fever are increasing due to chaotic urbanization, industrialization, poor hygienic conditions, and inappropriate water management. The morbidity rate is high due to lack of health care facilities, especially in developing countries. Organizations linked to the Government of Pakistan (e.g., Ministry of Environment, Ministry of Climate Change, Planning and Development, Ministry of Forest, Irrigation and Public Health, Pakistan Meteorological Department, National Disaster Management, Pakistan Agricultural Research Centre, Pakistan Council for Research in Water Resources, and Global Change Impact Study Centre), United Nation organizations, provincial government departments, non-governmental organizations (e.g., Global Facility and Disaster Reduction), research centers linked to universities, and international organizations (International Institute for Sustainable Development, Food and Agriculture, Global Climate Fund and World Bank) are trying to reduce the water-related impacts of climate change, but due to lack of public awareness and health care infrastructure, the death rate is steadily increasing. This paper critically reviews the scientific studies and reports both at national and at international level benefiting generalists concerned with environmental and public health challenges. The article underlines the urgent need for water conservation, risk management, and the development of mitigation measures to cope with the water-related impacts of climate change on agriculture and subsequently on public health. Novel solutions and bioremediation methods have been presented to control environmental pollution and to promote awareness among the scientific community. The focus is on diverse strategies to handle the forthcoming challenges associated with water resources management.

Keywords: bacteria; developing country; disease; environmental management; freshwater; pollution; sustainability; urbanization; wastewater; water resources

1. Introduction, Rationale, and Aim

Water-related disasters such as floods and droughts, changes in rainfall patterns, and increases in temperature are serious challenges, and their impacts on water quality and ultimately on human health have to be assessed and controlled [1]. About 50% of the recorded disasters are commonly due to floods and roughly 10% owing to high temperatures or heat waves [2]. Approximately 25% of all illnesses like diarrhea, malaria, and respiratory infection are due to change in climate and environmental degradation such as watercourse contamination from polluted agricultural runoff [3]. Challenges are particularly serious in developing countries. For example, according to the Global Facility for Disaster Reduction and Recovery, one-third of the people in Karachi lack clean water and health facilities [4].

With changing climate conditions such as rainfall, temperature, and humidity, water has great impacts both on agriculture and health. Water availability and quality are deteriorating and waterborne diseases are subsequently increasing, which impacts both sectors. Water quality in relation to climate change is not properly studied, especially the impact of climate change on water-related (both water- and vector-related) diseases. In Pakistan, waterborne diseases like cholera and vector borne diseases like malaria and dengue fever are prevailing with the changing rainfall pattern, temperature, humidity, etc. Water availability for agriculture is important as about 90% of water is used for irrigation purposes in many countries. With changing climatic conditions, water availability will affect agriculture and livestock production. There is a strong need to study these impacts with changing climatic scenarios.

Possible pathways through which climate change can affect multiple health outcomes are indicated in Figure 1. It follows that there is a need to assess water-related impacts of climate change on agriculture and subsequently on public health in general, but more particularly for developing countries, informing decision-makers with a wide range of professional backgrounds in environmental public health.

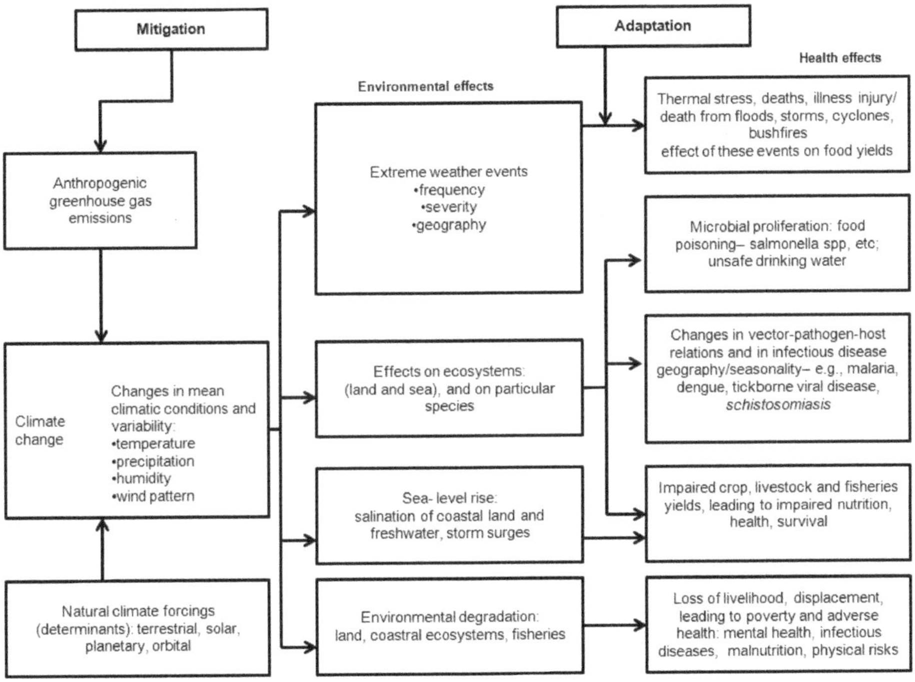

Figure 1. Overview of environmental and health effects linked to mitigation and adaptation strategies to climate change (after [5]).

Various research institutes, academia, and government organizations are working on collaborative projects such as the projects "Impacts of Climate Change on Pakistan's Water Sector Vulnerability

Assessment" and "Glacial Lakes Outburst Floods" (funded by the United Nations Development Program). Other climate and water conservation projects are conducted by different government institutions such as the Climate Change, Alternative Energy, and Water Resources Department of Pakistan; Agriculture Research Center and Global Change Impact Study Center; as well as international non-governmental organizations. There are many other organizations both at government level and in the private sector working on impacts of climate change, natural disasters, and their direct impacts human health. Private and government authorities are also working on water quality and other water related issues.

There is currently neither a framework nor detailed analytical work that has been implemented showing the specific state of water resources management, agriculture, water quality, and public health with reference to climate change in Pakistan. Therefore, this paper aims to critically review scientific studies to assess the need for water conservation, risk management, and the development of mitigation measures to cope with the water-related impacts of climate change on agriculture and subsequently on public health, particularly from the Pakistani perspective. Novel solutions and strategies benefiting a wide range of generalists and stakeholders will be presented to control environmental pollution and to promote public awareness, and deliver the basis for a conceptual framework for the assessment of current and future scenarios.

2. Methodology

A comprehensive literature review was performed between January 2015 and June 2016. References were identified using Google Scholar (in addition to the standard Google search engine), Web of Science, Scopus, and Science Direct. The key words and phrases climate change, water-related impact, agricultural pollution, vector-borne disease, waterborne disease, flooding impact, water quality, extreme event, public health, pollution control, water availability, water quality, and Pakistan were used in various combinations. The publication time period considered was between 1980 and early 2016.

The literature cited was selected based on a critical review of publications of greatest relevance to Pakistan and countries with similar environmental boundary conditions. Other criteria such as publication date, outlet type, and author (or institution) played less important roles during literature selection.

3. Flooding Impacts and Environmental Pollution

Floods bring biological and chemical pollutants, which might ultimately contaminate the groundwater. Flooding events often cause soil erosion associated with chemical pollutants such as organic and inorganic matter, including heavy metals and polycyclic aromatic compounds, which pose threats to groundwater sources and may be taken up by crops and other plants [6]. Both fertilizers and flooded soils are sources of polycyclic aromatic hydrocarbons [6].

Water-borne and health-related infections may increase after flooding. An increase in mold after extensive flooding of healthcare facilities and a simultaneous decrease in multi-drug-resistant organisms has been noted [7]. Contamination with enteric Gram-negative bacteria (e.g., *Aeromonas* species), *Legionella* species, and non-tuberculous *Mycobacterium* species in hospital water sources has also been reported [7]. The spread of water-borne diseases like cholera and dysentery may increase after diarrhea outbreaks. The risk of dysentery might increase after flooding events [8]. Floods may increase both water-borne and vector-borne diseases such as cholera, typhoid, dysentery, and malaria as well as dengue and yellow fever [9]. Flood-related events increase the risk of infectious diseases, including respiratory and vector-borne illnesses [10].

The intensity of floods and droughts adversely affect public health during both the event and immediately thereafter. Climate change can increase the frequency and intensity of floods, droughts, and heat waves within a country or at a regional level, and their appearance is uncertain [11]. A summary of relatively recent flood losses in Pakistan is given in Table 1.

Table 1. Summary of estimated flood losses over the past few years in Pakistan.

Year	Deaths	House Damages	Population Affected
2010	490	1,602,800	175,000,000
2011	69,890	15,977,500	9,345,000
2012	570	636,400	4,849,800
2013	330	46,200	1,489,100
2014	370	107,100	2,412,000
2015	150	4800	1,314,500

4. Water Quality and Public Health

Water pollution and associated public health implications belong to the most important challenges faced by humankind. Chemical (heavy metals such as lead, arsenic and iron), viral (hepatitis A, polio, and *Enteroviruses*) and bacterial (total and fecal coliforms along with *Streptococci*) pollution has profound effects on public health [12]. Various studies conducted in Bangladesh, China, and Pakistan reported on high concentrations of arsenic, but also on heavy metal pollutants like nickel, lead, chromium, cadmium, and mercury in groundwater, which directly affected public health [13,14]. One major source of water contamination is the improper disposal of sewage [15,16]. Both chemical and microbial pollution can affect aquatic life. Heavy metal pollution is a risk to fish, and subsequently to public health [17]. Improper management of sewage discharge and leakage of cesspool-influenced groundwater into coastal lagoons is responsible for some aquatic and environmental challenges [18,19].

Approximately 30% of the world population living in developing countries lacks access to sewage disposal [20]. *Escherichia coli* is often seen as the best indicator for fecal water pollution [21]. *Enteroviruses* are used as indicators to assess viral water contamination [22]. The diversity of antibiotic-resistant bacteria in aquatic environments can be enhanced by water pollution [23]. Heavy rainfall and floods associated with extreme weather and water supply contamination are responsible for waterborne disease outbreaks causing great risks for both developed and developing countries [24].

Climate change is often linked to an increase in occurrence of draughts and/or floods. Data relating floods with diarrheal patients in Dhaka (Bangladesh) during 1988, 1998 and 2004 have been discussed [25]. They reported that *Vibrio cholera* was the first and Rotavirus was the second most frequent cause of diarrhea. Other causes of diarrhea were enterotoxigenic *E. coli*, *Shigella*, and *Salmonella* species. Water-related pathogens cause diseases, their surveillance, and possible interventions are discussed in Table 2 [26–28]. No comprehensive published work has been reported on the relationship between water quality and fecal coliforms with special reference to climate change in Pakistan.

Table 2. Overview of water-related pathogens (both waterborne and vector-borne), diseases, and their impacts.

Pathogen Types and Typical Organisms	Typical Major Common Diseases	Surveillance	Interventions	References
Waterborne pathogens (examples)				
Salmonella spp.; *Escherichia coli*; *Vibrio cholera*; *Shigella* spp.; *Streptococci*; *Yersinia* spp.	Typhoid; abdominal cramps; Dysentery; Cholera; sore throat; Yersiniosis	Microbiological water quality; monitoring, especially during and after a monsoon	Track diseases; monitor water quality and health; diagnose and investigate waterborne and other infections outbreaks; apply health interventions	[26,27]
Water-based pathogens (examples)				
Poliovirus; *Enteroviruses*; Rotavirus; Hepatitis A and E viruses; *Helicobacter pylori*	Polio; diarrhoea; stomach ulcers; infections; respiratory illnesses	Microbiological water quality monitoring during and after a monsoon	Track diseases; monitor health; diagnose and investigate waterborne outbreaks; apply health interventions	[26,27]
Vector-borne pathogens (examples)				
Sand flies; dengue virus (mosquitoes); Plasmodium (mosquitoes); Flavivirus; Tsetse flies	*Leishmaniasis*; dengue fever; fever with shivering; Japanese encephalitis; West Nile virus; Yellow fever; Trypanosomiasis	Monitoring of vectors and their habitats; source identification and enhanced investigations	Diagnose and investigate vector-borne and other related outbreaks; apply the health interventions available	[26,28]

5. Overview of Agricultural Water Pollution Impacting on Human Health

This overview section is an introduction to this rather wide topic. Case study data usually depend on local and regional boundary conditions, which are often of little interest to the international reader. Therefore, the authors did not present numerical data, but provided a good number of references useful for readers requiring more information including data.

Agriculture can negatively affect water quality, especially in rural areas of both developing and developed countries [29]. Crops are often irrigated with wastewater polluted by domestic and industrial effluents containing heavy metals, which are potentially absorbed by vegetables and other cash crops, ultimately becoming part of the food chain. Literature [30] reported on potential toxicological risks of heavy metals on the public health using contaminated food. Urban agriculture has prominent effects on human health in terms of greenhouse gas emissions and spreading of water-related diseases such as malaria. Antonio-Nkondjio [31] pointed out that urban agriculture has a major role in spreading resistance to insecticides and malarial diseases. Chemical pollution can be minimized by applying natural fertilizers and sustainable agricultural principles in general.

Changes in temperature and rainfall due to climate change may influence the growth of fungi and increase in mycotoxins in agricultural food products, which are high risks to human health. Warm and humid climate is favorable for fungal growth where the average annual temperature is approximately 25 °C, but it varies depending upon season.

South Asian countries including Pakistan have been recognized as vulnerable regions subjected to the negative impacts of climate change in terms of public health [32]. A high population growth rate, deficiency in water availability, degradation of soil, urbanization, and an animal-based diet along with climate change are the global challenges, which are a threat to food security [33]. An increase in the demand for water in the agriculture sector for crops poses a severe threat to balanced water resources management. Only some crops such as wheat and barley are largely weather resistant, in particular, in a changing climate [34]. In general, the agriculture sector of most countries such as Pakistan has been adversely impacted by climate change, which may lead to a food shortage by 2030, resulting in an increase in food prices [35].

Droughts, floods, warming, and changes in precipitation can directly alter crop yields. This can threaten human life and cause long-term malnutrition and diseases. A study conducted on wheat production (Swat and Charsadda districts, Pakistan) suggests short duration and high yielding varieties should be introduced in hilly areas due to global warming [36].

Climate change has more profound impacts on agriculture and health as indicated in Table 3, which is based partly on literature and partly on expert opinion, because literature evidence is not conclusive in the interpretation of the strength of the case study relationships shown. Manure and animal waste contains pathogens, veterinary pharmaceuticals, and nutrients along with heavy metals, which are transported and spread into the environment, ultimately causing both environmental and human health hazards [37]. More intense storms due to climate change cause these contaminants to run-off and ultimately to enter the human food chain.

Table 3. Potentially strong relationships between exposure situations and health conditions relevant to agricultural food production and storage (based on this literature review and the expert opinions of the authors).

Health Conditions of Concern	Polluted Air	Excreta and Household Wastewater	Polluted Water or Deficiencies in Water Management	Polluted Food	Unsuitable Housing	Global Change of Environment
Acute respiratory infection	X		X		X	
Other infections		X		X	X	
Diarrheal diseases		X	X	X		X
Malaria and other vector-borne diseases			X			X
Injuries and poisonings	X	X	X	X	X	X
Mental health conditions					X	
Cardiovascular diseases	X			X	X	X
Cancer	X					X
Chronic respiratory diseases	X					X

6. Water Pollution Control and Detection Techniques

This section follows the logic of the three previous sections: Section 3 links climate change to flooding, which impacts the environment, usually increasing water pollution. Section 4 indicates how water quality is linked to public health. Finally, Section 5 links more specifically agricultural water pollution to human health. Raw and agricultural water pollution and its impacts on human health are discussed in Section 6. Commonly used detection techniques and strategies developed by scientists to control the current problems and the need to develop new techniques under changing climatic conditions are assessed.

Bacteria-based systems can help in the degradation of environmental pollutants [38]. Phytoremediation removes toxic metals from wastewater. Empirical studies have reported on the use of plants for the removal of heavy metals and dyes from wastewater and soil [39,40]. Among the conventional technologies, various plant parts are used as adsorbents and natural coagulants as well as in advanced oxidation processes for the removal of metallic nanoparticles, toxic metals, and bacterial pollution from wastewater [41,42]. Whole cell sensing systems as well as chemical and biosensors are applied for the detection of environmental pollutants like metals. Recent advancements have shown the conversion of toxic metals into useful metallic nanoparticles by using microbes [43,44].

Biosensors have specific interactions between enzymes and substrate, and are highly specific in their detection capabilities. Bio-sorption is another emerging and novel technique for the removal of toxic metals from wastewater. Zouboulis et al. [45] used *Bacillus laterosporus* and *Bacillus licheniformis* for cadmium and chromium removal. They reported that bacteria have a high surface area-to-volume ratio like metallic nanoparticles, and that they therefore provide a large contact interface, which interacts with metals from the surrounding environment. Pyridine is one of the most widespread heterocyclic industrial contaminants. A new strain of *Arthrobacter* has been found to be the best among all the known strains for the purification of industrial wastewater [46]. *Arthrobacter*, which is used for the removal of atrazine, has good bioremediation potential concerning contaminated soils and waters [47].

Some solutions for the removal of environmental pollutants are conventional such as synthetic and natural coagulation, adsorption, and anaerobic digestion of contaminants. In comparison, others are advanced such as emerging nanotechnology-based techniques (e.g., the use of silver nanoparticles, titanium dioxide, zinc oxide, iron nanoparticles, and carbon nanotubes) for the removal of contaminants [48,49]. Both conventional and advanced solutions aim to provide and maintain better solutions to environmental pollution. Reducing contaminants can help in improving both environmental and human health. Improved housing design and better pipe material used in water supply can assist in reducing environmental pollution and improving public health in developing countries [50].

Animal waste-containing fecal matter can cause contamination to water resources. Anaerobic digestion of animal waste rather than dumping of waste at different places (as it is a common practice in developing countries) can cause environmental and public health problems [51]. Animal waste can also be used as an alternative source of energy. Therefore, anaerobic digestion of animal waste could be applied for the production of biogas, and different methanogens can enhance the process of digestion [37].

Emerging nanotechnology-based methods and nano-materials with their unique physical and chemical properties have previously been applied to reduce environmental pollution [49]. Silver and other metallic nanoparticles (e.g., zinc oxide) have been developed against waterborne pathogens [48]. Carbon nanotubes have been utilized as adsorbents, because of their unique properties beneficial for the removal of organic and inorganic pollutants along with radionuclides [52]. Results compared with natural zeolites indicated that the adsorbents are highly efficient and economical. Magnetic graphene oxides have been tested as adsorbates for the removal of trace metals of polybrominated diphenyl ethers in water treatment. They are regarded as highly efficient for environmental remediation [53]. Moreover, magnetic nano-composites are used as adsorbents for the removal of heavy metals such as chromium, lead, mercury, and arsenic [54].

7. Water Pollution, Climate Change, and Population Increase

Climate change is expected to alter water quantity and quality [55–60], and is likely to be different between large and small basins [61,62]. The potential changes in temperature and precipitation may not uniformly distribute over large watersheds [63] and thus both regional and local scales as well as the extent of urbanization must be considered in climate change impact studies for water resources protection [59]. Climate change has dynamic impacts on surface watercourses such as rivers, streams, and lakes, which provide clean water. In order to protect water resources, policy makers should consider climate change impacts on the reduction of pollution for improving water quality [59].

Human and industrial (including agriculture) wastes are the main pollutants contaminating water bodies particularly during flood events. Bacterial pollutants of human origin such as *E. coli*, *Salmonella*, and *Vibrio* as well as heavy metals and pesticide-related carcinogens are originating from different industries and are discharged into water bodies, ultimately causing pollution [64], which puts farming communities particularly at risk. Both bacteriological and chemical water pollutants have negative effects on human health, but less information is available in relation to changing climatic conditions. An increase in population and urbanization is putting water resources in danger, negatively affecting public health, the economy, and the environment [65].

Extreme climatic conditions such as high temperature and heavy precipitation play significant roles in increasing water pollution. Urban runoff to rivers and streams pollute water resources [66]. Different waterborne pathogens such as *Giardia* cysts and Cryposporidium oocysts correlate positively with rainfall [67]. Vector- and waterborne diseases are enhanced by El Niño-related extreme climatic conditions [67]. Extreme weather events and climate change have momentous impacts on the hydrological cycle [68].

For example, in a drought-prone region in the Sindh Province (Pakistan), inhabitants either have no access to freshwater or use brackish water for drinking purposes [12]. Similarly, in the Baluchistan Province (Pakistan), the groundwater level is falling at a rate of 3.5 m annually, and it is predicted that groundwater will soon be exhausted [69].

Rainfall increases the fecal pollution in rivers and freshwater resources, and elevates the bacterial risk [70]. Warm temperatures and extreme rainfall are often contributing factors to waterborne disease outbreaks, for example, in Canada [71]. Heavy rainfall and floods are associated with extreme weather and may account for 55% and 53% of waterborne outbreaks, respectively [23]. Extreme weather events and changes in patterns increase the risk of gastrointestinal diseases. For example, in Japan (1999 to 2007), about 7.7% and 2.3% of infectious gastroenteritis case increases per week were recorded for a 1 °C increase in the average temperature and for every 1% decrease in relative humidity, respectively [72].

Changes in climatic conditions, precipitation, humidity, and wind pattern occur due to both natural and anthropogenic activities, which have environmental effects like changes in environmental factors, environmental degradation, and disturbance of ecosystems. Changes in environmental conditions, disturbances, and degradations may affect human health negatively [5].

8. Pollution and Public Health

About two-fifths of the global population (including the people of Pakistan) are facing water scarcity and waterborne diseases. One child dies approximately every eight seconds, because of waterborne diseases [73]. Farooq et al. [74] estimates that 44% of the global population is unable to access clean drinking water. Ren et al. [75] conducted a study in the Huai River basin (China). They reported that preventive measures and interventions to support hygiene should be adopted to improve surface water quality.

A study conducted in Pakistan by Nabeel et al. [42] indicated that about 71% and 58% of the reported samples across the country were found contaminated with total and fecal coliform which causes loss of 25–58 billion Pak Rupee annually. Similarly, Ahmed et al. [76] reported on the presence of coliforms and fecal coliforms in 67% of water samples tested from academic institutions at different parts of Abbottabad city. This study highlighted the prevalence of water-related diseases like diarrhea and typhoid.

Chemical pollution can cause several health problems. High nitrate levels in the water can be one of the co-factors for several cases of water-related Mathemoglobinemia, a condition in which methemoglobin (an oxygen-carrying metalloprotein hemoglobin type) cannot bind oxygen [77]. Both constructive and destructive impacts of climate change influence agriculture and public health, but destructive impacts have more devastating effects that need to be addressed (Table 4). The added word "potential" in the heading of Table 4 indicates that there is not necessarily consensus among all scientists. Therefore, expert opinion of the authors to make a judgement on the available evidence has been expressed.

Table 4. Potential impact of major climatic elements on agriculture and health (based on this literature review and the expert opinions of the authors).

Climatic Elements	Potential Impacts			
	Constructive		Destructive	
	Health	Agriculture	Health	Agriculture
Drought	Decrease in vectors and vector-borne diseases	Parasites and vector growths	Water quality and availability is affected; water-related diseases and death increase; hunger	Loss of water; reduction in crop productivity; economic growth
Flood	-	-	Poor water quality; injuries; increase in vectors, water-related vector-borne and zoonotic diseases; heat stress; cardiovascular failure; anxiety; depression	Reduction in crop productivity and economic growth; infrastructure destruction
Heat and humidity	-	May increase crop productivity	Decrease in water availability; skin infection; increase in vectors and vector-borne diseases like malaria, dengue fever, and Japanese encephalitis	Increase in vectors and pests, and related agricultural problems and crop diseases
Salt water intrusion	Decrease in the growth of pathogens and related diseases	-	Water quality and supply degradation; diseases,	Agricultural land loss; increase in soil salinity; water supply and quality deterioration

9. The Pakistani Scenario with Reference to Similar Countries

Water pollution is one of the major current problems affecting human health in Pakistan, because water quality is poorly monitored and managed [78]. Nabeela et al. [76] reported that 20% to 40% of all diseases are related to drinking water contamination resulting in annual economic losses between U.S. $0.25 and $0.58 billion.

In Pakistan, parallel water supply and sewage pipes currently lead to cross contamination and corrosion. In China, the situation is somehow similar to Pakistan where water pollution control, cross contamination between aquifers, and failure of the pipe network construction are the main concerns [14]. The public in Pakistan is unaware of pollutants such as iron, nitrates, and sulphates. Similarly, in Iran, 71% of the public are unaware of nitrates and 78% of people are largely ignorant of its corresponding health hazards [79].

Humid and warm conditions promote the growth of microbes, exaggerating water-related and waterborne diseases. In Pakistan, summers are longer than winters, and the temperature ranges between 30 °C and 45 °C in Islamabad as well as other cities of Punjab. The temperature in Pakistan is predicted to rise by about 3 °C by 2040, and between 5 °C and 6 °C by the end of this century [55,68,80]. Heavy rain and change in temperature and moisture conditions, especially in the monsoon season, encourage the spread of malaria, dengue fever, diarrhea, typhoid, and cholera [80]. Sterk et al. [81] studied the effect of climate on *Campylobacter* and *Cryptosporidium* under different climatic conditions and reported that climate change can increase the release but overall effect is limited.

Concerning Pakistan, the spread of dengue fever through viruses, which were imported into the country through tire trading and movement of travelers, is seen as a serious public health risk [82]. Climate change indirectly supports the growth of *Aedes aegyptei* larvae and adults, which cannot survive below 10 °C and below 5 °C, respectively [83].

Changes in temperature and humidity have disturbed the ecological equilibrium and contribute to new epidemics of malaria, dengue fever and other vector-related diseases [84]. There are a considerable number of studies correlating an increase in malaria with global warming. However, there is no sound evidence for this correlation [85]. Low temperature stops the growth of mosquitoes. An increase in temperature during the summer favors the growth of mosquitoes spreading malaria and dengue fever [84].

Dengue fever is endemic in Pakistan and spreads with an increase in temperature. As the temperature rises, the number of cases reported increase. Over-population as well as inadequate facilities in homes and towns, along with poor management of sewerage and water management, are the major reasons for the spread of dengue fever. Stagnant water in cities and towns provide breeding habitat for vector growth and its multiplication. Other reasons include travel and spread of viral infection from one region to another. Details of suspected cases, laboratory-confirmed cases, and deaths (confirmed by the World Health Organization in various unpublished reports) are given in Table 5.

Table 5. Dengue fever cases reported in Pakistan.

Year	Suspected Cases	Cases Laboratory-Confirmed	Deaths
2006	4961	1931	41
2007	2304	1226	18
2008	2792	2469	17
2009	1940	1085	13
2010	15,901	11,024	40
2011	252,935	17,057	219
2012	3913	639 (Karachi only)	-
2013	9037	8546	33
2014	-	504	6
2015	-	327 (Sindh)	-

Wang et al. [86] studied the variation in water quality in urban, suburban, and rural areas of Shanghai (China). They reported that well-managed urban areas have a better water quality compared to rural areas. Similarly, in Pakistan, rural areas have frequently poor water quality in comparison to the capital city Islamabad, as 90% of rural inhabitants lack access to clean water [87]. The country is facing plenty of challenges like a population boom, lack of natural resources, and no development of new reservoirs, which may lead to long-term water access per capita of less than 1000 m^3. This water shortage may get more severe in regions which are located outside the Indus basin, where the average per capita water demand is already less than this threshold [88].

According to numerous international standards, there should not be any fecal coliforms in 100-mL of drinking water. In Pakistan, the main challenge is bacteriological contamination. The years 2007 and 2011 have been the worst years in regard to dengue virus infection in Pakistan [89]. The dengue virus circulates in Pakistan throughout the year with a peak incidence in the post monsoon period. Recent floods in Pakistan made the situation worse [90]. Mashiatullah et al. [91] reported that the feeding streams of Rawal Lake in Islamabad are contaminated by bacteria. The lake provides drinking water to more than 1.5 million inhabitants in Rawalpindi. Similarly, Ahmed et al. [92,93] reported on different dams located in the Pothwar region showing contamination of water resources with fecal matter.

10. Approaches to Diminish Water-Related Impacts

This section focuses on current health challenges. Specific approaches proposed by the authors to mitigate water-related impacts partly due to climate change for countries comparable to Pakistan include the following:

1. Reducing water scarcity and pollution by changing lifestyles of individuals through education and by applying water conservation strategies, rain water harvesting, integrated sustainable water management, as the global water requirement is expected to increase by 55% in 2050. (In Pakistan, the annual water availability was 5260 m^3/capita in 1951. Due to increasing urbanization and anthropogenic activities, it is expected to be <800 m^3/capita in 2030. In comparison, the estimated figure is 1066 m^3/capita in 2015.).
2. Improving laws linked to the introduction of missing water valuation, surface water quality impacts due to climate change, groundwater challenges, and pollution control through awareness raising, and implementation of policies regarding water storage, water conservation, integrated water resources management, capacity building, and awareness raising that should be encouraged at various levels by introducing fines to reduce water scarcity and pollution problems should be encouraged [94,95].
3. Developing new and improved irrigation techniques and strategies (e.g., drip irrigation, site specific irrigation, micro-irrigation and sprinkling), crop rotation, introduction of new crop varieties, alternate crop selection [96], as well as applying innovative ideas for risk management, biodiversity enhancement, land and grazing management, water conservation, adaptation, and rehabilitation along with pollution control. Adaptation of strategies like crop management practices along soil fertility and water management are practiced due to a reduced availability of water and associated socio-economic effects [97]. Other strategies related to water management in agriculture include tunnel farming, alternate or renewable energy sources, especially pasteurized irrigation systems, gated piped irrigation, and laser land leveling [98].
4. Provision of more funds for research in biotechnology supporting the introduction of specific heat resistant, flood (or drought) tolerant, water efficient, and high yield crop varieties; adaptation of better strategies like water channels to conserve water by minimizing water evaporation and transpiration, water reuse strategies after consuming or using water, dam construction to enable water storage; minimizing the effects of water-related impacts of climate change on agriculture and health; and ensuring both water and food security [94]. Provision of funds to establish climate change research centers in agricultural departments to support highly efficient technologies to save labor and to increase yields along with optimized pollution control in the agriculture sector under changing climate scenarios is encouraged [95].

5 Involvement of national bodies and key local stakeholders, and securing their active engagement and contributions in adaptation and rehabilitation during and after disasters such as severe floods, earthquakes, heat waves, and storms. Educating farmers may be a considerable challenge when developing strategies to improve crop varieties and better breeds, which are tolerant to adverse climatic conditions like change in temperature, floods, and shift in rainfall patterns—as social barriers may limit the use of feasible measures by farmers [96,99].
6 Increasing transparent access to high quality information about water-related disasters and resulting impacts of climate change by national meteorology departments and disaster management control authorities along with provision of data for research-related projects to improve existing scenarios.
7 Increasing access to clean water sources subject to water quality assessments at specific periods, especially in flood-prone areas. This should be the top priority to avoid severe health challenges in flood affected areas.
8 Supporting the health system by improving surveillance and monitoring as well as proper disposal of sewage to avoid agricultural pollution, soil erosion, and sedimentation. Minimizing the impact and use of agriculture chemicals—like fertilizers, insecticides, pesticides, and leaching of other chemicals like toxic metals—on the enrichment of nutrients in ground water and its subsequent impacts on water quality and food security [100].
9 Improving health care facilities and availability of medicines and early responses to disasters to reduce casualties.

11. Recommendations for Further Work

To reduce the effects of climate change on health and agriculture, the following recommendations should be implemented:

1 To use this review as the basis for the development of a conceptual framework by which to consider the status of water-related impacts of climate change on agriculture and subsequently on public health in countries such as Pakistan.
2 To develop efficient and effective community-related projects to minimize the water-related impacts of climate change on agriculture and public health;
3 To build capacity and strengthen surveillance against waterborne disease outbreaks;
4 To enhance capacity and develop mechanisms for the diagnoses and control of water-related diseases;
5 To develop adaptation and mitigation strategies to improve the response to climate change-induced effects on health and agriculture;
6 To increase awareness among the general public through education, radio, TV programs, and print media;
7 To involve the community in the reduction of water and agriculture pollution, and to subsequently minimize the water-related infections originating due to climate change;
8 To develop an efficient drinking water quality monitoring scheme in order to mitigate water-related impacts of climate change and ensure a constant delivery of safe water;
9 To create assessment plans for the evaluation of community-related projects benefiting the public; and
10 To mobilize health professionals to protect the health and wellbeing of future generations via seminars, workshops, and training sessions for locals.

12. Conclusions

Climate change is likely to have a profound effect on public health, agriculture, and economy; especially on water-related impacts in terms of water quality, diseases, and changes in patterns of rain and droughts in some parts of the world including Pakistan. There is a strong link between agricultural pollution and public health.

This review highlights the need for water conservation, risk management, and the development of adaptation and mitigation strategies to cope with the water-related impacts of climate change. Different aspects regarding water-related impacts of climate change on health and agriculture have been discussed, and novel solutions and bioremediation methods have been presented to control environmental pollution and to promote public health awareness among the scientific community.

There is also a requisite to encourage regional and national authorities such as the Ministry of Climate Change and authorities working under the Ministry of Science and Technology and the Ministry of Food Security to intervene and to make changes in policies and laws with respect to climate change that affect the water, health, and agriculture sectors. Contradictory policy measures like electricity subsidies to farmers for tube wells in different provinces of Pakistan (especially in Baluchistan, where it is difficult to get water from aquifers due to low water tables) and loans for providing additional sugar mills, rather than improving existing ones, should be reconsidered. Introduction of heat resistant and flood (or drought) tolerant varieties as well as more yield- and water-efficient crop varieties, drought resistant grasses, and plants in urban areas (especially along the roadsides) should be introduced to conserve water. Development of better strategies like water channels to conserve water and dam constructions to enhance water storage are important to save Pakistan during both drought and flood events. The adaptation of more crops to the 'less drops strategy' to minimize the effects of water-related impacts due climate change on agriculture, water quality, and their subsequent health concerns should be encouraged.

Acknowledgments: The authors gratefully acknowledge the support provided by the Center for Climate Research and Development, COMSATS IIT, Islamabad, Pakistan.

Author Contributions: Wajeeha Niaz provided material considered for writing this article. Toqeer Ahmed initiated and provided the first paper draft with the support of Wajeeha Niaz, and contributed to the paper revisions. Furat Al-Faraj contributed to the first paper draft and revisions. Miklas Scholz wrote the final paper and edited all revisions.

Conflicts of Interest: The authors declare no conflict of interest. The founding sponsor had no role in the writing of the manuscript, and in the decision to publish the results.

References

1. Stanford, B.D.; Wright, B.; Routt, J.C.; Debroux, J.F.; Khan, S.J. *Water Quality Impacts of Extreme Weather-Related Events*; Water Research Foundation: Denver, CO, USA; Water Services Association of Australia: Melbourne, Australia, 2014.
2. Pollner, J.; Kryspin-Watson, J.; Nieuwejaar, S. *Disaster Risk Management and Climate Change Adaptation in Europe and Central Asia*; Global Facility for Disaster Reduction and Recovery: Washington, DC, USA; The World Bank: Washington, DC, USA, 2011.
3. Fang, C.M.; Chhetri, N. What have we learned about climate variability and human health? *Clim. Vulnerabil. Underst. Addressing Threat. Essent. Resour.* **2013**, *1*, 79–86.
4. Global Facility for Disaster Reduction and Recovery. *Building Resilience to Disasters—Delivering Results, Global Facility for Disaster Reduction and Recovery Annual Report 2011*; Global Facility for Disaster Reduction and Recovery: Washington, DC, USA, 2011.
5. McMichael, A.J.; Woodruff, R.E.; Hales, S. Climate change and human health: Present and future risks. *Lancet* **2006**, *367*, 859–869. [CrossRef]
6. Ciesielczuk, T.; Kusza, G.; Poluszyńska, J.; Kochanowska, K. Pollution of flooded arable soils with heavy metals and polycyclic aromatic hydrocarbons (PAHs). *Water Air Soil Pollut.* **2014**, *225*, 2145. [CrossRef] [PubMed]
7. Apisarnthanarak, A.; Mundy, M.L.; Khawcharoenporn, T.C.; Mayhall, C.G. Hospital infection prevention and control issues relevant to extensive floods. *Infect. Control Hosp. Epidemiol.* **2013**, *34*, 200–206. [CrossRef] [PubMed]
8. Ni, W.; Ding, G.; Li, H.; Liu, Q.; Jiang, B. Effects of the floods on dysentery in North Central Region of Henan Province, China from 2004 to 2009. *J. Infect.* **2014**, *69*, 430–439. [CrossRef] [PubMed]
9. World Health Organization. *Working Together for Health, the World Health Report*; World Health Organization: Geneva, Switzerland, 2006.

10. Ivers, L.C.; Ryan, E.T. Infectious diseases of severe weather-related and flood-related natural disasters. *Curr. Opin. Infect. Dis.* **2006**, *19*, 408–414. [CrossRef] [PubMed]
11. Greenough, G.; McGeehin, M.; Bernard, S.M.; Trtan, J.; Riad, J.; Engelberg, D. The potential impacts of climate variability and change on health impacts of extreme weather events in the United States. *Environ. Health Perspect.* **2001**, *109*, 191–198. [CrossRef] [PubMed]
12. Wright, J.; Gundry, S.; Conroy, R. Household drinking water in developing countries: A systematic review of microbiological contamination between source and point-of-use. *Int. J. Trop. Med. Health* **2004**, *9*, 106–117. [CrossRef]
13. Ullah, R.; Malik, R.N.; Qadir, A. Assessment of groundwater contamination in an industrial city, Sialkot, Pakistan. *Afr. J. Environ. Sci. Technol.* **2009**, *3*, 429–446.
14. Hu, H.; Jin, Q.; Kavan, P. A study of heavy metal pollution in China: Current status, pollution-control policies and countermeasures. *Sustainability* **2014**, *6*, 5820–5838. [CrossRef]
15. Rehman, A. Groundwater as source of contamination for water supply in rapidly growing megacities of Asia: Case of Karachi, Pakistan. *Water Sci. Technol.* **1996**, *34*, 285–292. [CrossRef]
16. Naseem, S.; Rafique, T.; Bashir, E.; Bhanger, I.M.; Laghari, A.; Usmani, H.T. Lithological influences on occurrence of high-fluoride groundwater in Nagar Parkar area, Thar Desert, Pakistan. *Chemosphere* **2010**, *78*, 1313–1321. [CrossRef] [PubMed]
17. Dahshan, H.; Abd-Elall, A.; Megahed, A. Trace metal levels in water, fish, and sediment from River Nile, Egypt: Potential health risks assessment. *J. Toxicol. Environ. Health* **2013**, *76*, 1183–1187. [CrossRef] [PubMed]
18. Vincent, P. Jeddah's environmental problems. *Geogr. Rev.* **2003**, *93*, 394–412. [CrossRef]
19. Furbey, A.K.; Apprill, A.; Cervino, M.J.; Ossolinski, E.J.; Hughan, A.K. Incidence of lesions on Fungiidae corals in the Eastern Red Sea is related to water temperature and coastal pollution. *Mar. Environ. Res.* **2010**, *98*, 29–38. [CrossRef] [PubMed]
20. McLellan, S.L.; Eren, A.M. Discovering new indicators of faecal pollution. *Trends Microbiol.* **2014**, *22*, 697–706. [CrossRef] [PubMed]
21. Edberg, S.C.; Rice, E.W.; Karlin, R.J.; Allen, M.J. *Escherichia coli*: The best biological drinking water indicator for public health protection. *J. Appl. Microbiol.* **2000**, *88*, 1068–1168. [CrossRef]
22. Wurtzer, S.; Prevost, B.; Lucas, F.S.; Moulin, L. Detection of *Enterovirus* in environmental waters: A new optimized method compared to commercial real-time RTqPCR kits. *J. Virol. Methods* **2014**, *209*, 47–54. [CrossRef] [PubMed]
23. Countinho, F.H.; Pinto, L.H.; Viera, R.P.; Martins, O.B.; Salloto, G.R.B.; Santoro, D.O.; Clementino, M.M.; Cardoso, A.M. Antibiotic resistance in aquatic environments of Rio de Janeiro, Brazil. In *INTECH Perspectives in Water Pollution 2013*; Ahmad, I., Dar, M.A., Eds.; Intech: Rijeka, Croatia, 2013.
24. Cann, K.F.; Thomas, D.R.; Salmon, R.L.; Wyn-Jones, A.P.; Kay, D. Extreme water-related weather events and waterborne disease. *Epidemiol. Infect.* **2013**, *141*, 671–686. [CrossRef] [PubMed]
25. Schwartz, B.S.; Harris, J.B.; Khan, A.I.; Larocque, R.C.; Sack, D.A.; Malek, M.A.; Faruque, A.S.G.; Qadri, F.; Calderwood, S.B.; Luby, S.P.; et al. Diarrheal epidemics in Dhaka, Bangladesh, during three consecutive floods: 1988, 1998, and 2004. *Am. J. Trop. Med. Hyg.* **2006**, *74*, 1067–1073. [PubMed]
26. Hunter, R.P. Climate change, waterborne and vector borne disease. *J. Appl. Microbiol.* **2013**, *94*, S37–S46. [CrossRef]
27. Luber, G. *Climate Change Adaptation in the Public Health Sector: The BRACE Framework. The Public Health Effects of Climate Change*; Centers for Disease Control and Prevention/National Center for Environmental Health: Atlanta, GA, USA, 2011.
28. Haines, A.; Kovats, R.S.; Campbell-Lendrum, D.; Corvalan, C. Climate change and human health: Impacts, vulnerability and public health. *Public Health* **2006**, *120*, 585–596. [CrossRef] [PubMed]
29. Crampton, A.; Ragusa, A.T. Perceived agricultural runoff impact on drinking water. *J. Water Health* **2014**, *2*, 484–491. [CrossRef] [PubMed]
30. Khan, Z.I.; Ahmad, K.; Ashraf, M. Assessment of potential toxicological risk for public health of heavy metals in wheat crop irrigated with wastewater: A case study in Sargodha, Pakistan. *Asian J. Chem.* **2013**, *25*, 9704–9706.
31. Antonio-Nkondjio, C.; Fossog, B.T.; Ndo, C.; Djantio, B.M.; Togouet, S.Z.; Awono-Ambene, P.; Costantini, C.; Wondji, C.S.; Ranson, H. *Anopheles gambiae* distribution and insecticide resistance in the cities of Douala and Yaoundé (Cameroon): Influence of urban agriculture and pollution. *Malar. J.* **2011**, *10*, 154–167. [CrossRef] [PubMed]

32. Biemans, H.; Speelman, L.H.; Ludwig, F.; Moors, E.J. Future water resources for food production in five South Asian river basins and potential for adaptation—A modeling study. *Sci. Total Environ.* **2013**, *468–469*, S117–S131. [CrossRef] [PubMed]
33. Lal, R. Food security in a changing climate. *Ecohydrol. Hydrobiol.* **2013**, *13*, 8–21. [CrossRef]
34. Ashofteh, P.; Haddad, O.; Mariño, M. Risk analysis of water demand for agricultural crops under climate change. *J. Hydrol. Eng.* **2015**, *20*, 04014060. [CrossRef]
35. Bandara, J.S.; Cai, Y. The impact of climate change on food crop productivity, food prices and food security in South Asia. *Econ. Anal. Policy* **2014**, *44*, 451–465. [CrossRef]
36. Hussain, S.S.; Mudasser, M. Prospects for wheat production under changing climate in mountain areas of Pakistan—An econometric analysis. *Agric. Syst.* **2007**, *94*, 494–501. [CrossRef]
37. Manyi-Loh, C.E.; Mamphweli, S.N.; Meyer, E.L.; Okoh, A.I.; Makaka, G.; Simon, M. Microbial anaerobic digestion (bio-digesters) as an approach to the decontamination of animal wastes in pollution control and the generation of renewable energy. *Int. J. Environ. Res. Public Health* **2013**, *10*, 4390–4417. [CrossRef] [PubMed]
38. Kabo-Bah, T.A.; Yuebo, X. The role of bacteria as a cure for polluted rivers in Africa. *J. Pure Appl. Microbiol.* **2013**, *7*, 2271–2275.
39. Salt, D.E.; Blaylock, M.; Kumar, N.P.B.A.; Dushenkov, V.; Ensley, B.D.; Chet, I.; Raskin, I. Phytoremediation: A novel strategy for the removal of toxic metals from the environment using plants. *Biotechnology* **1995**, *13*, 468–474. [CrossRef] [PubMed]
40. Ponnusami, V.; Vikram, S.; Srivastava, S.N. Guava (*Psidium guajava*) Leaf powder: Novel adsorbent for removal of methylene blue from aqueous solutions. *J. Hazard. Mater.* **2008**, *152*, 276–286. [CrossRef] [PubMed]
41. Ahmed, T.; Kanwal, R.; Hassan, M.; Ayub, N.; Scholz, M.; McMinn, W.R. Coagulation and disinfection in water treatment using *Moringa oleifera*. *Proc. ICE Water Manag.* **2010**, *163*, 381–388.
42. Ahmed, T.; Pervez, A.; Mehtab, M.; Sherwani, S.K. Assessment of drinking water quality and its potential health impacts in academic institutions of Abbottabad (Pakistan). *Desalin. Water Treat.* **2015**, *54*, 1819–1828. [CrossRef]
43. Belkin, S. Microbial whole-cell sensing systems of environmental pollutants. *Curr. Opin. Microbiol.* **2003**, *6*, 206–212. [CrossRef]
44. Edmundson, M.C.; Capeness, M.; Horsfall, L. Exploring the potential of metallic nanoparticles within synthetic biology. *New Biotechnol.* **2014**, *31*, 572–578. [CrossRef] [PubMed]
45. Zouboulism, A.I.; Loukidou, M.X.; Matis, K.A. Biosorption of toxic metals from aqueous solutions by bacteria strains isolated from metal-polluted soils. *Proc. Biochem.* **2004**, *39*, 909–916. [CrossRef]
46. Khasaeva, F.; Vasilyuk, N.; Terentyev, P.; Troshina, M.; Lebedev, A.T. A Novel soil bacterial strain degrading pyridines. *Environ. Chem. Lett.* **2011**, *9*, 439–445. [CrossRef]
47. Wang, Q.; Xie, S. Isolation and characterization of a high-efficiency soil atrazine-degrading *Arthrobacter* sp. Strain. *Inter. Biodeterior. Biodegrad.* **2012**, *71*, 61–66. [CrossRef]
48. Ahmed, T.; Imdad, S.; Ashraf, S.; Butt, N.M. Effect of size and surface ligands of silver (Ag) nanoparticles on waterborne bacteria. *Int. J. Theor. Appl. Trans.* **2013**, *1*, 111–116. [CrossRef]
49. Ahmed, T.; Imdad, S.; Butt, N.M. Bacteriological assessment of drinking water of Islamabad Capital Territory. *Desalin. Water Treat.* **2014**, 1–7. [CrossRef]
50. Haines, A.; Bruce, N.; Cairncross, S.; Davies, M.; Greenland, K.; Hiscox, A.; Lindsay, S.; Lindsay, T.; Satterthwaite, D.; Wilkinson, P. Promoting health and advancing development through improved housing in low-income settings. *J. Urban Health* **2012**, *90*, 810–831. [CrossRef] [PubMed]
51. Cordell, D.; Rosemarin, A.; Schröder, J.J.; Smit, L.A. Towards global phosphorus security: A systems framework for phosphorus recovery and reuse options. *Chemosphere* **2011**, *84*, 747–758. [CrossRef] [PubMed]
52. Ren, X.; Chen, C.; Nagatsu, M.; Wang, X. Carbon nanotubes as absorbent in environmental pollution management: A review. *Chem. Eng. J.* **2010**, *170*, 395–410. [CrossRef]
53. Gan, N.; Zhang, J.; Lin, S.; Long, N.; Cao, Y. A novel magnetic graphene oxide composite absorbent for removing trace residues of polybrominateddiphenyl ethers in water. *Materials* **2014**, *7*, 6028–6044. [CrossRef]
54. Zhu, J.; Wei, S.; Chen, M.; Gu, H.; Rapole, S.B.; Pallavkar, S.; Ho, T.C.; Hopper, J.; Guo, Z. Magnetic, nanocomposites for environmental remediation. *Adv. Powder Technol.* **2013**, *24*, 459–467. [CrossRef]
55. Bates, B.; Kundzewicz, Z.W.; Wu, S.; Palutikof, J. *Climate Change and Water WMO, Technical Paper VI*; Intergovernmental Panel on Climate Change: Geneva, Switzerland, 2008.

56. Delpa, A.V.; Jung, E.; Baures, M.; Clement, E.; Thomas, O. Impacts of climate change on surface water quality in relation to drinking water production. *Environ. Int.* **2009**, *35*, 1225–1233. [CrossRef] [PubMed]
57. Solheinm, A.L.; Austnes, K.; Eriksen, T.E.; Seifert, I.; Holen, S. *Climate Change Impacts on Water Quality and Biodiversity, Background Report for EEA European Environment State and Outlook Report*; European Topic Centre on Water: Prague, Czech Republic, 2010.
58. Vermeij, W.; van der Wiele, J.; van Moorselaar, I.; van der Grinten, E. *Impact of Climate Change on Water Quality in The Netherlands*; RIVM rapport 6078000072010; National Institute for Public Health and Environment: Bilthoven, The Netherlands, 2010.
59. Jalliffier-Verne, I.; Leconte, R.; Huaringa-Alvarez, U.; Madoux-Humery, A.S.; Galarneau, M.; Servais, P.; Prévost, M.; Dorner, S. Impacts of global change on the concentrations and dilution of combined sewer overflows in a drinking water source. *Sci. Total Environ.* **2015**, *508*, 462–476. [CrossRef] [PubMed]
60. Ghaleni, M.M.; Ebrahimi, K. Effects of human activities and climate variability on water resources in the Saveh Plain, Iran. *Environ. Monit. Assess.* **2015**, *187*, 35–39. [CrossRef] [PubMed]
61. Marengo, J.A.; Nobre, C.A.; Sampaio, G.; Salazar, L.F.; Borma, L.S. Climate change in the Amazon basin: Tipping points, changes in extremes, and impacts on natural and human systems. In *Tropical Rainforest Responses to Climatic Change*; Springer: Berlin/Heidelberg, Germany, 2011; pp. 259–283.
62. Driessen, A.L.T.; Ledden, V.M. The large-scale impact of climate change to Mississippi flood hazard in New Orleans. *Drink. Water Eng. Sci.* **2013**, *6*, 81–87. [CrossRef]
63. Allard, M.; Bourque, A.; Chaumont, D.; Des Jarlais, C.; Gosselin, P.; Houle, D.; Larrivée, C.; Lease, N.; Roy, R.; Savard, J.P.R.; et al. *Ouranos: Savoir S'adapter Aux Changements Climatiques*; Ouranos: Montréal, QC, Canada, 2010; p. 128.
64. Pall, E.; Niculae, M.; Kiss, M.T.; Sandru, C.D.; Spinu, M. Human impact on the microbiological water quality of the rivers. *J. Med. Microbiol.* **2013**, *62*, 1635–1640. [CrossRef] [PubMed]
65. Chou, R. Addressing watercourse sanitation in dense, water pollution-affected urban areas in Taiwan. *Environ. Urban* **2013**, *25*, 523–540. [CrossRef]
66. Scholz, M. *Wetlands for Water Pollution Control*, 2nd ed.; Elsevier: Amsterdam, The Netherlands, 2015.
67. Patz, J.A. Public health risk assessment linked to climatic and ecological change. *Hum. Ecol. Risk Assess.* **2001**, *7*, 1317–1327. [CrossRef]
68. Intergovernmental Panel on Climate Change. *Climate Change 2007: The Physical Science Basis. Contribution of Working Group I to the Fourth Assessment Report of the Intergovernmental Panel on Climate Change*; Cambridge University Press: Cambridge, UK, 2007.
69. Sajjad, M.; Rahim, S.; Tahir, S.S. Chemical quality of groundwater in Rawalpindi/Islamabad. *Water Eng. Dev. Cent.* **1998**, *24*, 271–274.
70. Tornevi, A.; Bergstedt, O.; Forsberg, B. Precipitation effects on microbial pollution in a river: Lag structures and seasonal effect modification. *PLoS ONE* **2014**, *9*, 98546–98556. [CrossRef] [PubMed]
71. Thomas, K.M.; Charron, D.F.; Waltner-Toews, D.; Schuster, C.; Maarouf, A.R.; Holt, J.D. A role of high impact weather events in waterborne disease outbreaks in Canada, 1975–2001. *Int. J. Environ. Health Res.* **2007**, *16*, 167–180. [CrossRef] [PubMed]
72. Onozuka, D.; Hashizume, M.; Hagihara, A. Effects of weather variability on infectious Gastroenteritis. *Epidemiol. Infect.* **2010**, *138*, 236–243. [CrossRef] [PubMed]
73. Cantor, K.P. Drinking water and cancer. *Cancer Causes Control* **1997**, *8*, 292–308. [CrossRef] [PubMed]
74. Farooq, S.; Hashmi, I.; Qazi, I.A.; Qaiser, S.; Rasheed, S. Monitoring of coliforms and chlorine residual in water distribution network of Rawalpindi, Pakistan. *Environ. Monit. Assess.* **2008**, *140*, 339–347. [CrossRef] [PubMed]
75. Ren, H.; Wan, X.; Yang, F.; Shi, X.; Xu, J.; Zhuang, D.; Yang, G. Association between changing mortality of digestive tract cancers and water pollution: A case study in the Huai River Basin, China. *Int. J. Environ. Res. Public Health* **2015**, *12*, 214–226. [CrossRef] [PubMed]
76. Nabeela, F.; Azizullah, A.; Bibi, R.; Uzma, S.; Murad, W.; Shakir, S.K.; Ullah, W.; Qasim, M.; Hader, D. Microbial contamination of drinking water in Pakistan—A review. *Environ. Sci. Pollut. Res.* **2014**, *21*, 13929–13942. [CrossRef] [PubMed]
77. Fewtrell, L. Drinking-water nitrate, Methemoglobinemia, and global burden of disease: A discussion. *Environ. Health Perspect.* **2004**, *112*, 1371–1374. [CrossRef]

78. Azizullah, A.; Khattak, K.N.M.; Richter, P.; Hader, D. Water pollution in Pakistan and its impact on public health—A review. *Environ. Int.* **2011**, *37*, 479–497. [CrossRef] [PubMed]
79. Azadegan, M.M.; Moghaddam, A.R.M.; Maknoon, R. Public awareness and performance regarding nitrate pollution in nitrate-polluted area of Tehran, Iran. *Environ. Eng. Manag. J.* **2014**, *13*, 611–617.
80. International Union for Conservation of Nature. *Climate Change: Vulnerabilities in Agriculture in Pakistan*; International Union for Conservation of Nature: Karachi, Pakistan, 2009.
81. Sterk, A.; Schijven, J.; de Roda Husman, A.M.; de Nijs, T. Effect of climate change on runoff of *Campylobacter* and *Cryptosporidium* from land to surface water. *Water Res.* **2016**, *95*, 90–102. [CrossRef] [PubMed]
82. Rasheed, S.B.; Butlin, R.K.; Boots, M. A review of Dengue as an emerging disease in Pakistan. *Public Health* **2013**, *127*, 11–17. [CrossRef] [PubMed]
83. Suleman, M.; Arshad, M.; Khan, K. Yellow fever mosquito (Diptera: Culicidae) introduced into Landi Kotal, Pakistan, by tire importation. *J. Med. Entomol.* **1996**, *33*, 689–693. [CrossRef] [PubMed]
84. Brower, V. Vector-borne diseases and global warming: Are both on an upward swing? *EMBO Rep.* **2001**, *2*, 755–757. [CrossRef] [PubMed]
85. Nabi, S.A.; Qader, S.S. Is global warming likely to cause an increased incidence of Malaria? *Libyan J. Med.* **2009**, *4*, 18–22. [CrossRef] [PubMed]
86. Wang, J.; Da, L.; Song, K.; Li, B. Temporal variations of surface water quality in urban, suburban and rural areas during rapid urbanization in Shanghai, China. *Environ. Pollut.* **2008**, *152*, 387–393. [CrossRef] [PubMed]
87. Pakistan Council for Research in Water Resources. *National Water Quality Monitoring Programme, Water Quality Report 2003–2004*; Pakistan Council for Research in Water Resources: Islamabad, Pakistan, 2005.
88. Pakistan Environmental Protection Agency. *State of Environment Report Pakistan*; Environmental Protection Agency, Ministry of Environment, Government of Pakistan: Islamabad, Pakistan, 2005.
89. Nasreen, S.; Arshad, M.; Ashraf, M.; Raza, A.; Bahar-e-Mustafa. The epidemiology of Dengue fever in district Faisalabad, Pakistan. *Int. J. Sci. Res. Publ.* **2015**, *5*, 1–6.
90. Idrees, S.; Ashfaq, U.A. A brief review on Dengue molecular virology, diagnosis, treatment and prevalence in Pakistan, Genet. *Vaccines Ther.* **2012**, *10*, 1–10.
91. Mashiatullah, A.; Chaudhary, M.Z.; Khan, M.S.; Javed, T.; Qureshi, R.M. Coliform bacterial pollution in Rawal Lake, Islamabad and its feeding streams/river. *Nucleus* **2010**, *47*, 35–40.
92. Ahmed, T.; Kanwal, R.; Hassan, M.; Ayub, N. Assessment of antibacterial activity of *Solanum surrattense* against water-borne pathogens isolated from surface water of Pothwar Region in Pakistan. *Int. J. Hum. Ecol. Risk Assess.* **2009**, *15*, 624–635. [CrossRef]
93. Ahmed, T.; Kanwal, R.; Tahir, S.S.; Rauf, N. Bacteriological analysis of water collected from different dams of Rawalpindi/Islamabad region in Pakistan. *Pak. J. Biol. Sci.* **2004**, *7*, 662–666.
94. Khan, M.A.; Khan, J.A.; Ahmad, Z.; Ahmad, M.N. The challenge of climate change and policy response in Pakistan. *Environ. Earth Sci.* **2016**, *75*, 412. [CrossRef]
95. Ministry of Environment. *National Climate Change Policy in Pakistan*; Government of Pakistan: Islamabad, Pakistan, 2011.
96. Evans, R.G.; Sadler, E.J. Methods and technologies to improve efficiency of water use. *Water Resour. Res.* **2008**, *44*, 1944–1973. [CrossRef]
97. Habib, N.; Anwer, M.Z.; Naheed, S.; Hassan, T. Identification of local climate change adaptation strategies for water management in districts Attock and Chakwal, Pakistan. *Sci. Technol. Dev.* **2015**, *34*, 255–259. [CrossRef]
98. South Asian Conservation Agriculture Network, Water Management Practices in Pakistan, Issue and Options for Productivity Enhancement. World Bank Resources. Available online: http://siteresources.worldbank.org/PAKISTANEXTN/Resources/WMPracticesinPakistan.pdf (accessed on 15 September 2016).
99. Iglesias, A.; Garrote, L. Adaptation strategies for agricultural water management under climate change in Europe. *Agric. Water Manag.* **2015**, *155*, 113–124.
100. FAO Cooperation Document Repository, Control of Water Pollution from Agriculture, Natural Resources Management and Environment Department. Available online: http://www.fao.org/docrep/w2598e/w2598e04.htm (accessed on 16 September 2016).

International Journal of
Environmental Research and Public Health

MDPI

Review

Climatic Conditions: Conventional and Nanotechnology-Based Methods for the Control of *Mosquito* Vectors Causing Human Health Issues

Toqeer Ahmed [1], Muhammad Zeeshan Hyder [2], Irfan Liaqat [1,2] and Miklas Scholz [3,4,5,*]

1 Centre for Climate Research and Development (CCRD), COMSATS University Islamabad, Park Road, Chak Shahzad, Tarlai Kalan 45550, Islamabad, Pakistan
2 Department of Biosciences, COMSATS University Islamabad, Park Road, Chak Shahzad, Tarlai Kalan 45550, Islamabad, Pakistan
3 Division of Water Resources Engineering, Faculty of Engineering, Lund University, P.O. Box 118, 221 00 Lund, Sweden
4 Department of Civil Engineering Science, School of Civil Engineering and the Built Environment, University of Johannesburg, Kingsway Campus, P.O. Box 524, Aukland Park 2006, Johannesburg, South Africa
5 Civil Engineering Research Group, School of Science, Engineering and Environment, The University of Salford, Newton Building, Salford M5 4WT, UK
* Correspondence: miklas.scholz@tvrl.lth.se; Tel.: +46-222-8920; Fax: +46-222-4435

Received: 10 July 2019; Accepted: 27 August 2019; Published: 30 August 2019

Abstract: Climate variability is highly impacting on *mosquito*-borne diseases causing malaria and dengue fever across the globe. Seasonal variability change in temperature and rainfall patterns are impacting on human health. *Mosquitoes* cause diseases like dengue fever, yellow fever, malaria, Chikungunya, West Nile and Japanese encephalitis. According to estimations by health organizations, annually one million human deaths are caused by vector-borne diseases, and dengue fever has increased about 30-fold over the past 50 years. Similarly, over 200 million cases of malaria are being reported annually. *Mosquito*-borne diseases are sensitive to temperature, humidity and seasonal variability. Both conventional (environmental, chemical, mechanical, biological etc.) and nanotechnology-based (Liposomes, nano-suspensions and polymer-based nanoparticles) approaches are used for the eradication of Malaria and dengue fever. Now green approaches are used to eradicate *mosquitoes* to save human health without harming the environment. In this review, the impact of climatic conditions on *mosquito*-borne diseases along with conventional and nanotechnology-based approaches used for controlling malaria and dengue fever have been discussed. Important recommendations have been made for people to stay healthy.

Keywords: climate change; dengue fever; environmental management; eradication of vectors; human health; *mosquito*-borne diseases; malaria; nanotechnology-based disease control approaches; traditional disease control; public health risk

---

1. Introduction

Vectors are the organisms responsible for the transmission of communicable diseases from faunas to human beings or among humans. The best-known vector for such diseases is the *mosquito*. Others may include flies, ticks, sand flies, triatomine bugs, fleas and aquatic snails [1]. The diseases caused by these vectors cause above one million of human deaths yearly. These diseases account for over 17% of the infectious/transmittable diseases [2]. In tropical countries, some vector-borne diseases are still ignored; e.g., lymphatic filariasis, dengue fever, Leishmaniasis, Human African Trypanosomiasis and Schistosomiasis [3]. There are about 3.9 billion people at risk of having dengue fever and 96 million cases of dengue are reported every year in 128 prevalent countries. It follows that almost half of the world's population is at risk [4]. The prevalence of dengue fever has increased by 30-fold in the past 50 years. In 2017, the estimated malaria cases and corresponding deaths occurred were 219 million and 435,000 respectively, comprising almost 90% of sub-Saharan Africa [5]. In the South-east Asia Region, many of the vector-borne diseases are prevalent, including some *mosquito*-borne diseases such as malaria, dengue, chikungunya, Japanese encephalitis and lymphatic filariasis, snail-transmitted disease (schistosomiasis) and the sand-fly borne disease (kalaazar). Malaria is prevalent in many tropical and subtropical regions of the world excluding the Maldives, which is officially stated as being malaria-free [6].

As the globe is continuously facing climate change challenges, *mosquitoes* are benefitting from this competition. As temperatures are getting warmer, the range of disease-carrying *mosquitoes* is increasing. The increased temperature allows them to breed quicker. *Mosquitoes* may breed all-year-round in warm areas. Warm temperatures facilitate the increase in hatching and reproduction rates of *mosquitoes* [7,8]. In South-east Asia, frequent epidemics with hundreds of thousands of reported and unreported cases have arisen during the past decade, resulting in significant numbers of deaths. Countries that are more severely affected such as Pakistan, India, Bangladesh and Sri Lanka can be seen as victims of climate change in terms of *mosquito* population increases. The risk factors of these vector-borne diseases that may cause corresponding epidemics are poor sanitation, low cleanliness, climate change and the lack of efficient vector control approaches [9,10].

An increase in epidemics of Dengue is due to the absence of active gene therapy or vaccines for its control. The only reliable control approach for these diseases is their prevention and control through source reduction and insecticides. As the *mosquitoes* are developing resistance against the insecticides, the prime focus of the scientific community is to find new ways of eradicating *mosquito* populations. The purpose of this study is to assess the existing conventional and novel eradication methods and techniques, which are being used in different countries of the world to eradicate or control vectors and diseases transmitted by such vectors. Moreover, this review identifies missing gaps in the management of vectors, especially malaria and dengue fever, and approaches to manage increases in temperature due to a changing climate.

2. Methodology

Peer-reviewed published research papers and reports along with grey literature were selected from 1981 to 2019 (39 Years). Literature was collected from the world-renowned databases ISI Web of Knowledge (http://isiknowledge.com), Science Direct (http://www.sciencedirect.com), Scopus (https://www.scopus.com) and Google Scholar (https://scholar.google.com.pk). Relevant literature was designated on the basis of inclusion and exclusion criteria; i.e., relevance of literature to the study area on the basis of keywords used. Preference was given to the publication years 1990–2019. The search was curtained by using the following keywords: malaria; dengue fever; Chikungunya; Zika virus; Yellow fever; climate change; health impacts of *mosquito*-borne diseases; temperature and precipitation effects; conventional control methods for *mosquito*; and nanotechnology-based methods.

According to the exclusion criterion, literature items, which did not fulfil the above criterion were deleted (Figure 1). Literature was reviewed and properly cited to acknowledge previous studies. The author followed all steps of the methodology proposed by The Preferred Reporting Items for Systematic Reviews and Meta-Analyses (PRISMA) Group [11]. PRISMA is an evidence-based minimum set of items for reporting in systematic reviews and meta-analyses. PRISMA can be used as a basis for reporting systematic literature reviews.

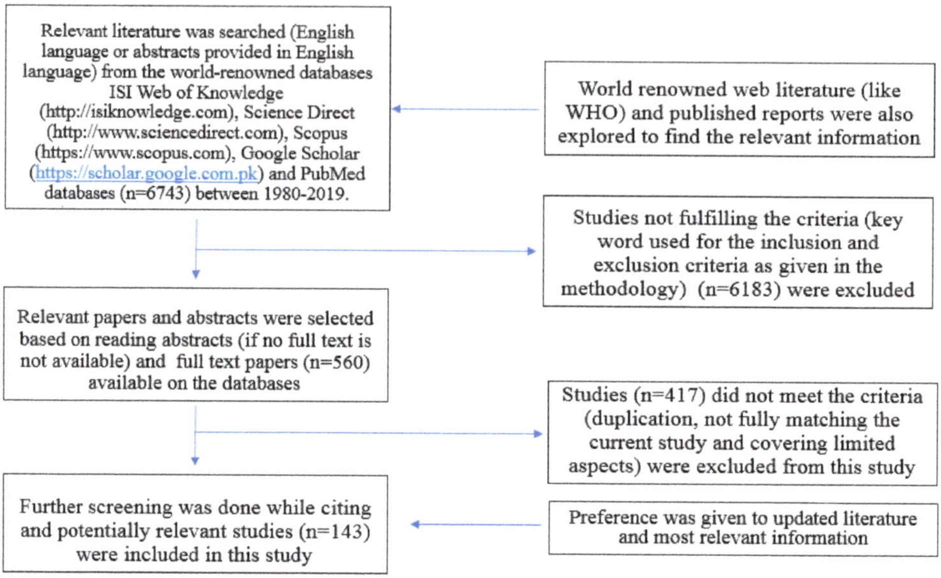

Figure 1. PRISMA Diagram showing the literature search strategy.

3. Results

3.1. Climatic Conditions Influence on Mosquito Vectors

3.1.1. Seasonality of Infectious Diseases

A high number of vector-borne diseases like dengue fever and malaria express substantial seasonal patterns around the world. Most of the insects including *mosquitoes* are poikilothermic ectotherm whose internal temperature is dependent on the ambient temperature of the environment [12]. Researchers described the relationship between water temperature and development rate that is analogous for eggs, larvae and pupae of the insects [13]. An increase in ambient temperature is linked to the increased metabolism of the *mosquitoes*. The transmission of the *mosquito*-borne diseases is at a maximum at higher temperature due to an increased rate of pupation, blood meals and a reduced extrinsic incubation period [12,14]. Similarly, optimum rainfall and precipitation is also linked to the growth and development of *mosquitoes*; and viral replication within the vector [14]. In Peru, a peak of infection with Cyclospora is seen in summer, which subsides in winter. During hot and dry seasons, other infections tend to rise, but decrease at the beginning of the rainy spell in, for example, Africa [15,16].

3.1.2. Vector-Borne Diseases

There are few vector-borne pathogens in the transmission of diseases [17] that may include:

- The reproduction and survival rates of vectors in a certain environment.
- The level and degree of vector-activity; typically, the rate of biting and the period of year.
- Reproduction and development rate of pathogens inside the vector.

The reproduction and survival of pathogens, hosts and vectors is dependent on specific climatic circumstances. Any fluctuation in such conditions may affect the rate of disease transmission. Among these finest environmental conditions for vector-borne diseases, temperature and humidity are the most significant climatic factors while the airstream, daylight duration and elevation of sea level are supplementary vital considerations [18]. Table 1 shows a summary of climatic change impacts to each biotic element of vector-borne illnesses.

3.1.3. Temperature Sensitivity

Extreme temperatures are mostly fatal for the survival and persistence of pathogens, but any incremental fluctuation in temperature could have varying effects. A slight rise in temperature may become deadly to the disease-causing agent, if a vector is subjected to an environmental condition such as mean temperature, which is approaching the edge of physiological tolerance for the infective agents or pathogens. On the other hand, if a vector lives in an atmosphere of comparatively lower mean temperature, an insignificant rise in temperature can accelerate the growth and replication of pathogens [19,20]. Temperature and development time are inversely correlated, and the optimum growth ranges from 22 to 32 °C [21,22].

The growth rate of a vector may also be modified by temperature due to changing their rates of biting and frequency of interaction with humans. Ultimately, a swing in temperature determines the span of transmission season [23]. Vectors can also adapt to the variations in temperature by shifting geographical distributions. The incidences of malaria in cooler environmental zones of African highlands can be the consequence of shifting habitats of *mosquitoes* to survive with augmented air temperatures [24]. Additionally, the vectors can also evolve in response to increase in temperatures. Recent evidence suggests that some vectors like the pitcher plant *mosquito* (*Wyeomyia smithii* Coquillett) has the ability to genetically adapt with climate change to survive for a longer period of time [8].

3.1.4. Precipitation Sensitivity

Changeability in precipitation has straight consequences on the outbreaks of infectious diseases. Increase in precipitation elevates the incidence of vectors by growing the magnitude of current larval habitation and generating new breeding lands [8]. In addition, this increase in precipitation can also favour the growth in food materials, which ultimately supports a larger population of vertebrate reservoirs. Flooding and decrease in vector population may be triggered by unusually heavy rainfall. On the other hand, flooding may increase the probability of vector human contact. In Brazil, leptospirosis (rodent-borne disease) outbreaks have been reported after extreme flooding [25]. Unexpected droughts may cause rivers to slow in wet tropics, creating additional areas of stagnant water, which is perfect for vector-breeding sites.

3.1.5. Humidity Sensitivity

The spreading of vector-borne illnesses can be greatly affected by humidity as well. The spreading of *mosquitoes*, which are also reliant on relative humidity, determines the extent of disease transmission [26]. The relative humidity is not only a limiting factor in those areas where it is more than 60%, but also temperature is considered as a main driver [27]. The survival rate of *mosquitoes* decreases in dry conditions as they can easily desiccate. Water saturation shortage as indicated by relative humidity remains the most critical factor in disease/climate models; e.g., Lyme disease models and dengue fever [23].

Table 1. Climate change impacts on vector-borne diseases [23].

Impacts of Temperature on Certain Vectors and Vector-Borne Pathogens	Impacts of Changes in Precipitation on Vector-Borne Pathogens	Impacts of Higher Sea Level on Vector-Borne Pathogens
Vector • Vector survival can increase or decrease depending on species [8]. • Some vectors have an increased survival rate at higher temperatures, higher altitudes and latitudes [28]. • Vector susceptibility to some pathogens varies (e.g., an increase in temperature lessens the size and lowers the activity of some vectors) [29]. • Vector population's growth rate can be changed [30]. • Fluctuations in rate of feeding and host contact can change the survival rate. • Alteration in population's seasonality [31].	*Vector* • Larval habitat and population size may increase due to the increased rain by providing new habitat. • Snowpack and excess rain can eradicate habitat due to flooding (declining vector population). • Lower rainfall can provide habitat by triggering rivers to dry into pools, resulting in dry season malaria. • Lower rainfall can lead to a rise of container-breeding *mosquitoes* by imposed increased water storage. [27,32] • Longer rainfall events can coordinate vector host-seeking and transmission of virus. • Increased humidity can influence vector survival. [33]	*Vector* Reducing or eradicating breeding sites of *mosquitoes* (e.g., *Cs. melanura*). The relationship between vector biology and climatic conditions is complex due to the natural capability of vectors to seek out appropriate microclimates for their survival such as hiding places under vegetation, pit toilets during hot or dry weather and tunnels during cold weather [23].
Pathogen • At higher temperatures, decrease in extrinsic incubation period of pathogens [34]. • Variations in transmission season. • Variations in distribution. • Lower viral replication [29].	*Pathogen* • Some direct effects but humidity significantly impacts on the malaria-causing parasite growth in the host (anopheline *mosquito*) [35].	
	Vertebrate host • High rainfall can influence vegetation, food accessibility. and size of population. • Elevated rainfall can cause flooding, which leads to a reduced population size but increases human contact.	

3.1.6. Sea Level Sensitivity

At the end of the 21st century, global warming is projected to increase sea levels by 18 to 59 cm through polar ice, melting of glaciers and the thermal expansion of seawater [36]. The increase in sea level related to the change in climate results in the elimination or reduction of breeding sites for coastal wetland *mosquitoes*. Mammalian and bird hosts that reside in such environmental niches can also be endangered, which support the removal of viruses prevalent in this environment [37]. Otherwise, local invasion of salty water may turn previous freshwater wetlands into coastal ones that help to host vector species evacuated from prior coastal wetland habitats [23].

Vector-borne microbes spend much of their life cycle in cold-blooded arthropods that are subjected to various environmental influences. The transmission of vector-borne diseases affected by climatic factors includes rainfall, temperature, extreme flooding, wind and sea level rise. Flooding can dislocate and lead them to seek out food and shelter [38].

3.2. *Mosquito-Borne Diseases and Health Impacts*

3.2.1. Vector-Host Relationships

It is necessary to understand the relationship between disease transmission and the connection of vectors/*mosquitoes* in the transmission of pathogens. Mechanical pathogen transmission is mainly accidental. In physically transmitted diseases, a pathogen that causes a disease needs support to move from one host to another. The arthropod obtains the pathogen from one host. The pathogen then grows in the body of the arthropod and is conveyed to another host. Within the invertebrate, the pathogen may or may not reproduce. If the parasite that causes the disease endures the sexual part of its lifecycle in a host, that host is known as the definitive or primary host (as in the case of *mosquitoes* that cause malaria). In case of malaria, a human is the transitional host in which the asexual phases of the parasite are found [39].

3.2.2. Diseases Transmitted by the *Mosquito* Vectors

Mosquitoes act as vectors for different diseases, which transfer them from one person to another. Some of these diseases have high mortality and wide distribution. Around 28 viruses, which have a major importance in public health, are transmitted by different *mosquitoes*. Arboviruses are transmitted by *mosquito* bites. Yellow fever and Dengue fever are transmitted by *Ae.* spp., while some kinds of Encephalitis are transmitted by *Culex* spp. and by *Ae.* spp. [40,41]. Malaria is a prime disease transmitted by several species of *Anopheles*, which carry an infective form of a protozoan parasite called *Plasmodium*. It may also be transmitted by *Anophels quadrimaculatus*. *Anophels hermsi* and *Anophels freeborni* are major vectors, while *Anophels Crucians* is a minor one. Malaria is one of the serious and lethal diseases around the globe affecting millions of people mostly in tropical and semi-tropical areas.

Five species of malarial parasites (*Plasmodium falciparum*, *Plasmodium malariae*, *Plasmodium vivax*, *Plasmodium ovale*, *Plasmodium knowlesi*) are responsible for malaria in humans. Most common signs include severe headache, fever, sweating, vomiting and chills nausea. Parasites first enter the liver and then destroy red blood cells causing anemia and weakness. In complicated cases, there could be kidney and brain damage resulting in renal catastrophe, encephalitis, shock, coma and death [37].

For dengue fever, *Ae. aegypti* and *Ae. albopictus* are central vectors in human-to-human transmission. Dengue viruses are endemic in tropical areas while its highly endemic in other areas. Symptoms of dengue fever include skin rash, pain behind the eyes, severe headache, fever as well as muscle and bone pain (thus also named as break bone fever). Recovery form dengue fever is long, but death is seldom. Each of the four strains provides lifelong immunity against the virus, but exposure to the second strain may result in the dengue shock syndrome and dengue haemorrhagic fever, which are much severe than dengue [38].

The Yellow fever virus is transmitted from some forest monkeys to humans by a vector. *Ae. aegypti* and *Ae. albopictus* can transmit the virus in urban areas, while *Oc. japonicus* may also act as potential vector. The symptoms it causes closely resemble those of the dengue fever, which includes fever, backache, headache, jaundice and internal bleeding, which can lead to death [39].

The West Nile Fever is caused by the West Nile virus and transmitted via *Culex* spp. (*mosquito*). It is a type of encephalitis and may also be called arboviral encephalitis. The virus is transmitted via the *mosquito* to their main reservoir host (usually birds). Horses and humans are rather accidental hosts. The symptoms of the West Nile fever include fever, vomiting, headache and swollen lymph nodes. In complicated cases, it may involve the central nerves system [39].

This is caused by the arbovirus, which is spread through *Culex tritaeniorhynchus* (*mosquito*). The virus is transferred from pigs or birds, which are their main hosts. Like the West Nile fever, horses and humans are accidental hosts. General symptoms include headache, fever, stupor, disorientation and loss of coordination. It may also lead to paralysis, seizures, coma and death [40].

These viruses may cause encephalitis and are transferred to humans by biting of humans accidently, and thus giving a dead-end host as the vectors cannot take the virus back form the human host. It involves a transmission cycle (similar to arboviruses) from birds or small mammals, which are the primary hosts. Some people are asymptomatic, some may get mild flu-like symptoms like headache and high fever. In some of the cases, people may get encephalitis disturbing the central nervous system, which may result in paralysis, seizures, coma and death [37].

The Alpha virus, which belongs to the family Togaviridae is the causing agent of Chikungunya. It is transmitted by bites of infected *mosquitoes* to humans. *Ae. aegypti* and *Ae. albopictus* are the main agents. Symptoms associated with Chikungunya include headache, nausea, vomiting, skin rash, fever and chills. Some patients may have pain in their joints [40].

3.2.3. Treatment and Vaccines for *Mosquito* Vectors

According to WHO, no specific treatment is available for dengue fever, but symptomatic treatment and the Dengvaxia® vaccine are used to decrease the severity of the diseases and decrease mortality rate. The Dengvaxia® (CYD-TDV) vaccine was developed in December 2015. In 2016, it was used in areas where dengue fever was highly endemic [40]. During the clinical trials, CYD-TDV was found effective in seropositive individuals. The main method to control dengue is to prevent the vector and to combat *mosquitoes*. Other vaccines developed by NIAID and Takeda are in the evaluation stage III [42]. Similarly, still no vaccines for Zika and Chikungunya virus have been found [43]. Other vaccines for Chikungunya and Zika are under clinical trials. Similarly, vaccines to provide broad protection against *mosquitoes* borne diseases like Malaria, Zika and West Nile Fever are under clinical trials by National Institute of Allergy and Infectious Diseases (NIAID) working under NIH [44]. As reported by WHO, yellow fever can be prevented by a single dose of effective vaccines, which are affordable and safe [45]. Effective drugs for malaria are easily available on the market. However, prescription is important before use.

3.3. *Conventional Methods Used to Control Mosquito Populations*

3.3.1. Overview

The purpose of monitoring *mosquito* populations is to lessen the potential for biting nuisance and disease transmission especially important for dengue and malaria. A number of effective methods are used in disease vector control and depend upon the targeted *mosquito* species. These approaches are classified into five classes: source reduction (environmental control), trapping (mechanical control), insecticides (chemical control), genetic control and biological control. An overview of conventional methods used for the eradication of *mosquitoes* is given in Figure 2.

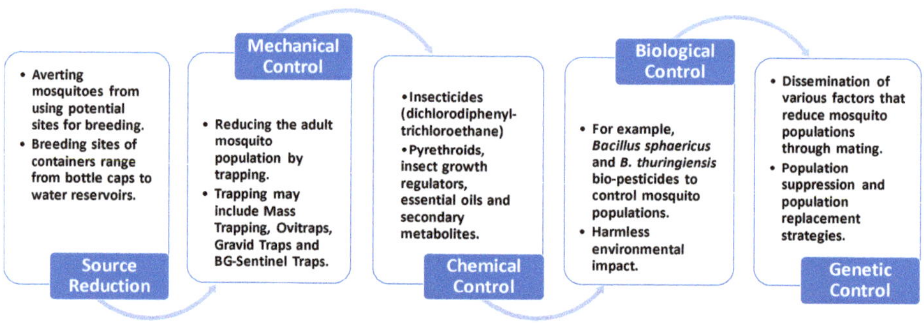

Figure 2. Overview of conventional methods used for the eradication of *mosquitoes*.

3.3.2. Source Reduction (Environmental Control)

Source reduction methods include averting *Aedes* spp. (*mosquito*) from using possible sites for breeding. These sites may consist of a varied range of containers or tanks from bottle covers to water reservoirs (Figure 2). This method is based on eradicating impermanent water tanks and closing permanent water reservoirs. This is frequently the first line of defence against *mosquitoes* such as *A. albopictus, Ae. aegypti* and *Ae. atropalpus* that favour small- and medium-sized artificial water containers and tires placed in or near homes. Source reduction also affects the dispersal of local *mosquitoes* like *Culex* spp. in the vicinity by restraining the existing sites for oviposition (process of laying eggs) [46–48].

Some breeding areas can be extremely fruitful for certain species. For example, the breeding sites for *A. albopictus* are catch sinks in northern Italy, ridged extension fountains in USA, and tank basins and tires in South Asia. Operative source reduction, specifically for *Aedes* spp., needs to be consistent and recurrent; e.g., washing or handling of water containers/vessels for daily use. Success depends largely on owner participation and public awareness. In a study in Brazil, a source lessening drive against *Ae. aegypti* was started using nylon nets to shelter the most productive sites such as water containers and metal barrels that resulted in a long-lasting drop in female *mosquito* populations, showing the usefulness of targeting preferable breeding sites. Regrettably, this method does not assist in tracing cryptic productive sites, which are often unseen or inaccessible such as natural reservoirs including leaf litter [49,50].

3.3.3. Trapping (Mechanical Control)

Mass trapping commonly uses odor to attract *mosquitoes*. For *Aedes*, trapping methods such as ovitraps or sticky/gravid traps target gravid females. For host-seeking females, the bio-agent-sentinel traps are used. Though the usage of bioagent-sentinel traps is commonly inadequate due to the necessity for electrical supply. Ovitraps uncover the tendency of *Aedes mosquito*es to lay their eggs in small containers. An autocidal or larvicide inclusion permits the long-standing use of ovitraps with minor danger of it becoming a major source of adult *mosquitoes*. Insecticide-treated egg-laying strips are also being used [51,52].

To improve the attractivity of ovitraps, organic infusions (grass, hay and oak) can be applied. Gravid/sticky ovitraps with adhesive surfaces have also been advanced. To improve *mosquito* collections, researchers developed a bulky autocidal gravid trap with a higher release rate of water vapours and other volatile attractants [53]. As push-pull approaches, combining a repellent with some attractive incentives in tandem, are an effective control method against various *mosquitoes*. It uses the spatial repellent and contact nuisance of insecticides through insecticide-treated materials or indoor residual spraying. Still, it is important to point out that insecticide-treated materials and indoor residual spraying methods do not target exophylic *mosquitoes* such as *Ae. albopictus* [53,54]. There are some other traps like bed net traps, entry and exit traps, sentinel traps, capture-kill traps, host seeking traps, light traps and chemical based traps used for the control of *Anophels* species. Similarly, CDC traps (CO_2 from dry ice) are used to catch 400–500% more *mosquitoes* [55,56].

3.3.4. Insecticides (Chemical Control)

Chemical control of *mosquitoes* is undertaken by using natural or synthetic chemicals (insecticides). This allows for instant *mosquito* reduction control when physical and biological methods are incapable to sustain *mosquito* numbers below certain thresholds. Larvicides are the compounds proposed to be applied directly to water to control larvae populations. Adulticides along with synergists are used in obscuring and spraying adult *mosquitoes* to control their numbers.

In the twentieth century, dichlorodiphenyltrichlroethane (commonly known as DDT) was the primary artificial organic insecticide that has been used for active malaria control by decreasing the life span of gravid female *mosquitoes*. Pyrethroids and insect growth regulators are the effective compounds used worldwide in *mosquito* control approaches, as adulticides and larvicides along with ovicidal properties possessed by some insect growth regulators such as methoprene pyriproxyfen and diflubenzuron [57].

A new strategy called auto-dissemination consists of manipulating female *mosquitoes* by contamination with insecticide (pyriproxyfen) through treated nets or diffusion stations designed from modified ovitraps. The method has proved to be effective in inducing high mortality rates of *Ae. aegypti* and *Ae. albopictus* at the pupal stage. Furthermore, production and hatchability of eggs were also seen to be affected. A new approach is to synergize the sterile insect technique (SIT) with auto-dissemination to release sterile male *mosquitoes* treated with pyriproxyfen to infect females during mating [58–60]. Common commercially available insecticides currently used are listed in Table 2.

Table 2. Commonly used pesticides on the market against vectors.

Name	International Union of Pure and Applied Chemistry Name	Molar Mass	Pack Size	Applications	Reference
Fendona 10% [$C_{22}H_{19}C_{12}NO_3$]	[cyano-(3-phenoxyphenyl) methyl] 3-(2,2-dichloroethenyl)-2, 2-dimethylcyclopropane-1-carboxylate	416.300 g/mol	100, 200 and 1000 mL	It has a broad action spectrum against a large variety of insect pests in households and public facilities.	[61]
Lambda Cyhalothrin [$C_{23}H_{19}ClF_3NO_3$]	cyano-(3-phenoxyphenyl) methyl] (1R,3R)-3-[(Z)-2-chloro-3,3,3-trifluoroprop-1-enyl]-2, 2 dimethylcyclopropane-1-carboxylate	449.854 g/mol	250 and 500 mL	Targets aphids, butterfly larvae, cockroaches, *mosquitoes* and flies.	[62]
Deltamethrin [$C_{22}H_{19}Br_2NO_3$]	Cyano (3-phenoxy-phenyl) methyl; 3-(2,2dibromoethenyl)-2, 2-dimethylcyclopropanecarboxylate (CA); [partial diff]-cyano-m-phenoxy benzyl, (1R,3R)-3-(2,2-dibromovinyl)-2,2-dimethyl -cyclopropanol-carboxylate, (S)-[partial diff]-cyano-3-phenoxybenzyl (1R)-cis-3-(2,2-dibromovinyl)-2, 2-dimethylcyclopropane-carboxylate	505.240 g/mol	25 g/L	Control of the malaria vector as a stomach poison for insects.	[63]
Fenpropathrin [$C_{22}H_{23}NO_3$]	2,2,3,3-Tetramethylcyclopropane carboxylic acid cyano(3-phenoxyphenyl) methyl ester	349.42 g/mol	1000 L (mini-mum order)	Controls a variety of pests; specifically, mites present in fruits and vegetables.	[64]

Plant-based insecticides received much attention, recently, due to their safe, cheap and environmentally friendly nature. Plants have a diversity of phytochemicals (used for defence) that can be applied to lessen insect outbreaks. In chemical ecology, the assessment of how specific chemicals (allelochemicals) are implicated in organism interactions with each other and with their environments is studied. These allelochemicals serve their purpose as defence mechanisms and effect molecular targets such as cellular proteins, enzymes, nervous system signal transduction (synthesis of neurotransmitter, their storage and release as well as receptor binding) and metabolic pathways in herbivores or microbes [65,66].

The secondary metabolites (phenols, alkaloids, slavanoids, sterols, terpenes, carotenoids etc.) of plants protect them against microbial parasites and arthropods; e.g., *Chloroxylon swietenia* against *Anopheles gambiae*, *Culex quinquefasciatus*, *Aedes aegypti* and *Calocedrus decurrens*, *Juniperus occidentalis* against adult *Ae. aegypti*, and *Eucalyptus tereticornis* against established *Anopheles stephensi*.

Plant extract-based larvicides such as essential oils, terpenes and their corresponding elements disturb biochemical processes, particularly effecting the endocrinological balance, neuromuscular fatigue, respiratory capability, neuroexcitation as well as neuro-inhibition, which results in energy depletion, oxygen deprivation, immobility and paralysis that ultimately leads to death (Table 3) [66–69].

Table 3. Plant-extracted essential oils and their mechanisms of action (after [65]).

System	Active Compound	Mechanism	Plant	References
Cholinergic system	Essential oils	Acetylecholinestrase (AChE) inhibition	*Azadirachtina indica*, *Lavendula* spp. and *Mentha* spp.	[70]
	Veratrin	Nerves sodium channels	*Schoenocaulon officinale*	[71]
	Nicotine	Cholinergic acetylcholine nicotinic receptor agonist/antagonist	*Nicotiana* spp., *Haloxylon salicornicum*, *Delphinium* spp. and *Stemona japonicum*	[72]
GABA system	Thymol and Silphinenes	GABA-gated chloride channel	*Thymus vulgaris*	[73]
Mitochondrial system	Pyrethrin	Potassium ion and sodium exchange disturbance	*Crysanthemum cinerariaefolium*	[74]
	Rotenone	Cellular respiration inhibitor (mitochondrial complex I electron transportinhibitor or METI)	*Lonchocarpus* spp.	[75]
	Ryanodine	Calcium channel disturbance	*Ryania* spp.	[76]
	Sabadilla	Alter nerve cell membrane action	*Schoenocaulon officinale*	[77]
Octopaminergic system	Essential oils	Octopaminergic receptors	*Cedrus* spp., *Pinus* spp., *Citronella* spp. and *Eucalyptus* spp.	[78,79]
	Thymol	Block octopamine receptors by functioning through tyramine receptors cascade	*Thymus vulgaris*	[78,80]
Miscellaneous	Azadirachtin	Anti-mitotic (G2/M Phase)	*Azadiractina indica*	[71]

However, it has been proposed that plant extracts, which comprise of several chemicals, are more complex in nature as compared to synthetic insecticides and, therefore, the mixture of physiological and behavioural actions of botanical insecticides prevents the development of resistance.

3.3.5. Biological Control

In recent years, bio-pesticides are receiving increased interest as an effective *mosquito* control program due to their role in promoting vertebrates' safety and lowered environmental impact. A number of organisms were discovered as potential bio-pesticides for *mosquito* control including bacteria, fungi, viruses, protozoa and fish. However, most of these organisms were not considered convenient for the development of an effective *mosquito* control program due to their limited supply. Some of the spore-forming bacteria such as *B. thuringiensis serovar israelensis* deBarjac (Bti) and *Bacillus sphaericus* Neide (Bs) were investigated against operational *Ae.*, *Anophels* and *Cx mosquito* populations as they already showed highly toxic effects to such dipteran species. Bti bacteria spores conduct a broader range of activities against *Ae.* spp., *Culex* and *Anophels* Bs is highly specific to certain species and acts only against some *Ae.* species and majorly effect *Culex* species [81].

In *B. sphaericus* (Bs) bacteria, two insecticidal proteins, BinA with 42 kDa and BinB with 51 kDa (known as Binary toxin btx) have shown to be highly toxic for *mosquitoes*. BinA Recombinant bacteria comprising these toxins separately confirmed that BinA is extremely toxic at high dose without any need of BinB, but BinB alone does not show any toxicity. However, their synergistic effect revealed that their equal concentrations have extreme toxicity to larvae. When the *mosquito* larvae ingest btx, BinA and BinB solubilize in the midgut, where the proteases process them into 39 kDa and 43 kDa proteins. After processing, btx-active proteins are coupled to receptors present on the brush border membrane of the midgut, where the internalization of active proteins occurs leading to the cell lysis, and ultimately, lysis and inflammation of midgut, which results in the insect's death. Another *mosquito*cidal toxin Mtx (100 kDa) appears to be highly toxic in protease negative Bs strains that has been synthesized in low toxicity strains [82–88].

In Bti bacteria, two insecticidal protein groups Cyt (cytolysins) and Cry (crystal delta-endotoxins) were also shown to be effective for *mosquito* control [50]. Bti toxins contain four polypeptides: Cry IVA (125 kDa), Cry IVB (135 kDa), Cry IVD (68 kDa) and Cyt A (28 kDa). They are assembled into crystals during sporulation. The genes encoding these Cry toxin proteins are present on the plasmid of the bacterium [89,90]. Cry proteins bind to definite receptors present on the midgut epithelium of the insect, while Cyt proteins do not distinguish specific sites present in the midgut. After ingestion, Bti crystals are processed into smaller fragments by proteases. The activated fragments interrupt the osmotic equilibrium of epithelium cells through making pores into the membrane causing cell death. Most of the *mosquitoes* die within hours due to a paralyzed gut [91–93].

However, there are some resistance problems with these insecticides, because of the insects' increased evolutionary rate. The factors linked to an increased evolutionary rate are elevated productive rates of species, increased and larger number of progenies, shorter generation times, and higher genetic variability among local species [94].

Recently, genetic engineering techniques are being used for improving bacterial larvicides for *mosquito* control. The recombinant bacteria of Bti and Bs strains are ten times more effective than wild strains that are also being used for larger scale larvicides production. The recombinant strains comprise all the endotoxins of Bti (Cry4A, Cry4B, Cry11A, and Cyt1A) along with Bs (Binary toxin). The synergy of these toxins will eradicate *mosquito* populations more effectively [95,96].

3.3.6. Genetic Control

Genetic approaches are attaining greater attention as alternatives to conventional methods for *mosquito* control. Dissemination of various factors that reduce *mosquito* damage by mating is defined as genetic control. Such heritable factors are introduced into target species so that the modified *mosquito* acts as biocontrol agent and their dependence on vertical capacity distinguishes them from biological control methods. Genetic strategies are classified based on their intended outcome into population suppression, population replacement and other key aspects of genetic element persistence [96].

Population suppression programs decrease the number of vectors in the target species, which is comparable to the purpose of insecticide-based strategies. For example, the sterile-male program is intended to suppress the target population when sufficient numbers of sterile males are released. These modified sterile males are disseminated in the environment to mate with unmodified females resulting in the death of the progeny of this mating, and can potentially lead to population eradication [87]. Additionally, population replacement methods diminish the midgut transmission capability of nearly all of the *mosquitoes'* present in the target population. For example, a new character (trait) like lower capability to spread a pathogen into the specific *mosquito* population will be advantageous for humans, while probably being lethal for the *mosquito* population [97,98].

Persistence or invasiveness is the ability to which the alteration (trait) will be present or disperse in the target group after its release. Concerning self-limiting strategy, the trait has the tendency to vanish from the target *mosquito* population until replaced by the release of further altered *mosquitoes'* periodically. In self-sustaining strategy (gene drive system), use of the proposed alteration can persevere forever and possibly even disperse inside the primary target species or to other species [99].

Regarding the self-limiting strategy, as through the use of sterile male systems, the mutations or inheritable lethal genes are introduced where only a females' offspring is affected [100]. Sterile insect techniques (SIT), where DNA-damaging agents like γ-radiations are used to introduce lethal mutations and nucleases in the germ line, are expressed to cause chromosomal breaks [101]. Another approach, release of insects carrying a dominant lethal (RIDL) genetic system can be applied to induce toxic gene expression in zygote relative to the father providing more flexibility (to act at a certain time in development), but at the same time make this strategy more vulnerable to the environment [102].

Sterility can also be introduced by diverse strains of *Wolbachia* bacteria by artificial infection. *Wolbachia* is maternally transmitted through the mother to her offspring. Female-killing systems can also offer "sterilization", where released male offspring are homozygous for a female-specific lethal gene that will result in inheritance of the female lethal gene copy; as an effect, offspring (daughters) would die. This approach is known as female-specific RIDL (fsRIDL). It provides *mosquito* population control much like classical SIT [102,103].

In self-sustaining systems, gene drive is the common phenomenon where all selfish-DNA constituents are introduced that can persist over a target population without giving a suitable benefit to the *mosquitoes'* carrying them. Many selfish-DNA elements are known that are being used such as invasive *Wolbachia, transposons*, synthetic *Medea*-like elements and the Homing Endonuclease Gene (HEG) [104,105]. The HEG is expressed either as separate genes within introns, as fusions with host proteins or lethal gene where they catalyse the genomic DNA hydrolysis within the cells that produce them.

Artificial *Medea*-like elements, originating from the naturally present selfish *Medea* elements of *Tribolium castaneum* have been created. The method uses reasonably intended synthetic elements that have the ability to replicate the inheritance pattern of *Medea* deprived of deriving its molecular components [106]. Furthermore, *Wolbachia* strains are selfish-DNA elements, which can spread by target *mosquito* species through altering their host's reproductive biology (generating CI to kill uninfected females).

Gene drive is another technology to propagate a particular gene by altering the probability from the natural to transmit a specific allele in the next generation. This can be performed in different ways to control *mosquito* species. However, a detailed discussion is beyond the scope of this review.

3.3.7. Integrative Vector Management Approach

This approach is used to achieve globally-set targets to control vector-borne diseases. This includes situation analysis, monitoring and evaluation, surveillance and capacity building. The overall purpose is to apply all strategies to control larvae, adults and bites from *mosquitoes*. The overall use of biological, chemical and physical methods for the control of *mosquitoes* is encouraged. Integrated practices are more advisable and a sustainable approach for lowering the *mosquito* population is advantageous. Appropriate ecofriendly plans and strategies should be adopted [8].

4. Nanotechnology-Based Methods

4.1. Overview

Nanotechnology-based methods have revolutionized a varied area of research fields including entomology. Nanotechnology has a good potential to combat climate change. There is a possibility to develop nanomaterials in the environment naturally. Temperature change can influence the reaction rate and disturb the formation and synthesis of nanoparticles [107]. Nanoparticles show a high antimicrobial activity against various microbes, because of their large surface to volume ratio that is responsible for their high catalytic activity. Nanoparticles have been testified as valuable when compared to chemical insecticides targeting adult *mosquitoes* and young larval instars. This is likely due to the fact that the overuse of insecticides has led to unfavorable consequences on the environment, plants and human health, along with the insecticide resistance development in targeted populations. Currently, a number of nanomaterials are being used to control *mosquito* vector-borne diseases.

4.2. Nanoliposomes

Liposomes are synthetic nano-assemblies up to few hundred nanometers in diameter comprising one or more outer phospholipid bilayers enclosed by an aqueous core. As a nano-carrier, both hydrophobic and hydrophilic particles can be captured within aqueous core and outer lipophilic layers, respectively. Nanoliposomes are also immunologically compatible due to their targeted uptake by cells through surface adjuvants such as antigens, antibodies and cell-associated specific ligands [108,109]. Nanoliposomes have been already used for malarial treatment as well as for the delivery of malaria vaccine. At present, efficient malarial therapy is restricted due to their deadly side effects and the potential for development of drug resistance. However, the encapsulation of a therapeutic drug (chloroquine) within nanoliposomes can effectively adjust the bioavailability and drug dose within the body that significantly lessen the drug toxic effects, and the risk of drug resistance [110].

Currently, innovative gel-core nanoliposomes that use a composite of polymer and lipid-based carrier systems have been designed and confirmed for the controlled delivery of Pfs25 along with CpGODN (immune-stimulatory adjuvant) as malarial vaccine. In gel-core nanoliposomes, the integration of a polymer into the interior aqueous part of the liposome increases its stability, permitting slower drug release. The slow diffusion through the polymer gel core and phospholipid bilayers actively controls the drug release rate, which enables the capability of nanoliposomes for lasting antigen persistence without the need of boosting [111].

4.3. Nanosuspensions

The biphasic approach containing drug particles of submicron-sized dissolved in an aqueous solution is defined as nano-suspensions, prepared through top-down and bottom-up techniques to lower the size of particles. The purpose of using nano-suspensions is that their lower size increases their surface area, providing higher bioavailability of the drug and lowers its toxicity [112].

The anti-malarial drug Lumefantrine is used to treat multi-drug resistant malaria by inhibiting the ability of *P. falciparum* to convert heme into toxic hemozoin. The increased accumulation of toxic heme in a parasite causes its death and stops the malarial infection. However, Lumefantrine has lower water solubility that can lead to impaired bioavailability through oral or dietary route [113,114]. Nano-suspensions based drug delivery can be useful to combat malarial infections. Improved antimalarial activity of lumefantrine-based nano-suspensions by reducing its size from 72 μm to 0.251 μm through in-vitro and in-vivo experiments against *P. Yoelii nigeriensis* and *P. falciparum* has been observed [115].

The antimalarial action of the dihydroartemisinin (DHA) drug against *P. falciparum* in in-vitro trials has been demonstrated. The lower concentration of drugs in nanosuspensions have decreased side effects other than antimalarial activity [108].

4.4. Polymer-Based Nanoparticles

Polymer-based nanoparticles are biodegradable and biocompatible solid-colloidal particles ranging from 1 to 1000 nm in size. The second most plentiful polysaccharide is chitin-derived. Chitosan nanoparticles have many advantages owing to their increased stability, biodegradability, biocompatibility, water solubility, controlled drug release, lower toxicity, non-immunogenic and ease-of-fabrication methods, which make them ideal candidates for *mosquito* control [116,117].

Primaquine (PQ) is a commonly used anti-malarial drug that opposes the relapsing form of malaria by *P. vivax* and *P. ovale* plasmodium parasites. However, PQ has some adverse effects due to non-specific targeting, its lower bioavailability and short half-life. Reformulation of PQ into chitosan-based nanoparticles can be a promising approach to overwhelm these side-effects. Scientists tested PQ-loaded solid lipid nanoparticles that showed effective vector reduction with increased half-life, reduced side effects and increased bioavailability compared to the conventional PQ drug [115–118].

Chitin is a major component of all insects including *mosquitoes*. It is part of their exoskeleton cuticle and other tissues like foregut, midgut, hindgut and trachea. Chitin biosynthesis is entirely dependent on the chitin synthases enzymes by catalysing the transmission of sugar from triggered sugar donors to definite acceptors present in *mosquitoes*. CHS-A is a chitin synthesis gene that is present in the cuticle and foregut, hindgut and trachea tissues, while the chitin synthesis gene CHS-B is specifically linked to the midgut. Epithelial cell's chitin biosynthesis is associated with the peritrophic matrix (PM) [119–121].

RNA interference (RNAi) technology is an eco-friendly targeted approach to control *mosquito* vectors through small interfering RNA (siRNA) activated post-transcriptional gene silencing [114]. Recently, scientists have developed chitosan/dsRNA-based nanoparticles against the African *mosquito Anopheles gambiae* to silence the chitin synthase genes CHS-A and CHS-B [117].

Mosquito growth and development mostly depends on chitin synthases. Consequently, chitin synthase genes are ideal targets to eradicate *mosquito* vector populations. Other polymeric nanoparticles such as poly glycolic acid (PGA), poly D, L-lactic acid (PLA), poly D, L, -lactic-co- glycolic acid (PLGA) and poly ε-caprolactone (PCL) are also being used to encapsulate drug active-compounds due to their increased drug stability, control drug release and lower toxicity [122,123].

The primaquine (PQ) drug can be encapsulated in polymeric nanoparticles to control malarial parasite infection [124,125]. Reseracherssynthesized nano-chloroquine (Nch) particles from 150–300 nm. Nch particles were tested against liver and spleen resulting in ~29% and ~37% reductions in liver and spleen damage, respectively, compared to conventional chloroquine [126].

4.5. Green-Synthesized Metallic Nanoparticles

The misuse of chemical insecticides is linked to major concerns regarding their toxicity and ecological problems, but green synthesized nanoparticles have reported to be advantageous, because they are eco-friendly and cost-effective compared to conventional methods. For an effective vector control approach, appropriate formulations of botanical-based insecticides need to be improved in terms of their persistence; green synthesized nanoparticles with suitable reducing and capping agents are employed to attain their optimal activity with reduced size and different shape. There are several biophysical techniques such as UV-vis spectroscopy for nano-synthesis monitoring over time, Fourier Transformed Infrared Spectroscopy (FTIR) for functional group studies involved in capping and reduction, Energy Dispersive X-ray (EDX) for elemental composition analysis and X-ray diffraction (XRD) spectroscopy for analysing crystalline structures of nanoparticles [127].

The efficacy of green-synthesized Ag nanoparticles obtained from Dicranopteris linearis, Chenopodium ambrosioides, Aristolochia indica, Gracilaria edulis, Couroupita guianensis and Phyllanthus niruri plant extracts was validated against Anopheline aedine and Culicinae spp. *mosquito* vectors. The LC_{50} values of these nano-larvicides was in the range of 1 to 30 μg/mL and the complete eradication of these larval species was recorded within 72 h after first treatment [128,129].

Egg hatchability of *Ae. aegypti* and *Culex Quinquefasciatus* was 100% decreased after exposure to green-synthesized Ag nanoparticles (30 μg/mL) from *Sargassum muticum*. Ag-nanoparticles from *D. linearis* and *S. maritima* also reduced the *Ae. aegypti* egg hatchability after their treatment with 25 μg/mL and 20 μg/mL concentrations, respectively. The *Culex Quinquefasciatus* eggs were resistant to larvicidal effect of green-synthesized nanoparticles in comparison to *Anophels stephensi* and *Ae. aegypti*. Lately, *Rubus ellipticus*-synthesized Ag nanoparticles showed no hatchability of *Ae. aegypti, Anophels stephensi* and *Culex Quinquefasciatus* with single dosage of 75 μg/mL, 90 μg/mL and 60 μg/mL, respectively [130].

Similarly, a number of leaf extract-based Ag nanoparticles have shown their adulticidal activity against *Ae. albopictus, Ae. Aegypti, Anophels stephensi and Culex Quinquefasciatus.* Unfortunately, no possible toxicity mechanism of ovicidal and adulticidal green-nanoparticles is known, yet [128]. However, it has been assumed that nanoparticle toxicity against *mosquito* young larvae is because of their ability to penetrate into exoskeleton and their binding to DNA phosphate groups and sulphur-rich proteins. Consequently, this results in DNA alterations, rapid protein degradation and a decrease in membrane permeability, which causes loss in cell function and cell death [129–131].

Recently, some studies reported that nanoparticle exposure to *Ae. Aegypti* and *Anophels Stephensi* results in adult longevity and female fecundity. *Hypnea musciformis*-fabricated Ag nanoparticles reduced the longevity of *Ae. Aegypti* males from 15.64 to 5.32 days and *Ae. Aegypti* female longevity from 26.87 to 17.34 days. Similarly, exposure of these nanoparticles to *Ae. Aegypti* results in the reduction of female fecundity from 150 eggs to 98 eggs after 50 ppm dosage.

P. aquilinum-fabricated Ag nanoparticles (50 ppm) reduced the longevity of *Anophels Stephensi* males and females from 21.44 to 9.90 days and from 37.18 to 20.90 days, respectively. While, post-treatment of 50 ppm nanoparticles reduced the *Anophels Stephensi* female fecundity from 145 to 66 eggs [132,133]. This method might indicate a way to control *mosquito*-borne diseases more effectively.

5. Drive to Transform Sick to Healthy Life under Changing Climatic Conditions

Mosquitoes are likely to benefit from climate change [8]. Apart from suitable *mosquito* breeding sites, temperature, precipitation and absolute humidity of more than 60% can affect parasite transmission in malaria. As the globe is continuously warming, more incidences of dengue and malaria as well as an increase in the distribution of *mosquitoes* have been related to climate change. The range of disease-vectors may not only increase in latitude but also in altitude. As the *mosquito* population is increasing globally with time, they will colonize new suitable areas where the temperature is warmer fulfilling their needs.

Due to warmer temperatures, the cell metabolism of *mosquitoes* will also increase as chemical reactions are increasing. In warm temperatures, mature females feed more frequently and digest blood rapidly, thus producing more progeny. Hard-freeze areas in the winter season have less *mosquitoes* as they cannot breed during this time and usually eggs are destroyed. However, some species are possibly able to live during the winter season, if the temperature is not too low. At higher temperatures, *mosquitoes* hatch at a higher rate, subsequently their rate of development and reproduction will rise exponentially [123], and the range of *mosquitoes*-borne diseases will increase as well [6].

As *mosquitoes* are poikilothermal, the development of parasites in the *mosquito* is reliant on the external temperature. For *P. vivax* and *P. falciparum*, the nominal temperature at which the development of parasites can be accomplished is 16.5 °C and 14.5 °C, respectively. Higher temperatures accelerate their development, because sporozoites are formed quickly. It follows that the life cycle is completed sooner. Therefore, the likelihood of malarial infection will increase with higher temperatures. There is an inverse relationship between the longevity of *mosquitoes* and temperature. At higher temperatures, *mosquitoes* and their parasites die. There is an optimum temperature range for Plasmodium transmission (22–28 °C for *P. vivax* and *A. messeae*, and 26–32 °C for *P. falciparum* and *A. gambiae*) [134].

The number of females that laid eggs and the number of eggs laid are influenced by both temperature and humidity (Figure 3). A reduction in oviposition rate was detected with increase in temperature, while the intensity of the reduction was affected by humidity. At high temperature (35 °C) and low humidity (relative humidity of 60%), a low oviposition rate (55 ± 4.8 eggs) was observed for adult females. On the other side, at a low temperature (25 °C) and high humidity (relative humidity of 80%), a high oviposition rate (99 ± 3.6 eggs) was noted (Table 4) [135].

A high humidity is suitable even up to saturation (80% or more of relative humidity) at 28 °C. At comparatively lower temperatures (18–20 °C), life expectation may be very substantial even at low humidity and *mosquitoes* can be kept alive if given water only (without any food) for several weeks. At a temperature of 25 °C and relative humidity of 70% with water provided, low mortality was observed among females earlier the seventh day either fed or not. The duration of life under such conditions without food is about 6 to 8 days. A maximum of 12 days of life expectancy was observed. However, at relatively high temperatures (28 °C) and in the absence of high humidity, a considerable mortality of males was observed even soon after emergence. After the seventh day of emergence, mortality among unfed males and females increased quickly and a high mortality by the tenth day was noted. Few *mosquitoes* were alive at the fourteenth day at 25 °C even at high humidity and with water given [123,135–137].

Table 4. Mean number of eggs laid by *Aedes aegypti* females at different temperature and humidity values (after [135]).

Temperature	Relative Humidity of 60%		Relative Humidity of 80%	
	Eggs (Sample Number)	Oviposition Variation	Eggs (Sample Number)	Oviposition Variation
25 °C	85.99 ± 3.16 (102)	4–160 (37.25%)	99.08 ± 3.56 (92)	4–155 (55.43%)
30 °C	82.89 ± 3.33 (111)	2–143 (37.84%)	75.75 ± 5.03 (75)	1–144 (45.33%)
35 °C	54.53 ± 4.81 (55)	1–126 (14.55%)	59.62 ± 3.41 (79)	2–132 (7.59%)
Total	78.25 ± 2.2 (268)		79.29 ± 2.53 (246)	

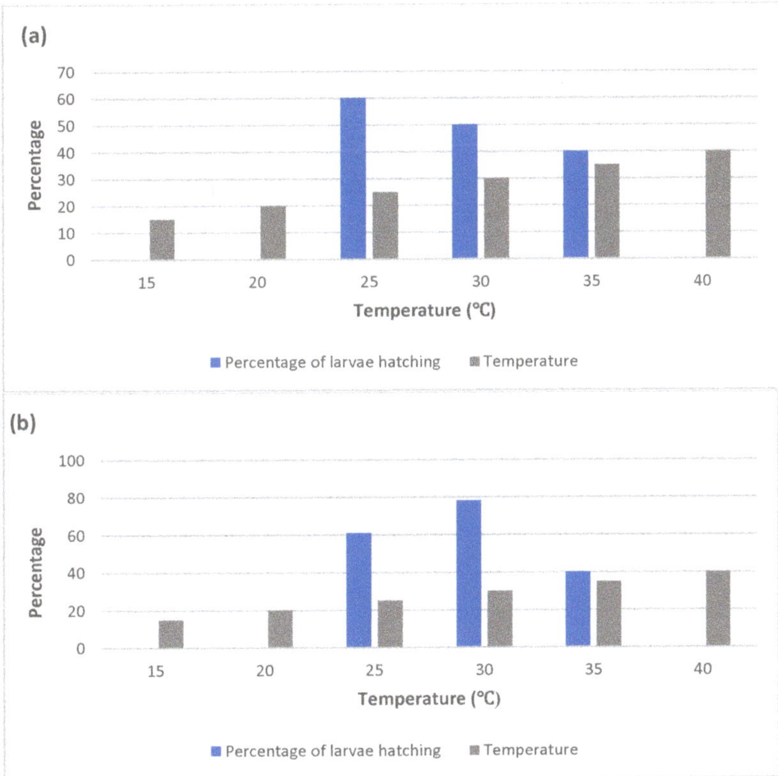

Figure 3. Fertility rates of eggs sustained at different temperatures and humidity values: (**a**) relative humidity (rh) of 60%; and (**b**) relative humidity (rh) of 80%; n = number of eggs (adopted from [135]).

A temperature below freezing appeared to be fatal for the adults, if continued for 24 h. At freezing temperature, the *mosquitoes* are completely immobilized. At 4 °C for 1 h, all *mosquitoes* survived, but extended exposures at 4 °C killed them. However, between 7 and 9 °C, *Ae. aegypti mosquitoes* were alive for about 82 days. Moreover, half of the females were alive after 30 days. The optimal temperature for *mosquitoes* is usually around 28 °C. An increase in temperature would be progressively disadvantageous for survival. More than 40 °C is lethal for *mosquitoes* [138,139].

In order to address climate change, there are two common strategies: mitigation and adaptation. These approaches are interrelated with each other, but the basic difference is that adaptation is linked to the response to the fluctuating climate changing the lifestyle in which humans live as a society, while mitigation means restraining climate change, mainly by lowering greenhouse gas emissions.

Scientists are working to improve the efficacy and availability of alternative energy approaches. To increase domestic energy efficiency, simple measures such as to drive less by biking and use of public transportation would play important roles in reducing climate change worldwide. To limit climate change, our priority should be on changing our own behaviour by replacing to energy sources that release greenhouse gases [140]. Alternative approaches to reduce emissions and lowering temperature can decrease the impacts on human health. Furthermore, adaptation to a changing climate is also important. There is a need for thoughtful planning to minimize hazards.

6. Pakistani Perspective with Reference to Other Countries

Climate change contributes to the spreading of diseases. Conferring to the World Health Organization (WHO), the most fatal vector-borne malarial disease claimed 627,000 lives worldwide in 2012. However, a fast-growing vector-borne disease is dengue; up to 30-fold rise in disease occurrence during the last 50 years [4,5].

Vector-borne diseases add to most health-related complications in developing countries. Since 2005/6, Pakistan is facing steady epidemics of dengue and dengue haemorrhagic fever (DHF). Since 2010, Pakistan has been severely impacted by dengue fever, which led to 16,580 confirmed cases and 257 deaths in Lahore alone. Almost 5,000 confirmed cases and 60 deaths in the other parts of the country have been reported. The entire country is susceptible to dengue through the changeable trends in climate. Pakistan has been categorized in "group three" (Eastern Mediterranean Region) by the World Health Organization together with countries such as Afghanistan, Djibouti and Somalia due to the current alarming situation of vector-borne diseases with an estimated impact of 1.5 million cases annually [7,140]. Worldwide statistical data on dengue cases and their mortality are shown in Table 5 [141].

Table 5. Statistical data on dengue cases and the corresponding mortality during the period between 2009 and 2017.

Reports	Saudi Arabia	Sri Lanka	Pakistan	Nepal	Malaysia	India	China	Bangladesh
Reported cases	1600	35,008	1085	30	41,486	17,000	322	510
Mortality	N/A	346	13	0	90	105	0	0
Reported cases	2200	34,188	11,024	917	46,171	28,000	260	405
Mortality	N/A	229	40	5	135	112	0	0
Reported cases	2400	28,473	17,057	79	19,884	19,000	160	1310
Mortality	N/A	246	219	0	38	171	0	8
Reported cases	800	44,461	639 (Karachi only)	183	21,900	50,000	610	750
Mortality	N/A	220	4	0	37	240	0	1
Reported cases	4200	32,063	4388	642	43,346	70,000	4779	1790
Mortality	N/A	N/A	32	0	95	140	0	3
Reported cases	1950	47,502	1400	355	108,698	40,571	47,056	355
Mortality	N/A	N/A	16	0	215	137	6	0
Reported cases	4200	29,777	3900	1500	120,836	99,913	4230	3162
Mortality	N/A	N/A	11	0	336	220	0	N/A
Reported cases	N/A	55,150	2500	594 till October	100,028	1,29,166	2098	6010
Mortality	N/A	N/A	3	N/A	231	245	N/A	N/A
Reported cases	N/A	185,688	N/A	854 till October	82,840	1,53,635	3195	N/A
Mortality	N/A	N/A	N/A	N/A	171	226	N/A	N/A

The underprivileged poor in exposed societies existing in distant rural areas with restricted access to health amenities suffer the most. Inappropriate settlements in slums that are without any satisfactory water and sanitation systems are also a challenge. Due to poor living environments, vector-borne diseases flourish. Increasing temperatures and humidity levels are likely to elevate vector-borne disease transmissions such as dengue, malaria, yellow fever and encephalitis. Different studies concluded that an increase in average temperature will enhance the reproduction cycle of the dengue fever virus.

Changing climatic conditions in terms of temperature, rainfall and humidity as well as low levels of immunity among poor populations enhance malaria outbreaks. A temperature range between 20 and 30 °C, a humidity level above 55% and the presence of breeding sites in standing water to rainfall are optimal parameters for development, longevity and transmission of malaria. In Pakistan, vector-borne diseases (predominantly dengue fever and malaria) proliferate after the monsoon. From July to September, more than 80% of total vector-borne diseases are reported every year. The highest numbers of incidences have been reported for the Punjab and followed by Balochistan, Federally Administered Tribal Areas and Khyber Pakhtunkhwa in this order [142]. The monthly rainfall (mm) in Pakistan and locations of meteorological stations are shown in Figure 4. The indicated monsoon zone corresponds to the most affected areas [143].

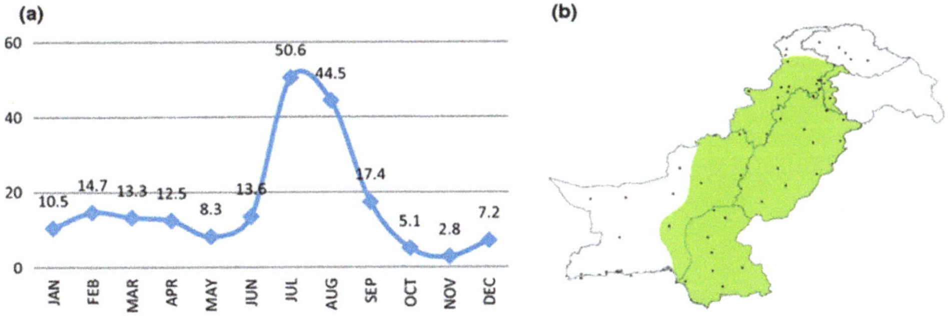

Figure 4. (**a**) Monthly area weighted rainfall (mm) for Pakistan; and (b) locations of meteorological stations that are available for climate data. Note that the *green color* shows the monsoon zone (adopted from [143]).

7. Conclusions

To fight drug and insecticide resistance of *mosquitoes* developed through conventional treatment methods to prevent dengue and malaria outbreaks, nano-based technology that is considered to be health- and eco-friendly such as food grade nanoparticles can be used. Food grade nanoparticles have no side effects compared to metallic nanoparticles. They are both eco- and human-friendly. In order to overcome complications, transgenic *mosquitoes* (genetically modified) and a combination of drugs have been tested. However, these methods are challenging, because *mosquito* trans-genes are destructed, and multi-drugs can be found in their bodies. Nanomedicines can be anticipated and might aid treatment for malaria and dengue fever. A multi-drug combination employing nanoparticles could be promising. Specific consideration should be given to metallic like Zno nanoparticles, food grade nanoparticles like Curcumin and biodegradable nanoparticles with multi-drug encapsulation to slow down the evolutionary progression. Especially food-based nanoparticles, which have low toxicity compared to metallic drugs, multi-drugs and bio-drugs, might help to eradicate vector-borne diseases in developing countries such as Pakistan in the future. Further investigations are required to test the larvicidal activity of food-based nanoparticles against the larvae of *mosquitoes* causing malaria and dengue fever.

Outlook

The following recommendations are made to people to stay healthy:

- An environmental management approach is very important for the control of breeding sites of *mosquitoes* especially during and after monsoons. These sites include open drainage, marshes and standing water in pots.
- Control of breeding sites as a result of increased rainfall and change in rainfall pattern due to climate change, which increases the vector population like *mosquitoes* and provide more breeding spaces.
- Awareness campaign among the general public at community level and in schools regarding the spread and control of malaria and dengue fever (especially the time period for the diseases).
- Personal protective approaches include use of proper clothing, nets, *mosquito* repellent lotions and other protective measures in homes, businesses, schools and offices.
- Allocation of enough funds by the authorities for health departments to control the spread of malaria and dengue fever in the community.
- Use of biological, chemical and physical methods to diminish *mosquito*-related diseases.

Author Contributions: T.A. project administration, funding acquisition, conceptualization and writing of the initial draft paper. I.L. writing of section drafts and data collection. M.Z.H. support in writing draft sections and data collection. M.S. writing and editing of the review paper.

Funding: This research was funded by the Higher Education Commission, Government of Pakistan; grant No: 5424/Federal/NRPU/R&D/HEC/2016.

Acknowledgments: The authors gratefully acknowledge funding and support received by the Higher Education Commission for the project entitled "Elucidation of Larvicidal Effects of Metallic Nanoparticles against Vectors Causing Malaria and Dengue Fever". The support received from Muhammad Usman (research associate), who worked with this project for few months, is highly acknowledged.

Conflicts of Interest: The authors declare no conflict of interest.

References

1. World Health Organization. Dengue Control. Geneva. Available online: http://www.who.int/denguecontrol/en (accessed on 28 March 2019).
2. World Health Organization. Neglected Tropical Diseases. Geneva. Available online: http://www.who.int/neglected_diseases/diseases/en (accessed on 28 March 2019).
3. World Health Organization. World Health Day—7 April 2014. Geneva. Available online: http://www.who.int/campaigns/world-health-day/2014/event/en (accessed on 28 March 2014).
4. World Health Organization. World Malaria Report 2013. Geneva. Available online: http://www.who.int/malaria/publications/world_malaria_report_2013/en (accessed on 28 March 2019).
5. WHO. Malaria vaccine: WHO position paper-January 2016. *Vaccine* **2018**, *36*, 3576–3577. [CrossRef] [PubMed]
6. Deichstetter, P. The Effect of Climate Change on *Mosquito*-Borne Diseases. *Am. Biol. Teach.* **2017**, *79*, 169–173. [CrossRef]
7. Githeko, A.K.; Lindsay, S.W.; Confalonieri, U.E.; Patz, J.A. Climate change and vector-borne diseases: A regional analysis. *Bull. World Health OrgAnophels* **2000**, *78*, 1136–1147.
8. Haider, Z.; Ahmad, F.Z.; Mahmood, A.; Waseem, T.; Shafiq, I.; Raza, T.; Qazi, J.; Siddique, N.; Humayun, M.A. Dengue fever in Pakistan: A paradigm shift; changing epidemiology and clinical patterns. *Perspect. Public Health* **2015**, *135*, 294–298. [CrossRef] [PubMed]
9. Yi, H.; Devkota, B.R.; Yu, J.; Oh, K.; Kim, J.; Kim, H. Effects of global warming on *mosquitoes* & *mosquito*-borne diseases and the new strategies for *mosquito* control. *Entomol. Res.* **2014**, *44*, 215–235. [CrossRef]
10. Mohammed, A.; Chadee, D.D. Effects of different temperature regimens on the development of *Aedes aegypti* (L.) (Diptera: *Culicidae*) *mosquitoes*. *Acta Trop.* **2011**, *119*, 38–43. [CrossRef] [PubMed]
11. Moher, D.; Liberati, A.; Tetzlaff, J.; Altman, D.G. Preferred Reporting Items for Systematic Reviews and Meta-Analyses: The PRISMA Statement. *J. Clin. Epidemiol.* **2009**, *62*, 1006–1012. [CrossRef]
12. Eisen, L.; Monaghan, A.J.; Lozano-Fuentes, S.; Steinhoff, D.F.; Hayden, M.H.; Bieringer, P.E. The Impact of Temperature on the Bionomics ofAedes (*Stegomyia*) *aegypti*, With Special Reference to the Cool Geographic Range Margins. *J. Med Èntomol.* **2014**, *51*, 496–516. [CrossRef] [PubMed]

13. Hamlet, A.; Jean, K.; Perea, W.; Yactayo, S.; Biey, J.; Van Kerkhove, M.; Ferguson, N.; Garske, T. The seasonal influence of climate and environment on yellow fever transmission across Africa. *PLoS Negl. Trop. Dis.* **2018**, *12*, e0006284. [CrossRef]
14. Madico, G.; McDonald, J.; Gilman, R.H.; Cabrera, L.; Sterling, C.R. Epidemiology and Treatment of Cyclospora cayetanensis Infection in Peruvian Children. *Clin. Infect. Dis.* **1997**, *24*, 977–981. [CrossRef]
15. Moore, P.S. Meningococcal Meningitis in Sub-Saharan Africa: A Model for the Epidemic Process. *Clin. Infect. Dis.* **1992**, *14*, 515–525. [CrossRef] [PubMed]
16. Magori, K.; Drake, J.M. The Population Dynamics of Vector-borne Diseases. *Nat. Educ. Knowl.* **2013**, *4*, 14.
17. Kovats, R.S.; Campbell-Lendrum, D.H.; McMichael, A.J.; Woodward, A.; Cox, J.S. Early effects of climate change: Do they include changes in vector-borne disease? *Philos. Trans. R. Soc. Lond. Ser. B. Biol. Sci.* **2001**, *356*, 1057–1068. [CrossRef] [PubMed]
18. Bradley, D.J. Human tropical diseases in a changing environment. *Ciba Found. Symp.* **1993**, *175*, 146–162. [PubMed]
19. Lindsay, S.W.; Birley, M.H. Climate change and malaria transmission. *Ann. Trop. Med. Parasitol.* **1996**, *90*, 573–588. [CrossRef] [PubMed]
20. Beserra, E.B.; Fernandes, C.R.M.; Silva, S.A.D.O.; Da Silva, L.A.; Santos, J.W. Efeitos da temperatura no ciclo de vida, exigências térmicas e estimativas do número de gerações anuais de *Aedes aegypti* (Diptera, *Culicidae*). *Iheringia. Série Zool.* **2009**, *99*, 142–148. [CrossRef]
21. Marinho, R.A.; Beserra, E.B.; Bezerra-Gusmão, M.A.; Porto, V.D.; Olinda, R.A.; dos Santos, C.A. Effects of temperature on the life cycle, expansion, and dispersion of *Aedes aegypti* (Diptera: *Culicidae*) in three cities in Paraiba, Brazil. *J. Vector Ecol.* **2016**, *41*, 1–10. [CrossRef] [PubMed]
22. Gubler, D.J.; Reiter, P.; Ebi, K.L.; Yap, W.; Nasci, R.; Patz, J.A. Climate variability and change in the United States: Potential impacts on vector- and rodent-borne diseases. *Environ. Health Perspect.* **2001**, *109*, 223–233. [PubMed]
23. Cox, J.; Craig, M.; Sueur, D.L.; Sharp, B. Mapping Malaria Risk in the Highlands of Africa. In *Mapping Climate Vulnerability and Poverty in Africa: Report to the Department for International Development*; ILRI: Nairobi, Kenya, 1999; p. 96.
24. Ko, A.I.; Galvão Reis, M.; Ribeiro Dourado, C.M.; Johnson, W.D., Jr.; Riley, L.W. Urban epidemic of severe leptospirosis in Brazil. Salvador Leptospirosis Study Group. *Lancet* **1999**, *354*, 820–825. [CrossRef]
25. Bai, L.; Morton, L.C.; Liu, Q. Climate change and *mosquito*-borne diseases in China: A review. *Glob. Health* **2013**, *9*, 10. [CrossRef]
26. Yang, G.J.; Gao, Q.; Zhou, S.S.; Malone, J.B.; McCarroll, J.C.; Tanner, M.; Vounatsou, P.; Bergquist, R.; Utzinger, J.; Zhou, X.N. Mapping and predicting malaria transmission in the People's Republic of China, using integrated biology-driven and statistical models. *Geospat. Health* **2010**, *5*, 11–22. [CrossRef] [PubMed]
27. Focks, D.A.; Daniels, E.; Haile, D.G.; Keesling, J.E. A Simulation Model of the Epidemiology of Urban Dengue Fever: Literature Analysis, Model Development, Preliminary Validation, and Samples of Simulation Results. *Am. J. Trop. Med. Hyg.* **1995**, *53*, 489–506. [CrossRef] [PubMed]
28. Reeves, W.C.; Hardy, J.L.; Reisen, W.K.; Milby, M.M. Potential Effect of Global Warming on *Mosquito*-Borne Arboviruses. *J. Med Èntomol.* **1994**, *31*, 323–332. [CrossRef] [PubMed]
29. Reiter, P. Weather, Vector Biology, and Arboviral Recrudescence. In *The Arboviruses: Epidemiology and Ecology*; Monath, T.P., Ed.; CRC Press: Boca Raton, FL, USA, 1988; pp. 245–255.
30. Reiter, P. Global-warming and vector-borne disease in temperate regions and at high altitude. *Lancet* **1998**, *351*, 839–840. [CrossRef]
31. Reisen, W.K. Effect of Temperature on *Culex tarsalis* (Diptera: *Culicidae*) from the Coachella and San Joaquin Valleys of California. *J. Med Èntomol.* **1995**, *32*, 636–645. [CrossRef] [PubMed]
32. Kramer, L.D.; Hardy, J.L.; Presser, S.B. Effect of Temperature of Extrinsic Incubation on the Vector Competence of Culex tarsalis for Western Equine Encephalomyelitis Virus. *Am. J. Trop. Med. Hyg.* **1983**, *32*, 1130–1139. [CrossRef] [PubMed]
33. Day, J.F.; Curtis, G.A. Influence of Rainfall on *Culex nigripalpus* (Diptera: *Culicidae*) Blood-Feeding Behavior in Indian River County, Florida. *Ann. Èntomol. Soc. Am.* **1989**, *82*, 32–37. [CrossRef]
34. Hardy, J.L.; Meyer, R.P.; Presser, S.B.; Milby, M.M. Temporal Variations in the Susceptibility of a Semi-Isolated Population of Culex tarsalis to Peroral Infection with Western Equine Encephalomyelitis and St. Louis Encephalitis Viruses. *Am. J. Trop. Med. Hyg.* **1990**, *42*, 500–511. [CrossRef]

35. Lansdowne, C.; Hacker, C.S. The Effect of Fluctuating Temperature and Humidity on the Adult Life Table Characteristics of Five Strains of *Aedes Aegypti*. *J. Med Èntomol.* **1975**, *11*, 723–733. [CrossRef]
36. United Nations (UN); Intergovernmental Panel on Climate Change (IPCC). *Fourth Assessment Report Climate Change 2007*; Intergovernmental Panel on Climate Change: Geneva, Switzerland, 2007.
37. Gratz, N.G. Emerging and resurging vector-borne diseases. *Annu. Rev. Èntomol.* **1999**, *44*, 51–75. [CrossRef]
38. Halstead, S.B. Dengue. *Lancet* **2007**, *370*, 1644–1652. [CrossRef]
39. Scholte, E.J.; Schaffner, F. Waiting for the Tiger: Establishment and Spread of the Ae. albopictus *Mosquito* in Europe. In *Emerging Pests and Vector-borne Disease in Europe*; Takken, W., Knols, B.G.J., Eds.; Wageningen Academic Publishers: Wageningen, The Netherlands, 2007; pp. 241–460.
40. Guerra, C.A.; Gikandi, P.W.; Tatem, A.J.; Noor, A.M.; Smith, D.L.; I Hay, S.; Snow, R.W. The Limits and Intensity of Plasmodium falciparum Transmission: Implications for Malaria Control and Elimination Worldwide. *PLoS Med.* **2008**, *5*, e38. [CrossRef] [PubMed]
41. WHO. Dengue and Severe Dengue. 2019 Report. Available online: https://www.who.int/news-room/fact-sheets/detail/dengue-and-severe-dengue (accessed on 2 July 2019).
42. Kantor, I.N. *Dengue, Zika, Chikungunya y el Desarrollo de Vacunas*; MEDICINA: Buenos Aires, Argentina, 2018; Volume 78, pp. 23–28, ISBN 1669-9106.
43. Paixão, E.S.; Teixeira, M.G.; Rodrigues, L.C. Zika, chikungunya and dengue: The causes and threats of new and re-emerging arboviral diseases. *BMJ Glob. Health* **2018**, *3*, 000530. [CrossRef] [PubMed]
44. NIH, NIH Begins Study of Vaccine to Protect Against *Mosquito*-Borne Diseases. 2017. Available online: https://www.nih.gov/news-events/news-releases/nih-begins-study-vaccine-protect-against-mosquito-borne-diseases (accessed on 18 August 2019).
45. WHO. Yellow Fever. Available online: https://www.who.int/news-room/fact-sheets/detail/yellow-fever (accessed on 18 August 2019).
46. Chebabi Abramides, G.; Roiz, D.; Guitart, R.; Quintana, S.; Guerrero, I.; Gimenez, N. Effectiveness of a multiple intervention strategy for the control of the tiger *mosquito* (*Ae. albopictus*) in Spain. *Trans. R. Soc. Trop. Med. Hyg.* **2011**, *105*, 281–288. [CrossRef] [PubMed]
47. Fonseca, D.M.; Unlu, I.; Crepeau, T.; Farajollahi, A.; Healy, S.P.; Bartlett-Healy, K.; Strickman, D.; Gaugler, R.; Hamilton, G.; Kline, D.; et al. Area-wide management of Ae. albopictus. Part 2, Gauging the efficacy of traditional integrated pest control measures against urban container *mosquitoes*. *Pest Manag Sci.* **2013**, *69*, 1351–1361. [CrossRef] [PubMed]
48. Dowling, Z.; Armbruster, P.; LaDeau, S.L.; Decotiis, M.; Mottley, J.; Leisnham, P.T. Linking *Mosquito* Infestation to Resident Socioeconomic Status, Knowledge, and Source Reduction Practices in Suburban Washington, DC. *EcoHealth* **2013**, *10*, 36–47. [CrossRef]
49. Petrić, D.; Bellini, R.; Scholte, E.-J.; Rakotoarivony, L.M.; Schaffner, F. Monitoring population and environmental parameters of invasive *mosquito* species in Europe. *Parasites Vectors* **2014**, *7*, 187. [CrossRef]
50. Jacups, S.P.; Rapley, L.P.; Johnson, P.H.; Benjamin, S.; Ritchie, S.A. Bacillus thuringiensis var. israelensis misting for control of Aedes in cryptic ground containers in North Queensland, Australia. *Am. J. Trop. Med. Hyg.* **2013**, *88*, 490–496. [CrossRef]
51. Kline, D.L. Semiochemicals, traps/targets and mass trapping technology for *mosquito* management. *J. Am. Mosq. Control. Assoc.* **2007**, *23*, 241–251. [CrossRef]
52. Mackay, A.J.; Amador, M.; Barrera, R. An improved autocidal gravid ovitrap for the control and surveillance of *Aedes aegypti*. *Parasites Vectors* **2013**, *6*, 225. [CrossRef]
53. Cook, S.M.; Khan, Z.R.; Pickett, J.A. The Use of Push-Pull Strategies in Integrated Pest Management. *Annu. Rev. Èntomol.* **2007**, *52*, 375–400. [CrossRef] [PubMed]
54. Paz-Soldan, V.A.; Plasai, V.; Morrison, A.C.; Rios-Lopez, E.J.; Guedez-Gonzales, S.; Grieco, J.P.; Mundal, K.; Chareonviriyaphap, T.; Achee, N.L. Initial assessment of the acceptability of a push-pull Ae. aegypti control strategy in Iquitos, Peru and Kanchanaburi, Thailand. *Am. J. Trop. Med. Hyg.* **2011**, *84*, 208–217. [CrossRef] [PubMed]
55. Lima, J.B.P.; Rosa-Freitas, M.G.; Rodovalho, C.M.; Santos, F.; Lourenço-De-Oliveira, R. Is there an efficient trap or collection method for sampling Anopheles darlingi and other malaria vectors that can describe the essential parameters affecting transmission dynamics as effectively as human landing catches? - A Review. *Memórias Do Inst. Oswaldo Cruz* **2014**, *109*, 685–705. [CrossRef] [PubMed]

56. Salazar, F.V.; Achee, N.L.; Grieco, J.P.; Prabaripai, A.; Ojo, T.A.; Eisen, L.; Dureza, C.; Polsomboon, S.; Chareonviriyaphap, T. Effect of Ae. aegypti exposure to spatial repellent chemicals on BG-Sentinel (TM) trap catches. *Parasit. Vect.* **2013**, *6*, 145. [CrossRef] [PubMed]
57. Suman, D.S.; Wang, Y.; Bilgrami, A.L.; Gaugler, R. Ovicidal activity of three insect growth regulators against *Aedes* and *Culex mosquitoes*. *Acta Trop.* **2013**, *128*, 103–109. [CrossRef] [PubMed]
58. Mulla, M.S. The future of insect growth regulators in vector control. *J. Am. Mosq. Control. Assoc.* **1995**, *11*, 269–273. [PubMed]
59. Ocampo, C.B.; Julieth, M.N.; Carabali, M.; Alexander, N.; Osorio, L. Reduction in dengue cases observed during mass control of *Aedes* (Stegomyia) in street catch basins in an endemic urban area in Colombia. *Acta Trop.* **2014**, *132*, 15–22. [CrossRef]
60. PubChem. U.S National library of medicine (NIH), National Center for Biotechnology Information. Available online: https://pubchem.ncbi.nlm.nih.gov/compound/Fendona#section=Depositor-Supplied-Synonyms (accessed on 29 August 2019).
61. PubChem. U.S National library of medicine (NIH), National Center for Biotechnology Information. Available online: https://pubchem.ncbi.nlm.nih.gov/compound/lambda-Cyhalothrin (accessed on 29 August 2019).
62. PubChem. U.S National library of medicine (NIH), National Center for Biotechnology Information. Available online: https://pubchem.ncbi.nlm.nih.gov/compound/deltamethrin (accessed on 29 August 2019).
63. PubChem. U.S National library of medicine (NIH), National Center for Biotechnology Information. Available online: https://pubchem.ncbi.nlm.nih.gov/compound/Fenpropathrin (accessed on 29 August 2019).
64. Regnault-Roger, C. The potential of botanical essential oils for insect pest control. *Integr. Pest Manag. Rev.* **1997**, *2*, 25–34. [CrossRef]
65. Roman, P. Essential oils for the development of eco-friendly *mosquito* larvicides: A review. *Ind. Crop. Prod.* **2015**, *76*, 174–187.
66. Dias, C.N.; Moraes, D.F. Essential oils and their compounds as *Ae. aegypti* L. (*Diptera: Culicidae*) larvicides: Review. *Parasitol. Res.* **2014**, *113*, 565–592. [CrossRef]
67. Maheswaran, R.; Ignacimuthu, S. A novel herbal formulation against dengue vector *mosquitoes* Ae. aegypti and Ae. albopictus. *Parasitol. Res.* **2012**, *110*, 1801–1813. [CrossRef] [PubMed]
68. Mikami, A.; Yamashita, N. The inhibitory effects of a neem formulation on emergence of Oc. japonicus and *Culex* pipiens pallens. *Med. Entomol. Zool.* **2004**, *55*, 239–242. [CrossRef]
69. Felipe, C.F.B.; Fonsêca, K.S.; Barbosa, A.L.R.; Bezerra, J.N.S.; Neto, M.A.; França Fonteles, M.M.; Barros Viana, G.S. Alterations in behavior and memory induced by the essential oil of Zingiber officinale Roscoe (ginger) in mice are cholinergic-dependent. *J. Med. Plants Res.* **2008**, *2*, 163–170.
70. Rameshwar, S.R. Mechanism of action of insecticidal secondary metabolites of plant origin. *Crop Prot.* **2010**, *29*, 913–920.
71. Federici, B.A.; Park, H.W.; Bideshi, D.K.; Wirth, M.C.; Johnson, J.J.; Sakano, Y.; Tang, M. Developing recombinant bacteria for control of *mosquito* larvae. *J. Am. Mosq. Control. Assoc.* **2007**, *23*, 164–175. [CrossRef]
72. Bloomquist, J.R.; Boina, D.R.; Chow, E.; Carlier, P.R.; Reina, M.; González-Coloma, A. Mode of action of the plant-derived silphinenes on insect and mammalian GABAA receptor/chloride channel complex. *Pestic. Biochem. Physiol.* **2008**, *91*, 17–23. [CrossRef]
73. Casida, J.E. *Pyrethrum, the Natural Insecticide*; Academic Press: New York, NY, USA, 1973.
74. Khambay, B.P.; Batty, D.; Jewess, P.J.; Bateman, G.L.; Hollomon, D.W. Mode of action and pesticidal activity of the natural product dunnione and of some analogues. *Pest Manag. Sci.* **2003**, *59*, 174–182. [CrossRef]
75. Copping, L.G.; Menn, J.J. Biopesticides: A review of their action, applications and efficacy. *Pest Manag. Sci.* **2000**, *56*, 651–676. [CrossRef]
76. Bloomquist, J.R. Ion Channels as Targets for Insecticides. *Annu. Rev. Ѐntomol.* **1996**, *41*, 163–190. [CrossRef]
77. Enan, E.E. Molecular and pharmacological analysis of an octopamine receptor from american cockroach and fruit fly in response to plant essential oils. *Arch. Insect Biochem. Physiol.* **2005**, *59*, 161–171. [CrossRef]
78. Kostyukovsky, M.; Rafaeli, A.; Gileadi, C.; Demchenko, N.; Shaaya, E. Activation of octopaminergic receptors by essential oil constituents isolated from aromatic plants: Possible mode of action against insect pests. *Pest Manag. Sci.* **2002**, *58*, 1101–1106. [CrossRef] [PubMed]
79. Enan, E.E. Molecular response of Drosophila melanogaster tyramine receptor cascade to plant essential oils. *Insect Biochem. Mol. Biol.* **2005**, *35*, 309–321. [CrossRef] [PubMed]

80. Subbiah, P. Current trends in the control of *mosquito* vectors by means of biological larvicides. *J. Biofertil. Biopestici.* **2012**, *3*. [CrossRef]
81. Mahmood, F. Laboratory bioassay to compare susceptibilities of Ae. aegypti and *Anophels* albimanus to Bacillus thuringiensis var. israelensis as affected by their feeding rates. *J. Am. Mosq. Control Assoc.* **1998**, *14*, 69–71. [PubMed]
82. Singh, G.J.; Gill, S.S. An electron microscope study of the toxic action of Bacillus sphaericus in *Culex* quinquefasciatus larvae. *J. Invertebr. Pathol.* **1998**, *52*, 237–247. [CrossRef]
83. Poopathi, S.; Mani, T.R.; Rao, D.R.; Baskaran, G.; Kabilan, L. Susceptibilty levels of resistance of *Culex* quinquefasciatus to the insecticidal toxin of Bacillus sphaericus (strain 2362). *Environ. Ecol.* **2000**, *18*, 703–710.
84. Poopathi, S.; Mani, T.R.; Raghunatha, R.D.; Baskaran, G.; Lalitha, K. Effect of Bacillus *sphaericus* and Bacillus thuringiensis yare israelensis on the ultrastructural changes in the midgut of *Culex* quinquefasciatus Say (Diptera: *Culicidae*). *J. Ent. Res.* **1999**, *23*, 347–357.
85. Charles, J.F.; Silva-Filha, M.H.; Nielsen-LeRoux, C.; Humphreys, M.J.; Berry, C. Binding of the 51- and 42-kDa individual components from the Bacillus sphaericus crystal toxin to *mosquito* larval midgut membranes from *Culex* and *Anophels* sp. (Diptera: *Culicidae*). *FEMS Microbiol. Lett.* **1997**, *156*, 153–159. [CrossRef]
86. Silva-Filha, M.H.; Nielsen-LeRoux, C.; Charles, J.F. Identification of the receptor for Bacillus sphaericus crystal toxin in the brush border membrane of the *mosquito Culex* pipiens (Diptera: *Culicidae*). *Insect Biochem. Mol. Biol.* **1999**, *29*, 711–721. [CrossRef]
87. Baumann, P.; A Clark, M.; Baumann, L.; Broadwell, A.H. Bacillus sphaericus as a *mosquito* pathogen: Properties of the organism and its toxins. *Microbiol. Rev.* **1991**, *55*, 425–436.
88. Ignoffo, C.M.; Couch, T.L.; Garcia, C.; Kroha, M.J. Relative activity of Bacillus thuringiensis var. kurstaki and B. thuringiensis var. israelensis against larvae of Ae. aegypti, *Culex* quinquefasciatus, Trichoplusia ni, Heliothis zea, and Heliothis virescens. *J. Econ. Entomol.* **1981**, *74*, 218–222. [CrossRef] [PubMed]
89. Höfte, H.; Whiteley, H.R. Insecticidal crystal proteins of Bacillus thuringiensis. *Microbiol. Rev.* **1989**, *53*, 242–255. [PubMed]
90. Delecluse, A.; Rosso, M.L.; Ragni, A. Cloning and expression of a novel toxin gene from Bacillus thuringiensis sub sp. jegathesan encoding a highly *mosquito*cidal protein. *Appl. Environ. Microbiol.* **1995**, *61*, 4230–4235. [PubMed]
91. Frutos, R.; Rang, C.; Royer, M. Managing Insect Resistance to Plants ProducingBacillus thuringiensisToxins. *Crit. Rev. Biotechnol.* **1999**, *19*, 227–276. [CrossRef]
92. Pimentel, D.; Burgess, M. Effects of Single Versus Combinations of Insecticides on the Development of Resistance. *Environ. Èntomol.* **1985**, *14*, 582–589. [CrossRef]
93. McGaughey, W.H.; Gould, F.; Gelernter, W. Bt resistance management. *Nat. Biotechnol.* **1998**, *16*, 144–146. [CrossRef] [PubMed]
94. Liu, Y.B.; Tabashnik, B.E. Experimental evidence that refuges delay insect adaptation to Bacillus thuringiensis. *Proc. R. Soc. B Biol. Sci.* **1997**, *264*, 605–610. [CrossRef]
95. Wirth, M.C.; Zaritsky, A.; Ben-Dov, E.; Manasherob, R.; Khasdan, V.; Boussiba, S.; Walton, W.E. Cross-resistance spectra of *Culex* quinquefasciatus resistant to *mosquito*cidal toxins of Bacillus thuringiensis towards recombinant Escherichia coli expressing genes from B. thuringiensis subsp. israelensis. *Environ. Microbiol.* **2007**, *9*, 1393–1401. [CrossRef]
96. Alphey, L. Genetic control of *mosquitoes*. *Annu. Rev. Entomol.* **2014**, *59*, 205–224. [CrossRef]
97. Alphey, L.; Benedict, M.; Bellini, R.; Clark, G.G.; Dame, D.A.; Service, M.W.; Dobson, S.L. Sterile-Insect Methods for Control of *Mosquito*-Borne Diseases: An Analysis. *Vector Borne Zoonotic Dis.* **2010**, *10*, 295–311. [CrossRef]
98. Lambrechts, L.; Koella, J.C.; Boëte, C. Can transgenic *mosquitoes* afford the fitness cost? *Trends Parasitol.* **2008**, *24*, 4–7. [CrossRef] [PubMed]
99. FAO/IAEA. Status and Risk Assessment of the Use of Transgenic Arthropods in Plant Protection. In Proceedings of the a Technical Meeting Organized by the Joint FAO/IAEA Programme of Nuclear Techniques in Food and Agriculture and the Secretariat of the International Plant Protection Convention, Rome, Italy, 8–12 April 2002.
100. Benedict, M. The first releases of transgenic *mosquitoes*: An argument for the sterile insect technique. *Trends Parasitol.* **2003**, *19*, 349–355. [CrossRef]

101. Dame, D.; Curtis, C.; Benedict, M.; Robinson, A.; Knols, B. Historical applications of induced sterilization in field populations of *mosquitoes*. *Malar. J.* **2009**, *8*, S2. [CrossRef] [PubMed]
102. Windbichler, N.; Papathanos, P.A.; Crisanti, A. Targeting the X chromosome during spermatogenesis induces Y chromosome transmission ratio distortion and early dominant embryo lethality in *Anophels* gambiae. *PLoS Genet.* **2008**, *4*, e1000291. [CrossRef] [PubMed]
103. Werren, J.H.; Baldo, L.; Clark, M.E. Wolbachia: Master manipulators of invertebrate biology. *Nat. Rev. Genet.* **2008**, *6*, 741–751. [CrossRef] [PubMed]
104. Burt, A.; Trivers, R. *Genes in Conflict: The Biology of Selfish Genetic Elements*; Belknap Press/Harvard University Press: Cambridge, MA, USA, 2006; p. 610.
105. Burt, A. Site-specific selfish genes as tools for the control and genetic engineering of natural populations. *Proc. R. Soc. B Biol. Sci.* **2003**, *270*, 921–928. [CrossRef]
106. Chen, C.H.; Huang, H.; Ward, C.M.; Su, J.T.; Schaeffer, L.V.; Guo, M.; Hay, B.A. A synthetic maternal-effect selfish genetic element drives population replacement in Drosophila. *Science* **2007**, *316*, 597–600. [CrossRef]
107. Lee, S.W.; Chang, S.H.; Lai, Y.S.; Lin, C.C.; Tsai, C.M.; Lee, Y.C.; Chen, J.C.; Huang, C.L. Effect of Temperature on the Growth of Silver Nanoparticles Using Plasmon-Mediated Method under the Irradiation of Green LEDs. *Materials* **2014**, *7*, 7781–7798. [CrossRef]
108. Santos-Magalhães, N.S.; Mosqueira, V.C.F. Nanotechnology applied to the treatment of malaria. *Adv. Drug Deliv. Rev.* **2010**, *62*, 560–575. [CrossRef]
109. Lasic, D.D. Novel applications of liposomes. *Trends Biotechnol.* **1998**, *16*, 307–321. [CrossRef]
110. Peeters, P.A.M.; Huiskamp, C.W.E.M.; Eling, W.M.C.; Crommelin, D.J.A. Chloroquine containing liposomes in the chemotherapy of murine malaria. *Parasitology* **1989**, *98*, 381–386. [CrossRef] [PubMed]
111. Agrawal, A.K.; Singhal, A.; Gupta, C. Functional drug targeting to erythrocytes in vivo using antibody bearing liposomes as drug vehicles. *Biochem. Biophys. Res. Commun.* **1987**, *148*, 357–361. [CrossRef]
112. Wu, Y.; Yang, W.; Wang, C.; Hu, J.; Fu, S. Chitosan nanoparticles as a novel delivery system for ammonium glycyrrhizinate. *Int. J. Pharm.* **2005**, *295*, 235–245. [CrossRef] [PubMed]
113. Nakache, E.; Poulain, N.; Candau, F.; Orecchioni, A.; Irache, J. Biopolymer and Polymer Nanoparticles and Their Biomedical Applications. In *Handbook of Nanostructured Materials and Nanotechnology*; Nalwa, H.S., Ed.; Academic Press: New York, NY, USA, 2000.
114. Baird, J.K.; Hoffman, S.L. Primaquine therapy for malaria. *Clin. Infect. Dis.* **2000**, *39*, 1336–1345. [CrossRef] [PubMed]
115. Omwoyo, W.N.; Ogutu, B.; Oloo, F.; Swai, H.; Kalombo, L.; Melariri, P.; Mahanga, G.M.; Gathirwa, J.W. Preparation, characterization, and optimization of primaquine-loaded solid lipid nanoparticles. *Int. J. Nanomed.* **2014**, *9*, 3865–3874.
116. Baird, J.; Rieckmann, K.H. Can primaquine therapy for vivax malaria be improved? *Trends Parasitol.* **2003**, *19*, 115–120. [CrossRef]
117. Dennis, E.; Peoples, V.A.; Johnson, F.; Bibbs, R.K.; Topps, D.; Bopda-Waffo, A.; Coats, M.T. Utilizing Nanotechnology to Combat Malaria. *J. Infect. Dis. Ther.* **2015**, *3*, 4. [CrossRef]
118. Ahmed, T.A.; Aljaeid, B.M. Preparation, characterization, and potential application of chitosan, chitosan derivatives, and chitosan metal nanoparticles in pharmaceutical drug delivery. *Drug Des. Dev. Ther.* **2016**, *10*, 483–507. [CrossRef]
119. Kilama, W.; Ntoumi, F. Malaria: A research agenda for the eradication era. *Lancet* **2009**, *374*, 1480–1482. [CrossRef]
120. Schwendener, R.A. Liposomes as vaccine delivery systems: A review of the recent advances. *Ther. Adv. Vaccines* **2014**, *2*, 159–182. [CrossRef]
121. Sen, G.L. A brief history of RNAi: The silence of the genes. *FASEB J.* **2006**, *20*, 1293–1299. [CrossRef] [PubMed]
122. Airs, P.M.; Bartholomay, L.C. RNA Interference for *Mosquito* and *Mosquito*-Borne Disease Control. *Insects* **2017**, *8*, 4. [CrossRef] [PubMed]
123. Zhang, X.; Zhang, J.; Zhu, K.Y. Chitosan/double-stranded RNA nanoparticle-mediated RNA interference to silence chitin synthase genes through larval feeding in the African malaria *mosquito* (*Anophels* gambiae). *Insect Mol. Biol.* **2010**, *19*, 683–693. [CrossRef] [PubMed]
124. Bennet, D.; Kim, S. Polymer Nanoparticles for Smart Drug Delivery. In *Application of Nanotechnology in Drug Delivery*; IntechOpen: London, UK, 2014.

125. Moon, J.J.; Suh, H.; Polhemus, M.E.; Ockenhouse, C.F.; Yadava, A.; Irvine, D.J. Antigen-Displaying Lipid-Enveloped PLGA Nanoparticles as Delivery Agents for a Plasmodium vivax Malaria Vaccine. *PLoS ONE* **2012**, *7*, e31472. [CrossRef] [PubMed]
126. Tripathy, S.; Das, S.; Chakraborty, S.P.; Sahu, S.K.; Pramanik, P.; Roy, S. Synthesis, characterization of chitosan–tripolyphosphate conjugated chloroquine nanoparticle and it's in vivo anti-malarial efficacy against rodent parasite: A dose and duration dependent approach. *Int. J. Pharm.* **2012**, *434*, 292–305. [CrossRef]
127. Tripathy, S.; Das, S.; Dash, S.K.; Chattopadhyay, S.; Roy, S. The impact of nanochloroquine on restoration of hepatic and splenic. *J. Nanopart.* **2013**, *9*, 106152. [CrossRef]
128. Benelli, G.; Maggi, F.; Pavela, R.; Murugan, K.; Govindarajan, M.; Vaseeharan, B.; Petrelli, R.; Cappellacci, L.; Kumar, S.; Hofer, A.; et al. *Mosquito* control with green nanopesticides: Towards the One Health approach? A review of non-target effects. *Environ. Sci. Pollut. Res.* **2017**, *25*, 10184–10206. [CrossRef]
129. Benelli, G. Plant-mediated biosynthesis of nanoparticles as an emerging tool against *mosquitoes* of medical and veterinary importance: A review. *Parasitol. Res.* **2016**, *115*, 23–34. [CrossRef]
130. Azarudeen, R.M.S.T.; Govindarajan, M.; Amsath, A.; Muthukumaran, U.; Benelli, G. Single-step biofabrication of silver nanocristals using Naregamia alata: A cost effective and eco-friendly control tool in the fight against Malaria, Zika virus and St Louis encephalitis *mosquito* vectors. *J. Clust. Sci.* **2017**, *28*, 179–203. [CrossRef]
131. Benelli, G. Green synthesized nanoparticles in the fight against *mosquito*-borne diseases and cancer—a brief review. *Enzym. Microb. Technol.* **2016**, *95*, 58–68. [CrossRef]
132. Panneerselvam, C.; Murugan, K.; Roni, M.; Aziz, A.T.; Suresh, U.; Rajaganesh, R.; Madhiyazhagan, P.; Subramaniam, J.; Dinesh, D.; Nicoletti, M.; et al. Fern-synthesize nanoparticles in the fight against malaria: LC/MS analysis of Pteridium aquilinum leaf extract and biosynthesis of silver nanoparticles with high *mosquito*cidal and antiplasmodial activity. *Parasitol. Res.* **2016**, *115*, 997–1013. [CrossRef] [PubMed]
133. Alto, B.W.; Juliano, S.A. Precipitation and temperature effects of populations of Ae. albopictus (Diptera: *Culicidae*): Implications for range expansion. *J. Med. Entomol.* **2001**, *38*, 646–656. [CrossRef] [PubMed]
134. Roni, M.; Murugan, K.; Panneerselvam, C.; Subramaniam, J.; Nicoletti, M.; Madhiyazhagan, P.; Dinesh, D.; Suresh, U.; Khater, H.F.; Wei, H.; et al. Characterization and biotoxicity of Hypnea musciformis-synthesized silver nanoparticles as potential eco-friendly control tool against Ae. aegypti and Plutella xylostella. *Ecotoxicol. Environ. Saf.* **2015**, *121*, 31–38. [CrossRef] [PubMed]
135. Costa, E.A.P.A.; Santos, E.M.; Correia, J.C.; Albuquerque, C.M.R. Impact of small variations in temperature and humidity on the reproductive activity and survival of *Aedes* aegypti (Diptera, *Culicidae*). *Rev. Bras. Entomol.* **2010**, *54*, 488–493. [CrossRef]
136. Becker, N. Influence of climate change on *mosquito* development and *mosquito*-borne diseases in Europe. *Parasitol. Res.* **2008**, *103*, 19–28. [CrossRef] [PubMed]
137. Canyon, D.V.; Hii, J.L.K.; Muller, R. Adaptation of *Aedes* aegypti (Diptera: *Culicidae*) oviposition behaviour in response to humidity and diet. *J. Insect Physiol.* **1999**, *45*, 959–964. [CrossRef]
138. Reiter, P.; Amador, M.A.; Anderson, R.A.; Clark, G.G. Short report: Dispersal of Ae. aegypti in an urban area after blood feeding as demonstrated by rubidium-marked eggs. *Am. J. Trop. Med. Hyg.* **1995**, *52*, 177–179. [CrossRef]
139. Mogi, M.; Miyagi, I.; Abadi, K.; Syafruddin. Inter- and intraspecific variation in resistance to desiccation by adult Aedes (Stegomyia) spp. (Diptera: *Culicidae*) from Indonesia. *Med. Vet. Entomol.* **1996**, *33*, 53–57.
140. Ahmed, T.; Scholz, M.; Al-Faraj, F.; Niaz, W. Water-Related Impacts of Climate Change on Agriculture and Subsequently on Public Health: A Review for Generalists with Particular Reference to Pakistan. *Int. J. Environ. Res. Public Health* **2016**, *13*, 1051. [CrossRef]
141. Kreft, S.; Eckstein, D.; Melchior, I. *Global Climate Risk Index 2017 Who Suffers Most from Extreme Weather Events? Weather-related Loss Events in 2015 and 1996 to 2015, 2017*; Germanwatch e.V.: Bonn, Germany, 2014.
142. Jahan, F. Short report: Dengue Fever (DF) in Pakistan. *Asia Pac. Fam. Med.* **2011**, *10*, 1. [CrossRef]
143. Kazmi, D.H.; Li, J.; Ruan, C.; Zhao, S.; Li, Y.; Sen, Z. A statistical downscaling model for summer rainfall over Pakistan. *Clim. Dyn.* **2016**, *47*, 2653–2666. [CrossRef]

International Journal of
Environmental Research and Public Health

MDPI

Review

Water-Related Impacts of Climate Change on Agriculture and Subsequently on Public Health: A Review for Generalists with Particular Reference to Pakistan

Toqeer Ahmed [1], Miklas Scholz [2,3,*], Furat Al-Faraj [2] and Wajeeha Niaz [1]

1 Centre for Climate Research and Development, COMSAS Institute of Information Technology, Islamabad Campus, Park Road, Chak Shahzad, Islamabad 45550, Pakistan; toqeer.ahmed@comsats.edu.pk (T.A.); wajeehaniax@gmail.com (W.N.)
2 Division of Water Resources Engineering, Faculty of Engineering, Lund University, P.O. Box 118, Lund 22100, Sweden; f.a.m.al-faraj@edu.salford.ac.uk
3 Civil Engineering Research Group, School of Computing, Science and Engineering, The University of Salford, The Crescent, Salford M5 4WT, UK
* Correspondence: miklas.scholz@tvrl.lth.se or m.scholz@salford.ac.uk; Tel.: +46-46-222-8920

Academic Editor: Yu-Pin Lin
Received: 30 June 2016; Accepted: 21 October 2016; Published: 27 October 2016

Abstract: Water-related impacts due to change in climatic conditions ranging from water scarcity to intense floods and storms are increasing in developing countries like Pakistan. Water quality and waterborne diseases like hepatitis, cholera, typhoid, malaria and dengue fever are increasing due to chaotic urbanization, industrialization, poor hygienic conditions, and inappropriate water management. The morbidity rate is high due to lack of health care facilities, especially in developing countries. Organizations linked to the Government of Pakistan (e.g., Ministry of Environment, Ministry of Climate Change, Planning and Development, Ministry of Forest, Irrigation and Public Health, Pakistan Meteorological Department, National Disaster Management, Pakistan Agricultural Research Centre, Pakistan Council for Research in Water Resources, and Global Change Impact Study Centre), United Nation organizations, provincial government departments, non-governmental organizations (e.g., Global Facility and Disaster Reduction), research centers linked to universities, and international organizations (International Institute for Sustainable Development, Food and Agriculture, Global Climate Fund and World Bank) are trying to reduce the water-related impacts of climate change, but due to lack of public awareness and health care infrastructure, the death rate is steadily increasing. This paper critically reviews the scientific studies and reports both at national and at international level benefiting generalists concerned with environmental and public health challenges. The article underlines the urgent need for water conservation, risk management, and the development of mitigation measures to cope with the water-related impacts of climate change on agriculture and subsequently on public health. Novel solutions and bioremediation methods have been presented to control environmental pollution and to promote awareness among the scientific community. The focus is on diverse strategies to handle the forthcoming challenges associated with water resources management.

Keywords: bacteria; developing country; disease; environmental management; freshwater; pollution; sustainability; urbanization; wastewater; water resources

1. Introduction, Rationale, and Aim

Water-related disasters such as floods and droughts, changes in rainfall patterns, and increases in temperature are serious challenges, and their impacts on water quality and ultimately on human health have to be assessed and controlled [1]. About 50% of the recorded disasters are commonly due to floods and roughly 10% owing to high temperatures or heat waves [2]. Approximately 25% of all illnesses like diarrhea, malaria, and respiratory infection are due to change in climate and environmental degradation such as watercourse contamination from polluted agricultural runoff [3]. Challenges are particularly serious in developing countries. For example, according to the Global Facility for Disaster Reduction and Recovery, one-third of the people in Karachi lack clean water and health facilities [4].

With changing climate conditions such as rainfall, temperature, and humidity, water has great impacts both on agriculture and health. Water availability and quality are deteriorating and waterborne diseases are subsequently increasing, which impacts both sectors. Water quality in relation to climate change is not properly studied, especially the impact of climate change on water-related (both water- and vector-related) diseases. In Pakistan, waterborne diseases like cholera and vector borne diseases like malaria and dengue fever are prevailing with the changing rainfall pattern, temperature, humidity, etc. Water availability for agriculture is important as about 90% of water is used for irrigation purposes in many countries. With changing climatic conditions, water availability will affect agriculture and livestock production. There is a strong need to study these impacts with changing climatic scenarios.

Possible pathways through which climate change can affect multiple health outcomes are indicated in Figure 1. It follows that there is a need to assess water-related impacts of climate change on agriculture and subsequently on public health in general, but more particularly for developing countries, informing decision-makers with a wide range of professional backgrounds in environmental public health.

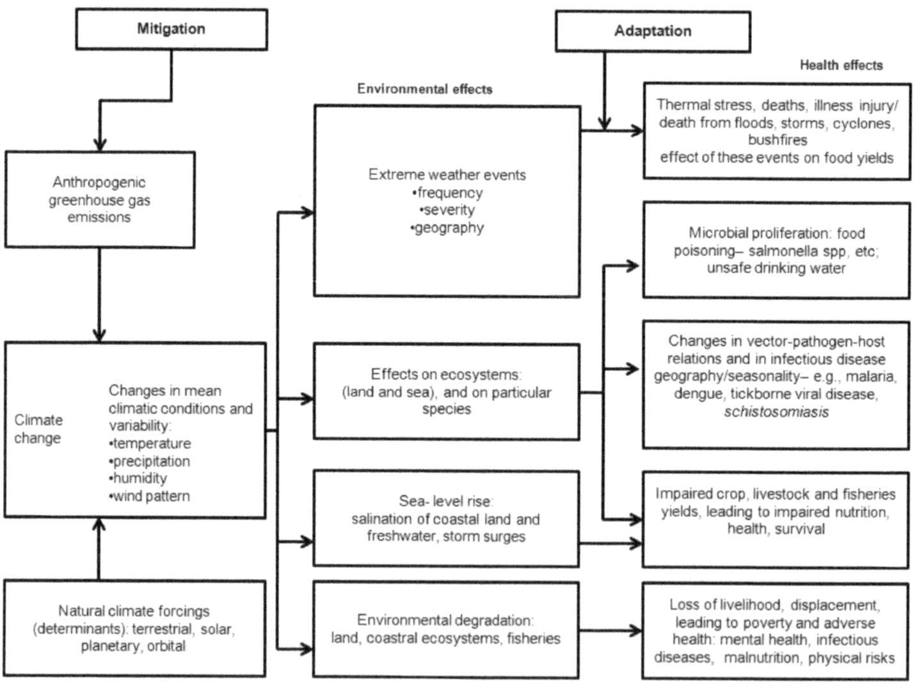

Figure 1. Overview of environmental and health effects linked to mitigation and adaptation strategies to climate change (after [5]).

Various research institutes, academia, and government organizations are working on collaborative projects such as the projects "Impacts of Climate Change on Pakistan's Water Sector Vulnerability

Assessment" and "Glacial Lakes Outburst Floods" (funded by the United Nations Development Program). Other climate and water conservation projects are conducted by different government institutions such as the Climate Change, Alternative Energy, and Water Resources Department of Pakistan; Agriculture Research Center and Global Change Impact Study Center; as well as international non-governmental organizations. There are many other organizations both at government level and in the private sector working on impacts of climate change, natural disasters, and their direct impacts human health. Private and government authorities are also working on water quality and other water related issues.

There is currently neither a framework nor detailed analytical work that has been implemented showing the specific state of water resources management, agriculture, water quality, and public health with reference to climate change in Pakistan. Therefore, this paper aims to critically review scientific studies to assess the need for water conservation, risk management, and the development of mitigation measures to cope with the water-related impacts of climate change on agriculture and subsequently on public health, particularly from the Pakistani perspective. Novel solutions and strategies benefiting a wide range of generalists and stakeholders will be presented to control environmental pollution and to promote public awareness, and deliver the basis for a conceptual framework for the assessment of current and future scenarios.

2. Methodology

A comprehensive literature review was performed between January 2015 and June 2016. References were identified using Google Scholar (in addition to the standard Google search engine), Web of Science, Scopus, and Science Direct. The key words and phrases climate change, water-related impact, agricultural pollution, vector-borne disease, waterborne disease, flooding impact, water quality, extreme event, public health, pollution control, water availability, water quality, and Pakistan were used in various combinations. The publication time period considered was between 1980 and early 2016.

The literature cited was selected based on a critical review of publications of greatest relevance to Pakistan and countries with similar environmental boundary conditions. Other criteria such as publication date, outlet type, and author (or institution) played less important roles during literature selection.

3. Flooding Impacts and Environmental Pollution

Floods bring biological and chemical pollutants, which might ultimately contaminate the groundwater. Flooding events often cause soil erosion associated with chemical pollutants such as organic and inorganic matter, including heavy metals and polycyclic aromatic compounds, which pose threats to groundwater sources and may be taken up by crops and other plants [6]. Both fertilizers and flooded soils are sources of polycyclic aromatic hydrocarbons [6].

Water-borne and health-related infections may increase after flooding. An increase in mold after extensive flooding of healthcare facilities and a simultaneous decrease in multi-drug-resistant organisms has been noted [7]. Contamination with enteric Gram-negative bacteria (e.g., *Aeromonas* species), *Legionella* species, and non-tuberculous *Mycobacterium* species in hospital water sources has also been reported [7]. The spread of water-borne diseases like cholera and dysentery may increase after diarrhea outbreaks. The risk of dysentery might increase after flooding events [8]. Floods may increase both water-borne and vector-borne diseases such as cholera, typhoid, dysentery, and malaria as well as dengue and yellow fever [9]. Flood-related events increase the risk of infectious diseases, including respiratory and vector-borne illnesses [10].

The intensity of floods and droughts adversely affect public health during both the event and immediately thereafter. Climate change can increase the frequency and intensity of floods, droughts, and heat waves within a country or at a regional level, and their appearance is uncertain [11]. A summary of relatively recent flood losses in Pakistan is given in Table 1.

Table 1. Summary of estimated flood losses over the past few years in Pakistan.

Year	Deaths	House Damages	Population Affected
2010	490	1,602,800	175,000,000
2011	69,890	15,977,500	9,345,000
2012	570	636,400	4,849,800
2013	330	46,200	1,489,100
2014	370	107,100	2,412,000
2015	150	4800	1,314,500

4. Water Quality and Public Health

Water pollution and associated public health implications belong to the most important challenges faced by humankind. Chemical (heavy metals such as lead, arsenic and iron), viral (hepatitis A, polio, and *Enteroviruses*) and bacterial (total and fecal coliforms along with *Streptococci*) pollution has profound effects on public health [12]. Various studies conducted in Bangladesh, China, and Pakistan reported on high concentrations of arsenic, but also on heavy metal pollutants like nickel, lead, chromium, cadmium, and mercury in groundwater, which directly affected public health [13,14]. One major source of water contamination is the improper disposal of sewage [15,16]. Both chemical and microbial pollution can affect aquatic life. Heavy metal pollution is a risk to fish, and subsequently to public health [17]. Improper management of sewage discharge and leakage of cesspool-influenced groundwater into coastal lagoons is responsible for some aquatic and environmental challenges [18,19].

Approximately 30% of the world population living in developing countries lacks access to sewage disposal [20]. *Escherichia coli* is often seen as the best indicator for fecal water pollution [21]. *Enteroviruses* are used as indicators to assess viral water contamination [22]. The diversity of antibiotic-resistant bacteria in aquatic environments can be enhanced by water pollution [23]. Heavy rainfall and floods associated with extreme weather and water supply contamination are responsible for waterborne disease outbreaks causing great risks for both developed and developing countries [24].

Climate change is often linked to an increase in occurrence of draughts and/or floods. Data relating floods with diarrheal patients in Dhaka (Bangladesh) during 1988, 1998 and 2004 have been discussed [25]. They reported that *Vibrio cholera* was the first and Rotavirus was the second most frequent cause of diarrhea. Other causes of diarrhea were enterotoxigenic *E. coli*, *Shigella*, and *Salmonella* species. Water-related pathogens cause diseases, their surveillance, and possible interventions are discussed in Table 2 [26–28]. No comprehensive published work has been reported on the relationship between water quality and fecal coliforms with special reference to climate change in Pakistan.

Table 2. Overview of water-related pathogens (both waterborne and vector-borne), diseases, and their impacts.

Pathogen Types and Typical Organisms	Typical Major Common Diseases	Surveillance	Interventions	References
Waterborne pathogens (examples)				
Salmonella spp.; *Escherichia coli*; *Vibrio cholera*; *Shigella* spp.; *Streptococci*; *Yersinia* spp.	Typhoid; abdominal cramps; Dysentery; Cholera; sore throat; Yersiniosis	Microbiological water quality; monitoring, especially during and after a monsoon	Track diseases; monitor water quality and health; diagnose and investigate waterborne and other infections outbreaks; apply health interventions	[26,27]
Water-based pathogens (examples)				
Poliovirus; *Enteroviruses*; Rotavirus; Hepatitis A and E viruses; *Helicobacter pylori*	Polio; diarrhoea; stomach ulcers; infections; respiratory illnesses	Microbiological water quality monitoring during and after a monsoon	Track diseases; monitor health; diagnose and investigate waterborne outbreaks; apply health interventions	[26,27]
Vector-borne pathogens (examples)				
Sand flies; dengue virus (mosquitoes); Plasmodium (mosquitoes); Flavivirus; Tsetse flies	*Leishmaniasis*; dengue fever; fever with shivering; Japanese encephalitis; West Nile virus; Yellow fever; Trypanosomiasis	Monitoring of vectors and their habitats; source identification and enhanced investigations	Diagnose and investigate vector-borne and other related outbreaks; apply the health interventions available	[26,28]

5. Overview of Agricultural Water Pollution Impacting on Human Health

This overview section is an introduction to this rather wide topic. Case study data usually depend on local and regional boundary conditions, which are often of little interest to the international reader. Therefore, the authors did not present numerical data, but provided a good number of references useful for readers requiring more information including data.

Agriculture can negatively affect water quality, especially in rural areas of both developing and developed countries [29]. Crops are often irrigated with wastewater polluted by domestic and industrial effluents containing heavy metals, which are potentially absorbed by vegetables and other cash crops, ultimately becoming part of the food chain. Literature [30] reported on potential toxicological risks of heavy metals on the public health using contaminated food. Urban agriculture has prominent effects on human health in terms of greenhouse gas emissions and spreading of water-related diseases such as malaria. Antonio-Nkondjio [31] pointed out that urban agriculture has a major role in spreading resistance to insecticides and malarial diseases. Chemical pollution can be minimized by applying natural fertilizers and sustainable agricultural principles in general.

Changes in temperature and rainfall due to climate change may influence the growth of fungi and increase in mycotoxins in agricultural food products, which are high risks to human health. Warm and humid climate is favorable for fungal growth where the average annual temperature is approximately 25 °C, but it varies depending upon season.

South Asian countries including Pakistan have been recognized as vulnerable regions subjected to the negative impacts of climate change in terms of public health [32]. A high population growth rate, deficiency in water availability, degradation of soil, urbanization, and an animal-based diet along with climate change are the global challenges, which are a threat to food security [33]. An increase in the demand for water in the agriculture sector for crops poses a severe threat to balanced water resources management. Only some crops such as wheat and barley are largely weather resistant, in particular, in a changing climate [34]. In general, the agriculture sector of most countries such as Pakistan has been adversely impacted by climate change, which may lead to a food shortage by 2030, resulting in an increase in food prices [35].

Droughts, floods, warming, and changes in precipitation can directly alter crop yields. This can threaten human life and cause long-term malnutrition and diseases. A study conducted on wheat production (Swat and Charsadda districts, Pakistan) suggests short duration and high yielding varieties should be introduced in hilly areas due to global warming [36].

Climate change has more profound impacts on agriculture and health as indicated in Table 3, which is based partly on literature and partly on expert opinion, because literature evidence is not conclusive in the interpretation of the strength of the case study relationships shown. Manure and animal waste contains pathogens, veterinary pharmaceuticals, and nutrients along with heavy metals, which are transported and spread into the environment, ultimately causing both environmental and human health hazards [37]. More intense storms due to climate change cause these contaminants to run-off and ultimately to enter the human food chain.

Table 3. Potentially strong relationships between exposure situations and health conditions relevant to agricultural food production and storage (based on this literature review and the expert opinions of the authors).

Health Conditions of Concern	Polluted Air	Excreta and Household Wastewater	Polluted Water or Deficiencies in Water Management	Polluted Food	Unsuitable Housing	Global Change of Environment
Acute respiratory infection	X		X		X	
Other infections		X		X	X	
Diarrheal diseases		X	X	X		X
Malaria and other vector-borne diseases			X			X
Injuries and poisonings	X	X	X	X	X	X
Mental health conditions					X	
Cardiovascular diseases	X			X	X	X
Cancer	X					X
Chronic respiratory diseases	X					X

6. Water Pollution Control and Detection Techniques

This section follows the logic of the three previous sections: Section 3 links climate change to flooding, which impacts the environment, usually increasing water pollution. Section 4 indicates how water quality is linked to public health. Finally, Section 5 links more specifically agricultural water pollution to human health. Raw and agricultural water pollution and its impacts on human health are discussed in Section 6. Commonly used detection techniques and strategies developed by scientists to control the current problems and the need to develop new techniques under changing climatic conditions are assessed.

Bacteria-based systems can help in the degradation of environmental pollutants [38]. Phytoremediation removes toxic metals from wastewater. Empirical studies have reported on the use of plants for the removal of heavy metals and dyes from wastewater and soil [39,40]. Among the conventional technologies, various plant parts are used as adsorbents and natural coagulants as well as in advanced oxidation processes for the removal of metallic nanoparticles, toxic metals, and bacterial pollution from wastewater [41,42]. Whole cell sensing systems as well as chemical and biosensors are applied for the detection of environmental pollutants like metals. Recent advancements have shown the conversion of toxic metals into useful metallic nanoparticles by using microbes [43,44].

Biosensors have specific interactions between enzymes and substrate, and are highly specific in their detection capabilities. Bio-sorption is another emerging and novel technique for the removal of toxic metals from wastewater. Zouboulis et al. [45] used *Bacillus laterosporus* and *Bacillus licheniformis* for cadmium and chromium removal. They reported that bacteria have a high surface area-to-volume ratio like metallic nanoparticles, and that they therefore provide a large contact interface, which interacts with metals from the surrounding environment. Pyridine is one of the most widespread heterocyclic industrial contaminants. A new strain of *Arthrobacter* has been found to be the best among all the known strains for the purification of industrial wastewater [46]. *Arthrobacter*, which is used for the removal of atrazine, has good bioremediation potential concerning contaminated soils and waters [47].

Some solutions for the removal of environmental pollutants are conventional such as synthetic and natural coagulation, adsorption, and anaerobic digestion of contaminants. In comparison, others are advanced such as emerging nanotechnology-based techniques (e.g., the use of silver nanoparticles, titanium dioxide, zinc oxide, iron nanoparticles, and carbon nanotubes) for the removal of contaminants [48,49]. Both conventional and advanced solutions aim to provide and maintain better solutions to environmental pollution. Reducing contaminants can help in improving both environmental and human health. Improved housing design and better pipe material used in water supply can assist in reducing environmental pollution and improving public health in developing countries [50].

Animal waste-containing fecal matter can cause contamination to water resources. Anaerobic digestion of animal waste rather than dumping of waste at different places (as it is a common practice in developing countries) can cause environmental and public health problems [51]. Animal waste can also be used as an alternative source of energy. Therefore, anaerobic digestion of animal waste could be applied for the production of biogas, and different methanogens can enhance the process of digestion [37].

Emerging nanotechnology-based methods and nano-materials with their unique physical and chemical properties have previously been applied to reduce environmental pollution [49]. Silver and other metallic nanoparticles (e.g., zinc oxide) have been developed against waterborne pathogens [48]. Carbon nanotubes have been utilized as adsorbents, because of their unique properties beneficial for the removal of organic and inorganic pollutants along with radionuclides [52]. Results compared with natural zeolites indicated that the adsorbents are highly efficient and economical. Magnetic graphene oxides have been tested as adsorbates for the removal of trace metals of polybrominated diphenyl ethers in water treatment. They are regarded as highly efficient for environmental remediation [53]. Moreover, magnetic nano-composites are used as adsorbents for the removal of heavy metals such as chromium, lead, mercury, and arsenic [54].

7. Water Pollution, Climate Change, and Population Increase

Climate change is expected to alter water quantity and quality [55–60], and is likely to be different between large and small basins [61,62]. The potential changes in temperature and precipitation may not uniformly distribute over large watersheds [63] and thus both regional and local scales as well as the extent of urbanization must be considered in climate change impact studies for water resources protection [59]. Climate change has dynamic impacts on surface watercourses such as rivers, streams, and lakes, which provide clean water. In order to protect water resources, policy makers should consider climate change impacts on the reduction of pollution for improving water quality [59].

Human and industrial (including agriculture) wastes are the main pollutants contaminating water bodies particularly during flood events. Bacterial pollutants of human origin such as *E. coli*, *Salmonella*, and *Vibrio* as well as heavy metals and pesticide-related carcinogens are originating from different industries and are discharged into water bodies, ultimately causing pollution [64], which puts farming communities particularly at risk. Both bacteriological and chemical water pollutants have negative effects on human health, but less information is available in relation to changing climatic conditions. An increase in population and urbanization is putting water resources in danger, negatively affecting public health, the economy, and the environment [65].

Extreme climatic conditions such as high temperature and heavy precipitation play significant roles in increasing water pollution. Urban runoff to rivers and streams pollute water resources [66]. Different waterborne pathogens such as *Giardia* cysts and Cryposporidium oocysts correlate positively with rainfall [67]. Vector- and waterborne diseases are enhanced by El Niño-related extreme climatic conditions [67]. Extreme weather events and climate change have momentous impacts on the hydrological cycle [68].

For example, in a drought-prone region in the Sindh Province (Pakistan), inhabitants either have no access to freshwater or use brackish water for drinking purposes [12]. Similarly, in the Baluchistan Province (Pakistan), the groundwater level is falling at a rate of 3.5 m annually, and it is predicted that groundwater will soon be exhausted [69].

Rainfall increases the fecal pollution in rivers and freshwater resources, and elevates the bacterial risk [70]. Warm temperatures and extreme rainfall are often contributing factors to waterborne disease outbreaks, for example, in Canada [71]. Heavy rainfall and floods are associated with extreme weather and may account for 55% and 53% of waterborne outbreaks, respectively [23]. Extreme weather events and changes in patterns increase the risk of gastrointestinal diseases. For example, in Japan (1999 to 2007), about 7.7% and 2.3% of infectious gastroenteritis case increases per week were recorded for a 1 °C increase in the average temperature and for every 1% decrease in relative humidity, respectively [72].

Changes in climatic conditions, precipitation, humidity, and wind pattern occur due to both natural and anthropogenic activities, which have environmental effects like changes in environmental factors, environmental degradation, and disturbance of ecosystems. Changes in environmental conditions, disturbances, and degradations may affect human health negatively [5].

8. Pollution and Public Health

About two-fifths of the global population (including the people of Pakistan) are facing water scarcity and waterborne diseases. One child dies approximately every eight seconds, because of waterborne diseases [73]. Farooq et al. [74] estimates that 44% of the global population is unable to access clean drinking water. Ren et al. [75] conducted a study in the Huai River basin (China). They reported that preventive measures and interventions to support hygiene should be adopted to improve surface water quality.

A study conducted in Pakistan by Nabeel et al. [42] indicated that about 71% and 58% of the reported samples across the country were found contaminated with total and fecal coliform which causes loss of 25–58 billion Pak Rupee annually. Similarly, Ahmed et al. [76] reported on the presence of coliforms and fecal coliforms in 67% of water samples tested from academic institutions at different parts of Abbottabad city. This study highlighted the prevalence of water-related diseases like diarrhea and typhoid.

Chemical pollution can cause several health problems. High nitrate levels in the water can be one of the co-factors for several cases of water-related Mathemoglobinemia, a condition in which methemoglobin (an oxygen-carrying metalloprotein hemoglobin type) cannot bind oxygen [77]. Both constructive and destructive impacts of climate change influence agriculture and public health, but destructive impacts have more devastating effects that need to be addressed (Table 4). The added word "potential" in the heading of Table 4 indicates that there is not necessarily consensus among all scientists. Therefore, expert opinion of the authors to make a judgement on the available evidence has been expressed.

Table 4. Potential impact of major climatic elements on agriculture and health (based on this literature review and the expert opinions of the authors).

Climatic Elements	Potential Impacts			
	Constructive		Destructive	
	Health	Agriculture	Health	Agriculture
Drought	Decrease in vectors and vector-borne diseases	Parasites and vector growths	Water quality and availability is affected; water-related diseases and death increase; hunger	Loss of water; reduction in crop productivity; economic growth
Flood	-	-	Poor water quality; injuries; increase in vectors, water-related vector-borne and zoonotic diseases; heat stress; cardiovascular failure; anxiety; depression	Reduction in crop productivity and economic growth; infrastructure destruction
Heat and humidity	-	May increase crop productivity	Decrease in water availability; skin infection; increase in vectors and vector-borne diseases like malaria, dengue fever, and Japanese encephalitis	Increase in vectors and pests, and related agricultural problems and crop diseases
Salt water intrusion	Decrease in the growth of pathogens and related diseases	-	Water quality and supply degradation; diseases,	Agricultural land loss; increase in soil salinity; water supply and quality deterioration

9. The Pakistani Scenario with Reference to Similar Countries

Water pollution is one of the major current problems affecting human health in Pakistan, because water quality is poorly monitored and managed [78]. Nabeela et al. [76] reported that 20% to 40% of all diseases are related to drinking water contamination resulting in annual economic losses between U.S. $0.25 and $0.58 billion.

In Pakistan, parallel water supply and sewage pipes currently lead to cross contamination and corrosion. In China, the situation is somehow similar to Pakistan where water pollution control, cross contamination between aquifers, and failure of the pipe network construction are the main concerns [14]. The public in Pakistan is unaware of pollutants such as iron, nitrates, and sulphates. Similarly, in Iran, 71% of the public are unaware of nitrates and 78% of people are largely ignorant of its corresponding health hazards [79].

Humid and warm conditions promote the growth of microbes, exaggerating water-related and waterborne diseases. In Pakistan, summers are longer than winters, and the temperature ranges between 30 °C and 45 °C in Islamabad as well as other cities of Punjab. The temperature in Pakistan is predicted to rise by about 3 °C by 2040, and between 5 °C and 6 °C by the end of this century [55,68,80]. Heavy rain and change in temperature and moisture conditions, especially in the monsoon season, encourage the spread of malaria, dengue fever, diarrhea, typhoid, and cholera [80]. Sterk et al. [81] studied the effect of climate on *Campylobacter* and *Cryptosporidium* under different climatic conditions and reported that climate change can increase the release but overall effect is limited.

Concerning Pakistan, the spread of dengue fever through viruses, which were imported into the country through tire trading and movement of travelers, is seen as a serious public health risk [82]. Climate change indirectly supports the growth of *Aedes aegyptei* larvae and adults, which cannot survive below 10 °C and below 5 °C, respectively [83].

Changes in temperature and humidity have disturbed the ecological equilibrium and contribute to new epidemics of malaria, dengue fever and other vector-related diseases [84]. There are a considerable number of studies correlating an increase in malaria with global warming. However, there is no sound evidence for this correlation [85]. Low temperature stops the growth of mosquitoes. An increase in temperature during the summer favors the growth of mosquitoes spreading malaria and dengue fever [84].

Dengue fever is endemic in Pakistan and spreads with an increase in temperature. As the temperature rises, the number of cases reported increase. Over-population as well as inadequate facilities in homes and towns, along with poor management of sewerage and water management, are the major reasons for the spread of dengue fever. Stagnant water in cities and towns provide breeding habitat for vector growth and its multiplication. Other reasons include travel and spread of viral infection from one region to another. Details of suspected cases, laboratory-confirmed cases, and deaths (confirmed by the World Health Organization in various unpublished reports) are given in Table 5.

Table 5. Dengue fever cases reported in Pakistan.

Year	Suspected Cases	Cases Laboratory-Confirmed	Deaths
2006	4961	1931	41
2007	2304	1226	18
2008	2792	2469	17
2009	1940	1085	13
2010	15,901	11,024	40
2011	252,935	17,057	219
2012	3913	639 (Karachi only)	-
2013	9037	8546	33
2014	-	504	6
2015	-	327 (Sindh)	-

Wang et al. [86] studied the variation in water quality in urban, suburban, and rural areas of Shanghai (China). They reported that well-managed urban areas have a better water quality compared to rural areas. Similarly, in Pakistan, rural areas have frequently poor water quality in comparison to the capital city Islamabad, as 90% of rural inhabitants lack access to clean water [87]. The country is facing plenty of challenges like a population boom, lack of natural resources, and no development of new reservoirs, which may lead to long-term water access per capita of less than 1000 m^3. This water shortage may get more severe in regions which are located outside the Indus basin, where the average per capita water demand is already less than this threshold [88].

According to numerous international standards, there should not be any fecal coliforms in 100-mL of drinking water. In Pakistan, the main challenge is bacteriological contamination. The years 2007 and 2011 have been the worst years in regard to dengue virus infection in Pakistan [89]. The dengue virus circulates in Pakistan throughout the year with a peak incidence in the post monsoon period. Recent floods in Pakistan made the situation worse [90]. Mashiatullah et al. [91] reported that the feeding streams of Rawal Lake in Islamabad are contaminated by bacteria. The lake provides drinking water to more than 1.5 million inhabitants in Rawalpindi. Similarly, Ahmed et al. [92,93] reported on different dams located in the Pothwar region showing contamination of water resources with fecal matter.

10. Approaches to Diminish Water-Related Impacts

This section focuses on current health challenges. Specific approaches proposed by the authors to mitigate water-related impacts partly due to climate change for countries comparable to Pakistan include the following:

1 Reducing water scarcity and pollution by changing lifestyles of individuals through education and by applying water conservation strategies, rain water harvesting, integrated sustainable water management, as the global water requirement is expected to increase by 55% in 2050. (In Pakistan, the annual water availability was 5260 m^3/capita in 1951. Due to increasing urbanization and anthropogenic activities, it is expected to be <800 m^3/capita in 2030. In comparison, the estimated figure is 1066 m^3/capita in 2015.).

2 Improving laws linked to the introduction of missing water valuation, surface water quality impacts due to climate change, groundwater challenges, and pollution control through awareness raising, and implementation of policies regarding water storage, water conservation, integrated water resources management, capacity building, and awareness raising that should be encouraged at various levels by introducing fines to reduce water scarcity and pollution problems should be encouraged [94,95].

3 Developing new and improved irrigation techniques and strategies (e.g., drip irrigation, site specific irrigation, micro-irrigation and sprinkling), crop rotation, introduction of new crop varieties, alternate crop selection [96], as well as applying innovative ideas for risk management, biodiversity enhancement, land and grazing management, water conservation, adaptation, and rehabilitation along with pollution control. Adaptation of strategies like crop management practices along soil fertility and water management are practiced due to a reduced availability of water and associated socio-economic effects [97]. Other strategies related to water management in agriculture include tunnel farming, alternate or renewable energy sources, especially pasteurized irrigation systems, gated piped irrigation, and laser land leveling [98].

4 Provision of more funds for research in biotechnology supporting the introduction of specific heat resistant, flood (or drought) tolerant, water efficient, and high yield crop varieties; adaptation of better strategies like water channels to conserve water by minimizing water evaporation and transpiration, water reuse strategies after consuming or using water, dam construction to enable water storage; minimizing the effects of water-related impacts of climate change on agriculture and health; and ensuring both water and food security [94]. Provision of funds to establish climate change research centers in agricultural departments to support highly efficient technologies to save labor and to increase yields along with optimized pollution control in the agriculture sector under changing climate scenarios is encouraged [95].

5 Involvement of national bodies and key local stakeholders, and securing their active engagement and contributions in adaptation and rehabilitation during and after disasters such as severe floods, earthquakes, heat waves, and storms. Educating farmers may be a considerable challenge when developing strategies to improve crop varieties and better breeds, which are tolerant to adverse climatic conditions like change in temperature, floods, and shift in rainfall patterns—as social barriers may limit the use of feasible measures by farmers [96,99].
6 Increasing transparent access to high quality information about water-related disasters and resulting impacts of climate change by national meteorology departments and disaster management control authorities along with provision of data for research-related projects to improve existing scenarios.
7 Increasing access to clean water sources subject to water quality assessments at specific periods, especially in flood-prone areas. This should be the top priority to avoid severe health challenges in flood affected areas.
8 Supporting the health system by improving surveillance and monitoring as well as proper disposal of sewage to avoid agricultural pollution, soil erosion, and sedimentation. Minimizing the impact and use of agriculture chemicals—like fertilizers, insecticides, pesticides, and leaching of other chemicals like toxic metals—on the enrichment of nutrients in ground water and its subsequent impacts on water quality and food security [100].
9 Improving health care facilities and availability of medicines and early responses to disasters to reduce casualties.

11. Recommendations for Further Work

To reduce the effects of climate change on health and agriculture, the following recommendations should be implemented:

1 To use this review as the basis for the development of a conceptual framework by which to consider the status of water-related impacts of climate change on agriculture and subsequently on public health in countries such as Pakistan.
2 To develop efficient and effective community-related projects to minimize the water-related impacts of climate change on agriculture and public health;
3 To build capacity and strengthen surveillance against waterborne disease outbreaks;
4 To enhance capacity and develop mechanisms for the diagnoses and control of water-related diseases;
5 To develop adaptation and mitigation strategies to improve the response to climate change-induced effects on health and agriculture;
6 To increase awareness among the general public through education, radio, TV programs, and print media;
7 To involve the community in the reduction of water and agriculture pollution, and to subsequently minimize the water-related infections originating due to climate change;
8 To develop an efficient drinking water quality monitoring scheme in order to mitigate water-related impacts of climate change and ensure a constant delivery of safe water;
9 To create assessment plans for the evaluation of community-related projects benefiting the public; and
10 To mobilize health professionals to protect the health and wellbeing of future generations via seminars, workshops, and training sessions for locals.

12. Conclusions

Climate change is likely to have a profound effect on public health, agriculture, and economy; especially on water-related impacts in terms of water quality, diseases, and changes in patterns of rain and droughts in some parts of the world including Pakistan. There is a strong link between agricultural pollution and public health.

This review highlights the need for water conservation, risk management, and the development of adaptation and mitigation strategies to cope with the water-related impacts of climate change. Different aspects regarding water-related impacts of climate change on health and agriculture have been discussed, and novel solutions and bioremediation methods have been presented to control environmental pollution and to promote public health awareness among the scientific community.

There is also a requisite to encourage regional and national authorities such as the Ministry of Climate Change and authorities working under the Ministry of Science and Technology and the Ministry of Food Security to intervene and to make changes in policies and laws with respect to climate change that affect the water, health, and agriculture sectors. Contradictory policy measures like electricity subsidies to farmers for tube wells in different provinces of Pakistan (especially in Baluchistan, where it is difficult to get water from aquifers due to low water tables) and loans for providing additional sugar mills, rather than improving existing ones, should be reconsidered. Introduction of heat resistant and flood (or drought) tolerant varieties as well as more yield- and water-efficient crop varieties, drought resistant grasses, and plants in urban areas (especially along the roadsides) should be introduced to conserve water. Development of better strategies like water channels to conserve water and dam constructions to enhance water storage are important to save Pakistan during both drought and flood events. The adaptation of more crops to the 'less drops strategy' to minimize the effects of water-related impacts due climate change on agriculture, water quality, and their subsequent health concerns should be encouraged.

Acknowledgments: The authors gratefully acknowledge the support provided by the Center for Climate Research and Development, COMSATS IIT, Islamabad, Pakistan.

Author Contributions: Wajeeha Niaz provided material considered for writing this article. Toqeer Ahmed initiated and provided the first paper draft with the support of Wajeeha Niaz, and contributed to the paper revisions. Furat Al-Faraj contributed to the first paper draft and revisions. Miklas Scholz wrote the final paper and edited all revisions.

Conflicts of Interest: The authors declare no conflict of interest. The founding sponsor had no role in the writing of the manuscript, and in the decision to publish the results.

References

1. Stanford, B.D.; Wright, B.; Routt, J.C.; Debroux, J.F.; Khan, S.J. *Water Quality Impacts of Extreme Weather-Related Events*; Water Research Foundation: Denver, CO, USA; Water Services Association of Australia: Melbourne, Australia, 2014.
2. Pollner, J.; Kryspin-Watson, J.; Nieuwejaar, S. *Disaster Risk Management and Climate Change Adaptation in Europe and Central Asia*; Global Facility for Disaster Reduction and Recovery: Washington, DC, USA; The World Bank: Washington, DC, USA, 2011.
3. Fang, C.M.; Chhetri, N. What have we learned about climate variability and human health? *Clim. Vulnerabil. Underst. Addressing Threat. Essent. Resour.* **2013**, *1*, 79–86.
4. Global Facility for Disaster Reduction and Recovery. *Building Resilience to Disasters—Delivering Results, Global Facility for Disaster Reduction and Recovery Annual Report 2011*; Global Facility for Disaster Reduction and Recovery: Washington, DC, USA, 2011.
5. McMichael, A.J.; Woodruff, R.E.; Hales, S. Climate change and human health: Present and future risks. *Lancet* **2006**, *367*, 859–869. [CrossRef]
6. Ciesielczuk, T.; Kusza, G.; Poluszyńska, J.; Kochanowska, K. Pollution of flooded arable soils with heavy metals and polycyclic aromatic hydrocarbons (PAHs). *Water Air Soil Pollut.* **2014**, *225*, 2145. [CrossRef] [PubMed]
7. Apisarnthanarak, A.; Mundy, M.L.; Khawcharoenporn, T.C.; Mayhall, C.G. Hospital infection prevention and control issues relevant to extensive floods. *Infect. Control Hosp. Epidemiol.* **2013**, *34*, 200–206. [CrossRef] [PubMed]
8. Ni, W.; Ding, G.; Li, H.; Liu, Q.; Jiang, B. Effects of the floods on dysentery in North Central Region of Henan Province, China from 2004 to 2009. *J. Infect.* **2014**, *69*, 430–439. [CrossRef] [PubMed]
9. World Health Organization. *Working Together for Health, the World Health Report*; World Health Organization: Geneva, Switzerland, 2006.

10. Ivers, L.C.; Ryan, E.T. Infectious diseases of severe weather-related and flood-related natural disasters. *Curr. Opin. Infect. Dis.* **2006**, *19*, 408–414. [CrossRef] [PubMed]
11. Greenough, G.; McGeehin, M.; Bernard, S.M.; Trtan, J.; Riad, J.; Engelberg, D. The potential impacts of climate variability and change on health impacts of extreme weather events in the United States. *Environ. Health Perspect.* **2001**, *109*, 191–198. [CrossRef] [PubMed]
12. Wright, J.; Gundry, S.; Conroy, R. Household drinking water in developing countries: A systematic review of microbiological contamination between source and point-of-use. *Int. J. Trop. Med. Health* **2004**, *9*, 106–117. [CrossRef]
13. Ullah, R.; Malik, R.N.; Qadir, A. Assessment of groundwater contamination in an industrial city, Sialkot, Pakistan. *Afr. J. Environ. Sci. Technol.* **2009**, *3*, 429–446.
14. Hu, H.; Jin, Q.; Kavan, P. A study of heavy metal pollution in China: Current status, pollution-control policies and countermeasures. *Sustainability* **2014**, *6*, 5820–5838. [CrossRef]
15. Rehman, A. Groundwater as source of contamination for water supply in rapidly growing megacities of Asia: Case of Karachi, Pakistan. *Water Sci. Technol.* **1996**, *34*, 285–292. [CrossRef]
16. Naseem, S.; Rafique, T.; Bashir, E.; Bhanger, I.M.; Laghari, A.; Usmani, H.T. Lithological influences on occurrence of high-fluoride groundwater in Nagar Parkar area, Thar Desert, Pakistan. *Chemosphere* **2010**, *78*, 1313–1321. [CrossRef] [PubMed]
17. Dahshan, H.; Abd-Elall, A.; Megahed, A. Trace metal levels in water, fish, and sediment from River Nile, Egypt: Potential health risks assessment. *J. Toxicol. Environ. Health* **2013**, *76*, 1183–1187. [CrossRef] [PubMed]
18. Vincent, P. Jeddah's environmental problems. *Geogr. Rev.* **2003**, *93*, 394–412. [CrossRef]
19. Furbey, A.K.; Apprill, A.; Cervino, M.J.; Ossolinski, E.J.; Hughan, A.K. Incidence of lesions on Fungiidae corals in the Eastern Red Sea is related to water temperature and coastal pollution. *Mar. Environ. Res.* **2010**, *98*, 29–38. [CrossRef] [PubMed]
20. McLellan, S.L.; Eren, A.M. Discovering new indicators of faecal pollution. *Trends Microbiol.* **2014**, *22*, 697–706. [CrossRef] [PubMed]
21. Edberg, S.C.; Rice, E.W.; Karlin, R.J.; Allen, M.J. *Escherichia coli*: The best biological drinking water indicator for public health protection. *J. Appl. Microbiol.* **2000**, *88*, 1068–1168. [CrossRef]
22. Wurtzer, S.; Prevost, B.; Lucas, F.S.; Moulin, L. Detection of *Enterovirus* in environmental waters: A new optimized method compared to commercial real-time RTqPCR kits. *J. Virol. Methods* **2014**, *209*, 47–54. [CrossRef] [PubMed]
23. Countinho, F.H.; Pinto, L.H.; Viera, R.P.; Martins, O.B.; Salloto, G.R.B.; Santoro, D.O.; Clementino, M.M.; Cardoso, A.M. Antibiotic resistance in aquatic environments of Rio de Janeiro, Brazil. In *INTECH Perspectives in Water Pollution 2013*; Ahmad, I., Dar, M.A., Eds.; Intech: Rijeka, Croatia, 2013.
24. Cann, K.F.; Thomas, D.R.; Salmon, R.L.; Wyn-Jones, A.P.; Kay, D. Extreme water-related weather events and waterborne disease. *Epidemiol. Infect.* **2013**, *141*, 671–686. [CrossRef] [PubMed]
25. Schwartz, B.S.; Harris, J.B.; Khan, A.I.; Larocque, R.C.; Sack, D.A.; Malek, M.A.; Faruque, A.S.G.; Qadri, F.; Calderwood, S.B.; Luby, S.P.; et al. Diarrheal epidemics in Dhaka, Bangladesh, during three consecutive floods: 1988, 1998, and 2004. *Am. J. Trop. Med. Hyg.* **2006**, *74*, 1067–1073. [PubMed]
26. Hunter, R.P. Climate change, waterborne and vector borne disease. *J. Appl. Microbiol.* **2013**, *94*, S37–S46. [CrossRef]
27. Luber, G. *Climate Change Adaptation in the Public Health Sector: The BRACE Framework. The Public Health Effects of Climate Change;* Centers for Disease Control and Prevention/National Center for Environmental Health: Atlanta, GA, USA, 2011.
28. Haines, A.; Kovats, R.S.; Campbell-Lendrum, D.; Corvalan, C. Climate change and human health: Impacts, vulnerability and public health. *Public Health* **2006**, *120*, 585–596. [CrossRef] [PubMed]
29. Crampton, A.; Ragusa, A.T. Perceived agricultural runoff impact on drinking water. *J. Water Health* **2014**, *2*, 484–491. [CrossRef] [PubMed]
30. Khan, Z.I.; Ahmad, K.; Ashraf, M. Assessment of potential toxicological risk for public health of heavy metals in wheat crop irrigated with wastewater: A case study in Sargodha, Pakistan. *Asian J. Chem.* **2013**, *25*, 9704–9706.
31. Antonio-Nkondjio, C.; Fossog, B.T.; Ndo, C.; Djantio, B.M.; Togouet, S.Z.; Awono-Ambene, P.; Costantini, C.; Wondji, C.S.; Ranson, H. *Anopheles gambiae* distribution and insecticide resistance in the cities of Douala and Yaoundé (Cameroon): Influence of urban agriculture and pollution. *Malar. J.* **2011**, *10*, 154–167. [CrossRef] [PubMed]

32. Biemans, H.; Speelman, L.H.; Ludwig, F.; Moors, E.J. Future water resources for food production in five South Asian river basins and potential for adaptation—A modeling study. *Sci. Total Environ.* **2013**, *468–469*, S117–S131. [CrossRef] [PubMed]
33. Lal, R. Food security in a changing climate. *Ecohydrol. Hydrobiol.* **2013**, *13*, 8–21. [CrossRef]
34. Ashofteh, P.; Haddad, O.; Mariño, M. Risk analysis of water demand for agricultural crops under climate change. *J. Hydrol. Eng.* **2015**, *20*, 04014060. [CrossRef]
35. Bandara, J.S.; Cai, Y. The impact of climate change on food crop productivity, food prices and food security in South Asia. *Econ. Anal. Policy* **2014**, *44*, 451–465. [CrossRef]
36. Hussain, S.S.; Mudasser, M. Prospects for wheat production under changing climate in mountain areas of Pakistan—An econometric analysis. *Agric. Syst.* **2007**, *94*, 494–501. [CrossRef]
37. Manyi-Loh, C.E.; Mamphweli, S.N.; Meyer, E.L.; Okoh, A.I.; Makaka, G.; Simon, M. Microbial anaerobic digestion (bio-digesters) as an approach to the decontamination of animal wastes in pollution control and the generation of renewable energy. *Int. J. Environ. Res. Public Health* **2013**, *10*, 4390–4417. [CrossRef] [PubMed]
38. Kabo-Bah, T.A.; Yuebo, X. The role of bacteria as a cure for polluted rivers in Africa. *J. Pure Appl. Microbiol.* **2013**, *7*, 2271–2275.
39. Salt, D.E.; Blaylock, M.; Kumar, N.P.B.A.; Dushenkov, V.; Ensley, B.D.; Chet, I.; Raskin, I. Phytoremediation: A novel strategy for the removal of toxic metals from the environment using plants. *Biotechnology* **1995**, *13*, 468–474. [CrossRef] [PubMed]
40. Ponnusami, V.; Vikram, S.; Srivastava, S.N. Guava (*Psidium guajava*) Leaf powder: Novel adsorbent for removal of methylene blue from aqueous solutions. *J. Hazard. Mater.* **2008**, *152*, 276–286. [CrossRef] [PubMed]
41. Ahmed, T.; Kanwal, R.; Hassan, M.; Ayub, N.; Scholz, M.; McMinn, W.R. Coagulation and disinfection in water treatment using *Moringa oleifera*. *Proc. ICE Water Manag.* **2010**, *163*, 381–388.
42. Ahmed, T.; Pervez, A.; Mehtab, M.; Sherwani, S.K. Assessment of drinking water quality and its potential health impacts in academic institutions of Abbottabad (Pakistan). *Desalin. Water Treat.* **2015**, *54*, 1819–1828. [CrossRef]
43. Belkin, S. Microbial whole-cell sensing systems of environmental pollutants. *Curr. Opin. Microbiol.* **2003**, *6*, 206–212. [CrossRef]
44. Edmundson, M.C.; Capeness, M.; Horsfall, L. Exploring the potential of metallic nanoparticles within synthetic biology. *New Biotechnol.* **2014**, *31*, 572–578. [CrossRef] [PubMed]
45. Zouboulism, A.I.; Loukidou, M.X.; Matis, K.A. Biosorption of toxic metals from aqueous solutions by bacteria strains isolated from metal-polluted soils. *Proc. Biochem.* **2004**, *39*, 909–916. [CrossRef]
46. Khasaeva, F.; Vasilyuk, N.; Terentyev, P.; Troshina, M.; Lebedev, A.T. A Novel soil bacterial strain degrading pyridines. *Environ. Chem. Lett.* **2011**, *9*, 439–445. [CrossRef]
47. Wang, Q.; Xie, S. Isolation and characterization of a high-efficiency soil atrazine-degrading *Arthrobacter* sp. Strain. *Inter. Biodeterior. Biodegrad.* **2012**, *71*, 61–66. [CrossRef]
48. Ahmed, T.; Imdad, S.; Ashraf, S.; Butt, N.M. Effect of size and surface ligands of silver (Ag) nanoparticles on waterborne bacteria. *Int. J. Theor. Appl. Trans.* **2013**, *1*, 111–116. [CrossRef]
49. Ahmed, T.; Imdad, S.; Butt, N.M. Bacteriological assessment of drinking water of Islamabad Capital Territory. *Desalin. Water Treat.* **2014**, 1–7. [CrossRef]
50. Haines, A.; Bruce, N.; Cairncross, S.; Davies, M.; Greenland, K.; Hiscox, A.; Lindsay, S.; Lindsay, T.; Satterthwaite, D.; Wilkinson, P. Promoting health and advancing development through improved housing in low-income settings. *J. Urban Health* **2012**, *90*, 810–831. [CrossRef] [PubMed]
51. Cordell, D.; Rosemarin, A.; Schröder, J.J.; Smit, L.A. Towards global phosphorus security: A systems framework for phosphorus recovery and reuse options. *Chemosphere* **2011**, *84*, 747–758. [CrossRef] [PubMed]
52. Ren, X.; Chen, C.; Nagatsu, M.; Wang, X. Carbon nanotubes as absorbent in environmental pollution management: A review. *Chem. Eng. J.* **2010**, *170*, 395–410. [CrossRef]
53. Gan, N.; Zhang, J.; Lin, S.; Long, N.; Cao, Y. A novel magnetic graphene oxide composite absorbent for removing trace residues of polybrominateddiphenyl ethers in water. *Materials* **2014**, *7*, 6028–6044. [CrossRef]
54. Zhu, J.; Wei, S.; Chen, M.; Gu, H.; Rapole, S.B.; Pallavkar, S.; Ho, T.C.; Hopper, J.; Guo, Z. Magnetic, nanocomposites for environmental remediation. *Adv. Powder Technol.* **2013**, *24*, 459–467. [CrossRef]
55. Bates, B.; Kundzewicz, Z.W.; Wu, S.; Palutikof, J. *Climate Change and Water WMO, Technical Paper VI*; Intergovernmental Panel on Climate Change: Geneva, Switzerland, 2008.

56. Delpa, A.V.; Jung, E.; Baures, M.; Clement, E.; Thomas, O. Impacts of climate change on surface water quality in relation to drinking water production. *Environ. Int.* **2009**, *35*, 1225–1233. [CrossRef] [PubMed]
57. Solheinm, A.L.; Austnes, K.; Eriksen, T.E.; Seifert, I.; Holen, S. *Climate Change Impacts on Water Quality and Biodiversity, Background Report for EEA European Environment State and Outlook Report*; European Topic Centre on Water: Prague, Czech Republic, 2010.
58. Vermeij, W.; van der Wiele, J.; van Moorselaar, I.; van der Grinten, E. *Impact of Climate Change on Water Quality in The Netherlands*; RIVM rapport 6078000072010; National Institute for Public Health and Environment: Bilthoven, The Netherlands, 2010.
59. Jalliffier-Verne, I.; Leconte, R.; Huaringa-Alvarez, U.; Madoux-Humery, A.S.; Galarneau, M.; Servais, P.; Prévost, M.; Dorner, S. Impacts of global change on the concentrations and dilution of combined sewer overflows in a drinking water source. *Sci. Total Environ.* **2015**, *508*, 462–476. [CrossRef] [PubMed]
60. Ghaleni, M.M.; Ebrahimi, K. Effects of human activities and climate variability on water resources in the Saveh Plain, Iran. *Environ. Monit. Assess.* **2015**, *187*, 35–39. [CrossRef] [PubMed]
61. Marengo, J.A.; Nobre, C.A.; Sampaio, G.; Salazar, L.F.; Borma, L.S. Climate change in the Amazon basin: Tipping points, changes in extremes, and impacts on natural and human systems. In *Tropical Rainforest Responses to Climatic Change*; Springer: Berlin/Heidelberg, Germany, 2011; pp. 259–283.
62. Driessen, A.L.T.; Ledden, V.M. The large-scale impact of climate change to Mississippi flood hazard in New Orleans. *Drink. Water Eng. Sci.* **2013**, *6*, 81–87. [CrossRef]
63. Allard, M.; Bourque, A.; Chaumont, D.; Des Jarlais, C.; Gosselin, P.; Houle, D.; Larrivée, C.; Lease, N.; Roy, R.; Savard, J.P.R.; et al. *Ouranos: Savoir S'adapter Aux Changements Climatiques*; Ouranos: Montréal, QC, Canada, 2010; p. 128.
64. Pall, E.; Niculae, M.; Kiss, M.T.; Sandru, C.D.; Spinu, M. Human impact on the microbiological water quality of the rivers. *J. Med. Microbiol.* **2013**, *62*, 1635–1640. [CrossRef] [PubMed]
65. Chou, R. Addressing watercourse sanitation in dense, water pollution-affected urban areas in Taiwan. *Environ. Urban* **2013**, *25*, 523–540. [CrossRef]
66. Scholz, M. *Wetlands for Water Pollution Control*, 2nd ed.; Elsevier: Amsterdam, The Netherlands, 2015.
67. Patz, J.A. Public health risk assessment linked to climatic and ecological change. *Hum. Ecol. Risk Assess.* **2001**, *7*, 1317–1327. [CrossRef]
68. Intergovernmental Panel on Climate Change. *Climate Change 2007: The Physical Science Basis. Contribution of Working Group I to the Fourth Assessment Report of the Intergovernmental Panel on Climate Change*; Cambridge University Press: Cambridge, UK, 2007.
69. Sajjad, M.; Rahim, S.; Tahir, S.S. Chemical quality of groundwater in Rawalpindi/Islamabad. *Water Eng. Dev. Cent.* **1998**, *24*, 271–274.
70. Tornevi, A.; Bergstedt, O.; Forsberg, B. Precipitation effects on microbial pollution in a river: Lag structures and seasonal effect modification. *PLoS ONE* **2014**, *9*, 98546–98556. [CrossRef] [PubMed]
71. Thomas, K.M.; Charron, D.F.; Waltner-Toews, D.; Schuster, C.; Maarouf, A.R.; Holt, J.D. A role of high impact weather events in waterborne disease outbreaks in Canada, 1975–2001. *Int. J. Environ. Health Res.* **2007**, *16*, 167–180. [CrossRef] [PubMed]
72. Onozuka, D.; Hashizume, M.; Hagihara, A. Effects of weather variability on infectious Gastroenteritis. *Epidemiol. Infect.* **2010**, *138*, 236–243. [CrossRef] [PubMed]
73. Cantor, K.P. Drinking water and cancer. *Cancer Causes Control* **1997**, *8*, 292–308. [CrossRef] [PubMed]
74. Farooq, S.; Hashmi, I.; Qazi, I.A.; Qaiser, S.; Rasheed, S. Monitoring of coliforms and chlorine residual in water distribution network of Rawalpindi, Pakistan. *Environ. Monit. Assess.* **2008**, *140*, 339–347. [CrossRef] [PubMed]
75. Ren, H.; Wan, X.; Yang, F.; Shi, X.; Xu, J.; Zhuang, D.; Yang, G. Association between changing mortality of digestive tract cancers and water pollution: A case study in the Huai River Basin, China. *Int. J. Environ. Res. Public Health* **2015**, *12*, 214–226. [CrossRef] [PubMed]
76. Nabeela, F.; Azizullah, A.; Bibi, R.; Uzma, S.; Murad, W.; Shakir, S.K.; Ullah, W.; Qasim, M.; Hader, D. Microbial contamination of drinking water in Pakistan—A review. *Environ. Sci. Pollut. Res.* **2014**, *21*, 13929–13942. [CrossRef] [PubMed]
77. Fewtrell, L. Drinking-water nitrate, Methemoglobinemia, and global burden of disease: A discussion. *Environ. Health Perspect.* **2004**, *112*, 1371–1374. [CrossRef]

78. Azizullah, A.; Khattak, K.N.M.; Richter, P.; Hader, D. Water pollution in Pakistan and its impact on public health—A review. *Environ. Int.* **2011**, *37*, 479–497. [CrossRef] [PubMed]
79. Azadegan, M.M.; Moghaddam, A.R.M.; Maknoon, R. Public awareness and performance regarding nitrate pollution in nitrate-polluted area of Tehran, Iran. *Environ. Eng. Manag. J.* **2014**, *13*, 611–617.
80. International Union for Conservation of Nature. *Climate Change: Vulnerabilities in Agriculture in Pakistan*; International Union for Conservation of Nature: Karachi, Pakistan, 2009.
81. Sterk, A.; Schijven, J.; de Roda Husman, A.M.; de Nijs, T. Effect of climate change on runoff of *Campylobacter* and *Cryptosporidium* from land to surface water. *Water Res.* **2016**, *95*, 90–102. [CrossRef] [PubMed]
82. Rasheed, S.B.; Butlin, R.K.; Boots, M. A review of Dengue as an emerging disease in Pakistan. *Public Health* **2013**, *127*, 11–17. [CrossRef] [PubMed]
83. Suleman, M.; Arshad, M.; Khan, K. Yellow fever mosquito (Diptera: Culicidae) introduced into Landi Kotal, Pakistan, by tire importation. *J. Med. Entomol.* **1996**, *33*, 689–693. [CrossRef] [PubMed]
84. Brower, V. Vector-borne diseases and global warming: Are both on an upward swing? *EMBO Rep.* **2001**, *2*, 755–757. [CrossRef] [PubMed]
85. Nabi, S.A.; Qader, S.S. Is global warming likely to cause an increased incidence of Malaria? *Libyan J. Med.* **2009**, *4*, 18–22. [CrossRef] [PubMed]
86. Wang, J.; Da, L.; Song, K.; Li, B. Temporal variations of surface water quality in urban, suburban and rural areas during rapid urbanization in Shanghai, China. *Environ. Pollut.* **2008**, *152*, 387–393. [CrossRef] [PubMed]
87. Pakistan Council for Research in Water Resources. *National Water Quality Monitoring Programme, Water Quality Report 2003–2004*; Pakistan Council for Research in Water Resources: Islamabad, Pakistan, 2005.
88. Pakistan Environmental Protection Agency. *State of Environment Report Pakistan*; Environmental Protection Agency, Ministry of Environment, Government of Pakistan: Islamabad, Pakistan, 2005.
89. Nasreen, S.; Arshad, M.; Ashraf, M.; Raza, A.; Bahar-e-Mustafa. The epidemiology of Dengue fever in district Faisalabad, Pakistan. *Int. J. Sci. Res. Publ.* **2015**, *5*, 1–6.
90. Idrees, S.; Ashfaq, U.A. A brief review on Dengue molecular virology, diagnosis, treatment and prevalence in Pakistan, Genet. *Vaccines Ther.* **2012**, *10*, 1–10.
91. Mashiatullah, A.; Chaudhary, M.Z.; Khan, M.S.; Javed, T.; Qureshi, R.M. Coliform bacterial pollution in Rawal Lake, Islamabad and its feeding streams/river. *Nucleus* **2010**, *47*, 35–40.
92. Ahmed, T.; Kanwal, R.; Hassan, M.; Ayub, N. Assessment of antibacterial activity of *Solanum surrattense* against water-borne pathogens isolated from surface water of Pothwar Region in Pakistan. *Int. J. Hum. Ecol. Risk Assess.* **2009**, *15*, 624–635. [CrossRef]
93. Ahmed, T.; Kanwal, R.; Tahir, S.S.; Rauf, N. Bacteriological analysis of water collected from different dams of Rawalpindi/Islamabad region in Pakistan. *Pak. J. Biol. Sci.* **2004**, *7*, 662–666.
94. Khan, M.A.; Khan, J.A.; Ahmad, Z.; Ahmad, M.N. The challenge of climate change and policy response in Pakistan. *Environ. Earth Sci.* **2016**, *75*, 412. [CrossRef]
95. Ministry of Environment. *National Climate Change Policy in Pakistan*; Government of Pakistan: Islamabad, Pakistan, 2011.
96. Evans, R.G.; Sadler, E.J. Methods and technologies to improve efficiency of water use. *Water Resour. Res.* **2008**, *44*, 1944–1973. [CrossRef]
97. Habib, N.; Anwer, M.Z.; Naheed, S.; Hassan, T. Identification of local climate change adaptation strategies for water management in districts Attock and Chakwal, Pakistan. *Sci. Technol. Dev.* **2015**, *34*, 255–259. [CrossRef]
98. South Asian Conservation Agriculture Network, Water Management Practices in Pakistan, Issue and Options for Productivity Enhancement. World Bank Resources. Available online: http://siteresources.worldbank.org/PAKISTANEXTN/Resources/WMPracticesinPakistan.pdf (accessed on 15 September 2016).
99. Iglesias, A.; Garrote, L. Adaptation strategies for agricultural water management under climate change in Europe. *Agric. Water Manag.* **2015**, *155*, 113–124. [CrossRef]
100. FAO Cooperation Document Repository, Control of Water Pollution from Agriculture, Natural Resources Management and Environment Department. Available online: http://www.fao.org/docrep/w2598e/w2598e04.htm (accessed on 16 September 2016).

water

MDPI

Article

The Effect of the El Nino Southern Oscillation on Precipitation Extremes in the Hindu Kush Mountains Range

Muhammad Umer Masood [1], Saif Haider [2,3], Muhammad Rashid [2], Muhammad Usama Khan Lodhi [2], Chaitanya B. Pande [3,4,5,*], Fahad Alshehri [3], Kaywan Othman Ahmed [6], Miklas Scholz [7,8,9,10,11,12,*] and Saad Sh. Sammen [13]

1 Geological Engineering Department, Montana Technological University, Butte, MT 59701, USA
2 Centre of Excellence in Water Resources Engineering, University of Engineering and Technology, Lahore 54890, Pakistan; m.rashid.6122@gmail.com (M.R.)
3 Abdullah Alrushaid Chair for Earth Science Remote Sensing Research, Geology and Geophysics Department, King Saud University, Riyadh 11451, Saudi Arabia
4 Institute of Energy Infrastructure, Universiti Tenaga Nasional, Kajang 43000, Malaysia
5 New Era and Development in Civil Engineering Research Group, Scientific Research Center, Al-Ayen University, Nasiriyah 64001, Thi-Qar, Iraq
6 Department of Civil Engineering, Faculty of Engineering, Tishk International University-Sulaimani, Sulaymaniyah 46001, Kurdistan Region, Iraq; kaywan.osman@tiu.edu.iq
7 Innovation Management Department, aconium GmbH (previously atene KOM), Invalidenstraße 91, 10115 Berlin, Germany
8 Department of Civil Engineering Science, School of Civil Engineering and the Built Environment, Kingsway Campus, University of Johannesburg, Aukland Park, P.O. Box 524, Johannesburg 2006, South Africa
9 Directorate of Engineering, School of Science, Engineering and Environment, The University of Salford, Newton Building, Greater Manchester M5 4WT, UK
10 Department of Town Planning, Engineering Networks and Systems, South Ural State University, 76, Lenin Prospekt, 454080 Chelyabinsk, Russia
11 Kunststoff-Technik Adams, Specialist Company According to Water Law, Schulstraße 7, 26931 Elsfleth, Germany
12 Nexus by Sweden, Skepparbacken 5, 722 11 Västerås, Sweden
13 Department of Civil Engineering, College of Engineering, University of Diyala, Diyala Coverenoate, Baqubah 32001, Diyala, Iraq; saad123engineer@yahoo.com
* Correspondence: chaitanay45@gmail.com (C.B.P.); m.scholz@salford.ac.uk (M.S.)

Citation: Masood, M.U.; Haider, S.; Rashid, M.; Lodhi, M.U.K.; Pande, C.B.; Alshehri, F.; Ahmed, K.O.; Scholz, M.; Sammen, S.S. The Effect of the El Nino Southern Oscillation on Precipitation Extremes in the Hindu Kush Mountains Range. *Water* **2023**, *15*, 4311. https://doi.org/10.3390/w15244311

Academic Editor: Paul Kucera

Received: 26 October 2023
Revised: 16 November 2023
Accepted: 13 December 2023
Published: 18 December 2023

Abstract: The El Nino Southern Oscillation (ENSO) phenomenon is devastating as it negatively impacts global climatic conditions, which can cause extreme events, including floods and droughts, which are harmful to the region's economy. Pakistan is also considered one of the climate change hotspot regions in the world. Therefore, the present study investigates the effect of the ENSO on extreme precipitation events across the Upper Indus Basin. We examined the connections between 11 extreme precipitation indices (EPIs) and two ENSO indicators, the Southern Oscillation Index (SOI) and the Oceanic Niño Index (ONI). This analysis covers both annual and seasonal scales and spans the period from 1971 to 2019. Statistical tests (i.e., Mann–Kendall (MK) and Innovative Trend Analysis (ITA)) were used to observe the variations in the EPIs. The results revealed that the number of Consecutive Dry Days (CDDs) is increasing more than Consecutive Wet Days (CWDs); overall, the EPIs exhibited increasing trends, except for the Rx1 (max. 1-day precipitation) and Rx5 (max. 5-day precipitation) indices. The ENSO indicator ONI is a temperature-related ENSO index. The results further showed that the CDD value has a significant positive correlation with the SOI for most of the UIB (Upper Indus Basin) region, whereas for the CWD value, high elevated stations gave a positive relationship. A significant negative relationship was observed for the lower portion of the UIB. The Rx1 and Rx5 indices were observed to have a negative relationship with the SOI, indicating that El Nino causes heavy rainfall. The R95p (very wet days) and R99p (extreme wet days) indices were observed to have significant negative trends in most of the UIB. In contrast, high elevated stations depicted a significant positive relationship that indicates they are affected by La Nina conditions. The PRCPTOT index exhibited a negative relationship with the SOI, revealing that the El Nino phase causes wet conditions in the UIB. The ONI gave a significant positive relationship for the UIB region, reinforcing the idea that both indices exhibit more precipitation during El Nino. The above observations imply that while policies are being developed to cope with climate change impacts, the effects of the ENSO should also be considered.

Keywords: ENSO; Upper Indus Basin; Mann–Kendall test; Innovative Trend Analysis

1. Introduction

Pakistan has regularly experienced a variety of meteorological disasters, including droughts and floods [1–3]. Environmental harm, deaths, financial losses, and population displacement were all results of these catastrophes [4–7]. These natural disasters cannot be avoided, but they may be managed well to reduce the risk that people will be exposed to them. The climate variability known as the El Nino Southern Oscillation (ENSO) is responsible for changes in ocean temperatures over the equatorial Pacific. Over time, the ENSO has had a significant influence on the world's climate and weather [8–10]. El Nino, or the warm phase, occurs when the ocean water is noticeably warmer than normal [11–13], and a cold phase, known as La Nina, occurs when the ocean water becomes significantly colder than usual, and it is thought to follow a roughly opposite pattern to that of El Nino [14–16]. Pakistan has had rainfall that has been above or below average at various times during the past few decades due to the ENSO [17–19]. When the ENSO is present, Pakistan has a weather anomaly that impacts both the summer and winter rains [17,18,20]. During El Nino episodes, the summer monsoon rainfall confronts shortfall across Pakistan and can result in meteorological droughts, which are conditions that can happen when precipitation is insufficient to support established human activities [17,19–23]. However, during La Nina years, which often cause floods, it receives near-normal to above-normal rainfall [18,24–26]. El Nino circumstances are frequently followed by La Nina conditions, albeit not always [8,27,28].

The Indus River Basin begins in China's Western Tibetan Plateau (TP), travels across India, reaches Pakistan in the north, and empties into the Arabian Sea in the south [29–31]. Pakistan is primarily an agricultural nation, and 85% of its wheat and rice obtain their water from the Indus River [32]. It is Pakistan's lifeblood [33]. Pakistan stores water from the Indus River at the Tarbela Reservoir for use in agricultural and electricity production. This region is referred to as the Upper Indus Basin (UIB) from its source at the Western TP to this reservoir [34,35]. In the UIB, the temperature changes mostly demonstrate regional and seasonal variability [36–38]. The UIB has previously emphasized differences in precipitation throughout time [39–41]. While the authors of [42] found different results between 1980 and 2006, the authors of ref. Archer et al. [40] found substantial rising trends in the winter, in the summer, and in the annual precipitation over the 1961–1999 period. In addition, ref. [30] noted an increase in precipitation in western UIB between 1995 and 2012. Additionally, higher elevations showed more pronounced decreasing precipitation, as seen in reference [43]. The historical records included in the UIB should be used to evaluate these divergent precipitation reactions seen by various researchers utilizing data from various time periods [44–46]. On the other hand, the regional climate of the UIB is significantly impacted by the North Atlantic Oscillation (NAO), the El Nino Southern Oscillation (ENSO), Indian Ocean Dipole (IOD), and Pacific Decadal Oscillations (PDOs) [47]. The Tmax, Tmin, and precipitation in this area need to be better understood for these four climatic indicators. Here, the NAO serves as a predictor of Atlantic Ocean oscillations (mid-latitude westerlies). The influence indices from the Pacific Oscillations and the Indian Ocean Dipole (IOD) are called the ENSO and PDO, respectively. Strong La Nina conditions in 2010 were linked to Pakistan's floods [48]. In the UIB [40], the authors of ref. [48] found a positive and negative connection between the NAO and the winter and summer precipitation levels, respectively. The winter precipitation level and ENSO linkages were described by the authors of ref. [49], where they discovered a consistent difference between heavier winter precipitation in El Nino years and condensed early winter precipitation in La Nina years. Additionally, ref. [50] discussed how the NAO affected winter precipitation and how the Southern Oscillation Index (SOI) affected the monsoon in the neighboring Himalayas [51–53]. The Indus River contributes water to the largest irrigation system in the world, providing water for 90% of food production in Pakistan, which furnishes 25% of the country [54,55]. However, the Indus Basin is prone to extreme events, i.e., floods and droughts, due to excess or limited stream flows, which affects the crop yields, and ultimately, the economic development of the country. The purpose of this study is to find the effect of the ENSO on the rainfall in the Upper Indus Region of Pakistan. The biggest impact of the ENSO was observed in Pakistan in the event of the 1998 El Nino, due to which a severe drought was experienced in the country for four years. Similarly, in the 2009 El Nino event, In 2010, a massive flood destroyed Pakistan, resulting in millions of dollars' worth of damage [56]. The primary objective of this research is to find the impact of ENSO on the Upper Indus Basin. To meet the requirement, several objectives include the evaluation of different extreme precipitation indices (EPIs) to analyze the extreme events, and an investigation of the spatiotemporal variations in the EPIs by using an Innovative Trend Analysis (ITA) and the Mann–Kendall test. Also, the phases of the ENSO indices and teleconnections of the ENSO-related index, SOI, with EPIs are analyzed using statistical methods.

2. Materials and Methods

2.1. Study Area and Data Sets

The Upper Indus Basin (UIB) is located at the spatial domain of 33°40′ to 37°12′ N and 70°30′ to 77°30′ E (Figure 1). The Indus Basin is considered to be one of the largest trans-boundary river basins in the world, shared by different countries including Pakistan (56%), India (26.6%), China (10.7%), and Afghanistan (6.7%) [57]. Due to its large boundary, it is a complex and entangled geopolitical region. It flows through the three mighty mountain ranges, including Karakoram, Hindukush, and the Himalayas, along with the Tibetan Plateau. As these are the highest mountain ranges in the world, they also encompass one of the world's largest glaciated systems, having almost 110,000 glaciers in number [16] with a massive area of about 16,000 km^2 of the surface area [58]. The annual average precipitation distribution varies from 1065 mm to 70 mm with elevation, while going from the direction of southeast to the northwest. The elevation of the area ranges between 8616 m and 140 m from the north to south direction of the UIB [59]. The water supplied by the UIB works as a lifeline for the socio-economic development of the country, and millions of inhabitants depend on it. The water demand in Pakistan is very high due to its utilization in agricultural and hydropower generation divisions; therefore, the Indus Basin is the most overstressed basin in the world [60]. Therefore, it is necessary to study the climatic changes in the UIB as it is considered the lifeline of the country.

2.2. Data Collection

The daily precipitation data were collected from PMD and WAPDA for 12 stations in the UIB. The data ranged from 15 to 49 years as there are some highly elevated areas whose gauge was installed later compared to other stations. The ENSO data including Nino 3.4 and ONI were taken from the Climate Prediction Center (CPC) www.cpc.ncep.noaa.gov (accessed on 12 July 2023). For SOI monthly pressure, data were taken for Tahiti and Darwin for 50 years from Climate Research Unit UK website https://crudata.uea.ac.uk/cru/data/soi/ (accessed on 10 September 2023). For the ONI, monthly and seasonal data were taken for 50 years. For Nino 3.4, 50-year SST data were taken. The stations and their characteristics are shown below in Table 1.

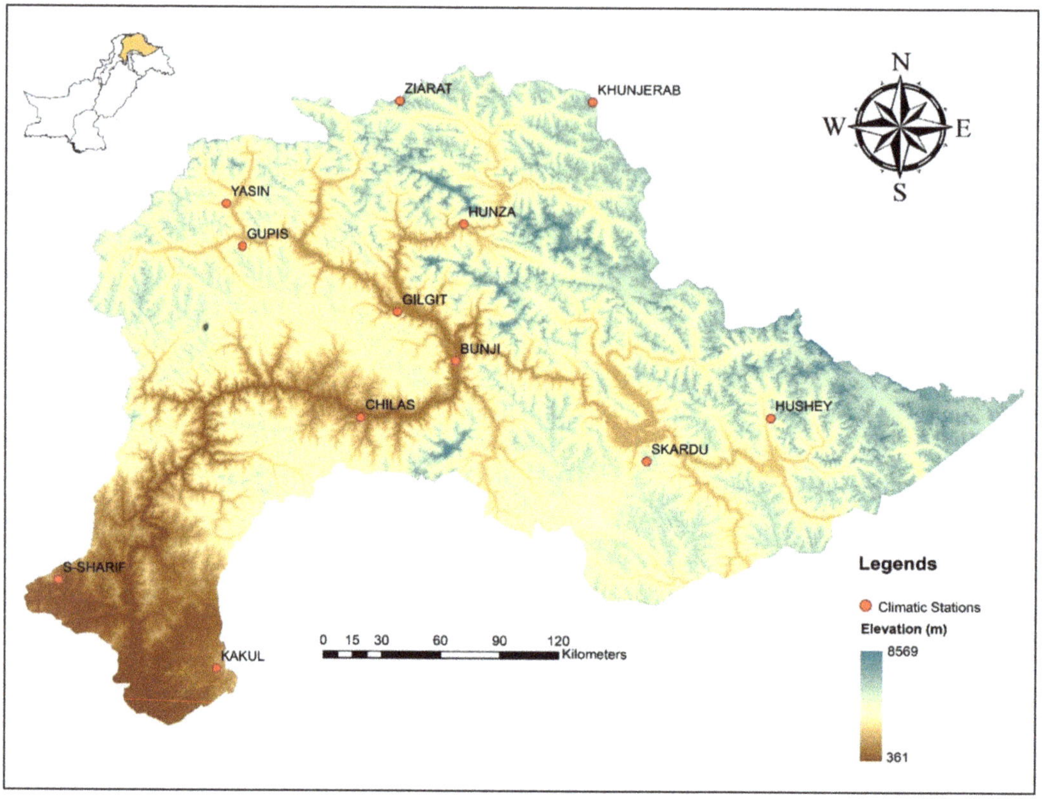

Figure 1. Study area (Upper Indus Basin) with climatic stations and elevation data.

Table 1. List of precipitation gauges.

Sr. No.	Stations	Longitude (Decimal Degrees)	Latitude (Decimal Degrees)	Elevation (m)	Mean Annual Precipitation (mm)	Available Data (Year)
1	Bunji	74.63	35.67	1372	164	1974–2020
2	Chilas	74.1	35.4	1251	215	1980–2020
3	Gilgit	74.3	35.9	1460	134	1975–2020
4	Gupis	73.4	36.2	2156	201	1972–2020
5	Hunza	74.67	36.32	2200	263	2007–2020
6	Hushey	76.4	35.4	3010	526	1995–2020
7	Kakul	73.3	34.2	1309	1242	1971–2020
8	Khunjerab	75.4	36.9	5182	280	1999–2020
9	Skardu	75.7	35.2	2210	237	1971–2020
10	S-Sharif	72.4	34.6	962	957	1974–2020
11	Yasin	73.3	36.4	3353	474	1999–2020
12	Ziarat	74.3	36.9	3688	395	1999–2020

2.3. *Precipitation Extreme Indices*

The Expert Team on Climate Change Detection and Indices (ETCCDI) standardized 27 extreme indices, out of which 11 indices were related to precipitation [61]. The indices were calculated using the package RClimDex 1.1 in R. The indices used are explained below in Table 2.

Table 2. Extreme precipitation indices recommended by ETCCDI.

Index	Name	Definition	Unit
CDD	Consecutive dry days	Maximum consecutive days having R < 1 mm	days
CWD	Consecutive wet days	Maximum consecutive days having R ≥ 1 mm	days
PRCPTOT	Annual total wet day precipitation	Total precipitation on wet days annually, i.e., R > 1 mm	mm
R10mm	Number of heavy precipitation days	Annual count of days when R ≥ 10 mm for the given period	days
R20mm	Number of very heavy precipitation days	Annual count of days when R ≥ 20 mm for the given period	days
R25mm	Number of extremely heavy precipitation days	Annual count of days when R ≥ 25 mm for the given period	days
R95p	Very wet days	Annual total precipitation when R > 95th percentile where R > 1 mm	mm
R99p	Extremely wet days	Annual total precipitation when R > 99th percentile where R > 1 mm	mm
Rx1 day	Max 1-day precipitation amount	Maximum 1-day precipitation for the given period.	mm
Rx5 day	Max 5-day precipitation amount	Maximum 5-day consecutive precipitation for the given period	mm
SDII	Simple daily precipitation intensity index	Total precipitation divided by the number of rainy days	mm/day

These extreme precipitation indexes are normally used around the world to measure the changes in precipitation patterns [62].

The daily precipitation data should be incorporated into the Excel file in comma-delimited format. The data which are missing are represented by −99.9 or −99.99. Once the file is uploaded, a simple quality control check is performed to find any missing data. The indices are calculated after the QC is performed.

2.4. Spatiotemporal Variation in Indices

To analyze the changes in spatiotemporal variation in extreme precipitation indices, we used the methods described in the methodology flowchart in Figure 2.

2.4.1. Mann–Kendall Test

The Mann–Kendall (M-K) test, also known as the M-K test, is widely used for trend analysis as it is a non-parametric test [63]. A non-parametric test means that the test is unaffected by the normal distribution [64]. The data should not have a serial correlation. If the data have normal distribution, linear regression should be used.

The Mann–Kendall statistics in S are given in the following equation:

$$S = \sum_{k=1}^{n-1} \sum_{j=k+1}^{n} sign(Y_j - Y_k) \quad (1)$$

$$sgn(Y_j - Y_k) = \begin{Bmatrix} if\left(Y_j - Y_k\right) < 0; & then & -1 \\ if\left(Y_j - Y_k\right) = 0; & then & 0 \\ if\left(Y_j - Y_k\right) > 0; & then & 1 \end{Bmatrix} \quad (2)$$

where Y_j and Y_k = successive data points of time series for the periods j and k, n = the number of data points, and sgn = the function that takes the values −1, 0, 1, as shown above.

The values of S represent the trend; if it is positive, the trend is increasing, and for negative values, it has a decreasing trend. The test is further followed by probability (E) and variance (Var), as suggested by Helsel and Hirsch, as shown below for a sample size of n > 10:

$$E[S] = 0 \quad (3)$$

$$Var(S) = \frac{n(n-1)(2n+5) - \sum_{p=1}^{q} t_p(t_p-1)(2t_p+5)}{18} \tag{4}$$

where q = tied groups, which represent observations of the same value but do not include the location of unique rank numbers, tp = the number of data values in the pth group, and sigma ($\sum$) = the sum of all tied groups.

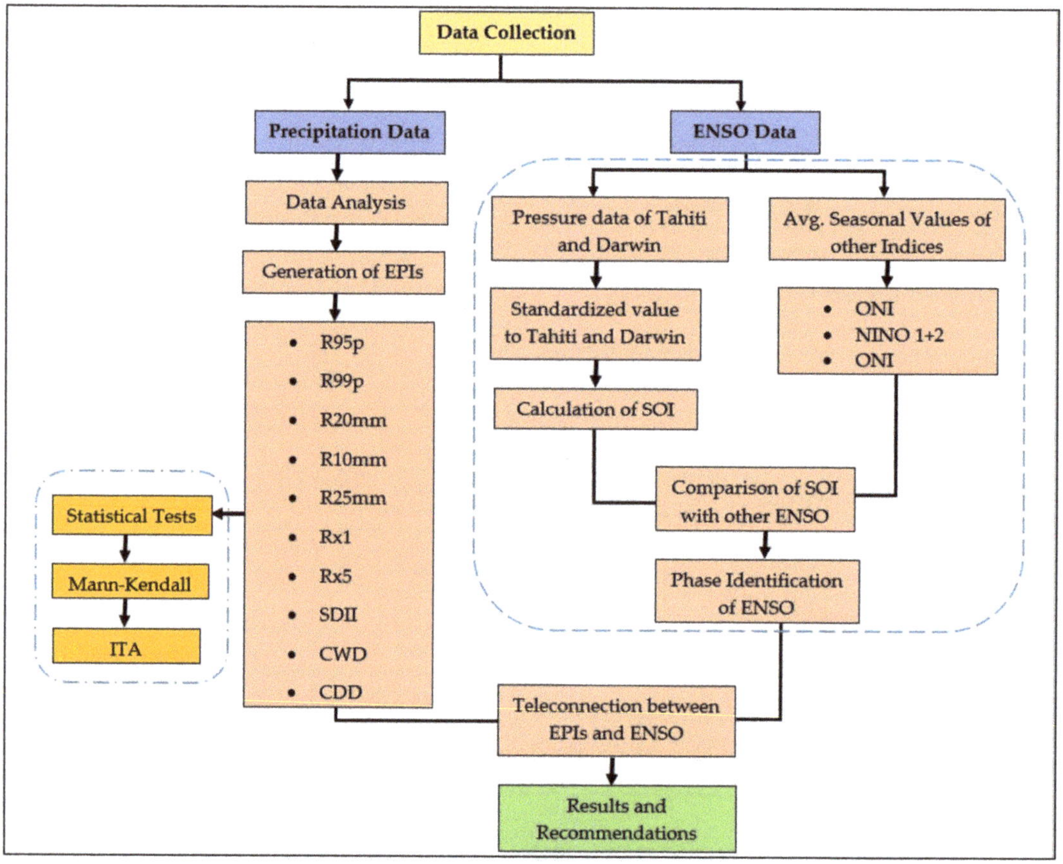

Figure 2. Schematic diagram of methodology.

However, if the data do not contain any tied classes, this description sequence can be overlooked. The standardized test statistics (Z_{MK}) value is determined using the equation below after manipulating the variance Var(S) from the above equation:

$$Z_{MK} = \begin{cases} \frac{S-1}{\sqrt{VAR(S)}}, & if \quad S > 0 \\ 0, & if \quad S = 0 \\ \frac{S+1}{\sqrt{VAR(S)}}, & if \quad S < 0 \end{cases} \tag{5}$$

The Z value calculates the magnitude of variation and obeys a normal distribution with a variance of "1" and a mean of "0". The null hypothesis, H0, is tested using the test statistics. When Z_{MK} is greater than Z $\alpha/2$, the data series shows a significant trend. At a confidence level of α = 10%, the computed value of Z_{MK} is compared to the usual distribution table of a two-tailed test. The null hypothesis (H0) for no trend is accepted in a two-tailed test if the computed value of Z_{MK} falls between $-Z1\text{-}\alpha/2$ and $Z1\text{-}\alpha/2$, and therefore, H1 is rejected. The patterns in the precipitation time series data are calculated at 1%, 5%, and 10% significance levels in this analysis.

2.4.2. Innovative Trend Analysis (ITA)

The trend analysis test, like the MK test, must meet certain criteria before being used, i.e., there should not be a serial correlation in the time series, and a normal distribution of data should not be present. A new method was proposed by Sen [65] that gives results as a graphical representation of trends without having any assumptions in the time series.

The basis of the ITA lies in the fact that if two time series are identical, their plot would be 45° with a 1:1 ratio in a Cartesian plane. The first half of the data is on the *X*-axis, and the second half is on the *Y*-axis. To categorize each half's variance, a sequence of clusters will be used. If all of the data sets in a scatter diagram are on the 45° (1:1) axis, the hydro-meteorological time series data has no trend.

In the first step of calculating the ITA, the data are equally divided into two halves and are arranged in ascending order. The two halves are arranged on the *X* axis and *Y* axis, respectively, and for their classification of the variance, a sequence of clusters is used. The trend is observed by looking at the scatter plot. If the data sets are completely placed on the 45° (1:1) line, it means there is no trend, and if the data points are distributed in the upward or downward portion of the triangular areas, it represents upward and downward trends, respectively. Figure 3 shows the graphical representation of the ITA. The equation used to estimate the magnitude of the trend is given by [66–68].

$$D = \frac{1}{n}\sum_{i=1}^{n} \frac{10(Y_j - Y_i)}{\mu} \quad (6)$$

where D = the trend indicator, n = the number of data values in each subseries, Y_i and Y_j = the first and second subseries data values, respectively, and μ = the first subseries' means. The negative or positive values of D represent a decreasing or increasing pattern, respectively.

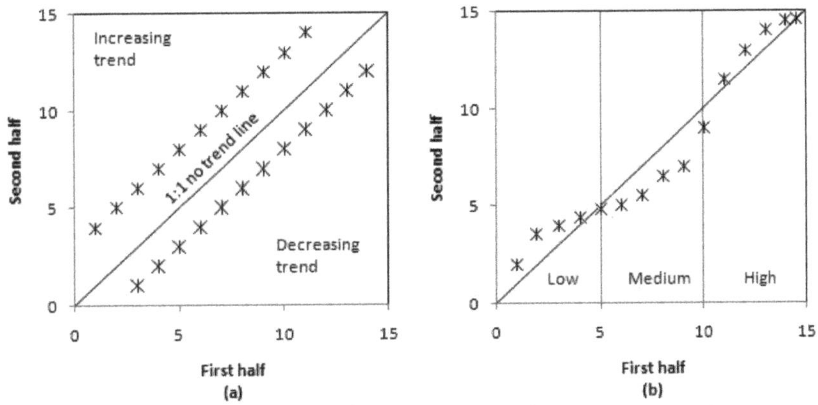

Figure 3. Representation of ITA graph and its components. (**a**) No trend, datasets, (**b**) upward and downward trend, datasets.

2.5. ENSO Index

The ENSO phenomenon, as described above, is a large-scale phenomenon that is observed through atmospheric and sea surface changes. Various indices are used for this purpose; these indices give the overall picture of global circulation patterns that are occurring in the atmosphere and oceanic surface. The index used for this study is mainly the SOI (Southern Oscillation Index). However, other indices are also incorporated to obtain a better picture of the ENSO phenomenon. The purpose of choosing the SOI is that it has the oldest record for pressure changes from 1866 to the present. Also, it can be used to find the changes in the Walker Circulation and predicts its strength; these changes in the WC further affect the rainfall [69] stream flows, agricultural production, etc.

The Southern Oscillation Index (SOI) mentioned above is a pressure-related index, so it oscillates between two phases known as El Nino and La Nina due to the pressure changes in the Tahiti and Darwin areas. The SOI gives stable values when the Tahiti minus Darwin index is calculated for the global phenomenon. (https://climatedataguide.ucar.edu/climate-data/southern-oscillation-indices-signal-noise-and-tahitidarwin-slp-soi (accessed on 12 July 2023)).

The SOI values move from −1 to 1, indicating El Nino and La Nina conditions, respectively. The threshold for the SOI is −0.5 and 0.5, i.e., if the SOI values go down from −0.5, this indicates an El Nino event, and if they move upward from 0.5, this indicates a La Nina event.

Derivation of SOI

The Southern Oscillation Index is a standardized index, which means its values are confined between −1 and 1 for a better understanding of the phenomenon. The NOAA used a method for calculating the SOI, which is shown below:

$$\text{Tahiti Anomaly} = \text{Actual Sea Level Pressure} - \text{Mean Sea Level Pressure} \tag{7}$$

$$\text{Darwin Anomaly} = \text{Actual Sea Level Pressure} - \text{Mean Sea Level Pressure} \tag{8}$$

The anomalies are calculated by using the climatology of the 1951–1980 period.

$$\text{Tahiti Standard Deviation} = \frac{\sqrt{\Sigma(\text{Tahiti Anomaly})^2}}{\text{N}} \tag{9}$$

$$\text{Darwin Standard Deviation} = \frac{\sqrt{\Sigma(\text{Darwin Anomaly})^2}}{\text{N}} \tag{10}$$

$$\text{Standardized Tahiti} = \frac{\text{Actual SLP} - \text{Mean SLP}}{\text{Standard Deviation Tahiti}} \tag{11}$$

$$\text{Standardized Darwin} = \frac{\text{Actual SLP} - \text{Mean SLP}}{\text{Standard Deviation Darwin}} \tag{12}$$

$$\text{MSD} = \frac{\sqrt{\Sigma(\text{Std. Tahiti} - \text{Std.Darwin})^2}}{\text{N}} \tag{13}$$

$$\text{SOI} = \frac{\text{Std. Tahiti} - \text{Std. Darwin}}{\text{MSD}} \tag{14}$$

2.6. Oceanic ENSO Indices

The ENSO comprises atmospheric as well as oceanic temperature indices. For this purpose, other indices dealing with sea surface temperature (SST) were also used, named Nino 3.4 SST and ONI.

For the sea surface temperatures, different regions are considered in the Pacific. These regions are termed Nino 1 + 2, Nino 3, Nino 3.4, and Nino 4. The locations of these regions are shown below in Table 3 and Figure 4.

For the current study, the Nino 3.4 SST Index is used. The Nino 3.4 Index uses a 5-month running mean, and El Nino and La Nina are considered when the Nino 3.4 SSTs exceed ±0.4 °C for six months or more.

The ONI is known as the Oceanic Nino Index, which uses the same region as Nino 3.4: 5 N-5 S, 170 W-120 W. The ONI uses a three-month running mean, and for El Nino or La Nina events, the anomalies must exceed ±0.5 °C for at least 5 consecutive months. It is defined by NOAA.

Table 3. Nino types.

SST Region	Location	Comments
Nino 1 + 2	0-10 S, 90 W-80 W	It is the most eastern part of Nino SST and is also the smallest.
Nino 3	5 N-5 S, 150 W-90 W	It was considered as the key region for ENSO but it was observed that the key region lies further in the west [70].
Nino 3.4	5 N-5 S, 170 W-120 W	SST anomalies for this region are considered average for the Pacific Ocean
Niño 4	5 N-5 S, 160 E-150 W	Nino 4 index captures SST anomalies in the central equatorial Pacific. It has less variance than the other SST regions.

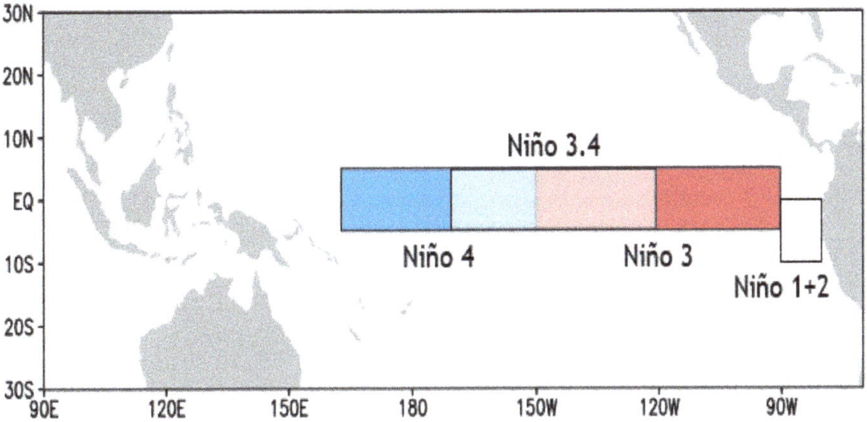

Figure 4. Sea surface temperature regions in the Pacific Ocean.

2.7. *Teleconnections of ENSO*

Teleconnections deal with large-scale atmospheric changes that occur globally. These patterns occur from weeks to months and can extend even to years. ENSO teleconnections mean that a change in one part of the globe can affect the other regions of the world.

The teleconnections of the SOI are found on annual and seasonal bases. For the annual time series, the SOI averaged values are calculated annually, and for seasonal values, 3-month averages are used to find 4 seasons denoted as DJF, MAM, JJA, and SON. The annual and seasonal SOI values are lagged and related to EPIs using the Pearson Correlation Method to find the Pearson coefficient. The correlation coefficient is further elaborated by finding the *p*-value [71].

Pearson Correlation Method

The Pearson Correlation Method, also known as the Pearson Product Moment Correlation Method, is used to find how much two variables are related to each other. The formula used for the Pearson Correlation Method is shown below:

$$r = \frac{\sum(xi - \overline{x})(yi - \overline{y})}{\sqrt{\sum(xi - \overline{x})^2 \sum(yi - \overline{y})^2}} \quad (15)$$

The Pearson Correlation Method is a widely used method for finding relationships between two entities. The Pearson coefficient ranges from −1 to 1, and it shows how strong or weak the relationship between two variables is; −1 shows that the two variables are inversely related, and +1 shows that the variables are positively related. The values near ±0.5 give a good correlation value. The Pearson correlation coefficient is further elaborated using a p-value. The p-value shows the significance of the relationship; if $p < 0.05$, it means the relationship is significant, and there is a strong probability of one variable affecting the other.

3. Results and Discussion

3.1. Spatiotemporal Variations in Precipitation over the Upper Indus Basin

The Upper Indus Basin is a complex region as it is affected by different climatic phenomena occurring in different regions. It can be seen that due to these climatic effects, such as monsoons, westerly winds, and orographic variations, there is a large variation in the precipitation of the Upper Indus Basin.

By observing the 12 stations in the UIB, it is seen that the variation in the monthly time series is not that significant. However, higher than average precipitation can be observed in the months of July and August, with about 40% more precipitation than in other months; this is because they lie in the monsoon period, as precipitation mainly occurs during the monsoon in Pakistan. Along with the monsoon effect on precipitation, an increase in precipitation is also observed from February to April; this can be attributed to the climate change that increases the temperature in the UIB, and abrupt changes are observed in the spring season, as discussed in [72].

Looking at the variation in the annual time series, a much larger diversification is observed compared to the monthly variation. This can be due to several reasons. As we know, the UIB is affected by different climate phenomena, such as monsoons and westerly winds, and orographic variations in different areas [73]. The monsoon is the main regime that causes precipitation in the country, and it is observed that the stations of Kakul and Saidu Sharif lie in the particular area of monsoons, due to which they depict high precipitation levels with increases of 60% and 56%, respectively, than the average precipitation levels of other stations. The stations in the northwest part of the Upper Indus Basin, like Ziarat and Yasin, displayed 10% more average precipitation than the stations situated between the Karakoram and Himalayas areas. This can be due to the effect of westerly disturbances that cause little precipitation. The stations situated between the Karakoram and Himalayas areas, such as Gilgit, Bunji, and Chilas, depicted the lowest precipitation, having 38%, 52%, and 35%, respectively, less precipitation than the average, which can be attributed to the orographic deviations that cause the least precipitation. Figure 5 shows the spatial mean annual variation in the Upper Indus Basin. Figures 6 and 7 show the temporal mean annual variation and the mean monthly variation, respectively.

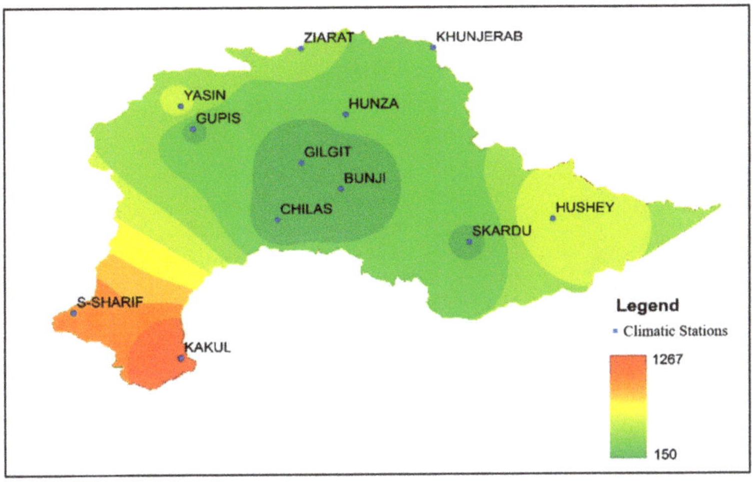

Figure 5. Spatial mean annual variation (mm).

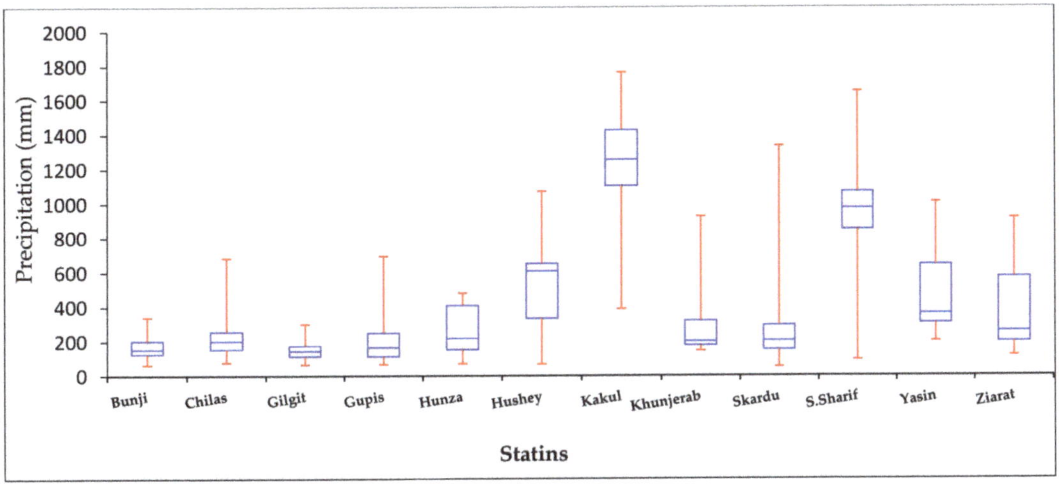

Figure 6. Temporal mean annual variation.

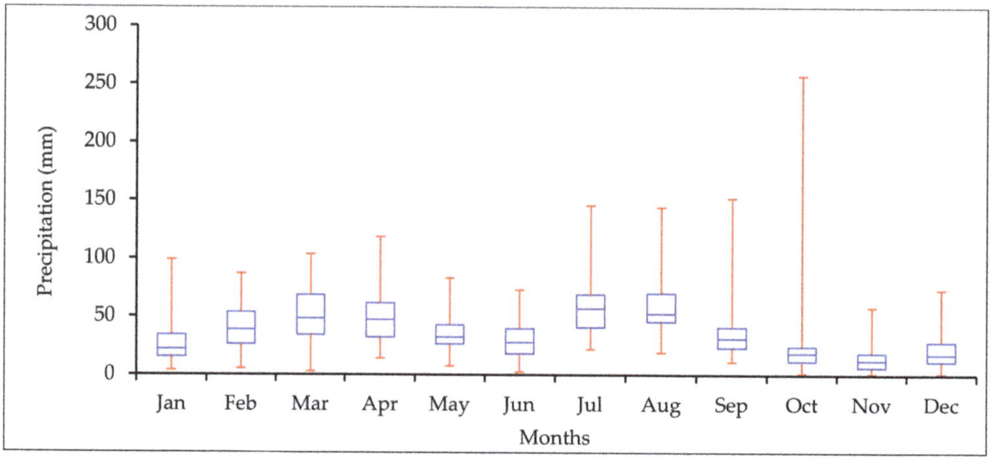

Figure 7. Temporal mean monthly variation.

3.2. Spatiotemporal Variation in EPI

The spatiotemporal variations are examined in the extreme precipitation indices (EPIs) using statistical methods. It is observed that both significant increasing and decreasing trends are displayed by different EPIs in the Upper Indus Basin. For most of the EPIs, two stations, Yasin and Ziarat, showed increasing trends. The total precipitation index (PRCPTOT), R10mm, R20mm, and R25mm gave significantly increasing trends for almost all of the stations, but three stations, Chilas, Kakul, and Skardu, gave decreasing trends.

The magnitude for PRCPTOT was found to be 5.23 mm/year, which shows an overall increase in precipitation. The index presented increasing and decreasing trends for nine and three stations, significant increasing trends were observed for six stations, and significant decreasing trends were observed for two stations (Chilas and Kakul), depicting an overall increase in precipitation.

The heavy precipitation days indices (R10mm, R20mm, and R25mm) had increasing magnitudes with the rates of 0.06 mm/year, 0.02 mm/year, and 0.00 mm/year. For the increased heavy precipitation indices, it was seen that the magnitude of precipitation was decreasing. R10mm and R25mm exhibited decreasing trends for eight stations and increasing trends for four stations, with significant increasing trends for two stations (Khunjerab and Ziarat). R20mm presented decreasing trends for seven stations and increasing trends for five stations, with significantly increasing trends for two stations (Khunjerab and Ziarat).

Indices like the CDD and CWD both gave significantly increasing results for four stations and significantly decreasing results at one station, which is Hushey. The magnitudes of CDD and CWD were 0.13 days/year and 0.09 days/year, respectively. As CDD was increasing more than CWD, dry conditions were the most likely to be observed.

R95p and R99p both had increasing magnitudes of 0.11 mm/year and 0.08 mm/year, but they both had decreasing trends for eight stations and increasing trends for four stations. The indices displayed that five stations had significantly decreasing trends. Hunza and Hushey both had significantly decreasing trends for R95p and R99p.

The Rx1 and Rx5 (maximum 1 and 5-day precipitation) indices presented decreasing and increasing trends for eight and four stations, respectively. A significant increasing trend was observed for only two stations, Khunjerab and Ziarat, and a significantly decreasing trend was only observed for Hushey. The indices were decreasing at the rates of 0.08 mm/year and 0.05 mm/year, respectively.

Along with the Rx1 and Rx5 indices, the SDII exhibited decreasing and increasing trends for nine and three stations, respectively, with significant decreasing trends for seven stations, and two stations displayed significantly positive trends, including Khunjerab and Ziarat. The magnitude of the SDII was found to be decreasing at the rate of 0.02 mm/day/year. The spatial patterns of the extreme precipitation indices are shown in Figure 8. The graphical representation of the ITA is shown in Figures A1–A10 in Appendix A. Most stations are within 10% variation of the (1:1) line of ITA. Some anomalous values were also observed, which were not included in the variance.

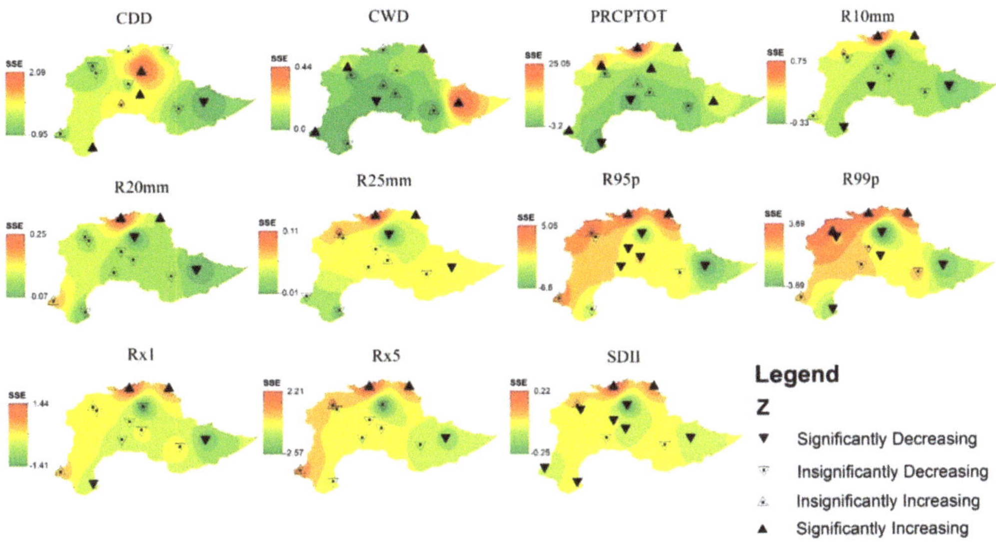

Figure 8. Spatial patterns of extreme precipitation indices in the Upper Indus Basin.

3.3. Comparison of MK and ITA

The results of the MK test and ITA are graphically represented by radial graphs in Figure 9. By analyzing the trends of both the MK test and ITA, it was observed that out of 132 time series, 47% and 52% of the trends were significant for the MK test and ITA, respectively. The results for almost all of the EPIs are comparable with very little difference. While analyzing the CDD values, it was observed that both had the same number of significant trends, but there was little difference in the overall trends. The MK test showed six stations with increasing and decreasing trends, whereas one station (Hushey) indicated a significantly decreasing trend. The ITA, on the other hand, had four and eight stations depicting decreasing and increasing trends, respectively. In the case of the CWD value, 10 stations had increasing trends and 2 stations had decreasing trends for the MK test, while the ITA had 9 stations showing increasing trends and 3 stations showing decreasing trends. Four stations, including Hushey, Khunjerab, Saidu Sharif, and Yasin, showed significantly increasing trends for the MK test, and five stations, including Hunza, Hushey, Khunjerab, Yasin, and Ziarat, exhibited significant positive trends for the ITA. Only one station (Chilas) showed a significantly decreasing trend for the MK test, and none were observed for the ITA.

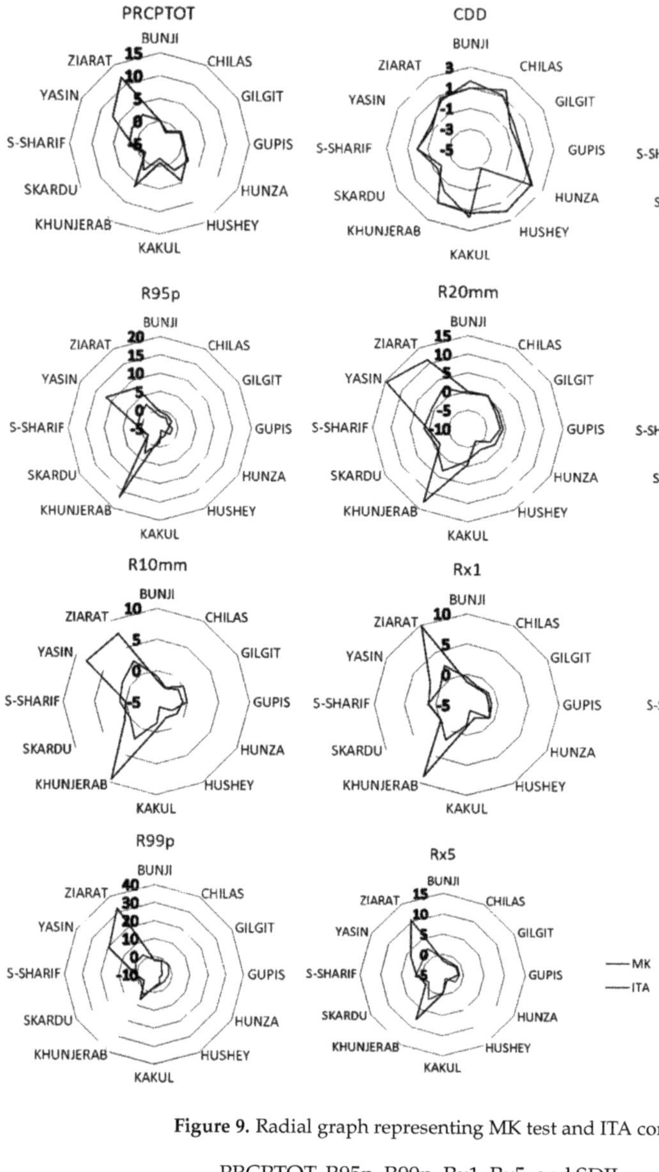

Figure 9. Radial graph representing MK test and ITA comparison.

PRCPTOT, R95p, R99p, Rx1, Rx5, and SDII gave exact increasing and decreasing trends for the MK test and ITA, with a small difference in the significant trends. In the case of PCPTOT, six stations exhibited significantly increasing trends, and two showed significantly decreasing trends, while the ITA had five stations exhibiting significantly increasing trends and only one station with a significantly decreasing trend. Hunza, Hushey, Khunjerab, Yasin, and Ziarat exhibited significantly increasing trends in both the MK test and ITA. The statistical tests indicate that Chilas manifested a decreasing trend for PRCPTOT.

While investigating the R10mm, R20mm, and R25mm indices, it was found that two stations gave significantly increasing trends for the MK test, including Khunjerab and Ziarat. In the case of the ITA, along with the aforementioned stations, Yasin also displayed a significantly positive trend. Hushey was the common station in the very heavy precipitation days indices that gave significantly decreasing trends for both the MK test and ITA.

The percentile indices, R95p and R99p, also depicted similar results for both the MK test and ITA, with eight stations presenting decreasing trends and four stations presenting increasing trends. Khunjerab, Ziarat, and Yasin showed significantly increasing trends for both the MK test and ITA, and Hunza and Hushey, along with Gilgit, exhibited significantly decreasing trends for both the MK test and ITA and for both percentile indices. Similarly, the maximum number of heavy precipitation days indices, i.e., Rx1 and Rx5, displayed comparable results, with eight stations showing decreasing trends and four stations showing increasing trends. Khunjerab and Ziarat showed significantly increasing trends, and Hushey and Hunza, along with Chilas, showed significantly decreasing trends.

The SDII index, on the other hand, exhibited nine stations with decreasing trends, and only three stations depicting increasing trends for both statistical tests, out of which only two stations, Khunjerab and Ziarat, exhibited significantly increasing trends. In the case of the MK test, seven stations displayed significantly decreasing trends, whereas five stations depicted significantly decreasing trends. The common stations depicting significantly decreasing trends consisted of the Hunza, Hushey, and Gilgit stations. It was seen that some of the stations, like Khunjerab and Ziarat, showed significantly increasing results for the maximum cases; this might be due to the stations being highly elevated. Other stations like Gilgit, Hushey, and Hunza showed significantly negative trends; this is similar to what was observed in [74]. The overall results reveal the compatibility between the MK test and ITA, but a difference was observed due to the nature of the two statistical tests. The MK test does not consider outliers while evaluating trends, whereas the ITA considers the outliers during the evaluation. The ITA has the ability to distribute the data into low, median, and high values, whereas the MK test has limitations such as the natural distribution of data, it and should be independent of any correlations.

3.4. Comparison of ENSO Indices

The ENSO indices are compared to one another, revealing that the ONI index exhibits contrasting relationships. For El Niño events, the ONI values are positive, whereas during La Niña events, the ONI values become negative. This relationship is consistent with the SST indices, as both are calculated for the same Nino 3.4 region. It is shown below in Figure 10.

3.5. Phase Identification

The phase of Nino 3.4 is found by calculating the 5-month running mean, and for the ONI, the 3-month running mean is considered. For the SOI average, the seasonal value is considered for the phase identification. The phase for the ENSO year is considered when the atmospheric and temperature indices give an El Nino, neutral, or La Nina phase. As it is known that the ENSO is a complex global phenomenon, it is better to observe the behaviors of different ENSO indices to identify the phase of the ENSO. The climatic departments of the world have a consensus that strong El Nino events occurred in 1982, 1983, 1997, 1998, 2015, and 2016, whereas strong La Nina events were observed in the years 1973, 1974, 1975, 1976, 1988, 1989, 1998, 1999, 2000, 2007, 2008, 2010, and 2011. The phases observed in the study also verify the phases of the ENSO. The graph below shows the different years of El Nino, La Nina, and neutral years for the SOI and ONI (Figure 11).

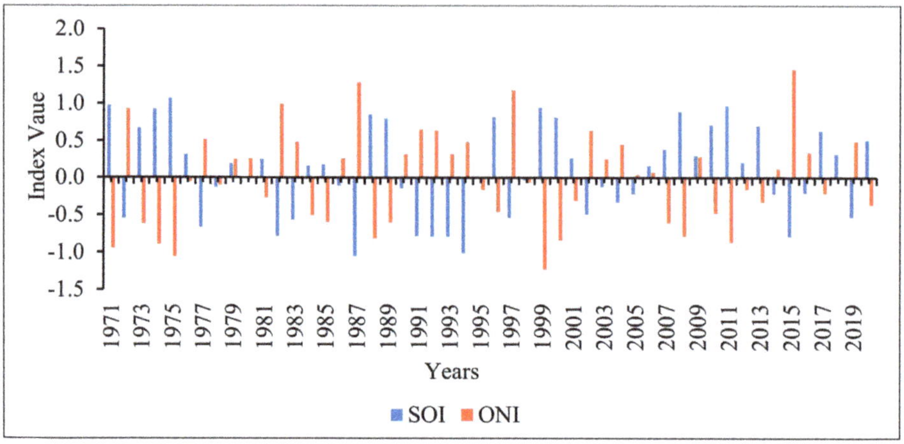

Figure 10. Comparison of SOI vs. ONI.

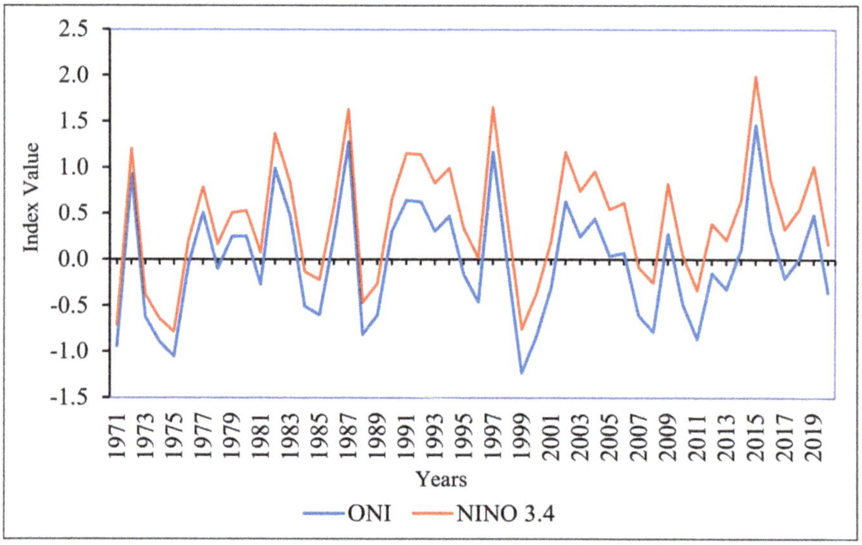

Figure 11. Comparison of ONI vs. NINO 3.4.

3.6. Precipitation Trend during ENSO Phase in UIB

A general pattern of precipitation was observed for 50 years in the UIB during different phases of the ENSO, and it exhibited that from 15 La Nina events occurring in 50 years with respect to the SOI, 8 events increased the average precipitation, with the index value of maximum increase being 0.6. Out of 13 El Nino events, on the other hand, 10 events increased the precipitation from the average, with the minimum increase being 0.1 and the maximum increase being 0.6 (Figure 12). By analyzing the ONI events for the UIB, it was observed that 10 out of 15 El Nino events increased the precipitation, with the maximum increase of 1 in the index, and a minimum increase of 0.1, and 6 out of 15 La Nina events increased the precipitation, with the maximum increase in the index value being 0.7, and the minimum index value being 0.1 (Figures 13 and 14). The pattern revealed that the increase in precipitation occurred during the El Nino phase of the ENSO (Figure 15), and decreased precipitation was observed during the La Nina phase of the ENSO [75].

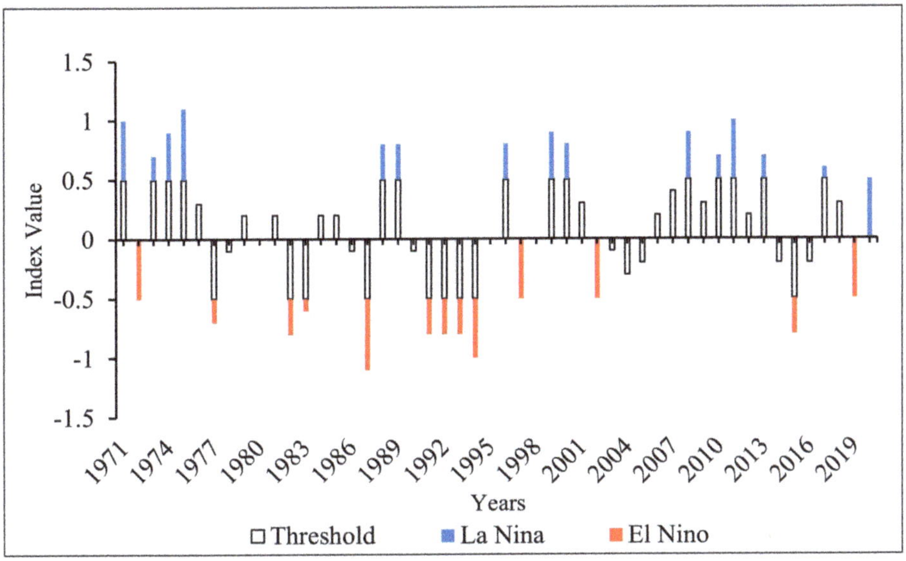

Figure 12. ENSO phases in SOI in the 1971–2020 period.

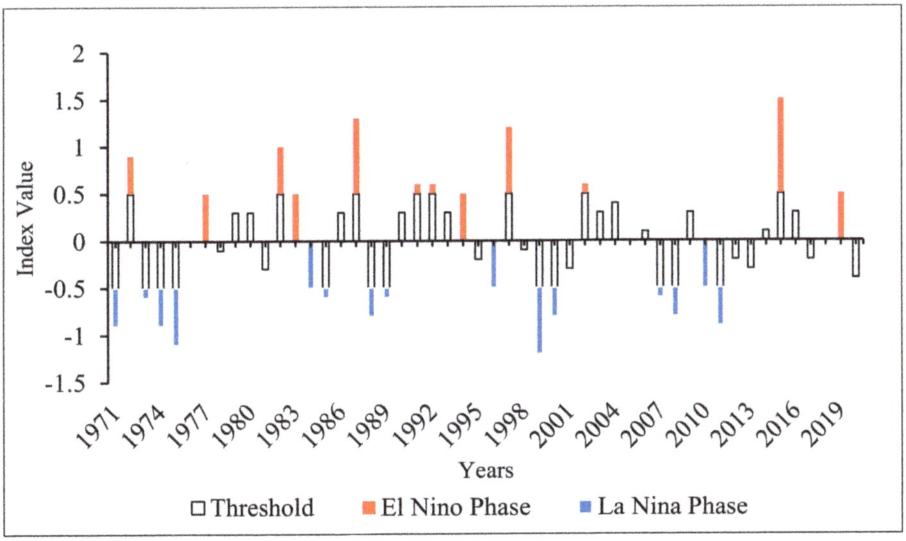

Figure 13. ENSO phases in ONI in the 1971–2020 period.

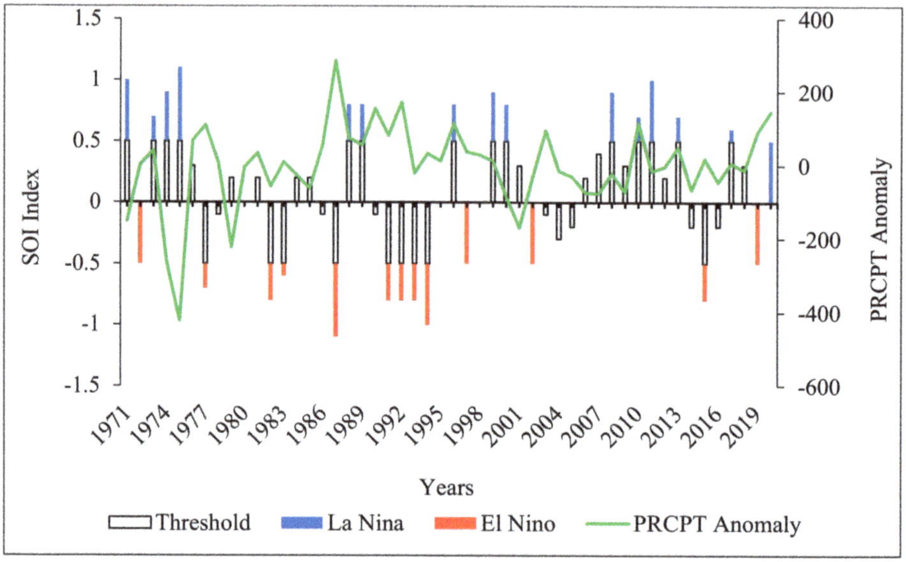

Figure 14. Precipitation in UIB during ENSO phases of SOI.

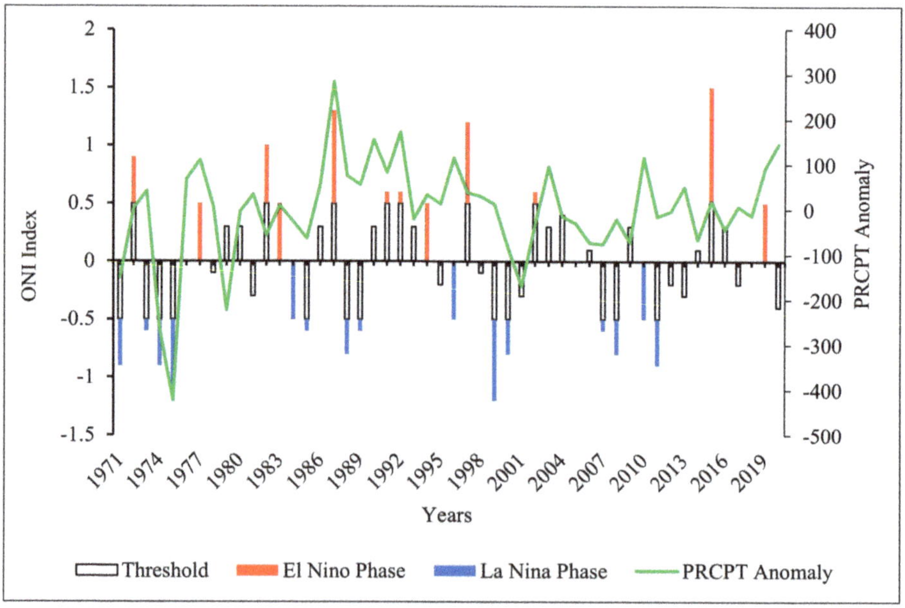

Figure 15. Precipitation in UIB during ENSO phases of ONI.

3.7. Correlation of ENSO Indices and EPIs

3.7.1. Annual Scale Correlations

Teleconnections between the ENSO indices and EPIs were analyzed using the Pearson Correlation Method. The seasonal and annual time series of the SOI and ONI were used to find the relationship between the ENSO indices and extreme precipitation indices (EPIs). For the annual time series, considering the CDD index, it was observed that five stations, Hunza, Hushey, Khunjerab, Kakul, and Gupis, were negatively correlated with the SOI, and the remaining seven stations were positively correlated with the SOI. In the case of the ONI, four of the above stations, Gupis, Hunza, Hushey, and Kakul, showed positive correlations, but Khunjerab showed anomalous behavior by exhibiting a positive correlation with the ONI. This might be due to Khunjerab being a highly elevated area, and it might be affected by La Nina conditions more than El Nino conditions. The other seven stations had a negative correlation with the ONI, depicting increases in dry days during the El Nino period.

In the case of the CWD index, inconsistent behavior was observed, as eight stations were positively correlated and four were negatively correlated with the SOI. The central stations of the region had a negative correlation, including the Gupis, Chilas, Hunza, and Bunji stations, while the other stations showed significant positive relationships with the SOI. While the ONI showed an opposite result, eight stations were negatively correlated, while four stations were positively correlated with the ONI. It was also seen that Bunji, Chilas, and Hunza depicted the same behaviors and had positive correlations with the ONI, showing that the precipitation in these central stations of the UIB increases during the El Nino phase.

While investigating the PRCPTOT index, six stations, Bunji, Chilas, Gupis, Hunza, Kakul, and Skardu, depicted negative correlations, in which three stations, Chilas, Gupis, and Hunza, had significant negative relationships with the PRCPTOT, and the remaining six stations had positive correlations, of which three stations, Khunjerab, Hushey, and Yasin, were significantly correlated with the SOI. On the other hand, the ONI also gave similar results, but four stations (Gilgit, Hunza, Hushey, and Khunjerab) had significant negative correlations, and two stations (Chilas and Gupis) had significant positive correlations.

The very heavy precipitation days indices show similar trends, with most stations having negative correlations with the SOI, and with Gupis and Hushey showing significant negative correlations with R10mm, R20mm, and R25mm. For the ONI Bunji, Hushey, Kakul, Khunjerab, and Saidu Sharif had positive correlations, but no significant correlation was found.

The extremely wet days indices (R95p and R99p) gave similar results, with five stations showing positive correlations, and seven stations showing negative correlations with the SOI. Gilgit, Gupis, and Hushey showed significant negative correlations, while Hunza, Yasin, and Ziarat showed significant positive correlations with the SOI. In the case of the ONI, Chilas and Skardu had positive significant results, while Yasin and Ziarat had significant negative correlations.

For the maximum 1-day and 5-day precipitation indices, Chilas, Gilgit, Gupis, Hushey, and Kakul had significant negative correlations with the SOI, and Hunza, Yasin, and Ziarat had significant positive correlations with the SOI. While investigating the ONI correlations with Rx1 and Rx5, it was found that Chilas, Gilgit, Gupis, Kakul, and Skardu had significant positive correlations, whereas Hunza had a significant negative correlation.

The SDII index had a negative correlation with the SOI for nine stations and a positive correlation with three stations. Chilas, Gupis, and Kakul had significant negative correlations, and no positive significant correlation was found. While observing the correlation with the ONI, heterogeneous results were found. Chilas and Skardu had significant positive correlations, while only Hunza had a significant negative relationship with the ONI.

R99p, Rx1, Rx5, and SDII consistently depicted significantly negative correlations for most of the stations in the annual time series for the SOI. These indices indicate an increase during the El Nino phase. Chilas, Gupis, and Hunza, the central areas of the UIB, exhibited increases in precipitation during the El Nino phase of the ENSO. Kakul also presented increased precipitation in the El Nino phase, whereas the high elevated areas like Khunjerab, Yasin, and Ziarat depicted increased precipitation in the La Nina phase of the ENSO; this might be because these stations have very high elevations that can cause the circulation of winds to change and increase precipitation during the La Nina phase. The ONI had a positive correlation, and the SOI had a negative correlation for most of the EPIs, and the same behavior was depicted in the Poyang Lake Basin in China [76].

3.7.2. Seasonal Scale Correlations

The investigation of the springtime series (MAM) relationship between the ENSO and EPIs exhibited almost the same pattern as the annual time series. The CDD index had heterogeneous results with Chilas, Gilgit, and Gupis, exhibiting a positive significant correlation with the SOI, and Hunza, Hushey, Yasin, and Ziarat showed negative significant correlations with the SOI. In the event of the ONI, mixed results were observed for the stations, but three stations, Gupis, Hunza, and Ziarat had significant positive correlations, and Gilgit had a significant negative correlation with the ONI. The CWD index had a negative correlation with the SOI for eight stations, and a positive correlation for four stations. Khunjerab, Skardu, and Ziarat had significant negative correlations with the SOI. Considering the correlation with the ONI, it was observed that nine stations were positively correlated, and three stations were negatively correlated with the ONI. Bunji, Kakul, Saidu Sharif, and Ziarat depicted significant positive correlations with the ONI.

For PRCPTOT, a negative relationship with the SOI was observed for nine stations, and three stations had negative correlations for the SOI in the UIB. Chilas, Gupis, Hunza, Kakul, and Saidu Sharif represented significant negative correlations with the SOI, while Hushey presented a significant positive correlation with the SOI. While investigating the correlation with the ONI, a noteworthy relationship was found, as 11 stations had positive relationships, and only Gilgit presented a negative correlation. Bunji, Gupis, Kakul, Khunjerab, Skardu, Saidu Sharif, and Ziarat had significant positive correlations, enforcing the idea that an increase in precipitation is observed during the El Nino phase of the ENSO.

R10mm, R20mm, and R25mm gave similar results, with maximum stations having negative correlations with the SOI. Gupis and Saidu Sharif displayed negative significant relationships for R10mm and R25mm. For the ONI and R10mm, nine stations presented positive correlations, and three presented negative correlations. Bunji, Hushey, Kakul, Khunjerab, Saidu Sharif, Yasin, and Ziarat exhibited positive significant correlations. R20mm and R25mm did not have significant correlations; however, R20mm showed peculiar behavior, as seven stations were negatively correlated, and four stations were positively correlated with the ONI, which is different from the other heavy precipitation days indices, and this was also in contrast to the results that were examined in California [77].

R95p and R99p had negative correlations with the SOI for seven and eight stations, with Gupis and Hushey having significant negative correlations, and Chilas and Ziarat exhibiting positive significant correlations with the SOI. When analyzing the correlation for the ONI, it was found that heterogeneous observations were conducted for the whole region, with Gupis, Hushey, and Khunjerab presenting significant positive correlations, and Chilas having a significant negative correlation with the ONI.

For Rx1 and Rx5, most stations presented negative correlations with the SOI; Chilas, Gupis, and Hushey had significant negative correlations, whereas no positive significant relationship was found. While observing the correlation for the ONI, it was found that Rx1 gave anomalous results, as most of the stations had negative correlations with the ONI, and only Gupis exhibited a significant positive correlation. Moreover, Rx5 had a positive correlation with nine stations, and Gupis, Hushey, and Khunjerab had significant positive correlations with the ONI. The SDII displayed a substantial correlation, with 10 stations having negative correlations, and 2 stations having negative correlations with the SOI. Bunji and Hushey had significant negative correlation with the SOI, while for the ONI, Hushey, Yasin, and Ziarat presented significant positive correlations.

When analyzing the results exhibited by the stations, it was observed that the central stations, Gupis, Hunza, and Chilas, are well correlated with the SOI and ONI. The monsoon region stations, i.e., Kakul and Saidu Sharif, also exhibited good relationships with the ENSO indices in the springtime series. The highly elevated stations, including Khunjerab, Yasin, and Ziarat, presented heterogeneous behavior with the ENSO indices. This was also observed in [78], where reduced precipitation was observed in highly elevated areas. Considering the summertime series (JJA) for the SOI, a constant pattern was represented for PRCPTOT, and the R10mm, R95p, and Rx1 EPIs had positive correlations with five stations and negative correlations for seven stations, with Gupis and Hunza exhibiting significant negative correlations, whereas no significant positive correlation was found in any stations for the SOI.

The CDD index had a significant negative relationship with five stations and a significant positive relationship with two stations. However, the SDII had an abnormal pattern, as seen in the annual and springtime series, and it had positive relationships with most of the stations but had significant negative relationships with two stations, with no positive significant trend. The ONI gave significantly positive correlation values for the maximum stations, showing an opposite trend with the SOI. When analyzing the stations of the study area, it can be seen that Hunza and Gupis are stations that give significant results for the ENSO indices, implementing a precipitation increase in the central region of the UIB, whereas no significant correlations were found for the La Nina conditions in the UIB. Furthermore, the pattern of summer rainfall is more aggressive, which might be due to the fact that monsoons also play roles in the summer (JJA), increasing the significant positive trends with the ONI and negative trends with the SOI.

For the Autumn Time Series (SON), the R10mm, R20mm, and Rx1 EPIs had positive correlations with three stations and negative correlations with nine stations, with very few significant trends for one or two stations. The other EPIs also exhibited similar results, with mostly negative correlations with the SOI, but very few significant trends. When investigating the ONI teleconnections, aggressive significant positive correlations were observed. PRCPTOT, R25mm, and R95p had positive correlations for all of the regions, with significant positive relations at five to eight stations. For the SDII, 10 stations showed positive trends, with 5 of them being significant. The overall autumn phase corresponded to JJA aggressively like the Indonesian region [79].

When analyzing the winter time series (DJF) for the SOI, significant trends were found between the CDD and SOI, with eight stations having negative significant correlations. The results depict dry conditions during the El Nino conditions; this, too, corresponds to the DJF behavior in the Indonesian region [79].

R10mm and R99p showed abnormal trends, with positive correlations for maximum stations depicting that these extremes were decreasing with a decreasing SOI, i.e., the El Nino phase is reducing the extremes, and the La Nina phase is increasing these extremes for winter. This can be because the La Nina phase is stronger in the winter time [80]. Other EPIs show the same negative correlations for the SOI, but significant trends are exhibited for fewer stations. The ONI shows an opposite trend to the SOI for most of the stations, that is, significant positive correlations are exhibited for almost all of the EPIs, but the CDD index shows anomalous behavior as it also shows a positive trend with the ONI, resulting in an increase in the CDD index for El Nino conditions and a decrease in La Nina conditions, which can be further elaborated as drought conditions may prevail in El Nino conditions. The dry conditions prevailing and other precipitation indices not giving up to the mark result are because in the winter, rainfall is suppressed and is influenced by La Nina, as it was confirmed by [56]. The spatial variation of the ENSO for various regions can be due to other phenomena at play, like the monsoons, the westerlies, and the orographic variations. Such phenomena can affect the impact of the ENSO on the UIB. Similarly, global warming is also affecting the ENSO anomalies, as there is an extension towards the east of the warm front pool of the western Pacific [81]. The spatial patterns of the ENSO correlations with the EPIs are represented in Figures 16–19.

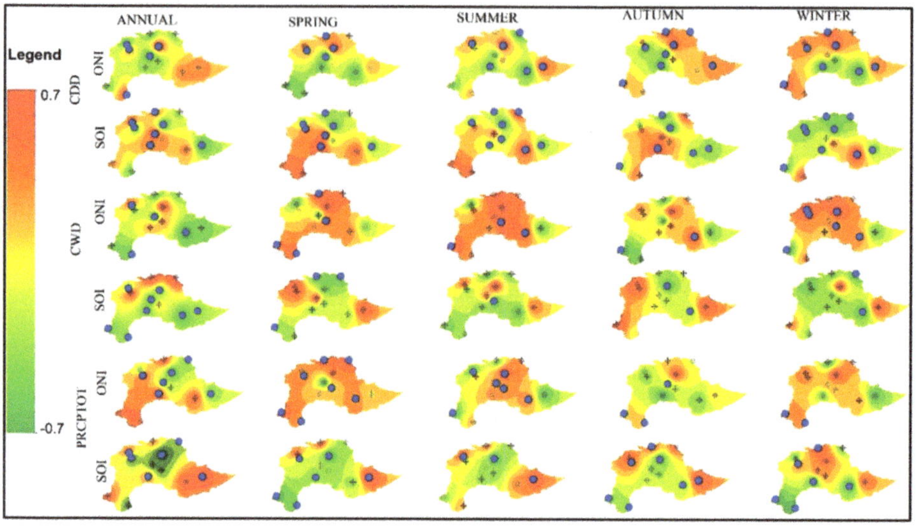

Figure 16. Spatial patterns of ENSO correlations with EPIs (PRCPTOT, CWD, CDD).

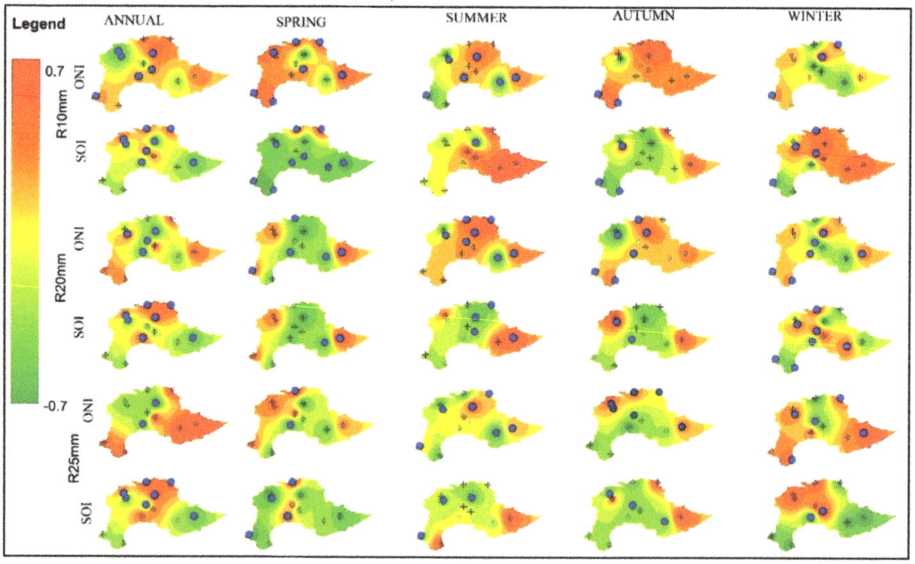

Figure 17. Spatial patterns of ENSO correlations with EPIs (R10 to R25).

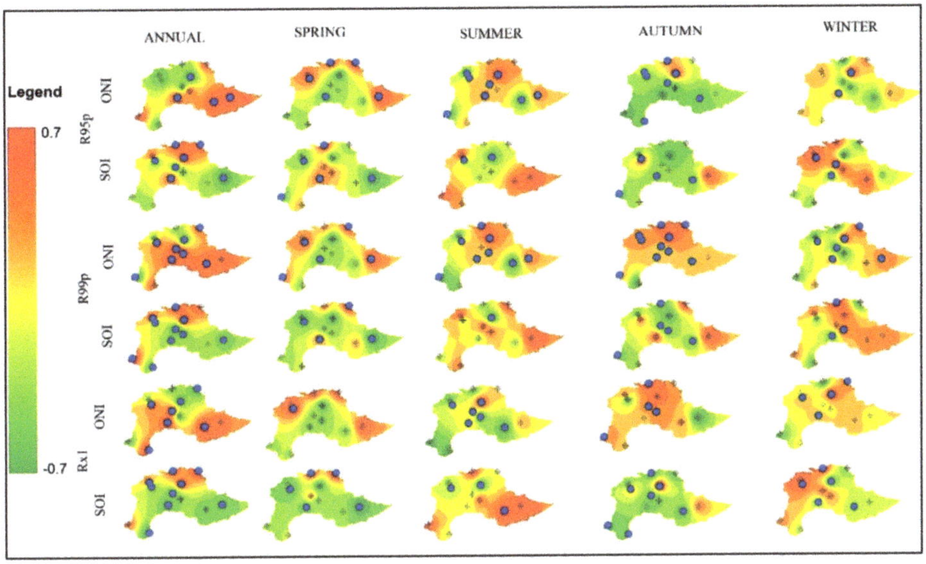

Figure 18. Spatial patterns of ENSO correlations with EPIs (Rx1, R99p and R95p).

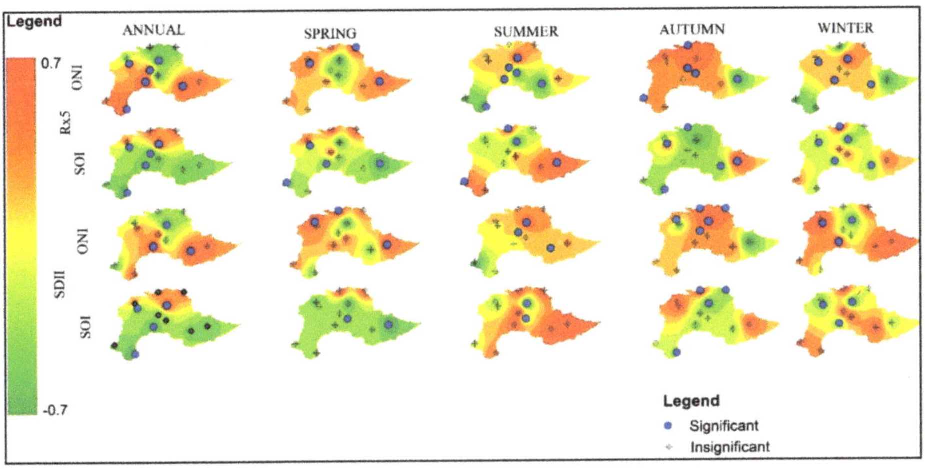

Figure 19. Spatial patterns of ENSO correlations with EPIs (SDII, Rx5).

3.8. Overall Trends in UIB

The impact of the ENSO was analyzed over the UIB in an annual time series. The three large-scale climate indices used include the SOI, ONI, and Nino 3.4 index, which were correlated with 11 extreme precipitation indices, giving an overall pattern of the ENSO's impact on the UIB. The results exhibited that the atmospheric index of the ENSO, i.e., the SOI, had a significant positive correlation with the CDD (36%) and CWD (37%) indices. The remaining nine indices had significant negative correlations with the SOI, emphasizing the fact that the El Nino phase of the SOI causes more extreme precipitation annually, whereas the La Nina phase of the SOI is followed by dry conditions. When investigating the correlation of the SST indices of the ENSO, i.e., the ONI and Nino 3.4, an opposite correlation was detected for the EPIs compared to the SOI. In the case of the ONI, all of the indices except for CWD exhibited significant negative correlations (36%)

with the ONI, whereas, on the other hand, Nino 3.4 had similar results as the ONI, with the CDD and CWD indices being negatively correlated, and the other 10 indices being positively correlated. The overall impact of the ENSO revealed that the atmospheric and sea surface temperature-related indices complement each other and form a coupled pattern in the climate, with a noteworthy impact on extreme events (Figure 20).

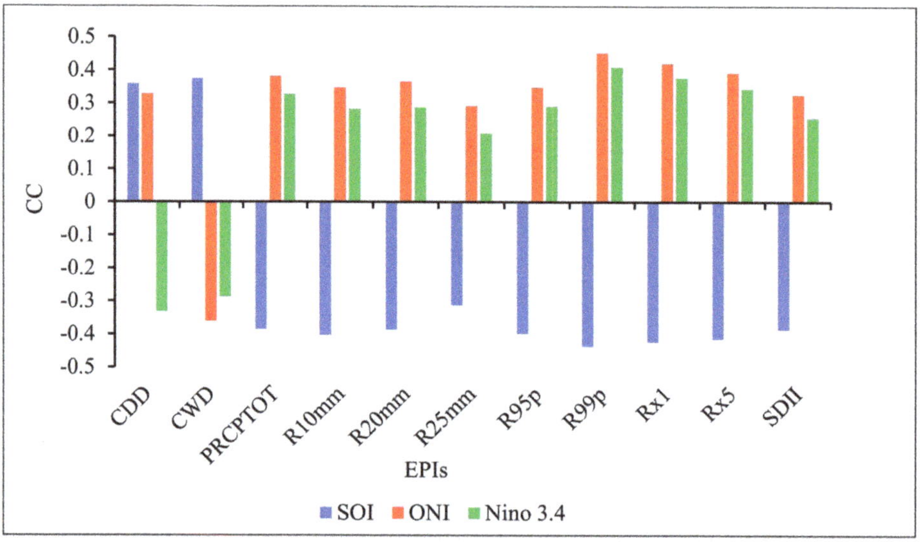

Figure 20. Overall correlation of ENSO with EPIs.

Highly Elevated Stations' Trends in UIB

It was observed that highly elevated stations, i.e., above a 3000 m elevation (Hushey, Khunjerab, Yasin, and Ziarat), exhibited different relationships with the ENSO indices. A further investigation revealed that for the SOI, all of the EPIs exhibited negative significant trends, except PRCPTOT, which depicted a positive insignificant trend. It was observed that PRCPTOT and CDD had opposite relationships with the SOI when observed during the overall study area correlation.

While investigating the trend of the ONI, it was observed that the correlations were not as significant as in the overall study area correlation. The CDD and Rx5 indices were the only two EPIs that had significant correlations with the ONI. It was also observed that the PRCPTOT and R25mm indices showed opposite results with the ONI when the correlation of the whole study area was analyzed.

Nino 3.4 gave insignificant results with the EPIs, except for R95p and R99p, and Rx5 had significant results with Nino 3.4. Further investigations revealed that CDD, PRCPTOT, and R25mm had opposite relationships compared to when it was observed for the whole study area (Figure 21).

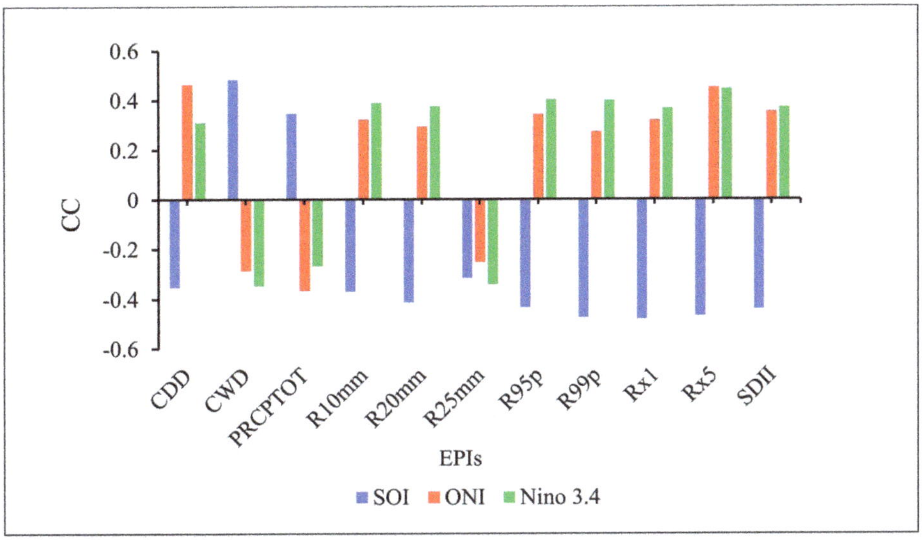

Figure 21. Highly elevated stations' correlations of ENSO with EPIs.

4. Conclusions

The purpose of this study was to analyze the effect of the ENSO on extreme rainfall in Pakistan. Based on a detailed analysis, the following conclusions are presented:

- An analysis of 132 time series revealed that 47% and 52% trends were significant for the MK test and ITA, respectively. CDD, CWD, and PRCPTOT showed mostly increasing significant trends for the EPIs.
- However, the CDD index is increasing by 0.13 days/year, whereas CWD is increasing by 0.09 days/year. This shows that the increase in CDD can cause drought conditions in the UIB.
- The very heavy precipitation days indices depicted decreasing trends for almost all of the regions and showed significant negative trends for two to four stations. However, it was seen that the overall magnitudes of R10 and R20mm were increasing with small rates of 0.06 and 0.02 days/year.
- Rx1 and Rx5 are decreasing at the rates of 0.08 and 0.05 mm/year, with eight stations showing decreasing trends, but only three to four stations showed significant trends.
- R95p and R99p also depicted decreasing trends for eight stations, but an overall increase in the magnitudes of 0.11 and 0.08 mm/days was observed.
- On the other hand, the SDII exhibited a decrease in magnitude by 0.02 mm/day/year. Nine stations displayed decreasing trends, with five stations showing significant trends.
- The climate indices revealed that there is a very slow increase in precipitation extremes for most of the indices, and decreasing trends in the Rx1, Rx5, and SDII indices.
- The correlation analysis revealed that the CDD index is significantly positively correlated with the ENSO indices during the winter period, and the inverse is true in the warm period. We can accept that the ENSO can reduce CDD in the warm phase and can increase CDD in the cold phase, as the warm phase, El Nino, increases precipitation.
- PRCPTOT exhibited a significant negative relationship with the SOI which indicates the increase in total precipitation during the El Nino phase of the ENSO.
- R95p and R99p also displayed negative relationships with the SOI in most of the stations, revealing that El Nino can cause more precipitation in the area.
- The maximum number of 1-day and 5-day precipitation indices also revealed that there is an increase in such days during the El Nino phase, causing more precipitation.

The ENSO is a global phenomenon that can have a significant effect on the climate of Pakistan. Therefore, it is recommended that the concerned departments should consider the impact of the ENSO while planning the water resources of the country. The ENSO impacts on temperature and elevation should also be measured to understand the ENSO better, as it can affect the climate of the country significantly.

Author Contributions: All authors were involved in the intellectual elements of this paper. M.U.M., S.H. and M.R. designed the research. S.H. and M.R. conducted the research and wrote the man-script, designed the methodology, and conducted the Investigation. S.H., F.A., K.O.A., M.S., S.S.S. and C.B.P. carried out writing—review and editing, writing—original draft, formal analysis, and validation, and helped with the data arrangement and analysis. All authors have read and agreed to the published version of the manuscript.

Funding: The research was supported by Abdullah Alrushaid Chair for Earth Science Remote Sensing Research.

Data Availability Statement: The data used to substantiate the findings of this research are accessible upon request from the corresponding author.

Acknowledgments: The authors extend their appreciation to Abdullah Alrushaid Chair for Earth Science Remote Sensing Research for funding.

Conflicts of Interest: The author Miklas Scholz is employed by aconium GmbH (previously atene KOM), Kunststoff-Technik Adams and Nexus by Sweden. The remaining authors declare that the research was conducted in the absence of any commercial or financial relationships that could be construed as a potential conflict of interest.

Appendix A

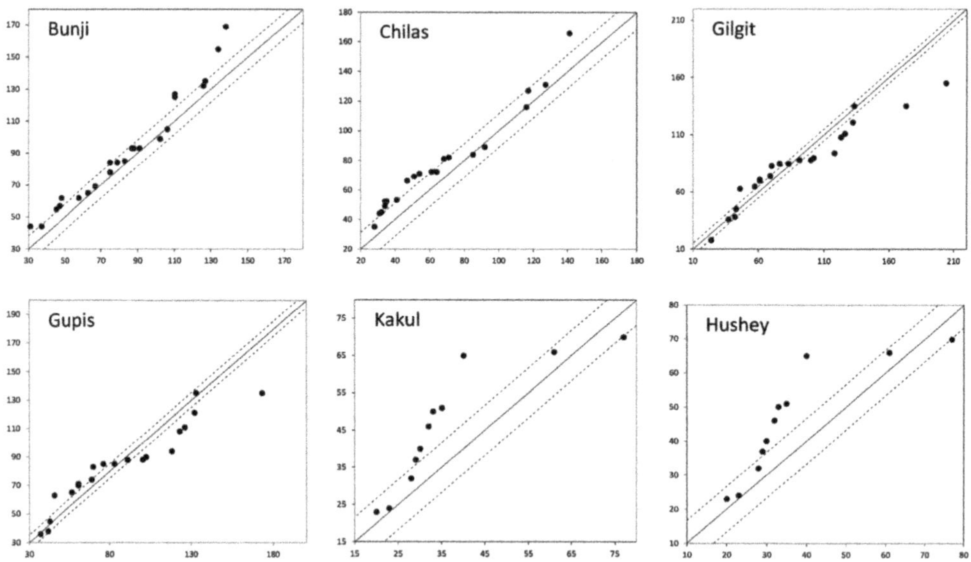

Figure A1. *Cont.*

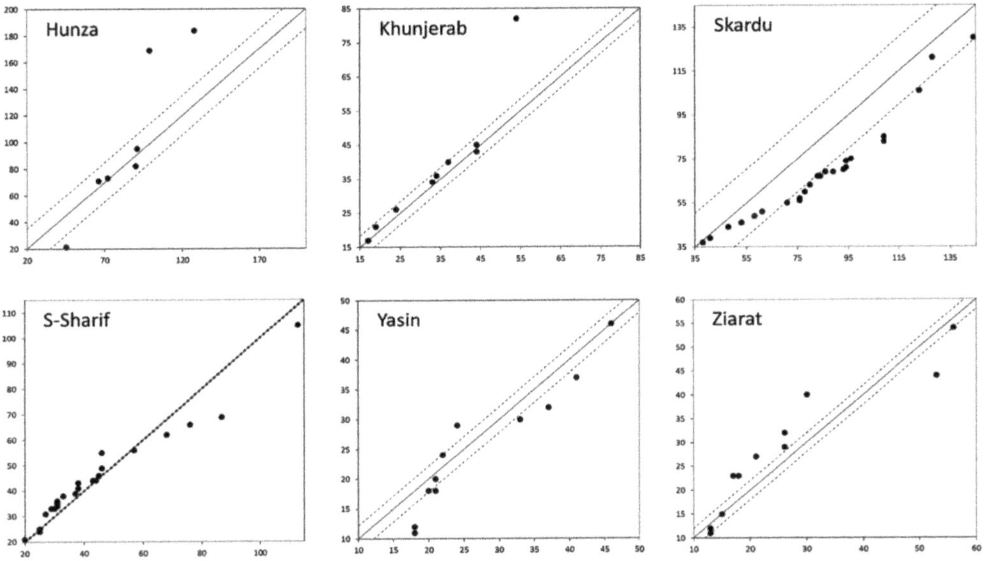

Figure A1. Results of CDD at 12 stations, obtained by using the ITA method.

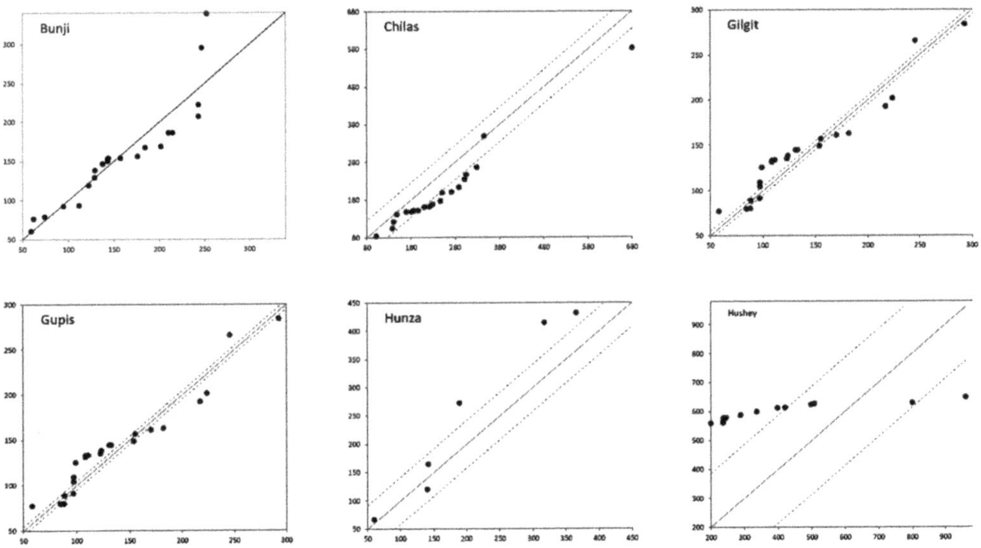

Figure A2. *Cont.*

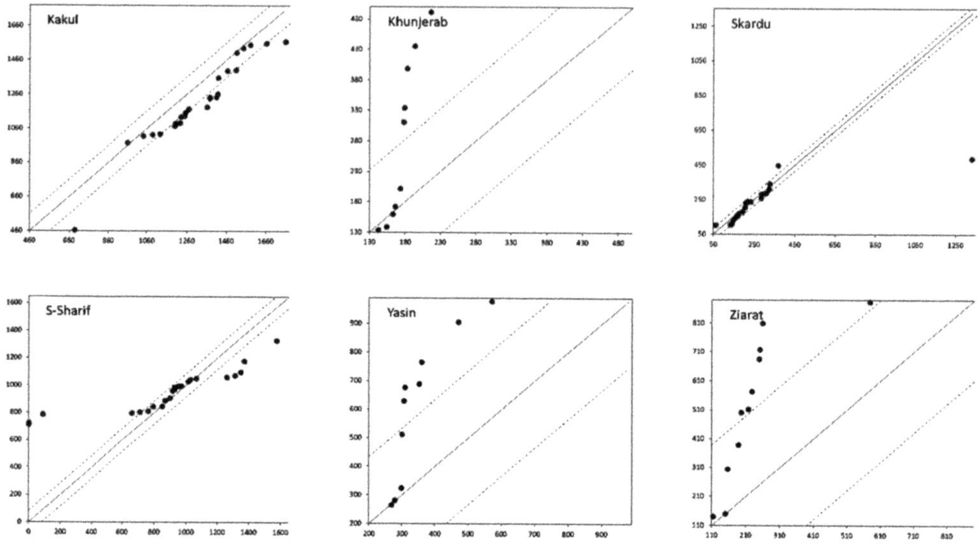

Figure A2. Results of PRCPTOT at 12 stations, obtained by using the ITA method.

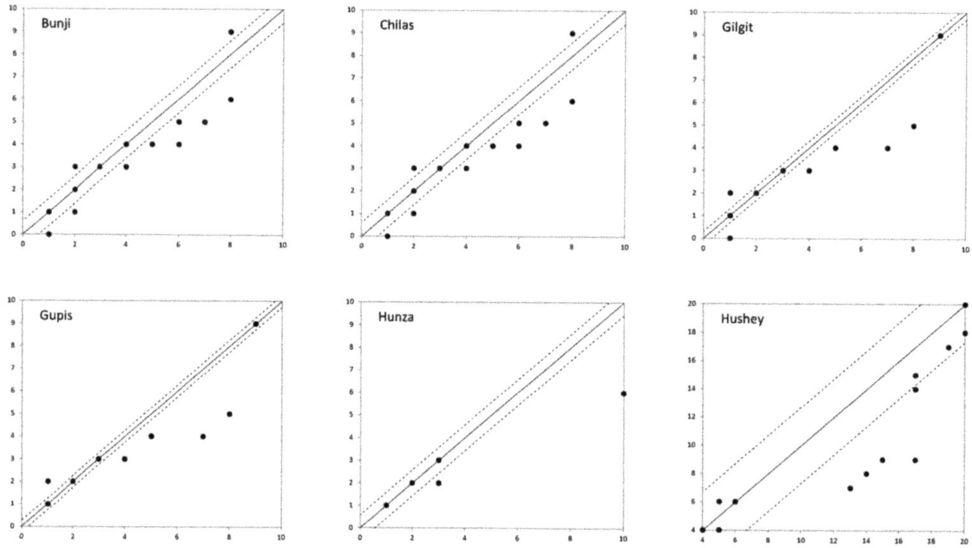

Figure A3. *Cont.*

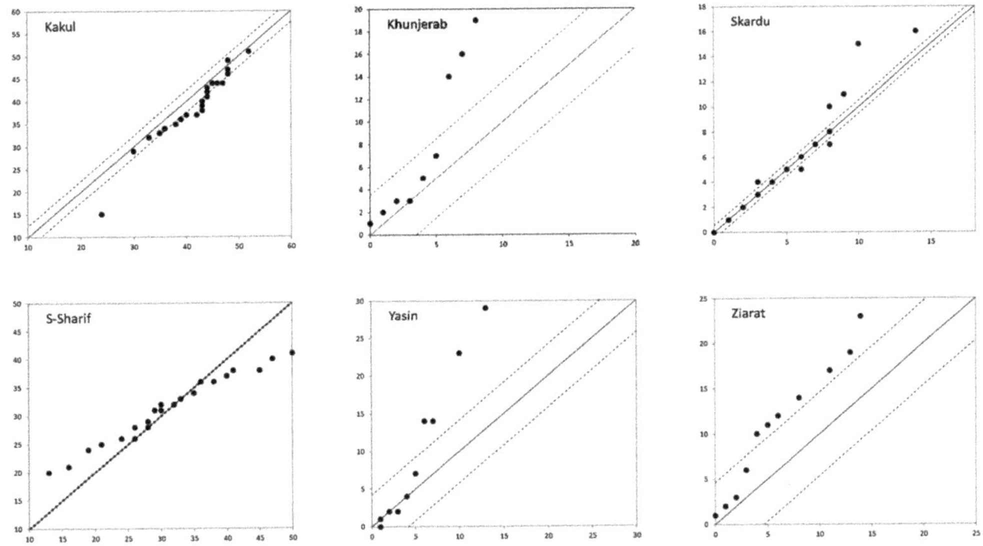

Figure A3. Results of R10mm at 12 stations, obtained by using the ITA method.

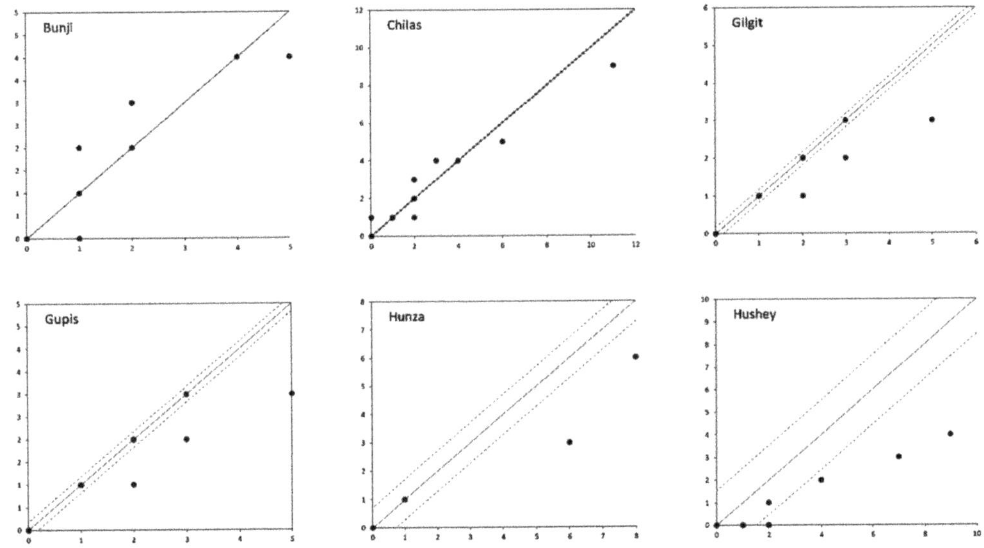

Figure A4. *Cont.*

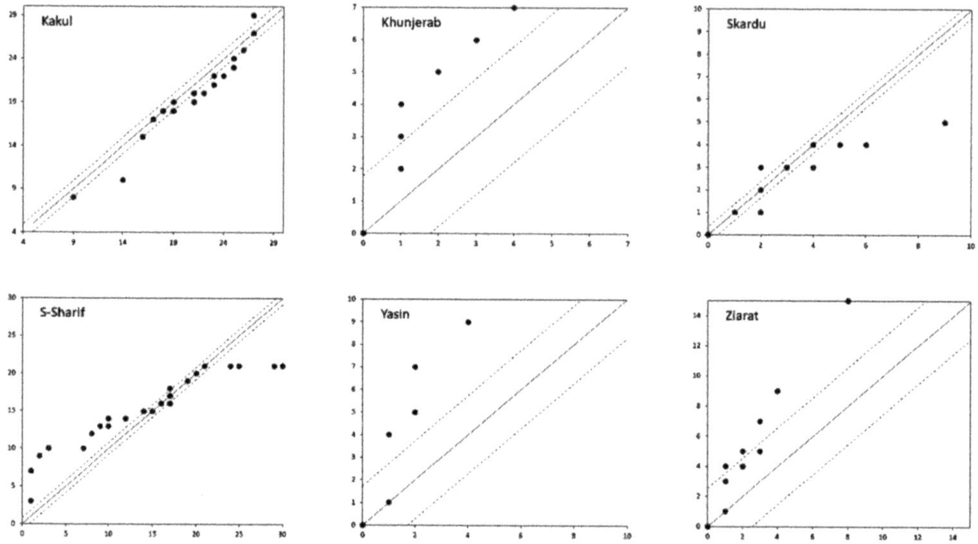

Figure A4. Results of R20mm at 12 stations, obtained by using the ITA method.

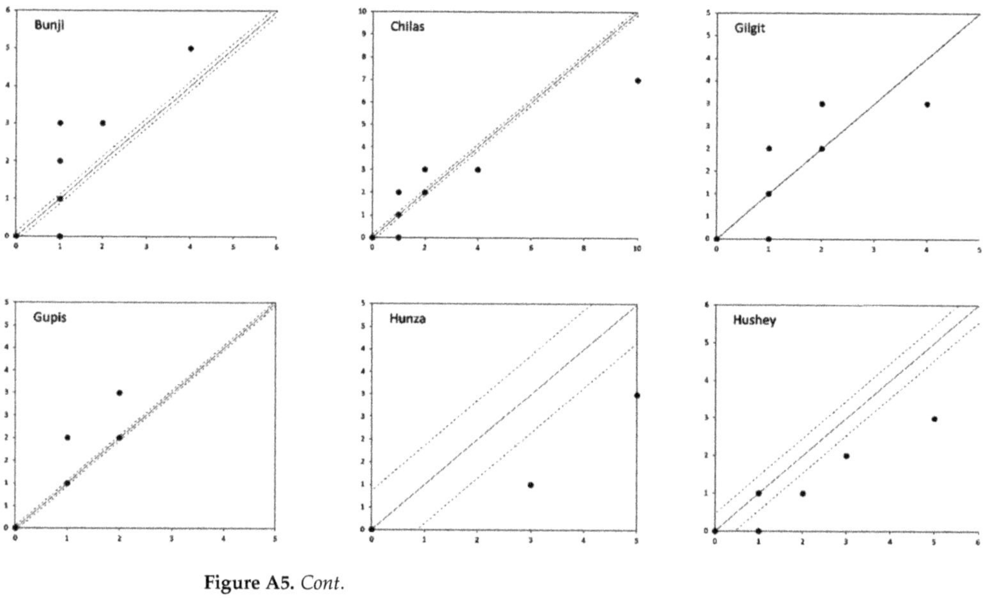

Figure A5. *Cont.*

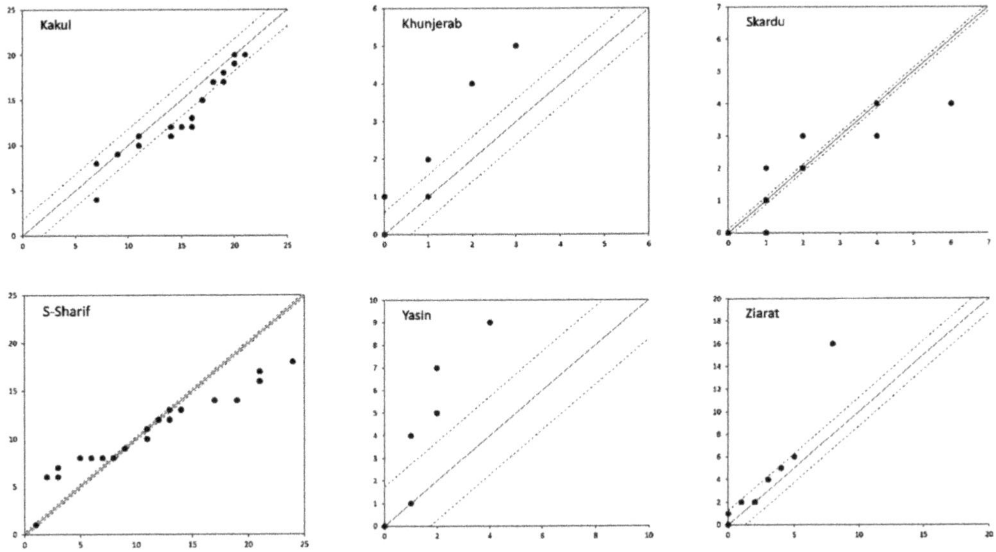

Figure A5. Results of R25mm at 12 stations, obtained by using the ITA method.

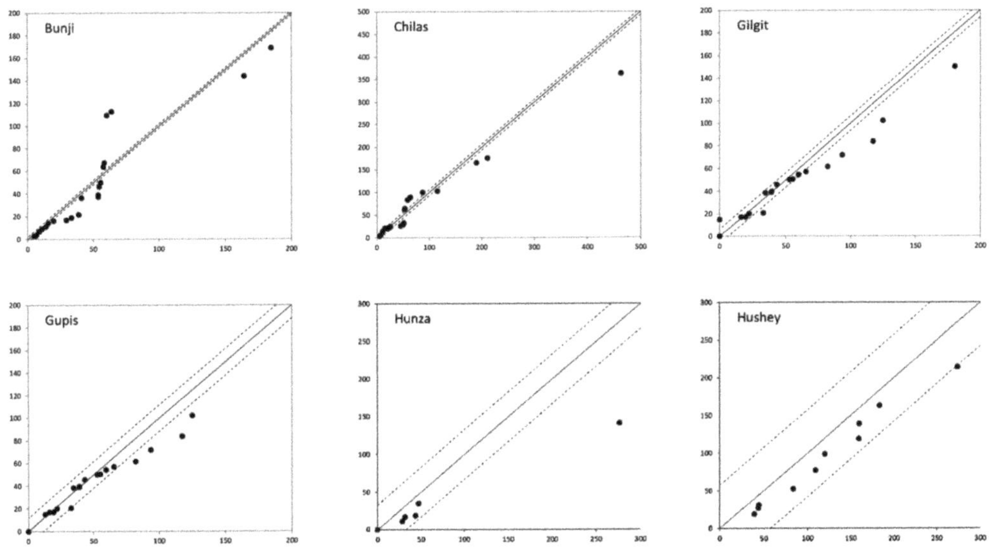

Figure A6. *Cont.*

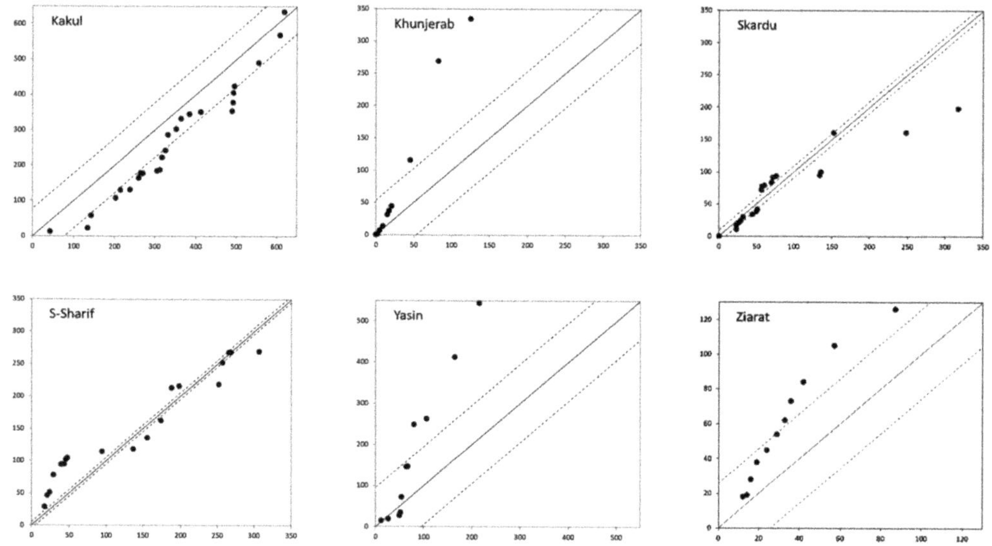

Figure A6. Results of R95p at 12 stations, obtained by using the ITA method.

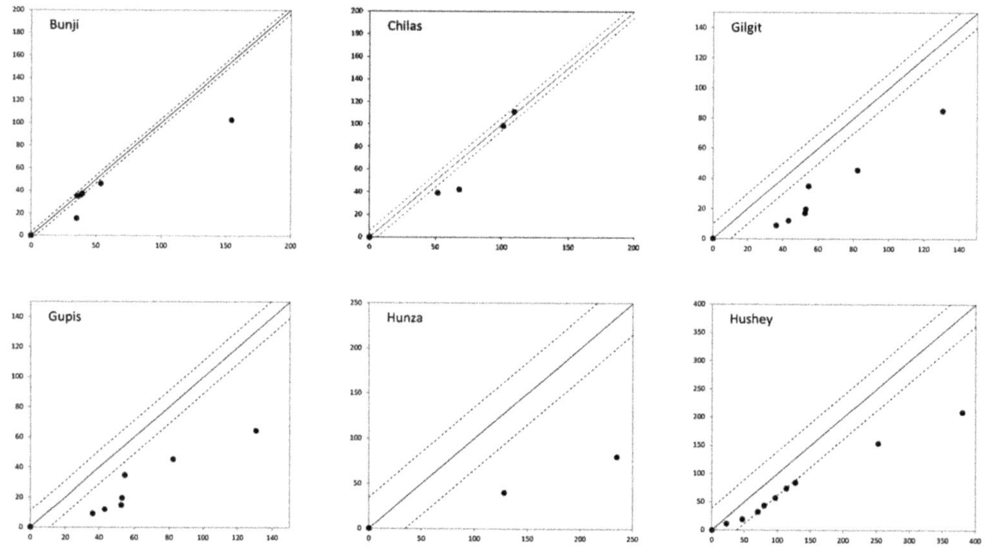

Figure A7. *Cont.*

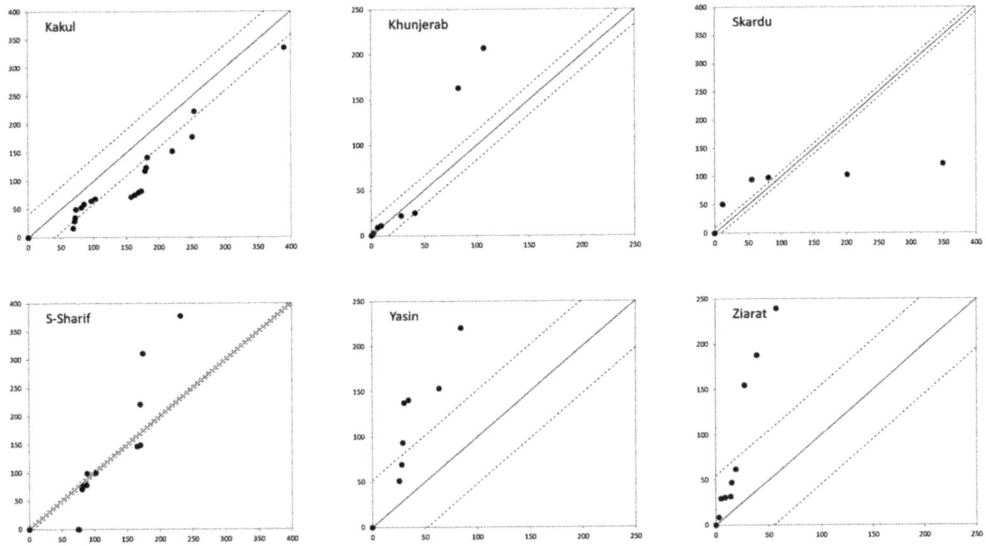

Figure A7. Results of R99p at 12 stations, obtained by using the ITA method.

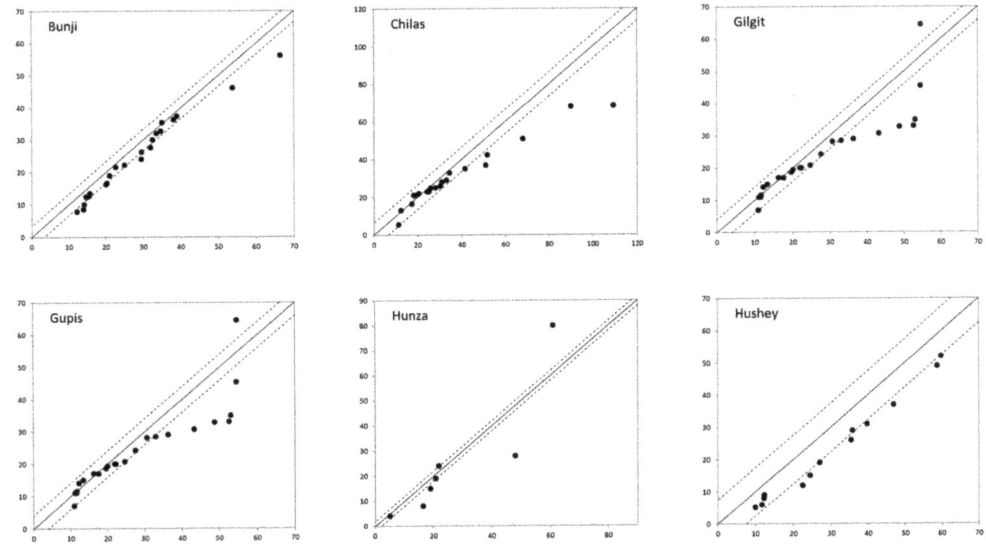

Figure A8. *Cont.*

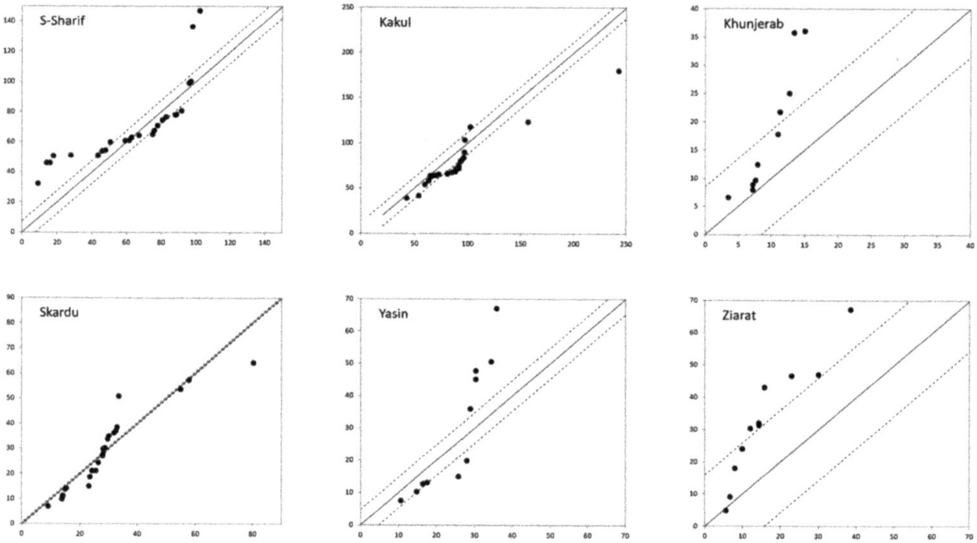

Figure A8. Results of Rx1 at 12 stations, obtained by using the ITA method.

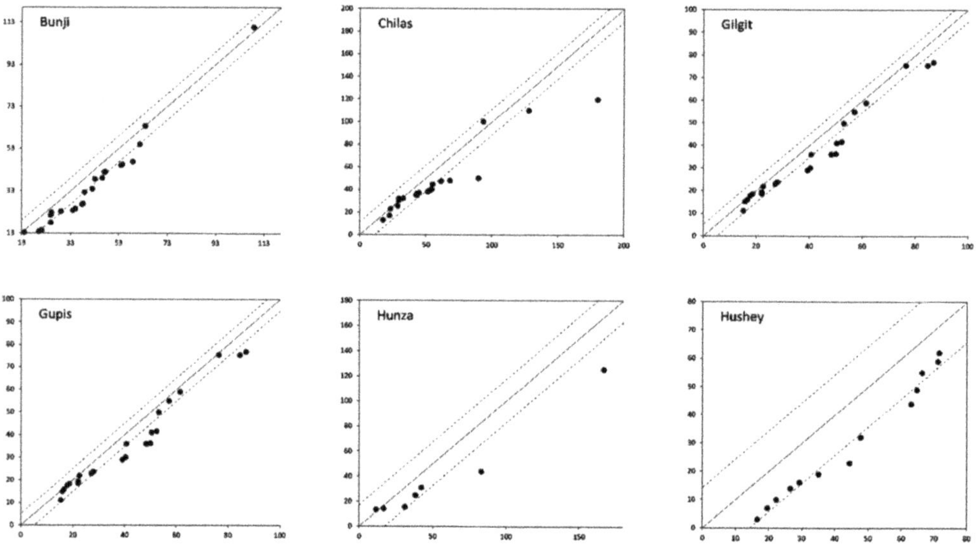

Figure A9. *Cont.*

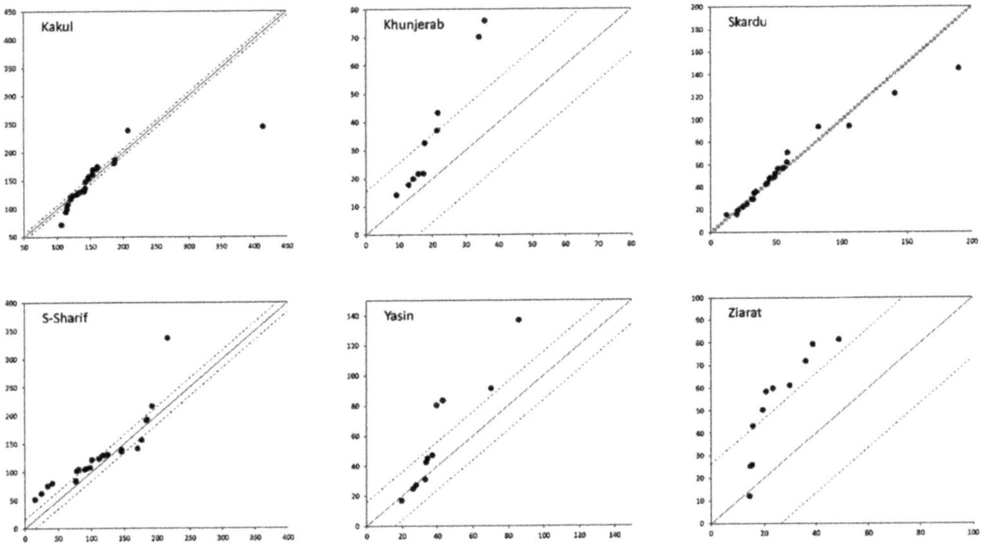

Figure A9. Results of Rx5 at 12 stations, obtained by using the ITA method.

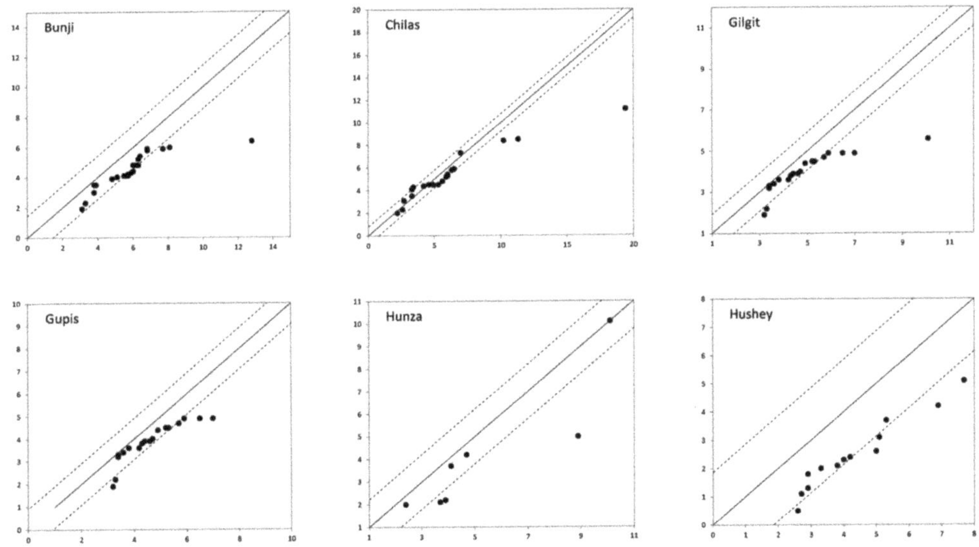

Figure A10. *Cont.*

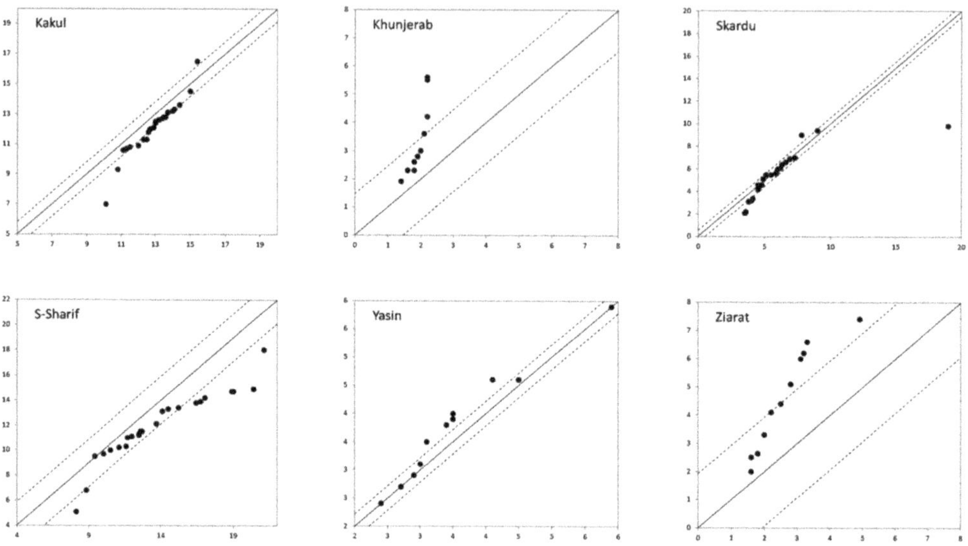

Figure A10. Results of SDII at 12 stations, obtained by using the ITA method.

References

1. Zhou, G.; Li, W.; Zhou, X.; Tan, Y.; Lin, G.; Li, X.; Deng, R. An innovative echo detection system with STM32 gated and PMT adjustable gain for airborne LiDAR. *Int. J. Remote Sens.* **2021**, *42*, 9187–9211. [CrossRef]
2. Zhou, G.; Deng, R.; Zhou, X.; Long, S.; Li, W.; Lin, G.; Li, X. Gaussian Inflection Point Selection for LiDAR Hidden Echo Signal Decomposition. *IEEE Geosci. Remote Sens. Lett.* **2021**, *19*, 6502705. [CrossRef]
3. Zhou, G.; Zhang, R.; Huang, S. Generalized Buffering Algorithm. *IEEE Access* **2021**, *9*, 27140–27157. [CrossRef]
4. Hashmi, H.N.; Siddiqui, Q.T.M.; Ghumman, A.R.; Kamal, M.A.; Mughal, H.U.R. A critical analysis of 2010 floods in Pakistan. *Afr. J. Agric. Res.* **2012**, *7*, 1054–1067. [CrossRef]
5. Gaurav, K.; Sinha, R.; Panda, P.K. The Indus flood of 2010 in Pakistan: A perspective analysis using remote sensing data. *Nat. Hazards* **2011**, *59*, 1815–1826. [CrossRef]
6. Carter, B.; Pozarny, P. *National Disaster Management Authorities*; GSDRC Helpdesk Research Report 1359; University of Birmingham: Birmingham, UK, 2016.
7. Khan, A.N.; Khan, S.N. Drought Risk and Reduction Approaches in Pakistan. In *Drought Risk and Reduction Approaches in Pakistan*; Springer: Berlin/Heidelberg, Germany, 2015; pp. 131–143.
8. Hirons, L.; Klingaman, N. La Niña 2016/2017: Historical Impact Analysis. 2016. Available online: https://www.gov.uk/research-for-development-outputs/la-nina-2016-2017-historical-impact-analysis (accessed on 12 December 2023).
9. Tian, H.F.; Huang, N.; Niu, Z.; Qin, Y.C.; Pei, J.; Wang, J. Mapping Winter Crops in China with Multi-Source Satellite Imagery and Phenology-Based Algorithm. *Remote Sens.* **2019**, *11*, 820. [CrossRef]
10. Tian, H.; Pei, J.; Huang, J.; Li, X.; Wang, J.; Zhou, B.; Qin, Y.; Wang, L. Garlic and Winter Wheat Identification Based on Active and Passive Satellite Imagery and the Google Earth Engine in Northern China. *Remote Sens.* **2020**, *12*, 3539. [CrossRef]
11. Yu, L.; Zhong, S.; Heilman, W.E.; Bian, X. A comparison of the effects of El Niño and El Niño Modoki on subdaily extreme precipitation occurrences across the contiguous United States. *J. Geophys. Res. Atmos.* **2017**, *122*, 7401–7415. [CrossRef]
12. Gao, C.; Hao, M.; Chen, J.; Gu, C. Simulation and design of joint distribution of rainfall and tide level in Wuchengxiyu Region, China. *Urban Clim.* **2021**, *40*, 101005. [CrossRef]
13. Xu, Z.; Li, X.; Li, J.; Xue, Y.; Jiang, S.; Liu, L.; Luo, Q.; Wu, K.; Zhang, N.; Feng, Y.; et al. Characteristics of Source Rocks and Genetic Origins of Natural Gas in Deep Formations, Gudian Depression, Songliao Basin, NE China. *ACS Earth Space Chem.* **2022**, *6*, 1750–1771. [CrossRef]
14. DeFlorio, M.J.; Pierce, D.W.; Cayan, D.R.; Miller, A.J. Western U.S. Extreme Precipitation Events and Their Relation to ENSO and PDO in CCSM4. *J. Clim.* **2013**, *26*, 4231–4243. [CrossRef]
15. Goly, A.; Teegavarapu, R.S.V. Individual and coupled influences of AMO and ENSO on regional precipitation characteristics and extremes. *Water Resour. Res.* **2014**, *50*, 4686–4709. [CrossRef]
16. Xu, J.; Lan, W.; Ren, C.; Zhou, X.; Wang, S.; Yuan, J. Modeling of coupled transfer of water, heat and solute in saline loess considering sodium sulfate crystallization. *Cold Reg. Sci. Technol.* **2021**, *189*, 103335. [CrossRef]
17. Rashid, A. Impact of el-nino on summer monsoon rainfall of pakistan. *Pak. J. Meteorol.* **2004**, *1*, 35–43.

18. Mahmood, A.; Khan, T.M.A.; Faisal, N. Correlation between multivariate enso index (mei) and pakistan's summer rainfall. *Pak. J. Meteorol.* **2004**, *1*, 53–64.
19. Hoyt, J.C. *Drought of 1936, with Discussion on the Significance of Drought in Relation to Climate*; U.S. Government Publishing Office: Washington, DC, USA, 1938. [CrossRef]
20. Zhu, X.; Xu, Z.; Liu, Z.; Liu, M.; Yin, Z.; Yin, L.; Zheng, W. Impact of dam construction on precipitation: A regional perspective. *Mar. Freshw. Res.* **2022**, *74*, 877–890. [CrossRef]
21. Kaskaoutis, D.; Houssos, E.; Solmon, F.; Legrand, M.; Rashki, A.; Dumka, U.; Francois, P.; Gautam, R.; Singh, R. Impact of atmospheric circulation types on southwest Asian dust and Indian summer monsoon rainfall. *Atmos. Res.* **2018**, *201*, 189–205. [CrossRef]
22. Masood, M.U.; Haider, S.; Rashid, M.; Aldlemy, M.S.; Pande, C.B.; Đurin, B.; Homod, R.Z.; Alshehri, F.; Elkhrachy, I. Quantifying the Impacts of Climate and Land Cover Changes on the Hydrological Regime of a Complex Dam Catchment Area. *Sustainability* **2023**, *15*, 15223. [CrossRef]
23. Haider, S.; Masood, M.U.; Rashid, M.; Alshehri, F.; Pande, C.B.; Katipoğlu, O.M.; Costache, R. Simulation of the Potential Impacts of Projected Climate and Land Use Change on Runoff under CMIP6 Scenarios. *Water* **2023**, *15*, 3421. [CrossRef]
24. Xie, X.; Xie, B.; Cheng, J.; Chu, Q.; Dooling, T. A simple Monte Carlo method for estimating the chance of a cyclone impact. *Nat. Hazards* **2021**, *107*, 2573–2582. [CrossRef]
25. Wu, X.; Guo, S.; Qian, S.; Wang, Z.; Lai, C.; Li, J.; Liu, P. Long-range precipitation forecast based on multipole and preceding fluctuations of sea surface temperature. *Int. J. Clim.* **2022**, *42*, 8024–8039. [CrossRef]
26. Yin, L.; Wang, L.; Li, T.; Lu, S.; Yin, Z.; Liu, X.; Li, X.; Zheng, W. U-Net-STN: A Novel End-to-End Lake Boundary Prediction Model. *Land* **2023**, *12*, 1602. [CrossRef]
27. Yin, L.; Wang, L.; Keim, B.D.; Konsoer, K.; Yin, Z.; Liu, M.; Zheng, W. Spatial and wavelet analysis of precipitation and river discharge during operation of the Three Gorges Dam, China. *Ecol. Indic.* **2023**, *154*, 110837. [CrossRef]
28. Gong, S.; Bai, X.; Luo, G.; Li, C.; Wu, L.; Chen, F.; Ran, C.; Xi, H.; Zhang, S. Climate change has enhanced the positive contribution of rock weathering to the major ions in riverine transport. *Glob. Planet. Chang.* **2023**, *228*, 104203. [CrossRef]
29. Hussain, D.; Kuo, C.-Y.; Hameed, A.; Tseng, K.-H.; Jan, B.; Abbas, N.; Kao, H.-C.; Lan, W.-H.; Imani, M. Spaceborne Satellite for Snow Cover and Hydrological Characteristic of the Gilgit River Basin, Hindukush–Karakoram Mountains, Pakistan. *Sensors* **2019**, *19*, 531. [CrossRef] [PubMed]
30. Hasson, S.U.; Böhner, J.; Lucarini, V. Prevailing climatic trends and runoff response from Hindukush–Karakoram–Himalaya, upper Indus Basin. *Earth Syst. Dyn.* **2017**, *8*, 337–355. [CrossRef]
31. Anjum, M.N.; Ding, Y.; Shangguan, D. Simulation of the projected climate change impacts on the river flow regimes under CMIP5 RCP scenarios in the westerlies dominated belt, northern Pakistan. *Atmos. Res.* **2019**, *227*, 233–248. [CrossRef]
32. Rashid, M.; Haider, S.; Masood, M.U.; Pande, C.B.; Tolche, A.D.; Alshehri, F.; Costache, R.; Elkhrachy, I. Sustainable Water Management for Small Farmers with Center-Pivot Irrigation: A Hydraulic and Structural Design Perspective. *Sustainability* **2023**, *15*, 16390. [CrossRef]
33. Forsythe, N.; Fowler, H.J.; Blenkinsop, S.; Burton, A.; Kilsby, C.G.; Archer, D.R.; Harpham, C.; Hashmi, M.Z. Application of a stochastic weather generator to assess climate change impacts in a semi-arid climate: The Upper Indus Basin. *J. Hydrol.* **2014**, *517*, 1019–1034. [CrossRef]
34. Bin Farhan, S.; Zhang, Y.; Aziz, A.; Gao, H.; Ma, Y.; Kazmi, J.; Shahzad, A.; Hussain, I.; Mansha, M.; Umar, M.; et al. Assessing the Impacts of Climate Change on the High Altitude Snow- and Glacier-Fed Hydrological Regimes of Astore and Hunza, the Sub-Catchments of Upper Indus Basin. *J. Water Clim. Chang.* **2018**, *11*, 479–490. [CrossRef]
35. Nagra, M.; Masood, M.U.; Haider, S.; Rashid, M. Assessment of Spatiotemporal Droughts through Machine Learning Algorithm over Pakistan. In Proceedings of the 2nd National Conference on Sustainable Water Resources Management (SWRM-22) at Center of Excellence in Water Resources Engineering, UET, Lahore, Pakistan, 16 November 2022; p. 8670.
36. Liu, Z.; Xu, J.; Liu, M.; Yin, Z.; Liu, X.; Yin, L.; Zheng, W. Remote sensing and geostatistics in urban water-resource monitoring: A review. *Mar. Freshw. Res.* **2023**, *74*, 747–765. [CrossRef]
37. Zhang, S.; Bai, X.; Zhao, C.; Tan, Q.; Luo, G.; Wang, J.; Li, Q.; Wu, L.; Chen, F.; Li, C.; et al. Global CO_2 Consumption by Silicate Rock Chemical Weathering: Its Past and Future. *Earth's Future* **2021**, *9*, e1938E–e2020E. [CrossRef]
38. Zhou, J.; Wang, L.; Zhong, X.; Yao, T.; Qi, J.; Wang, Y.; Xue, Y. Quantifying the major drivers for the expanding lakes in the interior Tibetan Plateau. *Sci. Bull.* **2021**, *67*, 474–478. [CrossRef] [PubMed]
39. Khattak, M.S.; Babel, M.S.; Sharif, M. Hydro-meteorological trends in the upper Indus River basin in Pakistan. *Clim. Res.* **2011**, *46*, 103–119. [CrossRef]
40. Archer, D.; Fowler, H. Spatial and temporal variations in precipitation in the Upper Indus Basin, global teleconnections and hydrological implications. *Hydrol. Earth Syst. Sci.* **2004**, *8*, 47–61. [CrossRef]
41. Ullah, S.; You, Q.; Ullah, W.; Ali, A. Observed changes in precipitation in China-Pakistan economic corridor during 1980–2016. *Atmos. Res.* **2018**, *210*, 1–14. [CrossRef]
42. Steinbauer, M.; Zeidler, J. Climate Change in the Northern Areas Pakistan: Impacts on Glaciers, Ecology and Livelyhoods. 2008. Available online: http://www.alfalter.org/wwfpakistan/Climate-change-in-the-Northern-Areas-Pakistan.pdf (accessed on 12 December 2023).

43. Latif, Y.; Yaoming, M.; Yaseen, M. Spatial analysis of precipitation time series over the Upper Indus Basin. *Theor. Appl. Clim.* **2016**, *131*, 761–775. [CrossRef]
44. Yin, L.; Wang, L.; Li, T.; Lu, S.; Tian, J.; Yin, Z.; Li, X.; Zheng, W. U-Net-LSTM: Time Series-Enhanced Lake Boundary Prediction Model. *Land* **2023**, *12*, 1859. [CrossRef]
45. Lin, X.; Zhu, G.; Qiu, D.; Ye, L.; Liu, Y.; Chen, L.; Liu, J.; Lu, S.; Wang, L.; Zhao, K.; et al. Stable precipitation isotope records of cold wave events in Eurasia. *Atmos. Res.* **2023**, *296*, 107070. [CrossRef]
46. Luo, J.; Niu, F.; Lin, Z.; Liu, M.; Yin, G.; Gao, Z. Abrupt increase in thermokarst lakes on the central Tibetan Plateau over the last 50 years. *CATENA* **2022**, *217*, 106497. [CrossRef]
47. Lüdecke, H.-J.; Müller-Plath, G.; Wallace, M.G.; Lüning, S. Decadal and multidecadal natural variability of African rainfall. *J. Hydrol. Reg. Stud.* **2021**, *34*, 100795. [CrossRef]
48. Shi, P.; Yang, T.; Xu, C.-Y.; Yong, B.; Shao, Q.; Li, Z.; Wang, X.; Zhou, X.; Li, S. How do the multiple large-scale climate oscillations trigger extreme precipitation? *Glob. Planet. Chang.* **2017**, *157*, 48–58. [CrossRef]
49. Fowler, H.J.; Archer, D.R. Hydro-Climatological Variability in the Upper Indus Basin and Implications for Water Resources. *IAHS-AISH Publ.* **2005**, *295*, 131–138.
50. Bhutiyani, M.R.; Kale, V.S.; Pawar, N.J. Climate change and the precipitation variations in the northwestern Himalaya: 1866–2006. *Int. J. Clim.* **2009**, *30*, 535–548. [CrossRef]
51. Wu, X.; Feng, X.; Wang, Z.; Chen, Y.; Deng, Z. Multi-source precipitation products assessment on drought monitoring across global major river basins. *Atmos. Res.* **2023**, *295*, 106982. [CrossRef]
52. Xiong, L.; Bai, X.; Zhao, C.; Li, Y.; Tan, Q.; Luo, G.; Wu, L.; Chen, F.; Li, C.; Ran, C.; et al. High-Resolution Data Sets for Global Carbonate and Silicate Rock Weathering Carbon Sinks and Their Change Trends. *Earth's Future* **2022**, *10*, e2022EF002746. [CrossRef]
53. Ma, S.; Qiu, H.; Yang, D.; Wang, J.; Zhu, Y.; Tang, B.; Sun, K.; Cao, M. Surface multi-hazard effect of underground coal mining. *Landslides* **2022**, *20*, 39–52. [CrossRef]
54. Basharat, M. Water Management in the Indus Basin in Pakistan: Challenges and Opportunities. *Indus River Basin* **2019**, *1*, 375–388.
55. Li, Q.; Lu, L.; Zhao, Q.; Hu, S. Impact of Inorganic Solutes' Release in Groundwater during Oil Shale In Situ Exploitation. *Water* **2022**, *15*, 172. [CrossRef]
56. Anwar, Z. El Nino and La Nina: Effects on Region and Pakistan; Islamabad. 2021. Available online: https://casstt.com/el-nino-and-la-nina-effects-on-region-and-pakistan (accessed on 12 December 2023).
57. Laghari, A.N.; Vanham, D.; Rauch, W. The Indus basin in the framework of current and future water resources management. *Hydrol. Earth Syst. Sci.* **2012**, *16*, 1063–1083. [CrossRef]
58. Shrestha, A.B.; Bajracharya, S.R.; Sharma, A.R.; Duo, C.; Kulkarni, A. Observed trends and changes in daily temperature and precipitation extremes over the Koshi river basin 1975–2010. *Int. J. Clim.* **2016**, *37*, 1066–1083. [CrossRef]
59. Zaman, M.; Ahmad, I.; Usman, M.; Saifullah, M.; Anjum, M.N.; Khan, M.I.; Qamar, M.U. Event-Based Time Distribution Patterns, Return Levels, and Their Trends of Extreme Precipitation across Indus Basin. *Water* **2020**, *12*, 3373. [CrossRef]
60. Lutz, A.F.; Immerzeel, W.W.; Kraaijenbrink, P.D.A.; Shrestha, A.B.; Bierkens, M.F.P. Climate Change Impacts on the Upper Indus Hydrology: Sources, Shifts and Extremes. *PLoS ONE* **2016**, *11*, e0165630. [CrossRef] [PubMed]
61. Karl, T.R.; Nicholls, N.; Ghazi, A. Clivar/GCOS/WMO Workshop on Indices and Indicators for Climate Extremes Workshop Summary. In *Weather and Climate Extremes: Changes, Variations and a Perspective from the Insurance Industry*; Springer: Berlin/Heidelberg, Germany, 1999; pp. 3–7.
62. Guo, J.; Guo, S.; Li, Y.; Chen, H.; Li, T. Spatial and temporal variation of extreme precipitation indices in the Yangtze River basin, China. *Stoch. Environ. Res. Risk Assess.* **2012**, *27*, 459–475. [CrossRef]
63. Mann, H.B. Nonparametric tests against trend. *Econometrica* **1945**, *13*, 245–259. [CrossRef]
64. Tabari, H.; Marofi, S.; Aeini, A.; Talaee, P.H.; Mohammadi, K. Trend analysis of reference evapotranspiration in the western half of Iran. *Agric. For. Meteorol.* **2011**, *151*, 128–136. [CrossRef]
65. Şen, Z. Innovative Trend Analysis Methodology. *J. Hydrol. Eng.* **2012**, *17*, 1042–1046. [CrossRef]
66. Pastagia, J.; Mehta, D. Application of innovative trend analysis on rainfall time series over Rajsamand district of Rajasthan state. *Water Supply* **2022**, *22*, 7189–7196. [CrossRef]
67. Körük, A.E.; Kankal, M.; Yıldız, M.B.; Akçay, F.; Şan, M.; Nacar, S. Trend analysis of precipitation using innovative approaches in northwestern Turkey. *Phys. Chem. Earth Parts A/B/C* **2023**, *131*, 103416. [CrossRef]
68. Alashan, S. An improved version of innovative trend analyses. *Arab. J. Geosci.* **2018**, *11*, 50. [CrossRef]
69. Ropelewski, C.F.; Halpert, M.S. The Southern Oscillation and Northern Hemisphere Temperature Variability. In *Developments in Atmospheric Science*; Elsevier: Amsterdam, The Netherlands, 1991; Volume 19, pp. 369–376, ISBN 0167-5117.
70. Trenberth, K.E.; Hoar, T.J. El Niño and climate change. *Geophys. Res. Lett.* **1997**, *24*, 3057–3060. [CrossRef]
71. Gupta, V.; Jain, M.K. Impact of ENSO, Global Warming, and Land Surface Elevation on Extreme Precipitation in India. *J. Hydrol. Eng.* **2020**, *25*, 05019032. [CrossRef]
72. Hussain, A.; Cao, J.; Hussain, I.; Begum, S.; Akhtar, M.; Wu, X.; Guan, Y.; Zhou, J. Observed Trends and Variability of Temperature and Precipitation and Their Global Teleconnections in the Upper Indus Basin, Hindukush-Karakoram-Himalaya. *Atmosphere* **2021**, *12*, 973. [CrossRef]

73. Anjum, M.N.; Ding, Y.; Shangguan, D.; Ahmad, I.; Ijaz, M.W.; Farid, H.U.; Yagoub, Y.E.; Zaman, M.; Adnan, M. Performance evaluation of latest integrated multi-satellite retrievals for Global Precipitation Measurement (IMERG) over the northern highlands of Pakistan. *Atmos. Res.* **2018**, *205*, 134–146. [CrossRef]
74. Salma, S.; Rehman, S.; Shah, M.A. Rainfall Trends in Different Climate Zones of Pakistan. *Pak. J. Meteorol.* **2012**, *9*, 37–47.
75. Magaña, V.O.; Vázquez, J.L.; Pérez, J.L.; Pérez, J.B. Geofísica Internacional. *Geofis. Int.* **2003**, *42*, 313–330.
76. Yang, X.; Wu, J.; Liu, J.; Ye, X. Changes of Extreme Precipitation and Possible Influence of ENSO Events in a Humid Basin in China. *Atmosphere* **2021**, *12*, 1522. [CrossRef]
77. Peña-Q, A.J.; Bermudez-F, L.N.; Ramírez-C, C.; Riaño-H, N.M. Oceanic Niño Index as a Tool to Determine the Effect of Weather on Coffee Plantation in Colombia. *Am. J. Exp. Agric.* **2015**, *7*, 395–404. [CrossRef]
78. Bhatti, A.S.; Wang, G.; Ullah, W.; Ullah, S.; Hagan, D.F.T.; Nooni, I.K.; Lou, D.; Ullah, I. Trend in Extreme Precipitation Indices Based on Long Term In Situ Precipitation Records over Pakistan. *Water* **2020**, *12*, 797. [CrossRef]
79. Supari; Tangang, F.; Salimun, E.; Aldrian, E.; Sopaheluwakan, A.; Juneng, L. ENSO modulation of seasonal rainfall and extremes in Indonesia. *Clim. Dyn.* **2017**, *51*, 2559–2580. [CrossRef]
80. Khan, A.H. The Influence of La-Nina Phenomena on Pakistan's Precipitation. *Pak. J. Meteorol.* **2004**, *1*, 23–31.
81. Cai, W.; Borlace, S.; Lengaigne, M.; van Rensch, P.; Collins, M.; Vecchi, G.; Timmermann, A.; Santoso, A.; McPhaden, M.J.; Wu, L.; et al. Increasing frequency of extreme El Niño events due to greenhouse warming. *Nat. Clim. Chang.* **2014**, *4*, 111–116. [CrossRef]

Section 2: Agricultural Water Management

Agricultural water management is covered in Section 2, comprised of Articles 6 to 17. Article 6 introduces water retention and nutrient management technologies. Experiments with recycled diesel spill-contaminated domestic wastewater treated by reed beds for the irrigation of sweet peppers are evaluated (Article 7). Linked to this are Article 8 on the contamination of soil used to grow two *Capsicum annuum* generations irrigated by reused urban wastewater treated by reed beds and Article 9 on the assessment of *C. annuum* grown in controlled and semi-controlled environments and irrigated with greywater treated by floating wetlands. Furthermore, this topic is supported by Article 10, which reports on the response of vegetables to cadmium-enriched soil, and Article 11 on the toxicity and bioaccumulation of heavy metals in spinach. Another set of articles deals with the water–energy–food nexus, addressing sustainable development goals (Article 12), nutrition security (Article 13) and gender vulnerability (Article 14). Furthermore, Article 15 is concerned with mitigating chilling stress by ozone pretreatment and the acclimation of sweet pepper. Article 16 reports on modifying walk-in tunnels through solar energy, fogging and evaporative cooling to mitigate heat stress on tomatoes. Finally, this section is concerned with delineating the crop–land dynamic due to extreme environments (Article 17).

Keywords: bioaccumulation of heavy metals; cadmium; *Capsicum annuum*; contaminated soil; crop–land dynamic; nutrient management; sustainable development goals; water–energy–food nexus; water retention; vegetable *water*

MDPI

Communication

Novel Water Retention and Nutrient Management Technologies and Strategies Supporting Agricultural Water Management in Continental, Pannonian and Boreal Regions

Miklas Scholz [1,2,3,4]

1 Division of Water Resources Engineering, Department of Building and Environmental Technology, Faculty of Engineering, Lund University, P.O. Box 118, 221 00 Lund, Sweden; miklas.scholz@tvrl.lth.se; Tel.: +46-703435270
2 Department of Civil Engineering Science, School of Civil Engineering and the Built Environment, University of Johannesburg, Kingsway Campus, Aukland Park, P.O. Box 524, Johannesburg 2006, South Africa
3 Institute of Environmental Engineering, Wroclaw University of Environmental and Life Sciences, ul. Norwida 25, 50-375 Wrocław, Poland
4 Department of Town Planning, Engineering Networks and Systems, South Ural State University, 76, Lenin Prospekt, 454080 Chelyabinsk, Russia

Abstract: Urgent water and food security challenges, particularly in continental and boreal regions, need to be addressed by initiatives such as the Horizon 2020-funded project WATer retention and nutrient recycling in soils and streams for improved AGRIcultural production (WATERAGRI). A new methodological framework for the sustainable management of various solutions resilient to climate change has been developed. The results indicate that the effect of the climate scenario is significantly different for peatlands and constructed wetlands. The findings also highlight that remote-sensing-based yield prediction models developed from vegetation indices have the potential to provide quantitative and timely information on crops for large regions or even at the local farm scale. Verification of remotely sensed data is one of the prerequisites for the proper utilization and understanding of data. Research shows that current serious game applications fall short due to challenges such as not clarifying the decision problem, the lack of use of decision quality indicators and limited use of gaming. Overall, WATERAGRI solutions improve water and food security by adapting agriculture to climate change, recycling nutrients and providing educational tools to the farming community. Farmers in small agricultural catchments benefit directly from WATERAGRI, but over the long-term, the general public does as well.

Keywords: agricultural water resources management; catchment hydrology; farm constructed wetland; field hydraulics; nature-based solutions; remote sensing pipeline; serious game; tracer methods; water and food nexus security; water scarcity; water quality control

Citation: Scholz, M. Novel Water Retention and Nutrient Management Technologies and Strategies Supporting Agricultural Water Management in Continental, Pannonian and Boreal Regions. *Water* **2022**, *14*, 1486. https://doi.org/10.3390/w14091486

Academic Editor: Xinchun Cao

Received: 19 April 2022
Accepted: 2 May 2022
Published: 5 May 2022

Publisher's Note: MDPI stays neutral with regard to jurisdictional claims in published maps and institutional affiliations.

1. Rationale, Structure and Objectives of the Communication

The rationale behind this communication was to collect scientific information concerning current WATERAGRI [1] outputs from all 23 partner organizations (see Section 3.2), evaluate its merit and discuss key findings in the wider context of water and food security challenges. The WATERAGRI concept aims to introduce a new framework for the use of small water retention approaches for managing the excess and shortage of water as well as improving the recovery of nutrients from agricultural catchments located in continental, Pannonian and boreal biogeographical regions by applying a multi-actor approach.

This paper communicates preliminary original research on potential impacts on water and food security in Europe. The published contributions of WATERAGRI that are of direct relevance to water retention and nutrient management in the context of agricultural water management are highlighted. Only the key published findings of WATERAGRI under this theme with a high impact potential are highlighted in Sections 4–8. These sections are preceded by sections on objectives (Section 1), challenges (Section 2) and potential solutions (Section 3). Sections 2 and 3 comprise motivating background information and the WATERAGRI consortiums' opinions on potential solutions to the outlined challenges, respectively. The communication ends with conclusions and recommendations (Section 9).

The scientific aim of this focused communication is to assess WATERAGRI water retention and nutrient management technologies and strategies supporting agricultural water management. The corresponding key objectives are to (a) assess nature-based solutions and wetland systems; (b) propose wetland system management strategies to mitigate climate change; (c) identify simplified models for wetland system design and performance prediction; (d) evaluate tracer methods linked to different key management practices; (e) demonstrate yield forecasting methods using remote sensing; and (f) develop serious games for decision support for end-users and other stakeholders.

2. Introduction to Challenges in Agricultural Water Management and Nutrient Recycling

A great upcoming societal challenge is to preserve water resources in view of the population increase and climate change [2]. In the European context, the Baltic Sea, the Danube and the Black Sea stand out as representing the end-recipients of agricultural wastewater and related eutrophication problems, as well as the loss of important ecosystems. Thus, integrated water management is linked to agricultural food production and water quantity and quality. Sustainable water resources management can support not only sustainable agricultural food production but also local ecosystems, in line with the bio-economy concept.

As most traditional agricultural areas in the Mediterranean regions of Europe become more unsustainable to farm due to their high water demands, there is a risk that fertile areas, particularly in continental climatic regions of Europe, will follow their fate in the next decades due to climate change. Therefore, Europe is likely to face a serious water and food security crisis in about 10 to 20 years. International projects such as WATERAGRI [1] address these challenges with technical and methodological innovations that have not reached the market yet and that require further development during field demonstrations.

During the 18th and 19th centuries, European wetlands acting as water and nutrient buffers to receiving waters were drained to a great extent. These areas were subsequently used for agricultural purposes. The result that can be seen today is large-scale water pollution and the loss of important wetland ecosystems. Reintroducing wetlands to the agricultural landscape means better retention of both water and nutrients, as previously reviewed by the author [3]. The local impact of climate change and variations in local micro-climate can, at the same time, be mitigated and introduce a sufficient supply of fresh or recycled water for sustainable crop production [4]. A number of underutilized techniques of water management, such as natural water retention and nutrient recovery, could be reintroduced to agricultural management for the benefit of farmers, local communities and the environment, according to a previous review by the author [5].

There is a need to introduce and test a new methodological framework for the use of small water retention approaches such as integrated constructed wetlands [3] for managing the excess and shortage of water and nutrient recovery from agricultural catchments. The link between agricultural land management and soil–sediment–water management for increased nutrient uptake, water quality improvement, water retention and groundwater replenishment will have to be assessed for different geographical regions, soils and climatic and particularly seasonal variations. The focus should be on affordable and easy-to-implement reviewed farm solutions, such as farm constructed wetlands [5]. Locally available eco-friendly materials for water storage such as clay and gravel should be used as a liner and substrate, respectively. All studies should also include an economic and sustainability analysis of the proposed measures and the maintenance of the infrastructure.

The analysis of sustainable techniques such as wetlands [5] for water management needs to consider the need for adaptation to climate change [6] and its impact on ecosystem services [7]. There is an obligation to evaluate long-term benefits for the farm and the local ecosystem from the implementation of small natural water retention measures.

Considerable nutrient loads are released to natural waterbodies due to inefficient fertilizer usage and insufficiently treated wastewater. There is a great economic and environmental potential to collect nutrients and reuse them in agricultural activities, for example, as fertilizer [4,8]. This will help to close the nutrient loop by promoting circular nutrient management. There is a need to investigate the probability of nutrient recovery for the use of growing crops and identify and test possible technologies for extracting nutrients from wetland sediments. There is a research gap in the development of innovative drainage systems to capture the nutrients from runoff and waste streams. These systems can also be applied for river restoration and any kind of water runoff. The captured nutrients can further be used directly with crops with high nutrient uptake and subsequently converted to biomass via composting.

To address these challenges in agricultural water management and nutrient recycling, WATERAGRI [1] has developed and tested the WATERAGRI concept (Figure 1) for the use of small water retention approaches focusing on integrated constructed wetlands [3,5] and innovative capture technologies for managing the excess and shortage of water and nutrient recovery from agricultural catchments.

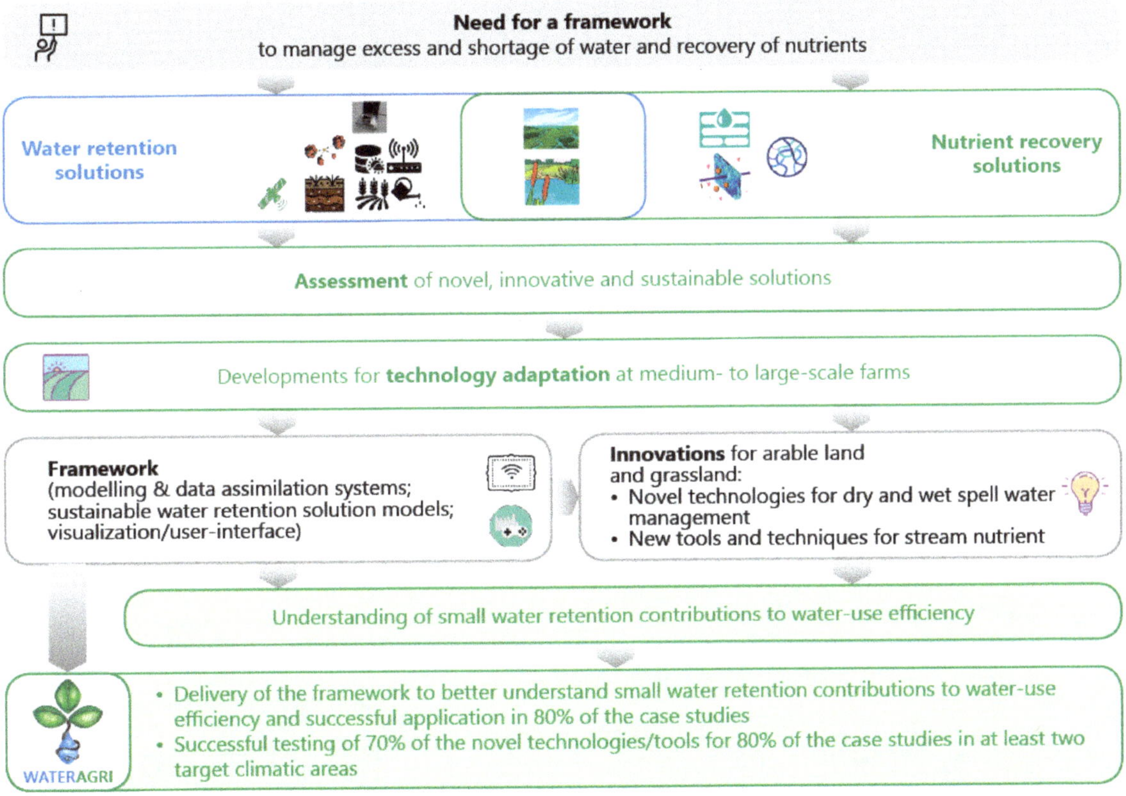

Figure 1. Methodological WATERAGRI concept outline of providing, assessing and adapting sustainable solutions for farmers in order to improve water and nutrient management.

3. Solutions and Their Expected Impacts

3.1. Potential Solutions and Their Direct Expected Impacts

Water and food security as well as climate change challenges may be addressed with various solutions, such as new technologies, methods, procedures, guidelines, models and educational tools. It is likely that there are many solutions that address these challenges. However, WATERAGRI focused only on promising innovations, which are summarized in Table 1. The purpose of the project was to evaluate them and to further develop the most promising solutions that are not ready to reach the market yet. The innovations in Table 1 are categorized into four groups: Framework and Modeling Tools (Group A), Sustainable Water Retention Solutions (Group B), Sustainable Water Retention and Nutrient Recovery Solutions (Group C) and Nutrient Recovery Solutions (Group D).

Table 1. Purpose of selected WATERAGRI solutions within the modeling framework and their corresponding technology readiness levels (TRLs).

ID	Solution	Initial TRL	Final TRL	Description of Purpose
A1	WATERAGRI Modeling Framework	3	6	The framework assesses small water retention approaches focusing on integrated constructed wetlands and innovative capture technologies for managing excess and shortage of water and nutrient recovery from agricultural catchments. The links between agricultural land and water management as well as soil–sediment–water management for increased nutrient uptake, water quality improvement, water retention and groundwater recharge are evaluated.
A2	Integrated Physically based Terrestrial System Models Combined with Data Assimilation	3.5	6.5	These models are used by the WATERAGRI Modeling Framework with the goal of providing near-real-time simulations of the terrestrial system, considering recent measurement data from online in situ and remote sensors. This allows for a significant increase in the efficiency of irrigation with optimal and joint use of surface and subsurface resources.
A3	Decision Support System Optimizing Irrigation Scheduling and Fertilization	3	6	This framework includes a decision support system, which optimizes irrigation scheduling and fertilization on the basis of the near-real-time updated model simulations.
A4	Irrigation Model	3	6	This model is part of the framework and supports farmers in the management of their farms by providing easy-to-use tools such as registration of crop operations and crop damages as well as seasonal weather forecasting.
A5	Water–Vapor Sorption Isotherm and Water Retention Characteristics (WVSI-WRC) Model	2	5	The framework integrates the novel physico-chemical WVSI-WRC model for unsaturated soils.
A6	WebGIS for Zoning Landscape Matrix	3	6	The matrix collects remote sensing data and assesses the impact of land use patterns for zoned agricultural lands and wetlands. The matrix incorporates digital elevation models, pedological maps, hydrology and vegetation status.
A7	Serious Game	2	5	This tool increases stakeholder acceptance of the simulation-assimilation-prediction, capacity building and real participative approaches.

Table 1. *Cont.*

ID	Solution	Initial TRL	Final TRL	Description of Purpose
B1	Remote Sensing Pipeline	3	6	The pipeline processes multiple types of high-resolution satellite data to obtain insights into numerous spectrally observable parameters.
B2	Irrigation Management and Agrometeorological Monitoring Solution	3	5	This innovation supports best management practices and monitoring of water requirements with particular reference to water retention and nutrient recovery.
B3	Precision Irrigation System	3	5	This system is integrated with a decision support system, which applies knowledge on weather and climate for the qualitative and quantitative improvement of agricultural production.
B4	Enhanced Water Retainer Product and Concept	5	8	The concept combines an existing water retainer product with other solutions.
B5	Advanced Tracer Methods	3	6	These methods assess water fluxes, residence times and groundwater recharge rates, which are parameters that cannot be directly measured in wetlands or many subsurfaces.
B6	Dewaterability Estimation Test (DET) Apparatus	3	6	The DET apparatus is used to test how easy it is to dewater mixtures of solids and liquids such as agricultural wastewater.
C1	Farm Constructed Wetland	3	7	This is a special type of integrated constructed wetland for water and nutrient control purposes.
C2	Biochar Adsorbents	3	6	Biochar is used for both water retention and nutrient adsorption.
D1	Bio-based Nutrient-Collecting Membrane	3	7	These membranes are applied to recycle nutrients such as phosphorus.
D2	Novel Drainage System	3	5	This system captures nutrients from farm yards, field runoff and various farm waste streams.
D3	Microfluidics	3	6	This innovation is efficient in the capture of various reagents from water.

The technology readiness levels (TRLs) referred to in Table 1 follow these definitions: TRL 1, basic principles observed; TRL 2, technology concept formulated; TRL 3, experimental proof of concept; TRL 4, technology validated in the laboratory; TRL 5, technology validated by a farm; TRL 6, technology demonstrated within a farm catchment; TRL 7, innovation prototype demonstrated in the operational environment; TRL 8, innovation complete and qualified; and TRL 9, actual innovation proven in the operational environment and manufactured. While the initial TRLs have been determined according to the above definitions, the final TRLs are only predictions for 2024/2025.

The paragraphs below further describe some of the key innovations (Table 1) and their expected impacts. The WATERAGRI Modeling Framework (Table 1; A1) is capable of simulating water, energy and nutrient cycles in the soil, groundwater, surface water, vegetation and engineering structures in a coupled manner, thus reflecting the complexity of agricultural systems. The measurement data from online and in situ sensors include soil moisture content, groundwater levels, stream discharge, crop state and water levels in retention reservoirs and drains. In addition, remotely sensed observations such as soil moisture content and leaf area index are also assimilated.

Near-real-time integrated model predictions informed by in situ and remote online measurements will allow farmers to take the best decisions to increase the efficiency of input use. The input efficiency increase generates economic benefits for farmers while increasing the sustainable use of water resources. Existing infrastructure can be integrated into the modeling system to maximize water retention and efficiency [9].

Figure 2 indicates the data gathering and analysis approaches within the WATERAGRI Modeling Framework. They integrate the key innovations developed (Table 1). Multiple sensors covering different temporal and spatial scales in the catchments have been developed. The data collected constitute, for example, hydraulic heads and soil moisture information as well as discharge and evapotranspiration measurements.

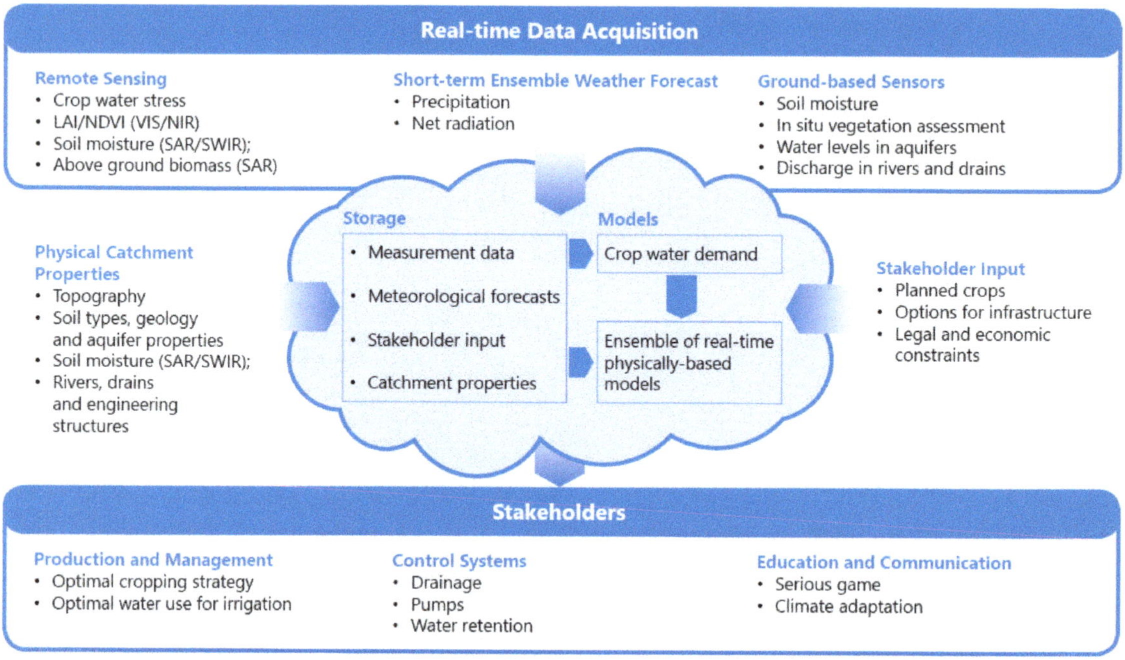

Figure 2. Data gathering and analysis approaches within the WATERAGRI Modeling Framework (A1) to support WATERAGRI solutions benefitting stakeholders in agriculture.

Within the cloud, data are stored within the framework, allowing for subsequent information extraction. Digital surface models of selected catchments have been generated using airborne laser scanning data and local data densification based on photogrammetric or laser scanning data collected with an unmanned aerial vehicle for selected sites. Relevant processes and catchment features have been implemented for selected catchments.

The Irrigation Model (Table 1; A4) integrates remote sensing technology to analyze crop development and variation over time. The model also integrates sensor data, networks, monitoring tools, forecast models and decision support functionalities. The Irrigation Model provides critical input to the integrated and physically based modeling system. The WVSI-WRC and hydraulic conductivity models provide well-defined groundwater conditions at varying water saturation degrees in relation to climate and crop farming, which play a key part in the whole Irrigation Model.

In contrast to conventional models used in unsaturated subsurface hydrology, which are empirical, the WVSI-WRC model (Table 1; A5) is based on the underlying physics of pore surface adsorption and capillary condensation. For this reason, the parameters in the model have physical meaning. This provides the advantage of using the model to optimize the implementation of the new technologies and the design of water retention products in terms of their underlying physics. On the other hand, the model can be validated using the data collected from laboratory tests and field observation.

The Serious Game (Table 1 (A7) and Section 8) can be used to facilitate decision making in real situations. This is possible because the interactive gaming environment enables different stakeholders to simulate and quantify the impact of their decisions on technical, economic and environmental aspects of the analyzed problem, should they choose to do so. Subsequently, stakeholders will learn to have a greater appreciation of trade-offs that exist between different water retention options and agricultural production, increasing framework acceptance [10].

The Remote Sensing Pipeline (Table 1 (B1), Figure 3 and Section 7) operates in the short-wave infrared spectrum to measure soil moisture and vegetation water stress, and it uses a combination of visible near-infrared light and radar observations to measure vegetation densities and phenological stages (where possible). These measurements are used to calibrate the WVSI-WRC model (Table 1). This helps farmers to decide upon and characterize the variation in the model parameters, which will be integrated into the database of the framework. The soil moisture and vegetation water stress data are integrated in the cloud (Figure 2) and can be used to inform real-time models for short-term predictions. The use of dense sub-weekly time series of multispectral imagery satellites (3–10 m spatial resolution) from both the Copernicus program and private actors makes the monitoring of crop biophysical parameters feasible.

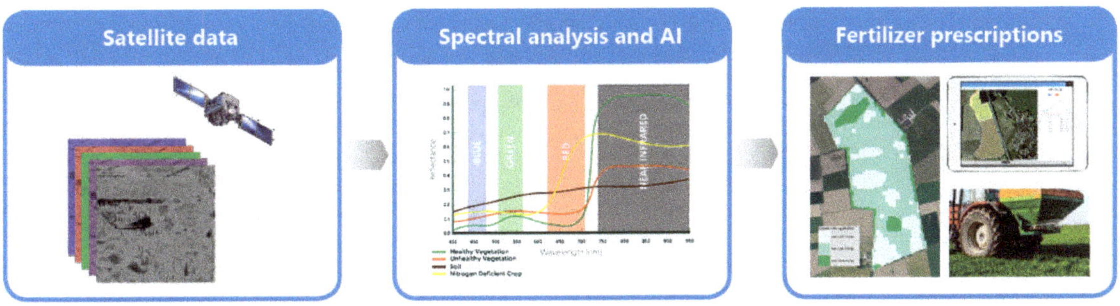

Figure 3. Impact example: Remote Sensing Pipeline (B1) application in farming (AI, artificial intelligence) to improve fertilizer application.

Remote sensing applications help to assign water and fertilizer demands for different crop and soil types. The pipeline B1 improves decision support by providing data. The overview quantifies and benchmarks changes. The identification of plant water leads to spatially optimized water use, supporting efficient water irrigation and lower costs. Remote sensing data will help to identify effective innovations. The data are cost-effective and useful in measuring important indicators during dry and wet spells, improving water management.

The analysis of remote sensing results has its limitations, as reported by WATERAGRI researchers. The assessment of output may show differences with, for example, different satellite image resolutions and spectral analysis methods. Moreover, it is sometimes hard to collect appropriate satellite images because of cloud obstructions.

The Irrigation Management and Agrometeorological Monitoring Solution (Table 1; B2) is used to help farmers, agronomists and farm advisers to manage irrigation scheduling and crop stress in real time, ensuring optimal production while reducing water use, energy consumption and environmental impact. Stress management and irrigation advice services have the purpose of covering the entire irrigation process, ensuring optimal production all season long and planning farm operation and management strategies based on current crop needs and weather conditions.

The Precision Irrigation System (Table 1; B3) is integrated with a decision support system. The irrigation plan encoded in the decision support system is based on the prediction of the soil water content in the root zone and daily crop water requirements using a water balance model, which combines crop, weather and soil databases as well as historical and forecast weather data. The main functions of the decision support system include real-time irrigation management, decision-making support, user-customized irrigation scheduling, simulation of soil water dynamics in the root zone, evaluation of the effect of certain irrigation schedules on crop yield reduction and database management.

The crop simulation model and the water requirement calculations of the decision support system work on a daily time step. The modeling approach is based on the continuity equation, which is applied to the soil layer explored by roots. Crop evapotranspiration losses are evaluated at the field level with an algorithm that simulates the reference crop evapotranspiration, the maximum crop evapotranspiration and the real crop evapotranspiration.

The Precision Irrigation System output, which is updated daily, includes the following information: crop water status and irrigation requirements, as well as temporal patterns of soil moisture levels compared to upper (optimal soil moisture status to be reached with irrigation) and lower (beginning of stress, when irrigation is mandatory) thresholds. Additional data output provided by the model includes the phenological phase, crop coefficient and water stress coefficient. Likewise, numerical models simulating the surface and subsurface resources can be linked to this decision support system. This allows end-users to analyze how providing irrigation water will affect water storage in surface and subsurface reservoirs in the short and long term. It also allows studying the effect of in-stream measures on soil moisture storage. This is a central precondition for improved water retention.

In general, the water retainer product helps the ground to maintain a steady water balance by reducing evaporation. Water retainers are often organic soil conditioner liquids helping plants to take up water and diminish the effects of drought and dehydration. WATERAGRI has used a water retainer product in different conditions and provided the research background to product development activities by investigating the effects of the water retainer on the soil ecosystem using molecular biology methods. Furthermore, the WVSI-WRC model was used to model and characterize the performance of the biodegradable water retainer product to help improve its design and quality. These actions resulted in the Enhanced Water Retainer Product and Concept (Table 1; B4).

The organic water retainer B4 reduces evaporation, regulates the water balance and stops water seepage deeper into the soil. The retainer effectively compensates for dry spells by increasing the soil's water storage capacity. Plants should then maintain an acceptable yield of high quality. Soil is then also more likely not to be water-repellent.

Advanced Tracer Methods (Table 1 (B5) and Section 6) are used to analyze the stable isotopes of water in the pore water of soils. Advanced water–vapor equilibration techniques allow measuring the isotopic composition of pore water in high-resolution soil cores. Corresponding data can be used to quantify water fluxes and improve the calibration of subsurface models (soil and groundwater), thus reducing their predictive uncertainties.

The DET Apparatus (Table 1; B6) data should allow for better management decisions regarding the selection of dewatering technology. The test can also be used to evaluate the water retention capacity of different soils and sludge within the agricultural industry [11]. Moreover, B6 will help in the identification of economically sustainable technologies and methods for the dry- and wet-spell water management of soil and sludge.

The DET is almost as simple as the capillary suction test, but it is more reliable, faster, flexible and informative in terms of the visual measurement data collected with modern image analysis software. The standard deviations associated with repeated measurements for the same sludge are lower for the DET than for the capillary suction test. In contrast to the capillary suction time test device, capillary suction in the DET test is linear and not radial, allowing for a straightforward interpretation of findings [11].

Farm Constructed Wetlands (Table 1 (C1) and Sections 4 and 5) can be used for sustainable water retention and nutrient recycling. The analysis and modeling of soil moisture retention with drainage level controls, vegetated buffer zones and nutrient retention in wetlands [5] for water management considered the need for adaptation to climate change and its impact on ecosystem services [7] such as flood control.

Wetland design recommendations taking variation into account should improve seasonal water retention. Modeling helps to identify the tools and techniques for successful waste stream nutrient recovery. The modeling results support the assessment of the economic impact and management strategies.

Considerable nutrient loads are released to semi-natural waterbodies such as wetlands due to inefficient (artificial) fertilizer usage and insufficiently treated agricultural wastewater. There is considerable economic and environmental potential to capture these nutrients and reuse them in agriculture [8]. Recovered nutrients from wetlands can be used to grow crops [4].

Biochar Absorbents (Table 1; C2) have been shown to increase both the soil water holding capacity and the available water capacity. Moreover, C2 acts as a nutrient adsorbent from the runoff water. However, the biochar's efficiency depends on its properties, soil texture, raw material(s) and pyrolysis conditions. Char activation should improve the nutrient adsorptive performance.

The WVSI-WRC model can be used to characterize the performance of the biochar's efficiency. This should result in a quantified assessment of surface adsorption and soil water holding capacity improvements. Such assessments can guide the improvement of current product design and manufacturing processes.

The Bio-based Nutrient-Collecting Membrane (Table 1; D1) is made of nano-cellulose. With numerous surface-tailoring options, the membrane has the potential for selective nutrient capture. The production method is green and up-scalable and can thus be produced for various catchment scales and corresponding configurations. The biological structure opens the possibility of using the nutrient-rich membrane material after recovery for soil amendment and/or fertilization.

The Novel Drainage System (Table 1; D2) is based on a low-cost bio-inspired drainage technology that captures nutrients from runoff and streams. Different layers of material act like a rhizosphere to absorb and store nutrients in the soil, metabolize them and make them accessible to crops. The captured nutrients can further be used directly with crops with high nutrient uptake and subsequently be converted to biomass. Moreover, active drainage management (e.g., closing drains during drought conditions) improves the efficiency of irrigation and fertigation.

Microfluidics (Table 1; D3) can be integrated with wastewater treatment systems (Figure 4) for agricultural activities targeting nutrients within the operational context. This innovation is energetically efficient and designed to permit reagent recovery on an agricultural farm scale. The device is suitable for circular nutrient management. Furthermore, D3 allows for the flow of large volumes of contaminated water.

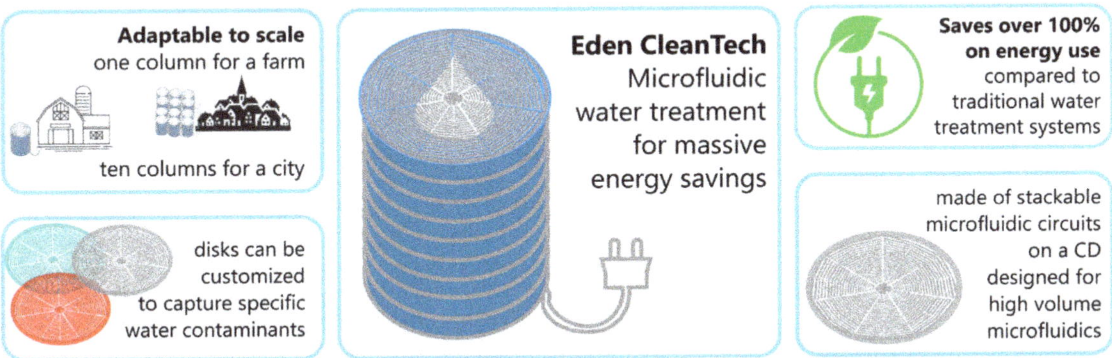

Figure 4. Impact example: Microfluidics (D3) application to produce clean water and recover nutrients at relatively low cost.

3.2. Expected Long-Term Case Study Impacts

Figure 5 provides an overview of all case study locations. The following paragraphs summarize the corresponding expected long-term impacts. The first Finnish case study may lead to the improvement of water regulation for potato farming and comprises the development of automatic drainage. Drainage water regulation for farming on mineral soils in the municipality of Tyrnävä, Northern Ostrobothnia, should be enhanced. The outcome comprises an integrated system for (a) automatic soil and drain water monitoring; (b) models of the soil water content; and (c) automatic control of drainage structures using in situ observations, remote sensing and control functions that should be operated by the farmer via a mobile phone. The monitoring, modeling and observation system is intended to optimize potato growth and water retention to limit irrigation and the leaching of nutrients. The system may detect flow in drain pipes to predict drain blockages and drain cleaning intervals.

The second Finnish site is used for grass production and is located in the municipality of Ruukki, Northern Ostrobothnia. The expected impact should be on water regulation to limit subsidence, nutrient leaching, acidity leaching (acid sulfate soils) and greenhouse gas emissions from organic soils, which are common in the boreal region.

In Sweden, Gårdstånga Nygård (GN; Figure 5) manages 200 ha of organic and 800 ha of conventional farmland, which is vulnerable to droughts. Conventional cultivation is undertaken according to FAO's three principles of conservation agriculture [12]. The expected impact of applying the framework (A1), in addition to improving the planting sequence and field management, may comprise improved soil health, reduced leaching of nutrients and decreased carbon dioxide emissions from the soil. Sustainable water retention management should also include the construction of dikes, wetlands and reservoirs.

In France, a 4000 ha catchment near Auxerre has challenges with water polluted by pesticides and nitrates. The arable land relies on drainage pipes pouring into sinkholes. WATERAGRI innovations (Table 1) are designed to help farmers to adjust their crop rotations, nutrient management, controlled drainage and wetland technology.

The Selhausen agricultural research station in Germany consists of 51 agricultural fields covering 1 km^2 and represents the heterogeneous rural area of the lower Rhine valley. The innovations should, with the help of field experiments, determine the drought stress responses of plants to optimize irrigation. The proposed framework (A1) may assist in the selection and management of crops such as sugar beet, winter wheat, winter barley, maize and rapeseed. The impact indicator is the expected production gain as a function of the amount of irrigation water.

In Poland, a farm of 500 ha is located in the lowland part of Lower Silesia and specializes in cereals. Despite having drainage system operations over the whole area, the farm struggles with both water shortages and local flooding. Online sensors to monitor soil moisture, the groundwater table, water outflow from the catchment and weather conditions should optimize water management. This should be achieved by identifying field locations with high water demand, assessing drainage conditions and implementing the framework (A1) for controlled drainage supported by small water retention solutions. Improved field nutrient doses may maintain high yields of cultivated crops and reduce the contamination of water within the catchment. The farm should benefit from improved water retention and quality. The expected impact should be on water management at the farm level to improve water availability, resulting in high yields of cultivated crops.

The framework (A1) was tested in collaboration with the largest vegetable farming association in Seeland, Switzerland. If current agricultural practices are continued, soil resources will be depleted in 50 years. The changing precipitation dynamics make future production targets vulnerable. The landscape in its current form is the result of a regional scale water correction and draining project. Through the drainage of the area, the upper soil layer in the region shrank drastically through mineralization. Furthermore, the growing population in the area makes it a challenge to develop new agricultural areas. The main requirement is the conservation of agricultural production.

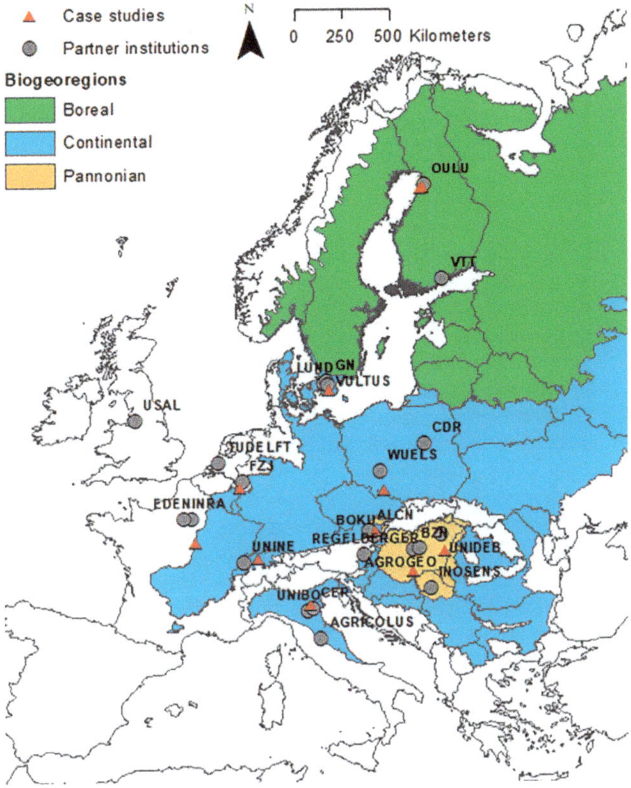

Figure 5. WATERAGRI case study demonstration sites and partner overview for all target regions (LUNDS UNIVERSITET, ULUND; EDEN TECH; EDEN; FORSCHUNGSZENTRUM JULICH GMBH; FZJ; TEKNOLOGIAN TUTKIMUSKESKUS VTT Oy, VTT; DEBRECENI EGYETEM, UNIDEB; ALCHEMIA-NOVA GMBH, ALCN; AGROGEO AGARFEJLESZTO-FOLDTANI-FOVALLALKOZO KORLATOLT FELELOSSEGU TATRSASAG, AGROGEO; UNIVERSITAET FUER BODENKULTUR WIEN, BOKU; ALMA MATER STUDIORUM UNIVERSITA DI BOLOGNA, UNIBO; THE UNIVERSITY OF SALFORD, USAL; COCONSORZIO DI BONIFICA DI SECONDO GRADO PER IL CANALE EMILIANO ROMAGNOLO CANALE GIANDOTTI, CER; CENTRUM DORADZTWA ROLNICZEGO W BRWINOWIE, CDR; INOSENS DOO NOVI SAD, INOSENS; UNIWERSYTET PRZYRODNICZY WE WROCLAWIU, WUELS; BAY ZOLTAN ALKALMAZOTT KUTATASI KOZHASZNU NONPROFIT KFT, BZN; VULTUS AB, VULTUS; TECHNISCHE UNIVERSITEIT DELFT, TUDELFT; UNIVERSITE DE NEUCHATEL, UNINE; AB GARDSTANGA NYGARD, GN; OULUN YLIOPISTO, OULU; AGRICOLUS SRL, AGRICOLUS; INSTITUT NATIONAL DE RECHERCHE POUR L'AGRICULTURE, L'ALIMENTATION ET L'ENVIRONNEMENT, INRA; MARTIN REGELSBERGER, TBR).

WATERAGRI innovations (Table 1) should maintain a high level of food production in the long term through intelligent water, soil and nutrient management. It may optimize drainage management through real-time management, which is currently conducted in an uncoordinated manner by individual farmers. Moreover, the efficiency of costly investments such as new drainage systems or irrigation systems can be assessed under the consideration of climate change.

Near Vienna, Austria, is an experimental agricultural field already equipped with soil water measurement devices, where WATERAGRI in collaboration with a vocational training school for farmers investigates water flows on the farm level for the improvement of irrigation of different crops and for the sustainable use of water resources. WATERAGRI uses tracer and mathematical modeling approaches to assess water fluxes, water retention times and groundwater recharge rates.

In Italy, a 12.5 ha experimental farm of the Land Reclamation Consortium is located near Bologna (northern Italy; continental climate zone), and different crops (winter wheat, soya, maize, fruits, vegetables, etc.) are grown. Drainage water coming from the farm is treated by a 0.4 ha surface flow constructed wetland before discharge to surface water bodies. WATERAGRI innovations (Table 1) should optimize irrigation, water retention, agricultural drainage water treatment (e.g., pesticide removal) and nutrient recovery.

A Hungarian farm comprises 16 ha of pasture with sprinkler irrigation for cattle grazing and 50 ha of irrigated arable land in a nitrate-sensitive area (based on European guidelines). Excess water and purified fermentation sludge should be utilized as an alternative water source. The framework (A1) may help to evaluate alternative water source applications in variable-rate sprinkler irrigation technology. Irrigation technology demonstration guidelines contribute to the reduction in artificial fertilizers to adapt to climate change and a reduction in available conventional water resources.

The guidelines developed cover conventional and state-of-the-art methods for field monitoring for irrigation practice. The methods proposed include technology for the utilization of excess water coming from small water retention measures and treated water obtained from biogas production, as well as smart technologies for vegetation surveys for the spatial optimization of irrigation. The innovations are designed to enhance irrigation sustainability by reducing water discharge to both groundwater and surface water and should contribute to the reduction in artificial fertilizers to adapt to climate change through a reduction in available conventional water resources.

4. Nature-Based Solutions including Wetland Systems

WATERAGRI has a strong focus on nature-based solutions [13,14], including physical ones such as the Farm Constructed Wetland (C1), Biochar Adsorbents (C2) and Bio-based Nutrient-Collecting Membrane (D1) (Table 1). This section briefly outlines key characteristics of nature-based solutions in preparation for Section 5.

The interest in nature-based solutions is growing since these kinds of systems can help to mitigate the negative impacts of climate change and water pollution with reduced operational and maintenance costs. One of these negative effects is certainly agricultural water pollution and especially the release of nitrogen into water ecosystems. Different types of nature-based solutions can be used to prevent diffuse nitrogen pollution, and it is important to understand which processes can take place in these systems and which influencing factors can affect nitrogen removal [13,14].

Constructed wetlands were found to be the nature-based solution type used for both diffuse pollution control and point-source contamination removal [3,5]. Although vegetation plays an important role, through the special property of macrophytes of pumping oxygen from the leaves to the roots, plant uptake is not the major nitrogen removal route, according to WATERAGRI project review findings [15]. The wetland substrate is an important factor since it can provide a carbon source needed for denitrification, which was identified as the most important nitrogen removal pathway [16,17]. In this context, the presence of certain microbial species in constructed wetlands is crucial since they can influence processes such as nitrification and denitrification [3,5].

The scientific community has proposed different ways to enhance nitrogen abatement efficiency. For example, the use of hybrid constructed wetlands, which combine surface and subsurface constructed wetland systems, can promote nitrogen removal by exploiting the advantages of different wetland types. Moreover, aeration has proved beneficial since it can control the presence of oxygen inside the system and keep it at the optimum level when it is required [18]. It is also important to adjust operational parameters (e.g., hydraulic loading rate and hydraulic retention type) since they control system behavior [5]. Other nature-based solution types, such as buffer strips, vegetated channels and water sediment control basins, were found to have lower applicability due to either their low efficiency or their inability to manage variable and high water flows, typical of agricultural drainage water, according to a WATERAGRI review [14,15,19].

Finally, different nitrogen recovery strategies were studied in the past. For example, biochar substrate or algae biomass previously used in constructed wetlands for water treatment could be rich in nitrogen content. These materials can be later used to produce compost or soil amendments and therefore reduce the need for chemical fertilizers [20,21].

5. Wetland System Management

5.1. Management to Mitigate Climate Change

WATERAGRI focuses on wetland management to adapt to climate change and secure clean and sufficient water resources for the future. The appropriate management of Farm Constructed Wetlands (C1) could both mitigate and help adapt to climate change [5]. The use of collected and stored water in wetland systems for subsequent reuse as irrigation water is an easy adaptation measure during hot summers [4]. However, the optimized management of these systems to mitigate climate change is the focus of the first two sub-sections.

Water purification is one of the most essential services provided by wetlands [19]. However, climate change has been identified as a major threat to wetlands. Altered hydrology and rising temperature can change the biogeochemistry and function of a wetland to the degree that some important services might be turned into disservices. This means that they will, for example, no longer provide a water purification service, and conversely, they may start to decompose and release nutrients to the surface water. This might lead to serious ecological challenges, e.g., eutrophication and acidification. Moreover, a higher rate of decomposition than primary production (photosynthesis) may lead to a shift in their function from being a sink for carbon to a source, according to WATERAGRI publications [22–25]. It can also endanger the well-being and livelihood of populations that depend on these systems [26].

Salimi et al. [24] reviewed, on behalf of WATERAGRI, the potential response of natural wetlands (peatlands) and constructed wetlands to climate change in terms of gas emissions and nutrient release. In addition, the impact of key climatic factors, such as temperature and water availability, on wetlands has been assessed. The authors identified methodological gaps and weaknesses in the literature and then introduced a new framework for conducting a comprehensive mesocosm experiment to address the existing gaps in the literature to support future climate change research on wetland ecosystems.

In the future, higher temperatures resulting in drought might shift the role of both constructed wetlands and peatlands from sinks to sources of carbon. However, higher temperatures accompanied by more precipitation can promote photosynthesis to a degree that might exceed respiration and maintain the carbon sink role of the wetland [19]. There might be a critical water level at which the wetland can preserve most of its services. In order to find that level, a WATERAGRI study of the key factors of climate change and their interactions using an appropriate experimental method was necessary [24,25].

Some contradictory results of past experiments may be associated with different methodologies, designs, time periods, climates and natural variability. Hence, a long-term simulation of climate change for wetlands according to the proposed framework is recommended. This framework provides relatively more accurate and realistic simulations, valid comparative results and comprehensive understanding and supports coordination between researchers. This can help to find a sustainable management strategy for wetlands to be resilient to climate change, according to WATERAGRI [24].

Salimi and Scholz [24,25] assessed the effect of climate change on water quality in peatland and constructed wetland ecosystems subject to water level management as part of the WATERAGRI project. For this purpose, the authors simulated the current climate scenario based on the database from Malmö station (Scania, Sweden) for 2016 and 2017, as well as future climate scenarios for the last 30 years of the century based on the representative concentration pathway (RCP) and different regional climate models for a region wider than Scania County. For future climate change, the authors simulated low (RCP 2.6), moderate (RCP 4.5) and extreme (RCP 8.5) climate scenarios. All simulations were conducted within climate chambers for experimental peatland and constructed wetland mesocosms.

The results demonstrated that the effect of the climate scenario is significantly different for peatlands and constructed wetlands (interactive effect) for the combined chemical variables. The warmest climate scenario, RCP 8.5, is linked to a higher water purification function for constructed wetlands but to a lower water purification function and the subsequent deterioration of peatland water qualities, even if subjected to water level management. The explanation for the different responses of constructed wetlands and peatlands to climate change could be due to the fact that the substrate in the constructed wetland mesocosms and peatlands was different in terms of the organic matter quality and quantity [19]. Plants and microbial communities within the constructed wetlands readily use up all easily available nutrients when the temperature rises. In contrast, concerning the extreme scenario RCP 8.5, peatlands have shown a tendency to exhibit the reverse process in WATERAGRI mesocosm experiments [24,25].

Salimi et al. [25] highlight that stress factors such as climate change and drought may switch the role of temperate peatlands from carbon dioxide sinks to sources, leading to positive feedback to global climate change. Water level management has been regarded as an important WATERAGRI climate change mitigation strategy, as it can sustain the natural net carbon dioxide sink function of a peatland. Little is known about how resilient peatlands are in the face of future climate change scenarios or how effectively water level management can sustain the carbon dioxide sink function to mitigate global warming [19].

Salimi et al. [25] assessed the effect of climate change on carbon dioxide exchange in south Swedish temperate peatlands, which were either unmanaged or subject to water level regulation. Climate chamber simulations described previously [24] were conducted as part of WATERAGRI.

Published WATERAGRI results show that all managed and unmanaged systems under future climate scenarios could serve as carbon dioxide sinks throughout the experimental period. However, the 2018 extreme drought caused unmanaged mesocosms under RCP 4.5 and RCP 8.5 to switch from a net carbon dioxide sink to a source during summer. Surprisingly, unmanaged mesocosms under RCP 2.6 benefited from the warmer climate and served as the best sink among the other unmanaged systems. Water level management had the greatest effect on the carbon dioxide sink function under RCP 8.5 and RCP 4.5, which improved their carbon dioxide sink capability by up to six and two times, respectively. Under the current climate scenario, water level management had a negative effect on the carbon dioxide sink function, and it had almost no effect under RCP 2.6. Therefore, the researchers concluded that water level management is necessary for RCP 8.5, beneficial for RCP 4.5 and unimportant for RCP 2.6 and the current climate [25].

5.2. Application of the Van Genuchten–Mualem Models to Peat Soils

Undisturbed peatlands are effective carbon sinks and provide a variety of ecosystem services, such as adaptation and mitigation regarding climate change. However, anthropogenic disturbances, especially land drainage, strongly alter peat soil properties and jeopardize the benefits of peatlands. The effects of disturbances were therefore assessed and predicted as part of the WATERAGRI project [23–25]. To support accurate modeling, Menberu et al. [27] determined the physical and hydraulic properties of intact and disturbed peat samples collected from 59 sites (in total, 3073 samples) in Finland and Norway.

The bulk density, porosity and specific yield values obtained indicated that the top layer (0–30 cm depth) at agricultural and peat extraction sites was most affected by land use change. The bulk density in the top layer at agricultural, peat extraction and forestry sites was 441, 140 and 92% higher, respectively, than that of intact peatlands. Porosity decreased with increasing bulk density, but not linearly. Agricultural and peat extraction sites had the lowest saturated hydraulic conductivity and porosity and the highest bulk density among the land use options studied by the WATERAGRI team [27].

The van Genuchten–Mualem soil water retention curve and hydraulic conductivity models proved to be applicable for the peat soils tested, providing values of soil water retention curve, hydraulic conductivity and van Genuchten–Mualem parameters (α and n) for peat layers (top, middle and bottom) under different land uses. A decrease in peat soil water content of $\geq$10% reduced the unsaturated hydraulic conductivity values by two orders of magnitude. This unique data set can be used to improve hydrological modeling in peat-dominated catchments and for fuller integration of peat soils into large-scale hydrological models [27].

The outcomes of the above study [27] were fed directly into the WATERAGRI Modeling Framework (A1). They are particularly relevant for boreal climates (Figure 5), where there is a serious risk of peatland degradation as the climate becomes warmer. On the other hand, some of these peatlands may be transformed in a sustainable manner into farmland if, for example, the water level is managed appropriately.

5.3. Assessment of Plants Irrigated with Wastewater Treated by Wetlands

Wetlands can also contribute to irrigation water provision, especially in terms of non-conventional water resources (e.g., treated wastewater). There is a high potential to reduce the agricultural water demand by recycling different types of wastewaters in the irrigation of crops [4,19]. However, there is a need for sufficient pre-treatment to reduce potentially negative impacts, such as the pollution of crops by, for example, heavy metals. Moreover, groundwater resources need to be protected.

Almuktar et al. [28] assessed *Capsicum annuum* L. (chili; an easy-to-grow example plant) grown in controlled and semi-controlled environments irrigated with greywater treated by floating wetland systems as part of the WATERAGRI project. The accumulation of trace elements, including heavy metals, was evaluated in the soil and fruits of chili plants grown under both laboratory-controlled and semi-controlled greenhouse location conditions. Chili plant biomass growth in different development stages and fruit productivity were evaluated and compared with each other for the impact of growth boundary conditions and water quality effects. Treated synthetic greywaters in different operational design set-ups of floating treatment wetland systems were recycled for watering chilies in both locations. The effluents of each individual group of treatment set-up systems were labeled to feed sets of three replicates of chili plants in both locations.

WATERAGRI results revealed that the treated synthetic greywater complied with thresholds for irrigation water, except for high concentrations of phosphates, total suspended soils and some harmful trace elements such as cadmium. Chili plants grew in both locations with different growth patterns in each development stage. First blooming and high counts of flowers were observed in the laboratory. Higher fruit production was noted for greenhouse plants: 2266 chili fruits with a total weight of 16.824 kg with an expected market value of GBP 176.22 compared to 858 chili fruits from the laboratory with a weight of 3.869 kg and an estimated price of GBP 17.61 [28].

Trace element concentrations were detected in chili fruits with the ranking order of occurrence as follows: Mg > Ca > Na > Fe > Zn > Al > Mn > Cu > Cd > Cr > Ni > B. The highest concentrations of accumulated Cd (3.82 mg/kg), Cu (0.56 mg/kg) and Na (0.56 mg/kg) were recorded in chili fruits from the laboratory. Accumulations of Ca, Cd, Cu, Mn and Ni with concentrations of 4.73, 1.30, 0.20, 0.21 and 0.24 mg/kg, respectively, were linked to fruits from the greenhouse. Trace elements in chili plant soils followed the trend: Mg > Fe > Al > Cr > Mn > Cd > Cu > B. The accumulated concentrations in either chili fruits or the soil were above the maximum permissible thresholds, indicating the need for further water quality improvements [28].

The WATERAGRI findings [28] helped to understand practical challenges with the recycling of wastewater in farming. However, there is uncertainty about farmers not actually knowing what they put on their fields in terms of potential pollution loads and when these loads may become a challenge in the future for certain plants [4,19].

5.4. Simplified Models for Wetland Systems

Constructed treatment wetlands are systems designed to optimize chemical, physical and biogeochemical processes occurring in wetland ecosystems to treat wastewater [19]. The type of treatment wetland typically used to treat agricultural runoff is the free water surface wetland because of its strong ability to cope with pulse flows [3]. According to WATERAGRI research, current design guidelines for these systems are based on empirical rules of thumb and/or simple first-order decay models, which are based on experimental data with pilot plants and specific boundary conditions such as climatic conditions or wastewater composition [5,29].

In addition, free water surface wetlands are designed and used according to the experiences and needs of each region [5,19]. For example, in boreal biogeographical areas (Figure 5), wetlands are mostly used for phosphorus retention, while in warmer bioclimatic regions, with optimal conditions for nitrifying bacteria, they are used to remove nitrogen. The design is mainly based on hydraulic criteria by improving the hydraulic efficiency or increasing the hydraulic retention time, i.e., adding obstacles, increasing the aspect ratio (length to width) or calculating the wetland surface area in relation to the catchment area.

Process-based modeling is also advanced, and there are many studies on wetland performance. However, these models require advanced modeling skills and specific parameters that are impossible to obtain if the wetland is not yet constructed. Therefore, some researchers encourage the development of simplified models where only a few parameters are required [5,19]. Current simplified design tools are only available for combined sewer overflow wetlands, i.e., RSF_Sim [30] and ORAGE [31]. These models have proven to be robust and reliable for design purposes [32].

As part of WATERAGRI [1], researchers [33] compared the performance of different simple models using data from a full-scale wetland monitored over the long term located in the Emilia-Romagna region, Italy. The models simulated the transport and removal of total nitrogen in two precipitation events with different characteristics. Moreover, the models were evaluated under steady- and unsteady-state conditions. The best performance was achieved with a tanks-in-series model coupled with a first-order degradation model with non-zero background concentration for pollutant degradation. The simulations under steady-state conditions were able to simulate outflow total nitrogen concentrations even though the inputs were discontinuous. In contrast, the piston flow with the dispersion model did not fit the wetland hydraulics in either event due to the nature of wetlands, which receive water in pulses following rainfall events.

A simplified model can be very useful for rough assessments and can be used for the upfront design, which would help decision making. The WATERAGRI findings will help to set performance ranges for certain conditions, which will provide insight into the real possibilities and limitations of free water surface wetlands. The adaptations have been incorporated into the WATERAGRI Modeling Framework (A1).

6. Tracer Methods

6.1. Background on Isotopes

Advanced Tracer Methods (B5; Table 1) have been developed as part of WATERAGRI [1] to assess more complex water retention challenges. Stable oxygen (O) and hydrogen (H) isotopes of water (δ18O and δ2H) can be applied as environmental and conservative tracers and are inherent compounds of the water cycle used to understand hydrological processes in agricultural soils. The isotopic composition of precipitation is modified by fractionation processes, resulting in distinct seasonal and geographical distributions, generating a global distribution map [34].

Seasonal tracer variations may still be observed in the pore water of soils, with the attenuation of the signal depending on transport processes (i.e., dispersion and diffusion).

Thus, the measurement of δ18O and δ2H in pore water allows for tracking water from different precipitation events in the unsaturated zone, providing integrative information about the sources, flow and transport of water at large scales and in long time series [35]. Combined with the analysis of soil water content, water fluxes such as mobile soil water or potential groundwater recharge can be quantified [36,37]. Using a water balance approach, other fluxes (e.g., evapotranspiration) can be estimated as well, which has been shown in WATERAGRI studies [38–40].

6.2. Standard Method Development

For analyzing isotopes in pore water, the water–vapor equilibration concept can be used. This method does not require the extraction of pore water like other methods, such as cryogenic water extraction. A rock or sediment sample is placed into a sealable, inflatable and leak-tight bag (usually a plastic Ziploc® bag or laminated Al-bags). The bag is inflated with dry air and equilibrated for up to three days. Within the closed system, water and vapor are in equilibrium (the water amount and the isotopic composition), and the isotopic composition of the vapor is analyzed with laser spectroscopy.

No standard protocols for this type of method currently exist; e.g., different laboratories have various equilibration times. It follows that it needs to be tested whether the equilibration time, soil texture and pore water saturation have effects on isotopic results using the water–vapor equilibration method. Therefore, stable water isotopes were analyzed as part of WATERAGRI in soil samples with different textures (sand, silty loam and clay (kaolinite)) and different soil saturation levels (40–100%) using different equilibration times (24 to 168 h) [41].

The findings showed that a 24 h equilibration time was sufficient for sandy soils at all tested saturation levels. For kaolinite, little variance with equilibration time was found. For silty loam containing organic carbon (2% and 4%), the method indicated that equilibration could only be obtained with difficulty. Nevertheless, disaggregation of samples generally improved the isotope analysis [41]. This means that further tests are required to understand the effect of the presence of organic carbon on water–vapor equilibration. It also means that the water–vapor equilibration method can be generally applied, and equilibration times can be adjusted according to the individual soil type and water content of the target farm.

6.3. Application in Agricultural Water Management

Sustainable agriculture should be based on management practices that improve resource usage efficiency and minimize harmful impacts on the environment while maintaining and stabilizing crop production [1]. Both tillage and irrigation can have a great influence on hydrological processes within agroecosystems. However, it remains difficult to directly assess the effect of various agricultural practices on water fluxes, which have been mainly indirectly quantified by complex numerical modeling methods in the past. Whether isotope approaches also allow for the assessment of the impact of management practices on water fluxes in agricultural soils still remains to be tested. It would serve as a simple approach to obtain basic information on hydrological processes in agroecosystems from single sampling campaigns that can be used even in remote farming areas.

As part of the WATERAGRI project [1], Canet-Marti et al. [42] assessed hydrological processes and water flux quantification in agricultural fields under different tillage and irrigation systems using stable water isotopes. In order to support sustainable agricultural water management practices, the objective of their study was to use a space-for-time concept and measure oxygen (O) and hydrogen (H) isotopes (δ18O, δ2H) in the pore water of soil profiles as well as moisture contents for quantifying the soil water balance and fluxes. Covering all combinations, soil profiles and isotope analysis was performed for 16 sites planted with winter wheat and managed with different tillage (conventional tillage, reduced tillage, minimal tillage and no-tillage) and irrigation systems (hose reel boom irrigation with nozzles, sprinkler irrigation, drip irrigation and no irrigation).

The results indicated that the more intense the tillage, the lower the water content. Among the irrigation systems, drip irrigation had the highest average water content. Tracing the minimum in the isotopic composition in the pore water within the depth profiles showed the deeper percolation of water in the conventional tillage fields, which indicates higher water flow velocity. Considering both water content and differences in water flow velocities resulted in water fluxes ranging from 46 to 91 mm per annum. The losses due to evapotranspiration varied between 80% and 91%. The resulting evapotranspiration within tillage and irrigation variants decreased in this order: conventional tillage > reduced tillage > minimal tillage > no-tillage, and sprinkler irrigation > hose reel boom irrigation with nozzles > drip irrigation > no irrigation.

The new method revealed that the lower water content in conventional tillage fields is a consequence of deeper water infiltration and higher evapotranspiration. Moreover, irrigation water contributed mostly to evapotranspiration, and drip irrigation showed the lowest evapotranspiration losses among irrigation systems. This WATERAGRI study demonstrated that stable water isotopes can be used as indicators and are a promising method to quantify water fluxes in agricultural fields with great potential for evaluating management practices [42].

7. Yield Forecasting Using Remote Sensing

Since global trading prices of agricultural commodities depend largely on their seasonal production levels, the total size of the cropping area and crop yields are important for export–import companies, agricultural agencies at national and international levels, government agencies and other crop marketing agencies. Furthermore, due to the increasing global demand for food grains, early and reliable information on crop production is important from a humanitarian point of view as well as to organize emergency response and food aid interventions [43].

WATERAGRI is further developing the Remote Sensing Pipeline (B1; Table 1) for the agricultural industry, because remote sensing has become a widespread technique used in agriculture and agronomy [44], and the interest in using remotely sensed satellite data for crop monitoring and crop production forecasting has increased, as it produces uniform data at the global scale, and modeling results can potentially be utilized in large regions. Reliable and early yield forecasts are also needed by farmers to implement adaptation measures (usually technical measures) to reduce the risk of potential yield loss at the farm level. Providing and developing a monitoring basis can be an important step forward in improving crop yields. Moreover, remote sensing is capable of providing temporal (and potentially real-time) and objective data on crop vigor, density, health and productivity, because remotely sensed data are in close relation to the canopy leaf area index and the fraction of absorbed photosynthetically active radiation [45].

Green vegetation can be monitored through its spectral reflectance properties [46]. The normalized difference vegetation index (NDVI) is an appropriate solution to monitor the total wheat dry-matter accumulation, since, in the growing season, the NDVI explains 79% of the wheat dry-biomass variations. Moreover, in minimizing the distribution of the effects on the relationships between vegetation spectral reflectance and crop yield, some researchers refer to distance-based vegetation indices, such as the soil-adjusted vegetation index [47]. This index is applied to correct the NDVI for the influence of soil brightness in areas where vegetative cover is low.

In the previous decades, the National Oceanic and Atmospheric Administration's advanced very high resolution radiometer has been the main data source since the 1980s for large-scale crop yield forecasting and monitoring. Recently, remote-sensing-based yield forecasting research has shifted to the National Aeronautics and Space Administration's moderate resolution imaging spectroradiometer and other satellites such as Landsat, SPOT (satellite for the observation of the earth) or Sentinel satellites, which provide data at a better spatial resolution. However, there are considerable limitations (i.e., information on crop rotation, small field sizes and the extension of locally calibrated models to other areas) of using remotely sensed satellite data in crop yield forecasting [43]. Information on long-term yield variability is important for tailoring farming practices to the needs of crops. In particular, remotely sensed vegetation indices such as the NDVI [48,49] and soil-adjusted vegetation index [50] have been widely utilized for agricultural mapping and monitoring. Several studies, including WATERAGRI, found that the soil-adjusted vegetation index achieved higher accuracies than the NDVI, suggesting that the former index reduced some of the effects of soil background reflectance [51–53].

The developed wheat yield forecasting model provides timely information on the production of wheat, as well as its status and yield, in a regular and standardized manner at field and catchment levels. From NDVI and soil-adjusted vegetation index forecasting models that were developed based on six training years, the yield can be predicted six weeks earlier before harvesting. These WATERAGRI findings can reduce the impacts of possible yield losses if delivered to farmers or decision makers in a timely and appropriate format, and if mitigation measures and preparedness plans are in place [51,54].

Nowadays, irrigation is one of the answers to drought mitigation. Irrigation is usually based on the measurement of soil water content or meteorological parameters to model or calculate evapotranspiration. In addition, the use of various proximal sensors is possible to measure pigment activity related to the photosynthetic activity [55,56], and multispectral cameras provide images with high spatial and temporal resolution, which are also suitable for assessing vegetation coverage and typology as well as biomass and vegetation monitoring data. Plant-based methods such as the plant water stress index have great potential for controlling irrigation, although there may be challenges in setting reference or threshold values [57]. The impact of irrigation management on the use of plant water is a practical consideration to improve yield and water productivity for plants. Based on the results, crop sensors equipped with linear irrigation equipment in the field are suitable for NDVI assessment and monitoring of the area in both irrigated and non-irrigated areas. Furthermore, pigments can be derived not only based on NDVI images but also based on the area ratio, and the biomass weight of maize can also be predicted. The use of virtual field sensors can help farmers to improve irrigation management for increased water savings and better crop production. According to WATERAGRI output, the verification of remotely sensed data is one of the prerequisites for the proper utilization and understanding of the data and their translation into leaf area, biomass amount, then evapotranspiration and eventually irrigation requirements [51,54].

8. Game for Decision Support and Stakeholder Engagement

Sustainable agricultural water management is a complex problem characterized by multiple alternatives, conflicting objectives and multiple uncertainties about key drivers such as climate change, land use change, legislative restrictions, population growth and increasing urbanization [1]. Serious games are becoming a popular means to support decision makers who are responsible for the planning and management of water systems. This is evident in the number of articles about serious games in recent years [58]. However, the effectiveness of these games in improving decision making and the quality of their design and evaluation approaches remains unclear.

In support of WATERAGRI, Mittal et al. [58] identified 41 serious games predominantly covering the urban water cycle and shortlisted 15 games for a detailed review. By using common rational decision-making and game design phases from the literature, the authors evaluated and mapped how the shortlisted games contribute to these phases. The findings show that current serious game applications fall short due to multiple limitations: (a) a lack of focus on executing the initial phases of decision making (phase 1 for problem structuring, phase 2 for defining objectives and attributes, and phase 3 for developing alternatives); (b) the limited use of storytelling and adaptive game elements; (c) the use of low-quality evaluation designs and explicit indicators to measure game outcomes; and (d) a lack of attention to the cognitive processes of players playing the game.

Addressing the above limitations and improving on them is critical to advancing a purposeful game design supporting agricultural water management. Therefore, WATERAGRI has developed a Serious Game (A7) that addresses these challenges and transfers existing knowledge from urban to rural areas.

A clear understanding of the needs and typical characteristics of target audiences, such as farmers or the general public, is an essential part of the WATERAGRI dissemination plan, which will ensure that communication channels are appropriate for the types of messages being sent. Table 2 gives an overview of the three levels of dissemination strategy impacts on stakeholder groups. The Serious Game directly supports dissemination for action as well as understanding and uptake.

Table 2. Overview of the levels of WATERAGRI dissemination strategy impacts on the main stakeholder groups and their relationship to the Serious Game (A7; Table 1).

Level	Target Stakeholder Group	Targeted Stakeholder Profiles (TO WHOM)	Expected Impacts (WHY)
Dissemination for Awareness	General audience not directly targeted by the Serious Game	1. Civil society interested in WATERAGRI [1] and benefitting from more water and food security 2. People interested in science and new water management technologies 3. Public initiatives linked to the farming society 4. Policy makers	• Awareness about WATERAGRI objectives, results and impacts • Increased awareness of the need for environmental protection • Enhanced water and food security • Raised awareness about new technologies and services
Dissemination for Understanding/Uptake	External audience directly related to the project results testing the Serious Game	1. Farmers or farm managers (not) directly involved in the project 2. Agricultural chambers, farmer associations, schools of farmers, extension services and water retention and nutrient recycling industry 3. Media Researchers 4. Municipalities 5. Local water management organizations 6. All-level policy makers directly involved in farm water and soil fertilization management	• Advancement in understanding of agricultural water management and nutrient recycling in soils • Enhancement and stimulation of further research and innovation activities between project partners • Creation of media interest to obtain their involvement and support • Increased support for the implementation of the framework
Dissemination for Action	Audience in connection with the project developing the Serious Game	1. Farmers and farm managers, agronomists and farm advisers 2. The WATERAGRI consortium members (Figure 5)	• Protection of crops • Improvement of water quality and nutrient uptake by crops • Increase in income • A strong brand image

9. Conclusions and Recommendations

This communication highlights research outputs linked to selected innovations that have been further developed as part of the Horizon 2020 WATERAGRI project to address water and food security challenges by optimizing sustainable agricultural water management and nutrient recycling strategies.

A review of factors that can influence nitrogen and phosphorus removal in different types of nature-based solutions was performed. The proposed framework for undertaking wetland experiments provides relatively more accurate and realistic simulations, valid comparative results and comprehensive understanding and supports coordination between researchers. This can help to find a sustainable management strategy for Farm Constructed Wetlands to increase resilience to climate change.

Our results using mesocosms in climate chambers demonstrate that the effect of the climate scenario is significantly different for peatlands and constructed wetlands (interactive effect) for combined chemical variables for a continental climate. The warmest climate scenario, RCP 8.5, is linked to a higher water purification function for constructed wetlands but to a lower water purification function and the subsequent deterioration of peatland water qualities, even if subjected to water level management.

The unmanaged mesocosms under RCP 2.6 benefited from the warmer climate and served as the best sink compared to other unmanaged systems. Water level management had the greatest effect on the carbon dioxide sink function under RCP 8.5 and RCP 4.5, which improved their carbon dioxide sink capability by up to six and two times, respectively. Water level management is necessary for RCP 8.5, beneficial for RCP 4.5 and unimportant for RCP 2.6 and the current climate. WATERAGRI encourages the development of simplified wetland models of systems where only a few parameters are needed or where there are insufficient data. Furthermore, similar wetland experiments should also be performed for boreal climate scenarios, and linked environmental impact assessments on natural resources on the field scale need to be undertaken.

Advanced Tracer Methods (B5) have the potential to compare the influence of different management practices on hydrological processes. Such practices may include tillage in agricultural land management, water level management and irrigation.

The Remote Sensing Pipeline (B5) uses remote-sensing-based yield forecasting models to provide estimations of wheat yield during the growing season well before the Biologische Bundesanstalt, Bundessortenamt und Chemische Industrie (BBCH) 41 development stage (i.e., when the flag leaf sheath is extending), which fosters preparedness for the mitigation of water shortage and for increased food security. The use of virtual field sensors can help practitioners to improve irrigation management for increased water savings and better vegetation production. The verification of remotely sensed data is one of the prerequisites for the proper utilization and understanding of the data and their translation into leaf area, biomass amount, then evapotranspiration and eventually irrigation requirements. The limitations of remote sensing technology linked to poor visibility due to, for example, cloud cover have been highlighted.

Our research shows that current serious game applications fall short due to a lack of attention to the initial phases of decision making, the limited use of storytelling and adaptive elements, low-quality evaluation of games without the use of explicit decision quality indicators and, lastly, a lack of attention to the cognitive processes of players playing the game. Improving these limitations is critical to advancing a purposeful Serious Game design for decision support in agricultural water management.

This communication has its limitations, as it predominantly assesses key findings of the WATERAGRI project and focuses heavily on the continental, boreal and Pannonian climatic regions of Europe and similar regions elsewhere. Therefore, the authors recommend assessing the same and other promising solutions to improve water and food security also for more climate zones. Moreover, further market development actions, including business modeling of the best innovations, need to be performed after the end of WATERAGRI.

Funding: This work was financially predominantly supported by WATERAGRI (European Union Horizon 2020 research and innovation program under Grant Agreement Number 858735) but also by other funding bodies, such as VINNOVA (Swedish government innovation agency), RainSolutions (Water JPI 2018 Joint Call project) and EcoDiver (Naturvårdsverket (Swedish Government Innovation Agency)).

Institutional Review Board Statement: Not applicable.

Informed Consent Statement: Not applicable.

Data Availability Statement: The data that support the findings of this communication are available from the corresponding author upon reasonable request. Most data and findings are also available as deliverables in the public domain via European Commission websites.

Acknowledgments: The support provided by all WATERAGRI partners is acknowledged. The following individuals provided small unedited text passages: Stevo Lavrnic (ALMA MATER STUDIORUM UNIVERSITA DI BOLOGNA), Attila Nagy (DEBRECENI EGYETEM), Tamara Avellán (OULUN YLIOPISTO), Christine Stumpp, Günter Langergraber and Alba Canet (all three from the UNIVERSITAET FUER BODENKULTUR WIEN) as well as Zoran Kapelan and Aashna Mittal (both from the TECHNISCHE UNIVERSITEIT DELFT).

Conflicts of Interest: Miklas Scholz is the Project Coordinator of WATERAGRI. He is also one of the official inventors of the dewaterability test apparatus. The funders had no role in the design of the study, in the collection, analyses or interpretation of data, in the writing of the manuscript or in the decision to publish the results.

References

1. WATERAGRI. WATer Retention and Nutrient Recycling in Soils and Streams for Improved AGRIicultural Production (WATERAGRI). 2022. Available online: https://wateragri.eu (accessed on 24 March 2022).
2. United Nations. *The Sustainable Development Goals Report*; United Nations: New York, NY, USA, 2021; Available online: https://www.un.org/en/desa/sustainable-development-goals-sdgs (accessed on 10 April 2022).
3. Scholz, M.; Harrington, R.; Carroll, P.; Mustafa, A. The Integrated Constructed Wetlands (ICW) concept. *Wetlands* **2007**, *27*, 337–354. [CrossRef]
4. Almuktar, S.A.A.-A.N.; Scholz, M. Mineral and biological contamination of soil and *Capsicum annuum* irrigated with recycled domestic wastewater. *Agric. Water Manag.* **2016**, *167*, 95–109. [CrossRef]
5. Carty, A.; Scholz, M.; Heal, K.; Gouriveau, F.; Mustafa, A. The universal design, operation and maintenance guidelines for Farm Constructed Wetlands (FCW) in temperate climates. *Bioresour. Technol.* **2008**, *99*, 6780–6792. [CrossRef] [PubMed]
6. Mohammed, R.; Scholz, M. Adaptation strategy to mitigate the impact of climate change on water resources in arid and semi-arid regions: A Case Study. *Water Resour. Manag.* **2017**, *31*, 3557–3573. [CrossRef]
7. Mak, C.; Scholz, M.; James, P. Sustainable Drainage System site assessment using urban ecosystem services. *Urban Ecosyst.* **2017**, *20*, 293–307. [CrossRef]
8. European Commission. Water Reuse—Proposal for a Regulation on Minimum Requirements for Water Reuse. Available online: http://ec.europa.eu/environment/water/reuse.htm (accessed on 24 March 2022).
9. Hendricks Franssen, H.-J.; Brunner, P. Integrating hydrological modelling, data assimilation and cloud computing for real-time management of water resources. *Environ. Model. Softw.* **2017**, *93*, 418–435. [CrossRef]
10. Reed, M.S.; Graves, A.; Dandy, N.; Posthumus, H.; Hubacek, K.; Morris, J.; Prell, C.; Quinn, C.H.; Stringer, L.C. 'Who's in and why? A typology of stakeholder analysis methods for natural resource management. *J. Environ. Manag.* **2009**, *90*, 1933–1949. [CrossRef]
11. Scholz, M.; Almuktar, S.; Clausner, C.; Antonacopoulos, A. Highlights of the novel Dewaterability Estimation Test (DET) device. *Environ. Technol.* **2019**, *41*, 2594–2602. [CrossRef]
12. Food and Agricultural Organization of the United Nations (FAO). The 3 Principles of Conservational Agriculture. 2014. Available online: https://www.fao.org/emergencies/fao-in-action/stories/stories-detail/en/c/216752/?msclkid=28c4e794ab5411ec8df29a742367c0d2 (accessed on 24 March 2022).
13. Food and Agricultural Organization of the United Nations (FAO). Nature-Based Solutions for Agricultural Water Management and Food Security. 2018. Available online: http://www.fao.org/3/CA2525EN/ca2525en.pdf (accessed on 24 March 2022).
14. European Commission. Nature-Based Solutions. 2019. Available online: https://ec.europa.eu/research/environment/index.cfm?pg=nbs (accessed on 24 March 2022).
15. Mancuso, G.; Bencresciuto, G.F.; Lavrnić, S.; Toscano, A. Diffuse water pollution from agriculture: A review of Nature-Based Solutions for nitrogen removal and recovery. *Water* **2021**, *13*, 1893. [CrossRef]
16. Reddy, K.R.; D'Angelo, E.M. Biogeochemical indicators to evaluate pollutant removal efficiency in constructed wetlands. *Water Sci. Technol.* **1997**, *35*, 1–10. [CrossRef]
17. Spieles, D.J.; Mitsch, W.J. The effects of season and hydrologic and chemical loading on nitrate retention in constructed wetlands: A comparison of low- and high nutrient riverine systems. *Ecol. Eng.* **2000**, *14*, 77–91. [CrossRef]
18. Wu, H.; Fan, J.; Zhang, J.; Ngo, H.H.; Guo, W.; Hu, Z.; Lv, J. Optimization of organics and nitrogen removal in intermittently aerated vertical flow constructed wetlands: Effects of aeration time and aeration rate. *Int. Biodeterior. Biodegrad.* **2016**, *113*, 139–145. [CrossRef]
19. Scholz, M. *Sustainable Water Management: Engineering Solutions for a Variable Climate*; Elsevier: Amsterdam, The Netherlands, 2018; ISBN 9780128162460.
20. Ghezzehei, T.A.; Sarkhot, D.V.; Berhe, A.A. Biochar can be used to capture essential nutrients from dairy wastewater and improve soil physico-chemical properties. *Solid Earth* **2014**, *5*, 953–962. [CrossRef]

21. Acién Fernández, F.G.; Gómez-Serrano, C.; Fernández-Sevilla, J.M. Recovery of nutrients from wastewaters using microalgae. *Front. Sustain. Food Syst.* **2018**, *2*, 59. [CrossRef]
22. Loisel, J.; Gallego-Sala, A.V.; Amesbury, M.J.; Magnan, G.; Anshari, G.; Beilman, D.W.; Benavides, J.C.; Blewett, J.; Camill, P.; Charman, D.J.; et al. Expert assessment of future vulnerability of the global peatland carbon sink. *Nat. Clim. Chang.* **2021**, *11*, 70–77. [CrossRef]
23. Salimi, S.; Scholz, M. Impact of future climate scenarios on peatland and constructed wetland water quality under water level management: A mesocosm experiment within climate chambers. *J. Environ. Manag.* **2021**, *289*, 112459. [CrossRef]
24. Salimi, S.; Almuktar, S.; Scholz, M. The impact of climate change on wetland ecosystems: A critical review of experimental wetland mesocosms. *J. Environ. Manag.* **2021**, *286*, 112160. [CrossRef]
25. Salimi, S.; Berggren, M.; Scholz, M. Response of the peatland carbon dioxide sink function to future climate change scenarios and water level management. *Glob. Chang. Biol.* **2021**, *27*, 5154–5168. [CrossRef]
26. Raihan, F.; Hossain, M.M. Livelihood vulnerability assessments and adaptation strategies to climate change: A case study in Tanguar haor Sylhet. *J. Water Clim. Chang.* **2021**, *12*, 3448–3463. [CrossRef]
27. Menberu, M.W.; Marttila, H.; Ronkanen, A.-K.; Haghighi, A.T.; Kløve, B. Hydraulic and Physical Properties of Managed and Intact Peatlands: Application of the Van Genuchten-Mualem Models to Peat Soils. *Water Resour. Res.* **2021**, *57*, e2020WR028624. [CrossRef]
28. Almuktar, S.; Abed, S.N.; Scholz, M.; Uzomah, V.C. Assessment of *Capsicum annuum* L. grown in controlled and semi-controlled environments irrigated with greywater treated by floating wetland systems. *Agronomy* **2021**, *11*, 1817. [CrossRef]
29. Langergraber, G. Numerical modelling: A tool for better constructed wetland design? *Water Sci. Technol.* **2011**, *64*, 14–21. [CrossRef] [PubMed]
30. Meyer, D.; Dittmer, U. RSF_Sim—A simulation tool to support the design of constructed wetlands for combined sewer overflow treatment. *Ecol. Eng.* **2015**, *80*, 198–204. [CrossRef]
31. Palfy, T.G.; Meyer, D.; Troesch, S.; Gourdon, R.; Olivier, L.; Molle, P. A single-output model for the dynamic design of constructed wetlands treating combined sewer overflow. *Environ. Model. Softw.* **2018**, *102*, 49–72. [CrossRef]
32. Langergraber, G. Applying process-based models for subsurface flow treatment wetlands: Recent developments and challenges. *Water* **2017**, *9*, 5. [CrossRef]
33. Canet-Marti, A.; Grüner, S.; Lavrnic, S.; Toscano, A.; Strech, T.; Langergraber, G. Comparison of simple models for total nitrogen removal in free-water surface wetlands. *Water Sci. Technol.* 2022, *in press*.
34. Rozanski, K.; Araguasaraguas, L.; Gonfiantini, R. Relation between long-term trends of O-18 isotope composition of precipitation and climate. *Science* **1992**, *258*, 981–985. [CrossRef]
35. Stumpp, C.; Bruggemann, N.; Wingate, L. Stable isotope approaches in vadose zone research. *Vadose Zone J.* **2018**, *17*, 1–7. [CrossRef]
36. Barbecot, F.; Guillon, S.; Pili, E.; Larocque, M.; Gibert-Brunet, E.; Helie, J.F.; Noret, A.; Plain, C.; Schneider, V.; Mattei, A.; et al. Using water stable isotopes in the unsaturated zone to quantify recharge in two contrasted infiltration regimes. *Vadose Zone J.* **2018**, *17*, 1–13. [CrossRef]
37. Chesnaux, R.; Stumpp, C. Advantages and challenges of using soil water isotopes to assess groundwater recharge dominated by snowmelt at a field study located in Canada. *Hydrol. Sci. J.* **2018**, *63*, 679–695. [CrossRef]
38. Boumaiza, L.; Chesnaux, R.; Walter, J.; Stumpp, C. Assessing groundwater recharge and transpiration in a humid northern region dominated by snowmelt using vadose-zone depth profiles. *Hydrogeol. J.* **2020**, *28*, 2315–2329. [CrossRef]
39. Boumaiza, L.; Chesnaux, R.; Walter, J.; Stumpp, C. Constraining a flow model with field measurements to assess water transit time through a vadose zone. *Groundwater* **2021**, *59*, 417–427. [CrossRef] [PubMed]
40. Liebhard, G.; Klik, A.; Stumpp, C.; Nolz, R. Partitioning evapotranspiration using water stable isotopes and information from lysimeter experiments. *Hydrol. Sci. J.* **2022**, *67*, 646–661. [CrossRef]
41. Vadibeler, D.; Stockinger, M.P.; Wassenaar, L.I.; Stumpp, C. Influence of equilibration time, soil texture, and saturation on the accuracy of porewater water isotope assays using the direct H_2O(liquid)-H_2O(vapor) equilibration method. *J. Hydrol.* **2022**, *607*, 127560. [CrossRef]
42. Canet-Marti, A.; Morales-Santos, A.; Nolz, R.; Langergraber, G.; Stumpp, C. Hydrological Processes and Water Flux Quantification in Agricultural Fields Under Different Tillage and Irrigation Systems Using Water Stable Isotopes. In Proceedings of the EGU General Assembly 2021, Online, 19–30 April 2021; p. EGU21-11039. [CrossRef]
43. Rembold, F.; Atzberger, C.; Rojas, O.; Savin, I. Using low resolution satellite imagery for yield prediction and yield anomaly detection. *Remote Sens.* **2013**, *11*, 1704–1733. [CrossRef]
44. Atzberger, C. Advances in remote sensing of agriculture: Context description, existing operational monitoring systems and major information needs. *Remote Sens.* **2013**, *5*, 949–981. [CrossRef]
45. Jacobs, C.; Berglund, M.; Kurnik, B.; Dworak, T.; Marras, S.; Mereu, V.; Michetti, M. Climate change adaptation in the agriculture sector in Europe. *EEA Rep.* **2019**, *4*, 112. [CrossRef]
46. Tucker, C. Red and photographic infrared linear combinations for monitoring vegetation. *Remote Sens. Environ.* **1979**, *8*, 127–150. [CrossRef]
47. Huete, A.R. A Soil-Adjusted Vegetation Index (SAVI). *Remote Sens. Environ.* **1988**, *25*, 295–309. [CrossRef]

48. Dempewolf, J.; Adusei, B.; Becker-Rehef, I.; Hansen, M.; Potapov, P.; Khan, A.; Barker, B. Wheat yield forecasting for Punjab Province from vegetation index time series and historic crop statistics. *Remote Sens.* **2014**, *6*, 9653–9675. [CrossRef]
49. Nagy, A.; Fehér, J.; Tamás, J. Wheat and maize yield forecasting for the Tisza river catchment using MODIS NDVI time series and reported crop statistics. *Comput. Electron. Agric.* **2018**, *151*, 41–49. [CrossRef]
50. Mokhtari, A.; Noory, H.; Vazifedoust, M. Improving crop yield estimation by assimilating LAI and inputting satellite-based surface incoming solar radiation into SWAP model. *Agric. For. Meteorol.* **2018**, *250–251*, 159–170. [CrossRef]
51. Nagy, A.; Szabó, A.; Adeniyi, O.D.; Tamás, J. Wheat yield forecasting for the Tisza River catchment using landsat 8 NDVI and SAVI time series and reported crop statistics. *Agronomy* **2021**, *11*, 652. [CrossRef]
52. Muller, S.J.; Sithole, P.; Singels, A.; Van Niekerk, A. Assessing the fidelity of Landsat-based fAPAR models in two diverse sugarcane growing regions. *Comput. Electron. Agric.* **2020**, *170*, 105248. [CrossRef]
53. Liaqat, U.M.; Cheema, M.J.M.; Huang, W.; Mahmood, T.; Zaman, M.; Khan, M.M. Evaluation of MODIS and Landsat multiband vegetation indices used for wheat yield estimation in irrigated. *Comput. Electron. Agric.* **2017**, *138*, 39–47. [CrossRef]
54. Nagy, A.; Szabó, A.; Farkasné Gálya, B.; Tamás, J. 51. Real-time spectral information to measure crop water stress for variable rate irrigation scheduling. In *Precision Agriculture '21*; Stafford, J.V., Ed.; Wageningen Academic Publishers: Wageningen, The Netherlands, 2021; pp. 427–433. ISBN 978-90-8686-363-1/978-90-8686-916-9. [CrossRef]
55. Pullanagari, R.R.; Yule, I.; King, W.; Dalley, D.; Dynes, R. The use of optical sensors to estimate pasture quality. *Int. J. Smart Sens. Intell. Syst.* **2011**, *4*, 125–137. [CrossRef]
56. Pallottino, F.; Antonucci, F.; Costa, C.; Bisagli, C.; Figorilli, S.; Menesatti, P. Optoelectronic proximal sensing vehicle-mounted technologies in precision agriculture: A review. *Comput. Electron. Agric.* **2019**, *162*, 859–873. [CrossRef]
57. Jones, H.G. Irrigation scheduling: Advantages and pitfalls of plant-based methods. *J. Exp. Bot.* **2004**, *407*, 2427–2436. [CrossRef]
58. Mittal, M.; Scholten, L.; Kapelan, Z. A narrative review of serious games for urban water management decisions: Current gaps and future research directions. *Water Res.* **2022**, *215*, 118217. [CrossRef]

International Journal of
Environmental Research
and Public Health

MDPI

Article

Experimental Assessment of Recycled Diesel Spill-Contaminated Domestic Wastewater Treated by Reed Beds for Irrigation of Sweet Peppers

Suhad A.A.A.N. Almuktar and Miklas Scholz *

Civil Engineering Research Group, School of Computing, Science and Engineering, The University of Salford, Greater Manchester, Salford M5 4WT, UK; s.a.a.a.n.almuktar@edu.salford.ac.uk
* Correspondence: m.scholz@salford.ac.uk; Tel.: +44-161-295-5921; Fax: +44-161-295-5575

Academic Editor: Yu-Pin Lin
Received: 2 November 2015; Accepted: 4 February 2016; Published: 6 February 2016

Abstract: The aim of this experimental study is to assess if urban wastewater treated by ten different greenhouse-based sustainable wetland systems can be recycled to irrigate *Capsicum annuum* L. (Sweet Pepper; California Wonder) commercially grown either in compost or sand within a laboratory environment. The design variables were aggregate diameter, contact time, resting time and chemical oxygen demand. The key objectives were to assess: (i) the suitability of different treated (recycled) wastewaters for irrigation; (ii) response of peppers in terms of growth when using recycled wastewater subject to different growth media and hydrocarbon contamination; and (iii) the economic viability of different experimental set-ups in terms of marketable yield. Ortho-phosphate-phosphorus, ammonia-nitrogen, potassium and manganese concentrations in the irrigation water considerably exceeded the corresponding water quality thresholds. A high yield in terms of economic return (marketable yield expressed in monetary value) was linked to raw wastewater and an organic growth medium, while the plants grown in organic medium and wetlands of large aggregate size, high contact and resting times, diesel-spill contamination and low inflow loading rate produced the best fruits in terms of their dimensions and fresh weights, indicating the role of diesel in reducing too high nitrogen concentrations.

Keywords: *Capsicum annuum*; hydrocarbon; marketable yield; nutrient; sustainable agricultural water resource; water reclamation; wetland; vegetable

---

1. Introduction

1.1. Background and Motivation

Since water resources are limited in dry climates, sustainable wastewater treatment and the recycling of the corresponding effluent is a good alternative to using potable water for irrigation [1]. Treated urban water can be recycled for irrigation in agriculture, urban landscape management, industry and ground water recharge [2]. Around 20M ha of land is irrigated by untreated and treated wastewater [3]. Advantages linked to urban wastewater recycling include the abundant supply of nutrients to crops, which could lead to higher marketable yields as well as a decrease in the need for commercial fertilizers [4].

1.2. Wastewater Recycling for Irrigation

Wastewaters can be treated with a wide range of standard (e.g., activated sludge process or trickling filters) and alternative (e.g., wetlands) technologies that can be selected based on criteria such as reliability, simplicity, efficiency, land requirement, affordability, social acceptability and sustainability [5]. Various practical and academic tools have been developed to assist decision-makers in selecting the most appropriate technology including expert opinion [6,7].

Treated wastewater can be recycled to irrigate crops in arid regions that are confronted by considerable water shortages, supporting renewable agriculture and food systems. However, pre-treated wastewaters might require disinfection before application to fields [6]. Irrigation by recycled wastewater can increase the productivity of farming by between 100% and 400%, allowing some crops to be grown in regions with unfavorable conditions [8].

The assessment of the impacts of wastewater reuse on agricultural products intended for consumption is important [9–11]. Either too high or too low concentrations of nutrients in the reused water are a potential problem to crops. Hydrocarbons within road runoff are a new challenge [12,13].

Researchers [12] studied the impact of treated urban wastewater on soil and Sweet Pepper. Recycling saved fertilizer. Moreover, hydrocarbons and heavy metals were low in the harvested fruits. The reuse of nutrients from settled primary urban wastewater on peppers was researched, previously [14]. The crops grown removed both nitrogen and phosphorous, and were healthy compared to the control using standard fertilizer. Nutrients such as ammonia have a negative effect on fruit, leaf and stem developments [15]. Moreover, the total yield increases as the nitrate-nitrogen to ammonia-nitrogen ratio increases. This can be explained by a reduction in fruit physiological disorders, which usually reduce fruit mean weight [16].

Research was undertaken to evaluate the impact of various growth media on Sweet Pepper yields, indicating that peat moss media benefited seedlings. Moreover, peat moss and coco-peat alone or mixed with sand led to a better harvest than other media [17]. The yield response of peppers to mineral and organic fertilization has been assessed, previously [18]. Findings indicate that no differences in yield were noted between organic and conventional farming practices. Another study was undertaken to assess the effects of only peat, and a mixture of peat, perlite and sand (volume ratio of 1:1:1) on yield-related parameters. Results indicated that mixed media increased length, diameter and weight of fruits in all cultivars in comparison to only peat media [19].

Wetland systems can be applied to treat urban wastewater well [13,20]. The treatment efficiency of constructed wetlands on wastewaters and their suitability for reuse in agriculture was also assessed elsewhere [21]. Only water quality variables with high removal efficiencies fulfilled the guidelines for recycling. However, parameters with rather low efficiencies such as solids and phosphorus limited the water reuse potential. Wetlands treating urban effluents to be reused in the agricultural sector were assessed previously [22]. Mean removal efficiencies for suspended solids, biochemical oxygen demand, chemical oxygen demand, total nitrogen and total phosphorus were 85%, 65%, 75%, 42% and 32%, respectively, indicating the possibility for ecological sanitation.

1.3. Nutrient and Mineral Requirements

The authors of this article focused on Sweet Pepper, because it is an easy-to-grow and cost-effective plant with good nutritional benefits [23]. The major elements influencing the growth of crops are nitrogen, phosphorus, potassium, calcium, magnesium and sulphur [24]. Heavy metals may be toxic for peppers.

Maximum concentrations for iron, manganese and potassium are 5.0 mg/L, 0.2 mg/L and 2.0 mg/L, respectively [25,26]. The application of various treated wastewaters for recycling has been classified [27]. Suitable ranges for ammonia-nitrogen and ortho-phosphate-phosphorous are 0 mg/L to 5 mg/L, and 0 mg/L to 2 mg/L in that order. Furthermore, no restriction for the reuse of pre-treated waters with a nitrate-nitrogen value below 5 mg/L has been proposed. Slight to moderate constraints exist for the range between 5 mg/L and 30 mg/L. However, severe restrictions are imposed for measurements greater than 30.0 mg/L [26].

1.4. Rationale, Aim and Objectives

Effluents from different wetlands treating urban wastewater were recycled to irrigate Sweet Pepper. Some wetlands received wastewater contaminated by diesel. The aim of this study is to evaluate if Sweet Pepper can be grown successfully using recycled urban wastewater treated by wetlands to obtain a high marketable yield.

The specific and measurable objectives related to the growing of peppers are to assess: (a) the appropriateness of treated (recycled) wastewater for irrigation compared to corresponding standards; (b) the impact of various waters as a function of the type of wetland; (c) the response of peppers in terms of growth when using recycled (pre-treated) wastewater streams (some contaminated by a diesel spill) subject to different growth media; (d) the effect of environmental boundary conditions on the yield; and (e) the economic return of various experimental systems in terms of marketable yield.

2. Materials and Methods

2.1. Wetlands Set-Up and Operational Arrangements

Ten vertical-flow wetland filters were operated between 27 June 2011 and 25 September 2014. The design variables were aggregate diameter, contact time, resting time and chemical oxygen demand. Contact time is defined as the period of time when the inflow water stays within the wetland. In comparison, resting time indicates the duration when the wetland is drained. The set-up includes two controls receiving clean de-chlorinated tap water (Table 1).

Table 1. Comparison of the experimental vertical-flow wetland set-up.

Filters [a]	Design variables			
	Aggregate Diameter (mm)	Contact Time (h)	Resting Time (h)	Chemical Oxygen Demand (mg/L)
Filter 1 [b]	20	72	48	123.3
Filter 2	20	72	48	123.3
Filter 3 [b]	10	72	48	123.3
Filter 4	10	72	48	123.3
Filter 5 [b]	10	72	48	244.7
Filter 6	10	72	48	244.7
Filter 7	10	36	48	123.3
Filter 8	10	36	24	123.3
Control A [b]	10	72	48	2.3
Control B	10	72	48	2.3

[a] Annually treated volumes of wastewater: Filters 1 to 6, 470 L/a; Filter 7, 624 L/a; Filter 8, 858 L/a; Control A and B, 470 L/a. [b] On 26 September 2013, 130 g of diesel (equivalent to an inflow concentration of 20 g/L) have been added to Filters 1, 3 and 5, and Control A.

The wetland filters were constructed from Pyrex tubes (inner diameter of 19.5 cm and height of 120 cm). The filters were filled with pea gravel up to 60 cm and planted with *Phragmites australis* (Cav.) Trin. ex Steud. (Common Reed)(*P. australis*). The outlet valve is located at the bottom of each filter [28].

Preliminary treated wastewater was obtained from the Davyhulme Sewage works in Manchester. In order to simulate diesel fuel spills, 130 gram of diesel were poured into Filters 1, 3 and 5, and into Control A on 26 September 2013. Chillers (Aquacadabra, Barnehurst Road, Bexleyheath, UK) were used to maintain the root system at 12 °C. All wetland columns received approximately 6.5 L of inflow [28]. All water quality parameters were recorded during or directly after harvesting the wastewater from the wetland filter.

2.2. Water, Soil and Pepper Quality Analysis

Routine water quality sampling was carried out according to standard methods [29]. The analysis of water samples for nutrients and trace element concentrations was undertaken using Varian 720-ES Inductively Coupled Plasma—Optical Emission Spectrometer technology (ICP–OES [30]) manufactured by Agilent Technologies UK (Wharfedale Road, Wokingham, Berkshire, UK).

Soil quality analysis was undertaken [31]. Pepper marketable yield was assessed according to Table 2 [32–34]. Microbial tests (total coliforms, *Escherichia coli*, fecal *Streptococcus* spp. and *Salmonella* spp.) for water and vegetables (skin, flesh and washing solution harvested at different distances from the soil: 0 to 50 cm, 50 to 100 cm and more than 100 cm) were performed using aseptic pour plate techniques according to standard methods [29]. Where relevant, sample numbers, sampling periods and replicate numbers for water, soil and plant samples have been identified in the illustrations shown in Section 3.

2.3. Light, Humidity and Temperature

Light measurements were undertaken using the LUX meter ATP-DT-1300 (TIMSTAR, Road Three, Winsford Industrial Estate, Winsford, Cheshire, UK). Humidity and temperature were recorded using wetterladen24.de (JM Handelspunkt, Geschwend, Germany). The humidity was controlled using Challenge 3.0L Ultrasonic Humidifiers (Argos, Avebury Boulevard, Central Milton Keynes, England, UK).

2.4. Sweet Pepper Growing

Sweet Pepper seeds were obtained from B&Q plc (Chandlers Ford, Hants SO53 3LE;) on 14 September 2013. The seeds were first planted in shallow seed trays for about one week, and subsequently replanted (second planting) in larger nursery pots. The third and final planting was undertaken 28 days after the second planting on 8 November 2013, following supplier instructions. The peppers were planted into 10-litre plastic and round plant pots sourced from scotplants (Hedgehogs Nursery, Crompton Road, Glenrothes, Scotland, UK).

Plant pots dimensions were: height of 22.0 cm, bottom diameter of 22.0 cm and top diameter of 28.5 cm. Compost and pure sand were used. The compost was supplied by B&Q plc as part of their verve brand (product code: 03717644). The sand (Play Pit Sand (silica), product code: 5060096123309) was provided by Deko-Pak Limited (Deco House, Halifax Road, Hipperholme, Brighouse HX3 8BW).

The basic soil properties are listed in Table 3. The top 2 cm were left unplanted for both sand- and soil-based pots. However, sand-based plants were planted to a depth of 20.0 cm, and soil-based plants were planted to a depth of 17.5 cm, and covered by 2.5 cm of bark (B&Q verve range, product code: 5397007188110), which was described by B&Q as ideal for pots, beds and borders to control weeds, retain moisture and insulate soil. The plant pots remained indoors under laboratory conditions characterized in Section 2.3.

Some peppers received fertilizer sourced from the B&Q plc verve range (product code: 5397007068245). The fertilizer had a nitrogen to phosphorus to potassium ratio of 4:4:4. Liquid fertilizer was added to the inflow water as specified.

2.5. Data Analysis

Microsoft Excel and IBM SPSS Statistics Version 20 were used. Significant findings have been highlighted, where appropriate.

Table 2. Sweet Pepper harvest classification scheme (partly adopted from elsewhere [32–34].

Variable	Class A	Class B	Class C	Class D	Class E
Quality class	Outstanding	Good	Good	Satisfactory	Unsatisfactory
European Union classification equivalent	"Extra" Class	Class I	Class II	Not applicable	Not applicable
Mean price estimate; pence (Sterling)/gram	0.28	0.22	0.16	0.10	0.00
Target market	Top restaurant	National supermarket	Independent retailer or market	Vegetable industry	Waste company
Product	Fresh vegetable	Fresh vegetable	Fresh vegetable	Frozen or canned	Waste
Contamination	Uncontaminated	Uncontaminated	Uncontaminated	Uncontaminated	Contaminated
Illnesses	None	None	None	Likely; no harm	Likely; harmful (rotten)
Length (L, mm)	Jumbo ($L \geqslant 110$)	Extra-large ($90 \leqslant L < 110$)	Large ($70 \leqslant L < 90$)	Medium ($40 \leqslant L < 70$)	Small ($L < 40$)
Diameter (D, mm)	Jumbo ($D \geqslant 90$)	Extra-large ($70 \leqslant D < 90$)	Large ($50 \leqslant D < 70$)	Medium ($30 \leqslant D < 50$)	Small ($D < 30$)
Weight (w, g)	Very Large ($w \geqslant 190$)	Large ($120 \leqslant w < 190$)	Medium ($70 \leqslant w \leqslant 120$)	Small ($20 \leqslant w < 70$)	Very Small ($w < 20$)
Tolerance by weight or number per plant (%)	5	10	10	10	10
Defect in shape (Damage (%) of surface area)	Damage $\leqslant 10$	$10 \leqslant$ Damage < 20	$20 \leqslant$ Damage < 30	$30 \leqslant$ Damage < 60	Too many damages (>60)
Defect of the skin (Damage (%) of surface area)	Damage $\leqslant 3$	$3 \leqslant$ Damage < 4	$4 \leqslant$ Damage < 5	$5 \leqslant$ Damage < 20	Too many damages (>20)

Table 3. Basic soil properties based on three replicates each (14 September 2013).

Parameter	Soil Type		Total Per Pot (mg)	
	Compost	Sand	Compost	Sand
pH	6.43	9.40	-	-
Redox potential (mV)	62.60	−79.20	-	-
Electrical conductivity (μs/cm)	2438.50	116.00	-	-
Total nitrogen (mg/kg)	998.75	7.60	3495.63	114.00
Total phosphor (mg/kg)	367.50	0.85	1286.25	12.75
Aluminium (mg/kg)	1118.38	1180.43	3914.33	17,706.45
Calcium (mg/kg)	18,421.96	174.16	64,476.86	2612.40
Iron (mg/kg)	6233.15	1196.48	21,816.03	17,947.20
Potassium (mg/kg)	2776.02	168.57	9716.07	2528.55
Magnesium (mg/kg)	5287.67	279.53	18,506.85	4192.95
Manganese (mg/kg)	201.59	8.09	705.57	121.35
Zinc (mg/kg)	26.59	1.95	93.07	29.25
Boron (mg/kg)	12.29	<0.0001	43.02	0.0015
Organic matter (%)	89.00	0.03	-	-
Bulk density(g/L)	350	1522	-	-

3. Results and Discussion

3.1. Comparison of Irrigation Water Qualities

3.1.1. Comparison of Hydrocarbon Values

Table 4 shows the inflow water quality. Total petroleum hydrocarbon values followed this order: Control A > Filter 8 > Filter 1 > Filter 3> Filter 5. Regarding filters contaminated by diesel (Filters 1, 3, 5 and Control A), the total petroleum hydrocarbon concentrations were 0.100 mg/L, 0.069 mg/L, 0.014 mg/L and 0.346 mg/L, respectively. These concentrations were in compliance with Chinese standards [35], indicating a maximum threshold of 1.0 mg/L. Note that Chinese standards were used, considering that China produces about 54% (estimated in 2008) of peppers in the world [36].

3.1.2. Comparison of Oxygen Demand Variables

Table 4 shows that chemical oxygen demand values were the highest for raw urban wastewater followed by filters contaminated with diesel following the order of F5 > F3 > F1 > Control A. Chemical oxygen demand concentrations were highly variable due to seasonal changes. Moreover, the standard deviation for Filter 8 was particularly high due to the low resting time (Table 1) resulting in insufficient biodegradation in some seasons. Statistically, no significant difference ($p > 0.05$) in chemical oxygen demand values of Filters 2 and 4 were found, indicating that aggregate size may not matter (Table 1). Filter 8 outflow water had chemical oxygen demand values, which were higher than those of Filter 7, highlighting the impact of long resting time on outflow water chemical oxygen demand (Table 1). In comparison, the lowest chemical oxygen demand values were recorded for Control B (no diesel contamination; Table 1).

The biochemical oxygen demand was the highest for raw urban wastewater and corresponding samples diluted with dechlorinated potable water followed by filters contaminated with diesel (Filters 1, 3 and 5). The biochemical oxygen demand values for Filter 8 (short resting time) outflow water were higher than those for Filter 7 (long resting time). The corresponding values for Control A (contaminated with diesel) were higher than those for Control B. Tap water had the lowest biochemical oxygen demand (Table 4).

Table 4. Comparison of the water quality of the inflow waters received by the vegetable pots (mean ± standard deviation (number of samples)) between 11 October 2013 and 25 September 2014.

Water Type	TPH [a] (μg/L)	COD [b] (mg/L)	BOD [c] (mg/L)	NH_4-N [d] (mg/L)	NO_3-N [e] (mg/L)	PO_4-P [f] (mg/L)	SS [g] (mg/L)	Turbidity (NTU) [h]	Ph (−)	EC [i] (μS/cm)	DO [j] (mg/L)	SAR [k] (me/L) [l]
Filter 1 outflow	100	77.7 ± 23.35 (18)	25.8 ± 16.74 (53)	4.8 ± 2.83 (22)	0.4 ± 0.22 (19)	4.0 ± 2.48 (18)	11.3 ± 10.42 (56)	9.0 ± 5.65 (54)	6.4 ± 0.26 (54)	336.5 ± 50.82 (22)	1.5 ± 1.03 (15)	2.4 ± 1.07 (5)
Filter 2 outflow	<10	34.9 ± 19.21 (15)	13.6 ± 8.11 (51)	6.2 ± 5.84 (20)	2.2 ± 2.72 (18)	3.3 ± 1.33 (18)	6.7 ± 9.49 (56)	5.4 ± 5.75 (53)	6.5 ± 0.21 (54)	328.6 ± 53.37 (22)	1.7 ± 1.10 (15)	1.8 ± 0.60 (5)
Filter 3 outflow	69	87.5 ± 26.00 (18)	22.8 ± 16.42 (51)	3.7 ± 2.53 (22)	0.4 ± 0.28 (19)	3.3 ± 2.04 (18)	11.7 ± 10.79 (56)	8.7 ± 6.09 (53)	6.5 ± 0.18 (54)	396.7 ± 76.59 (22)	1.7 ± 1.18 (15)	1.7 ± 0.53 (5)
Filter 4 outflow	<10	34.9 ± 23.77 (15)	12.8 ± .8.86 (50)	5.0 ± 10.53 (20)	1.8 ± 3.27 (18)	2.9 ± 1.06 (18)	7.4 ± 10.57 (56)	5.7 ± 5.46 (53)	6.5 ± 0.19 (54)	352.6 ± 67.56 (22)	2.0 ± 1.60 (15)	2.4 ± 0.39 (5)
Filter 5 outflow	14	100.8 ± 67.90 (18)	22.5 ± 16.35 (51)	9.7 ± 3.20 (21)	0.9 ± 0.86 (19)	4.4 ± 2.07 (18)	11.3 ± 12.76 (57)	8.6 ± 6.22 (53)	6.6 ± 0.19 (54)	564.1 ± 163.66 (22)	1.5 ± 0.81 (15)	2.2 ± 0.85 (5)
Filter 6 outflow	<10	35.6 ± 22.46 (14)	15.9 ± 12.68 (52)	9.0 ± 7.28 (20)	3.6 ± 4.68 (18)	4.6 ± 3.16 (18)	6.9 ± 8.68 (57)	5.4 ± 4.41 (53)	6.8 ± 0.19 (55)	524.3 ± 152.66 (22)	1.6 ± 1.09 (15)	3.1 ± 0.61 (5)
Filter 7 outflow	<10	32.5 ± 20.40 (14)	11.9 ± 8.01 (61)	3.6 ± 5.52 (24)	2.8 ± 2.98 (18)	3.6 ± 2.23 (17)	2.6 ± 3.86 (66)	3.4 ± 2.24 (62)	6.6 ± 0.18 (62)	355.0 ± 83.11 (28)	1.7 ± 0.86 (25)	2.4 ± 0.47 (5)
Filter 8 outflow	116	55.9 ± 86.05 (15)	13.9 ± 7.50 (69)	1.4 ± 1.35 (22)	2.8 ± 3.51 (16)	3.3 ± 1.90 (16)	2.9 ± 4.31 (76)	3.6 ± 2.48 (76)	6.5 ± 0.20 (78)	339.7 ± 104.74 (25)	1.9 ± 1.15 (22)	2.1 ± 0.44 (5)
Control A outflow	346	66.4 ± 44.32 (17)	12.0 ± 7.58 (51)	1.3 ± 1.79 (22)	0.4 ± 0.44 (19)	1.8 ± 0.56 (18)	9.0 ± 10.25 (56)	5.7 ± 4.31 (53)	6.7 ± 0.17 (55)	149.2 ± 32.47 (22)	1.4 ± 0.93 (15)	0.5 ± 0.15 (5)
Control B outflow	<10	16.0 ± 15.12 (15)	8.8 ± 7.58 (52)	1.3 ± 1.77 (21)	0.3 ± 0.35 (18)	1.9 ± 0.33 (18)	3.6 ± 8.18 (56)	4.1 ± 4.54 (53)	6.5 ± 0.20 (54)	153.9 ± 29.87 (22)	1.8 ± 1.04 (15)	0.5 ± 0.14 (5)
Deionised water	Nm [m]	3.5 ± 0.08 (3)	7.3 ± 1.84 (3)	0.1 ± 0.13 (3)	0.0 ± 0.00 (3)	0.0 ± 0.00 (3)	2.0 ± 2.31 (10)	1.3 ± 0.14 (10)	5.1 ± 0.58 (10)	1.5 ± 0.72 (10)	nm	0.1 ± 0.15 (5)
Tap water (100%)	Nm	6.2 ± 0.33 (3)	4.9 ± 1.13 (3)	0.1 ± 0.00 (3)	0.2 ± 0.00 (3)	0.8 ± 0.00 (3)	2.0 ± 2.31 (10)	1.4 ± 0.21 (10)	6.1 ± 1.06 (10)	95.8 ± 15.20 (10)	nm	0.8 ± 0.15 (5)
Tap water with fertiliser	Nm	8.6 ± 0.22 (3)	8.0 ± 2.62 (3)	16.0 ± 0.01 (3)	8.9 ± 0.38 (3)	14.9 ± 0.07 (3)	1.6 ± 0.46 (10)	3.0 ± 0.49 (10)	6.0 ± 0.28 (10)	204.0 ± 5.66 (10)	nm	0.8 ± 0.10 (5)
Wastewater (20%); tap water (80%)	Nm	47.6 ± 15.39 (17)	21.8 ± 15.99 (55)	6.7 ± 3.69 (22)	0.5 ± 0.64 (21)	3.0 ± 1.43 (21)	26.4 ± 18.48 (63)	16.2 ± 15.18 (56)	7.1 ± 0.07 (55)	122.1 ± 55.98 (22)	nm	1.7 ± 0.59 (5)
Wastewater (100%)	Nm	237.9 ± 76.96 (17)	105.3 ± 75.98 (55)	33.6 ± 18.46 (22)	2.4 ± 3.22 (21)	14.9 ± 7.15 (21)	131.9 ± 92.64 (63)	80.4 ± 75.97 (56)	7.5 ± 0.42 (55)	575.5 ± 181.66 (22)	5.2 ± 3.72 (16)	2.8 ± 0.62 (5)
Standard	1000	-	-	5	30	2			6.0–8.5	3000		⩽15

[a] TPH: total petroleum hydrocarbon; [b] COD: chemical oxygen demand; [c] BOD: five-day biochemical oxygen demand; [d] NH_4-N: ammonia-nitrogen; [e] NO_3-N: nitrate-nitrogen; [f] PO_4-P: ortho-phosphate-phosphorus; [g] SS: suspended solids; [h] NTU: turbidity; [i] EC: electrical conductivity; [j] DO: dissolved oxygen; [k] SAR: sodium adsorption ratio (sodium (calcium+magnesium)$^{-2}$)$^{-0.5}$); [l] me/L: milliequivalent per litre; [m] nm: not measured.

Dissolved oxygen values were higher for those filters without diesel (Table 4). Correlation analysis results indicated that dissolved oxygen was significantly negatively correlated with micro-organisms, total petroleum hydrocarbon and chemical oxygen demand in the treatment system. This negative correlation can be explained by an improvement of the chemical oxygen demand and the total petroleum hydrocarbon removal efficiencies as micro-organisms responsible for biodegradation acclimatized, resulting in a reduction of the amount of available dissolved oxygen [13].

3.1.3. Comparison of Nitrogen Compounds

The inflow water quality was highly variable for both nitrogen species, because of seasonal water quality variations in the wetland systems (Table 4). The inflow waters with a high chemical oxygen demand resulted in statistically significant ($p < 0.05$) differences between the ammonia-nitrogen concentrations of Filters 3 and 4 compared to those of Filters 5 and 6, respectively (Table 1). Elevated concentrations of ammonia-nitrogen exceeding the threshold of 5 mg/L [25,26] were recorded for raw wastewater, wastewater diluted with 80% of potable water, and outflow waters from Filters 5 and 6, which were fed with high inflow loads, followed by that from Filter 2, which had a large aggregate size (Table 4).

Moreover, the mean nitrate-nitrogen values of Filter 4 compared to those of Filters 7, and the concentrations for Filters 3 and 4 compared to those of Filters 5 and 6 were statistically significantly different from each other ($p < 0.05$), indicating the impact of contact time and inflow loading rate of wetland systems on outflow water nitrate-nitrogen values (Table 1). However, nitrate-nitrogen concentrations for all outflows (Table 4) were below 4 mg/L, which is considerably less than the threshold of 30 mg/L [25,26].

3.1.4. Comparison of Ortho-Phosphate-Phosphorus

Considering the threshold of 2 mg/L for ortho-phosphate-phosphorus [25], the outflow waters from all wetlands were associated with too high ortho-phosphate-phosphorus concentrations (Table 4). Statistical results did not show any significant differences in ortho-phosphate-phosphorus values of the outflow waters indicating that wetland aggregate diameter, contact and resting times as well as inflow loading rate do not matter (Table 1). However, phosphorus is difficult to remove by mature wetlands [37], because it is often present in particulate form [13].

3.1.5. Comparison of Trace Elements

Figure 1 shows an overview of the ICP–OES findings for selected elements determined in the irrigation water compared to standards. Figure 1a shows that sodium concentration for all irrigation waters did not exceed the standard for irrigation water of 920 mg/L [25,27]. However, statistical analysis showed that the sodium values of Filters 3 and 4 compared to those of Filters 5 and 6 outflow waters were significantly different from each other indicating the impact of the inflow loading rate of wetland systems on outflow water sodium concentrations (Table 1).

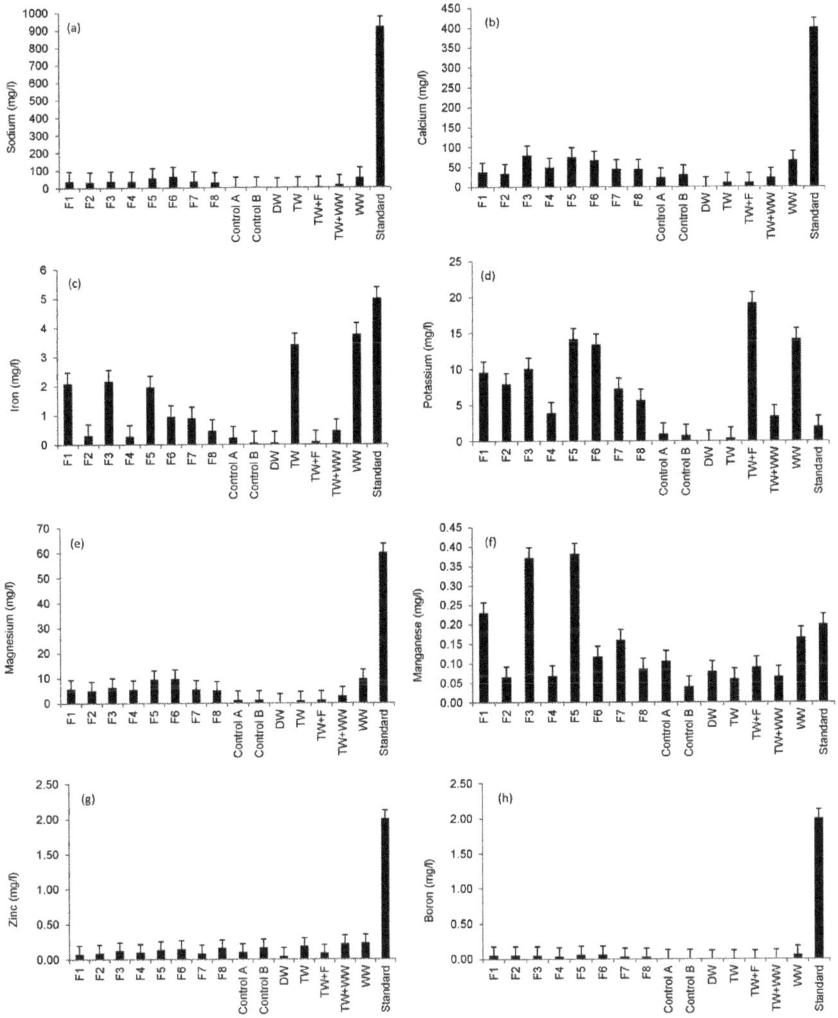

Figure 1. Overview of the Inductively Coupled Plasma—Optical Emission Spectrometer (ICP–OES) analysis (sample number: 10; 11 October 2013 to 25 September 2014) for detected elements compared with common standards for irrigation water [25,27]: (**a**) sodium; (**b**) calcium; (**c**) iron; (**d**) potassium; (**e**) magnesium; (**f**) manganese; (**g**) zinc; and (**h**) boron.

Figure 1b,c shows that the calcium and iron concentrations of all irrigation waters did not exceed the standards of 400 mg/L and 5 mg/L, respectively. Regarding the threshold of 2 mg/L for potassium [25,27], all irrigation water types (except for Controls A and B) had too high potassium concentrations. Statistical results showed that outflow water from Filter 4 had potassium concentrations, which were significantly different from those associated with Filter 7, indicating the impact of contact time on outflow water potassium concentrations (Table 1).

Moreover, a high inflow loading rate of the wetland system resulted in significant differences ($p < 0.05$) in outflow water potassium concentrations for Filter 4 compared with Filter 6 (Figure 1d). No magnesium concentrations exceeded the threshold of 60 mg/L [25,27] as shown in Figure 1e. However, statistical results showed that outflow waters from Filters 3 and 4 compared to those of

Filters 5 and 6 had magnesium concentrations, which were significantly ($p < 0.05$) different from each other, explaining the impact of inflow loading rate of wetland systems on outflow water magnesium concentrations (Table 1). Figure 1f shows that results for Filters 1, 3 and 5, which were contaminated with diesel, have elevated manganese concentrations exceeding the threshold of 0.2 mg/L [25,27]. Figure 1g,h show that zinc and boron concentrations in all irrigation water types did not exceed the threshold of 2 mg/L [25,27].

3.1.6. Comparison of Particles

The inflow water quality was highly variable for particles indicated by suspended solids and turbidity (Table 4). This can also be explained by the seasonal water quality variations in the wetland systems. For example, as above-ground *P. australis* plant parts decay in winter and early spring, more particles are created as by-products of the biodegradation process. Furthermore, the standard deviations for very clean waters such as tap water are high due to the random presence of larger particles.

Table 4 shows that the highest value for suspended solids was noted for raw wastewater and diluted wastewater followed by those for outflow waters from filters contaminated with diesel (Filters 1, 3 and 5, and Control A). Turbidity had the highest values for raw wastewater and diluted wastewater followed by outflow waters received from Filters 1, 3 and 5, which were contaminated with diesel. Filters 7 and 8 had the lowest turbidity values in spite of different resting times. Correlation analysis results showed that turbidity was significantly positively correlated with suspended solids and micro-organisms in treatment systems indicating a good relationship between turbidity and indicator micro-organisms activity due to degradation of organic matter and a subsequent increase in particles [28]. However, high values of suspended solids and turbidity associated with irrigation water will considerably increase the development of hydrophobicity in the soils, and subsequently affect plant growth.

3.1.7. Comparison of pH and Salinity

Table 4 shows that the pH values were normal [25]. Conductivity is the most important indirect measure of salinity, posing a great hazard to crops and determining the suitability of water for irrigation use. Salts negatively impact on the growth of plants, and the soil structure and permeability, indirectly affecting plant growth as well. However, the conductivity values for all filter outflow waters complied with the threshold of 3000 μs/cm [25,27]. Furthermore, the sodium adsorption ratio concentrations for all outflows were normal; *i.e.*, between 0 milliequivalents per liter (me/L) and 15 me/L [27].

3.1.8. Comparison of Microbial Content

Microbial characteristics of irrigation water are summarized in Figure 2. Based on the maximum value for total coliforms (1000 CFU per 100 mL) regarding the irrigation of crops [38], the outflow waters from all wetlands were associated with too high contamination by total coliforms. Furthermore, high contamination by total coliforms was also observed for raw wastewater and diluted wastewater.

Raw wastewater was associated with the highest contamination by *Escherichia coli* (8000 CFU per 100 mL) followed by outflow water from Filter 5 and wastewater. Outflow waters from Filters 1 and 3 had similar numbers of *Escherichia coli*. No contamination by *Escherichia coli* was detected for outflow waters from other wetlands.

The highest contamination by *Streptococcus* spp. was associated with Filter 1 outflow water followed by those for Filters 3 and 5, which were contaminated with hydrocarbons (Figure 2). Filter 4 had a higher *Streptococcus* spp. contamination than Filter 2, indicating the effect of aggregate size when comparing these filters with each other (Table 1). Furthermore, raw wastewater was more contaminated by *Streptococcus* spp. than diluted wastewater. The highest *Salmonella* spp. counting was observed in the outflow water from Filter 5 followed by raw wastewater (Figure 2). Filter 1 outflow water was associated with higher *Salmonella* spp. contamination than the water from Filter 3, highlighting the impact of aggregate size (Table 1). Furthermore, *Salmonella* spp. contamination in Control A outflow water was higher than that associated with Control B, explaining the effect of hydrocarbon contamination.

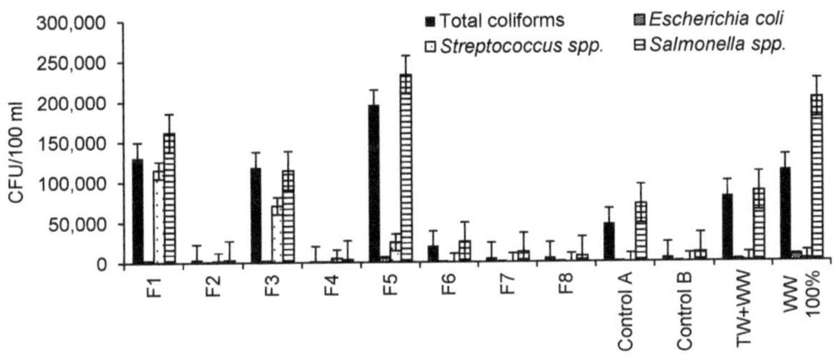

Figure 2. Microbiological characteristics of irrigation water (sample number: 20; 11 October 2013 to 25 September 2014).

Figure 2 showed that the microbial contamination of outflow water from wetland filters polluted with hydrocarbon was higher than those from standard filters (uncontaminated). This confirms previous findings [39], assessing the impact of long-term total petroleum hydrocarbon (TPH) on the structure of bacterial communities. The results indicated that a high concentration of TPH positively impacted on the diversity of hydrocarbon-degrading bacteria. Furthermore, wetland filters fed with undiluted inflow water showed higher microbial contamination levels than those fed with diluted inflow, confirming other findings [28], indicating that high-rate filters tend to be overloaded.

3.2. Environment Boundary Conditions

Table 5 shows environmental boundary conditions. The light intensity records for this experiment during the flowering and fruiting stage were below the proposed range from about 8600 lux to 17,200 lux [40]. Low light intensity may lead to flower inhibition or cause flower abscission [41]. Moreover, low light intensity applied to plants will produce leggy plants growing toward light, which is necessary for photosynthesis [42].

For the germination stage (Table 5), the temperature records complied with the optimal temperature for peppers during this phase [43]. Concerning the vegetative growth stage, the temperature records (Table 5) for this experiment were higher than the recommended optimum values of between 21 °C and 23 °C [44]. However, temperature records for this stage complied with the values associated with the highest photosynthesis rate, which can be achieved at temperatures between 24 °C and 29 °C [45,46].

Table 5 shows that the relative humidity before and after fruiting was low (37 $\pm$ 7.6% and 57 $\pm$ 7.8%, respectively). Humidity values below 50% could have a negative impact on the fruit development as humid atmosphere is necessary for flowers to successfully pollinate; otherwise, the unfertilized flowers will drop off as reported elsewhere [46].

3.3. Sweet Pepper Growth Comparisons

Figure 3a,f shows a growth comparison between pepper plants growing in organic and inorganic media in terms of plant overall height, number of leaves, buds, flowers and total weight of fruits harvested from each treatment. Findings indicate that compost compared to sand is associated with considerably greater plant growth and productivity. This is due to the elevated nutrient availability in the basic compost [17] compared to sand (Table 3). Furthermore, organic substrate decomposes, releasing nutrients [47,48].

Sweet Pepper prefers light and well-drained soil, which is rich in organic substances with a pH value from 6.5 to 7.5 (Table 3) [43]. However, under acid soil conditions (soil pH < 7), heavy metals could be a challenge to Sweet Pepper [49]. Figure 4 shows that plants grown in compost consume more water than those grown in sand and subsequently increase the nutrient load applied to plants via irrigation water, leading to higher foliage and yield production.

Regarding the overall height of plants growing in organic media, Figure 3a shows that the maximum height was associated with plants irrigated with raw wastewater followed by those irrigated with tap water spiked with fertilizer. This can be explained by the high nutrient load (Table 6) applied via irrigation water. Results were statistically significantly different ($p < 0.05$) for the overall height of plants irrigated with water harvested from Filter 7 and Control B.

Regarding the total number of leaves (Figure 3b) linked to peppers grown in organic media, findings indicated that peppers irrigated with tap water spiked by fertilizer produced the highest leave number followed by those plants irrigated with water harvested from Filter 4 and raw wastewater, while the lowest leave numbers were recorded for plants irrigated with deionized water followed by tap water and Controls A and B.

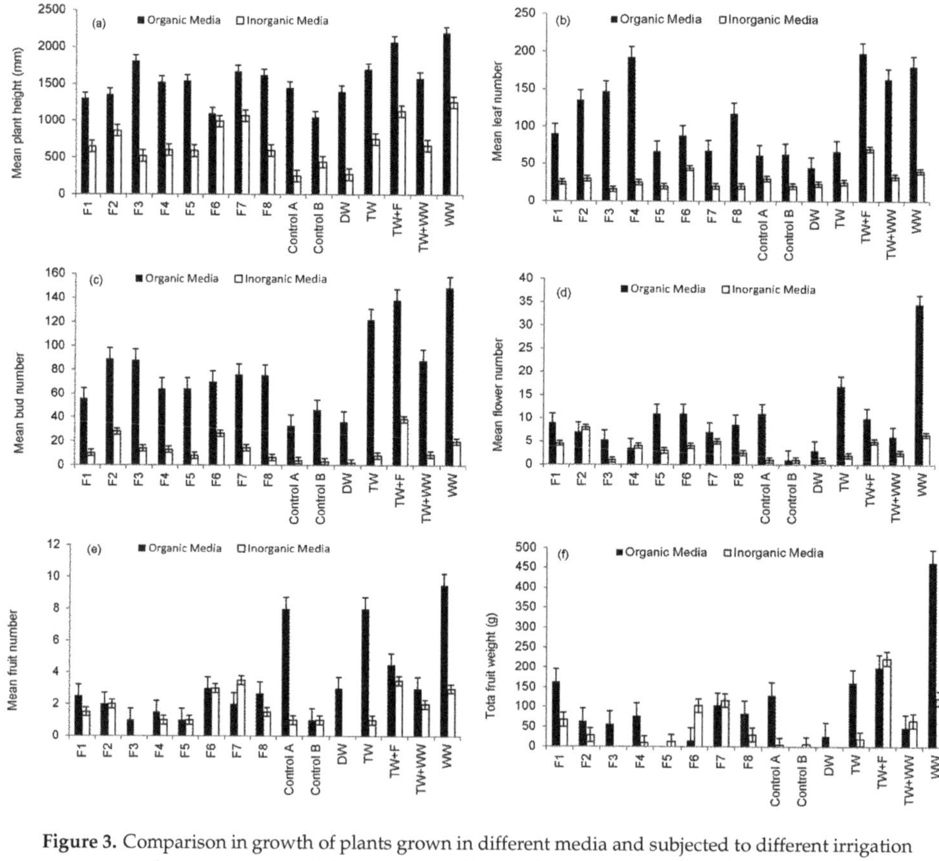

Figure 3. Comparison in growth of plants grown in different media and subjected to different irrigation water types (harvest between 20 January and 25 September 2014): (**a**) mean plant height; (**b**) mean leaf number; (**c**) mean bud number; (**d**) mean flower number; (**e**) mean fruit number; and (**f**) mean fruit weight.

Table 5. Overview of environmental boundary conditions associated with the vegetable pots (mean ± standard deviation (number of records)).

Parameter	Unit	A [a]	B [b]	C [c]	D [d]	E [e]	F [f]
Illuminance (one-off record during lab visit)	lux	5587 ± 5501.1 (918)	nm	4208 ± 2560.5 (36)	12316 ± 1823.3 (102)	3682 ± 3246.1 (513)	5877 ± 9262.2 (267)
Temperature (one-off record during lab visit)	°C	25.4 ± 2.12 (603)	20.5 ± 1.25 (13)	24.8 ± 1.17 (48)	25.0 ± 1.89 (102)	26.3 ± 2.32 (204)	25.0 ± 1.83 (236)
Temperature (minimum within a 24-hour period)	°C	20.8 ± 1.97 (75)	nm	nm	20.3 ± 1.87 (8)	21.2 ± 2.02 (33)	20.6 ± 2.05 (34)
Temperature (maximum within a 24-hour period)	°C	26.8 ± 2.59 (75)	nm	nm	25.3 ± 1.98 (8)	27.0 ± 2.83 (33)	26.6 ± 2.26 (34)
Relative humidity (one-off record during lab visit)	%	49 ± 11.7 (488)	nm	nm	42 ± 5.4 (96)	37 ± 7.6 (156)	57 ± 7.8 (236)
Relative humidity (minimum within a 24-hour period)	%	35 ± 7.1 (75)	nm	nm	36 ± 3.7 (8)	30 ± 3.5 (33)	38 ± 8.5 (34)
Relative humidity (maximum within a 24-hour period)	%	55 ± 12.5 (75)	nm	nm	46 ± 5.6 (8)	48 ± 10.5 (33)	63 ± 9.8 (34)

[a] A: Overall period (11 October 2013 to 25 September 2014); [b] B: Germination period (17 September 2013 to 22 September 2013); [c] C: First Planting period (23 September 2013 to 10 October 2013); [d] D: Second planting period (11 October 2013 to 7 November 2013); [e] E: Final planting period before fruiting (8 November 2013 to 19 January 2014); [f] F: Final planting period after fruiting (20 January 2014 to 25 September 2014); nm: not measured.

Figure 3c–f provides summaries of plant developments. Very high numbers of buds were recorded for peppers grown in organic media. Most flowers died before producing any fruits due to the elevated ammonia-nitrogen concentrations supplied to those plants grown in organic media and irrigated by wastewater [43].

Sweet Peppers grown in sand had less buds compared to those peppers grown in organic media. Most buds reached the fruiting stage (Figure 3e), because of a better balance in nutrients supplied to those plants by the irrigation water. The potential of a rather moderate diesel spill to function as stimulation for plant growth in clean water becomes apparent when comparing both controls with each other (Table 1).

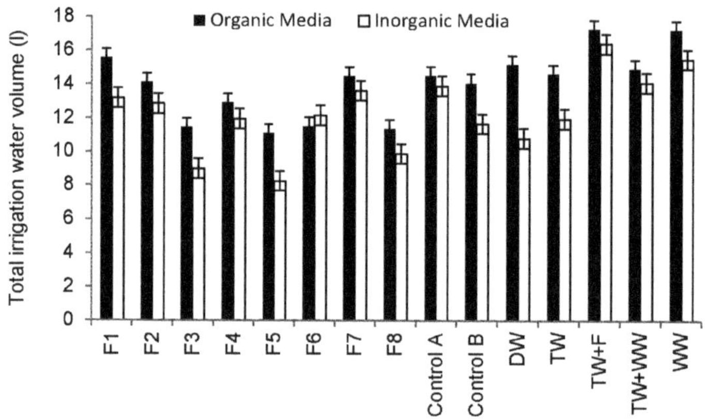

Figure 4. Overview of total irrigation water volumes for Sweet Pepper plants during the whole experiment period (11 October 2013 to 25 September 2014).

Figure 3f summaries a comparison of total weight. Fruits harvested from plants grown in organic media were heavier than those from plants raised in inorganic media. This confirms results obtained by other researchers [17,19] showing the impact of various growth media on pepper harvests.

Figure 5 summaries differences in fruit characteristics. Findings show that fruits harvested from plants irrigated with Filter 1 outflow water were greater than those obtained from peppers irrigated with waters from Filter 2 due to high element loads applied to plants associated with Filter 2 compared to Filter 1 (Table 6). Moreover, fruits belonging to Filter 1 had diameters, which were greater than others indicating the impact of nutrient (mainly nitrogen) and trace element loads provided by irrigation water obtained from Filter 1 compared to the other filters (Table 6).

Figure 5 shows that there is no statistically significant difference in mean fruit length harvested from plants irrigated with different irrigation water types. However, fruits harvested from plants irrigated with Filter 7 (low contact time) outflow water were the longest followed by those irrigated with water obtained from Filters 1 (large aggregate size) and 3 (small aggregate size), which were contaminated with hydrocarbons. The shortest fruit lengths were observed for those harvested from plants irrigated with Filter 6 (high inflow rate) outflow water.

Regarding mean fruit weight, statistical analysis showed that there are significant differences ($p < 0.05$) in fruit mean weight for plants irrigated with water harvested from Filter 6, tap water spiked with fertilizer and raw wastewater. Figure 5 indicates that Sweet Peppers irrigated with water harvested from Filter 1 produced fruits of the highest mean weight (54 g) followed by those harvested from plants irrigated with Filter 7 outflow water, which produced fruits of 52 g mean weight, while the lowest mean fruit weight was recorded for those plants irrigated with Filter 6 outflow water (16 g), explaining the negative impact of high nutrients and trace elements applied to plant fruit weight (Table 6).

Table 6. Overview of element mass applied on plants grown in organic media subjected to different irrigation water types (11 October 2013 to 25 September 2014).

Water Type	Total Applied Mass (mg)									
	NH_4-N [a]	NO_3-N [b]	PO_4-P [c]	Ca [d]	Fe [e]	K [f]	Mg [g]	Mn [h]	Zn [i]	B [j]
Filter 1 outflow	74.8	6.2	62.3	591.9	32.6	149.0	89.0	3.6	1.2	0.8
Filter 2 outflow	87.5	31.0	46.5	484.3	4.6	112.7	71.1	0.9	1.3	0.7
Filter 3 outflow	42.4	4.6	37.8	919.3	24.9	115.1	74.1	4.2	1.4	0.6
Filter 4 outflow	64.5	23.2	37.4	638.7	3.7	50.6	69.8	0.9	1.3	0.5
Filter 5 outflow	107.7	10.0	48.9	834.9	21.8	157.2	104.2	4.2	1.5	0.6
Filter 6 outflow	103.7	41.5	53.0	765.8	11.0	154.1	112.5	1.3	1.7	0.7
Filter 7 outflow	52.2	40.6	52.2	650.8	13.1	105.0	78.9	2.3	1.2	0.4
Filter 8 outflow	15.9	31.8	37.5	506.8	5.4	69.4	57.6	1.0	1.8	0.3
Control A outflow	18.9	5.8	26.1	342.7	3.4	14.5	17.2	1.5	1.5	0.1
Control B outflow	18.3	4.2	26.7	429.8	1.0	11.1	17.8	0.6	2.3	0.1
Deionised water	1.5	<0.1	<0.1	<0.1	1.0	<0.1	1.4	1.2	0.7	<0.1
Tap water (100%)	1.5	10.2	29.7	151.8	49.9	6.2	14.6	0.9	2.7	<0.1
Tap water with fertiliser	276.7	153.9	257.7	179.8	1.6	331.4	20.9	1.6	1.5	<0.1
Wastewater (20%); tap water (80%)	100.0	7.5	44.8	336.6	7.0	51.2	42.1	1.0	3.3	0.1
Wastewater (100%)	580.3	41.4	257.3	1149.9	65.0	244.4	169.1	2.9	4.0	1.0

[a] NH_4-N: ammonia-nitrogen; [b] NO_3-N: nitrate-nitrogen; [c] PO_4-P: ortho-phosphate-phosphorus; [d] Ca: calcium; [e] Fe: iron; [f] K: potassium; [g] Mg: magnesium. [h] Mn: manganese; [i] Zn: zinc; [j] B: boron.

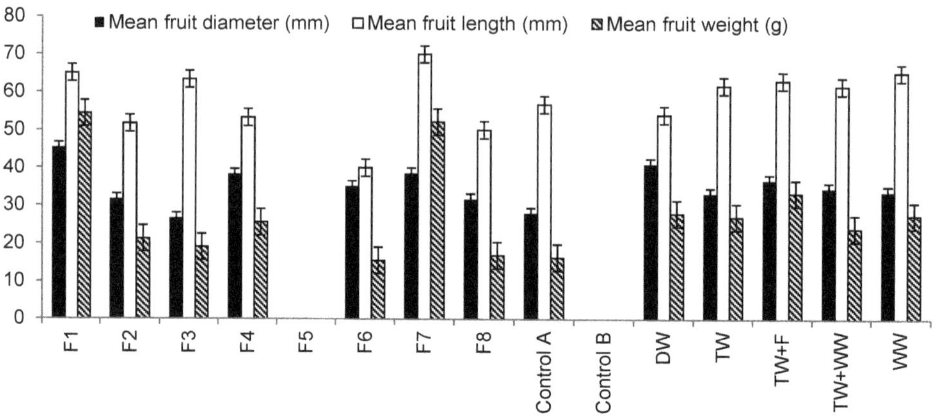

Figure 5. Differences in mean fruit diameter, mean fruit length and mean fruit weight linked to harvested plants (20 January to 25 September 2014) irrigated with different water types and grown in organic media. Notes: No fruit harvest has been noted for plants associated with Filter 5 and Control B.

Ammonia-nitrogen has a negative effect on plant fruit, leaf and stem developments [15,16]. However, the total yield increases as the nitrate-nitrogen to ammonia-nitrogen ratio increases. This can be explained by a reduction in fruit physiological disorders, which usually reduce fruit mean weight [15,16]. Moreover, high phosphorus levels are known to interfere with the normal metabolism of peppers. Also, it is known to promote manganese uptake by plants [50]. However, researchers [51] reported that high potassium concentration in irrigation water provides protection against stem damage from low night temperatures. Manganese is an essential trace element for most plants, intervening in several metabolic processes (mainly in photosynthesis). Nevertheless, an excess of this micronutrient is often toxic for plants. Manganese phyto-toxicity is exhibited in a reduction of biomass and photosynthesis, and biochemical disorders including oxidative stress [50].

Correlation analysis findings indicated that fruit weights were significantly positively correlated with total water volumes used for irrigation ($R = 0.821$, $p < 0.001$). Since the peppers irrigated with raw wastewater and grown in organic media had the highest number of fruits (Figure 3e), this helps to explain why the total weight of harvested fruits was associated with plants irrigated with raw urban wastewater (Figure 3g). The provision of plants with high nutrient and trace element loads leads to increases in the quantity at the expense of quality of yield.

3.4. *Sweet Pepper Quality*

Table 2 proposes a novel but conservative harvest classification scheme for Sweet Peppers. The lowest variable class entry for any individual pepper fruit assessment determined the final class. If a fruit is categorized, for example, as class A with respect to length, class B in terms of diameter and E regarding weight, then the final class for this fruit is class E. It follows that the corresponding price for this pepper sample will be zero pence (Table 2).

Figure 6 indicates the monetary value of the pepper harvest. No fruits from any plant were categorized as Class A, B or C. The highest number of fruits categorized as Class D was harvested from peppers grown in organic media and irrigated with raw wastewater followed by those irrigated with tap water, Control A and Filter 1 outflow waters. The highest number of fruits categorized as Class E was harvested also from plants grown in organic media and watered with raw wastewater. No microbial contamination was detected in fruits (skin, flesh and washing solution) harvested from any treatments. However, microbial contamination of peppers is rather unlikely due to the relatively long distance between the fruits and the contaminated soil.

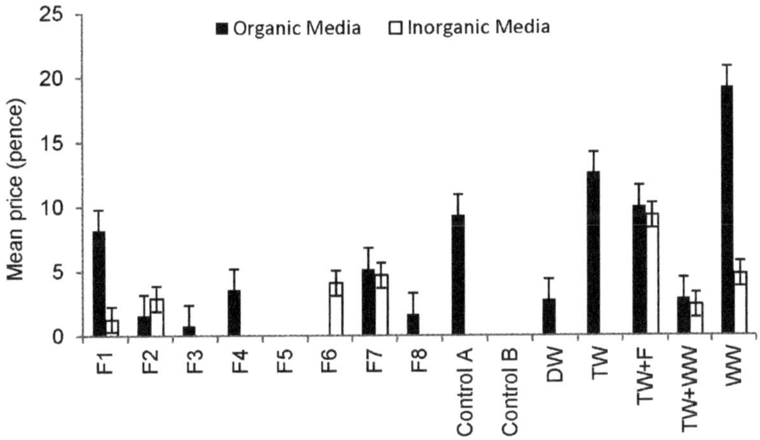

Figure 6. Comparison of the Sweet Pepper harvest outcome linked to plants grown in different media (after classification scheme (Table 2) application).

4. Conclusions and Further Research

The key research findings have been compared to what was promised in Section 1.4 stating the objectives. Sweet Peppers can be grown using wastewater treated by constructed wetlands. However, the marketable yield was too low to make a decent profit (addressing objective (a)).

The highest number of fruits was linked to raw wastewater and an organic growth medium, while the highest fruit quality indicated by diameter, length and weight was observed for peppers grown in organic media and irrigated with outflow water from wetlands with large aggregates, long contact and resting times, and low inflow loading rate. These results correspond to objectives (b) and (c).

As the nutrients within the degraded compost got depleted about ten months after the start of the experiment, the harvest increased for pots that received pre-treated wastewater in comparison to those depending only on the remaining nutrients obtained from the almost exhausted compost. These findings correspond to objectives (c) and (d).

Results show that nutrient concentrations supplied to the peppers by biodegrading compost and nutrient-rich wastewater were too high to produce a reasonable harvest, because Sweet Peppers are sensitive to too high nutrient concentrations leading to plant development challenges. A high marketable yield (harvest of Sweet Peppers, which are of good quality) related to the most suitable provision of nutrients to the peppers, addressing objectives (c) to (e)).

A good pepper harvest was linked to a wetland system with a large aggregate diameter and diesel spill. This can be explained by the fact that the degradation of hydrocarbon requires the presence of considerable nitrogen resources. In the absence of diesel, too much nitrogen increases leave and decreases fruit developments (addressing objectives (c) to (e)).

Considering that findings indicate the unsuitability for Sweet Peppers to be grown in the tested manner, further research will be undertaken with a mixture of different growth media, and different dilutions of outflow water from wetland filters to optimize the concentrations of nutrients applied to plants supporting the production of the highest yield and best quality. An assessment of the long-term impact of soil and fruit enrichment with minerals will be undertaken in the future. Finally, the authors recommend that field studies should complement experimental studies.

Acknowledgments: Suhad Almuktar obtained a PhD Studentship funded by the Iraqi government. Rawaa Al-Isawi, Abdulkadir Sani, Sai Aung, Marjorie Melac, Audrey Bouvier and Pauline Morereau helped with the data collection. Furthermore, Laurie Cunliffe, Chuxia Lin and Helen Bradshaw provided advice.

Author Contributions: Suhad A.A.A.N. Almuktar provided most of the data and the first paper draft. Miklas Scholz finalized the paper.

Conflicts of Interest: The authors declare no conflict of interest.

References

1. Asano, T. Reusing urban wastewater—An alternative and a reliable water resource. *Water Int.* **1994**, *19*, 36–42. [CrossRef]
2. Asano, T.; Burton, F.L.; Leverenz, H.; Tsuchihashi, R.; Tchobanoglous, G. *Waterreuse: Issues, Technologies, and Applications*; McGraw-Hill Education: Columbus, OH, USA, 2007.
3. Jiménez, B.; Asano, T. *Water Reclamation and Reuse Around the World, Water Reuse: An International Survey of Currentpractice, Issues and Needs*; International Water Association Publishing: London, UK, 2008; pp. 3–26.
4. Bichai, F.; Polo-López, M.I.; Fernández Ibañez, P. Solar disinfection of wastewater to reduce contamination of lettuce crops by *Escherichia coli* in reclaimed water irrigation. *Water Res.* **2012**, *46*, 6040–6050. [CrossRef] [PubMed]
5. Singhirunnusorn, W.; Stenstrom, M. Appropriate wastewater treatment systems for developing countries: Criteria and indictor assessment in Thailand. *Water Sci. Technol.* **2009**, *59*, 1873–1884. [CrossRef] [PubMed]
6. Curiel-Esparza, J.; Cuenca-Ruiz, M.A.; Martin-Utrillas, M.; Canto-Perello, J. Selecting a sustainable disinfection technique for wastewater reuse projects. *Water* **2014**, *6*, 2732–2747. [CrossRef]
7. Kalbar, P.P.; Karmakar, S.; Asolekar, S.R. The influence of expert opinions on the selection of wastewater treatment alternatives: A group decision-making approach. *J. Environ. Manage.* **2013**, *128*, 844–851. [CrossRef] [PubMed]
8. FAO. *The Wealth of Waste: The Economics of Wastewater Use in Agriculture*; Food and Agriculture Organisation (FAO) of the United Nations: Rome, Italy, 2010.
9. Aiello, R.; Cirelli, G.L.; Consoli, S. Effects of reclaimed wastewater irrigation on soil and tomato fruits: A case study in Sicily (Italy). *Agric. Water Manage.* **2007**, *93*, 65–72. [CrossRef]
10. Asano, T.; Levine, A.D. Wastewater reclamation, recycling and reuse: Past, present, and future. *Water Sci. Technol.* **1996**, *33*, 1–14. [CrossRef]
11. Cirelli, G.L.; Consoli, S.; Licciardello, F.; Aiello, R.; Giuffrida, F.; Leonardi, C. Treated municipal wastewater reuse in vegetable production. *Agric. Water Manage.* **2012**, *104*, 163–170. [CrossRef]
12. García-Delgado, C.; Eymar, E.; Contreras, J.; Segura, M. Effects of fertigation with purified urban wastewater on soil and pepper plant (*Capsicum annuum L.*) production, fruit quality and pollutant contents. *Span. J. Agric. Res.* **2012**, *10*, 209–221. [CrossRef]
13. Scholz, M. *Wetland Systems—Storm Water Management Control*; Springer Verlag: Berlin, Germany, 2010.
14. Boyden, B.H.; Rababah, A.A. Recycling nutrients from municipal wastewater. *Desalination* **1996**, *106*, 241–246. [CrossRef]
15. Bar-Tal, A.; Aloni, B.; Karni, L.; Oserovitz, J.; Hazan, A.; Itach, M.; Gantz, S.; Avidan, A.; Posalski, I.; Tratkovski, N. Nitrogen nutrition of greenhouse pepper. I. Effects of nitrogen concentration and NO_3: NH_4 ratio on yield, fruit shape, and the incidence of blossom-end rot in relation to plant mineral composition. *HortScience* **2001**, *36*, 1244–1251.
16. Bar-Tal, A.; Aloni, B.; Karni, L.; Rosenberg, R. Nitrogen nutrition of greenhouse pepper. II. Effects of nitrogen concentration and NO_3: NH_4 ratio on growth, transpiration, and nutrient uptake. *HortScience* **2001**, *36*, 1252–1259.
17. Rahimi, Z.; Aboutalebi, A.; Zakerin, A. Comparison of different medium for production of sweet pepper transplant. *Int. Res. J. Appl. Basic Sci.* **2013**, *4*, 307–310.
18. Del Amor, F.M. Yield and fruit quality response of sweet pepper to organic and mineral fertilization. *Renew. Agric. Food Syst.* **2007**, *22*, 233–238. [CrossRef]
19. Gungor, F.; Yildirim, E. Effect of different growing media on quality, growth and yield of pepper (*Capsicum annuum L.*) under greenhouse conditions. *Pak. J. Bot.* **2013**, *45*, 1605–1608.
20. Dong, Y.; Wiliński, P.R.; Dzakpasu, M.; Scholz, M. Impact of hydraulic loading rate and season on water contaminant reductions within integrated constructed wetlands. *Wetlands* **2011**, *31*, 499–509. [CrossRef]
21. Morari, F.; Giardini, L. Municipal wastewater treatment with vertical flow constructed wetlands for irrigation reuse. *Ecol. Eng.* **2009**, *35*, 643–653. [CrossRef]

22. Lopez, A.; Pollice, A.; Lonigro, A.; Masi, S.; Palese, A.M.; Cirelli, G.L.; Toscano, A.; Passino, R. Agricultural wastewater reuse in Southern Italy. *Desalination* **2006**, *187*, 323–334. [CrossRef]
23. Nickels, J. *Growing Chillies—A Guide to the Domestic Cultivation of Chilli Plants*; Jason Nickels: UK, 2012.
24. Jones, J.B. *Instructions for Growing Tomatoes in the Garden and Green-House*; CreateSpace Independent Publishing Platform: Anderson, SC, USA, 2013.
25. FAO. *Users Manual for Irrigation with Treated Wastewater*; FAO Regional Office of the Near East: Cairo, Egypt, 2003.
26. Pescod, M.B. Wastewater treatment and use in agriculture—FAO irrigation and drainage paper number 47. Available online: http://www.Fao.Org/docrep/t0551e/t0551e00.Htm (accessed on 26 May 2014).
27. Food and Agriculture Organization. *The State of Food and Agriculture*; Food and Agriculture Organization (FAO) of the United Nations: Rome, Italy, 1994.
28. Sani, A.; Scholz, M.; Bouillon, L. Seasonal assessment of experimental vertical-flow constructed wetlands treating domestic wastewater. *Bioresour. Technol.* **2013**, *147*, 585–596. [CrossRef] [PubMed]
29. American Public Health Association. Standard methods for the examination of water and wastewater. In *American Public Health Association (APHA), American Water Works Association, and Water and Environment Federation*, 21st ed.; American Public Health Association (APHA): Washington, DC, USA, 2005.
30. Environmental Protection Agency. *Determination Of Metals And Trace Elements In Water And Wastes By Inductively Coupled Plasma-Atomic Emission Spectrometry*; U.S. Environmental Protection Agency (EPA): Cincinnati, OH, USA, 1994.
31. Chary, N.S.; Kamala, C.T.; Raj, D.S.S. Assessing risk of heavy metals from consuming food grown on sewage irrigated soils and food chain transfer. *Ecotoxicol. Environ. Saf.* **2008**, *69*, 513–524. [CrossRef] [PubMed]
32. Commission Regulation No. 1455/1999 Laying Down the Marketing Standard for Sweet Peppers. Available online: http://faolex.fao.org/cgi-bin/faolex.exe?rec_id=028004&database=faolex&search_type=link&table=result&lang=eng&format_name=@ERALL (accessed on 6 January 2005).
33. Laying Down Detailed Rules for the Application of Council Regulation (EC) No.1234/2007 in Respect of the Fruits and Vegetables Sectors. Available online: http://eur-lex.europa.eu/legal-content/EN/TXT/?uri=CELEX%3A32011R054315 (accessed on June 2011).
34. Thai Agricultural Standard, National Bureau of Agricultural Commodity and Food Standards, Ministry of Agriculture and Cooperatives. Available online: http://www.acfs.go.th/standard/download/eng/peppers.pdf (accessed on 7 June 2004).
35. SEPA. *Standards for Irrigation Water Quality*; State Environmental Protection Administration: Beijing, China, 2005.
36. US Bell & Chile Pepper Statistics. Available online: http://usda.mannlib.cornell.edu/MannUsda/viewDocumentInfo.do?documentID=1659 (accessed on 2 November 2015).
37. Smith, E.; Gordon, R.; Madani, A.; Stratton, G. Year-round treatment of dairy wastewater by constructed wetlands in atlantic Canada. *Wetlands* **2006**, *26*, 349–357. [CrossRef]
38. US EPA. *Guidelines for Water Reuse*; United States Environmental Protection Agency (EPA): Washington, DC, USA, 2004.
39. Benedek, T.; Vajna, B.; Táncsics, A.; Márialigeti, K.; Lányi, S.; Máthé, I. Remarkable impact of PAHs and TPHs on the richness and diversity of bacterial species in surface soils exposed to long-term hydrocarbon pollution. *World J. Microbiol. Biotechnol.* **2013**, *29*, 1989–2002. [CrossRef] [PubMed]
40. Deli, J.; Tiessen, H. Interaction of temperature and light intensity on flowering of *Capsicum frutescens* var *grossum* cv. California Wonder. *J. Am. Soc. Hortic. Sci.* **1969**, *94*, 349–351.
41. Wein, H.C.; Zhang, Y. Prevention of flower abscission in bell pepper. *J. Am. Soc. Hortic. Sci.* **1991**, *116*, 516–519.
42. Ciju, R.J. *Bell Peppers—Growing Practices and Nutritional Value*; CreateSpace Independent Publishing Platform: Ridgmont, UK, 2013.
43. Chemicals, H. Nutritional Recommendations for Pepper. Available online: ttp://www.haifa-group.com/files/Guides/Pepper/Pepper.pdf (accessed on 3 February 2014).
44. Bakker, J.C.; Ufflen, V.J.A.M. The effect of diurnal temperature regimes on growth and yield of greenhouse sweet pepper. *Neth. J. Agric. Sci.* **1988**, *36*, 201–208.
45. Bhatt, R.; Srinivasa Rao, N. Photosynthesis and dry matter partitioning in three cultivars of *Capsicum annuum* L. grown at two temperature conditions. *Photosynthetica* **1989**, *23*, 21–26.

46. Nilwik, H.J.M. Photosynthesis of whole sweet pepper plants. I. Response to irradiance and temperature as influenced by cultivation conditions. *Photosynthetica* **1980**, *14*, 373–381.
47. Bakker, J.C. The effects of air humidity on flowering, fruit set, seed set and fruit growth of glasshouse sweet pepper (*Capsicum annuum* L.). *Sci. Hortic.* **1989**, *40*, 1–8. [CrossRef]
48. Olle, M.; Ngouajio, M.; Siomos, A. Vegetable quality and productivity as influenced by growing medium: A review. *Agriculture* **2012**, *99*, 399–408.
49. Baudoin, W.; Nono-Womdim, R.; Lutaladio, N.B.; Hodder, A. *Good Agricultural Practices for Greenhouse Vegetable Crops: Principles for Mediterranean Climate Areas*; Food and agriculture organization (FAO) of the United Nations: Rome, Italy, 2013.
50. Sillanpää, M. *Trace Elements in Soils and Agriculture*; Food and Agriculture Organisation (FAO) of the United Nations: Rome, Italy, 1972.
51. Cakmak, I. The role of potassium in alleviating detrimental effects of abiotic stresses in plants. *J. Plant Nutr. Soil Sci.* **2005**, *168*, 521–530. [CrossRef]

International Journal of
Environmental Research and Public Health

MDPI

Article

Contaminations of Soil and Two *Capsicum annuum* Generations Irrigated by Reused Urban Wastewater Treated by Different Reed Beds

Suhad A. A. N. Almuktar [1,2], Suhail N. Abed [1] and Miklas Scholz [1,3,4,*]

1 Civil Engineering Research Group, School of Computing, Science and Engineering, The University of Salford, Salford M5 4WT, UK; suhad.suhad81@yahoo.com (S.A.A.N.A.); suhail.najem@gmail.com (S.N.A.)
2 Department of Architectural Engineering, Faculty of Engineering, The University of Basrah, Al Basrah 61001, Iraq
3 Division of Water Resources Engineering, Department of Building and Environmental Technology, Faculty of Engineering, Lund University, P.O. Box 118, 22100 Lund, Sweden
4 Department of Civil Engineering Science, School of Civil Engineering and the Built Environment, University of Johannesburg, Kingsway Campus, P.O. Box 524, Aukland Park 2006, Johannesburg, South Africa
* Correspondence: miklas.scholz@tvrl.lth.se; Tel.: +46-46-22-28920

Received: 16 July 2018; Accepted: 17 August 2018; Published: 18 August 2018

Abstract: *Background*: In order to save potable water, this study aims to evaluate the contamination of soil and *Capsicum annuum* L. (chilli) watered with urban wastewater (sewage) pre-treated by various wetland systems. *Methods*: The appropriateness of wetland outflow for irrigation when applying reused wastewater with high contamination of minerals and pathogens was assessed. The impact of wastewaters pre-treated by various wetlands on soil and harvest was tested in terms of mineral and biological contamination risk. *Results*: The wetlands met the standards for irrigation water for most water quality variables. However, the thresholds for key water quality parameters were significantly ($p < 0.05$) exceeded. The highest values for total coliforms, ammonium-nitrogen, phosphorus and potassium were 157,072 CFU/100 mL, 8.5 mg/L, 5.0 mg/L, and 7.0 mg/L, respectively. The harvest was moderately polluted only by zinc according to vegetable quality standards (threshold of 50 mg/kg). Zinc concentrations for Filters 2, 4, 6, 7 and 8 were 35.8, 60.6, 65.1, 65.5 and 53.2 mg/kg, respectively. No bacterial contamination was detected. *Conclusions*: Treatment of domestic wastewater applying constructed wetlands and subsequent recycling of the treated wastewater for irrigation of crops is a good substitute to the traditional application of drinking water for irrigation purposes.

Keywords: constructed wetland; cultivar; ecological engineering; irrigation water quality; sewage treatment; sustainable development; zinc

1. Introduction

1.1. Background

Solutions for worldwide challenges including water and food scarcity as well as pollution of water are needed. In developing nations, there is much interest in using reused treated wastewater for producing food. Benefits related to wastewater reuse comprise the supply of trace minerals and nutrients to plants, possibly resulting in yield increases and a reduction in the inorganic fertilizer need. Nevertheless, there are numerous problems linked to irrigation with reused urban wastewater. For example, increase in soil salinity with soil permeability reduction as well as toxic element and nutrient accumulation within watered soil and plants [1,2]. Furthermore, the elevated microbial level in the wastewater may result in both reduced harvest and crop quality as well as crops potentially contaminated with microbes [3].

Constructed wetlands of various designs including horizontal-flow and vertical-flow systems can treat various types of wastewater [4–8]. The evaluation of the effect of recycling of treated wastewater on crops to be consumed by humans requires attention. In Italy, recycling of treated domestic wastewater using constructed wetlands for subsequent crop irrigation has been applied according to Cirelli et al. [9]. The research shows that the treated wastewater was linked to high levels of *Escherichia coli* that considerably exceeded the local standard (50 colony forming units (CFU) per 100 mL).

The assessment of reused urban wastewater effects on irrigated crop quality and soil properties was carried out by Aiello et al. [10]. The results indicated that the use of wastewater led to increasing microbial pollution on the irrigated soil surface (*E. coli*: 3000 most probable number (MPN) per 100 mL; faecal *Streptococci* spp.: 1200 MPN per 100 mL). The disturbed soil layer was of low porosity as well as of decreasing hydraulic conductivity and water retention.

Moreover, the application of wastewater on soil for the assessment of potential contamination with heavy metals was undertaken by Chary et al. [11]. Findings indicated relatively high zinc, chromium and copper concentrations linked to the irrigated soil, which was available for growing plants.

There is a need for research assessing the effect of various wetland designs (including aggregate composition and planting) on treating domestic wastewater for subsequent crop irrigation reuse. The pre-treated wastewater has to be safe for consumption and not lead to soil contamination.

1.2. Motivation, Aim and Objectives

The main motivation for this experiment is to evaluate the contamination of soil and plants concerning pathogens and minerals that may affect the human health due to consumption. This article is built on work formerly published by Almuktar et al. [12,13], Almuktar and Scholz [7,14] and Almuktar et al. [8] concentrating on growing chillies with success to obtain their seeds for producing a new cultivar used to domestic wastewater. Almuktar et al. [8] dealt with the growth of daughter plants compared to their mothers. However, this new paper is concerned with soil and fruit contamination of chilli daughter plants and also fills a gap in scientific knowledge regarding the use of wetland systems to treat wastewater for subsequent agricultural food production.

Therefore, this project aims to evaluate the pollution of soil and two chilli generations (mothers and daughters) in terms of minerals and microbes due to irrigation with wastewater treated via numerous wetland systems. The objectives of this study were to: (a) assess the treated wastewater long-term suitability for irrigation of plants, (b) evaluate the impact of different wetland designs, operations and management practices on treated wastewater used for watering soil and fruits, and (c) compare yield quality subject to mineral and biological pollution risk between mother and daughter (i.e., first generation of a new cultivar) plants.

2. Materials and Methods

2.1. Set-Up and Experimental Operation

The experimental system (Figure 1) tested follows a completely randomised design and has been described by Almuktar and Scholz [6,7,12,13]. The experiment ran between 27 June 2011 and 25 September 2015 to study the influence of aggregate size and inflow loading rate as well as contact time (time the treated wastewater is in contact with the substrate) and resting time (time the substrate is not in contact with the treated wastewater; i.e., air fills the empty space between aggregates). The impact of aggregate diameter was tested when comparing Filters 1 and 2 (20 mm) with Filters 3 and 4 (10 mm), respectively. All contact times were 72 h, except for Filters 7 and 8 (36 h). All resting times were 48 h, except for Filter 8 (24 h).

Figure 1. Experimental set-up of the experimental wetland system.

The COD loading rate was another design parameter. Undiluted wastewater represented the high inflow loading rate. Wastewater diluted by 50% was used for the low loading rate. The controls received just chlorinated tap water. Therefore, the mean chemical oxygen demand (COD) inflow concentrations for Filters 1 to 4, 5, 6, 7 and 8 as well as the controls were 123.3, 244.7, 244.7, 123.3, 123.3 and 2.3 mg/L, respectively. The corresponding annually treated volumes of wastewater were 470, 470, 470, 624, 858 and 470 L/a in this order.

The constructed wetland Pyrex tubes had an inner diameter and height of 19.5 cm and 120 cm, correspondingly. Inert pea gravel was used to fill the tubes up to a depth of 60 cm. The wetlands were planted with *Phragmites australis* (Cav.) Trin. ex Steud., which is also known as common reed. The cleaned wastewater was harvested from the tubes via an outlet valve at the bottom as described, previously [4,6,8,12,13]. The preliminary treated urban wastewater came from the Davyhulme Sewage works located in Greater Manchester. Aqua Medic Titan chillers (Aquacadabra, Bexleyheath, UK) kept the wetland rhizosphere at around 12 °C [4].

The mother chilli plants were established from seeds purchased from B&Q plc (Chandlers Ford, UK) with the product code 03623879 on 14 September 2013 (experiment No. 1). The subsequent daughter chilli plant generation (experiment No. 2) was obtained from experiment No. 1.

The seeds were initially planted in shallow trays between 16 September and 10 October 2013, and then replanted (second planting between 11 October–7 November 2013) in nursery pots. The third (final) planting took place between 8 November 2013 and 25 September 2014. The more mature chillies were transferred to 10-litre pots (Hedgehogs Nursery, Glenrothes, UK) with the following dimensions: height, 22.0 cm; bottom diameter, 22.0 cm; and top diameter, 28.5 cm. B&Q plc provided the compost (product code 03717644). The planting depth was 17.5 cm. The soil was topped by 2.5 cm of bark (B&Q verve range, product code 5397007188110). The basic raw soil (original soil from supplier before use) properties were as follows: pH of 6.43, total nitrogen 999 mg/kg, total phosphor 368 mg/kg, potassium 2776 mg/kg, zinc 26.59 mg/kg and organic matter 89%. Finally, irrigation waters were obtained from Filters 1 to 8 as well as from Controls A and B. Concerning the experiment

No. 2, the plants were grown in the compost using seeds randomly selected from the original mother plants obtained from experiment No. 1, which were irrigated with outflows from Filters 2, 4, 6, 7 and 8 only, because they had the best growth rate and yield quality [6,12–14].

The surface irrigation method was applied [1,15]. The soil moisture was constantly regulated using a graduated cylinder supplied by Fisher Scientific UK Ltd. (Loughborough, UK) according to Almuktar et al. [12,13] and Almuktar and Scholz [6,7]. The volume of treated waste water used for irrigating each plant was noted.

According to Almuktar et al. [12,13], a LUX meter ATP-DT-1300 (TIMSTAR, Winsford, UK) was used to regulate light. A thermometer-hygrometer-station supplied by wetterladen24.de (JM Handelspunkt, Geschwend, Germany) was applied to control temperature and humidity. The humidity was regulated using humidity meters (Challenge 3.0L Ultrasonic Humidifier; Argos, Central Milton Keynes, UK). Further details on the experimental methodology have been published by Almuktar et al. [8].

2.2. *Quality Analysis of Water, Soil and Plants*

All samples were tested according to APHA [16]. A Varian 720-ES Inductively Coupled Plasma—Optical Emission Spectrometer (ICP–OES; Agilent Technologies UK Ltd., Wokingham, UK) was applied to detect trace elements and nutrients in the samples [17]. A soil auger was used for soil sampling (to the depth of 20 cm) directly after the experiment. According to Chary et al. [11], the soil samples were assessed for mineral contents with the help of the Varian 720-ES Inductively Coupled Plasma—Optical Emission Spectrometer. Moreover, fruits were randomly selected for mineral content detection from each treatment after harvesting applying the Varian 720-ES Inductively Coupled Plasma—Optical Emission [18]. Faecal coliforms, total coliforms, faecal *Streptococcus* spp., *E. coli* and *Salmonella* spp. were detected for vegetables including flesh, skin and washing solution obtained from various spaces away from the irrigated soil as well as for the water and soil samples.

2.3. *Analysis of Data*

Microsoft Excel was used for simple analysis. The IBM-SPSS Statistics Version 23.0 software (IBM, Armonk, NY, USA) calculated 5% significance levels. The normality was checked applying the Shapiro-Wilk test. The independent *t*-test was used for normally distributed data. In contrast, non-normally distributed data were tested applying the Mann-Whitney U-test. The one-way analysis of variance and the Kruskal-Wallis H-test were applied for data that were normally and non-normally distributed, respectively. The Spearman's test helped with correlation studies.

3. Results and Discussion

3.1. *Overview Regarding Irrigation Water Quality*

3.1.1. Oxygen Demand Parameters

Table 1 indicates highest COD values for Filter 6 followed by Filter 8, and the lowest concentrations for Filter 7. Almuktar et al. [8] indicated no significant differences ($p > 0.05$) in COD values for Filters 2 and 4 compared to Filters 4 and 7 in this order. It follows that aggregate size and contact time did not really matter statistically with respect to COD removal. The COD values for Filters 7 and 4 were significantly ($p < 0.05$) different compared to the concentrations of Filters 8 and 6, correspondingly, explaining the impact of resting time and inflow loading rate.

The five-day biochemical oxygen demand (BOD) was the highest for Filter 6 followed by Filter 2. In comparison, Filter 7 had the lowest BOD. The BOD concentrations of Filters 2 and 4 were higher with respect to those of Filters 4 and 7, correspondingly. This showed the influence of aggregate size and contact time. Filter 7 had BOD values lower than those concerning Filter 8. This explains the impact of resting time. The BOD for Filter 6 was significantly ($p < 0.05$) higher compared to Filter 4 [8] supporting findings by Sani et al. [4], stating that high-load filters are commonly under-performing. The dissolved oxygen was highest for Filter 4 followed by Filters 8 and 7. In comparison, the Filters 2 and Filter 6 were deprived of oxygen. However, Almuktar et al. [8] did not reveal any significant differences between filters.

Table 1. Filter outflow (irrigation water for plants) water quality (mean ± standard deviation (number of samples)) compared to common standard values.

Filter	COD	BOD_5	DO	NH_4-N	NO_3-N
Filter 2	45.0 ± 18.14 (19)	18.9 ± 14.98 (41)	2.8 ± 1.56 (45)	4.6 ± 4.57 (23)	1.6 ± 2.06 (22)
Filter 4	43.3 ± 13.10 (18)	15.6 ± 15.10 (42)	3.1 ± 1.96 (44)	2.9 ± 2.86 (22)	0.4 ± 0.48 (21)
Filter 6	63.9 ± 36.81 (18)	29.4 ± 26.99 (41)	2.9 ± 1.53 (45)	8.5 ± 7.30 (24)	3.9 ± 3.57 (24)
Filter 7	42.2 ± 23.82 (16)	14.2 ± 12.76 (48)	3.1 ± 2.13 (46)	3.5 ± 4.23 (17)	4.0 ± 3.36 (15)
Filter 8	60.4 ± 34.41 (17)	17.2 ± 13.46 (53)	3.1 ± 2.39 (50)	1.6 ± 2.33 (18)	3.0 ± 2.29 (16)
Standards *	-	-	-	5.0	30.0
Filter	**PO_4-P**	**SS**	**NTU**	**pH**	**EC**
Filter 2	4.1 ± 1.47 (24)	12.1 ± 10.07 (53)	9.2 ± 8.07 (53)	6.6 ± 0.26 (52)	462.6 ± 146.89 (44)
Filter 4	3.7 ± 1.24 (23)	4.7 ± 6.25 (52)	3.5 ± 4.19 (51)	6.6 ± 0.28 (51)	483.4 ± 155 (43)
Filter 6	5.0 ± 2.01 (23)	11.0 ± 13.00 (53)	8.2 ± 9.05 (51)	6.8 ± 0.28 (52)	832.4 ± 298.17 (44)
Filter 7	4.3 ± 2.53 (19)	4.7 ± 8.16 (56)	3.8 ± 3.71 (55)	6.7 ± 0.32 (58)	582.9 ± 442.86 (44)
Filter 8	4.0 ± 2.09 (20)	3.1 ± 3.71 (56)	3.1 ± 2.76 (55)	6.6 ± 0.38 (61)	584.1 ± 459.11 (47)
Standards *	2.0			6.5-8.4	3000

Note: COD, chemical oxygen demand (mg/L); BOD_5, biochemical oxygen demand (mg/L); DO, dissolved oxygen (mg/l); NH_4-N, ammonia-nitrogen (mg/L); NO_3-N, nitrate-nitrogen (mg/L); PO_4-P, orthophosphate-phosphorus (mg/L); SS, suspended solids (mg/L); NTU, turbidity (NTU); EC, electrical conductivity (μS/cm); * Common standards such as FAO [1].

3.1.2. Irrigation Water Nutrients and Trace Elements

The highest ammonium-nitrogen values were recorded for Filter 6 followed by Filters 2 and 7 (Table 1). In comparison, the lowest values were linked to Filter 8 followed by Filter 4. Filter 2 concentrations were significantly ($p < 0.05$) higher than those for Filter 4 (Table 1 and [8]) showing the influence of aggregate diameter and nitrogen transformation processes. Ammonium-nitrogen values for Filter 4 were lower than for Filter 7, while the latter outflow water had ammonium-nitrogen concentrations significantly ($p < 0.05$) higher compared to those for Filter 8. This indicates a great impact of both contact and resting times on ammonium. Elevated COD inflow water led to significant ($p < 0.05$) differences between the ammonium-nitrogen concentrations between Filters 4 and 6 [8], indicating that high-load filters are underperforming [4]. High ammonium-nitrogen concentrations above standard thresholds were noted for Filter 6 (high inflow loading rate), impacting negatively on plant fruit, leaf and growth [8,19].

High nitrate-nitrogen concentrations were linked to Filter 6 and low ones to Filter 4 (Table 1). Almuktar et al. [8] indicated that nitrate-nitrogen values were significantly ($p < 0.05$) greater for Filter 2 in comparison to Filter 4. This can be explained by different aggregate diameters. Significant differences ($p < 0.05$) in nitrate-nitrogen outflows of Filters 4 and 7 were recorded. This can be explained by the influence of contact time. Filters with a higher inflow loading rate had nitrate-nitrogen concentrations that were significantly ($p < 0.05$) greater compared to those subjected to diluted inflow (i.e., Filter 4 compared to Filter 6) as shown previously by Sani et al. [4].

Nitrate-nitrogen for all filter outflows was below the threshold of 30 mg/ L [1,20]. The total yield increases as the nitrate-nitrogen to ammonium-nitrogen ratio elevates. This can be explained by a reduction in fruit physiological disorders decreasing fruit weights [19].

The highest orthophosphate-phosphorus concentrations were noted for Filter 6 followed by Filter 7. In contrast, the lowest corresponding concentrations were obtained for Filter 4 (Table 1). Filter 2 had orthophosphate-phosphorus concentrations higher than those for Filter 4 (Table 1). This can be explained by a lower removal rate due to less active biomass within the spaces between aggregates. Filter 4 had lower orthophosphate-phosphorus concentrations than Filter 7. However,

Filter 7 had concentrations higher than the ones for Filter 8 due to the influences of different wetland contact and resting times on orthophosphate-phosphorus concentrations.

Irrigation water linked to Filter 6 had orthophosphate-phosphorus concentrations that were significantly ($p < 0.05$) higher compared to those of Filter 4 [8]. This can be explained by the impact of the inflow loading rate on orthophosphate-phosphorus, which is difficult to remove [5,19,21]. Compared to the standard threshold of 2 mg/ L, all recycled outflow waters had orthophosphate-phosphorus values exceeding the threshold [1,20]. Findings indicate that phosphorus deficiency limits crop yields and enhances the uptake of manganese [22,23].

An ICP—OES analysis for the irrigation water based on a sample number of 15 has been performed, previously [8]. Elements such as arsenic, barium, bismuth, cadmium, cobalt, chromium, copper, nickel, lead, strontium and titanium were below the detection limits. High iron for Filter 7 followed by Filter 6 was noted. The lowest concentrations were recorded for Filter 4. In comparison, Filter 2 had iron values higher than those for Filter 4. This can be explained by the impact of wetland aggregate diameter on the removal of iron. Filters 4 and 7 had iron concentrations significantly ($p < 0.05$) different from those of Filters 7 and 8, respectively [8], indicating the impacts of contact and resting times on iron removal. Filter 6 had iron values that were significantly ($p < 0.05$) higher than those of Filter 4 [8]. However, all concentrations were below the threshold of 5.0 mg/ L [1,20].

Iron is removed by oxidative processes and iron hydroxide creation [24,25]. However, biotic processes involving bacteria in iron oxidation can also be important [25]. Oxygen and pH are essential variables for iron removal processes influenced by photosynthesis.

Magnesium concentrations were highest for Filter 7 followed by Filter 6. Low numbers were observed for Filter 2. Filter 4 had manganese concentrations, which were significantly ($p < 0.05$) lower compared to Filter 7. Moreover, Filter 7 values were significantly ($p < 0.05$) higher than those for Filter 8, highlighting the impact of both contact and resting times on manganese reductions. An elevated loading rate significantly ($p < 0.05$) impacted on the outflow water iron concentration. This can be seen when comparing Filter 4 to 6 (Supplementary Materials Table S1). Manganese concentrations were usually below the corresponding threshold of 0.2 mg/ L [1,20].

Manganese reductions are due to oxygenic photosynthesis particularly during summer. However, iron should be removed first to support manganese elimination [25]. High manganese values are linked to low plant growth [26]. Manganese phyto-toxicity reduces biomass and photosynthesis [27].

Zinc within irrigation waters was highest for Filter 6 followed by Filter 2. The lowest concentrations were linked to Filter 4. However, Almuktar et al. [8] indicated that there were no significant differences in zinc concentrations associated with different aggregate diameters, contact times, resting times and inflow loading rates [6,7], complementing similar results published elsewhere [28]. All zinc outflow concentrations were below the standard of 2.0 mg/ L [1,20].

The highest boron concentrations for Filter 6 were followed by Filter 2. In comparison, the lowest boron concentrations were noted for Filter 7. Nevertheless, Almuktar et al. [8] showed no significant ($p > 0.05$) differences for boron concerning all wetlands [6,7]. Moreover, all boron concentrations were lower than the standard of 0.75 mg/L [1,15].

Filters 6 and 4 had the highest and lowest potassium values, respectively. Filter 2 (large aggregates) had potassium concentrations greater than those for Filter 4 (small aggregates). Filter 7 had potassium values greater than those for Filters 4 and 8 due to differences in contact and resting time in this order. This can be explained by the influence of aggregate diameter, contact time and resting time on potassium removal [6,7]. Wetlands with undiluted wastewater had potassium concentrations that were significantly ($p < 0.05$) greater than those of diluted inflow (e.g., comparison between Filters 6 and 4). This observation agrees with the literature [4] highlighting that filters of elevated inflow loading rate are commonly overloaded. All outflows exceeded the potassium threshold of 2.0 mg/L [1,15].

Relatively high potassium concentrations protect plant stems from damage during cold nights [29]. Furthermore, frost reduces the harvest and increases leaf damage, which can be addressed by increasing the potassium concentrations in the irrigation waters. Furthermore, elevated potassium lowers seedling death rates during cold periods [29].

Sodium values were highest for Filter 6 followed by Filter 7, and lowest for Filter 8. Drain waters from Filters 2, 4, 7 and 8 had rather similar concentrations. Almuktar et al. [8] indicated that there were significantly ($p < 0.05$) lower values for Filter 4 compared to Filter 6, because of differences in terms of the inflow loading rate [4]. All wetland sodium concentrations were below the standard of 920 mg/ L [1,20].

Calcium values were highest for Filter 6 followed by Filter 4. In contrast, the lowest concentrations were recorded for Filter 2. Filter 2 (large gravel) had calcium concentrations lower than the values for Filter 4 (small gravel). Moreover, Filter 4 had calcium values higher than those for Filter 7 due to different contact times. Filter 4 was fed with diluted wastewater, and had calcium values lower than those for Filter 6 (high inflow load). All irrigation waters had calcium values lower than the threshold of 400 mg/ L [1,20].

The highest magnesium concentrations were associated with Filter 6 and the lowest ones with Filter 8. Almuktar et al. [8] showed that Filter 6 had magnesium values, which were significantly ($p < 0.05$) higher compared to those obtained from Filter 4. All irrigation waters had values that were below the standard of 60 mg/ L for magnesium [1,20]. The removal can be explained by processes such as sorption by sediment, adsorption, complexation, cation and anion exchange, oxidation and reduction, chemical precipitation, co- precipitation as insoluble salts and phyto-accumulation as well as microbial and plant uptake [30–33].

3.1.3. Particles, pH and Salinity

The highest suspended solids and turbidity values were noted for Filter 2 followed by Filter 6 (Table 1). In contrast, lowest numbers were noted for Filter 8. Irrigation waters obtained from Filter 2 had suspended solids and turbidity values that were significantly ($p < 0.05$) greater than those for Filter 4 [8]. This is due to the impact of wetland aggregate size on processes such as filtration [4]. Filter 7 had suspended solids and turbidity values greater than those of Filter 8. This can be explained by differences in resting time. The loading rate significantly ($p < 0.05$) impacted on the particle content (e.g., Filter 6 compared to Filter 4 [8]).

High suspended solids and turbidity increase soil hydrophobicity [6,7,12,13,33]. Previous studies [34–37] indicated that solids can be removed via sedimentation, settling, adsorption and biological degradation processes. Furthermore, in surface flow systems, suspended solids may be reduced via flocculation, sedimentation and filtration processes [38]. Suspended solids also interact with heavy metals, nutrients, pathogens and organic matter, which lead to combined removal processes [39]. In sub-surface vertical-flow constructed wetlands, substrate, hydraulic load and microorganisms determine solids removal [40].

Recorded pH values were normal [1,20]. Filter 6 had the highest pH values followed by Filter 7. In contrast, the lowest numbers were recorded for Filter 2 (Table 1). Almuktar et al. [8] showed that there were significant ($p < 0.05$) differences in pH recordings of outflow waters subject to contact time, resting time and the inflow loading rate.

The pH commonly impacts on nitrogen and organic matter removal. The reduction of alkalinity during nitrification will lead to a drop in pH, which affects the denitrification rate [34]. The optimum pH for denitrification ranges from 6 to 8. The highest rate has commonly been observed at a pH value between 7.0 and 7.5 [41].

Electrical conductivity correlates well with salinity [15]. The highest conductivity was noted for Filter 6 followed by Filter 8 (Table 1). In contrast, the lowest numbers were recorded for Filter 2. Filter 6 had salinity values that were significantly ($p < 0.05$) greater than those for Filter 4. This is due to overloading [4]. Nevertheless, all recorded salinity values were below the standard of 3000 μS/cm [1,20]. An elevated electrical conductivity results in saline soil, which is negative for plant growth, soil structure and soil permeability [42].

3.1.4. Microbial Indicators within the Irrigation Water

The key indicators of microbial contamination detected in the irrigation water have been discussed, previously [8]. The highest total coliform recordings are associated with Filter 6 followed by Filter 2. The lowest ones were noted for Filter 8. Filter 4 had total coliform numbers that were significantly ($p < 0.05$) different from the ones for Filters 6 and 7 [8]. Differences in filter loading rate and contact time are responsible for this observation. Filter 7 had total coliforms higher than those for Filter 8, explaining the impact of resting time on the wetland system. All irrigation waters exceeded the standard of 1000 CFU per 100 mL [43].

Escherichia coli contamination followed this order: Filter 6 > Filter 2 > Filter 8 [8]. Irrigation water harvested from Filter 2 (large aggregates) had *E. coli* values (71 CFU per 100 mL) greater than those (0 CFU per 100 mL) for Filter 4 (small aggregates). Filter 6 had *E. coli* numbers (5572 CFU per 100 mL) greater than those (0 CFU per100 mL) for Filter 4. Furthermore, Filter 8 (long resting period) had *E. coli* numbers (59 CFU per 100 mL) higher than those for Filter 7 (0 CFU per 100 mL) of short resting periods. Filters 4 and 7 were not contaminated by *E. coli*, which was not expected [9].

Salmonella spp. counts were high for Filter 6 followed by Filter 2 [8]. The lowest numbers were recorded for Filter 7. Filter 4 counts were significantly ($p < 0.05$) higher compared to Filter 7 [8] indicating the influence of contact and resting times on microbial contamination. Furthermore, Filter 6 had significantly ($p < 0.05$) higher counts than Filter 4 due to different loading rates [8], which confirms previous findings [4,14].

Wetlands with large aggregate diameters had higher *Salmonella* spp. counts than those with small aggregates. This is due to large aggregate diameters permitting more organisms to colonies the space between stones [6,7,14].

3.2. *Analysis of Soil Quality*

3.2.1. pH and Redox Potential Comparison

Figure 2 illustrates qualities for soils irrigated with wastewater treated by wetland filters. Ten soil samples were tested. All soil pH values showed acidic conditions, impacting on plant trace element uptake [1,23]. Supplementary Materials Table S2 indicates that compared with raw soil (pH = 6.2), irrigation with pre-treated wastewater did not cause significant ($p < 0.05$) changes with the exception of soil irrigated with Filter 4 outflow, which showed the highest pH values of 6.7 tailed by those of Filter 2 (pH = 6.4), while minimum values were reported for soils watered with Filter 6 effluent showing a pH value of 6.0.

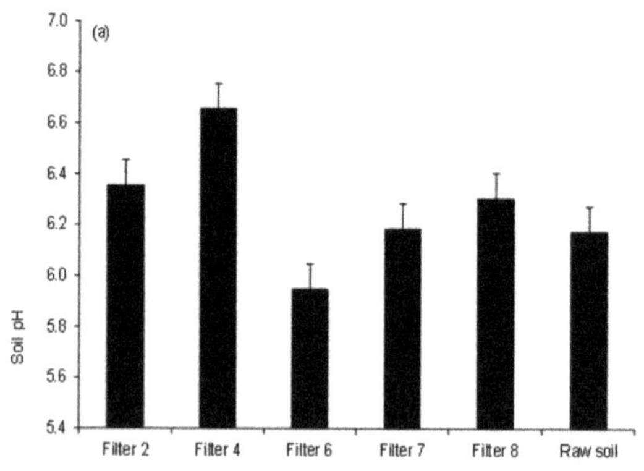

Figure 2. *Cont.*

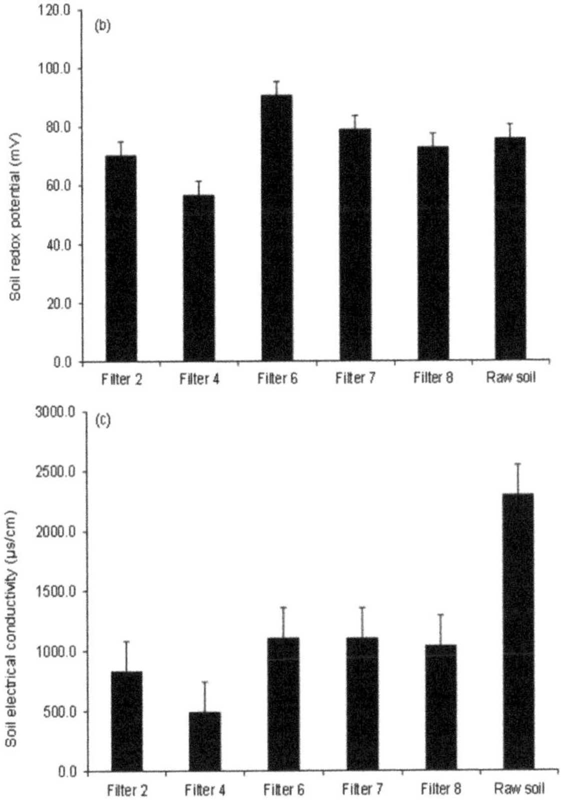

Figure 2. Soil qualities subject to irrigation water: (**a**) pH; (**b**) redox potential, and (**c**) electrical conductivity.

Furthermore, irrigation with Filter 4 drain water showed pH values that were significantly ($p < 0.05$) greater compared to those for Filters 2, 6 and 7, while no significant differences ($p > 0.05$) were observed, if pH values of soil watered with Filters 7 and 8 drain waters are compared with each other. However, all soil pH entries were within the optimal range of from 6.0 to 7.5 for growth of many plants and soil microbes [1,23].

Regarding soil redox potential values, soil can be classified as moderately reduced soil (+100 to +400 mV), reduced soil (−100 to +100 mV) and highly reduced soil (−100 to −300 mV), according to Husson [44]. Figure 2 indicates that all soil could be interpreted as reduced. The highest redox potentials were noted for soils watered with Filter 6 effluent followed by those linked to Filter 7 showing values of 90.8 mV and 79.1 mV, respectively, while the lowest values were associated with soils irrigated with water harvested from Filter 4 (redox potential value of 56.8 mV). Results showed that irrigation with treated wastewaters did not change soil redox potential values significantly ($p > 0.05$) compared with the raw soil (Supplementary Materials Table S2).

Moreover, soils watered with Filter 4 effluent showed redox potential values that were significantly different ($p < 0.05$) from those of Filters 2, 6 and 7, while no dissimilarities ($p > 0.05$) were calculated when making a comparison between redox potential values of soil watered with Filter 7 with those corresponding ones linked to Filter 8. High redox potentials can impact on the health of plants [43]. Furthermore, correlation analysis results showed that both pH and redox potential values were significantly negatively ($R = -0.986$, $p < 0.001$) correlated with each other, as reported by FAO [23] and Essington [45].

3.2.2. Soil Salinity Comparison

Figure 2 shows that irrigation with pre-treated wastewater did not result in an increase of the soil salinity, if compared to the raw soil. However, among the irrigated soils, application of outflow water from Filter 6 (high inflow loading) resulted in the highest electrical conductivity value of 1108 µS/cm, while soil linked to Filter 4 showed the lowest value of 493.8 µS/ cm. Moreover, salinity values for soil irrigated with Filters 2 and 7 effluents were greater than those of Filters 4 and 8, respectively. Irrigation with Filters 6 and 7 effluents resulted in soil salinity values, which were significantly ($p < 0.05$) greater than those for Filter 4 (Supplementary Materials Table S2), highlighting the impact of wetland system design in terms of both contact time and inflow loading rate on the salinity of the outflow water (Table 1). Furthermore, correlation analysis results showed that soil electrical conductivity values were significantly negatively correlated with soil pH values ($R = -0.899$, $p = 0.015$). For example, in acidic conditions of low pH value, the dissolution of elements such as calcium, potassium, sodium and magnesium will increase resulting in elevated soil salinity. However, excessive soil salinity could result in nutrient imbalances [1,23].

3.2.3. Soil Microbes

Figure 3 shows that total coliforms were detected with the highest values in the soil watered with Filter 6 effluent (4818 CFU/g) followed by those linked to Filter 4 showing a value of 3846 CFU/g. *Streptococci* spp. and *E. coli* were not detected in the tested soils. Ten soil samples were analyzed. The lowest values were associated with soils irrigated with Filter 8 (2000 CFU/g). Supplementary Materials Table S2 highlights that soil watered with Filter 4 effluent had total coliform colonies significantly ($p < 0.05$) higher than those soils irrigated with Filters 2 and 7 effluents, showing the impact of stone diameter and contact time of the filter on outflow water total coliforms and subsequently on the irrigated soils. Irrigation with outflow water from an undiluted inflow wetland filter significantly ($p < 0.05$) increased soil total coliform levels compared with those of diluted inflow wastewater as shown when comparing soils irrigated with Filter 6 with those irrigated with Filter 4 effluent (Supplementary Materials Table S2).

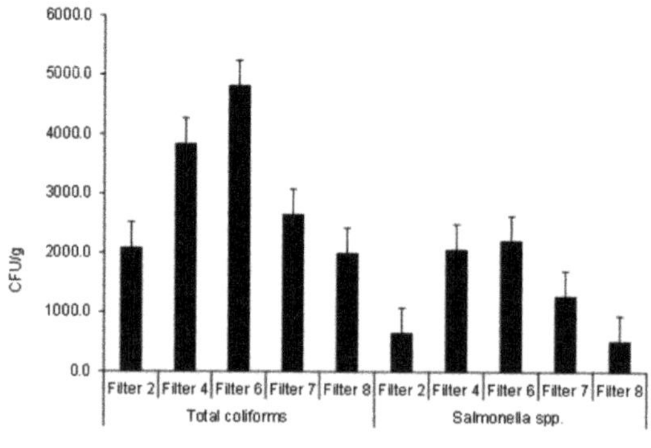

Figure 3. Soil microbial content.

Similar to the total coliform development, Figure 3 shows that the highest *Salmonella* colonies were detected in soil watered with Filter 6 followed by those irrigated with the effluent of Filter 4, showing values of 2214 CFU/g and 2062 CFU/g, respectively. The lowest values were noted for soils irrigated with Filer 8 outflow water (524 CFU/g). Statistically, soil watered with water drained from Filter 2 of large aggregate size had *Salmonella* counts significantly ($p < 0.05$) lower than those linked to Filter 4 of small aggregate diameter, in spite of their high abundancy in the outflow waters of the former [8]. Significant differences ($p < 0.05$) in irrigated soil *Salmonella* counts were also observed when comparing soils associated with Filters 4 and 7 with those of Filters 7 and 8, respectively, due to differences in contact time and resting time design variables for the corresponding filters in the wetland system (see above). Correlation analysis findings indicated that both total coliforms and *Salmonellae* were significantly positively correlated with each other ($R = 0.954$ and p value of less than 0.001), confirming results reported by Almuktar and Scholz [14]. The survival time of soil bacteria in crops and water is less than 70, 30 and 60 days in this order [46].

3.2.4. Soil Aluminum

The solubility of aluminum is influenced by pH, organic compounds and clay content of the soil. When the soil pH decreases, exchangeable aluminum will instantly increase. The findings showed that watering with wetland treatment system drain water significantly ($p < 0.05$) increased aluminum levels, if compared to the raw soil (Figure 4 and Supplementary Materials Table S2) due to its rather low biological availability [47]. Concerning Figure 4, the sample number was 24. Note that other elements such as arsenic, barium, bismuth, cadmium, chromium, cobalt, copper, nickel, lead, strontium and titanium were below the detection limit. Results showed that the maximum aluminum concentrations were detected in soil watered with Filter 8 (followed by Filter 6) effluent, while minimum values were recorded for soils irrigated from waters obtained from Filters 4 and 7. Filter 4 outflow water irrigation resulted in mean aluminum concentrations lower than those for soils linked to Filters 2 and 6, showing the impact of wetland filter aggregate diameter and inflow loading rate on outflow water aluminum concentrations and subsequently on its levels in the watered soil. Furthermore, soils watered with Filter 7 drain water had aluminum values, which were significantly ($p < 0.05$) lower than those for Filter 8 (Figure 4 and Supplementary Materials Table S2), probably due to the difference in applied volumes of irrigation water [8]. Correlation analysis results (Supplementary Materials Table S3) show that aluminum concentrations in the irrigated soil were significantly ($p < 0.001$) positively correlated with calcium, iron, potassium, magnesium, manganese and zinc values, while adversely correlated with boron levels in the soil, as informed by Essington [45].

3.2.5. Soil Zinc

Figure 4 indicates that maximum zinc values were recorded for the soil watered with water drained from Filters 2 and 7. In comparison, minimum concentrations were noted for those soils watered with Filter 6 effluent. Compared to the raw soil, no significant ($p > 0.05$) increase in the irrigated soil zinc levels were noted (Supplementary Materials Table S2). Irrigation with outflow water from Filter 2 (large stones) caused higher soil zinc values compared to those soils watered with from Filter 4 (small stones) as can be seen in Figure 4. Moreover, soils watered with effluents from Filters 4 and 7 had zinc levels, which were dissimilar from those linked to Filters 7 and 8, correspondingly, because of differences in their contact time and resting time variables of the systems (see above). However, no significant differences ($p < 0.05$) in mean soil zinc concentrations among soils irrigated with differently treated wastewaters were noted (Supplementary Materials Table S2). These results indicate the effect of wetland system design variables on the treated water zinc concentrations [8] leading to differences in the distribution of this element in the irrigated soils. Zinc concentrations in the irrigated soil were significantly ($p < 0.001$) positively correlated with calcium, iron, potassium, magnesium, manganese and aluminum values (Supplementary Materials Table S3), while negatively correlated with boron levels in the soil [45]. Nonetheless, concentrations of zinc in watered soil were below the threshold of 300 mg/kg [48].

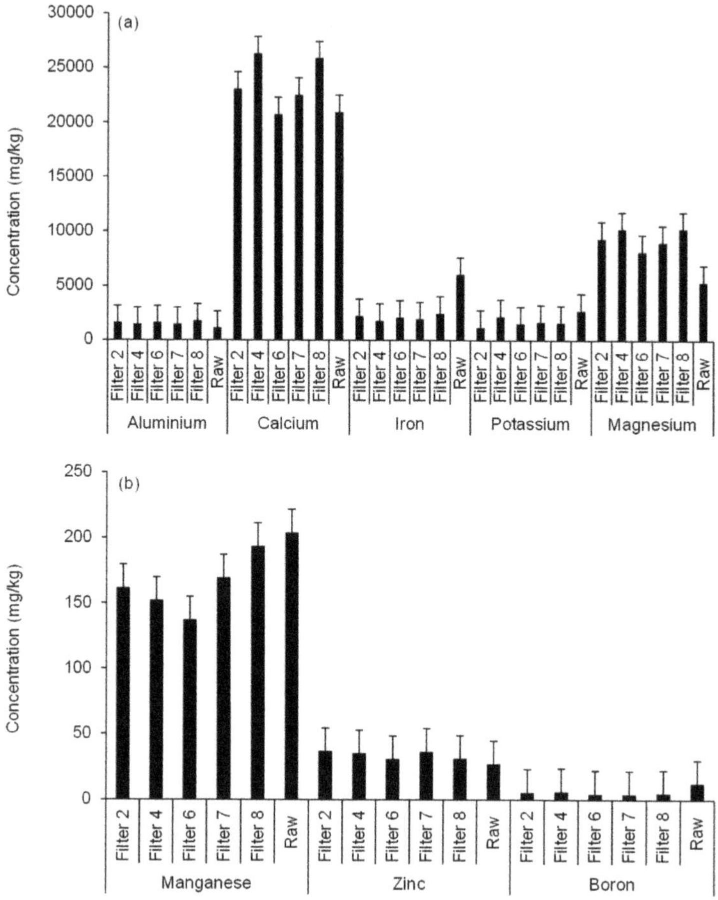

Figure 4. Inductively coupled plasma optical emission spectrometer analysis for elements in the irrigated soil: (**a**) aluminum, calcium, iron, potassium and magnesium; and (**b**) manganese, zinc and boron.

3.2.6. Soil Boron

There are numerous factors that may affect boron soil availability like soil texture, nature of the soil minerals, source of the irrigation water, organic matter content, soil pH, environmental conditions (mainly high light intensity and dry weather) and the relationships of boron with other elements [23]. Figure 4 illustrates that the maximum boron concentrations were detected in soil watered with Filter 4 followed by Filter 2 effluent. Minimum concentrations were reported for soil watered with effluent from Filter 7. In comparison with raw soil, watering with treated wastewaters did not elevate the soil boron levels (Figure 4). Findings indicate no significant ($p < 0.05$) differences in irrigated soil boron values (Supplementary Materials Table S2). However, soil watered with effluent from Filter 4 had higher boron concentrations compared to those soils watered with Filters 2, 6 and 7 outflows. Also, soils watered with Filter 7 drain water had boron levels lower than those watered with effluent from Filter 8. This indicates the effect of wetland system design variables on treated water boron concentrations [8], which caused differences in the element distribution, when applied to soils. Correlation analysis (Supplementary Materials Table S3) showed that boron concentrations in the soil correlated negatively with other elements in the soil, as discussed by Essington [45].

3.2.7. Other Elements

Refer to Almuktar et al. [8] concerning total element masses in general and calcium, iron, potassium, magnesium and manganese contaminants in particular, which are usually not a problem in soil.

3.3. *Chilli (First Generation) Microbial and Mineral Contents*

3.3.1. Overview

Harvested chillies (both skin and flesh) as well as the corresponding washing solution were free from microbial contamination. This is due to the relative long distance between the potentially contaminated soil and the harvested fruits [9]. This confirms previous results [14]. Regarding chilli mineral contamination, Figure 5 and Supplementary Materials Table S4 show the detected element concentrations in chillies obtained from first generation plants and the associated statistical analysis results, respectively. The bioavailability of each element was indicated by calculating the concentration factor (CF) value. This factor, as a percentage, is defined as the relationship between element concentration in the plant organ and its concentration in the soil [49] as shown in Equation (1):

$$CF = 100^{*}\ (C\ \text{fruit}\ C\ \text{soil}^{-1}) \quad (1)$$

where CF is concentration factor (%), C fruit is the element concentration in the fruit (mg/kg), and C soil is the element concentration in the soil (mg/kg)

Findings showed that the CF values in the chillies followed the order potassium > boron > zinc > magnesium > manganese > calcium > iron, with percentage values of 3819, 314, 169, 30, 14, 3 and 1, respectively. More details on fruit element content are shown below.

3.3.2. Aluminum

The solubility of aluminum depends on the soil pH and its content in terms of clay and organic material. Figure 5 shows that aluminum was not observed in any of the harvested fruits from the first generation plants watered with different water types [6]. According to Husson [44], aluminum concentrations can be increased at low pH. Findings indicated that an abundancy of aluminum was detected in the irrigated soils (Figure 4). Despite of this, the transfer of aluminum to the tissue of fruits was limited. This is possibly due to the great abundance of calcium (see below) in the watered soil, which limited aluminum transportation to the plants [23]. Regarding human health, Stahl et al. [47] showed that there is no risk linked to the presence of too much aluminum due to its low bioavailability [50].

3.3.3. Calcium

Figure 5 indicates that maximum calcium values were detected in fruits obtained from chillies watered with Filter 8 effluent, trailed by those irrigated with Filter 6 harvested water. On the other hand, minimum calcium concentrations were noted for the fruits of chillies watered with Filter 2 effluent. However, calcium levels in all tested chilli fruits (except for those of Filters 2 and 4) were above 45 mg per 100 g [51]. Supplementary Materials Table S4 shows that plants watered with Filter 2 (large stones) drain water produced chillies of calcium concentrations, which were similar to those associated with Filter 4 (small stones). Moreover, irrigation with the effluent of the high-load Filter 6 resulted in fruit calcium concentrations, which were significantly ($p < 0.05$) greater than those associated with Filter 4 (subjected to diluted wastewater) as shown in the Supplementary Materials Table S4. Furthermore, chillies linked to Filter 7 had calcium concentrations that were significantly ($p < 0.05$) different from those linked to Filters 4 and 8. No significant ($p > 0.05$) correlation was calculated for calcium values between soil and fruits (Figure 6a).

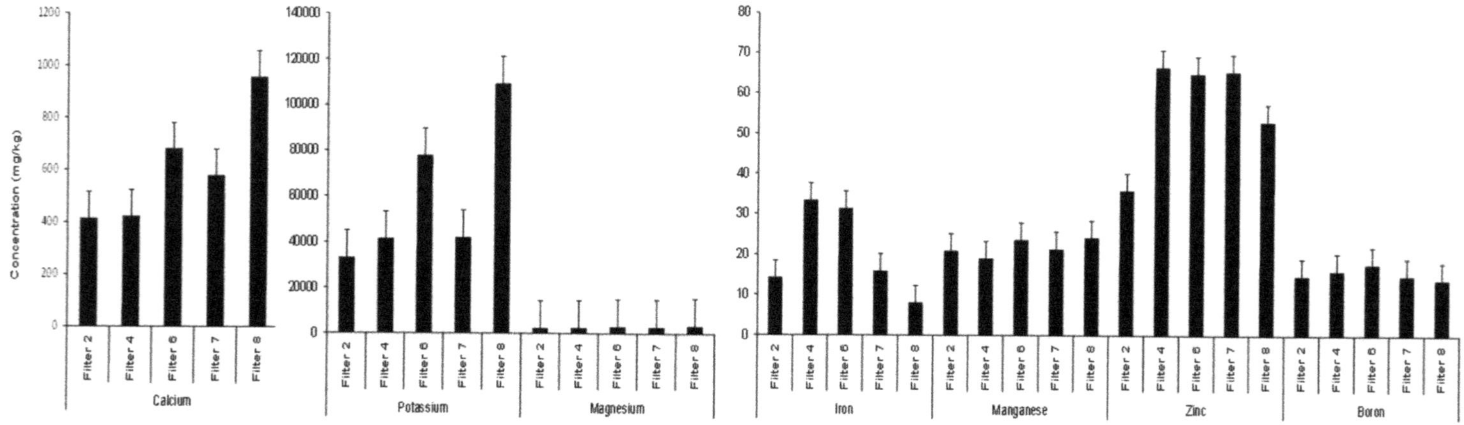

Figure 5. Elemental analysis within harvested chili daughter generations.

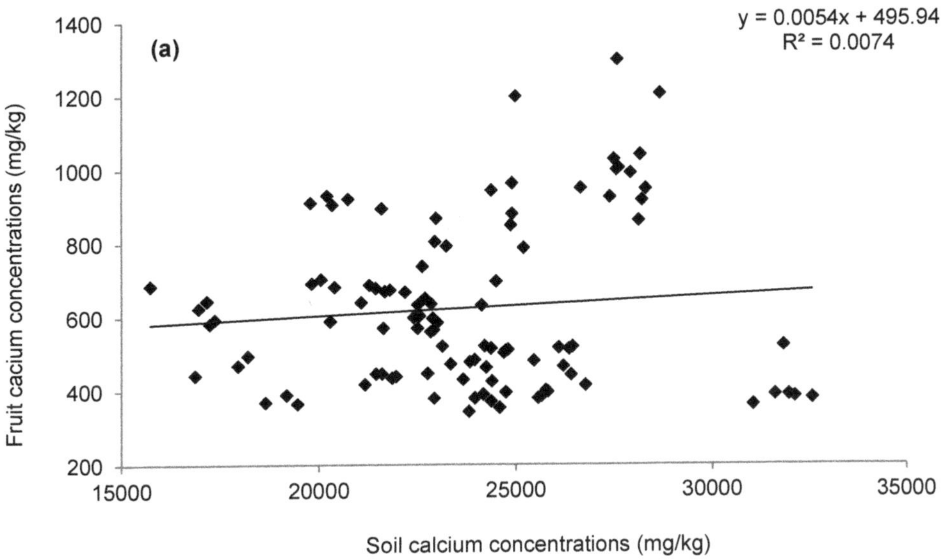

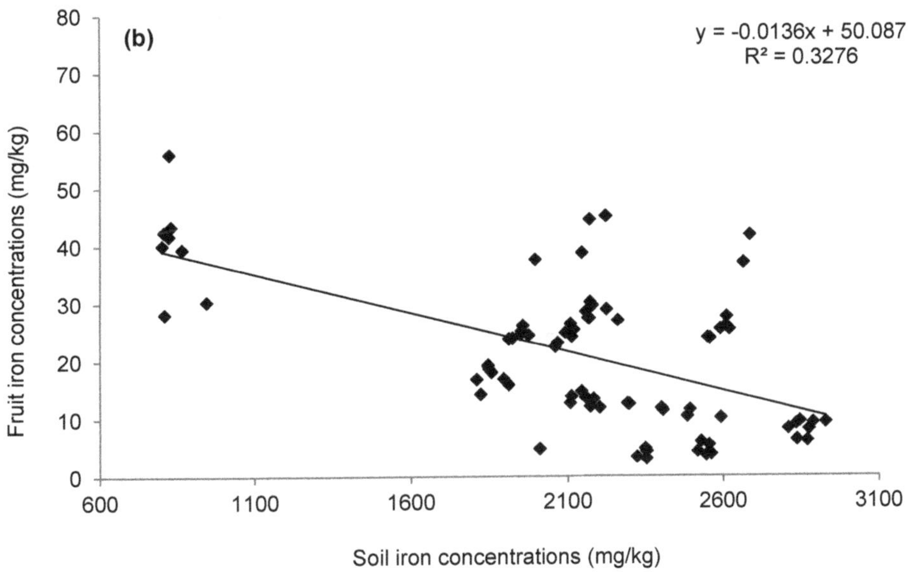

Figure 6. *Cont.*

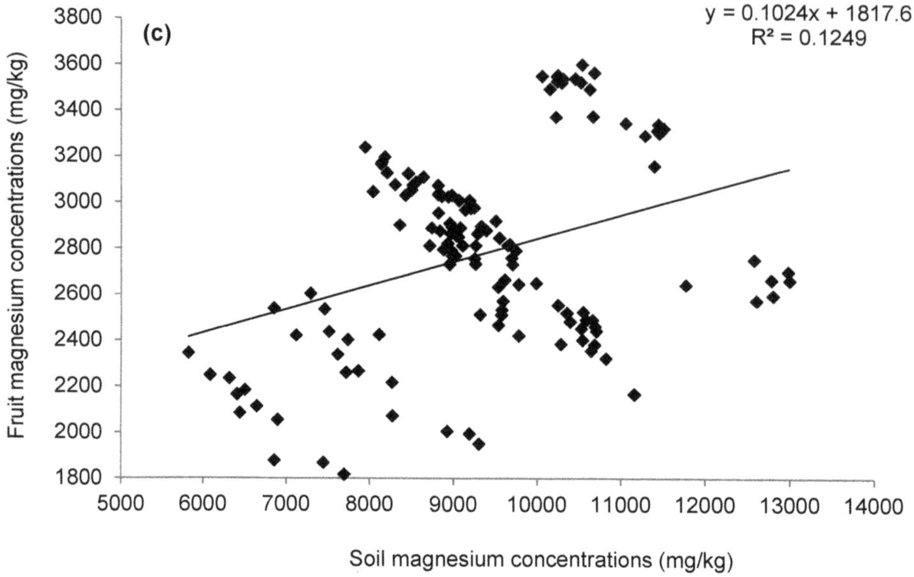

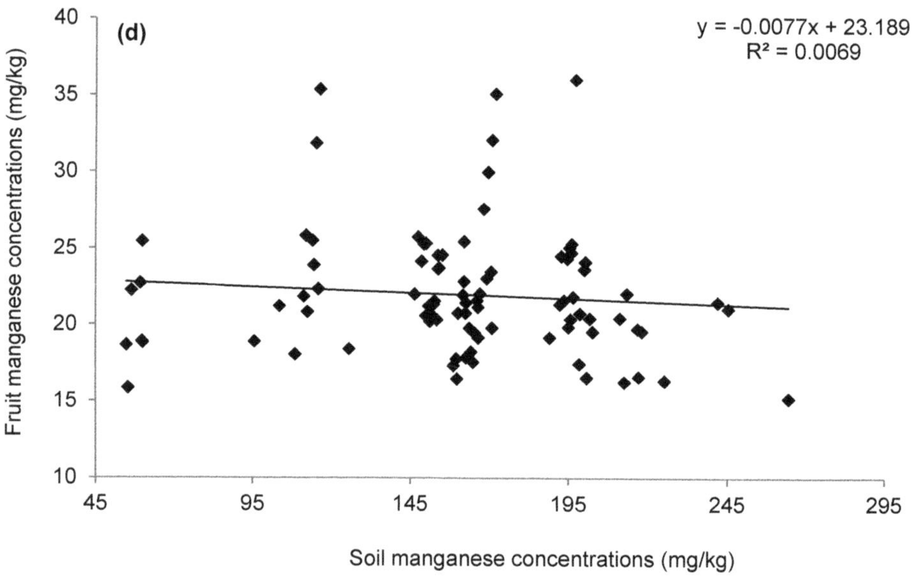

Figure 6. *Cont.*

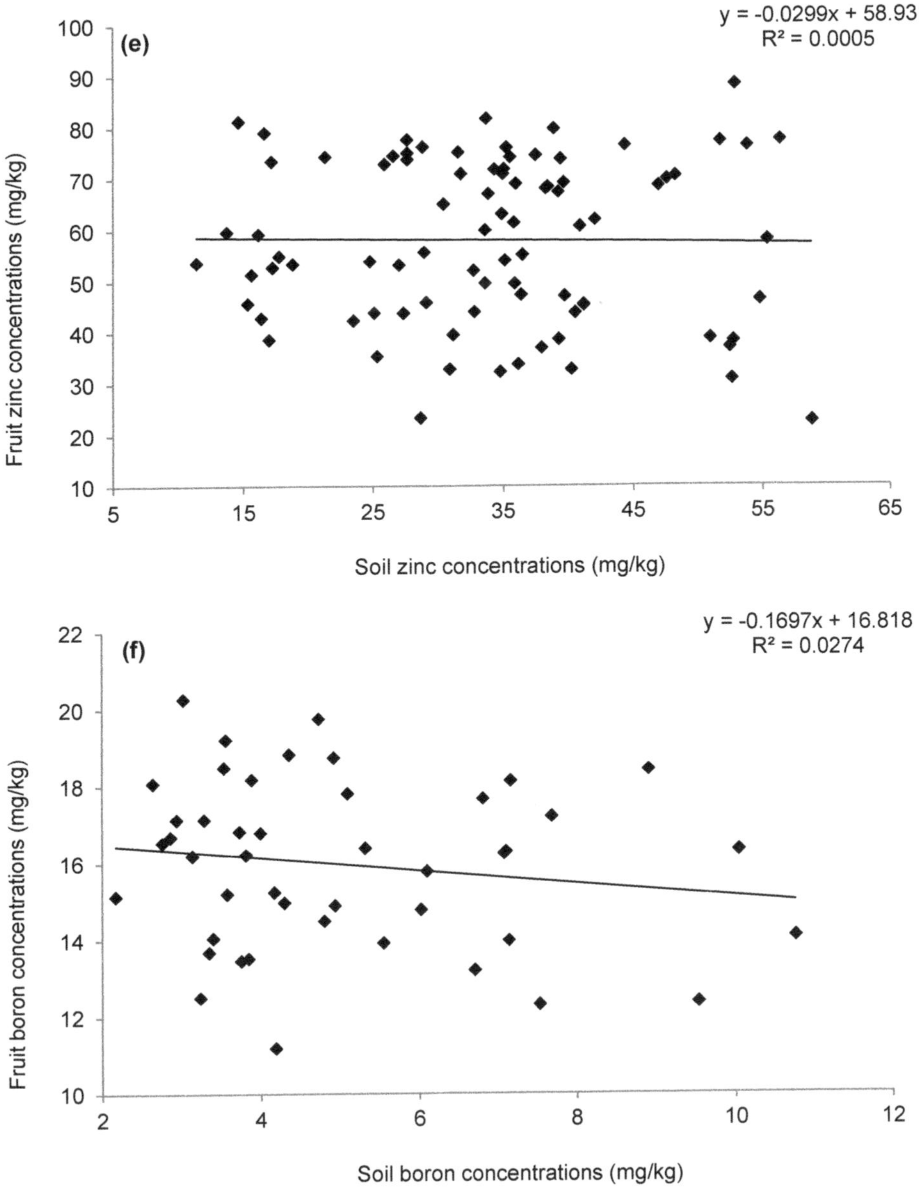

Figure 6. Influence of soil on fruits concerning the elements (**a**) calcium; (**b**) iron, (**c**) magnesium, (**d**) manganese, (**e**) zinc, and (**f**) boron.

Moreover, the calcium CF in the tested fruits had this order: Filter 8 > Filter 6 > Filter 7 > Filter 2 > Filter 4 with percentages of 3.7%, 3.3%, 2.6%, 1.8% and 1.6%, respectively. Compared with their mothers, the first chilli generation fruits had calcium concentrations that were significantly ($p < 0.05$) less (Supplementary Materials Table S4 and Figure 7a), explaining the impact of higher irrigation water amounts applied to mother plants than those used for the first generation plants [8]. However, calcium in the soil competes with other major cations such as sodium, potassium, magnesium, ammonium, iron, and aluminum for the uptake by crops [23]. High potassium loads lower the calcium uptake in plants [52].

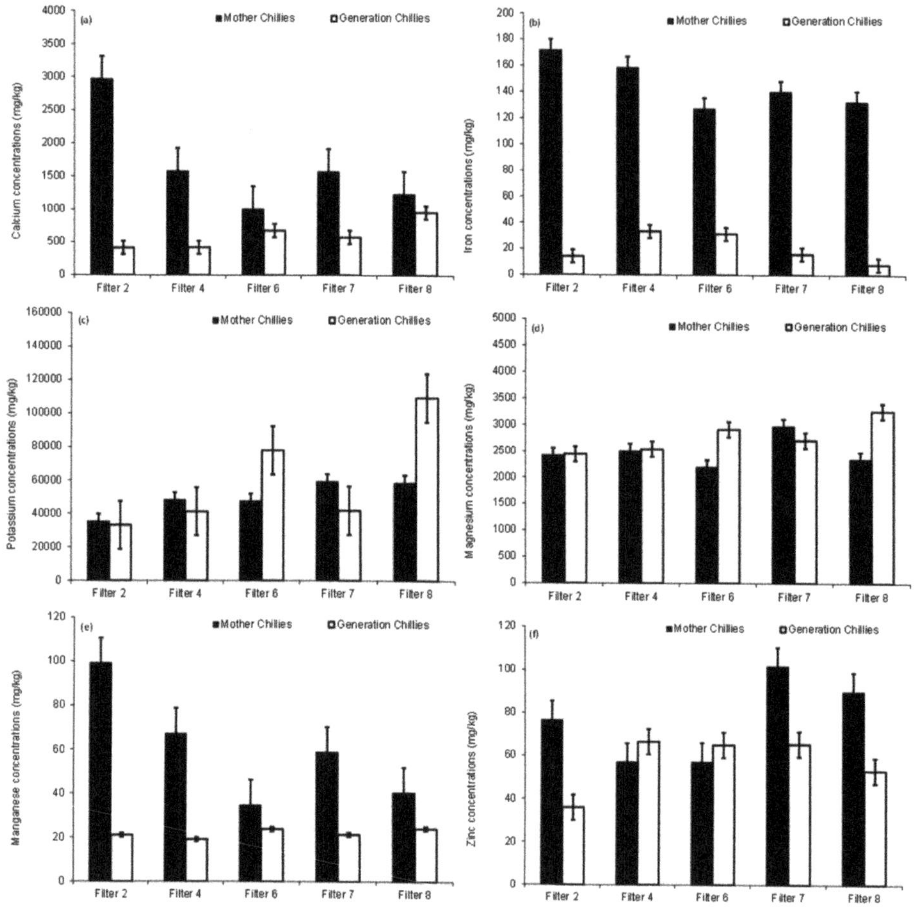

Figure 7. Chilli generations: (**a**) calcium, (**b**) iron, (**c**) potassium, (**d**) magnesium, (**e**) manganese, and (**f**) zinc.

As the soil pH goes down, mainly iron (Fe^{2+}) and aluminum (Al^{3+}) become soluble and react with calcium to form insoluble compounds [52]. High calcium levels may inhibit boron uptake. Calcium is essential for many plant functions [23]. From a human health point of view, calcium plays a main role in bone structure, metabolism processes, muscle and nerve function control as well as balancing of blood streams as reported by Zhu and Prince [53].

3.3.4. Iron

Figure 5 illustrates that maximum iron values were detected in fruits from chillies receiving effluent from Filter 4, followed by those fruits irrigates with Filter 6 effluent. Minimum iron numbers were noted in fruits of chilies watered with Filter 8 outflow. The detected iron levels in fruits obtained from all treatments were considerably lower than 6.04 mg per 100 g of dried chillies as reported by Ciju [51]. Statistical results (Supplementary Materials Table S4) indicate that the effect of the wetland aggregate diameter was significant ($p < 0.05$), if compared to the mean iron values in fruits harvested from chillies irrigated with outflow from Filters 2 and 4.

Fruits taken from chillies watered with effluent from Filters 4 and 7 had mean iron values that were significantly ($p < 0.05$) different from those for fruits linked to Filters 7 and 8, respectively, due to the effect of wetland contact and resting time variables. Mean iron concentrations in soil and fruits were significantly negatively correlated with each other ($R = -0.475$, $p < 0.001$). Moreover, regression analysis findings (Figure 6b) indicated that iron concentrations in the fruits decreased linearly but not significantly with the corresponding values in the soil due to their low bioavailability to the plants, as reported by FAO [23].

The iron CF in the tested fruits followed the order Filter 4 > Filter 6 > Filter 7 > Filter 2 > Filter 8 with percentage points of 1.8%, 1.5%, 0.8%, 0.6% and 0.3%, respectively. Compared with their mothers, chilli generation fruits had iron concentrations that were significantly ($p < 0.05$) lower (Supplementary Materials Table S4 and Figure 7b), highlighting the effect of higher irrigation volumes applied to the mother plants than those for the first generation plants [8]. Furthermore, iron levels in assessed fruits were below the standard of 425 mg/kg [48]. This metal is a vital element for human health, but excessive quantities may result in damage to tissues as reported by Abbaspour et al. [54].

3.3.5. Potassium

Figure 5 shows that maximum mean potassium values were detected in fruits linked to Filter 8 effluent trailed by Filter 6 drain waters. In comparison, minimum concentrations were noted for fruits linked to Filter 2. However, potassium levels in fruits exceeded those numbers published previously [51]; 1870 mg per 100 g of sun-dried chillies. Fruits obtained from plants watered with Filter 2 (big gravel) outflow water had potassium values less than those of Filter 4 (small gravel). Fruits obtained from the latter filter had potassium concentrations that were similar to those of Filter 7 (Figure 5). Moreover, the Supplementary Materials Table S4 highlights that fruits obtained from chillies irrigated with effluent from Filters 4 and 7 had potassium values that were significantly ($p < 0.05$) lower than those of Filters 6 and 8 in this order.

The potassium CF in the tested fruits had this sequence: Filter 8 > Filter 6 > Filter 2 > Filter 7 > Filter 4 with points of 6826%, 5103%, 2768%, 2503% and 1897%, respectively. Compared with their mother plants (Figure 7), the first generation fruits showed some significant ($p < 0.05$) differences in mean potassium values (Supplementary Materials Table S4), possibly due to differences in element masses subjected to both plants [8] via irrigation water leading to differences in corresponding soil potassium concentrations available for uptake by pants. Potassium has an important role to play for plants, as it takes part in many physiological processes [23]. Moreover, this element is vital for human health, as it can maintain human blood pressure and water balance [48].

3.3.6. Magnesium

Figure 5 illustrates that magnesium in the harvest was higher than 88 mg per 100 g of dried chillies as reported, previously [51]. The maximum magnesium values were detected in fruits obtained from chillies watered with Filter 8 effluent followed by Filter 6 effluent. In contrast, minimum concentrations were associated with Filter 2 effluent. Fruits picked from plants irrigated with Filter 2 effluent water had average magnesium values similar to those of plants associated with Filter 4, while the latter plants produced fruits of mean concentrations, which were less than those linked to Filter 7.

A statistical analysis (Supplementary Materials Table S4) indicated that there were significant ($p < 0.05$) dissimilarities in average magnesium values of chillies watered with Filter 7 outflow in comparison to those irrigated with effluent from Filter 8, indicating the importance of resting time on the wetland system. A significant ($p < 0.05$) dissimilarity was noted between fruit average values related to Filter 4 outflow compared to those corresponding ones linked to Filter 6. Moreover, regression analysis findings indicated that fruit magnesium concentrations linearly increased but not significantly with their corresponding levels in the soil (Figure 6c).

Furthermore, the magnesium CF in the tested fruits had this order: Filter 6 > Filter 8 > Filter 7 > Filter 2 > Filter 4 with corresponding percentages of 36%, 32%, 30%, 26% and 25%. Moreover, first chilli generation magnesium mean concentrations were observed to be different from their mother ones, as illustrated in Figure 1 and Supplementary Materials Table S4. However, the uptake of magnesium mainly depends on calcium and potassium as well as their levels in the soil. Plant magnesium uptake is usually a minor portion of the overall exchangeable magnesium available in the soil, which means that magnesium depletion from the soil by plant uptake is a minor factor, as discussed by Barber [52]. Magnesium is an essential plant nutrient as it is important for the photosynthesis process, because it is a building block of chlorophyll. The deficiency of magnesium in soil limits crop production [23]. Magnesium is an essential element for human health, as it is necessary for bone development. According to Musso [55], excessive magnesium in food may not cause any risk linked to the health of humans.

3.3.7. Manganese

Manganese average values in the harvested plants are shown in Figure 5. Maximum levels were detected in fruits linked to Filter 8 effluent followed by Filter 6 drain water, while minimum concentrations were noted for those fruits linked to chillies watered with Filter 4 outflow. Supplementary Materials Table S4 indicates that fruit average manganese concentration values linked to plants irrigated with effluents from Filters 4 and 7 were significantly ($p < 0.05$) different from those irrigated with outflows associated with Filters 2 and 8, highlighting the impact of aggregate diameter and wetland resting time on corresponding soil element distribution available for uptake by plants [19]. Furthermore, fruits of plants irrigated with Filter 4 had average magnesium values, which were significantly ($p < 0.05$) dissimilar from those of Filter 6, indicating the effect of loading rate for the wetland system. However, differences in fruit manganese levels resulted from variations in this element within the corresponding soils (Figure 4). Correlation analysis results showed that manganese concentrations in the soil and fruits were negatively correlated with each other ($R = -0.135$, $p = 0.206$). Moreover, regression analysis results (Figure 6d) indicated that fruit manganese concentrations linearly decreased but not significantly with their corresponding values in the soil due to their low bioavailability as reported by Barber [52].

The manganese CF in the tested fruits had this sequence: Filter 6 > Filter 4 = Filter 2 = Filter 7 > Filter 8 with values of 17%, 13%, 13%, 13% and 12% in this order. In comparison to their mother chillies, the first generation chilli fruits showed mean manganese numbers that were significantly ($p < 0.05$) lower (Figure 7 and Supplementary Materials Table S4). Manganese is essential for chilli physiological processes, particularly photosynthesis. Manganese deficiencies lead to less yield, weak resistance against pathogens and lowered tolerance to droughts [56]. According to the threshold value of 500 mg/kg [48,57], findings indicate no exceedance in manganese of harvested fruits.

3.3.8. Zinc

Figure 5 illustrates that maximum zinc values were noted in fruits obtained from chillies fed with Filter 4 effluent, while minimum values were recorded in chilli fruits watered with Filter 2 effluent. However, the observed zinc values were higher than 1.02 mg for 100 g of dried chillies, which was reported by Ciju [51]. The findings (Supplementary Materials Table S4) indicated that average zinc values in fruits linked to Filters 4 and 8 were significantly ($p < 0.05$) dissimilar from those for Filters 2 and 7, correspondingly, highlighting the effect of the gravel diameter and resting time on the associated soil zinc values, which subsequently resulted in considerable fruit zinc variation levels (Figure 4). No significant ($p > 0.05$) negative correlation relationship was found for zinc concentrations when comparing soils and fruits (Figure 6e).

The zinc CF order in the tested fruits was as follows: Filter 6 > Filter 4 > Filter 7 > Filter 8 > Filter 2 with values of 210%, 189%, 178%, 170% and 97%, respectively. However, first generation chilli plants had average zinc values, which were significantly ($p < 0.05$) unlike from their corresponding values obtained from their mothers (Figure 7 and Supplementary Materials Table S4). Zinc is an important micronutrient for chillies and controls gene expression [58]. Results showed that zinc levels in fruits obtained from all irrigated plants (with exception of those fed with Filter 2 effluent) exceeded the standard of 50 mg/kg [48,57]. The contamination/pollution ($C\ P^{-1}$) ratio was evaluated using the tested fruit metal values divided by the corresponding standard values [59]. Based on listed intervals of $C\ P^{-1}$ by Lăcătuşu [59], findings indicated that all tested chilli fruits for zinc were observed to be marginally polluted as $C\ P^{-1}$ showed values from 1.1 to 2.0. According to FAO/WHO [48], zinc is important for human health. However, consuming high doses of zinc for a long time may cause toxicity effects.

3.3.9. Boron

Figure 5 indicates that boron was detected at maximum levels in the fruits obtained from plants watered with effluent from Filter 6 (trailed by Filter 4). Minimum concentrations were determined for fruits from Filter 8-related plants. Chillies from Filters 2 and 7 had average boron concentrations that were lower than those of Filter 4, which was associated with boron concentrations lower than those for Filter 6. Moreover, chilli fruits irrigated with effluent from Filters 7 and 8 drain were different from each other (Figure 5). Results showed that boron concentrations in fruits and soils were negatively but not significantly correlated with each other as shown in Figure 6f, which indicates that boron in the fruits decreased linearly with their corresponding soil values.

The boron CF order in the tested fruits was like this: Filter 6 > Filter 7 > Filter 8 > Filter 2 > Filter 4 with values of 408%, 355%, 281%, 267% and 257%, correspondingly. These results contradict those reported by Diana [60] indicating that soil can contain various boron concentrations. However, only a small amount of boron can be obtained by plants. Therefore, it was not detected in the mother chillies. This is possibly due to the higher calcium concentrations in soils associated with the mother plants compared to those of the first generation plants, because of the higher irrigation water volume applied to the former [8], which will inhibit boron uptake and utilization [52]. Nevertheless, boron is a key micronutrient for chilli growth, as it has an important role in metabolism processes, mainly related to the stabilization of cell membranes [61,62]. Considering human health, boron positively affects the growth of bones and reducing the risk of getting cancer [63].

4. Conclusions

This work indicates that wetlands can be applied successfully for domestic sewage treatment. Moreover, the corresponding system effluent can subsequently be recycling for irrigating chillies used to treated wastewater, when grown in organic growth media. Total coliforms, ammonium-nitrogen, phosphorus and potassium significantly ($p < 0.05$) surpassed standards (1000 CFU/100 mL, 5 mg/L, 2 mg/L and 2 mg/L, respectively) set for irrigation. The highest corresponding values were 157,072 CFU/100 mL, 8.5 mg/L, 5.0 mg/L, and 7.0 mg/L in that order. No microbial content was observed in the harvested fruits. Reuse of treated wastewater for irrigation resulted in increases of some minerals like zinc, aluminum and magnesium in the soil compared to the raw materials. Recycling of purified wastewater for irrigation did not cause any significant soil mineral contamination. Slight contamination by zinc was noticed in the harvested chillies according to vegetable quality standards (threshold of 50 mg/kg). Zinc concentrations for Filters 2, 4, 6, 7 and 8 were 35.8, 60.6, 65.1, 65.5 and 53.2 mg/kg, respectively.

The element concentrations in the harvested fruits depended greatly on the corresponding concentrations and element bioavailability in the soil. Results indicated, for example, high concentration factor values for potassium (6826%) followed by zinc (210%), and a low value of 2% for iron.

The mother plants required a lot of irrigation water (pre-treated wastewater), because they were much taller (due to the plants not being adapted to high nitrogen loads in the irrigation water) and had higher biomass compared to the corresponding daughter plants, which also received the same type of irrigation water, but were apparently adapted to the high nitrogen load compared to their mother plants. This reduction in irrigation volumes concerning the first generation chillies (daughter plants) compared to their mothers led to a lowering in total element mass and consequently a reduction in first generation chilli fruit mineral content compared to their mother plants, increasing safety for human consumption.

Domestic wastewater treatment using reed beds and subsequent recycling of the treated wastewater for irrigation of crops such as chilli is a good substitute to the traditional use of drinking water in irrigation. This recycling approach helps to overcome the worldwide water scarcity problem by saving drinking water and reducing fertilizer application due to the various nutrients and minerals available in the treated wastewater.

The authors recommend long-term field studies on soil property changes as well as on plant growth, productivity and food safety using pre-treated wastewater from large-scale wetland systems. More replicates should be used for all plant generations.

Supplementary Materials: The following are available online at http://www.mdpi.com/1660-4601/15/8/1776/s1, Table S1: Statistically significant differences in properties of soil subjected to different irrigation water types, Table S2: Correlation coefficients and associated significances between soil elements using the non-parametric Spearman correlation, Table S3: Overview of the statistically significant differences for elements within the harvested fruits, Table S4: Differences in Chilli fruit mean element concentrations harvested from mother and generation plants.

Author Contributions: Conceptualization, M.S.; Methodology, M.S. and S.A.A.A.N.A.; Formal Analysis, S.A.A.A.N.A.; Investigation, S.A.A.A.N.A., M.S. and S.N.A.; Resources, M.S.; Data Curation, S.A.A.A.N.A., M.S. and S.N.A.; Writing-Original Draft Preparation, S.A.A.A.N.A.; Writing-Review & Editing, M.S.; Visualization, S.A.A.A.N.A.; Supervision, M.S.; Project Administration, M.S.; Funding Acquisition, S.A.A.A.N.A., S.N.A. and M.S.

Funding: Suhad A.A.A.N. Almuktar received a PhD Studentship funded by the Government of Iraq.

Acknowledgments: Laurie Cunliffe, Chuxia Lin and Furat Al-Faraj gave technical and scientific advice.

Conflicts of Interest: The authors declare no conflict of interest.

References

1. FAO. *User's Manual for Irrigation with Treated Wastewater*; Food and Agriculture Organization (FAO) of the United Nations, FAO Regional Office of the Near East: Cairo, Egypt, 2003.
2. Pinto, U.; Maheshwari, B.L.; Grewal, H.S. Effects of greywater irrigation on plant growth, water use and soil properties. *Resour. Conserv. Recycl.* **2010**, *54*, 429–435. [CrossRef]
3. Zavadil, J. The effect of municipal wastewater irrigation on the yield and quality of vegetables and crops. *Soil Water Res.* **2009**, *4*, 91–103. [CrossRef]
4. Sani, A.; Scholz, M.; Bouillon, L. Seasonal assessment of experimental vertical-flow constructed wetlands treating domestic wastewater. *Bioresour. Technol.* **2013**, *147*, 585–596. [CrossRef] [PubMed]
5. Scholz, M. *Wetland System—Storm Water Management Control*; Springer: Berlin, Germany, 2010.
6. Almuktar, S.A.A.A.N.; Scholz, M. Mineral and biological contamination of soil and *Capsicum annuum* irrigated with recycled domestic wastewater. *Agric. Water Manag.* **2016**, *167*, 95–109. [CrossRef]
7. Almuktar, S.A.A.A.N.; Scholz, M. Experimental assessment of recycled diesel spill-contaminated domestic wastewater treated by reed beds for irrigation of Sweet Peppers. *Int. J. Environ. Res. Public Health* **2016**, *13*, 208. [CrossRef] [PubMed]
8. Almuktar, S.A.A.A.N.; Abed, S.N.; Scholz, M. Recycling of domestic wastewater treated by vertical-flow wetlands for irrigation of two consecutive *Capsicum annuum* generations. *Ecol. Eng.* **2017**, *107*, 82–98. [CrossRef]
9. Cirelli, G.L.; Consoli, S.; Licciardello, F.; Aiello, R.; Giuffrida, F.; Leonardi, C. Treated municipal wastewater reuse in vegetable production. *Agric. Water Manag.* **2012**, *104*, 163–170. [CrossRef]
10. Aiello, R.; Cirelli, G.L.; Consoli, S. Effects of reclaimed wastewater irrigation on soil and tomato fruits: A case study in Sicily (Italy). *Agric. Water Manag.* **2007**, *93*, 65–72. [CrossRef]
11. Chary, N.S.; Kamala, C.T.; Raj, D.S.S. Assessing risk of heavy metals from consuming food grown on sewage irrigated soils and food chain transfer. *Ecotoxicol. Environ. Saf.* **2008**, *69*, 513–524. [CrossRef] [PubMed]

12. Almuktar, S.A.A.A.N.; Scholz, M.; Al-Isawi, R.H.K.; Sani, A. Recycling of domestic wastewater treated by vertical-flow wetlands for irrigating Chillies and Sweet Peppers. *Agric. Water Manag.* **2015**, *149*, 1–22. [CrossRef]
13. Almuktar, S.A.A.A.N.; Scholz, M.; Al-Isawi, R.H.K.; Sani, A. Recycling of domestic wastewater treated by vertical-flow wetlands for watering of vegetables. *Water Pract. Technol.* **2015**, *10*, 445–464. [CrossRef]
14. Almuktar, S.A.A.A.N.; Scholz, M. Microbial contamination of *Capsicum annuum* irrigated with recycled domestic wastewater treated by vertical-flow wetlands. *Ecol. Eng.* **2015**, *82*, 404–414. [CrossRef]
15. FAO. *The State of Food and Agriculture*; FAO Agriculture Series Number 27; Food and Agriculture Organization (FAO) of the United Nations: Rome, Italy, 1994.
16. APHA. *Standard Methods for the Examination of Water and Wastewater*, 21st ed.; American Public Health Association (APHA), American Water Works Association, and Water and Environment Federation: Washington, DC, USA, 2005.
17. EPA. *Determination of Metals and Trace Elements in Water and Wastes by Inductively Coupled Plasma-Atomic Emission Spectrometry*; Method 200.7, Revision 4.4 (EMMC Version); US Environmental Protection Agency (EPA): Cincinnati, OH, USA, 1994.
18. Plank, C.O. *Plant Analysis Reference Procedures for the Southern Region of the United States*; Southern Cooperative Series Bulletin Number 368; University of Georgia: Athens, GA, USA, 1992.
19. Bar-Tal, A.; Aloni, B.; Karni, L.; Rosenberg, R. Nitrogen nutrition of greenhouse pepper. II. Effects of nitrogen concentration and NO3: NH4 ratio on growth, transpiration, and nutrient uptake. *HortScience* **2001**, *36*, 1252–1259.
20. Pescod, M.B. Wastewater treatment and use in agriculture. In *FAO Irrigationand Drainage Paper Number 47*; Food and Agriculture Organisation (FAO): Rome, Italy, 1992.
21. Scholz, M. *Wetlands Systems to Control Urban Runoff*; Elsevier: Amsterdam, The Netherlands, 2006.
22. McCauly, A.; Jones, C.; Jacobsen, J. *Plant Nutrient Functions and Deficiency and Toxicity Symptoms*; Nutrient Management Module No. 9; Montana State University: Bozeman, MT, USA, 2011.
23. FAO. *Trace Elements in Soils and Agriculture*; FAO Water Report 17; Food and Agriculture Organisation (FAO) of the United Nations: Rome, Italy, 1972.
24. Wiseman, I.M.; Edwards, P.J. Constructed wetlands for minewater treatment: Performance and sustainability. *Water Environ. J.* **2004**, *18*, 127–132. [CrossRef]
25. Lesley, B.; Daniel, H.; Paul, Y. Iron and manganese removal in wetland treatment systems: Rates, processes and implications for management. *Sci. Total Environ.* **2008**, *394*, 1–8. [CrossRef] [PubMed]
26. Rahimi, Z.; Aboutalebi, A.; Zakerin, A. Comparison of different medium for production of sweet pepper transplant. *Int. Res. J. Appl. Basic Sci.* **2013**, *4*, 307–310.
27. Millaleo, R.; Reyes-Díaz, M.; Ivanov, A.; Mora, M.; Alberdi, M. Manganese as essential and toxic element for plants: Transport, accumulation and resistance mechanisms. *J. Soil Sci. Plant Nutr.* **2010**, *10*, 470–481. [CrossRef]
28. Yeh, T.Y.; Chou, C.C.; Pan, C.T. Heavy metal removal within pilot-scale constructed wetlands receiving river water contaminated by confined swine operations. *Desalination* **2009**, *249*, 368–373. [CrossRef]
29. Cakmak, I. The role of potassium in alleviating detrimental effects of abiotic stresses in plants. *J. Plant Nutr. Soil Sci.* **2005**, *168*, 521–530. [CrossRef]
30. Deng, H.; Ye, Z.H.; Wong, M.H. Accumulation of lead, zinc, copper and cadmium by 12 wetland plant species thriving in metal-contaminated sites in China. *Environ. Pollut.* **2004**, *132*, 29–40. [CrossRef] [PubMed]
31. Galletti, A.; Verlicchi, P.; Ranieri, E. Removal and accumulation of Cu, Ni and Zn in horizontal subsurface flow constructed wetlands: Contribution of vegetation and filling medium. *Sci. Total Environ.* **2010**, *408*, 5097–5105. [CrossRef] [PubMed]
32. Guittonny-Philippe, A.; Masotti, V.; Höhener, P.; Boudenne, J.L.; Viglione, J.; Laffont-Schwob, I. Constructed wetlands to reduce metal pollution from industrial catchments in aquatic Mediterranean ecosystems: A review to overcome obstacles and suggest potential solutions. *Environ. Int.* **2014**, *64*, 1–16. [CrossRef] [PubMed]
33. Travis, M.J.; Wiel-Shafran, A.; Weisbrod, N.; Adar, E.; Gross, A. Greywater reuse for irrigation: Effect on soil properties. *Sci. Total Environ.* **2010**, *408*, 2501–2508. [CrossRef] [PubMed]
34. Kadlec, R.; Knight, R. *Treatment Wetlands*; Lewis Publishers: Boca Raton, FL, USA, 1996.

35. Green, M.; Friedler, E.; Ruskol, Y.; Safrai, I. Investigation of alternative method for nitrification in constructed wetlands. *Water Sci. Technol.* **1997**, *35*, 63–70. [CrossRef]
36. Garcia, J.; Rousseau, D.P.; Morato, J.; Lesage, E.L.S.; Matamoros, V.; Bayona, J.M. Contaminant removal processes in subsurface-flow constructed wetlands: A review. *Crit. Rev. Environ. Sci. Technol.* **2010**, *40*, 561–661. [CrossRef]
37. Hua, G.F.; Li, L.; Zhao, Y.Q.; Zhu, W.; Shen, J.Q. An integrated model of substrate clogging in vertical flow constructed wetlands. *J. Environ. Manag.* **2013**, *119*, 67–75. [CrossRef] [PubMed]
38. Kadlec, R.H.; Wallace, S.D. *Treatment Wetlands*, 2nd ed.; CRC Press: Boca Raton, FL, USA, 2009.
39. Sundaravadivel, M.; Vigneswaran, S. Constructed wetlands for wastewater treatment. *Crit. Rev. Environ. Sci. Technol.* **2001**, *31*, 351–409. [CrossRef]
40. Manios, T.; Stentiford, E.I.; Millner, P. Removal of total suspended solids from wastewater in constructed horizontal flow subsurface wetlands. *J. Environ. Sci. Health Part A* **2003**, *38*, 1073–1085. [CrossRef]
41. Saeed, T.; Sun, G. A review on nitrogen and organics removal mechanisms in subsurface flow constructed wetlands: Dependency on environmental parameters, operating conditions and supporting media. *J. Environ. Manag.* **2012**, *112*, 429–448. [CrossRef] [PubMed]
42. Maas, E.V.; Grattan, S.R. Crop yields as affected by salinity. *Agronomy* **1999**, *38*, 55–110.
43. USEPA. *Guidelines for Water Reuse*; United States (US) Environmental Protection Agency (EPA): Washington, DC, USA, 2004.
44. Husson, O. Redox potential (Eh) and pH as drivers of soil/plant/microorganism systems: A transdisciplinary overview pointing to integrative opportunities for agronomy. *Plant Soil* **2013**, *362*, 389–417. [CrossRef]
45. Essington, M.E. *Soil and Water Chemistry: An Integrative Approach*; CRC Press: Boca Raton, FL, USA, 2015.
46. EPA. *Guidelines for Water Reuse: Manual*; US Environmental Protection Agency (EPA) and US Agency for International Development: Cincinnati, OH, USA, 1992.
47. Stahl, T.; Taschan, H.; Brunn, H. Aluminium content of selected foods and food products. *Environ. Sci. Eur.* **2011**, *23*, 37. [CrossRef]
48. FAO/WHO. *Report on the 32nd Session of the Codex Committee on Food Additives and Contaminants*; Joint Food and Agriculture Organization (FAO) and World Health Organization (WHO) Food Standard Programme Codex Alimentarius Commission: Geneva, Switzerland, 2001.
49. Li, Q.; Chen, Y.; Fu, H.; Cui, Z.; Shi, L.; Wang, L.; Liu, Z. Health risk of heavy metals in food crops grown on reclaimed tidal flat soil in the Pearl River Estuary, China. *J. Hazard. Mater.* **2012**, *227–228*, 148–154. [CrossRef] [PubMed]
50. Kidd, P.S.; Proctor, J. Effects of aluminum on the growth and mineral composition of *Betula pendula* Roth. *J. Exp. Bot.* **2000**, *51*, 1057–1066. [CrossRef]
51. Ciju, R.J. *Chile Peppers*; Amazon: Ridgmont, UK, 2013.
52. Barber, S.A. *Soil Nutrient Bioavailability: A Mechanistic Approach*; John Wiley & Sons: Hoboken, NJ, USA, 1995.
53. Zhu, K.; Prince, R.L. Calcium and bone. *Clin. Biochem.* **2012**, *45*, 936–942. [CrossRef] [PubMed]
54. Abbaspour, N.; Hurrell, R.; Kelishadi, R. Review on iron and its importance for human health. *J. Res. Med. Sci.* **2014**, *19*, 164–174.
55. Musso, C. Magnesium metabolism in health and disease. *Int. Urol. Nephrol.* **2009**, *41*, 357–362. [CrossRef] [PubMed]
56. Hakala, M.; Rantamäki, S.; Puputti, E.M.; Tyystjärvi, T.; Tyystjärvi, E. Photoinhibition of manganese enzymes: insights into the mechanism of photosystem II photoinhibition. *J. Exp. Bot.* **2006**, *57*, 1809–1816. [CrossRef] [PubMed]
57. European Commission. *Setting Maximum Levels for Certain Contaminants in Food Stuffs*; Commission Regulation No. 466/2001; European Commission: Brussels, Belgium, 2001; p. L77/1.
58. Brown, P.H.; Cakmak, I.; Zhang, Q. Form and function of zinc plants. In *Zinc in Soils and Plants*; Springer: New York, NY, USA, 1993; pp. 93–106.
59. Lăcătuşu, R. Appraising levels of soil contamination and pollution with heavy metals. In *Land Information Systems*; Developments for Planning the Sustainable Use of Land Resources, EUR 17729; European Soil Bureau: Brussels, Belgium, 1998.
60. Diana, G. Boron in the soil, from deficit to toxicity. *Informatore Agrario* **2006**, *62*, 54–58.
61. Cakmak, I.; Römheld, V. Boron deficiency-induced impairments of cellular functions in plants. *Plant Soil* **1997**, *193*, 71–83. [CrossRef]

62. Blevins, D.G.; Lukaszewski, K.M. Boron in plant structure and function. *Annu. Rev. Plant Biol.* **1998**, *49*, 481–500. [CrossRef] [PubMed]
63. Nielsen, F.H. Update on human health effects of boron. *J. Trace Elem. Med. Biol.* **2014**, *28*, 383–387. [CrossRef] [PubMed]

agronomy

MDPI

Article

Assessment of *Capsicum annuum* L. Grown in Controlled and Semi-Controlled Environments Irrigated with Greywater Treated by Floating Wetland Systems

Suhad A. A. A. N. Almuktar [1,2,3], Suhail N. Abed [1], Miklas Scholz [1,2,4,5,6,*] and Vincent C. Uzomah [1]

1 Civil Engineering Research Group, School of Science, Engineering and Environment, The University of Salford, Newton Building, Salford M5 4WT, UK; suhad.almuktar@tvrl.lth.se (S.A.A.A.N.A.); s.n.abed@edu.salford.ac.uk (S.N.A.); v.uzomah@salford.ac.uk (V.C.U.)

2 Division of Water Resources Engineering, Department of Building and Environmental Technology, Faculty of Engineering, Lund University, P.O. Box 118, 221 00 Lund, Sweden

3 Department of Architectural Engineering, Faculty of Engineering, The University of Basrah, Al-Basrah 61001, Iraq

4 Department of Civil Engineering Science, School of Civil Engineering and the Built Environment, Kingsway Campus, University of Johannesburg, P.O. Box 524, Aukland Park, Johannesburg 2006, South Africa

5 Department of Town Planning, Engineering Networks and Systems, South Ural State University, 76, Lenin prospekt, 454080 Chelyabinsk, Russia

6 Institute of Environmental Engineering, Wroclaw University of Environmental and Life Sciences, ul. Norwida 25, 50-375 Wrocław, Poland

* Correspondence: miklas.scholz@tvrl.lth.se; Tel.: +46-(0)462228920; Fax: +46-(0)462224435

Citation: Almuktar, S.A.A.A.N.; Abed, S.N.; Scholz, M.; Uzomah, V.C. Assessment of *Capsicum annuum* L. Grown in Controlled and Semi-Controlled Environments Irrigated with Greywater Treated by Floating Wetland Systems. *Agronomy* **2021**, *11*, 1817. https://doi.org/10.3390/agronomy11091817

Academic Editor: Jose Beltrao

Received: 9 August 2021
Accepted: 7 September 2021
Published: 10 September 2021

Abstract: Accumulation of trace elements, including heavy metals, were evaluated in soil and fruits of chilli plants (*Capsicum annuum* L.) grown under both laboratory-controlled and semi-controlled greenhouse location conditions. Chilli plant biomass growth in different development stages and fruit productivity were evaluated and compared with each other for the impact of growth boundary conditions and water quality effects. Treated synthetic greywaters by different operational design set-ups of floating treatment wetland systems were recycled for watering chillies in both locations. Effluents of each individual group of treatment set-up systems were labelled to feed sets of three replicates of chilli plants in both locations. Results revealed that the treated synthetic greywater (SGW) complied with thresholds for irrigation water, except for high concentrations (HC) of phosphates, total suspended soils, and some trace elements, such as cadmium. Chilli plants grew in both locations with different growth patterns in each development stage. First blooming and high counts of flowers were observed in the laboratory. Higher fruit production was noted for greenhouse plants: 2266 chilli fruits with a total weight of 16.824 kg with an expected market value of GBP 176.22 compared to 858 chilli fruits from the laboratory with a weight of 3.869 kg and an estimated price of GBP 17.61. However, trace element concentrations were detected in chilli fruits with the ranking order of occurrence as: Mg > Ca > Na > Fe > Zn > Al > Mn > Cu > Cd > Cr > Ni > B. The highest concentrations of accumulated Cd (3.82 mg/kg), Cu (0.56 mg/kg), and Na (0.56 mg/kg) were recorded in chilli fruits from the laboratory, while greater accumulations of Ca, Cd, Cu, Mn, and Ni with concentrations of 4.73, 1.30, 0.20, 0.21, and 0.24 mg/kg, respectively, were linked to fruits from the greenhouse. Trace elements in chilli plant soils followed the trend: Mg > Fe > Al > Cr > Mn > Cd > Cu > B. The accumulated concentrations in either chilli fruits or the soil were above the maximum permissible thresholds, indicating the need for water quality improvements.

Keywords: greywater recycling; constructed floating wetland; *Capsicum annuum* L.; soil pollution; agricultural water management; heavy metal accumulation

1. Introduction

Some of the challenges facing water resource management include climate change phenomena, such as droughts linked to global warming. Anthropogenic activities have negatively affected natural resources, such as freshwater, in terms of its quality compared to international standards for safe usage [1,2]. Severe climate and environmental challenges have been predicted for Australia, the Middle East, North Africa, and the southern USA [3,4]. The world population in 2050 might hit 9.7 billion; this number could reach 11.0 billion by 2100 [5]. Furthermore, the population growth rate increase might also lead to mass migration. More than 67% of the world population could face water shortages by 2025 [6,7]. At least 50% will be under serious high water stress by 2030, as predicted by Scheierling et al. [8]. Water consumption is expected to increase by 40% in 2030 [9]. Consequently, more wastewater contaminated with organic, inorganic, and biological pollutants will be generated [1]. Discharging inadequately treated wastewater to watercourses could have serious effects on soil, aquatic ecosystems, and the public health [10,11]. Therefore, recycling treated wastewater for non-potable purposes is regarded as a feasible technique to mitigate water shortage. Thus, it is strongly recommended to treat wastewater before discharge or recycling [1].

Wastewater treatment and recycling are encouraged due to the rapid increase in the demand for water availability and the desire to protect the environment/public health. Agricultural irrigation is one of several options used to recycle processed wastewater for non-drinking usage [12]. Sustainability principles and concepts of organic farming systems have been introduced to industrial agriculture to improve environmental quality and human dietary needs [13]. Wastewater is one of the most important potential sources of recycled nutrients, reducing the need for fertilizers [14]. Irrigation within agriculture requires more than 70% of available water resources [15]. This proportion is likely to increase by around 14% in 2030, according to predictions by the Food and Agriculture Organization (FAO) [1].

In the 16th and 17th centuries, wastewater was already utilized as a water source for irrigation practices in Germany, Poland, and Scotland [16]. In the 20th century, governments, international originations, and agencies had issued legislation and standards to regulate the safe reuse of wastewater for irrigation purposes [4]. The intricacies associated with reusing or recycling wastewater for irrigation are linked to the community's health and wider environmental risks, as discussed by Dalahmeh and Baresel [17]. Health risk concerns are associated with recycling wastewater for irrigation of plants of freshly edible roots, foliage, and fruits. Faecal pathogen contamination could spread in soil and adhere to plant tissues [18]. Safety, hygiene, aesthetics, environmental tolerance, as well as economic and technical feasibilities, are important assessment criteria [19].

In general, domestic wastewater has faecal constituents from toilet discharge, which is classified as black wastewater (BW), while wastewater generated from domestic activities is known as grey wastewater or greywater (GW). The majority of GW generated from laundry, showers, washing basins, dishwashers, and kitchens constitutes about 75% of the total domestic wastewater [20]. Therefore, recycling GW for agricultural irrigation has gained wide popularity, in terms of the low level of pathogens and nutrient contaminants [21,22].

There is a risk of accumulation of contaminants, such as metals in both soil and plant tissues [23,24], negatively effecting human and animal health [14]. Some plant species are able to grow in contaminated soils with elevated metal concentrations through hyperaccumulation processes [25]. Accumulated trace elements can significantly change soil enzymes, increase microorganism metabolic activities, and threaten bacterial functional diversity [26]. All metals in crops should be lower than the allowable concentration limits to reduce human health risks [27,28].

The allowable trace element concentrations in crops are stated according to their fresh weight and based on the daily intake. International regulations vary; e.g., India [29], China [30], European Union [31], United States Environmental Protection Agency [11], and the Food and Agriculture Organization (FAO)/World Health Organization (WHO) of the United Nations [27,32]. Leafy and root vegetables represent higher health risks than fruits, since metals accumulate in roots and leaves of crops rather than their fruits or nutrient storage organs [33,34]. Some vegetable cultivars have a high ability to accumulate nutrients compared to other species [35]. However, other studies have indicated an accumulation of arsenic (As), cadmium (Cd), lead (Pb), and chromium (Cr) in fruits, such as chillies [36,37]. Trace element levels in vegetable biomass vary, because of differences in application of contaminated water for irrigation (wastewater), contaminated soil (sewage sludge), fertilizer, pesticides, contaminated organic waste manure, industrial by-products, and inadequate water management strategies [28]. Some heavy metals are classified as biologically beneficial elements including cobalt (Co), copper (Cu), nickel (Ni), and zinc (Zn), which are required to build cellular and human organ tissues. However, elevated levels cause toxicity [34,38,39].

Practical and scientific efforts crucially focus on efficient and sustainable non-conventional wastewater treatment methods, which are low in capital expenditure, operation, and maintenance costs, and are environmentally friendly, such as wetland systems. Constructed wetlands (CW) are recognised as vital engineering solutions for conservation of water resources, not only for arid and semi-arid regions, but also internationally [40,41]. Wetland systems as ecological treatment technology for wastewater enhance sustainable water resources and produce effluents that could be used for recycling purposes by the agricultural irrigation industry [42]. Constructed wetlands remove pollutants by biological, chemical, and physical processes with moderate capital expenditures, consuming low energy, and requiring low efforts for maintenance and operation [43–45]. To avoid claiming too much expensive land for CW, the engineering innovation free water surface constructed wetland (FWS-CW) has led to the introduction of floating treatment wetlands (FTW) [46]. These floating systems are innovative ecological approaches to control water quality from point and non-point source pollution [47]. Aquatic macrophytes are cultivated hydroponically on water surfaces by artificial floating mats. Large surface areas within the water column are provided for microorganisms. Biofilms are attached to macrophyte roots and rhizomes, which are not grown in substrate [48]. Free-floating plants usually have high efficiencies in uptake of heavy metals from water compared to submerged and emergent macrophytes, due to their high growth rate and specific morphology [49].

The main objective of this study is to assess the suitability of processed greywater by FTW to be recycled for the irrigation of chilli plants grown in two different environmental conditions (laboratory and greenhouse). The corresponding objectives linked to achieve the main target are to assess (a) the effect of the environmental boundary conditions on plant growth and fruit productivity; (b) the economic benefit of different operational design variables of the FTW for fruit productivity; (c) the accumulated trace elements in soil; and (d) the accumulated trace elements in chilli fruits.

2. Materials and Methods

2.1. *Operational Design of Floating Treatment Wetlands*

Greywater was created artificially under laboratory-controlled conditions using analytical-grade chemicals obtained from Fisher Scientific Co., Ltd., Bishop Meadow Road, Loughborough, UK [50]. Two chemical formulas of different recipes were selected to represent synthetic greywater (SGW) in low and high pollutant concentrations, LC-SGW and HC-SGW, respectively, see Supplementary Material (Table S1). Concentrated stock solutions for both recipes were prepared separately, and diluted later as one part to 100 parts of tap water at each experimental treatment cycle.

The experimental treatment systems comprised 72 mesocosm-scale plastic buckets of 14-L with a depth of 0.3 m and a diameter of 0.25 m, filled with 10 L of SGW, which was operated to resemble natural floating reed islands [51]. The experiment was operated under authentic weather conditions on an open flat roof of the Newton Building, The University of Salford, Manchester, UK. Bare-rooted *Phragmites australis (Cav.) Trin. ex Steud.* (Common reed) plants provided by VESI Environmental, Ltd. (Little Island, Co. Cork, Ireland) were utilised to float on the mesocosm water surface [52].

Mine water sludge (ochre) collected from North Rochdale at the Deerplay Coal Mine (OL13 8RD), UK, was included in some of the treatment systems as adsorbent substances to enhance the performance of FTW. Three parts of Ordinary Portland Cement (OPC) were added to seven parts of raw ochre sludge to create cement–ochre pellets [53].

The water quality tests commenced on 1 September 2014, and ended on 1 November 2016. However, assessments only started on 1 November 2014, to allow two months for biofilm growth (September and October, 2014).

There were four operational design variables for the FTW systems: strength of greywater pollutants (LC-SGW and HC-SGW), hydraulic retention time (HRT; 2 and 7 days), presence or absence of macrophytes (*Phragmites australis*), and presence or absence of cement–ochre pellets [51]. The general experimental set-up of FTW systems consisted of two groups of mesocosms treating SGW for 2 and 7 days of HRT. The experiment had three groups of mesocosms: first group for treatment of HC-SGW (T1, T2, T3, and T4 for 2 days HRT; T9, T10, T11, and T12 for 7 days HRT); the second group for LC-SGW (T5, T6, T7, and T8 for 2 days HRT; T13, T14, T15, and T16 for 7 days HRT); and the third group for tap water (TW), which was considered for control purposes (C1 and C2 for 2 days HRT; C3 and C4 for 7 days HRT). Each set in the first and second group had four replicates, except for the third set of controls, which had two replicates of mesocosms. The treatment systems of T1, T2, T5, T6, T9, T10, T13, T14, C1, and C3 contained floating *Phragmites australis*, while 300 g of cement–ochre pellets were used to treat 10 L of SGW in the mesocosms T2, T4, T6, T8, T10, T12, T14, and T16. Afterward, a combination of *Phragmites australis* and ochre pellets was used in the systems T2, T6, T10, and T13, while systems of only SGW were linked to mesocosms T3, T7, T11, and T15 (Table 1). Treated SGW (effluents) was replaced by freshly created SGW (influents) after the specific HRT, without disturbance of the biofilm that was attached to the macrophyte roots/rhizomes and on the vessel interior walls [51].

Table 1. Operational parameters in the experimental set-up supporting the irrigation of chilli plant *Capsicum annuum* L. with treated greywater by different designs of floating wetland systems [51].

Treatment System	HRT		SGW		TW	Vegetation		Cement–Ochre		Plant Receiving the Effluent
	2-Day	7-Day	HC	LC		With	Without	With	Without	
T1	♦		♦			♦			♦	P1
T2	♦		♦			♦		♦		P2
T3	♦		♦				♦		♦	P3
T4	♦		♦				♦	♦		P4
T5	♦			♦		♦			♦	P5
T6	♦			♦		♦		♦		P6
T7	♦			♦			♦		♦	P7
T8	♦			♦			♦	♦		P8
T9		♦	♦			♦			♦	P9
T10		♦	♦			♦		♦		P10
T11		♦	♦				♦		♦	P11
T12		♦	♦				♦	♦		P12
T13		♦		♦		♦			♦	P13
T14		♦		♦		♦		♦		P14
T15		♦		♦			♦		♦	P15
T16		♦		♦			♦	♦		P16
C1	♦				♦	♦			♦	P1c
C2	♦				♦		♦		♦	P2c
C3		♦			♦	♦			♦	P3c
C4		♦			♦		♦		♦	P4c

Note: ♦, selection mark; T1–T16, treatment systems with four replicates; C1–C4, control treatment systems with two replicates; HRT, hydraulic retention time; SGW, synthetic greywater; HC, high pollutant concentration of SGW; LC, low pollutant concentration of SGW; TW, tap water; and P1–P4c, chilli plant with three replicates.

2.2. Material Selection and Chilli Planting Processes

The effluent from each FTW type was designated to be recycled for watering one set of chilli plants, which consisted of the three replicates a, b, and c (Table 1). Planting media, bark, and chilli pepper seeds "Verve Brand" (www.diy.com; accessed on 9 August 2021) were purchased from a local B&Q plc warehouse in Salford, Greater Manchester, UK (unless mentioned otherwise). Multipurpose peat-based compost soil (product code: 03717644) was selected as a planting media [54]. The dry composition of raw compost (before planting) comprised organic matter (89%), total phosphorus (368 mg/kg), total nitrogen (999 mg/kg), potassium (2776 mg/kg), and zinc (26.59 mg/kg) [4]. Small chipped bark (product code: 5397007188110) of mixed wood was applied on the top of the compost soil to maintain moisture and insulate the soil within the pots.

According to the supplier, the compost soil contained 42% of non-peat compost, which was a mixture of composted green waste and spent brewery grains. While the majority (58%) was sustainably sourced material in terms of ecological, archaeological, and conservation criteria. This product contained green compost, wood fibre, coir (natural fibre extracted from the husk (outer shell of coconuts) and oyster shells), *Sphagnum* moss peat, and unspecified amounts of composted bark, vermiculture, perlite, loam, charcoal, sand, grit, wetting agent (to retain moisture better; 200–400 mL/m^3), essential nutrients, and trace minerals. The fertilizer and dolomitic limestone content were up to 3 kg/m^3 and up to 7 kg/m^3, respectively. However, the exact combination of all ingredients is confidential for commercial purposes. Therefore, the compost soil had a variable content with a complex structure and a bulk density between 200 and 450 g/L. A low bulk density and a high organic content proportion of compost provides a substrate with a high total porosity, stable soil structure, good hydraulic conductivity, as well as a high water retention time. A good compost water holding potential and water retention capacity is linked to high soil porosity. In addition, the authors reduced water evaporation and increased the moisture content of the compost by covering the top compost layer with small-chipped bark [3].

Chilli pepper seeds (*De Cayenne*; *Capsicum annuum* L. Longum Group; product code: 03623879) were purchased on 19 November 2014, to assess their growth when irrigated with artificial greywater pre-treated by differed designs of floating wetland systems. On 21 November 2014, about 180 single seeds were sown into a propagator, which was semi-filled with compost. One or two seeds were put in each propagated cell and covered with a thin compost soil layer of 6 mm thickness. On 19 December 2014, all propagators were protected by transparent covers to maintain the moisture content of the soil. The plants were kept in a dark incubation room at 20.8 °C until the seeds germinated. The recommended range by the supplier was 18–25 °C. After seed germination, all propagators were relocated to a laboratory fitted with the grow lights OSRAM HQL (MBF-U), which were high-pressure mercury lamps (400 W; Base E40) purchased from OSRAM (North Industrial Road, Foshan, Guangdong, China). The lamps were linked to a H4000 Gear Unit provided by Philips (London Road, Croydon, CR9 3QR).

The germination time was between 5 and 14 days, while the sowing to cropping period was 18 weeks [54]. All lights were electrically controlled by timers to simulate both sunrise and sunset times (http://www.timeanddate.com; accessed on 9 August 2021). The temperature near to the plants was around 19.3 to 26.3 °C with an average of 24.2 °C. On 13 February, 2015, true stems and more than two leaves were observed for almost germinated seedlings (Figure 1a). The strongest 150 chilli pepper plants were transplanted individually in round plastic pots of 10 litres (220 mm height, 220 mm bottom diameter, and 285 mm top diameter) purchased from ScotPlants Direct (Hedgehogs Nursery Ltd., Crompton Road, Glenrothes, Scotland, UK). Seedlings were transplanted in pots filled with moist multipurpose compost soil up to a height of 175 mm and topped-up with a layer of small chip bark of 25 mm thickness, while the remaining height of the pot (20 mm) was left as free space for irrigation water and litter. Another 10 chilli plants were also prepared in the same manner to serve as spare plants; i.e., substitutes (Figure 1b). Weak stems were initially supported by small bamboo sticks, and all plants were subjected to the same laboratory-controlled conditions.

Figure 1. *Cont.*

Figure 1. Photographs (taken by Suhad Almuktar) of chilli plants (*Capsicum annuum* L.) stages: (**a**) seedlings grown in propagators; (**b**) seedlings transplanted in large pots; (**c**) laboratory-controlled experiment; and (**d**) greenhouse-based semi-controlled experiment.

The healthiest 120 chilli plants were selected from the grown plants to be part of the experiment: 60 plants were left in the laboratory (Figure 1c), while the remaining 60 plants were transported to the greenhouse (Figure 1d). On 20 March 2015, treated greywater (effluents of the FTW) was applied for watering chilli plants in the laboratory and greenhouse simultaneously. Since, the FTW system designs consisted of 20 mesocosm sets, effluent from each mesocosm set irrigated 20 chilli plant sets of three replicates in both the laboratory and greenhouse (Table 1).

2.3. Growth Environment Monitoring and Recording

Laboratory and greenhouse environmental boundary conditions, such as light intensity, relative humidity, and temperature, were monitored. The effect of these two different growing environments on chilli plant growth and fruit quality was also investigated, and comparisons between them were made to highlight any possible significant differences.

In both the laboratory and greenhouse, light intensity measurements were indicated by the LUX meter ATP-DT-1300 for the measurement range 200 l× to 50,000 l× (TIMSTAR, Road Three, Winsford Industrial Estate, Winsford, Cheshire, UK). The temperature and relative humidity were measured using a thermometer hygrometer station obtained from wetterladen24.de (JM Handelspunkt, Gschwend, Germany).

In the laboratory, room temperature was controlled using electric heaters (Rhino H029400 TQ3 2.8 kW Thermo Quartz Infrared Heater 230 V) provided by Express Tools Ltd. (Alton Road, Bournemouth, UK). The humidity was regulated by operating humidifiers

(Challenge 3.0 L Ultrasonic Humidifier; Argos, Avebury Boulevard, Central Milton Keynes, England, UK). The provided lights were set on electric-powered timers to mimic sunshine hours.

2.4. Justification of Chilli Plant Selection

Chilli pepper plants (*De Cayenne; C. annuum* (*Linnaeus*) Longum Group) grown with recycled treated greywater were selected due for public health and safety, environmental, and economic reasons. Chilli fruits usually hang far above (at least 45 cm) the soil surface; therefore, they are subjected less to microbial contamination in comparison to plants with edible parts, such as salad or strawberries grown in potential contact with the soil [55]. According to the supplier (B&Q plc)—chilli has slender and hot fruits and can be grown easily in pots at various locations. The environmental growth conditions of chilli plants are comparable to those of warm geographical areas, but they can also be grown in British greenhouses [55,56]. Chilli prefers moist and loamy nutrient-rich soil with a pH range between 7.0 and 8.5 [54]. In addition, chillies are mostly perennial in tropical and subtropical regions (for at least three years). Commercial growing of chillies is easy, popular, and cost-effective. The plants are easy to obtain, have a high nutritional value, and are perfect for general cooking. The chilli growth time from sowing to cropping is only around 18 weeks. The germination time is between 5 and 14 days. Approximately 100 days are required for the plants to reach maturity.

2.5. Water Quality, Soil, and Chilli Fruit Analysis

Water samples were obtained from the effluents of FTW after specific HRT of treatment to assess water quality according to the standard methods for the examination of water and wastewater [57], unless stated otherwise (Table 2). Non-ionic detergents were used for cleaning and washing water collection kits, rinsed with tap water, soaked overnight into a 10% nitric acid solution, and then rinsed with deionised water before application. A wide range of parameters were evaluated by operating a spectrophotometer DR 2800 Hach Lange (www.hach.com; accessed on 9 August 2021): colour, total suspended solids (TSS), ortho-phosphate-phosphorus ($PO_4{}^{-}P$), nitrate-nitrogen ($NO_3{}^{-}N$), ammonia-nitrogen ($NH_4{}^{-}N$), and chemical oxygen demand (COD). The five-day biochemical oxygen demand (BOD_5) was calculated form a mono-metric measurement device (OxiTop IS 12-6 System) supplied by the Wissenschaftlich-Technische Werkstätten (WTW), Weilheim, Germany.

The conductivity meter METTLER TOLEDO FIVE GOTM (Keison Products, Chelmsford, Essex, England, UK) was used for electric conductivity (EC) measurements. Turbidity was determined with a TurbiCheck Turbidity Meter (Lovibond Water Testing, Tintometer Group), while hydrogen ion (pH) and redox potential (Eh) were measured with a SensION+ benchtop multi-parameter meter (Hach Lange, Düsseldorf, Germany). Digital Electrochemistry (HQ30d Flexi Meter; Hach Lange, Düsseldorf, Germany) was used for measuring Dissolved Oxygen (DO).

Trace elements were examined according to SW-846: TEST Method 6010D [58]. Inductively Coupled Plasma-Optical Emission Spectrometry (ICP-OES) applying a Varian 720-ES provided by Agilent Technologies UK Ltd. (Wharfedale Road, Wokingham, Berkshire, UK) was used for water mineral analysis (Table 2). Following USEPA (1994) [59], triplicate water samples of 10 mL each were acidified and filtered through a 0.45 µm cellulose filter paper before analysis.

Table 2. Influent and effluent (irrigation water) properties of synthetic greywater (SGW) treated by floating treatment wetland systems (FTW).

Parameter [57]	Unit	Influent	2-Day HRT (HC-SGW Effluent)				Influent	2-Day HRT (LC-SGW Effluent)			
		HC-SGW	T1	T2	T3	T4	LC-SGW	T5	T6	T7	T8
pH	–	8.4 ± 1.61	7.4 ± 1.09	8.8 ± 1.69	7.8 ± 1.37	8.7 ± 1.73	6.9 ± 0.48	7.0 ± 0.71	10.5 ± 1.12	7.5 ± 0.70	10.6 ± 0.99
Redox potential	mV	−36.6 ± 74.22	8.1 ± 52.68	−54.8 ± 83.66	−3.0 ± 62.95	−49.9 ± 83.61	34.1 ± 21.23	27.5 ± 32.18	−137.4 ± 54.91	4.2 ± 30.40	−143.5 ± 51.01
Turbidity	NTU	188.9 ± 47.22	175.9 ± 59.61	223.8 ± 97.40	192.1 ± 50.87	191.3 ± 84.41	22.9 ± 7.14	28.2 ± 37.09	39.2 ± 45.10	20.2 ± 14.20	35.6 ± 18.11
Total suspended solids	mg/L	317.0 ± 58.35	302.9 ± 75.19	422.5 ± 152.77	321.8 ± 56.68	337.4 ± 109.45	39.9 ± 15.94	41.7 ± 43.57	62.0 ± 49.93	30.0 ± 12.12	66.2 ± 36.63
Electronic conductivity	µS/cm	988.5 ± 196.09	987.4 ± 107.25	1174.5 ± 282.81	965.2 ± 106.68	1178.4 ± 264.41	164.6 ± 63.24	145.9 ± 30.41	371.5 ± 260.12	138.5 ± 23.26	344.5 ± 287.03
Dissolved oxygen	mg/L	10.5 ± 1.39	9.0 ± 1.03	9.0 ± 1.24	10.2 ± 0.73	10.0 ± 0.52	10.4 ± 1.24	9.3 ± 1.08	8.8 ± 0.87	10.5 ± 0.82	10.1 ± 0.73
Colour	Pa/Co	1587.8 ± 379.89	1525.6 ± 411.54	2150.8 ± 864.04	1527.6 ± 326.28	1935.6 ± 702.18	214.5 ± 64.07	183.7 ± 74.89	308.2 ± 134.65	164.5 ± 40.93	331.7 ± 119.34
Temperature	°C	16.9 ± 5.40	17.1 ± 4.92	17.4 ± 4.87	17.1 ± 4.75	17.2 ± 4.73	17.7 ± 4.58	17.0 ± 4.84	16.6 ± 4.55	16.0 ± 4.59	16.3 ± 4.24
Biochemical oxygen demand	mg/L	34.7 ± 12.99	17.7 ± 6.40	11.1 ± 5.89	14.7 ± 7.78	11.7 ± 7.71	17.6 ± 8.00	9.9 ± 5.49	5.4 ± 4.36	5.6 ± 3.60	4.4 ± 5.13
Chemical oxygen demand	mg/L	129.2 ± 34.68	96.3 ± 32.01	109.2 ± 24.38	106.6 ± 22.68	100.3 ± 21.08	28.9 ± 14.47	32.4 ± 14.55	29.6 ± 16.67	26.8 ± 6.18	24.0 ± 4.99
Ammonia–nitrogen	mg/L	0.4 ± 0.19	0.4 ± 0.21	0.4 ± 0.13	0.4 ± 0.16	0.4 ± 0.09	0.2 ± 0.22	0.1 ± 0.07	0.2 ± 0.14	0.09 ± 0.05	0.1 ± 0.04
Nitrate–nitrogen	mg/L	8.9 ± 6.38	14.1 ± 6.40	14.3 ± 5.02	9.4 ± 4.67	12.9 ± 7.03	1.3 ± 1.21	1.7 ± 1.13	0.4 ± 0.33	1.2 ± 0.71	0.6 ± 0.54
Ortho-phosphate–phosphorus	mg/L	59.1 ± 14.16	52.0 ± 14.87	21.1 ± 5.81	46.2 ± 10.74	19.5 ± 4.98	8.4 ± 4.36	7.6 ± 3.90	3.2 ± 1.16	7.0 ± 3.89	3.9 ± 1.25
Element [58,59]											
Aluminium (Al)	mg/L	2.13 ± 0.869	1.54 ± 1.479	2.02 ± 1.624	2.41 ± 1.016	2.98 ± 2.087	0.52 ± 0.528	0.08 ± 0.054	1.07 ± 0.874	0.34 ± 0.180	0.76 ± 0.347
Boron (B)	mg/L	0.57 ± 0.068	0.53 ± 0.086	0.41 ± 0.079	0.54 ± 0.060	0.50 ± 0.078	0.14 ± 0.067	0.11 ± 0.010	0.09 ± 0.011	0.11 ± 0.009	0.10 ± 0.024
Calcium (Ca)	mg/L	36.08 ± 8.750	42.50 ± 4.561	81.39 ± 23.641	43.02 ± 2.411	104.13 ± 32.868	10.54 ± 0.853	11.51 ± 0.926	45.13 ± 11.676	11.25 ± 0.773	70.99 ± 33.166
Cadmium (Cd)	mg/L	7.36 ± 2.981	4.90 ± 2.730	4.10 ± 1.839	7.69 ± 1.064	7.14 ± 2.429	0.09 ± 0.056	0.04 ± 0.020	0.03 ± 0.019	0.05 ± 0.031	0.04 ± 0.030
Chromium (Cr)	mg/L	3.20 ± 0.918	2.48 ± 2.060	2.74 ± 2.021	3.76 ± 1.203	3.99 ± 1.806	0.04 ± 0.063	0.03 ± 0.036	0.03 ± 0.033	0.04 ± 0.049	0.05 ± 0.039
Copper (Cu)	mg/L	1.44 ± 0.435	0.95 ± 0.561	0.90 ± 0.375	1.45 ± 0.113	1.55 ± 0.308	0.16 ± 0.058	0.04 ± 0.029	0.04 ± 0.035	0.06 ± 0.049	0.05 ± 0.043
Iron (Fe)	mg/L	6.41 ± 2.476	4.31 ± 2.928	4.71 ± 2.744	6.35 ± 2.423	7.11 ± 2.934	0.21 ± 0.102	0.15 ± 0.118	0.21 ± 0.202	0.21 ± 0.157	0.48 ± 0.447
Potassium (K)	mg/L	60.16 ± 1.684	52.79 ± 1.322	54.03 ± 11.214	55.68 ± 4.486	60.47 ± 15.561	4.04 ± 0.448	3.40 ± 0.675	10.78 ± 10.185	3.87 ± 0.364	12.77 ± 15.139
Magnesium (Mg)	mg/L	17.16 ± 2.119	17.32 ± 1.296	11.01 ± 2.533	17.76 ± 1.392	13.33 ± 4.526	1.45 ± 0.191	1.36 ± 0.157	0.63 ± 0.310	1.35 ± 0.133	0.70 ± 0.336
Manganese (Mn)	mg/L	0.98 ± 0.257	0.48 ± 0.320	0.51 ± 0.255	1.19 ± 0.063	0.89 ± 0.396	0.17 ± 0.084	0.01 ± 0.012	0.04 ± 0.031	0.08 ± 0.056	0.08 ± 0.069
Sodium (Na)	mg/L	62.68 ± 14.538	58.54 ± 11.080	56.95 ± 9.494	58.19 ± 10.620	58.54 ± 11.630	14.32 ± 1.662	14.74 ± 1.282	15.90 ± 1.869	13.82 ± 1.175	15.35 ± 3.197
Nickel (Ni)	mg/L	0.05 ± 0.065	0.02 ± 0.019	0.02 ± 0.019	0.03 ± 0.018	0.03 ± 0.033	0.04 ± 0.065	0.004 ± 0.006	0.01 ± 0.010	0.01 ± 0.007	0.01 ± 0.012
Zinc (Zn)	mg/L	4.25 ± 1.500	2.86 ± 1.680	2.58 ± 1.114	4.30 ± 0.524	4.52 ± 0.961	0.21 ± 0.159	0.06 ± 0.066	0.04 ± 0.054	0.09 ± 0.083	0.07 ± 0.084
Parameter [57]	**Unit**	**Influent**	**7-day HRT (HC-SGW effluent)**				**Influent**	**7-day HRT (LC-SGW effluent)**			
		HC-SGW	**T9**	**T10**	**T11**	**T12**	**LC-SGW**	**T13**	**T14**	**T15**	**T16**
pH	–	8.4 ± 1.61	7.3 ± 0.82	9.8 ± 1.34	7.7 ± 1.21	9.8 ± 1.54	6.9 ± 0.48	6.9 ± 0.61	10.3 ± 1.33	7.5 ± 0.72	10.5 ± 1.05
Redox potential	mV	−36.6 ± 74.22	12.2 ± 40.30	−100.1 ± 66.45	−4.4 ± 59.67	−95.5 ± 88.21	34.1 ± 21.23	31.0 ± 28.12	−130.8 ± 63.74	1.8 ± 33.00	−131.3 ± 72.36
Turbidity	NTU	188.9 ± 47.22	154.8 ± 86.08	178.8 ± 98.79	185.7 ± 49.24	245.8 ± 96.29	22.9 ± 7.14	18.9 ± 11.05	25.1 ± 16.21	16.5 ± 7.27	40.9 ± 25.03
Total suspended solids	mg/L	317.0 ± 58.35	267.8 ± 110.05	342.9 ± 125.33	302.6 ± 61.44	423.4 ± 114.04	39.9 ± 15.94	27.7 ± 16.48	37.5 ± 15.62	25.0 ± 10.96	55.2 ± 24.85
Electronic conductivity	µS/cm	988.5 ± 196.09	1137.4 ± 471.09	1191.1 ± 343.72	1003.0 ± 306.88	1107.1 ± 299.47	164.6 ± 63.24	161.4 ± 42.91	306.8 ± 118.32	144.0 ± 32.28	290.2 ± 135.74

Table 2. *Cont.*

Parameter [57]	Unit	Influent	2-Day HRT (HC-SGW Effluent)				Influent	2-Day HRT (LC-SGW Effluent)			
		HC-SGW	T1	T2	T3	T4	LC-SGW	T5	T6	T7	T8
Dissolved oxygen	mg/L	10.5 ± 1.39	8.8 ± 0.89	8.3 ± 1.03	10.5 ± 0.91	9.8 ± 1.19	10.4 ± 1.24	9.3 ± 1.24	8.7 ± 0.94	11.0 ± 1.11	10.1 ± 0.84
Colour	Pa/Co	1587.8 ± 379.89	1448.1 ± 647.98	1593.5 ± 761.50	1644.8 ± 489.96	2040.5 ± 757.57	214.5 ± 64.07	159.1 ± 56.83	250.6 ± 120.15	152.6 ± 41.05	283.8 ± 115.21
Temperature	°C	16.9 ± 5.40	16.8 ± 4.03	18.0 ± 4.14	16.6 ± 3.87	17.7 ± 4.20	17.7 ± 4.58	15.9 ± 4.18	17.3 ± 4.31	15.3 ± 4.23	17.0 ± 4.15
Biochemical oxygen demand	mg/L	34.7 ± 12.99	23.1 ± 9.35	12.1 ± 7.32	16.6 ± 7.07	8.3 ± 4.23	17.6 ± 8.00	13.4 ± 5.63	5.5 ± 6.00	6.7 ± 4.85	5.4 ± 3.95
Chemical oxygen demand	mg/L	129.2 ± 34.68	94.0 ± 31.13	90.7 ± 29.89	100.8 ± 27.65	103.1 ± 16.10	28.9 ± 14.47	31.3 ± 11.95	29.2 ± 10.71	17.2 ± 6.95	19.9 ± 7.28
Ammonia–nitrogen	mg/L	0.4 ± 0.19	0.5 ± 0.23	0.3 ± 0.14	0.3 ± 0.13	0.3 ± 0.11	0.2 ± 0.22	0.1 ± 0.07	0.1 ± 0.07	0.1 ± 0.04	0.1 ± 0.15
Nitrate–nitrogen	mg/L	8.9 ± 6.38	10.7 ± 7.92	16.3 ± 4.89	8.5 ± 8.42	15.0 ± 8.59	1.3 ± 1.21	1.3 ± 0.77	0.7 ± 0.77	1.0 ± 0.64	0.3 ± 0.28
Ortho-phosphate–phosphorus	mg/L	59.1 ± 14.16	48.0 ± 13.76	16.3 ± 3.00	43.0 ± 13.78	17.3 ± 5.63	8.4 ± 4.36	11.9 ± 6.36	3.0 ± 1.77	8.5 ± 4.03	3.7 ± 1.29
Element [58,59]											
Aluminium (Al)	mg/L	2.13 ± 0.869	2.33 ± 1.321	1.56 ± 0.880	2.98 ± 1.218	3.61 ± 2.306	0.52 ± 0.528	0.12 ± 0.094	0.37 ± 0.232	0.36 ± 0.189	0.73 ± 0.420
Boron (B)	mg/L	0.57 ± 0.068	0.55 ± 0.211	0.44 ± 0.202	0.54 ± 0.160	0.39 ± 0.078	0.14 ± 0.067	0.13 ± 0.069	0.08 ± 0.005	0.12 ± 0.064	0.08 ± 0.006
Calcium (Ca)	mg/L	36.08 ± 8.750	42.49 ± 4.386	77.22 ± 42.765	37.39 ± 4.030	145.67 ± 92.506	10.54 ± 0.853	11.44 ± 0.944	60.11 ± 13.881	10.74 ± 0.739	65.46 ± 37.361
Cadmium (Cd)	mg/L	7.36 ± 2.981	5.82 ± 2.238	4.61 ± 2.126	6.40 ± 1.984	6.87 ± 2.628	0.09 ± 0.056	0.08 ± 0.097	0.02 ± 0.021	0.09 ± 0.083	0.05 ± 0.046
Chromium (Cr)	mg/L	3.20 ± 0.918	3.22 ± 1.736	2.86 ± 1.328	4.76 ± 1.215	4.75 ± 2.021	0.04 ± 0.063	0.05 ± 0.069	0.04 ± 0.031	0.07 ± 0.074	0.06 ± 0.054
Copper (Cu)	mg/L	1.44 ± 0.435	1.15 ± 0.385	0.98 ± 0.308	1.30 ± 0.301	1.47 ± 0.247	0.16 ± 0.058	0.07 ± 0.081	0.04 ± 0.032	0.10 ± 0.091	0.06 ± 0.057
Iron (Fe)	mg/L	6.41 ± 2.476	5.45 ± 1.657	5.03 ± 1.475	7.02 ± 1.801	8.69 ± 2.012	0.21 ± 0.102	0.14 ± 0.080	0.39 ± 0.218	0.20 ± 0.100	0.93 ± 0.759
Potassium (K)	mg/L	60.16 ± 1.684	44.90 ± 2.827	56.58 ± 19.919	45.77 ± 5.160	59.62 ± 20.132	4.04 ± 0.448	2.99 ± 0.216	17.59 ± 16.141	3.62 ± 0.438	20.16 ± 19.003
Magnesium (Mg)	mg/L	17.16 ± 2.119	17.77 ± 3.477	12.84 ± 6.124	16.24 ± 1.971	12.97 ± 3.785	1.45 ± 0.191	1.55 ± 0.195	0.84 ± 0.224	1.38 ± 0.161	0.78 ± 0.330
Manganese (Mn)	mg/L	0.98 ± 0.257	0.35 ± 0.249	0.46 ± 0.212	1.01 ± 0.223	0.86 ± 0.457	0.17 ± 0.084	0.05 ± 0.077	0.04 ± 0.033	0.06 ± 0.074	0.10 ± 0.094
Sodium (Na)	mg/L	62.68 ± 14.538	55.09 ± 11.391	55.85 ± 12.850	55.22 ± 11.852	55.59 ± 12.232	14.32 ± 1.662	13.91 ± 1.648	15.42 ± 3.280	13.15 ± 1.199	15.69 ± 5.272
Nickel (Ni)	mg/L	0.05 ± 0.065	0.10 ± 0.091	0.05 ± 0.077	0.09 ± 0.081	0.04 ± 0.033	0.04 ± 0.065	0.05 ± 0.081	0.00 ± 0.012	0.05 ± 0.080	0.01 ± 0.010
Zinc (Zn)	mg/L	4.25 ± 1.500	3.12 ± 0.872	2.78 ± 0.859	3.90 ± 0.972	4.32 ± 0.787	0.21 ± 0.159	0.11 ± 0.094	0.06 ± 0.050	0.13 ± 0.068	0.11 ± 0.089

Parameter [57]	Unit	2-day HRT (TW effluent)		7-day HRT (TW effluent)	
		C1	C2	C3	C4
pH	–	6.7 ± 0.39	7.4 ± 0.60	6.6 ± 0.39	7.1 ± 0.52
Redox potential	mV	42.2 ± 16.50	9.6 ± 28.10	44.1 ± 17.06	25.1 ± 24.68
Turbidity	NTU	9.3 ± 6.61	4.2 ± 4.37	12.7 ± 12.56	3.7 ± 3.47
Total suspended solids	mg/L	14.3 ± 8.16	3.9 ± 2.93	17.8 ± 13.69	4.3 ± 5.79
Electronic conductivity	µS/cm	84.4 ± 12.15	81.5 ± 9.94	92.9 ± 27.28	87.1 ± 20.83
Dissolved oxygen	mg/L	9.0 ± 0.87	10.4 ± 0.70	8.9 ± 1.09	10.8 ± 1.07
Colour	Pa/Co	44.3 ± 30.56	8.6 ± 7.66	56.1 ± 31.45	12.7 ± 9.73
Temperature	°C	16.5 ± 3.76	16.8 ± 4.04	15.1 ± 4.20	15.5 ± 4.17
Biochemical oxygen demand	mg/L	7.3 ± 3.45	5.4 ± 4.03	9.1 ± 5.05	6.7 ± 4.65
Chemical oxygen demand	mg/L	15.9 ± 7.74	6.3 ± 2.84	17.6 ± 6.74	7.0 ± 2.48

Table 2. *Cont.*

Parameter [57]	Unit	Influent	2-Day HRT (HC-SGW Effluent)				Influent	2-Day HRT (LC-SGW Effluent)			
		HC-SGW	T1	T2	T3	T4	LC-SGW	T5	T6	T7	T8
Ammonia–nitrogen	mg/L		0.1 ± 0.12		0.1 ± 0.14			0.1 ± 0.04		0.1 ± 0.05	
Nitrate–nitrogen	mg/L		1.1 ± 0.75		0.8 ± 0.53			0.9 ± 0.42		0.8 ± 0.54	
Ortho-phosphate–phosphorus	mg/L		2.8 ± 1.82		2.4 ± 0.63			3.4 ± 1.47		2.4 ± 0.86	
Element [58,59]											
Aluminium (Al)	mg/L		0.01 ± 0.006		0.01 ± 0.007			0.08 ± 0.092		0.09 ± 0.101	
Boron (B)	mg/L		0.02 ± 0.018		0.03 ± 0.009			0.05 ± 0.061		0.05 ± 0.059	
Calcium (Ca)	mg/L		9.96 ± 0.549		9.78 ± 0.552			9.67 ± 0.591		9.51 ± 0.476	
Cadmium (Cd)	mg/L		0.01 ± 0.006		0.00 ± 0.006			0.04 ± 0.071		0.05 ± 0.071	
Chromium (Cr)	mg/L		0.00 ± 0.005		0.00 ± 0.005			0.03 ± 0.063		0.03 ± 0.063	
Copper (Cu)	mg/L		0.01 ± 0.006		0.01 ± 0.008			0.04 ± 0.073		0.05 ± 0.078	
Iron (Fe)	mg/L		0.02 ± 0.007		0.02 ± 0.009			0.05 ± 0.069		0.05 ± 0.066	
Potassium (K)	mg/L		0.35 ± 0.049		0.69 ± 0.261			0.50 ± 0.492		0.52 ± 0.127	
Magnesium (Mg)	mg/L		1.10 ± 0.123		1.10 ± 0.138			1.20 ± 0.119		1.16 ± 0.120	
Manganese (Mn)	mg/L		0.01 ± 0.010		0.00 ± 0.009			0.04 ± 0.070		0.04 ± 0.069	
Sodium (Na)	mg/L		6.62 ± 0.721		6.69 ± 0.869			6.80 ± 0.085		6.35 ± 0.105	
Nickel (Ni)	mg/L		0.01 ± 0.023		0.01 ± 0.023			0.04 ± 0.075		0.04 ± 0.075	

Note: Values in mean ± SD. SD, standard deviation; NTU, nephelometric turbidity unit; HRT, hydraulic retention time; HC, high pollutant concentrations; T9, treatment system with only *Phragmites australis*; T10, treatment system with *Phragmites australis* and ochre pellets; T11, treatment system without *Phragmites australis* or ochre pellets; T12, treatment system with ochre pellets only; LC, low pollutant concentrations; T13, treatment system with only *Phragmites australis*; T14, treatment system with *Phragmites australis* and ochre pellets; T15, treatment system without *Phragmites australis* or ochre pellets; and T16, treatment system with only ochre pellets. TW, tap water; C1 and C3, treatment system with TW and floating *Phragmites australis*; C2 and C4, treatment system with only TW.

Multipurpose compost soil and chilli fruits were analysed for minerals using ICP-OES and following the USEPA Method 200.7 [59]. Soil samples were obtained by a soil sampler kit reaching a depth of up to 20 cm [60]. Samples of chilli fruits were randomly selected from each group of plants separately. Both soil and fruit samples were analysed for mineral content following the USEPA Method 3050B [61]. Samples were dried overnight in an oven at 105 °C, which is required for enzymatic reactions and to stabilise the sample weight [62]. About 10 mL of aqua regia was mixed with one part of nitric acid (HNO_3). Three parts of hydrochloric acid (HCl) were added to 300 mg of oven-dried samples, which were weighed on a digital balance at an accuracy of 0.1 mg. Samples were subsequently digested in a CEM Mars Xpress microwave. Thereafter, they were analysed using ICP-OES. Results were noted in mg/kg for the contents of aluminium (Al), boron (B), calcium (Ca), cadmium (Cd), chromium (Cr), copper (Cu), iron (Fe), potassium (K), magnesium (Mg), manganese (Mn), sodium (Na), nickel (Ni), and zinc (Zn).

Blank samples were analysed at the beginning of each test to identify contamination due to either the reagents or equipment during the test process, and were periodically tested to confirm that values were within the detection limits. Furthermore, three standard calibration solutions were regularly run between the samples to address instrumental drifts.

2.6. Data Statistical Analysis

A statistical assessment of the collected data was performed for significant differences with confidence level of 95% throughout IBM-SPSS (Statistical Package for the Social Sciences) statistical software program version 23. Before deciding on a comparison technique, distribution patterns of independent sets of data were investigated using the Shapiro–Wilk test for normality [63]. The independent sample parametric T-test is used when the hypothesis of normal distribution of data is correct, otherwise, the non-parametric Mann–Whitney U-test is executed for the rejected normality hypothesis of data distribution [64]. The homogeneity of variances was examined by using Levene's test for parametric and non–parametric data. Significant differences between the means of at least three independent data groups were evaluated by a one-way analysis of variance (ANOVA) of normally distributed data. In comparison, the Kruskal–Wallis H-test was applied for the assessment of non-normally distributed data [65]. Furthermore, the correlations between variables were assessed using Spearman's test at 99% confidence level [66].

3. Results and Discussion

3.1. Irrigation Water Quality

The effluents from different set-up designs of FTW (Table 2) were recycled to irrigate potted chilli plants grown in the laboratory and greenhouse. The irrigation regime followed the experiment set-up design shown in Table 1. The pH of the effluents was greater than 6.5, which complied with the minimum limitation stated by FAO [1] to be used for irrigation. Compared to the maximum allowed water pH limit of 8.5 for irrigation [1], the treatment systems with cement–ochre pellets produced effluents of pH values higher than 8.5 (Tables 1 and 2). However, an Italian decree reported that irrigation water of pH up to 9.5 could be allowed [67].

The electric conductivity (EC) of wastewater has been limited when reused as agricultural water, since it is a measurement of water salinity. It affects crop productivity, soil structure, and capacity of water and air transport into the soil. According to FAO [1] and WHO [2], EC values of all effluents were much lower than 3000 µS/cm.

It was observed that TSS values of all LC-SGW effluents were below 100 mg/L, which is the lower limit of the range recommended by WHO [2]. While TSS figures of HC-SGW effluents were within the recommended range (100–350 mg/L), except effluent of the treatment system T12 (HC-SGW with only ochre pellets for 7-day HRT), as in Table 2. High TSS values could cause soil clogging, negatively effecting soil composition and porosity [4].

Organic matter was evaluated by measuring the five-day biochemical oxygen demand (BOD_5) of the SGW effluents (Table 2). All BOD_5 values were significantly ($p < 0.05$) less than the recommended range of 110–400 mg/L [2]. This could be a positive indication of a low level of microbiological contamination. Crop productivity, plant biomass, soil structure, and nutritious content could be positively impacted with an increase in the organic matter content. In contrast, a too high organic loading rate could clog the soil causing an anaerobic condition in the root-zone, thereby depleting nitrogen through denitrification in organic biodegradation processes [3]. Therefore, the low organic matter content in greywater recycling could address this serious concerns compared to recycling of blackwater or mixed-resource wastewater for irrigation [21].

Measurements showed that NH_4-N and NO_3-N in effluents of both types of SGW were less than the thresholds of 5 mg/L and 30 mg/L, respectively [1]. The presence of too much nitrogen rather leads to more foliage than fruits. However, exceeding the NO_3-N to more than 30 mg/L could lead to a delay in grain crop ripening, reducing the sugar content in beets and canes [2]. Furthermore, Bar-Tal et al. [68] stated that a low NO_3: NH_4 ratio leads to a decrease in yield productivity in terms of the reduction in fruit weights due to physiological disorders in chilli pepper plants.

According to the recommended $PO_4^{-}P$ level of 2 mg/L [1] and 5 mg/L [11], the PO_4-P concentrations were around the threshold limit in effluents from treatments with cement–ochre pellets compared to others treatment systems, especially for LC-SGW systems. However, WHO [2] stated that the total phosphorus of irrigation water between 6 and 20 mg/L could increase crop productivity without a destructive effect on soil. The bioavailability of copper, zinc, and iron could be limited in alkaline soils when phosphorus concentrations of agricultural water are over 20 mg/L [2]. Furthermore, it was indicated that a deficiency in phosphorus content could limit the crop yields and enhance plant uptake for manganese [69,70].

Table 2 shows the heavy metal concentrations and other trace elements of the effluents of FTW. Aluminium (Al) and iron (Fe) concentrations were lower than the threshold of 5 mg/L for long-term irrigation in all effluents (Table 3). For short-term irrigation, Al and Fe were limited, up to 20 mg/L [1,11]. High concentrations of Al and Fe could reduce the phosphorus mobilization in soil effecting crops due to phosphorus deficiency [2]. The boron (B) content was less than the allowed lower limits (0.5–0.75 mg/L) for crops of high sensitivity [2].

Table 3. Permissible concentrations of chemical elements in agricultural water, soil, and crops for safe human health and environment.

Sample	Aluminium (Al)	Boron (B)	Calcium (Ca)	Cadmium (Cd)	Chromium (Cr)	Copper (Cu)	Iron (Fe)	Potassium (K)	Magnesium (Mg)	Manganese (Mn)	Sodium (Na)	Nickel (Ni)	Zinc (Zn)	Reference
Water (mg/L)	5	3	20	0.01	0.1	0.2	5	2	5	0.2	40	0.2	2	[1]
	–	–	–	–	0.55	0.017	0.5	–	–	–	–	1.4	0.2	[2]
	5-20	–	–	0.01–0.05	0.1–1	0.2–5	5–20	–	–	0.2–10	–	0.2–2	10	[11]
	–	–	–	0.01	0.1	0.2	–	–	–	0.2	–	0.2	2	[71]
Soil (mg/kg)	–	–	–	3–6	–	270	–	–	–	–	–	150	600	[29]
	–	–	–	3	150	140	–	–	–	–	–	75	300	[31]
	–	–	–	–	100	30	–	–	–	–	–	80	200	[32]
	–	–	3	–	100	100	50,000	–	–	2000	–	50	300	[72]
	–	–	–	100	100	–	–	–	–	–	–	–	1500	[73]
	–	–	–	100	20	0.3	–	–	–	–	–	140	–	[74]
Crops (mg/kg)	–	–	–	0.1	2.3	73.3	425	–	–	500	–	67	100	[27]
	–	–	–	0.05	–	20	–	–	–	–	–		50	[31]
	–	–	–	0.02	1.3	10	–	–	–	–	–	10	0.6	[32]

Calcium (Ca) was present at high levels within effluents treated by systems with cement–ochre pellets, such as T2, T4, T6, T8, T10, T12, T14, and T16 (Tables 1 and 2). Concentrations of Ca in LC-SGW effluents from treatment without cement–ochre pellets (T5, T7, T13, and T15) complied with the recommended range between 0 and 20 mg/L [1]. However, corresponding concentrations were between 37.39 and 43.02 mg/L for HC-SGW effluents of treatment systems without cement–ochre pellets (T1, T3, T9, and T11), as shown in Tables 2 and 3. Alkalinity caused by carbonates and bicarbonates of wastewater reused for irrigation was between 50 and 200 mg of $CaCO_3$/L, which has no negative effect on soil and crops. In contrast, wastewater with $CaCO_3$ higher than 500 mg/L could negatively impact the soil structure by precipitation of calcium and burnt plant leaves in a warm climate [2].

Cadmium (Cd) concentrations for HC-SGW effluents (4.10–7.69 mg/L) were higher than the recommended thresholds of 0.01 to 0.05 mg/L [1,11], while Cd concentrations of LC-SGW effluents were between 0.02 and 0.09 mg/L (Tables 2 and 3). Plant uptake of cadmium increases with time depending on the pH and cadmium content in soil [2].

Concentrations of chromium (Cr), potassium (K), magnesium (Mg), and sodium (Na) were higher for HC-SGW effluents compared to the recommended concentrations in wastewater used for irrigation: 0.1–1.0 mg/L, 0.0–2.0 mg/L, 0.0–5.0 mg/L, and 0.0–40.0 mg/L, respectively [1,11]. In comparison, corresponding concentrations complied with the above thresholds for effluents of LC-SGW. Copper (Cu), manganese (Mn), nickel (Ni), and zinc (Zn) concentrations were lower than the threshold ranges: 0.2–5.0 mg/L, 0.2–10.0 mg/L, 0.2–2.0 mg/L, and 5.0–10.0 mg/L, respectively [1,11].

The potential for water reuse might be limited due to low water irrigation quality in terms of high total phosphorus and total suspended solids. An unfavourable sodium adsorption ratio (SAR) of compost soil is associated with irrigation water of elevated Ca, Mg, and Na concentrations, leading to a poor soil structure [75]. Overall yields of chillies irrigated by treated greywater were low, indicating challenges with elevated salinity [76]. However, irrigation with greywater had no negative effect on the plant dry biomass, number of leaves, and water demand [3]. Water stress might cause low fruit productivity in terms of weight, diameter, and length [77]. Since the salinity and organic matter content becomes elevated in soil with increased irrigation time, the plant growth rate is affected. However, glasshouse research indicated that greywater irrigation had no significant impact on the reduction of dry biomass, number of leaves, and water use [78].

3.2. Growth Environmental Conditions

A comparison between the environmental boundary conditions in the laboratory and greenhouse associated with chilli plants grown in pots is shown in Figure 2. Temperature measurements complied with the recommended limits for different growth stages of chilli plants [55,75]. The observed temperature in the laboratory was slightly higher than in the greenhouse, especially for the summer season (Figure 2a). The recorded temperature in both locations met to the suggested range (24–29 °C) by Bhatt and Srinivasa [79] for the highest photosynthesis rate for various growth stages of chilli plants.

The mean values of relative humidity in the laboratory varied between 40 and 60%, and were lower than the humidity measurements in the greenhouse reaching 80% in July 2015 (Figure 2b). Low relative humidity may negatively impact the pollination process and the corresponding fruit development progress. In contrast, a high humidity causes fruit degradation and rotting [80]. High fluctuations of light intensity were monitored in the greenhouse compared to the steady light intensity in the laboratory at around 20,000 Lux (Figure 2c). An insufficient light intensity during the blossoming stage could seriously affect plant health and fruit productivity and quality, such as flower abscission [54]. Deli and Tiessen [81] recommended a light density range between 8600 and 17,200 Lux to avoid inhibition/detachment of flowers and other syndromes in plants.

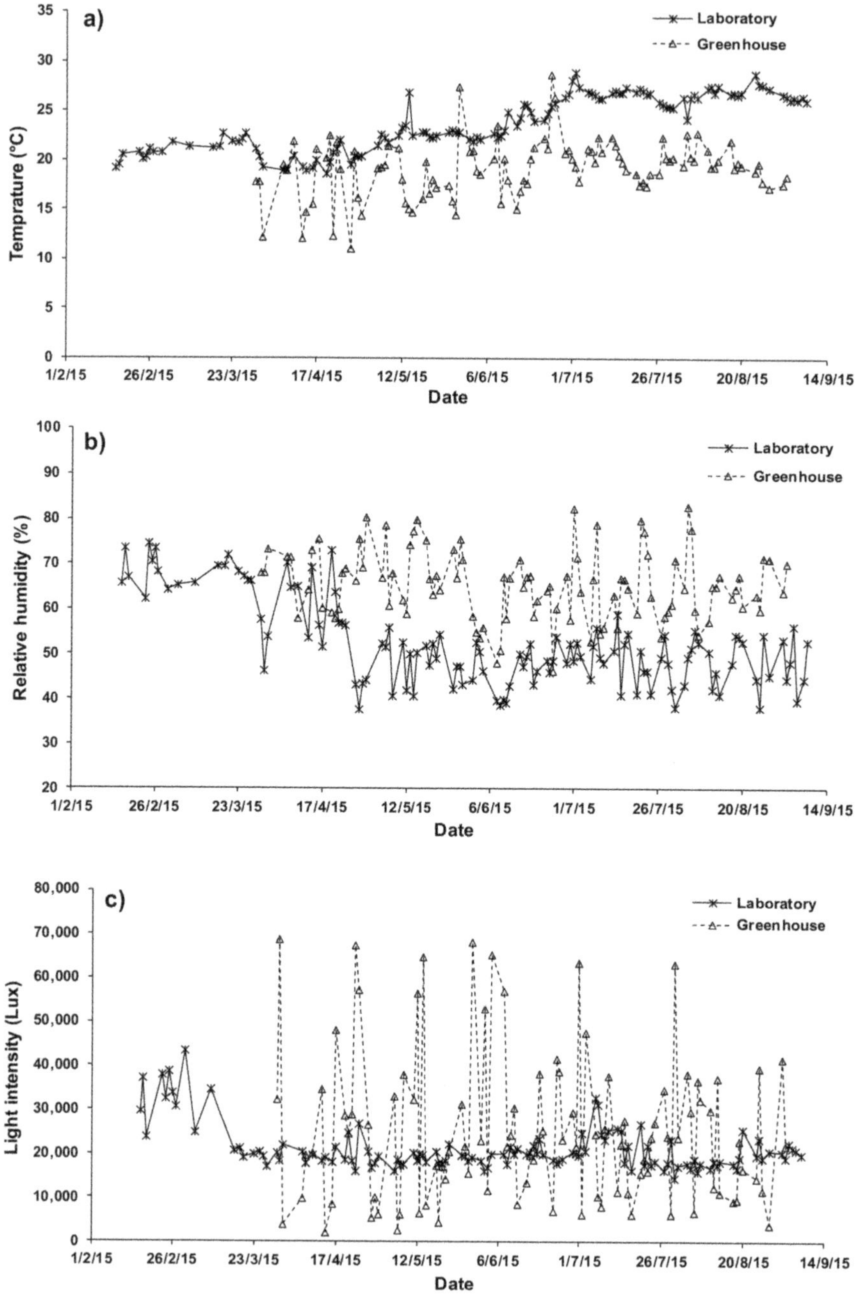

Figure 2. Monitoring growth environmental condition for growth chilli plant in laboratory and greenhouse in terms of (**a**) temperature; (**b**) relative humidity; and (**c**) light intensity.

3.3. Growth Monitoring

Chilli plant biomass development was recorded in April and August 2015. Plant height and number of leaves considerably increased in April, while no significant increase ($p > 0.05$) in heights were observed after August. Old "fallen down" leaves and the growth of new ones were noticed in August.

In April 2015, the average heights of chilli plants grown in the laboratory were greater than the heights of the corresponding chilli group receiving the same irrigation water, but grown in the greenhouse (Figure 3a). The tallest plant in the laboratory was P8 with a height of 423 mm (watering by treated LC-SGW with only cement–ochre pellets; 2 days of HRT), while the shortest plant was P3c with a height of 283 mm (watering by tap water with only *Phragmites australis*; 2 days of HRT). In August 2015, chilli plants in the greenhouse showed a non-significant increase ($p > 0.05$) in height compared to corresponding plant heights in the laboratory. An exception was chilli plants receiving tap water. Chilli plants in both locations showed significant ($p < 0.05$) growth with good health in August compared to their growth rate measured in April.

The maximum average height in the greenhouse was recorded as 695 mm for P4c (receiving from system retaining tap water; 7 days HRT), which is significantly ($p < 0.05$) differed compared with other plants in the same location ranging between 420 and 695 mm. Only one significant record ($p < 0.05$) was linked to the height (637 mm) of the chilli plant P9 in the laboratory (watering by treated HC-SGW with only *Phragmites australis*; 7 days of HRT), which was greater than the corresponding plant height (490 mm) in the greenhouse, as shown in Figure 3a. The plant heights were between 333 and 637 mm with significant ($p < 0.05$) differences compared to each other.

In April, the counted numbers of chilli plant leaves were significantly ($p < 0.05$) greater than the number of leaves for plants grown in the greenhouse, except for P3, P7, P13, P1c, P2c, and P3c (Figure 3b). The number of leaves increased significantly ($p > 0.05$) for chilli plants in both places in August compared to April. A significant ($p < 0.05$) leaf count number in the greenhouse was noted for the plants P1, P2, P14, P15, P16, and P3c, which was greater than in the laboratory. In contrast, plants P3, P4, P5, P6, P7, P8, P10, and P13 had significantly ($p < 0.05$) less leaf numbers than in the laboratory (Figure 3b). The plant height measurements showed that the variation of irrigation water quality had significant effects on the development patterns for different weather conditions. Furthermore, the greenhouse conditions enhanced the plant biomass, particularly for plants receiving nutrients complying with the irrigation thresholds. These findings are in agreement with García-Delgado et al. [77], who stated that leaves, stems, and biomass productions of chilli plants significantly improved when irrigated with treated wastewater compared to other plants using other types of irrigation water with added mineral fertilizers in a greenhouse environment.

In April 2015, the number of chilli buds in the laboratory were significantly ($p < 0.05$) higher compared to the corresponding plants in the greenhouse, except for chilli plant P8 (Figure 3c). Then the number of buds fluctuated in both locations due to transformation to flowers or failure in growth (either slowly dying or even dropping), which was frequently noticed in the laboratory experiment. In May 2015, the bud numbers decreased approximately to half in both locations. In June 2015, chilli plants in the greenhouse showed new bud production. The bud numbers were significantly ($p < 0.05$) elevated compared to the laboratory plants, except for chilli plant P8, where the bud numbers were greater in the laboratory (Figure 3c). In July 2015, the counted number of buds decreased significantly ($p < 0.05$) in both locations compared to previous months, because of the production of flowers, except for plants P8 and P12, which still contained buds (Figure S1).

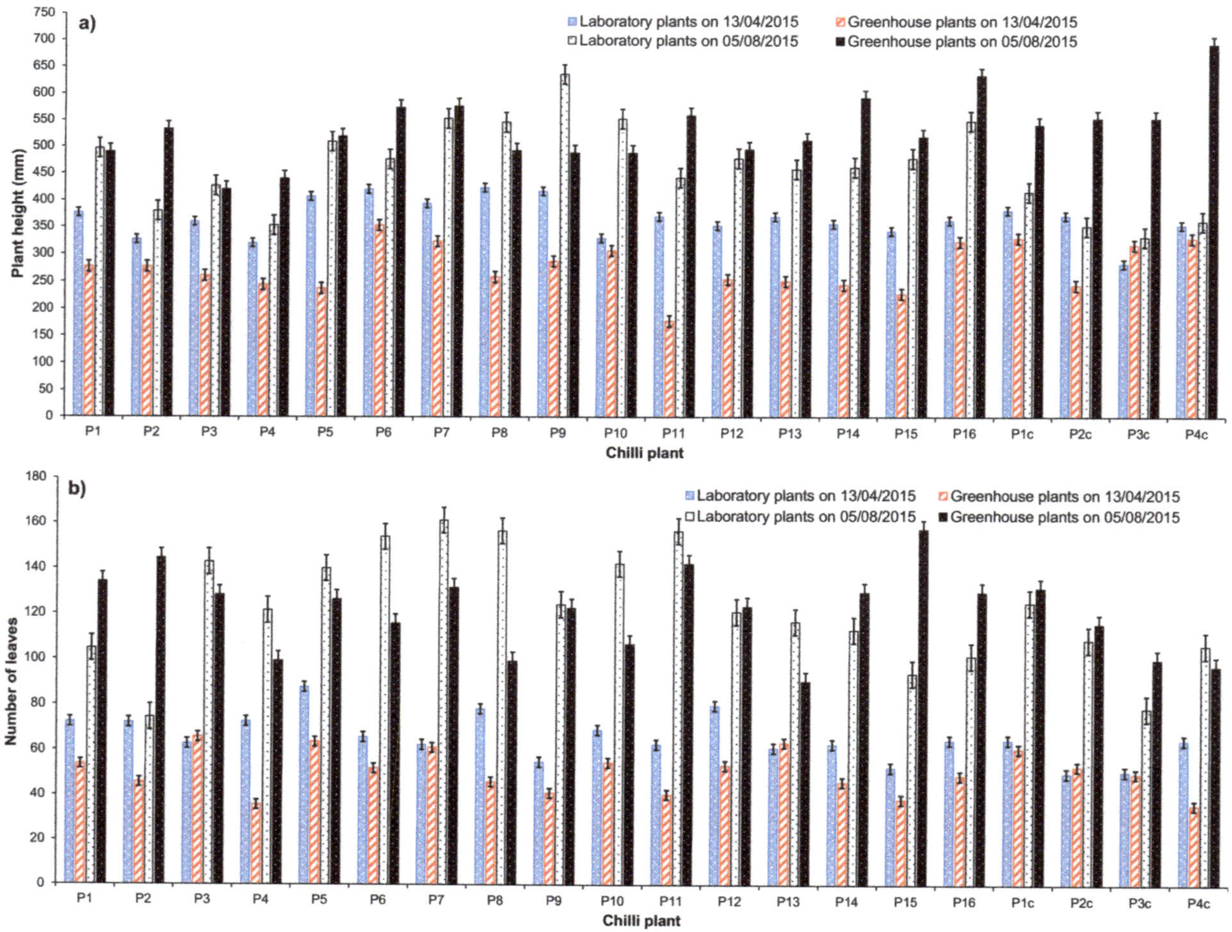

Figure 3. *Cont.*

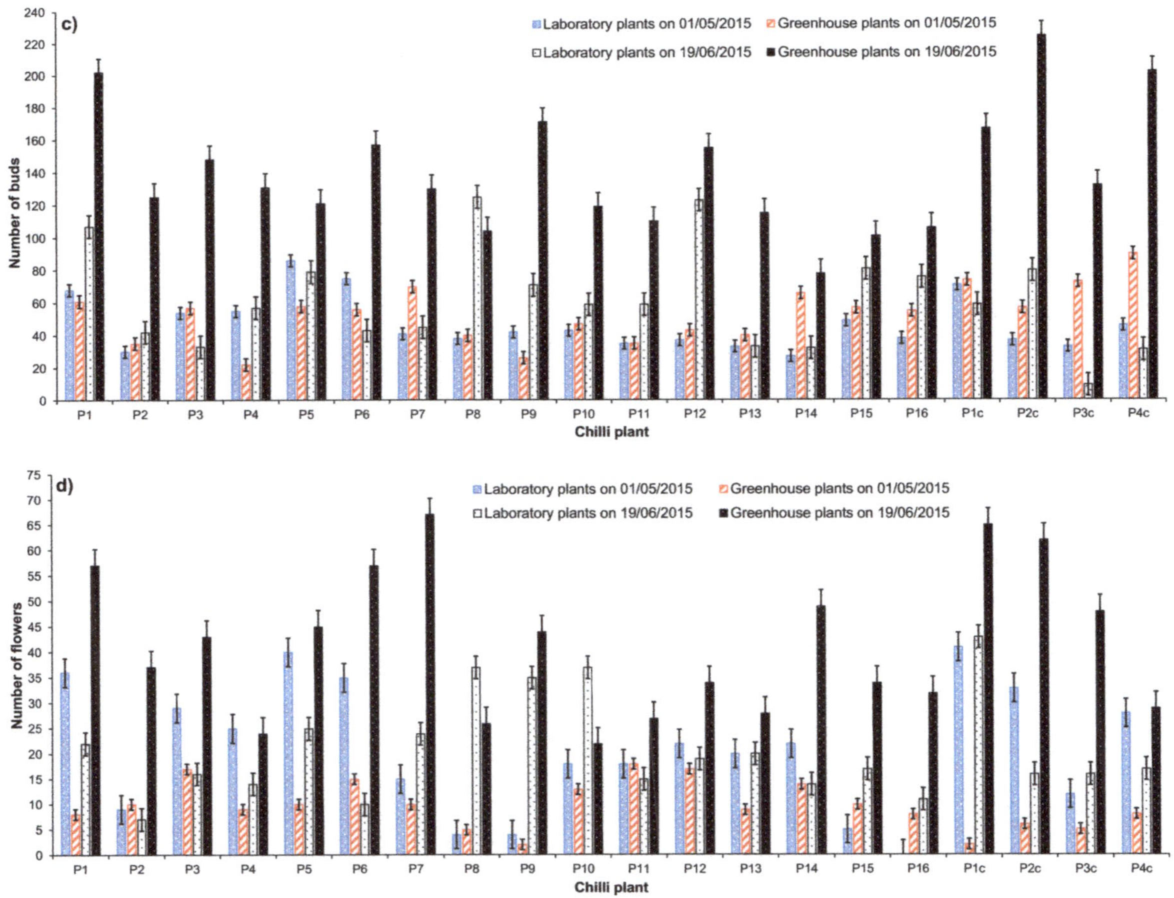

Figure 3. Monitoring of chilli plant growth in terms of (**a**) plant height; (**b**) number of leaves; (**c**) number of buds; and (**d**) number of flowers.

Blooming was observed first in the laboratory-based chilli plants by the middle of April 2015; a week later, it was also apparent for greenhouse plants. In May 2015, the counted flower numbers for plants located in the laboratory were significantly ($p < 0.05$) higher than in the greenhouse, except for plants P2, P8, P11, P15, and P16, where there were lower numbers. The maximum significant ($p < 0.05$) average number of flowers was recorded for plant P1c followed by plants P5 and P1 compared to other plants in the laboratory. In contrast to June 2015, greenhouse chilli plants produced significant ($p < 0.05$) numbers of flowers compared to the plants in the laboratory, with the exception of plants P8 and P10. The average flower number of plant P7 was significantly ($p < 0.05$) greater than the corresponding number of the other plants in the greenhouse (Figure 3d). In both locations, it was observed that the stage of producing flowers from buds was very rapid and it might occur within a few days, which agreed with previously published findings [54,78].

3.4. Chilli Fruit Production, Quality, and Classification

The production of chilli fruits was monitored from the ripening stage until the harvesting season. Following Almuktar et al. [54], chilli fruits were classified according to their quality, such as weight, length, width, and shape bending (Table 4). Therefore, the productivity of the chilli planting experiment was assessed depending on the number of produced fruits, their weight, and price. The chilli fruit price was estimated in pound sterling (GBP).

Table 4. Classification scheme for quality of the harvested chilli fruit [54].

Parameter	Class A	Class B	Class C	Class D	Class E
Quality class	Outstanding	Very good	Good	Satisfactory	Unsatisfactory
Approximate Codex Standard	"Extra" Class	Class I	Class II	Not applicable	Not applicable
Length (L, mm)	Very long ($L \geq 80$)	Long ($80 > L \geq 60$)	Medium ($60 > L \geq 40$)	Short ($40 > L \geq 20$)	Very short ($L < 20$)
Width (W, mm)	Very wide ($W \geq 20$)	Wide ($20 > W \geq 16$)	Medium ($16 > W \geq 12$)	Slim ($12 > W \geq 8$)	Very slim ($W < 8$)
Fresh weight (w, gram)	Very large ($w \geq 9$)	Large ($9 > w \geq 7$)	Medium ($7 > w \geq 5$)	Small ($5 > w \geq 3$)	Very small ($w < 3$)
Bending (L/W)	Characteristically ($L/W \geq 3.5$)	Characteristically ($L/W \geq 3.5$)	Characteristically ($L/W \geq 3.5$)	Uncharacteristically ($L/W < 3.5$)	Uncharacteristically ($L/W < 3.5$)
Price (Sterling, pence/g)	2.00	1.00	0.50	0.25	0.00

In both laboratory and greenhouse environments, harvesting of chilli fruits was commenced in June 2015 and finalised in January 2016. The monthly record showed that the maximum number of chilli fruits from both locations was harvested in July. The chilli fruit quantity in the greenhouse was 1512 fruits (12.024 kg), which was significantly ($p < 0.05$) higher than in the laboratory (254 fruits (1.384 kg)), as shown in Figure 4a,b. Plant P7 in the greenhouse and plant P8 in the laboratory contributed with the highest production of fruits in July: 104 (0.646 kg) and 29 (0.188 kg) chilli fruits, respectively. Plant P4c located in the greenhouse had the highest harvested weigh of fruits in July (0.787 kg for 86 chilli fruits) compared to all other plants in the greenhouse (Figure 4c,d). Furthermore, the chilli price in July linked to plant P8 in the laboratory was GBP 1.39 in comparison to the total price in July of GBP 6.57, which was significantly ($p < 0.05$) lower compared to the chilli price (GBP 10.75) associated with plant P1c in the greenhouse and to the total price of chilli fruits (GBP 135.58) gained only in July (Figure 4e,f).

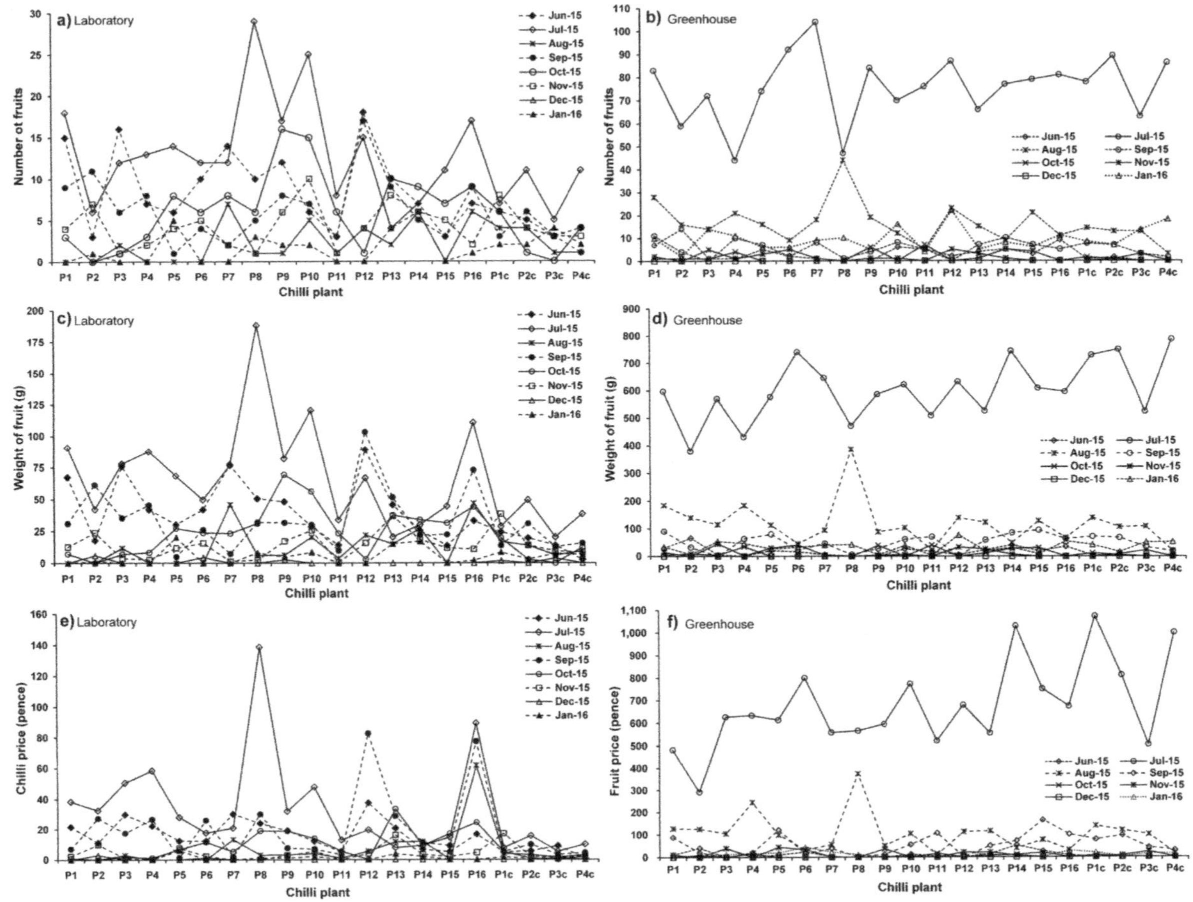

Figure 4. Monthly fruit harvest and productivity of chilli plants grown in laboratory and greenhouse environments in terms of (**a**,**b**) number of fruits; (**c**,**d**) weight of fruit; and (**e**,**f**) fruit price.

The highest number of Class A produce was linked to plant P1c in the greenhouse (36 chillies of 0.449 kg worth GBP 8.97) compared to plant P16 in the laboratory (5 chillies), as shown in Figure 5 and Figure S2. Plant P1 grown in the greenhouse had a greater number of chilli fruits of Class B (47 chillies of 0.459 kg worth GBP 4.59) compared to plant P16 (13 chillies). Plants P12 and P2c in the greenhouse had the highest number of Class C fruits (35 chillies of total weight (price) of 0.214 kg (GBP 1.07) and 0.260 kg (GBP 1.33), respectively), compared to highest number of Class C fruits obtained in the laboratory from plant P8 (24 chillies). Class D chilli fruits was the dominant class for almost plants in both locations (Table 4). The highest number of Class D fruits was produced by plant P7 in greenhouse (52 chillies of 0.230 kg worth GBP 0.57) compared to the Class D fruits (33 chillies) from plant P10 located in the laboratory (Figure 5 and Figure S2). All plants in both locations produced Class E chilli fruits, which were deemed unsatisfactory, because they are very short, small and slim with little value on the market as fresh fruits (Table 4). Plant P11 in the greenhouse gave 31 chillies of Class E with a weight of 0.052 kg compared to 19 chillies from P10 in the laboratory.

A large number (142) of chilli fruits was produced from plant P1 in greenhouse; 47 fruits were labelled as Class B compared to 70 chillies from plant P10 in the laboratory (Figure 5a and Figure S2a). Plant P1c in the greenhouse produced the heaviest harvest of 0.998 kg; 0.449 kg was labelled as Class A fruits compared to 0.322 kg from plant P16 in the laboratory with 0.110 kg of Class B chillies (Figure 5b and Figure S2b). Regarding the chilli price, the highest income was obtained from P1c (GBP 13.25), where the majority of plants was linked to Class A produce (GBP 8.97), as shown in Figure 5c and Figure S2c. García-Delgado et al. [80] stated that chilli plants irrigated with treated wastewater produced a significantly high number of fruits, classified as large (70–90 mm in diameter) and very large (>90 mm in diameter) compared to groundwater and untreated wastewater with and without mineral fertilizer.

The total production of chilli fruits in the laboratory was 858 fruits where plants P10 and P9 gave large fruit numbers of 70 and 63 chillies, respectively, compared to other plants. These findings were greater than the average production number published by Almuktar et al. [54,82]. However, plants P16 and P8 in the laboratory produced the highest weights of 0.323 and 0.319 kg, respectively. The total chilli weight of 3.869 kg is linked to the laboratory planting experiment. The total produced quantity of chilli could be sold for GBP 17.61, where plants P16 and P8 chillies were priced as GBP 2.74 and GBP 2.16, respectively.

In the greenhouse, the total number of chill fruits harvested in the whole experiment was 2266 fruits with a total weight of 16.824 kg, which could be marketed for GBP 176.22. Plants P1 and P7 in the greenhouse produced the highest number of chillies of 142 and 141 fruits, respectively, but the highest chilli prices were indicated for plants P1c and P14 of GBP 13.25 and GBP 12.24 in this order. These figures are significantly higher than the ones published by Al-Isawi et al. [78].

A high fruit productivity in the greenhouse reflects the effect of real sunlight intensity, high relative humidity, and temperature, which contributed to enhanced soil and plant health, converting flowers to fruits more successfully compared to the boundary conditions of the laboratory [77].

The highest weight of chilli fruits was harvested from plants P1c, P14, P2c, and P8 with 0.997, 0.986, 0.958, and 0.905 kg, respectively. The highest chilli fruit numbers were associated with high nutrient availability for plant biomass production harvested from plants receiving effluent from T1 (floating wetland system treating greywater of high contamination level with a 2-day HRT in the presence of floating *Phragmites australis*), which agreed with findings reported by Al-Isawi et al. [78], in terms of nutrient load and hydraulic retention time. The results obtained from the greenhouse planting experiment were significantly better compared to the findings from the laboratory experiment in terms of chilli fruit quantity, quality, productivity, and marketability. However, chilli plants in the laboratory continued to produce fruits even after the usual harvest season.

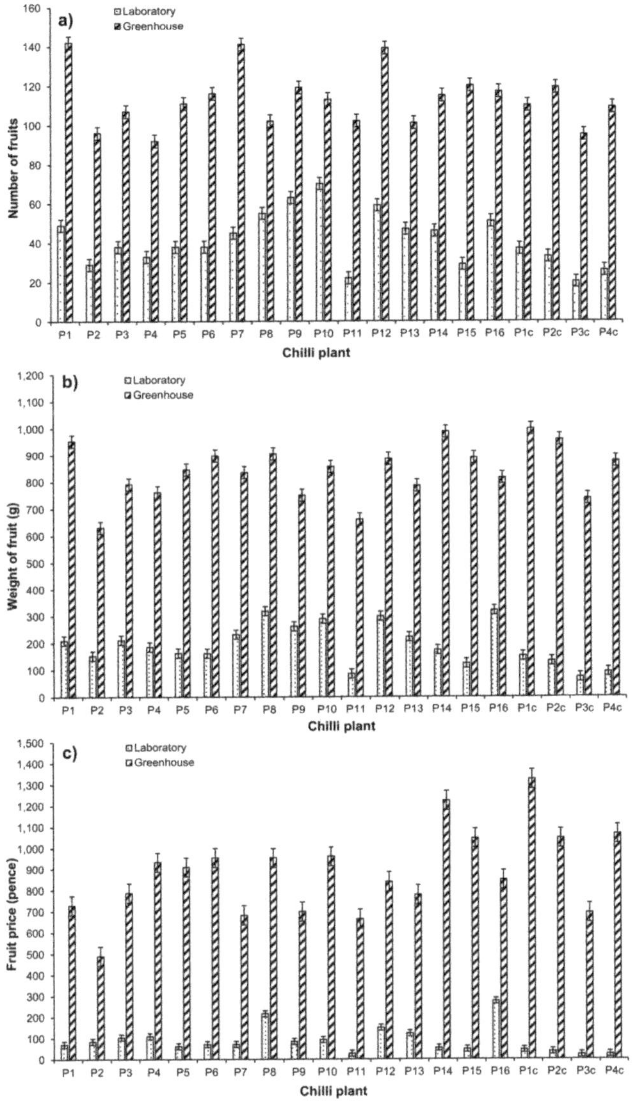

Figure 5. Overall fruit productivity of chilli plants grown in laboratory and greenhouse environments in terms of (**a**) number of fruits; (**b**) weight of fruits; and (**c**) fruit price.

Nutrients provided to the chilli plants by treated greywater and compost soil could be considered efficient for good harvesting. However, plant water consumption is related to the environmental weather conditions and growth stage, it is not strongly linked to the fruit productivity [3]. It was indicated that there was no significant difference in plant water consumption when comparing the laboratory to greenhouse plants [82].

Nutrients provided to the chilli plants by treated greywater and compost soil could be considered beneficial for a good harvest. However, the plant water consumption is related to the environmental and weather conditions as well as growth stage. It is not strongly linked to the fruit productivity [3]. Findings indicated that there was no significant difference in plant water consumption between laboratory and greenhouse plants [76].

3.5. Accumulated Trace Elements in Soil

The findings of a comparison of detected trace elements for the collected soil samples from the laboratory and greenhouse experiments are illustrated in Figure 6. The chilli plant soils were fed with two different pollutant strengths of recycled greywater (Section 2.1). The chemical analysis of chilli plant soils for trace elements showed that significant changes happened in element concentrations compared to the raw soil. As described in Section 3.1, almost all water quality samples complied with irrigation water thresholds in terms of trace element concentrations, especially for the LC-SGW effluents. However, some samples related to HC-SGW effluents were not in compliance [1,11].

In general, the concentrations of accumulated trace elements in chilli plant soils for both the laboratory and greenhouse locations followed this trend: Mg > Fe > Al > Cr > Mn > Cd > Cu > B, with some variations in Cd, Cr, Cu, and Mn. The changes in trace element concentrations of organic media-based soil could be problematic to detect due to a high cation exchange capacity, leading to a high variety in chemical composition [83]. Furthermore, the bioavailability of the chemical elements as well as soil pH and organic content affect and govern plant uptake of soil elements [3]. The measured pH values of the chilli soil samples were around 6.5 to 8.5, especially for soils irrigated with LC-SGW. However, pH values less than 6.0 or greater than 8.5 were rarely recorded in soils, which were irrigated with tap water or HC-SGW, respectively. The allocated trace element ions from soil to plant tissue could be limited at a pH of around 7.0 or decreased at a pH greater than 6.5 [84].

Concentrations of Al in the laboratory plant soils irrigated with effluents of T9 (7-days HRT; HC-SWG; *Phragmites australis*), T10 (7-days HRT; HC-SWG), and T14 (7-days HRT; LC-SWG; *Phragmites australis*; cement–ochre pellets) were significantly higher ($p < 0.05$) than the Al concentrations of the other soils in both locations (Figure 6a). These effluents have relatively high pH values between 7.3 and 10.3. The soils of the control chilli plants that were irrigated with tap water (P1c, P2c, P3c, and P4c (Table 1)) showed Al concentrations between 6000 and 8000 mg/kg. Organic matter and clay proportions in agricultural soil govern the aluminium mobility and solubility at different soil pH conditions. A negative correlation was calculated between decreasing pH values and increasing aluminium ion exchange in soil. Then, Al mobility becomes limited to plant biomass with an abundance of Ca ions in soil [66]. There is no toxicity threat to human health and the environment associated with the accumulation of Al in soil or plants due to its low bioavailability. This element is present in high abundancy in organic soils, except for acid soils [3]. However, mineral contamination might be a risk when recycling wastewater in the agricultural environment. The build-up of chemicals, soil salinization, and mobilisation of pollutants from soil to cultivated crops should be monitored to protect the environment and consumers [38,80].

Traces of B were detected in all soils linked to chilli plants grown in the greenhouse, except for soil of chilli plant P7. In comparison, only eight of twenty soils with traces of B were found for plants grown in the laboratory (Figure 6b). A significantly higher concentration of B was observed in the soil of plants P3 (229.3 mg/kg) and P9 (180.7 mg/kg) grown in the laboratory and greenhouse, respectively. Soil samples of control plants, which were irrigated only with tap water, showed no trace of B. However, 55.3 mg/kg was detected in soil samples of P3c, which received water from the treatment system C3 (7-days HRT; tap water; *Phragmites australis* present). Planted soils irrigated with effluents from systems of 7-day HRT showed a high fluctuation in B concentration, in particular, those chillies grown in the greenhouse. Boron is present in soils associated with recycled effluents of treatment systems with long hydraulic retention times.

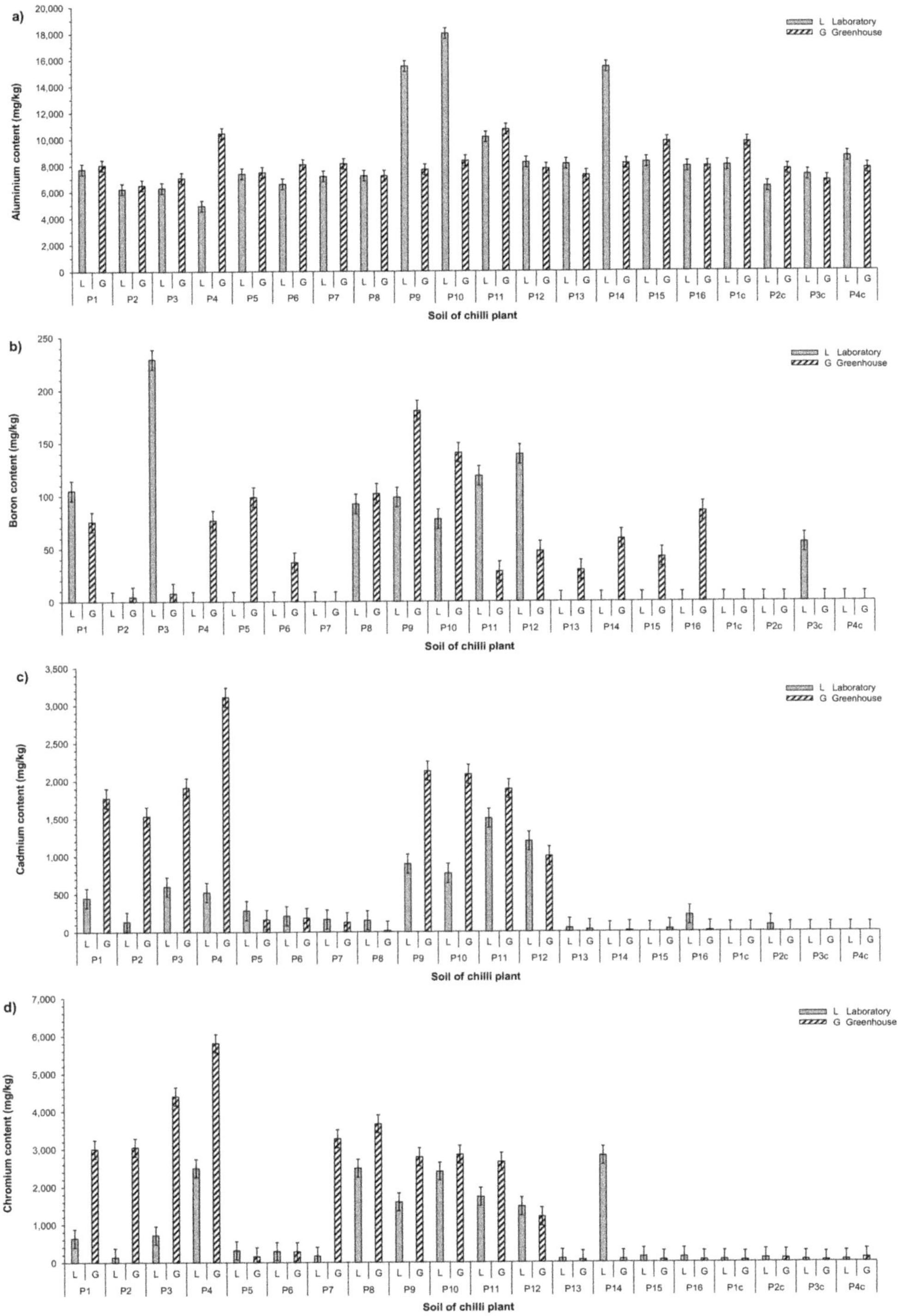

Figure 6. *Cont.*

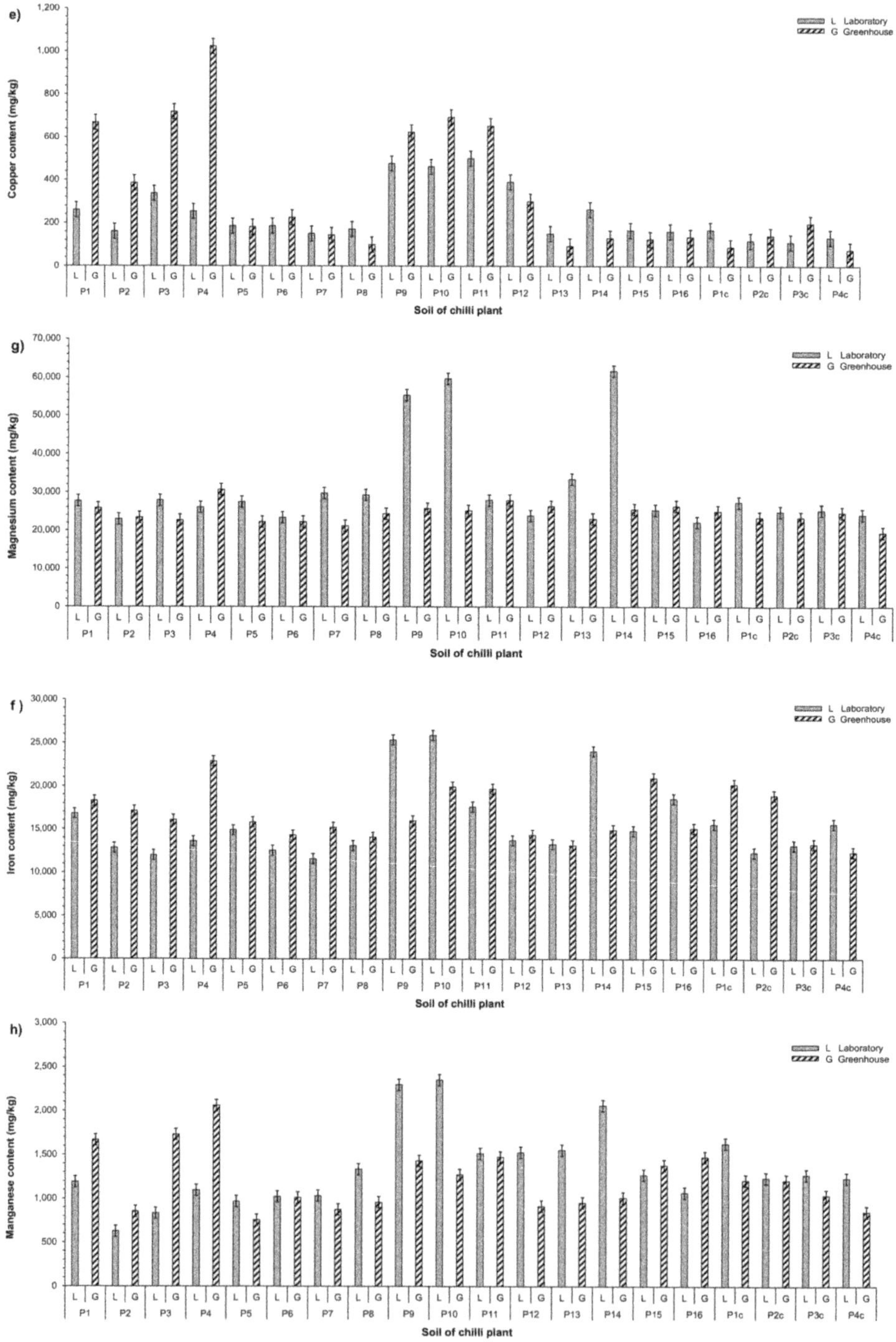

Figure 6. Comparison between the content of accumulated trace elements in the soil of chilli plants grown in the laboratory and greenhouse environments in terms of (**a**) aluminium; (**b**) boron; (**c**) cadmium; (**d**) chromium, (**e**) copper; (**f**) iron; (**g**) magnesium; and (**h**) manganese.

Significantly ($p < 0.05$) higher Cd, Cr, and Cu concentrations were detected in soils of chilli plants irrigated with effluents of HC-SGW compared to planted soils irrigated with LC-SGW. This is especially the case for those plants grown in the greenhouse. Recycling of effluents treated for longer hydraulic retention times showed less Cd, Cr, and Cu accumulations in soils irrigated with LC-SGW (Figure 6c–e). The accumulation of Cd, Cr, and Cu in soils watered with highly contaminated greywater was significant in greenhouse chilli plant soil. Concentrations were higher than the corresponding thresholds (Table 3).

The identified concentrations of Fe, Mg, and Mn in planted soils located in the laboratory and greenhouse were variable and fluctuated without a clear trend between 11,572 and 25,856 mg/kg for Fe, 19,455 and 61,667 mg/kg for Mg, and 626 and 2352 mg/kg for Mn. No significant effects were noted concerning the accumulations of Fe, Mg, and Mn in planted soil. However, the highest mineral concentrations were recorded for soil samples of plants P9, P10, and P14 grown in the laboratory: Fe (25,313, 25,856, and 24,023 mg/kg, respectively), Mg (55,376, 59,662, and 61,667 mg/kg, respectively) and Mn (2298, 2352, and 2063 mg/kg, respectively).

In comparison, Fe (22,871 mg/kg), Mg (mg/Kg), and Mn (2059 mg/kg) of soil linked to P4 grown in the greenhouse (Figure 6f–h) had the highest values (Table 3). A positive correlation between Fe and Mg was recorded, since Mg was consumed during plant photosynthesis. However, high Mg levels cause a low plant growth rate [66]. The build-up of chemicals, soil salinization, and soil pollutant mobilisation by cultivated crops negatively affect consumer health [38,80]. Oxygen and soil pH are crucial parameters for metal (e.g., Fe) bioavailability in terms of plant uptake and accumulation processes in their tissues influencing photosynthesis. Nevertheless, involving microorganisms in metal oxidative processes and metal hydroxide creation could limit metal consumption by plants [69,70].

Transfer rates of metals from soil to cultivated plants have been reported. They vary according to the following rank order: Cd > Cr > Ni > Zn > Cu > Mn [39]. The proportionate accumulation of trace elements in soil increases with irrigation of treated wastewater: Cd (109%), Cu (152%), Zn (32%), Ni (161%), and Cr (52.8%), crossing the maximum permissible threshold limits for long-term irrigation [85,86].

3.6. Accumulated Trace Elements in Chilli Fruits

Chilli fruits were analysed chemically for the accumulated concentrations of several minerals, including heavy metals (Table S2 and Figure 7). The statistical comparison of accumulated trace elements in chilli fruits is based on the effect of environmental growth conditions between the plants grown in the laboratory and greenhouse, and the effects of irritation water quality supplied to chilli plants (Tables 1 and 2). The ranking order of occurrence for the trace element concentrations accumulated in chilli fruits grown in both the laboratory and greenhouse was as follows: Mg > Ca > Na > Fe > Zn > Al > Mn > Cu > Cd > Cr > Ni > B. The statistical analysis showed that the total accumulated chemical elements in chilli fruits of plants P11, P8, P12, and P1 grown in the laboratory were significantly ($p < 0.05$) higher than the accumulated concentrations in fruits of all chilli plants, and compared to, in particularly, plants grown in the greenhouse receiving water of the same quality (Table S2, Figure 7a,b). A greater accumulation of trace elements in the greenhouse was observed for chilli fruits of plant P15 (irrigated with effluent of treatment system T15; treating LC-SGW for 7-days HRT). The variation in environmental growth conditions affects the accumulation of trace elements in fruits. A high temperature was recorded in the laboratory and both high relative humidity and natural sunlight characterised the greenhouse environment [3,54,66,78,82,86,87]. Furthermore, chilli fruits of plant P15 grown in the greenhouse indicated a greater accumulation of Ca, Cd, Cu, Mn, and Ni with concentrations of 4.73, 1.30, 0.20, 0.21, and 0.24 mg/kg, respectively (Table S2).

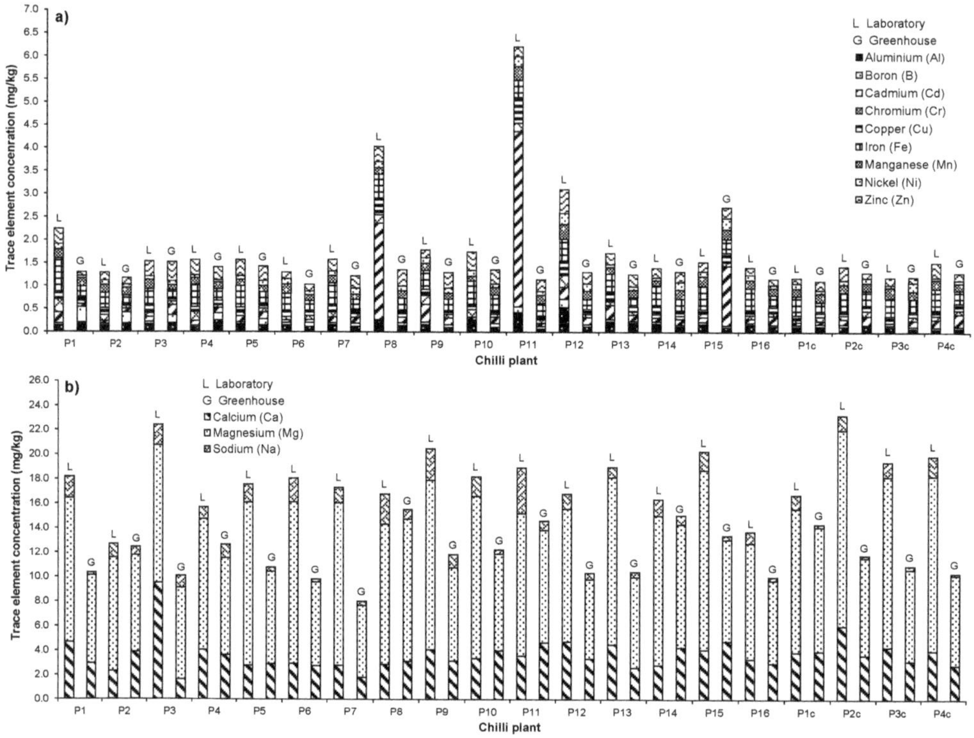

Figure 7. Comparison between trace element concentrations identified in chilli fruits grown in laboratory and greenhouse environments for (**a**) aluminium, boron, cadmium, chromium, copper, iron, manganese, nickel and zinc; and (**b**) calcium, magnesium, and sodium.

Chilli fruits harvested from plant P12 in the laboratory (receiving water from treatment system T12; treating HC-SGW for 7-days HRT with cement–ochre pellets) showed greater accumulation of Al, B, Mn, Ni, and Zn with concentrations of 0.54, 0.18, 0.32, 0.24, and 0.52 mg/kg, respectively (Figure 7a,b). The highest concentrations of accumulated Cd (3.82 mg/ kg), Cu (0.56 mg/ kg), and Na (0.56 mg/ kg) were recorded in chilli fruits of plant P11 grown in the laboratory (receiving water from treatment system T11; treating HC-SGW for 7-days HRT). The notable accumulations of Cr and Fe with 0.28 and 0.75 mg/kg, correspondingly (Table S2), were found in the analysis of chilli fruits of plant P1 in the laboratory (irrigated with effluent of treatment T1; Treating HC-SGW for 2-days with *Phragmites australis*).

The maximum accumulated Al, B, Ca, Mg, and Na concentrations in chillies were 0.54, 0.33, 9.5, 16.02, and 3.72 mg/kg, respectively (Table S2). However, almost international guidelines and standards have not stated recommended limits for accumulated concentrations of Al, B, Ca, K, Mg, and Na (Table 3). Macronutrients (N, P, K, S, Ca, and Mg) and micronutrients, including heavy metals (Co, Cu, Fe, Mn, Mo, Ni, and Zn), must be provided to plants for healthy growth and are vital in human food. Soil deficiency could affect plant metabolism and biomass productivity [69]. However, high levels of micronutrients may cause plant toxicity and subsequently human and animal diseases [70]. In comparison with permissible chemical element concentrations (Table 3), the maximum detected concentrations of Cr, Cu, Fe, Mn, Ni, and Zn (0.28, 3.82, 0.75, 0.32, 0.25, and 0.52 mg/kg, as shown in Table S2) were significantly ($p < 0.05$) lower than the higher permissible limits for safe consumer health [27,31,32].

A significant maximum accumulated Cd concentration (3.82 mg/kg) was detected in chilli fruits of plant P11 grown in the laboratory. This plant received effluent from system T11 (storying high contamination greywater for 7days HRT). In comparison, the Cd concentration accumulated in chilli fruits grown in greenhouse and irrigated with the same water was only 0.06 mg/kg. The thresholds of allowable Cd concentrations accumulated in crops are 0.02 mg/kg [32], 0.05 mg/kg [31], and 0.1 mg/kg [27], as shown in Table 3. Therefore, fruits of the laboratory-grown plants P1, P8, P9, P11, P12, and P13 crossed the allowable Cd limits significantly ($p < 0.05$): 0.24, 2.10, 0.39, 3.82, 0.26, and 0.31 mg/kg, respectively. In the greenhouse, chilli fruits of P3, P15, P16, and P4c (control plant receiving tap water) showed Cd level significantly ($p < 0.05$) higher than the corresponding thresholds with accumulated concentrations of 0.22, 1.30, 0.21, and 0.27 mg/kg in that order. It follows that greenhouse plants much less accumulated Cd and were safer for human health. The fixation of Cd in soils (similar for F, Hg, and Pb, which were not considered in this study) is often associated with contaminated air, applying certain phosphoric fertilizers to agricultural soils, and Cd being present in irrigation water [86]. Accumulated trace element concentrations may be greater than the safe thresholds for soils, vegetable leaves, and fruits due to irrigation with treated wastewater [39,86] or cultivated in contaminated soil associated with mining areas [73].

4. Conclusions and Recommendations

Greywater and wastewater treatment systems, such as all types of constructed wetlands, can provide effluents to be recycled for irrigation. The best crop yield results and plant health could be achieved by following the international guidelines to control microbial and mineral pollutions associated with recycling of wastewater to protect human health and the environment. Total suspended and dissolved solids in irrigation water cause problems for both soil and cultivated plants.

Environmental conditions had a significant effect on plant growth, fruit quality, productivity, and marketability. Greenhouse-grown chilli plants had more acceptable yields, since the corresponding environmental boundary conditions (mainly humidity and sunlight) were more optimal than in the laboratory. Chilli plants irrigated with the same greywater in terms of quality and quantity gave significantly different yields for the two different weather conditions. The trace element accumulation in plant soil was reduced, except for cadmium and chromium. There was also less accumulation of trace elements in chilli fruits grown in the greenhouse. However, accumulated cadmium concentrations were above the permissible maximum thresholds.

The percentage of buds that developed to chilli fruits in the greenhouse was significantly higher in comparison to the laboratory experiment. Irrigation of chillies planted in the greenhouse achieved high marketability with high physical quality of fruits compared to laboratory-grown plants. The accumulation of some metals within the soil threatens plants and subsequently human health. Nevertheless, the accumulation of almost all heavy metals in the soil and plant tissues was less than the permissible thresholds. The trace element accumulation in chilli fruits grown in the laboratory was greater than in the greenhouse. The accumulated Cd in chilli fruits of plants grown in the laboratory was higher than the threshold. However, the risk of mineral contamination by accumulation of heavy metals in soils and chilli fruits must be reduced by optimising the greywater treatment system.

Treatment technology designated for irrigation water should comprise of stages for heavy metal removal. It is recommended to allow up to 12 h for solids in effluents to settle, when the total suspended solid concentration is above 20 mg/L in the irrigation water and the relatively low microbial growth is determined. High total suspended and dissolved solids concentrations could cause clogging of soil and negatively affect the soil structure and permeability. Floating treatment systems could be improved by increasing the macrophyte density. Furthermore, it is recommended to assess organic contaminations, such as toxic polycyclic aromatic hydrocarbons in chilli fruits.

Supplementary Materials: The following are available online at https://www.mdpi.com/article/10.3390/agronomy11091817/s1. Table S1: Chemical recipes of synthetic greywaters (SGW) for low (LC) and high (HC) pollutant concentrations. Table S2: Trace element concentrations (mg/kg) accumulated in fruits of chilli plants grown in (a) laboratory, and (b) greenhouse environments. Figure S1: Monitoring of chilli plant growth in terms of number of buds. Figure S2: Overall fruit productivity classes of chilli plants grown in laboratory and greenhouse environments in terms of (a) number of fruits; (b) weight of fruits; and (c) fruit price.

Author Contributions: Conceptualization, S.A.A.A.N.A., S.N.A., M.S., and V.C.U.; methodology, S.N.A. and M.S.; software, S.A.A.A.N.A. and V.C.U.; validation, S.A.A.A.N.A., S.N.A., M.S., and V.C.U.; formal analysis, S.N.A. and V.C.U.; investigation, S.A.A.A.N.A. and S.N.A.; resources, S.A.A.A.N.A., M.S., and S.N.A.; supervision, M.S.; data curation, S.A.A.A.N.A. and S.N.A.; writing—original draft preparation, S.A.A.A.N.A. and S.N.A.; writing—review and editing, M.S.; visualization, S.A.A.A.N.A., S.N.A., M.S., and V.C.U. All authors have read and agreed to the published version of the manuscript.

Funding: The experimental work did not receive any specific grant from funding agencies in the public, commercial, or not-for-profit sectors. However, data analysis and writing in terms of work time was financially supported by WATERGRI (https://wateragri.eu; accessed on 9 August 2021), which is a project funded by the European Union's Horizon 2020 research and innovation Programme under grant agreement no. 858735.

Institutional Review Board Statement: Not applicable.

Informed Consent Statement: Not applicable.

Data Availability Statement: The data can be made available by the authors on reasonable request.

Acknowledgments: Furat Al-Faraj and Matthew Dennis provided advice and technical support. Guillaume Drouin, Pauline Francois, Rubén García, Guillaume Gourdikian, Claire Guillin, Elena Manjon Alfaro, César Moya, Anita Paul, and Carlos Verdú helped with data collection.

Conflicts of Interest: The authors declare that they have no known competing financial interest or personal relationships that could have appeared to influence the work reported in this paper.

References

1. FAO. *User Manual for Irrigation with Treated Wastewater*; Food and Agriculture Organization (FAO) of the United Nations, Regional Office for Near East: Cairo, Egypt, 2003.
2. WHO. *Guidelines for the Safe Use of Wastewater, Excreta and Greywater: Wastewater Use in Agriculture*; World Health Organization (WHO): Geneva, Switzerland, 2006; Volume 2.
3. Almuktar, S.A.A.A.N.; Abed, S.N.; Scholz, M. Contaminations of Soil and Two *Capsicum annuum* Generations Irrigated by Reused Urban Wastewater Treated by Different Reed Beds. *Int. J. Environ. Res. Public Health* **2018**, *15*, 1776. [CrossRef]
4. Almuktar, S.A.A.A.N.; Abed, S.N.; Scholz, M. Wetlands for wastewater treatment and subsequent recycling of treated effluent: A review. *Environ. Sci. Pollut. Res.* **2018**, *25*, 23595–23623. [CrossRef] [PubMed]
5. DESA-UN. *World Population Prospects 2019: Highlights*; Report (ST/ESA/SER.A/423); United Nations, Department of Economic and Social Affairs, Population Division: New York, NY, USA, 2019.
6. Alcamo, J.; Döll, P.; Kaspar, F.; Stefan, S. *Global Change and Global Scenarios of Water Use and Availability: An Application of WaterGAP 1.0*; Centre for Environmental Systems Research, University of Kassel: Kassel, Germany, 1997.
7. Alcamo, J.; Henrichs, T.; Rösch, T. *World Water in 2025: Global Modelling and Scenario Analysis for the World Commission on Water for the 21st Century*; Centre for Environmental Systems Research, University of Kassel: Kassel, Germany, 2000.
8. Scheierling, S.M.; Bartone, C.R.; Mara, D.D.; Drechsel, P. Towards an agenda for improving wastewater use in agriculture. *Water Int.* **2011**, *36*, 420–440. [CrossRef]
9. WWAP-UN. *The United Nations World Water Development Report 4: Managing Water Under Uncertainty and Risk*; UNESCO, World Water Assessment Programme (WWAP): Paris, France, 2012.
10. WHO. *Health Guidelines for the Use of Wastewater in Agriculture and Aquaculture*; Technical Report Series No. 77; World Health Organization (WHO): Geneva, Switzerland, 1989.
11. USEPA. *Guidelines for Water Reuse*; Report (EPA/600/R-12/618); United States Environmental Protection Agency (USEPA): Washington, DC, USA, 2012.
12. Cirelli, G.L.; Consoli, S.; Licciardello, F.; Aiello, R.; Giuffrida, F.; Leonardi, C. Treated municipal wastewater reuse in vegetable production. *Agric. Water Manag.* **2012**, *104*, 163–170. [CrossRef]
13. Willer, H.; Lernoud, J. *The World of Organic Agriculture. Statistics and Emerging Trends*; Research Institute of Organic Agriculture (FiBL), Frick, and IFOAM–Organics International: Bonn, Germany, 2019.

14. Weissengruber, L.; Möller, K.; Puschenreiter, M.; Friedel, J.K. Long-term soil accumulation of potentially toxic elements and selected organic pollutants through application of recycled phosphorus fertilizers for organic farming conditions. *Nutr. Cycl. Agroecosyst.* **2018**, *110*, 427–449. [CrossRef]
15. UNESCO. *Water for People-Water for Life: A Joint Report by the Twenty-Three United Nations Agencies Concerned with Freshwater*; United Nations Educational, Scientific and Cultural Organization (UNESCO): Barcelona, Spain, 2003.
16. Shuval, H.I.; Adin, A.; Fattal, B.; Rawitz, E.; Yekutiel, P. *Wastewater Irrigation in Developing Countries: Health Effects and Technical Solutions*; Technical Paper No. 51; World Bank: Washington, DC, USA, 1986.
17. Dalahmeh, S.; Baresel, C. *Reclaimed Wastewater Use Alternatives and Quality Standards from Global to Country Perspective: Spain versus Abu Dhabi Emirate*; IVL Swedish Environmental Research Institute: Uppsala/Stockholm, Sweden, 2014.
18. Toze, S. Reuse of effluent water–Benefits and risks. *Agric. Water Manag.* **2006**, *80*, 147–159. [CrossRef]
19. Nolde, E. Greywater reuse systems for toilet-flushing in multi-storey buildings-over ten years' experience in Berlin. *Urban Water* **1999**, *1*, 275–284. [CrossRef]
20. Christova-Boal, D.; Eden, R.E.; McFarlane, S. An investigation into greywater reuse for urban residential properties. *Desalination* **1996**, *106*, 391–397. [CrossRef]
21. Eriksson, E.; Auffarth, K.; Henze, M.; Ledin, A. Characteristics of grey wastewater. *Urban Water* **2002**, *4*, 85–104. [CrossRef]
22. Al-Jayyousi, O.R. Greywater reuse: Towards sustainable water management. *Desalination* **2003**, *156*, 181–192. [CrossRef]
23. Edogbo, B.; Okolocha, E.; Maikai, B.; Aluwong, T.; Uchendu, C. Risk Analysis of Heavy Metal Contamination in Soil, Vegetables and Fish around Challawa Area in Kano State, Nigeria. *Sci. Afr.* **2020**, *17*, e00281. [CrossRef]
24. Hussain, M.I.; Qureshi, A.S. Health risks of heavy metal exposure and microbial contamination through consumption of vegetables irrigated with treated wastewater at Dubai, UAE. *Environ. Sci. Pollut. Res.* **2020**, *27*, 11213–11226. [CrossRef]
25. Osmani, M.; Bani, A.; Hoxha, B. Heavy Metals and Ni Phytoextraction in the Metallurgical Area Soils in Elbasan. *Albanian J. Agric. Sci.* **2015**, *14*, 414–419.
26. Mkhinini, M.; Boughattas, I.; Alphonse, V.; Livet, A.; Giusti-Miller, S.; Banni, M.; Bousserrhine, N. Heavy metal accumulation and changes in soil enzymes activities and bacterial functional diversity under long-term treated wastewater irrigation in East Central region of Tunisia (Monastir governorate). *Agric. Water Manag.* **2020**, *235*, 106–150. [CrossRef]
27. FAO/WHO. Codex Committee on Contaminants in Foods 10th Session; Working Document for Information and Use in Discussions Related to Contaminants and Toxins in the GSCTFF Volume 4; Food and Agriculture Organization, Rome, Italy 2016. Available online: http://www.fao.org/fao-who-codexalimentarius (accessed on 9 August 2021).
28. Hadayat, N.; De Oliveira, L.M.; Da Silva, E.; Han, L.; Hussain, M.; Liu, X.; Ma, L.Q. Assessment of trace metals in five most-consumed vegetables in the US: Conventional vs. organic. *Environ. Pollut.* **2018**, *243*, 292–300. [CrossRef] [PubMed]
29. Awashthi, S.K. *Prevention of Food Adulteration Act No 37 of 1954*; Central and State Rules as Amended for 1999; Ashoka Law House: New Delhi, India, 2000.
30. NHFPC. *GB 2762-2012 China Food Safety National Standard for Maximum Levels of Contaminants in Foods*; NHFPC-National Health and Family Planning of People's Republic of China: Beijing, China, 2012.
31. European Union (EU). *Heavy Metals in Wastes, European Commission on Environment*; European Union: Brussels, Belgium, 2002; Available online: http://ec.europa.eu/environment/waste/studies/pdf/heavymetalsreport.pdf (accessed on 9 August 2021).
32. WHO. *Permissible Limits of Heavy Metals in Soil and Plants*; World Health Organization (WHO): Geneva, Switzerland, 1996.
33. Douay, F.; Pelfrêne, A.; Planque, J.; Fourrier, H.; Richard, A.; Roussel, H.; Girondelot, B. Assessment of potential health risk for inhabitants living near a former lead smelter. Part 1: Metal concentrations in soils, agricultural crops, and home grown vegetables. *Environ. Monit. Assess.* **2013**, *185*, 3665–3680. [CrossRef]
34. Hu, J.; Wu, F.; Wu, S.; Cao, Z.; Lin, X.; Wong, M.H. Bioaccessibility, dietary exposure and human risk assessment of heavy metals from market vegetables in Hong Kong revealed with an in vitro gastrointestinal model. *Chemosphere* **2013**, *91*, 455–461. [CrossRef]
35. Zhou, H.; Yang, W.T.; Zhou, X.; Liu, L.; Gu, J.F.; Wang, W.L.; Zou, J.L.; Tian, T.; Peng, P.Q.; Liao, B.H. Accumulation of heavy metals in vegetable species planted in contaminated soils and the health risk assessment. *Int. J. Environ. Res. Public Health* **2016**, *13*, 289. [CrossRef] [PubMed]
36. Bigdeli, M.; Seilsepour, M. Investigation of metals accumulation in some vegetables irrigated with waste water in Shahre Rey-Iran and toxicological implications. *Am.-Eurasian J. Agric. Environ. Sci.* **2008**, *4*, 86–92.
37. Shaheen, N.; Irfan, N.M.; Khan, I.N.; Islam, S.; Islam, M.S.; Ahmed, M.K. Presence of heavy metals in fruits and vegetables: Health risk implications in Bangladesh. *Chemosphere* **2016**, *152*, 431–438. [CrossRef] [PubMed]
38. Khan, S.; Cao, Q.; Zheng, Y.M.; Huang, Y.Z.; Zhu, Y.G. Health risks of heavy metals in contaminated soils and food crops irrigated with wastewater in Beijing, China. *Environ. Pollut.* **2008**, *152*, 686–692. [CrossRef]
39. Khan, K.; Lu, Y.; Khan, H.; Ishtiaq, M.; Khan, S.; Waqas, M.; Wei, L.; Wang, T. Heavy metals in agricultural soils and crops and their health risks in Swat District, northern Pakistan. *Food Chem. Toxicol.* **2013**, *58*, 449–458. [CrossRef]
40. Scholz, M.; Lee, B.H. Constructed wetlands: A review. *Int. J. Environ. Stud.* **2005**, *62*, 421–447. [CrossRef]
41. Vymazal, J. Removal of nutrients in various types of constructed wetlands. *Sci. Total Environ.* **2007**, *380*, 48–65. [CrossRef] [PubMed]
42. Scholz, M. *Sustainable Water Treatment: Engineering Solutions for a Variable Climate*; Elsevier Inc.: Amsterdam, The Netherlands, 2019.
43. Brix, H. Use of constructed wetlands in water pollution control: Historical development, present status, and future perspectives. *Water Sci. Technol.* **1994**, *30*, 209–224. [CrossRef]

44. Vymazal, J. Horizontal sub-surface flow and hybrid constructed wetlands systems for wastewater treatment: Review. *Ecol. Eng.* **2005**, *25*, 478–490. [CrossRef]
45. Scholz, M. *Wetland Systems–Storm Water Management Control*; Springer: Berlin, Germany, 2010.
46. Borne, K.E.; Fassman-Beck, E.A.; Tanner, C.C. Floating treatment wetland retrofit to improve stormwater pond performance for suspended solids, copper and zinc. *Ecol. Eng.* **2013**, *54*, 173–182. [CrossRef]
47. Wang, C.Y.; Sample, D.J. Assessment of the nutrient removal effectiveness of floating treatment wetlands applied to urban retention ponds. *J. Environ. Manag.* **2014**, *137*, 23–35. [CrossRef]
48. Keizer-Vlek, H.E.; Verdonschot, P.F.M.; Verdonschot, R.C.M.; Dekkers, D. The contribution of plant uptake to nutrient removal by floating treatment wetlands. *Ecol. Eng.* **2014**, *73*, 684–690. [CrossRef]
49. Rezania, S.; Taib, S.M.; Din, M.F.M.; Dahalan, F.A.; Kamyab, H. Comprehensive review on phytotechnology: Heavy metals removal by diverse aquatic plants species from wastewater. *J. Hazard. Mater.* **2016**, *318*, 587–599. [CrossRef]
50. Abed, S.N.; Scholz, M. Chemical simulation of greywater. *Environ. Technol.* **2016**, *37*, 1631–1646. [CrossRef] [PubMed]
51. Abed, S.N.; Almuktar, S.A.A.A.N.; Scholz, M. Phytoremediation performance of floating treatment wetlands with pelletized mine water sludge for synthetic greywater treatment. *J. Environ. Health Sci. Eng.* **2019**, *372*, 1–28. [CrossRef]
52. Abed, S.N.; Almuktar, S.A.A.A.N.; Scholz, M. Remediation of synthetic greywater in mesocosm-scale floating treatment wetlands. *Ecol. Eng.* **2017**, *102*, 303–319. [CrossRef]
53. Abed, S.N.; Almuktar, S.A.A.A.N.; Scholz, M. Treatment of contaminated greywater using pelletised mine water sludge. *J. Environ. Manag.* **2017**, *197*, 10–23. [CrossRef]
54. Almuktar, S.A.A.A.N.; Scholz, M.; Al-Isawi, R.; Sani, A. Recycling of domestic wastewater treated by vertical-flow wetlands for watering of vegetables. *Water Pract. Technol.* **2015**, *10*, 445–464. [CrossRef]
55. Nickels, J. *Growing Chillies—A Guide to the Domestic Cultivation of Chilli Plants*; Jason Nickels: London, UK, 2012.
56. Jones, J.B., Jr. *Instructions for Growing Tomatoes in the Garden and Greenhouse*; GroSystems: Anderson, SC, USA, 2013.
57. APHA. *Standard Methods for the Examination of Water and Wastewater*, 21st ed.; American Public Health Association (APHA), American Water Works Association, and Water and Environment Federation: Washington, DC, USA, 2005.
58. USEPA. *SW–846: Test method 6010D: Inductively Coupled Plasma-Optical Emission Spectrometry (ICP-OES)*; Revision 4; United States Environmental Protection Agency (USEPA): Washington, DC, USA, 2014.
59. USEPA. *Method 200.7: Determination of Metals and Trace Elements in Water and Wastes by Inductively Coupled Plasma-Atomic Emission Spectrometry*; Revision 4.4; United States Environmental Protection Agency (USEPA): Washington, DC, USA, 1994.
60. Chary, N.S.; Kamala, C.T.; Raj, D.S.S. Assessing risk of heavy metals from consuming food grown on sewage irrigated soils and food chain transfer. *Ecotoxicol. Environ. Saf.* **2008**, *69*, 513–524. [CrossRef]
61. USEPA. *Method 3050B: Acid Digestion of Sediments, Sludges, and Soils*; Revision 2; United States Environmental Protection Agency (USEPA): Washington, DC, USA, 1996.
62. Plank, C.O. *Plant Analysis Reference Procedures for the Southern Region of the United States.*; Southern Cooperative Series Bulletin number 368; University of Georgia: Athens, GA, USA, 1992.
63. Shapiro, S.S.; Wilk, M.B. An analysis of variance test for normality (complete samples). *Biometrika* **1965**, *52*, 591–611. [CrossRef]
64. Kasuya, E. Mann-Whitney U test when variances are unequal. *Anim. Behav.* **2001**, *61*, 1247–1249. [CrossRef]
65. Stoline, M.R. The status of multiple comparisons: Simultaneous estimation of all pairwise comparisons in one-way ANOVA designs. *Am. Stat.* **1981**, *35*, 134–141.
66. Almuktar, S.A.A.A.N.; Scholz, M. Mineral and biological contamination of soil and *Capsicum annuum* irrigated with recycled domestic wastewater. *Agric. Water Manag.* **2016**, *167*, 95–109. [CrossRef]
67. Decreto Ministeriale. *Regulating Technical Standards for Wastewater Reuse*; Decreto Ministeriale: Rome, Italy, 2003; Volume 185.
68. Bar-Tal, A.; Aloni, B.; Karni, L.; Rosenberg, R. Nitrogen nutrition of greenhouse pepper. II. Effects of nitrogen concentration and NO_3:NH_4 ratio on growth, transpiration, and nutrient uptake. *HortScience* **2001**, *36*, 1252–1259. [CrossRef]
69. Millaleo, R.; Reyes-Díaz, M.; Ivanov, A.; Mora, M.; Alberdi, M. Manganese as essential and toxic element for plants: Transport, accumulation and resistance mechanisms. *J. Soil Sci. Plant Nutr.* **2010**, *10*, 470–481. [CrossRef]
70. McCauly, A.; Jones, C.; Jacobsen, J. *Plant Nutrient Functions and Deficiency and Toxicity Symptoms*; Nutrient Management Module No. 9; Montana State University: Bozeman, MT, USA, 2011.
71. BOE. *Royal Decree 140/2003 That Establish Health Criteria of Water Quality for Human Consumption*; Boletín Oficial de Estado (BOE) No 45, 21/02/2003; BOE: Madrid, Spain, 2003.
72. Ewers, U. Standards, guidelines and legislative regulations concerning metals and their compounds. In *Metals and Their Compounds in the Environment: Occurrence, Analysis and Biological Relevance*; Merian, E., Ed.; VCH: Weinheim, Germany, 1991; pp. 458–468.
73. NJDEP. *Soil Cleanup Criteria*; Proposed Cleanup Standards for Contaminated Sites, NJAC 7:26D; New Jersey Department of Environmental Protection: Tuckerton, NJ, USA, 1996.
74. DPR-EGASPIN. *Environmental Guidelines and Standards for the Petroleum Industry in Nigeria (EGASPIN)*; Department of Petroleum Resources: Lagos, Nigeria, 2002.
75. Almuktar, S.A.A.A.N.; Scholz, M.; Al-Isawi, R.H.K.; Sani, A. Recycling of domestic wastewater treated by vertical-flow wetlands for irrigating Chillies and Sweet Peppers. *Agric. Water Manag.* **2015**, *149*, 1–22. [CrossRef]

76. Pinto, U.; Maheshwari, B.L.; Grewal, H.S. Effects of greywater irrigation on plant growth, water use and soil properties. *Resour. Conserv. Recycl.* **2010**, *54*, 429–435. [CrossRef]
77. García-Delgado, C.; Eymar, E.; Contreras, J.I.; Segura, M.L. Effects of fertigation with purified urban wastewater on soil and pepper plant (*Capsicum annuum* L.) production, fruit quality and pollutant contents. Span. *J. Agric. Res.* **2012**, *10*, 209–221. [CrossRef]
78. Al-Isawi, R.H.; Scholz, M.; Al-Faraj, F.A. Assessment of diesel-contaminated domestic wastewater treated by constructed wetlands for irrigation of chillies grown in a greenhouse. *Environ. Sci. Pollut. Res.* **2016**, *23*, 25003–25023. [CrossRef] [PubMed]
79. Bhatt, R.M.; Rao, N.K.S. Photosynthesis and dry matter partitioning in three cultivars of *Capsicum annuum* L. grown at two temperature conditions. *Photosynthetica* **1989**, *23*, 21–26.
80. Almuktar, S.A.A.A.N.; Abed, S.N.; Scholz, M. Recycling of domestic wastewater treated by vertical-flow wetlands for irrigation of two consecutive *Capsicum annuum* generations. *Ecol. Eng.* **2017**, *107*, 82–98. [CrossRef]
81. Deli, J.; Tiessen, H. Interaction of temperature and light intensity on flowering of *Capsicum frutescens var grossum cv.* California Wonder. *J. Am. Soc. Hortic. Sci.* **1969**, *94*, 349–351.
82. Al-Isawi, R.H.; Almuktar, S.A.A.A.N.; Scholz, M. Monitoring and assessment of treated river, rain, gully pot and grey waters for irrigation of Capsicum annuum. *Environ. Monit. Assess.* **2016**, *188*, 287. [CrossRef] [PubMed]
83. Ding, Z.; Li, Y.; Sun, Q.; Zhang, H. Trace elements in soils and selected agricultural plants in the Tongling mining area of China. *Int. J. Environ. Res. Public Health* **2018**, *15*, 202. [CrossRef]
84. Sharma, R.K.; Agrawal, M.; Marshall, F. Heavy metal contamination in vegetables grown in wastewater irrigated areas of Varanasi, India. *Bull. Environ. Contam. Toxicol.* **2006**, *77*, 312–318. [CrossRef] [PubMed]
85. Singh, A.; Sharma, R.K.; Agrawal, M.; Marshall, F.M. Risk assessment of heavy metal toxicity through contaminated vegetables from waste water irrigated area of Varanasi, India. *Trop. Ecol.* **2010**, *51*, 375–387.
86. Wuana, R.A.; Okieimen, F.E. Heavy metals in contaminated soils: A review of sources, chemistry, risks and best available strategies for remediation. *Int. Sch. Res. Net. ISRN Ecol.* **2011**, *2011*, 1–20. [CrossRef]
87. Chemicals, H. *Crop Guide: Peppers*; Haifa Group: Haifa, Israel, 2019; Available online: https://www.haifa-group.com/articles/crop-guide-peppers/ (accessed on 9 August 2021).

Water **2014**, *6*, 1246-1256; doi:10.3390/w6051246

OPEN ACCESS

water

ISSN 2073-4441

www.mdpi.com/journal/water

Article

Response of Vegetables to Cadmium-Enriched Soil

Babak Ebrazi Bakhshayesh [1], Madjid Delkash [1] and Miklas Scholz [2,*]

[1] Department of Civil and Environmental Engineering, University of Delaware, Newark, DE 19716, USA; E-Mails: babakeb@udel.edu (B.E.B.); delkash@udel.edu (M.D.)

[2] Civil Engineering Research Group, School of Computing, Science and Engineering, The University of Salford, Newton Building, Salford M5 4WT, England, UK

* Author to whom correspondence should be addressed; E-Mail: m.scholz@salford.ac.uk; Tel.: +44-161-295-5921; Fax: +44-161-295-5575.

Received: 13 January 2014; in revised form: 29 April 2014 / Accepted: 29 April 2014 / Published: 7 May 2014

Abstract: Environmental and water pollution through heavy metals is a growing concern. The recycling of untreated wastewater, which is often contaminated with heavy metals, for agricultural applications is becoming more popular. However, information on the amount of absorption and accumulation of cadmium (Cd) at variable concentrations by different crops is limited. This study aims to analyze the impact of various Cd concentrations (0, 30, 60 and 120 mg/kg) in the root zone on the quantity of its absorption as well as accumulation in various parts of seven different types of common vegetables. The experiments were carried out under laboratory-like controlled conditions. Four treatments and three replicates were selected. Cadmium accumulation exceeded the permissible limits for human consumption, and its accumulation in different plant parts followed this order: Leaves: broccoli > spinach > basil > garlic > carrot > tarragon > dill. Stems: broccoli > spinach > basil > garlic > tarragon > carrot > dill. Roots: broccoli > garlic > basil > spinach > carrot > dill > tarragon. Therefore, the authors recommend the reuse of treated wastewater, which should be virtually free of contaminants such as heavy metals, to irrigate farm lands in the future.

Keywords: basil; broccoli; cadmium; carrot; garlic; irrigation; metal accumulation; spinach; tarragon; treated wastewater

---

1. Introduction

An increase in the rate of population growth and changing water usage patterns have led to the production of high volumes of wastewater and depleting freshwater resources. Reusing wastewater can be considered as a potential solution to save freshwater resources for drinking consumption and getting rid of wastewater at the same time. One of the sectors in which non-conventional water resources are recycled is the agricultural sector. However, there are concerns regarding public health and environmental pollution as well as cultural and religious barriers hindering the widespread use of wastewater for irrigation purposes [1,2].

Irrigating agricultural farm land provides food for humans, alleviating poverty [3]. Artificial irrigation is associated with the lion share of water consumption in some regions of the world such as the Middle East and Northern Africa [1,2,4]. Despite intense droughts in some regions, about 67% to 90% of water resources are allocated to agricultural practices [5]. The reuse of wastewater in irrigation systems seems a promising method to provide the essential need for the agricultural industry. In addition to resolving the water shortage problem, irrigating with nutrient-rich wastewater provides free fertilizer to potentially poor soil. However, long-term usage of wastewater, which is mainly prevalent for cultivation of leafy vegetables, has resulted in relatively high heavy metal (e.g., Cd) accumulation in the soil and their subsequent transfer to the crops under cultivation [6,7].

Cadmium is used widely in industry; colour pigment, nickel-cadmium battery, anticorrosive agent, stabilizer in plastics. Unfortunately, the consumption of this potentially dangerous metal is increasing in developing countries such as Iran, because people often discharge this pollutant into the wastewater stream carelessly. Cadmium is often associated with fine clay particles within the raw water. The current concentration of Cd in wastewater received by the wastewater treatment plant of Tehran is comparatively elevated, and varies between 0.05 and 0.018 mg/L [8].

Taking appropriate measures to prevent Cd accumulation in the environment seems vital, because Cd may be easily absorbed by some plants used for human consumption and accumulates in agricultural products in concentrations that can even be considered toxic for some plant species. Excessive accumulation of Cd in soil can reduce the growth of plants [9]. The consumption of vegetables containing accumulated Cd is a known pathway for the entry of toxic metals into humans. Contaminated food can deplete some essential nutrients in the body. This could result in reduced immunological defence and some disabilities associated with malnutrition [10].

Several studies have been undertaken concerning the impact of wastewater containing Cd used for irrigation on plants and particularly vegetables in the south of Tehran (Iran). Table 1 indicates corresponding bioaccumulation findings for different plants [11]. Other vegetables such as broccoli, basil, garlic, tarragon, carrot and dill have not been studied with respect to their tolerance to Cd. Cadmium contamination levels in farm lands are fairly high; for example, between 0.01 and 7.54 mg/kg for soil and between 0.398 and 1.437 mg/kg dry weight for the corresponding crops growing on the contaminated soil south of Tehran [12].

Introducing Cd to soil by irrigation with wastewater containing Cd enhances the level of Cd in the corresponding topsoil. It follows that there is a need to assess the responses of different vegetables and their individual parts to Cd bioaccumulation to prevent humans eating vegetable parts that are too contaminated. Furthermore, the most Cd-tolerant vegetable should be promoted for further cultivation.

Table 1. Cadmium bioaccumulation in plant parts for a relevant case study south of Tehran, Iran [11].

Plant	Part	Concentration (ppm)
Corn	Seed	3.22
Alfalfa	Shoot	4.9
Lettuce	Leaf	2.8
Radish	Leaf	1.9
Bean	Seed	1.6
Cotton	Root	1.1
Mung bean	Seed	53.5
Sunflower	Seed	0.48
Squash	Root	6.2
Spinach	Leaf	1.3
Turnip	Tuber	1.1

The key aim of this research is to assess the potential of different vegetables and their corresponding parts in absorbing Cd at various concentration levels within the Cd-enriched soils. The paper is concerned with growing edible vegetables in contaminated soil. However, the treatment of the contaminated soil is beyond the scope of this study. The findings will help to identify the most appropriate vegetable parts of selected vegetables for human consumption.

2. Materials and Methods

2.1. Site Description

The research was conducted in the Varamin Valley near Tehran. This is an agricultural area producing about 40% of Tehran's crop needs according to the authors' estimation. At the first stage of the experiment, an appropriate experimental farm site, which includes essential facilities such as water, electricity and a proper protection to prevent animals and people from entering the site, was selected.

The experiments were carried out at the Abureyhan Campus of Tehran University located in the Varamin Valley (about 40 km south of Tehran). The maximum monthly rainfall in this region is about 40 mm in March compared to and less than 5 mm in July, representing minimum precipitation. The temperature varies between 25 and 37 °C in July, which is known as the hottest month, and between 1 and 8 °C in January, which is usually the coldest month.

Soil with a texture and structure similar to the dominant soil texture and structure of the whole region, was collected by gathering soil samples from different parts of the Abureyhan Campus. In order to avoid contaminating the soil samples utilized in the experiments and the entire experimental site, planting pots with a diameter and height of 80 cm and 100 cm, respectively, were located in a vegetable farm area of about 1000 m^2. The soil texture comprised silt (42%), sand (35%) and clay (23%). The soil was almost neutral (pH = 7.4) with a background Cd concentration of 0.03 mg/kg (Table 2).

Table 2. Physical and chemical characteristics of soil samples (meq/L, milliequivalent of solute per litre).

Variable	Unit	Value
Sand	%	35
Silt	%	42
Clay	%	23
Organic carbon	%	1.25
Phosphorus (available by plants)	mg/kg	3.2
Total nitrogen	%	0.04
Potassium (available by plants)	mg/kg	105
pH	-	7.4
Cation-exchange capacity	meq/100g	11
Cadmium	mg/kg	0.03
Sodium	meq/L	2.72
Magnesium	meq/L	3.31
Calcium	meq/L	4.12
Sulphate	meq/L	3.8
Chloride	meq/L	3.32
Bicarbonate	meq/L	3.2

2.2. Cultivation and Measurements

All experiments were carried out under laboratory-like conditions using a factorial testing plan as part of the random block model design with four different treatments and three replicates to assess the influences of dissimilar Cd concentrations within soil samples on three plant parts (root, zone and stem) for seven vegetables (spinach, garlic, carrot, dill, tarragon, basil and broccoli) representative of a wide section of available vegetable plant species. The Cd concentration was the only variable parameter between these treatments to reduce noise in the findings, and to obtain statistically valid results. Details of the four treatments are presented in Table 3.

Due to the high variability of Cd in real wastewater and the presence of other contaminants, the effect of wastewater contaminated with Cd used for irrigation of soil was simulated by using soil already contaminated by Cd. Therefore, cadmium nitrate was powdered and mixed entirely to gain a homogenous mixture, which was used to prepare soil samples with three different Cd concentrations (30, 60 and 120 mg/kg; Table 3). Finally, to check for the uniformity of Cd concentrations at different levels of the prepared soil sample, various samples were taken and their Cd concentrations were analysed in the laboratory. It should be mentioned that the soil samples were collected from different levels of the soil column using stainless steel sampling tools and clean plastic buckets. Samples were immediately sent to the laboratory in clean standard soil containers.

Considering that real wastewater is highly variable in its chemical composition, groundwater, which is relatively stable in its composition and which is the dominant water resource in the Varamin Valley, was used as a substitute to irrigate the example vegetable species during the growing season. The groundwater had an electrical conductivity of 635 dS/m. The chemical traits of the groundwater are shown in Table 4. The Penman-Monteith equation [13] was utilized to accurately determine the crops' water demand during different growth stages.

Table 3. Characteristics of the studied treatments.

Treatment number	Description	Comment
1	Soil with 0 mg/kg cadmium (Cd)	Control
2	Soil with 30 mg/kg Cd	None
3	Soil with 60 mg/kg Cd	None
4	Soil with 120 mg/kg Cd	None

Table 4. Chemical configurations of Varamin Valley groundwater (meq/L, milliequivalent of solute per litre).

Variable	Unit	Value
Electric conductivity	dS/m	635
pH	-	7.3
Calcium	meq/L	3.2
Magnesium	meq/L	3.8
Sodium	meq/L	1.69
Potassium	meq/L	0
Carbonate	meq/L	0
Bicarbonate	meq/L	3.64
Sulphate	meq/L	2.87
Chloride	meq/L	2.05
Cadmium	meq/L	0

Cultivation of the investigated species was done according to the local cropping schedule using pots. No pesticides and fertilizers were used during the cultivation season to eliminate their potentially problematic impact on the outcome of the research. Any weeds were removed manually if and when appropriate.

At the end of the cultivation season, different sections of the investigated crops (root, stem and leaf) were used to assess Cd accumulation within these plant parts. After cutting the samples, they were washed with distilled water. They were subsequently dried at 100 °C and then burnt to gain their ashes, which were put in 100 mL of aqua regia (3 parts in volume of 12 M HCl to 1 part of 16 M HNO_3) and diluted (1 in 20) with distilled water. Finally, the Cd concentrations were measured by graphite furnace atomic absorption spectroscopy (Perkins-Elmer model 4100ZL, Cupertino, CA, USA) for the prepared crop samples [12].

2.3. Statistical Analysis

An analysis of variance (ANOVA) was carried out on the data obtained from the measurements to analyse the differences between group means and their associated procedures such as the variation among and between groups. The observed variance in a particular variable was partitioned into components that can be attributed to various sources of variation. The ANOVA was used to assess whether or not the means of several groups were equal, and to compare at least three means of group or variables for statistical significance.

The common software package IBM SPSS Statistics was used. Moreover, the results obtained from the data analysis were then statistically compared with each other using the Duncan's Multiple Range test at 1% and 5% probably levels. This multi-comparison procedure provides significance levels for the difference between any pair of means. For graphical representation, common Microsoft Excel software was used.

3. Results and Discussion

3.1. Effect of Species on Cadmium Accumulation

The ANOVA table for Cd accumulation levels in different parts of the vegetables is presented in Table 5. The findings were significant at 0.01 probability level for all plant parts. It follows that it would make sense to distinguish between different vegetables and associated plant parts when regulating the agricultural market regarding contaminated products in the future.

Table 5. Variance analysis of the investigated characteristics in studied species.

Sources of variation	Degrees of freedom	Mean square (MS)		
		Stem	Leaf	Root
Species (S)	6	15.14**	4.98**	4.13**
Treatment (T)	3	51.32**	30.143**	15.16**
S × T	18	2.36**	0.627**	0.373**
Error	56	0.07	0.021	0.007
Coefficient of variation	not applicable	15.72	10.68	8.85

Note: **Significant at 0.01 probability level.

Cadmium pollution in water and soil has been a great challenge for a long time, and several suggestions regarding the maximum allowable concentrations have been recommended in the literature [9,14,15]. In addition to these recommendations, some standards have been presented concerning permissible Cd accumulations in various herbs, concentrations in sewage used for irrigation of farm land and human diet. A few representative and relevant maximum threshold recommendations are tabulated in Table 6.

Table 6. Maximum allowable concentrations of cadmium (Cd).

Organization	Reference	Maximum Cd	Application threshold
World Health Organization	[16]	0.1 mg/L	Drinking water
American Food Industries	[17]	92 μg/day	Solid food intake
United States Environmental Protection Agency	[17]	85 ppm	Ooze deposition onto farm land
United Nations	[18]	7 μg/kg of body weight	Solid food intake

Cadmium concentrations for the tested vegetable species are presented in Table 7. The maximum concentration of Cd within leaves, stems and roots were always associated with broccoli. The corresponding minimum concentrations were linked to dill, dill and tarragon, respectively. However, the root concentration for dill was also relatively low.

3.2. Effect of Treatment on Cadmium Accumulation

The effect of different Cd concentrations in soil samples on the corresponding Cd accumulation level of the selected vegetables is presented in Figure 1. The highest amount of Cd concentration corresponds usually to leaves, while the lowest amount of Cd concentration has been determined for the roots. This poses a problem for those vegetables such as broccoli, spinach and basil where the leaves are consumed by humans and not the roots. On the other hand, a relatively low root contamination is advantageous for vegetables such as carrots where the roots are eaten by consumers.

Table 7. Average cadmium (Cd) concentrations for the studied dried plants.

Species	Cd concentration (mg/kg)		
	Leaf	Stem	Root
Carrot	2.67	1.28	1.83
Tarragon	2.51	1.68	0.71
Basil	3.23	1.96	1.98
Garlic	2.82	1.94	2.16
Broccoli	4.25	3.21	2.52
Spinach	3.54	2.47	1.86
Dill	1.83	1.03	0.84

Figure 1. Comparison of the mean total cadmium (Cd) concentrations for different parts of the vegetables and for different treatments (1: 0 mg/kg Cd; 2: 30 mg/kg Cd; 3: 60 mg/kg Cd; 4: 120 mg/kg Cd).

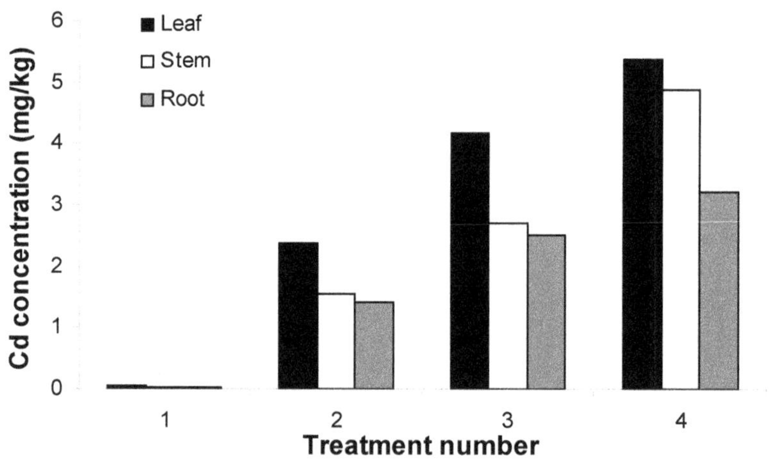

Table 8 compares the responses of different plant parts to various Cd treatments, indicating that the accumulated Cd is the highest for the fourth treatment (Table 3). Moreover, there is a direct positive correlation relationship between Cd concentration levels in all plant organs of the tested vegetables and the Cd concentrations in soil, simulating previously irrigated land with wastewater containing high levels of Cd. It follows that a continuation of the historic practice of irrigation with wastewater needs to be regulated to prevent further permanent soil contamination.

The Cd accumulation results can be summarized as follow: Leaves; broccoli > spinach > basil > garlic > carrot > tarragon > dill. Stems: broccoli > spinach > basil > garlic > tarragon > carrot > dill. Roots: broccoli > garlic > basil > spinach > carrot > dill > tarragon. These relationships are useful when deciding on what vegetables to grow in the future.

Table 8. Comparison of Cd concentrations (mg/kg) within different plant parts as a response to various cadmium (Cd) treatments (Table 3). Sample number n = 3.

Species	Treatment	Mean			Standard deviation		
		Leaf	Stem	Root	Leaf	Stem	Root
Carrot	Treatment 1	0.053	0.026	0.037	0.020	0.004	0.006
	Treatment 2	2.136	1.024	1.464	0.942	0.295	0.451
	Treatment 3	3.738	1.792	2.562	0.939	0.625	0.955
	Treatment 4	4.806	2.304	3.294	0.961	0.406	0.403
Tarragon	Treatment 1	0.050	0.034	0.014	0.010	0.012	0.002
	Treatment 2	2.008	1.344	0.566	0.230	0.44	0.130
	Treatment 3	3.514	2.352	0.990	0.606	0.901	0.056
	Treatment 4	4.518	3.024	1.273	1.106	1.563	0.055
Basil	Treatment 1	0.065	0.039	0.042	0.013	0.009	0.025
	Treatment 2	2.584	1.568	1.586	0.198	0.254	0.225
	Treatment 3	4.522	2.744	2.776	1.161	0.829	0.731
	Treatment 4	5.814	3.528	3.569	0.796	1.098	1.190
Garlic	Treatment 1	0.056	0.039	0.043	0.010	0.011	0.011
	Treatment 2	2.256	1.552	1.728	0.568	0.350	0.585
	Treatment 3	3.948	2.716	3.024	1.063	1.631	0.225
	Treatment 4	5.076	3.492	3.888	1.844	0.747	0.982
Broccoli	Treatment 1	0.085	0.064	0.051	0.020	0.021	0.013
	Treatment 2	3.400	2.568	2.568	1.198	0.601	0.759
	Treatment 3	5.950	4.494	4.494	1.805	1.103	0.630
	Treatment 4	7.650	5.778	5.778	2.141	0.799	1.264
Spinach	Treatment 1	0.071	0.049	0.037	0.011	0.013	0.006
	Treatment 2	2.832	1.976	1.488	0.699	0.871	0.358
	Treatment 3	4.956	3.458	2.604	1.888	0.777	0.438
	Treatment 4	6.372	4.446	3.348	0.808	0.518	0.936
Dill	Treatment 1	0.030	0.021	0.017	0.011	0.008	0.002
	Treatment 2	1.464	0.824	0.672	0.477	0.226	0.338
	Treatment 3	2.562	1.442	1.176	0.723	0.568	0.375
	Treatment 4	3.294	1.854	1.512	0.891	0.911	0.198

The simulated treatments are representative of future soil conditions if the practice of using irrigation wastewater containing Cd is not discontinued. The evaluation of vegetable responses to each treatment may lead to an informed decision about future plant selection. Table 8 indicates that dill and tarragon are possibly the best planting options in contrast to broccoli, which planting should not be encouraged anymore.

3.3. Consequences of Findings

The Cd accumulations in the selected plant species exceeded the permissible limit (0.5 mg/kg as discussed by [9]) for human food intake. It follows that the studied example vegetables should not be consumed anymore. This could be regulated for the agricultural industry. However, small farmers and poor families who support their diet with food grown in their garden are likely to continue producing and eating contaminated vegetables due to economic pressure.

Cultivating vegetables on farms where the Cd concentration in the corresponding soil is more than 30 mg/kg leads to Cd accumulations in vegetables likely to exceed existing permissible thresholds recommended for human consumption. This is the case for large areas of the case study region, and representative for other countries in North Africa and the Middle East.

In areas where the soil is heavily contaminated due to decades of wastewater application and where wastewater is the only available and economic water source, farmers have either the option to continue farming and to produce contaminated crops or to stop farming. A political decision needs to be made by the responsible authorities to come to a realistic solution that does not harm public health and agricultural exports. Subsidies for the installation of (better) wastewater treatment systems and soil remediation programmes might be an option for oil-rich countries such as Iran. In contrast, economically poor countries in the same region such as Yemen and Jordan might not be able to afford potentially expensive treatment systems [1,2]. However, there is well-established guidance on how to irrigate farms with treated wastewater in a sustainable manner without undertaking expensive land remediation programmes [19].

3.4. Limitations

Uncontaminated soil to which increasing concentrations of Cd was added was used in this experiment. Alternatively, freshwater spiked with different Cd concentrations could have been used. This would have resulted in long-term accumulation of Cd. However, it would have taken many years to reach the desired concentrations within the soil before the experiment could have been started. Moreover, Cd is easily adsorbed by clay located within the soil matrix, which makes the argument for long-term adsorption less relevant.

The usefulness of the findings is limited to arid countries where irrigation with heavy metal-enriched wastewater has been practiced for many years or even decades. However, the study is also relevant for countries wishing to recycle wastewater for irrigation in the future. They could learn from the mistakes of those countries with contaminated soil due to poor irrigation strategies.

A further limitation is the lack of a high number of replicates. Three replicates were assessed in Table 8. The findings would have been more significant if at least 30 replicates would have been used. However, there were resource restrictions in terms of work force and funding.

4. Conclusions and Recommendations

Wastewater recycling for the irrigation of crops is a possibility for countries with low freshwater availability. However, studies have shown that relatively high concentrations of Cd in soil samples resulted in high Cd accumulations in plant parts. The maximum average Cd concentrations of 4.25, 3.12 and 2.52 mg/kg were observed in leaves, stems and roots of broccoli, respectively. There is a positive correlation between the amount of Cd in soil samples and its accumulation in plant parts. Considering that most of the selected plants such as broccoli and spinach absorbed and accumulated relatively high Cd quantities in their stems and leaves, which are consumed by humans, it is recommended to prevent cultivation of these vegetables on farm lands, which are irrigated with essentially untreated urban and industrial wastewater containing high levels of heavy metals such as Cd. Moreover, vegetables should not be grown on farm land, which has already a Cd concentration of more than 30 mg/kg.

The authors recommend the reuse of treated wastewater to irrigate farm lands in the future. This should result in edible vegetables. Treatment technology such as integrated vertical-flow constructed wetlands might offer a cost-effective and sustainable solution.

Acknowledgments

The authors thank Tehran University for provision of experimental facilities and Bahman Yargholi (Agricultural Engineering Research Institute, Karaj, Iran) for advice. The collaborative work would not have been possible without the support of the University of Delaware and The University of Salford.

Author Contributions

Babak Bakhshayesh and Madjid Delkash undertook the experimental work. Miklas Scholz wrote the article based on a first draft paper provided by Madjid Delkash.

Conflicts of Interest

The authors declare no conflict of interest.

References

1. Almas, A.A.M.; Scholz, M. Potential for wastewater reuse in irrigation: Case study from Aden (Yemen). *Int. J. Environ. Stud.* **2006**, *63*, 131–142.
2. Almas, A.A.M.; Scholz, M. Agriculture and water resources in Yemen: Need for sustainable agriculture. *J. Sustain. Agric.* **2006**, *28*, 55–75.
3. Mohammadi, Y.; Sabouhi, M. Analysis of effective components on agricultural water management in Zarindasht County from farmers viewpoint. *J. Agric. Sci. Nat. Resour.* **2009**, *16*, 9–18. (In Persian)
4. Brooks, D.B. An operational definition of water demand management. *Int. J. Water Resour. Dev.* **2006**, *23*, 227–241.
5. Rezadoost, B.; Allahyari, M.S. Farmers opinions regarding effective factors on optimum agricultural water management. *J. Saudi Soc. Agric. Sci.* **2013**, *13*, 15–21.
6. Hashem, H.A.; Hassanein, R.A.; Shouman, A.I. Irrigation with industrial wastewater activates antioxidant system and osmoprotectant accumulation in lettuce, turnip and tomato plants. *Ecotoxicol. Environ. Safety* **2013**, *95*, 144–152.
7. Torabian, A.; Mahjouri, M. Heavy metals uptake by vegetable crops irrigated water in south Tehran. *J. Environ. Study* **2002**, *16*, 34. (In Persian)
8. Harati, M.; Varavi Pour, M.; Tamadon Rastegar, M.; Foghi, B. Effect of urban wastewater usage and problems of accumulation of heavy metals in agricultural lands (south of Tehran). *Afr. J. Agric. Res.* **2011**, *6*, 3224–3231.

9. Miller, R.W.; Al-Khazraji, M.L.; Sisson, D.R.; Gardiner, D.T. Alfalfa growth and absorption of cadmium and zinc from soils amended with sewage sludge. *Agric. Ecosyst. Environ.* **1994**, *23*, 33–45.
10. Arona, M.; Kiran, B.; Rani, S.; Rani, A.; Kaur, B.; Mittal, N. Heavy metal accumulation in vegetables irrigated with water from different sources. *Food Chem.* **2008**, *111*, 811–815.
11. Hashemi, S.A. The investigation of irrigation with wastewater on trees (*Populus deltoids* L.). *Toxicol. Ind. Health* **2013**, *29*, 711–715.
12. Izadiyar, M.H.; Yargholi, B. Study of cadmium absorption and accumulation in different parts of four forages. *Am. Eurasian J. Agric. Environ. Sci.* **2010**, *9*, 231–238.
13. Monteith, J.L. Evaporation and environment. *Symp. Soc. Exp. Biol.* **1965**, *19*, 205–224.
14. Okoronkwo, N.E.; Igwe, J.C.; Onwuchekwa, E.C. Risk and health implications of polluted soils for crop production. *Afr. J. Biotechnol.* **2005**, *4*, 1521–1524.
15. Kabatta, A.; Pendis, H. *Trace Elements in Soils and Plants*, 3rd ed.; CRC Press: Boca Raton, FL, USA, 1992.
16. Sauerbeck, D.R. Uptake and bioavailability of heavy metals. *J. Water Air Soil Pollut.* **1991**, *57–58*, 227–237.
17. United States Environmental Protection Agency. *Process Design Manual: Land Application of Sewage Sludge and Domestic Sewage*; Office of Research and Development: Washington, DC, USA, 1995.
18. Ernst, A. *Bioavailability of Heavy Metals and Decontaminations of Soils by Plants*; World Health Organization: Geneva, Switzerland, 1996.
19. Food and Agriculture Organization. *Users Manual for Irrigation with Treated Wastewater*; Food and Agriculture Organization of the United Nations, Food and Agriculture Organization Regional Office of the Near East: Cairo, Egypt, 2003.

Int. J. Environ. Res. Public Health **2015**, *12*, 7400-7416; doi:10.3390/ijerph120707400

OPEN ACCESS

International Journal of
Environmental Research and Public Health
ISSN 1660-4601
www.mdpi.com/journal/ijerph

Article

Toxicity and Bioaccumulation of Heavy Metals in Spinach (*Spinacia oleracea*) Grown in a Controlled Environment

Naz Alia [1,2], Khan Sardar [2], Muhammad Said [3], Khalid Salma [4], Alam Sadia [5], Siddique Sadaf [6], Ahmed Toqeer [7] and Scholz Miklas [8,*]

1 Department of Environmental Sciences, University of Haripur, Haripur 21120, Pakistan; E-Mail: aliaawkum@gmail.com
2 Department of Environmental Sciences, University of Peshawar, Peshawar 25120, Pakistan; E-Mail: sardar.khan2008@yahoo.com
3 Department of Earth Sciences, COMSATS Institution of Information Technology, Abbottabad 22060, Pakistan; E-Mail: saidmuhammad1@gmail.com
4 Prime Institute of Public Health, Peshawar 25120, Pakistan; E-Mail: anagalious_79@yahoo.com
5 Department of Microbiology, University of Haripur, Haripur 21120, Pakistan; E-Mail: sadia.alam2004@gmail.com
6 Department of Forestry and Wildlife Management, University of Haripur, Haripur 21120, KPK, Pakistan; E-Mail: dua632@yahoo.com
7 Centre for Climate Research and Development (CCRD), COMSATS Institute of Information Technology (CIIT), Chak Shahzad, Islamabad 45550, Pakistan; E-Mail: toqeer.ahmed@comsats.edu.pk
8 Civil Engineering Research Group, School of Computing, Science and Engineering, The University of Salford, Salford M5 4WT, UK

* Author to whom correspondence should be addressed; E-Mail: m.scholz@salford.ac.uk; Tel.: +44-161-2955-921; Fax: +44-161-2955-575.

Academic Editor: Paul B. Tchounwou

Received: 20 April 2015 / Accepted: 23 June 2015 / Published: 30 June 2015

Abstract: The impact of heavy metal toxicity on the shoot and root lengths, total protein, fiber characteristics, moisture content and nutrient composition of spinach (*Spinacia oleracea*) was evaluated. Plants were grown in pots containing soil and treated with different concentrations (mg/kg) of lead (Pb; 300, 400 and 500), cadmium (Cd; 0.5, 1 and 1.5) and zinc (Zn; 250, 500, and 700) as well as mixtures of Cd and Pb (0.5/300, 1/400, 1.5/500), Cd and Zn

(0.5/250, 1/500, 1.5/700), and Pb and Zn (300/250, 400/500, 500/700). Soil contaminated by long-term irrigation with wastewater containing heavy metals was simulated. An increase in concentrations of heavy metals both individually and as mixtures significantly ($p < 0.05$) reduced the growth parameters and nutrient contents of *S. oleracea.* The uptake patterns of heavy metals in mixtures showed antagonistic impacts on each other. The toxicities of the mixtures Cd and Pb, Cd and Zn as well as Pb and Zn were higher than those observed in separate heavy metal applications but less than their additive sums. The toxicity caused by individual heavy metals was the highest for Cd followed by Pb and Zn. The highest toxicity was observed in plants grown in soil contaminated by Cd and Pb.

Keywords: bioaccumulation; cadmium; contamination; irrigation; lead; nutrient; spinach; toxicity; water resources management; zinc

---

1. Introduction

Heavy metal accumulation in soil interrupts the normal functioning of soil ecosystems and plant growth [1,2]. Plants absorb various kinds of heavy metals when available in the soil or irrigation water [3]. Metals like manganese (Mn), magnesium (Mg), copper (Cu) and iron (Fe) is classified as plant essential metals. These metals are required in specific amount and their deficiency or elevated concentrations will result in toxic effects and reduce the plant productivity. For example, Mn is involved in splitting water molecules necessary for photosynthesis. Other metals like magnesium deficiency is responsible for cholorosis in plant leaves [4,5] and also induces oxidative stress [6]. Zinc (Zn) is essentially required for plants. However, too high concentrations can damage plants [4] and inhibit their growth. Zinc is responsible for chlorosis in leaves by reducing chlorophyll [7]. However, heavy metals including Cd and Pb are toxic metal and influence the plant growth adversely by affecting the leaves and root growth and inhibit enzymatic activities and resulted in reduce production [8,9].

Cadmium is considered as phytotoxic as it inhibits plant growth parameters including respiration, photosynthesis and water and nutrient uptake [10]. Further it reduces the rate of new cell production and root growth [11], inhibits the ant oxidative enzymes activities [12] and induces oxidative stress in cells [13]. Moreover, Cd induces changes in plants at all biochemical, physical and genetic levels, which are responsible for the reduction in the growth of plants [14], leaf chlorosis, and leaf or root necrosis [15] and ultimately plant death occurred [16]. Like Cd, Pb is also phytotoxic in nature. It affects the plants photosynthesis by reducing the chlorophyll content. This is because Pb reduces the uptake of chlorophyll-essential elements such as Mg and Fe, affecting chloroplast, changing essential enzymatic processes for photosynthesis and disturbing the closing of stomata [17]. Lead has significant impacts on seedling dry mass, root and shoot length, and weight [18,19]. It adversely affects the process of respiration and metabolism of plants [20].

Soils are contaminated in the environment with a number of heavy metals by natural (weathering and erosion of parent rock material or ore deposits) or artificial (wastewater irrigation, mining activities) sources. The presence of one contaminant can increase or decrease the impacts of others. To date, majority of studies have focused or investigated the effects of a single metal on plant species [21–23]. However, the study of plant to a mixture of heavy metals requires more attention throughout the world.

Human exposure via the oral pathway (*i.e.*, eating food) is one the major routes for heavy metal exposure [24]. *Spinacia oleracea* is a member of the Caryophyllales order, comprising broad, green and leafy vegetables possessing large surface areas, relatively high growth rates and rather elevated heavy metal absorption rates. Recently, due to these unique characteristics, *S. oleracea* and other members of the Caryophyllales order have been researched in a number of scientific studies to observe their growth and toxicity responses to heavy metal contaminations [25–28]. *Spinacia oleracea* has an imperative position in the order due to large and expanded leafs, fast growth and by being a common part of the human diet. Nevertheless, there is a lack of information regarding growth behavior, metal accumulation, total protein content, fiber characteristics, moisture content and inorganic nutrients response to individual and combined heavy metals with respect to this plant. Therefore, it is necessary to unravel the response of *S. oleracea* to a range of individual and combined heavy metals.

2. Materials and Methods

2.1. Experimental Design

Spinacia oleracea was taken as a representative plant for broad leafy vegetables. Soil contaminated by long-term irrigation with wastewater containing heavy metals was simulated. This is a common practice considering that a field experiment with contaminated irrigation water would otherwise take years or even decades to complete [26]. Soil used was characterized by the following parameters: pH (6.7), organic matter content (2%) and electric conductivity (2.1 dS/m). The soil particle size distribution was as follows: <20 μm (8.15%), ≥20–62 μm (47.3%), ≥62–250 μm (44.0%) and ≥250 μm–1mm (0.34%).

Figure 1 shows a diagrammatic representation of the experimental design and key procedures undertaken. Soil from an uncontaminated site was analyzed for physicochemical properties and selected heavy metals to establish a baseline. Representative soil samples were freshly spiked with salt solutions of heavy metals (Cd, Pb and Zn) and thoroughly mixed (all concentrations in mg/kg) according to Figure 1.

Plastic pots were filled with 1 kg of freshly spiked soil having four replicates of each treatment and a control, and marked properly. The disinfected (30% (w/w) hydrogen peroxide solution for 10 min) seeds were germinated in Petri dishes inside the folds of wet filter papers at 28 ± 1 °C. After four days, five uniform seedlings were cultivated in each plastic pot. This experiment was performed in a greenhouse with a day temperature of 25 ± 4 °C and a night temperature of 19 ± 3 °C. The plants were kept under sunlight for 12 h and at a relative humidity of 65% ± 2%. The positions of pots were changed on a regular basis to ensure similar light and temperature readings. The plants were irrigated with deionized water (100 mL) twice per day and were harvested after maturation at 40 days. The plants were washed with tap water and then deionized water and were cut down into shoots and roots. Fresh weights as well as length and shoot diameters and other physical appearance were recorded. Roots and shoots were oven dried at 70 °C for 48 h and powdered with grinder and sieved through 2 mm mesh size [24,29].

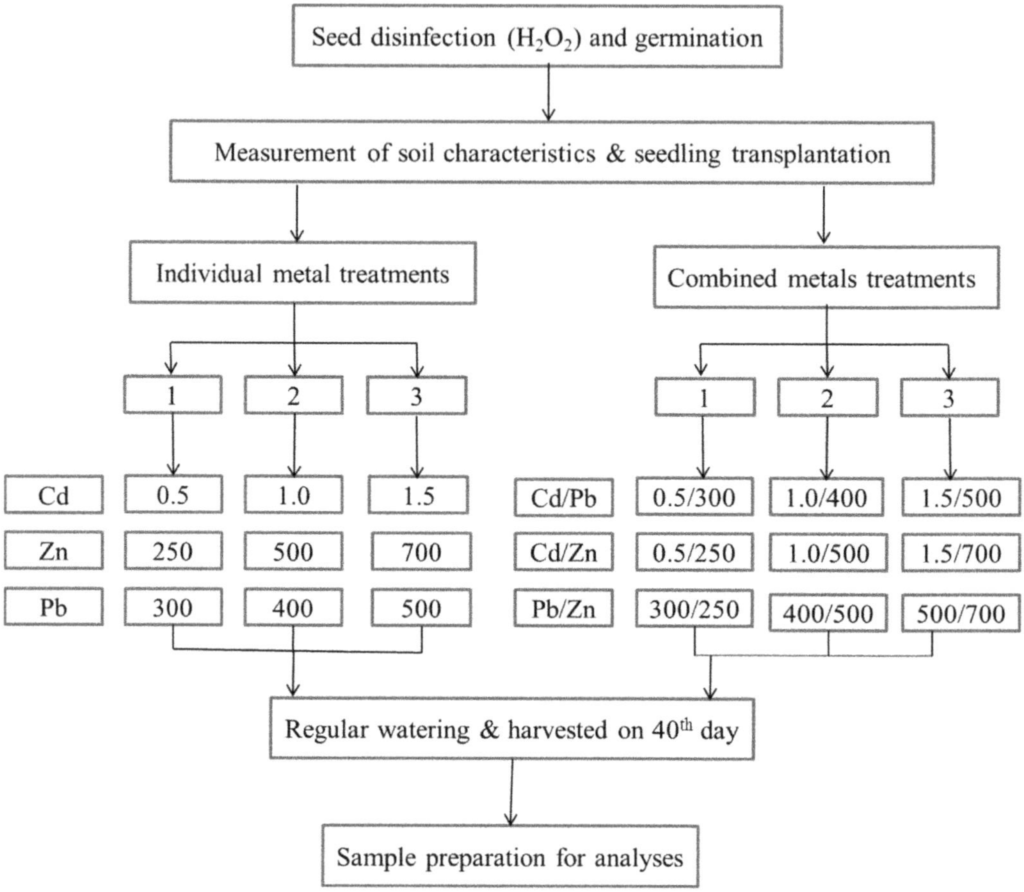

Figure 1. Diagrammatic representation of experimental design and procedure (Cd, cadmium; Pb, lead; Zn, zinc).

Moisture, fiber and protein contents were determined using standard methods [30]. Moisture was analyzed by using the dry oven method. A plant sample was dried in an oven at 105 °C for 3 h. The Kjeldahl method was used for evaluating nitrogen and subsequently the protein content by calculation. The crude fiber content was estimated according to Aldwairji *et al.* [31], who developed a method based on a procedure by the Association of Official Analytical Chemists [32]. The total protein and fiber content of each treatment (including the control group) were determined. Reductions of protein and fiber contents subject to treatments were compared with the control group to assess the impact of the corresponding treatment.

2.2. Metal Extraction and Analysis

Plants were weighed and samples of 0.5 g were put in acid-washed and dried digestion tubes. Powdered plant parts were mixed with (15 mL) of nitric, perchloric and sulfuric acids (5:1:10) overnight to prevent next day foaming. On the following day, the digestion tubes were placed on a digestion block at 80 °C for one hour and then raised to between 120 °C and 130 °C until a clear solution was obtained [24]. Although nitric acid alone can be used as an oxidizing agent, however, the advantage of this method is due to complete degradation of organic material and safety reasons (reduction of hazards linked to perchloric acid). On the other hand, disadvantages are due to handling of three hazardous acids and higher costs. The digested and transparent solutions were filtered through Whatman (0.45 μm) filter paper into acid-washed volumetric flasks. Double deionized water was used to increase the volume to 50 mL. An Analyst 700 atomic absorption spectrometer (PerkinElmer, Waltham, MA, USA) was used.

2.3. Quality Control

For verification purposes and to achieve a high accuracy and precision, a reagent blank sample as well as standard reference soil and vegetable samples (NIST-SRM, 1570a for spinach leaves and SRM 2709 for soil) were included in the digestion procedure [24]. Plant and soil were first analyzed for selected heavy metals according to standard optimum conditions of each metal (Table 1). All chemicals and reagents used in the experiments were of analytical grade and purchased from Merck (Darmstadt, Germany). All glassware used for digestion and preservation of the digested samples were washed with a solution of 10% of nitric acid followed by washing with double deionized water. An average value of triplicates was used to support the interpretation of findings.

Table 1. Instrumental analytical conditions associated with the analyses of selected elements.

Element	Acetylene (L/min)	Air (L/min)	Wave Length (nm)	Slit Width (nm)	Lamp Current (Ma)	Detection Limit (μg/L)
Calcium	2.0	17.0	422.7	0.7	10.0	1.5
Cadmium	2.0	17.0	228.8	0.7	4.0	0.8
Iron	2.3	17.0	288.3	0.2	30.0	5.0
Potassium	2.0	17.0	766.5	0.7	12.0	3.0
Magnesium	2.0	17.0	285.2	0.7	6.0	0.2
Manganese	2.0	17.0	279.5	0.2	20.0	1.5
Sodium	2.0	17.0	589.0	0.2	8.0	0.3
Lead	2.0	17.0	283.3	0.7	30.0	5.0
Zinc	2.0	17.0	213.9	0.7	15.0	1.5

2.4. Statistical Analysis

All data were statistically analyzed using the statistical software package SPSS 17 (International Business Machines Corporation, Armonk, NY, USA). One-way analysis of variance to confirm the variability and validity of results was performed. The Duncan's multiple range test was applied to determine significant differences among treatments at a significance level of $p < 0.05$. A linear regression analysis was performed to establish the relationships between heavy metal concentrations in the plant tissue and the corresponding concentrations in the soil.

3. Results and Discussion

3.1. Effects of Heavy Metals on Plant Biomass

The toxicological effects of Cd, Pb and Zn individually and in combination on the biomass of shoots and roots (fresh and dry weights) of *S. oleracea* were assessed. Results revealed that these heavy metal concentrations have significantly ($p < 0.05$) impacted on the biomass of *S. oleracea*. Shoot and root (fresh and dry) weights were decreased by 25.3, 42.4, 10.1 and 35.1% at the highest dose of Cd exposure as compared to controls treatment, respectively (Table 2). Similarly, the shoot and root (fresh and dry) weights decreased by 25, 47, 8 and 28% at highest dose of Pb exposure as compared to the control treatment, respectively (Table 2). Similar to Cd and Pb, exposure to higher doses of Zn the shoot and root (fresh and dry) weights decreased by 23, 44, 6 and 14% as compared to the controls, respectively (Table 2).

Table 2. Reduction (%) in growth parameters of Spinach (*Spinacia oleracea*) due to different heavy metal (cadmium (Cd), Pb (lead) and Zn (zinc)) treatments (in comparison to the controls).

Treatment	Shoot Fresh Weight	Root Fresh Weight	Shoot Dry Weight	Root Dry Weight	Shoot Length	Root Length
Cd 1	7.0 ± 0.10	23.5 ± 0.20	2.5 ± 0.08	21.1 ± 0.19	8.2 ± 0.10	15.9 ± 0.10
Cd 2	18.6 ± 0.11	27.1 ± 0.30	6.3 ± 0.09	28.1 ± 0.20	13.1 ± 0.30	17.7 ± 0.2
Cd 3	25.3 ± 0.09	42.4 ± 0.33	10.1 ± 0.10	35.1 ± 0.30	18.0 ± 0.30	19.7 ± 0.22
Pb 1	5.4 ± 0.12	20.0 ± 0.12	1.90 ± 0.09	9.0 ± 0.17	6.6 ± 0.21	10.8 ± 0.20
Pb 2	18.3 ± 0.20	21.2 ± 0.21	5.9 ± 0.06	14.0 ± 0.25	11.5 ± 0.10	13.3 ± 0.23
Pb 3	24.7 ± 0.31	47.1 ± 0.30	7.6 ± 0.10	28.1 ± 0.40	13.0 ± 0.20	15.8 ± 0.30
Zn 1	3.0 ± 0.01	18.9 ± 0.22	1.8 ± 0.08	8.1 ± 0.20	4.6 ± 0.19	6.0 ± 0.01
Zn 2	17.7 ± 0.13	20.5 ± 0.25	3.8 ± 0.10	10.1 ± 0.21	4.9 ± 0.30	8.8 ± 0.01
Zn 3	23.0 ± 0.38	43.5 ± 0.28	5.7 ± 0.10	14.4 ± 0.12	3.0 ± 0.10	12.7 ± 0.11
Cd 1/Pb 1	10.5 ± 0.19	30.9 ± 0.20	3.5 ± 0.09	28.1 ± 0.30	10.1 ± 0.10	17.1 ± 0.20
Cd 2/Pb 2	27.4 ± 0.20	32.5 ± 0.25	12.1 ± 0.14	35.1 ± 0.32	14.3 ± 0.20	20.9 ± 0.23
Cd 3/Pb 3	30.1 ± 0.29	78.8 ± 0.27	13.9 ± 0.13	42.1 ± 0.23	20.9 ± 0.30	22.0 ± 0.23
Cd 1/Zn 1	6.8 ± 0.12	25.9 ± 0.33	3.0 ± 0.10	25.1 ± 0.11	6.4 ± 0.29	16.1 ± 0.12
Cd 2/Zn 2	19.2 ± 0.22	29.4 ± 0.40	10.6 ± 0.14	32.1 ± 0.12	8.0 ± 0.10	18.6 ± 0.23
Cd 3/Zn 3	28.7 ± 0.38	58.8 ± 0.38	12.2 ± 0.20	43.2 ± 0.30	18.0 ± 0.10	20.0 ± 0.33
Zn 1/Pb 1	6.5 ± 0.12	23.5 ± 0.22	2.5 ± 0.08	15.1 ± 0.15	2.0 ± 0.09	11.5 ± 0.10
Zn 2/Pb 2	20.4 ± 0.23	27.1 ± 0.35	9.7 ± 0.09	17.1 ± 0.23	6.2 ± 0.11	14.6 ± 0.21
Zn 3/Pb 3	26.5 ± 0.30	54.7 ± 0.44	11.4 ± 0.10	32.1 ± 0.33	14.1 ± 0.20	16.2 ± 0.23

The reductions in shoot and root (fresh and dry) weights were 30, 79, 14 and 42%, respectively, if compared to controls, under the influence of the highest dose of Cd mixed with Pb. Similarly, at highest dose of Cd mixed with Zn the shoot and root (fresh and dry) weights decreased by 29, 59, 12 and 43% (Table 2), respectively, as compared to the control. Addition of a high dose of Pb mixed with Zn decreased shoot and root (fresh and dry) weights by 27, 55, 11 and 32%, respectively, if compared to controls (Table 2).

With both Cd and Pb added to soil, the toxicity of spinach biomass was further increased, but was less than the sum of the toxicity for Cd and Pb, when added separately. Toxicity in the biomass of seedlings under the influence of combined Cd and Zn was more than the individual toxicities of Cd and Zn. The combined toxicity of Zn and Pb was less than the toxicity associated with separate Zn and Pb on *S. oleracea* biomass. The dry weights of both shoots and roots were more affected than their fresh seedling weights. The (fresh and dry) root weights were affected more than the (fresh and dry) shoot weights.

3.2. Impact of Heavy Metals on Plant Length

Shoot and root lengths of *S. oleracea* were significantly ($p < 0.05$) affected by the addition of individual Cd, Pb and Zn concentrations as well as their mixtures. The increasing concentrations of heavy metals in the soil resulted in a decrease of the shoot and root lengths of *S. oleracea* (Table 2). At highest dose of Cd, the shoot and root lengths decreased by 18 and 20%, respectively, if compared to controls (Table 2). Similarly, at the highest dose of Pb, the shoot and root lengths decreased by 13 and 16%, respectively (Table 2), as compared to controls. At highest dose of Zn, the shoot and root lengths decreased by 3 and 13%, respectively, as compared to controls (Table 2). This reduction in the shoot and root lengths were 21 and 22%, respectively, as compared to control under influence of the highest dose of Cd/Pb. The combined toxicity of Cd and Zn in the shoot and root lengths were 18 and 20%, respectively, if compared to controls. This reduction in shoot and root lengths were 14 and 16%, respectively, under the influence of Pb and Zn combined. Generally, the root lengths were more affected than shoot lengths.

3.3. Effects of Heavy Metals on Total Protein, Fiber Characteristic and Moisture Content

Heavy metal concentrations had a significant ($p < 0.05$) adverse impacts on protein, fiber and moisture contents of *S. oleracea*. At highest dose of Cd, the total protein, fiber and moisture contents of *S. oleracea* decreased by 31, 29 and 33%, respectively (Figure 2), if compared to controls. Similarly, at highest dose of Pb, the total protein, fiber and moisture contents decreased by 23, 22 and 29%, respectively (Figure 2), as compared to controls. Addition of a high dose of Zn decreased the total protein, fiber and moisture contents by 16, 16 and 20%, respectively, if compared to controls. This reductions in total protein, fiber and moisture contents were 36, 37 and 43%, respectively, if compared to controls under the influence of the highest dose of combined Cd and Pb. Similarly, at highest dose of Cd and Zn, the total protein, fiber and moisture contents decreased by 27, 26 and 31%, respectively, if compared to controls (Figure 2). Addition of a high dose of combined Pb and Zn decreased the total protein, fiber and moisture contents by 26, 28 and 40%, respectively (Figure 2), as compared to controls. Toxic effects to mixture of Cd and Pb on the total protein, fiber, sodium, potassium, calcium, iron and manganese are more than their individual effects.

In case of moisture content, the combined toxicity of Cd and Pb is less severe than the toxicity due to Pb and more severe than the toxicity associated with Cd. Concerning the calcium and magnesium content of plant, the mixture of Cd and Pb had a less severe impact compared to individual Cd and Pb treatments. The combined toxicity due to Cd and Zn was less severe than the toxicity due to Cd and more than the toxicity of Zn for almost all nutrient components of *S. oleracea*. The toxicity due to Pb combined with Zn was more severe than the toxicity due Pb and Zn alone in case of their influence on the nutrient content.

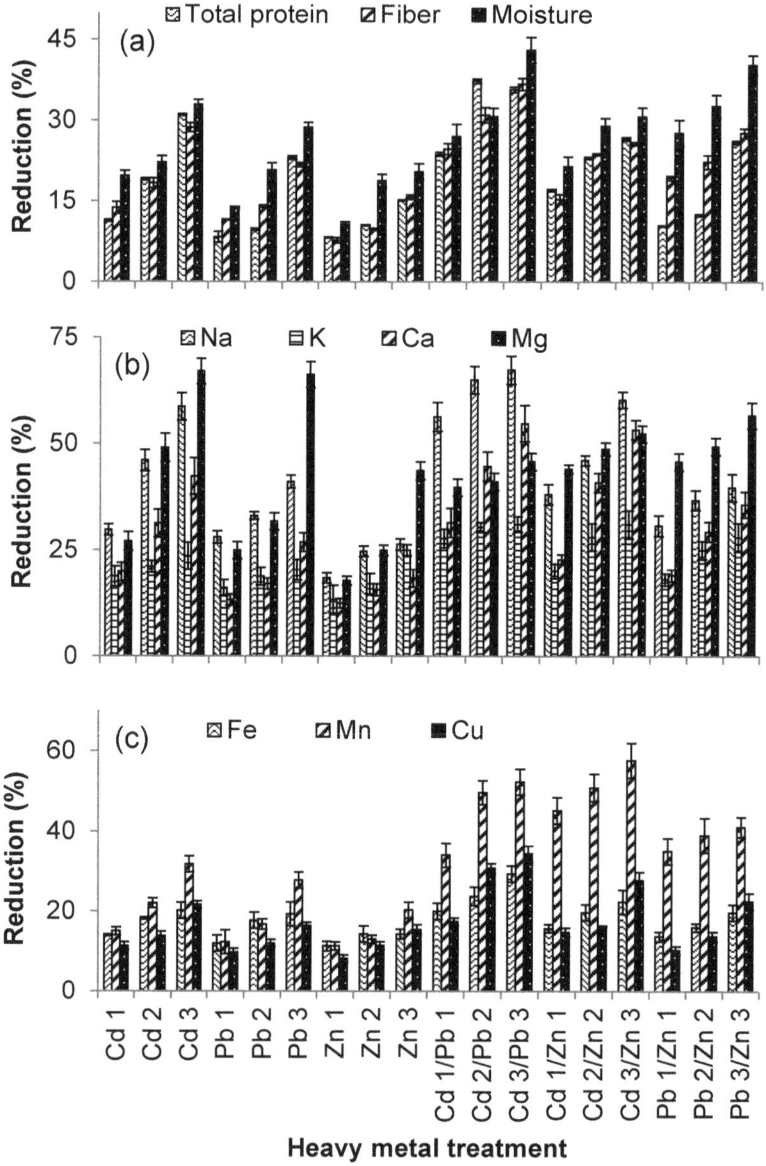

Figure 2. Reduction (%) in (**a**) total protein, total fiber and moisture; (**b**) sodium (Na), potassium (K), calcium (Ca) and magnesium (Mg); and (**c**) of iron (Fe), manganese (Mn) and copper (Cu) determined for Spinach (*Spinacia oleracea*) due to different heavy metal (cadmium (Cd), Pb (lead) and Zn (zinc)) treatments (in comparison to the controls).

3.4. Effects of Heavy Metals on Nutrient Uptake

The increasing concentrations of heavy metals resulted in the decrease of sodium, potassium, calcium, iron, magnesium, manganese and copper in *S. oleracea* (Table 2). These reductions in concentrations within *S. oleracea* were significant ($p < 0.05$). At the highest dose of Cd, the concentrations of sodium, potassium, calcium, iron, magnesium, manganese and copper reduced to 59, 24, 42, 21, 67, 32 and 22%, respectively (Table 2), as compared to the controls. Similarly, at the highest dose of Pb, the concentrations of these elements showed corresponding reductions of 41, 20, 27, 19, 66, 28 and 16% (Table 2). At the highest dose of Zn, the concentrations of sodium, potassium, calcium, iron, magnesium, manganese and copper showed reductions of 26, 25, 18, 44, 20 and 15%, respectively (Table 2), if compared to the controls. The reductions in concentrations of these elements were 67, 31, 55, 29, 46, 52 and 34%, respectively, if compared to the control under the influence of the highest combined dose of Cd and Pb. The concentrations of sodium, potassium, calcium, iron, magnesium, manganese and copper were 60, 31, 53, 22, 52, 58 and 30%, respectively, if compared to the controls under the influence of the highest combined dose of cadmium and zinc. Similarly, at the highest combined dose of lead and zinc, concentrations of these elements were 40, 28, 36, 20, 57, 41 and 23%, respectively, as compared to the controls.

3.5. Up take of Heavy Metals

Increasing concentrations of Cd in soil (whether as a single contaminant or as part of a mixture with another element) resulted also in a corresponding increase of Cd in the roots (Table 3). Root accumulation of Cd follows the order Cd alone > Cd and Pb combined > Cd and Zn combined (Figure 3). Similarly, it was found that with an increase in concentration of Cd within the roots, its corresponding concentration in the shoots also increased.

The concentrations of Pb within roots showed an increase with increasing Pb concentrations within the soil. The regression analysis showed positive relationships between the concentrations of Pb within the soil and roots for all three treatments; *i.e.*, Pb alone, Pb mixed with Cd and Pb mixed with Zn (Table 3). All correlation relationships for Pb concentrations within roots and shoots are positive. The increasing concentrations of Pb within roots also correspond to increasing concentrations within the shoots.

The regression analysis showed strong positive relationships among the Zn concentrations in soil and roots for Zn alone, combined Zn and Cd and combined Zn and Pb treatments (Table 3). Root- accumulated Zn follows this order: Zn alone > Zn combined with Cd > Zn combined with Pb (Figure 4). Table 3 shows relationships between the Zn concentrations within the roots and shoots of *S. oleracea* concerning zinc alone, Cd combined with Zn and Pb combined with Zn treatments. All relationships were positive. An increasing concentration of Zn within roots increases the concentration in the corresponding shoots as well.

Plants grow on metal-contaminated soils simulating soils that have been irrigated with contaminated water for a long time, and accumulate heavy metals in their body tissues [1,2,27,28]. Heavy metals are toxic to plants, subsequently reducing plant yield, affecting leaf and root growths, and inhibiting enzymatic activities [8].

Table 3. Linear regressions model for heavy metal concentrations in soils, roots and shoots.

Heavy Metal Uptake	Heavy Metal Treatment	Medium	Coefficient of Determination
Cadmium (Cd)	Cd	Soil to root	0.8037
		Root to shoot	0.9999
	Cd/Pb	Soil to root	0.9671
		Root to shoot	1.0000
	Cd/Zn	Soil to root	0.9976
		Root to shoot	0.9995
Lead (Pb)	Pb	Soil to root	0.9001
		Root to shoot	0.9991
	Pb/Cd	Soil to root	0.8150
		Root to shoot	0.9075
	Pb/Zn	Soil to root	0.9450
		Root to shoot	0.9830
Zinc (Zn)	Zn	Soil to root	0.7076
		Root to shoot	1.0000
	Zn/Cd	Soil to root	0.8283
		Root to shoot	0.9995
	Zn/Pb	Soil to root	0.9340
		Root to shoot	0.9994

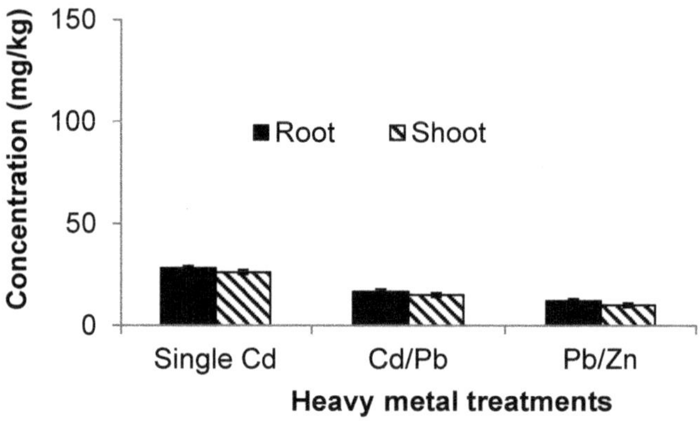

Figure 3. Comparison of cadmium (Cd) uptake subject to different treatments.

Cadmium inhibits plant growth, and its toxicity increases with increasing Cd concentration in soil. In the present study, increasing concentrations of Cd significantly ($p < 0.05$) reduced shoot and root fresh and dry weights. The results of this study support previous research [25,33–38]. However, the results of the present study are not consistent with other published findings [39,40]. Increasing concentrations of Cd in soil led to toxicity in plant biomass and plant lengths of *S. oleracea*, which is in agreement with previous work [25,37]. Cadmium toxicity was more severe within roots in terms of both biomass and length. Roots are more sensitive than shoots, because they are part of plants, which come into contact with toxic substances first. Researchers [11] reported that a reduction in the formation of new cells under the influence of Pb and Cd leads to a reduction in shoot and root lengths.

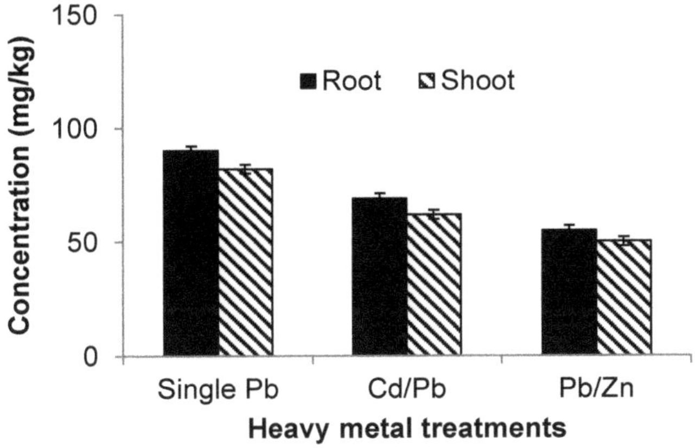

Figure 4. Comparison of lead (Pb) uptake subject to different treatments.

Spinach was suffering from toxicity with increasing concentrations of Pb in terms of plant biomass and length. Increasing concentrations of Pb significantly ($p < 0.05$) reduced plant biomass and length. Other researchers [25,35,36] observed decreases in plant shoot and root growths with increasing concentrations of Pb in the growth medium.

Zinc is an essential element for plants, but its excess can significantly damage plants [4]. This study indicated that increasing concentrations of Zn are responsible for increased toxicity in *S. oleracea*. Shoot and root (fresh and dry) weights reduced with increasing concentrations of Zn. Zinc reduced plant biomass, because it led to a deficiency of macro-nutrients such as phosphorus [34]. Researchers [36] also found reductions in growth of corn with increasing concentrations of Zn.

The combined toxicity of Cd and Pb in terms of biomass and length was found to be more severe than the toxicity of Cd and Pb alone, but was less than the additive toxicity of the two heavy metals alone. The uptake results showed that in combination, Cd decreased the uptake of Pb (Figure 5) and Pb lowered the uptake of Cd (Figure 4). Although both Cd and Pb are toxic on their own, they decrease the uptake of each other if combined. It follows that the combined toxicity does not equal the additive of both toxicities. Some studies [37] have reported similar results for broccoli at low Cd concentrations, while others [33] produced the same result in studying Cucumber. The combined toxicity of Cd and Zn is more severe than the individual toxicity of Cd and Zn, but less than the additive toxicity of the two heavy metals alone. The combined toxicity is not the sum of both toxicities, because Zn and Cd both reduce the uptake of each other by plants [38].

The combined toxicity of Cd and Zn is more than the individual toxicities of Zn and Cd in terms of biomass plant length. The result is consistent with previous findings [39]. The combined toxicity of Pb and Zn in terms of total biomass and length is more than the corresponding individual toxicities, but less than the sum of the individual toxicities of Zn and Pb. The reason for the reduction in toxicological effect of combined Pb and Zn is the antagonistic effects of Zn and Pb. Lead decreases the uptake of Zn (Figure 5) and Zn reduces the uptake of Pb (Figure 4).

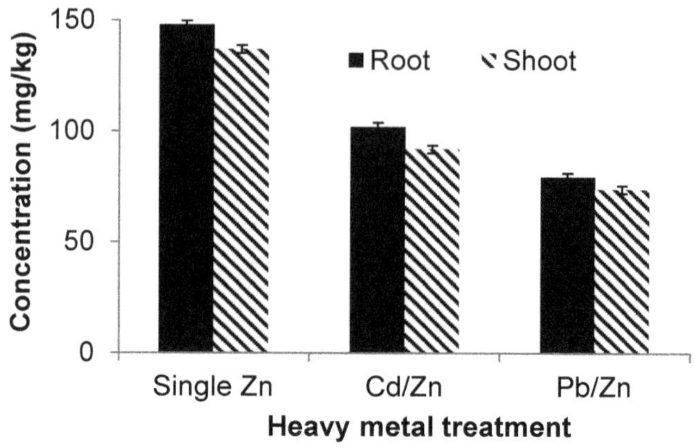

Figure 5. Comparison of zinc (Zn) uptake subject to different treatments.

As the concentration of Cd increases, Pb and Zn decrease the total protein contents in plants. The results of this study show a drop in the total protein content in plant shoots with increasing concentrations of Cd, Pb and Zn alone and also with respect to their mixtures; *i.e.* combinations of Cd and Pb, Cd and Zn and Pb and Zn. The results are consistent with those of previous studies [4,40,41]. Other researchers [40,42] found a reduction in protein content for *Daucus carota* (carrot) and *Helianthus annuus* (sunflower) with increasing concentration of Cd in the growth medium. A high dose (1500 μM) of Pb was responsible for 77% reduction in protein content in *Brassica juncea* (mustard greens) [43].

Previous studies reported a reduction in protein content in algae and *Brassica napus* (rapeseed) as Zn increased [4,44,45]. There are many reasons for the drop in protein content with heavy metals. A drop may be due to the accelerating degradation of protein with increasing protease activity [46] or disturbance of nitrogen metabolism in the presence of heavy metals such as Cd and Pb. The protease activity increases in stress conditions [43] like the presence of heavy metals in the growth medium. According to previous work [47], heavy metals such as Cd and Pb disturb nitrogen metabolism, which further decreases the synthesis of protein. Heavy metals including Cd are responsible for the reduction in photosynthesis, which reduces the synthesis of protein [40].

The results of the present study showed that an increase in the concentrations of heavy metals resulted in a decrease of sodium, potassium, calcium, iron, magnesium, manganese and copper in *S. oleracea*. The results are consistent with previous findings. An excess of Zn decreased the uptake of elements like magnesium, manganese, copper and iron in plants [4]. An increasing concentration of Cd interfered with other elements like potassium, calcium and magnesium by disturbing their distribution in plant parts and also decreasing their content in plant tissue [40].

Scientists [48] found a decrease in manganese concentration in barley plants with increasing concentrations of Cd. Cadmium decreased the uptake of iron [49], potassium, manganese and calcium [44]. The toxicity in terms of reduction uptake rates of essential elements by Cd is more severe than the individual toxicity due to Pb and Zn. This might be attributed to a higher toxicity and rate of accumulation of Cd in plants, especially in roots.

Others [45] found bioaccumulation coefficients for Cd of up to 1100 in shoots and 6700 in roots at a concentration of 0.1 μg Cd/mL in soil. The reduction in the uptake of elements was greater for a combination of Cd and Pb treatments in comparison to their individual treatments, but it was less than the sum of both toxicities. This might be due to a reduction in the uptake of both heavy metals. Similarly, the combined toxicity in terms of reduction of metals uptake for combined Cd and Zn treatment was less severe than due to Cd alone, but more than for Zn alone. Zinc reduced Cd uptake [40], so that the corresponding toxicity is also reduced. Similarly, the combined toxicity due to Pb and Zn was less than the individual one for Pb.

High concentrations of Cd, Pb and Zn were found in roots. These results are in agreement with previous reports [50] indicating the presence of high concentrations of Cd in *Solanum lycopersicum* (tomato) roots. Similarly, others [32] observed high concentrations of Pb in roots of plants. Roots showed high concentrations of heavy metals if compared to other plant parts, because heavy metals come into contact with the roots of plants first [51].

4. Conclusions and Recommendations

Plant exposure to heavy metal contamination resulted in severe toxicity of *S. oleracea*. Results revealed that Cd and Pb treatments even at low concentrations and Zn at high concentration induces a significant ($p < 0.05$) reduction in all growth parameters (shoot and root lengths, biomass and number of leaves) as well as total protein content, fiber, moisture content and minerals (Na, K, Ca, Fe, Mg, Mn and Cu) of *S. oleracea.* The impacts of all selected heavy metals significantly depended on their concentrations in the plant tissues. The results of the combined toxicity showed antagonistic affects. The uptake rate of Cd by *S. oleracea* was higher compared to previous studies. This was reflected in the growth of the plants. Further work in the field using real and not simulated wastewater contaminated by heavy metals is recommended. A greater variety of crops grown in different geographical regions would be helpful. However, such studies are likely to result in highly variable data and may take years or even decades to conclude.

Acknowledgments

The authors express thank to their institutions supporting the international collaborative research.

Author Contributions

Alia Naz, Sardar Khan, Said Muhammad, Salma Khalid, Sadia Alam, Sadaf Siddique designed the experimnetal work and subsequently carried out the experiments and corresponding analysis. Alia Naz and Toqeer Ahmed helped by writing the first draft. Miklas Scholz wrote the final draft and facilitated the submission process as the coresponding author.

Conflicts of Interest

The authors declare no conflict of interest.

References

1. Khan, S.; Aijun, L.; Zhang, S.; Hu, Q.; Zhu, Y.G. Accumulation of polycyclic aromatic hydrocarbons and heavy metals in lettuce grown in the soils contaminated with long-term wastewater irrigation. *J. Hazard. Mater.* **2008**, *152*, 506–515.
2. Khan, S.; Cao, Q.; Zheng, Y.M.; Huang, Y.Z.; Zhu, Y.G. Health risks of heavy metals in contaminated soils and food crops irrigated with wastewater in Beijing, China. *Environ. Pollut.* **2008**, *152*, 686–692.
3. Fusconi, A.; Repetto, O.; Bona, E.; Massa, N.; Gallo, C.; Dumas-Gaudot, E.; Berta, G. Effects of cadmium on meristem activity and nucleus ploidy in roots of *Pisum sativum* L. cv. Frisson seedlings. *Environ. Exp. Bot.* **2006**, *58*, 253–260.
4. Wang, C.; Zhang, S.H.; Wang, P.F.; Hou, J.; Zhang, W.J.; Li, W.; Lin, Z.P. The effect of excess Zn on mineral nutrition and ant oxidative response in rapeseed seedlings. *Chemosphere* **2009**, *75*, 1468–1476.
5. Jiang, H.M.; Yang, J.C.; Zhang, J.F. Effects of external phosphorus on the cell ultrastructure and the chlorophyll content of maize under cadmium and zinc stress. *Environ. Pollut.* **2007**, *147*, 750–756.
6. Tewari, R.K.; Kumar, P.; Sharma, P.N. Magnesium deficiency induced oxidative stress and antioxidant responses in mulberry plants. *Sci. Horticult.* **2006**, *108*, 7–14.
7. Lo'pez-Mosquera, M.E.; Moiro'n, C.; Carral, E. Use of dairy-industry sludge as fertilizer for grasslands in northwest Spain: heavy metal levels in the soil and plants. *Res. Conserv. Recycl.* **2000**, *30*, 95–109.
8. Zeng, X.; Li, L.; Mei, X. Heavy metals content in Chinese vegetable plantation land soils and related source analysis. *Agricul. Sci. China* **2008**, *7*, 1115–1126.
9. Lai, Y.; Xu, B.; He, L.; Lin, M.; Cao, L., Wu, Y., Mou, S.; He, S. Cadmium uptake by and translocation within rice (*Oryza sativa* L.) seedlings as affected by iron plaque and Fe_2O_3. *Pakistan J. Bot.* **2012**, *44*, 1557–1561.
10. Kuo, C.Y.; Wong, R.H.; Lin, J.Y.; Lai, J.C.; Lee, H. Accumulation of chromium and nickel metals in lung tumors from lung cancer patients in Taiwan. *J. Tox. Environ. Health* **2006**, *69*, 1337–1344.
11. Liu, W.J.; Zhu, Y.G.; Smith, F.A.; Smith, S.E. Do iron plaque and genotypes affect arsenate uptake and translocation by rice? *J. Exp. Bot.* **2004**, *55*, 1707–1713.
12. Correa, A.D.; Rorig, R.; Verdinelli, L.R.; Cotelle, M.A.; Ferard, S.; Radetski, C.M. Cadmium phytotoxicity: quantitative sensitivity relationships between classical endpoints and antioxidative enzyme biomarkers. *Sci. Total Environ.* **2006**, *357*, 120–127.
13. Sandalio, L.M.; Dalurzo, H.C.; Gomez, M.; Romero-Puertas, M.C.; del Rio, L.A. Cadmium-induced changes in the growth and oxidative metabolism of pea plants. *J. Exp. Bot.* **2001**, *52*, 2115–2126.
14. Nouariri, I.; Ammar, B.W.; Youssef, N.B.; Miled Daoud, D.B.; Ghorbel, M.H.; Zarrouk, M. Comparative study of cadmium effects on membrane lipid composition of *Brassica juncea* and *Brassica napus* leaves. *J. Plant. Physiol.* **2006**, *170*. 511–519.

15. Baryla, A.; Carrier, P.; Franck, F.; Coulomb, C.; Sahut, C.; Havaux, M. Leaf chlorosis in oil seed rape (*Brassica napus*) grown on cadmium polluted soil causes and consequences for photosynthesis and growth. *Planta* **2001**, *212*, 606–709.
16. Toppi, S.L.; Gabrielli, R. Response to cadmium in higher plants. *Environ. Exp. Bot.* **1999**, *41*, 105–130.
17. Sharma, P.; Dubey, R.S. Lead toxicity in plants. *Braz. J. Plant. Physiol.* **2005**, *17*, 35–52.
18. Joseph, L.U.; Andrea, L.C.; Mal, T.K. Effects of lead contamination on the growth of *Lythrum salicaria*. *Environ. Pollut.* **2002**, *120*, 319–323.
19. Farooqi, Z.R.; Iqbal, M.Z.; Kabir, M.; Shafiq, M. Toxic effects of lead and cadmium on germination and seedling growth of *Albizia lebbeck* Benth Pakistan. *J. Bot.* **2009**, *41*, 27–33.
20. Paolacci, A.R.; Badiani, M.; Damnibale, A.; Fusari, A.; Matteucci, G. Antioxidants and photosynthesis in the leaves of *Triticum durum* Desf seedlings acclimated to non-stressing high temperature. *J. Plant. Physiol.* **1997**, *150*. 381–387.
21. Cao, H.; Jiang, Y.; Chen, J.; Zhang, H.; Huang, W.; Li, L.; Zhang, W. Arsenic accumulation in *Scutellaria baicalensis* Georgi and its effects on plant growth and pharmaceutical components. *J. Hazard. Mater.* **2009**, *171*, 508–513.
22. Yang, Y.; Zhang, F.; Li, H.; Jiang, R. Accumulation of cadmium in the edible parts of six vegetable species grown in Cd-contaminated soils. *J. Environ. Manag.* **2009**, *90*, 1117–1122.
23. He, J.Y.; Zhu, C.; Ren, Y.F.; Yan, Y.P.; Cheng, C.; Jiang, D.A.; Sun, Z.X. Uptake, sub cellular distribution, and chemical form of cadmium in wild-type and mutant rice. *Pedosphere* **2008**, *18*, 371–377.
24. Khan, M.U; Malik, R.N; Muhammad, S. Human risk from heavy metal via food crops consumption with wastewater irrigation practices in Pakistan. *Chemoshere.* **2013**, *93*, 2230–2238.
25. Naz, A.; Khan, S.; Qasim, M.; Khalid, S.; Muhammad, S.; Tariq, M. Metal toxicity and its bioaccumulation in pursolane seedlings grow in controlled environment. *Natur. Sci.* **2013**, *5*, 573–579.
26. Alexander, P.D.; Alloway, B.J.; Dourado, A.M.I. Genotypic variations in the accumulation of Cd, Cu, Pb and Zn exhibited by six commonly grown vegetables. *Environ. Pollut.* **2006**, *144*, 736–745.
27. Dhongade, S.; Nandkar, P.B. The phytotoxicity of heavy metals on growth and metal uptake by spinach. *Agr. Biol. Res.* **2011**, *27*, 78–90.
28. Yizong, H.; Ying, H.; Yunxia, L. Combined toxicity of copper and cadmium to six rice genotypes (*Oryza sativa* L.). *J. Environ. Sci.* **2009**, *21*, 647–653.
29. Khan, S.; Cao, Q.; Chen, B.-B.; Zhu, Y.-G. Humic acids increase the phytoavailability of Cd and Pb to wheat plants cultivated in freshly spiked, contaminated soil. *J. Soils Sedim.* **2006**, *6*, 236–*242.*
30. Muhammad, S.; Shah, M.T.; Khan, S. Heavy metal concentrations in soil and wild plants growing around Pb-Zn sulfide terrain in the Kohistan region, northern Pakistan. *Microchem. J.* **2011**, *99*, 67–75.
31. Aldwairji, M.A.; Chu, J.; Buley, V.J.; Orfila, C. Analysis of dietary fibre of boiled and canned legumes commonly consumed in the United Kingdom. *J. Food Comp. Anal.* **2014**, *36*, 111–116.
32. Association of Official Analytical Chemists (AOAC). *Official Method of Analysis*, 16th ed.; AOAC International: Arlington, VA, USA, 1995.
33. Ebrazi Bakhshayesh, B.; Delkash, M.; Scholz, M. Response of vegetables to cadmium-enriched soil. *Water* **2014**, *6*, 1246–1256.

34. Sun, Y.; Li, Z.; Guo, B.; Chu, G.; Wei, C.; Liang, Y. Arsenic mitigates cadmium toxicity in rice seedlings. *Environ. Exp. Bot.* **2008**, *64*, 264–270.
35. Lingua, G.; Franchin, C.; Todeschini, V.; Castiglione, S.; Biondi, S.; Burlando, B.; Parravicini, V.; Torrigiani, P.; Berta, G. *Arbuscular mycorrhizal* fungi differentially affect the response to high zinc concentrations of two registered poplar clones. *Environ. Pollut.* **2008**, *153*, 137–147.
36. An, Y.; Kim, Y.; Kwon, T.; Jeong, S. Combined effect of copper, cadmium, and lead upon *Cucumis sativus* growth and bioaccumulation. *Sci. Total Environ.* **2004**, *326*, 85–93.
37. Shukla, V.C.; Singh, J.; Joshi, PC; Kakkar, P. Effect of bioaccumulation of cadmium on biomass productivity, essential trace elements, chlorophyll biosynthesis and macromolecules of wheat seedlings. *Biol. Trace Elem. Res.* **2003**, *92*, 257–273.
38. Devi, R.; Munjral, N.; Gupta, A.K.; Kaur, N. Cadmium induced changes in carbohydrate status and enzymes of carbohydrate metabolism, glycolysis and pentose phosphate pathway in pea. *Environ. Exp. Bot.* **2007**, *61*, 167–174.
39. Vogel-Mikus, K.; Pongrac, P.; Kump, P.; Necemer, M.; Regvar, M. Colonisation of a Zn, Cd and Pb hyperaccumulator *Thlaspi praecox* Wulfen with indigenous *Arbuscular mycorrhizal* fungal mixture induces changes in heavy metal and nutrient uptake. *Environ. Pollut.* **2006**, *139*, 362–337.
40. Lin, R.Z.; Wang, X.R.; Luo, Y.; Du, W.C.; Guo, H.Y.; Yin, D.Q. Effects of soil cadmium on growth, oxidative stress and antioxidant system in wheat seedlings (*Triticum aestivum* L.). *Chemosphere* **2007**, *69*, 89–98.
41. Marschner, H. Mineral Nutrition of Higher Plants, 2nd ed.; Academic Press: San Diego, CA, USA, 1995.
42. Mahmood, S.; Hussain, A.; Saeed, Z.; Athar, M. Germination and seedling growth of corn (*Zea mays* L.) under varying levels of copper and zinc. *Int. J. Environ. Sci. Technol.* **2005**, *2*, 269–274.
43. Weihong, X.; Wenyi, L.; Jianping, H.; Singh, B.; Zhiting, X. Effects of insoluble Zn, Cd, and EDTA on the growth, activities of antioxidant enzymes and uptake of Zn and Cd in *Vetiveria zizanioides*. *J. Environ. Sci.* **2009**, *21*, 186–192.
44. Khudsar, T.; Iqbal, M.; Sairam, R.K. Zinc-induced changes in morpho-physiological and biochemical parameters in *Artemisia annua*. *Biol. Plant.* **2004**, *48*, 255–260.
45. John, R.; Ahmad, P.; Gadgil, K.; Sharma, S. Heavy metal toxicity: Effect on plant growth, biochemical parameters and metal accumulation by *Brassica juncea*. *Int. J. Plant. Prod.* **2009**, *3*, 65–75.
46. Xu, J.; Yang, L.; Wang, Z.; Dong, G.; Huang, J.; Wang, Y. Toxicity of copper on rice growth and accumulation of copper in rice grain in copper contaminated soil. *Chemosphere* **2006**, *62*, 602–607.
47. Auda, A.M.; Ali, E.S. Cadmium and zinc toxicity effects on growth and mineral nutrients of carrot (*Daucus carota*). *Pakistan J. Bot.* **2010**, *42*, 341–351.
48. Kastori, R.; Petrovic, M.; Petrovic N. Effect of excess lead, cadmium, copper and zinc on water relations in sunflower. *J. Plant. Nutr.* **1992**, *15*, 2427–2439.
49. Zengin, F.K.; Munzuroglu, O. Toxic effects of cadmium (Cd) on metabolism of sunflower (*Helianthus annuus* L.) seedlings. *Soil Plant. Sci.* **2006**, *56*, 224–229.
50. Palma, J.M.; Sandalio, L.M.; Javier Corpas, F.; Romero-Puertas, M.C.; McCarthy, I.; del Río, L.A. Plant proteases protein degradation and oxidative stress: role of peroxisomes. *Plant. Physiol. Biochem.* **2002**, *40*, 521–530.

51. Odjegba, V.J.; Fasidi, I.O. Effects of heavy metals on some proximate composition of *Eichhornia crassipes*. *J. Appl. Sci. Environ. Manag.* **2006**, *10*, 83–87.

water

MDPI

Article

Water-Energy-Food Accessibility and Tracking Progress towards Achieving Sustainable Development Goals in the Savannah Region of Katsina State, Nigeria

Yahaya Sani [1] and Miklas Scholz [1,2,3,4,*]

1 Division of Water Resources Engineering, Department of Building and Environmental Technology, Faculty of Engineering, Lund University, P.O. Box 118, 221 00 Lund, Sweden; yahaya.sani@tvrl.lth.se
2 Department of Civil Engineering Science, School of Civil Engineering and the Built Environment, University of Johannesburg, Kingsway Campus, P.O. Box 524, Aukland Park, Johannesburg 2006, South Africa
3 Department of Town Planning, Engineering Networks and Systems, South Ural State University, 76, Lenin Prospekt, 454080 Chelyabinsk, Russia
4 Institute of Environmental Engineering, Wroclaw University of Environmental and Life Sciences, ul. Norwida 25, 50-375 Wrocław, Poland
* Correspondence: miklas.scholz@tvrl.lth.se; Tel.: +46-(0)-462228920; Fax: +46-(0)-462224435

Abstract: Although remarkable progress has been achieved in reducing hunger and poverty and improving people's health in the past couple of decades, humanity still faces considerable socio-economic and sustainability challenges. Ensuring sustainable access to safe and sufficient water, improved sanitation facilities, clean energy sources and healthy food is a necessary requirement for ending hunger and poverty, advancing health and achieving all the goals of the sustainable development agenda. Socio-economic variables are determinant factors of water, energy and food accessibility. Ecological region, income and education are measures used in this study, which aims to examine a pairwise comparison of water and energy sources, sanitation facilities and food accessibilities in six sampling communities and tracking progress towards achieving the sustainable development goals (SDG) at a local scale using nine specific SDG indicators. A study involving questionnaire administration covering 1785 households across the three ecological regions of Katsina state was performed. Two communities representing urban and rural households from each of the ecological regions were selected. An analysis of variance was used to test the equality of resource accessibility across the investigated communities followed up by a post hoc analysis to identify significant mean groups. The results showed that the overall access level to safely manage water and sanitation facilities were 16.5% and 28.1%, respectively. Access indices of 1.83 and 1.24 for electricity and cooking fuel, respectively, were calculated in the study area. The study revealed that location, education and income are the key drivers of water, energy and food access and choice.

Keywords: water; energy; food; sanitation facility; socio-ecology; sustainable development

Citation: Sani, Y.; Scholz, M. Water-Energy-Food Accessibility and Tracking Progress towards Achieving Sustainable Development Goals in the Savannah Region of Katsina State, Nigeria. *Water* **2021**, *13*, 3595. https://doi.org/10.3390/w13243595

Academic Editor: Adriana Bruggeman

Received: 27 October 2021
Accepted: 9 December 2021
Published: 14 December 2021

1. Introduction

The SDG are comprehensive international guidelines that are adopted by the United Nations member states aiming to move the world towards a more sustainable future, balancing economic growth, social development and environmental protection [1,2]. The SDG can be viewed as a successor to the millennium development goals and are set to be achieved by 2030. Each of the 17 goals has well-defined targets; for instance, goal 2 is about ending hunger, achieving food security, improving nutrition and promoting sustainable agriculture. Goals 6 and 7 are concerned with security in terms of water and energy, respectively. All goals are interlinked, and progress to one goal is best achieved in conjunction with progress towards others [3]. The achievement of the SDG is particularly relevant to low- and middle-income countries (LMIC) such as Nigeria, where more progress towards meeting these goals is necessary.

The water-energy-food nexus is being promoted as a conceptual tool for achieving sustainable development. The nexus addresses the connections between these three resource sectors and deals with their potential conflicts, synergies, trade-offs and resource-use efficiencies that arise from how they are managed. These three resources have long been recognised as essential to human life and socio-economic progress. The nexus approach perspectives emphasise the multiple inter-reliance among water, energy and food security and the underlying natural resources. It also stresses the need to adopt a socio-ecological perspective and the need for a conceptual framework connecting water, energy and food to sustainable development [4–7]. Everyone has the right to good quality water, clean energy and healthy food to support active and healthy lives. However, these crucial resources are under pressure. With the current world population at over 7 billion inhabitants, it has been reported that 900 million people live without access to clean drinking water, 2.7 billion live without access to proper sanitation, 1.3 billion live without electricity and 1.02 billion are undernourished [8,9]. Population growth, urbanisation, economic prosperity and climate change are considered as major driving factors for the global increase in demand for water, energy and food [8–10]. Increased urbanisation and a high population growth rate put additional pressure on the resources in sub-Saharan Africa to meet the basic demand of the population in the region [8–10]. The water-energy-food nexus is being endorsed as central to achieving sustainable development [8].

Due to their interdependencies, potential conflicts, synergies and trades-off among the various systems of water, energy and food have raised the corresponding nexus to prominence in development. New policy frameworks for addressing the scarcities and sustainability of water, energy and food are required [11–14]. Even though general awareness concerning the water-energy-food nexus approach has increased over the past decades, there is minimal attention on the nexus at household scale [15–17]. Even when there were attempts to investigate the nexus at the household level, the focus was often only on one or two elements of the nexus [17]. For example, the water and energy nexus has been studied in the Beijing-Tiajin-Hebei region of China [18,19].

In addition, Zouh et al. and Viera et al. [19,20] investigated single elements of the nexus. For instance, Vieira et al. [19] appraised the effectiveness of household water consumption. Furthermore, they related household water efficiency to socio-demographic variables. Vieira et al. [19] studied water related to energy use in low-income households of Brazil. They focused on the water sector's sustainability, which is principally connected to the decrease of waste matters generated in centralised systems. They further suggested that to lessen the impacts associated with a rise in energy consumption in the water sector, a reduction in the production of household effluents should be implemented.

The nature of climatic regions play an important role in access to water, energy and food. For instance, rainfall determines the most significant meteorological trend on earth for natural and human life [21]. The variability in the amount of rainfall has resulted in prevalent droughts in the central Maghreb nations [22], causing a substantial challenge to the availability and accessibility of water and food resources [23–25]. Rainfall is linked to global climate change. Thus, the analysis of rainfall at various spatial-temporal scales is crucial [26]. It is evident that climate has a wide range of impacts on natural resources including freshwater ecosystems, household energy and food resources [27,28]. It has been reported that the less-privileged developing regions of the world, especially rural communities, are the most exposed ones to severe impacts of climate change [26].

The impact of variability in household socio-economic and demographic characteristics on water, energy and food accessibility are widely addressed in various studies [29–31]. In addition, Phoebe and Lydia [32] identified the impact of climate as the main driver for physical access to water, energy and food. Furthermore, previous studies highlighted the relationship between rainfall variability as well as water demand and quality. Calow et al. [33] and Friel et al. [34] revealed that during drought seasons access to good quality water and healthy food can be crucial due to availability and accessibility challenges. Several studies [35–38] on the impact of rainfall variability on water and food resources have been carried out. A solid connection between socio-economic and ecological characteristics with regards to water, energy and food accessibilities is still lacking.

The availability of water, energy (biomass) and food is strongly dependent on the amount of rain. Furthermore, water, energy and food supplies at household level depend on the sources and quantity, which directly depend on rainfall variability and its spatial-temporal processes that comprise rainfall time, duration and location. There is insufficient evidence signifying the extent of the impact of socio-ecological water, energy and food accessibilities. The water-energy-food nexus perspective draws awareness to the need to implement socio-ecological perspectives, and the need for a broad conceptual framework linking the water-energy-food nexus to larger sustainable development issues.

The aim of this study is to analyse water, energy and food accessibility across the three ecological case study regions (isohyets) connected to socio-economic variables and progress towards the achievement of the relevant SDG in an example case study (Katsina state, northern Nigeria). Findings were compared with global indicators, where possible. This comparison will help to identify data gaps and areas for potential research and development, as well as stimulate discussions about the types of data required for SDG targets and index computation for other sub-Saharan regions with similar socio-ecological characteristics.

This research paper is structured as follows: after a brief introduction and a review of the scientific literature concerning the nexus and its relation to sustainable development in Section 1, Section 2 is dedicated to the research methodology, and it covers a full description of the materials and methods used to conduct the research, which involves the study area description, conceptual model, selection of the studied communities data and statistical analysis. Section 3 is dedicated to the research findings, and it highlights results on the socio-economic characteristics of the household heads, access to household water sources, sanitation facilities as well as energy and food items. Moreover, findings were used to assess specific indicators towards achieving the SDG at a local scale. Finally, Section 4 concludes the main research findings and highlights the relevance of this paper.

2. Materials and Methods

2.1. Study Area

The study was conducted in Katsina state, which is located in the north-western part of Nigeria between latitude 11°08′ N and 13°22′, and longitude 6°52′ E and 9°20′ E. It covers an area of approximately 24,000 km^2. The state shares political boundaries with Kaduna state to the south, Jigawa and Kano states to the east, Zamfara state to the west and the Republic of Niger to the north [39].

On the basis of seasonality, the state is classified into two different climatic zones, tropical continental and semi-arid continental. The state experiences a hot dry season from March to May and a warm wet season from June to September. A less distinct season is identified by decreasing rainfall and a gradual decline in temperature during the months of October and November. The months of December to February are characterised by a cold dry season, which is popularly referred to as the harmattan.

Furthermore, based on the longitudinal pattern of rainfall influence, the state is categorised into three extensive rainfall regions. These isohyets match up with the three existing ecological regions of the Guinea, Sudan and Sahel savannah regions in the south, central and north, respectively [40]. Figure 1a shows Africa comprising Nigeria including Katsina state; Figure 1b shows six investigated communities across the three different ecological (rainfall) regions in the state. The southern region of the state receives rainfall in the region of above 900 mm, while the central and northern regions receive between 700 and 900 mm, and below 700 mm, respectively.

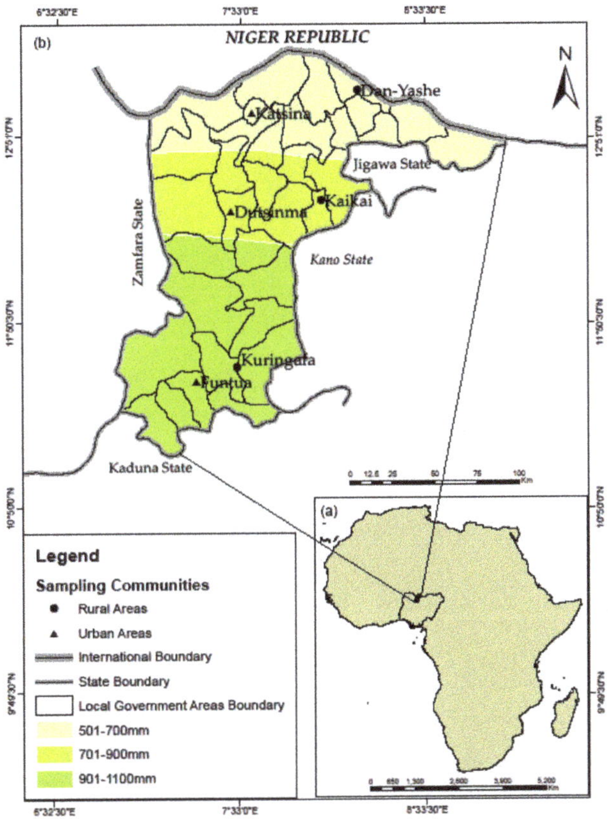

Figure 1. Maps of (**a**) Africa; and (**b**) Katsina state showing sampling communities across the isohyets.

The state population projected data issued by the National Population Commission indicated that the total population for the year 2019 was about 8,613,100, out of which 4,565,000 (53%) and 4,048,100 (47%) are located in rural and urban communities, respectively.

The study was carried out in six sampling communities located in Katsina state (Figure 1), which were selected based on urban and rural criteria. The urban communities surveyed across the respective isohyets of the northern, central and southern regions were Katsina, Dutsinma and Funtua, and the corresponding rural communities surveyed were Dan-Yashe, Kaikai and Kuringafa. These communities are characterised below.

Katsina: The community of Katsina is based in one of the ancient cities of Hausaland, emerging in the 15th century. The ancient city is the administrative and commercial capital and the largest settlement of the state. It has a heterogeneous setting of mixed formal and informal (traditional African) settlement settings. In contrast to the traditional settlements, the formal settlement is well-planned and accessible. The residents are connected to electricity and a piped water supply, and they have access to basic sanitation facilities.

Dutsinma and Funtua: Both settlements are local government and zonal administrative headquarters of the Katsina state. Furthermore, Funtua is the second largest urban community and commercial centre after urban Katsina. Politically, it is also a southern senatorial zone of the state. These two urban communities are similar to urban Katsina in terms of settlement patterns. They are also characterised by a mixture of traditional African and formal (modern) settings. Both Dutsinma and Funtua urban communities are connected to the national electricity grid. Zobe and Mairuwa are multi-purpose dams constructed in the respective central and southern isohyets to supply water for various uses. Therefore, both settlements are connected to the water supply systems and have access to various sanitation facilities.

Dan-Yashe, Kaikai and Kuringafa: These three communities are typical rural African communities. They are characterised by lower population densities compared to urban communities. In addition, the communities are unplanned and without adequate energy, water and sanitation facilities.

The map of the study area showing the sampling communities was obtained through a cartographical analysis and geographical information system investigations. Global positioning system coordinates of the sampling communities were recorded during the field survey and incorporated into the existing digital map database available at the Geographical Information System and Remote Sensing Unit of the Department of Geography at Umaru Musa Yarádua University.

2.2. Conceptual Model

The study attempted to uncover several layers of influence which determine accessibility to various water and energy sources, sanitation facilities and food resources. The socio-ecological model (Figure 2) illustrates these various layers.

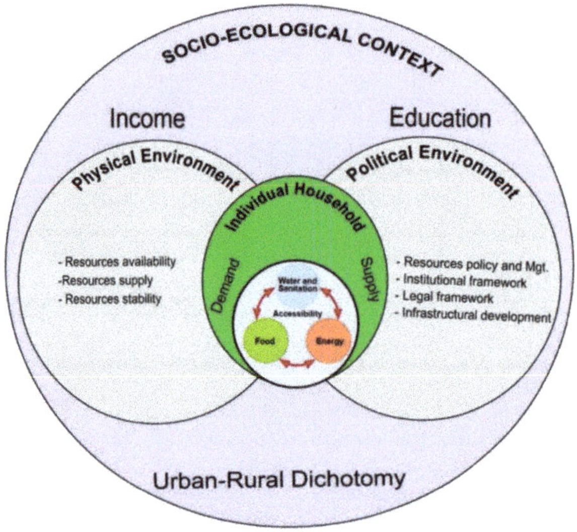

Figure 2. Socio-ecological model of water, energy and food access.

The model is constructed of four inter-related characteristics: individual household as well as socio-economic, physical and political environments. Socio-ecological parameters are not the only dominant ones, but they intersect with all of the other layers of influence; for example, the effects of location on urban–rural dichotomy influence access to household resources across the communities. Hence, it is constructed in accordance with the nexus perspective, which also draws attention to the need to adopt an integrated landscape or socio-ecological perspective, and the need for a broad conceptual framework linking the water-energy-food nexus to the larger sustainable development agenda.

The model helps to assess the role of various parameters related to different water and energy sources, sanitation facilities and food access at various households in the sampling communities. It also demonstrates the vital role of physical environment, political environment and the socio-economic (income and education level) characteristics of the household's heads as determinant factors of water, sanitation, energy and food accessibility at household scale.

In the natural environment, there is a strong linkage among water, energy and food. Water is fundamental for agriculture, and consequently food production, and certainly for the functioning of all terrestrial ecosystems including biomass production and other agricultural ecosystems. Insufficient amounts or variability in the availability of water has severe impacts on agricultural yields and vegetation cover (biomass). Thus, climatic (isohyets) regions of the world with an inadequate amount of water and with a large number of poor people also face the most serious challenges in terms of the availability of water for food production, biomass burning and other household usages.

The political environment plays a leading role in the control and regulation of water, energy and food production in the region. It also provides an institutional and legal framework, which contains the rules, regulations, laws and the role of the public and private sectors in terms of water, energy and food supplies. Moreover, in order to maintain a sustainable access to good quality water, clean energy and healthy food, a sound socio-economic infrastructure is crucial. Thus, governments have to invest huge amounts of resources for the development of overhead capital including power, energy, agricultural inputs and transportation facilities.

An urban household usually has access to improved water sources, improved sanitation facilities, clean cooking fuels and secure food sources, in contrast to their rural counterparts. Similarly, a highly educated household is likely to earn more income than a household characterised by members with a low education level. Thus, an educated household is more likely to consume safe and sufficient water from the improved sources, has access to enhanced sanitation facilities and benefits from clean cooking energy and healthy food.

2.3. Selection of the Studied Communities

A qualitative research design was conducted across six communities in Katsina state, Nigeria. A stratified random sampling method was used to get a full and clear representation of the state, which was stratified into regions based on three existing rainfall zones (i.e., the southern, central and the northern zones). Furthermore, each region was further stratified into rural and urban communities in accordance with the Katsina State Urban and Regional Planning Board guidelines [41], which stratified the whole state into urban and rural areas. One settlement was selected from each sub-stratum representing urban and rural areas in the study area. The sample size of 1785 households was determined adopting a method by Israel [42] at a 95% confidence level (see Table 1).

Table 1. Format of questionnaire distribution.

Isohyet	Stratum	Sampling Community	Estimated Population in 2019	Estimated Number of Households	Number of Questionnaires Administered
South	Urban	Funtua	190,092	31,682	397
	Rural	Kurigafaa	2874	479	222
Central	Urban	Dutsinma	78,275	13,682	390
	Rural	Kaikai	1179	197	134
North	Urban	Katsina	714,543	119,090	400
	Rural	Dan-Yashe	3914	652	242
	Total		1,114,494	185,750	1785

Due to unavailable data on the number of households in the study area, an average of six persons per household was assumed according to the Katsina state Primary Health Care Development Agency [43] estimations based on their routine immunisation programmes. A purposive (non-probability) sampling method was used in selecting households for the administration of questionnaires in the sampling communities. The estimated 2019 population figures were obtained from the National Population Commission, Katsina state.

2.4. Data Collection

Primary and secondary data sources were used for this study. The primary data were produced through the administration of structured and pre-tested questionnaires. The English version of the questionnaire was adapted and translated into Hausa, which is the regional language. The questionnaires were administered in person by 16 field assistants, who are familiar with Hausa and the sampling communities, in addition to receiving training in questionnaire administration. Furthermore, all interviews and discussions were conducted in Hausa. The questionnaire design and guidance for interviews followed common standards in terms of sections on household, characteristics, composition and socio-economic status [44]. The questionnaire is available as Supplementary Material SM1.

Data were collected over a period of two months (July and August 2019). The number of houses investigated was a reflection of the estimated sample size in each investigated community. Katsina (north-urban), which had 22.4% of the sampled households, was linked to 400 copies of questionnaires. Dan-Yashe (north-rural), which had 13.6% of the sampled households, received 242 copies of questionnaires. Dutsinma (central-urban), representing 21.8% of the sampled households, obtained 390 copies of questionnaires. Kaikai (central-rural) had 7.5% of the sampled households, representing 134 copies of questionnaires. Funtua (south-urban) had 22.2% of the sampled households (397 copies of questionnaires). Finally, Kuringafa (south-rural), which represents 12.4% of the sampled households, had 222 copies of questionnaires. At the end of the exercise, 1785 copies of questionnaires were served to the household heads in Katsina state.

2.5. Statistical Analysis

The data were analysed using IBM SPSS version 24. In order to determine the proportion of the households' accessibility level regarding food purchase frequencies as well as water and energy sources, descriptive statistics were computed. The relationship between household educational status and monthly income was assessed using the Pearson Product Moment Correlation (PPMC) coefficient r. A one-way analysis of variance was used to determine if there were any differences in the mean amount of water sources, sanitation facilities, energy sources and food purchase frequencies across the six sampling communities. After rejection of the hypothesis of equality, significant group means (pair-wise) of water, energy and food accessibility levels across the six sampling communities were compared with each other. A post hoc analysis using Duncan's method for $\alpha = 0.05$ was applied using pairwise comparisons of water, sanitation, energy and food access across the sampling communities.

In addition, the information captured by the multi-tier matrix was compiled into a single number representing the level of access to electricity and cooking fuels in a study area. A simple index was calculated by weighting the tiers and arriving at a weighted average. Equation (1) showing the index of access to electricity supply and cooking fuels was applied [45].

$$\text{Index} = \sum (P_T \times T) \quad (1)$$

where P_T represents the proportion of households at tier T with tier number {0,1,2,3,4,5}.

2.6. Study Variables

The key variables for the study area were access to household water source, sanitation facilities, energy (cooking fuel) source and access to households' food resources. Each household in the respective urban and rural communities across the isohyets was investigated regarding access to the various water and energy sources as well as sanitation facilities. Water sources and sanitation facilities were classified into improved and unimproved sources based on Joint Monitoring Programme (JMP) categorisation [46] and energy access was classified according to WHO [47]. Food access frequency was grouped according to Frongillo and Gittelsohn [48,49]. Table 2 shows from the bottom to the top a progressive improvement in terms of resource security.

Table 2. Classification of household water, energy and food based on secure and unsecure access informing the questionnaire.

Variable	Secured	Unsecured
Access to water source (UNICEF and WHO [46])	Piped water into dwelling Piped water to yard Public tap/standpipe Borehole/tube well Protected dug well Protected spring Rainwater	Unprotected spring Unprotected dug well Cart with tank or drum (water vending) Tanker truck Surface water
Access to sanitation facility (UNICEF and WHO [46])	Flush toilet Pipe sewer system Septic tank Flush/pour to pit latrine Ventilated improved pit latrine Pit latrine with slab Compositing toilet	Flush/pour elsewhere Pit latrine without slab Bucket Hanging toilet No facility (open defecation)
Access to energy sources (WHO [47])	Electricity Natural gas Liquefied petroleum gas Ethanol and methanol Kerosene	Coal Charcoal Fuelwood Agricultural residue Dung
Access to food flow and economic access [48,49]	Food security Bulk purchase Less frequent purchase	Food insecurity Small-quantity purchase High-frequency purchase

Furthermore, to determine the water service access level, water quality tests were performed using the standard JMP portable kit for *Escherichia coli* as described by [46]. The water testing quality was carried out in 20% of the surveyed households and was tested proportionate to their accessibility to various water sources. The testing was carried out in collaboration with the Water Laboratory, Department of Geography, Umaru Musa Yarádua University.

A multi-tier framework [45,50,51] was adopted to measure the proportion of the households' access level to electricity and cooking energy. The Multi-Tier Framework (MTF) of the Global Traffic Framework (GTF) was developed to address the limitations of a binary energy access tool whereby a household was either categorised as having access or not [48,49]. The framework measures the level of electricity access and usage on the basis of these indicators: peak capacity, duration, reliability, quality, affordability, health and environmental safety. To measure cooking energy access, the framework was designed to analyse data in multiple dimensions of access and consists of six equal attributes: exposure and efficiency formed the two technical attributes while the other four contextual attributes capture the user's experience in terms of convenience, affordability, safety and reliability. In order to measure progress, each attribute has six tiers ranging from 0 to 5, designated as no access, very low access, low access, limited access, high access and very high access, respectively. The method for assessing cooking energy with an overall tier rating is designed to be technology and fuel neutral, while reflecting the broad range of cooking solutions. Cooking solutions in the household are assessed based on the combination of six attributes of energy across six tiers (0–5), starting with access to basic solutions and increasing gradually to modern cooking solutions that deliver the highest results for all attributes. Each attribute is assessed independently and the overall tier for a household's access to cooking solutions is obtained by summing-up the entire index of the six attributes using Equation (1).

In addition, to assess household food security, food purchase frequency was used to determine food poverty linked to purchasing power. The following socio-ecological factors were considered in this study: ecological (isohyets) and social (rural/urban) location of the residence as well as the income and education level of the household's head.

Moreover, local progress towards SDG achievement was compared with the global indicator framework. Using data from the study, the global indicator framework for the SDG was applied to calculate indicators for the study area cumulatively. Responses to questionnaires, which aligned with SDG indicators were used to calculate a specific index. Where responses matched SDG indices, a direct comparison was possible. This was mostly the case for relative indices, e.g., the percentage of population living below the international poverty line, proportion of population using safely managed drinking water services and proportion of population with access to electricity among others.

3. Results

3.1. Socio-Economic Characteristics of the Households' Heads

In total, 1785 households were surveyed across the six studied communities of Katsina state. The main socio-economic characteristics of the respondents are based on the frequency analysis shown in Table 3. In all communities, more than half of the respondents were from urban communities (66%). Only 34.5% of the respondents were from rural communities. An advanced university degree was the highest level of education found only in the urban communities. The highest percentage of advanced degrees was 17.3% in the northern urban areas and the lowest was 5.9% in the central urban areas. The majority of household heads that had no formal education were also found in the rural communities. The northern rural community was found to have the highest percentage (80.1%) of respondents with no formal education and the lowest percentage (61.9%) was found in the central rural community. The majority of the high-income earning household heads were located in urban communities across the isohyets. The highest proportion of household heads that earned above N180,000 ($500) were found in the northern urban community. The highest percentage (72.3%) of low-income earning household heads (<N18,000 ($50)) was linked to the northern rural region.

Table 3. Educational level and income of the household heads in the six sampling communities.

Variable	Item	Location Category											
		Katsina		Dan-Yashe		Dutsinma		Kaikai		Funtua		Kuringafa	
		N	%	N	%	N	%	n	%	n	%	n	%
Educational status	No education	44	11.0	194	80.1	119	30.5	83	61.9	119	30.0	149	67.1
	Primary school	55	13.7	35	14.5	81	20.8	25	18.7	42	10.6	40	18.0
	Secondary school	47	11.7	12	5.0	62	15.9	23	17.2	54	13.6	24	10.8
	Ordinary National Diploma/National Certificate of Education	90	22.5	1	0.4	48	12.3	3	2.2	58	14.6	7	3.2
	University degree	95	23.8	-	-	57	14.6	-	-	95	23.9	2	0.9
	Advanced university degree	69	17.3	-	-	23	5.9	-	-	29	7.3	-	-
	Total	400	100	242	100	390	100	134	100	397	100	222	100
Income/month	<N18,000 ($50)	45	11.3	175	72.3	88	22.5	103	76.9	85	21.4	62	28.0
	N18,000–36,000 ($50–100)	59	14.7	43	17.8	69	17.7	15	11.2	40	10.1	60	27.0
	N36,001–72,000 (>$100–200)	75	18.7	24	9.9	89	22.8	16	11.9	48	12.1	76	34.2
	N72,001–144,000 (>$200–300)	39	9.8	-	-	23	5.9	-	-	39	9.8	22	9.9
	N144,001–180,000 (>400–500)	60	15.0	-	-	79	20.3	-	-	61	15.4	2	0.9
	Above 180,000 (>$500)	122	30.5	-	-	42	10.8	-	-	124	31.2	-	-
	Total	400	100	242	100	390	100	134	100	397	100	222	100

Table 4 indicates the association between household head income and educational level. The PPMC was calculated to determine the direction and strength of association between the variables. At the community level, the table revealed stronger associations between household head income and educational level in the urban communities. The highest r value was found for Katsina (northern urban region) and the lowest one for Kaikai (central rural region) with the respective values of 0.782 and 0.238. Generally, the PPMC results indicated strong associations between household head educational status and monthly income across the urban communities. The table also revealed weak associations across the rural investigated communities.

Table 4. Correlation between household head educational status and income.

Isohyet	Stratum	Sampling Community	Number of Household Heads	PPMC (r Value)	p-Value
South	Urban	Funtua	397	0.640	0.000
	Rural	Kurigafaa	222	0.458	0.000
Central	Urban	Dutsinma	390	0.532	0.000
	Rural	Kaikai	134	0.238	0.001
North	Urban	Katsina	400	0.782	0.000
	Rural	Dan-Yashe	397	0.366	0.000

PPMC, Pearson Product Moment Correlation.

3.1.1. Access to Household Water Sources

Table 5 indicates access to various water sources, which include piped water into a dwelling, piped water to a yard, public tap (standpipe), private borehole, public borehole, protected dug well, unprotected dug well, water vendor, surface water and tanker truck (fuel truck or tanker) for different households across the six investigated communities. Overall, the use of water vendors and public boreholes are recorded across the six areas.

Table 5. Various household water sources across the sampling areas.

Water Source	Community											
	Katsina		Dan-Yashe		Dutsinma		Kaikai		Funtua		Kuringafa	
	N	%	n	%	n	%	n	%	n	%	n	%
Pipe water into dwelling	26	6.5	-	-	-	-	-	-	7	1.7	-	-
Pipe water to yard	1	0.2	-	-	-	-	-	-	27	6.8	-	-
Public tap	7	1.8	-	-	3	0.8	-	-	1	0.3	-	-
Private borehole	143	35.8	-	-	80	20.5	-	-	117	29.5	1	0.4
Public borehole	30	7.5	12	5.0	31	8.0	18	13.4	46	11.6	52	23.4
Protected dug well	20	5.0	-	-	22	5.6	7	5.2	21	5.3	29	13.1
Unprotected dug well	1	0.2	24	9.9	45	11.5	8	6.0	77	19.4	64	28.8
Water vendor	161	40.2	108	44.6	133	34.1	55	41.1	72	18.1	7	3.2
Surface water	-	-	-	-	-	-	-	-	-	-	69	31.1
Tanker truck	11	2.8	98	40.5	76	19.5	46	34.3	29	7.3	-	-
Total	400	100	242	100	390	100	134	100	397	100	222	100

n, sample number.

Access to a water vendor has dramatically decreased in six sampling communities from the northern to the southern isohyets. The highest proportion of water vendor users was found in the Dan-Yashe (northern rural area) community at 44.6% followed by Kaikai (central rural area) at 41.1%, and the lowest proportion was found at 3.2% in the Kuringafa (southern rural) community. Access to a water vendor followed a similar pattern for the rural communities. In the urban communities, Katsina (northern urban area) was associated with 40.2%, followed by Dutsinma (central urban area) at 34.1% and 18.1% for Funtua (urban south). Accessibilities to two different types of boreholes (public and private) were found in the study. The highest accessibility level to a public borehole was found in the rural south at 23.4% and the lowest one was found in northern rural areas at 7.5%. Access to a private borehole was only recorded in urban communities across the three isohyets and in the rural south. The highest proportion of private borehole access was found at 35.8% in the urban north and the lowest one at 0.4% in the southern rural region. Among the ten different water sources that were utilised in the sampling communities, utilisation of piped water into dwellings, piped water to yard and public tap were recorded at the lowest utilisation level. Piped water into a dwelling and piped water to a yard were found in two urban communities. Piped water into a dwelling was found at 6.5% and 1.7% for the urban north and urban south, respectively. Proportions of 0.2% and 6.8% of piped water to yard were found in the urban north and urban south, respectively. About 1.8%

of public tap supply was only recorded in the urban community of the north. Similarly, surface water source access was only recorded in the southern rural community at 31.1%. Significant proportions of tanker truck utilisation were found in the sampling communities with the exception of southern rural communities. The highest figures were recorded at 40.5% in the northern rural area, while the lowest proportion of access to tanker trucks was recorded at 2.8% in the urban north.

Similarly, two types of dug wells were accessed at various households across the sampling communities. Unprotected dug wells were utilised in all six communities, where the highest accessibility level was recorded in the rural south at 28.8% and the lowest level was found at 0.2% in the urban north. While the protected dug well was used in all communities (except in the rural north), the highest proportion of users was found in southern rural areas at 13.1% and a rather low proportion was recorded at 5.0% for the northern urban communities.

Generally, the study revealed that 39.3% of the households have access to various improved water sources in contrast to the 60.7% that lack access to improved sources. In addition to the design nature and construction of water sources, having a potential of delivering safe drinking water in line with JMP [46], the investigated households using the water sources were subdivided into these three groups: accessible to premises, available when needed and free from contamination (Figure 3).

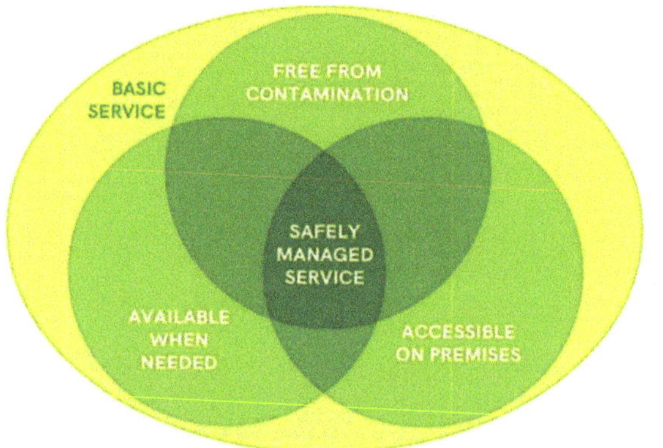

Figure 3. Elements of access to safely managed household water services.

Table 6 revealed that 16.5% of the investigated households have access to safely managed water sources, 10.3% have basic access and 12.5% have limited-service access.

Table 6. The household water access service ladder.

Service Level	Definition	Proportion (%)
Safely Managed	Access to water from an improved source that is located on premises, available when needed and free from faecal and priority chemical contaminant.	16.5
Basic	Access to household water from an improved source, AND provided collection time is not more than 30 min for a round trip, including queuing.	10.2
Limited	Access to household water from an improved source, for which collection time exceeds 30 min for a round trip, including queuing.	12.5
Unimproved	Access to household water from an unprotected dug well, tanker truck and water vending.	56.9
Surface Water	Access to household water directly from surface water.	3.9

An analysis of variance was performed on the results of the overall access to household water sources, which revealed that all of the group means were not equal at $p < 0.05$. Hence, the hypothesis of equality was rejected. However, to compare water source accessibility across the sampling communities, a post hoc analysis was performed. The results indicated that household water source mean access in the urban communities of northern (Katsina) and southern (Funtua) isohyets were similar. In addition, rural communities in the southern (Kuringafa) isohyet and urban communities (Dutsinma) in the central isohyet were similar. However, the respective rural areas in the central (Kaikai) and northern (Dan-Yashe) isohyets were different.

3.1.2. Household Sanitation Facilities

Table 7 indicates a variety of household sanitation facilities, which include a septic tank, pit latrine with a slab, pit latrine without a slab and no facility (open defecation), across the six sampling communities. Overall, pit latrines with slabs and pit latrines without slabs were found across urban and rural areas within the isohyets.

Table 7. Household sanitation facilities across the sampling areas.

Sanitation Facility	Community											
	Katsina		Dan-Yashe		Dutsinma		Kaikai		Funtua		Kuringafa	
	n	%	n	%	n	%	N	%	n	%	N	%
Septic tank	215	53.7	-	-	109	27.9	-	-	178	44.8	1	0.4
Pit latrine with slab	133	33.3	18	7.4	157	40.3	22	16.4	143	36.0	96	43.2
Pit latrine without slab	52	13.0	206	85.2	124	31.8	112	83.6	75	18.9	122	55.0
No facility (open defecation)	-	-	18	7.4	-	-	-	-	1	0.3	3	1.4
Total	400	100	242	100	390	100	134	100	397	100	222	100

n, sample number.

Findings show substantial access to septic tanks in all three urban communities across the isohyets (Table 7). A high level of septic tank accessibility at 53.7% was found in the northern urban community (Katsina) and low-level accessibility in the urban communities was recorded in the central urban community (Dutsinma) at 27.9%. The analysis further reveals the high accessibility of pit latrines with slabs in the respective urban communities across the isohyets, contrasting the high use of pit latrines in the corresponding rural communities. In rural communities, access to septic tanks was recorded only in the south (Kuringafa) at 0.4%. In urban areas, access to a septic tank was highest in the northern (Katsina) isohyets at 53.7%, it dropped considerably to 27.9% in the central region and rose to 36.0% in the southern region. Moreover, access to pit latrines with slabs was highest at 43.2% in the southern rural areas, followed by 40.3% in the central areas (Dutsinma) and 7.4% in the northern rural areas. The accessibility level of pit latrines without slabs was highest in the rural north (Dan-Yashe) at 85.2% and the lowest level was found at 55.0% for the southern rural community (Kuringafa). Furthermore, a substantial proportion of households without sanitation facilities (open defecation) was recorded in rural communities at 7.4% and 0.4% in Dan-Yashe (rural north) and Kuringafa (rural south), respectively. While 0.3% of open defecation was recorded for the Funtua community (urban south).

Furthermore, household access to sanitation facilities was in line with JMP [46] for the investigated households. As defined by UNICEF and WHO [46], Table 8 illustrates the five access service levels for adequate sanitation facilities, outlining the specific characteristics for each to provide a more in-depth understanding.

Table 8. The households' sanitation facilities access services ladder.

Service Level	Definition	Proportion (%)
Safely managed	Access to improved facilities not shared with households, and excretes are safely disposed either in situ or transported and treated offsite.	28.1
Basic	Access to improved facilities that are not shared with households.	26.7
Limited	Access to improved facilities that are shared with households.	5.3
Unimproved	Access to pit latrines without a slab, bucket or hanging latrines.	38.7
Open defecation	Disposal of human faeces in the open field/spaces.	1.2

Findings revealed that 28.1% of the investigated households have access to safely managed services, 26.7% have basic access, 5.3% have limited-service access, 38.7% have unimproved and 1.2% have open defecation service levels. An analysis of variance ($p > 0.05$) indicated access to various sanitation facilities across the sampling communities. A post hoc analysis revealed that mean access to household sanitation facilities in the three urban areas across the isohyets was different compared to each other: 3.9800, 4.4005 and 5.200 for the north, central and south, respectively. Rural communities in the southern and central isohyets had similar access figures related to household sanitation (6.5586 and 6.8358, respectively). Moreover, rural communities in the central and northern isohyets also had similar mean values of 6.8358 and 7.0000, respectively.

3.2. *Access to Household Energy*

3.2.1. Proportion of Household Access to Electricity

Access to electricity was equated to the proportion of households connected to both grid or off-grid electric supply for lighting and other household services. A multi-tier framework was employed to measure the level of electricity access based on the specified indicators. The results are illustrated in Figure 4.

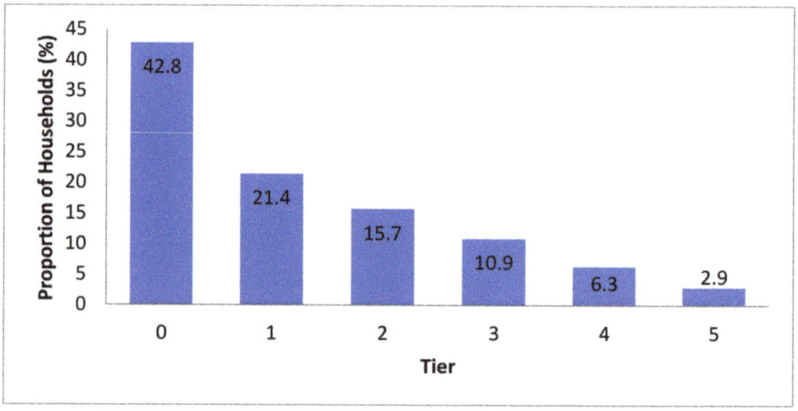

Figure 4. Overall electricity access.

Figure 4 revealed that 42.8% of the investigated households were classified as having no access to electricity. The SE4ALL Global Tracking Framework [45] defines these households as having access to less than 5 watts of electricity per day. In addition, 21.4% of the surveyed households were categorised as tier 1 of the multi-tier framework. These households are characterised by a low electric power supply (5–50 watts with less than four hours of supply daily) and have basic access to electricity for lighting and phone charging. This level also corresponds to the one for electricity supply linked to solar panels. The study further shows that 15.7% of the surveyed households are part of tier 2. These households are characterised by a low electric power supply (a minimum of 50 watts with at least four hours of daily supply) and have beyond basic access and applications of electricity for household appliances such as televisions, videos and fans in addition to lighting and phone charging. This level also corresponds to the one for electricity supply associated with solar panels. Furthermore, the findings revealed that 10.9% of the investigated households belong to tier 3 of the multi-tier framework. These are households characterised by a daily electrical supply of at least 200 watts and enjoyed all the services of tier 2 in addition to the use of other electrical appliances such as refrigerators. It was found that only 6.3% of the investigated households were reported to have a high electric power supply of a minimum capacity of 800 watts daily. These households were characterised by services from tier 3 in addition to the use of other appliances such as heaters and pressing irons. Only 2.1% of the surveyed households were reported having access to all of the services in tier 4. Finally, only 0.8% was recorded for tier 5 of the framework. This tier consists of households with the use of all services linked to tier 4 plus the use of other appliances such as air conditioners, submersible pumps and other gadgets that require a high electric supply. Moreover, the overall household electricity access index for the study area was low (1.83), implying that the majority of households in Katsina state are constrained in receiving reliable and efficient energy for lighting and other appliances.

3.2.2. Access to Household Cooking Energy

Table 9 indicates a variety of energy sources, which include electricity, cooking gas (usually liquefied petroleum gas (LPG)), kerosene, charcoal, sawdust, fuelwood (or wood fuel), agricultural residue and dung. The table summarises household energy sources for cooking in the study area.

Table 9. Various household energy sources across the sampling areas.

Energy Source	Community											
	Katsina		Dan-Yashe		Dutsinma		Kaikai		Funtua		Kuringafa	
	n	%	n	%	N	%	n	%	n	%	n	%
Electricity	15	3.7	-	-	-	-	-	-	-	-	-	-
Cooking gas (liquefied petroleum gas)	180	45.0	-	-	100	25.6	-	-	160	40.3	-	-
Kerosene	2	0.5	-	-	1	0.3	-	-	-	-	-	-
Charcoal	17	4.2	-	-	11	2.8	2	1.5	5	1.2	9	4.1
Sawdust	3	0.8	-	-	1	0.3	-	-	-	-	-	-
Fuelwood	180	45.0	131	54.1	276	70.7	125	93.3	221	55.7	145	65.3
Agricultural residue	3	0.8	104	43.0	1	0.3	7	5.2	11	2.8	62	27.9
Dung	-	-	7	2.9	-	-	-	-	-	-	6	2.7
Total	400	100	242	100	390	100	134	100	397	100	222	100

n, sample number.

Findings show overall use of fuelwood and agricultural residue across the six communities of the three isohyets (Table 9). The highest proportion of fuelwood access was found in the central rural community at 93.3%. The lowest utilisation level was found in the northern rural community. Similarly, the accessibility pattern followed the same trend among the urban communities. The highest accessibility level of fuelwood was estimated at 70.7% for the central urban region. The lowest corresponding level was recorded for the northern rural community at 45.0%. A high level of agricultural residue access was found for the rural communities, where 43.0% was recorded in the north and 5.2%, which was the lowest proportion, in the central rural community.

Table 9 reveals a trend of access to cooking gas (LPG) within all urban communities. The highest accessibility level of 45.0% was recorded in Katsina (urban north) and the least was found in Dutsinma (central urban region) at 25.6%. Access to electricity as a cooking energy source was only found in Katsina (urban north) at 3.7%. In addition, dung was only found in the poor rural households across the northern and southern isohyets at 2.9% and 2.7%, respectively. Furthermore, kerosene and sawdust were only accessed in the urban communities of the northern and central isohyets. The highest accessibility levels of kerosene and sawdust were recorded at 0.5% and 0.8%, respectively, in the north, while the lowest level of both energy sources was recorded at 0.3% each in the central region.

An analysis of variance revealed an inequality in access to various cooking energy sources. Furthermore, a post hoc analysis indicates that urban areas in the central and southern isohyets were found to be at the same range with energy mean usages of 3.3769 and 3.5088, respectively. In addition, the analysis shows an overlap between the southern and northern urban areas in the third group with household mean usages of 3.5088 and 3.6100 in the respective communities. Moreover, rural areas in the southern and northern isohyets are found within the same range at means of 3.8829 and 4.0331, respectively.

Access to sustainable energy for cooking is usually equated with the use of clean fuels as primary energy sources. The study categorised the access level into three groups: no access, which is aligned with tier 0 of the multi-tier framework; basic access, which is aligned with tiers 1–3, representing the use of self-made and manufactured non-BLEN cook stoves; and advanced access, which is aligned with tiers 4–5 corresponding to BLEND cook stoves. Figure 5 indicates that 75.1% of households had basic access to cooking fuels, these households made up tiers 1–3 and the majority of them had a low-grade technical performance. These are mostly cooking stoves (e.g., three-stone stove) whose efficiency and performance are unknown.

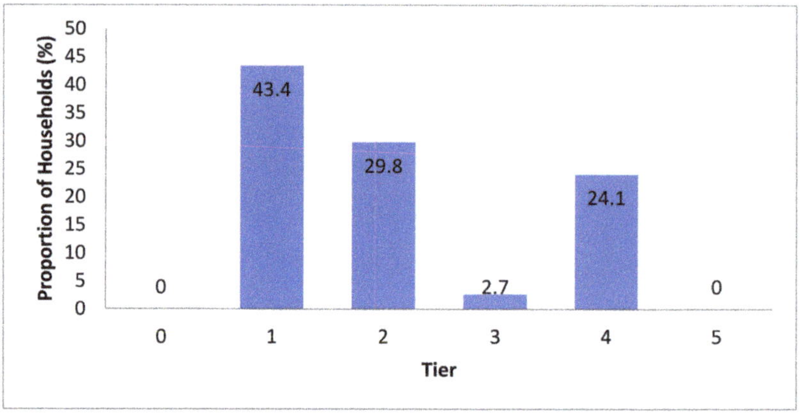

Figure 5. Overall cooking energy access index.

Figure 5 further indicates that 24.1% of the investigated households had advanced access to cooking fuels. They are households with access to electricity and stoves run on cooking gas, which are graded high in terms of efficiency and performance of primary cooking solutions. These households were aligned to tiers 4 and 5 of the multi-tier framework. Moreover, the overall household electricity access index for the study area was low (1.24), which implies that the majority of households in Katsina state are associated with deficient access to sustainable cooking energy.

3.3. *Economic Access to Household Food*

Table 10 indicates variable food purchase frequency in various households across the six communities. A considerable variety of patterns of household food purchases was found: daily, weekly and monthly purchases.

Table 10. Frequency of household food purchase.

Frequency of Food Purchase	Community											
	Katsina		Dan-Yashe		Dutsinma		Kaikai		Funtua		Kuringafa	
	N	%	n	%	n	%	n	%	n	%	n	%
Produced own food	37	9.2	60	24.7	43	11.0	37	27.6	81	20.4	77	34.7
Daily	54	13.5	82	33.9	125	32.1	69	51.5	79	20.0	49	22.1
Weekly	55	13.8	96	39.7	84	21.5	20	14.9	71	17.8	74	33.3
Monthly	254	63.5	4	1.7	138	35.4	8	6.0	166	41.8	22	9.9
Total	400	100	242	100	390	100	134	100	397	100	222	100

n, sample number.

Moreover, households that accessed their food through their own production were also identified. Disparities exist in household food accessibility among the six sampling communities. Table 8 shows a substantial proportion of monthly purchases of food in all three urban communities across the isohyets. This is in contrast to substantial proportions of daily purchases of staple food (defined as food that is eaten routinely and in considerable quantities) in the corresponding rural communities. The highest proportion of monthly food purchases was recorded in the northern urban area at 63.5% followed by 35.4% in the central urban region, whereas the lowest proportion of monthly purchases among the urban areas is found in the south at 9.9%. In rural communities, monthly food purchases were recorded in all three rural communities. The highest proportion was found in the rural south at 9.9%, while the lowest proportion of monthly food purchases linked to rural communities was recorded in the rural north at 1.7%. The highest proportion of daily food purchases was determined at 33.9% for the urban-rural category, while the lowest proportion was found in the rural south at 22.1%. In urban communities, the highest proportion of daily food purchases was found in the central-urban region at 32.1%, and the lowest proportion was recorded in the urban north at 13.5%. Own production of food was high in the rural communities. The highest production was recorded for southern rural communities (34.7%). Proportions of 27.6% and 9.2% were found in the south-central and northern rural communities, respectively. In urban communities, the highest proportion of own food production was found in the southern urban (20.4%) category, while the lowest value of 9.2% was noted for the urban communities in the north.

An analysis of variance was performed to compare several means of household major food-type usages among the six sampling communities. The statistical test performed on the results of overall household food accessibility shows that all of the group means are not equal at $p < 0.05$. However, in order to identify which particular differences between pairs are significant, post hoc tests using the Duncan method were performed to explore the six group means of food access in the study area. Results revealed that inequality in food access existed in the study area. The analysis further revealed that central-rural, north-rural and central-urban areas were found within the same range with the respective access mean values of 2.0970, 2.1736 and 2.2538, while the remaining three studied communities were found within the same range of mean access at 2.5721, 2.6045 and 2.6850 for south-rural, south-urban and north-urban areas, respectively.

3.4. Comparison of the Study Findings with SDG Targets and Indices

Table 11 compares data collected from the investigated households across the six communities in Katsina state with relevant SDG indicators falling under the SDG 1, 2, 3, 6, 7 and 11 covering issues of no poverty, zero hunger, health and well-being, clean water and sanitation, clean and affordable energy and sustainable cities, respectively.

Table 11. Tracking progress towards achieving sustainable development goals (SDG) using relevant indicators in Katsina state.

SDG	SDG Indicator	Indicator's Description	Context
SDG 1: End poverty	1.1.1	"Proportion of population below the international poverty line, sex, age, employment status and geographical region (urban/rural)"	At least 31.3% of respondents lived below the 2020 international poverty line at the time of the survey ($1.90/person/day). Precise data for respondents' incomes were not obtainable, as data on income were collected as an ordinal variable.
	1.2.1	Population living below the national poverty thershhold	22.9% of respondents lived below the national poverty line of N137,430 ($381)/person/year. The proportion of people living below the poverty line could be marginally higher, considering that precise figures for respondents' incomes were not available as data on income were collected as an ordinal variable.
SDG 2: Zero hunger	2.1.2	"Prevalence of moderate or severe food insecurity in a population based on the Food Insecurity Experience Scale"	25.7% and 22.4% of the surveyed households bought food stuff on a daily (severe food insecurity) or weekly (moderate food insecurity) basis, respectively.
SDG 3: Health and well-being	3.9.1	"Mortality attributed household and ambient air pollution"	72.3% of households were using solid fuels (fuel wood, saw dust, charcoal, agricultural residue and dung). 1078 households accessed fuel wood for cooking. 40.2% and 49.8% households used modern moulded (higher burning efficiency stove) and traditional three stone stoves, respectively.
	3.9.2	"Mortality attributed to unsafe water, sanitation and lack of hygiene"	Results indicated that 60.7% and 39.9%) of the surveyed households reported to have various sources of unimproved water, and sanitation facility access, respectively.
SDG 6: Clean water and sanitation	6.1.1	"Proportion of population using safely managed drinking water services"	39.3% of households had access to a basic drinking water source. This includes piped water into dwellings, yards or plots, public taps or standpipes, boreholes, protected dug wells and rainwater.
SDG 7: Affordable and clean energy	7.1.1	"Proportion of population with access to electricity"	76.5% of the surveyed households were connected to the national electricity grid (erratic and unsustainable supply of the electricity) relevant to indicator 7.1.1. The access to electricity index was 1.84.
	7.1.2	"Proportion of population with primary reliance on clean fuels and technology	27.2% of households were using non-solid fuel (electricity, cooking gas and electricity), contrary to 72.3% of households relying on various solid fuel sources (fuel wood, saw dust, charcoal, agricultural residue and dung) for cooking.
SDG 11: Sustainable cities and communities	11.1.1	"Proportion of urban population living in slums, informal settlements or inadequate housing"	Only 39.2% of the investigated urban households lived in formal dwellings.

Table 11 is directly relevant to SDG 1 (no poverty), particularly indicators 1.1.1 and 1.2.1. About 31.3% of the households lived below the 2020 international poverty line at the time of the survey ($1.90/person/day), and 22.9% of respondents lived below the national poverty line of N137,430 ($381)/person/year. In addition, relevant to SDG 2 (zero hunger), particularly indicator 2.1.2, the study further indicated that 25.7% and 22.4% of the surveyed households economically accessed household food stuff on a daily (severe food insecurity) and a weekly (moderate food insecurity) basis, respectively. Moreover, related to SDG 6, 7 and 3, Table 9 indicated that 60.7% and 39.9% of the surveyed households reported to have access to various sources of unimproved water and sanitation facility respectively. Results further revealed that 72.3% of the households were using solid fuels of mainly biomass (fuel wood, saw dust, charcoal, agricultural residue and dung) and 49.8% used less efficient cooking stoves.

Table 11 also showed that 60.7% and 39.9% of the surveyed households were vulnerable to certain health issues caused by either pollutants from various water sources or due to the inaccessibility of basic sanitation facilities. It further revealed that 72.3% of the investigated households were also vulnerable to various health issues as a result of indoor air pollutants due to the burning of fuels. In relation to SDG 11, the table shows that 39.2% of the investigated urban households lived in formal dwellings.

4. Discussion

There has been growing global concern around the need to provide universal access to safe and sufficient water, clean energy and healthy food for all. In Nigeria, efforts are underway to achieve water, energy and food security for most communities by about 2030.

In the investigated communities, the hypothesis of equality to household water sources, energy sources and food accessibility varied significantly ($p < 0.05$). Several sources of household water, cooking energy and food accessibility were identified. Access to both improved (piped water into dwelling, piped water to yard, public tap/stand pipe, private borehole, public borehole and protected dug well) and unimproved water sources (unprotected dug well, water vendor, surface water and tanker truck) was recorded. Both improved (septic tank and pit latrine with a slab) and unimproved sanitation facilities (pit latrine without a slab and open defecation) facilities were noted. Clean energy sources (electricity, liquefied petroleum gas and kerosene) and unclean energy sources (fuelwood, agricultural residue, charcoal, saw dust and dung) were also recorded. Finally, food access (including production of own food) and purchase frequency (monthly, weekly and daily purchases) were documented.

The technologies and corresponding accessibilities regarding water, sanitation and energy are inadequate. The results of the study showed that more than half (60.7%) of all households in the investigated communities lack access to improved water sources. More than one third (40.0%) of households lack access to improved sanitation facilities. About 74.3% of households lack access to clean cooking energy sources. About half (48.0%) of the households frequently had only smaller food quantities either on a daily or weekly basis, indicating food insecurity.

Dan-Yashe (north-rural), Kaikai (central-rural) and Kuringafa (south-rural) are communities where households have lower access to improved water sources. In rural communities, accessibility to improved water sources decreased from north to south. The results revealed that only 5.0% of households in the rural north have access to improved water sources, while 18.7% of the central-rural category were found to have access to various improved water sources. For the south-rural category, 34.9% of households have access to various improved water sources.

Restricted access to improved water sources and sanitation facilities in rural communities has also been reported elsewhere [52–54]. Both high poverty and population growth have been identified as major factors for the inaccessibility of improved water sources. In urban communities, accessibility to improved water sources was higher in Katsina (urban north, 56.8%) compared to 36.9% in Dutsinma (urban central region) and 55.2% in Funtua (urban south). In the Dan-Yashe (north-rural) and Kaikai (central-rural) communities, 5.0% and 13.4%, respectively, of the surveyed households had access to public boreholes as the only improved source. In the Kuringafa (rural south) community, 0.5%, 23.4% and 13.1% of the households accessed private boreholes, public boreholes and protected dug wells, respectively. Rural households were associated with restricted access to improved water sources. In addition, southern rural households had higher proportions of people with access to improved water sources, which include private boreholes, public boreholes and protected dug wells. This indicated the influence of isohyets regarding water access [55]. Unlike for the rural households, the study revealed that urban households were more likely to access improved water sources. For the Katsina community in the urban north, 56.8% of households had access to various improved water sources, followed by the Funtua (urban south) community, where 55.2% of the households had access to various improved water sources, and the lowest proportion was recorded for the Dutsinma (central-urban category) community, where 34.9% of the households had access to improved water sources. This is in contrast to rural communities, where the trend of accessibility to improved water sources increased from north to south. In urban communities, the study revealed the highest accessibility level to various water sources in the urban community located in the northern isohyets.

The likely reason for Katsina (urban north) having a higher proportion of access to improved water sources and sanitation facilities is that it is the administrative capital and the informal commercial capital of Katsina state. Although Funtua (urban south) cannot be matched with Katsina in terms of political priorities, it was next in terms of the accessibility level. Concerning the surveyed communities in the southern isohyets, their higher level of physical accessibility to improved water sources can be linked to the higher levels and durations of rainwater received [56–58]. A post hoc analysis showed that Katsina (urban north) and Funtua (urban south) were on the same sub-set group with corresponding means of water accessibility at 7.0925 and 7.2670, respectively.

An increase in the amount of rainfall across rural areas positively impacts on agricultural production, which also results in higher incomes and household welfare [56,57]. Thus, higher accessibility to improved water and more access to food purchases can be attributed to higher earnings as a result of increased economic activities. The findings match those of other studies [58,59]. The study showed comparable trends of access to both improved water sources and sanitation facilities for rural communities. The accessibility increased from north to south in rural communities. In rural communities in general, the overwhelming majority of households do not have access to improved sanitation facilities. In Dan-Yashe (north-rural), Kaikai (central-rural) and Kuringafa (south-rural) communities, 95% 81.3% and 56.3% of the respective households did have access to improved sanitation facilities. Moreover, access to various water sources, sanitation facilities and results obtained from water quality tests supported SDG 6.1 and 6.2, and thus enable the examination of inequalities in service levels across the investigated communities.

Geographical location, income and education were found to be among the determinant factors that force the majority of households to access unimproved sanitation facilities in Nigeria [54,60,61]. A post hoc analysis revealed that Dan-Yashe (north-rural) and Kuringafa (south-rural) were grouped in different sub-sets with access means of sanitation facilities of 7.000 and 6.5586, respectively. Though there was an overlap between both the rural north and the rural south with Kaikai (rural central region) in the transition. The analysis revealed that urban communities across the three isohyets are significantly different from rural areas.

The study showed strong associations between similar categories of water sources and sanitation facilities. Thus, an increase in improved water accessibility corresponds to an associated increase in improved sanitation facilities [62]. Generally, the results are in line with another study [63,64] showing little or no access to improved water sources and improved sanitation facilities in poor households, especially in rural developing countries.

The accessibility of household energy sources for cooking in the surveyed communities varied significantly ($p < 0.05$) from one community to another. Several sources of energy were identified. In rural communities, access to (solid) biomass (mainly fuelwood), agricultural residue, charcoal and dung were identified. This implies the inaccessibility of non-solid (clean) energy sources and a total dependence on solid fuel sources in these communities. In contrast, in urban communities, access to various sources of cooking energy from solid and non-solid categories were identified. In the Katsina (north-urban) community, the highest proportion of households having access to clean (non-solid) energy sources was found to be 49.3%, 25.9% and 43.7% for Katsina (north-urban), Dutsinma (central-urban) and Funtua (south-urban) communities, respectively. The highest accessible level of biomass, which includes fuelwood and charcoal in urban and rural communities across the isohyets, showed a significant level of access to fuelwood in developing countries [65]. The inaccessibility of clean cooking fuels and socio-economic status were identified as the major determinants responsible for the high utilisation level of biomass in developing countries [65–68].

Access to clean cooking fuels, which include electricity and cooking gas among the urban households, is a clear indication of elevated educational level and financial capabilities [62,68]. In addition, access to electricity as a source of household energy for cooking was only recorded in the Katsina (north-urban) community. Results from the interviews indicated that an overwhelming majority of urban households was connected to electricity systems. However, the distribution of electricity in the state is unreliable. A low electricity accessibility level in this study showed an insufficient and erratic supply. This forced the majority of urban households to use other cooking fuels for easy accessibility.

Economic access to various food types through purchasing frequencies, which include monthly, weekly and daily purchases, alongside those that produced their food items through agricultural practices varied significantly ($p < 0.05$) from one surveyed community to another. The study revealed a high proportion of households that produced their own food in the rural communities where mostly subsistence farming is practiced. Subsistence farming plays a crucial role in ensuring food security [69]. Moreover, the study coincided with other studies [70,71] which revealed food purchase frequencies as measures of food security. In addition, the study supports other findings [72,73] revealing that socioeconomic parameters are drivers to food access.

Tracking progress towards achieving the SDG in the study area was compared with relevant indicators. The general indicator framework for sustainable development was formulated by the Inter Agency and Expert group on sustainable development goal indicators and was unanimously adopted at the 48th session of the United Nations General Assembly on 6 July 2017. The official SDG indicator framework presently consists of 231 indicators, which are divided into three tiers (1—method established and data widely available, 2—method established but limited data, 3—no internationally agreed-upon method). Furthermore, 123 indicators (53%) belong to tier 1, and the rest are assigned to tier 2 [74,75]. As a result, the official global SDG indicator framework is only partly effective, particularly in countries that have weak official data compilation systems. Identifying the difficulties of adopting a global indicator framework that works for all countries, the 2030 Agenda states that members will develop their national indicators in line with the principles of the 2030 Agenda and that targets are defined as aspirational and global, with each government setting its own national targets guided by the global level of ambition, but taking into account national circumstances [76].

The income of about one third (31.3%) of the surveyed population ranks below the international and the national poverty lines (Table 9). The results further revealed that the Katsina state population (33.1%) has an income below the international poverty line, exceeding the national proportion (22.9%). Food purchase was being employed as a measure of food security through assessing purchase frequencies. Table 9 revealed that 25.7% and 22.4% of the surveyed households bought food stuff on a daily (severe food insecurity) and a weekly (moderate food insecurity) basis, respectively. The definition of access to clean and affordable drinking water and sanitation is outlined by UNICEF and WHO [46]. Concerning Katsina state, many households had access to piped water. However, household water supply was erratic. Households often had extended periods of time without running water, thus relying on water storage, leading to other health-related risks (e.g., bacteriological contamination causing diarrheal disease). The study revealed that 39.3% and 60.0% of the surveyed households reported to have some form of water access and sanitation, respectively. Generally, it seems that more people living in Katsina state have formal dwellings compared to the rest of the country. Fewer people (24.2%) were reported having access to the Internet in the study areacompared to the rest of the country (51.4%). Given the definition of access to electricity, clean cooking fuels and cooking energy access [47,48], the study revealed that the electricity and cooking energy access indexes were low at 1.83 and 1.24, respectively.

Table 9 showed that 72.3% of households were using solid fuels (fuel wood, saw dust, charcoal, agricultural residue and dung). Furthermore, 1078 households accessed fuel wood for cooking; 40.2% and 49.8% of them used modern molded (higher burning efficiency stove) and traditional three-stone stoves respectively. Relevant to indicators 3.9.1 and 3.9.2, the lack of access to improved water sources and sanitation facilities led to water-borne illnesses such as cholera and stunted child growth. [77,78]. In addition, indoor air pollution caused by burning solid fuels using inefficient cooking stoves is another cause of deadly acute respiratory infections as well as pulmonary- and cardiovascular-related diseases [79]. Findings revealed that 49.2% of the investigated households lived in formal dwellings (Table 9). This means that more people in Katsina state, especially in the rural communities, lived in informal dwellings.

5. Conclusions

Access to improved sources of water, basic sanitation facilities, clean energy and food remains a challenge for poor households in sub-Saharan African countries, particularly in rural communities. There is a need for inventive planning approaches based within a socio-ecological context to provide equitable access to improved water sources, basic sanitation facilities, clean energy sources and healthy food within this decade. The study revealed the existence of a strong relationship between socio-ecological characteristics and access to the household resources and the amount of seasonal rainfall in the respective isohyets, especially across the rural communities. The findings indicated a progressive trend of access to improved water sources and improved sanitation facilities from the rural north to the rural south. A corresponding clear trend could not be detected for the urban investigated communities. However, a similar pattern to energy access was identified in the urban communities, where access to clean energy was the highest at 49.2% for Katsina (north-urban), followed by 40.3% for Funtua (south-urban) and only 25.9% for Dutsinma (central-urban). No access to clean (non-solid) energy sources was recorded in any of the three rural communities.

The study indicated a progressive trend of access to food regarding monthly purchases from 1.7% in Dan-Yashe (north-rural) to 6.0% in Kuringafa (south-rural). In the urban investigated communities, there was no clear trend.

A significant proportion of access to improved water sources, basic sanitation facilities, clean energy and food was found in the urban communities, particularly in Katsina (urban north), where a high proportion of educated and high-income households were found. Education and income were key determinants of living standard. Hence, accessibilities to household water, sanitation facilities, energy and food correlate well with the standard of living.

6. Limitations and Future Research

Data collected on socio-economic variables yielded insights on various households' water-energy-food access issues connected to specific SDG indicators. The original study survey was not designed for the primary purpose of tracking progress towards achieving

SDG e, and so the data were mostly not useful according to common calculation methodologies. This is frequently a drawback in project-specific surveys; they are often not created with other assessments in mind.

As data gaps represent one of the main reasons why progress towards the SDG in Katsina state cannot be adequately computed or expressed, it is advisable that researchers be mindful of the opportunity for data compatibility between the SDG framework and survey data, for example, with respect to socio-economic characteristics and access to water-energy-food. If this is addressed, survey data can contribute to the understanding of local as well as national progress towards SDG achievement. This is particularly important for countries that lack resources focusing on socio-economic surveys, which leads to large data gaps.

Future research should take into account more household characteristics such as family size, gender, age and occupation. Furthermore, the research should be continued and extended to other low- and middle-income developing countries. The current data of the surveyed communities on census and the number of households have not been published previously, and they are available from the Katsina state office of the National Population Commission (NPC). Therefore, projections based on the available data were made and households in the communities were also estimated adopting World Health Organisation estimates for the study area. An overwhelming majority of the population in Katsina state, especially in the rural communities, is facing the ever increasing threat of banditry, a type of organised crime that includes kidnapping, murder, rape and cattle rustling. Thus, this limits the study to access more communities especially in the rural areas.

The authors also recommend that future surveys should be formulated in such a way that the survey results can be directly used for the calculation of relevant SDG target indicators. This would help to assess progress in meeting the SDG at both macro- and micro-levels. Moreover, decision-makers would be guided by carefully structured surveys to introduce tailored interventions and awareness campaigns.

Supplementary Materials: The following are available online at https://www.mdpi.com/article/10.3390/w13243595/s1. The questionnaire used in the survey is accessible as supplementary material SM1.

Author Contributions: Conceptualisation, Y.S. and M.S.; methodology, Y.S. and M.S.; formal analysis, Y.S.; investigation, Y.S.; data curation, Y.S.; writing—original draft preparation, Y.S.; writing—review and editing, M.S.; visualisation, Y.S.; supervision, M.S. All authors have read and agreed to the published version of the manuscript.

Funding: This research was funded by the Tertiary Education Tax Fund (TETFUND), Nigeria.

Institutional Review Board Statement: Ethical review and approval were waived for this study by the collaborating authorities in Nigeria.

Informed Consent Statement: Informed consent was obtained from all subjects involved in the study.

Data Availability Statement: Data are available on reasonable request following Nigerian state law.

Acknowledgments: The author would like to acknowledge the advice provided by Magnus Persson on methodology and conceptualisation. Aminu Yahaya El-Ladan supported the data curation and helped with the statistical analysis. Practical contributions by Nura Umar and other laboratory and field assistants were welcome. We would like to recognise the support of the Katsina State Government as well as the local authorities in the respective investigated communities.

Conflicts of Interest: The authors declare that they have no known competing financial interest or personal relationships that could have appeared to influence the work reported in this paper.

References

1. Sarvajayakesavalu, S. Addressing challenges of developing countries in implementing five priorities for sustainable development goals. *Ecosyst. Health Sustain.* **2015**, *1*, 1–4. [CrossRef]
2. Dhimal, M.; Dhimal, M.L.; Karki, K.; Montag, D.; Groneberg, D.A.; Kuch, U. Tracking health-related Sustainable Development Goals (SDGs) in Nepal. *J. Health Soc. Sci.* **2017**, *2*, 143–148.

3. United Nations. IAEG-SDGs, Tier Classification for Global SDG Indicators. Available online: https://unstats.un.org/sdgs/iaeg-sdgs/tier-classification/ (accessed on 15 September 2020).
4. Rasul, G.; Sharma, B. The nexus approach to water–energy–food security: An option for adaptation to climate change. *Clim. Policy* **2016**, *16*, 682–702. [CrossRef]
5. Petrariu, R.; Constantin, M.; Dinu, M.; Pătărlăgeanu, S.R.; Deaconu, M.E. Water, Energy, Food, Waste Nexus: Between Synergy and Trade-Offs in Romania Based on Entrepreneurship and Economic Performance. *Energies* **2021**, *14*, 5172. [CrossRef]
6. Nkiaka, E.; Okpara, U.T.; Okumah, M. Food-energy-water security in sub-Saharan Africa: Quantitative and spatial assessments using an indicator-based approach. *Environ. Dev.* **2021**, *40*, 100655. [CrossRef]
7. Li, J.; Cui, J.; Sui, P.; Yue, S.; Yang, J.; Lv, Z.; Wang, D.; Chen, X.; Sun, B.; Ran, M.; et al. Valuing the Synergy in the Wa-ter-Energy-Food Nexus for Cropping Systems: A Case in the North China Plain. *Ecol. Indic.* **2021**, *127*, 107741. [CrossRef]
8. Bonn Nexus Conference, the Water Energy and Food Security Nexus Solutions for the Green Economy. Bonn, Germany. 2011. Available online: https://library.wmo.int/index.php?lvl=notice_display&id=9202#.YbhUI55ByUk (accessed on 8 December 2021).
9. Bazilian, M.; Rogner, H.; Howells, M.; Hermann, S.; Arent, D.; Gielen, D.; Steduto, P.; Mueller, A.; Komor, P.; Tol, R.; et al. Considering the energy, water and food nexus: Towards an integrated modelling approach. *Energy Policy* **2011**, *39*, 7896–7906. [CrossRef]
10. FAO. *The Water-Energy-Food Nexus: A New Approach in Support of Food Security and Sustainable Agriculture*; Food and Agriculture Organization of the United Nations: Rome, Italy, 2014.
11. World Economic Forum. *Water Security: The Water-Food-Energy-Climate Nexus*; Island Press: Washington, DC, USA, 2011.
12. Hoff, H. Understanding the nexus. In Proceedings of the Bonn 2011 Conference: The Water, Energy and Food Security Nexus, Bonn, Germany, 16–18 November 2011; pp. 16–18.
13. Leck, H.; Conway, D.; Bradshaw, M.; Rees, J. Tracing water-energy-food nexus: Description, theory and practice. *Geogr. Compass* **2015**, *9*, 445–460. [CrossRef]
14. Simpson, G.B.; Jewitt, G. The Development of the Water-Energy-Food Nexus as a Framework for Achieving Resource Security: A Review. *Front. Environ. Sci.* **2019**, *7*, 1–7. [CrossRef]
15. Chen, B.; Lu, Y. Urban nexus: A new paradigm for urban studies. *Ecol. Model.* **2015**, *318*, 5–7. [CrossRef]
16. Wakeel, M.; Chen, B.; Hayat, T.; Alsaedi, A.; Ahmad, B. Energy consumption for water use cycles in different countries: A review. *Appl. Energy* **2016**, *178*, 868–885. [CrossRef]
17. Hussien, W.A.; Memon, F.A.; Savic, D.A. An integrated model to evaluate water-energy-food nexus at a household scale. *Environ. Model. Softw.* **2017**, *93*, 366–380. [CrossRef]
18. Wang, S.; Chen, B. Energy–water nexus of urban agglomeration based on multiregional input–output tables and ecological network analysis: A case study of the Beijing–Tianjin–Hebei region. *Appl. Energy* **2016**, *178*, 773–783. [CrossRef]
19. Vieira, P.; Jorge, C.; Covas, D. Assessment of household water use efficiency using performance indices. *Resour. Conserv. Recycl.* **2017**, *116*, 94–106. [CrossRef]
20. Abdullah; Zhou, D.; Shah, T.; Ali, S.; Ahmad, W.; Din, I.U.; Ilyas, A. Factors affecting household food security in rural northern hinterland of Pakistan. *J. Saudi Soc. Agric. Sci.* **2019**, *18*, 201–210. [CrossRef]
21. Kipkorir, E. Analysis of rainfall climate on the Njemps Flats, Baringo District, Kenya. *J. Arid. Environ.* **2002**, *50*, 445–458. [CrossRef]
22. Zeineddine, N.; Ovidiu, M. Rainfall Variability and Trend Analysis of Annual Rainfall in North Africa. *Int. J. Atmos. Sci.* **2016**.
23. Daryanto, S.; Wang, L.; Jacinthe, P.-A. Global Synthesis of Drought Effects on Food Legume Production. *PLoS ONE* **2015**, *10*, e0127401. [CrossRef]
24. Twongyirwe, R.; Mfitumukiza, D.; Barasa, B.; Naggayi, B.R.; Odongo, H.; Nyakato, V.; Mutoni, G. Perceived effects of drought on household food security in South-western Uganda: Coping responses and determinants. *Weather. Clim. Extremes* **2019**, *24*, 100201. [CrossRef]
25. Peña-Guerrero, M.D.; Nauditt, A.; Muñoz-Robles, C.; Ribbe, L.; Meza, F. Drought impacts on water quality and potential implications for agricultural production in the Maipo River Basin, Central Chile. *Hydrol. Sci. J.* **2020**, *65*, 1005–1021. [CrossRef]
26. IPCC Summary for Policymakers. Climate change. The physical science basis. In *Contribution of Working Group I to the Fifth Assessment Report of the Intergovernmental Panel on Climate Change*; Stocker, T.F., Boschung, J., Nauels, A., Xia, Y., Bex, V., Midgley, P.M., Eds.; Cambridge University Press: Cambridge, UK; New York, NY, USA, 2013; pp. 1–30.
27. Ketlhoilwe, M.J.; Kanene, K.M. Access to energy sources in the face of climate change: Challenges faced by women in rural communities. *Jàmbá J. Disaster Risk Stud.* **2018**, *10*, 8. [CrossRef]
28. Afshar, N.R.; Fahmi, H. Impact of climate change on water resources in Iran. *Int. J. Energy Water Resour.* **2019**, *3*, 55–60. [CrossRef]
29. Romano, G.; Salvati, N.; Guerrini, A. Estimating the Determinants of Residential Water Demand in Italy. *Water* **2014**, *6*, 2929–2945. [CrossRef]
30. Harrisfry, A.H.; Azad, K.; Kuddus, A.; Shaha, S.; Nahar, B.; Hossen, M.; Younes, L.; Costello, A.; Fottrell, E. Socio-economic determinants of household food security and women's dietary diversity in rural Bangladesh: A cross-sectional study. *J. Health Popul. Nutr.* **2015**, *33*, 1–12. [CrossRef]
31. Fuerst, F.; Kavarnou, D.; Singh, R.; Adan, H. Determinants of energy consumption and exposure to energy price risk: A UK study. *Zeitschrift für Immobilienökonomie* **2019**, *6*, 65–80. [CrossRef]

32. Koundouri, P.; Papadaki, L. *Integrating Water-Food-Energy Nexus with Climate Services: Modelling and Assessment for a Case Study in Africa*; Sustainability Concept in Developing Countries; Kulshreshtha, S.N., Ed.; Intech Open, 2020; Available online: https://www.intechopen.com/chapters/70971 (accessed on 8 December 2021). [CrossRef]
33. Calow, R.; MacDonald, C.; Nicol, M.; Robins, N.S. Groundwater security and drought in Africa linking availability, access and demand. *J. Ground Water* **2010**, *48*, 246–256. [CrossRef]
34. Friel, S.; Berry, H.; Dinh, H.; O'Brien, L.; Walls, H.L. The impact of drought on the association between food security and mental health in a nationally representative Australian sample. *BMC Public Health* **2014**, *14*, 1102. [CrossRef]
35. Onyenechere, E.; Azuwike, D.; Enwereuzor, A. Effect of Rainfall Variability on Water Supply in Ikeduru L.G.A. of Imo State, Nigeria. *Afr. Res. Rev.* **2011**, *5*, 223–241. [CrossRef]
36. Nyakundi, R.; Makokha, M.; Mwangi, J.; Obiero, C. Impact of rainfall variability on groundwater levels in Ruiru municipality, Kenya. *Afr. J. Sci. Technol. Innov. Dev.* **2015**, *7*, 1–7. [CrossRef]
37. Pearson, A.L.; Zwickle, A.; Namanya, J.; Rzotkiewicz, A.; Mwita, E. Seasonal Shifts in Primary Water Source Type: A Comparison of Largely Pastoral Communities in Uganda and Tanzania. *Int. J. Environ. Res. Public Health* **2016**, *13*, 169. [CrossRef]
38. Kinda, S.R.; Badolo, F. Does rainfall variability matter for food security in developing countries? *Cogent Econ. Financ.* **2019**, *7*, 1640098. [CrossRef]
39. *Katsina State Diary*; Government Printers: Katsina, Nigeria, 2019.
40. El-Tantawi, A. The Effects of Climate on Human's Comfort and Health in North Western Region of Nigeria. *Katsina J. Nat. Appl. Sci.* **2012**, *3*, 161–174.
41. *Katsina State Urban and Regional Planning Board (KTURPB)*; Government Printers: Katsina, Nigeria, 2018.
42. Isreal, G.D. *Determining Sample Size*; Institute of Food and Agricultural Science (IFAS), University of Florida: Gainesville, FL, USA, 2018.
43. *Katsina State Primary Health Care Development Agency (KTPHCDA)*; Government Printers: Katsina, Nigeria, 2019.
44. Angelsen, A.; Lund, J.F. Designing the household questionnaire. In *Measuring Livelihoods and Environmental Dependence Analytical Report at the National Level, Methods for Research and Fieldwork*; Angelsen, A., Larsen, H.O., Lund, J.F., Smith-Hall, C., Wunder, S., Eds.; Earthscan Publications: Oxford, UK, 2011; pp. 107–126.
45. Sustainable Energy for All. Global Tracking Framework: Workshop on Capacity Development for Mainstreaming Energy Sustainable Development Goals (SDGs), Target and Indicators into Statistical Programmes in Selected Latin Countries. 2015. Available online: https://sustainabledevelopment.un.org/content/documents/13139Global%20Tracking%20Framework_World%20Bank.pdf (accessed on 26 October 2021).
46. United Nations Children's Fund; World Health Organisation. *Integrating Water Quality Testing into Household Survey: Thermatic Report on Drinking Water*; UNICEF: New York, NY, USA, 2020.
47. World Health Organisation (WHO). Fuel for Life: Household Energy and Health; WHO Library Cataloguing in Publication Data. 2006. Available online: http://www.who.int/indoorair/publications/fuelforlife.pdf?ua=1 (accessed on 12 February 2020).
48. Frongillo, E.A.; Chowdhury, N.; Ekstrom, E.-C.; Naved, R.T. Understanding the Experience of Household Food Insecurity in Rural Bangladesh Leads to a Measure Different from That Used in Other Countries. *J. Nutr.* **2003**, *133*, 4158–4162. [CrossRef] [PubMed]
49. Gittelsohn, J.; Mookherji, S.; Pelto, G. Operationalizing Household Food Security in Rural Nepal. *Food Nutr. Bull.* **1998**, *19*, 210–222. [CrossRef]
50. Bhatia, M.; Angelou, N. *Capturing Multi-Dimensionality of Energy Access*; Live Wire; World Bank: Washington, DC, USA, 2014.
51. Bhatia, M.; Angelou, N. *Beyond Connections: Energy Access Redefined, ESMAP Technical Report, 008/15*; World Bank: Washington, DC, USA, 2015; Available online: https://openknowledge.worldbank.org/handle/10986/24368 (accessed on 15 April 2020).
52. Gomez, M.; Perdiguero, J.; Sanz, À. Socioeconomic factors affecting water access in rural areas of low and middle income countries. *Water* **2019**, *11*, 202. [CrossRef]
53. Abubakar, I.R. Exploring the determinants of open defecation in Nigeria using demographic and health survey data. *Sci. Total. Environ.* **2018**, *637–638*, 1455–1465. [CrossRef]
54. Armah, F.A.; Ekumah, B.; Yawson, D.O.; Odoi, J.O.; Afitiri, A.-R.; Nyieku, F.E. Access to improved water and sanitation in sub-Saharan Africa in a quarter century. *Heliyon* **2018**, *4*, e00931. [CrossRef]
55. Moylan, H.G. *The Impact of Rainfall Variability on Agricultural Production and Household Welfare in Rural Malawi*; Graduate College of the University of Illinois: Champaign, IL, USA, 2012; Available online: http://www.illinois.edu/bitstream/handle/2142/3447/Moylan_Heather.pdf?sequence=1 (accessed on 14 November 2020).
56. Sekela, T.; Manfred, F.B. Seasonal and Annual Rainfall Variability and Their Impact on Rural Water Supply Services in Wami River Basin, Tanzania. *Water* **2019**, *11*, 2055. [CrossRef]
57. Tabari, H. Climate change impact on flood and extreme precipitation increases with water availability. *Sci. Rep.* **2020**, *10*, 13768. [CrossRef]
58. Animashaun, I.M.; Oguntunde, P.G.; Akinwumiju, A.S.; Olubanjo, O.O. Rainfall Analysis over the Niger Central Hydrological Area, Nigeria: Variability, Trend, and Change point detection. *Sci. Afr.* **2020**, *8*, e00419. [CrossRef]
59. De Janvry, A.; Sadoulet, E. Agricultural Growth and Poverty Reduction: Additional Evidence. *World Bank Res. Obs.* **2009**, *25*, 1–20. [CrossRef]

60. Mahama, A.M.; Anaman, K.A.; Osei-Akoto, I. Factors influencing householders' access to improved water in low-income urban areas of Accra, Ghana. *J. Water Health* **2014**, *12*, 318–331. [CrossRef]
61. Simelane, M.S.; Shongwe, M.C.; Vermaak, K.; Zwane, E. Determinants of Households' Access to Improved Drinking Water Sources: A Secondary Analysis of Eswatini 2010 and 2014 Multiple Indicator Cluster Surveys. *Adv. Public Health* **2020**, *2020*, 6758513. [CrossRef]
62. Folayan, M.O.; Obiyan, M.; Olaleye, A.O. Association between water, sanitation, general hygiene and oral hygiene practices of street-involved young people in Southwest Nigeria. *BMC Oral Health* **2020**, *20*, 1–11. [CrossRef]
63. Van Der Bruggen, B.; Borghgraef, K.; Vinckier, C. Causes of Water Supply Problems in Urbanised Regions in Developing Countries. *Water Resour. Manag.* **2009**, *24*, 1885–1902. [CrossRef]
64. Lorenzo, T.E.; Kinzid, A.P. Double Exposure: Future Water Security across Urban Southeast Asia. *Water* **2020**, *12*, 116. [CrossRef]
65. Win, Z.C.; Mizoue, N.; Ota, T.; Kajisa, T.; Yoshida, S. Consumption Rates and Use Patterns of Firewood and Charcoal in Urban and Rural Communities in Yedashe Township, Myanmar. *Forest* **2018**, *9*, 429. [CrossRef]
66. Hussain, A.; Dasgupta, S.; Bargali, H.S. Fuelwood consumption patterns by semi-nomadic pastoralist community and its implication on conservation of Corbett Tiger Reserve, India. *Energy Ecol. Environ.* **2017**, *2*, 49–59. [CrossRef]
67. Heltberg, R. Factors determining household fuel choice in Guatemala. *Environ. Dev. Econ.* **2005**, *10*, 337–361. [CrossRef]
68. Miah, M.D.; Kabir, R.R.; Mohammad, S.; Koihe, M.; Akther, S.; Shin, M.Y. Rural household energy consumption pattern in disregarded villages of Bangladesh. *Energy Policy* **2010**, *38*, 997–1003. [CrossRef]
69. Hlophe-Ginindza, S.N.; Mpandeli, N. The Role of Small-Scale Farmers in Ensuring Food Security in Africa. *Food Secur. Afr.* **2021**. [CrossRef]
70. Ambikapathi, R.; Rothstein, J.D.; Yori, P.P.; Olortegui, M.P.; Lee, G.; Kosek, M.; Caulfield, L.E. Food purchase patterns indicative of household food access insecurity, children's dietary diversity and intake, and nutritional status using a newly developed and validated tool in the Peruvian Amazon. *Food Secur.* **2018**, *10*, 999–1011. [CrossRef]
71. French, S.A.; Tangney, C.C.; Crane, M.; Wang, Y.; Appelhans, B.M. Nutrition quality of food purchases varies by household income: The SHoPPER study. *BMC Public Health* **2019**, *19*, 1–7. [CrossRef]
72. French, A.S.; Wall, M.; Mitchell, N.R. Household income differences in food sources and food items purchased. *Int. J. Behav. Nutr. Phys. Act.* **2010**, *7*, 77–78. [CrossRef]
73. Ogunniyi, A.I.; Omotoso, S.O.; Salman, K.K.; Omotayo, A.O.; Olagunju, K.O.; Aremu, A.O. Socio-economic Drivers of Food Security among Rural Households in Nigeria: Evidence from Smallholder Maize Farmers. *Soc. Indic. Res.* **2021**, *155*, 583–599. [CrossRef]
74. IAEG-SDGs. Report of the Inter-Agency and Expert Group on Sustainable Development Goal Indicators; 2016. Available online: https://unstats.un.org/unsd/statcom/47th-session/documents/2016-2-IAEG-SDGs-Rev1-E.pdf (accessed on 15 July 2020).
75. IAEG-SDGs. Tier Classification for Global SDG Indicators as of 17 July 2020; 2020. Available online: https://unstats.un.org/sdgs/files/Tier%20Classification%20of%20SDG%20Indicators_17%20July%202020_web.v2.pdf (accessed on 20 July 2020).
76. United Nations. Transforming Our World: The 2030 Agenda for Sustainable Development 2015. Available online: https://sustainabledevelopment.un.org/post2015/transformingourworld (accessed on 24 September 2021).
77. Prüss-Ustün, A.; Bartram, J.; Clasen, T.; Colford, J.M., Jr.; Cumming, O.; Curtis, V.; Bonjour, S.; Dangour, A.; De France, J.; Fewtrell, L.; et al. Burden of disease from inadequate water, sanitation and hygiene in low- and middle-income settings: A retrospective analysis of data from 145 countries. *Trop. Med. Int. Health* **2014**, *19*, 894–905. [CrossRef]
78. Bekele, T.; Rahman, B.; Rawstorne, P. The effect of access to water, sanitation and handwashing facilities on child growth indicators: Evidence from the Ethiopia Demographic and Health Survey 2016. *PLoS ONE* **2020**, *15*, e0239313. [CrossRef]
79. Van Tran, V.; Park, D.; Lee, Y.-C. Indoor Air Pollution, Related Human Diseases, and Recent Trends in the Control and Improvement of Indoor Air Quality. *Int. J. Environ. Res. Public Health* **2020**, *17*, 2927. [CrossRef]

sustainability

MDPI

Article

Interplay of Water–Energy Security and Food Consumption Patterns towards Achieving Nutrition Security in Katsina State, North-Western Nigeria

Yahaya Sani [1] and Miklas Scholz [1,2,3,4,*]

1 Division of Water Resources Engineering, Department of Building and Environmental Technology, Faculty of Engineering, Lund University, P.O. Box 118, 22100 Lund, Sweden; yahaya.sani@tvrl.lth.se
2 Department of Civil Engineering Science, School of Civil Engineering and the Built Environment, University of Johannesburg, Kingsway Campus, P.O. Box 524, Aukland Park, Johannesburg 2006, South Africa
3 Department of Town Planning, Engineering Networks and Systems, South Ural State University, 76, Lenin Prospekt, 454080 Chelyabinsk, Russia
4 Institute of Environmental Engineering, Wroclaw University of Environmental and Life Sciences, ul. Norwida 25, 50-375 Wrocław, Poland
* Correspondence: miklas.scholz@tvrl.lth.se; Tel.: +46-(0)4-6222-8920; Fax: +46-(0)4-6222-4435

Abstract: Everyone has the right to secure water, energy, and food supplies. These essential resources are stressed in many countries. With the current population growth rate and urbanisation, especially in sub-Saharan Africa, there is a need for more food, water, and energy to sustain the increasing population. The aim of this study was to assess the inter-relationship among water and energy in various urban and rural households to support food and nutrition security. Considering the social-economic peculiarities of the region, a specific framework and questionnaire were developed for the study. A survey involving 1785 questionnaires was conducted. Urban and rural stratification methods were used in selecting settlements across the regions. The household's nutritional status was measured in relation to protein-rich foods as well as vegetable and fruit consumption. In addition to the Person's correlation coefficient, which was applied to measure the association between two categories of food consumption, the chi-squared test of interdependence to determine the effect of the urban–rural dichotomy on resource utilisation was calculated. The findings indicate a high risk of undernourishment associated with insufficient sources of water and energy, as well as inappropriate sanitation facilities, especially in rural communities.

Keywords: sustainable development; water sources; energy sources; energy crisis; scarcity; sanitation facilities; nutrition assessment; resource access; urban–rural dichotomy; urbanisation

Citation: Sani, Y.; Scholz, M. Interplay of Water–Energy Security and Food Consumption Patterns towards Achieving Nutrition Security in Katsina State, North-Western Nigeria. *Sustainability* **2022**, *14*, 4478. https://doi.org/10.3390/su14084478

Academic Editors: Aled Jones and Vasilis Kanakoudis

Received: 30 December 2021
Accepted: 7 April 2022
Published: 9 April 2022

1. Introduction

The water–energy–food nexus has been promoted as a theoretical tool for achieving sustainable development. The nexus perspective tackles the links connecting the essential resources of water, food, and energy [1–3]. These three resources have long been recognised as essential to human life and socio-economic progress. The nexus approach perspectives highlight the multiple inter-reliance among water, energy, and food security and the underlying natural resources. It also draws attention to the potential synergies and trade-offs, as well as complicit and efficient utilisation [4–9]. The future securities of water, energy, and food are of major global concern [10]. Major challenges are inaccessibility, rapidly growing global demand, resource constraints, disparity in regional availability, and variations in demand and supply. Population growth, urbanisation, climate change, economic growth, land use, and technological developments have been identified as major drivers of rapidly growing demand of water, energy, and food [2,8,10]. The demands for water, energy, and food have exceeded the available supplies in some regions of the world such as sub-Saharan Africa, characterised by poverty as well as rapid population and particularly urban growth [11–13].

Access to safe water and sanitation is a universal need and a basic human right. It is an essential element of human development and poverty alleviation and constitutes a necessary component of primary health care. Inadequate water and sanitation result in sickness and potentially death, as well as in higher health costs, lower workforce productivity, overall school enrolment decline, and low retention rates of schoolgirls [14,15].

The availability to good and sufficient water resources influences production and is a major criterion for the sustainable development of the agricultural sector in Nigeria. Although the country is rich in both surface and groundwater resources, it has been estimated that the total precipitation of 1062.336 km^3/y for the whole country is linked to an average total precipitation of 1150 mm/y. However, spatio-temporal variations in rainfall across different regions of the country indicate surplus in some regions and scarcity in other regions. This results in challenges for effectiveness in utilisation and productivity improvement in water-scarce regions [16].

The northern region of Nigeria, which comprises both arid and semi-arid belts, is an area characterised by little rainfall. The annual rainfall declines northwards to an average of less than 500 mm in a season of 60 days, with the upper and lower confidence limits being 635 and 389 mm, respectively [16]. Over the years, there has been evidences of prevalence of events of drought in the region with increasing pressure on available water resources and a requirement for better resource management [17]. The increasing desertification in the northern region is also attributed to the persistent deforestation of the savannah woodland and bushes having been converted into open agricultural land with no protection during the heavy rain downpours, leading to erosion and soil degradation [18].

Considering the fast-growing population in Nigeria, arable land is also required for food production and wood for energy generation, thus resulting in trees being cut down and leaving the fields open during the dry seasons when there are no crops on the field. This leads to erosion of the topsoil layer during heavy and frequent rain downpours [19]. Energy is a vital input for the socio-economic growth for any country. Despite the enormous endowments of renewable and non-renewable primary energy resources, Nigeria is still faced with many electricity challenges linked to generation, transmission, distribution, and marketing. This has hampered its economic development. The total installed capacity of power generation in Nigeria in August 2015 was 12,522 MW, but only 7141 MW were available [20]. According to the World Bank [21] in 2020, 85 million Nigerians do not have access to grid electricity. This corresponds to 43% percent of the country's population and makes Nigeria the country with the greatest energy access deficit in the world. The lack of reliable power is a significant constraint for many communities in terms of socio-economic progress, resulting in an annual economic loss estimated at USD 26.2 billion (NGN 10.1 trillion), which is equivalent to about 2% of the GDP. The report further revealed that, Nigeria's position is only 171 out of 190 countries in terms of obtaining electricity. Electricity access is seen as one of the major limitations for the private sector development. Water and energy are critical components of the food system as well. Energy type, price, and availability are key factors that influence growers and manufacturers [22].

At household level, water, energy, and food securities are described as states when people almost always have economic and/or physical access to safe and sufficient water, clean energy, and nutritious food, enabling healthy and productive lives. On the other hand, household water insecurity is defined as the inability to access and utilise safe, reliable, and sufficient corresponding resources for a healthy life and good well-being [23]. Low access to food has been identified as a major contributing factor to chronic under-nutrition, which has been estimated to negatively impact on 793 million individuals globally [24]. Ensuring accessibility and ability to afford adequate and modern forms of household energy is crucial for maintaining public and individual health and well-being. Yet, millions of households globally lack access to clean energy sources [25]. Therefore, the concepts of water, energy and food securities include three key dimensions: availability, accessibility, and utilisation [26–29].

A single household has been identified as a unit of demand and is seen as the most appropriate component in influencing consumption practices [9]. Relevant to household resource use, a household comprises those who live and eat together. Household energy consumption is defined as the amount of energy spent on various household appliances, which include all energy type of use in the household [30]. In addition, household water consumption is characterised as the amount of water used for all usual household applications including drinking, food preparation, and bathing, as well as related household utility needs of the inhabitants [31]. Furthermore, the FAO [32] defined household food consumption as the entire sum of food available for consumption, which excludes the food taken outside except when prepared at home. Relevant to dietary diversity, household food consumption has been defined as the frequency of unique foods or categories of food consumed over a period of time, which has been considered as a measure to determine nutritional status [33]. A considerable proportion of water, energy, and food consumption in the municipalities can be ascribed to domestic use. For example, energy consumption at households in Nigeria and Burkina Faso account for approximately 65% and 75% of the overall consumption, respectively [34–36].

Many studies have assessed the relationship among water, energy, and food at the regional, national, and international levels. However, limited work has been undertaken on the interaction between water, energy, and food at the domestic level [9]. Individual constituents of the nexus have been examined in some research projects. Similarly, other studies [36–38] assessed individual elements such as water, energy, or food as a separate entity. Vieira et al. [37] evaluated the efficacy of household water utilisation. Furthermore, they linked household water efficiency and socio-demographic variables with each other. In addition, Ogwumike and Ozughalu [38] analysed household energy poverty and highlighted its implications for achieving sustainable development in Nigeria. They found that most Nigerian households did not have adequate access to clean energy sources. Moreover, Zouh et al. [34] evaluated the rural food security at household level in northern Pakistan. Their findings revealed that among some factors impacting on household food security, gender played a dominant role.

Effective and sustainable accessibility to safe and sufficient water, clean cooking energy, and healthy food is critical towards achieving sustainable development in any society [39–41]. According to the FAO [42], nutritious security can only be achieved when all people at all time have access to nutritious diets, comprising all vital nourishments and water, combined with sanitary environment and sufficient health services that guarantee a healthy and active life for all household members. Consequently, access to clean cooking fuels is paramount to a healthy and active life. Therefore, accessibility to these essential resources should be unbiased between urban and rural communities. Accessibility to water, energy, and food resources are driving forces in the urban–rural context. Their sources are basic commodities for both urban and rural communities in terms of household services [43–45]. The variability in household characteristics (family size, socio-economic variables, and seasonality) and appliances for water, energy, and food consumption patterns is enormous [46,47].

The main aim of this study is hence to examine the accessibility of water sources, cooking energy sources, and various food consumption patterns across the representative urban and rural households in Katsina state, north-western Nigeria. The objectives were to (a) explore the interplay of water–energy security and food consumption patterns towards achieving nutrition security; (b) examine effects of water and energy scarcities on nutrition and food security; (c) evaluate accessibility to various household food and consumption patterns; and (d) compare food consumption patterns related to accessibility to various sources of water and energy in urban and rural households. Given that 47% and 53% of the region's approximate 8.6 million people (as of 2020) live in urban and rural areas, respectively, and that their water, energy, and food accessibility situation reflects that of most of the urban and rural households of other sub-Saharan African regions, it is presumed that selecting Katsina state as a case study would make the findings also relevant to other regions, especially to those with similar socio-economic and ecological characteristics.

This research paper is structured as follows: Section 1 briefly introduces and reviews the scientific literature concerning the nexus at household scale. Section 2 describes the methodology, which consists of a full description of the materials and methods used to carry out the research, involving the study area description, conceptual framework, and selection of the surveyed communities; data collection; and statistical analysis. Section 3 is dedicated to the research findings, as well as the discussion of findings, which highlights the strong connection between water and energy security towards achieving nutrition and food security and lastly concludes the article.

2. Materials and Methods

2.1. Description of the Study Area

Katsina state is situated in the north-western part of Nigeria between latitude 11°08′ N and 13°22′, and longitude 6°52′ E and 9°20′ E, comprising an area of 23,938 km^2. This state has territorial boundaries with Kano and Jigawa states to the east, Kaduna state to the south, and Zamfara state to the west. The Republic of Niger is located to the north. The state is part of the large high plains of Hausa land [48].

Katsina is classified into two distinct climatic zones on the basis of seasonal variations and months: tropical continental and semi-arid continental. The state is characterised by a hot dry season between March and May, as well as a warm wet season between June and September. Generally, the annual rainfall figures diminish northwards. The extreme northern region of the state, which is categorised as Sahel Savannah zone, is an area characterised by low rainfall of between 501 and 700 mm. In the central region of Katsina state, which consists of the Sudan Savannah zone, the region is characterised by rainfall between 701 and 900 mm. The southern part of the state consists of the Guinea Savannah with rainfall above 900 mm (Figure 1). A less characteristic season is identified by decreasing rainfall and a gradual decrease in temperature during October and November. The months between December and February are characterised by a cold and dry (harmattan) season. The proportions of urban and rural populations within Katsina state were 47% and 53%, respectively, in 2019 [48].

2.2. Conceptual Framework

The study is based on an assessment of the interrelationships among the three household's essential resources, which are water, energy, and food. A generic conceptual framework provides a basic overview of potential pathways through which water and energy securities can have an impact on food security (Figure 2).

Household water and energy access influence cooking practices and dietary choices. The lack of access to safe and sufficient water sources and clean cooking energy can potentially negatively impact dietary choices, cooking practices, and sanitation. It can result in skipping meals and reduced cooking times by switching to food types that are less water and fuel demanding. Generally, a few of the major food types consumed in developing countries can be completely digested unless cooked. Protein-rich foods such as meat and beans are more water and energy demanding. Thus, the protein intake can be reduced when alternative faster cooking food types are chosen, resulting in unbalanced and poor nutrition. Water and energy scarcity can therefore influence the quantity, quality, and the type of food consumed and digested, and could be a cause of reduced nutrition leading to poor health conditions.

Lack of access to improved water and energy sources may lead to switches to inferior water and energy sources. Water and energy source ladders were designed as hierarchical relationships between household location and economic prosperity. Thus, poor access to improved water and clean energy compels households to come down from superior to inferior sources of various sources of water and energy. Consequently, consumption of insecure and inadequate water and increased air pollution leads to uncompromised health issues.

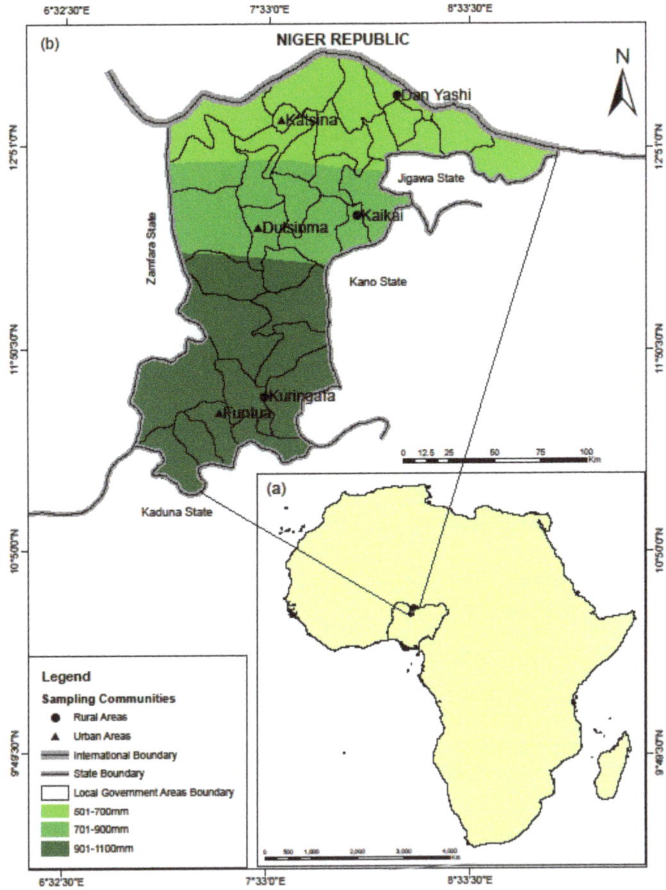

Figure 1. (**a**) Map of Africa showing Nigeria; and (**b**) map of the study area outlining the surveyed communities across the three isohyets.

Poor access to safe and sufficient water and clean energy sources may also lead to the reallocation of household resources from other productive activities and preparations for water and energy procurements. Water and energy scarcity may compel household members to spend less time on being productive, hence reducing income-earning activities. Insufficient income may be spent on water and fuel purchases rather than on nutritious food. Data on household consumption can be collected either by questionnaire administration or interviews consisting of retrospective questions, or by the use of a household diary where records on household consumption and expenditure on a daily basis are recorded. This diary method lessens the reliance on respondent's memory. However, data acquisition using the dairy method is particularly suitable for developed regions of the world where keeping records is part of the daily routines. In rural communities, where a substantial fraction of the population is illiterate, the diary method is likely to fail. Hence, the authors administered a questionnaire (see the Supplementary Materials), and interviews were conducted where necessary.

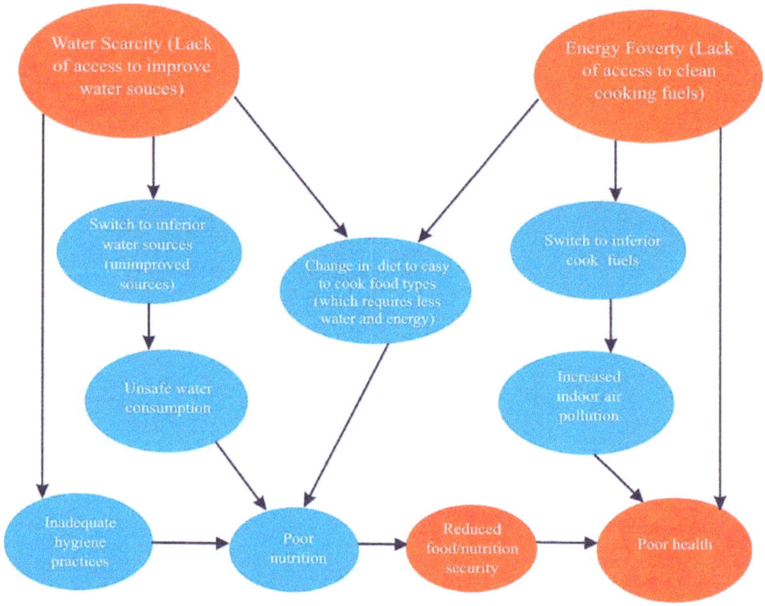

Figure 2. Links between household water and energy access on one side and nutrition and poor health on the other side.

2.3. Research Design

This study was undertaken in Katsina state located in north-western Nigeria. A stratified and random sampling technique was employed. The state has been stratified into urban and rural areas as adopted from the Katsina State Urban and Regional Planning Board format [49]. Three settlements were selected from each stratum representing urban and rural areas in the study area as indicated in Figure 1b.

The sample size was determined according to Isreal [50] at a 95% confidence level for each investigated community, which resulted in a total of 1785 respondents. Data on the number of households located in the case study region were not available. Therefore, household numbers in each of the targeted sampling communities were estimated by using an average of six persons per household as a standard, which has been estimated and adopted by the state Primary Health Care Development Agency in its routine immunisation programmes [51]. Furthermore, estimates informed the sampling frame, and then streets and households were selected for the administration of questionnaires (see the Supplementary Materials) across the respective communities (Table 1).

Table 1. Questionnaire distribution across the study area.

Stratum	Sampling Community	Estimated Population in 2019	Estimated Number of Households	Number of Questionnaires Administered
Urban	Katsina	714,543	119,090	400
	Dutsinma	78,275	13,682	390
	Funtua	190,092	31,682	397
Rural	Dan-Yashe	3914	652	242
	Kaikai	1179	197	134
	Kurigafaa	2874	479	222
Total		1,114,494	185,750	1785

The estimated population of the state in 2019 was about 8,613,100, out of which 47% (4,048,100) and 53% (4,565,000) were located in urban and rural areas, respectively.

2.4. Data Collection

Both primary and secondary data were utilised in this evaluation. The primary data were generated through the administration of structured and pre-tested questionnaires. The English version of the questionnaire was adapted and translated into Hausa, which is the main local language. The questionnaires were administered face-to-face by 16 field assistants, who are conversant with the local language and familiar to the respective sampling communities, in addition to receiving training in questionnaire administration. Furthermore, all conversations and interviews were performed using local languages. The designs of questionnaires and guides for interviews were in line with various standards covering sections on household characteristics and compositions as well as socioeconomic status [52].

2.5. Study Variable

The variable outputs of the study were household nutritional security related to households' water security. Food consumptions patterns (of mainly protein-containing food items, vegetables, and fruits) related to various water and energy sources across the respective households. To assess the nutritional security level, each household was asked about protein-containing foods (of mainly animal protein foods, which include meat, fish, and egg consumption) as well as vegetable and fruit consumption frequencies within a month using the Household Dietary Diversity Score for measuring household food access designed by Swindale et al. [53]. Questions related to the household nutritional status had three domain responses of either rare (consumption of one or twice per month), sometimes (consumption of 3 to 10 times per month), or often (consumption of more than 10 times per month) adopting the Household Food Insecurity Access Scale response [54]. In addition to questions related to nutrition, each household was also asked about household water and energy sources for cooking.

Water sources and sanitation facilities in the respective households were also classified as improved or unimproved sources adopting the WHO/UNICEF Joint Monitoring Programme for Water Supply, Sanitation and Hygiene classification [55]. In addition, and in line with the energy ladder concept promoted by World Health Organisation [56], energy sources were also classified as non-solid (clean) and solid (unclean) sources in this research.

2.6. Data Analysis

IBM SPSS (version 24) was selected to analyse data. To identify the proportion of household consumption for various food types as well as water and energy sources, descriptive statistics (percentages) were calculated. Person product moment correlations were applied to determine possible associations among protein-rich foods as well as vegetable and fruit consumption among the urban and rural dwellers. Chi-squared tests of independence were undertaken to determine whether food consumption as well as water and energy source usages at household level are dependent on location.

3. Results

3.1. Overview of Survey Findings

A total of 1785 households participated in the study; 1187 (66.5%) and 598 (33.5) of participants lived in urban and rural areas, respectively. Figure 3 reveals that 470 (39.6%) and 2 (0.3%) households often consume protein-rich foods in the surveyed communities of urban and rural strata, respectively. A total of 539 (45.4%) and 550 (92.0%) households in the urban and rural areas, respectively, rarely consume protein-rich foods. In addition, the study revealed that 546 urban and 59 rural households rarely consume vegetables and fruits, representing 46.0% and 9.9% in the areas, respectively. Furthermore, 158 (13.3%) and 191 (31.9%) households only sometimes consume vegetables and fruits in the corresponding urban and rural areas in this order. The results revealed that 40.7% and 58.2 of households often consume vegetables and fruits in the urban and rural households, respectively.

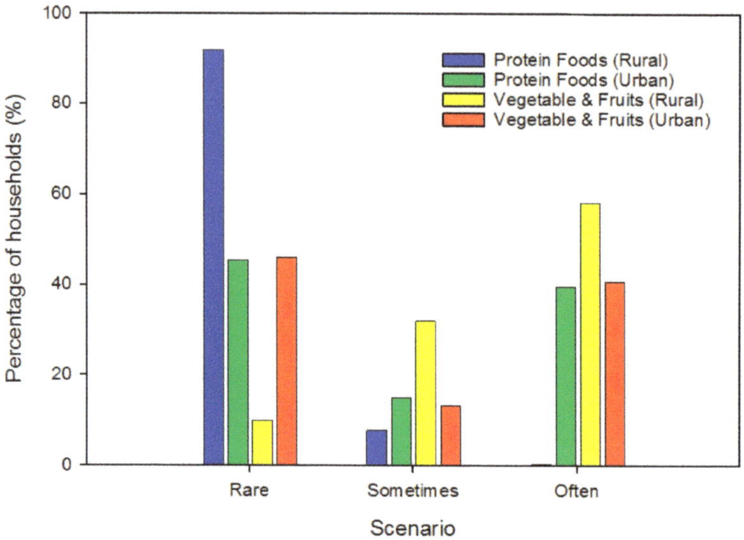

Figure 3. Consumption pattern of protein-rich foods and vegetables/fruits in the respective urban and rural households.

Results from the study revealed that high consumption of vegetables and fruits in the rural stratum (in contrary to low intake of protein-rich foods) was due to the local production of the commonly edible leafy vegetables that are mostly consumed either fresh or after storage using traditional preservation methods such as dehydration and drying. The most common leafy vegetables produced and consumed in rural areas include *Moringa oleifera*, *Leptadenia hastate*, *Cassia tora* (previously *Senna tora*), *Spinach oleracea*, and *Rumex acetosa*.

Okro (also known as ochro), tomatoes, onion, pumpkin, eggplant, and cucumber were among the non-leafy vegetables that are mostly consumed, while plum (prune) desert date (*Balanites aegyptiaca*), shea (*Vitellaria*), doum fruit (*Hyphaene thebaica*), African fan palm (*Barassus aethiopum*), jackalberry (*Diospyros mespiliformis*), sweet detar (*detarium senegalense*), and African locust bean (*Parkia biglobosa*) were local fruits consumed in addition to mango, cashew, and guava. In urban areas, bananas, orange, pineapples, apple, pawpaw, watermelon, and grapes constitute major fruits that are consumed in addition to those in rural areas. Furthermore, in urban areas, lettuce, carrots, green bean, cabbage, and avocado constitute major vegetables on top of vegetable types that are consumed in rural areas.

The chi-squared analyses for protein food consumption ($\chi^2 = 390.046$, $p = 0.00$) and vegetable/fruit consumption ($\chi^2 = 249.925$, $p = 0.01$) of the households indicated that the accessibility and utilisation of the various food types that constitute the nutritional standard of the household dietary pattern were statistically significant. To determine the strength and direction of association between protein-rich food and vegetable/fruit consumption, the Pearson product moment correlation (PPMC) r was calculated. Concerning urban stratum, the Pearson's r data analysis indicated that there is a strong association ($r = 0.988$). On the other hand, a weak association was revealed in the rural stratum ($r = 0.146$). However, the p-value for both was less than 0.05, indicating significance of the measure of association.

3.2. Effect of Water and Energy Scarcities on Households' Cooking Habits

Our findings uncovered households' water and energy scarcities as the influencing factor determining the households' nutritional and health status. The study conceptual framework (Figure 1) demonstrates the inter-linkages between water and energy scarcities and food security. Moreover, the study indicated that scarce water and energy supplies affected the pattern and preference of food consumption across the urban and rural households. Findings from the study on the consequences of water and energy scarcities were reduced cooking sessions and eating inadequately cooked foods. Foods rich in essential nutrients but which require more water and cooking fuels such as beans and cowpeas were avoided due to water and energy scarcities.

The study further revealed that 52.3% and 54.8% of the urban households responded that water and energy scarcities, respectively, affect the pattern and preference of food intake. The study further revealed that for the rural households, 76.2% and 42.1% responded that water and energy scarcities, respectively, affect the pattern and preference of food intake.

Table 2 indicates a variety of coping strategies adopted in the events of water and energy scarcities. There is a significant ($p < 0.005$) difference between urban and rural strata in the strategies adopted. The table revealed that in an event of water scarcity, various coping strategies were adopted to save water and cooking fuels across the affected households; 29.2% and 31.9% of the households in the urban and rural households, respectively, cooked single meals, and 34.3% and 45.2% of the surveyed households in the urban and rural households, respectively, cooked composite meals. A composite meal is made up of many different food types such as lasagne. The table further revealed that 36.5% and 22.9% prepared meals with less water requirements in the urban and rural households, respectively, to save water in the households.

Table 2. Effects of water and energy scarcities on food consumption patterns and nutrition in the urban and rural households, respectively.

Stratum	Reason for Meal Cooked	Proportion of Type of Meal Cooked (%)				
		Single Meals	Composite Meals	Cooked Meals That Require Less Water	Cooked Meals That Require Less Energy	Total
Urban	Save water	29.2	34.3	36.5	-	52.3
	Save cooking energy	31.1	32.9	-	36.0	54.8
Rural	Save water	31.9	45.2	22.9	-	76.2
	Save cooking energy	19.4	52.7	-	27.9	42.1

Moreover, the findings show that similar coping strategies in an event of energy scarcity were adopted. Table 2 shows that 31.1% and 31.9% in the urban and rural households, respectively, cooked a single meal, 32.9% and 57.7% prepared composite meals, and 36.0 and 27.9% cooked meals that require less energy requirement to save on cooking fuels.

The findings revealed that more than 60% of respondents preferred cooked meals that require less water and energy including roots and tuber crops (such as potatoes, cassava (also known as manioc), cocoyam (also called dasheen), and yam (various species of the genus *Dioscorea*)). Furthermore, a disparity between urban and rural households exists, whereby a high proportion of Irish potato and yam are consumed in urban households, whereas cassava, sweet potato, and cocoyam are highly consumed in the rural counterparts. In addition, the food called fura (millet ball or millet porridge) was found to be widely prepared and consumed in the rural areas; it is a culturally popular meal requiring composite cooking (prepared from cereals, mostly millet, and commonly mixed with milk). This traditional food (often characterised as a drink as well) is rich in both carbohydrates and minerals, being seen as the most common food in rural communities. It is often consumed during every mealtime of the day.

3.3. Household Feeding Habits, Nutritional Disorder, and Poor Health Conditions

Data from local health clinics in the urban and rural communities revealed the following common prevalent nutritional disorders in children, respectively: kwashiorkor (23% and 42.7%), marasmus (12% and 26%), and rickets (3.2% and 4.6%). Although there were no empirical data available, the noticeable lack of nutritious foods in routine diets could be a principal factor in the nutrition disorders identified at the local health clinics. For instance, the prevalence of kwashiorkor among children, especially in the rural households, seems to be partly due to vitamin-deficient but carbohydrate-rich food such as fura.

3.4. Households' Water Sources Related to Protein-Rich Food as Well as Vegetable and Fruit Consumption

Access to secure, sufficient, and dependable sources of household water supply is crucial. Table 3 shows different kinds of household water sources related to protein-rich food in the respective urban and rural communities. The data indicate a variety of water sources for domestic use in the study. The chi-squared analyses for access to various household water sources related to various food consumption patterns ($\chi^2 = 417.840$) across the urban and rural surveyed households indicated that there is a significant ($p < 0.005$) difference among the urban and rural dwellers.

Table 3. Frequency of protein-rich food related to household water sources in urban and rural areas.

Water Source	**Urban Scenario**						**Rural Scenario**					
	Rare		**Sometimes**		**Often**		**Rare**		**Sometimes**		**Often**	
	Freq.	**%**	**Freq.**	**%**	**Freq.**	**%**	**Freq.**	**%**	**Freq.**	**%**	**Freq.**	**%**
Piped water into dwelling	-	-	16	9.0	17	3.6	-	-	-	-	-	-
Piped water to yard		-	1	0.6	27	5.7	-	-	-	-	-	-
Public tap	7	1.2	4	2.2	-	-	-	-	-	-	-	-
Private borehole	-	-	25	14.0	315	67.0	-	-	-	-	1	50.0
Public borehole	86	16.0	7	4.0	14	3.0	59	10.7	22	47.8	1	50.0
Protected dug well	51	9.5	12	6.7	3	0.6	20	3.6	16	34.8	-	-
Unprotected dug well	118	21.9	2	1.1	-	-	93	16.9	3	6.5	-	-
Water vendor	203	37.7	77	43.3	86	18.3	167	30.4	3	6.5	-	-
Surface water	-	-	-	-	-	-	67	12.2	2	4.3	-	-
Tanker truck	74	13.7	34	19.1	8	1.7	144	26.2	-	-	-	-
Total	539	100	178	100	470	100	550	100	46	100	2	100

The study revealed that privately or publicly owned boreholes are found across the scenarios in the respective urban and rural strata. In urban strata, the overall use of boreholes witnessed an upward trend across the three scenarios, whereas the utilisation level of water vendor use as a source of household water supply fluctuated. An initial increase was followed by a rapid decrease across the scenarios. There was a drastic rise of urban household-owned private boreholes from 14.0% to 67.0% for households that occasionally and often consume protein-rich foods. Piped water to the yard had the lowest proportion (0.6%) of utilisation in the urban strata. Meanwhile, for the rural stratum, the utilisation level of public boreholes at various households increased significantly across the scenarios.

Table 4 shows the utilisation levels of different sources of household water supply in relation to vegetable and fruit consumption in the respective urban and rural areas.

Sources of domestic water supply related to vegetable and fruit consumption in urban areas follow the same pattern compared to those related to protein-rich food intake in the same area, whereas a disparity exists in rural areas. Water vendors and tanker trucks are major sources of water supply across the three scenarios in rural areas. Unlike the common scenario of protein-rich food consumption, where boreholes as improved sources of water supply are utilised, a variety of water sources are used by households that often consume vegetables and fruits. The lowest utilisation level of private boreholes was 0.3%, whereas the level was 18.7% for public boreholes. An unprotected dug well was found to be at the highest level of utilisation for the often scenario at 19.8% of the rural stratum. High proportions (67.0% and 65.0%) of private boreholes (an improved water source) was found for the often scenario for protein-rich food as well as vegetable and fruit consumption, respectively, in the urban areas. In rural areas, the study revealed a similar trend in the respective rural areas, where the highest (100%) proportion of boreholes (50% of private borehole and 50% of public borehole usage) was found within the often scenario of protein-rich food intake.

Table 4. Frequency of the intake of vegetables and fruits related to household water sources in urban and rural areas.

Water Source	Urban Scenario						Rural Scenario					
	Rare		Sometimes		Often		Rare		Sometimes		Often	
	Freq.	%	Freq.	%	Freq.	%	Freq.	%	Freq.	%	Freq.	%
Piped water into dwelling	-	-	1	0.6	32	6.6	-	-	-	-	-	-
Piped water to yard	-	-	1	0.6	27	5.6	-	-	-	-	-	-
Public tap	7	1.2	4	2.5	-	-	-	-	-	-	-	-
Private borehole	-	-	26	16.5	314	65.0	-	-	-	-	1	0.3
Public borehole	86	15.8	8	5.1	13	2.7	2	3.4	15	7.9	65	18.7
Protected dug well	51	9.3	12	7.6	-	-	-	-	1	0.5	35	10.1
Unprotected dug well	118	21.6	2	1.3	3	0.6	8	13.6	19	9.9	69	19.8
Water vendor	210	38.5	70	44.3	86	17.8	30	50.8	76	39.8	64	18.4
Surface water	-	-	-	-	-	-	3	5.1	4	2.1	62	17.8
Tanker truck	74	13.6	34	21.5	8	1.7	16	27.1	76	39.8	52	14.9
Total	546	100	158	100	483	100	59	100	191	100	348	100

Furthermore, higher proportions of unimproved sources, including 37.7% and 38.5% of water vendors (usually equipped with a cart and small drum), and 21.9% and 21.6% of unprotected dug wells, were found for the rare scenario of protein-rich food and vegetable/fruit consumption, respectively, in urban areas. In rural communities, the study revealed similar trends of higher proportions of unimproved water source usage among various households that rarely consume protein-rich foods, vegetables, and fruits. Water vendors (30.4% and 50.8%), tanker trucks (26.2% and 27.1%), and unprotected dug wells (13.6% and 16.9%) were utilised as sources of household water supply for protein-rich food as well as vegetable and fruit consumptions, respectively.

3.5. Household Sanitation Facilities Related to Protein-Rich Food as Well as Vegetable and Fruit Consumption

Tables 5 and 6 demonstrate utilisation levels of various sanitation facilities in relation to protein-rich food and vegetable/fruit consumption, respectively, in the urban and rural areas. Sanitation facilities related to protein-rich food intake in urban areas follow similar patterns to those related to vegetable and fruit consumption in the same area, whereas a disparity exists in rural areas. Overall household sanitation facility use related to protein-rich food intake the study shows that there is a significant ($p < 0.005$) difference between urban and rural strata. Similarly, related to vegetable and fruit consumption, a significant difference in sanitation facilities between urban and rural households exists ($p < 0.005$).

The chi-squared analyses for access to various sanitation facilities related to various food consumption patterns ($\chi^2 = 594.259$) across the urban and rural surveyed households indicated that there is a significant ($p < 0.005$) difference among the urban and rural dwellers. Improved sanitation facilities including septic tanks and pit latrines with slabs were found across the three scenarios of protein-rich foods, vegetable consumption, and fruit consumption. However, pit latrines without slabs, which are categorised as an unimproved sanitation facility, were also found across the three scenarios in the urban communities. Table 6 shows a progressive increase of septic tanks from 0.9% for the rare scenario to 32.9% for the sometimes scenario and subsequently to 92.1% for the often scenario with respect to both vegetable and fruit consumption. In the case of protein-rich food intake, Table 5 illustrates a progressive increase of septic tank utilisation from 38.2% for the sometimes scenario to 92.3% for the often scenario, while for the rare scenario, no septic tank was found.

Table 5. Frequency of protein-rich food related to household sanitation facilities in urban and rural areas.

Sanitation Facilities	Urban Scenario						Rural Scenario					
	Rare		Sometimes		Often		Rare		Sometimes		Often	
	Freq.	%	Freq.	%	Freq.	%	Freq.	%	Freq.	%	Freq.	%
Septic tank	-	-	68	38.2	434	92.3	-	-	-	-	1	50.0
Pit latrine with slab	319	59.1	90	50.6	24	5.1	89	16.2	46	100	1	50.0
Pit latrine without slab	219	40.6	20	11.2	12	2.6	440	80.0	-	-	-	-
No facility (open defecation)	1	0.2	-	-	-	-	21	3.8	-	-	-	-
Totals	539	100	178	100	470	100	550	100	46	100	2	100

Table 6. Frequency of intake of vegetables and fruits related to household sanitation facilities in urban and rural areas.

Water Source	Urban Scenario						Rural Scenario					
	Rare		Sometimes		Often		Rare		Sometimes		Often	
	Freq.	%	Freq.	%	Freq.	%	Freq.	%	Freq.	%	Freq.	%
Septic tank	5	0.9	52	32.9	445	92.1	-	-	-	-	1	0.3
Pit latrine with slab	320	58.6	87	55.1	26	5.4	7	11.9	23	12.0	106	30.5
Pit latrine without slab	220	40.3	19	12.0	12	2.5	45	76.2	158	82.7	237	68.1
No facility (open defecation)	1	0.2	-	-	-	-	7	11.9	10	5.2	4	1.1
Total	546	100	158	100	483	100	59	100	191	100	158	100

Table 5 shows a drastic decrease in utilisation pattern of pit latrines with and without slabs related to protein-rich food and vegetable/fruit consumptions across the three scenarios. A decrease of pit latrines with slabs and without slabs from 59.1% and 40.6% for the rare scenario to 5.1% and 2.6%, respectively, for the often scenario concerning protein-rich food consumption in urban areas was observed. Additionally, the respective decreases of pit latrines with and without slabs follow similar patterns in relation to vegetable and fruit consumptions. For the rare scenario, 58.8% and 40.3% of pit latrines with slabs and without slabs, respectively, were found. Regarding the often scenario, 5.4% and 2.5% of pit latrines with and without slabs, respectively, were recorded. These show a significant drop across the three scenarios in urban communities.

In rural communities, the utilisation of sanitation facilities related to protein-rich food intake follows different patterns to those related to vegetable/fruit consumption. Pit latrines with slabs (an improved facility) were found across the three scenarios of protein-rich food consumption. In relation to vegetable/fruit consumption, various types of sanitation facilities, which include pit latrine with slab, open defecation (no facility), and pit latrine without slab, have the highest level of utilisation across the three scenarios. In contrast, septic tanks were only found for the often scenario. In relation to protein consumption, different utilisation levels of sanitation facilities were found. There was a significant increase of pit latrines with slabs from 16.2% for the rare scenario to 100% for the sometimes scenario, while for the often scenario, the utilisation level of pit latrines with slabs dropped to 50%. In addition, 50% of septic tank utilisation was witnessed for the rare scenario of protein-rich food consumption. The highest proportion of unimproved sanitation household-level facilities was found for the rare scenario: 3.8% without sanitation facility (open defecation) and 40.6% of pit latrines without slabs.

3.6. Household Energy Sources Related to Protein-Rich Food as Well as Vegetable and Fruit Consumption

The chi-squared analyses for access to various household cooking fuels related to different food consumption patterns ($\chi^2 = 555.592$) across the urban and rural surveyed households indicated that there is a significant ($p < 0.005$) difference among the urban and rural dwellers. Tables 7 and 8 indicate a great variety of household energy utilisation across the three scenarios in the respective urban and rural strata. Overall, the utilisation of fuelwood witnessed a downward trend across the scenarios in urban stratum, whereas the utilisation level of cooking gas witnessed an upward trend from households that sometimes consume vegetables and fruits as well as protein-rich foods compared to the often scenarios. In relation to vegetable/fruit consumption, fuel wood utilisation was found to be 91.9%, 62.0%, and 15.9% for the rare, sometimes, and often scenarios, respectively. Similar trends were also found related to protein-rich food intake, where 92.0%, 65.2%, and 13.8% were recorded for the rare, sometimes, and often scenarios. In terms of cooking gas utilisation across the three scenarios, the highest level of utilisation (82.6%) was recorded for the often scenario, followed by 29.2% for the sometimes scenario. The findings also revealed that the majority of households in the rural stratum utilised fuel wood as a household energy source for cooking across the three scenarios of protein-rich food consumption; the highest level of utilisation (67.8%) was found for both the rare and often scenarios, and 65.4% was recorded for the sometimes scenario. Electricity and kerosene were utilised only in urban areas. Only 3.2% and 3.1% of households used electricity as a source of household energy for cooking concerning the often scenario in the urban stratum for protein-rich food and vegetable/fruit intakes, respectively. In addition, 0.6% and 0.4% of households that occasionally and often consume protein-rich food utilised kerosene as a source of cooking energy, respectively. Furthermore, dung was only utilised in rural areas, with the highest level of utilisation (11.9%) for the rare scenario, followed by 3.6% for the sometimes scenario concerning vegetable/fruit intake. Only 2.4% of dung utilisation was recorded for the rare scenario regarding protein-rich food consumption in rural areas.

Table 7. Frequency of protein-rich food intake related to urban and rural energy sources.

Energy Source	Urban Scenario						Rural Scenario					
	Rare		Sometimes		Often		Rare		Sometimes		Often	
	Freq.	%	Freq.	%	Freq.	%	Freq.	%	Freq.	%	Freq.	%
Electricity	-	-			15	3.2	-	-	-	-	-	-
Gas	-	-	52	29.2	388	82.6	-	-	-	-		-
Kerosene	-	-	1	0.6	2	0.4	-	-	-	-	-	-
Charcoal	25	4.6	8	4.5	-	-	9	1.6	2	4.3	-	-
Sawdust	3	0.6	1	0.6	-	-	-	-	-	-	-	-
Fuel wood	496	92.0	116	65.1	65	13.8	363	66.0	36	78.3	2	100
Agricultural residue	15	2.8	-	-	-	-	165	30.0	8	17.4	-	-
Dung	-	-	-	-	-	-	13	2.4	-	-	-	-
Total	539	100	178	100	470	100	550	100	46	100	2	100

Table 7 shows a slight decrease in charcoal utilisation across the scenarios in the urban stratum, whereas an upward trend of charcoal use was recorded in the rural stratum across the scenarios for protein-rich food consumption. Results within each stratum showed 4.6% and 1.6% for rare cases as well as 4.5% and 4.3% for the sometimes scenario in the urban and rural strata, respectively. Table 8 shows similar patterns among various households in relation to protein-rich food consumption and vegetable/fruit intake in the urban stratum, whereas a disparity exists among various households located in the rural stratum. Only 3.2% of charcoal utilisation was found for the often scenario consumption in rural areas.

Table 8. Intake of vegetables and fruits related to urban and rural energy sources.

Energy Source	Urban Scenario						Rural Scenario					
	Rare		Sometimes		Often		Rare		Sometimes		Often	
	Freq.	%	Freq.	%	Freq.	%	Freq.	%	Freq.	%	Freq.	%
Electricity	-	-	-	-	15	3.1	-	-	-	-	-	-
Gas	-	-	51	32.3	389	80.5	-	-	-	-	-	-
Kerosene	-	-	1	0.6	2	0.4	-	-	-	-	-	-
Charcoal	26	4.8	7	4.4	-	-	-	-	-	-	11	3.2
Sawdust	3	0.5	1	0.6	-	-	-	-	-	-	-	-
Fuel wood	502	91.9	98	62.0	77	16.0	40	67.8	125	65.4	236	67.8
Agricultural residue	15	2.7	-	-	-	-	12	20.3	60	31.4	101	29.0
Dung	-	-	-	-	-	-	7	11.9	6	3.1	-	-
Total	456	100	158	100	483	100	59	100	191	100	158	100

A significant downward trend of dung use was witnessed for the rural stratum across the rare and sometimes scenarios for vegetable/fruit consumption. For the rare case, 11.9% was recorded, while 3.1% was found for the sometimes scenario. In addition, only 2.4% of dung utilisation was recorded for the rare scenario concerning protein-rich food intake.

The findings revealed an energy switch from fuelwood to either agricultural residue or dung in the study area as a result of reduced access to forest resources. This is the case as most forests in the study area are serving as camping sites for insurgent groups that kidnap people and lunch attacks on the local population.

In contrast to dung, only 0.5% and 0.6% of sawdust use was noted for the rare and sometimes scenarios, respectively, in the urban areas. The study shows that the overwhelming majority of households that rarely consume protein-rich foods utilise solid (unclean) cooking energy sources.

4. Discussion

Good nutrition is an essential component of a healthy and productive life [57,58]. Nahla et al. [57,59] proposed that with regard to availability, accessibility, utilisation, and stability of food, nutrition should also form an integral part of all pillars of food security. Various food types that are associated with rich protein content are associated with eminent beneficial effects. In addition to molecule transport, protein helps in building and repair of cells.

Jager et al. [60] indicated that for building and maintaining mass muscles, an overall daily protein intake of between 1.4 and 2.0 g/kg body weight is required. Additionally, vegetables and fruits are regarded as a best source of fibre, minerals, and nutrients. Fibre intake is linked to lower incidences of cardiovascular diseases and obesity. Minerals and vitamins supplied from vegetables and fruits to diets are sources of phytochemicals that serve as antioxidants and anti-inflammatory agents [60,61]. In addition, Noorwali et al. [62] attributed a substantial weight of global disease and mortality to a low intake of vegetables and fruits. Moreover, Micha [63] identified dietary intake as a major factor associated with mortality from various cardiovascular-related diseases. In order to achieve food security at a household level, the quality of food consumed has to be considered. This is determined by the nutritional value of the food, in addition to the physical availability of food items.

The type of cooking in relation to the corresponding nutrient release and the overall appeal of the food can never be over-emphasised [64,65]. From work conducted in the camps for internally displaced people, it was eminent that while cooking diminishes disease prevalence, improves nutrition, and enhances food taste, the fuel necessary for cooking the hard-to-cook food (usually maize and beans) is not easily within reach, and the task of obtaining fuel for cooking is placed on women and children [66]. Thus, the choice of women to under-cook meals to save water and cooking fuels leads to an increase in the threat of food-borne illnesses. Therefore, the increasing scarcity of water and cooking fuels are likely to lead to families consuming less nutritious or even under-cooked meals. These findings are coincided by those of Sola et al. [67,68], who noted that diminishing availability of cooking fuel affects nutrition security.

In line with the Household Food Insecurity Access Scale response based on the three scenarios of food consumption [54], there were 39.4% and 0.3% of households that were nutrition-secure in urban and rural areas, respectively. In comparison, more households were severely nutrition-insecure: 45.4% of the urban and 9.9% of the rural households. Significant differences between urban and rural communities related to their nutritional status were found. The findings support several studies [69–72], which found great disparity in the nutritional status between urban and rural residences in various low- and medium-income countries. Consumption patterns in urban households were characterised by a high frequency of availability concerning dairy products and meat intake, which is contrary to rural households. In addition, Walbel and Hohfeld [73–76] found that undernutrition continues to be a challenge in rural areas. They found that various socio-economic factors such as income, educational status, employment, location, and food prices are the main factors influencing undernutrition.

On the basis of the WHO/UNICEF Joint Monitoring Programme for Water Supply and Sanitation classification of water sources [55], the study showed a significant association between the food consumption pattern and various water sources across the strata. High proportions of improved sources were found at the often scenario for protein-rich food and vegetable/fruit consumption, respectively. The findings revealed strong relationships between nutrition and access to safe and sufficient water in the study area, which coincides with similar findings by Li et al. [77]. Their study indicated that improved water sources decreased child malnutrition. Furthermore, Mabhaudhi et al. [78] attributed inadequate poor nutrition to water scarcity in poor sub-Saharan rural communities. Additionally, Mbwana et al. [79] attributed distance to a household water source among the significant determinants of nutrition status in the Dodoma rural community of Tanzania.

Gao et al. [80] investigated the links among household water, dietary diversity, and nutrition status in poor rural households of central and western China. They found that access to unimproved water sources was connected to lower likelihood of achieving dietary diversity. In addition, water inaccessibility shapes nutritional intake well beyond the cleanliness of the corresponding physical environment via many other non-production pathways, which include preparation of food techniques and dietary diversity [81]. The majority of households that access groundwater through private boreholes are high-income earners living in urban areas. The capacity to drill private boreholes for household water supply is within the financial reach of such individuals [82]. The findings reveal that the majority of public boreholes are constructed by the state government, especially in rural communities. This could be attributed to the fact that most rural areas in the state are not linked up with piped water. Generally, the study revealed a high utilisation of various sources of groundwater, which is comparable to findings in other low-income regions of South-East Asia, where groundwater sources play a critical role as sources for drinking water [83].

This study compares well with findings by Waibel and Hohfeld [73], who found that poor sanitation practices among other factors are linked to under-nutrition in various rural households of Vietnam. Furthermore, the study was in line with the work of Spears and Haddad [84]. Their findings reveal strong relationships between nutrition and sanitation. They found that the overwhelming majority of stunted children (reduced in their growth development) in India were found in various households with no sanitation facilities (open defecation). Furthermore, Mahmud and Mbuya [85] linked poor sanitation to diarrhoea, which consequently leads to undernutrition and compromises child growth. Their nutritional status has a significant relationship with water, sanitation, and hygiene (also known as WASH) practices. Chattopadhyay et al. [86] revealed that open defecation and non-use of sanitary napkins (menstrual pads) were among the key predicators of stunting among the adolescence girls in eastern India. Therefore, proper sanitation and hygiene can support good nutrition and reduce stunting in children and teenagers. Additionally, Zavala et al. [87] and Momberg [88] associated the nutritional status including stunting with access to water and sanitation facilities.

The strong link between food security and energy has been established by FAO [89]. The inaccessibility to enough and suitable energy sources for cooking may compel people to change their cooking and eating practices by shifting to foods that demand less energy and cooking time or by reducing the number of meals. In addition, a direct linkage between household cooking energy and food security is shown by Makungwa et al. [90]. They suggested that food security cannot be achieved without due consideration of availability and accessibility of cooking energy of vulnerable households. A high proportion of charcoal utilisation in the urban stratum coincides with studies conducted by Ajoa [91]. In comparison, Win et al. [92] revealed a higher level of charcoal utilisation in various developing countries for urban compared to rural areas.

This suggests that nutrition security cannot be achieved without access to clean energy sources [93]. Consequently, Amare et al. [94] found a link between unsuitable household cooking energy sources and malnutrition among children. They discovered that children in households with conventional (solid) cooking fuel types were more likely to be stunted compared to those with non-solid (cleaner) types. Furthermore, ensuring a provision of clean energy source is a prerequisite for reducing food insecurity for the overwhelming majority of the sub-Saharan African population [67].

5. Conclusions

The interrelationships between household food consumption patterns as well as water and energy security among urban and rural households were assessed. The proposed generic framework was successfully tested in Katsina state, northern Nigeria. The study revealed that scarcities of water and cooking energy resulted in changes in cooking habits, whereby households decided to cook composite meals contrary to single meals. Households also reduced their cooking sessions from the usual three meals per day to two, or sometimes only one meal per day. Foods with shorter cooking times were favoured to those that took longer to cook. This was due to firewood scarcity. This compromised the nutritional status of especially children.

The study further revealed that there is a clear dichotomy between urban and rural households on food consumption patterns as well as sanitation facilities and sources of water and energy. Protein-rich food consumption patterns were the strong determinants on the various sources of water and energy use. A high consumption of protein-rich foods was highly associated with the utilisation of improved water and clean energy sources in urban households. Similarly, a low consumption frequency of protein-rich foods in rural areas was strongly associated with a high utilisation level of unimproved sources of water and sanitation facilities and unclean (solid) energy. The findings show that those households that often consume protein-rich foods are associated with 66.7% of private boreholes, 92.3% of septic tanks as sanitation facilities, and 82.6% use of liquefied petroleum gas as a source of cooking energy with respect to urban households. In comparison, for rural communities, the findings show 30.4% of water vendor use, 80.0% of pit latrines without slabs, and 66.0% of fuel wood utilisation for households that rarely consume protein-rich foods. Overall, the questionnaire produced results that validated the study conceptual framework, revealing the effects of water and energy scarcities on food and nutritional security. This led to both poor nutrition and health.

6. Limitations and Future Research

The community census data including household numbers have not been published previously, but are available from the Katsina state office of the National Population Commission. Furthermore, household numbers in the communities were also estimated on the basis of data from the World Health Organisation for the study area. Consequently, the projections in our paper are limited by available support data.

A vast majority of the rural inhabitants in Katsina state are facing the ever-increasing threat of banditry, a type of organised crime that includes murder, rape, kidnapping, and cattle rustling. Therefore, these circumstances have limited access to more households as the security of our survey team could not be guaranteed.

Data collected on the households' food security were only related to the nutritional status of mainly protein, vegetable, and fruit consumption and their associations with various households' water–energy source utilisation level. Other elements of food security, which include availability, accessibility, and stability, could also have been more incorporated in the study. Therefore, future studies should take into account other elements of food security. Moreover, the research should be extended and continued to other low- and middle-income developing countries to evaluate the progress towards achieving sustainable food–energy–water security.

Supplementary Materials: The following supporting information can be downloaded at https://www.mdpi.com/article/10.3390/su14084478/su14084478/s1, Questionnaire.

Author Contributions: Conceptualisation, Y.S. and M.S.; methodology, Y.S. and M.S.; investigation, Y.S.; formal analysis, Y.S.; writing the original draft, Y.S.; visualisation, Y.S.; writing, review and editing, M.S.; supervision, M.S. All authors have read and agreed to the published version of the manuscript.

Funding: This research was funded by the Tertiary Education Tax Fund (TETFUND), Nigeria.

Institutional Review Board Statement: Ethical review and approval were waived for this study by the local authorities and community leaders in Nigeria.

Informed Consent Statement: Informed consent was obtained from all subjects involved in the study.

Data Availability Statement: Not applicable.

Acknowledgments: Aminu Yahaya El-Ladan supported the data curation and helped with the statistical analysis. Practical contributions by Nura Umar and other field assistants are acknowledged. We would like to thank for the support by Katsina state Government, the local authorities, and the traditional leaders in the respective investigated communities.

Conflicts of Interest: The authors declare that they have no known competing financial interest or personal relationships that could have appeared to influence the work reported on in this paper.

References

1. Biggs, E.M.; Bruce, E.; Boruff, B.; Duncan, J.M.A.; Horsley, J.; Pauli, N.; McNeill, K.; Neef, A.; Van Ogtrop, F.; Curnow, J.; et al. Sustainable development and the water–energy–food nexus: A Perspective on Livelihoods. *Environ. Sci. Policy* **2015**, *54*, 389–397. [CrossRef]
2. Hoff, H. Understanding the nexus. In Proceedings of the Bonn 2011 Conference. The Water, Energy and Food Security Nexus, Bonn, Germany, 11 November 2011; pp. 16–18.
3. Bonn Nexus Conference. *The Water Energy and Food Security Nexus Solutions for the Green Economy: Bonn Germany*; Stockholm Environment Institute: Stockholm, Sweden, 2011.
4. Rasul, G.; Sharma, B. The nexus approach to water–energy–food security: An Option for Adaptation to Climate Change. *Clim. Policy* **2016**, *16*, 682–702. [CrossRef]
5. Petrariu, R.; Constantin, M.; Dinu, M.; Pătărlăgeanu, S.R.; Deaconu, M.E. Water, Energy, Food, Waste Nexus: Between Synergy and Trade-Offs in Romania Based on Entrepreneurship and Economic Performance. *Energies* **2021**, *14*, 5172. [CrossRef]
6. Nkiaka, E.; Okpara, U.T.; Okumah, M. Food-energy-water security in sub-Saharan Africa: Quantitative and Spatial Assessments using an Indicator-Based Approach. *Environ. Dev.* **2021**, *40*, 100655. [CrossRef]
7. Li, J.; Cui, J.; Sui, P.; Yue, S.; Yang, J.; Lv, Z.; Wang, D.; Chen, X.; Sun, B.; Ran, M.; et al. Valuing the Synergy in the Water-Energy-Food Nexus for Cropping Systems: A Case in the North China Plain. *Ecol. Indic.* **2021**, *127*, 107741. [CrossRef]
8. Bazilian, M.; Rogner, H.; Howells, M.; Hermann, S.; Arent, D.; Gielen, D.; Steduto, P.; Mueller, A.; Komor, P.; Tol, R.; et al. Considering the energy, water and food nexus: Towards an Integrated Modelling Approach. *Energy Policy* **2011**, *39*, 7896–7906. [CrossRef]
9. FAO. *The Water-Energy-Food Nexus: A New Approach in Support of Food Security and Sustainable Agriculture*; Food and Agriculture Organization of the United Nations: Rome, Italy, 2014.
10. Hussein, W.A.; Memon, F.A.; Savic, D.A. An integrated model to evaluate water-energy-food nexus at a household scale. *Environ. Model. Softw.* **2017**, *93*, 366–380. [CrossRef]

11. World Economic Forum. *Water Security: The Water-Food-Energy-Climate Nexus*; Island Press: Washington, DC, USA, 2011.
12. Dos Santos, S.; Adams, E.; Neville, G.; Wada, Y.; de Sherbinin, A.; Mullin, B.E.; Adamo, S. Urban growth and water access in sub-Saharan Africa: Progress, Challenges and Emerging Research Directions. *Sci. Total Environ.* **2014**, *607*, 497. [CrossRef]
13. Warner, K.; Jones, G. Environment and population in sub-Saharan Africa: Energy for Four Billions? *Environments* **2018**, *5*, 107. [CrossRef]
14. Chauvin, N.D.; Mulangu, F.; Porto, G. *Food Production and Consumption Trends in Sub-Saharan Africa: Prospects for the Transformation of the Agricultural Sector*; United Nations Development Program, WP 2012-011; Regional Bureau for Africa: New York City, NY, USA, 2012.
15. Blackett, I.; Hawkins, P.; Heymans, C. *The Missing Link in Sanitation Service Delivery: A Review of Fecal Sludge Management in 12 Cities*; Water and Sanitation Program Research Brief; World Bank: Washington, DC, USA, 2014.
16. Adukia, A. Sanitation and Education. *Am. Econ. J. Appl. Econ.* **2017**, *9*, 23–59. [CrossRef]
17. NIMET, State of the Climate in Nigeria. *The Weather and Climate Research Centre*; Nigerian Meteorological Agency: Abuja, Nigeria, 2021.
18. FAO. *The State of Food Insecurity in the World*; Food and Agricultural Organisation (FAO) of the United Nations: Rome, Italy, 2015.
19. Nwa, E.U. *History of Irrigation, Drainage and Flood Control in Nigeria from Precolonial Time to 1999*; Spectrum Books Limited: Ibadan, Nigeria, 2003.
20. Abdulrashid, L.; Yahaya, Z.I. Communities Pattern of Fuel Wood Exploitation and the Perceived Impact of Afforestation Programme in Northern Katsina State, Nigeria. *Int. J. Innov. Hum. Ecol. Nat. Stud.* **2018**, *6*, 5–25.
21. Adeyanju, G.C.; Osobajo, O.A.; Otitoju, A.; Ajide, O. Exploring the potentials, barriers and option for support in the Nigeria renewable energy industry. *Discov. Sustain.* **2020**, *1*, 7. [CrossRef]
22. World Bank. Press Release No: 2021/088/AFR. 2021. Available online: https://www.worldbank.org/en/news/press-release/2021/02/05/nigeria-to-improve-electricity-access-and-services-to-citizens (accessed on 23 February 2022).
23. Oyedepo, S.O. Energy and sustainable development in Nigeria: The Way Forward. *Energy Sustain. Soc.* **2012**, *2*, 15. [CrossRef]
24. Jepson, W.E.; Wutich, A.; Collins, S.M.; Boateng, G.O. Progress in household water insecurity metric: A Cross Disciplinary Approach. *WIREs Water* **2017**, *4*, e1214. [CrossRef]
25. FAO. *The State of Food Insecurity in the World*; Food and Agricultural Organisation (FAO) of the United Nations: Rome, Italy, 2021.
26. Adusei, L.A.; Energy Poverty. Exploring Household Energy Constraint and Coping Strategies—Epsilon Archive for Student Projects. Swedish University of Agricultural Sciences. 2012. Available online: https://stud.epsilon.slu.se/5105 (accessed on 29 December 2021).
27. Birol, F. Energy economics: A Place for Energy Poverty in the Agenda? *Energy J.* **2007**, *28*, 1–6. Available online: www.jstor.org/stable/41323106 (accessed on 6 August 2021).
28. Ericksen, P.J.; Ingram, J.S.I.; Liverman, D.M. Food security and global environmental change: Emerging Challenges. *Environ. Sci. Pol.* **2009**, *12*, 373–377. [CrossRef]
29. UN-Water Task Force on Water Security. Water Security and the Global Water Agenda: A UN-Water Analytical Brief. Prepared by Harriet Bigas, 2013, United Nations (UN) University-INWEH on behalf of the UN-Water Task Force on Water Security. Available online: https://sustainabledevelopment.un.org/content/unosd/documents/1482013-03-%20UN-Water%20-%20Water%20Security%20Analytical%20Brief.pdf (accessed on 29 December 2021).
30. Winzer, C. *Conceptualising Energy Security*; Electricity Policy Group Working Paper 1123, Cambridge Working paper in Economics 1151; University of Cambridge: Cambridge, UK, 2011.
31. Silviconsult. *Northern Nigeria Household Energy Studies*; Federal Forestry Management Evaluation and Coordinating Unit: Ibadan, Nigeria, 2014.
32. Reynaud, A.; Pons, M.; Pesado, C. Household water demand in Andorra: Impact of Individual Metering and Seasonality. *Water* **2018**, *10*, 321. [CrossRef]
33. FAO. *Driving Food Security Information from National Household Budget Surveys: Experiences, Achievement, and Challenges*; Food and Agricultural Organisation (FAO) of the United Nations: Rome, Italy, 2008.
34. Zouh, D.; Shah, T.; Ali, S.; Ahmad, W.; Ud Din, I.; Ilyas, A. Factors affecting household food security in rural northern hinterland of Pakistan. *J. Saudi Soc. Agric. Sci.* **2019**, *18*, 201–210. [CrossRef]
35. Energy Commission of Nigeria. *Renewable Energy Master Plan. Energy Commission of Nigeria*; Federal Republic of Nigeria: Abuja, Nigeria, 2005.
36. Hermann, S.; Welsch, M.; Ericsdotter Segerstrom, R.; Howells, M.I.; Ypung, C.; Alfstad, T.; Roger, H.H.; Steduto, P. Climate, land, energy and water (CLEW) interlinkages in Burkina Faso: An Analysis of Agricultural Intensification and Bioenergy Production. *Nat. Resour. For.* **2012**, *36*, 245–262. [CrossRef]
37. Vieira, P.; Jorge, C.; Covas, D. Assessment of household water use efficiency using performance indices. *Resour. Conserv. Recycl.* **2017**, *116*, 94–106. [CrossRef]
38. Ogwumike, O.F.; Ozughalu, M.U. Analysis of energy poverty and its implication for sustainable development. *Environ. Dev. Econ.* **2016**, *21*, 273–290. [CrossRef]
39. Sani, Y.; Scholz, M. Water-Energy-Food Accessibility and Tracking Progress towards Achieving Sustainable Development Goals in the Savannah Region of Katsina State, Nigeria. *Water* **2021**, *13*, 3595. [CrossRef]

40. Golam, R. Managing the food, water, and energy nexus for achieving the Sustainable Development Goals in South Asia. *Environ. Dev.* **2016**, *18*, 14–25. [CrossRef]
41. Isha, R.; Kirk, R.S. Towards safe drinking water and clean cooking for all. *Lancet Glob. Health* **2021**, *9*, e361–e365. [CrossRef]
42. FAO. *Committee on World Food Security: Coming to Terms and Terminology*; Food and Agricultural Organisation (FAO) of the United Nations: Rome, Italy, 2012.
43. Steibuks, J.; Hertel, T. Energy prices will play an important role in determining global land use in the twenty first century. *Environ. Res. Lett.* **2013**, *8*, 014014. [CrossRef]
44. Zhang, B.; Fang, K.; Bearenklau, K. Have Chinese water pricing reforms reduced urban residential water demand? *Water Resour. Res.* **2017**, *53*, 5057–5069. Available online: https://ui.adsabs.harvard.edu/link_gateway/2017WRR....53.5057Z/doi:10.1002/2017WR020463 (accessed on 29 December 2021).
45. Anna, H.O.; Harald, U.S. Defining conceptual model for market mechanism in food supply chains, and parameterising price functions for coffee, wheat, soybeans and beef. *Int. J. Food Syst. Dyn.* **2019**, *10*, 224–247.
46. Romano, G.; Salvati, N.; Guerrini, A. Estimating the determinants of residential water demand in Italy. *Water* **2014**, *6*, 2929–2945. [CrossRef]
47. Some, J.W.; Jones, A.D. The influence of crop production and socioeconomic factors on seasonal household dietary diversity in Burkina Faso. *PLoS ONE* **2018**, *13*, e01195685. [CrossRef]
48. Katsina Diary. *The Diary of Katsina State, Nigeria*; Government Printers: Katsina, Nigeria, 2019.
49. KTURPB. *A Profile of Katsina State Urban and Regional Planning Board*; Government Printers: Katsina, Nigeria, 2014.
50. Isreal, G.D. *Determining Sample Size*; Institute of Food and Agricultural Science, University of Florida: Gainesville, FL, USA, 2018.
51. KTPHCDA. *A Profile of Katsina State Primary Health Care Development Agency*; Government Printers: Katsina, Nigeria, 2019.
52. Angelsen, A.; Lund, J.F. Designing the household questionnaire. In *Measuring Livelihoods and Environmental Dependence. Methods for Research and Fieldwork*; Analytical Report at the National Level; Angelsen, A., Larsen, H.O., Lund, J.F., Smith-Hall, C., Wunder, S., Eds.; Earthscan Publications: Oxford, UK, 2011; pp. 107–126.
53. Swindale, A.; Bilinsky, P. *Household Dietary Diversity Score (HDDS) for Measurement of Household Food Access: Indicator Guide (v. 2)*; FHI 360/FANTA: Washington, DC, USA, 2006.
54. Coates, J.; Swindale, A.; Bilinsky, P. *Household Food Insecurity Access Scale (HFIAS) for Measurement of Household Food Access: Indicator Guide (v.3)*; FHI 360/FANTA. Food and Nutrition Technical Assistance Project, Academy for Educational Development: Washington, DC, USA, 2007.
55. WHO; UNICEF. *Progress on Sanitation and Drinking-Water—2014 Update*; World Health Organisation and the United Nations Children's Fund: Geneva, Switzerland, 2014.
56. World Health Organisation. *Fuel for Life: Household Energy and Health*; WHO Library Cataloguing in Publication Data, World Health Organisation: Geneva, Switzerland, 2006. Available online: http://www.who.int/indoorair/publications/fuelforlife.pdf?ua=1 (accessed on 12 February 2020).
57. Nahla, H.; Sibelle, E.; Richard, A. Nutrition security is an integral component of food security. *Front. Life Sci.* **2016**, *9*, 167–172. [CrossRef]
58. Ohlhorst, S.D.; Russell, R.; Bier, D.; Klurfeld, D.M.; Li, Z.; Mein, J.R.; Milner, J.; Ross, A.C.; Stover, P.; Konopka, E. Nutrition research to affect food and a healthy life span. *Adv. Nutr.* **2013**, *4*, 579–584. [CrossRef] [PubMed]
59. Francesco, B.; Pasquale, D.M. From food availability to nutritional capabilities: Advancing Food Security Analysis. *Food Policy* **2016**, *60*, 10–19. [CrossRef]
60. Jäger, R.; Mohr, A.E.; Carpenter, K.C.; Kerksick, C.M.; Purpura, M.; Moussa, A.; Townsend, J.R.; Lamprecht, M.; West, N.P.; Black, K.; et al. International Society of Sports Nutrition position stand: Probiotics. *J. Int. Soc. Sports Nutr.* **2019**, *16*, 62. [CrossRef] [PubMed]
61. Dhalaria, R.; Verma, R.; Kumar, D.; Puri, S.; Tapwal, A.; Kumar, V.; Nepovimova, E.; Kuca, K. Bioactive Compounds of Edible Fruits with Their Anti-Aging Properties: A Comprehensive Review to Prolong Human Life. *Antioxidants* **2020**, *9*, 1123. [CrossRef] [PubMed]
62. Noorwali, E.; Hardie, L.; Cade, J. Bridging the gap reciprocal between sleep and fruit and vegetable consumption: A Review of the Evidence, Potential Mechanisms, Implications and Directions for Future Work. *Nutrients* **2019**, *11*, 1382. [CrossRef]
63. Micha, R.; Peñalvo, J.L.; Cudhea, F.; Imamura, F.; Rehm, C.D.; Mozaffarian, D. Association Between Dietary Factors and Mortality from Heart Disease, Stroke, and Type 2 Diabetes in the United States. *JAMA* **2017**, *317*, 912–924. [CrossRef]
64. Aju, P.C.; Uwalaka, R.E. *Forest Resources and Economy of Rural Nigerians*; Ijeoma, H.M., Aiyeloja, A.A., Eds.; Practical Issues in Forest and Wildlife Resources Management, Green Canopy Consultants: Choba, Bulgaria; Port Harcourt, Nigeria, 2010; pp. 172–191.
65. Lee, S.; Choi, Y.; Jeong, H.S.; Lee, J.; Sung, J. Effect of different cooking methods on the content of vitamins and true retention in selected vegetables. *Food Sci. Biotechnol.* **2017**, *27*, 333–342. [CrossRef]
66. Clean Cooking Alliance. Food Security & Nutrition. 2019. Available online: https://www.safefuelandenergy.org/issues/food-security-nutrition.cfm (accessed on 2 June 2021).
67. Sola, P.; Ochieng, C.; Yila, J.; Ilyama, M. Link between energy access and food security in sub Saharan Africa: An Exploration Review. *Food Secur.* **2016**, *8*, 635–642. [CrossRef]

68. Waswa, F.; Mcharo, M.; Mworia, M. Declining wood fuel and implications for household cooking and diets in tigania sub-county Kenya. *Sci. Afr.* **2020**, *8*, e00417. [CrossRef]
69. Cesani, M.F.; Garraza, M.; Bergel Sanchis, M.L.; Luis, M.A.; Torres, M.F.; Quintero, F.A.; Oyhenart, E.E. A comparative study on nutritional status and body composition of urban and rural schoolchildren from Brandsen District (Argentina). *PLoS ONE* **2013**, *8*, e52792. [CrossRef]
70. Cordeiro, L.S.; Otis, N.P.; Sibeko, L.; Nelson-Peterman, J. Rural-urban disparities in the nutritional status of younger adolescents in Tanzania. *PLoS ONE* **2021**, *16*, e0261480. [CrossRef] [PubMed]
71. Berheto, T.M.; Mikitie, W.K.; Argaw, A. Urban-rural disparities in the nutritional status of school adolescent girls in the Mizan district, south-western Ethiopia. *Rural Remote Health* **2015**, *15*, 2687.
72. Fagbamigbe, A.F.; Kandala, N.B.; Uthman, A.O. Demystifying the factors associated with rural–urban gaps in severe acute malnutrition among under-five children in low- and middle-income countries: A Decomposition Analysis. *Sci Rep.* **2020**, *10*, 11172. [CrossRef] [PubMed]
73. Waibel, H.; Hohfeld, L. *Poverty and Nutrition: A Case Study of Rural Households in Thailand and Vietnam*; ADBI Working paper, No. 623; Asian Development Bank Institute (ADBI): Tokyo, Japan, 2016.
74. Muraya, K.W.; Jones, C.; Berkley, J.A.; Molyneux, S. Perceptions of childhood undernutrition among rural households on the Kenyan coast—A qualitative study. *BMC Public Health* **2016**, *16*, 693. [CrossRef]
75. Fotso, J.C. Child health inequities in developing countries: Differences Across Urban and Rural Areas. *Int. J. Equity Health* **2006**, *5*, 9. [CrossRef] [PubMed]
76. Abdel Wahed, W.Y.; Hassan, S.K.; Eldessouki, R. Malnutrition and its associated factors among rural school children in Fayoum Governorate Egypt. *J. Environ. Public Health* **2017**, *2017*, 4783791. [CrossRef] [PubMed]
77. Li, W.; Liu, E.; BeLue, R. Household water treatment and the nutritional status of primary-aged children in India: Findings from India Human Development Survey. *Glob. Health* **2018**, *14*, 37. [CrossRef]
78. Mabhaudhi, T.; Chibaradada, T.; Modi, A. Water-food-nutrition-health nexus: Linking Water to Improving Food, Nutrition and Health in Sub-Saharan Africa. *Int. J. Environ. Res. Public Health* **2016**, *13*, 107. [CrossRef]
79. Mbwana, H.A.; Kinabo, J.; Lambert, C.; Bieselki, H.K. Determinants of household dietary practices in rural Tanzania: Implications for Nutrition Interventions. *Cogent Food Sci. Tech.* **2016**, *2*, 1224046. [CrossRef]
80. Gao, Y.; Sheng, J.; Mi, X.; Zhou, M.; Zou, S.; Zhou, H. Household Water Access, Dietary Diversity and Nutritional Status among Preschoolers in Poor, Rural Areas of Central and Western China. *Nutrients* **2022**, *14*, 458. [CrossRef]
81. Sera, L.Y. Viewpoint: The Measurement of Water Access and Use is Key for more Effective Food and Nutrition Policy. *Food Policy* **2021**, *104*, 102138. [CrossRef]
82. Capstick, S.; Whitmarsh, L.; Healy, A.; Bristow, G. *Resilience in Groundwater Supply Systems: Findings from a Survey of Private Households in Lagos, Nigeria. RIGSS Working Paper*; Cardiff University: Cardiff, UK, 2017. Available online: https://www.cardiff.ac.uk/__data/assets/pdf_file/0009/1149741/rigss_final_report.pdf (accessed on 8 August 2021).
83. Carrard, N.; Foster, T.; Willets, J. Groundwater as a source of drinking water in Southeast Asia and the Pacific: A Multi-Country Review of Current Reliance and Resource Concerns. *Water* **2010**, *11*, 1605. [CrossRef]
84. Spearse, D.; Haddad, L. Why sanitation matter for nutrition. In *The Power of WASH*; International Food Policy Research Institute: Washington, DC, USA, 2016; pp. 19–29.
85. Mahmud, I.; Mbuya, N. Water, Sanitation, Hygiene, and Nutrition in Bangladesh: Can Building Toilets Affect Children's Growth? World Bank Publication. 2015. Available online: https://openknowledge.worldbank.org/bitstream/handle/10989/22800/9781464806988.pdf (accessed on 20 May 2021).
86. Chattopadhyay, A.; Sethi, V.; Nagargoje, V.P.; Saraswat, A.; Surani, N.; Agarwal, N.; Bhatia, V.; Ruikar, M.; Bhattacharjee, S.; Parhi, R.N.; et al. WASH practices and its association with nutritional status of adolescent girls in poverty pockets of eastern India. *BMC Women's Health* **2019**, *19*, 89. [CrossRef] [PubMed]
87. Zavala, E.; King, S.E.; Sawadogo-Lewis, T.; Roberton, T. Leveraging water, sanitation and hygiene for nutrition in low-and middle-income countries: A Conceptual Framework. *Matern Child Nutr.* **2021**, *17*, e13202. [CrossRef]
88. Momberg, D.J.; Ngandu, B.C.; Voth-Gaeddert, L.E.; Cardoso Ribeiro, K.; Norris, S.A.; Said-Mohamed, R. Water, sanitation and hygiene (WASH) in sub-Saharan Africa and associations with undernutrition, and governance in children under five years of age: A Systematic Review. *J. Dev. Orig. Health Dis.* **2021**, *12*, 6–33. [CrossRef]
89. FAO. *Safe Access to Firewood and Alternative Energy in Humanitarian Setting in Emergencies Guidelines Note*; Food and Agricultural Organisation of the United Nations: Rome, Italy, 2013.
90. Makungwa, S.D.; Epulani, F.; Woodhouse, I.H. Fuelwood supply: A Missed Essential Component in a Food Security Equation. *J. Food Secur.* **2013**, *1*, 49–51. [CrossRef]
91. Ajoa, A.O. Determinants of urban charcoal demand in Ogbomosho Metropolis. *Acad. Arena* **2011**, *3*, 41–48.
92. Win, Z.C.; Mizoue, N.; Ota, T.; Kajisa, T.; Yoshida, S. Consumption rates and pattern of firewood and charcoal in urban and rural communities in Yadashe township, Myanmar. *Forest* **2018**, *9*, 429. [CrossRef]
93. Bogdanski, A. Integrated food-energy systems for climate-smart agriculture. *Agric. Food Secur.* **2012**, *1*, 9. [CrossRef]
94. Amare, Z.Y.; Ahmed, M.E.; Mehari, A.B. Determinants of nutritional status among children under age 5 in Ethiopia: Further Analysis of the 2016 Ethiopia Demographic and Health Survey. *Glob. Health* **2019**, *15*, 62. [CrossRef]

sustainability

MDPI

Article

Gender and Other Vulnerabilities to Water–Energy Accessibility in Rural Households of Katsina State, Northern Nigeria

Yahaya Sani [1] and Miklas Scholz [2,3,4,*]

1 Division of Water Resources Engineering, Department of Building and Environmental Technology, Faculty of Engineering, Lund University, P.O. Box 118, 221 00 Lund, Sweden; yahaya.sani@tvrl.lth.se
2 Directorate of Engineering the Future, School of Science, Engineering and Environment, The University of Salford, Newton Building, Greater Manchester M5 4WT, UK
3 Department of Civil Engineering Science, School of Civil Engineering and the Built Environment, University of Johannesburg, Kingsway Campus, P.O. Box 524, Auckland Park, Johannesburg 2006, South Africa
4 Department of Town Planning, Engineering Networks and Systems, South Ural State University, 76, Lenin Prospekt, 454080 Chelyabinsk, Russia
* Correspondence: m.scholz@salford.ac.uk

Abstract: Water and energy are essential resources for all people. However, despite the availability of sufficient water and energy resources, men and women continue to be subject to unequal rights to both water and energy in terms of access, allocation, gathering, and quality of resources. Socio-economic parameters, which include gender, income, and location, are determinant factors of water and cooking energy accessibility in this study. The research aims to assess the accessibility of water and cooking fuels across female-headed households, and evaluate particular vulnerabilities and challenges faced by women and children in rural areas of Katsina State in circumstances of water and energy insecurities. A study involving a questionnaire covering 550 rural households across 11 areas in Katsina State, north-western Nigeria, was conducted. A Pearson product correlation analysis was performed to measure the strength of association between the respondents educational level and income. A chi-square test of independence was carried out to measure the degree of dependence of the households' resources accessibility. The authors assessed the disproportionate threats and health risks linked to fetching water and gathering of fuel resources. The research findings indicate that water and energy uncertainty among women in rural households is due to unequal responsibilities associated with water- and energy-related household duties that are potentially linked to disadvantages for females, including violence, security threats, diseases, and disempowerment. To address these challenges, water and energy interventions, and important pathways for beneficial change, are proposed for rural regions in sub-Saharan Africa. This should lead to more gender equity associated with water and energy.

Keywords: water resources access; cooking energy access; gender-based resource access; socio-economic sustainability; sustainable development goals; traditional rural practices; vulnerability; water; energy; food nexus

Citation: Sani, Y.; Scholz, M. Gender and Other Vulnerabilities to Water–Energy Accessibility in Rural Households of Katsina State, Northern Nigeria. *Sustainability* **2022**, *14*, 7499. https://doi.org/10.3390/su14127499

Academic Editor: Thomas A. Clark

Received: 17 April 2022
Accepted: 13 June 2022
Published: 20 June 2022

1. Introduction

A significant fraction of rural households in low- and middle-income countries, particularly of sub-Saharan Africa, have no access to piped water in their neighbourhood [1,2]. There are long walking distances to collect water, as well as cooking fuel, especially from an "improved" source of water for potable use and other household activities. The collection of water and cooking fuels can be a considerable physical and economic load that particularly impacts on women and mainly female children [3–5]. Households linked to water collection journey times of greater than 30 min commonly collect progressively less water [6,7]. Restricted water and energy availabilities often lead to a reduction in the amount of water and energy that are used for drinking, hygiene, and cooking in the household.

Residents' access to clean potable water and cooking fuels is imperative for appropriate development, and addressed in the Sustainable Development Goals (SDGs) [8]. The Joint Monitoring Program of the World Health Organization on water highlights that "Access to drinking water means that the source is less than 1 km away from its place of use and that it is possible to reliably obtain at least 20 L per member of a household per day." [1]. For the post-2015 SDGs, access to basic drinking water is defined as "using an improved source with a total fetching time of 30 min or less for a round trip including queuing" [9].

Access to good-quality water and a clean energy supply is an essential requirement for the reduction of poverty, and sustainable human development [10–12]. Despite impressive accomplishments towards sustainable access to safe water and clean energy sources, billions of people still lack access to sustainable resources nowadays. The Joint Monitoring Program (JMP) states that 26% of the global population (2.6 billion people) safely manages potable water, and that 2.3 billion people reside in water-stressed regions of the world [13]. Furthermore, at least 20% of the global population (about 1.4 billion people) are still denied access to electricity sources, and around 40% of the global population (roughly 2.7 billion people) depend on traditional biomass as their major source of energy for cooking [14]. Universal sustainable access to both clean water and energy are key priorities of the global development agenda, which is the foundation for the SDGs. Without sustainable water and energy provisions, large proportions of the world's population are denied access to essential amenities. As a consequence, the poor are forced to live and work in unhealthy circumstances.

Two-thirds of the world's poor people are female. They typically reside in water-scarce regions, with limited access to a secure and permanent supply of water for productive and household uses [15]. The majority of these poor people rely on agriculture for their livelihood, and reside in regions of south Asia and sub-Saharan Africa. These areas are linked to the world's water-poorest communities [16].

The SDGs were unanimously accepted by the member states of the United Nations in September 2015, providing a comprehensive framework for global cooperation to achieve a sustainable prospect for the planet. The 17 SDGs and their 169 targets define a path to fight long-standing inequality and injustice, end extreme poverty, and protect the planet's environment. Sustainable access to clean water and energy, as well as gender equality, are central to the success of the SDGs. The global goal on water (SDG6) consists of key elements such as ensuring availability to clean water and safe sanitation for all, as well as safe and affordable drinking water. The global goal on energy (SDG7) comprises three key targets: affordable, reliable, and common access to contemporary energy services; a substantial share of renewable energy in the overall energy mix; and doubling up the rate of improvement in global energy productivity [17]. It is imperative to highlight that inequality in accessing water and energy resources is intensified among some communities. For instance, women in rural communities often represent a marginalized group, which is unjustifiably burdened with inaccessibility to good-quality water and clean energy sources [13]. Females excessively serve as water and energy suppliers, collecting water and cooking fuels across many households. Frequently, women and girls need to walk long distances to fetch water and energy supplies [18].

Consequently, in low- and medium-income countries, water and energy inaccessibility is typically characterized by insufficient household access to both good-quality water and energy sources. This is particularly the case for electricity, leading to a reliance on unimproved water sources and unclean fuels for heating, cooking, and lighting, which can be harmful for human health and welfare [13,19–22].

Concerning the gender dimension, the understanding of 'gender' by the authors needs to be defined in the context of this article. The authors agree with Risman [23], and view gender as a social structure that identifies and legitimatizes certain behaviours, roles, and responsibilities as masculine or feminine, which is subsequently linked to social actions. As people usually act in accordance with their predefined gender roles, the social structure is remodelled [24]. Gender is typically associated with differences in what people can actually perform, the services and resources they may access, and their potentials and prospects for their own development [25]. Concerning the study region in rural Nigeria, gender is traditionally seen as binary. However, the authors are aware of, and accept, a more modern view of gender as not being binary.

There are considerable inter-linkages between water, energy, gender, and health-worsening imbalances among females, which cause health challenges. Amid other challenges, inaccessibility to safe and sufficient water, as well as clean energy, increases the risk for related waterborne and respiratory illnesses including, for example, cholera, which is a bacterial infection transmitted by polluted water, and cardiovascular illnesses, due to indoor air pollution [26–30]. Considering the position of females in providing water and energy for their households, women and girls are particularly exposed to the contraction and transmission of several diseases [26,30].

A number of conceptual frameworks of vulnerability are significant for directing multiple disciplines [31–35]. To evaluate the various vulnerabilities experienced, the study used the vulnerability concept, based on resource accessibility. This refers to a state of being exposed to the possibility of being assaulted, or otherwise harmed, either emotionally or/and physically, due to an incapacity to protect affected individuals' personal interests in the course of resource accessibility [36–38].

Since 2015, gender equality and the empowerment of women are seen as crucial in attaining the SDGs. Adhering to these development obligations, a considerable number of studies focus on the impacts of inequality experienced by females, with women and girls regularly experiencing a greater proportion of the detrimental effects of water and energy inaccessibility. However, limited work has been undertaken on the interaction between gender, water, and energy at the household level, particularly in rural areas. Remarkably, the Sustainable development Goals (SDGs) highlight the significance of equal rights to resource accessibility across gender in target 5.a. Thus, water and energy are crucial resources, which women should have the same right to as their male counterparts. Moreover, the importance of ending all forms of gender-based discrimination against women is enshrined in target 5.1 of the Sustainable Development Goals (SDGs) [39]. The series of connections between gender, water, and energy arise from the conventional roles played by women and girls on a household scale, which includes the collection of water and cooking fuel, as well as cooking [40].

Across several nations, women are prohibited from working, for social and cultural reasons. According to the World Bank, there are over 100 economies with labour regulations that limit the types of employment women can embark on, as well as where and when they are allowed to work [41]. It further assesses that this has an effect on the employment options of about three billion women. Furthermore, the report points out that 18 countries give husbands legitimate rights to prevent their spouses from working. Correspondingly, International Labour Organization (ILO) reports disclose that 14% of the women in Africa are household workers, and women represent an estimated 83% of household workers globally [42]. In 2018, the work force involvement rate of women was 48%, in contrast with that of men, which was 75% in the matching year [43]. This situation is more common in rural areas of Nigeria, where more than 50% of Nigerian women reside [44]. Despite the gender-based employment marginalisation faced by women in many regions of the world, studies show that women contribute immensely to households' resources accessibility. Studies [45,46] reveal that women in many rural Nigerian households contribute significantly from what they earn towards running daily activities, and securing households' food security [45,46].

Individual constituents (either water or energy) are examined in some research projects. For instance, other studies [26–30] assess individual elements, such as water or energy, as a separate entity. Pouramin et al. [26] find that females experience barriers towards accessing basic water provisions. They discover that women, due to their responsibilities as water providers, are at risk of exposure to polluted water, thereby suffering from various negative health effects. Wu [29] investigates the influence of the choice of household cooking energy source on female's health from various dimensions, including health and common activities. The study intends to assess energy transition and health enhancement concerning developing countries. Findings for individual households indicate that cooking energy selection switches from solid fuel to clean energy sources, which improves female health.

Regardless of these gender-related inequalities, research evaluating the intersection between gender on one side, and water and energy on the other, is still in progress. Successfully addressing gendered water–energy inequities requires considerable focused resources. Thus, this study aims to examine women's accessibility to households' water and energy; it also explores the various vulnerabilities experienced due to water and energy collection in rural areas of Katsina State, northern Nigeria.

This research article is structured in the following way: after a concise overview and a critical review of the scientific literature related to water–energy accessibility in Section 1, Section 2 summarises the methodology covering a description of the materials and methods applied to conduct the work, which involves the description of the study area, conceptual framework, a selection of the rural surveyed communities, as well as statistical analysis of the data. Section 3 is devoted to the results, highlighting socio-economic characteristics of the female household heads, access to water and energy across the identified income groups, physical distances covered, and time taken to collect water and cooking fuel. Moreover, key findings are discussed in Section 4. Section 5 concludes on the main results, and emphasizes the wider importance of this work. Finally, Section 6 summarises limitations and recommends future studies.

2. Materials and Methods

2.1. Study Area Description

The project was carried out in Katsina State, located within latitude 11°08′ N and 13°22′, and longitude 6°52′ E and 9°20′ E, with an area of about 24,000 km^2 (Figure 1). The state consists of 34 local government areas. The average literacy proportions are 59% for males, and 29% for females. In 2019, 56.42% of people in the state were below the poverty threshold [47]. The state population estimated census data released by the National Population Commission states that the total population for the year 2021 was 9,145,600, of which 4,664,256 (51%) and 4,481,344 (49%) were males and females, respectively.

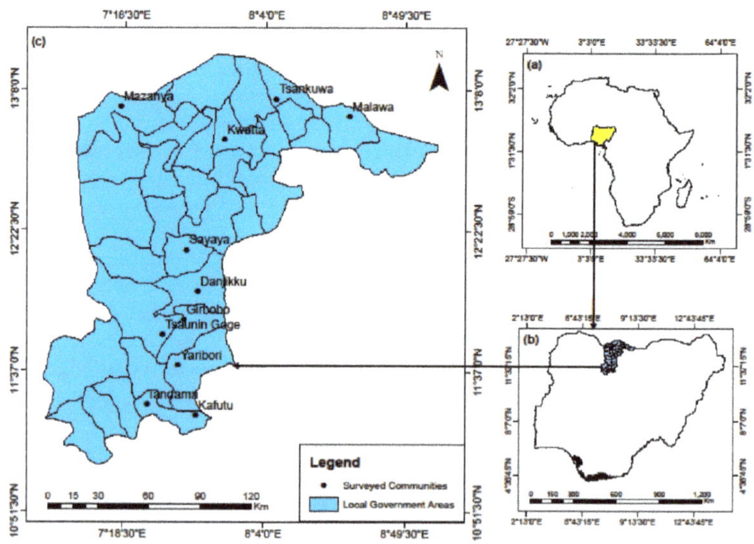

Figure 1. (**a**) Map of Africa indicating Nigeria; (**b**) map of Nigeria highlighting Katsina State; and (**c**) map of Katsina State outlining the surveyed rural communities.

The map of the study region highlighting the surveyed communities was created using a geographical information system application and subsequent cartographical analysis. Global positioning system coordinates of the sampled communities were noted during the field study, and integrated into the existing digital map database, accessible at the Geographical Information System and Remote Sensing Unit (Department of Geography, Umaru Musa Yarádua University).

2.2. Conceptual Framework

To investigate the inter-linkages between gender and accessibility to households' resources (water and energy), and to understand the different intensities of vulnerabilities as a result of water and cooking energy accessibility among rural, women-headed households, a conceptual framework for the study was designed. In rural, women-headed households of low- and medium-income countries, water and energy insecurities typically manifest themselves as a deficiency in household access to both safe drinking water and cooking fuels, leading to a reliance on unclean water and cooking fuels (biomass), which can be detrimental for health and well-being.

Fetching water and gathering biomass is commonly the responsibility of females. They can be asked by their husbands to perform this task for many hours per day, resulting in less productive time and energy for formal employment, education, as well as social and political interactions in public. Water and cooking fuel (biomass) collections may also be unsafe, due to grievances from carrying heavy loads and other health impacts (see above). In some contexts, women also face an increased exposure to both physical and sexual attacks. Consequently, old-fashioned gender divisions of household labour mean that females commonly spend considerable time at home, and prepare almost all household meals. This leaves females more vulnerable to the negative impacts of indoor air contamination and accidents. The associated impacts are felt disproportionately between males and females, with women experiencing a higher percentage of the harmful effects of water and energy insecurity.

2.3. Research Design

The study was designed based on the conceptual framework, illustrated in Figure 2, to explore women's access to households' water and cooking fuels, as well as the associated vulnerabilities experienced by accessing these resources. A semi-structured questionnaire was specifically designed for this study, including a socio-economic section, and questions about the physical and economic access to water and energy sources, as well as the considerable vulnerabilities and burdens experienced by females in rural communities. The focus was on conditions linked to water and cooking fuel accessibility, considering particularly the unequal dangers, physical security threats, and health risks, as well as time and energy losses, linked with water and energy access.

In order to explore the characteristics of socio-economic classification, the collected information included household heads' educational level, monthly income, and occupation. To understand the accessibility to water and energy sources, respondents were first questioned about the leading sources of drinking water and cooking energy in the surveyed area. Sources specified were grouped into enhanced and unimproved water sources [48]. The improved sources are piped water into dwelling, piped water to yard, public tap/standpipe, borehole/tube well, protected dug well, protected spring, and rainwater; original water sources are unprotected spring, unprotected dug well, cart with tank or drum (water vending), tanker truck, and surface water.

The cooking energy sources were also categorised, based on the World Health Organization (WHO) [49], into clean and unclean fuels. The clean fuel sources are electricity, natural gas, liquefied petroleum gas, ethanol/methanol, and kerosene; the unclean sources are coal, charcoal, sawdust, fuelwood, agricultural residue, and animal dung. To measure the distance covered to access various water sources, and the time taken to collect the corresponding water, WHO and the United Nations Children's Fund (UNICEF) recommend thresholds of 1000 m and 30 min, respectively [18]. The authors adopted these values in this study for categorisation purposes.

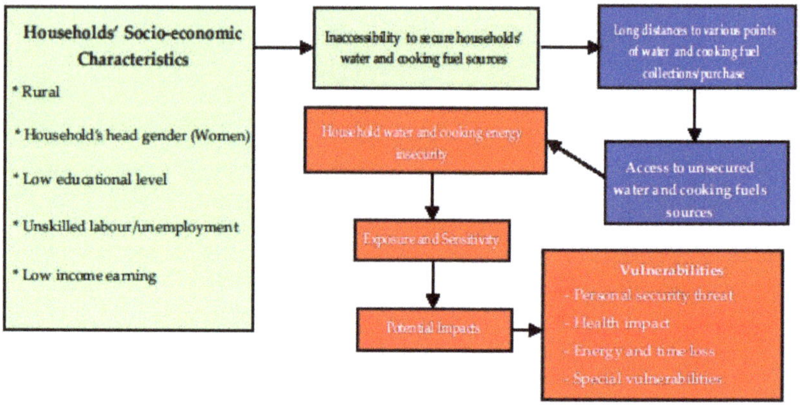

Figure 2. A conceptual framework connecting households' socio-economic characteristics, water and energy insecurity, and various associated vulnerabilities.

2.4. Selection of the Surveyed Households

A qualitative study design was carried out in Katsina State. The state has been stratified into urban and rural areas. Hence, this format was adopted in selecting ten surveyed communities that were chosen considering rural norms [50]. The selected surveyed rural communities are Mazanya, Tsankuwa, Kwalla, Malawa, Sayaya, Danjanku, Girbobo, Tsaunin Goge, Tandama, Yari bori, and Kafutu, as indicated in Figure 1.

Only households that are headed by a female were considered for the study. Respondents were questioned on the estimation of distance and time taken for a round trip to fetch water, quantity of water collected from the various sources, availability of cooking fuels at the point of purchase or collection, and who is responsible for water and energy collections. Information on vulnerabilities such as personal security threats, health impact of the water and energy collection trip, and energy and time loss, as well as special vulnerabilities, were also gathered and analysed.

2.5. Data Collection

Primary and secondary sources of data were applied for this study. The primary data were generated through the structured questionnaire administration. The survey was conducted in person by ten field assistants, who are conversant with the surveyed rural communities.

Data were collected over a period of one month (between mid-March to mid-April 2022). Due to unavailable data on the number of female-headed households in the study area, the number of households surveyed is a reflection of the available female-headed households across the surveyed communities. Mazanya has 11.8% of the surveyed households (65 households), Sayaya has 12.7% (70 households), Kwalla and Malawa each have 10.2% (56 households each), Danjanku has 9.1% (50 households), Tsankuwa has 7.3% (40 households), Girbobo has 7.6% (42 households), Tsaunin Goge has 9.5% (52 households), Tandama has 8.4% (46 households), and Kafutu has 6.7% (37 households). Finally, Yari bori, which represents 6.5% of the surveyed households, has 36 households. At the end of the exercise, 550 copies of questionnaires were served to the female-headed households across the selected rural communities.

2.6. Statistical Data Analysis

IBM SPSS version 24 was applied for data entry and analysis. Descriptive statistics were used to assess the household heads' socio-economic and demographic variables, as well as their access to various water and energy sources. Summary statistics in terms of proportions, expressed in percentages, were calculated. To determine the association and direction of the water and energy crisis, the Pearson product-moment correlation (PPMC) was employed to determine the relationships between the socio-economic variables of the female household heads. The corresponding key variables are educational status and monthly income. Simple bivariate correlations were adopted. Chi-square tests of independence were undertaken, to determine whether there is relationship between access to households' water and energy and the households' income groups. The authors only considered a minimum degree of significance at 95% confidence level ($p = 0.05$).

3. Results

3.1. Framework and Household Characteristics

The empirical study context, through the administration of a well-constructed questionnaire, generates dependable results, which authenticates the study's theoretical framework, which discloses the consequences of water and energy insecurity across the income groups of women-headed households within the rural context, and the various vulnerabilities associated with insecurities.

In total, 550 households were assessed among the ten surveyed rural communities of Katsina State. The study data are based on the responses of the female household heads across the investigated communities. Results indicate that most of the household heads are widows (61%), 20% are divorcees, and 18% are married. Overall, 56% of the female household heads are housewives, 33% are farmers, and 5% of them are traders. Regarding household income, the majority, representing 51%, earn less than NGN 30,000 (USD 72.8)/month, while 27% receive between NGN 30,000 and NGN 50,000 (USD 78.2–121.3)/month.

Three income groups are classified, based on the household monthly income, as follows:

- Group 1 (low-income-earning) includes illiterate people and those who have a monthly income of less than NGN 30,000. This group is classified as low by the socio-economic categorisation, because it comprises 51% of household heads characterised by no formal education level, and low monthly income;
- Group 2 (medium-income-earning) is formed by 27% of respondents with a low educational level (mostly below secondary school certificate), and a medium monthly income between NGN 30,000 and 50,000;
- Group 3 (high-income-earning) corresponds to the household heads with an income above NGN 50,000. This group represents 21% of the respondents with a high educational level (mostly secondary school certificate).

To determine the strength and direction of association between educational status of the women household heads and various income groups, the Pearson product-moment correlation (PPMC) r was calculated. The Pearson's r analysis indicates that there is a strong association ($r = 0.82$). The p value is less than 0.05, which implies the significance of the measure of association.

3.2. Accessibility to Water Sources

The sources of water accessible for household applications, and in the studied communities, are presented in Table 1. The overall result reveals that public borehole and public dug wells are the major sources of water across the surveyed households, representing 44% and 23%, respectively. It is observed that 3% of the households rely on privately owned boreholes and tanker trucks.

Table 1. Sources of water related to household income groups.

Main HH Water Source	Monthly Income of the Household Heads							
	<NGN 30,000 (USD 78.2)		NGN 30,000–50,000 (USD 78.2–121.3)		Above NGN 50,000 (USD 121.3)		Total	
	n	%	n	%	n	%	n	%
Public tap	-	-	31	21.1	-	-	31	5.6
Private borehole	-	-	-	-	15	12.6	15	2.7
Public borehole	102	36.4	72	48.6	65	54.6	239	43.5
Protected dug well	55	19.4	-	-	13	10.9	68	12.4
Unprotected dug well	126	44.5	-	-			126	22.9
Water vending	-	-	26	17.5	26	21.8	52	9.5
Tanker truck	-	-	19	12.8	-	-	19	3.4
Total	283	100	148	100	119	100	550	100

Across the income groups, there are not too many main water sources for household purposes. Most of the households from low-income groups access unprotected dug wells (45%), protected dug wells (19%), and a remaining 36% access public boreholes. In the medium-income group, access to various water sources are public borehole (48%), public tap (21%), tanker truck (13%), and water vending (18%). In the case of high-income groups, 12% access private boreholes, 55% public boreholes, and 11% protected dug wells. Finally, 22% of household water is provided through water vending. The chi-square analyses for income groups and access to water indicate a high statistical significance ($p < 0.01$).

After analysing the physical access to the water sources, Table 2 describes the distance to various water sources. Households that access privately owned (located in dwellings) boreholes have easy physical access to water sources, which also represent a total proportion (100%) of households that access private boreholes, and 21% of households that have their various water sources located in their respective dwellings. Households that access protected and unprotected boreholes represent 18% and 61%, respectively. These frequencies also represent 19% and 34% of the households accessing both protected and unprotected dug wells, respectively. Furthermore, these households have an average distance to the nearest water source of less than 1000 m (1 km).

Table 2. Household physical accessibility to various water sources.

Main Water Source	Average Distance to Water Source							
	In Dwelling		<1000 m		1000 m and above		Total	
	n	%	n	%	n	%	n	%
Public tap			24	10.6	7	2.8	31	5.6
Private borehole	15	21.1	-	-	-	-	15	2.7
Public borehole	-	-	112	49.6	127	50.2	239	43.5
Protected dug well	13	18.3	25	11.0	30	11.9	68	12.4
Unprotected dug well	43	60.6	54	23.9	29	11.4	126	22.9
Water vendor	-	-	11	4.9	41	16.2	52	9.5
Tanker truck	-	-	-	-	19	7.5	19	3.4
Totals	71	100	226	100	253	100	550	100

Table 2 reveals that households that access water through public boreholes represent the highest proportion (50%) of households that access it within less than 1000 m, while the lowest proportion (5%) of households within the same distance range access their household water supply through water vending. Various water sources are identified with a physical access with average distance of more than 1000 m across the surveyed households. The highest record is for public boreholes (50%). Public taps have the lowest proportion (3%) linked to the same average physical distance. The chi-square analyses for average distance covered to access various water sources indicates statistically highly significant ($p < 0.01$) findings.

3.3. Time Required to Collect Water from Various Sources

Table 3 indicates the time taken to fetch household water sources from various points of collection. Findings show that 13% of the total households surveyed have their various sources located in their respective dwellings. Hence, they spend no time on water collection. Findings further reveal that 14% of households spend less than 30 min collecting household water. The study further reveals that 90% of households collect water from a distance of at least 1000 m, and spend more than 30 min collecting water from various sources. Moreover, Table 3 reveals that 76% of the households have various water sources located within less than 1000 m, and spend more than 30 min on water collection, including queuing.

Table 3. Time required to fetch water from various sources.

Time Taken for a Round Trip Including Queuing	Location of Water Source							
	Within the Dwelling		<1000 m		1000 m and above		Total	
	N	%	n	%	n	%	n	%
No time spent	71	100	-	-	-	-	71	12.9
Less than 30 min	-	-	54	23.9	23	9.1	77	14.0
30 min and above	-	-	172	76.1	230	90.1	402	73.1
Total	71	100	226	100	253	100	550	100

3.4. Responsibility for Water Collections

Table 4 shows the division of responsibility for water fetching among the family members related to the distance to various points of water sources. Findings indicate that 80% of the total surveyed households collect water from different sources, across various distances. Furthermore, for 47% of the households, water collection is only the responsibility of women (household heads). For 27% of households, collection is a shared responsibility among women and children, while 22% of households only involve children.

Table 4. Responsibility of water collection across the availability.

Various Distances of Water Sources	Responsibility for Water Collection							
	Household Head (Women)		Women and Children		Children		Total	
	n	%	n	%	n	%	n	%
Less than 1000 m	80	32.8	71	55.5	75	70.1	226	47.2
1000 m and above	164	67.2	57	44.5	32	29.9	253	52.8
Total	244	100	128	100	107	100	479	100

3.5. Household Cooking Energy Sources across Income Groups

The overall portfolio of cooking fuel across the households is overshadowed by conventional solid biomass fuels, and the majority (59%) access fuelwood as the main fuel for cooking, as indicated in Table 5. This is followed by agricultural residues (28%) and charcoal (6%). This contrasts with 5% of the surveyed households accessing non-solid fuels (cooking gas and kerosene) as their core fuels for cooking. Furthermore, the usage of animal dung-cakes and sawdust for cooking is normally insignificant at 2% and 1%, respectively.

Across the income groups, most of the surveyed households from low-income groups access fuelwood (58%) and agricultural residue (38%). The remaining 4% access dung-cakes as their main cooking fuel source. In the medium-income group, access to various cooking fuel sources are fuelwood (64%), agricultural residue (31%), and charcoal (5%). In the case of the high-income group, 11% of households access liquefied petroleum gas, 18% kerosene, 21% charcoal, 3% sawdust, and 54% use fuelwood. Furthermore, the chi-square analyses for income groups and access to cooking fuel consumption indicate high statistical significance ($p < 0.01$).

Table 5. Sources of cooking energy related to household income groups.

Energy Sources	Monthly Income of the Household Heads							
	<NGN 30,000 (USD 78.2)		NGN 30,000–50,000 (USD 78.2–121.3)		Above NGN 50,000 (USD 121.3)		Total	
	n	%	n	%	n	%	n	%
Cooking gas (liquefied petroleum gas)	-	-	-	-	6	10.9	6	1.1
Kerosene	-	-	-	-	21	17.6	21	3.8
Charcoal	-	-	7	4.7	25	21.0	32	5.8
Sawdust	-	-	-	-	4	3.3	4	0.7
Fuelwood	165	58.3	95	64.2	64	53.7	324	58.9
Agricultural residue	107	37.8	46	31.1	-	-	152	27.6
Dung	11	3.7	-	-	-	-	11	2.0
Totals	283	100	148	100	119	100	550	100

3.6. Household Physical Accessibility and Availability to Cooking Fuel Sources

Table 6 reveals that only 8% of households cannot access their various cooking fuel sources locally. Findings further show that most of the cooking fuels that are readily available when needed are biomass, which constitutes fuelwood (61%), agricultural residue (37%), and dung cakes (3%). Household cooking fuel that is readily available on market days within the access location include kerosene (14%), charcoal (8%), and fuelwood (79%). Additionally, cooking fuel sources that are not locally available consist of non-solid fuel sources, which include cooking gas (14%) and kerosene (19%). The solid fuel sources within the physical access location involve sawdust (4%) and charcoal (58%). The chi-square analyses for cooking energy availability at various points of collection is also highly statistically significant ($p < 0.01$).

Table 6. Availability of various cooking energy sources.

Energy Source	Availability of Cooking Fuels at the Point of Purchase or Collection							
	Always Available When Needed		Available at the Local Periodic Market		Not Locally Available		Total	
	n	%	n	%	N	%	n	%
Cooking gas (liquefied petroleum gas)	-	-	-	-	6	13.9	6	1.1
Kerosene	-	-	13	14.0	8	18.6	21	3.8
Charcoal	-	-	7	7.5	25	58.1	32	5.8
Sawdust	-	-	-	-	4	9.3	4	0.7
Fuelwood	251	60.6	73	78.5	-	-	324	58.9
Agricultural residue	152	36.7	-	-	-	-	152	27.6
Dung	11	2.7	-	-	-	-	11	2.0
Total	414	100	93	100	43	100	550	100

3.7. Time Taken to Collect Cooking Energy Sources from Various Sources

Table 7 provides an overview of the time taken to collect various available cooking energy sources from different points of purchase or collection. Results indicate that 40% of households surveyed spend less than 30 min on cooking energy collection. Moreover, 33% of households spend between 30 min and 1 h on collecting cooking fuels, while 27% of households spend more than 1 h on similar tasks. Table 7 also reveals that 49% of the households have various sources of cooking fuel, and spend less than 30 min on the cooking energy source collection, while 47% of households that use cooking energy sources spend 30 min on their collection.

Table 7. Time taken to collect cooking energy sources from various points of purchase or collection.

Average Time Taken for Cooking Energy Collection Round Trip	Location of Cooking Energy Sources							
	Always Available When Needed		Available at the Local Periodic Market		Not Locally Available		Total	
	N	%	n	%	N	%	n	%
Less than 30 min	201	48.5	15	16.2	4	9.3	220	40.0
30 min to 1 h	121	29.3	41	44.0	19	44.2	181	32.9
Above 1 h	92	22.2	37	39.8	20	46.5	149	27.0
Total	414	100	93	100	43	100	550	100

3.8. Responsibility for Cooking Fuel Collections

Table 8 shows that the responsibility of cooking fuel collection is distributed among the household members related to the fuel availability at the various points of purchase or collection. Findings indicate that across 129 households, which represent 23.4% of the households surveyed, it is exclusively the role of women to collect or buy cooking fuels from various points. The table further shows that for 145 households, which represent 26.3% of the total households surveyed, it is a shared responsibility among women and children to either buy or collect the fuel sources from various locations, while for the remaining half of the surveyed households, only children take on this responsibility of energy collection. Moreover, Table 8 further shows that for 88% of households, it is an exclusive role of children to collect fuel when it is always available when needed. For only 5% of households, there is a shared responsibility among women and children to collect fuels that are not locally available.

Table 8. Responsibility for cooking fuel collection.

Availability of Cooking Fuels at the Point of Purchase or Collection	Responsibility for Cooking Fuel Collection							
	Household Head (Women)		Women and Children		Children		Total	
	N	%	n	%	N	%	n	%
Always available when needed	76	58.9	95	65.5	243	88.1	414	75.3
Available at the local periodic market	22	17.1	43	29.7	28	10.1	93	16.9
Not locally available	31	24.0	7	4.8	5	1.8	43	7.8
Total	129	100	145	100	276	100	550	100

3.9. Vulnerabilities Associated with Water and Cooking Energy Collection

Table 9 shows various vulnerabilities that are mostly experienced during water and energy collection across the surveyed households. Findings indicate that 35% and 34% of the responsible people experience energy and time loss (e.g., physical exhaustion) during water and energy collections, respectively. Furthermore, 30% and 31% of the respective people experience personal security threats during the collection round trips, while 9% and 21% suffer from various vulnerabilities linked to adverse health impacts during the water and energy collection trips, correspondingly. Small proportions of the respective energy (14%) and water (16%) access challenges are linked to various special vulnerabilities, due to disabilities, old age, and pregnancy.

Table 9. Various vulnerabilities linked to water collection.

Vulnerabilities Experienced	Various Vulnerabilities Related to Water Collection									
	Security Challenge and Threat		Health Impact		Energy and Time Loss		Special Vulnerabilities		Total	
	n	%	N	%	n	%	n	%	n	%
Due to water collection	166	30.1	105	9.1	194	35.3	85	15.5	550	100
Due to energy collection	169	30.7	117	21.3	188	34.2	76	13.8	550	100

4. Discussion

This investigative study adds hard data evidence to the ongoing discussion towards achieving sustainable equitable access to clean water and energy, regardless of gender, socio-economic status, or location in sub-Saharan, rural African settings. Ending all forms of discrimination against women is not only a fundamental human right, but is central for the sustainable future of these regions. Empowering women and girls helps economic growth and development. Thus, ensuring equitable rights to economic resources and accessibility to household resources, which include water and energy, is key to empowering women.

The study observes that physical and economic inaccessibility to good-quality water and clean energy is prevalent in many of the surveyed rural households. Poor water and energy access is more widespread in low-income households, whereas poor accessibility to these essential household resources is associated with various vulnerabilities experienced across the affected households.

The investigation, across 550 households headed by females, reveals a low level of household head education, which implies that women are denied access to the same education as men. The study also reveals that the relationship between the educational status of female household heads with their various income groups is strong. In addition, high-income households with a household head with a relatively higher educational level tend to have easy access to enhanced water and clean energy sources. This finding reveals the water access situation where low-income households have access to various unimproved water sources. Consequently, the study shows the prevalence of access to different sources of unclean (solid) cooking fuels across the surveyed households. This is directly associated with a low-income level and location. Previous articles indicate that income is important for rural household water and energy preferences in developing states [51–60].

The results show that the accessibility to various water sources, availability of fuels, and the various distances to either points of collections or purchases varies across the investigated households. Several households (52.8% of the surveyed households) obtain water by walking more than 1000 m from their households, which coincides with some studies conducted in other sub-Saharan African countries [61,62]. The distances are above the maximum threshold recommended by WHO and UNICEF [18].

The study further reveals the frequent unavailability of many high-value fuel sources from local supplies, which include cooking gas, kerosene, charcoal, and saw dust, across the surveyed rural communities. This can be explained by poorly developed markets and distribution problems [63]. Conversely, households that access low-value energy sources made of biomass, which include dung, agricultural residue (post-harvest waste), and fuelwood, find these readily available either at the point of collection or via purchase.

The findings support international investigations by Rahut et al. [54] and Zhou et al. [64] in rural households of Pakistan and northern China, respectively. They find that the availability of biomass energy sources in the respective rural households are a major factor in energy choice. Furthermore, Gaur [57] finds that in rural areas of India, closeness to the market is one of the reasons that positively affects domestic use of modern fuel sources.

The study reveals the average distance travelled and time taken to collect water from various sources remains high for most households, which indicates that a large proportion of women and children live in families where the burden of collection is both over 1000 m and 30 min, which means that the distance covered and time taken are higher than the respective WHO and UNICEF thresholds for a safe journey [18]. Consequently, the study finds that rural women and children spend unreasonable time periods collecting cooking energy sources. This finding is supported by Heltberg [65], who finds that household responses to fuel scarcity leads to increased fuel collection times in rural India.

Moreover, the findings reveal that the majority of the surveyed households travel long distances to collect water and cooking fuels. On their daily trips to collect water and cooking fuel, rural women across the investigated households are vulnerable to dangers threatening their personal security. As the water and cooking fuel collection sources are located at various different places away from their households, women and children commonly walk very long distances, and have to trek via unsecured paths, often on their own and defenceless. Women and girls fetching water and cooking fuel everyday often became the target of threats to their personal security, sexual violence, and physical attacks.

Pommells et al. [66] report that travelling long distances, intensified by the regularity of community women's water-fetching habits, gives attackers the chance to target women who are alone, isolated, and defenceless. In addition, other studies [66–68] reveal that beyond the physical threats, which include sexual assaults, women are also subjected to psychological stress linked to panic attacks and general anxiety, intensified by the lack of confidence among females. On the same paths to water and fuel collection locations, physical violence linked to animal attacks is also reported [66,67,69]. Sharing the same water resource and foot paths with dangerous hungry animals also contributes to physical insecurity.

The study reveals that women and children collecting large quantities of water and cooking fuel multiple times per day report considerable physiological health impacts attributed to their trips. These health impacts are outside of those linked to water quality or safe cooking fuel. Women are often executing collection activities from an early age when good physical development is critical. Other studies [69,70] state that adverse health impacts linked to collecting water and cooking fuels include lasting back injuries, fatigue, micronutrient shortages due to a high number of calories being burned, body parts scratched and wounded by shrubs, attacks by wild dogs, and bites by venomous snakes.

Combining health effects with security fears, a broader scope of health risks appear. As an example, sexual attacks may not only damage the attacked person physically and psychologically, but may also result in long-term sexually transmitted diseases, such as the human immunodeficiency virus, potentially leading to the acquired immunodeficiency syndrome. Animal strikes are also a considerable health threat. Inflicted injuries are either hard to cure in remote rural locations and/or are liable to infection, potentially leading to mortality. The consequential health effects as a result of these experiences not only damage the physical advancement of women and children, but also obstruct their capability to take part in or achieve other daily activities and tasks, which include school education and professional work. As a consequence, some women remain uneducated, and without qualified jobs.

While collecting water and fuels for various household activities including cooking, hygiene, drinking, cleaning, and other fundamental actions is not a waste of time, the way in which most women and children across the investigated households fetch the resources often pose a great loss of time for them. In most of the surveyed households, access to water and cooking fuel sources is remote. It follows that women spend many hours making their daily collection round trips. The time spent could be used differently, for other productive or recreational activities.

The challenges highlighted in this study are also common to other rural settings, for example in Somalia, where women devote an average of 11.3 h weekly to the fetching of water [68]. The time spent on water and cooking fuel collection is accompanied by an opportunity cost [5], linked to 'trade-offs' [68]. Fetching water, collecting fuelwood, and other household responsibilities performed by women cause trade-offs including reduced security, nourishment deficiencies, and insufficient schooling [68].

In addition to time loss, the intensity of energy required to carry out water and fuel collections leaves little energy to accomplish other productive pursuits in the remaining daytime hours. Therefore, enhancing access to water, as well as cooking fuel, and reducing the distant trips to collect water and fuel allows women to participate in other productive activities, such as education and professional work.

This study reveals the influence of various income groups on access to household resources. For instance, high-income groups are linked to a lower average distance to the water sources than the other groups. However, this is not the case for collecting water from improved sources. The insecurity is related to the time taken and distance covered, which show the vulnerability of all respondents, regardless of their income group. There is a very high level of health concern common to all individuals who need to walk more than 1000 m to a water source, or require more than 30 min for total collection time.

The research reveals that across all investigated households, rural women and children are exclusively accountable for the collection of water and cooking fuels. Geere and Cortobius [68] also highlight that the women and children are principally in charge of fetching water. Moreover, women with special vulnerabilities are at an even greater disadvantage in accessing water. The study indicates that older adults, pregnant women, orphans, individuals with long-term illnesses, disabled females, and women coping with social stigma are in a more difficult position to access, and subsequently carry, water. It follows that these people are especially vulnerable, and their households face severe water insecurity [66,68]. Respondents report that pregnant women are extremely exposed to water uncertainty because of their physical constraints in undertaking the water collection activities. These groups have diverse physical or incidental constraints, and their incapability to perform the trip of water collection effectively broadens the challenge of inequitable access to water sources. This may either force them to take more dangerous journeys to other water resources, reduce their opportunity to successfully meet their basic needs for water, or force them to make other more costly arrangements.

The study findings reveal that it is a major role of women to collect cooking fuel across the investigated households; this coincides with the findings of the African Development Bank [69], which indicate that the typical rural energy predicament is linked to traditional gender role separation, with women spending considerably more time than men addressing energy supply needs for family survival [71]. This renders them vulnerable to wounds, including attacks by feral animals [70]. Moreover, addressing the challenges of women's access to water and energy is critical towards achieving SDGs 5, 6, and 7. Females are disadvantaged concerning water and energy governance in rural societies in sub-Saharan Africa, because they are not participating in the decisions concerning water and energy access, control, and utilisation. In order to proceed positively on SDG 6.B ("stakeholders participation") and SDG 7.1.2 ("proportion of population with primary reliance on clean fuels and technology"), a clear focus on addressing SDGs 5.1 ("end all forms of discrimination against all women and girls everywhere"), 5.2 ("eliminate all forms of violence against all women and girls in the public and private spheres, including trafficking and sexual and other types of exploitation"), and 5.5 ("ensure women's full and effective participation and equal opportunities for leadership at all levels of decision-making in political, economic and public life") is required [17]. Therefore, it is necessary to include women in local water and energy management decision-making, in order to lessen discrimination and violent behaviour linked to water and energy collection.

The struggles faced by rural women can be addressed if there is improved ownership by women, and a reduction in power held by men who traditionally manage key components of the household income, which also concerns water and energy management. Safeguarding women, so they have the same opportunities as men, would encourage them, and add invaluable understanding to basic processes that they are personally connected to, such as water and energy organisation.

5. Conclusions

The study examined gender accessibility to household water and energy supply in varied income households in rural communities in the Sahel Savannah region of Katsina State. There is a strong relationship between water and energy access and household income ($r = 0.67$ and $r = 0.74$ for water and energy, respectively). The results show that access to unimproved water and unclean energy sources for cooking are dominant across the surveyed households. Based on the distance to various water sources and the time taken to fetch water, findings reveal high levels of water insecurity. The majority of the families obtain water outside the specified WHO maximum standard in terms of time spent on collection. The study suggests that households are susceptible to water-borne diseases based on closeness to unimproved resources. Households depend on unclean cooking fuels with inefficient technologies (stoves), together with less healthy kitchen arrangements including the lack of a chimney, exhaust fan, or general ventilation. Access to solid cooking fuel sources, alongside inefficient cooking arrangements, further reveals that households are also prone to lethal diseases, as a result of indoor air pollution.

6. Limitations and Future Research

A vast majority of the rural inhabitants in Katsina State are confronting the growing risk of banditry, which is organised crime including murder, rape, kidnapping, and cattle rustling. Hence, due to these circumstances, the researchers had limited access to more rural households, as the security of the survey team could not be guaranteed at all times.

The data collected on the household water and energy accessibility and availability only relate to female-headed households. Other elements of water and cooking energy securities, which include affordability, safety, and stability should also be assessed in future studies. Moreover, the research should be extended to other rural households of low- and middle-income regions, and could evaluate the progress towards achieving sustainable gender equality for the most vulnerable social classes.

Author Contributions: Conceptualisation, Y.S. and M.S.; methodology, Y.S. and M.S.; investigation, Y.S.; formal analysis, Y.S.; writing the original draft, Y.S.; visualisation, Y.S.; writing, review, and editing, M.S.; supervision, M.S. All authors have read and agreed to the published version of the manuscript.

Funding: This research was sponsored by the Tertiary Education Tax Fund (TETFUND), Nigeria.

Institutional Review Board Statement: Ethical review and approval were waived for this study by the local authorities and community leaders in Nigeria.

Informed Consent Statement: Informed consent was obtained from all subjects involved in the study.

Data Availability Statement: Not applicable.

Acknowledgments: Aminu Yahaya El-Ladan supported the data curation and helped with the statistical analysis. Practical contributions by Nura Umar and other field assistants are acknowledged. The authors would like to acknowledge the support of the Katsina State government, the local authorities, and traditional leaders in the respective investigated communities.

Conflicts of Interest: The authors declare that they have no known competing financial interest or personal relationship that could appear to influence the work reported in this paper.

References

1. World Health Organisation (WHO); United Nations Children's Fund (UNICEF). Joint Water Supply and Sanitation Monitoring Programme 2014. In *Progress on Drinking Water and Sanitation*; WHO: New York, NY, USA; UNICEF: New York, NY, USA, 2013.
2. United Nations. *The Millennium Development Goals Report 2014*; United Nations: New York, NY, USA, 2014.
3. Blackden, C.M.; Wodon, Q. *Gender, Time Use, and Poverty in Sub-Saharan Africa*; World Bank: Washington, DC, USA, 2006. Available online: http://siteresources.worldbank.org/INTAFRREGTOPGENDER/Resources/gender_time_use_pov.pdf (accessed on 15 April 2022).
4. Goetz, A.M. *Who Answers to Women? Gender and Accountability*; United Nations Development Fund for Women: New York, NY, USA, 2008.
5. Sorenson, S.B.; Morssink, C.; Campos, P.A. Safe access to safe water in low income countries: Water fetching in current times. *Soc. Sci. Med.* **2011**, *72*, 1522–1526. [CrossRef] [PubMed]
6. Pickford, J. (Ed.) *Developing World Water*; Grosvenor Press: London, UK, 1987.
7. Tumwine, J.K. *Drawers of Water II: 30 Years of Change in Domestic Water Use & Environmental Health in East Africa*; International Institute for Environment and Development: London, UK, 2002.
8. United Nations. The Post 2015 Water Thematic Consultation: Recognition of Outcomes, High. Level Forum–World Water Day. 2013. Available online: http://www.unwater.org/downloads/Final9Aug2013_WATER_THEMATIC_CONSULTATION_REPORT.pdf (accessed on 15 April 2022).
9. Water Supply and Sanitation Collaborative Council. In *WASH Post-2015: Proposed Targets and Indicators for Drinking-Water, Sanitation and Hygiene*; 2014; pp. 1–12. Available online: http://www.unicef.org/wash/files/2_WSSCC_JMP_Fact_Sheets_2_UK_LoRes.pdf (accessed on 15 April 2022).

10. Swe, K.T.; Rahman, M.M.; Rahman, M.S.; Teng, Y.; Abe, S.K.; Hashizume, M.; Shibuya, K. Impact of poverty reduction on access to water and sanitation in low and lower-middle income countries: Country: Country-specific Bayesian projections to 2030. *Trop. Med. Int. Health* **2021**, *26*, 760–774. [CrossRef] [PubMed]
11. Christine, W.N.; Sammy, C.L. Energy Poverty and Its Implication on Standard of Living in Kirinyaga. *J. Energy* **2018**, *2018*, 3196567. [CrossRef]
12. Peter, H. Poverty Reduction Strategies: Opportunities and threats for sustainable rural water services in sub-Saharan Africa. *SAGE* **2008**, *8*, 115–128. [CrossRef]
13. World Health Organisation (WHO); United Nations Children's Fund (UNICEF). *Progress on Household Drinking Water, Sanitation, and Hygiene 2000–2017: Special Focus on Inequalities*; WHO: New York, NY, USA; UNICEF: New York, NY, USA, 2019.
14. United Nations Development Programme (UNDP). *Delivering Sustainable Energy in a Changing Climate—Strategy Note on Sustainable Energy 2017–2021*; UNDP: New York, NY, USA, 2017. Available online: http://www.undp.org/content/undp/en/home/librarypage/climate-and-disaster-resilience-/undp-s-enery-strategy-.html (accessed on 15 April 2022).
15. International Fund for Agricultural Development (IFAD). *Rural Poverty Report 2001: The Challenges of Ending Rural Poverty*; Oxford University Press for IFAD: Oxford, UK, 2001.
16. Molden, D. (Ed.) *Water for Food, Water for Life: A Comprehensive Assessment of Water Management in Agriculture*; International Water Management Institute: London, UK; Earthscan: Colombo, Sri Lanka, 2007. Available online: http://www.iwmi.cgiar.org/assessment/index.htm (accessed on 15 April 2022).
17. United Nations Inter-Agency and Expert Group on SDG Indicators. Tier Classification for Global SDG Indicators. Available online: https://unstats.un.org/sdgs/iaeg-sdgs/tier-classification (accessed on 27 March 2022).
18. World Health Organisation (WHO); United Nations Children's Fund (UNICEF). *Progress on Drinking Water, Sanitation, and Hygiene: 2017 Update and SDG Baselines*; UNICEF: Geneva, Switzerland, 2017.
19. Seckler, D.; Barker, R.; Amarasnghe, U. Water Scarcity in the Twenty-first Century. *Int. J. Wat. Resour. Developm.* **2010**, *15*, 29–42. [CrossRef]
20. Pachauri, S.; Spreng, D. Measuring and monitoring energy poverty. *Energy Pol.* **2011**, *39*, 7497–7504. [CrossRef]
21. Pachauri, S.; Spreng, D. Energy use and energy access in relation to poverty. *Econom. Politic. Wkly.* **2004**, *39*, 271–278.
22. Cecelski, E.; Dunkerley, J.; Ramsay, W. *Household Energy and the Poor in the Third World*; Routledge: London, UK; New York, NY, USA, 2015.
23. Risman, B.J. Gender as a Social Structure: Theory Wrestling with Activism. *Gend. Soc.* **2004**, *18*, 429–450. [CrossRef]
24. Dicke, A.; Safavian, N.; Eccles, J.S. Traditional Gender Role Beliefs and Career Attainment in STEM: A Gendered Story. *Front. Psychol.* **2019**, *10*, 1053. [CrossRef]
25. Makama, G.A. Patriarchy and Gender Inequality in Nigeria: The Way Forward. *Europ. Scientif. J.* **2013**, *9*, 17.
26. Pouramin, P.; Nagabhatla, N.; Miletto, M.A. Systematic Review of Water and Gender Interlinkages: Assessing the Intersection with Health. *Front. Wat.* **2020**, *2*, 6. [CrossRef]
27. Mahamud, A.S.; Ahmed, J.A.; Nyoka, R.; Auko, E.; Kahi, V.; Ndirangu, J.; Nguhi, M.; Burton, J.W.; Muhindo, B.Z.; Breiman, R.F.; et al. Epidemic cholera in Kakuma Refugee Camp, Kenya, 2009: The importance of sanitation and soap. *J. Infect. Dev. Ctries.* **2011**, *6*, 234–241. [CrossRef] [PubMed]
28. Fletcher, A.J.; Schonewille, R. United Nations World Water Assessment Programme Gender and Water Series Resource Paper United Nations World Water Assessment Programme. 2015. Available online: http://www.unesco.org/open-access (accessed on 15 April 2022).
29. Wu, S. The health impact of household cooking fuel choice on women: Evidence from China. *Sustainability* **2021**, *13*, 12080. [CrossRef]
30. Beulah, S.J.; Ranjitha, S.S.; Asha, K.; Avinash, S. Household cooking fuel use and its health effects among rural women in southern India—A cross-sectional study 2020. *PLoS ONE* **2020**, *5*, e0231757. [CrossRef]
31. Andrews, G.; Skinner, D.; Zuma, K. Epidemiology of health and vulnerability among children orphaned and made vulnerable by HIV/AIDS in sub- Saharan Africa. *AIDS Care* **2006**, *18*, 8. [CrossRef] [PubMed]
32. Galea, S.; Ahern, J.; Karpati, A. A model of underlying socioeconomic vulnerability in human populations: Evidence from variability in population health and implications for public health. *Soc. Sci. Med.* **2005**, *60*, 2417–2430. [CrossRef] [PubMed]
33. Leavitt, F.J. Is any medical research population not vulnerable? *Camb. Q. Healthc. Ethics* **2006**, *15*, 81–88. [CrossRef]
34. Montes, J.J.; Johnston, L.L. Eliminating health disparities for vulnerable populations through health education interventions within health services programs. *J. Health Educ.* **1998**, *29*, 2. [CrossRef]
35. Ramanna, H.; DeBakker, J.M.; Elvan, A.; Hauer, R.N. On the atrial response to focal discharges in man. *J. Cardiovas. Electrophysiol.* **2004**, *15*, 629–636. [CrossRef]
36. Hurst, S.A. Vulnerability in research and health care: Describing the elephant in the room? *Bioethics* **2008**, *22*, 191–202. [CrossRef]
37. Rio Political Declaration on Social Determinants of Health: A Snapshot of Canadian Actions 2015. Ottawa: Public Health Agency of Canada. 2015. Available online: https://www.healthycanadians.gc.ca/publications/science-research-sciences-recherches/rio/alt/rio2015-eng.pdf (accessed on 15 April 2022).
38. Brown, K. "Vulnerability": Handle with care. *Ethics Soc. Welf.* **2011**, *5*, 313–321. [CrossRef]
39. United Nations General Assembly. Transforming our World: The 2030 agenda for Sustainable Development. 2015. Available online: https://sdgs.un.org/2030agenda (accessed on 15 April 2022).

40. MacArthur, J.; Carrard, N.; Willetts, J. WASH and gender: A critical review of the literature and implications for gender-transformative WASH research. *J. Water Sanit. Hyg. Dev.* **2020**, *10*, 818–827. [CrossRef]
41. World Economic Forum. 104 Countries Have Laws that Prevent Women from Working in Some Jobs. 2018. Available online: https://www.weforum.org/agenda/2018/08/104-countries-have-laws-that-prevent-women-from-working-in-some-jobs/ (accessed on 15 April 2022).
42. International Labour Organization. *Domestic Workers across the World: Global and Regional Statistics and the Extent of Legal Protection*; International Labour Office Geneva: Geneva, Switzerland, 2013.
43. International Labour Organization (ILO). World Employment Social Outlook: Trends 2019. Available online: https://www.ilo.org/wcmsp5/groups/public/---dgreports/---dcomm/-publ/documents/publication/wcms_670542.pdf (accessed on 15 April 2022).
44. Abdullahi, F.G.; Ghani, N.A.; Dalhatu, S. Rural women's economic contribution towards community development in rural communities of Kano State, Nigeria. *Mediterr. J. Soc. Sci.* **2015**, *6*, 250–259. [CrossRef]
45. Opata, P.I.; Ezeiba, A.B.; Ume, C.O. Impact of women's share of income on household expenditure in southeast Nigeria. *Afr. J. Agric. Res. Econ.* **2020**, *15*, 51–64. [CrossRef]
46. Adepoju, A.A.; Ogunniyi, L.T.; Agbedeyi, D. The role of women in household food security in Osun state, Nigeria. *Int. J. Agric. Policy Res.* **2015**, *3*, 104–113. [CrossRef]
47. *Katsina State Diary*; Government Printers: Katsina, Nigeria, 2022.
48. United Nations Children's Fund (UNICEF); World Health Organisation (WHO). *Integrating Water Quality Testing into Household Survey: Thematic Report on Drinking Water*; UNICEF: New York, NY, USA, 2020.
49. World Health Organisation (WHO). *Fuel for Life: Household Energy and Health*; WHO Library Cataloguing in Publication Data: New York, NY, USA, 2006. Available online: http://www.who.int/indoorair/publications/fuelforlife.pdf?ua=1 (accessed on 12 February 2022).
50. *Katsina State Urban and Regional Planning Board (KTURPB)*; Government Printers: Katsina, Nigeria, 2018.
51. Gebremichael, S.G.; Yismaw, E.; Tsegaw, B.D.; Shibeshi, A.D. Determinants of water source use, quality of water, sanitation and hygiene perceptions among urban households in North-West Ethiopia: A cross-sectional study. *PLoS ONE* **2021**, *16*, e0239502. [CrossRef]
52. Gomez, M.; Perdiguero, J.; Sanz, À. Socioeconomic factors affecting water access in rural areas of low and middle income countries. *Water* **2019**, *11*, 202. [CrossRef]
53. Adamu, B.; Ndi, H.N. Changing trends in water sources and related pathologies in small to medium size African cities. *Geojournal* **2017**, *83*, 885–896. [CrossRef]
54. Rahut, D.B.; Khondoker, A.A.A.; Jeetendra, P.A. Wealth, education and cooking-fuel choices among rural households in Pakistan. *Energy Strat. Rev.* **2019**, *24*, 236–243. [CrossRef]
55. Hussain, A.; Dasgupta, S.; Bargali, H.S. Fuelwood consumption patterns by semi-nomadic pastoralist community and its implication on conservation of Corbett Tiger Reserve, India. *Energy Ecol. Environ.* **2017**, *2*, 49–59. [CrossRef]
56. Heltberg, R. Factors determining household fuel choice in Guatemala. *Environ. Dev. Econ.* **2005**, *10*, 337–361. [CrossRef]
57. Gaur, V. Determinants of household's modern cooking and lighting energy transition in rural India- exploring household's activities and its interactions with other households. In *ZEF-Discussion Papers on Development Policy No. 256*; University of Bonn—Center for Development Research (ZEF): Bonn, Germany, 2018. [CrossRef]
58. Rahut, D.B.; Behera, B.; Ali, A. Factors determining household use of clean and renewable energy sources for lighting in sub-saharan Africa. Renew. *Sustain. Energy Rev.* **2017**, *72*, 661–672. [CrossRef]
59. Sani, Y.; Scholz, M. Water-energy-food accessibility and tracking progress towards achieving sustainable development goals in the Savannah region of Katsina State, Nigeria. *Water* **2021**, *13*, 3595. [CrossRef]
60. Sani, Y.; Scholz, M. Interplay of water-energy security and food consumption patterns towards achieving nutrition security in Katsina State, Nigeria. *Sustainability* **2022**, *14*, 4478. [CrossRef]
61. Demie, G.; Bekele, M.; Seyoum, B. Water accessibility impact on girl and women's participation in education and other development activities: The case study of Wuchale and Jidda Woreda, Ethiopia. *Environ. Syst. Res.* **2016**, *5*, 11. [CrossRef]
62. Benjamin, L.; Nygren, C.E.O.; Eric, D.M. The relationship between distance to source and moderate-to-severe diarrhoea in the Global Enterics Multi-Center Study in Kenya, 2008–2011. *Am. J. Trop. Med. Hyg.* **2016**, *94*, 1143–1149. [CrossRef]
63. Basu, A.; James, D.; Marett, J.D. Access to Clean Energy in Rural Kenya through Innovative Market Based solutions. Available online: http://www.ss.undp.org/content/dam/LECB/docs/pubs-namas/undp-lecb-Kenya_Clean-Energy-NAMA-2016.pdf (accessed on 12 March 2022).
64. Zhou, Z.; Wu, W.; Chen, Q.; Chen, S. Study on sustainable development of rural household energy in northern China. *Renew. Sust. Energ. Rev.* **2008**, *12*, 2227–2239. [CrossRef]
65. Heltberg, T.; Arndt, T.C.; Sekhar, N.U. Fuelwood consumption and degradation: A household model for domestic energy substitution in rural India. *Land Econ.* **2000**, *76*, 213–232. [CrossRef]
66. Pommells, M.; Schuster-Wallace, C.; Watt, S.; Mulawa, Z. Gender violence as a water, sanitation, and hygiene risk: Uncovering violence against women and girls as it pertains to poor WaSH access. *Viol. Against Women* **2018**, *24*, 1851–1862. [CrossRef]
67. Kyayesimira, J.; Muheirwe, F. Health concerns and use of biomass energy in households: Voices of women from rural communities in Western Uganda. *Energ. Sustain. Soc.* **2021**, *11*, 42. [CrossRef]

68. Geere, J.; Cortobius, M. Who Carries the Weight of Water? Fetching Water in Rural and Urban Areas and the Implications for Water Security. *Wat. Alternativ.* **2017**, *10*, 513–540.
69. Njenga, M.; Mendum, R.; Gitau, J.; Jamnadass, R.; Watson, C. Trees on farms could satisfy household's firewood needs. Miti. *Tree Busin. Magaz. Afr.* **2017**, *33*, 20–23. Available online: http://apps.worldagroforestry.org/downloads/Publications/PDFS/NA17373.pdf (accessed on 15 April 2022).
70. African Development Bank. *Kenya Country Gender Profile*; Human Development Department (OSHD): Abidjan, Ivory Coast, 2007.
71. Fathallah, J.; Pyakurel, P. Addressing gender in energy studies. *Energy Res. Soc. Sci.* **2020**, *65*, 101461. [CrossRef]

horticulturae

MDPI

Article

Mitigation of Chilling Stress by Ozone Pretreatment and Acclimation of Sweet Pepper Grown under Unheated Greenhouse Conditions

Mohamed A. Sharaf-Eldin [1], Abdelwahab A. Etman [1], Ali Mahmoud Yassin [1], Salah Elsayed [2], Miklas Scholz [3,4,5,*] and Zaher Mundher Yaseen [6,*]

1 Horticulture Department, Faculty of Agriculture, Kafrelsheikh University, Kafr Elsheikh 33516, Egypt
2 Agricultural Engineering, Evaluation of Natural Resources Department, Environmental Studies and Research Institute, University of Sadat City, Minufiya 32897, Egypt
3 Directorate of Engineering the Future, School of Science, Engineering and Environment, the University of Salford, Newton Building, Greater Manchester M5 4WT, UK
4 Department of Civil Engineering Science, School of Civil Engineering and the Built Environment, Kingsway Campus, University of Johannesburg, Aukland Park, P.O. Box 524, Johannesburg 2006, South Africa
5 Department of Town Planning, Engineering Networks and Systems, South Ural State University, 76, Lenin Prospekt, 454080 Chelyabinsk, Russia
6 Civil and Environmental Engineering Department, King Fahd University of Petroleum & Minerals, Dhahran 31261, Saudi Arabia
* Correspondence: m.scholz@salford.ac.uk (M.S.); z.yaseen@kfupm.edu.sa (Z.M.Y.)

Citation: Sharaf-Eldin, M.A.; Etman, A.A.; Yassin, A.M.; Elsayed, S.; Scholz, M.; Yaseen, Z.M. Mitigation of Chilling Stress by Ozone Pretreatment and Acclimation of Sweet Pepper Grown under Unheated Greenhouse Conditions. *Horticulturae* **2022**, *8*, 1189. https://doi.org/10.3390/horticulturae8121189

Academic Editor: Luigi De Bellis

Received: 17 November 2022
Accepted: 9 December 2022
Published: 13 December 2022

Abstract: Ozone is an important air pollutant that causes many challenges for human health, such as lung diseases. The negative impacts of exogenous ozone on cultivated plants have been discussed in several publications, but the positive impacts are less investigated. The current study is an attempt to answer the following question: is there any positive contribution of ozone pretreatment in growing plants under stress? Plants grown in unheated plastic greenhouses suffer from cold stress during the winter when the temperature drops to 5–10 °C. This stress can also be enhanced under saline soil conditions in arid regions. Treatments involving different ozone application methods (seed priming and seedling foliar application) and cold pretreatment (4 °C for 36 h) were compared with untreated controls of two sweet pepper hybrids (Zidenka and Lirica) in an unheated plastic greenhouse. In general, the Lirica hybrid outperformed the Zidenka hybrid in growth and fruit yield and showed good adaptation to cold stress resulting from ozone treatment through foliar application on seedlings. Moreover, cold treatment was associated with higher values of the studied parameters compared to the control (untreated). A concentration of 20 ppm of ozone in the first season and as 30 ppm of ozone in the second season increased plant leaf area, proline content, and APX activity, all of which improved the plant's defense mechanisms against cold stress. These benefits contributed to high fruit sets; early, total, and marketable fruit yields; and fruit quality under cold stress. The highest yield (16.52 kg m^{-2}) was attained with 30 ppm ozone applied as a seedling spray, compared with 10.07 kg m^{-2} in the control. Therefore, the foliar application of ozone up to 30 ppm can be recommended for sweet pepper hybrids of Lirica under unheated plastic greenhouse conditions. Further investigations are needed to study the interaction of combined ozone and cold stress, as well as various levels of soil salinity.

Keywords: proline; ascorbate peroxidase; membrane permeability; yield and quality; cold pretreatment

1. Introduction

Global climate change has a negative impact on the agricultural sector, especially in arid regions [1–3]. Cold temperatures are a serious factor limiting the survival, productivity, and geographical distribution of plants in large areas worldwide [4,5]. Exposure to a low, non-lethal temperature usually has a significant adverse effect on the biochemical and physiological characteristics of plants through photosynthesis, antioxidant activity, uptake of water and nutrients, plant growth and productivity, and the quality of many economically important crops, such as fruits of loquat [6], zucchini [7], tomato [1], and pepper [2]. The inability to increase membrane fluidity and suppress photosynthetic processes results in membrane leakiness and negatively affects pepper productivity [3,8]. As reported by El-Aidy and Sharaf-Eldin [3], in the same experimental location and under the same conditions as those of the current study, low temperature in an unheated plastic greenhouse during the winter limited growth and significantly reduced fruit yield and quality, causing significant economic loss of sweet pepper in Egyptian.

Environmentally friendly approaches for overcoming biotic and abiotic stresses to crops play a crucial role in improving plant production and quality. One of the most common and effective approaches is plant breeding [9]. Additionally, protected cultivation successfully protects plants from various kinds of stresses in several regions [10]. Changing agricultural practices is essential for managing stress. Grafting is considered a valuable practice for increasing crop yield under stress conditions [11]. In a recent study, Consentino et al. [11] reported that the combined application of grafting and biostimulants (growth-promoting bacteria from *Azospirillum brasilense* DSM 2298) is a sustainable agronomic practice that significantly enhanced eggplant growth, yield, and quality under protected cultivation conditions.

The production of vegetable crops under stress is a challenge for sustainable agricultural systems under greenhouse conditions [12]. In places with mild, sunny winters, such as the Mediterranean, it is common to grow crops that require elevated temperatures in unheated greenhouses in the winter; however, the plants still suffer from cold stress, which negatively affects production. This strategy can reduce high cost associated with heating energy, especially given the high energy expenses brought on by the war between Russia and Ukraine. However, this strategy would be more effective if combined with adaptation techniques for cold stress. Cold adaptation requires early exposure to non-lethal low temperatures for a brief period [13]. Modifications in morphological, physiological, and biochemical processes involving antifreeze proteins, cell membrane inflexibility, compatible solutes, and epigenetic mechanisms enhance cold stress tolerance [14]. Moreover, antifreeze activity (enzymatic antioxidants, phenolics, and proline) and molecular changes in plants can result in an acclimation response that is characterized by a increased ability to resist low-temperature stress [15].

Ozone (O_3), a natural gas in the atmosphere, is considered one of the most damaging air pollutants [16] to cultivated plants at the ground level (30–100 $\mu g\ m^{-3}$) because of its phytotoxicity. It may be toxic in agricultural and rural regions at high concentrations (300–800 $\mu g\ m^{-3}$) [17]. Many adverse impacts of ozone on plant growth (e.g., reducing biomass production, inhibiting photosynthetic processes, and the formation of oxidative stress) have been reported for many crops, such as tomato, spinach, chard [18], common bean [19], maize [20], soybean [21], and wheat [22]. On the other hand, ozone could be used as an antimicrobial agent, owing to its strong oxidative ability in both aqueous and gaseous phases, and is useful for fruit preservation because it has no side effects on nutritional values and quality of products [23]. Hence, ozone has a distinguished role in extending the shelf life of postharvest fruits and vegetables [24] such as strawberry [25], tomato [26], and cantaloupe [16].

In addition to its crucial role in enhancing secondary metabolites and bioactive properties, the role of ozone in promoting plant growth and yield against many pathogens and abiotic stress has attracted considerable attention [27]. Some studies have reported on the role of exogenous ozone in pomegranate under stressful conditions, such as salinity [28], drought on *Phillyrea angustifolia* [29], and cold stress on cantaloupe [20]. When plants are exposed to nontoxic doses of ozone, their phytochemical parameters, including the antioxidant defense system and bioactive compounds, change as a typical initial stress response [30]. This modification of the plant biochemical system can contribute to mitigation of other kinds of stresses in the future.

Sweet pepper (*Capsicum annuum* L.) is one of the most important horticultural plants, owing to its nutritional value (ascorbic acid or vitamin C, antioxidants, and carotenoids), color, and flavor [31]. Pepper plants originate in tropical or subtropical regions of the world, so they require an elevated temperature for development that ranges from 25 to 30 °C [32]. Thus, sweet pepper commonly suffers from chilling stress in the winter season, and dramatic damage can occur in association with salt stress under in unheated plastic greenhouses in the winter season. Seed priming and foliar antistressors are crucial methods for mitigating stress on cultivated plants such as salinity stress [33] and water-deficit stress [34]. Several antistressors have been used in seed priming to overcome many stresses, such as potassium nitrate or salicylic acid under water-deficit stress [34] and salicylic acid under salinity–alkalinity stress [33]. Methyl salicylate was applied for the production of sweet pepper under stress [2]. Moreover, exogenous zeaxanthin was used on pepper seedlings to mitigate chilling injury.

The first published data about the positive role of ozone in improving sweet pepper resistance to cold stress only considered the plant growth in the seedling stage [8]. However, no articles on the role of ozone in the production of sweet pepper under cold conditions have been published to date. Nevertheless, such high stress commonly occurs in unheated plastic greenhouses in arid regions. Hence, the aim of this study is to answer the following questions: Which method is better for sweet pepper production in an unheated plastic greenhouse under cold stress: ozone or cold pretreatments with seed priming and/or seedling spraying? Which application method is better: seed priming or foliar spraying of seedling? Is the growth stage a factor in determining the appropriate application of ozone or chilling for sweet pepper acclimation? This study was carried out to evaluate the tolerance of sweet pepper hybrids to cold stress and saline soil conditions through ozone and cold pretreatments of seed priming or foliar spray of seedlings in an unheated plastic greenhouse. The impacts of different treatments on physiological and biochemical characteristics, as well as productivity, during plant growth were also investigated.

2. Materials and Methods

This work was carried out on two sweet pepper hybrids (Zidenka and Lirica) under plastic greenhouse conditions at the International Protected and Smart Agriculture Center, Faculty of Agriculture, Kafrelsheikh University, Egypt, during the two seasons of 2017/2018 and 2018/2019.

2.1. Climatic and Microclimatic Conditions

During the experimental period from September until June in both growing seasons, the maximum and minimum air temperatures for the inside and outside of the plastic greenhouse were recorded using RH/Temp data loggers (model BESANTEK BST-DL13, Nanjing, Jiangsu, China), as presented in Figure 1.

2.2. Treatments

The treatments included:

(A) Two sweet pepper hybrids (Zidenka and Lirica)

The plants were bought from the seed company Rijk Zwaan (The Netherlands). Healthy seeds with consistent in size and shape were chosen and sterilized for 5 min with 1% sodium hypochlorite.

(B) Four concentrations of ozonated water were compared to cold treatment and an untreated control.

An ozone generator (Matra—GL—2186, China) was used to make ozone-enriched water with different concentrations. Four O_3 concentrations (1, 5, 10, and 20 mg L^{-1}) were applied for the first season. However, the lower concentrations (1 and 5 mg L^{-1}) were replaced by two higher concentrations (30 and 60 mg L^{-1}) in the second season. Ozone concentrations were compared to cold stress treatment and an untreated control during both growing seasons.

(C) Two application methods in two separate experiments (seed soaking and seedling spraying)

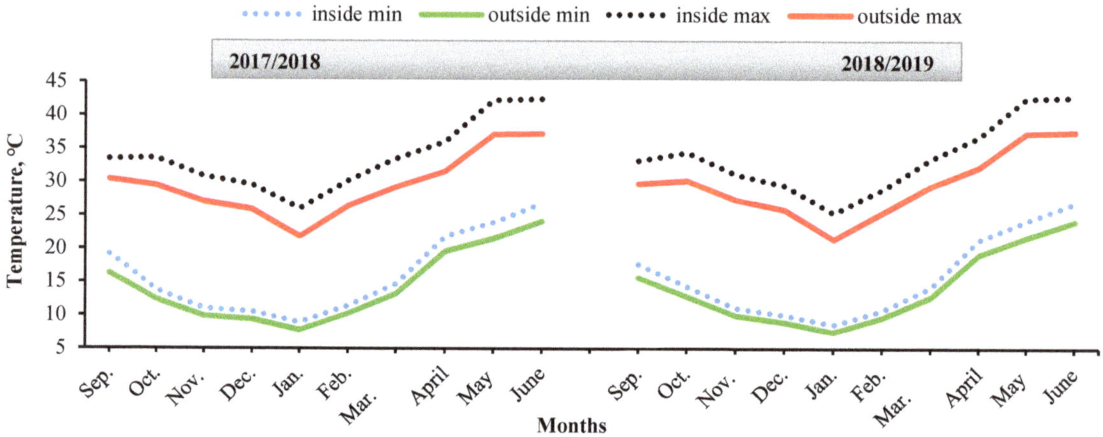

Figure 1. Maximum and minimum temperature for the inside and outside of the plastic greenhouse during the seasons of 2017/2018 and 2018/2019.

Seed soaking treatment:

The seeds were soaked in distilled water for 24 h and dried for 30 min at room temperature. Then, they were deep-soaked in the abovementioned concentrations of concentrated O_3 solution at room temperature for 1 h, followed by washing in running tap water for about 1 min (to avoid damage by ozone), were left to dry on the surface of paper towels under ambient conditions (22 °C and 65% relative humidity), then planted. For untreated seeds (control), the same procedures were followed, but water alone was used in place of the ozone solution. After germination, a chilling treatment was conducted on the seeds at 4 ± 1 °C for 36 h in the light [35]. The treated seeds were sown in seedling trays, which were filled with a mixture of peat moss and vermiculite (1:1 v/v). Untreated seeds (control) were sown at the same time as the treated seeds. In brief, this experiment comprised three groups. The first group was the untreated control (without ozone treatment or cold treatment). The second group was treated with ozone concentrations. The third group was subjected to cold treatment to induce cold resistance.

Seedling spray treatment:

Another separate experiment was conducted on another group of seeds. Untreated seeds were sown in seedling trays until they grew three real leaves. In this stage, the studied O_3 concentrations were foliar-sprayed as a seedling treatment. The seedlings were sprayed with O_3 solutions three times within three-day intervals. The chilling treatment was conducted at 4 ± 1 °C for 36 h in the light at the same age as the seedlings were treated with O_3. Untreated seedlings were considered the control. Thus, this experiment contained comprised groups of seedlings; untreated control (without cold or ozone treatments), ozone as a foliar spray, and cold treatment.

Pepper seeds were sown in seedling trays on 25 September in the first season and 5 September in the second season. After sowing, the trays were covered by black plastic for 3–4 days, then removed. Subsequently, the common practices of irrigation, fertilization, and pest management were performed in the nursery. The seedlings from each of the previously mentioned experiments were transplanted separately to same greenhouse. Each experiment had a separate untreated control (without ozone or cold treatment). The greenhouse comprises 1200 m^2 of land, with a length of 40 m, a width of 30 m, and a height of 3.5. The greenhouse was covered by a 200 μm thick polyethylene plastic film, and the he ventilation openings were covered by an insect-proof net sheet. The treatments were carried out on seeds and seedlings. The evaluated parameters were determined in mature plants under greenhouse conditions to consider the plant behavior during the production period.

2.3. *Studied Data*

2.3.1. Plant Leaf Area

Thirty and sixty days after transplanting, vegetative growth parameters were measured, i.e., leaf area per plant (m^2), using a portable leaf area meter (model LI-3000A, Lincoln, NE, USA).

2.3.2. Plant Biochemical and Physiological Parameters

Some biochemical assessments were conducted three times: (1) at the beginning of cold stress, (2) during the extreme cold stress period, and (3) after the cold period (i.e., after 30, 60, and 90 days, respectively).

(A) The relative chlorophyll content (SPAD) or green color content in the first fully expanded leaves was determined (without destroying them) using an SPAD501 apparatus (Minolta Corp, Ramsey, NJ, USA) for greenness measurements.

(B) Membrane permeability (MP), a measure of semipermeability loss of the plasma membrane, was determined by assessing electrolyte leakage according to the method described by Valentovic et al. [36]. Five plants were randomly chosen per replicate and cut into uniformly sized discs; then, 0.5 g of the disc was taken from the middle portion of the youngest fully developed leaf, which was washed with distilled water to remove surface contamination. The discs were placed in closed tubes containing 20 mL of deionized water and incubated at 25 °C for 24 h. The electrical conductivity (EC) of the bathing solution (EC1) was determined. The samples were then boiled in a water bath at 120 °C for 20 min, and the electrical conductivity (EC2) was determined after cooling the solution to room temperature. Membrane permeability was calculated as a ratio as follows:

$$(\mathrm{EC1}/\mathrm{EC2}) \times 100$$

(C) The relative water content (RWC) estimates the water content of fresh sampled leaf tissue relative the maximal water content it can hold at full turgidity (condition of being swollen). It was measured in fully developed leaves, which were cut and weighed immediately to determine the fresh weight (FW) and then immersed in double-distilled water for 16 h. The excess surface water was removed by drying with paper towels to determine the turgid weight (TW) of the leaves. The leaves were then oven-dried until a constant weight was recorded as the dry weight (DW). The RWC was determined according to Anjum [37]:

The RWC was determined according to the following Equation:

$$\mathrm{RWC}\ (\%) = \frac{\mathrm{FW} - \mathrm{DW}}{\mathrm{TW} - \mathrm{DW}} \times 100$$

(D) The proline (an amino acid) content was determined according to the method developed by Bates et al. [38], which involves filtering 0.5 g fresh leaf material homogenized in 10 mL of 3% aqueous sulfosalicylic acid through Whitman's No. 1 filter paper. Then, 2 mL of filtered extract was taken for the analysis, and 2 mL acid ninhydrin and 2 mL glacial acetic acid were added. The reaction mixture was incubated in a boiling water bath for 1 h, and the reaction was finished in an ice bath. Then, 4 mL of toluene was added to the reaction mixture, and the organic phase was extracted and read at 520 nm by UV-visible spectrophotometer, using toluene as a blank.

(E) Ascorbate peroxidase (APX) was measured in plants according to [39] using a spectrophotometer (model UV—160A, Shimadzu, Japan).

(F) The chemical composition of samples of five fruits from each plot was determined 90 days after transplanting in both seasons by measuring the total soluble solids (TSS) and vitamin C (mg 100 g^{-1} FW) in fruit juice according to the methods described by the AOAC [40].

2.3.3. Flowering and Fruit Set Parameters

The number of flowers/plant, the number of fruits/plant, fruit set percentage, and number of seeds/fruit were recorded during the coldest period of the season in December and January to determine the most beneficial treatment for mitigating cold stress during this period.

2.3.4. Fruit Yield and Quality

Full-colored red fruits from the Zidenka hybrid and yellow fruits from the Lirica hybrid were selected to determine yield parameters. Early yield was defined as the number and weight of all harvested fruits during the first 45 days of picking. Data on the early and total yields include fruit yield per square meter (kg) and fruit number. Ten fruits were randomly taken from each plot to measure the average fruit length and diameter (cm), as well as the average fruit weight (g). Damaged and deformed fruits were considered unmarketable. All studied parameters of fruit yield and quality were measured at the Physiology and Breeding of Horticultural Crops Laboratory, Dept. of Horticulture, Fac. of Agric., Kafrelsheikh University, Kafr El-Sheikh, Egypt, an accredited lab according to the ISO/IEC 17025-2017 standard.

2.4. *Soil Analysis*

Soil samples were randomly collected at a depth of a 0–30 cm before conducting the experiments in both growing seasons. The soil texture was clayey, with pH values of 7.86 and 8.20 (in extract 1:2.5), 1.71 and 1.75 Mg/m^3 bulk density, 1.7 and 1.5% organic matter percentage, ESP 7.37% and 10.21%, water holding capacity of 37.3% and 36.7%, infiltration rate of 0.23 and 0.25 cm/h, 40.2% and 39.1% field capacity, and 3.94 and 4.38 dS m^{-1} EC (in extract 1:5) in the first and second season, respectively, indicating that the experimental soil had a high salinity level. Other values were previously determined in a soil and water suspension according to [41] at the Central Lab for Environmental Studies at Kafrelsheikh Uni., which is accredited under ISO/IEC 17025-2017.

2.5. *Agricultural Practices*

The seedlings were transplanted in soil in a Spanish-style unheated plastic greenhouse with 30 m width, 40 m length, and 3.5 m height on 10 November in the first season and October 15th in the second season. Two side ridges with a width of 1.5 m width and a length of 30 m were prepared with plant spacing of 50 cm. The plant density was 2.66 plants per m^2, and the experimental plot area was 6.25 m^2. Pruning was carried out on two branches 60 days after transplanting and continuously during the growing season. All missing plants were replaced within two weeks of transplanting. Common agricultural practices for drip irrigation, pest control, and fertilization were applied.

2.6. *Statistical Analyses*

Two factors in three replicates were studied in a split-plot design. The first factor was two pepper hybrids, which were assigned as main plots. The second factor included six treatments (chilling treatments with ozone levels of 0, 10, 20, 30, and 60 mg L^{-1}), which was assigned as a subplot. Statistical analysis was performed using the Assistats statistical software version 7.7 (2016). The main values of the treatments were compared according to Duncan's multiple range test at 0.05 levels for each season separately.

3. Results

3.1. Climatic and Microclimatic Conditions

Data presented in Figure 1 indicate that the air temperature in the studied greenhouse was higher than the outside temperature during all the experimentation periods from September until June. However, the temperature inside the greenhouse reached its minimum during January, with values of 7.8 and 7.5 °C in the first and second season, respectively. The minimum temperature also dropped to approximately 9–10 °C from November to February (about 120 days), indicating that the plants grown in the unheated greenhouse suffered from chilling stress for an extended period.

3.2. Relative Water Content of Leaves (RWC)

It is reasonable to follow up the changes in RWC in relation to the studied treatments because these changes have an impact on other important parameters, such as physiological characteristics, membrane permeability, enzyme activity, and solute concentrations. Overall, the RWC increased during the later sampling dates (60 and 90 days after transplanting (DAT)) compared with younger plant ages (Table 1). On all sampling dates during both growing seasons, the RWC was significantly affected by chilling tolerance pretreatments, with minor variations between the studied hybrids. Therefore, increasing the ozone concentration up to 20 or 30 ppm (in the first and second season, respectively) significantly increased the RWC in leaves. In comparison with cold pretreatment, it was higher than the untreated control, with intermediate values. With respect to the ozone application method, we did not find any significant differences between any sampling dates in either season, except after 60 DAT in the second season, for which the soaking method caused a much higher RWC than ozone seedling spraying.

Table 1. Effect of ozone and chilling tolerance pretreatments on relative water content of two sweet pepper hybrids 30, 60, and 90 days after transplanting during the 2017/18 and 2018/19 seasons.

Treatment		Relative Water Content (%)					
		30 Days after Transplanting		60 Days after Transplanting		90 Days after Transplanting	
		Seed Soaking	Seedling Spray	Seed Soaking	Seedling Spray	Seed Soaking	Seedling Spray
2017/2018							
Zidenka cv.	Control	72.43 d	71.50 f	81.10 c	79.46 e	81.00 b	81.13 b
	* Cold	75.46 b	76.13 b	82.06 b	81.90 bc	81.20 b	81.30 b
	1 ppm O_3	72.60 d	71.40 f	81.16 c	79.40 e	81.30 b	81.20 b
	5 ppm O_3	72.10 d	71.50 f	81.23 c	79.56 e	81.50 b	81.40 b
	10 ppm O_3	74.26 c	73.06 e	81.56 c	81.66 c	81.40 b	81.50 b
	20 ppm O_3	75.20 b	75.70 bc	82.30 b	82.03 b	82.06 a	82.16 a
Lirica cv.	Control	74.30 c	74.40 d	82.00 bc	81.00 c	81.06 b	80.96 ab
	* Cold	74.26 c	76.13 b	82.56 b	81.33 c	81.06 b	81.26 b
	1 ppm O_3	74.06 c	74.36 d	82.00 bc	81.10 c	81.26 b	81.06 bc
	5 ppm O_3	74.30 c	74.50 d	82.03 b	81.43 c	81.80 ab	81.73 b
	10 ppm O_3	75.46 b	75.06 c	84.43 a	84.20 a	81.73 ab	81.80 b
	20 ppm O_3	78.63 a	78.33 a	85.23 a	85.13 a	82.06 a	82.33 a
Significance		*	*	*	*	*	*
2018/2019							
Zidenka cv.	Control	71.20 i	71.50 g	79.60 e	79.63 f	81.00 cd	81.13 c
	* Cold	76.60 e	76.13 d	81.90 d	81.20 c	81.20 c	81.30 c
	10 ppm O_3	73.33 g	73.06 f	82.00 cd	79.86 f	81.40 c	81.50 c
	20 ppm O_3	76.23 e	75.70 e	83.26 c	80.03 e	82.06 b	82.16 b
	30 ppm O_3	81.36 b	81.00 b	89.73 a	81.93 bc	83.00 a	83.13 ab
	60 ppm O_3	77.20 d	81.13 b	84.63 b	82.56 b	82.93 b	83.23 a

Table 1. *Cont.*

Treatment		Relative Water Content (%)					
		30 Days after Transplanting		60 Days after Transplanting		90 Days after Transplanting	
		Seed Soaking	Seedling Spray	Seed Soaking	Seedling Spray	Seed Soaking	Seedling Spray
		2018/2019					
Lirica cv.	Control	74.30 fg	74.40 ef	80.86 e	79.83 f	81.06 cd	80.96 d
	* Cold	76.70 e	76.50 d	82.66 c	81.16 c	81.06 cd	81.26 c
	10 ppm O_3	75.46 f	75.06 e	84.53 b	80.70 e	81.73 c	81.80 c
	20 ppm O_3	78.63 cd	78.23 c	85.20 b	81.36 c	82.06 b	82.33 b
	30 ppm O_3	83.83 a	82.90 a	91.76 a	83.70 ab	84.06 a	84.40 a
	60 ppm O_3	79.30 c	82.20 a	84.66 b	84. 93 a	83.60 a	83.23 a
Significance		*	*	*	*	*	*

Means followed by a lowercase letter in the same column are not significantly different according to Duncan's multiple range test at 0.05 levels for each season separately. * Cold stress treatment was performed at 4 °C for 36 h. Ozonated water applied as seed soaking or seedling spray compared to the untreated control.

3.3. Plant Leaf Area

The results presented in Table 2 show that the plant leaf area almost doubled from 30 to 60 (DAT). The interaction between the hybrids and chilling tolerant treatments was significant in both growing seasons, except in the first season on the early sampling date (30 DAT). It was observed that regardless the hybrid, the untreated control and cold pretreatment obtained the lower values than ozone pretreatment. However, the higher ozone concentrations either with seed soaking or seedling spray significantly increased plant leaf area. Ozone at 20 ppm produced the highest plant leaf area in the first season, followed by 10 ppm, whereas in the second season, 30 ppm of ozone achieved the highest values. Moreover, data show insignificant differences between the application methods of seed soaking and seedling spray in terms of plant leaf area, except at 60 DAT in the first season, when seedling spray had a better effect than seed soaking. However, the plant leaf area of the Lirica's hybrid was somewhat greater than that of the Zidenka hybrid, with maximum values recorded when exposed to ozone levels of 20 or 30 ppm.

Table 2. Effect of ozone and chilling tolerance pretreatments on plant leaf area of two sweet pepper hybrids 30 and 60 days after transplanting during the 2017/18 and 2018/19 seasons.

Treatment		Leaf Area (m^2 $Plant^{-1}$)			
		30 Days after Transplanting		60 Days after Transplanting	
		Seed Soaking	Seedling Spray	Seed Soaking	Seedling Spray
		2017/2018			
Zidenka cv.	Control	15.68 a	15.47 a	30.01 e	31.09 d
	* Cold	15.00 a	15.00 a	33.62 b	31.40 d
	1 ppm O_3	15.88 a	15.31 a	30.56 e	31.58 d
	5 ppm O_3	15.88 a	16.03 a	30.64 e	31.25 d
	10 ppm O_3	16.86 a	17.01 a	32.43 c	34.15 bc
	20 ppm O_3	17.51 a	17.29 a	36.58 a	35.73 b
Lirica cv.	Control	15.90 a	15.27 a	31.09 d	33.57 c
	* Cold	15.34 a	15.42 a	31.40 d	35.72 b
	1 ppm O_3	16.19 a	16.00 a	31.58 d	33.31 c
	5 ppm O_3	16.26 a	17.32 a	31.25 d	33.62 c
	10 ppm O_3	17.03 a	17.37 a	34.15 b	40.39 a
	20 ppm O_3	17.95 a	15.84 a	35.75 a	36.37 b
Significance		ns	ns	*	*

Table 2. *Cont.*

Treatment		Leaf Area (m^2 $Plant^{-1}$)			
		30 Days after Transplanting		60 Days after Transplanting	
		Seed Soaking	Seedling Spray	Seed Soaking	Seedling Spray
		2018/2019			
Zidenka cv.	Control	18.50 cd	17.55 d	26.12 h	28.77 f
	* Cold	15.92 e	18.07 cd	31.55 g	42.42 c
	10 ppm O_3	19.13 c	19.49 b	34.00 f	38.26 d
	20 ppm O_3	19.77 bc	19.64 b	41.32 d	44.20 b
	30 ppm O_3	21.59 a	19.28 b	43.96 c	47.03 a
	60 ppm O_3	19.92 bc	18.77 c	45.04 b	34.09 e
Lirica cv.	Control	16.85 d	16.71 e	25.73 h	26.84 g
	* Cold	15.98 de	15.89 e	30.38 g	27.80 f
	10 ppm O_3	20.18 b	19.13 bc	37.55 e	33.34 e
	20 ppm O_3	20.96 ab	21.94 a	43.91 c	37.75 d
	30 ppm O_3	21.65 a	20.83 ab	49.36 a	48.33 a
	60 ppm O_3	21.05 a	18.20 c	44.93 b	38.84 d
Significance		*	*	*	*

Means followed by a lowercase letter in the same column are not significantly different according to Duncan's multiple range test at 0.05 levels for each season separately. * Cold stress treatment performed at 4 °C for 36 h. Ozonated water applied as seed soaking or seedling spray compared to the untreated control.

3.4. Relative Chlorophyll Content of Leaves (SPAD)

The relative chlorophyll content (SPAD) seemed to rise with plant age until 90 DAT (Table 3). Lirica leaves tended to have the highest relative chlorophyll content when exposed to high ozone concentrations (20 and 30 ppm). Increasing the ozone concentration to 20 ppm (in the first season) or 30 ppm (in the second season) significantly increased SPAD values during the first three months of plant life. However, the control and cold pretreatment resulted in the lowest values. Except at early sampling dates (30 and 60 DAT) in the second season, the differences between the two application methods (seed soaking or seedling spray) were not statistically detectable, and seed soaking was superior to seedling spray. In both growing seasons at all sampling dates, the interaction between the hybrids and chilling tolerance pretreatments was significant (Table 2).

Table 3. Effect of ozone and chilling tolerance pretreatments on relative chlorophyll content (SPAD) of two sweet pepper hybrids 30, 60, and 90 days after transplanting during the 2017/18 and 2018/19 seasons.

Treatment		Relative Chlorophyll Content (SPAD)					
		30 Days after Transplanting		60 Days after Transplanting		90 Days after Transplanting	
		Seed Soaking	Seedling Spray	Seed Soaking	Seedling Spray	Seed Soaking	Seedling Spray
		2017/2018					
Zidenka cv.	Control	43.06 e	41.43 e	49.46 e	49.30 e	58.30 c	58.46 b
	* Cold	49.10 c	46.60 c	52.20 c	54.60 bc	58.33 c	58.13 bc
	1 ppm O_3	42.56 ef	41.50 e	49.63 e	49.36 e	58.13 c	58.33 b
	5 ppm O_3	43.86 e	41.30 e	49.76 e	49.40 e	58.13 c	58.13 bc
	10 ppm O_3	48.13 d	43.46 d	54.10 b	51.46 d	58.13 c	58.13 bc
	20 ppm O_3	53.20 ab	47.13 bc	54.83 b	55.13 b	59.10 b	59.10 ab
Lirica cv.	Control	48.50 cd	48.13 b	52.06 c	53.90 c	58.80 bc	58.50 b
	* Cold	48.03 d	47.60 bc	52.60 c	55.60 b	59.70 ab	59.70 b
	1 ppm O_3	48.50 cd	48.30 b	52.33 c	55.13 b	59.70 ab	59.70 a
	5 ppm O_3	48.40 cd	48.60 b	52.36 c	56.40 a	60.13 a	60.13 a
	10 ppm O_3	52.73 b	49.50 a	54.70 b	56.13 a	60.13 a	60.13 a
	20 ppm O_3	54.76 a	50.13 a	57.40 a	56.20 a	60.13 a	61.06 a

Table 3. *Cont.*

Treatment		Relative Chlorophyll Content (SPAD)					
		30 Days after Transplanting		60 Days after Transplanting		90 Days after Transplanting	
		Seed Soaking	Seedling Spray	Seed Soaking	Seedling Spray	Seed Soaking	Seedling Spray
Significance		*	*	*	*	*	*
2018/2019							
Zidenka cv.	Control	41.20 e	42.30 e	51.20 g	51.30 e	58.30 c	58.46 c
	* Cold	41.80 e	46.60 c	51.80 g	56.60 c	58.33 c	58.13 c
	10 ppm O_3	48.13 d	43.66 d	58.13 e	53.46 d	58.13 c	58.13 c
	20 ppm O_3	49.10 c	47.13 b	59.10 d	57.13 b	59.10 b	59.10 bc
	30 ppm O_3	53.13 ab	48.76 a	63.13 b	58.76 a	60.13 a	60.13 ab
	60 ppm O_3	48.20 d	45.66 cd	58.20 e	55.66 c	59.76 ab	59.23 bc
Lirica cv.	Control	48.50 cd	48.13 ab	58.50 de	58.13 ab	58.80 c	58.80 c
	* Cold	44.60 e	47.60 ab	54.60 f	57.60 b	59.70 ab	59.70 b
	10 ppm O_3	52.73 b	45.90 cd	62.73 bc	55.90 c	60.13 a	60.13 ab
	20 ppm O_3	53.20 ab	47.13 b	63.20 b	57.13 b	60.13 a	61.06 a
	30 ppm O_3	54.76 a	49.10 a	64.76 a	59.10 a	60.36 a	60.36 a
	60 ppm O_3	52.13 b	48.56 a	62.13 c	58.56 a	60.00 a	59.83 b
Significance		*	*	*	*	*	*

Means followed by a lowercase letter in the same column are not significantly different according to Duncan's multiple range test at 0.05 levels for each season separately. * Cold stress treatment was performed at 4 °C for 36 h. Ozonated water applied as seed soaking or seedling spray compared to the untreated control.

3.5. Membrane Permeability

The data presented in Table 4 indicate that the membranes were more efficient during early plant growth (30 DAT), and their effectiveness then declined. In general, at all sampling dates during both growing seasons, the studied pretreatments had a significant impact on the permeability of the leaf cell membrane, and slight differences between the application methods (seed soaking and seedling spray) were noticed. The treatments increased the membrane stability compared to the untreated control. However, the results with respect to the studied hybrids are in conflict. In the first season at early sampling dates, the control did not significantly differ from the plants treated with low ozone concentrations. Later, at 90 DAT, all ozone concentrations were significantly higher than the untreated control. Regardless of the treated hybrid, plants treated with higher ozone concentrations (20 ppm in the first season and 30 and 60 ppm in the second season) had the highest values, whereas the cold pretreatment had intermediate values.

Table 4. Effect of ozone and chilling tolerance pretreatments on membrane permeability of two sweet pepper hybrids 30, 60, and 90 days after transplanting during the 2017/18 and 2018/19 seasons.

Treatment		Membrane Permeability (%)					
		30 Days after Transplanting		60 Days after Transplanting		90 Days after Transplanting	
		Seed Soaking	Seedling Spray	Seed Soaking	Seedling Spray	Seed Soaking	Seedling Spray
2017/2018							
Zidenka cv.	Control	18.23 a	18.23 a	22.13 a	22.56 a	21.06 a	21.20 a
	* Cold	16.36 c	16.36 c	19.63 c	19.70 c	19.96 b	20.66 ab
	1 ppm O_3	18.30 a	18.23 a	21.50 b	22.53 a	17.13 e	16.66 cd
	5 ppm O_3	18.03 a	18.36 a	21.76 ab	22.60 a	17.96 e	16.43 d
	10 ppm O_3	17.23 b	17.23 b	21.76 ab	21.53 b	19.66 b	19.50 b
	20 ppm O_3	15.20 d	15.20 d	26.60 e	21.40 b	19.03 b	18.80 bc

Table 4. *Cont.*

Treatment		Membrane Permeability (%)					
		30 Days after Transplanting		60 Days after Transplanting		90 Days after Transplanting	
		Seed Soaking	Seedling Spray	Seed Soaking	Seedling Spray	Seed Soaking	Seedling Spray
Lirica cv.	Control	17.93 ab	17.93 ab	20.32 bc	19.73 c	18.60 c	19.73 b
	* Cold	16.56 c	16.56 c	18.90 cd	18.66 d	18.50 c	18.60 bc
	1 ppm O_3	18.13 a	17.56 ab	21.06 b	19.70 c	18.26 c	18.13 c
	5 ppm O_3	18.26 a	17.86 ab	20.53 bc	19.60 c	17.40 e	17.23 c
	10 ppm O_3	17.40 b	17.40 b	17.73 d	17.93 de	18.03 c	18.03 c
	20 ppm O_3	15.66 d	15.66 d	17.00 d	17.13 e	17.60 e	17.60 cd
Significance		*	*	*	*	*	*
2018/2019							
Zidenka cv.	Control	18.23 a	18.23 a	22.13 a	22.56 a	21.06 a	21.20 a
	* Cold	16.36 c	16.36 c	19.63 d	19.70 c	19.96 ab	20.06 b
	10 ppm O_3	17.23 b	17.23 b	21.50 b	22.53 a	19.66 b	19.50 b
	20 ppm O_3	15.20 d	15.20 d	21.76 ab	22.60 a	19.03 b	18.80 bc
	30 ppm O_3	14.46 e	14.46 e	21.70 ab	21.53 b	18.26 c	18.13 c
	60 ppm O_3	16.30 c	14.96 d	20.60 c	21.40 b	17.40 d	17.23 cd
Lirica cv.	Control	17.93 a	17.93 a	20.23 c	22.53 a	18.60 bc	19.73 b
	* Cold	16.56 c	16.56 c	18.90 de	18.66 e	18.50 bc	18.60 bc
	10 ppm O_3	17.40 b	17.40 ab	21.06 b	19.73 c	18.03 c	18.03 c
	20 ppm O_3	15.66 d	15.66 d	20.53 c	19.60 c	17.60 d	17.60 c
	30 ppm O_3	14.06 e	14.06 e	17.73 e	17.93 f	17.13 d	16.66 d
	60 ppm O_3	17.23 b	14.80 e	17.00 e	17.13 e	17.96 cd	16.43 d
Significance		*	*	*	*	*	*

Means followed by a lowercase letter in the same column are not significantly different according to Duncan's multiple range test at 0.05 levels for each season separately. * Cold stress treatment was performed at 4 °C for 36 h. Ozonated water applied as seed soaking or seedling spray compared to the untreated control.

3.6. Proline Content of Leaves

At 60 DAT, proline content jumped to almost three times more than that at 30 DAT, then slightly decreased at 90 DAT (Figures 2 and 3). The proline content in Lirica leaves was significantly higher than that in Zidenka leaves. Lirica leaves had the highest proline content under 20 or 30 ppm ozone in the first and second season, respectively. Chilling tolerance pretreatment significantly affected leaf proline content at all sampling dates (30, 60, and 90 DAT) in both seasons. Proline content increased gradually as O_3 concentration was increased to 30 or 60 ppm. At all tested sampling dates in both seasons, cold pretreatment ranked second, whereas the control recorded the lowest value. Seedling spray was better than seed soaking at 30 DAT, increased from 0.806 to 1.645 and from 0.874 to 0.993 μmol g^{-1}FW in the first and second season, respectively, with increases from 0.911 to 1.75 and from 1.761 to 1.874 μmol g^{-1} in the first and second season, respectively, at 60 DAT, whereas the differences were not statistically detectable at 90 DAT.

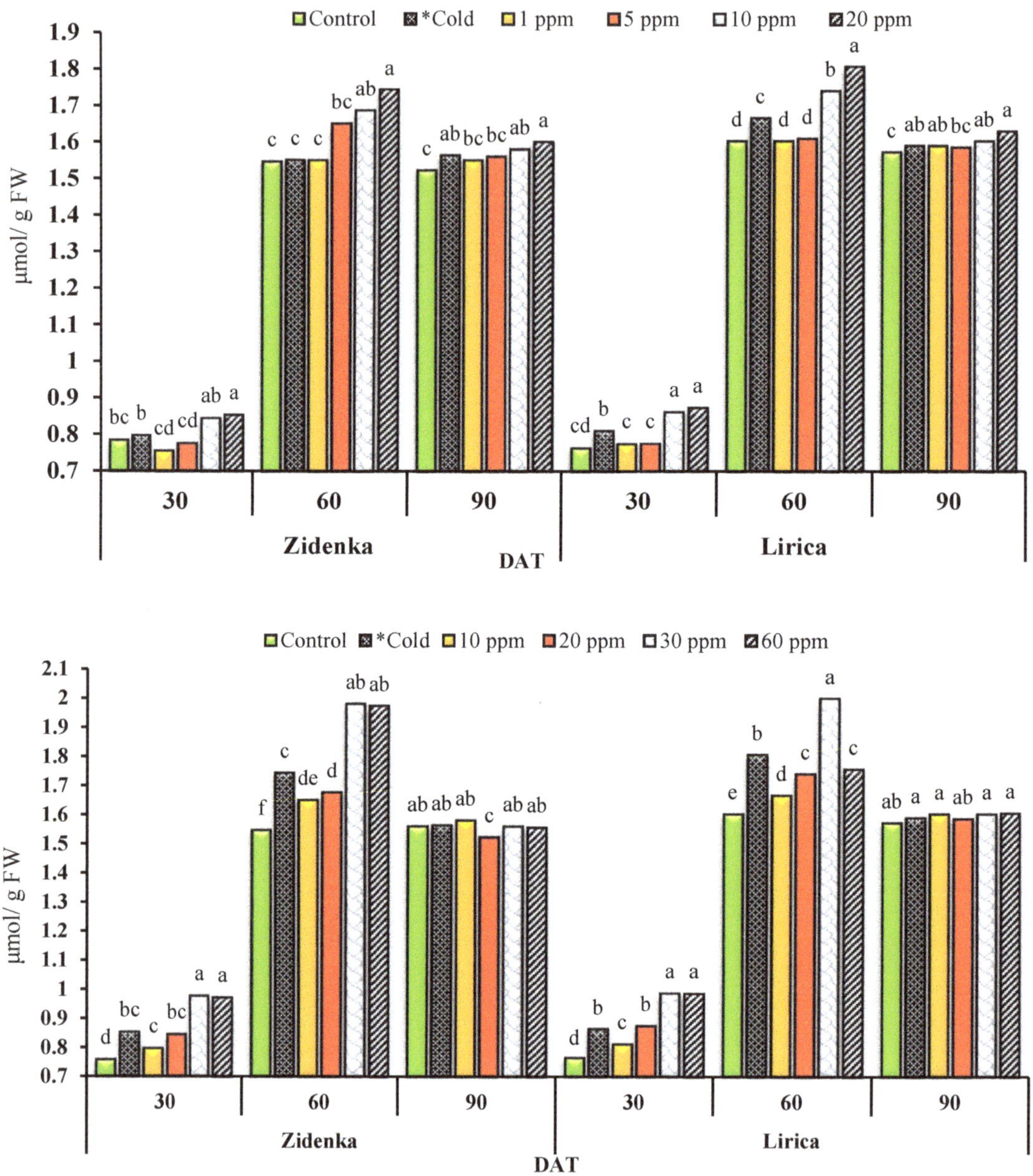

Figure 2. Effect of seed soaking with different ozonated water concentrations and cold pretreatments on the proline content of two pepper hybrids 30, 60, and 90 days after transplanting during the 2017/2018 (**upper** figure) and 2018/2019 (**lower** figure) seasons. Columns labeled with a lowercase letter are not significantly different according to Duncan's multiple range test at 0.05 levels for the same sampling date in each season and each hybrid separately. * Cold stress treatment was performed at 4 °C for 36 h. Ozonated water was applied as seed soaking. The average value of three biological and three technical replicates is reported.

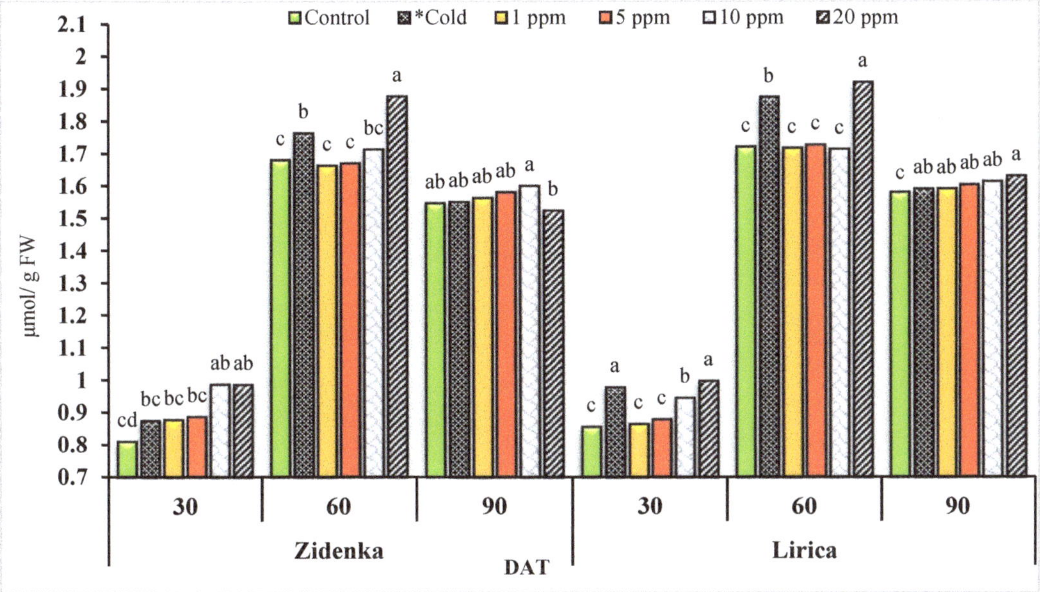

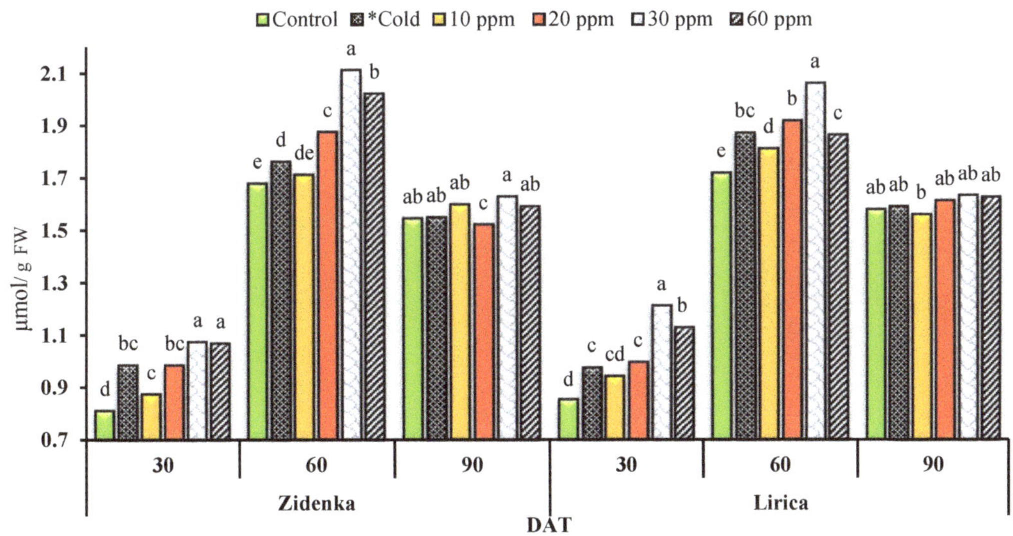

Figure 3. Effect of seedlings spray with different ozonated water concentrations and cold pretreatments on proline content of two pepper hybrids 30, 60, and 90 days after transplanting during the 2017/2018 (**upper** figure) and 2018/2019 (**lower** figure) seasons. The columns labeled with a lowercase letter are not significantly different according to Duncan's multiple range test at 0.05 levels for the same sampling date in each season and each hybrid separately. * Cold stress treatment was performed at 4 °C for 36 h. The average value of three biological and three technical replicates is reported.

3.7. Ascorbate Peroxidase (APX)

According to the data shown in Figures 4 and 5, APX almost doubled 60 days after transplanting compared to after 30 days, then slightly decreased after 90 days. Data indicate that ozone and cold pretreatments had a significant impact on APX activity in both hybrid leaves at all tested sample dates during both growing seasons. In general, Lirica leaves had the highest APX activity when treated with higher ozone-induced concentrations. However, the Zidenka control had the lowest values. APX activity increased with increasing ozone concentration and reached the maximum value in Lyrica leaves with 20 or 30 ppm O_3 (in the first and second season, respectively). The cold treatment resulted in intermediate values between the higher concentrations of ozone and the control. With respect to the application method, it was found that APX activity was significantly higher when seedlings were sprayed by ozone than when the seeds were soaked in ozonated water at a young plant age 30 and 60 days after transplanting. The enzyme activity increased from 0.333–0.362 to 0.378–0.412 μmol min^{-1}g at 30 DAT and from 0.683–0.731 to 0.731–0.778 μmol min^{-1}g at 60 DAT in the first and second season, respectively. However, the differences were not statistically detectable at 90 DAT in either growing season.

3.8. Flowering and Fruit Set Parameters

To investigate the efficiency of treatments in mitigating cold stress, flowering and fruit set parameters were monitored during the coldest period of the year in December and January (Table 5). Among all examined flowering and fruit set characteristics, the interaction between the hybrids and prime treatments was significant. Additionally, a considerable increase in pollination and fertilization over the control and cold treatment was suggested. It was noticed that Lirica hybrid's flowering was extremely sensitive to cold treatment, as reflected by the poor flower production of the plant (3.66–4.20 flower/plant) during the coldest period of December and January. However, it produced the most flowers (6.66 to 7.33 flowers/plant) when primed by high ozone concentrations. Furthermore, when exposed to increased ozone concentrations, Larica had a higher fruit set percentage, more fruits per plant, and more seeds inside each fruit (Table 5). Ozone pretreatment had a superior effect in terms of pollination and fertilization processes under cold stress, as evidenced by the considerable increases in the number of flowers per plant (from 4.76–5.20 to 6.33–7.33 flowers) and fruit set percentage (from 34.86–45.50 to 93.19–99.24%), which resulted from increasing the ozone concentration up to 20 ppm in the first season and 30 ppm in the second season. It was apparent that the trend in the number of fruits formed by each plant followed that of flowers. Cold treatment and the control had the lowest values in both seasons. As an indicator of fertilization efficacy, we counted the seeds inside the fruit. When the seeds and seedlings were previously primed by ozonated water with concentrations of 20 and 30 ppm, the fruits had high seed counts. The control and the cold treatment plants recorded had the lowest values in both seasons. Regarding application techniques, we found no significant variations in any of the blooming and fruit set features investigated in either growing season.

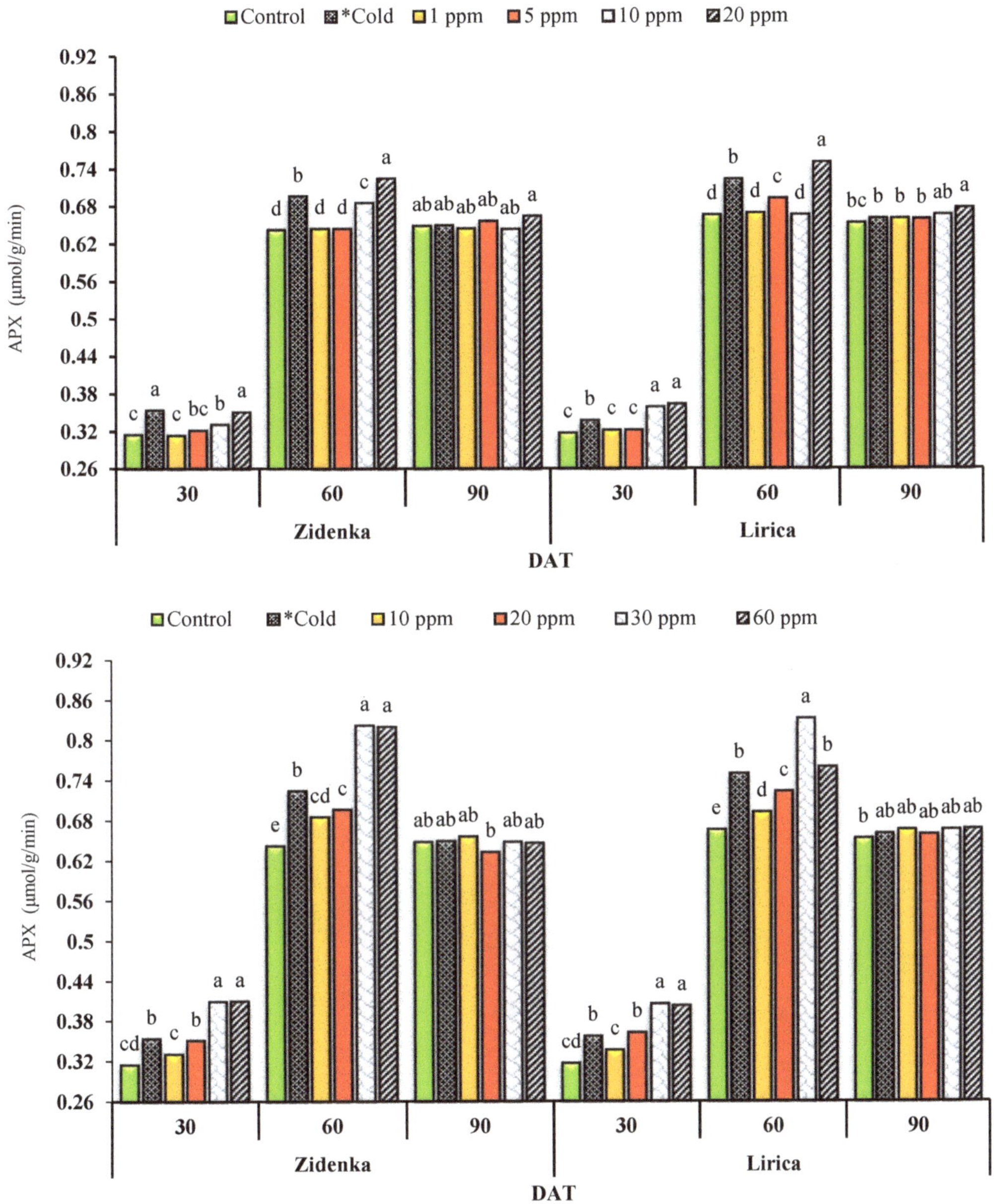

Figure 4. Effect of seed soaking in different ozonated water concentrations and cold pretreatments on APX activity of two pepper hybrids 30, 60, and 90 days after transplanting during the 2017/2018 (**upper** figure) and 2018/19 (**lower** figure) seasons. The column followed by a lowercase letter are not significantly different according to Duncan's multiple range test at 0.05 levels for the same sampling date of each season and each hybrid separately. * cold treatment was performed at 4 °C for 36 h. The average value of three biological and three technical replicates is reported.

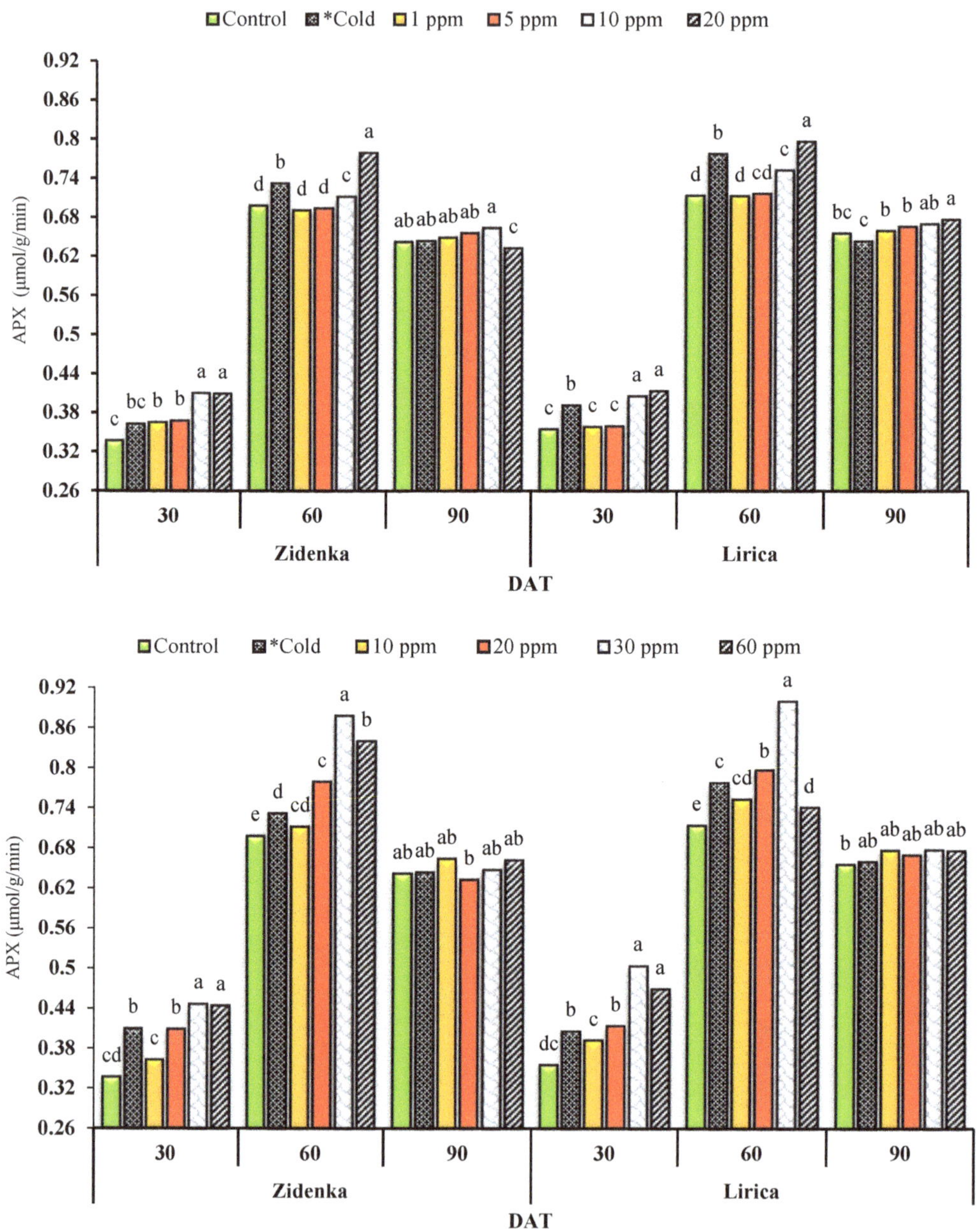

Figure 5. Effect of seedlings spray with different ozonated water concentrations and cold pretreatments on APX activity of two pepper hybrids 30, 60, and 90 days after transplanting during the 2017/2018 (**upper** figure) and 2018/2019 (**lower** figure) seasons. Columns labeled with a lowercase letter are not significantly different according to Duncan's multiple range test at 0.05 levels for the same sampling date in each season and each hybrid separately. * Cold stress treatment was performed at 4 °C for 36 h. Ozonated water applied as seedling spray compared to the untreated control. The average value of three biological and three technical replicates is reported.

Table 5. Effect of ozone and chilling tolerance pretreatments on flowering and fruit set parameters of two sweet pepper hybrids during December and January of the 2017/18 and 2018/19 seasons.

Treatment		No. Flowers/Plant		No. Fruits/Plant		No. Seeds/Fruit		Fruits Set %	
		Seed Soaking	Seedling Spray	Seed Soaking	Seedling Spray	Seed Soaking	Seedling Spray	Seed Soaking	Seedling Spray
2017/2018									
Zidenka cv.	Control	5.00 c	5.00 bc	1.66 e	1.66 d	261 e	261 d	38.77 e	34.86 f
	* Cold	4.66 cd	4.66 c	3.00 c	3.00 bcd	263 e	263 d	65.00 c	65.00 d
	1 ppm O_3	4.33 d	5.33 b	2.66 cd	3.66 bc	307 cd	254 d	65.41 c	69.44 c
	5 ppm O_3	5.33 bc	5.00 bc	2.33 d	3.00 bcd	290 d	277 cd	55.16 d	69.11 c
	10 ppm O_3	4.66 cd	5.00 bc	3.00 c	3.66 bc	315 c	303 bc	56.00 d	93.65 a
	20 ppm O_3	6.00 ab	5.66 b	4.33 ab	5.33 a	322 b	339 c	73.40 b	88.29 b
Lirica cv.	Control	4.66 cd	4.66 c	3.00 c	3.33 bc	280 d	280 cd	63.44 bc	79.65 b
	* Cold	3.66 e	3.66 d	2.33 d	2.33 cd	313 c	313 c	66.60 b	68.33 c
	1 ppm O_3	5.66 b	5.00 bc	4.33 ab	2.33 cd	311 c	360 b	78.66 b	50.62 e
	5 ppm O_3	5.33 bc	5.00 bc	5.66 a	4.66 b	314 c	356 b	57.93 d	83.45 b
	10 ppm O_3	6.33 ab	5.66 b	3.66 b	5.33 a	341 ab	412 a	77.98 b	91.62 ab
	20 ppm O_3	7.00 a	7.33 a	5.66 a	6.00 a	364 a	403 a	99.16 a	97.77 a
Significance		*	*	*	*	*	*	*	*
2018/2019									
Zidenka cv.	Control	5.20 bc	4.76 bc	2.06 d	2.16 de	283 d	283 d	40.47 e	45.50 e
	* Cold	4.86 c	4.93 b	2.96 cd	3.13 cd	276 d	276 de	60.83 cd	63.82 c
	10 ppm O_3	4.53 cd	5.53 ab	2.66 d	3.23 cd	322 c	268 e	59.37 cd	59.55 d
	20 ppm O_3	5.26 bc	5.43 ab	2.66 d	3.13 cd	304 c	324 c	52.45 d	59.56 d
	30 ppm O_3	5.93 ab	6.50 a	4.60 d	4.86 b	348 b	355 bc	78.28 b	75.30 b
	60 ppm O_3	5.93 ab	5.80 a	4.53 b	5.53 ab	329 b	318 c	74.08 bc	92.13 a
Lirica cv.	Control	5.03 c	5.20 ab	3.33 c	3.46 bc	294 d	294 d	65.99 c	73.13 bc
	* Cold	4.20 d	4.20 c	2.66 d	2.73 d	328 bc	328 c	64.42 c	63.97 c
	10 ppm O_3	5.53 b	4.86 b	4.53 b	2.66 d	327 bc	374 b	79.69 b	54.80 d
	20 ppm O_3	5.20 bc	5.53 ab	5.83 a	4.86 b	329 b	376 b	81.92 b	88.21 ab
	30 ppm O_3	7.26 a	6.66 a	5.80 a	6.16 a	382 a	423 a	99.24 a	93.19 a
	60 ppm O_3	6.66 a	6.33 a	4.06 bc	5.76 ab	358 a	421 a	61.26 c	91.50 a
Significance		*	*	*	*	*	*	*	*

Means followed by a lowercase letter in the same column are not significantly different according to Duncan's multiple range test at 0.05 levels for each season separately. * Cold stress treatment was performed at 4 °C for 36 h. Ozonated water applied as seed soaking or seedling spray compared to the untreated control.

3.9. Fruit Yield and Its Components

Full-colored red fruits from the Zidenka hybrid and yellow fruits from the Lirica hybrid were ready for picking on 20 February in the first season and 10 February in the second season, and picking continued until July in both seasons. The studied yield parameters were significantly affected by the interaction between hybrids and priming treatments (Table 6). In comparison with the control and cold treatment, ozone-induced pretreatment of Lirica seeds or seedlings, particularly at concentrations of 20 and 30 ppm in the first and second seasons, provided the highest early yield with the highest average fruit weight and fruit numbers. However, the control and cold treatment had the lowest values in both seasons. The early yield increased from 4.95 kg m^{-2} (control average) to 7.34 kg m^{-2} (average with 20 and 30 ppm ozone). Lirica provided the maximum early yield when primed by ozone at 30 ppm (9.87 kg m^{-2}), as well as the maximum fruits per m^2 (29.19 fruit), and average fruit weight (234 g). In contrast, the lowest obtained values were obtained in the Lirica control (4.56 kg m^{-2} early yield and 16.81 fruits m^{-2}), whereas the Zidenka control produced the lowest average fruit weight (164 g). We did not detect any significant changes between plants treated with ozone by either foliar spray or seed soaking (Table 6).

Table 6. Effect of ozone and chilling tolerance pretreatments on fruit yield parameters of two sweet pepper hybrids during the 2017/18 and 2018/19 seasons.

Treatment		+ Early Yield (kg m^{-2})		Fruits per m^{-2} for Early Yield		Average Fruit Weight (g) for Total Yield	
		Seed Soaking	Seedling Spray	Seed Soaking	Seedling Spray	Seed Soaking	Seedling Spray
2017/2018							
Zidenka cv.	Control	4.76 d	5.75 bc	24.44 ab	26.41 ab	164 cd	172 cd
	* Cold	4.80 d	5.49 c	24.53 ab	21.60 c	175 c	173 cd
	1 ppm O_3	4.63 d	4.52 c	19.75 d	25.82 b	177 c	172 cd
	5 ppm O_3	5.04 c	4.88 d	24.83 b	21.98 cd	169 c	186 c
	10 ppm O_3	5.05 c	5.23 c	23.60 bc	23.84 c	179 c	169 d
	20 ppm O_3	5.89 bc	5.14 cd	26.44 a	23.55 c	175 c	171 cd
Lirica cv.	Control	4.36 e	4.80 d	16.81 e	19.75 d	220 a	205 b
	* Cold	4.57 de	5.50 c	17.60 e	22.03 cd	212 a	206 b
	1 ppm O_3	5.24 c	5.90 bc	21.27 d	20.99 d	200 b	206 b
	5 ppm O_3	6.04 b	5.36 c	23.26 bc	19.56 de	209 ab	207 b
	10 ppm O_3	6.11 b	6.69 b	22.63 c	23.35 c	206 ab	218 a
	20 ppm O_3	7.71 a	8.98 a	25.37 a	28.24 a	222 a	229 a
Significance		*	*	*	*	*	*
2018/2019							
Zidenka cv.	Control	5.11 c	5.64 d	25.55 b	25.39 b	173 c	175 d
	* Cold	5.14 c	5.61 d	25.36 b	26.70 ab	184 c	180 cd
	10 ppm O_3	5.04 c	4.92 e	20.43 e	22.34 c	183 c	176 d
	20 ppm O_3	5.49 cd	5.32 d	25.67 b	22.73 c	178 c	196 c
	30 ppm O_3	6.61 b	6.08 c	27.91 a	26.30 ab	184 c	179 d
	60 ppm O_3	5.01 cd	5.38 d	22.23 d	23.20 c	187 c	181 d
Lirica cv.	Control	4.56 d	4.59 e	17.72 e	18.99 de	230 a	212 b
	* Cold	4.97 cd	5.93 cd	17.38 f	22.78 c	223 ab	215 b
	10 ppm O_3	5.71 bc	6.42 c	21.99 de	21.70 d	211 b	213 b
	20 ppm O_3	6.58 b	4.98 e	24.05 c	17.33 e	220 ab	218 b
	30 ppm O_3	8.49 a	9.87 a	26.23 ab	29.19 a	234 a	241 a
	60 ppm O_3	6.65 b	7.28 b	23.39 cd	24.14 b	203 b	230 a
Significance		*	*	*	*	*	*

+ The early yield was determined during the first 45 days of picking. Means followed by a lowercase letter in the same column are not significantly different according to Duncan's multiple range test at 0.05 levels for each season separately. * Cold stress treatment was performed at 4 °C for 36 h. Ozonated water applied as seed soaking or seedling spray compared to the untreated control.

During both growing seasons, the total and marketable yields of the examined hybrids significantly responded to pretreatments for chilling tolerance; however, the nonmarketable yield did not exhibit any significant response (Figures 6 and 7). All ozone pretreatments resulted in a significant increase in total and marketable fruit yield compared with the control and cold treatment in both seasons. Lirica had higher total and marketable yields than Zidenka. The total yield increased from 11.57–12.29 to 14.76–16.13 kg/m^2 when Lirica was treated by 20 ppm in the first season and from 12.64–13.36 to 16.04–16.52 kg/m^2 in the second season, with an increased in the marketable yield from 11.21–11.83 to 14.33–15.56 and from 12.24–12.85 to 15.43–16.10 kg/m^2, in the first and second seasons, respectively. The total and marketable yields of Zidenka were lowest, especially in the control and the plant treated with slow ozone concentration. Therefore, there were non-significant differences between the application methods, i.e., seed soaking and seedling spray.

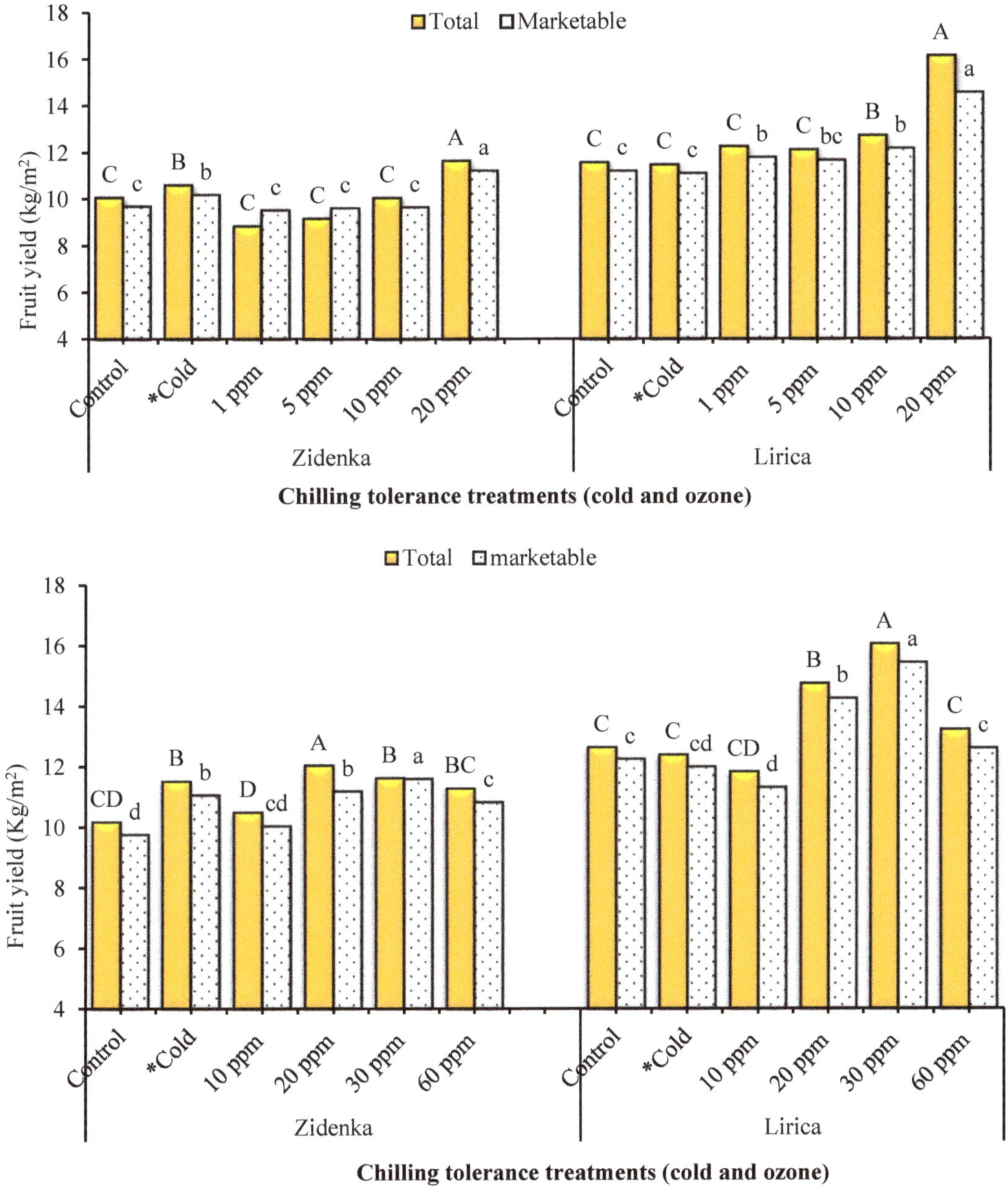

Figure 6. Effect of seed soaking in different ozonated water concentrations and cold pretreatments on total and marketable fruit yields of two sweet pepper hybrids during the 2017/2018 (**upper** figure) and 2018/2019 (**lower** figure) seasons. The columns labeled with different letters with in the same case are significantly different according to Duncan's multiple range test at 0.05 levels. * Cold stress treatment was performed at 4 °C for 36 h.

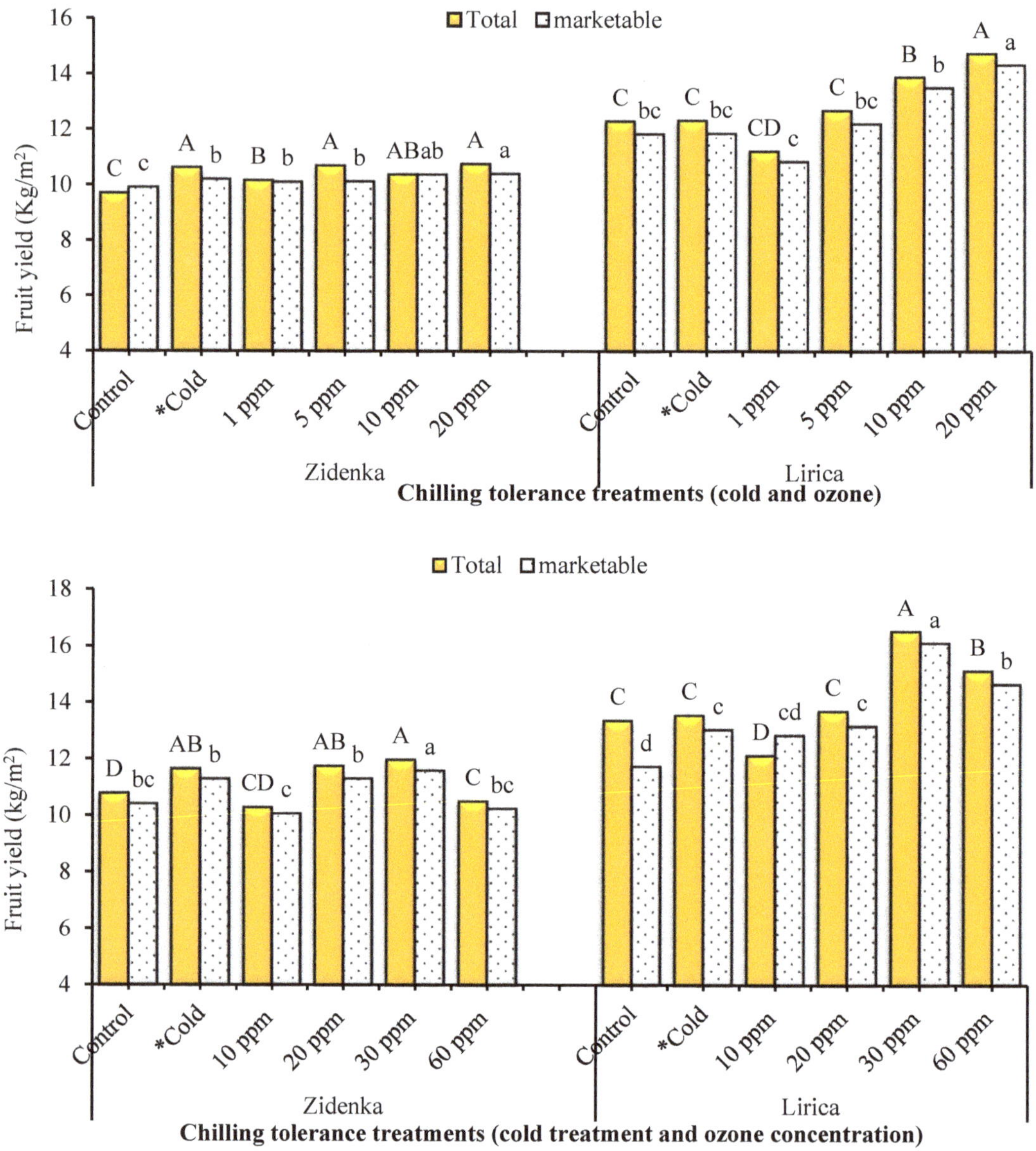

Figure 7. Effect of seedlings spray with different ozonated water concentrations and cold pretreatments on total and marketable fruit yields of two sweet pepper hybrids during the 2017/2018 (**upper** figure) and 2018/2019 (**lower** figure) seasons. The columns labeled with different letters in the same case are significantly different according to Duncan's multiple range test at 0.05 levels. * Cold treatment was performed at 4 °C for 36 h.

3.10. Fruit Quality

The results presented in Table 7 indicate that increasing ozone concentrations significantly increased fruit length of both hybrids during both seasons. The fruit of the Lirica hybrid longest, increasing from 8.46–9.83 cm in the control to 12.00–12.33 cm with 200 ppm ozone in the first season and from 9.60 to 11.73–11.76 cm in the second season with 30 ppm. Cold treatment did not significantly differ relative to the control. Fruit diameter was significantly affected by the interaction, except in seeds soaked in the second season. The evaluated hybrids slightly differed in fruit diameter, with insignificant differences between the application methods of ozone. In the case of total soluble solids vitamin C contents in fruits, the differences were statistically detectable only in the first season. A slight increase due to high ozone concentration was attained, with a favorable effect of seedlings spray compared to seed soaking.

Table 7. Effect of ozone and chilling tolerance pretreatments on morphological and chemical quality characteristics of the fruits of two sweet pepper hybrids during the 2017/18 and 2018/19 seasons.

Treatment		Length (cm)		Diameter (cm)		TSS (%)		Vitamin C (mg 100 g^{-1} FW)	
		Seed Soaking	Seedling Spray	Seed Soaking	Seedling Spray	Seed Soaking	Seedling Spray	Seed Soaking	Seedling Spray
2017/2018									
Zidenka cv.	Control	9.10 c	8.00 cd	8.33 ab	8.00 b	10.00 a	10.00 ab	650 ab	650 ab
	* Cold	9.60 bc	8.63 c	8.00 b	8.63 ab	10.06 a	10.06 ab	654 a	654 ab
	1 ppm O_3	10.16 ab	8.16 c	9.00 a	8.16 b	9.26 b	9.60 bc	607 b	627 b
	5 ppm O_3	9.00 c	9.03 b	9.00 a	8.06 b	9.10 b	10.06 ab	593 b	654 ab
	10 ppm O_3	9.70 bc	10.13 ab	8.00 a	8.00 b	9.00 bc	10.33 a	585 b	671 a
	20 ppm O_3	13.00 a	11.86 a	9.00 a	9.00 a	10.16 a	10.06 ab	661 a	654 ab
Lirica cv.	Control	8.83 cd	8.46 c	6.50 c	7.00 c	9.10 b	9.10 c	591 b	602 c
	* Cold	8.33 d	9.00 bc	8.00 b	7.00 c	9.50 b	9.50 bc	619 b	621 bc
	1 ppm O_3	10.00 b	10.00 b	8.00 b	9.00 a	10.00 a	10.20 a	650 ab	663 a
	5 ppm O_3	10.00 b	12.00 a	8.10 ab	8.16 b	9.96 ab	9.46 bc	647 ab	615 bc
	10 ppm O_3	10.00 b	11.00 ab	8.83 ab	8.66 ab	10.00 a	10.40 a	650 ab	670 a
	20 ppm O_3	12.33 a	12.00 a	9.00 a	9.33 a	10.26 a	10.40 a	661 a	678 a
Significance		*	*	*	*	*	*	*	*
2018/2019									
Zidenka cv.	Control	10.20 b	10.20 b	7.60 a	7.60 b	8.06 a	8.06 a	645 a	645 a
	* Cold	10.66 ab	9.40 c	8.66 a	7.80 b	7.90 a	8.26 a	632 a	657 a
	10 ppm O_3	9.33 c	10.33 b	8.20 a	8.06 ab	8.06 a	8.83 a	648 a	657 a
	20 ppm O_3	9.66 bc	10.53 b	8.26 a	8.60 a	8.30 a	8.53 a	660 a	658 a
	30 ppm O_3	9.33 c	11.53 a	8.36 a	8.66 a	8.53 a	8.43 a	682 a	679 a
	60 ppm O_3	11.26 a	11.00 ab	8.10 a	7.86 b	8.03 a	9.09 a	680 a	675 a
Lirica cv.	Control	9.60 bc	9.60 c	8.06 a	8.06 ab	8.80 a	8.80 a	656 a	656 a
	* Cold	9.90 b	10.10 bc	8.96 a	8.30 a	8.50 a	8.70 a	665 a	665 a
	10 ppm O_3	10.80 ab	9.76 c	8.73 a	8.66 a	8.50 a	8.43 a	661 a	661 a
	20 ppm O_3	11.13 a	10.20 b	8.76 a	9.00 a	8.70 a	8.80 a	661 a	676 a
	30 ppm O_3	11.73 a	11.76 a	9.13 a	9.26 a	9.23 a	9.30 a	696 a	702 a
	60 ppm O_3	11.66 a	11.30 a	8.20 a	8.46 a	8.83 a	9.53 a	686 a	699 a
Significance		*	*	ns	*	ns	ns	ns	ns

Means followed by a lowercase letter in the same column are not significantly different according to Duncan's multiple range test at 0.05 levels for each season separately. * Cold stress treatment was performed at 4 °C for 36 h. Ozonated water applied as seed soaking or seedling spray compared to the untreated control.

4. Discussion

Cold stress is a serious threat to plant production science. It plays a significant role in crop losses. Harmful effects on plants include poor germination, poor seedling health index, leaf chlorosis, reduced leaf area, wilting, and death of tissue [42]. Pepper plants suffer from cold stress even if they are grown in unheated plastic greenhouses during the cold season [3]. The inside temperature of the plastic greenhouse can reach 5–10 °C during January (Figure 1), owing to the characteristics of polyethylene cover, which allow for rapid loss of stored heat (during daytime) at night [4]. Hence, the morphological, physiological, and biochemical properties of the plants are strongly affected, as reflect by low yield and poor quality. The results obtained in the current study confirm the results reported in [43]. Excessive harm can occur if plants are grown under other stressful conditions, such as salinity, which commonly occurs during winter in arid regions [44]. High soil salinity was shown at the experiment site. Furthermore, the studied hybrids have high yields with good quality when grown in plastic greenhouses and have recently received increased attention from growers. However, their yield and quality are strongly affected by cold stress during January, which can extend from December to February (Figure 7); therefore, they require additional acclimation to cold stress.

Plants exposed to cold stress generally exhibit water stress symptoms [41,45]. Our results indicate that the plants exposed to chilling stress displayed a low percentage of relative water content compared to the control (Table 1), which is considered a good quantitative indicator of water status in the plant. Low RWC values were detected in the control compared to the plants pretreated with cold or ozone before transplanting in the unheated plastic greenhouse. Thus, the pretreatments helped the plant to maintain high RWC valued when the plants were later grown under cold stress. As a result, cell membranes gradually lost their properties and ability to normally transition, which was accompanied by high membrane permeability (Table 4). These results confirm those reported in [46], in which it was found that the grown plants under stress showed low water content, and the cells membranes had high electrolyte leakage.

Plants were reported to suffer from highly stressful conditions when they were exposed to high ozone concentrations [47]. In this case, ozone caused damage in the cellular membrane, altering gene expression and metabolic activities and ultimately causing the death of plant tissues [48]. Wilkinson et al. [49] suggested that such exposure to ozone can cause a decline in carbon transport to the roots and a decrease in nutrient and water uptake, affecting plant stability and leading to a reduction in growth and processes of biomass production. Peng et al. [20] reported the negative impact of O_3 on the productivity of maize crop, with O_3 sensitivity in the following order: photosynthetic physiology > biomass > yield components. The results of the present study indicate that cold acclimation through seed merging or seedling spray by ozonated water at a low dose (30–60 ppm) had several, benefits including a decrease MP (Table 4). Although ozone has been extensively studied as a phytotoxic air pollutant with a harmful effects on the environment and biodiversity [50], little attention has been paid to its beneficial effects on plants. Recently, hormesis, the "dose-dependent response" of different stressors such as temperature and salinity in relation to biological and physiological activities, has been considered [51,52]. However, hormesis of air pollutant generally and ozone specifically in plants requires additional investigations. Hormesis greatly depends on plant species and stressor dose [53]. A low dose of stressor induces defense mechanisms, leading to a positive effect on plant health and performance [52]. Some studies have considered ozone a "eustressor", which, if applied in a suitable concentration and at the appropriate time for a constant period, should improve plant nutritional quality, as reflected by an increase in antioxidant capacity, secondary metabolites, and bioactive compounds, as a tool to cope with the increase in reactive oxygen species (ROS) and oxidative stress as a result to exposure to ozone [30,54]. Marchica et al. [54] reported ozone application in a low dose and for a short period of exposure as an effective method for priming purposes by activation of the phenolic pathway, leading to an increase in the production of phenolic metabolites and increased total antioxidant activity. These outcomes support the concept of ozone as a "eustressor" when applied at a low dose for a short period and reported ozone as a potential tool to improve the quality of sage leaf extracts. These results are supported by those reported by Pellegrini [30], who reported ozone prime as a potential method to increase the beneficial properties of the medicinal herb *Hypericum perforatum* plants at different stages by enhancing upregulation of the reduced/oxidized glutathione ratio (up to about 2-fold higher than the untreated plants), which is related to an increase in peroxidase activity, as well as the accumulation of total phenols, flavonoids and anthocyanins and an increase in antioxidant potential. These potential benefits of ozone in low concentrations on plants were also reported for the development of a rapid and non-destructive method using reflectance spectroscopy for early detection of the responses of crops to ozone [53]. This method was developed to measure the adaptation mechanism of the plant to cope with the ozone effect (in the absence of visible symptoms) by estimating related parameters of photosynthesis, oxidative pressure, and antioxidant capacity. Our results support these findings; most importantly, we used a simple, cost-effective, and ecofriendly method to mitigate cold stress of sweet pepper grown in an unheated plastic greenhouse, which improved fruit productivity and quality. Ozone is considered an ecofriendly and natural method in several fields, including medicine and agriculture, without negative impacts on the environment [55]. The present study indicates that cold acclimation through seed merging or seedling spray by ozonated water at a low dose (30–60 ppm) had several physiological and biochemical benefits. We attempted to explain physiological changes related to ozone priming by estimating the changes in membrane permeability (Table 4). The reduction in electrolyte leakage could protect the cells from damage under environmental stresses, including cold stress. Hence, MP is considered a sensitive stress marker due to the sensitivity of the cellular membrane to various environmental stresses that always cause oxidative damage accompanied by increasing permeability [56]. Plants grown under stress produce ROS through the induction of antioxidant defense systems, which conserve the membranes and other essential substances [57]. Nali et al. [58] suggested that increasing antioxidant levels (both enzymatic and non-enzymatic) taking part in cellular repair processes increases cell wall strength, reducing MP and increasing cell content of water, as reported in our study (Table 4), to reduce stress caused by ROS [59]. A similar response was observed in some leguminous plants [60] and a considerable number of herbaceous species [61]. Plants accumulate additional proline under cold stress (Figure 3) to maintain osmotic adjustment and membrane stability and protect cells from the disruptive effect of free radicals [62,63]. Sufficient indices could explain the favorable effect of low ozone concentration on proline accumulation under cold stress (Figures 2 and 3). Zhang et al. [64] reported that proline accumulates in response to biotic and abiotic stresses. In this case, proline contributes to conserving tissue water, as well as protection of proteins and cellular membranes from osmotic and oxidative stresses [65]. Furthermore, proline helps to maintain osmotic adjustment and membrane stability and decreases the effects of ROS damage as a free radical scavenger [66], improving resistance against chilling [67] and helping to protecting enzymes, biological membranes, and photosynthetic apparatus from oxidative damage [68]. Consequently, the increase in proline content can be considered a good indicator of cold stress resistance.

Moreover, chilling induces oxidative damage in both root and leaf tissues [48]. Ozone can provide acclimation protection against oxidative stress by increasing ascorbate peroxidase (APX) activity (Figures 4 and 5). Yan et al. [69] reported that APX activity depended on ozone dose and the exposure period. In our study, APX activity increased when the seed or seedlings were acclimated to a low ozone dose (30–60 ppm) for a short time, i.e., seed soaking for 1 h or seedling spray by ozonated water. These results are in accordance with the findings of Liu et al. [70], who reported that cold acclimation effectively alleviates oxidative damage and increases photosynthetic capacity. Flowers et al. [71] reported excess bean growth and yield as a result of increasing photosynthesis intensity when the plants were exposed to low ozone concentrations for a short time (15 ppb O3 for 12 h weekly until harvest) in comparison to ozone-free plants. Similarly, an increase in photosynthesis was achieved with low exposure time for 1 h/day (compared to the control), which then decreased with increased exposure time to 4 h/day [72]. The present study supports these findings, confirming that exposure to low ozone concentrations for a short period causes an increase in chlorophyll intensity (Table 3), which is closely connected to photosynthesis [73].

It was noted that pepper plants have a severe problem with pollination and fertilization, as well as a severe reduction in fruits yield and quality under cold stress [3,74]. To solve such a problem, fruit set percentage and seed count inside the fruit were investigated during the coldest time of the season in December and January to determine whether the acclimation effect lasted until the flowering and fruiting stages. Furthermore, we could not find any publications regarding the role of ozone acclimation in the production of sweet pepper under double stresses of cold and salinity in an unheated plastic greenhouse. Our results show that the favorable effect of ozone acclimation exceeded the physiological and biochemical properties during vegetative growth and was prolonged throughout the productivity stage. Accordingly, ozone acclimation significantly augmented flower and fruit numbers, as well as fruit set percentage (Table 5). Additionally, the formed fruits had high seeds count and consequently produced larger fruits with higher quality, in addition to a significant increase in the marketable and total yields compared to the control (Table 6 and Figure 7).

5. Conclusions

The present work provides evidence that ozone plays a beneficial role in plant resistance to cold, which be achieved when ozone is applied in a low concentration for a brief period during early plant development as seed soaking or seedling foliar spray. Ozonated water with concentrations ranging from 0 to 60 ppm was applied to two hybrids of sweet pepper. The effectiveness of treatments was evaluated during plant production under unheated greenhouse conditions in the winter season. The results indicate that ozone treatment at 30 ppm as seed soaking or seedling spray is a promising, simple, practical, and ecofriendly strategy without harmful effects on the environment.

Ozone significantly increased plant leaf area, the contents of proline, and ascorbate peroxides activity, which promote the mechanism of plant defense against cold stress, as reflected by increased contents of chlorophyll (SPAD) and relative water content but reduced and preferable membrane permeability. Furthermore, vegetative growth and fruit set were increased, subsequently improving, early, total, and marketable pepper fruit yields, as well as fruit quality under cold stress. Finally, the appropriate application of ozone with the correct right dose, application time/period, and plant type could contribute to enhanced plant resistance to stresses and lead to improved adaption to climate changes in different regions. Additional detailed studies are needed to examine the role of ozone application to different plant species under various stress conditions.

Author Contributions: Conceptualization, M.A.S.-E., S.E., M.S. and Z.M.Y.; Data curation, M.A.S.-E., A.M.Y., M.S. and Z.M.Y.; Formal analysis, M.A.S.-E., A.A.E., A.M.Y., S.E. and Z.M.Y.; Investigation, A.M.Y., M.S. and Z.M.Y.; Methodology, A.M.Y.; Project administration, Z.M.Y.; Resources, M.A.S.-E.; Software, A.A.E.; Supervision, S.E., M.S. and Z.M.Y.; Validation, A.A.E., S.E., M.S. and Z.M.Y.; Visualization, A.M.Y., S.E. and Z.M.Y.; Writing—original draft, M.A.S.-E., A.A.E., A.M.Y., S.E., M.S. and Z.M.Y.; Writing—review and editing, A.A.E. All authors have read and agreed to the published version of the manuscript.

Funding: This work was financially supported predominantly by WATERAGRI (European Union Horizon 2020 research and innovation programme under Grant Agreement Number 858735).

Institutional Review Board Statement: Not applicable.

Informed Consent Statement: Not applicable.

Data Availability Statement: Not applicable.

Conflicts of Interest: The authors declare no conflict of interest.

References

1. Bai, C.; Fang, M.; Zhai, B.; Ma, L.; Fu, A.; Gao, L.; Kou, X.; Meng, D.; Wang, Q.; Zheng, S.; et al. Regulations of M6A Methylation on Tomato Fruit Chilling Injury. *Hortic. Plant J.* **2021**, *7*, 434–442. [CrossRef]
2. Rehman, R.N.U.; Malik, A.U.; Khan, A.S.; Hasan, M.U.; Anwar, R.; Ali, S.; Haider, M.W. Combined Application of Hot Water Treatment and Methyl Salicylate Mitigates Chilling Injury in Sweet Pepper (*Capsicum annuum* L.) Fruits. *Sci. Hortic.* **2021**, *283*, 110113. [CrossRef]
3. El-Aidy, F.A.; Sharaf-Eldin, M.A. Modifying Microclimatic Conditions in Plastic Walk-in Tunnels through Solar Energy System for Improving Yield and Quality of Four Sweet Pepper Hybrids. *Plasticulture* **2015**, *134*, 6–22.

4. Zhang, L.; Hao, X.; Li, Y.; Jiang, G. Response of Greenhouse Tomato to Varied Low Pre-Night Temperatures at the Same Daily Integrated Temperature. *HortScience* **2010**, *45*, 1654–1661. [CrossRef]
5. Sharma, P.; Sharma, N.; Deswal, R. The Molecular Biology of the Low-Temperature Response in Plants. *BioEssays* **2005**, *27*, 1048–1059. [CrossRef]
6. Zhang, Y.; Jin, P.; Huang, Y.; Shan, T.; Wang, L.; Li, Y.; Zheng, Y. Effect of Hot Water Combined with Glycine Betaine Alleviates Chilling Injury in Cold-Stored Loquat Fruit. *Postharvest Biol. Technol.* **2016**, *118*, 141–147. [CrossRef]
7. Zhang, M.; Liu, W.; Li, C.; Shao, T.; Jiang, X.; Zhao, H.; Ai, W. Postharvest Hot Water Dipping and Hot Water Forced Convection Treatments Alleviate Chilling Injury for Zucchini Fruit during Cold Storage. *Sci. Hortic.* **2019**, *249*, 219–227. [CrossRef]
8. Sharaf-Eldin, M.A.; Alshallash, K.S.; Alharbi, K.R.; Alqahtani, M.M.; Etman, A.A.; Yassin, A.M.; Azab, E.S.; El-Okkiah, S.A.F. Influence of Seed Soaking and Foliar Application Using Ozonated Water on Two Sweet Pepper Hybrids under Cold Stress. *Sustainability* **2022**, *14*, 13453. [CrossRef]
9. Giudice, G.; Moffa, L.; Varotto, S.; Cardone, M.F.; Bergamini, C.; De Lorenzis, G.; Velasco, R.; Nerva, L.; Chitarra, W. Novel and emerging biotechnological crop protection approaches. *Plant Biotechnol. J.* **2021**, *19*, 1495–1510. [CrossRef]
10. FAO. Good Agricultural Practices for Greenhouse Vegetable Crops: Principles for Mediterranean Climate Areas. 2013. Available online: www.fao.org/3/a-i3284e (accessed on 1 October 2022).
11. Consentino, B.B.; Sabatino, L.; Vultaggio, L.; Rotino, G.L.; La Placa, G.G.; D'Anna, F.; Leto, C.; Iacuzzi, N.; De Pasquale, C. Grafting of aubergines on underutilized solane species and the biostimulating action of Azospirillum brasilense modulate growth, yield, NUE and nutritional and functional traits. *Horticulturae* **2022**, *8*, 722. [CrossRef]
12. Lefèvre, A.; Perrin, B.; Lesur-Dumoulin, C.; Salembier, C.; Navarrete, M. Challenges of Complying with Both Food Value Chain Specifications and Agroecology Principles in Vegetable Crop Protection. *Agric. Syst.* **2020**, *185*, 102953. [CrossRef]
13. Tan, S.; Cao, J.; Xia, X.; Li, Z. Advances in 5-Aminolevulinic Acid Priming to Enhance Plant Tolerance to Abiotic Stress. *Int. J. Mol. Sci.* **2022**, *23*, 702. [CrossRef] [PubMed]
14. Satyakam; Zinta, G.; Singh, R.K.; Kumar, R. Cold adaptation strategies in plants—An emerging role of epigenetics and antifreeze proteins to engineer cold resilient plants. *Front. Genet.* **2022**, *13*, 909007. [CrossRef] [PubMed]
15. Zhang, W.; Jiang, H.; Cao, J.; Jiang, W. Advances in Biochemical Mechanisms and Control Technologies to Treat Chilling Injury in Postharvest Fruits and Vegetables. *Trends Food Sci. Technol.* **2021**, *113*, 355–365. [CrossRef]
16. Zhang, X.; Tang, N.; Zhang, H.; Chen, C.; Li, L.; Dong, C.; Cheng, Y. Comparative Transcriptomic Analysis of Cantaloupe Melon under Cold Storage with Ozone Treatment. *Food Res. Int.* **2021**, *140*, 109993. [CrossRef] [PubMed]
17. Chaudhary, I.J.; Rathore, D. Assessment of Ozone Toxicity on Cotton (*Gossypium hirsutum* L.) Cultivars: Its Defensive System and Intraspecific Sensitivity. *Plant Physiol. Biochem.* **2021**, *166*, 912–927. [CrossRef]
18. González-Fernández, I.; Elvira, S.; Calatayud, V.; Calvo, E.; Aparicio, P.; Sánchez, M.; Alonso, R.; Bermejo Bermejo, V. Ozone Effects on the Physiology and Marketable Biomass of Leafy Vegetables under Mediterranean Conditions: Spinach (*Spinacia oleracea* L.) and Swiss Chard (*Beta vulgaris* L. Var. Cycla). *Agric. Ecosyst. Environ.* **2016**, *235*, 215–228. [CrossRef]
19. Sharps, K.; Hayes, F.; Harmens, H.; Mills, G. Ozone-Induced Effects on Leaves in African Crop Species. *Environ. Pollut.* **2021**, *268*, 115789. [CrossRef]
20. Peng, J.; Shang, B.; Xu, Y.; Feng, Z.; Calatayud, V. Effects of Ozone on Maize (*Zea mays* L.) Photosynthetic Physiology, Biomass and Yield Components Based on Exposure- and Flux-Response Relationships. *Environ. Pollut.* **2020**, *256*, 113466. [CrossRef]
21. Zhang, X.; Zhang, X.; Wang, T.; Li, C. Metabolic Response of Soybean Leaves Induced by Short-Term Exposure of Ozone. *Ecotoxicol. Environ. Saf.* **2021**, *213*, 112033. [CrossRef]
22. Yadav, D.S.; Agrawal, S.B.; Agrawal, M. Ozone Flux-Effect Relationship for Early and Late Sown Indian Wheat Cultivars: Growth, Biomass, and Yield. *Field Crops Res.* **2021**, *263*, 108076. [CrossRef]
23. Chen, C.; Zhang, H.; Dong, C.; Ji, H.; Zhang, X.; Li, L.; Ban, Z.; Zhang, N.; Xue, W. Effect of Ozone Treatment on the Phenylpropanoid Biosynthesis of Postharvest Strawberries. *RSC Adv.* **2019**, *9*, 25429–25438. [CrossRef]
24. Shezi, S.; Samukelo Magwaza, L.; Mditshwa, A.; Zeray Tesfay, S. Changes in Biochemistry of Fresh Produce in Response to Ozone Postharvest Treatment. *Sci. Hortic.* **2020**, *269*, 109397. [CrossRef]
25. Chen, C.; Zhang, X.; Zhang, H.; Ban, Z.; Li, L.; Dong, C.; Ji, H.; Xue, W. Label-Free Quantitative Proteomics to Investigate the Response of Strawberry Fruit after Controlled Ozone Treatment. *RSC Adv.* **2019**, *9*, 676–689. [CrossRef]
26. Rodrigues, A.A.Z.; de Queiroz, M.E.L.R.; Neves, A.A.; de Oliveira, A.F.; Prates, L.H.F.; de Freitas, J.F.; Heleno, F.F.; Faroni, L.R.D.A. Use of Ozone and Detergent for Removal of Pesticides and Improving Storage Quality of Tomato. *Food Res. Int.* **2019**, *125*, 108626. [CrossRef] [PubMed]
27. Agathokleous, E.; Belz, R.G.; Calatayud, V.; De Marco, A.; Hoshika, Y.; Kitao, M.; Saitanis, C.J.; Sicard, P.; Paoletti, E.; Calabrese. Predicting the effect ofozone on vegetation via linear non-threshold (LNT), threshold and hormetic dose-response models. *Sci. Total Environ.* **2019**, *649*, 61–74. [CrossRef] [PubMed]
28. Calzone, A.; Podda, A.; Lorenzini, G.; Maserti, B.E.; Carrari, E.; Deleanu, E.; Hoshika, Y.; Haworth, M.; Nali, C.; Badea, O.; et al. Cross-Talk between Physiological and Biochemical Adjustments by *Punica granatum* cv. Dente di Cavallo Mitigates the Effects of Salinity and Ozone Stress. *Sci. Total Environ.* **2019**, *656*, 589–597. [CrossRef]
29. Pellegrini, E.; Cotrozzi, L.; Neri, L.; Baraldi, R.; Carrari, E.; Nali, C.; Lorenzini, G.; Paoletti, E.; Hoshika, Y. Stress Markers and Physiochemical Responses of the Mediterranean Shrub Phillyrea Angustifolia under Current and Future Drought and Ozone Scenarios. *Environ. Res.* **2021**, *201*, 111615. [CrossRef]

30. Pellegrini, E.; Campanella, A.; Cotrozzi, L.; Tonelli, M.; Nali, C.; Lorenzini, G. Ozone primes changes in phytochemical parameters in the medicinal herb *Hypericum perforatum* (St. John' s wort). *Ind. Crops Prod.* **2018**, *126*, 119–128. [CrossRef]
31. Endo, H.; Miyazaki, K.; Ose, K.; Imahori, Y. Hot Water Treatment to Alleviate Chilling Injury and Enhance Ascorbate-Glutathione Cycle in Sweet Pepper Fruit during Postharvest Cold Storage. *Sci. Hortic.* **2019**, *257*, 108715. [CrossRef]
32. Airaki, M.; Leterrier, M.; Mateos, R.M.; Valderrama, R.; Chaki, M.; Barroso, J.B.; Del Rio, L.A.; Palma, J.M.; Corpas, F.J. Metabolism of Reactive Oxygen Species and Reactive Nitrogen Species in Pepper (*Capsicum annuum* L.) Plants under Low Temperature Stress. *Plant Cell Environ.* **2011**, *35*, 281–295. [CrossRef] [PubMed]
33. Hongna, C.; Leyuan, T.; Junmei, S.; Xiaori, H.; Xianguo, C. Exogenous Salicylic Acid Signal Reveals an Osmotic Regulatory Role in Priming the Seed Germination of *Leymus chinensis* under Salt-Alkali Stress. *Environ. Exp. Bot.* **2021**, *188*, 104498. [CrossRef]
34. Kulak, M.; Jorrín-Novo, J.V.; Romero-Rodriguez, M.C.; Yildirim, E.D.; Gul, F.; Karaman, S. Seed Priming with Salicylic Acid on Plant Growth and Essential Oil Composition in Basil (*Ocimum basilicum* L.) Plants Grown under Water Stress Conditions. *Ind. Crops Prod.* **2021**, *161*, 113235. [CrossRef]
35. Korkmaz, A.; Korkmaz, Y.; Demirkiran, A.R. Enhancing chilling stress tolerance of pepper seedlings by exogenous application of 5-aminolevulinic acid. *Environ. Exp. Bot.* **2010**, *67*, 495–501. [CrossRef]
36. Valentovič, P.; Luxová, M.; Kolarovič, L.; Gašparíková, O. Effect of Osmotic Stress on Compatible Solutes Content, Membrane Stability and Water Relationsin Two Maize Cultivars. *Plant Soil Environ.* **2011**, *52*, 186–191. [CrossRef]
37. Anjum, S.A.; Farooq, M.; Xie, X.; Liu, X.; Ijaz, M.F. Antioxidant Defense System and Proline Accumulation Enables Hot Pepper to Perform Better under Drought. *Sci. Hortic.* **2012**, *140*, 66–73. [CrossRef]
38. Bates, L.S.; Waldren, R.P.; Teare, I.D. Rapid Determination of Free Proline for Water-Stress Studies. *Plant Soil* **1973**, *39*, 205–207. [CrossRef]
39. Nakano, Y.; Asada, K. Hydrogen Peroxide Is Scavenged by Ascorbate-Specific Peroxidase in Spinach Chloroplasts. *Plant Cell Physiol.* **1981**, *22*, 867–880. [CrossRef]
40. AOAC. *Official Methods of Analysis. Association of Official Analytical Chemists*, 15th ed.; AOAC: Washington, DC, USA, 1990.
41. Bottomley, P.J.; Angle, J.S.; Weaver, R.W. *Methods of Soil Analysis, Part 2: Microbiological and Biochemical Properties*; John Wiley & Sons: Hoboken, NJ, USA, 2020; Volume 12, ISBN 089118810X.
42. Yadav, S.K. Cold Stress Tolerance Mechanisms in Plants. A Review. *Agron. Sustain. Dev.* **2010**, *30*, 515–527. [CrossRef]
43. İşeri, Ö.D.; Körpe, D.A.; Sahin, F.I.; Haberal, M. Hydrogen Peroxide Pretreatment of Roots Enhanced Oxidative Stress Response of Tomato under Cold Stress. *Acta Physiol. Plant.* **2013**, *35*, 1905–1913. [CrossRef]
44. Shalaby, T.A.; Abd-Alkarim, E.; El-Aidy, F.; Hamed, E.-S.; Sharaf-Eldin, M.; Taha, N.; El-Ramady, H.; Bayoumi, Y.; dos Reis, A.R. Nano-Selenium, Silicon and H_2O_2 Boost Growth and Productivity of Cucumber under Combined Salinity and Heat Stress. *Ecotoxicol. Environ. Saf.* **2021**, *212*, 111962. [CrossRef] [PubMed]
45. Aliabadi, F.; Hussein, L.; Mohammad, H.; Shiranirad, A.H.; Valadabadi, A.R.; Daneshian, J. Effects of Arbuscular Mycorrhizal Fungi, Different Levels of Phosphorus and Drought Stress on Water Use Efficiency, Relative Water Content and Proline Accumulation Rate of Coriander (*Coriandrum sativum* L.). *J. Med. Plants Res.* **2008**, *2*, 125–131.
46. Filek, M.; Walas, S.; Mrowiec, H.; Rudolphy-Skórska, E.; Sieprawska, A.; Biesaga-Kościelniak, J. Membrane Permeability and Micro- and Macroelement Accumulation in Spring Wheat Cultivars during the Short-Term Effect of Salinity- and PEG-Induced Water Stress. *Acta Physiol. Plant.* **2011**, *34*, 985–995. [CrossRef]
47. Chaudhary, I.J.; Rathore, D. Assessment of Dose–Response Relationship between Ozone Dose and Groundnut (*Arachis hypogaea* L.) Cultivars Using Open Top Chamber (OTC) and Ethylenediurea (EDU). *Environ. Technol. Innov.* **2021**, *22*, 101494. [CrossRef]
48. Schmidt, R.; Kunkowska, A.B.; Schippers, J.H.M. Role of Reactive Oxygen Species during Cell Expansion in Leaves. *Plant Physiol.* **2016**, *172*, 2098–2106. [CrossRef]
49. Wilkinson, S.; Mills, G.; Illidge, R.; Davies, W.J. How Is Ozone Pollution Reducing Our Food Supply? *J. Exp. Bot.* **2011**, *63*, 527–536. [CrossRef]
50. Ainsworth, E.A. Understanding and improving global crop response to ozone pollution. *Plant J.* **2017**, *90*, 886–897. [CrossRef]
51. Agathokleous, E.; Kitao, M.; Harayama, J.; Calabrese, E.J. Temperature-induced hormesis in plants. *J. For. Res.* **2019**, *30*, 13–20. [CrossRef]
52. Jalal, A.; de Oliveira Junior, J.C.; Ribeiro, J.S.; Fernandes, G.C.; Mariano, G.G.; Trindade, V.D.R.; dos Reis, A.R. Hormesis in plants: Physiological and biochemical responses. *Ecotox. Environ. Saf.* **2021**, *207*, 111225. [CrossRef]
53. Marchica, A.; Loré, S.; Cotrozzi, L.; Lorenzini, G.; Nali, C.; Pellegrini, E.; Remorini, D. Early Detection of Sage (*Salvia officinalis* L.) Responses to Ozone Using Reflectance Spectroscopy. *Plants* **2019**, *8*, 346. [CrossRef]
54. Marchica, A.; Ascrizzi, R.; Flamini, G.; Cotrozzi, L.; Tonelli, M.; Lorenzini, G.; Nali, C.; Pellegrini, E. Ozone as eustress for enhancing secondary metabolites and bioactive properties in Salvia officinalis. *Ind. Crops Prod.* **2021**, *170*, 113730. [CrossRef]
55. Modesti, M.; Baccelloni, S.; Brizzolara, S.; Aleandri, M.P.; Bellincontro, A.; Mencarelli, F.; Tonutti, P. Effects of treatments with ozonated water in the vineyard (cv Vermentino) on microbial population and fruit quality parameters. *BIO Web Conf.* **2019**, *13*, 04011. [CrossRef]
56. Liheng, H.; Zhiqiang, G.; Runzhi, L. Pretreatment of Seed with H_2O_2 Enhances Drought Tolerance of Wheat (*Triticum aestivum* L.) Seedlings. *Afr. J. Biotechnol.* **2009**, *8*, 6151–6157. [CrossRef]
57. Ali, B.; Hasan, S.A.; Hayat, S.; Hayat, Q.; Yadav, S.; Fariduddin, Q.; Ahmad, A. A Role for Brassinosteroids in the Amelioration of Aluminium Stress through Antioxidant System in Mung Bean (*Vigna radiata* L. Wilczek). *Environ. Exp. Bot.* **2008**, *62*, 153–159. [CrossRef]

58. Nali, C.; Paoletti, E.; Marabottini, R.; Della Rocca, G.; Lorenzini, G.; Paolacci, A.R.; Ciaffi, M.; Badiani, M. Ecophysiological and Biochemical Strategies of Response to Ozone in Mediterranean Evergreen Broadleaf Species. *Atmos. Environ.* **2004**, *38*, 2247–2257. [CrossRef]
59. Bailly, C.; El-Maarouf-Bouteau, H.; Corbineau, F. From Intracellular Signaling Networks to Cell Death: The Dual Role of Reactive Oxygen Species in Seed Physiology. *Comptes Rendus Biol.* **2008**, *331*, 806–814. [CrossRef]
60. Sanz, J.; Muntifering, R.B.; Bermejo, V.; Gimeno, B.S.; Elvira, S. Ozone and Increased Nitrogen Supply Effects on the Yield and Nutritive Quality of Trifolium Subterraneum. *Atmos. Environ.* **2005**, *39*, 5899–5907. [CrossRef]
61. Lin, J.C.; Nosal, M.; Muntifering, R.B.; Krupa, S.V. Alfalfa Nutritive Quality for Ruminant Livestock as Influenced by Ambient Air Quality in West-Central Alberta. *Environ. Pollut.* **2007**, *149*, 99–103. [CrossRef]
62. Yadegari, L.Z.; Heidari, R.; Carapetian, J. The Influence of Cold Acclimation on Proline, Malondialdehyde (MDA), Total Protein and Pigments Contents in Soybean (*Glycine max*) Seedlings. *J. Biol. Sci.* **2007**, *7*, 1436–1441. [CrossRef]
63. Esra, K.O.Ç.; İŞLEK, C.; Üstün, A.S. Effect of Cold on Protein, Proline, Phenolic Compounds and Chlorophyll Content of Two Pepper (*Capsicum annuum* L.) Varieties. *Gazi Univ. J. Sci.* **2010**, *23*, 1–6.
64. Zhang, Z.J.; Li, H.Z.; Zhou, W.J.; Takeuchi, Y.; Yoneyama, K. Effect of 5-Aminolevulinic Acid on Development and Salt Tolerance of Potato (*Solanum tuberosum* L.) Microtubers in Vitro. *Plant Growth Regul.* **2006**, *49*, 27–34.
65. Farooq, M.; Wahid, A.; Kobayashi, N.; Fujita, D.; Basra, S.M.A. Plant Drought Stress: Effects, Mechanisms and Management. In *Sustainable Agriculture*; Springer: Dordrecht, The Netherlands, 2009; pp. 153–188, ISBN 9789048126651.
66. Farooq, M.; Wahid, A.; Lee, D.-J.; Ito, O.; Siddique, K.H.M. Advances in Drought Resistance of Rice. *Crit. Rev. Plant Sci.* **2009**, *28*, 199–217. [CrossRef]
67. Farooq, M.; Aziz, T.; Wahid, A.; Lee, D.-J.; Siddique, K.H.M. Chilling Tolerance in Maize: Agronomic and Physiological Approaches. *Crop Pasture Sci.* **2009**, *60*, 501. [CrossRef]
68. Parida, A.K.; Dagaonkar, V.S.; Phalak, M.S.; Aurangabadkar, L.P. Differential Responses of the Enzymes Involved in Proline Biosynthesis and Degradation in Drought Tolerant and Sensitive Cotton Genotypes during Drought Stress and Recovery. *Acta Physiol. Plant.* **2008**, *30*, 619–627. [CrossRef]
69. Yan, K.; Chen, W.; He, X.; Zhang, G.; Xu, S.; Wang, L. Responses of Photosynthesis, Lipid Peroxidation and Antioxidant System in Leaves of *Quercus mongolica* to Elevated OZONE. *Environ. Exp. Bot.* **2010**, *69*, 198–204. [CrossRef]
70. Liu, W.; Zheng, C.; Chen, J.; Qiu, J.; Huang, Z.; Wang, Q.; Ye, Y. Cold acclimation improves photosynthesis by regulating the ascorbate–glutathione cycle in chloroplasts of *Kandelia obovate*. *J. For. Res.* **2019**, *30*, 755–765. [CrossRef]
71. Flowers, M.D.; Fiscus, E.L.; Burkey, K.O.; Booker, F.L.; Dubois, J.-J.B. Photosynthesis, Chlorophyll Fluorescence, and Yield of Snap Bean (*Phaseolus vulgaris* L.) Genotypes Differing in Sensitivity to Ozone. *Environ. Exp. Bot.* **2007**, *61*, 190–198. [CrossRef]
72. Han, Y.J.; Gharibeshghi, A.; Mewis, I.; Förster, N.; Beck, W.; Ulrichs, C. Plant Responses to Ozone: Effects of Different Ozone Exposure Durations on Plant Growth and Biochemical Quality of Brassica Campestris L. Ssp. Chinensis. *Sci. Hortic.* **2020**, *262*, 108921. [CrossRef]
73. Khan, M.I.R.; Iqbal, N.; Masood, A.; Per, T.S.; Khan, N.A. Salicylic Acid Alleviates Adverse Effects of Heat Stress on Photosynthesis through Changes in Proline Production and Ethylene Formation. *Plant Signal. Behav.* **2013**, *8*, e26374. [CrossRef]
74. Rajametov, S.N.; Lee, K.; Jeong, H.-B.; Cho, M.-C.; Nam, C.-W.; Yang, E.-Y. The Effect of Night Low Temperature on Agronomical Traits of Thirty-Nine Pepper Accessions (*Capsicum annuum* L.). *Agronomy* **2021**, *11*, 1986. [CrossRef]

horticulturae

Article

Modifying Walk-In Tunnels through Solar Energy, Fogging, and Evaporative Cooling to Mitigate Heat Stress on Tomato

Mohamed A. Sharaf-Eldin [1], Zaher Mundher Yaseen [2,*], Adel H. Elmetwalli [3], Salah Elsayed [4], Miklas Scholz [5,6,7,*], Zainab Al-Khafaji [8] and Genesia F. Omar [9]

1 Horticulture Department, Faculty of Agriculture, Kafrelsheikh University, Kafr Elsheikh 33516, Egypt
2 Civil and Environmental Engineering Department, King Fahd University of Petroleum & Minerals, Dhahran 31261, Saudi Arabia
3 Department of Agricultural Engineering, Faculty of Agriculture, Tanta University, Tanta 31527, Egypt
4 Agricultural Engineering, Evaluation of Natural Resources Department, Environmental Studies and Research Institute, University of Sadat City, Minufiya 32897, Egypt
5 Directorate of Engineering the Future, School of Science, Engineering and Environment, The University of Salford, Newton Building, Salford M5 4WT, UK
6 Department of Civil Engineering Science, School of Civil Engineering and the Built Environment, University of Johannesburg, Kingsway Campus, P.O. Box 524, Johannesburg 2006, South Africa
7 Department of Town Planning, Engineering Networks and Systems, South Ural State University, 76 Lenin Prospekt, 454080 Chelyabinsk, Russia
8 Department of Building and Construction Techniques Engineering, Al-Mustaqbal University College, Hillah 51001, Iraq
9 Horticulture Department, Faculty of Agriculture, Suez Canal University, Ismailia 8366004, Egypt
* Correspondence: z.yaseen@kfupm.edu.sa (Z.M.Y.); m.scholz@salford.ac.uk (M.S.)

Abstract: Global warming is by far the most significant issue caused by climate change. Over the past few decades, heat stress has intensified into a serious issue that has a negative impact on crop production. Hence, it is crucial to modify cultivation systems to cope with this kind of stress, particularly in arid dry regions. In comparison to open-field cultivation, tomato production under protected cultivation techniques in walk-in tunnels that are suited for different farmers' financial abilities was evaluated during the late summer season. The studied tunnels included a shaded net tunnel with natural ventilation, net tunnel with a fogging system and plastic tunnel with evaporative cooling (wet pad and fans). For the operation of fogging and evaporative cooling systems, solar energy was used as a sustainable, eco-friendly energy source. The results indicated that the solar energy system successfully operated the studied cooling systems. All studied protective cultivation techniques mitigated heat stress on tomato plant and improved the microclimate under walk-in tunnels. Moreover, evaporative cooling and fogging systems significantly increased plant leaf area, cell membrane efficiency and the contents of chlorophyll, relative water and proline compared to the net tunnel with natural ventilation. Furthermore, a marked reduction in physiological disorders was noticed. Improved physiological and biochemical parameters and limited physiological diseases led to higher fruit set, marketable fruit yield and total productivity. The percentage of marketable fruit yield increased by around 31.5% with an evaporative cooling system, 28.8% with a fogging system and 17% with a shaded net tunnel with no positive cooling as compared to an open field. However, the plants grown in open-field cultivation without protection significantly deteriorated from heat stress and had a high incidence of physiological disorders. The most incident physiological disorders were blossom-end rot, cracking, internal white tissues, sunscald, puffiness, blotchy ripening, cat face and exserted stigma. It is recommended to use a solar energy system to modify microclimate conditions through fogging or evaporative cooling under walk-in tunnels to ameliorate heat stress on grown tomato in the late summer season for higher fruit yield and fewer physiological disorders.

Keywords: *Solanum lycopersicon*; protected cultivation; fogging; pad–fan cooling; microclimate; physiological disorders; productivity

Citation: Sharaf-Eldin, M.A.; Yaseen, Z.M.; Elmetwalli, A.H.; Elsayed, S.; Scholz, M.; Al-Khafaji, Z.; Omar, G.F. Modifying Walk-In Tunnels through Solar Energy, Fogging, and Evaporative Cooling to Mitigate Heat Stress on Tomato. *Horticulturae* **2023**, 9, 77. https://doi.org/10.3390/horticulturae9010077

Academic Editor: Domenico Ronga

Received: 1 November 2022
Revised: 4 December 2022
Accepted: 12 December 2022
Published: 6 January 2023

1. Introduction

The growing global population accompanied by climate change has increased food and energy demand. Moreover, the war between Russia and Ukraine has pushed the world to seriously secure food and renewable energy sources. The use of solar energy systems in protected cultivation is one of the most promising solutions for the development of the agricultural sector to address the issues posed by traditional energy sources and climate change, hence reducing environmental pollution and securing food [1]. Climate change has become the core focus of the world in the last decades due to the observed risks to human life [2]. Human activity through burning fossil fuels, cutting down forests and farming livestock are the main causes of gas emissions and global warming, which is known as the "greenhouse effect" [3]. Global warming negatively affects human life and food security. The Mediterranean region's climate, as a "hot spot" of climate change, is described by hot summer with high solar radiation and low relative humidity that is accompanied by limited water resources [4]. Global warming extremely affects ecosystems, including the quantity and quality of food supply [5]. As one of the most important vegetable crops, tomato is not far from these adverse impacts since its yield and quality are affected by heat stress [6]. Fruit set percentage is a crucially sensitive indicator for heat stress since it can fall by 40% with just 2.5 °C over the ideal temperature (about 25 °C) [7]. Reduced fruit set directly correlates with poor yield and quality [8,9]. The harmful effects of heat stress include the production of reactive oxygen species enzymes such as superoxide dismutase and ascorbate peroxidase which negatively affect CO_2 fixation, pollen grain viability, pollen tube growth, pollination and fertilisation function [10–12]. Moreover, a wide range of physiological disorders, including blossom-end rot, cracking, puffiness, cracking and sunscald, are common in incidence under heat stress in open-field cultivation, causing a significant loss in fruit productivity [13,14].

It is necessary to adjust cultivation strategies for better adaptation to climate change. Protected agriculture is suggested to play a crucial part in coping with the adverse effects of climate change and achieving farm sustainability [15,16]. Numerous forms of protected growing facilities, including greenhouses, net houses, tunnels and others, are created based on the needs of the various plant species and climatic conditions. Protected farming has several benefits, such as a reduction in weather-related yield loss, protection from pests, weeds, and diseases, more effective use of resources, improved crop yield and quality and higher farmer incomes [17]. Despite being the best option for changing the microclimate, fully controlled greenhouses face considerable challenges. These include expensive costs and technology as well as energy challenges that cannot be widely applied, particularly for poor farmers and developing countries [1]. In sunny regions, it is common to use unheated plastic greenhouses during the cool season and shaded net houses in the hot ones. However, these methods are still more expensive and need more practical experience than open-field growing. Besides heat stress in these regions, grown tomatoes in the open field in the late summer season suffer from water stress and insect attacks that are critical reasons for viruses transfer and which all increase physiological and biological diseases [18]. These reasons encourage the farmers to establish various kinds of protected cultivation. Low and high tunnels are preferred by the small-holder growers as they are easier and lower-cost options than the greenhouses. According to KC et al. [19], tunnel farming is an efficient low-cost strategy for fending off the effects of climate change, such as severe rainfall and temperature variations, and it enhanced productivity by 32 tons/year/hectare. The walk-in tunnel is appropriate for farmers since it is less expensive than high tunnels and easier for implementing agricultural practices due to its adequate height compared to low tunnels. Mainly, it relies on natural ventilation rather than artificial heating or cooling, which reduces the cost of both construction and maintenance [8,20]. There is a need to incorporate renewable energy systems to modify the microclimate under these types of tunnels to accommodate different farming financial capacities and environments and then to compare the products' productivity and quality. Under hot and sunny conditions, some strategies can be used for cooling the microclimate under protected cultivation, including two techniques. The first does not need energy (passive cooling), including the use of a net cover with different shading levels that provide natural ventilation [21,22] and various kinds of screens and materials to reflect sunlight [23,24]. The second technique needs energy, including forced ventilation [25], evaporative cooling [26] and the use of fogging systems [27].

Shading houses are commonly used by small farmers as a low-cost solution to protect the plants from high summer solar radiation and temperature [19]. El-Bassiony et al. [28] confirmed that shading during the late summer season was effective to boost tomato growth, yield and quality. Under Mediterranean regional conditions, it was also reported that shading during the summer cultivation of tomato was an excellent tool for enhancing the phytochemical quality [29]. Controlling the elevated temperature and low relative humidity around noon, however, is insufficient. Pad–fan evaporative cooling is a low-energy-cost option in hot and dry climates with a favourable effect on plant growth under greenhouse conditions and no negative impact on the environment [30]. Another option is a fog system, which produces small water droplets of 10–20 microns in diameter that are floated in the air before falling onto the crop canopy, causing a reduction in air temperature [31]. Baudoin [32] suggested fogging systems as a cooling method to mitigate the negative impacts of high evapotranspiration and elevated temperatures. According to Leyva et al. [33], using a fogging system on cherry tomatoes grown under a screen house reduced incident radiation by between 30 and 37%, while increasing relative humidity by between 16 and 20% to reduce the occurrence of physiological stress that would have a negative impact on yield and final quality.

Greenhouse modifications for high productivity have been extensively investigated, but for the modification of walk-in tunnels to be suitable for small-holder farmers during the hot summer season, there need to be more studies. Additionally, it is important to compare simple negative cooling with a forced one under these kinds of tunnels, especially when employing a renewable energy source. The evaluation of protected and non-protected tomato growing, as well as the impact of various tunnel covers and cooling techniques that are suitable for different financial abilities of small-holder farmers, were the main goals of this study. Furthermore, we aimed to investigate how far these strategies can modify the microclimate under the low-cost walk-in tunnels. We investigated how far these modifications can alleviate heat stress on grown tomatoes in the late summer season and affect the physiological and biochemical responses as well as the final productivity and physiological disorders in comparison with open-field cultivation.

2. Materials and Methods

2.1. Field Experimental Description

The current experiment was carried out on tomato plant (*Solanum lycopersicon* L.) F1 hybrid of 023 (Sakata seeds Co., Yokohama, Japan) at the International Protected Cultivation Centre, Faculty of Agriculture, Kafrelsheikh Univ., Egypt during the late summer seasons of 2020 and 2021 in silty clay soil (7.8 pH, EC 2.19 ds m^{-1} and 1.9 % organic matter). On the 3rd of June, 35-day-old seedlings were transplanted into rows that were 175 cm wide and had 50 cm between plants. The Agriculture Ministry's recommendations for tomato production including drip irrigation, fertilisers and pest control were followed.

The plants were transplanted in the open field and three walk-in tunnels with the same land area. The tunnels were 2.20 m tall, 6 m wide and 30 m long in the east/west orientation. Galvanised iron pipes were used as a frame. Two tunnels were covered by a white mesh insect-proof net with 35% shade level, 274.3 μm thread diameter, 0.345 m^2 m^{-2} porosity, 236.6 μm diameter of the inside circumference of the pore, 0.171 mm^2 area of the pore and 0.69 ventilation efficiency. The net cover was washed every four weeks to remove the dust. One of these tunnels was equipped with a fogging system under 405 KPa pressure. Three fog lines with 100 cm in between were placed 50 cm below the tunnel roof. The last tunnel was covered by polyethylene plastic film with 200 μm thickness, and a cooling evaporative system with a wet pad and fans was constructed (Figures 1 and S1).

Three fans (1 m in diameter, 300 m^3 per minute capacity) were installed in the tunnel on the east side to exchange the tunnel air once each minute (Figure 1). On the west side, a cooling bed with a pump that circulates water through (30 L/min) and over a porous pad was installed (Figures S1 and S2). To supply the required water, a water tank with a 300 L capacity was placed underground to reduce water temperature (Figure 1). The cooling system was adjusted to work when the outside temperature increases over 25 °C and stop when it reaches 22 °C.

Figure 1. Solar energy cells used in the experiment (**left**), front side of the walk-in tunnel with evaporative cooling system (**right**).

A solar energy system with 2.115 kW photovoltaic was used as an energy source for fogging and evaporative cooling systems (Figure 1).

2.2. Treatments

Four treatments were arranged as follows:

I. Open-field planting (OF).
II. Net house (NH).
III. Fogging under the net house (NF). The system was adjusted to work from 10 p.m. to 4 p.m. for 10 min/h at a rate of 6 S/36 S to lower the energy consumption.
IV. Evaporative cooling system under the plastic house (EP).

2.3. Microclimate Data

RH/Temp data loggers (model BESANTEK BST-DL13, Nanjing, Jiangsu, China) were placed 50 cm above the plant canopy to monitor the minimum, maximum and average air temperatures as well as the relative humidity (RH%). Three devices were randomly distributed in every treatment, and the sensors were shielded from direct sunlight. Additionally, three data loggers—one for each replicate—were dispersed across the open field. The monthly average and the hourly data during the day (3rd July) of peak flowering and fruit set were presented. Since the flowering and fruit set stage extended for two weeks and there were only minor changes (few days) among the studied treatments, an intermediate day was chosen to evaluate the effect of the studied modifications on the microclimate conditions and the related parameters.

2.4. Physiological and Biochemical Measurements

The physiological and biochemical parameters were taken 60 days after transplanting from five random plants from each replicate, and the measurements were carried out for three technical replicates.

2.4.1. Plant Leaf Area

A portable leaf area meter (model LI-3000A, Lincoln, NE, USA) was used to estimate the leaf area per plant (m^2) in the first completely opened leaves of five different random plants from each plot. The leaf area of the first completely developed leaf was multiplied by the overall number of plant leaves to determine the total plant leaf area.

2.4.2. The Relative Water Content (RWC)

The RWC determines a fresh sampled leaf tissue's water content in relation to the maximum amount of water the tissue can contain at full turgidity (condition of being swollen). It was determined for fully formed leaves that had been cut, directly weighed to determine the fresh weight (FW) and then submerged in double-distilled water for 16 h. To calculate the turgid weight (TW) of leaves, extra surface water was removed and dried with paper towels. The leaves were then dried in an oven until the dry weight remained unchanged (DW). According to the following equation [34]:

$$RWC\ (\%) = \frac{FW - DW}{TW - DW} \times W - D$$

2.4.3. Membrane Permeability (MP)

MP is a measurement of the plasma membrane's semi-permeability loss. According to the adopted research [35], it was determined by evaluating electrolyte leakage by selecting five plants randomly per replicate, cutting them into uniformly sized discs and taking 0.5 g of the discs from the middle of the youngest fully developed leaf. After that, the discs were cleansed with distilled water to eliminate any surface contaminants. The discs were incubated at 25 °C for 24 h in closed tubes containing 20 mL of deionised water. The bathing solution's electrical conductivity (EC1) was calculated. The samples were then heated to 120 °C in a water bath for 20 min, and when the solution had cooled to room temperature, the electrical conductivity (EC2) was measured. The MP (%) value was calculated as (EC1/EC2) 100.

2.4.4. Relative Chlorophyll Content

Relative chlorophyll content (SPAD) in the first fully developed leaves of five different plants was measured using the SPAD501 equipment (Minolta Corp, Ramsey, NJ, USA), which was used for measuring greenness without destroying the tissues [36].

2.4.5. Proline Content

The method suggested by Bates et al. [37] for determining proline content involved extracting 0.5 g of fresh leaf material, homogenising it in 10 mL of 3% aqueous sulfosalicylic acid and filtering the mixture through Whitman's No. 1 filter paper. Subsequently, 2 mL of the filtered extract was obtained for analysis along with 2 mL of acid ninhydrin and 2 mL of glacial acetic acid. The reaction mixture was first incubated in a bath of boiling water for one hour, and then it was completed in an ice bath. The reaction mixture was given 4 mL of toluene, and the organic phase was extracted and read at 520 nm, using toluene as a blank on a UV-visible spectrophotometer.

2.4.6. Flowering and Fruit Set

Fruit set percentage was taken during two weeks of the peak flowering and fruit set stage. The fully opened flowers of five plants from every replicate were counted and marked, and then the number of flowers converted into fruits was counted daily during this period. Fruit set percentage was calculated as follows:

$$\text{Fruit set\%} = (\text{Number of set flowers}/\text{Total number of marked flowers}) \times 100$$

The percentage of stigma exsertion during this period for the identical plants was also estimated as a sensitive reaction to heat stress damage on flowers according to the following formula:

$$\text{Stigma exertion \%} = (\text{Number of flowers with exserted stigma}/\text{Total number of flowers}) \times 100$$

2.5. Fruit Yield and Quality Parameters

All fruits from the studied plants were picked in the full mature pink stage to estimate the total and marketable yields per plant (kg) and average fruit weight (g). All picked fruits were sorted at every picking to determine the morphological disorders, and 20 fruits from each treatment were cut to estimate the internal defects. The following incident physiological disorders were expressed individually as an average of all pickings:

- Cracking: radial or concentric cracking.
- Sunscald: yellow, sunken areas.
- Blossom-end rot (BER): water-soaked areas at or near the blossom end.
- Puffiness: flat-sided, puffy and/or inside cavities lacking seed gel.
- Internal white tissue (IWT): internal white, hard areas in the outer walls and/or in the cross-wall, without outer symptoms.
- Blotchy ripening: outer uneven ripening or yellow shoulders.
- Cat face shape: brown deep cavities at the blossom end.

2.6. Statistical Analyses

Four treatments were used in three replicates of a complete block randomised design, with three rows in each tunnel and three rows in the open field. One-way analysis of variance was used to analyse the data using the statistical programme SPSS 18.0 for Windows. Duncan's multiple range test was used to compare the main values of the treatments at the $p \leq 0.05$ level.

3. Results

3.1. Microclimate Data

During the peak blooming and fruit set stage of the season, daytime hourly temperature and RH% were registered under the studied tunnels and the open field (Figures 2 and 3). The maximum temperature was extremely high in the open field since it reached 42.1 °C at 2 pm and 41.1 °C at 1 p.m. in the first and second seasons, respectively (Figure 2). In contrast, it dropped, achieving values of 38.8, 35.5 and 25.5 under the uncooled net tunnel, net tunnel with fogging and plastic tunnel with evaporative cooling, respectively. It is obvious that the protection techniques were successful in lowering the temperature during the hot part of the day between the hours of 8 a.m. and 6 p.m. At 8 p.m., the temperature in the open field and all studied tunnels dropped to below 27.5 °C and stayed around 20 °C until sunrise, which was suitable for tomato plant.

Except for when the fogging system was in operation (10 a.m.–4 p.m.) under the net tunnel, where RH% values were higher than those of the evaporative cooling system, the RH% under the plastic tunnel with evaporative cooling was higher than that of the other tunnels and the open field (Figure 3). While the RH% was extremely low in the open field, which dropped to the lowest values of 23.6–24.7% at 2 pm, the other protection techniques successfully improved RH% values. RH% ranged between 33.9 and 36.6% under the uncooled net house, between 60.1 and 62.7% under the net house with fogging and between 82.4 and 86.6% under the plastic house with evaporative cooling in the first and second seasons, respectively. Except for the plastic tunnel, the open field and the net tunnels had close RH% values that ranged between 78 and 80% and 64 and 71% in the first and second growing seasons, respectively. From 6 pm to 12 am, the two studied net tunnels either with or without cooling had close RH% values that ranged between 45 and 81% and 50 and 67% in the first and second seasons, respectively.

The average monthly maximum temperature during the experiment periods from June to September is shown in Figure 4. The open field had the highest values, recording 33.3–35.0 °C and 34.2–36.2 °C in the first and second seasons, respectively. Meanwhile, the studied cooling techniques of walk-in tunnels successfully reduced the maximum temperatures by 2.4–3.1 and 2.3–1.9 °C with the uncooled net tunnel, 5.3–5.0 and 5.5–6.2 °C with fogging under the net tunnel and 8.3–9.5 and 9.2–10.4 °C with evaporative cooling under the plastic tunnel.

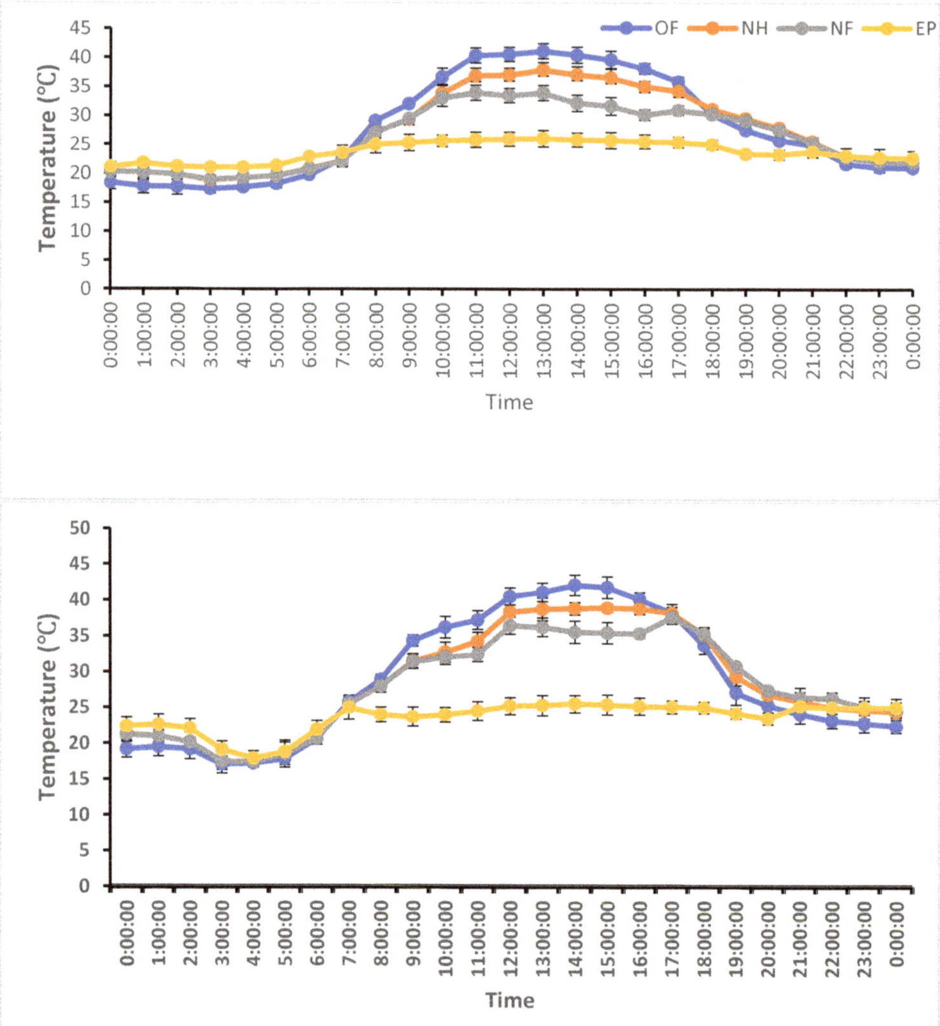

Figure 2. Hourly temperature changes during the peak of flowering and fruit set on 3 August 2020 (**upper figure**) and 5 August 2021 (**lower figure**) registered in the open field (OF), net house (NH), net house with fogging (NF, operating 6 S/36 S from 10 a.m. to 4 p.m.) and evaporative cooling under plastic house (EP). Standard error of the means was derived from three biological replicates.

The average monthly minimum temperature during the experiment period is presented in Figure 5. In the first season, the plastic tunnel kept the lowest minimum temperature ranging between 23 and 24 °C with 1.5–2.2 °C more than the open field, whereas the two studied net tunnels either with or without fogging had intermediate values with slight differences in between them. In the second season, the monthly average in the open field was higher than in the first season and increased up to 26 °C, hence the control system under the plastic tunnel worked to keep the temperature around 25 °C. As a result of the adjustment of the fogging system under the net tunnel to work only during the hottest period of the day (10 a.m.−4 p.m.) to lower the consumed energy, the minimum temperature had almost the same values in the cooled and uncooled tunnels, and it was at an acceptable level (24.5–28 °C).

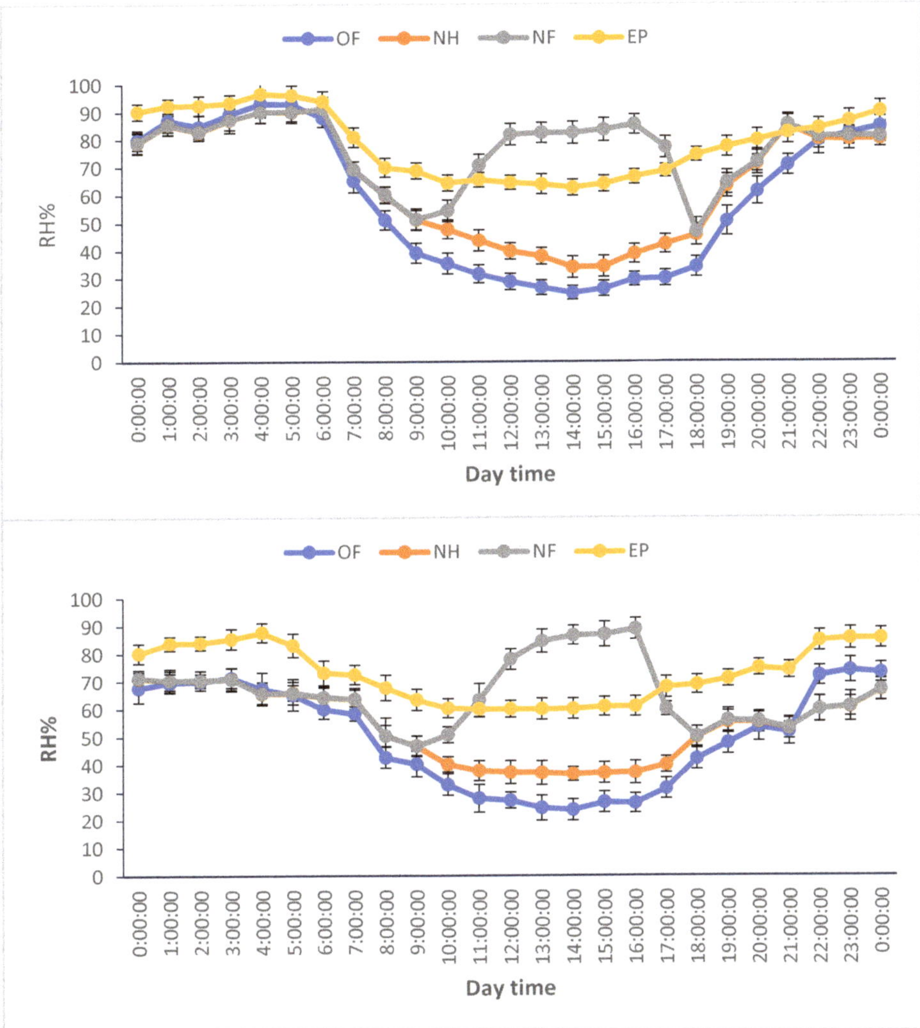

Figure 3. Hourly RH% changes during the peak of flowering and fruit set on 3 August 2020 (**upper figure)** and 5 August 2021 (**lower figure**) registered in the open field (OF), net house (NH), net house with fogging (NF, operating 6 S/36 S from 10 a.m. to 4 p.m.) and evaporative cooling under plastic house (EP). Standard error of the means was derived from three biological replicates.

Water cooling through fogging or evaporative systems enhanced the average monthly maximum RH% under net and plastic tunnels compared with the open field and uncooled net tunnel (Figure 6). Evaporative cooling increased the maximum RH% to 91.2–92.8%; however, fogging increased it to 81.6–89.5%. Meanwhile, the lowest values (81.7–82.2%) were obtained from the open field in the first season, and they were obtained from the uncooled net tunnel in the second one (75.6–77.9%).

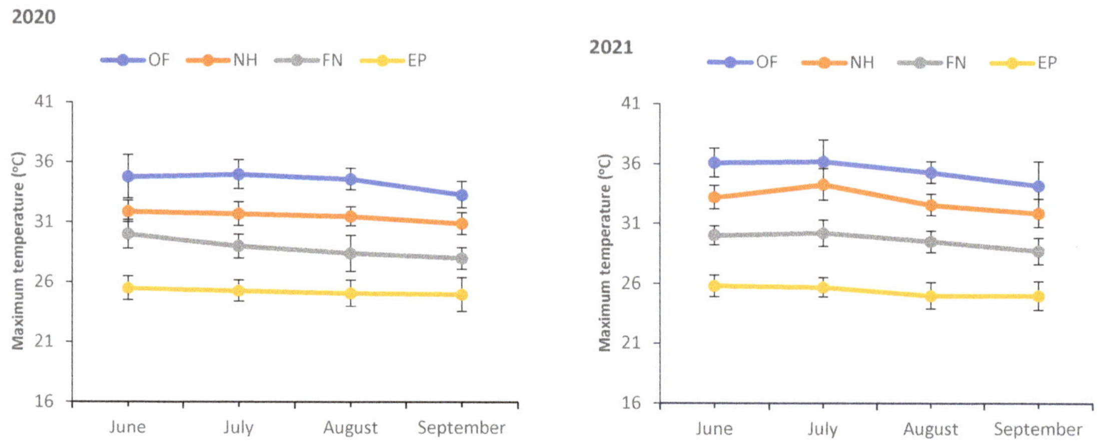

Figure 4. Average monthly maximum temperature during the experiment periods of 2020 and 2021 seasons, registered in the open field (OF), net house (NH), net house with fogging (NF, operating 6 S/36 S from 10 a.m. to 4 p.m.) and evaporative cooling under plastic house (EP). Standard error of the means was derived from three biological replicates.

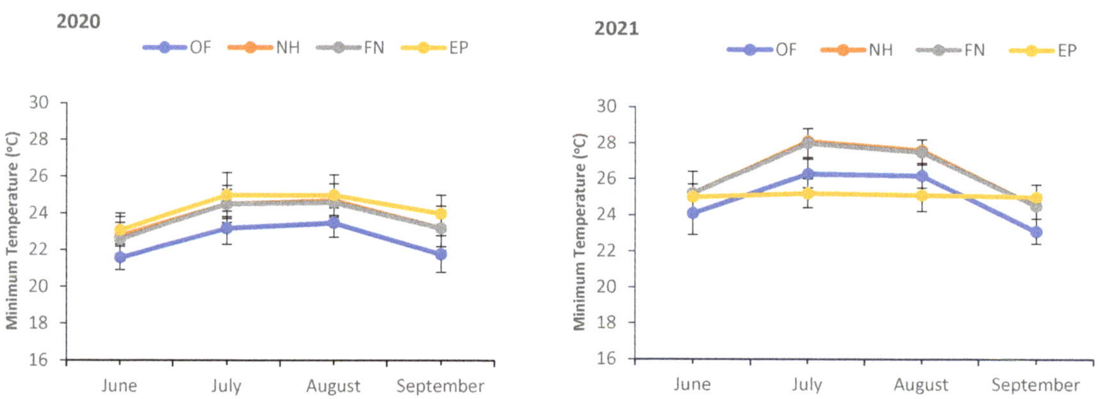

Figure 5. Average monthly minimum temperature during the experiment periods of 2020 and 2021 seasons, registered in the open field (OF), net house (NH), net house with fogging (NF, operating 6 S/36 S from 10 a.m. to 4 p.m.) and evaporative cooling under plastic house (EP). Standard error of the means was derived from three biological replicates.

The monthly average of minimum RH% during the experimental period in Figure 7 indicated that the plastic tunnel with evaporative cooling registered the highest values (65.2–74.2%) followed by the net tunnel with fogging (60.8–70.1%), net tunnel without cooling (49.3–59.0%) and finally the open field (46.3–58.2%).

3.2. Physiological and Biochemical Characteristics

Table 1 indicates that, in comparison to open-field cultivation, all studied physiological and biochemical characteristics of tomato plants including plant leaf area, RWC, MP, relative chlorophyll content and proline content significantly responded to the modification techniques in walk-in tunnels. When the plants were grown under the plastic modified tunnel with the evaporative cooling system, their leaf area was nearly doubled (223.8% and 214.8% in the first and second seasons, respectively, compared with the open field), recording the highest values. Additionally, modifying the net tunnel with a fogging system that operated throughout the hottest period of the day, from 10 a.m. to 4 p.m., was successful in enhancing leaf growth more than the un-fogged net tunnel. Meanwhile, plants grown in the open field without any protection produced the lowest leaf area.

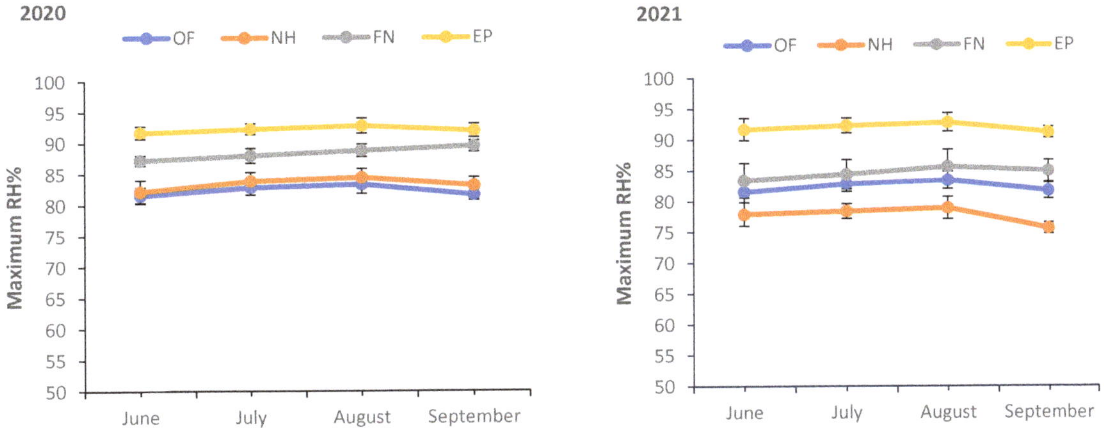

Figure 6. Average monthly maximum relative humidity percentage (RH%) during the experiment periods of 2020 and 2021 seasons, registered in the open field (OF), net house (NH), net house with fogging (NF, operating 6 S/36 S from 10 a.m. to 4 p.m.) and evaporative cooling under plastic house (EP). Standard error of the means was derived three biological replicates.

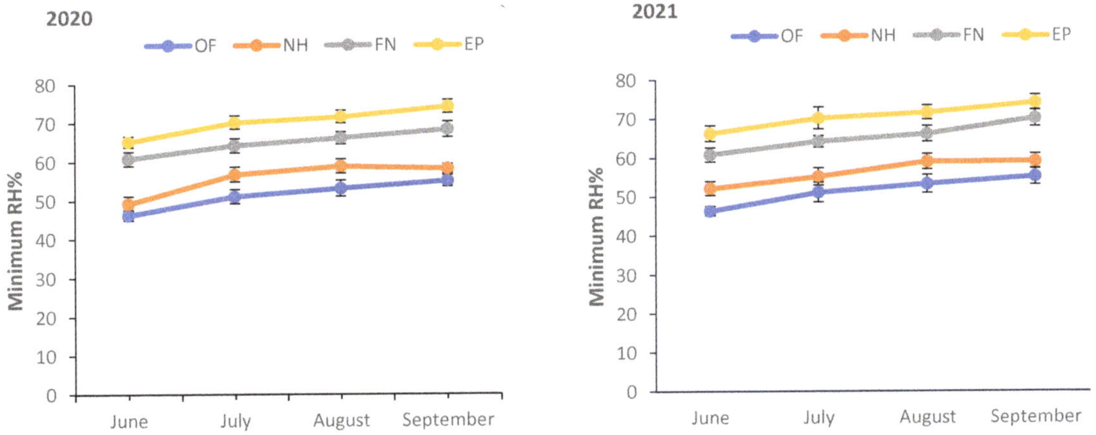

Figure 7. Average monthly minimum relative humidity percentage during the experimental periods of 2020 and 2021 seasons, registered in the open field (OF), net house (NH), net house with fogging (NF, operating 6 S/36 S from 10 a.m. to 4 p.m.) and evaporative cooling under plastic house (EP). Standard error of the means was derived from three biological replicates.

Plant leaf tissue showed a greater ability to hold more water when the microclimate under the tunnels was provided with moisture through fogging or evaporative systems or even with a plastic cover or net cover compared to the unmodified net tunnel or open-field growth (Table 1). Meanwhile, plant leaves that grew in the open field contained the lowest water content compared to the maximum water a leaf can retain (RWC). In the second season only, the differences between the open-field treatment and the un-fogging net tunnel were insignificant.

Leaf cells of the plants grown in the open field showed high membrane permeability compared to in the other studied cultivation protections (Table 1). It was highly effective to protect plants from heat stress to prevent damage to the membrane that could influence their permeability and result in the loss of their internal contents. In comparison to open-field growing, it showed up as decreased membrane permeability in plants cultivated under the net tunnel, net tunnel with fogging and plastic tunnel with an evaporative system, in that sequence.

Table 1. Changes in some physiological and biochemical traits in relation to reduced heat stress on grown tomato under modified walk-in tunnels compared to open-field growing.

Treatment #	Plant Leaf Area (m^2)	Relative Water Content (%)	Membrane Permeability (%)	Chlorophyll (SPAD)	Proline Content ($\mu mol\ g^{-1}$)
			2020 season		
Open field (OF)	7.02 ± 0.16 d	41.70 ± 0.25 d	15.62 ± 0.22 a	45.24 ± 0.04 d	0.72 ± 0.02 d
Net house (NH)	8.16 ± 0.75 c	53.20 ± 0.47 c	13.34 ± 0.17 b	46.19 ± 0.08 c	0.87 ± 0.03 c
NF	13.57 ± 0.43 b	62.99 ± 0.73 b	11.45 ± 0.06 c	47.29 ± 0.08 b	1.31 ± 0.05 b
EP	15.71 ± 0.19 a	69.65 ± 0.17 a	10.08 ± 0.06 d	49.02 ± 0.43 a	1.46 ± 0.02 a
			2021 season		
Open field (OF)	7.43 ± 0.19 d	41.15 ± 0.42 d	14.28 ± 0.04 a	44.74 ± 0.07 d	0.63 ± 0.01 d
Net house (NH)	8.45 ± 0.09 c	49.94 ± 0.03 c	13.69 ± 0.79 a	46.66 ± 0.09 c	0.75 ± 0.02 c
NF	14.20 ± 0.36 b	56.94 ± 0.81 b	11.41 ± 0.16 b	47.49 ± 0.17 b	0.85 ± 0.03 b
EP	15.96 ± 0.12 a	66.25 ± 0.59 a	10.04 ± 0.10 c	48.43 ± 0.23 a	1.36 ± 0.03 a

NH = net house covered by white mesh insect-proof net with 35% shade level, NF = net house with fogging (operating 6 S/36 S from 10 a.m. to 4 p.m.) and EP = evaporative cooling under plastic house. Different letters in the same column indicate that means are significantly different ($p \leq 0.05$). Standard error of the means was derived from three biological replicates.

In the case of the proline content of the leaf as an indicator of stress resistance, there was a significant increase in its content in the plants grown under the plastic tunnel with an evaporative cooling system, net tunnel with a fogging system and net tunnel without fogging, in order, whereas the lowest content was found in the plants grown under open-field conditions. These results were true for both growing seasons.

3.3. *Flowering and Fruit Yield*

As a sensitive indicator of the impact of heat stress on the flower, stigma exsertion was considered (Figures 8 and 9). Although exserted stigmas were not detectable in the modified tunnels by fogging under net cover and evaporative cooling under plastic cover, they were clearly observable under open-field conditions without any protection from the elevated temperature. They appeared in plants grown under the net tunnel without positive cooling with a lower incidence compared to the open-field plants. In the open field, their percentage ranged between 10.3 and 11.4%, whereas in the plants cultivated in net tunnels without cooling, they were between 0.95 and 1.02%.

An increase in fruit set percentage during the peak blooming and fruit set stages was observed from the cultivated plants under different modified tunnels compared to open-field cultivation in both growing seasons (Table 2). This increase reached about 33.5% with evaporative cooling under the plastic tunnel, 30% with fogging cooling under the net tunnel and 17.5% with the uncooled net tunnel more than the open field. The differences were significant ($p \leq 0.05$) in both growing seasons.

Positive cooling (requiring an energy source, which was solar energy in the current study) throughout evaporative or fogging systems effectively enhanced fruit weight when compared to the uncooled net tunnel and open-field cultivation (Table 2), since evaporative cooling under the plastic tunnel had the highest value (87.6–89.1 g). Nevertheless, open-field cultivation produced the lowest fruit weight (71.6–72.3 g). These results are true and significant in both growing seasons.

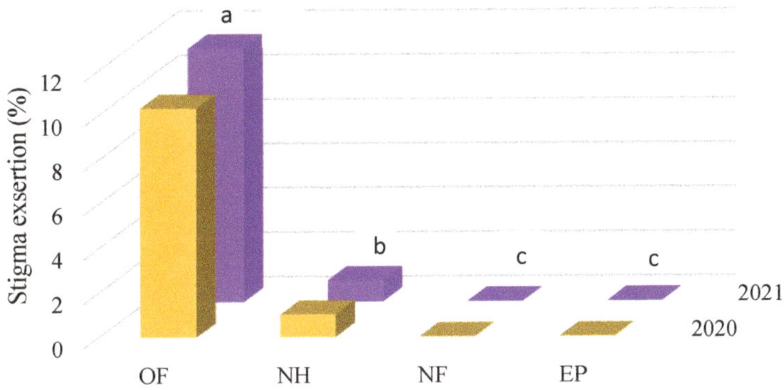

Figure 8. The percentage of flowers with exserted stigmas during the peak flowering period in relation to reduced heat stress by modifying walk-in tunnels (net house, NH; net house with fogging, NF, operating 6 S/36 S from 10 a.m. to 4 p.m.; and evaporative cooling under plastic house, EP) compared to open-field growing (OF). Different letters above the bars indicate that means are significantly different ($p \leq 0.05$). Presented data are the mean of 3 biological replicates, each with 5 plants.

Figure 9. Common physiological diseases during the experiment ((**A**) cracking, (**B**) sunscald, (**C**) blossom-end rot, (**D**) puffiness, (**E**) white internal tissue, (**F**) blotchy ripping, (**G**) cat face and (**H**) exserted stigma).

Cooling treatments using evaporative and fogging techniques reflected a significant increase in marketable fruit yield as a percentage of the total yield compared to open-field cultivation in both growing seasons (Table 2). However, the differences between the two cooling methods were significant only in the second season. When compared to an open field, the percentage of marketable yield rose by around 31.5% with an evaporative cooling system and by 28.8% with a fogging system. With no positive cooling, the shaded net tunnel had intermediate values that were 17% higher than the open field. Modifying microclimate conditions by evaporative or fogging cooling or shade significantly reduced the percentage of physiological diseases in both growing seasons (Table 2). Compared to the open field, the percentage was decreased by 19.4, 17.3 and 12.4%, respectively.

Table 2. Modified walk-in tunnels compared to open-field cultivation to reduce heat stress on tomato plant affecting fruit set, fruit weight, percentages of marketable yield and fruit disorders of tomato.

Treatment #	Fruit Set %	Average Fruit Weight (g)	Marketable Yield	Disorder Fruits
			As Percentage of the Total Yield	
		2020 season		
Open field (OF)	51.0 ± 0.52 d	71.6 ± 0.94 c	55.7 ± 1.19 c	25.0 ± 0.82 a
Net house (NH)	69.2 ± 0.43 c	77.2 ± 1.07 b	72.7 ± 0.72 b	12.7 ± 0.27 b
NF	80.7 ± 0.76 b	84.7 ± 0.56 a	85.0 ± 0.98 a	8.0 ± 0.19 c
EP	84.9 ± 1.63 a	87.6 ± 1.28 a	86.9 ± 0.52 a	6.0 ± 0.33 d
		2021 season		
Open field (OF)	51.9 ± 0.14 d	72.3 ± 0.49 c	55.4 ± 0.38 d	24.7 ± 0.19 a
Net house (NH)	69.0 ± 0.55 c	78.1 ± 0.49 b	72.8 ± 0.61 c	12.2 ± 0.32 b
NF	83.7 ± 1.09 b	86.8 ± 0.86 a	83.7 ± 1.77 b	7.1 ± 0.26 c
EP	85.4 ± 1.48 a	89.1 ± 1.19 a	87.0 ± 0.73 a	5.1 ± 0.06 d

NH = net house covered by white mesh insect-proof net with 35% shade level, NF = net house with fogging (operating 6 S/36 S h from 10 a.m. to 4 p.m.) and EP = evaporative cooling under plastic house. Different letters in the same column indicate that means are significantly different ($p \leq 0.05$). Standard error of the means was derived from three biological replicates.

The most common physiological diseases that were detected in the experiment are shown in Figure 9. They can be summarised as follows: fruit cracking, sunscald, blossom-end rot, puffiness, white internal tissue, blotchy ripping, cat face and exserted stigma. In both growing seasons, heat stress under open-field conditions led to a significant increase in all abovementioned physiological disorders in comparison to the other types of protection techniques (Table 3). The highest incident disorders in the open field were sunscald, blossom-end rot, cracking, white internal tissue, cracking, puffiness, blotchy ripping and cat face, in order, whereas the studied treatments did not significantly differ in the incidence of the cat face defect. Under the uncooled net tunnel, they appeared as follows: blossom-end rot, white internal tissue, cracking, sunscald, puffiness, blotchy ripping and finally cat face. All fruit disorders were the lowest under positive cooling via evaporative and fogging either with a plastic or net cover, with no visible signs of sunscald, and the incidence of fruit physiological disorders was lower under evaporative than fogging cooling. The covered tunnel with a white mesh net had intermediate values between open-field cultivation and the cooled tunnels.

3.4. Fruit Yield

Data about total and marketable fruit yields are shown in Figure 10. All protected cultivation techniques significantly increased total and marketable yields compared with open-field cultivation in both growing seasons. The plastic tunnel with an evaporative cooling system produced the highest yield, reaching 3.6 kg/plant as the marketable yield and 4.2 kg/plant as the total yield, compared to 1.1 kg/plant as the marketable yield and 2.1 as total kg/plant in open-field cultivation. Plant marketable yield increased by 1.0 kg and total yield increased by 1.2 kg when the net tunnel was supplied with the fogging system.

Table 3. Effect of modified walk-in tunnels compared to open field on common fruit disorders of tomato (as a percentage of total yield).

Treatment #	Cracking	Sunscald	BER *	Puffiness	IWT ^	Blotchy	Cat Face
			2020 season				
Open field (OF)	3.20 ± 0.06 a	8.47 ± 0.46 a	6.33 ± 0.06 a	1.58 ± 0.20 a	3.26 ± 0.04 a	1.17 ± 0.02 a	1.00 ± 0.01 a
Net house (NH)	1.68 ± 0.13 b	1.43 ± 0.04 b	4.11 ± 0.05 b	1.11 ± 0.01 b	2.31 ± 0.01 b	1.03 ± 0.03 b	1.00 ± 0.01 a
NF	0.78 ± 0.02 c	0.00 ± 0.00 c	2.20 ± 0.05 c	1.10 ± 0.01 b	1.88 ± 0.08 c	0.81 ± 0.03 c	1.02 ± 0.01 a
EP	0.49 ± 0.15 c	0.00 ± 0.00 c	1.94 ± 0.03 d	1.00 ± 0.03 b	0.81 ± 0.09 d	0.71 ± 0.06 d	0.92 ± 0.03 a
			2021 season				
Open field (OF)	2.65 ± 0.08 a	10.96 ± 0.03 a	3.27 ± 0.20 a	1.78 ± 0.23 a	2.64 ± 0.14 a	2.99 ± 0.09 a	1.04 ± 0.02 a
Net house (NH)	2.63 ± 0.02 a	0.00 ± 0.00 b	3.07 ± 0.04 a	1.47 ± 0.05 a	2.55 ± 0.06 a	2.91 ± 0.05 a	1.04 ± 0.02 a
NF	1.66 ± 0.06 b	0.00 ± 0.00 b	1.79 ± 0.05 b	0.98 ± 0.02 b	1.90 ± 0.05 b	1.68 ± 0.10 b	1.00 ± 0.01 a
EP	1.44 ± 0.06 c	0.00 ± 0.00 b	1.61 ± 0.05 b	0.79 ± 0.07 b	1.72 ± 0.03 b	1.35 ± 0.07 c	1.02 ± 0.01 a

NH = net. house covered by white mesh insect-proof net with 35% shade level, NF = net house with fogging (operating 6 S/36 S from 10 a.m. to 4 p.m.) and EP = evaporative cooling under plastic house. * BER = blossom-end rot. ^ IWT = internal white tissue. Different letters in the same column indicate that means are significantly different ($p \leq 0.05$). Standard error of the means was derived from three biological replicates.

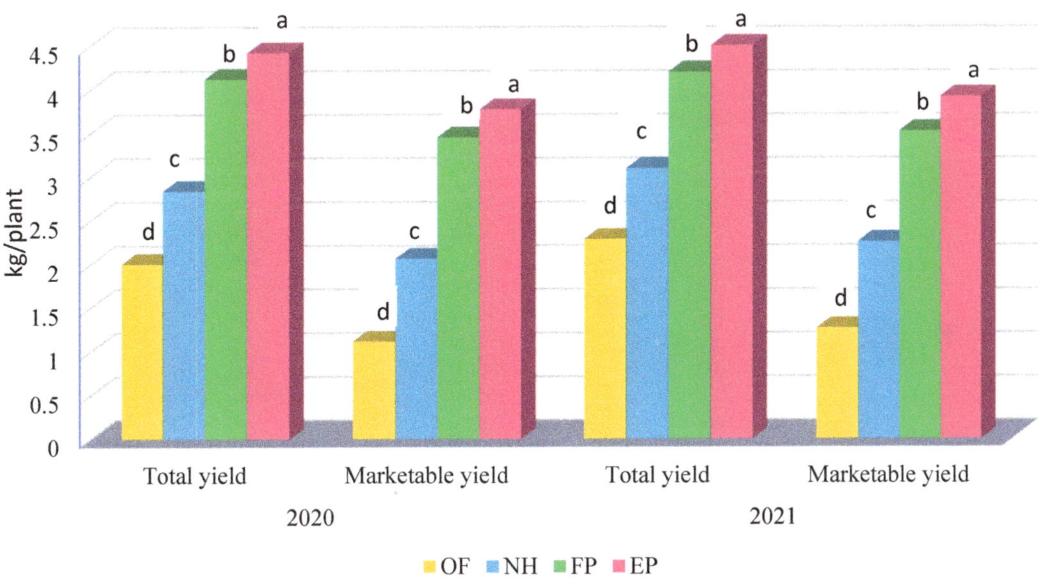

Figure 10. Total and marketable fruit yields of tomato in the open field (OF), net house (NH), net house with fogging (NF) operating 6 S/36 S from 10 a.m. to 4 p.m. and evaporative cooling under plastic house (EP). Different letters above the bars indicate that means are significantly different ($p \leq 0.05$). Presented data are the mean of 3 biological replicates.

4. Discussion

In the current study, we tried to suggest various solutions for the reduction in tomato growth, productivity and quality during the late summer season due to abiotic and biotic stresses, particularly with the severe effects of climate change. Since protected cultivation is the most crucial agricultural technique to protect grown plants from adverse climate changes and pest attacks, it contributes to improving the quality and productivity of plants. Although greenhouses offer the optimum solution to cope with these challenges, they require high technology and financial ability, which are unsuitable for small farmers and developing countries. Low and high tunnels produce a low-cost option without complex technologies compared to greenhouses, but we still need to develop agricultural production strategies to accommodate different farmers' abilities and maximise resource utilisation. Walk-in tunnels have an intermediate height between low and high tunnels that is enough for the workers to manage agricultural practices inside them at a lower cost than in high tunnels. In order to protect the plants from heat and biotic stresses in the late summer season, we investigated tomato production in our study under three types of walk-in tunnels, which are thought to suit different farmers' abilities in comparison with open-field cultivation.

The current results indicate that the shaded tunnel, which is suitable for small farmers, successfully reduced the inside temperature and increased RH% compared to open-field cultivation. However, the fogging system under the shaded tunnel had more efficiency in modifying microclimate conditions. These results are supported by those of [31]. In the hot-summer regions, it was reported that shade alone cannot lower the interior temperature and raise the humidity to levels that are appropriate for plants [8]. According to Abdel-Ghany et al. [23], the shading method effectively reduces solar radiation, but it also reduces photosynthetic radiation, which is important for plant development. It can be the reason for the lower growth and yield of the shaded tunnel without cooling techniques than the modified ones. Sethi and Sharma [38] demonstrated that ventilation systems can operate effectively in conditions of moderate air temperature. In contrast, ventilation systems (natural or forced) cannot function well in areas with high air temperatures and low humidity because they replace the interior air with the hotter ambient air. As a result, ventilation systems rarely cool greenhouses or provide good conditions for plant development [23]. The effectiveness of evaporative cooling systems (wet pad and fans), which are suitable for farmers with higher financial ability, in lowering ambient temperatures and raising air humidity to the desired range for the plant can be linked to the current study's positive outcomes. Evaporative cooling has been proven as the most effective cooling system for regulating the temperature and humidity under protected cultivation in arid regions [39,40]. The alternative is a fogging system, which is also successfully used in arid regions [28,41]. However, in order to wet the pad or create fog, they both need fresh water [27]. Here, we effectively utilised solar energy system for tunnel cooling, which has future prospects in protected cultivation in hot arid climates with minimal environmental effects and maximum utilisation of natural resources [30].

The improvement of physiological and biochemical parameters in relation to protected cultivation methods could be attributed to the amelioration of heat stress compared to open-field cultivation. When plants suffer from extremely high air temperature and low humidity under an open field without protection, it could harm the plants' biochemical and physiological functions [42,43]. Some research stated that tomato photoinhibition can happen between 30 and 40 °C and elevated radiation can occur between 1500 and 1800 mol m^{-2} s^{-1} [44,45]. The damage in physiological and biochemical processes could be attributed to the correlation between high temperature and accelerated senescence [46]. Thus, mesophyll cells underwent considerable damage from heat stress, and the increased permeability of the plasma membrane led to a decrease in stomatal conductance [47]. It is also reported that proline content, chlorophyll (SPAD) and the photosynthetic rate of tomato leaf were reduced under heat stress (45 °C) compared to under an un-stressful temperature of 25 °C; however, electrolyte leakage (membrane permeability) was increased [43]. In response to biotic and abiotic stressors, proline, a non-enzymatic antioxidant, accumulates, playing a beneficial role in metal chelation, antioxidant defense and signalling [48]. It also assists in maintaining membrane stability, osmotic adjustment or cell turgor and protects essential enzymes while reducing the negative effects of ROS and electrolyte leakage [49,50]. Our results support these findings since the higher concentration of protein under protected cultivation helps to maintain water content and cellular membrane permeability as preventing electrolyte leakage is associated with high leaf area and chlorophyll content.

Our results about the favourable effect of cooling the tunnels on tomato growth are supported by those of Sharaf-Eldin [51] and Leyva et al. [33] with shading and fogging techniques on tomato plant and Al-Helal [40] with evaporative cooling. It was also noted that reduced light intensity improved tomato growth and yield in the summer season. Mist application has an effective role in alleviating the negative effect of the double stress of salinity and high temperature on tomato plant, consistent with Romero-Aranda et al.'s [52] finding that intermittent misting for grown tomato under salinity and high-temperature conditions enhanced total leaf area and plant biomass. These findings can help to explain the beneficial effects of fog cooling on plant growth, which were also observed at our experiment site under salinity and elevated temperature. While under open-field cultivation without protection, the plants' leaf area reduced dramatically, indicating a drop in plant growth (Table 1). This reduction can be attributed to the physiological and biological leaf rolls due to severe heat stress and pest infection under unprotected cultivation, which were reflected in small leaf size. The curled, small-size leaf is a reaction from the plant to decrease water transpiration, thus ameliorating the negative impact of heat, light and drought [53,54].

The indirect response to heat stress was tomato flower stigma exsertion (Figure 8). These findings are supported by those of [55–57]. Stigma exsertion obviously appeared in open-field growing under severe heat stress and decreased under shaded, fogged and evaporative cooling tunnels, in order. The severity of this phenomenon relates to the reaction between the genotype and heat stress harshness as an indirect response of pistil development where the style is forced out of the anther tube and results in stigma insertion. In this situation, the stigma cannot be reached by the pollen, preventing successful fertilisation [58]. This is because the male function of tomato flower is generally more exposed to damage than the female one under heat stress [59–61]. Furthermore, Ozores-Hampton [62] indicated that stigma-drying of tomato female flower can also happen when the plants suffer from heat stress. Moreover, it was stated that the initial stages of stamen development are most susceptible to heat stress. In this way, heat inhibits pollen release and transfer to the stigma surface, pollen tube development and fertilisation, which all have a negative impact on pollen viability and quantity, leading to poor fruit set [63,64]. Accordingly, the suppression of fertilisation activity was caused by a decrease in the consistency of seeds, which are thought to be the source of auxin, which increases fruit size through cell division and enlargement [65].

A high occurrence of physiological diseases was obviously noticed in the open field without protection from heat stress compared to the modified tunnels throughout cooling systems (Table 3). The high incidence of sunscalds in the open field may be related to the limited plant leaf area (Table 1), which is unable to adequately cover the fruits and protect them from the intense sun radiation. The leak of fertiliser besides the heat stress in the open field was reported as a reason for puffiness and cat face as per the reported research [66], and the authors monitored tomato physiological disorders in relation to climate warming in Turkey as cat face, scalded, blossom-end rot and cracks increased under non-protected cultivation. However, in the current study, the noticed diseases were blossom-end rot, cracking, internal white tissues, sunscald, puffiness, blotchy ripening and cat face (Figure 9). In Swaziland, blossom-end rot, cat face, cracking, internal white tissue, irregular ripening, puffiness, pox and fleck, rain check, zippering and sunscald were encountered [67]. When pepper plants were irrigated with saline water, a high percentage of blossom-end rot was reported; however, fogging application increased the relative humidity, causing a considerable decrease in infected fruits [31]. These results are in harmony with the current results. In contrast, Gazquez et al. [68] obtained a higher percentage of blossom-end rot with fogging application than un-fogging, which was accompanied by a lower respiration rate under fogging. High air humidity can cause the respiration rate to slow down, which can lead to calcium deficiencies in the fruit, which are known to induce blossom-end rot [69]. The variable salinity conditions that might enhance calcium deficiency when heat and water stresses are present may be the cause of these conflicting findings.

The increased fruit production under tunnel cultivation can be attributed to the high use efficiency of resources and their role in protecting the plant against pest attacks and indirect viral infection. Additionally, with the proper modifications, the tunnels shield plants from the harmful effects of elevated temperatures and low humidity, which can lead to better growth and fruiting with less physiological diseases [19,51]. It is possible that the beneficial effects of fogging and evaporative cooling on tomato production are owed to the high relative humidity's ability to counteract the adverse effects of the salinity that was present at the experiment location and is common in the Mediterranean region. This trend is supported by the obtained results of Romero-Aranda et al. [52] who reported that fruit yield increased by 18% when intermittent misting was applied on grown tomato under saline conditions and high air temperature (36 °C as maximum) with respect to non-misted application, which was attributed to the increase in relative humidity with the mist treatment. Otherwise, Moreno-Teruel et al. [70] indicated that providing a greenhouse with a fogging system along with natural ventilation decreased the yield in comparison to a pad–fan cooling system and only natural ventilation without a cooling system. However, the pad–fan cooling system achieved the highest fruit yield.

5. Conclusions

The obtained findings lead to the following conclusions:

- A solar energy system, which can be used in arid dry regions, successfully operated the cooling systems under the modified walk-in tunnels via fogging and evaporative cooling.
- The studied cooling techniques effectively improved the microclimate conditions by significantly reducing the average monthly maximum temperatures by 2.5 °C with the uncooled net tunnel, 5.6 °C with fogging under the net tunnel and 9.4 °C with evaporative cooling under the plastic tunnel. Moreover, evaporative cooling kept the temperature around 25 °C.
- The tunnels with evaporative cooling and fogging systems significantly improved plant leaf area, water relative content, chlorophyll, membrane functions and proline content compared to the uncooled net tunnel. Moreover, better pollination and fertilisation functions with high fruit set were gained. In constrast, unprotected cultivation had the worst values.
- The percentage of marketable fruit yield increased by around 31.5% with evaporative cooling, 28.8% with the fogging system and 17% with the shaded net tunnel with no positive cooling as compared to an open field. Moreover, the physiological disease percentage decreased by 19.4, 17.3 and 12.4%, respectively.

In brief, the current study developed different eco-friendly techniques for tomato production that are suitable for various farmers' abilities to cope with climate warming. Further studies are needed to adapt agriculture techniques for various crops for climate change.

Supplementary Materials: The following supporting information can be downloaded at: https://www.mdpi.com/article/10.3390/horticulturae9010077/s1, Figure S1. Back-side of walk-in tunnel with evaporative cooling system (left) and air cycle system (right). Figure S2. Evaporative cooling system design.

Author Contributions: Conceptualisation, M.A.S.-E., Z.M.Y. and S.E.; Data curation, A.H.E. and G.F.O.; Formal analysis, M.A.S.-E., Z.M.Y., A.H.E., S.E., M.S. and Z.A.-K.; Investigation, A.H.E., S.E. and G.F.O.; Project administration, Z.M.Y.; Resources, G.F.O.; Supervision, Z.M.Y. and M.S.; Validation, M.A.S.-E., Z.M.Y., A.H.E., S.E., M.S. and Z.A.-K.; Visualisation, Z.M.Y., A.H.E., S.E. and G.F.O.; Writing—original draft, M.A.S.-E., A.H.E., S.E., M.S. and Z.A.-K.; Writing—review & editing, M.A.S.-E., Z.M.Y., M.S., Z.A.-K. and G.F.O. All authors have read and agreed to the published version of the manuscript.

Funding: This work was financially supported predominantly by WATERAGRI (European Union Horizon 2020 research and innovation programme under Grant Agreement Number 858735). In addition, the authors acknowledge the facility support by Al-Mustaqbal University College for providing technical and financial support for this research through the Grant Number: MUC-E-0122.

Data Availability Statement: Not applicable.

Conflicts of Interest: The authors declare no conflict of interest.

References

1. Hassanien, R.H.E.; Li, M.; Dong Lin, W. Advanced applications of solar energy in agricultural greenhouses. *Renew. Sustain. Energy Rev.* **2016**, *54*, 989–1001. [CrossRef]
2. Arias, P.; Bellouin, N.; Coppola, E.; Jones, R.; Krinner, G.; Marotzke, J.; Naik, V.; Palmer, M.; Plattner, G.K.; Rogelj, J. Climate Change 2021: The Physical science basis contribution of working group14 I to the sixth assessment report of the intergovernmental panel on climate change; technical summary. *Tech. Summ.* **2021**, 33–144. [CrossRef]
3. Al-Ghussain, L. Global warming: Review on driving forces and mitigation. *Environ. Prog. Sustain. Energy* **2018**, *38*, 13–21. [CrossRef]
4. Alessandri, A.; De Felice, M.; Zeng, N.; Mariotti, A.; Pan, Y.; Cherchi, A.; Lee, J.-Y.; Wang, B.; Ha, K.-J.; Ruti, P. Robust assessment of the expansion and retreat of Mediterranean climate in the 21st century. *Sci. Rep.* **2014**, *4*, 7211. [CrossRef]
5. Mahato, A. Climate change and its impact on agriculture. *Int. J. Sci. Res. Publ.* **2014**, *4*, 1–6.
6. Islam, M.T. Effect of temperature on photosynthesis, yield attributes and yield of tomato genotypes. *Int. J. Expt. Agric.* **2011**, *2*, 8–11.
7. Harel, D.; Fadida, H.; Slepoy, A.; Gantz, S.; Shilo, K. The effect of mean daily temperature and relative humidity on pollen, fruit set and yield of tomato grown in commercial protected cultivation. *Agronomy* **2014**, *4*, 167–177. [CrossRef]
8. El-Aidy, F.A.; Sharaf-Eldin, M.A. Modifying microclimatic conditions in plastic walk-in tunnels through solar energy system for improving yield and quality of four sweet pepper hybrids. *Plasticulture* **2015**, *134*, 6–22.
9. El-Tantawy, E.M.; El-Shatoury, R.S. Improving Tomato Productivity under High Temperature Conditions. *Hortscience J. Suez Canal Univ.* **2017**, *6*, 15–29.
10. Kafizadeh, N.; Carapetian, J.; Khosrow, K. Effects of heat stress on pollen viability and pollen tube growth in pepper. *Res. J. Biol. Sci.* **2008**, *3*, 1159–1162.
11. Hu, W.H.; Xiao, Y.A.; Zeng, J.J.; Hu, X.H. Photosynthesis, respiration and antioxidant enzymes in pepper leaves under drought and heat stresses. *Biol. Plant.* **2010**, *54*, 761–765. [CrossRef]
12. Zhou, R.; Kjaer, K.H.; Rosenqvist, E.; Yu, X.; Wu, Z.; Ottosen, C.-O. Physiological Response to Heat Stress During Seedling and Anthesis Stage in Tomato Genotypes Differing in Heat Tolerance. *J. Agron. Crop Sci.* **2016**, *203*, 68–80. [CrossRef]
13. Milenkovic, L.; Ilic, Z.S.; Sunic, L.; Trajkovic, R.; Kapoulas, N.; Durovka, M. Reducing of tomato physiological disorders by photoselective shade nets. In Proceedings of the 47th Croatian and 7th International Symposium on Agriculture, Opatija, Croatia, 13–17 February 2012; Volume 419, p. 423.
14. Shehata, S.; Elsagheer, A.A.; El-Helaly, M.A.; Saleh, S.A.; Abdallah, A.M. Shading effect on vegetative and fruit characters of tomato plant. *J. Appl. Sci. Res.* **2013**, *9*, 1434–1437.
15. Yohannes, H. A Review on Relationship between Climate Change and Agriculture. *J. Earth Sci. Clim. Chang.* **2015**, *7*, 335.
16. Liao, P.A.; Liu, J.Y.; Sun, L.C.; Chang, H.H. Can the Adoption of Protected Cultivation Facilities Affect Farm Sustainability? *Sustainability* **2020**, *12*, 9970. [CrossRef]
17. Magray, M.M.; Wani, K.P.; Chatto, M.A.; Ummyiah, H.M. Synthetic Seed Technology. *Int. J. Curr. Microbiol. Appl. Sci.* **2017**, *6*, 662–674. [CrossRef]
18. Rahman, M.S.; Acharjee, D.C. Impact of off-season summer tomato cultivation on income and food security of the growers. In *Agricultural Economics*; IntechOpen: London, UK, 2020; pp. 1–11.
19. KC, D.; Jamarkattel, D.; Maraseni, T.; Nandwani, D.; Karki, P. The Effects of tunnel technology on crop productivity and livelihood of smallholder farmers in Nepal. *Sustainability* **2021**, *13*, 7935. [CrossRef]
20. Janke, R.R.; Altamimi, M.E.; Khan, M. The use of high tunnels to produce fruit and vegetable crops in North America. *Agric. Sci.* **2017**, *8*, 692–715. [CrossRef]
21. Zaki, M.S.; AboaSedera, F.A.; Badr, L.A.; Sadek, I.I.; El-Sawy, A.M. Effect of some climatic factors and irrigation regimes on tomato growth and chemical constituents. *Ann. Agric. Sci. Moshtohor* **2014**, *52*, 1–9.
22. Statuto, D.; Abdel-Ghany, A.M.; Starace, G.; Arrigoni, P.; Picuno, P. Comparison of the efficiency of plastic nets for shading greenhouse in different climates. In Proceedings of the International Mid-Term Conference of the Italian Association of Agricultural Engineering, 12–13 September 2019; Springer: Cham, Switzerland, 2019; pp. 287–294.
23. Abdel-Ghany, A.M.; Al-Helal, I.M.; Alzahrani, S.M.; Alsadon, A.A.; Ali, I.M.; Elleithy, R.M. Covering materials incorporating radiation-preventing techniques to meet greenhouse cooling challenges in arid regions: A review. *Sci. World J.* **2012**, *2012*, 906360. [CrossRef]
24. Puglisi, R.; Statuto, D.; Picuno, P. Effects of greenhouse lime shading on filtering the solar radiation. In Proceedings of the 48th Symposium "Actual Tasks on Agricultural Engineering", Zagreb, Croatia, 2–4 March 2021.
25. Kittas, C.; Karamanis, M.; Katsoulas, N. Air temperature regime in a forced ventilated greenhouse with rose crop. *Energy Build.* **2005**, *37*, 807–812. [CrossRef]
26. Al-Helal, I.M. Effects of ventilation rate on the environment of a fan-pad evaporatively cooled, shaded greenhouse in extreme arid climates. *Appl. Eng. Agric.* **2007**, *23*, 221–230. [CrossRef]
27. Arbel, A.; Barak, M.; Shklyar, A. Combination of forced ventilation and fogging systems for cooling greenhouses. *Biosyst. Eng.* **2003**, *84*, 45–55. [CrossRef]

28. El-Bassiony, A.M.; Ghoname, A.A.; El-Awadi, M.E.; Fawzy, Z.F.; Gruda, N. Ameliorative effects of brassinosteroids on growth and productivity of snap beans grown under high temperature. *Gesunde Pflanz.* **2012**, *64*, 175–182. [CrossRef]
29. Formisano, L.; Ciriello, M.; El-Nakhel, C.; Poledica, M.; Starace, G.; Graziani, G.; Ritieni, A.; De Pascale, S.; Rouphael, Y. Pearl grey shading net boosts the accumulation of total carotenoids and phenolic compounds that Accentuate the antioxidant activity of processing tomato. *Antioxidants* **2021**, *10*, 1999. [CrossRef]
30. Merabti, L.; Abbas, M.; Taane, W. Applicability of Solar Evaporative Cooling in Greenhouses productivity Improvement. In Proceedings of the 7th International Renewable and Sustainable Energy Conference (IRSEC), Agadir, Morocco, 27–30 November 2019.
31. Montero, J.I. Evaporative cooling greenhouse: Effect on microclimate, water use efficiency and plant respons. *Acta Hortic.* **2006**, *719*, 373–384. [CrossRef]
32. Baudoin, W.; Nono-Womdim, R.; Lutaladio, N.; Hodder, A.; Castilla, N.; Leonardi, C.; De Pascale, S.; Qaryouti, M.; Duffy, R. *Good Agricultural Practices for Greenhouse Vegetable Crops: Principles for Mediterranean Climate Areas*; FAO: Rome, Italy, 2013; ISBN 9251076499.
33. Leyva, R.; Constán-Aguilar, C.; Blasco, B.; Sánchez-Rodríguez, E.; Romero, L.; Soriano, T.; Ruíz, J.M. Effects of climatic control on tomato yield and nutritional quality in Mediterranean screenhouse. *J. Sci. Food Agric.* **2013**, *94*, 63–70. [CrossRef]
34. Anjum, S.A.; Farooq, M.; Xie, X.; Liu, X.; Ijaz, M.F. Antioxidant defense system and proline accumulation enables hot pepper to perform better under drought. *Sci. Hortic.* **2012**, *140*, 66–73. [CrossRef]
35. Valentovič, P.; Luxová, M.; Kolarovič, L.; Gašparíková, O. Effect of osmotic stress on compatible solutes content, membrane stability and water relationsin two maize cultivars. *Plant Soil Environ.* **2011**, *52*, 186–191. [CrossRef]
36. Coste, S.; Baraloto, C.; Leroy, C.; Marcon, É.; Renaud, A.; Richardson, A.D.; Roggy, J.-C.; Schimann, H.; Uddling, J.; Hérault, B. Assessing foliar chlorophyll contents with the SPAD-502 chlorophyll meter: A calibration test with thirteen tree species of tropical rainforest in French Guiana. *Ann. For. Sci.* **2010**, *67*, 607. [CrossRef]
37. Bates, L.S.; Waldren, R.P.; Teare, I.D. Rapid determination of free proline for water-stress studies. *Plant Soil* **1973**, *39*, 205–207. [CrossRef]
38. Sethi, V.P.; Sharma, S.K. Survey of cooling technologies for worldwide agricultural greenhouse applications. *Sol. Energy* **2007**, *81*, 1447–1459. [CrossRef]
39. Ganguly, A.; Ghosh, S. Modeling and analysis of a fan–pad ventilated floricultural greenhouse. *Energy Build.* **2007**, *39*, 1092–1097. [CrossRef]
40. Al-Helal, I.M.; Abdel-Ghany, A.M. Energy partition and conversion of solar and thermal radiation into sensible and latent heat in a greenhouse under arid conditions. *Energy Build.* **2011**, *43*, 1740–1747. [CrossRef]
41. Handarto, H.; Hayashi, M.; Kozai, T. Air and leaf temperatures and relative humidity in a naturally ventilated single-span greenhouse with a fogging system for cooling and its evaporative cooling efficiency. *Environ. Control Biol.* **2005**, *43*, 3–11. [CrossRef]
42. Ayenan, M.A.T.; Danquah, A.; Hanson, P.; Ampomah-Dwamena, C.; Sodedji, F.A.K.; Asante, I.K.; Danquah, E.Y. Accelerating breeding for heat tolerance in tomato (*Solanum lycopersicum* L.): An Integrated Approach. *Agronomy* **2019**, *9*, 720. [CrossRef]
43. Guo, T.; Gull, S.; Ali, M.M.; Yousef, A.F.; Ercisli, S.; Kalaji, H.M.; Telesiński, A.; Auriga, A.; Wróbel, J.; Radwan, N.S.; et al. Heat stress mitigation in tomato (*Solanum lycopersicum* L.) through foliar application of gibberellic acid. *Sci. Rep.* **2022**, *12*, 11324. [CrossRef]
44. Gent, M.P.N.; Seginer, I.D.O. A carbohydrate supply and demand model of vegetative growth: Response to temperature and light. *Plant Cell Environ.* **2012**, *35*, 1274–1286. [CrossRef]
45. Masabni, J.; Sun, Y.; Niu, G.; Del Valle, P. Shade effect on growth and productivity of tomato and chili pepper. *Horttechnology* **2016**, *26*, 344–350. [CrossRef]
46. Hlaváčová, M.; Klem, K.; Rapantová, B.; Novotná, K.; Urban, O.; Hlavinka, P.; Smutná, P.; Horáková, V.; Škarpa, P.; Pohanková, E.; et al. Interactive effects of high temperature and drought stress during stem elongation, anthesis and early grain filling on the yield formation and photosynthesis of winter wheat. *Field Crop. Res.* **2018**, *221*, 182–195. [CrossRef]
47. Zhang, J.H.; Huang, W.-D.; Liu, Y.P.; Pan, Q.H. Effects of temperature acclimation pretreatment on the ultrastructure of mesophyll cells in young grape plants (*Vitis vinifera* L. cv. Jingxiu) under cross-temperature stresses. *J. Integr. Plant Biol.* **2005**, *47*, 959–970. [CrossRef]
48. Hayat, S.; Hayat, Q.; Alyemeni, M.N.; Wani, A.S.; Pichtel, J.; Ahmad, A. Role of proline under changing environments: A review. *Plant Signal. Behav.* **2012**, *7*, 1456–1466. [CrossRef] [PubMed]
49. Kavi Kishor, P.B.; Sangam, S.; Amrutha, R.N.; Sri Laxmi, P.; Naidu, K.R.; Rao, K.R.S.S.; Rao, S.; Reddy, K.J.; Theriappan, P.; Sreenivasulu, N. Regulation of proline biosynthesis, degradation, uptake and transport in higher plants: Its implications in plant growth and abiotic stress tolerance. *Curr. Sci.* **2005**, *88*, 424–438.
50. Desoky, E.-S.M.; Mansour, E.; Yasin, M.A.T.; El-Sobky, E.-S.E.A.; Rady, M.M. Improvement of drought tolerance in five different cultivars of Vicia faba with foliar application of ascorbic acid or silicon. *Span. J. Agric. Res.* **2020**, *18*, e0802. [CrossRef]
51. Sharaf-Eldin, M.A. Mitigation heat stress on tomato plant by shading and fogging system: Influence microclimate, fruit set, yield and physiological disorders. *Egypt. J. Hortic.* **2015**, *42*, 865–881.
52. Romero-Aranda, R.; Soria, T.; Cuartero, J. Greenhouse mist improves yield of tomato plants grown under saline conditions. *J. Am. Soc. Hortic. Sci.* **2002**, *127*, 644–648. [CrossRef]

53. Zhang, G.H.; Xu, Q.; Zhu, X.D.; Qian, Q.; Xue, H.W. Shallot-like1 is a KanadiA transcription factor that modulates rice leaf rolling by regulating leaf abaxial cell development. *Plant Cell* **2009**, *21*, 719–735. [CrossRef]
54. Faisal, S.; Guo, Y.; Du, C.; Zhang, D.; Lv, J.; Channa, S.A.; Qu, G.; Hu, S. Morphological, physiological and genetic analysesof an upward-curling leaf mutant in *Brassica napus* L. *Acta Physiol. Plant.* **2020**, *42*, 46. [CrossRef]
55. Fernández-Muñoz, R.; Cuartero, J. Effect of temperature and irradiance on stigma exsertion, ovule viability and embryo development in tomato. *J. Hortic. Sci.* **1991**, *66*, 395–401. [CrossRef]
56. Sato, S.; Kamiyama, M.; Iwata, T.; Makita, N.; Furukawa, H.; Ikeda, H. Moderate increase of mean daily temperature adversely affects fruit set of *Lycopersicon esculentum* by disrupting specific physiological processes in male reproductive development. *Ann. Bot.* **2006**, *97*, 731–738. [CrossRef]
57. Farinon, B.; Picarella, M.E.; Mazzucato, A. Dynamics of fertility-related traits in tomato landraces under mild and severe heat stress. *Plants* **2022**, *11*, 881. [CrossRef] [PubMed]
58. Riccini, A.; Picarella, M.E.; De Angelis, F.; Mazzucato, A. Bulk RNA-Seq analysis to dissect the regulation of stigma position in tomato. *Plant Mol. Biol.* **2020**, *105*, 263–285. [CrossRef] [PubMed]
59. Levitt, J. Responses of Plants to Environmental Stresses. In *Water, Radiation, Salt, and Other Stresses*; Academic Press: Cambridge, MA, USA, 1980; Volume 2, ISBN 0124455026.
60. Picken, A.J.F. A review of pollination and fruit set in the tomato (*Lycopersicon esculentum* Mill.). *J. Hortic. Sci.* **1984**, *59*, 1–13. [CrossRef]
61. Hoshikawa, K.; Pham, D.; Ezura, H.; Schafleitner, R.; Nakashima, K. Genetic and molecular mechanisms conferring heat stress tolerance in tomato plants. *Front. Plant Sci.* **2021**, *12*, 786688. [CrossRef] [PubMed]
62. Ozores-Hampton, M.; Kiran, F.; McAvoy, G. Blossom drop, reduced fruit set, and post-pollination disorders in tomato. *EDIS* **2012**, *2012*, 1–6. [CrossRef]
63. Pressman, E.; Shaked, R.; Firon, N. Tomato (*Lycopersicon esculentum*) response to heat stress: Focus on pollen grains. *Plant Stress* **2007**, *1*, 216–227.
64. Hanson, P.M.; Chen, J.; Kuo, G. Gene action and heritability of high-temperature fruit set in tomato line CL5915. *HortScience* **2002**, *37*, 172–175. [CrossRef]
65. Serrani, J.C.; Ruiz-Rivero, O.; Fos, M.; García-Martínez, J.L. Auxin-induced fruit-set in tomato is mediated in part by gibberellins. *Plant J.* **2008**, *56*, 922–934. [CrossRef]
66. Guner, U.; Akbas, B.; Oksal, D.; Degirmenci, K. Abiotic diseases of tomato plants (*Lycopersicum esculentum* L.) in Ankara and Eskişehir Provinces. *Acta Hortic.* **2009**, *808*, 423–430. [CrossRef]
67. Masarirambi, M.T.; Chingwara, V.; Shongwe, V.D. The effect of irrigation on synchronization of coffee (*Coffea arabica* L.) flowering and berry ripening at Chipinge, Zimbabwe. *Phys. Chem. Earth Parts A/B/C* **2009**, *34*, 786–789. [CrossRef]
68. Gazquez, J.C.; Lopez, J.C.; Baeza, E.; Saez, M.; Sanchez-Guerrero, M.C.; Medrano, E.; Lorenzo, P. Yield response of a sweet pepper crop to different methods of greenhouse coolin. *Acta Hortic.* **2006**, *719*, 507–514. [CrossRef]
69. Holder, R.; Cockshull, K.E. Effects of humidity on the growth and yield of glasshouse tomatoes. *J. Hortic. Sci.* **1990**, *65*, 31–39. [CrossRef]
70. Moreno-Teruel, M.Á.; Molina-Aiz, F.D.; López-Martínez, A.; Marín-Membrive, P.; Peña-Fernández, A.; Valera-Martínez, D.L. The Influence of different cooling systems on the microclimate, photosynthetic activity and yield of a tomato crops (*Lycopersicum esculentum* Mill.) in Mediterranean greenhouses. *Agronomy* **2022**, *12*, 524. [CrossRef]

agronomy

MDPI

Article

Delineating the Crop-Land Dynamic due to Extreme Environment Using Landsat Datasets: A Case Study

Bijay Halder [1], Jatisankar Bandyopadhyay [1], Haitham Abdulmohsin Afan [2], Maryam H. Naser [3], Salwan Ali Abed [4], Khaled Mohamed Khedher [5,6], Khaldoon T. Falih [7], Ravinesh Deo [8], Miklas Scholz [9,10,11,*] and Zaher Mundher Yaseen [12,13,*]

[1] Department of Remote Sensing and GIS, Vidyasagar University, Midnapore 721102, India; halder06bijay@gmail.com (B.H.); jatib@mail.vidyasagar.ac.in (J.B.)
[2] Department of Civil Engineering, Al-Maarif University College, Ramadi 31001, Iraq; haitham.afan@uoa.edu.iq
[3] Building and Construction Techniques Engineering Department, AL-Mustaqbal University College, Hillah 51001, Iraq; maryamhameed@mustaqbal-college.edu.iq
[4] College of Science, University of Al-Qadisiyah, Al Diwaniyah 58001, Iraq; salwan.abed@qu.edu.iq
[5] Department of Civil Engineering, College of Engineering, King Khalid University, Abha 61421, Saudi Arabia; kkhedher@kku.edu.sa
[6] Department of Civil Engineering, High Institute of Technological Studies, Mrezgua University Campus, Nabeul 8000, Tunisia
[7] New Era and Development in Civil Engineering Research Group, Scientific Research Center, Al-Ayen University, Thi-Qar 64001, Iraq; khaldoon@alayen.edu.iq
[8] USQ's Advanced Data Analytics Research Group, School of Mathematics, Physics and Computing, University of Southern Queensland, Springfield, QLD 4300, Australia; ravinesh.deo@usq.edu.au
[9] Directorate of Engineering the Future, School of Science, Engineering and Environment, The University of Salford, Newton Building, Greater Manchester M5 4WT, UK
[10] Department of Civil Engineering Science, School of Civil Engineering and the Built Environment, University of Johannesburg, Kingsway Campus, P.O. Box 524, Aukland Park, Johannesburg 2006, South Africa
[11] Department of Town Planning, Engineering Networks and Systems, South Ural State University, 76, Lenin prospekt, 454080 Chelyabinsk, Russia
[12] Department of Earth Sciences and Environment, Faculty of Science and Technology, Universiti Kebangsaan Malaysia, Bangi 43600, Selangor, Malaysia
[13] Adjunct Research Fellow, USQ's Advanced Data Analytics Research Group, School of Mathematics Physics and Computing, University of Southern Queensland, Springfield, QLD 4350, Australia
* Correspondence: m.scholz@salford.ac.uk (M.S.); yaseen@ukm.edu.my (Z.M.Y.)

Citation: Halder, B.; Bandyopadhyay, J.; Afan, H.A.; Naser, M.H.; Abed, S.A.; Khedher, K.M.; Falih, K.T.; Deo, R.; Scholz, M.; Yaseen, Z.M. Delineating the Crop-Land Dynamic due to Extreme Environment Using Landsat Datasets: A Case Study. *Agronomy* **2022**, *12*, 1268. https://doi.org/10.3390/agronomy12061268

Academic Editors: Syed Tahir Ata-Ul-Karim, Saadatullah Malghani and Muhammad Ishaq Asif Rehmani

Received: 30 March 2022
Accepted: 17 May 2022
Published: 25 May 2022

Abstract: Extreme climatic conditions and natural hazard-related phenomenon have been affecting coastal regions and riverine areas. Floods, cyclones, and climate change phenomena have hammered the natural environment and increased the land dynamic, socio-economic vulnerability, and food scarcity. Saltwater intrusion has also triggered cropland vulnerability and, therefore, increased the area of inland brackish water fishery. The cropland area has decreased due to low soil fertility; around 252.06 km^2 of cropland area has been lost, and 326.58 km^2 of water bodies or inland fishery area has been added in just thirty years in the selected blocks of the North 24 Parganas district, West Bengal, India. After saltwater intrusion, soil fertility appears to have been decreased and crop production has been greatly reduced. The cropland areas were 586.52 km^2 (1990), 419.92 km^2 (2000), 361.67 km^2 (2010) and 334.46 km^2 (2020). Gradually the water body areas were increased 156.21 km^2 (1990), 328.15 km^2 (2000), 397.77 km^2 (2010) and 482.78 km^2 (2020). The vegetated land area also decreased due to it being converted into inland fishery areas, and around 79.15 km^2 were degraded during the last thirty years. The super cyclone Aila, along with other super cyclones and other environmental stresses, like water-logging, soil salinity, and irrigation water scarcity were the reasons for the development of the new fishery areas in the selected blocks. There is a need for proper planning for sustainable development of this area.

Keywords: extreme climatic condition; crop land vulnerability; fishery area identification; remote sensing and GIS; North 24 Parganas district

1. Introduction

Climate change and environmental degradation have influenced the land dynamic, caused ecosystem damage, and resulted in unexpected life-threatening conditions [1,2]. The land use and land cover (LU/LC) classification and estimation, or LU/LC change, have been the most important factors for earth surface change analysis [3,4]. The classification of land use, land cover, and land alteration were used for studying the earth's surface change and estimating environmental degradation. The coastal areas, such as South 24 Parganas, North 24 Parganas, and Purba Medinipur of West Bengal state, India, are the most vulnerable, and natural extreme hazard events like floods and super cyclones, have affected the land and coastal area. The results have been shoreline change, saltwater intrusion, increased soil salinity, changed cropland dynamics, and socio-economic losses. The potential zones for surface water or groundwater and their quality assessment, organization, and investigation have continuously been of high importance; subsequently, it is important to communal, anthropological, environmental, health, and economic development [5]. The water quality assessment and water related research activities are the most significant in the present period [6–8]. The water organization methodologies are not solely about stopping water contamination or other problems, nevertheless, they aim towards forecasting the technical needs for sustainable water resource management through decision-making or policy-making by the water pollution regulators, and to teach suitable preparation methods to control water shortage or scarcity associated problems [9].

Strong tidal actions, wave, and long-shore tidal currents have continuously adapted, shaped, and redesigned the coastal shorelines in the alternating estuarine or riverine delta region by the hydro-geomorphological processes of erosion and accretion [10–12]. The coastal region is the area most vulnerable to cyclones, natural disasters that influence the earth's surface processes [13,14]. Cropland dynamics influence the food production of this local region because rice is the main food and fish production has high economic values, but ecological degradation has been hammering the local environment with associated rice production losses. Previously, in the early 1980s, cropland categories were good using temporal and supernatural physiognomies [15,16]. The estimation of the time periods having the maximum alteration for cropland categories has been frequently acknowledged [17–20]. The most common method for this purpose is an image classification constructed using the geo-spatial index like the normalized difference vegetation index (NDVI) [21,22]. Much research has used machine learning methods to categorize the cropland types, such as decision trees [23], support vector machines [24,25], random forest [26] or hidden Markov models [27]. The land dynamics of the selected study blocks are most affected by saltwater intrusion and climatic conditions as croplands and inland fisheries are located there. Therefore, land degradation measurement using the Remote Sensing and GIS procedures are more useful. The area most affected by land dynamics is the southern parts of the North 24 Parganas, which is the area most affected by these problems, so those blocks of North 24 Parganas were selected as the study area.

The North 24 Parganas district is generally impacted by natural disasters and environmental degradation every year, e.g., the Odisha super cyclone (1999), Phyan (2009), Nilam (2012), Phailin (2013), Helen (2013), Hudhud (2014), Vardah (2016), Ockhi (2017), Titli (2018), Fani (2019), Bulbul (2019), Amphan (2020) and Yass (2021). Many cyclones and floods have been associated with extreme climate events [28–31]. Many cyclone events have occurred like, Aila, Fani, Bulbul, Amphan, and Yash. These cyclones and the deformation of landforms have, therefore, increased the saltwater intrusion over the region. Mainly, the southern parts of the districts like Sandeshkhali-I, Minakhan, Haroa, Barasat-I, Barasat-II, and Hasnabad have been the most affected by saltwater intrusion. The Central inland fishery research institute (http://www.cifri.res.in/ (accessed on 21 February 2022)), which is situated in Barrackpore, influences inland fishery-related awareness, training (water quality and fish production). The satellite-based Remote sensing (RS) and Geographic Information System are influential methods for mapping, monitoring, and measuring the LU/LC alteration analysis using moderate and high resolution of temporal satellite-based imageries, which is cheaper and more effective than the methods used in the traditional procedure [32–35]. Many researchers have used the LU/LC classification and geospatial indicators for delineating the LU/LC classes and social impacts [36,37]. The Normalized Different Vegetation Index (NDVI) has been widely used for delineating the vegetation condition using a red and near-infrared band of satellite data [38,39]. For water area identification and area estimation, the Normalized Different Water Index (NDWI) has been used [40]. For land use alteration examination, previous studies have used multi-temporal Landsat datasets, and numerous procedures, like Cellular Automata (CA), Markov Chain (MC), regression analysis, and Artificial Neural Network (ANN) [41–43]. The CA procedure has been used aimed at changeover algorithms and historical circumstances of dissimilar LU/LC classes of the earth's surface. The distance from the road, distance from the river area, DEM, slope, and many other earth surface features have been used for the CA model to inaugurate the future LU/LC prediction [44]. Prediction of future land cover change can help gather valuable information about land degradation and future disaster related activities. It is also true that the North 24 Parganas areas have a vital role for rice paddy production and appear to be contributing a large amount of paddy per year. However, inland fisheries transformation has decreased the crop production and, therefore, the results of this study can be helpful for the future investigation, awareness, planning and management purposes.

The RS and GIS methods were extensively used for the LU/LC classification and identifying the land area alteration and monitoring the changes and environmental aspects. The Landsat 5 TM and 8 OLI/TIRS datasets for different years were used for mapping the LU/LC classification of the southern parts of North 24 Parganas. The Normalized Different Water Index (NDWI) and the Normalized Different Vegetation Index (NDVI) were used for monitoring the water and vegetation covered area of the study region. The foremost impartial objectives of this study were to: (i) make the LU/LC classification for different years 1990, 2000, 2010, and 2020; (ii) conduct land alteration analysis for different time periods; (iii) identify cropland dynamics and development of inland fishery areas using field data and classification maps; (iv) conduct vegetation and water condition analysis use two different geospatial indicators. The study results will be helpful for local planners, administrative departments like the agricultural department, inland fishery department, policymaker, researchers, and other stakeholders aimed at the development of this study blocks.

2. Study Area

The North 24 Parganas district is situated in West Bengal, which state is located in the eastern portion of India, and the study blocks are in the tropical zone from latitude 22°11′6″ to 23°15′2″ North, and longitude 88°20′ to 89°5′ East. The western parts are in the Kolkata, Howrah, and Hooghly districts. The total area of North 24 Parganas is 4094 km^2 and the total population of this district is 10,009,781 (Census of India and North 24 Parganas District handbook, 2011, https://www.census2011.co.in/census/district/11-north-twenty-four-parganas.html (accessed on 23 February 2022)). The headquarters of North 24 Parganas is located at Barasat. The annual average precipitation, or rainfall, is 1550 to 1600 mm. The main urban areas are Barasat, Habra, Madhyamgram, Basirhat, Rajarhat-Newtown, Hasnabad, Dum Dum etc. The average temperatures of this district are 41 °C in the month of May and 10 °C in the month of January, and the relative humidity varies from 50% in the month of March to 90% in the month of July in each year (http://imdkolkata.gov.in/districts/north-24-parganas (accessed on 28 February 2022), Indian Methodological Department, India).

In this study identifying of the area of crop land vulnerability and the area of the inland fishery, six blocks of the North 24 Parganas district were used (there are 22 blocks in the North 24 Parganas district) and the names of those blocks are Haroa, Minakhan, Sandeshkhali-I, Hasnabad, Basirhat-I, and Basirhat-II. Those areas were taken for this study because crop land has been converted into inland fishery in those areas. In the thirty years

1990 to 2020, many crop lands have been converted into brackish water inland fishery use. Gradually, food scarcity has increased due to crop production losses. Farmers are economically building a strong position (http://north24parganas.gov.in/blocks/gaighata/schemes (accessed on 3 March 2022)); however, the land use and land cover (LU/LC) change has been the main reason for crop vulnerability in this study area. The total study area was 927.55 km^2 (Figure 1) and it is situated in the southern parts of North 24 Parganas district. The study blocks of North 24 Parganas district are located in the Ganga-Brahmaputra-Meghna delta where extreme environmental events and ecological disturbances have been observed like floods, super cyclones, and manmade disasters. Those climatic conditions are the reason for saltwater intrusion. Saltwater intrusion is the main reason for land use and land cover change and cropland vulnerability. The salt water from the Bay of Bengal has inundated the riverine area and the crop lands are affected by this natural phenomenon. After super cyclone Aila, these areas were affected by saltwater creating huge soil fertility loss related problems. After that, the local farmers, or agriculturalists, have gradually converted the cropland area into inland fisheries.

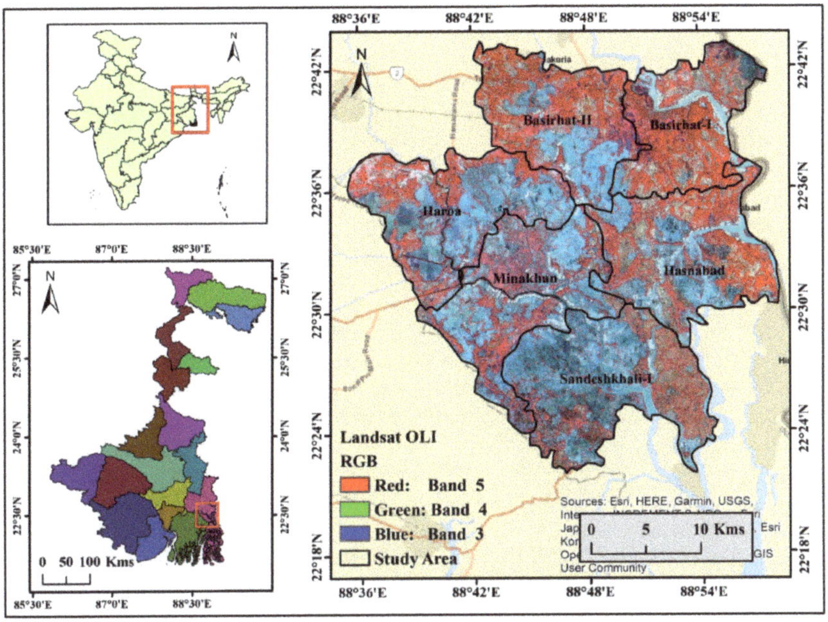

Figure 1. Location map of the selected study area. The red frame shows the identification of the study location.

3. Materials and Method

The water body and cropland dynamics were significantly influenced by the local natural conservation situation and the reserve parts were identified in the study blocks (Figure 2). The areas of inland fishery were increased gradually as the croplands were decreased due to extreme environmental condition and climatic phenomenon in the study area.

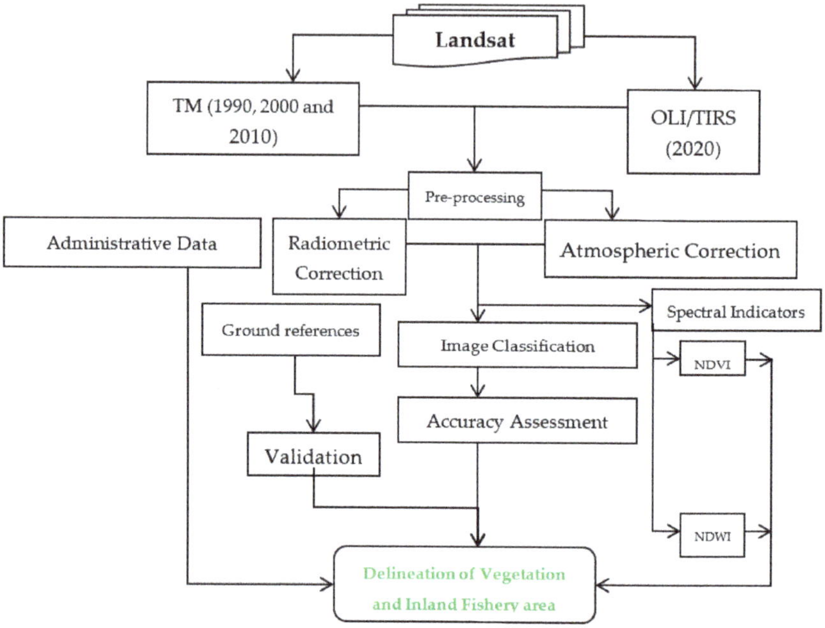

Figure 2. Entire methodology of the study area.

3.1. Data Used

Four Landsat 5 Thematic Mapper (TM) and 8 Operational Land Imager/Thermal Infrared Sensor (OLI/TIRS) datasets were used for mapping and monitoring the land dynamic and cropland dynamic in southern selected blocks of North 24 Parganas. The Landsat multi-temporal satellite datasets with less than 10% cloud cover were downloaded from the USGS earth explorer website (https://earthexplorer.usgs.gov/ (accessed on 2 February 2022)). Table 1 shows the sensor, path, row, and data details of different years. The 1990, 2000, 2010 and 2020 Landsat data were used for cropland dynamic and inland fishery area identification over the southern blocks of North 24 Parganas. The administrative boundary of each block and the population data were obtained from Census of India (https://censusindia.gov.in/ (accessed on 5 February 2022)). The ArcGIS 10.4 software (ESRI, Redlands, CA, USA)was used for image classification and monitoring of the inland fishery and cropland situation.

Table 1. Details of satellite data and acquisition dates.

Satellite	Sensor	Date	Path and Row	Data Source
Landsat 5	TM	14 November 1990	138,044	https://earthexplorer.usgs.gov/ (accessed on 2 February 2022)
		9 November 2000	138,044	
		6 February 2010	138,044	
Landsat 8	OLI/TIRS	18 December 2020	138,044	

3.2. Satellite Data Pre-Processing

The main objective of this study was to analyse the land alteration due to natural extreme environmental events and climate change. The Landsat data for the four years 1990, 2000, 2010, and 2020 were used for mapping and monitoring the LU/LC change. The satellite datasets were obtained from the earth explorer (USGS website) with minimal alteration in geometric accuracy. The pre-processing of satellite datasets is necessary for

LU/LC classification, mapping, and monitoring land dynamic and others earth surface-related work [45]. Geometric correction, atmospheric correction, and radiometric correction are needed for image classification. The ERDAS Imagine version 14 software was used for band combination or layer stacking or band composition, geo-referencing or rectification, masking, and sub-setting or clipping the Area of Interest (AOI). Histogram equalization was used for the enhancement and development of satellite images [46].

3.3. Image Classification and Post Classification

The LU/LC classification of the earth's surface is the main way to capture the impact of humans on the environment. The ecological balance and environmental conditions are important aspects of our earth's surface. But the urban expansion, overwhelming population pressure, and hazards such as natural extreme events like cyclones and floods, have influenced the local climatic disorder and environmental degradation [47]. The physical parts like, vegetation, water, soil, and other features have been destroyed by anthropogenic activities. Digital image classification techniques were used for the LU/LC classification [48]. The supervised classification technique with a maximum likelihood algorithm was used for the LU/LC maps classification [49,50]. Land cover was categorised as vegetation area, water bodies, agricultural land, and forest area. Land use/land cover change analysis was used for mapping and monitoring the land dynamic or alteration during the different time periods [51]. After the LU/LC classification, the change detection analysis, accuracy assessment, and the kappa coefficient estimation were the main aspects of the study. The selected blocks of the North 24 Parganas were classified into four classes, agricultural land, water body, vegetation land, and built-up area.

After land use/land cover classification, maps were subjected to an accuracy assessment. The kappa coefficient identification (Table 2) was used for monitoring the error matrix of LU/LC classification [52]. The ERDAS Imagine version 14 software was used for the accuracy assessment and the kappa coefficient. The accuracy valuation of each classified image was carried out by field survey and the data were obtained from Google Earth software. The accuracy assessment and kappa coefficient were calculated used those formulas (Equations (1) and (2)).

$$OA = \left(\frac{\sum_{i=1}^{k} n_{ij}}{n}\right) \quad (1)$$

$$K_i = \frac{(\text{Observed accuracy} - \text{Chance accuracy})}{(1 - \text{Chance accuracy})} \quad (2)$$

where, n_{ij} is representative of the slanting fundamentals in the error matrix, k is the total number of classes in the land use/land cover classification of the selected parts, n is the total number of samples in the error.

Table 2. Scale of Kappa coefficient and the strength of agreement.

Sl No.	Value of K	Strength of Agreement
1	<0.20	Poor
2	0.21–0.40	Fair
3	0.41–0.60	Moderate
4	0.61–0.80	Good
5	0.81–1.00	Very good

3.4. Validation of the Results

The LU/LC classifications derived from different Landsat images had problems due to the difficulty of identifying the proper area and validating the result. Because Landsat data has 30-m resolution, pixel mixing, and alteration were the main problems when identifying the land transformation. For validation of the classification results and accuracy assessment, 300 Google Earth sample collections were verified, and the classification results and the kappa coefficient scale were used for finding the suitable classification (Table 2). Field datasets were used aimed at validating the imagery classification results. The accuracy assessments were estimated at 90.33%, 90.67%, 88.00%, and 86.67% in the years of 1990, 2000, 2010, and 2020, respectively. The kappa coefficients were estimated as 0.86 (1990), 0.87 (2000), 0.83 (2010), and 0.80 (2020) correspondingly.

3.5. Image-Based Geo-Spatial Indices

3.5.1. Normalized Difference Vegetation Index (NDVI)

The delineation of green area is the major work for understanding the vegetated area and the health of the vegetation. Satellite-based RS data from the Landsat 5 TM and 8 OLI/TIRS datasets were used for vegetation monitoring of this area. Many indicators or methods have been extensively used for delineating the forest land area over the earth's surface, but the normalized difference vegetation index (NDVI) has been the most used for identifying the vegetation area [50]. The vegetation index (NDVI) map was used to identify the area of vegetation cover and its reduction over different time scales from 1990 to 2020. The following formula (Equation (3)) was used for delineating the NDVI maps using satellite images.

$$\text{NDVI} = \left(\frac{\text{NIR} - \text{Red}}{\text{NIR} + \text{Red}}\right) \tag{3}$$

where Red was denoting that the red band and the second band NIR represented the near infrared band of satellite images. The NDVI map shows -1 to +1. The 0 to +1 represented the densely green space or vegetation, and low index values (<) represented the other LU/LC classes of the study location.

3.5.2. Normalized Difference Water Index (NDWI)

The Normalized Difference Water Index (NDWI) was firstly established by McFeeters in 1996 to detect surface water bodies such as the pond, wetland, river, and lake, that is, the water body environments, and to express the measurement or documentation of their duration [53]. The NDWI index was estimated for use with the Landsat TM and OLI/TIRS Multi-spectral satellite images and it has been positively used with additional satellite sensors anywhere the magnitude of the water areas are desirable [54]. The NDWI was calculated using the Equation (4):

$$\text{NDWI} = \left(\frac{\text{Green} - \text{NIR}}{\text{Green} + \text{NIR}}\right) \tag{4}$$

This formula uses the Green band and the NIR, or Near Infrared band, of the Landsat 5 TM and 8 OLI/TIRS satellite images. The NDWI index values more than zero were identified as those parts that were actual water surfaces, while values less than or equivalent to zero represented the other LU/LC classes or surfaces in the selected region. Values of the NDWI were estimated in ArcGIS version 10.4 software.

3.5.3. LU/LC Feature Prediction

The LU/LC is a fluctuating earth's surface feature which is changing gradually but the prediction of future classes of LU/LC features is an additional problem to contemplate. Numerous approaches have been used for LU/LC features forecast like Cellular Automata (CA), Artificial neural network (ANN), regression techniques and Markov Chain (MC) [55,56]. The QGIS software and the MOLUSCE plugin were used for the LU/LC prediction investigation in the selected blocks of the North 24 Parganas district. The MOLUSCE plugin tool was used for LU/LC features prediction and for various types of LU/LC, NDVI, LST, and NDWI forecast and simulation. The well-known algorithms like CA, multi-criteria decision analysis, ANN, and logistic regression were used for the earth's surface. The DEM, distance from river, distance from road, domination lands water bodies, other LU/LC classes, and slope (LU/LC prediction) and Normalized Difference Water Index (NDWI), Normalized Difference Vegetation Index (NDVI), Normalized Difference Salinity Index (NDSI), and Normalized Difference Built-up Index (NDBI) were used for land use and land cover prediction. The 1990 and 2020 classification year images were used for forecasting the 2050-year LU/LC of these selected blocks. For approximating the reproduction of the LU/LC classes, the geometry requirements had similar resolution and the same geographic projection system. Using the Cellular Automata-Artificial neural network method (CA-ANN), a forecast was created for this study location.

4. Result and Discussion

Remote sensing-based Landsat datasets were used for this study to identify the cropland dynamic and inland fishery area using land use and land cover classification, field data collection, and geospatial indicators. The NDWI maps were used for delineating water body area and NDVI maps were used for vegetation area monitoring from 1990 to 2020 over the southern parts of North 24 Parganas. Supervised classification techniques with maximum likelihood algorithms were used for the LU/LC classification. The results show that quantifiable values of land alteration occurred during the last thirty years and the LU/LC maps and geospatial indicators (NDVI and NDWI) shows that the alteration of land and the socio-economic values also increased.

4.1. Land Dynamic Analysis

The Landsat 5 TM and 8 OLI/TIRS data of dissimilar years (1990, 2000, 2010, and 2020) were used for this study. A supervised classification technique with maximum likelihood algorithms was used for the LU/LC classification in southern parts of the North 24 Parganas block. Four types of LU/LC classes were identified in this study area, which were built-up land, agricultural land/ cropland water body, and vegetation. The built-up land and water bodies were increased progressively, whereas agricultural land and vegetation areas have been reduced due to several cyclonic floods and extreme environmental conditions over selected blocks of North 24 Parganas. Land transformation is the main occurring result for the LU/LC classification and the LU/LC transformation was augmented by the ecological susceptibility of the study location. The ecosystem was mostly affected by aspects due of land alteration. Agricultural land or croplands were converted into inland fishery areas and the riverine areas were mostly affected by several extreme natural events (Tables 3 and 4).

Table 3. LU/LC area change examination.

Class Name	Area in Sq. km				Area in Percentage (%)			
	1990	2000	2010	2020	1990	2000	2010	2020
Built-up Land	2.23	3.75	5.43	6.86	0.24	0.40	0.59	0.74
Water Body	156.21	328.15	397.77	482.78	16.84	35.38	42.88	52.05
Vegetation	182.61	175.74	162.69	103.46	19.69	18.95	17.54	11.15
Agricultural Land	586.52	419.92	361.67	334.46	63.23	45.27	38.99	36.06
Total	927.55	927.55	927.55	927.55				

Table 4. Loss and gain analysis of the LU/LC classes.

Class Name	Area Change (Sq. km)			
	(1990–2000)	(2000–2010)	(2010–2020)	(1990–2020)
Built-up Land	1.52	1.68	1.43	4.63
Water Body	171.94	69.62	85.02	326.58
Vegetation	−6.86	−13.06	−59.23	−79.15
Agricultural Land	−166.60	−58.25	−27.21	−252.06

The area of built-up lands in the four years were 2.23 km^2 (1990), 3.75 km^2 (2000), 5.43 km^2 (2010), and 6.86 km^2 (2020). The areas of built-up land were mainly located in the Rampur, Sorberia, Basirhat, Hasnabad, Rameswarpur, Taki, and Haroa areas. Basically, area of built-up lands became less in the study area. Areas of croplands and inland fishery mostly fluctuated in the terms of the land use classes in the study blocks (Table 3). Vegetation land area also decreased due to anthropogenic activities and natural extreme events over the study area. Basirhat-I and Basirhat-II were the two blocks most vegetated in the year 1990, but after that, the vegetation area decreased (Figure 3). A total area of 1852.61 km^2 (19.69%) of vegetation land was identified in the year 1990, but after that vegetation area was gradually decreased, as shown by the LU/LC classification results of 175.74 km^2 (2000), 162.69 km^2 (17.54%), and 103.46 km^2 (11.15%) (Figure 3).

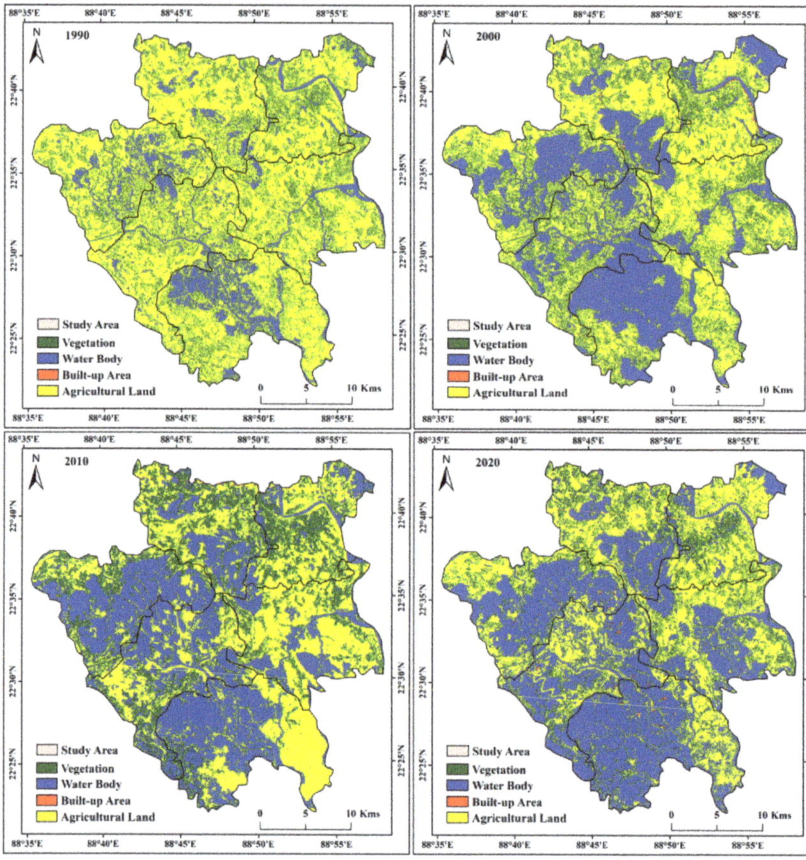

Figure 3. Land use and land cover classification maps of different time periods in the study area like 1990, 2000, 2010, and 2020.

The area of agricultural land or croplands identified in the classification maps were 582.52 km^2 (63.23%), 419.92 km^2 (45.27%), 361.67 km^2 (38.99%), and 334.46 km^2 (36.06%) in the years 1990, 2000, 2010 and 2020, respectively (Figure 4a,b). Agricultural cropland was the most affected LU/LC class of this region because of natural extreme events and man-made hazards. The water bodies were mainly river and inland fishery areas. The Landsat data for these four years were used for this study to identify the increased water area over the study area. The bodies of inland fishery areas were located in the Hatgachi, Sandeshkhali, Bayar Mari Abad, Khariat Abad, Sankardaha Abad, Matbari Abad, Bhurkunda, Mallick Gheri, Ramjay Gheri, and Ranigacchi areas. Those areas were mostly converted to inland fishery areas and the local names of those inland fisheries are 'Bheri'.

The water bodies occupied 156.21 km^2 (16.84%), 328.15 km^2 (35.38%), 397.77 km^2 (42.88%), and 482.78 km^2 (52.05%) in the years 1990, 2000, 2010, and 2020, respectively.

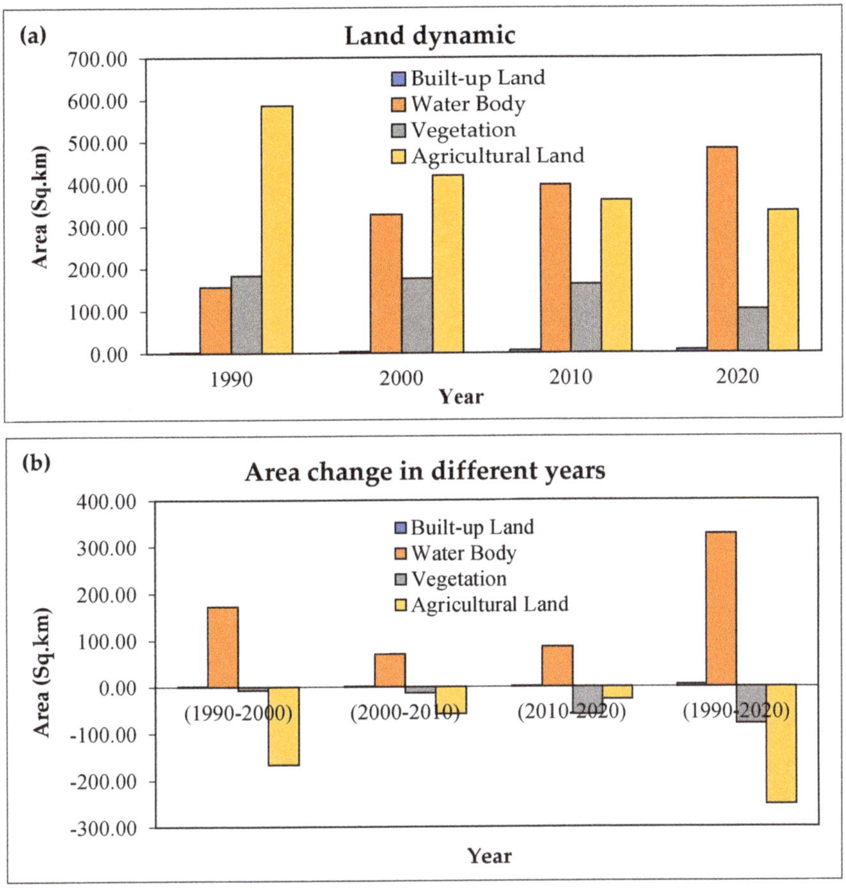

Figure 4. LU/LC classification area calculation; (**a**) total LU/LC classes in different time periods; (**b**) loss/gain analysis of different years.

Land alteration or transformation also occurred in the study area and the changed areas for different years were calculated to monitor the yearly land alteration in the study area. From the year 1990 to 2020, the built-up area was increased by 1.52 km^2, water body area was increased by 171.94 km^2, vegetation and agricultural land were decreased by 6.86 km^2 and 166.60 km^2, respectively (Table 4). Land-use change and land alteration phenomena are natural conditions, but identification of the reason for land alteration is the most effective way of monitoring the land dynamic [57,58]. From the year 2000 to 2010, the land classes areas were 1.68 km^2 for built-up land, 69.62 km^2 for water bodies which were increased, and 13.06 km^2 for vegetation and 58.25 km^2 for agricultural cropland which were both decreased (Figure 5). The same situation was identified by the study area. Many portions of the study area were rehabilitated into the inland fisheries areas due to cyclones and other extreme environmental conditions (Figure 6). Over the thirty years (1990–2020), the built-up area and water bodies areas were increased 4.63 km^2 and 326.58 km^2, respectively, also the vegetation and agricultural cropland areas were decreased around 79.15 km^2 and 252.06 km^2, accordingly (Figure 7a–d). The accuracy assessments were estimated at 90.33%, 90.67%, 88.00%, and 86.67% in the years of 1990, 2000, 2010, and 2020, respectively. The kappa coefficients were identified as 0.86 (1990), 0.87 (2000), 0.83 (2010), and 0.80 (2020), correspondingly (Tables 5–8).

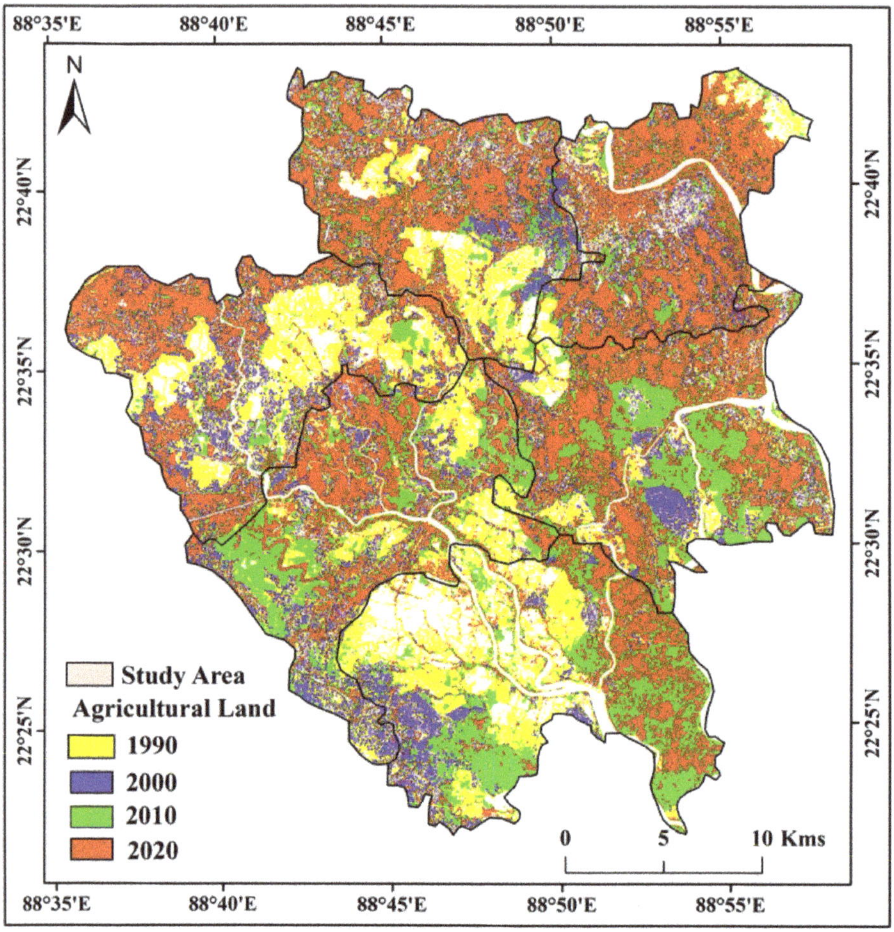

Figure 5. Agricultural Land dynamic in different time periods.

Table 5. Accuracy assessment and kappa coefficient in the year of 1990.

Class Name	Ground Truth/References				Row Total	Commission Error	User Accuracy
	Water Body	Agricultural Land	Vegetation	Built-Up Land			
Water body	68	3	3	1	75	9.33%	90.67%
Agricultural Land	3	99	6	2	110	10.00%	90.00%
Vegetation	2	6	96	1	105	8.57%	91.43%
Built-up Land	0	1	1	8	10	20.00%	80.00%
Column Total	73	109	106	12	300		
Omission Error	6.85%	9.17%	9.43%	33.33%			
Producer Accuracy	93.15%	90.83%	90.57%	66.67%			
Overall Accuracy	**90.33%**			Kappa Coefficient	**0.86**		

Bold indicates the variaiton.

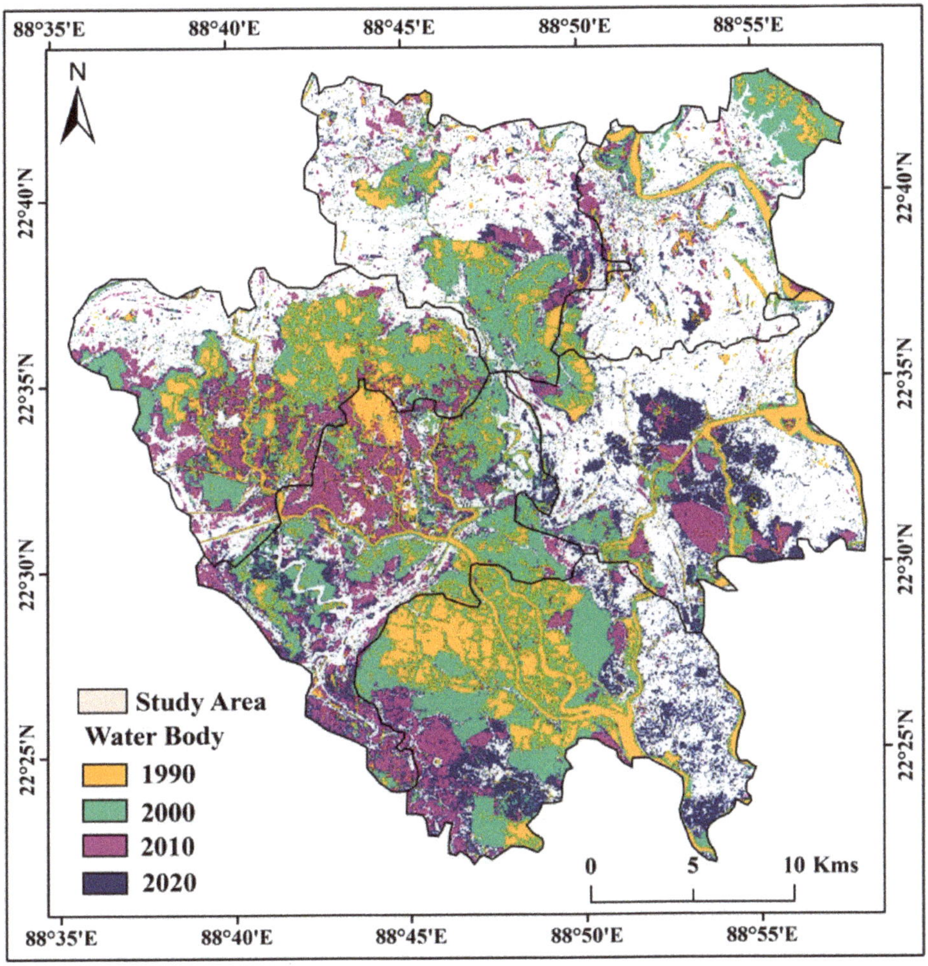

Figure 6. Water body change analysis of different study time.

Table 6. Accuracy assessment and kappa coefficient in the year of 2000.

Class Name	Ground Truth/References				Row Total	Commission Error	User Accuracy
	Water Body	**Agricultural Land**	**Vegetation**	**Built-Up Land**			
Water body	90	4	3	1	98	8.16%	91.84%
Agricultural Land	2	94	5	1	102	7.84%	92.16%
Vegetation	1	5	79	2	87	9.20%	90.80%
Built-up Land	1	1	2	9	13	30.77%	69.23%
Column Total	94	104	89	13	300		
Omission Error	4.26%	9.62%	11.24%	30.77%			
Producer Accuracy	95.74%	90.38%	88.76%	69.23%			
Overall Accuracy	**90.67%**			Kappa Coefficient	**0.87**		

Bold indicates the variaiton.

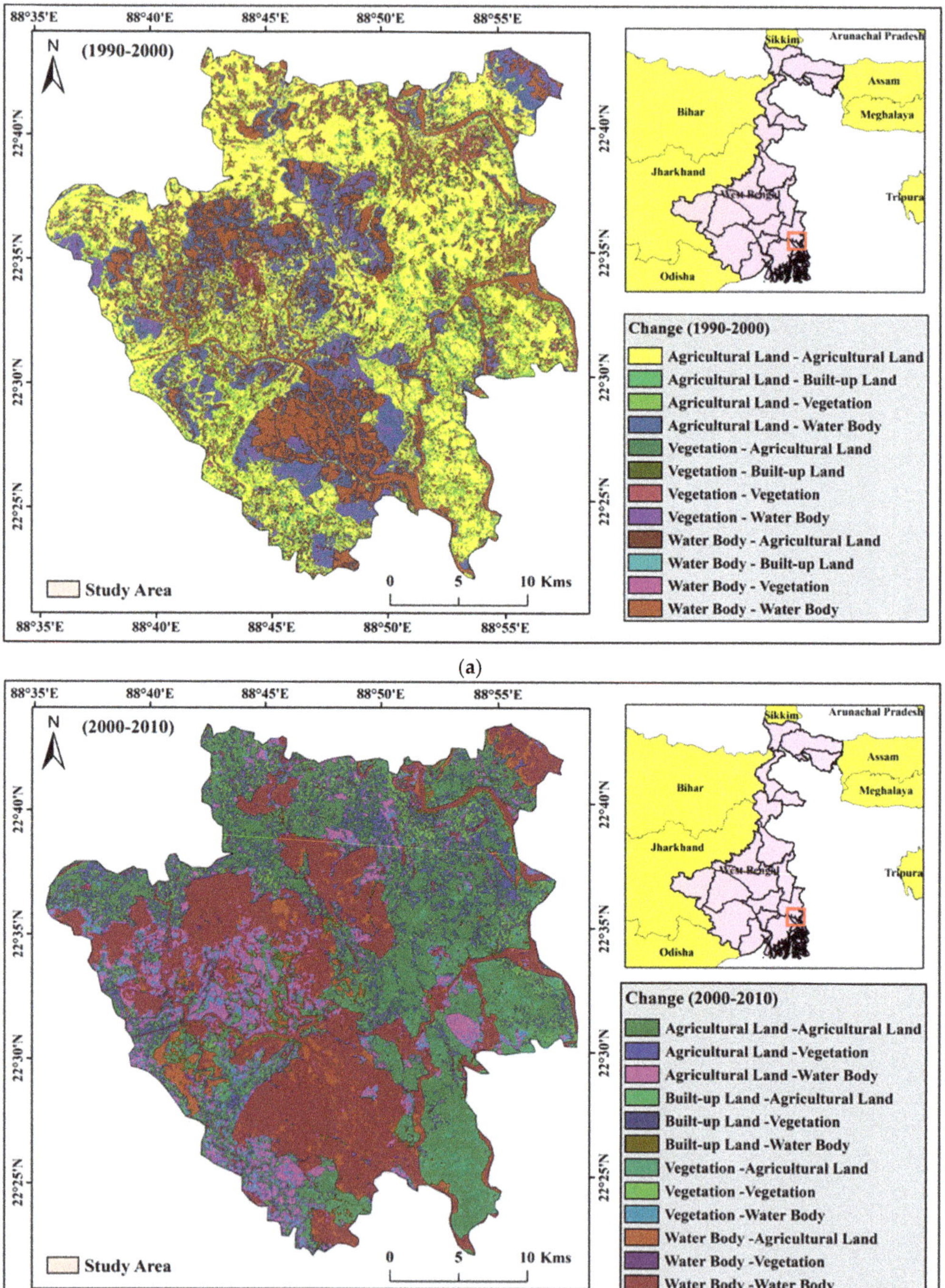

(**a**)

(**b**)

Figure 7. *Cont.*

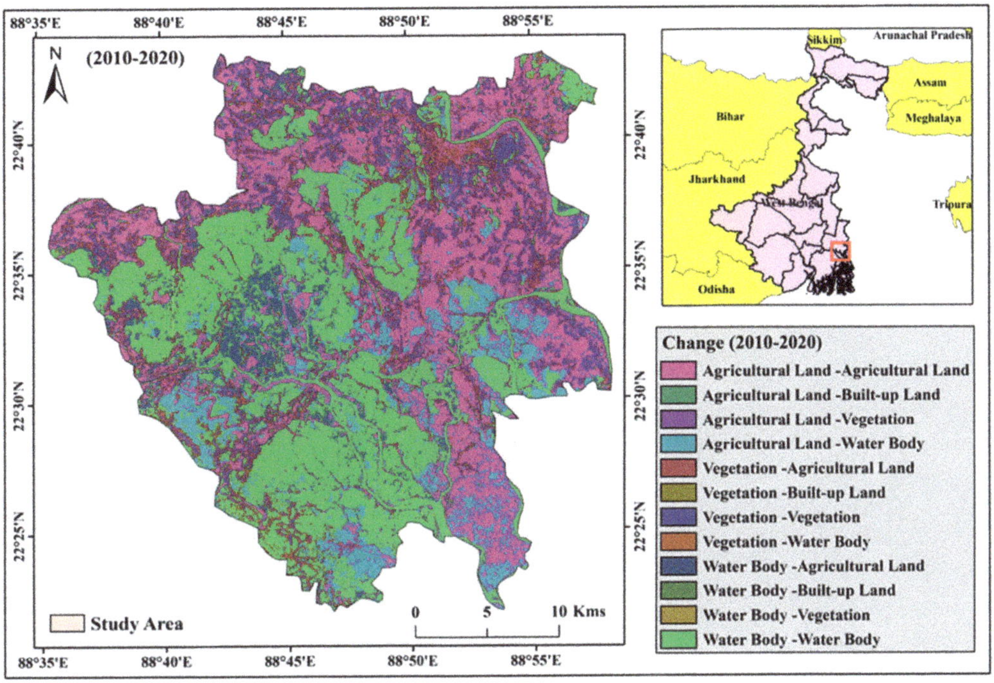

(**c**)

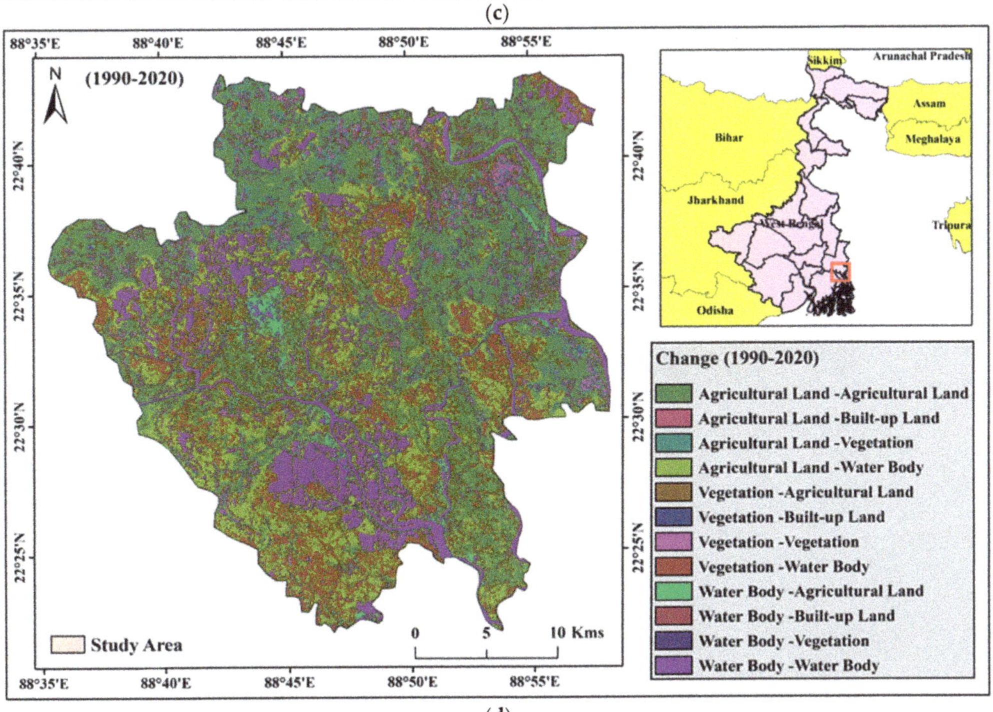

(**d**)

Figure 7. Change detection analysis of different time periods. (**a**) 1990–2000; (**b**) 2000–2010; (**c**) 2010–2020; and (**d**) 1990–2020. The red frame shows the identification of the study location.

Table 7. Accuracy assessment and kappa coefficient in the year of 2010.

Class Name	Ground Truth/References				Row Total	Commission Error	User Accuracy
	Water Body	Agricultural Land	Vegetation	Built-Up Land			
Water body	101	9	5	2	117	13.68%	86.32%
Agricultural Land	3	82	4	2	91	9.89%	90.11%
Vegetation	3	4	69	1	77	10.39%	89.61%
Built-up Land	0	1	2	12	15	20.00%	80.00%
Column Total	107	96	80	17	300		
Omission Error	5.61%	14.58%	13.75%	29.41%			
Producer Accuracy	94.39%	85.42%	86.25%	70.59%			
Overall Accuracy	**88.00%**			Kappa Coefficient	**0.83**		

Bold indicates the variaiton.

Table 8. Accuracy assessment and kappa coefficient in the year of 2020.

Class Name	Ground Truth/References				Row Total	Commission Error	User Accuracy
	Water Body	Agricultural Land	Vegetation	Built-Up Land			
Water body	115	6	7	1	129	10.85%	89.15%
Agricultural Land	6	73	4	2	85	14.12%	85.88%
Vegetation	3	6	59	1	69	14.49%	85.51%
Built-up Land	3	0	1	13	17	23.53%	76.47%
Column Total	127	85	71	17	300		
Omission Error	9.45%	14.12%	16.90%	23.53%			
Producer Accuracy	90.55%	85.88%	83.10%	76.47%			
Overall Accuracy	**86.67%**			Kappa Coefficient	**0.80**		

Bold indicates the variaiton.

4.2. Geospatial Indicator

Geospatial indicators have been widely used for delineating the different index-based maps. The Landsat 4–5 TM, 7 ETM+, 8 OLI/TIRS, and Sentinel-2A/B datasets have been used for identification of different geospatial indicators. The most used indicators have been the Normalized Difference Water Index (NDWI), Normalized Difference Vegetation Index (NDVI), Soil-Adjacent Vegetation Index (SAVI), Ratio Vegetation Index (RVI), Transformed Normalized Difference Vegetation Index (TNDVI), Enhance Vegetation Index (EVI), Modified Normalized Difference Water Index (MNDWI), Water Ratio Index (WRI) and Normalized Difference Salinity Index (NDSI) for vegetation, water body, and salinity identification of an area. This study used two geospatial indicators (NDVI and NDWI) for delineating the vegetation scenario and water area identification. Moreover, the indices were used for the validation of the classification. Agricultural land and water area, mainly the area of inland fishery, dominated land classes of the southern parts of North 24 Parganas. Figures 8 and 9 show that the NDVI and NDWI maps for different time periods of the southern parts of North 24 Parganas. In the year 1990, the vegetation area occupied a huge amount in the south, north and north-east parts of the study area. After that, the green space area was greatly reduced by human modification and saltwater intrusion over the study area. The green colour shows the vegetated area, and the blue colour indicates the water area. The high values of NDVI were 0.83 (1990), 0.63 (2000), 0.54 (2010), and 0.47 (2020). The NDVI maps show that the vegetation area was degraded, and water bodies increased (Figure 8). Normalized Different Water Index (NDWI) maps were used for defining the area of water bodies in the study location. In the initial phase, the areas of water bodies or inland fisheries, were less and only showed in the Sandeshkhali-I and Haroa blocks, but after the saltwater intrusion, extreme environmental conditions, and disaster-related work, those areas had a huge amount of water area change. The highest values of NDWI were, 0.27 (1990), 0.31 (2000), 0.38 (2010), and 0.46 (2020) (Figure 9). The

Aila, Fani, Bulbul, Amphan, and Yash cyclones have destroyed the region and similarly, the inland fishery areas were increased.

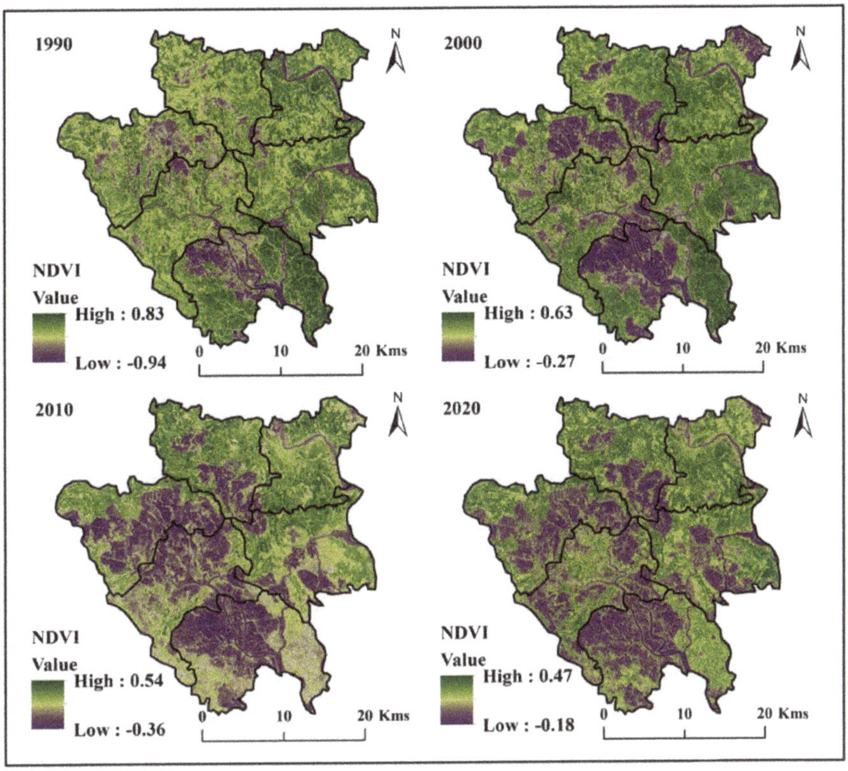

Figure 8. Normalized Different Vegetation Index (NDVI) maps of the study area.

4.3. Impact of Cropland Dynamic

Crop production is very important for West Bengal because many people are dependent on rice. Rice is the main food in West Bengal, but it was the rice-growing areas that have been converted into inland fishery areas. Farmers are economically well off for cultivating the fish, but the resultant rice scarcity has increased due to loss of crop land. It was mainly the riverine areas that were converted from cropland into inland fishery use. An administrative awareness program, planning and water quality related information and training was given by the government. The number of markets and preservative companies were increased due to inland fish cultivation, but crop production was decreased on this study area. Around 586.52 km^2 (63.23%) of agricultural cropland area was identified in the year 1990, and the most cropped production block was Sandeshkhali-I. After several natural disasters and environmental changes, these blocks were almost all converted from cropland to inland fishery area (Figure 7). In 2020, the agricultural cropland was identified 334.46 km^2 (36.06%).

4.4. Impact of Inland Fishery Alteration

Inland fisheries are a more profitable use of this area because of food production and the international demand for fish. Mainly the southern parts of North 24 Parganas are farming different shrimp and crabs for their livelihood. The southern parts of the West Bengal and Odisha coast are regularly affected by several cyclones and natural disasters yearly, that is why those areas are mainly facing a huge amount of saltwater intrusion and the associated decreased soil fertility rate and soil pH, which were the most significant parameters for crop production. But this problem has been widely affected over the area. Several natural disasters like the Aila, Fani, Bulbul, Amphan, and Yash cyclones have affected the riverine area and influence the land dynamic. Fish cultivation is more profitable for the farmers, but the overwhelming land alteration has affected the natural environment and the flora and fauna. The ecosystem of the rural areas has been affected by this type of land alteration.

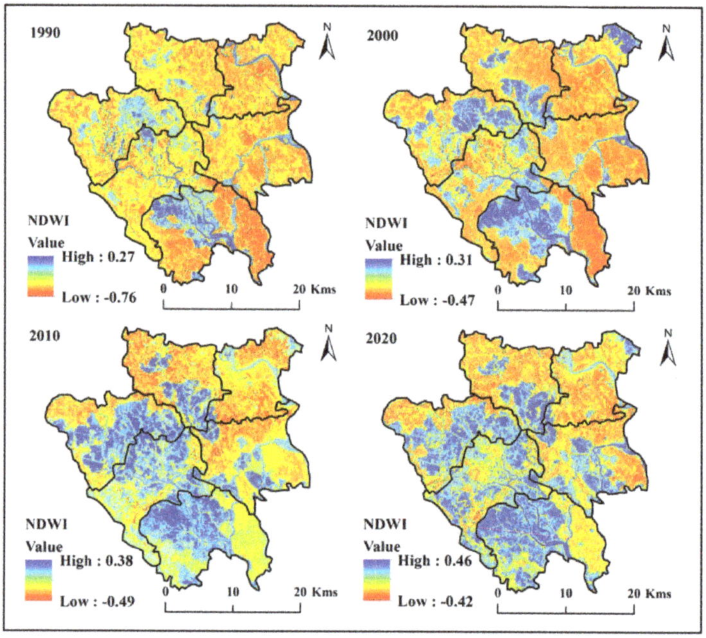

Figure 9. Normalized Difference Water Index (NDWI) maps of the study area.

In the year 1990, 156.21 km^2 (16.84%) of the land was identified as water bodies, but several years of cyclonic activities changed the areal conditions over the study area. Most of the inland fishery areas were identified in Sandeshkhali-I and Haroa during 1990 (Figure 6). But after that, several cyclones and environmental disasters have affected the area and influenced land alteration. The Sandeshkhali-I block was the most affected area and had the maximum amount of terrestrial land that was rehabilitated cropland altered to inland fisheries lands. In the year 2020, 482.78 km^2 (52.05%) area was under water bodies. This change influenced the land alteration and crop area dynamic. People were mostly building their economic development due to fish production and high international demands for fish-related food production, but the land alteration has degraded the local ecology and environment. Mangrove areas are a natural barrier, which protects the land from extreme environmental and natural disasters. Only the Sandeshkhali-II block has some parts of the mangrove area remaining; the rest of the area is not covered by mangrove forest. The reason for floodwater intrusion is that low land areas and the Ganga delta have a huge amount of high tide related problems. During high tides, many land areas are cover by water. The cyclonic condition has triggered this phenomenon and decreased the soil fertility rate.

4.5. Socio-Economic Values due to Land Alteration

The surface water body change analysis and crop vulnerability area identification was the most effective research work for delineating food scarcity and land dynamic identification. Furthermore, the causes of land dynamics and mitigation strategies are more essential for forthcoming development and sustainable expansion of this area. The southern parts of North 24 Parganas are a riverine area, and those six blocks were the most affected by the natural extreme environment. Cyclones Aila, Bulbul, Fani, Amphan, Yash, and many other natural disasters have triggered the changes in the natural environment and reduced local soil fertility. Good soil fertility and soil quality (pH, nitrogen, etc.) are essential for crop production, but the floods have affected that region, and low soil fertility has triggered the conversion of cropland into inland fishery area over the southern parts of North 24 Parganas. Sandeshkhali-I is the most affected block of North 24 Parganas, with most of the land now covered in inland fisheries. In the initial phase or year of this study, 1990, the area did not support this type of inland fishery, but after Aila, those regions were where the cropland was converted into an inland fishery area. The Kanmari, Chunchura, Matbari Abad, Malancha, Kachurhula, Muchikhola, and Ramchakir Gheri zones then supported an enormous quantity of inland fisheries area.

This remote sensing (RS) and geographic information system (GIS) based study has indicated that the land dynamic over thirty years in southern parts of North 24 Parganas has changed. The Landsat 5 TM and 8 OLI/TIRS datasets were used for this study from 1990 to 2020 at 10-year intervals. The NDVI and NDWI geospatial indices were used for green space or vegetation degradation and water area change analysis. The geospatial indicator was widely used for monitoring the land-related study and different NDWI maps for the four years show that the water areas have changed due to climate change and extreme environmental conditions. The Sandeshkhali-I, Haroa, and Minakhan blocks have been most affected by the saltwater interruption because the river areas were situated only on those blocks. This study has identified that the area of cropland has changed, and the inland fishery area has increased, which has developed the local farmer's economic well-being and they are building their life towards a sustainable healthy livelihood. Government and policymakers also build such type of planning for the overall development of those areas.

West Bengal is the highest rice-producing state of India, but with the overwhelming population pressure and urban expansion towards rural and fringe areas, the areas of cropland and vegetation has decreased. The vegetation area was converted by the local people for building the settlement. The natural extreme environmental conditions and methodological conditions have affected the coastal area, which was the most demanded parts for crop production, by saltwater intrusion and reduced soil fertility rate. But the natural environment and man-made disasters have affected the selected blocks of North 24 Parganas and increased the inland fishery area due to saltwater intrusion. Farmers are mostly economically stronger because of fish production. National and international fish cultivation demands are very high, and farmers have increased their profit by farming fish and crabs. Mainly, the selected blocks of North 24 Parganas were farming brackish water inland fish after conversion of cropland to fishery areas, and farmers were most economically strong and built proper environmental conditions over the study area. The Central Inland Fishery Research Institute (http://www.cifri.res.in/ (accessed on 28 February 2022)), which is situated in Barrackpore, runs an awareness program for farmers, training, and a water quality monitoring centre for the development of fish production, for the general improvement of this study location.

4.6. Land Use/Land Cover Prediction for 2050

For the LU/LC forecast for the year 2050, the two different image classification maps of 1990 and 2020, distance from road and the digital elevation model (DEM) were used with the QGIS software MOLUSCE plugin toolbar or algorithm. The forecast map shows that the natural disaster connected phenomena will augment the agricultural land alteration and control the water bodies or inland fisheries location. The soil salinity of the land and the inland fisheries lands will both be increased in forthcoming years. In the predicted LU/LC map for the year 2050, the water body or inland fishery was identified as 614.73 km^2 (66.27%), agricultural land as 217.38 km^2 (23.44%), vegetation as 76.85 km^2 (8.28%), and built-up land as occupying 18.58 km^2 or 2% of the total area (Figure 10). The water bodies or inland fishery area will have increased gradually and the agricultural cropland and vegetation significantly been decreased. Due to urban expansion and overwhelming population pressure, the settlements land will be likewise increased [59]. The reduced agricultural cropland and vegetation land combined with the local climatic disorder will result in a degraded environmental condition. The fishery area will be increased gradually and the area along the river side will be the most affected by this LU/LC change. The Sandeshkhali-I, Minakhan, Haroa and Basirhat-II blocks will be the most affected by 2050.

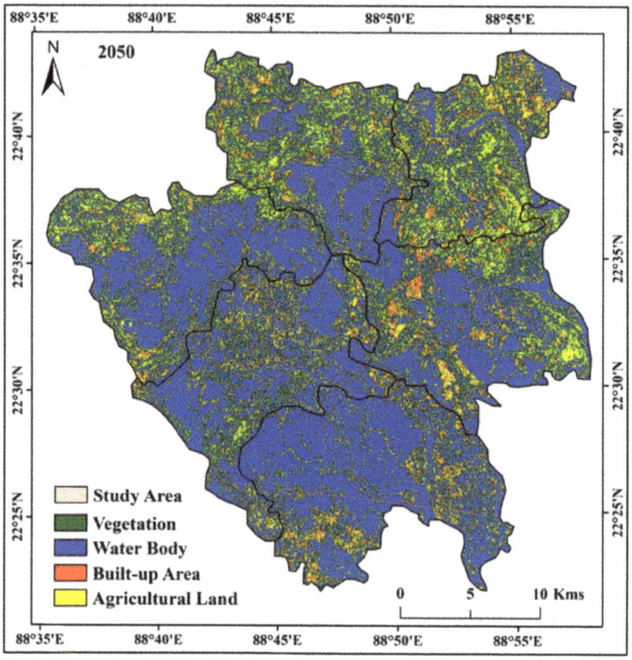

Figure 10. Prediction map of the study area in the year 2050.

5. Limitation and Recommendation

The Landsat 5 TM and 8 OLI/TIRS datasets were used for calculating the LU/LC change, then geospatial indicators (NDVI and NDWI) were used for identification in the selected blocks of North 24 Parganas district, West Bengal, India. Four multi-temporal datasets were used for this cropland dynamic and inland fishery area identification (1990, 2000, 2010 and 2020). Due to resolution problems and pixel mixing problems, the area identification was more difficult for and is a limitation of the Landsat data. Additionally, the area of cloud cover and pixel identification were the most important limitations of these images. But the Landsat data have been widely used for earth surface change analysis. The CA-ANN model was used for the LU/LC prediction of the study location [42]. The QGIS software was used for the purpose of the LU/LC prediction, where some of the most significant variables for prediction such as the road density, elevation, slope, and residential areas were used. The CA-ANN model is not used for established designated standards in the structure of each weighting contribution criterion contributing to their significance [60]. The LU/LC did not forecast 100% correctly through several models, therefore better prediction is desirable for future development and management in the study location. This study was also accommodating for the administrators, policymakers, local planners, other stakeholders and researchers for their study and development of this area. The future research scope for this area, are flood susceptibility mapping, soil salinity identification, cropland losses estimation, green space decreased identification, groundwater potential zone and groundwater quality assessment, socio-economic impact study, and improvement of farmers income study.

6. Conclusions

Land dynamics has increased the land scarcity for some areas like urban, peri-urban, and fringe areas, because vegetation and agricultural land has been converted into built-up or industrial land. The North 24 Parganas district is the most land dynamic district of West Bengal because of croplands being converted into inland fisheries due to extreme weather conditions. The Western parts of this district are joint with the megacity Kolkata and the southern parts are mangrove forests. The southern parts of this area have some important rivers, which are the main water source for some time. The Bay of Bengal is situated in the southern part of this area. Every year, the natural environment has been destroyed by the changing climate conditions, floods, cyclones, and many other natural and manmade hazards. This location has been subjected to an enormous volume of saltwater intrusion due to the riverine area that has damaged the cropland over these study areas. The Sandeshkhali, Basirhat, Haroa, Hasnabad, and Minakhan areas are the most affected by natural phenomena and the cyclonic storms that have hammered the natural environment. Due to saltwater intrusion, the land conversion has occurred in the land use and land cover classification map. In 1990, the agricultural land, or mainly the cropland occupied a large area in the selected blocks but after that, the extreme events of climatic change have destroyed the cropland and increased the inland fisheries areas over the study region.

Cropland vulnerability assessment is the most recent work for this study area because most of the people of West Bengal are dependent on rice cultivation and the main food is rice and related items. But the natural cyclones have increased cropland vulnerability over the southern parts of North 24 Parganas. The most affected blocks are the Sandeshkhali-I, Hasnabad, and Haroa. After the super cyclone, Aila, the South, and North 24 Parganas were most affected, and saltwater intrusion has damaged the soil fertility and crop production capacity. The soil is now mostly saline and rice cultivation is not suitable for those areas. Because of this natural climatic condition, many farmers have converted the cropland into brackish water inland fishery areas, resulting in increased crop vulnerability and reduced food security for this location. The cropland area was reduced around 252.06 km^2 (1990 to 2020) due to saltwater intrusion and man-made hazards. Gradually the water area was increased by 326.58 km^2 (1990 to 2020). Vegetated land area also decreased due to anthropogenic activities and salinity incensement of this area. Around 79.15 km^2 of vegetation portions have been lost due to climatic conditions and human activities. There is a need for proper planning, management, and an increased awareness for this problem, and for some mitigation strategies to figure out the sustainable development goals for the study location. Otherwise, saltwater intrusion and land dynamics will increase the crop vulnerability and inland fishery over the study area. The study results can accommodate the policymakers, local administrators, and other stakeholders in building proper planning for those blocks and increasing a better healthy life. Future study is required for the development of this area, such as the identification of areas of flood susceptibility, soil salinity, crop production and fish production, and the socio-economic conditions of this area, and agricultural application. This study method can also be used for future study over some other areas with or without suitable modification.

Author Contributions: Conceptualization, B.H., S.A.A., R.D., M.S. and Z.M.Y.; data curation, B.H., R.D., M.S. and Z.M.Y.; formal analysis, B.H., J.B., H.A.A., M.H.N., S.A.A., K.M.K., K.T.F., R.D., M.S. and Z.M.Y.; investigation, J.B., H.A.A., M.H.N., K.M.K., K.T.F., R.D. and Z.M.Y.; methodology, B.H., M.H.N., K.M.K., K.T.F. and M.S.; project administration, Z.M.Y.; resources, Z.M.Y.; software, B.H.; supervision, K.M.K.; validation, B.H., J.B., M.H.N., S.A.A., R.D. and M.S.; visualization, B.H., J.B., H.A.A., K.T.F., R.D. and Z.M.Y.; writing—original draft, B.H., J.B., H.A.A., M.H.N., S.A.A., K.M.K., K.T.F., R.D., M.S. and Z.M.Y. All authors have read and agreed to the published version of the manuscript.

Funding: This work was financially supported predominantly by WATERAGRI (European Union Horizon 2020 research and innovation programme under Grant Agreement Number 858735).

Data Availability Statement: Data are presented in the article.

Acknowledgments: The first two authors are thankful to the Vidyasagar University for this research opportunity and truly thankful to the local government body for field survey and data collection. This work was supported by the King Khalid University, Abha, Saudi Arabia (by grant number R.G.P. 3/237/43). We express our gratitude to the Deanship of Scientific Research, King Khalid University, for its support of this study.

Conflicts of Interest: The authors declare no conflict of interest.

References

1. Choudhury, D.; Das, K.; Das, A. Assessment of Land Use Land Cover Changes and Its Impact on Variations of Land Surface Temperature in Asansol-Durgapur Development Region. *Egypt. J. Remote Sens. Space Sci.* **2019**, *22*, 203–218. [CrossRef]
2. Kumar, D.; Pfeiffer, M.; Gaillard, C.; Langan, L.; Scheiter, S. Climate Change and Elevated CO_2 Favor Forest over Savanna under Different Future Scenarios in South Asia. *Biogeosciences* **2021**, *18*, 2957–2979. [CrossRef]
3. Siddique, M.A.; Dongyun, L.; Li, P.; Rasool, U.; Khan, T.U.; Farooqi, T.J.A.; Wang, L.; Fan, B.; Rasool, M.A. Assessment and Simulation of Land Use and Land Cover Change Impacts on the Land Surface Temperature of Chaoyang District in Beijing, China. *PeerJ* **2020**, *8*, e9115. [CrossRef] [PubMed]
4. Salman, S.A.; Shahid, S.; Sharafati, A.; Salem, G.S.A.; Bakar, A.A.; Farooque, A.A.; Chung, E.-S.; Ahmed, Y.A.; Mikhail, B.; Yaseen, Z.M. Projection of Agricultural Water Stress for Climate Change Scenarios: A Regional Case Study of Iraq. *Agriculture* **2021**, *11*, 1288. [CrossRef]
5. Sun, F.; Sun, W.; Chen, J.; Gong, P. Comparison and Improvement of Methods for Identifying Waterbodies in Remotely Sensed Imagery. *Int. J. Remote Sens.* **2012**, *33*, 6854–6875. [CrossRef]
6. Meng, X.; Zhang, Y.; Yu, X.; Zhan, J.; Chai, Y.; Critto, A.; Li, Y.; Li, J. Analysis of the Temporal and Spatial Distribution of Lake and Reservoir Water Quality in China and Changes in Its Relationship with GDP from 2005 to 2010. *Sustainability* **2015**, *7*, 2000–2027. [CrossRef]
7. Khaleefa, O.; Kamel, A.H. On The Evaluation of Water Quality Index: Case Study of Euphrates River, Iraq. *Knowl.-Based Eng. Sci.* **2021**, *2*, 35–43. [CrossRef]
8. Yaseen, Z.M. An Insight into Machine Learning Models Era in Simulating Soil, Water Bodies and Adsorption Heavy Metals: Review, Challenges and Solutions. *Chemosphere* **2021**, *277*, 130126. [CrossRef]
9. Tiyasha, T.; Bhagat, S.K.; Fituma, F.; Tung, T.M.; Shahid, S.; Yaseen, Z.M. Dual Water Choices: The Assessment of the Influential Factors on Water Sources Choices Using Unsupervised Machine Learning Market Basket Analysis. *IEEE Access* **2021**, *9*, 150532–150544. [CrossRef]
10. Adarsa, J.; Shamina, S.; Arkoprovo, B. *Morphological Change Study of Ghoramara Island, Eastern India Using Multi Temporal Satellite Data*; International Science Congress Association: Indore, India, 2012.
11. Ghosh, A.; Mukhopadhyay, S. Quantitative Study on Shoreline Changes and Erosion Hazard Assessment: Case Study in Muriganga–Saptamukhi Interfluve, Sundarban, India. *Model. Earth Syst. Environ.* **2016**, *2*, 75. [CrossRef]
12. Raju, D.K.; Santosh, K.; Chandrasekar, J.; Tiong-Sa, T. Coastline Change Measurement and Generating Risk Map for the Coast Using Geographic Information System. In Proceedings of the Joint International Conference on Theory, Data Handling and Modelling in GeoSpatial Information Science, Hong Kong, China, 26–28 May 2010.
13. Ghosh, M.K.; Kumar, L.; Roy, C. Monitoring the Coastline Change of Hatiya Island in Bangladesh Using Remote Sensing Techniques. *ISPRS J. Photogramm. Remote Sens.* **2015**, *101*, 137–144. [CrossRef]
14. Tao, H.; Al-Bedyry, N.K.; Khedher, K.M.; Shahid, S.; Yaseen, Z.M. River Water Level Prediction in Coastal Catchment Using Hybridized Relevance Vector Machine Model with Improved Grasshopper Optimization. *J. Hydrol.* **2021**, *598*, 126477. [CrossRef]
15. Odenweller, J.B.; Johnson, K.I. Crop Identification Using Landsat Temporal-Spectral Profiles. *Remote Sens. Environ.* **1984**, *14*, 39–54. [CrossRef]
16. Badhwar, G.D. Automatic Corn-Soybean Classification Using Landsat MSS Data. I. Near-Harvest Crop Proportion Estimation. *Remote Sens. Environ.* **1984**, *14*, 15–29. [CrossRef]
17. Bargiel, D. A New Method for Crop Classification Combining Time Series of Radar Images and Crop Phenology Information. *Remote Sens. Environ.* **2017**, *198*, 369–383. [CrossRef]
18. Blaes, X.; Vanhalle, L.; Defourny, P. Efficiency of Crop Identification Based on Optical and SAR Image Time Series. *Remote Sens. Environ.* **2005**, *96*, 352–365. [CrossRef]
19. Conrad, C.; Dech, S.; Dubovyk, O.; Fritsch, S.; Klein, D.; Löw, F.; Schorcht, G.; Zeidler, J. Derivation of Temporal Windows for Accurate Crop Discrimination in Heterogeneous Croplands of Uzbekistan Using Multitemporal RapidEye Images. *Comput. Electron. Agric.* **2014**, *103*, 63–74. [CrossRef]
20. Waldhoff, G.; Lussem, U.; Bareth, G. Multi-Data Approach for Remote Sensing-Based Regional Crop Rotation Mapping: A Case Study for the Rur Catchment, Germany. *Int. J. Appl. Earth Obs. Geoinf.* **2017**, *61*, 55–69. [CrossRef]

21. Simonneaux, V.; Duchemin, B.; Helson, D.; Er-Raki, S.; Olioso, A.; Chehbouni, A.G. The Use of High-resolution Image Time Series for Crop Classification and Evapotranspiration Estimate over an Irrigated Area in Central Morocco. *Int. J. Remote Sens.* **2008**, *29*, 95–116. [CrossRef]
22. Wardlow, B.; Egbert, S.; Kastens, J. Analysis of Time-Series MODIS 250 m Vegetation Index Data for Crop Classification in the U.S. Central Great Plains. *Remote Sens. Environ.* **2007**, *108*, 290–310. [CrossRef]
23. Peña-Barragán, J.M.; Ngugi, M.K.; Plant, R.E.; Six, J. Object-Based Crop Identification Using Multiple Vegetation Indices, Textural Features and Crop Phenology. *Remote Sens. Environ.* **2011**, *115*, 1301–1316. [CrossRef]
24. Duro, D.C.; Franklin, S.E.; Dubé, M.G. A Comparison of Pixel-Based and Object-Based Image Analysis with Selected Machine Learning Algorithms for the Classification of Agricultural Landscapes Using SPOT-5 HRG Imagery. *Remote Sens. Environ.* **2012**, *118*, 259–272. [CrossRef]
25. Mathur, A.; Foody, G.M. Crop Classification by Support Vector Machine with Intelligently Selected Training Data for an Operational Application. *Int. J. Remote Sens.* **2008**, *29*, 2227–2240. [CrossRef]
26. Long, J.A.; Lawrence, R.L.; Greenwood, M.C.; Marshall, L.; Miller, P.R. Object-Oriented Crop Classification Using Multitemporal ETM+ SLC-off Imagery and Random Forest. *GIScience Remote Sens.* **2013**, *50*, 418–436. [CrossRef]
27. Siachalou, S.; Mallinis, G.; Tsakiri-Strati, M. A Hidden Markov Models Approach for Crop Classification: Linking Crop Phenology to Time Series of Multi-Sensor Remote Sensing Data. *Remote Sens.* **2015**, *7*, 3633–3650. [CrossRef]
28. Behera, M.D.; Prakash, J.; Paramanik, S.; Mudi, S.; Dash, J.; Varghese, R.; Roy, P.S.; Abhilash, P.C.; Gupta, A.K.; Srivastava, P.K. Assessment of Tropical Cyclone Amphan Affected Inundation Areas Using Sentinel-1 Satellite Data. *Trop. Ecol.* **2022**, *63*, 9–19. [CrossRef]
29. Halder, B.; Bandyopadhyay, J. Monitoring the Tropical Cyclone 'Yass' and 'Amphan' Affected Flood Inundation Using Sentinel-1/2 Data and Google Earth Engine. *Model. Earth Syst. Environ.* **2022**, 1–16. [CrossRef]
30. Hassan, M.M.; Ash, K.; Abedin, J.; Paul, B.K.; Southworth, J. A Quantitative Framework for Analyzing Spatial Dynamics of Flood Events: A Case Study of Super Cyclone Amphan. *Remote Sens.* **2020**, *12*, 3454. [CrossRef]
31. Halder, B.; Das, S.; Bandyopadhyay, J.; Banik, P. The Deadliest Tropical Cyclone 'Amphan': Investigate the Natural Flood Inundation over South 24 Parganas Using Google Earth Engine. *Saf. Extrem. Environ.* **2021**, *3*, 63–73. [CrossRef]
32. Bhatta, B.; Saraswati, S.; Bandyopadhyay, D. Urban Sprawl Measurement from Remote Sensing Data. *Appl. Geogr.* **2010**, *30*, 731–740. [CrossRef]
33. Belal, A.A.; Moghanm, F.S. Detecting Urban Growth Using Remote Sensing and GIS Techniques in Al Gharbiya Governorate, Egypt. *Egypt. J. Remote Sens. Space Sci.* **2011**, *14*, 73–79. [CrossRef]
34. Srivastava, A.; Sahoo, B.; Raghuwanshi, N.S.; Singh, R. Evaluation of Variable-Infiltration Capacity Model and MODIS-Terra Satellite-Derived Grid-Scale Evapotranspiration Estimates in a River Basin with Tropical Monsoon-Type Climatology. *J. Irrig. Drain. Eng.* **2017**, *143*, 4017028. [CrossRef]
35. MohanRajan, S.N.; Loganathan, A.; Manoharan, P. Survey on Land Use/Land Cover (LU/LC) Change Analysis in Remote Sensing and GIS Environment: Techniques and Challenges. *Environ. Sci. Pollut. Res.* **2020**, *27*, 29900–29926. [CrossRef] [PubMed]
36. Mishra, K.; Prasad, P.R.C. Automatic Extraction of Water Bodies from Landsat Imagery Using Perceptron Model. *J. Comput. Environ. Sci.* **2015**, *2015*, 903465. [CrossRef]
37. Awadh, S.M.; Al-Sulttani, A.H.; Yaseen, Z.M. Temporal Dynamic Drought Interpretation of Sawa Lake: Case Study Located at the Southern Iraqi Region. *Nat. Hazards* **2022**, *112*, 619–638. [CrossRef]
38. Gascon, M.; Cirach, M.; Martínez, D.; Dadvand, P.; Valentín, A.; Plasència, A.; Nieuwenhuijsen, M.J. Normalized Difference Vegetation Index (NDVI) as a Marker of Surrounding Greenness in Epidemiological Studies: The Case of Barcelona City. *Urban For. Urban Green.* **2016**, *19*, 88–94. [CrossRef]
39. Hashim, B.M.; Al Maliki, A.; Sultan, M.A.; Shahid, S.; Yaseen, Z.M. Effect of Land Use Land Cover Changes on Land Surface Temperature during 1984–2020: A Case Study of Baghdad City Using Landsat Image. *Nat. Hazards* **2022**, *112*, 1223–1246. [CrossRef]
40. McFeeters, S.K. The Use of the Normalized Difference Water Index (NDWI) in the Delineation of Open Water Features. *Int. J. Remote Sens.* **1996**, *17*, 1425–1432. [CrossRef]
41. Balzter, H. Markov Chain Models for Vegetation Dynamics. *Ecol. Modell.* **2000**, *126*, 139–154. [CrossRef]
42. Santé, I.; García, A.M.; Miranda, D.; Crecente, R. Cellular Automata Models for the Simulation of Real-World Urban Processes: A Review and Analysis. *Landsc. Urban Plan.* **2010**, *96*, 108–122. [CrossRef]
43. Zenil, H. Compression-Based Investigation of the Dynamical Properties of Cellular Automata and Other Systems. *Complex Syst.* **2010**, *19*, 1–28. [CrossRef]
44. Ménard, A.; Marceau, D.J. Exploration of Spatial Scale Sensitivity in Geographic Cellular Automata. *Environ. Plan. B Plan. Des.* **2005**, *32*, 693–714. [CrossRef]
45. Halder, B.; Bandyopadhyay, J.; Banik, P. Assessment of Hospital Sites' Suitability by Spatial Information Technologies Using AHP and GIS-Based Multi-Criteria Approach of Rajpur–Sonarpur Municipality. *Model. Earth Syst. Environ.* **2020**, *6*, 2581–2596. [CrossRef]
46. Meshesha, T.W.; Tripathi, S.K.; Khare, D. Analyses of Land Use and Land Cover Change Dynamics Using GIS and Remote Sensing during 1984 and 2015 in the Beressa Watershed Northern Central Highland of Ethiopia. *Model. Earth Syst. Environ.* **2016**, *2*, 1–12. [CrossRef]

47. Halder, B.; Haghbin, M.; Farooque, A.A. An Assessment of Urban Expansion Impacts on Land Transformation of Rajpur-Sonarpur Municipality. *Knowl.-Based Eng. Sci.* **2021**, *2*, 34–53. [CrossRef]
48. Shahkooeei, E.; Arekhi, S.; Kani, A.N. Remote Sensing and GIS for Mapping and Monitoring Land Cover and Land Use Changes Using Support Vector Machine Algorithm (Case Study: Ilam Dam Watershed). *Int. Res. J. Appl. Basic Sci.* **2014**, *8*, 464–473.
49. Cohen, J.L.; Furtado, J.C.; Barlow, M.; Alexeev, V.A.; Cherry, J.E. Asymmetric Seasonal Temperature Trends. *Geophys. Res. Lett.* **2012**, *39*, 1–7. [CrossRef]
50. Halder, B.; Banik, P.; Bandyopadhyay, J. Mapping and Monitoring Land Dynamic Due to Urban Expansion Using Geospatial Techniques on South Kolkata. *Saf. Extrem. Environ.* **2021**, *3*, 27–42. [CrossRef]
51. Ramachandra, T.V.; Bharath, S.; Gupta, N. Modelling Landscape Dynamics with LST in Protected Areas of Western Ghats, Karnataka. *J. Environ. Manag.* **2018**, *206*, 1253–1262. [CrossRef]
52. Cheruto, M.C.; Kauti, M.K.; Kisangau, P.D.; Kariuki, P. Assessment of Land Use and Land Cover Change Using GIS and Remote Sensing Techniques: A Case Study of Makueni County, Kenya. *J. Remote Sens. GIS* **2016**, *5*, 1000175. [CrossRef]
53. McFeeters, S. Using the Normalized Difference Water Index (NDWI) within a Geographic Information System to Detect Swimming Pools for Mosquito Abatement: A Practical Approach. *Remote Sens.* **2013**, *5*, 3544–3561. [CrossRef]
54. Chowdary, V.M.; Chandran, R.V.; Neeti, N.; Bothale, R.V.; Srivastava, Y.K.; Ingle, P.; Ramakrishnan, D.; Dutta, D.; Jeyaram, A.; Sharma, J.R.; et al. Assessment of Surface and Sub-Surface Waterlogged Areas in Irrigation Command Areas of Bihar State Using Remote Sensing and GIS. *Agric. Water Manag.* **2008**, *95*, 754–766. [CrossRef]
55. Yaseen, Z.M.; Sulaiman, S.O.; Deo, R.C.; Chau, K.-W. An Enhanced Extreme Learning Machine Model for River Flow Forecasting: State-of-the-Art, Practical Applications in Water Resource Engineering Area and Future Research Direction. *J. Hydrol.* **2018**, *569*, 387–408. [CrossRef]
56. Yaseen, Z.M.; Shahid, S. Drought Index Prediction Using Data Intelligent Analytic Models: A Review. In *Intelligent Data Analytics for Decision-Support Systems in Hazard Mitigation*; Springer: Berlin/Heidelberg, Germany, 2020; pp. 1–27.
57. Alsharif, A.A.A.; Pradhan, B. Urban Sprawl Analysis of Tripoli Metropolitan City (Libya) Using Remote Sensing Data and Multivariate Logistic Regression Model. *J. Indian Soc. Remote Sens.* **2013**, *42*, 149–163. [CrossRef]
58. Silk, J. *Book Reviews: The Restless Urban Landscape*; Knox, P., Ed.; Prentice Hall: Englewood Cliffs, NJ, USA, 1993; pp. 9, 285. ISBN 0137554141.
59. Mehr, A.D.; Akdegirmen, O. Estimation of Urban Imperviousness and Its Impacts on Flashfloods in Gazipaşa, Turkey. *Knowl.-Based Eng. Sci.* **2021**, *2*, 9–17. [CrossRef]
60. Shatnawi, N.; Qdais, H.A. Mapping Urban Land Surface Temperature Using Remote Sensing Techniques and Artificial Neural Network Modelling. *Int. J. Remote Sens.* **2019**, *40*, 3968–3983. [CrossRef]

Section 3: Sustainable Flood Retention Basins and Drainage Systems

Large sustainable flood retention basins and other smaller drainage systems are analyzed and assessed in the third section (Articles 18 to 23). Article 18 reports on novel methods to estimate the risk of dam failure. The study promotes a new rapid screening tool developed to estimate the dam condition and the corresponding dam failure hazard and dam failure risk. Article 19 deals with computing air demand using the Takagi–Sugeno Model for dam outlets. Furthermore, the prediction of multiple functions of sustainable flood retention basins under uncertainty via multi-instance, multi-label learning is covered. A strategic framework for the sustainable management of drainage systems has also been proposed (Article 20). Article 22 is more concerned with selecting sustainable drainage structures based on ecosystem service variables estimated by different stakeholder groups. An innovative decision support tool based on the rapid estimation of novel ecosystem service variables at a low cost and with acceptable uncertainty has been proposed. Finally, Article 23 critically reviews water quality improvement performances of geotextiles within permeable pavement systems. The presence of geotextiles leads only to minor water quality improvements. For example, suspended solids are being held back by geotextiles and these solids sometimes also contain organic matter, nutrients and heavy metals.

Keywords: dam risk failure; ecosystem services; geotextile; multi-instance multi-label learning; permeable pavement; stakeholder assessment; suspended solids; sustainable management; uncertainty analysis; water quality control

Sustainability **2011**, *3*, 2200-2216; doi:10.3390/su3112200

OPEN ACCESS

sustainability

ISSN 2071-1050

www.mdpi.com/journal/sustainability

Article

Novel Method to Assess the Risk of Dam Failure

Miklas Scholz [1,2,*] and Qinli Yang [2]

[1] Civil Engineering Research Centre, School of Computing, Science and Engineering, The University of Salford, Newton Building, Salford M5 4WT, UK

[2] Institute for Infrastructure and Environment, School of Engineering, The University of Edinburgh, William Rankine Building, Mayfield Road, The King's Buildings, Edinburgh EH9 3JL, UK; E-Mail: Q.Yang-7@sms.ed.ac.uk

* Author to whom correspondence should be addressed; E-Mail: m.scholz@salford.ac.uk; Tel.: +44-161-29-55921.

Received: 11 November 2011 / Accepted: 14 November 2011 / Published 16 November 2011

Abstract: A new flexible, rapid and affordable risk assessment procedure was developed and verified for dams based on case studies in Scotland (UK) and the region of Baden (Germany). A database of six different sustainable flood retention basin (SFRB) types with varying flood control potential has been developed. In Scotland, there are a relatively high number of current and former large drinking water reservoirs which could contribute to flood management control. In comparison, purpose-built and relatively small SFRB, which are predominantly used for flood control, dominate the landscape in Baden. Moreover, 13 out of 149 SFRB have recently been upgraded, and 11 new SFRB have been built since 2006. Both the estimated hazard and risk are small in comparison to those found in the flood infrastructure in Scotland. The study assesses a rapid screening tool developed to estimate the Dam Condition and the corresponding Dam Failure Hazard and Dam Failure Risk. Most SFRB in Baden have a relatively poor Dam Condition, high Dam Failure Hazard but low Dam Failure Risk compared to those in Scotland. Findings show that Baden is more advanced in flood defence management as well as adaptation to climate change.

Zusammenfassung: Eine neue, flexible, schnelle und preisgünstige Methode zur Risokobeurteilung von Dämmen wurde entwickelt und getestet, die auf Fallbeispielen in Schottland (Vereinigtes Königreich) und der Region Baden (Deutschland) basiert. Eine Datenbank von sechs verschiedenen Typen nachhaltiger Hochwasserrückhaltebecken

(NHRB) mit unterschiedlichem Hochwasserrückhaltevermögen wurde entwickelt. Eine relativ hohe Anzahl von gegenwärtigen und ehemaligen großen Trinkwassertalsperren, die zur Hochwasserschutzkontolle verwandt werden könnten, befinden sich in Schottland. Zweckmäßig gebaute und relativ kleine NHRB, die hauptsächlich für den Hochwasserschutz verwendet werden, dominieren hingegen die Landschaft in Baden. Darüber hinaus wurden 13 von 149 NHRB kürzlich renoviert und seit 2006 wurden 11 neue NHRB gebaut. Sowohl die geschätzte Gefahr als auch das Risiko sind im Vergleich zu den Parametern, die für die Hochwasserschutzinfrastruktur in Schottland gefunden worden sind, klein. Die Studie untersucht ein zeitsparendes Instrument zur Beurteilung des Dammzustandes, der Dammbruchgefahr und des Dammbruchrisikos. Die meisten NHRB in Baden haben relativ geringe Werte bezüglich des Dammzustandes, hohe Werte für Dammbruchgefahr und niedrige Werte bezüglich des Dammbruchrisikos im Vergleich zu NHRB in Schottland. Die Ergebnisse zeigen, dass Baden im Hochwasserschutz vorne liegt und daher dem Klimawechsel besser angepasst ist.

Keywords: water resources management; dam dondition; dam failure hazard; dam railure risk; reservoir; adaptation to climate change; classification system; safety

1. Einführung

Die Europäische Gemeinschaft hat die Hochwasserrichtlinie 2007/60 EC [1] eingeführt, welche vorsieht, dass alle Mitgliedsstaaten nachhaltige Hochwasserrisikopläne erstellen. Die schottische Regierung hat daher den Flood Risk Management (Scotland) Act 2009 [2] erlassen. Dieses Gesetz ergänzt den Reservoirs Act 1975 [3]. Betreiber von Talsperren, die mehr als 10000 m^3 Kapazität haben, sollen in Zukunft stärker reguliert werden. In Deutschland hat man das Konzept von Risikobeurteilung schon wesentlich früher erkannt und in deutsche Maßstäbe eingearbeitet [4].

Die Benutzung des Begriffes Nachhaltiges Hochwasserrückhaltebecken (NHRB) ist relativ neu (2006) und lehnt sich an den englischen Begriff Sustainable Flood Retention Basin (SFRB) an, der von der Forschungsgruppe der Autoren [5,6] geprägt wurde, an. Ein NHRB ist als ein künstlicher oder natürlicher Wasserkörper (z.B. Talsperre oder Feuchtgebiet) definiert, welches eine direkte oder mögliche Rolle im Hochwasser- und Umweltschutz hat. Diese Schutzfunktionen können kostengünstig durch umweltfreundliche Unterhaltungspläne, welche nachhaltige Dränage, Verschmutzungsreduktion, Artenvielfaltsteigerung und Freizeitwertsteigerung fördern, erreicht werden. Dies ist eine neue und holistische Definition, die nicht mit den deutschen Definitionen für Begriffe wie Talsperre oder Hochwasserrückhaltebecken verwechselt werden sollte.

Die Europäische Gemeinschaft unterstützt Mitgliedsstaaten bei regionalen und länderübergreifenden Förderungsprogrammen wie der Strategic Alliance for Water Management Actions (SAWA) [7]. Ein wichtiges Ziel von SAWA ist es, neue und holistische Richtlinien für die Entwicklung von Maßnahmen und Konzepten wie die NHRB zu erstellen.

Mehr Regenfälle im Frühling und Sommer aufgrund des Klimawechsel werden zu mehr Abfluss in Teilen von Großbritannien und Deutschland führen. Höhere Wasserspiegel in Rückhaltebecken und daher mehr Druck auf die Dämme werden erwartet. Das unkontrollierte Brechen von Dämmen aufgrund von extremen Naturereignissen kann zu Überflutungen und Umweltverschmutzungen führen. Dies kann katastrophale Folgen wie Todesfälle und Infrastrukturschäden haben [7–9]. Es ist daher notwendig, eine schnelle Methode zur Beurteilung des Dammbruchrisikos für zahlreiche Wasserkörper zu entwickeln.

Der Hauptzweck dieses Forschungsartikels besteht darin, eine holistische, schnelle und kostengünstige Methode zur Beurteilung von Dammbruchrisiken bei NHRB vorzustellen. Die folgenden Punkte sind damit verbundene Nebenzwecke:

- Klassifizierung von NHRB mit Dämmen in sechs Gruppen (NHRB Typen);
- Entwicklung einer schnellen und kostengünstigen Methode zur Identifizierung von Dammbruchgefahr und Dammbruchrisiko;
- Unterscheidung von verschiedenen Gefahren- und Risikostufen für verschiedene NHRB-Typen;
- Gewährleistung der weiten Anwendbarkeit der Methode durch das Prüfen von möglichst vielen internationalen Fallstudien;
- Untersuchung von NHRB-Datenbanken, um zu ermitteln, wieviele NHRB dem Klimawechsel schon angepasst wurden; und
- Beurteilung der räumlichen Variabilität bezüglich des Quotienten Dammbruchrisiko über Dammbruchgefahr.

Diese Arbeit beruht auf internationalen Erfahrungen und sollte als eine holistische Ergänzung zu der deutschen Sichtweise [10] von Hochwasser- und Umweltschutz angesehen werden. Die vorgestellte Methode beschränkt sich daher nicht auf hydrologische und hydraulische Parameter, deren genaue Ermittlung häufig sehr kostspielig und in der Praxis schwer ausführbar ist. Darüberhinaus schlagen die Autoren keinesfalls vor, nützliche Normen (zum Beispiel die DIN 4,048 für Hochwasserrückhaltebecken oder die DIN 19,700 für Stauanlagen) vollständig zu ersetzen.

2. Methodik

In Schottland wurden 199 NHRB identifiziert (Abbildung 1). Im Vergleich dazu wurden 165 NHRB in Baden aufgenommen (Abbildung 2). Diese Abbildungen geben einen guten Überblick über die große räumliche Verteilung der Becken. Die Beurteilungen beruhten auf einer Literaturstudie und einer Ortsbegehung. Die Literaturstudie in Schottland beruft sich weitgehend auf die Quellen [11–15]. Informationen bezüglich der badischen Fallstudien wurden durch zahlreiche Gemeinden und Wasserverbände geliefert.

Die Definitionen der Autoren für die unterschiedlichen Typen von NHRB wurden in Tabelle 1 zusammengefasst. Diese Beschreibungen beruhen auf umfangreichen Literaturstudien und Expertenmeinungen [16]. Die Bestimmung der einzelnen Standardvariablen beruht auf einer ehemaligen Veröffentlichung [5] für NHRB in Baden. Eine ausführliche Beschreibung dieser Begriffe wäre für diese Zeitschrift zu umfangreich, kann jedoch von den Autoren angefordert werden [17].

Abbildung 1. Studiengebiet, administrative Grenzen und die 199 Nachhaltigen Hochwasserrückhaltebecken (NHRB) mit Dämmen im Großraum Zentral-Schottland (Vereinigtes Königreich).

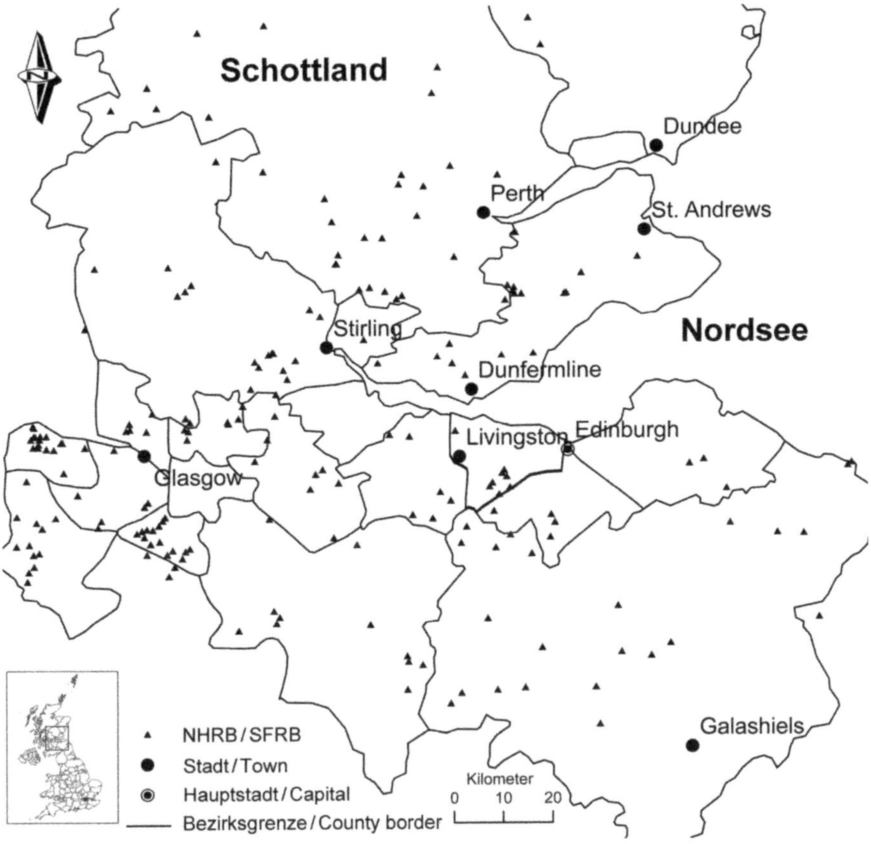

Abteilung 2. Studiengebiet, administrative Grenzen und die 165 Nachhaltigen Hochwasserrückhaltebecken (NHRB) mit Dämmen in Süd-Baden (Deutschland).

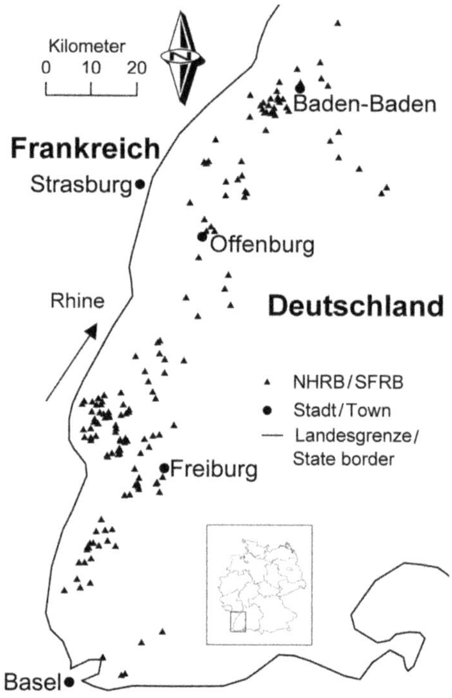

Tabelle 1. Definitionen für verschiedene Typen von nachhaltigen Hochwasserrückhaltebecken (NHRB).

Typ	Name	Definition von NHRB Typ	Typische Beispiele	Gefahr/ Risiko
1	Hydraulisches Hochwasserrück-haltebecken (HHRB)	Bewirtschaftetes NHRB, welches hydraulisch (oder sogar automatisch) optimiert ist, und Sedimente kontrolliert anhäuft	Einige Trinkwassertalsperren; große zweckmäßige Hochwasserrückhaltebecken	Hohe Gefahr und niedriges Risiko
2	Traditionelles Hochwasserrück-haltebecken (THRB)	Ästhetisches Rückhaltebecken, welches für Hochwasserrückhaltung benötigt wird; nachhaltige Dränage ist möglich	Ehemalige Trinkwassertalsperre; traditionelles Hochwasserrück-haltebecken	Moderate Gefahr und moderates Risiko
3	Nachhaltiges Hochwasserrück-haltefeuchtgebiet (NHRF)	Ästhetisches Rückhaltebecken und Behandlungsfeuchtgebiet, welches für einen passiven Hochwasserschutz verwendet wird; nachhaltige Dränage ist möglich	Nachhaltige Dränageanlage (zum Beispiel ein Rückhaltebecken, Einstaubecken, großer Teich oder Feuchtgebiet)	Niedrige Gefahr und niedriges Risiko
4	Ästhetisches Hochwasserbe-handlungsfeucht-gebiet (ÄHBF)	Behandlungsfeuchtgebiet für die Rückhaltung von verschmutztem Ablauf, welches ästhetisch in die Landschaft integriert ist; einige soziale Vorteile; Freizeitswertsteigerung	Einige moderne künstliche und integrierte Feuchtgebiete	Hohe Gefahr und niedriges Risiko
5	Integriertes Hochwasserrück-haltefeuchtgebiet (IHRF)	Integrierte Hochwasserrückhaltefeuchtgebiete für passive Behandlung von Ablauf; Förderung von Freizeitwerten	Künstliche Gewässer innerhalb von Parks oder in der Nähe von Straßen, welche klare Mehrzwecke haben (zum Beispiel: Wassersport und Angeln)	Hohe Gefahr und niedriges Risiko
6	Natürliches Hochwasserrück-haltefeuchtgebiet (NHRF)	Passive und natürliche Hochwasserrüchhaltebecken, welche möglicherweise Naturschutzgebiete werden könnten	Seen und Teiche (möglicherweise mit Zugangseinschränkung)	Moderate Gefahr und niedriges Risiko

Tabelle 2 beinhaltet eine Kurzbeschreibung der neuen Parameter Dammzustand, Dammbruchgefahr und Dammbruchrisiko bezüglich deren Komponenten und Gewichtungen. Eine Gefahr (zum Beispiel: unerwünschter Baumbewuchs und Nagetieraktivitäten auf einem Damm) kann entweder mit einem niedrigen (fast immer leeren Rückhaltebecken) oder hohem (fast immer vollen Becken) Risiko verknüpft sein. Beispielbeschreibungen für die Extremwerte bezüglich aller Komponenten sollen den Ingenieuren und Wissenschaftlern helfen, möglichst genaue Abschätzungen vorzunehmen. Alle Werte basieren auf Vergleichsabschätzungen und Expertenmeinungen. In dem Parameter Dammbruchrisiko werden unabhängigen Parameter wie das Versagensrisiko und das Schadenrisiko zusammengefasst. Dies kann zu Verzerrungen bei der Bewertung und wesentlichem Informationsverlust führen. Experten müssen daher die Gewichtungswerte für die einzelnen Parameter vorher der Region anpassen.

Weitere Informationen wie das NHRB Handbuch (56 Seiten [17]) zur Bestimmung der einzelnen Parameter können von den Autoren angefordert werden. Dieses Material ist für eine Veröffentlichung in dieser Zeitschrift jedoch zu umfangreich.

Tabelle 2. Kurzbeschreibung der Summenparameter Dammzustand (%), Dammbruchgefahr (%) und Dammbruchrisiko (%) bezüglich deren Komponenten und Gewichtungen.

Dammzustand (%)			***Dammbruchgefahr (%)***			***Dammbruchrisiko (%)***		
Komponente	Obere Gewichtungsbeschreibung (Beispiel)	Untere Gewichtungsbeschreibung (Beispiel)	Komponente	Obere Gewichtungsbeschreibung (Beispiel)	Untere Gewichtungsbeschreibung (Beispiel)	Komponente	Obere Gewichtungsbeschreibung (Beispiel)	Untere Gewichtungsbeschreibung (Beispiel)
Dammaufbau (30%)	Sehr guter Dammaufbau; sehr ordentlich; wahrscheinlich gute Bewirtschaftung durch einen Wasserverband oder eine Gemeinde (>80%)	Sehr schlechter Dammaufbau; Oberflächenrisse möglich; Sickerwasser gesichtet; Damm ist wahrscheinlich nicht mehr in Betrieb (<20%)	*Kraft auf den Damm* (30%)	Dammhöhe größer als 35 m; hohe permanente Wasserkraft; schlechte Konstruktion bezüglich des mineralischen Kernes, der Uferböschung oder der Grundabdichtung; Wasserwellenschaden; Verstopfung der Überlaufabdeckung wahrscheinlich (>80%)	Dammhöhe häufig kleiner als 18 m; sehr selten Druck auf den Damm (zum Beispiel: leere Talsperre); sehr gute Konstruktion (<20%)	*Statisches Dammbruchrisiko* (20%)	Sehr hoher Dammdruck; schlechte Unterhaltung; risikoreicher Betrieb; sehr dünner, hoher und langer Damm mit vielen potentiellen Schwachstellen (>80%)	Niedriger Druck auf den Damm; sehr gute Unterhaltung; sichere Struktur durch sehr weiten, flachen und kurzen Damm (<10%)
Überlaufzustand (30%)	Normalerweise eine Hochwasserentlastungsanlage; verstärkte Grasssoden möglich; keine ungewollte Vegetation; gut gepflegt und unterhalten (>80%)	Kein kontrollierter Überlauf; fehlende Bausteine; Bauelement sollte repariert werden (<5%)	*Mögliche Tote durch Sperrenbruch* (35%)	Sehr großer Wasserkörper; sehr hohe permanente Bevölkerungsdichte im Einzugsbebiet unterhalb des Dammes; Personen kommen höchst wahrscheinlich ums Leben (>80%)	Sehr kleiner Wasserkörper; ländlicher Raum; nur wenige Menschen leben unterhalb des Dammes (<10%)	*Risiko bezüglich Tote durch Sperrenbruch* (50%)	Sehr hohe Bevölkerungsdichte; permanente Wohneinheiten; kein Sicherheits- und Evakuationsplan vorhanden (>80%)	Dünn besiedelt; niedriger Anteil an dauerhafter Bevölkerung; kleiner Damm; kein Sicherheitskonzept notwendig (<10%)
Zustand der Wellenabfangmauer (20%)	Gut unterhaltene Wellenabfangmauer; Betonmauer, Steinmauer oder große Findlinge; keine ungewollte Vegetation (>90%)	Stellenweise Erosion des Erd-dammes; keine regelmäßige Unterhaltung; fehlende Bausteine (<10%)	*Wichtigkeit der Infrastruktur unter Einfluß eines Dammversagens* (25%)	Wichtige Flugplätze, Bahnstrecken, Straßen und Brücken, Gasleitungen, Industriegebiete und Elektrizitätsversorgungsstationen sind sehr beinträchtigt; hoher Wasserverlust (>80%)	Signifikante ländliche Gebiete; keine wichtige Infrastruktur; nur einspurige Straßen sind beinflusst (<5%)	*Infrastrukturschädigungsrisiko* (20%)	Sehr dürftiger Hochwasserschutz; niedrige Seitenbefestigungen; nahe eines Wasserkörpers; sehr hohe Überflutungstiefe; keine Anpassung an den Klimawechsel offensichtlich (>80%)	Sehr gut vor Überflutung geschützt; Damm befindet sich im Gebirge; hohe Dammseiten; fern von anderen Gewässern; Niedrigwasser; voll an den Klimawechsel angepasst (<15%)

Tabelle 2. *Fortsetzung.*

	Dammzustand (%)			***Dammbruchgefahr (%)***			***Dammbruchrisiko (%)***	
Einfluss des Operations-volumens (10%)	Stau- und Betriebsraumvolumen größer als 20 km^3; großer Einfluß auf den Damm durch hohe und lang anhaltende Wasserkraft im Falle eines Dammdurchbruches (>80%)	Stau- und Betriebsraumvolu-men häufig kleiner als 0.5 km^3; sehr selten mit Wasser gefüllt; wenig Druck auf den Damm (<20%)	*Andere Faktoren, welche die Dammbruchgefahr beeinflussen könnten* (10%)	Ernsthafte Erosion and Dammschäden; trübes Sickerwasser in Bohrlöchern; Bäume und Sträucher wachsen auf dem Damm (Gefahr auf Grund von interner Erosion); verstopfter oder beschädigter Überlauf (Gefahr des Überströmens); Schäden durch Nagetiere und Krustentiere; wichtiges Naturschutz-gebiet unterhalb des Dammes (>80%)	Naturnaher Wasserkörper ohne offensichtliche Gefahrenquellen; öffentlicher Park (<10%)	*Andere Faktoren, welche das Dammbruchrisiko beeinflussen könnten* (10%)	Damm- und Seitenbefestigungsschäden besonders in feuchten Jahren wahrscheinlich; Risiko von schadstoffhaltigen Sedimentationsablagerungen in bevölkerungsreichen Gebieten; Kettenefekt bezüglich Dammbrüchen; Klimawechsel sorgt für unvorhersehbare meteorologische Ereignisse; hohes Zerstörungsrisiko durch Terrorismus, Sabotage und Erbeben (>80%)	Gute und sichere Unterhaltung; kein Risiko identifiziert (<10%)
Andere Faktoren, welche den Dammzustand beeinflussen (10%)	Becken werden derzeit von einem Wasserverband verwaltet; Trinkwasserversorgungszweck und/oder Hochwasserschutznutzung (>85%)	Naturnaher Wasserkörper (See oder Feuchtgebiet); keine regelmäßige Unterhaltung (<10%)						

Um eine Gruppenanalyse (cluster analysis) der NHRB durchzuführen [18], wurde Matlab 7.1 [19] verwendet. Die Ergebnisse dieser Methode können graphisch in Form von Dendogramms gezeigt werden. Die NHRB-Daten wurden in sechs Gruppen sortiert (Tabelle 1), welche den einzelnen NHRB-Typen entsprechen.

3. Aufarbeitung der Ergebnisse

Abbildung 3 zeigt das Dendrogramm für die kombinierte Datenbank. Die Gruppen A, B and C repräsentieren fast ausschließlich die schottischen NHRB. Im Gegensatz dazu enthalten die Gruppen D, E und F fast nur badische NHRB. Wenig Übereinstimmung besteht zwischen den schottischen und badischen Daten auf Grund von geringen Ähnlichkeiten (Y-Achse) zwischen den NHRB Gruppen (X-Achse). Abbildung 3 ist auch notwendig, um verschiedene Typen von NHRB (Tabelle 1) in beiden Fallstudien zu bestimmen. Die NHRB des Typs 2 dominieren in Schottland. Typen 1 and 4 sind charakteristisch für Baden.

Abbildung 3. Dendrogramm basierend auf 43 Parametern für die kombinierte Datenbank, welche 197 schottische und 160 badische Nachhaltige Hochwasserrückhaltebecken (NHRB; Einträge auf der X-Achse) enthält.

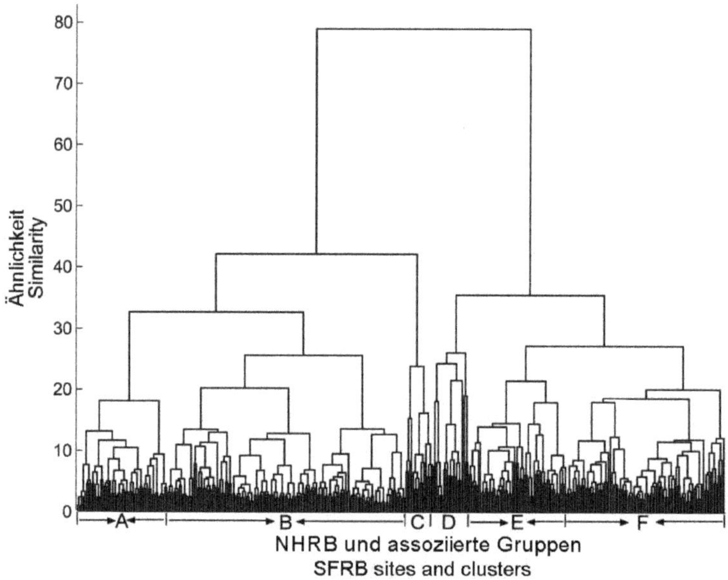

Tabelle 3 zeigt eine Übersicht der wichtigsten physikalischen Variablen, die für die Bestimmung der Risikosummenparameter relevant sind. Die Variablen wurden während Begehungen der Becken aufgenommen und durch Literaturstudien bestätigt. Die Dateninterpretation zeigt, dass wenig Übereinstimmung zwischen den schottischen und badischen Daten besteht. Tabelle 3 bestätigt daher Abbildung. 3. Das maximale Stauvolumen für schottische im Vergleich zu badischen NHRB ist zum Beispiel viel größer. Dies ist auch der Fall für ähnliche Einzugsgebiete. Schottische NHRB sind fast ausschließlich randvoll. Badische NHRB sind dagegen so gut wie immer leer.

Tabelle 3. Statistische Informationen für die wichtigsten Variablen, die für die Bestimmung der risikorelevanten Parameter von nachhaltigen Hochwasserrückhaltebecken (NHRB) relevant sind.

Land	Gruppe (NHRB Typ)	Statistische Parameter	*Damm-höhe* m	*Damm-länge* m	*Speicherlängs-gefälle* %	*Maximales Rückhalte-volumen* Million m^3	*Jährlicher Regenfall* mm/a	*Einzugs-gebietsgröße* km^2	*Mittlere Beckentiefe* m
Schottische Becken	Gruppe A (51 Becken; Typ 3)	Durchschnitt	2,91	127,82	0,02	0,32	949,4	3,08	2,70
		Mittlere Abweichung	2,62	133,13	0,01	0,51	236,21	3,59	1,08
		Zuversichtswert	80,8	82,8	67,5	66,4	75,1	80,7	61,3
	Gruppe B (130 Becken; Typ 2)	Durchschnitt	9,64	259,62	0,02	1,96	1.102,8	8,16	5,70
		Mittlere Abweichung	2,27	199,74	0,02	2,84	289,26	14,45	2,70
		Zuversichtswert	78,7	84,6	72,3	71,0	76,9	84,1	64,70
	Gruppe C (15 Becken; Typ 5)	Durchschnitt	30,16	318,50	0,08	20,57	1.039,30	38,58	15,10
		Mittlere Abweichung	16,33	169,30	0,25	18,38	350,52	40,12	6,69
		Zuversichtswert	86,9	90,2	68,3	81,0	79,0	85,6	73,3
	Gruppe D (1 Becken; Typ 6)	Durchschnitt	32,1	240,0	1,0	5,1	900,0	74,0	25,0
		Zuversichtswert	99,0	99,0	60,0	99,0	60,0	60,0	70,0
	Total (197 Becken)	Durchschnitt	9,4	229,4	0,0	3,0	1.057,8	11,4	5,5
		Mittlere Abweichung	9,57	192,48	0,02	7,68	288,42	38,70	4,02
		Zuversichtswert	79,8	84,6	70,7	70,6	76,6	83,3	64,6

Tabelle 3. *Fortsetzung.*

Land	Gruppe (NHRB Typ)	Statistische Parameter	*Damm-höhe*	*Damm-länge*	*Speicherlängs-gefälle*	*Maximales Rückhalte-volumen*	*Jährlicher Regenfall*	*Einzugs-gebietsgröße*	*Mittlere Beckentiefe*
			m	m	%	Million m^3	mm/a	km^2	m
Badische Becken	Gruppe D (18 Becken; Typ 6)	Durchschnitt	3,53	1.862,32	1,42	0,87	764,20	95,42	2,50
		Mittlere Abweichung	2,34	1801,12	2,43	1,34	78,55	130,14	1,94
		Zuversichtswert	74,3	74,7	56,1	66,5	68,3	50,8	51,7
	Gruppe E (54 Becken; Typ 1)	Durchschnitt	5,66	451,48	1,67	0,20	808,30	8,72	3,30
		Mittlere Abweichung	3,23	852,50	1,16	0,39	80,61	12,72	1,83
		Zuversichtswert	70,7	71,8	56,5	66,7	74,3	61,6	53,6
	Gruppe F (87 Becken; Typ 4)	Durchschnitt	4,29	147,93	2,22	0,04	739,80	2,44	2,80
		Mittlere Abweichung	2,60	251,56	2,22	0,14	74,47	3,77	1,52
		Zuversichtswert	74,9	74,0	62,3	64,6	79,7	61,8	60,6
	Gruppe C (1 Becken; Typ 5)	Durchschnitt	8,0	65,0	0,1	0,3	870,0	490,0	3,0
		Zuversichtswert	80,0	98,0	70,0	70,0	80,0	80,0	75,0
	Total (160 Becken)	Durchschnitt	4,8	455,1	1,9	0,2	766,0	13,0	3,1
		Mittlere Abweichung	3,60	965,05	1,97	0,69	83,03	38,08	2,43
		Zuversichtswert	73,5	73,5	59,6	65,7	76,4	60,2	57,3

Das Forschungsprojekt versuchte die oben beschriebenen Methoden zum Risikomanagement in einem zeitsparenden Instrument zur Risikobeurteilung zu vereinigen. Tabelle 4 zeigt die wichtigsten statistischen Parameter für die Variablen, welche Risikoszenarien beschreiben könnten. Die Variablen wurden mit der Hilfe von Tabelle 2 und dem mehr ausführlicheren NHRB Handbuch [17] bestimmt. Die individuellen Dammbruchrisikodaten helfen Entscheidungsträgern bei der schnellen Identifizierung von Dämmen für die Handlungsbedarf besteht.

Risikowerte sind im Allgemeinen viel kleiner als Gefahrenwerte. Dies kann mit direkten (z.B. stabiler Damm) und indirekten (z.B. dünne Besiedelung unterhalb des Dammes) Massnahmen zur Risikobeschränkung erklärt werden. Tabelle 4 bestätigt Tabelle 3 in der Behauptung, dass zwischen den schottischen und badischen Fallbeispieldaten wenig Überlappung zu erkennen ist.

Tabelle 4. Statistische Informationen bezüglich der risikorelevanten Parameter für nachhaltige Hochwasserrückhaltebecken (NHRB).

Land	**Gruppe (NHRB Typ)**	**Statistische Parameter**	***Damm-zustand*** %	***Dammbruch-gefahr*** %	***Dammbruch-risiko*** %
Schottische Becken	Gruppe A (51 Becken; Typ 3)	Durchschnitt	55,4	2,6	4,4
		Mittlere Abweichung	17,47	3,48	3,35
		Zuversichtswert	62,2	71,1	63,3
	Gruppe B (130 Becken; Typ 2)	Durchschnitt	77,7	8,6	6,3
		Mittlere Abweichung	7,40	11,67	3,80
		Zuversichtswert	66,0	67,2	60,3
	Gruppe C (15 Becken; Typ 5)	Durchschnitt	88,7	21,6	4,9
		Mittlere Abweichung	8,44	16,70	3,43
		Zuversichtswert	76,9	67,0	66,3
	Gruppe D (1 Becken; Typ 6)	Durchschnitt	85,9	1,8	8,5
		Zuversichtswert	61,8	60,0	55,6
	Total (197 Becken)	Durchschnitt	72,8	8,0	5,7
		Mittlere Abweichung	15,35	11,57	3,74
		Zuversichtswert	68,3	68,3	63,1
Badische Becken	Gruppe D (18 Becken; Typ 6)	Durchschnitt	51,7	11,9	2,6
		Mittlere Abweichung	16,38	12,15	2,55
		Zuversichtswert	64,2	56,4	61,1
	Gruppe E (54 Becken; Typ 1)	Durchschnitt	52,3	18,3	2,4
		Mittlere Abweichung	11,64	11,87	1,46
		Zuversichtswert	63,2	56,1	59,4
	Gruppe F (87 Becken; Typ 4)	Durchschnitt	46,7	12,7	2,5
		Mittlere Abweichung	11,46	9,93	2,06
		Zuversichtswert	66,4	59,7	63,7
	Gruppe C (1 Becken; Typ 5)	Durchschnitt	78,0	26,1	2,4
		Zuversichtswert	65,0	60,0	70,0
	Total (160 Becken)	Durchschnitt	49,1	14,6	2,4
		Mittlere Abweichung	12,28	11,15	1,87
		Zuversichtswert	64,6	57,5	61,3

Der Dammzustand für NHRB in Schottland ist normalerweise besser (73% verglichen mit 49%) als in Deutschland. Dies kann damit erklärt werden, dass Schottland viele Trinkwassertalsperren besitzt. Es ist daher interessant, daß die Dammbruchrisiken für Baden im Allgemeinen wesentlich geringer sind als für Schottland. Dies liegt daran, dass deutsche NHRB meistens leer sind (Tabelle 4). Die angeführten Werte sind relative Vergleichsgrößen und sollten daher nur im gültigen Zusammenhang miteinander verglichen und interpretiert werden. Ein hoher Wert (zum Beispiel für Dammbruchgefahr) bedeutet nicht, dass der jeweilige Damm kurz vor dem Zusammenbruch steht. Nur wenn der dazugehörige Wert für Dammbruchrisiko ebenfalls hoch ist, besteht Grund zur Besorgnis.

Abbildung 4 zeigt die räumliche Verteilung des Quotienten Dammbruchrisiko über Dammbruchgefahr für Zentral-Schottland. Je höher dieser Quotient ist, desto grösser ist im Allgemeinen das Risiko eines Dammbruches mit hohen Sachschäden und gegebenenfalls auch mit Todesopfern. Niedrige Werte sind die Regel, da Risikowerte meisstens viel kleiner sind als Gefahrenwerte. Die vergleichbare Verteilung für Süd-Baden ist in Abbildung 5 zu sehen. Die Kartenwerte sind keine Modellierungswerte und basieren lediglich auf einem einfachen Interpolationsverfahren; sie dienen daher nur der generellen Übersicht. Es ist jedoch deutlich für Ortskundige, dass NHRB, die sich im Gebirge und oberhalb von Ortschaften befinden, einen hohen Risikoquotienten haben.

Abbildung 4. Räumliche Verteilung des Verhältnisses von Dammbruchrisiko zu Dammbruchgefahr für 197 nachhaltige Hochwasserrückhaltebecken im Großraum Zentral-Schottland

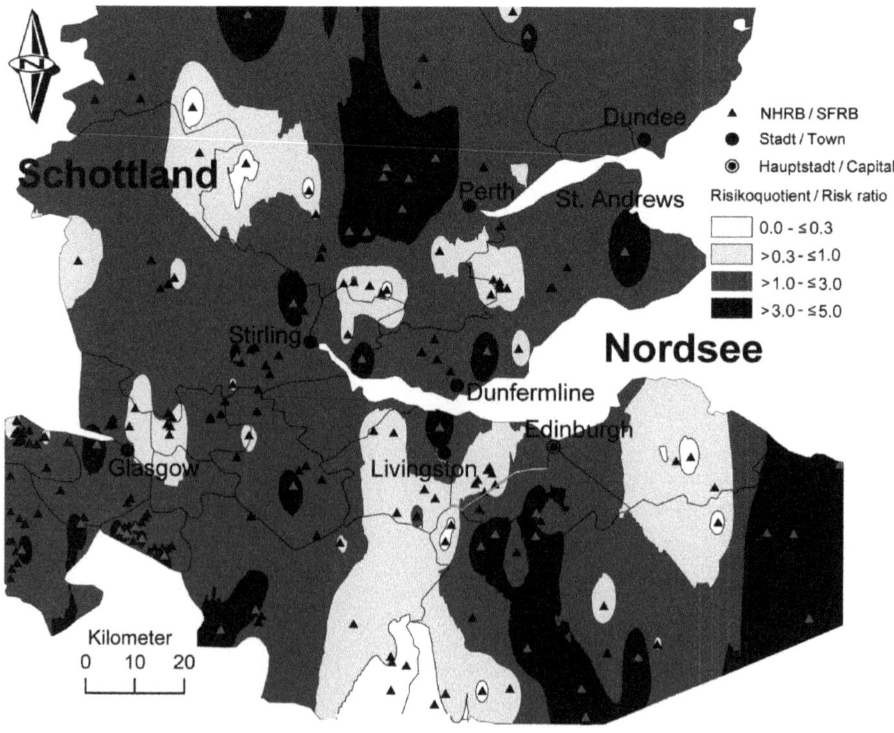

Abbildung 5. Räumliche Verteilung des Verhältnisses von Dammbruchrisiko zu Dammbruchgefahr für 160 nachhaltige Hochwasserrückhaltebecken in Süd-Baden

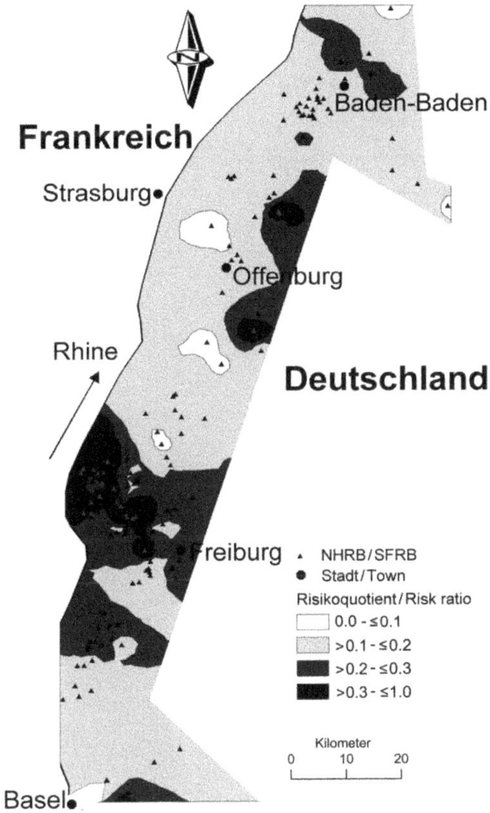

Abbildung 4 zeigt deutlich, daß der Quotient von Gefahr über Risiko für die schottischen Fallstudien zwischen 0 und 5 liegt. Fast 40% der Quotienten sind kleiner als 1. Vergleichbare Werte für Baden liegen jedoch nur zwischen 0 und 1 (Abbildung. 5). Ungefähr 80% der badischen NHRB haben Quotienten zwischen 0 und 0,3. Diese Erbebnisse deuten an, dass das Sicherheitskonzept in Baden viel erfolgreicher zu sein scheint. Die schottische Wasserfirma Scottish Water sollte also das Hochwasserschutzrisiko für ihre Anlagen besser kontrollieren.

Verschiedene NHRB Typen gehören unterschiedlichen Gefahren- und Risikokategorien an (Tabelle 4), welches in Tabelle 1 (letzte Spalte) angedeutet ist. Die größte Gefahr sollte für NHRB vom Typ 2 bestehen. Diese Wasserkörper werden zumeist von Scottish Water nach einem Betriebsplan betrieben, der nicht von den ursprünglichen Designingenieuren als Standardoperation vorgesehen war. Viele dieser manuell betriebenen und häufig kleineren Talsperren sind immer randvoll, und laufen ständig über. Aus Kostengründen wird auf einen aktiven Betrieb verzichtet. Diese unsachgemäße Praxis birgt ein zusätzliches Risiko für die Sicherheit dieser Bauwerke.

Ein Vergleich bezüglich der Nutzungskategorien der untersuchten NHRB zeigt, dass sich die deutschen Becken durch Vielseitigkeit und großes Hochwasserrückhaltevermögen (62%) auszeichnen.

Die schottischen NHRB dienen derzeitig dem Hochwasserschutz nur zu 3%, da sie hauptsächlich für die Trinkwasserversorgung (40%) Verwendung finden. Scottish Water hat derzeit keine rechtliche Verpflichtung NHRB für den Hochwasserschutz zur Verfügung zu stellen. Die ausschließliche Verwendung für die Langzeitspeicherung von Wasser (13%) für die Trinkwasserversorgung und aus erholungsförderlichen Gründen ist relativ eindeutig. Die badischen Becken hingegen haben (abgesehen vom Hochwasserschutz) eher umweltschutzsteigernde (11%) und landschaftsbereichernde (8%) Nebenzwecke.

Ein Vergleich von wichtigen Parametern, die gezielt durch bauliche Maßnahmen verbessert worden sind, um der Anpassung an den Klimawechsel zu dienen, zeigt, dass Baden Schottland in dieser Hinsicht weit voraus ist: 24 deutsche NHRB im Vergleich zu nur einem schottischen NHRB wurden innerhalb von vier Jahren (Sommer 2006 bis Sommer 2010) entweder aufgerüstet (13 NHRB) oder neu gebaut (11 NHRB). Aufrüstungsmassnahmen schliessen die folgenden Arbeiten ein: Erhöhung des Dammes, Verbreitung des Dammes und Vergrösserung der Lehmschicht. Nur ein Überlauf in Zentral-Schottland wurde in diesem Zeitraum um einiges umgebaut. Diese Massnahmen führen zu höheren Stauvolumen und reduzieren die Gefahr von Dammbrüchen auf Grund von häufigeren und stärkeren Regenfällen.

Die Untersuchungen zeigen, dass Deutschland im Vergleich zum Vereinigten Königreich Hochwasserschutz in der Praxis ernster nimmt. Dies wird deutlich auf Grund der folgenden Beobachtungen bezüglich der schottischen Fallstudien:

- Der schottische Wasserversorger scheint den praktischen Hochwasserschutz derzeit nicht vorrangig zu behandeln.
- Schottische Gemeinden erhalten normalerweise nur wenig Zuschüsse für Hochwasserschutzmaßnahmen.
- Es gibt in Schottland eine verhältnismäβig geringe Anzahl von zweckgebundenen NHRB (3% verglichen mit 62%).
- Kein NHRB ist dort in der Regel trocken (0% verglichen mit 99%). Die meissten NHRB sind immer voll, and haben daher nur ein beschränktes Hochwasserrückhaltevolumen.
- Viele NHRB in Schottland werden nur selten renoviert (1% verglichen mit 9% in Baden).

4. Fazit und Vorschläge für weitere Forschungen

Die drei NHRB Typen 1, 4 und 6 wurden mit einer Gruppenanalyse für Baden identifiziert. Diese NHRB sind vornehmlich Hochwasserrückhaltebecken, die jedoch auch weitere Funktionen wie Umwelterhaltung und Landschaftsbereicherung haben können. Die schottischen NHRB sind jedoch überwiegend vom Typ 2, 3 and 5. Die Überlappung zwischen schottischen und badischen NHRB ist ausgesprochen gering. Traditionelle Hochwasserrückhaltebecken (Typ 2) sind im Wesentlichen ehemalige Trinkwasserspeicher, die die schottische Landschaft bestimmen. Diese Anlagen könnten einem kostengünstigen Hochwasserschutz dienen. Ihr Wasserstand ist jedoch derzeit nicht optimal reguliert.

Im Vergleich zu Schottland haben NHRB in Baden schlechtere Dammzustände und daher hohe Dammbruchgefahrenwerte, aber niedrige Dammbruchrisikowerte. Dies kann damit erklärt werden, dass schottische NHRB vergleichsweise hohe Dämme und große Wasservolumen haben. Badische

NHRB sind hingegen meistens leer. Darüber hinaus sind in Schottland viele Anlagen in städtischen Räumen zu finden. Auf Grund von räumlichen Einschränkungen haben viele NHRB in verbauten Gegenden hohe Quotienten von Dammbruchrisiko über Dammbruchgefahr. Ungefähr 9% aller deutschen NHRB wurden zwischen 2006 und 2010 renoviert. Darüber hinaus wurden viele neue NHRB in Baden gebaut. Schottland hingegen ist noch nicht auf den Klimawechsel vorbereitet.

Das vorgestellte Verfahren zur Beurteilung von Dämmen ist schnell, kostengünstig und kann hohe Dammbruchrisiken effizient bestimmen. Die hohe potenzielle Ungenauigkeit der Expertenmethode ist jedoch ein Nachteil.

Die Wirkung von Dammbrüchen bezüglich des Schadenspotenzials weit unterhalb der Becken wurde in diesem Artikel nicht berücksichtigt. Es ist davon eventuell auszugehen, dass ein Dammbruch mit Hochwasserwellen anderer Gewässer unterhalb des Beckens zusammentrifft. Dies bedeutet, dass ein Dammversagen, je nach Größe des Damms, sich sehr weit unterhalb noch auswirken kann. Weitere Forschungen zu dieser Problematik sind erwünscht.

Dank

Das 'Europäische Regionale Entwicklungsprojekt IVB 2007-2013 Nordsee Region Programm' unterstützt finanziell das Forschungsprojekt 'Nachhaltige Hochwasserrückhaltebecken zur Kontrolle von Überflutungen und diffusen Einträgen', welches Teil der Gruppe 'Strategische Allianz für Wasserunterhaltungsaktionen' ist. Die Alexander von Humboldt Stiftung förderte Miklas Scholz in den Jahren 2006 und 2010 mit einem Forschungsaufenthalt an der Albert-Ludwigs-Universität Freiburg. Die Autoren danken Ihren Gastgebern, insbesondere Herrn Werner Konold und Herrn Reiner Dietrich.

Literatur

1. EC. Hochwasserrichtlinie 2007/60/EC des Europäischen Parlamentes vom 23.10.2007. *Official Journal of the European Community* (EC) (Eur Lex) **2007**, Ref L 288/27-34.
2. Flood Risk Management (Scotland) Act 2009 (asp 6). Scottish Government, Edinburg, Schottland, Vereinigtes Königreich, 2009.
3. Office of Public Sector Information: Revised Statute from the UK Statute Law Database. Reservoirs Act 1975 (c.23). Office of Public Sector Information, London, England, Vereinigtes Königreich, 2010. http://www.opsi.gov.uk/RevisedStatutes/Acts/ukpga/1975/cukpga_19750023_en_1.
4. DIN. Deutsche Norm DIN 19700 Stauanlagen. Deutsches Institut für Normung (DIN), Beuth Verlag GmbH, Berlin, Deutschland, 2000.
5. Scholz, M.; Sadowski, A.J. Conceptual classification model for sustainable flood retention basins. *Journal of Environmental Management* **2009**, 90, 624–633.
6. Scholz M. *Wetland Systems – Storm Water Management Control*. Springer, Berlin, Deutschland, 2010.
7. SAWA. SAWA - A Strategic Alliance in the North Sea Region. – Strategic Alliance for Water Management Actions (SAWA) project information. SAWA, Hamburg, Deutschland, 2010. Available online: http://www.sawa-project.eu/ (accessed on 1 November 2011).

8. ATV-DVWK. *Hochwasserrückhaltebecken – Probleme und Anforderungen aus wasserwirtschaftlicher und ökologischer Sicht.* Deutsche Vereinigung für Wasserwirtschaft, Abwasser und Abfall e.V. (ATV-DVWK) und Gesellschaft zur Förderung der Abwassertechnik e.V., Hennef, Deutschland, 2001.
9. Evans, S.Y.; Hohl, A. Reservoir inundation mapping and emergency planning. In *Proceedings of Water and Environment 2010*, The Chartered Institution of Water and Environmental Management's Annual Conference. Olympia Conference Centre, London, England, Vereinigtes Königreich, 2010.
10. Merz, B. *Hochwasserrisiken – Möglichkeiten und Grenzen der Risikoabschätzung.* Schweizerbart'sche Verlagsbuchhandlung, Stuttgart, Deutschland, 2006.
11. Bassett, D.; Pettit, A.; Anderson, C.; Grace, P. Scottish Flood Defence Asset Database – Final Report. Jeremy Benn Associates Consulting for the Scottish Government, Edinburg, Schottland, Vereinigtes Königreich, 2007. Available online: http://www.scotland.gov.uk/ Publications/2007/08/20111904/0 (accessed on 1 November 2011).
12. Meteorological Office. Fact Sheet 4. Climate of the United Kingdom. Meteorological Office, Exeter, England, Vereinigtes Königreich. S. 17, 2007.
13. Foster, G.C.; Chiverrell, R.C.; Harvey, A.M.; Dearing, J.A.; Dunsford, H. Catchment hydro-geomorphological responses to environmental change in the Southern Uplands of Scotland. *Holocene* **2008**, 18, 935–950.
14. EDINA. Various maps and datasets. EDINA, Edinburgh, Schottland, Vereinigtes Königreich, 2010. www.edina.ac.uk.
15. SEPA. Indicative River and Coastal Flooding Map. Scottish Environmental Protection Agency (SEPA), Edinburg, Schottland, Vereinigtes Königreich, 2010. http://www.multimap.com/clients/ browse.cgi?client=sepa&X=312000&Y=723000&width=550&height=450&scale=25000&coords ys=gb&nosnap=true&overlay=layer1 (accessed on 1 November 2011).
16. McMinn, W.R.; Yang, Q.; Scholz, M. Classification and assessment of water bodies as adaptive structural measures for flood risk management planning. *Journal of Environmental Management* **2010**, 91, 1855-1863.
17 Scholz, M. *Guidance Manual: Rapid Assessment Methodology for Survey of Water Bodies including Sustainable Flood Retention Basins (SFRB).* The University of Salford, Salford, England, Vereinigtes Königreich, 2011.
18. Kaufman, L.; Rousseeuw, P.J. *Finding Groups in Data – An Introduction to Cluster Analysis.* John Wiley and Sons, New York, New York, Vereinigte Staaten von Amerika, 2005.
19. Pratap, R. *Getting Started with MATLAB: A Quick Introduction for Scientists and Engineers.* Oxford University Press, Oxford, England, Vereinigtes Königreich, 2002.

Water **2013**, *5*, 1441-1456; doi:10.3390/w5031441

OPEN ACCESS

water

ISSN 2073-4441
www.mdpi.com/journal/water

Article

Computing Air Demand Using the Takagi–Sugeno Model for Dam Outlets

Mohammad Zounemat-Kermani [1] and Miklas Scholz [2,*]

[1] Department of Water Engineering, Shahid Bahonar University of Kerman, Kerman, Iran; E-Mail: zounemat@uk.ac.ir

[2] Civil Engineering Research Group, The University of Salford, School of Computing, Science and Engineering, Newton Building, Salford, Greater Manchester M5 4WT, UK

* Author to whom correspondence should be addressed; E-Mail: m.scholz@salford.ac.uk; Tel.: +44-161-295-5921; Fax: +44-161-295-5575.

Received: 12 July 2013; in revised form: 13 August 2013 / Accepted: 13 September 2013 / Published: 23 September 2013

Abstract: An adaptive neuro-fuzzy inference system (ANFIS) was developed using the subtractive clustering technique to study the air demand in low-level outlet works. The ANFIS model was employed to calculate vent air discharge in different gate openings for an embankment dam. A hybrid learning algorithm obtained from combining back-propagation and least square estimate was adopted to identify linear and non-linear parameters in the ANFIS model. Empirical relationships based on the experimental information obtained from physical models were applied to 108 experimental data points to obtain more reliable evaluations. The feed-forward Levenberg-Marquardt neural network (LMNN) and multiple linear regression (MLR) models were also built using the same data to compare model performances with each other. The results indicated that the fuzzy rule-based model performed better than the LMNN and MLR models, in terms of the simulation performance criteria established, as the root mean square error, the Nash–Sutcliffe efficiency, the correlation coefficient and the *Bias*.

Keywords: dam; fuzzy model; outlet works; reservoir; subtractive clustering; Takagi-Sugeno; vent air discharge

Nomenclature

a_i	=	parameter of the consequent part of a rule
A	=	Area of gate (cm^2)

A_n^i	=	membership function
ANFIS	=	adaptive neuro-fuzzy inference system
ANN	=	artificial neural network, also neural network
b_i	=	parameter of the consequent part of a rule
Bias	=	statistic test representing the mean of all the individual errors
β	=	aeration coefficient
c	=	parameter of the consequent part of a rule
D_i	=	density measure
D_1^*	=	first cluster center
Fr	=	Froude number
H	=	Head of water (cm)
k	=	index of each fold in the *K*-fold cross-validation
K	=	total number of folds in the *K*-fold cross-validation, and the number of fuzzy 'if-then' rules
LMNN	=	Feed-forward Levenberg-Marquardt artificial neural network
Mallows CP	=	coefficient of the Mallows statistic
MLR	=	multiple linear regression
$\mu_{A_j^i}(x_j)$	=	membership degree of the *j*th input x_j for the *i*th rule
N	=	number of observations
NSE	=	Nash–Sutcliffe efficiency (%)
O	=	opening (%)
Q_a	=	air flow rate (L/s), also called air demand
O_i	=	measured values of a variable
Q_w	=	Water discharge (L/s)
r	=	Pearson product moment correlation coefficient, also called correlation coefficient
R_0	=	positive constant called the cluster radius
r_a	=	influential radius for clustering the data space
r_b	=	positive constant; $r_b > r_a$, typically $r_b = 1.5\ r_a$, where r_a is another positive constant
RMSE	=	root mean square error
S_i	=	computed (by model) values of a variable
Te	=	true error
TS	=	Takagi–Sugeno model
u_i	=	normalized degree of fulfilment of the antecedent clause of a rule
V_a	=	air velocity (cm/s)
X	=	Input vector
x_1^*	=	data point with the highest density measure
x_n	=	Input variable
x_j	=	*j*th input variable in the *n* dimensional input data space
y_i	=	output variable

1. Introduction

1.1. Background

Gated tunnels in dams can be used for various purposes, such as regulating the surface of reservoir water, drawdown of the reservoir, sediment flushing, and flood release [1]. For most dams, flow regulation can be performed from a low level outlet consisting of a closed conduit with a slide gate or valve. Outlet works are devices used to release and regulate water flow from a dam usually for irrigational purposes. Such devices may consist of one or more pipes or tunnels through the embankment of the dam, directing water, often under high pressure, to the river downstream [2]. When the outlet gate is placed inside the conduit, reduced pressure, which may causes cavitation, is often measured just downstream of the gate.

Diffusing air into the flow can eliminate cavitation damages. Aeration will also improve the mean pressure and reduce the intensity of hydrodynamic pressure fluctuations [3]. Therefore, to minimize these effects, aerators are recommended just downstream of gates to introduce air into the flow [4].

A proper size for the air-vent pipe should be considered to allow for the sufficient amount of air flow rate. The air flow rate Q_a refers to the amount of air drawn into the air vent. Air flow can be diffused into the water flow through turbulent mixing. The process of air and water mixing can be applied by utilizing a separate air phase above the water surface of the pipe outlet [4].

Insufficient research has been conducted on the air and water flow properties of high-velocity waters discharging at the downstream end of tunnels. Kalinske and Robertson [5] were one of the first researchers who have studied the air demand in closed conduits as a function of the Froude number. Other researchers proposed related but alternative methods for predicting air demand discharge [6–11].

1.2. Purpose, Rationale, Objectives, and Boundary Conditions

The purpose of this study is to apply an adaptive network-based model for air demand estimations regarding low-level outlet works. This work also aims to determine if the use of artificial neural networks (ANN) and simpler models, such as multiple regression models for air demand estimations, could be justified.

In this study, a fuzzy rule-based model was developed for estimating air flow rate in two stages. In the first stage, local sub-regions were determined by analysing the pattern of input data. The regions can be determined intuitively, requiring often too many trial and error attempts. Therefore, alternative clustering techniques were used in this study to find the sub-sets of an input space that characterized possible occurrences of the data. In the second stage, a local model was built for each cluster. The Mamdani's model, the Takagi–Sugeno's (TS) model, and the standard additive model can be applied at this stage. In this study, the TS model was chosen, because it can solve complex and high-dimensional problems relying only on a few rules.

In general, artificial intelligence models such as an adaptive neuro-fuzzy inference system (ANFIS) and ANN do not need any *a priori* assumptions to be made on the nature (linear or non-linear) of the relationship between the response variable and explanatory variables. However, the successful application of artificial intelligence in modelling requires good comprehension of the effect of some internal parameters related to the input variables, model structure, training steps, and decision-making process. The dam geometries considered in this research involved a slide gate installed on the sloping upstream face of an embankment dam, followed by a vertical elbow where the flow entered the conduit, as shown in Figure 1. The air demand varied with gate and conduit geometry, gate opening, and water discharge passing through the gate. Hence, these parameters were considered potential input variables for the ANFIS, ANN, and multiple regression models.

Figure 1. Typical representation of a low-level outlet works.

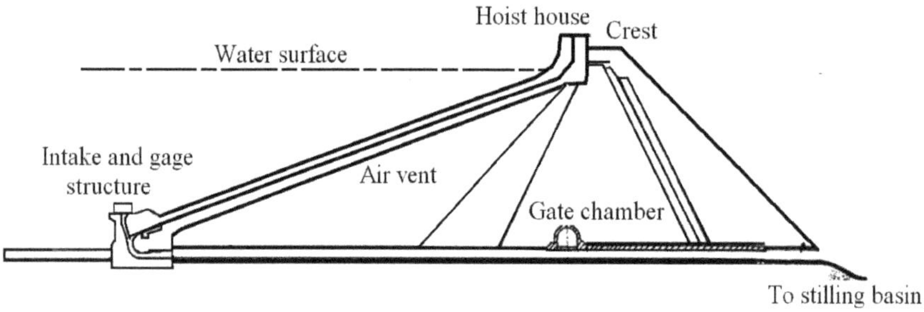

2. Materials and Methods

2.1. Experimental Data

The 108 data used in this study were obtained from a study published by Tullis and Larchar [4]. In an effort to develop a better understanding of head-discharge relationships and air-venting requirements for inclined slide gates, a laboratory-scale model (Figure 2) of low-level outlet works representative of small- to medium-sized embankment dam applications was constructed at the Utah Water Research Laboratory, Utah State University. A schematic representation of the experimental set-up is shown in Figure 2b. The model shown in Figure 2a consisted of an elevated steel tank (approximately 1.8 m long, 1.8 m tall and 0.9 m wide). Two acrylic slide gates (round and rectangular) were constructed and subsequently tested. The gate designs were based on commercially available slide gates. The data collected for each test condition included the area of gate (A), opening percentage (O%), head of water (H), and water discharge (Q_w) for outlet conditions and the air velocity (V_a) in the supply line (vented only).

Table 1. Design parameters after [4].

Extremes	Area (cm^2)	Gate Opening (%)	Head (cm)	Water Discharge (L/s)	Air Discharge (L/s)
Minimum	45.6 (round gate)	10	13.8	0.3	0.0
Maximum	58.1 (rectangular gate)	100	168.5	25.3	7.3

In the experiment, three different flow conditions at the downstream end of the discharge pipe were considered: (1) non-vented flow; (2) vented flow with a free-discharging pipe outlet; and (3) vented flow with a submerged pipe outlet [4]. The data were collected at 10%, 30%, 50%, 60%, 70%, 90%, and 100% gate openings. A gate opening value represents the proportion (%) of the total linear travel distance of the gate. Table 1 summarizes the minimum and maximum design parameters.

Figure 2. (**a**) Schematic of lab-scale low-level outlet works; and (**b**) experimental set-up after [4].

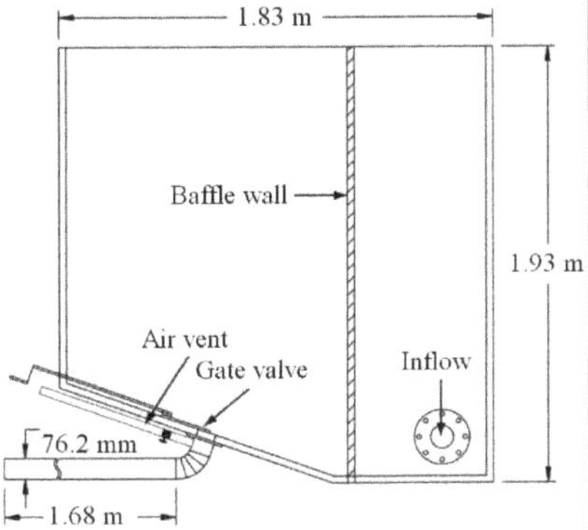

(**a**)

(**b**)

2.2. Empirical Relationships for Estimating Discharge Air Vents

Research has traditionally concentrated on the flow aeration downstream of bottom outlet gates. Studies are usually based on experimental information obtained from physical models. Most of the published air-venting studies are limited to large-dam outlet geometries [4]. In order to validate the experimental relationships for low-level outlets, formulas related to large dam outlets were considered for determining the air demand in this study.

The Froude Number is a dimensionless parameter defined as the ratio of a characteristic velocity to a gravitational wave velocity [Equation (1)]. Kalinske and Robertson [5] reported results on air demand for situations where a hydraulic jump was formed in the downstream conduit. Based on their results, the aeration coefficient (β) for the condition of a hydraulic jump was suggested as a function of the Froude number (Fr) as shown in Equation (2).

$$Fr = \frac{V}{\sqrt{g.Y_c}} \tag{1}$$

where Fr is the Froude number; V is the mean velocity of water; Y_c is the flow depth at the contracted section; and g is the gravitational acceleration.

$$\beta = 0.0066\left(Fr - 1\right)^{1.4} \tag{2}$$

The aeration coefficient (β) can also be expressed as the vent air discharge over the water flow discharge ($\beta = Q_a/Q_w$). Campbell and Guyton [6] presented Equation (3) for the air demand ratio using the Froude number in the contracted section downstream of the gate [12].

$$\beta = 0.04\left(Fr - 1\right)^{0.85} \tag{3}$$

The U.S. Army Corps of Engineers [7] published Equation (4), which is based on prototype observations. Equation (4) is rather similar to Equation (3).

$$\beta = 0.03\left(Fr - 1\right)^{1.06} \tag{4}$$

In another experiment, Sharma [10] verified prototype data and compared results with the empirical equations in the water flow of conduits. Equation (5) directly relates the aeration coefficient to the Froude number according to Sharma's experiments.

$$\beta = 0.09Fr \tag{5}$$

2.3. Adaptive Network-Based Fuzzy Inference System

The ANFIS integrates the features of fuzzy systems and neural networks. Thereafter, it has the potential to capture the benefits of both in a single framework. Membership functions are the central concept of fuzzy set theory, which numerically represents the degree to which a given element belongs to a fuzzy set [13].

In order to avoid over-fitting of the ANFIS model, an early stopping technique has been applied. In this method, the validation set can be used to detect the time in which over-fitting starts during the supervised training. At this stage, training is stopped before convergence to avoid over-fitting [14].

2.4. Takagi–Sugeno's Model

The TS model was published by Takagi and Sugeno in 1985 [15]. A TS fuzzy model consists of four major elements of member functions, internal functions, rules, and outputs [16]. The TS fuzzy models are quasi-linear in nature, resulting in smooth transitions between linear sub-models [17]. Figure 3a illustrates the typical structure of the ANFIS model. For a multi-input and single-output model, the typical fuzzy rule of a TS model is shown in Equation (6).

Figure 3. Schematic representation of the (**a**) adaptive neural-based fuzzy inference system; and the (**b**) feed-forward Levenberg-Marquardt artificial neural network structure.

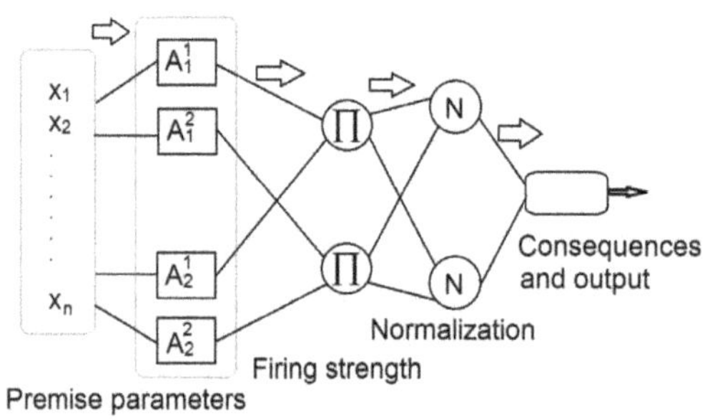

(**a**)

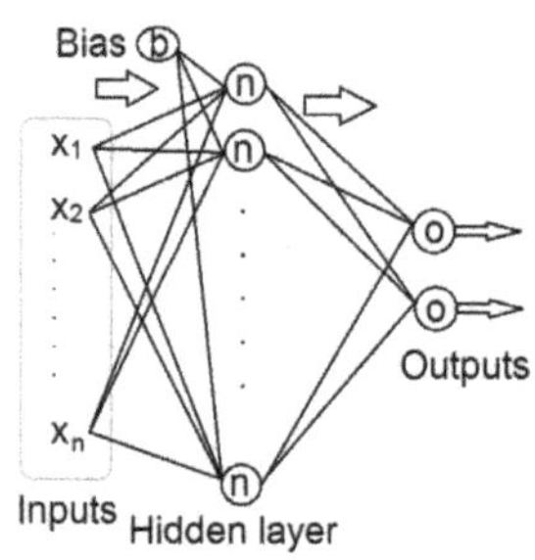

(**b**)

$$\begin{aligned} &Rule_i : If\left((x_1 \; is \; A_1^i) \; and \; (x_2 \; is \; A_2^i) \; and \ldots (x_n \; is \; A_n^i)\right) \\ &Then\left(y_i = f_i(x_1, x_2, \ldots, x_n)\right) \; for \; i = 1, 2, \ldots, K \end{aligned} \tag{6}$$

where x_n is the input variable, A_n^i is the membership function (MF) and K is the number of fuzzy if-then rules. The consequent part of the rule base shows the rule output. In a TS fuzzy model, rule consequents are usually taken to be either crisp numbers or linear functions of the input parameters [Equation (7); layer 1].

$$y_i = f_i(x_1, x_2, \ldots, x_n) = a_1^i x_1 + a_2^i x_2 + \ldots + a_n^i x_n + c^i$$
$$y_i = a_1^i x_1 + a_2^i x_2 + \ldots + a_n^i x_n + c^i \tag{7}$$

where y_i is the output variable, and a_i and c are parameters of the consequent parts of the rule shown in Equation (6). The number of rules is indicated by K, and A_i is the antecedent fuzzy set of the i-th rule defined by the membership function $\mu_{A_j^i}$ (premise parameters in Figure 3a). The degree of matching between the input parameters and rule [Equation (6)] is called the rule firing strength (Figure 3a), which is normally defined as an and-conjunction by means of the product operator [Equation (8); layer 2].

$$\alpha_i = \prod_{j=1}^{n} \mu_{A_j^i}(x_j) \tag{8}$$

where x_j is the j-th input variable in the n dimensional input data space and $\mu_{A_j^i}(x_j)$ is the membership degree of the j-th input x_j for the i-th rule. For the input x, the total output y of the TS model is computed by aggregating the contributions of individual rules [17]. Therefore, the overall fuzzy system output can be obtained by Equation (9). Consequents and outputs are shown in Figure 3a.

$$y = \sum_{i=1}^{K} u_i(x).y_i \tag{9}$$

where u_i is the normalized degree of fulfilment of the antecedent clause of rule shown in Equation (6) [13,18]. The normalized degree of fulfilment can be expressed by Equation (10). The normalization layer is shown in Figure 3a.

$$u_i(x) = \frac{\alpha_i(x)}{\sum_{i=1}^{K} \alpha_i(x)} \tag{10}$$

2.5. Hybrid Algorithm

Two learning methods are generally used in the adaptive TS model to specify the relationship between input and output and to determine the optimized distribution of MF. The TS model utilizes a combination of the least-square method and the back-propagation gradient descent method for training the FIS membership function parameters to identify patterns hidden in a given training dataset [19–22].

Several methods can be utilized for setting up the MF of the ANFIS (e.g., grid partition and subtractive clustering). Regarding the combination of grid partition and ANFIS, grid partition divides the input vector into a number of fuzzy regions using paralleled axis. However, in this method, fuzzy rules increase exponentially when the amount of input variables increases. Therefore, the application of grid partition in ANFIS is not recommended for large input variable problems [23].

In this study, a subtractive clustering method was used to initialize the Gaussian type of MF. The simulation begins by generating the fuzzy rules using subtractive clustering, which is based on a measure of the density of data points in the feature space. This approach is applied to determine the number of rules and antecedent membership functions by considering each cluster centre as a fuzzy rule. An example of how the clusters are identified in the second (gate opening) and the fourth (water discharge) input dimensions as well as the third (head of water) and fourth (water discharge) input dimensions of the input space is shown in Figure 4.

Figure 4. Cluster centres using the centre of gravity method in (**a**) input 2 [gate opening (*O*)] and input 4 [water discharge (Q_w)]; and in (**b**) input 3 [head of water (*H*)] and input 4 (Q_w).

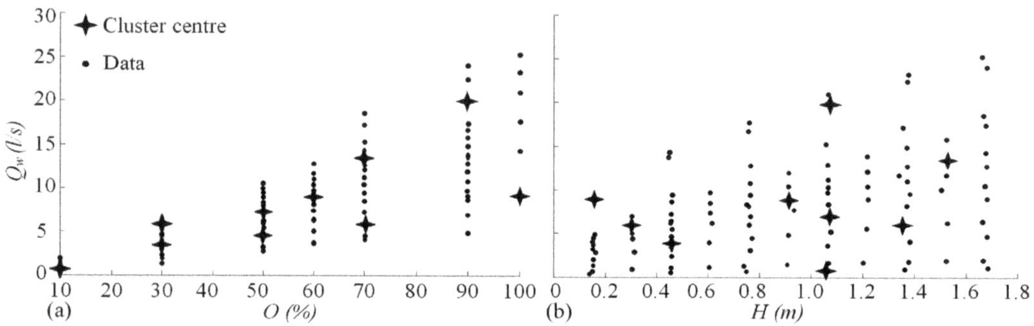

Desirable variables of the membership functions are optimized for the identification data set through the back-propagation procedure while a linear least squares method is used for calculating the consequent parameters. Parameters associated with membership functions change through the learning process and the gradient vector facilitates the calculation of these parameters. Each time when the gradient vector is obtained, an optimization procedure is performed to adjust parameters for reducing errors [24].

2.6. Input Data Determination

The selection of appropriate input variables is an important consideration in heuristic modeling. Inappropriate input variable selection may cause unsuitable effects on the modelling results. Several remedies were reported to overcome these problems including autocorrelation and partial autocorrelation function analysis, linear and non-linear cross-correlation analysis, spectral analysis, and partial mutual information [25,26].

In the study, input variables are selected using a stepwise selection procedure. A stepwise regression method (*i.e.*, step-by-step iterative construction of a regression model that involves automatic selection of independent variables) was applied to explore relationships among the collected data. The Mallows statistic was used as a criterion to select a suitable multiple regression model. Mallows CP is a powerful selection procedure in stepwise regression [27]. The result of stepwise regression according to Mallows CP coefficient is tabulated in Table 2.

According to findings shown in Table 2, the area representing the shape of the slide gate (round or rectangular) was found to be the most significant variable for explaining air discharge demand.

Table 2. Stepwise regression results for the four independent variables area of gate (*A*), head of water (*H*), opening percentage (*O*) and water discharge (Q_w) against the dependent parameter of air flow rate (Q_a).

Step	**1**	**2**	**3**	**4**
Parameter	*A* (cm^2)	*H* (cm)	Q_w (L/s)	*O* (%)
Mallows CP	35.3	25.2	17.9	5.0

However, water head and water discharge followed by gate opening percentage were also found to be significant as input variables. Therefore, both artificial intelligence models (fuzzy and ANN) as well as the regression model were tested using all available explanatory variables.

2.7. Comparing Model Performance

The performance of the developed models can be evaluated using several statistical tests that describe the errors associated with the model. After calibrating each model structure using the testing data set, the performance can then be evaluated in terms of statistical measures of goodness of fit. In order to provide an indication of goodness of fit between the observed and estimated values, the root mean square error (*RMSE*), correlation coefficient (*r*), Nash–Sutcliffe efficiency (*NSE*), and *Bias* were calculated and evaluated. The *RMSE* evaluates the variance of errors independently from the sample size, which is given by Equation (11).

$$RMSE = \sqrt{\tfrac{1}{N}\sum_{i=1}^{N}(S_i - O_i)^2} \tag{11}$$

where S_i and O_i represent the model computed and measured values of the variable; and N indicates the number of observations. The smaller the *RMSE*, the better is the performance of the model. The *Bias* represents the mean of all the individual errors and indicates whether the model overestimates or underestimates the dependent variable. This statistic is calculated as shown in Equation (12) [28,29].

$$Bias = \frac{1}{N}\sum_{i=1}^{N}(S_i - O_i) \tag{12}$$

The *NSE*, which is a normalized statistic, determines the relative magnitude of residual variance compared to the observed variance and gives an indication of how well the observed and simulated results fit to a 1:1 line (line of agreement). This statistic can be obtained via Equation (13) [30].

$$NSE = 1 - \left[\sum_{i=1}^{n}(S_i - O_i)^2 / \sum_{i=1}^{n}(O_i - \bar{O}_i)^2\right] \tag{13}$$

NSE ranges from $-\infty$ to 1. Essentially, the closer *NSE* is to 1, the more accurate the model is likely to be. The correlation coefficient (*r*) is based on the Pearson product moment correlation coefficient of the simulated and observed flow series, which is obtained via Equation (14).

$$r = \left[\frac{\sum_{i=1}^{n}(O_i - \bar{O}_i)(S_i - \bar{S}_i)}{\sqrt{\sum_{i=1}^{n}(O_i - \bar{O}_i^{o})^2}\sqrt{\sum_{i=1}^{n}(S_i - \bar{S}^{s})^2}}\right] \tag{14}$$

The correlation coefficient is a measure of strength of the model in developing a relationship between input and output variables. The higher the *r* value (with 1 being the maximum value), the better is the performance of the model.

2.8. K-fold Cross-Validation

Cross validation techniques tend to focus on not using the entire data set when building a model. They are applied for assessing how the results of statistical analysis would generalize to an independent data set. In addition, they are applied for the settings in which the goal is estimating how accurately a predictive model would perform in practice. In *K*-fold cross-validation, the data are split into *K* parts (folds) with *K*-1 parts as the training set and one part as the testing set.

The cross-validation process is then repeated *K* times. Once the model is built using the left cases (often called the training data set), the cases that are removed (referred to as the testing data set) can be used to test the performance of the model on the 'unseen' data (*i.e.*, the testing set). The *K* results from the folds can then be averaged (or otherwise combined) to produce a single estimation [31].

The advantage of this strategy is that all data have the chance to be trained and evaluated, giving the true error (T_e) for each error criterion (*RMSE*, *Bias*, *NSE*, and *r*). Equation (15) shows the true error of the *RMSE*:

$$RMSE_{Te} = \frac{1}{K}\left(\sum_{k=1}^{K} RMSE_k\right) \tag{15}$$

where *K* is the total number of folds and *k* is the index of each fold. In this study, the data set was divided randomly into four training and testing sub-sets by the cross validation method as a systematic process to obtain effective and sensitive modelling results.

3. Results and Discussion

3.1. Applications

It is expected that training data sets should cover all the characteristics of the scientific problem to obtain correct model estimations. Therefore, the data set was divided into four training and testing sub-sets by using the cross validation method as a systematic methodology to obtain effective and sensitive model findings. To get more reliable evaluations of performance of the ANFIS model, MLR given in Equation (16) was established for the 108 experimental data [32]. As with the fuzzy approach, the four-fold cross validation method was used again.

$$Q_a = \left[-5.63 - 0.216\,Q_w + 1.87\,H + 0.033\,O\% + 883\,A\right] \tag{16}$$

The best model structure having four input variables was also trained and tested by ANN. The feed-forward Levenberg-Marquardt ANN network (LMNN) was used in this study. The LMNN model was trained and tested using the same non-transformed data set. The error back-propagation algorithm and tangent activation function were used for the training/testing of the LMNN model. Figure 3b shows the typical schematic representation of a LM back-propagation neural network. The number of hidden layers and the hidden neurons within a layer, the learning rate (0.1), the coefficient of momentum (0.5) and epochs (1000) were selected by applying a trial and error method during the model training phase. The structure of the LMNN model consisted of eleven hidden neurons within one hidden layer. Details on the development of the LMNN model were presented in previous reports [14,33]. Table 3 summarizes the comparison of results of the ANFIS, LMNN, MLR, and empirical models.

Comparing the estimation models from Table 3, it can be seen that *RMSE* values with respect to the ANFIS model were much lower compared to the MLR and empirical models for each fold. The *RMSE* values of the ANFIS model were also lower than those for the LMNN model. In addition, values for the *NSE* efficiency and correlation coefficients of the ANFIS model were higher than those for the

LMNN, MLR and empirical models for each fold. However, it should be noted that a trial and error procedure had to be performed for the LMNN model to develop the best network structure while such a procedure was not required for developing the ANFIS model. Moreover, in this study, the ANFIS model was trained using just 30 epochs while the LMNN model required 60 epochs. The results suggest that the ANFIS method was superior to the LMNN method in estimating the vent air discharge.

Table 3. Values of model performance indices and error functions for the testing.

Error Criteria	Testing Data Set	ANFIS	LMNN	MLR	Sharma	U.S. Army	Campbell	Kalinske and Robertson
RMSE	1st fold	0.242	0.359	1.024	6.628	2.233	2.03	3.325
	2nd fold	0.221	0.315	0.734	5.957	1.912	1.669	3.147
	3rd fold	0.286	0.469	0.867	7.291	2.272	1.992	3.661
	4th fold	0.265	0.436	1.361	5.608	2.096	1.963	2.976
NSE	1st fold	0.959	0.912	0.269	−29.608	−2.474	−1.873	−6.707
	2nd fold	0.912	0.871	0.453	−52.135	−4.48	−3.175	−13.834
	3rd fold	0.923	0.855	0.326	−78.614	−9.233	−6.868	−25.577
	4th fold	0.923	0.850	0.440	−9.777	−0.506	−0.321	−2.036
Bias	1st fold	−0.025	0.021	−0.193	4.994	1.142	0.965	2.083
	2nd fold	−0.091	−0.183	0.236	4.497	1.210	1.023	2.152
	3rd fold	0.123	−0.338	0.053	5.357	1.321	1.119	2.358
	4th fold	−0.072	−0.099	−0.131	4.099	0.763	0.588	1.668
r	1st fold	0.981	0.949	0.546	−0.137	−0.145	−0.134	−0.16
	2nd fold	0.981	0.965	0.678	0.063	0.046	0.068	0.009
	3rd fold	0.962	0.942	0.654	−0.182	−0.174	−0.164	−0.188
	4th fold	0.972	0.93	0.632	0.139	0.142	0.145	0.125

Notes: ANFIS, adaptive neural-based fuzzy inference system; LMNN, feed-forward Levenberg-Marquardt artificial neural network; MLR, multiple linear regression; *RMSE*, root mean square error; *NSE*, Nash–Sutcliffe efficiency; *Bias*, test statistic representing the mean of all the individual errors; *r*, Pearson product moment correlation coefficient.

Scatter plots are displayed in Figures 5 and 6 for the training and testing data sets, respectively. Figure 6 shows the observed vent air discharge on the x-axis against the simulated vent air discharge on the *y*-axis for the Campbell and Kalinske-Robertson's empirical relationships.

In each of the scatter plots, a perfect estimation was placed on the 1:1 line. The ANFIS simulation (Figure 6) fell relatively close to the 1:1 line, except for two points of the testing data set. It is interesting to note that air discharges below 1 L/s were over-simulated by empirical and MLR models whereas air discharges above 2 L/s were under-simulated. The LMNN (no figures shown) and ANFIS estimated air discharges were distributed evenly on both sides of the line of agreement. However, the data spread was more pronounced for the LMNN than for the ANFIS method.

Figure 5. Comparing the results of Campbell and Kalinske-Robertson's empirical models *versus* the observations (1st fold).

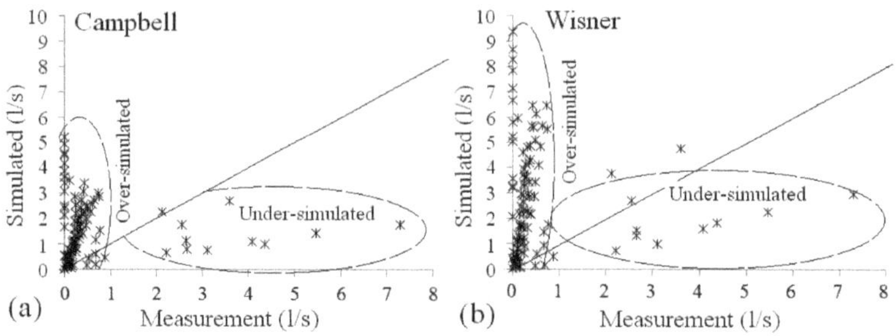

Figure 6. Comparing the results of adaptive neural-based fuzzy inference system (ANFIS) and multiple linear regression (MLR) models *versus* the observations (testing set of 1st fold).

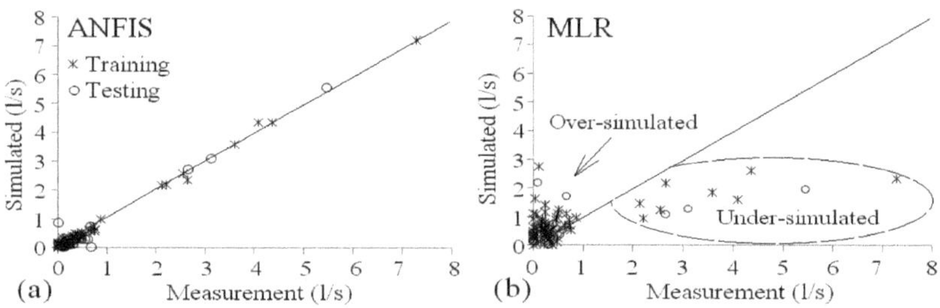

3.2. Assessing Empirical, ANFIS, MLR, and LMNN Models

For comparison, performance data of the ANFIS model against the corresponding MLR and empirical models are presented in Table 4 using true error values. It is evident that the ANFIS model was by far more accurate than the empirical models and considerably more accurate than the MLR and LMNN models in terms of their simulation accuracy of the true error criteria. The ANFIS model simulated the significant air discharge parameters with an acceptable accuracy. The result of the *Bias* index indicated that all empirical relationships highly overestimated air discharges (e.g., $Bias_{TE}$ for Sharma = 4.7) while the LMNN model slightly underestimated air discharges ($Bias_{TE} = -0.15$). ANFIS and MLR had normal tendencies with negligible magnitude for *Bias*. The overall average values for *NSE* were slightly negative.

Comparing the estimation models with each other, it can be seen that the values of $RMSE_{Te}$ for the ANFIS model (test/0.254 and train/0.186) were lower than those for the LMNN (0.395/0.192) and MLR (0.997/0.907) models and much lower than those for the empirical models (e.g., Sharma: 6.37) for both the testing and training data sets. It appears that the NSE_{Te} of the ANFIS model (test/0.929 and train 0.982) was higher compared to the LMNN, MLR, and empirical models. In addition, the correlation coefficients of the ANFIS model (0.974/0.991) were higher than those of the LMNN (0.946/0.987), MLR (0.627/0.612) and empirical (e.g., Sharma: −0.029) models for both the testing and training sets. It should be noted that a trial and error procedure has to be performed for the LMNN model in order to develop the best network structure, while such a procedure is not required when developing the ANFIS model.

Table 4. Performance statistics for the adaptive neural-based fuzzy inference system (ANFIS), feed-forward Levenberg-Marquardt artificial neural network (LMNN), multiple linear regression (MLR), and empirical models using true error (T_e).

Model	Testing set				Training set			
	$RMSE_{Te}$	NSE_{Te}	$Bias_{Te}$	r_{Te}	$RMSE_{Te}$	NSE_{Te}	$Bias_{Te}$	r_{Te}
ANFIS	0.254	0.929	−0.016	0.974	0.186	0.982	−0.0003	0.991
LMNN	0.395	0.872	−0.150	0.946	0.192	0.971	−0.0007	0.987
MLR	0.997	0.372	−0.009	0.627	0.907	0.375	−0.003	0.612
Sharma	6.371	−42.534	4.737	−0.029				
U.S. Army	2.128	−4.173	1.109	−0.033				
Campbell	1.914	−3.059	0.924	−0.021				
Kalinske and Robertson	3.277	−12.039	2.065	−0.053				

Notes: *RMSE*, root mean square error; *NSE*, Nash–Sutcliffe efficiency; *Bias*, test statistic representing the mean of all the individual errors; *r*, Pearson product moment correlation coefficient.

For the ANFIS model, NSE_{Te} is 0.93, which corresponds to a perfectly modeled match to the observed data, indicating the superiority of the ANFIS model compared to both the LMNN and MLR approaches. Negative values of *NSE* indicated that the observed mean was a better predictor than the model. Thereafter, all the empirical models failed to simulate the air discharges properly according to the *NSE* criteria. In general, the results suggested that the ANFIS method is superior to the LMNN, MLR, and empirical methods for the purpose of simulating vent air discharges.

3.3. Comparison between Empirical and Computational Methods

According to empirical relationships, the air demand flow at different gate opening scenarios was determined as function of the Froude number at a contracted section according to Equations (2–5). Findings have subsequently been compared with computational relations.

Results indicate that there are considerable differences between empirical and computational methods. This could be explained by differences in the input variables used by each method. The Froude number [Equation (1)], which is used by all empirical methods as the basic parameter for estimating the air demand, includes velocity (V) as a dependent parameter of water discharge, gate opening, and vent area ($V = Q_w/A \cdot O$) and the flow depth at the contracted section, which is a dependent parameter of water depth and gate opening ($Y_c = Y \cdot O$). Therefore, the empirical relationships are a function of four parameters: $f(Q_w, A, O, Y)$. According to the stepwise regression results (Table 2), the second most effective input variable of estimating air flow rate is head of water (H), which is not an input variable for the empirical relationships. This could be the reason for inferior results associated with the empirical relationships in comparison to the computational methods.

In addition to the empirical relationships, experimental data were used to assess the relationship based on non-linear regression between the Froude number (Fr) and the aeration coefficient (β). Equation (17) shows the best power relationship for the applied experimental data (Figure 7).

$$\beta = 0.08(Fr - 1)^{1.85} \tag{17}$$

Figure 7. Illustration of the power relationship between the Froude number (*Fr*) and the aeration coefficient (*β*) of the applied experimental data.

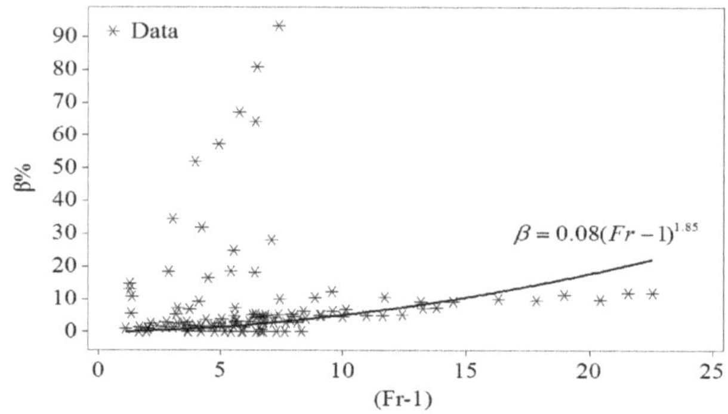

In order to evaluate the validity of the above relationships, the statistical measures *RMSE, NSE, Bias* and *r* were calculated. Results show that the *RMSE* = 1.24, *NSE* = −0.14, *Bias* = −0.00036 and *r* = −0.045. Comparing the performance of the obtained relationships to the empirical ones [Equations (2–5)] indicates their superiority (lower *RMSE*, *r* and normal tendency for *Bias*) to other empirical power relationships discussed in this study. However, it should be noted that artificial intelligence models (e.g., ANFIS and ANN) do not provide an explicit expression relating the independent with the dependent variables.

4. Conclusions

Fuzzy modelling and identification of measured data are effective tools for the approximation of uncertain non-linear systems. In this paper, a TS fuzzy inference system was successfully developed and applied for the simulation of air demand discharge in low-level dam outlet works. The subtractive clustering algorithm was utilized to extract the fuzzy model structure. In order to verify the performance of the proposed approach, empirical methods (Shrama, Campbell, Kalinske-Robertson, and U.S. Army), a traditional MLR model and the more recent LMNN model were successfully built using the same data and subsequently compared with each other. The data were randomly separated into four sub-sets using the *K*-fold cross validation method.

The performances of the empirical models were inferior to the MLR model. The *Bias* index values indicated that empirical methods highly over-estimated the air demand discharges while the ANFIS model had a normal tendency. The average *RMSE* of four folds was 0.25 for the ANFIS model compared to 0.40 for the LMNN model, which was considered acceptable. The performance of the ANFIS model was satisfactory, considering that the average *NSE* efficiency values of 0.98 and 0.93 were recorded for the training and testing data sets, respectively. Lower corresponding values of *NSE* efficiency were computed for the LMNN (0.97/0.87) and MLR (0.38/0.37) models.

The considerable difference between the results of empirical and computational methods indicates the high degree of a non-linear relationship between water discharge and air flow rate. The use of only the Froude number as an input parameter for estimating the air flow rate was unreliable. Alternatively, the proposed fuzzy rule-based model can be used at least complementary to the empirical relationships,

MLR, and artificial neural network models to assess the interactions between air demand discharge and hydro-structural parameters of low-level outlet works for dams.

Conflicts of Interest

The authors declare no conflict of interest.

References

1. Vischer, D.L.; Hager, W.H. *Dam Hydraulics*; John Wiley & Sons: Chichester, UK, 1998.
2. Larchar, J.A. Air Demand in Low-level Outlet Works. MSc Thesis, Utah State University, Logan, UT, USA, 12 January 2011.
3. Kavianpour, M.R.; Rajabi, E. Application of neural network for flow aeration downstream of outlet leaf gates. *Iran Water Resour. Res.* **2005**, *1*, 1–8.
4. Tullis, B.P.; Larchar, J. Determining air demand for small- to medium-sized embankment dam low-level outlet works. *J. Irrig. Drain. Eng.* **2011**, *137*, 793–800.
5. Kalinske, A.A.; Robertson, J.W. Closed conduit flow. *ASCE Trans.* **1943**, *108*, 1435–1447.
6. Campbell, F.B.; Guyton, B. Air demand in gated outlet works. In Proceedings of the 5th International Association for Hydraulic Research (IAHR) and American Society of Civil Engineers (ASCE) Joint, Reston, VA, USA, 1–4 September 1953; pp. 529–533.
7. U.S. Army Corps of Engineers (USACE). *Hydraulic Design Criteria: Air Demand-regulated Outlet Works*; USACE: Washington, DC, USA, 1964.
8. Wisner, P. On the role of the froude criterion for the study of air entrainment in high velocity flows. In Proceedings of the 11th International Association for Hydraulic Research (IAHR Congress), Madrid, Spain, 6–11 September 1965.
9. U.S. Bureau of Reclamation (USBR). *Hydraulic Model Studies of the Silver Jack Outlet Works Bypass*; Bostwick Park Project; USBR: Denver, CO, USA, 1966.
10. Sharma, H.R. Air-entrainment in high head gated conduits. *J. Hydraul. Div.* **1976**, *102*, 1629–1646.
11. Ozkan, F.; Baylar, A.; Ozturk, M. Air entrainment and oxygen transfer in high-head gated conduits. *Proc. Inst. Civ. Eng. Water Manag.* **2006**, *159*, 139–143.
12. Yazdi, J.; Zarrati, A.R. An algorithm for calculating air demand in gated tunnels using a 3D numerical model. *J. Hydro Environ. Res.* **2011**, *5*, 3–13.
13. Vernieuwe, H.; Georgieva, O.; de Baets, B.; Pauwels, V.R.N.; Verhoest, N.E.C.; de Troch, F.P. Comparison of data-driven Takagi-Sugeno models of rainfall-discharge dynamics. *J. Hydrol.* **2005**, *302*, 173–186.
14. Zounemat-Kermani, M. Hourly predictive Levenberg-Marquardt ANN and multi linear regression models for predicting of dew point temperature. *Meteorol. Atmos. Phys.* **2012**, *117*, 181–192.
15. Takagi, T.; Sugeno, M. Fuzzy identification of systems and its applications to modeling and control. *IEEE Trans. Syst. Man Cybern.* **1985**, *15*, 116–132.
16. Kwong, C.K.; Chan, K.Y.; Wong, H. Takagi-Sugeno neural fuzzy modeling approach to fluid dispensing for electronic packaging. *Exp. Syst. Appl.* **2008**, *34*, 2111–2119.

17. Lohani, A.K.; Goel, N.K.; Bhatia, K.K.S. Takagi-Sugeno fuzzy inference system for modeling stage-discharge relationship. *J. Hydrol.* **2006**, *331*, 146–160.
18. Torun, Y.; Tohumoglu, G. Designing simulated annealing and subtractive clustering based fuzzy classifier. *Appl. Soft Comput.* **2011**, *11*, 2193–2201.
19. Talebizadeh, M.; Moridnejad, A. Uncertainty analysis for the forecast of lake level fluctuations using ensembles of ANN and ANFIS models. *Exp. Syst. Appl.* **2011**, *38*, 4126–4135.
20. Pulido-Calvo, I.; Gutiérrez-Estrada, J.C. Improved irrigation water demand forecasting using a soft-computing hybrid model. *Biosyst. Eng.* **2009**, *102*, 202–218.
21. Zhang, G.P. Time series forecasting using a hybrid ARIMA and neural network model. *Neurocomputing* **2003**, *50*, 159–175.
22. Zounemat-Kermani, M.; Teshnehlab, M. Using adaptive neuro-fuzzy inference system for hydrological time series prediction. *Appl. Soft Comput.* **2008**, *8*, 928–936.
23. Cobaner, M. Evapotranspiration estimation by two different neuro-fuzzy inference systems. *J. Hydrol.* **2011**, *398*, 299–302.
24. Wu, X.J.; Zhu, X.J.; Cao, G.Y.; Tu, H.Y. Nonlinear modeling of a SOFC stack based on ANFIS identification. *Simul. Model. Pract. Theory* **2008**, *16*, 399–409.
25. Pulido-Calvo, I.; Gutiérrez-Estrada, J.C.; Savic, D. Heuristic modelling of the water resources management in the Guadalquivir River Basin, Southern Spain. *Water Resour. Manag.* **2012**, *26*, 185–209.
26. Fernando, T.M.K.G.; Maier, H.R.; Dandy, G.C. Selection of input variables for data driven models: An average shifted histogram partial mutual information estimator approach. *J. Hydrol.* **2009**, *367*, 165–176.
27. Kadane, J.B.; Lazar, N.A. Methods and criteria for model selection. *Am. Statist. Assoc.* **2004**, *99*, 279–290.
28. Singh, K.P.; Basant, A.; Malik, A.; Jain, G. Artificial neural network modeling of the river water quality—A case study. *Ecol. Modell.* **2009**, *220*, 888–895.
29. Adamowski, J.; Karapataki, C. Comparison of multivariate regression and artificial neural networks for peak urban water-demand forecasting: Evaluation of different ANN learning algorithms. *J. Hydrol. Eng.* **2010**, *15*, 729–743.
30. Katambara, Z.; Ndiritu, J.G. A hybrid conceptual-fuzzy inference streamflow modelling for the Letaba River system in South Africa. *Phys. Chem. Earth* **2010**, *35*, 582–595.
31. Firat, M.; Güngör, M. River flow estimation using adaptive neuro fuzzy inference system. *Mathem. Comput. Simul.* **2007**, *75*, 87–96.
32. Dursun, O.F.; Kaya, N.; Firat, M. Estimating discharge coefficient of semi-elliptical side weir using ANFIS. *J. Hydrol.* **2012**, *426–427*, 55–62.
33. Zounemat-Kermani, M. Hydrometeorological parameters in prediction of soil temperature by means of artificial neural network: Case study in Wyoming. *J. Hydrol. Eng.* **2013**, *18*, 707–718.

Water **2015**, *7*, 1359-1377; doi:10.3390/w7041359

OPEN ACCESS

water

ISSN 2073-4441

www.mdpi.com/journal/water

Article

Predicting Multiple Functions of Sustainable Flood Retention Basins under Uncertainty via Multi-Instance Multi-Label Learning

Qinli Yang [1,3], Christian Boehm [4], Miklas Scholz [5], Claudia Plant [6] and Junming Shao [2,3,*]

1 School of Resources and Environment, University of Electronic Science and Technology of China, No. 2006, Xiyuan Avenue, West High-Tech Zone, Chengdu 611731, China; E-Mail: qinli.yang@uestc.edu.cn

2 School of Computer Science and Engineering, University of Electronic Science and Technology of China, No. 2006, Xiyuan Avenue, West High-Tech Zone, Chengdu 611731, China

3 Big Data Research Center, University of Electronic Science and Technology of China, No. 2006, Xiyuan Avenue, West High-Tech Zone, Chengdu 611731, China

4 Institute for Computer Science, University of Munich, Munich 80937, Germany; E-Mail: boehm@dbs.ifi.lmu.de

5 Civil Engineering Research Group, School of Computing, Science and Engineering, The University of Salford, Salford M5 4WT, UK; E-Mail: m.scholz@salford.ac.uk

6 Helmholtz Zentrum Munich, German Research Center for Environmental Health, Neuherberg 85764, Germany; E-Mail: claudia.plant@helmholtz-muenchen.de

* Author to whom correspondence should be addressed; E-Mail: junmshao@uestc.edu.cn; Tel.: +86-182-8009-6713; Fax: +86-028-6183-1571.

Academic Editor: Enedir Ghisi

Received: 16 December 2014 / Accepted: 13 March 2015 / Published: 26 March 2015

Abstract: The ambiguity of diverse functions of sustainable flood retention basins (SFRBs) may lead to conflict and risk in water resources planning and management. How can someone provide an intuitive yet efficient strategy to uncover and distinguish the multiple potential functions of SFRBs under uncertainty? In this study, by exploiting both input and output uncertainties of SFRBs, the authors developed a new data-driven framework to automatically predict the multiple functions of SFRBs by using multi-instance multi-label (MIML) learning. A total of 372 sustainable flood retention basins, characterized by 40 variables associated with confidence levels, were surveyed in Scotland, UK. A Gaussian model with Monte Carlo sampling was used to capture the variability of variables (*i.e.*, input uncertainty), and the MIML-support vector machine (SVM) algorithm was subsequently applied to predict the potential functions of SFRBs that have not yet been assessed, allowing for one basin belonging to different types (*i.e.*, output uncertainty). Experiments demonstrated that the proposed approach enables effective automatic prediction of the potential functions of SFRBs (e.g., accuracy >93%). The findings suggest that the functional uncertainty of SFRBs under investigation can be better assessed in a more comprehensive and cost-effective way, and the proposed data-driven approach provides a promising method of doing so for water resources management.

Keywords: sustainable flood retention basin; function assessment; uncertainty; multi-instance multi-label learning; classification

1. Introduction

There is a wide range of natural watercourses and traditional engineering solutions that can be applied for flood protection in urban and rural areas, such as barriers and dykes. The concept of sustainability has recently been introduced to flood defenses [1]. As an adaptive structural measure, sustainable flood retention basins (SFRBs) have been proposed to facilitate the implementation of the Flood Directive [2,3]. An SFRB is internationally defined as a natural or artificial impoundment or integrated wetland, which has a pre-defined or potential role in flood defense and diffuse pollution control that can be accomplished cost-effectively through best management practices, achieving sustainable flood risk management and enhancing sustainable drainage, pollution reduction, biodiversity, green space, and recreational opportunities for society [4]. In reality, different SFRBs usually perform diverse functions such as flood control, irrigation, drinking water supply and electricity generation. Ambiguity between these functions may lead to conflict or risk for decision-makers in charge of water resources management and planning. Therefore, methods to assess and distinguish the functions of water bodies have been attracting increased attention in the field of water resources research.

During past decades, many typological approaches for various kinds of water bodies have been proposed [5–8]. For instance, the Ramsar classification system [9] divides wetlands into three main categories (*i.e.*, marine and coastal wetlands, inland wetlands and man-made wetlands) and 43 associated wetland types. This classification system is complicated and requires detailed data sets that are frequently not available. The system also does not show direct relationships between the types and diverse functions of water bodies.

In the United States, a hierarchical classification system has been proposed for wetlands and deep water habitats [5]. The highest level consists of five classes (Marine, Estuarine, Riverine, Lacustrine, and Palustrine), and each class has different sub-classes. This classification scheme also hardly considers the functions of water bodies.

Under the European Water Framework Directive [10], a classification scheme for surface water bodies has been established by incorporating ecological status and chemical status classification [11]. However, the monitoring program is mainly based on biological and chemical elements and is extremely time-consuming and costly. Moreover, the classification system assesses the status of water bodies instead of the functions of water bodies.

In Florida, surface waters are classified into six types. Designated uses and water quality criteria were established for each type [12]. However, this functional assessment of water bodies is mainly based on water quality rather than comprehensive properties. Therefore, to better assess and distinguish the functions of a large number of basins, a rapid and efficient classification method based on comprehensive properties is greatly needed.

One strategy is to build a data-driven environmental model. The basic idea is to first collect and integrate different types of data to characterize the system under study, and then apply pattern classification approaches such as a support vector machine [13], artificial neural networks [14], a self-organizing map [15,16] and multi-label classification [17] to solve real, practical problems. Recently, to handle the input and output ambiguity, Zhou and Zhang [18] further proposed multi-instance multi-label learning for image classification, which performs well compared to traditional pattern classification or multi-instance learning or multi-label learning. Therefore, in this study, to capture the ambiguities of SFRBs from aspects of input and output, the team investigates them using multi-instance multi-label learning.

According to the practical functions, six types of SFRBs based on various indicators are defined by different professions [2]. Uncertainty is one of the most challenging problems in SFRB system analysis, and here the authors focus on its associated input and output uncertainty. Input uncertainty mainly originates from estimation bias and measurement error concerning some SFRB properties during rapid data acquisition. For output, one basin usually has multiple potential functions and satisfies multiple demands and thus belongs to multiple types. As a result, output uncertainty is here regarded as ambiguity in type determination for SFRBs. Function uncertainty caused by hydrological uncertainty is out of the scope of this paper. To gain deeper insight into the multiple functions of SFRBs, in this study, the authors investigate the input and output uncertainties of basins simultaneously.

In recent years, many studies have focused on uncertainty analysis of water resources, specifically for water resources management and planning [19–21], hydrologic modeling [22,23], distributed watershed modeling [24], decision making [25,26], water allocation [27,28], and water quality [29]. Various uncertainty analysis techniques have been developed. For instance, regression, Monte Carlo analysis, multiple modeling and the moment equation approach are all strategies for uncertainty analysis applied in ground water modeling [30]. For watershed modeling, five uncertainty analysis techniques are widely used: Generalized Likelihood Uncertainty Estimation (GLUE) [31], Parameter Solution (ParaSol) [32], the Sequential Uncertainty Fitting algorithm (SUFI-2) [33], and a Bayesian framework implemented using Markov Chain Monte Carlo (MCMC) and Importance Sampling (IS) techniques [34]. Furthermore, a framework and guide for uncertainty in the environmental modeling process has been proposed, and 14 uncertainty assessment methods were reviewed [35]. Different techniques with different concepts give users some freedom to formulate functions as required. However, most of the abovementioned work concentrated on model structure and parameter uncertainties, while the input and output uncertainties of water bodies were of less concern [36,37].

In this paper, the authors propose a new data-driven framework to optimize the multi-criteria analysis of SFRBs with uncertainty. The objective of this study is to identify potential multiple functions of water bodies under uncertainty by using multi-instance multi-label learning. In detail, to characterize the intrinsic properties of water bodies, a Gaussian model with Monte Carlo sampling is used to capture its input data uncertainty. Thereafter, one basin is represented by multiple instances. To further investigate the functional ambiguity of water bodies (output uncertainty), the MIML-SVM algorithm has been applied to automatically predict the potential functions of SFRBs that have not yet been assessed.

2. Methodology

2.1. Data Acquisition

In Scotland, there is a high number of water bodies with diverse functions. The sites of interest are those where the water level can be controlled either manually or automatically. In total, 372 SFRBs situated in central Scotland have been selected and surveyed in this study (Figure 1). To characterize the properties of water bodies, 40 variables (see Table 1) were proposed based on a literature review and field experience [38]. To analyze the functions of SFRBs, based on international expert judgment, empirical studies, statistical analysis and feedback from collaborators, six SFRB types were defined [39]. Namely, hydraulic flood retention basins (Type 1, Figure 2A), traditional flood retention basins (Type 2, Figure 2B), sustainable flood retention wetland (Type 3, Figure 2C), aesthetic flood treatment wetland (Type 4, Figure 2D), integrated flood retention wetland (Type 5, Figure 2E) and natural flood retention wetland (Type 6, Figure 2F). In addition, Table 2 shows the relationships among SFRB types, dominant functions of SFRBs, and the typical examples of each type of SFRB.

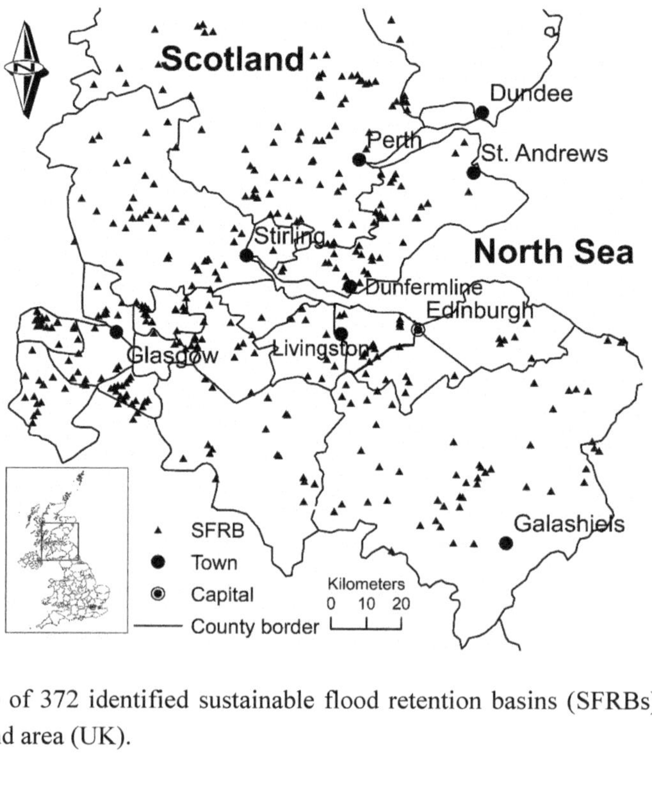

Figure 1. Map of 372 identified sustainable flood retention basins (SFRBs) in the wider Central Scotland area (UK).

Table 1. Classification variables used for the assessment of sustainable flood retention basins.

ID	Variable and Unit	ID	Variable and Unit
1	Engineered (%)	21	Impermeable Soil Proportion (%)
2	Dam Height (m)	22	Seasonal Influence (%)
3	Dam Length (m)	23	Site Elevation (m)
4	Outlet Arrangement and Operation (%)	24	Vegetation Cover (%)
5	Aquatic Animal Passage (%)	25	Algal Cover in Summer (%)
6	Land Animal Passage (%)	26	Relative Total Pollution (%)
7	Floodplain Elevation (m)	27	Mean Sediment Depth (cm)
8	Basin and Channel Connectivity (m)	28	Organic Sediment Proportion (%)
9	Wetness (%)	29	Flotsam Cover (%)
10	Proportion of Flow within Channel (%)	30	Catchment Size (km^2)
11	Mean Flooding Depth (m)	31	Urban Catchment Proportion (%)
12	Typical Wetness Duration (day/year)	32	Arable Catchment Proportion (%)
13	Estimated Flood Duration (d/year)	33	Pasture Catchment Proportion (%)
14	Basin Bed Gradient (%)	34	Viniculture Catchment Proportion (%)
15	Mean Basin Flood Velocity (cm/s)	35	Forest Catchment Proportion (%)
16	Wetted Perimeter (m)	36	Natural Catchment Proportion (%)
17	Maximum Flood Water Volume (m^3)	37	Groundwater Infiltration (%)
18	Flood Water Surface Area (m^2)	38	Mean Depth of the Basin (m)
19	Mean Annual Rainfall (mm)	39	Length of Basin (m)
20	Drainage (cm/day)	40	Width of Basin (m)

Figure 2. Typical examples for six different types of sustainable flood retention basins. (**A**): Hydraulic Flood Retention Basin; (**B**): Traditional Flood Retention Basin; (**C**): Sustainable Flood Retention Wetland; (**D**): Aesthetic Flood Treatment Wetland; (**E**): Integrated Flood Retention Wetland; (**F**): Natural Flood Retention Wetland.

Table 2. The relationships among sustainable flood retention basin types and functions.

SFRB Type	Type Name	Dominant Function	Typical Examples
1	Hydraulic Flood Retention Basin (HFRB)	Hydroelectricity generation and drinking water supply	Hydropower reservoir; highly engineered and large-scale drinking water reservoir (Figure 2A)
2	Traditional Flood Retention Basin (TFRB)	Flood control	Former drinking water reservoir; traditional flood retention basin (Figure 2B)
3	Sustainable Flood Retention Wetland (SFRW)	Retention and drainage	Sustainable drainage systems or best management practices such as some retention and detention basins (Figure 2C)
4	Aesthetic Flood Treatment Wetland (AFTW)	Integrated floodwater treatment	Some modern constructed treatment wetlands and integrated constructed wetlands (Figure 2D)
5	Integrated Flood Retention Wetland (IFRW)	Multiple recreation functions (e.g., fishing, water sports)	Some artificial water bodies within parks or near motorways; Reservoirs providing recreational activities (Figure 2E)
6	Natural Flood Retention Wetland (NFRW)	Nature conservation	Natural or semi-natural lakes and large ponds, potentially with restricted access (Figure 2F)

The data collection for each SFRB consisted of a two-stage process: a desk study and a field visit. The desk study (each site usually takes 30 to 60 min) provided a rapid estimate of most variables by checking information from the Scottish Flood Defense Asset Database [40], digital maps and relevant regional references such as the Meteorological Office and the Scottish Environment Protection Agency [41]. For instance, during the desk study, the catchment size, land use types in the catchment (urban, arable, forestry and natural grassland proportion), wetted perimeter, length of the dam and elevation could be measured using 1:50,000 or 1:25,000 digital maps.

The field visit was conducted to verify the attributes determined during the desk study. Each visit required three to five experts to attend. With the agreement of all experts, data for 40 characteristic variables and functions of SFRB were recorded. The photographic records of water body inflows and outflows are documented. For more details of how to rapidly survey a water body, please refer to the published guidance [38].

In this study, due to environmental and human factors, the estimation or measurement of each variable is usually not 100% accurate. For instance, the variable "Engineered" determines whether the SFRB is natural or man-made and how pronounced these tendencies are. The estimation depends greatly on the experts' knowledge. Dam structures with full engineering control such as a modern drinking water supply reservoir or a hydraulic flood retention basin would typically receive values of between 70% and 95%. The variable "Vegetation Cover" can only be estimated but not measured accurately. Dry SFRB covered by short grass can achieve a vegetation cover value between 20% and 70%, while mature vegetation such as a full basin covered with trees is associated with a value close to 100%. Even for the measured data, inherent errors exist despite following strict quality assurance and quality control guidelines [31]. To quantify the input data uncertainty, during data collection, a confidence level (*i.e.*, Low: 1% to 40%; Medium: 40% to 60%; High: 60% to 100%) was introduced and attributed to each variable to reflect how confident the assessors were of their estimations. Data with low confidence levels were subsequently improved by a further literature review or a follow-up field visit.

2.2. Evaluation of Uncertainty

To assess the multiple functions of SFRBs, in this study, the team proposes a data-driven framework, which is simply illustrated in Figure 3. To deal with the input uncertainty, the authors use a Gaussian model and Monte Carlo sampling technique to capture the variability of each variable. Following that, each water body is represented by multiple instances. To further assess the ambiguity of SFRB functions, the MIML-SVM algorithm is applied to automatically identify the potential multiple types of water bodies.

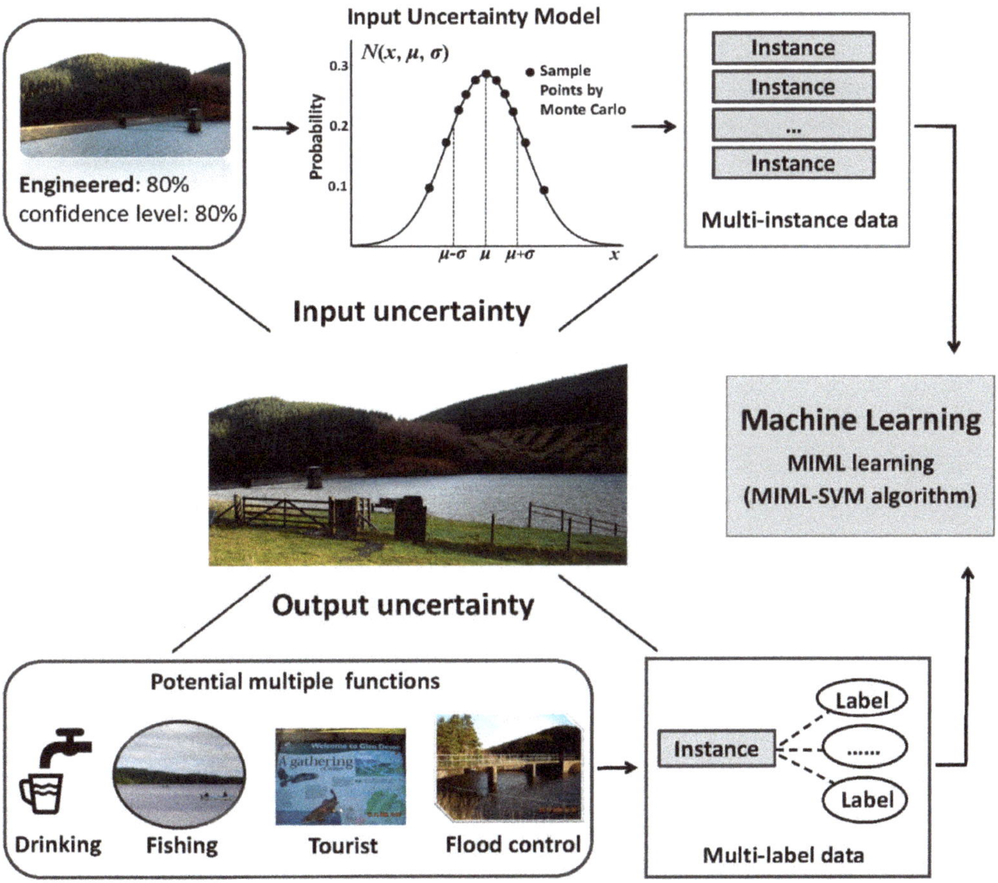

Figure 3. Schema of the proposed framework.

2.2.1. Evaluation of Input Uncertainty

To objectively represent the status of the SFRB to some extent, a confidence level is assigned to each variable data point. However, uncertainty still remains and makes it difficult to know the true values of SFRB properties. An interesting question is as follows: how can one integrate the confidence level into SFRB analysis so as to get closer to the intrinsic properties of the SFRB? For this purpose, the team proposes a simple yet effective model to determine the input data uncertainty originating from data acquisition (see Section 2.1).

The basic idea is intuitive. The authors use a set of values sampled from a Gaussian distribution using the Monte Carlo method to represent each variable of each SFRB, instead of the original single value. The rationale is that if the acquired value of one variable associated with an SFRB is associated with a high confidence level, the potential true value is expected to be closer to its current value and falls into a relatively narrow range around it, and vice versa. In such a situation, the mean and standard deviation parameters denote the acquired value and the variability estimated with confidence levels, respectively.

One can generate a number of values according to the corresponding Gaussian probability distribution with Monte Carlo sampling. Formally, let x_i be one sample of SFRB data, and x_{ij} be the *j-th* variable of the sample x_i, a set of values (*K*) following the Gaussian probability distribution function N (x, μ, σ) (Equation (1)) are generated to represent each variable x_{ij}.

$$N(x,\mu,\sigma) = \frac{1}{\sigma\sqrt{2\pi}} e^{-\frac{(x-\mu)^2}{2\sigma^2}} \quad (1)$$

The expected value μ is the original data of each variable, and the standard deviation σ of the Gaussian distribution function is defined in Equation (2).

$$\sigma = (1-\alpha)^{\beta} \cdot std \quad (2)$$

where α is the confidence level, β is the control factor and a positive constant, and *std* indicates the standard deviation value of the *j*-th variable in the original data (Equation (3)).

$$std = \sqrt{\frac{1}{N}\sum_{i=1}^{N}(x_{ij} - \overline{x_j})^2} \quad (3)$$

where N is the total number of SFRB samples, $\overline{x_j}$ presents the average value of each variable, which is calculated in Equation (4).

$$\overline{x_j} = \frac{1}{N}\sum_{i=1}^{N} x_{ij} \quad (4)$$

According to the uncertainty model, each sample can be represented by a set of instances sampled from a Gaussian distribution, which is denoted as $X_i = \{X_i^1, X_i^2, \ldots, X_i^K\}$. Hence, the variability or uncertainties of the variables of each SFRB are well-modeled by a set of values, which provides a potential way to capture the real and intrinsic properties of input data in an intuitive and effective fashion. Namely, the true value of each variable is well-estimated by a set of values instead of a single potential error (bias) value.

To illustrate this, take Glensherup Reservoir (56°7'48" N, 3°24'3" W; The reservoir example shown in Figure 3). Table 3 gives the thirty instances that were generated followed by the Gaussian distribution function according to its confidence levels. Figure 4 further plots the distribution of the first variable ("Engineered") on the newly generated data based on the uncertainty model. One can observe that the set generated values fit Gaussian (Normal) distribution well, and provide a good way to estimate the true value of "Engineered" with different probabilities.

Table 3. The generated new data based on the uncertainty model (taking Glensherup Reservoir (Figure 3) as a representative example).

Variable	Engineered (%)	Dam Height (m)	Dam Length (m)	Outlet Operation (%)	Width of Basin (m)
X_i	80.00	20.00	250.00	75.00	200.00
C.I.	0.80	0.70	0.80	0.85	0.90
σ	1.25	0.81	7.54	0.71	2.63
X_i^1	80.02	19.34	250.34	74.50	200.24
X_i^2	80.55	19.99	249.71	75.26	202.46
X_i^3	79.82	20.26	250.50	75.05	200.29
X_i^4	79.87	20.09	244.95	74.94	201.56
X_i^5	81.23	20.32	248.35	75.30	199.40
X_i^K	79.80	20.08	250.55	75.37	198.02

Notes: X_i: Original data; and C.I.: Confidence level.

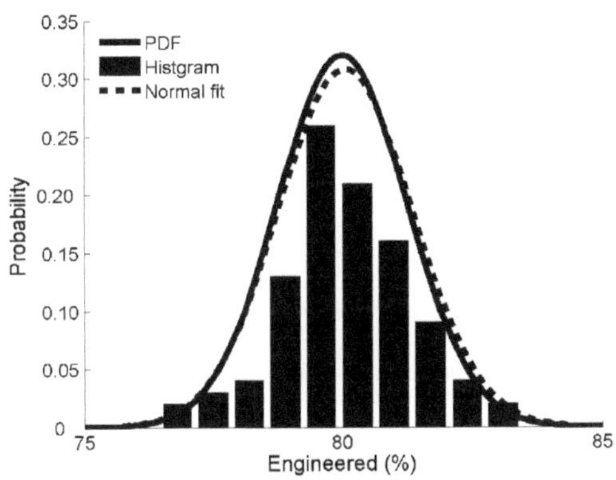

Figure 4. The histogram of the newly generated data for the variable "Engineered" (%) for Glensherup Reservoir based on the uncertainty model ($\mu = 80$, $\sigma = 1.25$ and $K = 100$); Normal fit ($\mu' = 80.06$ and $\sigma' = 1.29$); PDF, probability density function.

In this study, the authors model and encode the potential true values using the set of values, which allows for the provision of more accurate information to assess the multiple functions of water bodies. As each SFRB is represented as a set of values with uncertainty (input uncertainty) and it usually performs multiple functions and is associated with multiple SFRB types (output uncertainty), the task of multi-label classification of water bodies is naturally transferred into a multi-instance multi-label learning problem.

2.2.2. Evaluation of Output Uncertainty

2.2.2.1. Preliminaries

In traditional supervised learning, an object is represented as one instance and associated with only one class label. The task is to learn a function $l = f(x)$ from a given data set $D = \{(x_1, l_1), (x_2, l_2), ..., (x_m, l_m)\}$, where $x_i \in x$ is an example and $l_i \in l$ is the corresponding label.

For multi-instance learning, each example associated with one label is represented by several instances. The goal is to find a function $l = f(x)$ from a given data set $D = \{(x_1, l_1), (x_2, l_2), ..., (x_m, l_m)\}$, where $X_i = \{x_i^1, x_i^1, ..., x_i^{ni}\}$ is a set of instances (e.g., X_i is the set of instances generated by the uncertainty model in this study), ni is the number of corresponding instances and $l_i \in l$ is its label.

In contrast, multi-label learning studies the problem where an example described by one instance is associated with multiple labels. Formally, the task is to gain knowledge of a function $L = f(x)$ from a given data set $D = \{(x_1, l_1), (x_2, l_2), ..., (x_m, l_m)\}$, where $x_i \in x$ is an example, $L_i = \{l_i^1, l_i^2, ..., l_i^{li}\}$ is a set of labels (e.g., L_i is the multiple types of one SFRB), l_i is the number of labels of the example and $l_i \in l$ is the corresponding label.

However, the multi-instance or multi-label frameworks cannot capture all real-world problems. For example, take an image containing many regions represented as many instances, and belonging to multiple semantic classes. Therefore, a more complicated problem is to determine a function $L = f(X)$ from a given data set $D = \{(X_1, L_1), (X_2, L_2), ..., (X_m, L_m)\}$, where X_i is represented by a set of instances $\{x_i^1, x_i^1, ..., x_i^{ni}\}$ and $L_i = \{l_i^1, l_i^2, ..., l_i^{li}\}$. $L_i = \{l_i^1, l_i^2, ..., l_i^{li}\}$ is a set of labels of the example X_i. This is a combinational problem of multi-instance learning and multi-label learning, which is called a multi-instance multi-label problem. To deal with such challenges, the multi-instance multi-label learning (MIML) was introduced. Zhou and Zhang [18] first formalized multi-instance multi-label learning by transferring it into a typical multi-instance learning or multi-label learning problem, which resulted in the algorithm MIML-SVM. In this study, each SFRB is represented by a set of instances modeled by the proposed uncertainty function, and it usually exhibits multiple functions simultaneously, which naturally fits the multi-instance multi-label learning scheme.

2.2.2.2. Multi-Instance Multi-Label Support Vector Machine

Let $D = \{(X_1, L_1), (X_2, L_2), ..., (X_N, L_N), \}$ be a data set, where $X_i = \{x_i^1, x_i^2, ..., x_i^K\}$ is the i-th example consisting of K instances, and L_i are the corresponding class labels. MIML-SVM learning [18] is involved in the following four phases:

(1). Data modeling: Construct a data set Γ_{MIML} consisting of MIML examples (X_i, L_i) according to the proposed uncertainty model.

(2). Clustering: Perform k-medoids clustering on the MIML examples to obtain k-medoids: M_k.

(3). Transformation: Transform the MIML learning task into a multi-label learning task by calculating the distance between each MIML example and M_k medoids, and a new data set (Γ_{ML}) is further generated.

(4). Multi-label learning: Learn the newly generated data set Γ_{ML} based on the multi-label SVM classification scheme [42].

For step 4, multi-label SVM transforms the multi-label learning problem into multiple independent binary classification problems. In making predictions, the T-Criterion [42] was used.

2.3. Evaluation Metrics for Assessing the Performance of the MIML-SVM Algorithm

To evaluate the performance of the MIML-SVM algorithm, the authors applied several metrics, which were widely used for multi-label tasks in previous studies [43,44]. These selected evaluation measures are Average Precision, Coverage, One-Error, Ranking-Loss and Hamming-Loss. These measures attempt to evaluate the performance of classification algorithms from different aspects and they are defined separately. In addition, for comparison, the widely used measures Precision, Recall and F_1 are applied to evaluate the performance of traditional supervised learning (*i.e.*, SVM in this study).

Formally, let $D = \{(X_i, L_i), i = 1, 2,\ldots, m\}$ be a multi-instance multi-label evaluation data set and L is the set of labels, where $X_i = \{x_i^1, x_i^2, \ldots, x_i^K\}$ is the i-th sample consisting of K number of instances, and L_i is the corresponding class labels and $L_i \subseteq L L_i \subseteq L$. Given $P_i = \{p_1, p_2, \ldots, p_n\}$ is the set of labels predicted by the multi-instance multi-label learning algorithms, $r_i(p_j)$ indicates the rank of a predicted label p_j by the ranking method. Average Precision (Avg. Pre., Equation (5)) is used to evaluate the document ranking performance for query retrieval. When average precision equals one, it means that the ranking runs perfectly.

$$\text{Average Precision} = \frac{1}{m}\sum_{i=1}^{m}\frac{1}{|L_i|}\sum_{p_j \in L_i}\frac{|\{p_j \in L_i : r_i(p) \leq r_i(p_j)\}|}{r_i(p_j)} \quad (5)$$

where m is the number of instances in the evaluated data set D; L_i is the set of actual labels of a given instance X_i; $r_i(p_j)$ indicates the rank of a predicted label p_j by the ranking method; p indicates the class label, where the rank is higher than that of class label p_j.

Coverage (Equation (6)) is designed to assess how far one must go, on average, down the list of labels to cover all the possible labels that the instances actually belong to. The smaller the value of *Coverage* is, the better the performance.

$$\text{Coverage} = \frac{1}{m}\sum_{i=1}^{m}\max_{p_j \in L_i} r_i(p_j) - 1 \quad (6)$$

One-Error (Equation (7)) evaluates how many times the top-ranked label does not appear in the set of ground truth labels. The smaller the value of One-Error is, the better the performance.

$$\text{One-Error} = \frac{1}{m}\sum_{i=1}^{m}\delta(\arg\max_{p_j \in L_i} r_i(p_j) \quad (7)$$

where $\delta(p_j)$ equals to one, if $p_i \notin L_i$, otherwise it equals to zero.

Ranking-Loss (Ran.-Loss, Equation (8)) expresses how many times the relevant labels are reversely ordered. The performance is perfect when Ranking-Loss equals zero.

$$\text{Ran.-Loss} = \frac{1}{m}\sum_{i=1}^{m}\frac{1}{|L_i||\overline{L_i}|}|\{(p_a, p_b): r_i(p_a) > r_i(p_b), (p_a, p_b) \in L_i \times \overline{L_i}\}| \quad (8)$$

where $\overline{L_i}$ denotes the complementary set of L_i in L. p_a and p_b indicate the predicted class labels.

Hamming-Loss (Ham.-L.^{ml}, Equation (9)) evaluates how many times an instance-label pair is classified incorrectly [43].

$$\text{Ham.-L.}^{ml} = \frac{1}{m}\sum_{i=1}^{m}\frac{|L_i \Delta P_i|}{|Q|} \tag{9}$$

where $L_i \Delta P_i$ stands for the symmetric difference between the set of actual labels and the set of predicted labels. Q indicates the size of the label set.

Moreover, to investigate the sensitivity of parameter K of the uncertainty model on SFRB classification, a series of settings (K = 10, 30, 50, 70 and 100) were applied to generate different sizes of data sets. Afterwards, the MIML-SVM algorithm was performed on all these generated data sets based on 10-fold cross-validation. In contrast to the traditional method of splitting data into only two parts (*i.e.*, training data and testing data), cross-validation is performed using different partitions on multiple rounds. Specifically, all data instances are split into ten folds, and one fold is selected as the testing data, and then the remaining nine folds are used as the training data. It runs for ten rounds and the results are averaged.

For comparison, the traditional support vector machine (SVM) algorithm was also performed on the same SFRB data set without considering uncertainty. All experiments have been implemented on a workstation with 2.4 GHz CPU and 2.0 GB RAM.

3. Results and Discussion

To investigate the ambiguity of the functions of a specific group of water bodies called SFRBs in terms of input and output uncertainties, an intuitive Gaussian probability function has been proposed to model the input data uncertainty to reflect their intrinsic properties. Then, a multi-instance multi-label learning algorithm (MIML-SVM) was used to assess the multiple potential functions of SFRBs (output uncertainty). The performances were further evaluated by using the metrics discussed above.

The experimental results of the MIML learning algorithm and traditional SVM learning algorithm are summarized in Table 4. Generally, the MIML-SVM classifier achieved great prediction results, and outperformed the traditional classification scheme [2]. In other words, the multi-criteria analysis of SFRBs under uncertainty has been optimized. Furthermore, with different K values, MIML-SVM achieved similar classification results, which indicated that the classification was not very sensitive to the parameter K in the uncertainty model. Specifically, the mean value of *average precision* for MIML-SVM was above 93%. In comparison, SVM obtained an *accuracy* of 84.7%.

Take Glensherup Reservoir (56°7'48" N, 3°24'3" W, Figure 5) as a case study. It is located on a tributary of the River Devon, operated by Scottish Water. The reservoir was built in 1883, and has a catchment size of 5.5 km^2. It provides drinking water to the city Glendevon, which indicates that the water body belongs to SFRB type 2. Furthermore, it allows the community to undertake recreational activities such as fishing and walking, which shows that the reservoir also belongs to SFRB type 5. The traditional classifier SVM predicted the reservoir to be SFRB type 2. After integrating uncertainty, the reservoir was predicted to belong to SFRB types 2 and 5 (Table 2).

Table 4. Classification results of sustainable flood retention basins by using a multi-instance multi-label learning algorithm-support vector machine (MIML-SVM) and SVM. (mean ± standard deviation).

Algorithm	K	Evaluation Criteria				
		Ham.-L. [ml]	Ran.-Loss	One-Error	Coverage	Avg. Pre.
MIML-SVM	10	0.094 ± 0.029	0.051 ± 0.027	0.097 ± 0.057	0.768 ± 0.057	0.935 ± 0.031
	30	0.092 ± 0.022	0.049 ± 0.020	0.082 ± 0.060	0.761 ± 0.149	0.935 ± 0.029
	50	0.091 ± 0.018	0.049 ± 0.018	0.087 ± 0.033	0.750 ± 0.120	0.935 ± 0.020
	70	0.093 ± 0.028	0.049 ± 0.024	0.087 ± 0.058	0.758 ± 0.191	0.934 ± 0.029
	100	0.089 ± 0.023	0.048 ± 0.015	0.087 ± 0.048	0.753 ± 0.119	0.936 ± 0.024
	Mean	0.092 ± 0.024	0.049 ± 0.021	0.088 ± 0.051	0.758 ± 0.157	0.935 ± 0.027
SVM		Accuracy	Precision	Recall	F_1	
		0.847 ± 0.023	0.842 ± 0.025	0.847 ± 0.013	0.843 ± 0.024	

Notes: Ham.-L.[ml]: Hamming-loss; Ran.-Loss: Ranking-Loss; Avg. Pre.: Average Precision.

Figure 5. Glensherup Reservoir (56°7'48" N, 3°24'3" W) is a typical example of a sustainable flood retention basin (SFRB) belonging to SFRB types 2 and 5.

Type 5 is closer to the reality, recognizing the dual function of the reservoir: drinking water provision and multiple recreation functions. This has implications on policy. For example, Scottish Water has the obligation to manage the reservoir in terms of health and safety, taking responsibility for visitors by creating safe paths and parking spaces. On the other hand, visitors might not be allowed to swim in parts of the reservoir, particular if the water level is low.

Take Garnqueen Loch (55°53'24" N, 4°3'5" W, Figure 6) located in North Lanarkshire as another example. The loch (Scottish for "lake") is a natural water body without a man-made dam and supports a healthy variety of aquatic plants and many other reed grasses. Furthermore, various birdlife (e.g., mute swan, moorhen and tufted duck) and fish life (e.g., perch and roach) also live on and under the surface of the loch, respectively. The loch is located in the Glenboig Village Park and has been developed for recreational activities and drainage of the surrounding area. Based on the above prior knowledge, experts judge the loch to fall under SFRB types 3, 5 and 6. The original estimations of some representative variables for Garnqueen Loch are recorded as follows (variable data, confidence level): engineered (10%, 90%); dam height (0 m, 100%), drainage (1.2 cm/day, 75%), vegetation cover (20%, 85%) and urban catchment proportion (40%, 80%). Without considering the uncertainty issue, the loch was predicted to belong to SFRB type 5 by the SVM classifier. After the input uncertainty was modeled, the proposed new classification scheme predicted it to be SFRB types 3, 5 and 6 (Table 2), which is consistent with expert judgment.

Figure 6. Garnqueen Loch (55°53'24" N, 4°3'5" W) is a typical example of a sustainable flood retention basin (SFRB) belonging to SFRB types 3, 5 and 6.

The new classification methodology recognizes the multi-functionality of the loch not just for recreational purposes but also for sustainable drainage and nature conservation. It follows that the municipality has the obligation to manage the loch for multiple stakeholders. In practice, this means managing potentially conflicting interests fairly and appropriately. For example, recreational activities might have to be limited during the bird nesting season. On the other hand, wildlife has to cope with visitors during the summer.

The improved classification performance is mainly due to the uncertainty model as it is effective in encoding the intrinsic properties of water bodies into an intuitive probability function. Modeling the uncertainty with a set of instances using Monte Carlo sampling means one instance among them should be closer to the true values, and it will be automatically selected and educated by multi-instance multi-label learning. Therefore, it is evident that input uncertainty and output uncertainty are closely correlated, and performance in predicting multiple functions of SFRBs highly depends on whether someone can effectively model the input data uncertainty.

The function of a water body such as an SFRB may change over time due to a changing environment. For instance, one basin might have initially been designed for hydropower generation (SFRB type 1) in a sub-urban area. However, after several decades, urban expansion and population growth in the downstream area may demand much more drinking water. Thereby, the SFRB previously used for hydropower generation may be requested to perform an additional new function, *i.e.*, drinking water supply. It follows that the basin now belongs to SFRB types 1 and 2. Except for human activities, climate change can also result in SFRB type change via precipitation-runoff pattern alterations. Therefore, to adaptively manage water resources, the function assessment of SFRBs needs to be updated, allowing for multiple functions (types).

In this study, to characterize SFRBs, 40 easy, accessible variables have been collected to support a rapid and efficient classification model. However, this general data-driven model is not restricted to a fixed number of input variables, and more variables can be investigated such as ecological and sustainability parameters like habitats or rare species, adapting to the requirements of practical problems.

Moreover, the framework might also be extended and applicable to other related environmental studies, considering that the authors provide a general model for classification under uncertainty based on multi-instance multi-label learning. The proposed tool should be of particular interest to policy makers and implementers, because it provides an unbiased framework for decision-makers balancing the interests of different stakeholders such as the water industry, municipalities, agriculture, forestry, fisheries and the public.

4. Conclusions and Recommendations

To assess the functions of a large number of SFRBs in a relatively short time period with a limited number of experts is a challenge for water resources managers and planners. To rapidly assess and distinguish the multiple functions of sustainable flood retention basins (SFRBs) under uncertainty, the authors have developed a data-driven framework based on multi-instance multi-label learning scheme. A Gaussian-based model with Monte Carlo sampling was proposed to reflect the intrinsic uncertainty of the properties of SFRBs. Multi-instance multi-label learning was further introduced to predict the multiple potential functions of basins.

The study shows that by taking uncertainty into account, the prediction of MIML-SVM achieves an average precision as high as 93.5%, outperforming that of the traditional SVM algorithm (84.7%). The more accurate prediction is due to the superior characterization of water bodies with the proposed uncertainty model, which investigates the input and output uncertainties simultaneously. The proposed framework will help water resources managers and planners to better understand the diverse potential functions of SFRBs, which has been demonstrated by two case study examples.

Case studies demonstrated that the proposed framework provides an intuitive way to model uncertain data. For example, the classification of SFRBs is more accurate after taking confidence levels into account. It thus helps to better study the diverse potential functions of SFRBs based on pattern classification.

The major knowledge contributions from this study are as follows: (a) Taking uncertainty into account, the proposed model provides a rapid and effective tool to predict the multiple potential functions of SFRBs in a comprehensive way; (b) The input and output uncertainty are investigated simultaneously, and the multi-instance multi-label learning scheme is naturally introduced to handle a case study problem; and (c) The proposed framework not only complements the study of SFRBs but also has the potential to be applicable to many other water and environmental studies, as this novel and timely approach provides a generic method to handle input and output uncertainty simultaneously.

In the future, the authors will further integrate more variables to characterize SFRBs, and consider the distinct roles of variables for classification via some weighting schemes. The team also recommends that the Environment Agency's current project entitled "Design, Operation and Adaptation of Flood Storage Reservoirs" should consider the SFRB concept and its associated classification methods when updating the existing national guidance for flood storage reservoirs in 2015 and 2016.

Acknowledgments

The European Regional Development Fund Interreg IVB 2007–2013 North Sea Region Program funded the Sustainable Flood Retention Basins to Control Flooding and Diffuse Pollution research project, which is the British contribution to the Strategic Alliance for Water Management Actions consortium. The authors also acknowledge funding received from The University of Edinburgh, The University of Salford, the Natural Science Foundation of China (61403062), the Fundamental Research Funds for the Central Universities (ZYGX2014J091), and the Postdoctoral Science Foundation of China (2014M552344).

Author Contributions

The research topic was discussed and decided by Qinli Yang, Junming Shao and Christian Boehm. Junming Shao also made important recommendations regarding the paper structure. Miklas Scholz contributed expertise in the SFRB concept as well as water resources management and planning, and made significant paper modifications; Claudia Plant gave valuable recommendations on paper structure and formatting; The major part of this manuscript was completed by the first author.

Conflicts of Interest

The authors declare no conflict of interest.

References

1. Shih, S.C.; Nicholls, R.J. Urban managed realignment: Application to the Thames Estuary, London. *J. Coast. Res.* **2007**, *23*, 1525–1534.
2. Scholz, M. Classification methodology for sustainable flood retention basins. *Landsc. Urban Plan.* **2007**, *81*, 246–256.

3. European Parliament and Council (EPC). Directive 2007/60/EC of the European Parliament and of the Council of 23 October 2007 on the assessment and management of flood risks with EEA relevance. *Off. J.* **2007**, *288*, 27–34.
4. McMinn, W.R.; Yang, Q.; Scholz, M. Classification and assessment of water bodies as adaptive structural measures for flood risk management planning. *J. Environ. Manag.* **2010**, *91*, 1855–1863.
5. Cowardin, L.M.; Carter, V.; Golet, F.C.; LaRoe, E.T. *Classification of wetlands and deepwater habitats of the United States*; US Department of the Interior, Fish and Wildlife Service: Washington, DC, USA, 1979; p. 131. Available online: http://www.npwrc.usgs.gov/resource/wetlands/classwet/index.htm (accessed on 20 September 2014).
6. Dodkins, I.; Rippey, B.; Harrington, T.J.; Bradley, C.; Chathain, B.N.; Kelly-Quinn, M.; McGarrigle, M.; Hodge, S.; Trigg, D. Developing an optimal river typology for biological elements within the Water Framework Directive. *Water Res.* **2005**, *39*, 3479–3486.
7. Kowalkowski, T.; Zbytniewski, R.; Szpejna, J.; Buszewski, B. Application of chemometrics in river water classification. *Water Res.* **2006**, *40*, 744–752.
8. Dahl, M.; Nilsson, B.; Langhoff, J.H.; Refsgaard, J.C. Review of classification systems and new multi-scale typology of groundwater–surface water interaction. *J. Hydrol.* **2007**, *344*, 1–16.
9. Ramsar Convention Secretariat. *The Ramsar Convention Manual: A Guide to the Convention on Wetlands (Ramsar, Iran, 1971)*, 4th ed.; Ramsar Convention Secretariat: Gland, Switzerland, 1971.
10. European Parliament and Council (EPC). Directive 2000/60/EC of the European Parliament and of the Council of 23 October 2000 establishing a framework for Community action in the field of water policy. *Off. J.* **2000**, *L327*, 1–72.
11. Environmental Agency (EA). Method Statement for the Classification of Surface Water Bodies (Version 3.0). EA Monitoring Strategy Briefing Note. Available online: https://www.gov.uk/government/uploads/system/uploads/attachment_data/file/290506/LIT_5769_ed4e2b.pdf (accessed on 20 September 2014).
12. Florida. Available online: Https://www.gov.uk/government/uploads/system/uploads/attachment_data/file/290506/LIT_5769_ed4e2b.pdf (accessed on 20 September 2014).
13. Yang, Q.; Shao, J.; Scholz, M.; Plant, C. Feature selection methods for characterizing and classifying adaptive Sustainable Flood Retention Basins. *Water Res.* **2011**, *45*, 993–1004.
14. Wieland, R.; Mirschel, W.; Zbell, B.; Groth, K.; Pechenick, A.; Fukuda, K. A new library to combine artificial neural networks and support vector machines with statistics and a database engine for application in environmental modeling. *Environ. Model. Softw.* **2010**, *25*, 412–420.
15. Hedmark, Å.; Zhang, L.; Scholz, M.; Aronsson, P.; Elowson, T. Self-organizing map analysis of planted soil infiltration systems for treatment of log yard runoff. *For. Sci.* **2009**, *55*, 183–188.
16. Yang, Q.; Shao, J.; Scholz, M. Self-organizing map to estimate sustainable flood retention basin types and variables. *Environ. Eng. Manag. J.* **2014**, *13*, 129–134.
17. Yang, Q.; Shao, J.; Scholz, M.; Boehm, C.; Plant, C. Multi-label classification models for sustainable flood retention basins. *Environ. Model. Softw.* **2012**, *32*, 27–36.
18. Zhou, Z.H.; Zhang, M.L. Multi-instance multi-label learning with application to scene classification. *Adv. Neural Inf. Process. Syst.* **2007**, *18*, 1609–1616.

19. Li, Y.P.; Huang, G.H.; Nie, S.L. Water Resources Management and Planning under Uncertainty: An Inexact Multistage Joint-Probabilistic Programming Method. *Water Resour. Manag.* **2009**, *23*, 2515–2538.
20. Nazemi, A.; Wheater, H.S. How can the uncertainty in the natural inflow regime propagate into the assessment of water resource systems? *Adv. Water Res.* **2014**, *63*, 131–142.
21. Korteling, B.; Dessai, S.; Kapelan, Z. Using Information-Gap Decision Theory for Water Resources Planning Under Severe Uncertainty. *Water Resour. Manag.* **2013**, *27*, 1149–1172.
22. Montanari, A.; Baldassarreb, G.D. Data errors and hydrological modelling: The role of model structure to propagate observation uncertainty. *Adv. Water Res.* **2013**, *51*, 498–504.
23. Hughes, D.A.; Kapangaziwiri, E.; Sawunyama, T. Hydrological model uncertainty assessment in southern Africa. *J. Hydrol.* **2010**, *387*, 221–232.
24. Yang, J.; Reichert, P.; Abbaspour, K.C.; Xia, J.; Yang, H. Comparing uncertainty analysis techniques for a SWAT application to the Chaohe Basin in China. *J. Hydrol.* **2008**, *358*, 1–23.
25. Harrison, K.W. Two-stage decision-making under uncertainty and stochasticity: Bayesian Programming. *Adv. Water Res.* **2007**, *30*, 641–664.
26. Madani, K.; Lund, J.R. A Monte-Carlo game theoretic approach for Multi-Criteria Decision Making under uncertainty. *Adv. Water Res.* **2011**, *34*, 607–616.
27. Chen, H.W.; Chang, N.B. Using fuzzy operators to address the complexity in decision making of water resources redistribution in two neighboring river basins. *Adv. Water Res.* **2010**, *33*, 652–666.
28. Wang, S.; Huang, G.H. Identifying Optimal Water Resources Allocation Strategies through an Interactive Multi-Stage Stochastic Fuzzy Programming Approach. *Water Resour. Manag.* **2012**, *26*, 2015–2038.
29. Shen, Z.Y.; Hong, Q.; Yu, H.; Niu, J.F. Parameter uncertainty analysis of non-point source pollution from different land use types. *Sci. Total Environ.* **2010**, *408*, 1971–1978.
30. Refsgaard, J.C.; Christensen, S.; Sonnenborg, T.O.; Seifert, D.; Højberg, A.L.; Troldborg, L. Review of strategies for handling geological uncertainty in groundwater flow and transport modeling. *Adv. Water Res.* **2012**, *36*, 36–50.
31. Beven, K.; Binley, A. The future of distributed models—Model calibration and uncertainty prediction. *Hydrol. Process.* **1992**, *6*, 279–298.
32. Van Griensven, A.; Meixner, T. Methods to quantify and identify the sources of uncertainty for river basin water quality models. *Water Sci. Technol.* **2006**, *53*, 51–59.
33. Abbaspour, K.C.; Johnson, C.A.; van Genuchten, M.T. Estimating uncertain flow and transport parameters using a sequential uncertainty fitting procedure. *Vadose Zone J.* **2004**, *3*, 1340–1352.
34. Kuczera, G.; Parent, E. Monte Carlo assessment of parameter uncertainty in conceptual catchment models: The Metropolis algorithm. *J. Hydrol.* **1998**, *211*, 69–85.
35. Refsgaard, J.C.; van der Sluijs, J.P.; Hojberg, A.L.; Vanrolleghem, P.A. Uncertainty in the environmental modelling process—A framework and guidance. *Environ. Model. Softw.* **2007**, *22*, 1543–1556.
36. Howden, N.J.K.; Burt, T.P.; Mathias, S.A.; Worrall, F.; Whelan, M.J. Modelling long-term diffuse nitrate pollution at the catchment-scale: Data, parameter and epistemic uncertainty. *J. Hydrol.* **2011**, *403*, 337–351.

37. Wu, S.; Li, J.; Huang, G.H. Characterization and evaluation of elevation data uncertainty in water resources modeling with GIS. *Water Resour. Manag.* **2008**, *22*, 959–972.
38. Scholz, M.; Yang, Q. Guidance on variables characterizing water bodies including sustainable flood retention basins. *Landsc. Urban Plan.* **2010**, *98*, 190–199.
39. Scholz, M. Expert system outline for the classification of Sustainable Flood Retention Basins (SFRBs). *Civ. Eng. Environ. Syst.* **2007**, *24*, 193–209.
40. Bassett, D.; Pettit, A.; Anderton, C.; Grace, P. Scottish Food Defence Asset Database Final Report. JBA Consulting. Available online: Http://www.scotland.gov.uk/Resource/Doc/195446/0052419.pdf (accessed on 7 September 2014).
41. Scottish Environment Protection Agency (SEPA). Available online: Http://www.sepa.org.uk/default.aspx (accessed on 20 September 2014).
42. Boutell, M.R.; Luo, J.; Shen, X.; Brown, C.M. Learning multi-label scene classification. *Pattern Recognit.* **2004**, *37*, 1757–1771.
43. Schapire, R.E.; Singer, Y. Boostexter: A boosting-based system for text categorization. *Mach. Learn.* **2000**, *39*, 135–168.
44. Tsoumakas, G.; Katakis, I.; Vlahavas, I. Mining multi-label data. In *Data Mining and Knowledge Discovery Handbook*, 2nd ed.; Maimon, O., Rokach, L., Eds.; Springer: New York, NY, USA, 2010; pp. 667–685.

water

MDPI

Article

Strategic Framework for Sustainable Management of Drainage Systems in Semi-Arid Cities: An Iraqi Case Study

Mohammed Nanekely [1], Miklas Scholz [1,2,*] and Furat Al-Faraj [1]

[1] Civil Engineering Research Group, School of Computing, Science and Engineering, The University of Salford, Newton Building, Salford M5 4WT, UK; m.a.a.nanekely@edu.salford.ac.uk (M.N.); f.a.m.al-faraj@edu.salford.ac.uk (F.A.-F.)

[2] Division of Water Resources Engineering, Faculty of Engineering, Lund University, P.O. Box 118, Lund 221 00, Sweden

* Correspondence: miklas.scholz@tvrl.lth.se or m.scholz@salford.ac.uk; Tel.: +46-222-8920; Fax: +46-222-4435

Academic Editor: Athanasios Loukas

Received: 20 June 2016; Accepted: 12 September 2016; Published: 19 September 2016

Abstract: For the purpose of this paper, Erbil city, located in the northern part of Iraq, has been chosen as a representative case study for a large number of cities, particularly in semi-arid areas, lacking sustainable drainage systems (SuDS). The study assesses (a) the role of SuDS as a measure in areas with a water shortage; (b) water scarcity in decision-making processes; (c) the lack of legislation to implement SuDS; (d) the adverse effects of climate change on the urban drainage system; and (e) the effects of an increased population on SuDS implementation. An integrated methodology that incorporates a self-administrated questionnaire, workshops, face-to-face communication and interviews, as well as electronic media interactions, were used to achieve the objectives. A generic platform that consists of thirteen pillars, supporting the short to long-term national policies and strategies towards a sustainable urban drainage system, has been developed. Results showed that environmental laws need to be introduced. Findings also indicate that a growing population, which is partly due to an increase of internally displaced people, is a major challenge to an early application of SuDS, due to a rise in land demand and a lack of financial resources.

Keywords: climate change; flooding; legislation; population growth; sanitation; socio-economic; sustainable framework; sustainable drainage system; urban inundation; urban ecology

1. Introduction

1.1. Background

Decades of wars combined with economic sanctions, armed conflicts, and the current insecure atmosphere has left deep scars on Iraq's environment, socio-economic features and infrastructure. A large proportion of the water supply and sanitation services are malfunctioning, which greatly intensified water-related challenges and exacerbated the size of the problems [1,2]. This has threatened human life, the environment, and the safe access to water supply and basic sanitation practices. Most people have limited or inadequate access to safe drinking water and basic sanitation facilities. Poorly trained personnel, an intermittent power supply, a sharp decrease in spare parts availability and chemicals needed to maintain the safe running of water treatment plants, inefficient operation and maintenance programmes, and a prolonged tendency that relies on curative rather than long-term sustainable solutions have intensified the problems of the water-related service delivery systems, particularly the sustainable governance of drainage systems [2–4].

Management of the water supply and sanitation installations in a sustainable manner in Iraq has become a crucial issue. Due to decades of armed conflicts and violence associated with loss of skills and institutional weakness, Iraq became one of the vulnerable and water insecure countries that have fragile water and sanitation services [5]. Appropriately designed and operated urban drainage systems associated with the proper operation of other urban water facilities such as domestic water supply, are fundamental parts of healthy and safe urban environments [6].

The main drivers adding to the elevated vulnerability include but are not limited to: (a) growing water demands at local, country-wide and transboundary levels; (b) a considerable decrease in yearly flow volume entering the case study country Iraq from upstream riparian countries (in particular, Turkey and Iran); (c) an impairment of water quality due to effluents of untreated contaminated wastewater and considerable return flows from large-scale irrigation projects that discharge directly into watercourses; (d) non-rational water consumption use in different sectors (particularly in agriculture); (e) inadequate water supply and sanitation practices; (f) fragmented responsibilities between different actors; (g) weakness of dynamic and functional coordination among relevant stakeholders; (h) a lack or even absence of transparency in the exchange of information including data; (i) a significant and drastic decline in groundwater level; and (j) the absence of water withdrawal monitoring networks [4–6].

Al-Faraj et al. [5] indicated that the level of vulnerability has been exacerbated by the negative implications of decades of conflict and the associated unstable economic situation and political crisis, which weakened and delayed stakeholders' responses. Moreover, some key hydraulic structures (i.e., barrages and regulators) on the Euphrates, Tigris and Diyala rivers have been controlled by "Daesh" (also known as Islamic State) several times, which impaired the daily operational policies and water resources management strategies [7,8].

1.2. Addressing the Challenges

Sustainable drainage systems have been increasingly considered as promising techniques to alleviate three major water-related challenges. The problems are: (a) flash flooding; (b) imbalance between water demand and supply; and (c) water pollution [9,10].

Like many other countries, Iraq has experienced the consequences of a changing climate [11–14]. Since 2010, the Iraqi people have witnessed both severe droughts and extreme rainfall events combined with flash floods that have adversely impacted on the existing water supply and sanitation systems. According to the Fifth Assessment Report of the Inter-governmental Panel on Climate Change [15], more frequent and more extreme weather events are anticipated in the years to come.

In this paper, Erbil city (capital of Kurdistan region) in the northern part of Iraq has been chosen as a representative case study for a large number of cities in semi-arid areas, which have an inadequate water supply distribution network and ineffective conventional combined urban drainage facilities. In 2014, Iraq's Kurdistan Regional Government requested that the local communities reduce their water use due to the largest shortages of water since 2000. The municipality of Erbil has imposed mandatory water rationing and indicated that it will fine those individuals violating this restriction. The washing of vehicles with drinking water has also been restricted. The increasing demand due to the rapid growth of population, increased number of internally displaced people, and the systematic squandering of fresh water, combined with frequent power outages, are the key drivers of the current water shortages [16,17].

In conjunction with the recent shortage of water, abrupt torrential rains of 28 mm, 59 mm and 42 mm in Erbil on 9 November 2015, 30 December 2015 and 29 March 2016, respectively, have resulted in flash floods [18]. Many sewers overflowed, which led sewage to escape and mix with storm water. Flooding also contributed to more power outages as many local, small power generators were flooded. Roads were damaged and drainage systems got blocked even days after it had stopped raining (Figure 1). Figure 2 shows some photos that demonstrate the failure of the drainage system in Erbil city between 1936 and 1970.

Figure 1. Failure scenarios of the existing conventional drainage system at different sites in Erbil city: (**a**) Kirkuk Road flooded on 28 January 2014 (photo obtained from Erbil Governorate; (**b**) Gulan District flooded on 28 January 2014 (photo taken by Mohammed A. Nanekely); (**c**) 60 m of the Ring Road flooded on 11 September 2015 (photo obtained from Erbil Sewerage Directorate); (**d**) Zhiyan District flooded on 30 December 2015 (photo taken by Mohammed A. Nanekely); (**e**) Saidawa District flooded on 30 December 2015 (photo obtained from Erbil Sewerage Directorate) and (**f**) Ministry's Council Gate flooded on 30 December 2015 (photo obtained from Erbil Governorate).

Figure 2. Historic drainage system under-performances in Erbil city: (**a**) City center of Khanaqahin 1936 (Erbil Governorate archive); (**b**) City center of Tayrawain 1960 (Erbil Governorate archive); (**c**) City center of Tayrawain 1967 (Erbil Governorate archive); and (**d**) City center of Tayrawain 1970 (Erbil Governorate archive).

1.3. Aim, Objectives and Application

This paper aims to develop a generic platform supporting strategic plans for sustainable drainage system (SuDS) implementation and management in Erbil city and elsewhere. The objectives of this study are to assess (a) the role of SuDS as a compensatory measure in water scarce areas; (b) water scarcity in decision-making processes; (c) the lack of legislation and regulations to implement SuDS; (d) adverse effects of climate change and variability on the existing urban drainage system; and (e) potential effects of increased population and a growing number of displaced people on the implementation of SuDS.

The proposed platform can also be adopted by other cities and regions that have similar characteristics and conditions such as Jinancity in China [19], Xàtiva and Benaguasill (Valencia region) in Spain [20–22], the Gaza Strip in Palestine [23], Haifaand Tel Aviv in Israel [24], Greater Mendoza in Argentina [25], and The South Fork of Chollas Creek, which is located southeast of downtown San Diego (California and Colorado) in the USA [26,27].

2. Materials and Methods

2.1. Erbil City as a Case Study

Erbil city (also known as Hawler) is located in the northern part of Iraq and is the capital of the Kurdistan region. Erbil province covers an area of 14,873 km^2 [28]. The governorate had a population of about 2,062,380 people in 2015, which included roughly 358,260 internally displaced people. Erbil city spans an area of about 491 km^2 (about 3.3% of the Erbil province) with a population of approximately 1,341,130 including about 232,870 internally displaced people [29].

2.2. Methodology

A solid integrated and joint methodology was used to achieve the objectives and appropriately demonstrate the results. The methodology is a combination between a self-administrated questionnaire, face-to-face communication and interviews, and electronic media interaction. An on-line questionnaire was designed and five workshops, targeting multidisciplinary cohorts (hydrologists, ecologists, civil engineers and ecologists), were conducted in 2015. Mitchell [30] pointed out that "using a self-administered questionnaire can be a cheap and easy way to get honest answers". Similarly; Mbaofficial.com [31] stated that the advantages are low-cost, high reliability, time-saving and high suitability for collecting large samples. Face-to-face communication and interviews (including the exchange of ideas, information, feedback and constructive comments) and electronic media (i.e., direct e-mails and LinkedIn professional networking) were used to target a high number of potentially authoritative responders such as academics and Ph.D. students at universities, researchers at research institutes and decision-makers in relevant industries.

The main reason for selecting particular categories of cohorts is that they usually comprise professionals with good knowledge and experience, which is likely to lead to more objective and scientific results. Questions were grouped into a solid set of classes (Appendix A). The statistical analysis was performed using the International Business Machines software package for statistical analysis version 20 (IBM SPSS 20; IBM Corporation, Armonk, NY, USA) [32] in an attempt to convert the responses to informative output.

In 2015, 337 individuals, representing 35% of "various" organisations, 30% of local councils, 17% of government commissions, 12% of the local community and 6% from the private sector participated in the interviews and workshops undertaken for this study. Participants were involved in the project via either individual face-to-face interviews and/or telephone conversations. The interviews were used to investigate current and future foreseeable water scarcity, as well as impacts of water scarcity on ecosystems, agriculture, industry and domestic users. The relationship between water scarcity and sustainable management of water and drainage practices, as well as the socio-economic drivers and their influences on water resources management in a sustainable manner, were also assessed.

Moreover, the study examined the likelihood of growing conflicts among multi-water use stakeholders as a consequence of a water shortage.

The interviews and the workshops were structured to identify individuals who can offer good insight and who represent a spectrum of experiences and opinions. Semi-structured interview techniques [33] were adopted in this study. The interviews were undertaken by a number of well-designed inter-connected specific questions (Appendix A) to effectively engage diverse groups of people and to ensure integrity, consistency and comparability of the data gained through the questionnaire, interview and workshop processes.

Prior to conducting the interviews and workshops, ethical approvals from the Ministry of Municipalities and Tourism (Kurdistan Region, Iraq) were obtained. The questions listed in the questionnaire were categorized into six themes (Figure 3): (a) challenges to decision-makers; (b) business management; (c) strategic planning, legislation and regulation; (d) sustainability; (e) climate change and variability; and (f) social and environmental aspects.

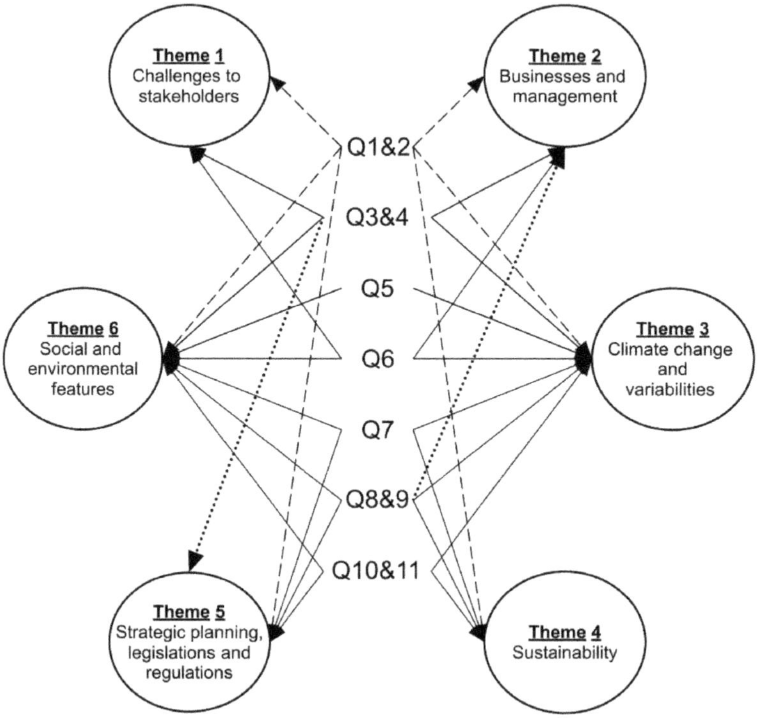

Figure 3. Spectrum of adopted themes.

Table 1 lists the meteorological stations, and their corresponding coordinates and altitudes. Annual precipitation and temperature data between 1980 and 2014 observed at seven meteorological stations located within or in close proximity to Erbil city (Figure 4). Data analysis using Microsoft Office (Excel) was conducted to demonstrate the long-term trend in precipitation and temperature data between 1980 and 2014. The analysis allows the user to add trend lines. The correlation coefficient relevant to each equation was calculated using the least squares method. This was achieved by asking the interviewees to rank their responses for each question entry on a scale, for example, from 1 to 4, where 1 may represent the lowest and 4 the highest characterization (e.g., threat or impact) as shown in Appendix A. Statistical significance was also tested using the software Excel.

Table 1. Coordinates and altitude of the meteorological stations.

Stations	Longitudes	Latitudes	Altitudes (masl)
1	43.7500	36.3747	401
2	44.0625	36.3747	507
3	44.3750	36.3747	977
4	44.0400	36.1950	414
5	43.7500	36.0624	278
6	44.0625	36.0624	439
7	44.3750	36.0624	605

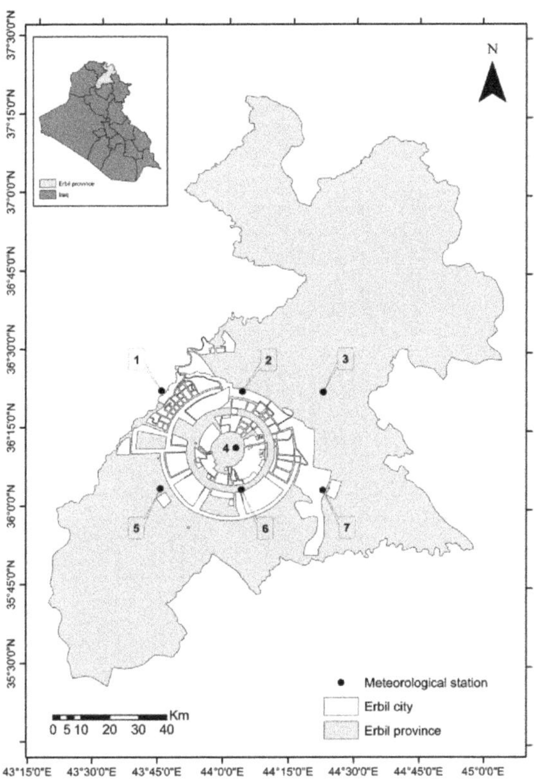

Figure 4. Erbil city and locations of corresponding meteorological stations.

3. Results and Discussion

The long-term total annual precipitation and the mean annual temperature observed between 1980 and 2014 were about 595 mm and 20.0 °C, respectively. The maximum and minimum total annual rainfall of 1552 mm and 128 mm were observed in 2013 and 2008 in this order. The maximum and minimum mean annual temperatures of about 24.0 °C and 16.0 °C were recorded in 2014 and 1992 in this order. A negative trend (Figure 5) was associated with total annual precipitation observed between 1980 and 2014 in all stations except station 3, indicating a drop in the amount of precipitation. As far as the rate of temperature is concerned, a positive trend (Figure 6) was perceived in all stations, showing growth in the rate of temperature.

Table 2 shows the Pearson's correlation coefficients between the themes. The values of the correlation coefficient fall between 0.728 and 0.967. The lowest correlation coefficient of 0.728 was observed between Theme 1 and Theme 4, while the highest value of correlation coefficient of 0.964 was witnessed between Theme 3 and Theme 6.

Results indicate that the normal condition was associated with 51% of the water years, and 26% were wet years, while the remaining 23% were dry years. The lowest annual precipitation of 130 mm was recorded in 2008, accounting for about 23% of the long-term average annual precipitation. The years 1999, 2000 and 2009 were associated with considerably lower precipitation than what can be considered as average: 36%, 42% and 53%, respectively.

Questionnaire results reveal the following challenges to decision-making: conflicts (45.5%) > health (23.1%) > economic growth (19.8%) > social poverty (11.6%). No significant differences were observed (p-value of 0.083) between the influences of these challenges in the decision-making process. Dynamic involvement of the local community in planning, decision-making and monitoring is essential. The beneficiaries (local authorities, environment agencies and local communities) should enjoy sufficient flexibility to choose the service level that responds well to their needs and capacities. Ownership or, at least, co-ownership of sustainable drainage infrastructure by the local community is crucial for long-term management in a sustainable manner. Moreover, effective participation of the local community at all age stages of a sustainable drainage project will positively contribute to a sense of ownership, helping to ensure that the services provided to the community are based on their needs, priorities and affordability.

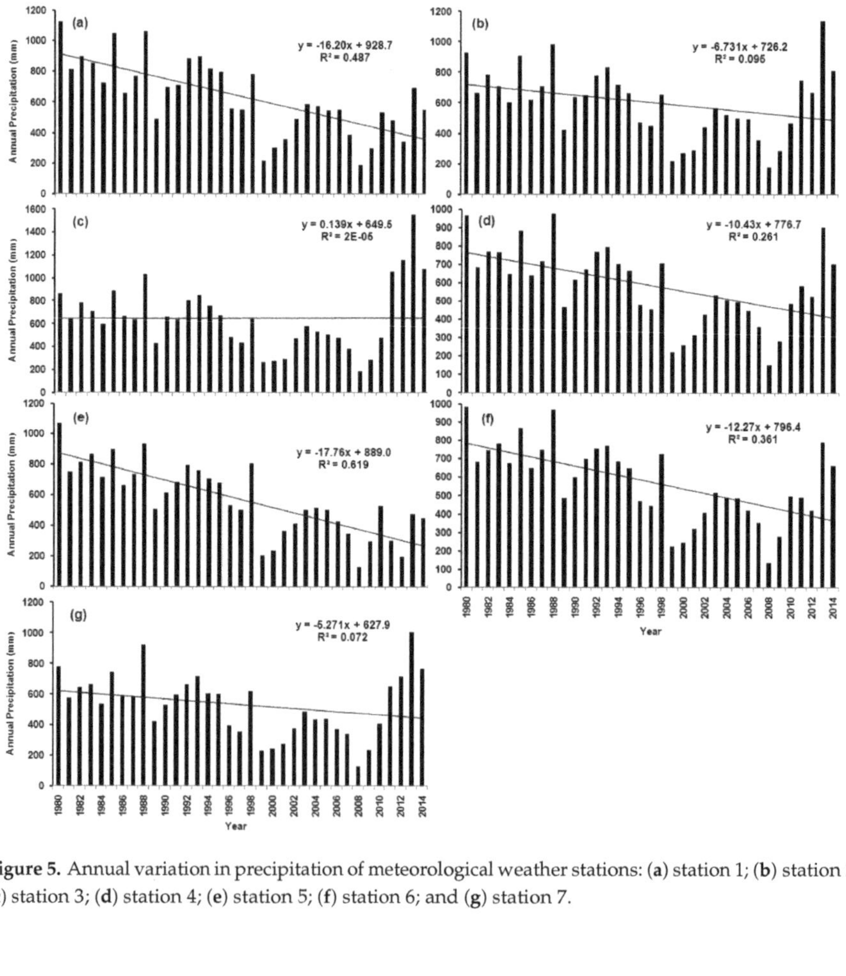

Figure 5. Annual variation in precipitation of meteorological weather stations: (**a**) station 1; (**b**) station 2; (**c**) station 3; (**d**) station 4; (**e**) station 5; (**f**) station 6; and (**g**) station 7.

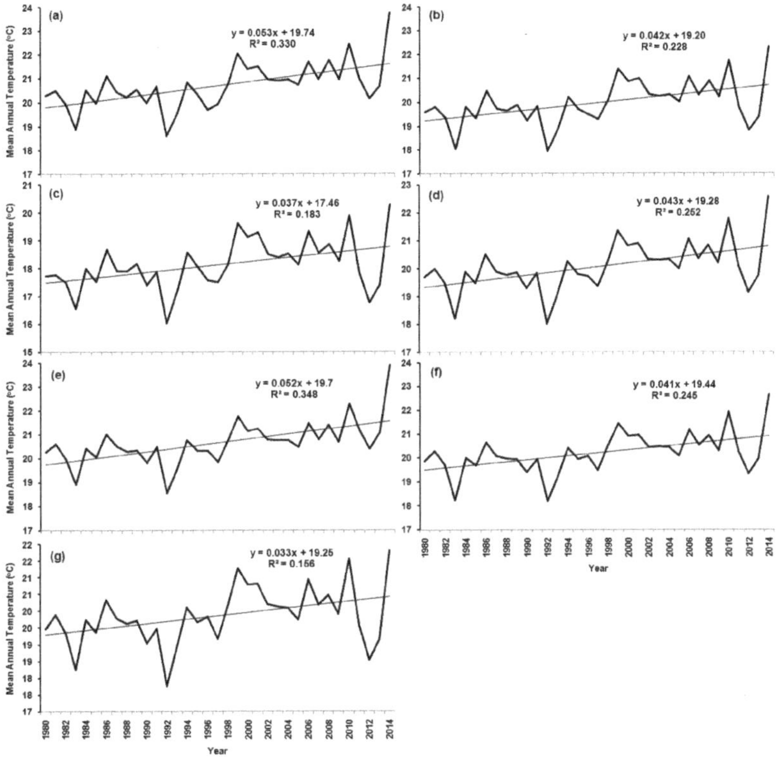

Figure 6. Annual variation in mean annual temperature at the meteorological weather stations: (**a**) station 1; (**b**) station 2; (**c**) station 3; (**d**) station 4; (**e**) station 5; (**f**) station 6; and (**g**) station 7.

The financial and physical influences were of similar importance, accounting for approximately 85% of the total influence on business wellness and productivity. The collective risks related to the regulation and business reputation features accounted for around 15%.

The private sector should be actively supported in initiating capacities for investment, building and coherent service delivery. Creating a public-private partnership would be effective, particularly during the initial stage, which supports the rehabilitation of the existing infrastructure, improves efficiency and service quality of utilities as well as setting-up new sustainable drainage projects. Moreover, economic water scarcity is an outstanding issue that has to be avoided. Accordingly, there is a need for regulatory and enhancement measures to secure the proper engagement of the private sector and provide an appropriate atmosphere for safe investment.

Regulations of water supply and sanitation services are dispersed between several ministries and agencies bringing challenges and difficulties associated with complex coordination mechanisms and consistency. In this regard, effort is required to introduce incentives to encourage solidarity among the various regulatory bodies with diverse responsibilities (e.g., public health management, drinking water quality and licensing of water utilities) and to advance regulatory capacity at various levels. Moreover, outdated or restrictive regulations need to be identified and updated.

Results drawn from the questionnaire (questions 3 and 6) and outcomes from discussions during workshops (academics and decision-makers) show that the construction of water and sanitation facilities contributes to an increase in man-power and reduces the unemployment proportion. This is not limited to the implementation period, but further to the long-term management, operation and maintenance needs.

Table 2. Correlation coefficients between themes (correlations are significant at the 0.01 level).

Theme Number	Theme 1	Theme 2	Theme 3	Theme 4	Theme 5	Theme 6
1	1.000	0.953	0.835	0.728	0.914	0.894
2	–	1.000	0.895	0.832	0.964	0.947
3	–	–	1.000	0.890	0.920	0.967
4	–	–	–	1.000	0.908	0.882
5	–	–	–	–	1.000	0.963
6	–	–	–	–	–	1.000

Findings also indicate that climate change will pose an enormous challenge to the current combined conventional drainage system in terms of capacity while coping with increasing runoff. Urban drainage facilities should be developed in cooperation with water resources management stakeholders and utilities, using an integrative approach. Water use should be sustainable and abide by environmental guidelines. Wastewater disposal should be planned and managed with a view to minimising environmental impact and ensuring water resources protection.

Concerning the tested environment-related issues pollution increase, green area reduction, dust storm increase and wilderness increase, the highest mark (40.4%) was associated with the increase in pollution followed by shrinkage in green areas (31.5%), while the increase in dust storm and wilderness were found to be about 14.1%. The results indicate that perceptions regarding environmental phenomena are influenced by the scarcity of water and its mismanagement. An increase of pollution is attributed to the advancement of industry and agriculture, which has led to an increase in population and the demand by most people for a higher standard of living, all triggering an increase in water consumption. At the same time, wastewater discharges also worsen the situation.

The indifference for the sustainable management of water, rainwater harvesting, the use of SuDS techniques, and source control of storm water and groundwater conservation has led to water shortages. As a consequence, decreases in water supply for irrigation in agriculture have been observed.

4. Conclusions and Recommendations

The results are based on an integrated methodology, incorporating a self-administrated questionnaire, workshops, face-to-face communication and interviews coupled with electronic media interactions. Concerning challenges to decision-making, findings point out that the highest rate was given to conflicts accounting for nearly 46%, while the lowest proportion was linked to social poverty (12%). About 23.1% and 19.8% were associated with health and economic growth, respectively. Results indicated that nearly 85% of the total risks were related to financial and physical attributes. Approximately 15% of the risks were associated with both regulations and business reputation features. Findings also show that Erbil city tends to experience drier and warmer weather conditions.

Revisions and amendments of environmental acts, laws and regulations are essential to promote water conservation and investments in integrated water resources management. Urban drainage systems face an increased challenge to meet the demands linked to a growing population, including an increase of internally displaced people. Therefore, a capacity assessment should be conducted to identify the current capacity gaps and potential future needs, develop a solid action plan for short- to long-term capacity building programmes, and put into practice a coherent monitoring and evaluation process and measures to ensure that the implementation is thoroughly followed-up.

It is also recommended to prepare an inclusive curriculum on primary health care, which highlights the importance of hygiene and the urgent need to access safe drinking water and basic sanitation facilities. This should be incorporated into short-, medium- and long-term media campaigns that utilise all possible measures including the internet, television, radio and newspapers.

Acknowledgments: Some material has been provided by the Kurdistan Regional Government of Iraq (Ministry of Municipality) and Shuokor Q. Aziz (Civil Engineering Department, Salahaddin University, Erbil, Iraq). The University of Salford supported the upload of the questionnaire via the Bristol online survey tool. The Kurdistan Regional Government is also supporting a Ph.D. studentship for the lead author.

Author Contributions: Mohammed Nanekely undertook the questionnaire campaign and held seminars. He also provided the first paper draft. Miklas Scholz and Furat Al-Faraj edited various paper versions including the final one.

Conflicts of Interest: The authors declare no conflict of interest.

Appendix A

(The questionnaire form)

I am Mohammed A. Nanekely, currently studying for a Ph.D. degree at The University of Salford, United Kingdom. The Kurdistan Region was used as a case study to conduct a research project on Sustainable Drainage Systems (SuDS). You are invited to address a number of questions. There are no right or wrong answers. These questions are used for purely academic and scientific purposes. The interviewee's names and any information you give will be anonymous, and would be treated with professionalism and strict confidentiality. Answering all questions accurately will help the researcher in this area.

Many thanks for your co-operation and efforts to serve the scientific process.

Q1: Are you interested in water issues or belong to one of the following cohorts? If yes, please answer the rest of questions. If no, thank you so much for your well-intention and generosity.

- Civil Engineers
- Hydrologists
- Environmentalists
- Ecologists

Q2: Give your view on the seriousness of water scarcity in the 21st century.

Please indicate, on a scale from 1 to 5, where 1 is not at all serious and 5 is extremely serious.
Insert your entry here: ___

Q3: Which aspect is most related to water scarcity, resulting in a challenge to government?

Please indicate, on a scale from 1 to 4, where 1 is least and 4 is most related.

☐ Conflict
☐ Economic growth
☐ Health
☐ Social poverty

Q4: Which risk does water scarcity pose to business?

Please indicate, on a scale from 1 to 4, where 1 is lowest and 4 is the highest threat.

☐ Financial risk (e.g., rise of prices and low investment)
☐ Physical risk (e.g., drought and/or flooding)
☐ Regulatory risk (e.g., change of laws due to water scarcity)
☐ Reputational risk (e.g., loss of customers)

Q5: Which environmental phenomenon is most related to water scarcity?

Please indicate, on a scale from 1 to 4, where 1 is least and 4 is most related.

☐ Dust storm increase
☐ Green area reduction
☐ Pollution rate increase
☐ Wilderness increase

Q6: Which of the following risk has the greatest impact on human life?

Please indicate, on a scale from 1 to 3, where 1 is fewest and 4 is the greatest impact.

☐ Risk to business
☐ Risk to environment
☐ Risk to government

Q7: Which sustainable urban storm water management benefits are important for you?

Please indicate, on a scale from 1 to 5, where 1 is not at all serious and 5 is extremely serious.

Groundwater recharge: ___
Increase in public amenity: ___
Increase in biodiversity: ___
Supporting sustainability: ___
Water quality improvement: ___
Water quantity management: ___
Water recycling: ___
Other benefits (please state and rate):

Q8: Do you think that the use of Sustainable Drainage Systems will contribute to addressing the issue of water scarcity?

☐ Yes
☐ No

Q9: In your opinion, to what extent can the use of Sustainable Drainage Systems be considered as an influential factor in water re-use?

Please select only one option or indicate your estimation below:

☐ about 25% (i.e., *one of many important factors)*
☐ about 50%
☐ about 75%
☐ about 100% (i.e., *the most and virtually only factor)*

Alternatively, insert your entry here: ___ %

Q10: Do you believe that the use of sustainable drainage systems in semi-arid regions will be successful, despite of global climate change challenges?

☐ *Yes*
☐ *No*

Q11: In your opinion, to what extent is the use of sustainable drainage systems likely to be successful in cities that have not yet taken these systems into consideration (i.e., not yet part of the master planning or design sector planning)?

Please select only one option or indicate your estimation below:

☐ about 25% (i.e., *one of many potentially successful options)*
☐ about 50%
☐ about 75%
☐ about 100% (i.e., *absolutely certain to be successful)*

Alternatively, insert your entry here: ___ %

Thank you for your valuable time.

References

1. Al Obaidy, A.H.M.J.; Al-Khateeb, M. The challenges of water sustainability in Iraq. *Eng. Technol. J.* **2013**, *31*, 828–840.
2. Tokyo Engineering Consultants Co., Ltd.; Nippon Koei Co., Ltd. *The Feasibility Study on Improvement of the Water Supply System in Al-Basrah City and Its Surroundings in the Republic of Iraq*; Japan International Cooperation Agency: Tokyo, Japan, 2007; pp. 13–124.
3. Al-Ansari, N. Management of Water Resources in Iraq: Perspectives and Prognoses. *Engineering* **2013**, *5*, 667–684. [CrossRef]
4. United States Government Accountability Office. Rebuilding Iraq. Report to Congressional Committees. GAO-05-872 Iraq Water and Sanitation. 2005. Available online: http://www.gao.gov/new.items/d05872.pdf (accessed on 14 September 2016).
5. Al-Faraj, F.; Scholz, M.; Tigkas, D.; Boni, M. Drought indices supporting drought management in transboundary watersheds subject to climate alterations. *Water Policy* **2015**, *17*, 865–886. [CrossRef]
6. United Nations Educational, Scientific and Cultural Organization—International Research and Training Centre on Erosion and Drainage. *Urban Drainage in Specific Climates*; Technical Documents in Hydrology; UNESCO: Paris, France, 2011; Volume 3, No. 40.
7. Isis Closes Ramadi Dam Gates, Cutting off Water to Pro-Government Towns. Available online: https://www.theguardian.com/world/2015/jun/03/isis-closes-ramadi-dam-gates-cutting-off-water-to-pro-government-towns (accessed on 16 June 2016).
8. In Their Latest Outrage, Islamic State Fighters Are Using Water as a Weapon in Iraq. Available online: https://www.washingtonpost.com/world/middle_east/islamic-state-jihadists-are-using-water-as-a-weapon-in-iraq/2014/10/06/aead6792–79ec-4c7c-8f2f-fd7b95765d09_story.html (accessed on 16 June 2016).
9. Ghani, A.; Zakaria, N.; Chang, C.; Ainan, A. Sustainable Urban Drainage System (SUDS)—Malaysian Experience. In Proceedings of the 11th International Conference on Urban Drainage, Edinburgh, UK, 31 August–5 September 2008; pp. 1–10.
10. Zakaria, N.; Ghani, A.; Ayub, K.; Ramli, R. Sustainable Urban Drainage System. In Proceedings of the 2nd International Conference on Managing Rivers in 21st Century: Solutions towards Sustainable River Basins, Kuching, Sarawak, Malaysia, 6–8 June 2007; pp. 21–26.
11. Al-Faraj, F.; Scholz, M.; Tigkas, D. Sensitivity of Surface Runoff to Drought and Climate Change: Application for Shared River Basins. *Water* **2014**, *6*, 3033–3048. [CrossRef]
12. Al-Faraj, F.; Tigkas, D.; Scholz, M. Irrigation efficiency improvement for sustainable agriculture in changing climate: A transboundary watershed between Iraq and Iran. *Environ. Process.* **2016**. [CrossRef]
13. Al-Faraj, F.; Scholz, M. Impact of basin-wide dry climatic conditions and non-climatic drivers: An isolation approach. *J. Water Clim. Chang.* **2016**. [CrossRef]
14. Modesto Gonzalez Pereira, M.G.; Sanches Fernandes, L.F.; Barros Macário, E.M.; Gaspar, S.M.; Pinto, J.G. Climate change impacts in the design of drainage systems: Case study of Portugal. *J. Irrig. Drain. Eng.* **2015**, *141*, 05014009. [CrossRef]
15. Intergovernmental Panel on Climate Change. Long-Term Climate Change: Projections, Commitments and Irreversibility. Available online: http://www.ipcc.ch/pdf/assessment-report/ar5/wg1/WG1AR5_Chapter12_FINAL.pdf (accessed on 2 January 2016).
16. KRG Draft Water and Sanitation Policy. Available online: http://www.watsan-krg.org/ (accessed on 15 March 2014).
17. سەرۆکایەتیشارەوانیهەولێر (English Site Under Construction). Available online: http://www.pom-erbil.org (accessed on 13 May 2016).
18. Directorate General of Meteorology and Seismology. *The Annual Weather Report for Iraqi Kurdistan Region Cities*; Ministry of Communication and Transportation-KRG: Erbil, Iraq, 2016.
19. Yang, R.; Cui, B. Framework of Integrated Stormwater Management of Jinan City, China. *Procedia Environ. Sci.* **2012**, *13*, 2346–2352. [CrossRef]
20. Perales-Momparler, S.; Andres-Domenech, I.; Andreu, J.; Escuder-Bueno, I. A Regenerative Urban Stormwater Management Methodology: The Journey of a Mediterranean City. *J. Clean. Prod.* **2015**, *109*, 174–189. [CrossRef]

21. Casal-Campos, A. Selecting SUDS in the Valencia Region of Spain. *Water Pract. Technol.* **2012**, *7*, 1–9. [CrossRef]
22. Perales-Momparler, S.; Jefferies, C.; Perigüell-Ortega, E.; Peris-García, P.; Muñoz-Bonet, J. Inner-City SUDS Retrofitted Sites to Promote Sustainable Stormwater Management in the Mediterranean Region of Valencia: AQUAVAL (Life+ EU Programme). In Proceedings of the 8e Conference Internationale NOVATECH, Lyon, France, 24–26 June 2013; pp. 1–10.
23. Khalaf, A.R. Assessment of Rainwater Losses Due to Urban Expansion of Gaza Strip. Master's Thesis, The Islamic University of Gaza, Gaza City, Palestine, 2005.
24. Carmon, N.; Shamir, U. Water-Sensitive Planning: Integrating Water Considerations into Urban and Regional Planning. *Water Environ. J.* **2009**, *24*, 181–191. [CrossRef]
25. Vich, A.; Rodríguez, M.; Lauro, C.; Vaccarino, E. Proposals for Flashflood Management in Western Argentina. Case Study: The Metropolitan Area of Greater Mendoza. *Curr. Urban Stud.* **2014**, *2*, 37–48. [CrossRef]
26. Hawley, R.; Bledsoe, B. How Do Flow Peaks and Durations Change in Suburbanizing Semi-Arid Watersheds? A Southern California Case Study. *J. Hydrol.* **2011**, *405*, 69–82. [CrossRef]
27. Urbonas, B. Effectiveness of Urban Stormwater BMPs in Semi-Arid Climates. In Proceedings of the Regional Conference on Experience with Best Management Practices, Denver, CO, USA, 9 April 2003; pp. 1–13.
28. Kurdistan Region Statistics Office. *Report on Population Projections for the Kurdistan Region for the Period 2009–2020*; Ministry of Planning-KRG: Erbil, Iraq, 2014; p. 16.
29. Iraq Mission, International Organization for Migration. Erbil Governorate Profile, May 2015. Available online: http://iomiraq.net/reports/erbil-governorate-profile-may-2015 (accessed on 28 January 2016).
30. Mitchell, M.; Jolley, J. *Research Design Explained*, 8th ed.; Jon-David Hague: New York, NY, USA, 2012.
31. Mbaofficial.com. What Are the Types of Questionnaire? Available online: http://www.mbaofficial.com/mba (accessed on 22 April 2015).
32. Wheeler, A. Why I Feel SPSS (or Any Statistical Package) Is Better Than Excel for This Particular Job. Available online: https://andrewpwheeler.wordpress.com/2013/03/30/why-i-feel-spss-or-any-statistical-package-is-better-than-excel-for-this-particular-job/ (accessed on 26 February 2016).
33. Newton, N. The Use of Semi-Structured Interviews in Qualitative Research: Strengths and Weaknesses. Available online: http://www.academia.edu/1561689/The_use_of_semi-structured_interviews_in_qualitative_research_strengths_and_weaknesses (accessed on 5 March 2015).

Water **2013**, *5*, 1741-1759; doi:10.3390/w5041741

OPEN ACCESS

water

ISSN 2073-4441

www.mdpi.com/journal/water

Article

Selecting Sustainable Drainage Structures Based on Ecosystem Service Variables Estimated by Different Stakeholder Groups

Miklas Scholz *, Vincent C. Uzomah, Suhad A.A.A.N. Almuktar and Julie Radet-Taligot

Civil Engineering Research Group, School of Computing, Science and Engineering, The University of Salford, Newton Building, Salford M5 4WT, United Kingdom;
E-Mails: v.c.uzomah@edu.salford.ac.uk (V.C.U.); s.a.a.a.n.almuktar@edu.salford.ac.uk (S.A.A.A.N.A); julie.radet-taligot@ensil.unilim.fr (J.R.-T.)

* Author to whom correspondence should be addressed; E-Mail: m.scholz@salford.ac.uk; Tel.: +44-161-2955921; Fax: +44-161-2955575.

Received: 17 August 2013; in revised form: 30 September 2013 / Accepted: 17 October 2013 / Published: 25 October 2013

Abstract: In times of recession, expert systems supporting environmental managers undergo a revival. However, the retrofitting of sustainable water structures is currently undertaken *ad hoc* using engineering experience supported by minimal formal guidance. There is a lack of practical decision tools that can be used by different professions for the rapid assessment of ecosystem services that can be created when retrofitting water structures. Thus the aim was to develop an innovative decision support tool based on the rapid estimation of novel ecosystem service variables at low cost and acceptable uncertainty. The tool proposes the retrofitting of those sustainable drainage systems that obtained the highest ecosystem services score for a specific urban site subject to professional bias. The estimation of variables was undertaken with high confidence and manageable error at low cost. In comparison to common public opinion, statistically significant differences between social scientists and the general public for the estimation of *land costs* using the non-parametric Mann-Whitney U-test were found. It was also surprising to find no significant differences in the estimation of *habitat for species* by civil engineers and ecologists. The new methodology may lead to an improvement of the existing urban landscape by promoting ecosystem services.

Keywords: aesthetics; best management practice; civil engineering; ecology; expert judgment; habitat for species; land size; safety; social science; uncertainty

---

1. Introduction

Traditional drainage often creates flooding and pollution problems in the lower catchment. The implementation of sustainable drainage systems (SuDS; UK) [1], which has similar characteristics to best management practices (USA) and water-sensitive urban design (Australia) [2], can help to solve these problems. The philosophy of SuDS is to promote infiltration of (partially) treated runoff into the ground [1]. Most SuDS techniques support attenuation of runoff before entering the watercourse, storage of water in natural contours, infiltration of partially treated runoff into the ground and evapotranspiration of surface water by vegetation [3–5].

The traditional objective of SuDS is to reduce the negative impact of urbanization on the quantity and quality of surface runoff, while simultaneously increasing amenity and biodiversity opportunities, where possible. SuDS are capable of managing and controlling surface runoff through techniques such as infiltration, detention/attenuation, conveyance and/or rain harvesting [1,6]. Potential improvement opportunities in terms of ecosystem services including aesthetics, amenity and biodiversity by introducing SuDS are often neglected by engineers and planners in practice [5]. Ecosystem services can be integrated within water-sensitive urban design [2] and multi-functional land use planning to maximize wider value opportunities for the benefit of humans and the environment.

The benefits human beings may obtain from the semi-natural (managed) environment can be referred to as ecosystem services [7–9]. Ecosystem services are often defined as the benefits individuals gain from the goods and services produced by nature and its natural systems [10]. The natural resources such as food, timber and water, and functioning natural systems such as healthy fertile soils, clean water [11] and air, and a regulated climate are essential for human wellbeing, security and economic prosperity [7]. A high biodiversity helps to sustain the natural environment and is thus an important factor for ecosystem service provision.

A list of 17 ecosystem service variables and their respective categories is provided in Table 1. The listed ecosystem services have been reinterpreted to make them relevant to SuDS retrofitted in urban areas and are categorized in broad agreement with other guidelines [9,12].

The aim of this article is to outline an innovative decision support tool based on the rapid estimation of novel ecosystem service variables at low cost and acceptable uncertainty. The key objectives to achieve this aim are: (1) to assess the uncertainties of the rapidly estimated SuDS variables based on drainage engineering expert opinion; (2) to evaluate the variability of estimated example variables and the learning process of estimation by different stakeholder groups; and (3) to support the development of a decision support tool for SuDS retrofitting taking into account the perspectives of drainage engineers, developers, ecologists, planners, social scientists and the general public.

The introduction of a transparent weighting system as a function of different professional bias allows for the investigations of "what if" scenarios giving decision-makers more flexibility to test the likely acceptance of various SuDS treatment trains. The tool will improve the urban landscape for the benefit of humans and nature.

Table 1. Ecosystem service variables.

Services	Number	Variable	Abbreviation
Supporting	1	*Habitat for species*	*HS*
	2	*Maintenance of genetic diversity*	*MGD*
Regulating	3	*Local climate and air quality regulation*	*LCAR*
	4	*Carbon sequestration and storage*	*CSS*
	5	*Moderation of extreme events*	*MEE*
	6	*Storm runoff treatment*	*SRT*
	7	*Erosion prevention and soil fertility*	*EPSF*
	8	*Pollination*	*P*
	9	*Biological control*	*BC*
Provisioning	10	*Food*	*F*
	11	*Raw materials*	*RM*
	12	*Fresh water*	*FW*
	13	*Medicinal resources*	*MR*
Cultural	14	*Recreation, and mental and physical health*	*RMPH*
	15	*Tourism and area value*	*TAV*
	16	*Aesthetics, education, culture and art*	*AECA*
	17	*Spiritual experience and sense of place*	*SESP*

2. Methodology

2.1. Site Assessment

A total of 100 sites and corresponding catchment areas that were large enough for the retrofitting of SuDS to have a positive urban drainage impact were identified by studying Ordnance Survey and Google maps of Greater Manchester. Moreover, discussions with local authorities, United Utilities (water authority) and major private land owners regarding suitable SuDS sites were held. The main areas targeted within Greater Manchester were Salford and Manchester.

The standard site assessment template was based on a combination of the frameworks developed by Scholz and his team for retrofitting of SuDS techniques in Glasgow, Edinburgh and elsewhere [4,6], and the Construction Industry Research and Information Association guidelines [1,13]. Each potential SuDS site was assessed during a site visit by a group of experts (2 to 5 team members) to reduce subjectivity [14]. A desk study subsequently supplemented the site visit. The following key information was collected:

1. General site information such as site number and name, postcode, grid reference numbers, location name, names of the inspection team members, site acceptability for SuDS and presence of existing SuDS. Photos of the key site features were taken for each potential SuDS site and its catchment;
2. Land ownership information such as number of owners, ownership type (private or public) and estimated site value (£);
3. Proportions (%) of site classification categories including development, regeneration, retrofitting and recreation;

4. Surrounding area characteristics such as descriptions of the neighborhood to the North, South, East and West, current and future site use, total area of the catchment (m^2), and catchment shape;
5. Location description and distance (m) to the nearest sewer, storm pipe, stream, river, canal, pond, lake and sea, if located within a reasonable distance within or at the border of the catchment;
6. Estimated current and future surface permeability (%) for the land categories grass, trees, shrubs and impermeability of the proposed SuDS site and its catchment;
7. Estimated proportions (%) of current and future roof runoff for the categories institutional, commercial, industrial, high density housing, medium density housing, low density housing and other;
8. Estimated proportions (%) of current and future road runoff for the categories car park, motorway, primary road (or dual carriageway), A road, B road, tertiary road and other.
9. For each sub-catchment, area (m^2) and gradient in the two main directions having an angle of 90° to each other in the horizontal plain;
10. Hydro-geological information such as contaminated land (present or absent), soil infiltration (low, medium or high) and groundwater level (below or above 2 m depth);
11. Additional remarks regarding current drainage techniques and potential problems regarding the implementation of future SuDS techniques.

The information collected with the standard site assessment template supports the assessment team in determining the variables required for the ecosystem services approach.

2.2. Ecosystem Service Variable Assessments

Table 2 shows an overview of the new ecosystem services assessment approach. The potentials of new quantitative and qualitative approaches to assessing ecosystem services have been explored by others [8]. Table 1 shows an overview of the proposed 17 new ecosystem service variables that were also determined for the 100 potential SuDS sites. These variables belong to the established four ecosystem service categories of supporting, regulating, provisioning and cultural (Table 1).

2.3. Uncertainties of the Rapidly Estimated Variables

A relative measure of certainty expressed in percentage points was given to each variable to indicate the reliability of the assessment; the higher the value given, the more certain was the group of assessors. Only values greater than 50% were considered to be acceptable to progress to the next estimation without conducting further studies. Inconsistencies were removed after discussion within the assessment team.

2.4. Variability of Estimated Variables and Learning Process

The approach for evaluating the variability of the randomly selected estimated example variables *aesthetics*, *land cost*, *land size*, *habitat for species* (Figure 1) and *safety* is outlined in this section. Furthermore, the learning process of estimation undertaken by a relevant civil engineering student cohort example is explained with the help of a three-stage questionnaire survey based on a PowerPoint presentation.

Table 2. Overview of the new ecosystem services assessment approach.

Step	Step Description	Comment
1	Select potential sustainable drainage system (SuDS) sites in a case study area	Essential
2	Undertake site visits and note general variables	Essential
3	Desk study for each potential SuDS site	Essential
4	Determine all ecosystem service variables (Table 1) and associated confidence values	Essential
5	Decide on application of a weighting system (if appropriate) for a specific profession (Table 3)	Recommended
6	Decide on dropping variables where the confidence values are too low or undertake further field and/or desk studies	Optional
7	Assess the feasibility of at least the top three proposed SuDS techniques	Recommended

For each variable tested, six corresponding relevant pictures representing virtually the whole numerical spectrum (*i.e.*, very low to very high values; e.g., Figure 1) of possible answers were selected for the questionnaire. The pictures were taken from actual case study sites in Greater Manchester, and did not contain any misleading or irrelevant information such as distracting objects of random occurrence (e.g., an ice cream van or a pedestrian) in the foreground.

A mixture of 51 full-time BSc, BEng and MEng civil engineering students, who were broadly familiar with the overall case study area and studying water resources technology in their third year at The University of Salford, were asked on 19 March 2013 to assign values to each picture associated with a particular variable.

The questionnaire was split into three different stages to test progressive learning. For each stage, the same pictures had to be assessed. However, the order was changed at random. Approximately 15 seconds were allocated for each picture. At Stage 1, students had to assign values that they had to benchmark against their personal perception. They had to make reasonable assumptions about what is a low or high value for a particular variable. In comparison, at Stage 2, students were aware of the range of possible scenarios for each variable, and had the opportunity to refine their first choices purely based on their memory. In the third and final stage, all pictures associated with a particular variable were shown at the same time. Direct picture comparisons and value readjustments were possible.

Each mean score per picture provided by the student cohort was compared to a target score, which was determined by the research team based on professional drainage engineering perception (e.g., Figure 1). The target score is also subjective (expert opinion) and should therefore only be seen as a guideline to the reader.

2.5. Comparison of Variability with Other Cohorts

The variables *aesthetics*, *land cost*, *habitat for species* and *safety*, which were estimated in Section 2.4 by civil engineers, were also approximated by ecologists and social scientists for comparison. On 3 May 2013, 42 undergraduate students studying ecology at The University of Salford were tested. Furthermore, 31 undergraduate social science students were questioned at the same university on 1 May 2013. The same methodology as presented in Section 2.4 was applied. However, Stage 2 of the learning process was omitted.

Figure 1. Relative ranking values for the variable *habitat for species* (%). Ascending order (*i.e.*, from highly inadequate to highly adequate habitat) based on the authors' expertise: (**a**) 9%; (**b**) 23%; (**c**) 45%; (**d**) 62%; (**e**) 70%; and (**f**) 82%. All photographs were taken by the authors and Nathan Somerset in 2012 and 2013 (The University of Salford).

(**a**) (**b**) (**c**) (**d**) (**e**) (**f**)

The variables *aesthetics*, *land cost*, *habitat for species* and *safety* were also estimated by 49 randomly chosen members of the general public between 26 June and 25 July 2013. However, only Stage 3 (see Section 2.4) was applied; *i.e.*, all subjects were only presented with six pictures per variable in random order on a single sheet. The questionnaire survey can be found on the web [15]. The questionnaire will remain live at least until 25 December 2013, and further participation is still welcome.

The general public sample comprised subjects with the following backgrounds or professions: unidentified students (10%), civil engineering students (10%), engineers (33%), ecology students (0%), ecologists (12%), social science students (0%); developers (2%), planners (2%) and others (31%). Engineers and students are overrepresented in this sample. In contrast, members of the public with a below-average education are underrepresented.

2.6. Decision Support Tool for Different Professions

This section outlines the methodology for the development of a decision support tool for SuDS retrofitting taking into account the perspectives of drainage engineers, developers, ecologists, planners, social scientists and the general public as defined elsewhere [16]. A weighting system specific to the needs of a particular stakeholder group was introduced by providing weights for individual variables (Table 3) after consultation with different teams of academics representing different professions within The University of Salford.

Table 3. Weights for ecosystem service variables (Table 1).

Variable	Weights subject to bias					
	Drainage Engineer	**Developer**	**Ecologist**	**Planner**	**Social Scientist**	**General Public**
1	1	1	3	2	2	1
2	1	1	3	1	1	1
3	1	1	3	2	3	2
4	1	1	3	1	1	1
5	3	3	2	3	2	3
6	3	2	2	2	2	2
7	2	2	2	2	2	2
8	1	1	3	1	1	1
9	1	1	3	2	2	2
10	1	1	1	1	2	1
11	1	1	1	1	2	1
12	3	1	2	2	2	2
13	1	1	1	1	2	1
14	2	2	1	2	3	2
15	1	3	1	2	3	3
16	1	2	1	2	3	1
17	1	2	1	2	3	2

Variables of low relevance for a drainage engineer such as *MR* (see Table 1) in Greater Manchester were assigned with a low weight, while variables with a medium (e.g., *RMPH*) or high (e.g., *MEE*) relevance were assigned with a medium or high weight, respectively. Table 3 proposes weights from the viewpoint of different professionals (drainage engineer, developer, ecologist, planner, social scientist and the general public). A simple weighting system with only three categories (1, low; 2, normal; 3, high) has been proposed to keep the case study example simple. A maximum weight of 3 signifies that one variable is three times more important than a variable scoring only 1. However, the reader may wish to replace the proposed system by a more differentiated weighting system based on, for example, ten categories. Depending on the case study location and associated boundary conditions, end-users of the proposed tool may wish to select different weights, which will subsequently impact on the results. It is up the group of experts to decide if a weighting scale should be used and what weights may be appropriate for a particular case study. However, transparency in decision-making is essential.

2.7. Data Analysis

Microsoft Excel [17] was used for data storage and the general data analysis. The non-parametric Mann-Whitney U-test was computed using IBM SPSS Statistics Version 20 [18] and used to compare the medians of two (unmatched) independent samples. This was required because virtually all sample data (even after data transformation) were not normally distributed, so that an analysis of variance could not be applied.

3. Results and Discussion

3.1. Findings of the Assessment Method

Table 2 summarizes the new ecosystem services assessment approach applied to 100 potential example SuDS sites in Greater Manchester. Most ecosystem service variables did relate well to the natural environment such as biologically diverse parks (41% of all sites) and not to the built environment like impermeable car parks (33% of all sites). This relationship reduces the number of sites suitable for retrofitting of most SuDS, as car parks usually only perform well with respect to three ecosystem service variables [*moderation of extreme events* (*MEE*), *storm runoff treatment* (*SRT*) and *fresh water* (*FW*); Table 1]. The presence of public parks did not pull up the overall suitability of retrofitting sites, because they were usually small in size (30% of sites were <25,000 m^2), low in tree coverage (7%) and the presence of surface water [stream (0%), river (11%), canal (21%) and standing water (8%)] of the associated catchment was limited. However, the introduction of a weighting system (Table 3) that puts bias towards what a drainage engineer would perceive as more important variables for SuDS (e.g., flood control as part of *MEE* and water quality control considered by SRT) could increase the suitability of sites for retrofitting.

Table 4 shows the assessment approach in terms of proposed SuDS techniques for Greater Manchester. The relative proportions for each SuDS technique have been expressed in percentage points for all selected professions. Note that there were many occasions where more than one SuDS technique had the same order of preference.

Table 5 shows a comparison of the inter-site variability for a given sustainable drainage technique for Greater Manchester, and helps to interpret the preference distributions in Table 4. The relatively high variability for most variables such as ponds and constructed wetlands cannot be explained by factors relating to specific planning policies for Greater Manchester. Ponds are associated with the greatest inter-site variability because of their potentially relatively small size and great popularity [5,6,19].

Table 4. Drainage system preferences*.

Profession	Sustainable Drainage System	First	Second	Third
Drainage engineer	Permeable pavement	43	9	4
	Filter strip	2	7	12
	Swale	0	2	12
	Green roof	0	0	3
	Pond	33	11	4
	Constructed wetland	11	1	2
	Infiltration trench	5	9	44
	Soakaway	0	4	15
	Infiltration basin	1	4	8
	Belowground storage	5	44	13
	Water playground	3	17	9
Developer	Permeable pavement	42	13	12
	Filter strip	11	23	14
	Swale	1	13	11
	Green roof	0	0	1
	Pond	36	9	1
	Constructed wetland	8	6	1
	Infiltration trench	2	32	23
	Soakaway	3	1	34
	Infiltration basin	1	1	8
	Belowground storage	0	11	23
	Water playground	1	2	6
Ecologist	Permeable pavement	39	7	12
	Filter strip	13	22	22
	Swale	2	13	22
	Green roof	0	1	2
	Pond	30	13	5
	Constructed wetland	10	1	3
	Infiltration trench	8	33	26
	Soakaway	1	8	17
	Infiltration basin	2	8	12
	Belowground storage	1	13	32
	Water playground	5	19	8
Planner	Permeable pavement	39	8	6
	Filter strip	8	11	29
	Swale	1	6	17
	Green roof	0	1	1
	Pond	31	12	1
	Constructed wetland	10	1	1
	Infiltration trench	0	6	25
	Soakaway	0	3	16
	Infiltration basin	0	2	9
	Belowground storage	5	42	14
	Water playground	5	19	7

Table 4. *Cont.*

Profession	Sustainable Drainage System	First	Second	Third
	Permeable pavement	39	7	6
	Filter strip	12	24	19
	Swale	0	1	11
	Green roof	0	1	0
	Pond	33	10	0
Social scientist	Constructed wetland	10	0	1
	Infiltration trench	0	9	31
	Soakaway	0	2	20
	Infiltration basin	0	2	3
	Belowground storage	2	33	18
	Water playground	5	20	5

Note: * Proportion (%) of sites at which sustainable drainage system techniques are given first, second or third order of preference based on different professional perspectives (weights in Table 3). Note that numbers not necessarily add-up to 100, because some techniques received the same preferences.

Table 5. Inter-site variability* comparison for a given sustainable drainage technique.

Sustainable Drainage System	Drainage engineer	Developer	Ecologist	Planner	Social Scientist
Permeable pavement	21	17	16	19	16
Filter strip	16	18	19	19	18
Swale	15	17	17	17	13
Green roof	5	0	6	5	5
Pond	31	36	33	32	31
Constructed wetland	21	25	23	21	19
Infiltration trench	13	9	13	12	11
Soakaway	7	5	9	6	5
Infiltration basin	13	16	12	12	11
Belowground storage	17	15	13	15	13
Water playground	18	17	17	19	20

Note: * indicated by the standard deviation based on relative percentage points awarded.

It may come as a surprise that permeable pavements scored relatively highly on ecosystem service variables (Table 4), which contradicts the common belief among some engineers that there has to be a strong bias towards natural and soft techniques when using ecosystem service assessment techniques [5,20]. However, permeable pavements are likely to attract high values for variables such as *SRT* and *MEE*, respectively, if properly designed and managed.

3.2. Expert Judgment

The estimation of certainties associated with expert judgment needs to be undertaken consistently to be informative. Human judgment may vary considerably, and involves an appreciation of reality and what is a realistic solution to a given problem and an understanding of the importance of making the right choice about what action to take [21]. Confidence estimations are affected by ones familiarity of a topic, experience with probabilistic assessments, the level of difficulty of a task, and the environmental context in which the task is performed [22].

Research has proven that a group's level of judgment usually outperforms that of an average individual due to the sharing of responsibility between the group members. This sharing, in turn, leads to an increase in their confidence to communicate judgments [23].

Knowledge used by engineers to make judgments is not entirely of scientific nature, although a substantial part is derived by science, but is based on experimental evidence and on empirical observations of materials and systems. Understanding is built-up over time as a result of continuous unquantifiable but improving judgments and choices [24,25]. The introduction of a weighting system can address differences between assessor groups with different scientific backgrounds.

Previous studies indicate that good expert judgment performance can be observed when both the scientific validity of an estimated observation and the learnability of the estimation by the assessor are high. Poor expert opinion may occur if at least one of these factors is low [26]. Most variables (Table 1) to be estimated in the proposed SuDS retrofitting tool are strongly scientifically valid, and their estimation is uncontroversial and easy to learn (e.g., *SRT* and *FW*). Therefore, this paper focuses on the estimation of some of those more controversial variables that are highly subject to personal opinion and taste (*aesthetics* and *safety*), difficult to learn due to their highly dynamic nature in terms of time and space (*land cost*), and scientific complexity (*habitat for species*).

For example, the indirect assessment of biodiversity predominantly through the supporting ecosystem service variables *habitat for species* and *maintenance of genetic diversity* is difficult due to its scientific complexity in terms of sustainability assessment and ecosystem valuation. Any rapid and cost-effective screening method should preferably be undertaken by experts in order to avoid obtaining poor results based on guesses. In comparison, traditional biodiversity assessments are time-consuming and costly. Therefore, this paper assesses this challenge by researching to what degree users with different experience and scientific background (see Section 3.4) come up with similar findings.

3.3. Variability and Learning Process

An estimation tool has to be relatively simple to learn and apply [26], and should be based more on intuition than on expert understanding to limit the variability associated with estimations for the same variable by different assessors with potentially diverse backgrounds. Table 6 shows the findings of the questionnaire analysis. Figure 1 shows the relative ranking values for the variable *habitat for species* (%) in ascending order (*i.e.*, from highly inadequate to highly adequate habitat).

The example variables *aesthetics* and *land costs* were determined relatively well (Table 6). In comparison, *habitat for species* (Figure 1 and Table 1) and *safety* were associated with higher but still acceptable estimated errors. This can be explained by the high complexity of these variables (see Section 3.2). The cohort had serious difficulties in estimating *land size*. Nevertheless, this is not considered to be a problem, because *land size* can be easily measured in the field or estimated using maps.

Considering that the concept of "estimation" was new to the students, and they were neither briefed nor trained in advance of the questionnaire, someone might expect considerable progressive learning from stage to stage. However, learning only improved clearly for *land size* estimation between all stages (Table 6). Moreover, the authors expected to identify a clear reduction in variability (indicated by the standard deviation) as learning progressed. Nevertheless, this was not the case (Table 6).

Table 6. Summary of the questionnaire analysis* for the civil engineering student cohort.

Picture number	Target score	Stage 1		Stage 2		Stage 3	
		Mean	STDEV[a]	Mean	STDEV[a]	Mean	STDEV[a]
Aesthetics (%), which is part of variable 16 (*Aesthetics, education, culture and art*; Table 1)							
1	30	36	20.9	29	22.0	31	24.4
2	43	35	18.3	36	18.8	40	17.8
3	49	48	22.4	41	27.2	39	24.2
4	62	55	10.6	57	15.5	63	14.8
5	74	58	21.1	65	19.4	69	22.2
6	82	64	23.9	61	22.0	69	20.5
Land size (m^2), which influences all variables (Table 1)							
1	3240	6370	11,613	8510	19,523	8400	14,302
2	4600	8540	11,621	14,630	25,144	10,990	18,423
3	8200	11,560	23,187	10,790	23,532	21,100	59,486
4	9440	57,010	216,610	16,040	35,940	21,690	48,024
5	10,350	49,520	69,104	63,160	149,055	56,650	91,580
6	70,000	123,470	436,125	84,940	159,947	70,790	101,090
Land cost (%), which is part of variable 15 (*Tourism and area value*; Table 1)							
1	27	27	24.9	25	20.0	25	21.9
2	35	42	15.0	45	17.7	44	17.4
3	54	53	22.4	58	21.6	59	22.4
4	60	58	19.3	62	17.1	60	20.3
5	69	65	19.7	63	19.0	64	18.9
6	78	71	17.9	68	18.5	70	20.2
Habitat for species (%), which is variable 1 (Table 1)							
1	9	10	13.2	16	21.5	16	20.6
2	23	30	17.5	29	18.9	28	20.4
3	45	35	22.0	38	20.3	40	19.5
4	62	52	24.4	53	16.7	56	17.5
5	70	67	19.4	62	21.3	64	20.0
6	82	69	23.2	68	23.8	74	23.3
Safety (%); which is part of variable 14 (*Recreation, and mental and physical health*; Table 1)							
1	20	21	20.7	22	20.0	26	32.2
2	29	24	22.6	27	21.6	27	21.2
3	34	33	20.4	32	20.6	31	22.9
4	40	46	24.3	45	22.8	47	32.3
5	62	46	23.9	45	25.2	53	22.5
6	74	59	35.7	61	30.4	64	32.7

Notes: * indicating the variability for example variables and progressive learning; [a] standard deviation.

Figures 2–4 show the findings for the ecology students, social science students and the general public, respectively. The standard deviations associated with variable estimations were usually lower for the ecology compared to the civil engineering students. In comparison, the same was the case for social science students (except for *aesthetics* and *habitat for species*). The standard deviations for ecology and social science students and the general public were rather similar.

Table 7 shows an assessment of the statistically significant differences between different cohorts of estimators for selected SuDS characterization variables using the non-parametric Mann-Whitney U-test. There were five relationships that could be considered as unexpected with respect to commonly hold public opinions. Civil engineering compared to ecology students had similar views regarding *habitat for species* (P = 0.994; Table 7) and *safety* (P = 0.494; Table 7). However, one might assume that *habitat for species* would be much more important to ecologists than engineers. On the other hand, engineers are usually more aware of health and *safety* matters than ecologists.

Figure 2. Stage 3 estimations (%) by ecology students for the variables (**a**) *aesthetics*; (**b**) *land cost*; (**c**) *habitat for species*; and (**d**) *safety* based on different pictures represented by numbers on the x-axis. SD, standard deviation; AV, average.

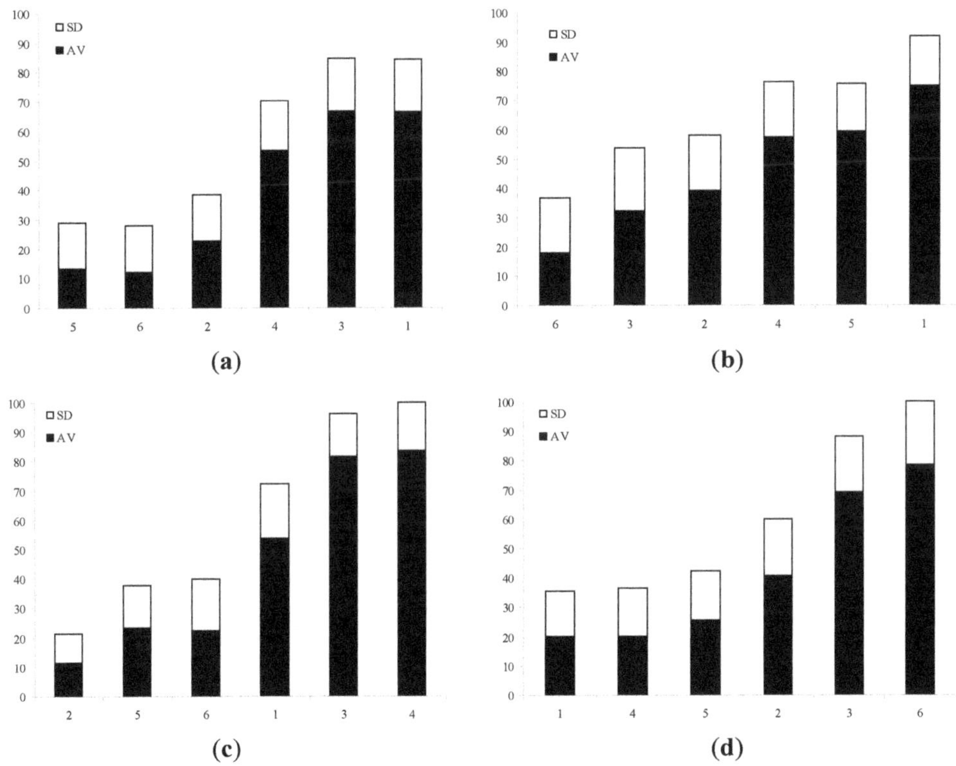

Someone might expect that civil engineering and social science students might have different views regarding *habitat for species*. However, the study showed that the data were rather similar (P = 0.379; Table 7). It could be expected that ecology students would have a different opinion regarding *habitat for species* compared to the general public. However, their assessments were rather similar (P = 0.072; Table 7), which is surprising considering that ecologist should have a better understanding of the associated science and might therefore have different assessment criteria. Finally, social scientists and the general public might be expected to have similar opinions with respect to the estimation of *land*

costs. However, their estimations were significantly different ($P = 0.006$; Table 7), which could be explained by the dominance of engineers in the general public sample.

Figure 3. Stage 3 estimations (%) by social science students for the variables (**a**) *aesthetics*; (**b**) *land cost*; (**c**) *habitat for species*; and (**d**) *safety*. based on different pictures represented by numbers on the x-axis. SD, standard deviation; AV, average.

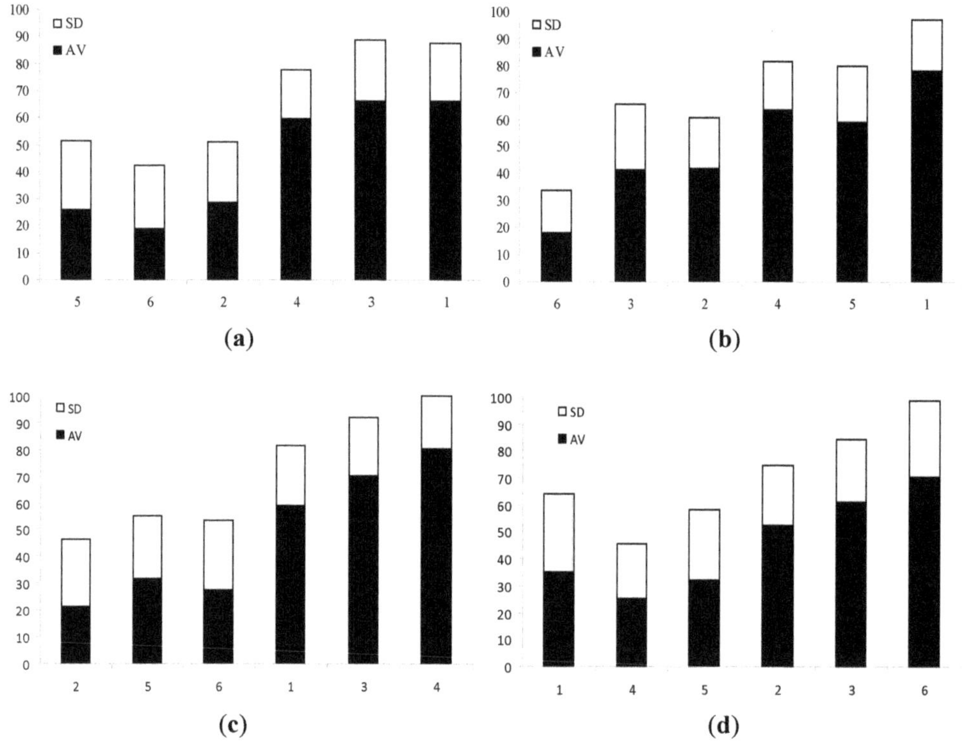

3.4. Different Professional Perspectives

Different professions will want to assign a higher importance to those variables that are of greater relevance to their interests (Table 4). Therefore, the new tool takes into account the diversity of professional opinions by giving any user the opportunity to select a weighting system (Table 3) of greatest relevance to his or her line of thought. However, the introduction of associated bias can be avoided by not selecting any weighting system.

In case a result that is free of any bias and error associated with the estimation by a specific cohort is preferable, the findings in Section 3.3 can be used to adjust the estimation results. For example, if an estimation is made by cohort A for a variable x, and it is known that A consistently overestimates x by 10% compared to all other relevant cohorts, x could be reduced by 10%, which would result in an estimation more acceptable by the majority of stakeholders. With respect to this study, the general public sample is dominated by engineers (at least 43%; Section 2.5). Considering that engineers consistently overestimate *aesthetics* for less beautiful (<50% for aesthetics) SuDS sites in comparison to, for example, ecologists and social scientists (Table 6; Figures 2 and 3), their estimations could be reduced by at least 15% and 5%, respectively, to bring them in line with those made by ecologists and social scientists. Such relationships can be formalized in numerical models based on uncertainty estimations associated with different cohorts and variables [27].

Figure 4. Stage 3 estimations (%) by the general public for the variables (**a**) *aesthetics*; (**b**) *land cost*; (**c**) *habitat for species*; and (**d**) *safety.* based on different pictures represented by numbers on the x-axis. SD, standard deviation; AV, average.

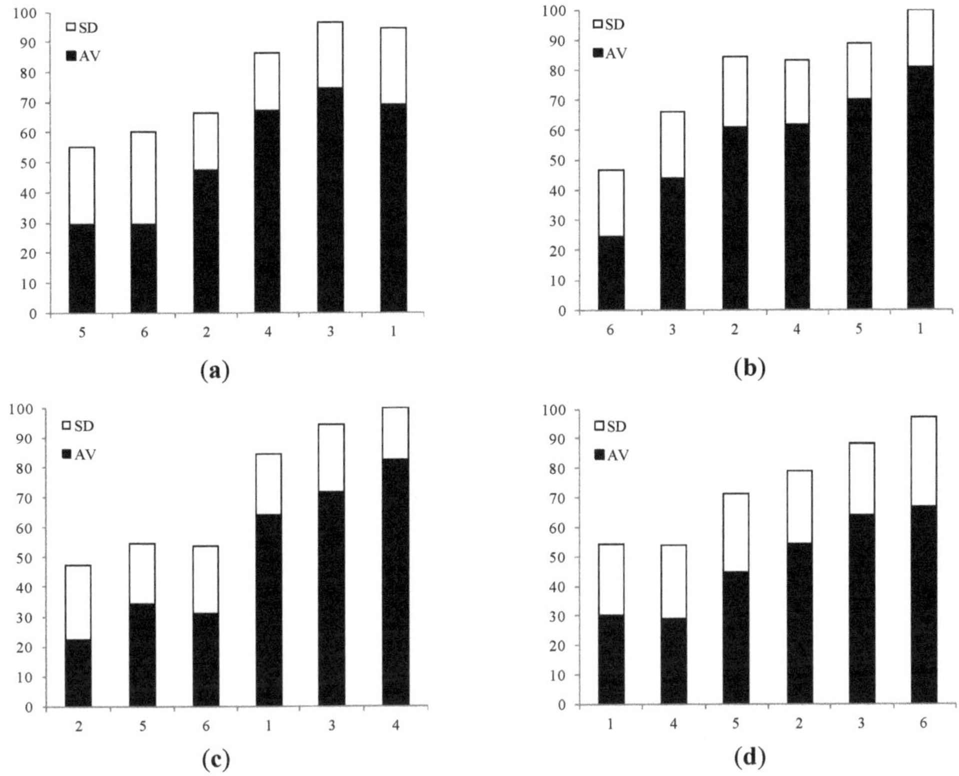

3.5. Strengths and Limitations

The strengths of the new ecosystem services approach to SuDS retrofitting, particularly in comparison to the community and environment methodology adopted by others [13,28], are as follows:

- Generic retrofitting approach based on universal ecosystem service variables;
- Recognition that various professions have different priority variables;
- Expert judgment may be more accurate than prediction models if the science base is strong, the learnability high and sufficient information is available [21,26];
- Inexpensive, user-friendly and easy-to-understand evaluation; and
- Overall ecosystem service potential of a site expressed through an individual value.

The potential weaknesses of the ecosystem services assessment approach are:

- Subjectivity and aggregation are generic limitations of an expert-based system, which can be addressed by involving expert groups and determination of uncertainty values for all estimations [14,29,30];
- Some ecosystem service variables are not always applicable;
- Strong perceived (often falsely; see below) bias towards natural sites and "soft" SuDS (e.g., ponds and wetlands) in contrast to urban sites and "hard" SuDS (e.g., permeable pavements and belowground storage systems); and
- Possibility of multicollinearity among variables due to potential dependencies between some of them [31].

Table 7. Assessment of the statistically significant differences between different cohorts of estimators (civil engineering, ecology *and* social science students, and the general public) for selected SuDS characterization variables (*aesthetics*, *land cost*, *habitat for species* and *safety*) using the non-parametric Mann-Whitney U-test (see also Section 2.7).

Cohort comparisons	Statistic	*Aesthetics*	*Land cost*	*Habitat for species*	*Safety*
Civil engineers and ecologists	*P*	0.000	0.004	0.994	0.494
	H	1	1	0	0
Civil engineers and social scientists	*P*	0.004	0.157	0.379	0.027
	H	1	0	0	1
Civil engineers and the general public	*P*	0.396	0.094	0.050	0.002
	H	0	0	0	1
Ecologists and social scientists	*P*	0.070	0.183	0.500	0.175
	H	0	0	0	0
Ecologists and the general public	*P*	0.000	0.000	0.072	0.018
	H	1	1	0	1
Social scientists and the general public	*P*	0.002	0.006	0.311	0.453
	H	1	1	0	0

Notes: *P* value, probability of obtaining a test statistic at least as extreme as the one that was actually observed, assuming that the null hypothesis is true; H, response indicator; if H = 1, filters are statistically significantly different ($P < 0.05$) for the corresponding water quality parameter; if H = 0, the difference is not significant.

Some of the above limitations such as subjectivity are also inherent in traditional assessment approaches [1,13]. However, multicollinearity might be a more relevant problem with the proposed ecosystem services approach due to the use of a high number of variables. In order to avoid artificial dependencies between some variables that could be considered as similar by the inexperienced assessor, all assessors need to be clear about their differences, which require training by more experiences evaluators. Considering that any tests for multicollinearity is case study-dependant, the inevitable bias associated with a case study does not allow for objective testing unless the number of case studies is very high and there is an adequate geographical spread to reduce bias. Nevertheless, a principal component analysis was carried out to identify redundant variables in order to reduce the risk of multicollinearity [31]. Findings indicate that all ecosystem services variables (Table 1) were considered to be necessary for the proposed expert system.

4. Conclusions and Recommendation for Further Research

A rapid estimation-based assessment methodology for retrofitting of SuDS was successfully introduced. This tool can be used together with water-sensitive urban design, multi-functional land use planning and regeneration strategies to prioritize sites for SuDS retrofitting, which is particularly important during difficult financial times.

The variable estimations and the assignment of associated confidence figures were based on expert judgment. However, findings show that estimation errors and variability are relatively low even for virtually untrained example cohorts. The introduction of a transparent and justified weighting system as a function of different professional bias leads to the preferred selection of some SuDS techniques by several professions. This methodology allows for the investigations of various "what if" scenarios giving decision-makers more flexibility to test the likely acceptance of various SuDS treatment trains.

Statistically significant differences between different cohorts of estimators for selected SuDS characterization variables using the non-parametric Mann-Whitney U-test were not found for about half of the possible combinations of cohorts. However, there were four of these relationships that could be considered as unexpected with respect to commonly hold public opinions. Civil engineering compared to ecology students had similar views regarding *habitat for species* and *safety*. Someone might also expect that civil engineering and social science students might have different views regarding *habitat for species*. However, the study showed that the data were rather similar. It could also be expected that ecology students would have a different opinion regarding *habitat for species* compared to the general public. However, their assessments were rather similar.

In comparison, statistically significant differences between cohorts for SuDS characterization variables using the non-parametric test that were surprising, were only found for social scientists compared to the general public, where someone might expect similar opinions concerning the estimation of *land costs*. However, corresponding estimations were significantly different.

More research on estimation adjustments to eliminate cohort bias, variability and errors would be welcome. Moreover, larger data sets would be beneficial in making judgments with higher confidence. It is therefore recommended to test the tool in different towns and cities to prove its validity for other case study scenarios.

Acknowledgments

Nathan Somerset (student at The University of Salford) supported the fieldwork activities. The Association of Greater Manchester Authorities, Salford City Council and United Utilities made access to sites and case study information available. More than 170 volunteers answered the questionnaires.

Conflicts of Interest

The authors declare no conflict of interest.

References

1. Construction Industry Research and Information Association (CIRIA). *The SuDS Manual*; CIRIA: London, UK, 2007.
2. Ashley, R.; Lundy, L.; Ward, S.; Shaffer, P.; Walker, L.; Morgan, C.; Saul, A.; Wong, T.; Moore, S. Water-sensitive urban design: Opportunities in the UK. *Proc. Inst. Civ. Eng. Munic. Eng.* **2003**, *166*, 65–76.
3. Construction Industry Research and Information Association (CIRIA). *Planning for SuDS—Making It Happen*; CIRIA: London, UK, 2010.
4. Scholz, M. *Wetland Systems to Control Urban Runoff*; Elsevier: Amsterdam, The Netherlands, 2006.
5. Scholz, M. *Wetland Systems—Storm Water Management Control*; Springer: Berlin, Germany, 2010.
6. Scholz, M.; Corrigan, N.L.; Yazdi, S.K. The Glasgow sustainable urban drainage system management project: Case studies (Belvidere Hospital and Celtic FC Stadium Areas). *Environ. Eng. Sci.* **2006**, *23*, 908–922.
7. Millennium Ecosystem Assessment. *Ecosystems and Human Well-Being*; United Nations Environment Programme: Washington, DC, USA, 2005.
8. Busch, M.; Notte, A.L.; Laporte, V.; Erhard, M. Potentials of quantitative and qualitative approaches to assessing ecosystem services. *Ecol. Indic.* **2012**, *21*, 89–103.
9. Moore, T.L.C.; Hunt, W.F. Ecosystem service provision by stormwater wetlands and ponds—A means for evaluation? *Water Res.* **2012**, *46*, 6811–6823.
10. Her Majesty's Government. *Overarching Impact Assessment for the Natural Environment White Paper*; Department of the Environment, Food and Rural Affairs: London, UK, 2011. Available online: http://www.archive.defra.gov.uk/environment/natural/documents/newp-ia-110607.pdf (accessed on 22 October 2013).
11. Walsh, C.J.; Fletcher, T.D.; Burns, M.J. Urban stormwater runoff: A new class of environmental flow problem. *PLoS ONE* **2012**, *7*, e45814.
12. Economics of Ecosystems and Biodiversity (TEEB). *TEEB Manual for Cities*: *Ecosystem Services in Urban Management*; TEEB: Leipzig, UK, 2011. Available online: http://www.teebweb.org (accessed on 25 March 2013).
13. Construction Industry Research and Information Association (CIRIA). *Sustainable Drainage Systems. Hydraulic, Structural and Water Quality Advice*; Report C609; CIRIA: London, UK, 2004.
14. Munoz-Pedreros, A. Landscape evaluation: An environmental management. *Rev. Chil. Hist. Nat.* **2004**, *77*, 139–156.
15. Uzomah, V.C.; Almuktar, S.A.A.A.N. *SUDS Questionnaire*: *Visual Assessment of Urban Sites*; The University of Salford: Salford, UK.
16. Blockley, D. *The New Penguin Dictionary of Civil Engineering*; Penguin Books: New York, NY, USA, 2005.
17. Microsoft. Microsoft Office. http://office.microsoft.com/en-gb (accessed on 23 October 2013).
18. IBM. Downloading IBM SPSS Statistics 20. http://www-01.ibm.com/support/docview.wss?uid=swg24029274 (accessed on 23 October 2013).
19. Scholz, M. Case study: Design, operation, maintenance and water quality management of sustainable storm water ponds for roof run-off. *Bioresour. Technol.***2004**, *95*, 269–279.

20. Butler, D.; Davies, J.W. *Urban Drainage*, 2nd ed.; Spon Press: London, UK, 2004.
21. Stewart, T.R.; Roebber, P.J.; Bosart, L.F. The importance of the task in analyzing expert judgment. *Organ. Behav. Hum. Decis. Process.* **1997**, *69*, 205–219.
22. O'Connor, M. Models of human behaviour and confidence in judgment: A review. *Inter. J. Forecast.* **1989**, *5*, 159–169.
23. Schultze, T.; Mojzisch, A.; Schulz-Hardt, S. Why groups perform better than individuals at quantitative judgment tasks: Group to individual transfer as an alternative to differential weighting. *Organ. Behav. Hum. Decis. Process.* **2012**, *118*, 24–36.
24. Ferguson, E. *Engineering and the Minds Eye*; Massachusetts Institute of Technology Press: Cambridge, MA, USA, 1992.
25. Holt, J.E. The designer's judgment. *Des. Stud.* **1997**, *18*, 113–123.
26. Bolger, F.; Wright, G. Assessing the quality of expert judgment—Issues and analysis. *Decis. Support Sys.* **1994**, *11*, 1–24.
27. Refsgaard, J.C.; van der Sluijs, J.P.; Højberg, A.L.; Vanrolleghem, P.A. Uncertainty in the environmental modelling process—A framework and guidance. *Environ. Model. Softw.* **2007**, *22*, 1543–1556.
28. Ellis, J.B.; Shutes, R.B.E.; Revitt, M.D. *Constructed Wetlands and Links with Sustainable Drainage Systems*. Technical Report P2-159/TR1; Environment Agency: Bristol, UK, 2003.
29. Scholz, M.; Yang, Q. Guidance on variables characterising water bodies including Sustainable Flood Retention Basins. *Landsc. Urban Plan.* **2010**, *98*, 190–199.
30. Danso-Amoako, E.; Kalimeris, N.; Scholz, M.; Yang, Q.; Shao, J. Predicting dam failure risk for sustainable flood retention basins: A generic case study for the wider Greater Manchester area. *Comput. Environ. Urban Sys.* **2012**, *36*, 423–433.
31. McMinn, W.R.; Yang, Q.; Scholz, M. Classification and assessment of water bodies as adaptive structural measures for flood risk management planning. *J. Environ. Manag.* **2010**, *91*, 1855–1863.

Water **2013**, *5*, 462-479; doi:10.3390/w5020462

OPEN ACCESS

water

ISSN 2073-4441

www.mdpi.com/journal/water

Review

Water Quality Improvement Performance of Geotextiles Within Permeable Pavement Systems: A Critical Review

Miklas Scholz

Civil Engineering Research Group, School of Computing, Science and Engineering, The University of Salford, Newton Building, Salford M5 4WT, England, UK; E-Mail: m.scholz@salford.ac.uk; Tel.: +44-161-2955-921; Fax: +44-161-2955-575

Received: 21 February 2013; in revised form: 20 March 2013 / Accepted: 8 April 2013 / Published: 18 April 2013

Abstract: Sustainable drainage systems (SuDS; or best management practices) are increasingly being used as ecological engineering techniques to prevent the contamination of receiving watercourses and groundwater. Permeable paving is a SuDS technique, which is commonplace in car parks, driveways and minor roads where one of their functions is to improve the quality of urban runoff. However, little is known about the water quality benefits of incorporating an upper geotextile within the paving structure. The review focuses on five different categories of pollutants: organic matter, nutrients, heavy metals, motor oils, suspended solids originating from street dust, and chloride. The paper critically assesses results from previous international tests and draws conclusions on the scientific rigour and significance of the data. Findings indicate that only very few studies have been undertaken to address the role of geotextiles directly. All indications are that the presence of a geotextile leads only to minor water quality improvements. For example, suspended solids are being held back by the geotextile and these solids sometimes contain organic matter, nutrients and heavy metals. However, most studies were inconclusive and data were often unsuitable for further statistical analysis. Further long-term research on industry-relevant, and statistically and scientifically sound, experimental set-ups is recommended.

Keywords: best management practice; car park; clogging; heavy metals; oil; paving block; pollutant removal; salt; suspended solids; sustainable drainage system

1. Introduction

1.1. Background

The runoff from urban areas carries various pollutants including organic matter, nutrients, heavy metals, oils and suspended solids, which have previously been deposited onto impermeable surfaces. The majority of pollution in urban runoff originates from diffuse sources (often difficult to identify) including traffic emissions, decomposing litter, salts, building materials and soil losses [1,2]. These pollutants pose a risk to the urban watercourse quality and to the soil, if they remain untreated.

The management of storm water with Sustainable drainage systems (SuDS) such as permeable pavements, ponds and swales can have a positive effect in reducing these pollutants and delaying the volume of water discharging to the sewer or receiving water body. However, SuDS are frequently difficult to retrofit and implement on a large scale due to space and cost constraints. The change from permeable to impermeable land (e.g., roofs, roads and pavements) reduces groundwater recharge and creates a large volume of runoff and a higher peak flow rate in the drainage system. This can often lead to urban flooding, particularly during heavy rainfall and when sewers operate at their full capacity [1,2].

The SuDS technique 'permeable pavement' has become a popular solution in reducing the burden of increased runoff by restoring the infiltration treated runoff (if desired), water quality improvement and hydraulic functions of natural systems [3]. Permeable pavement systems vary greatly in terms of type, construction, dimensions, operation and management. An example of a permeable pavement system is shown in Figure 1.

Figure 1. Schematic outline of the main design components of a permeable pavement system.

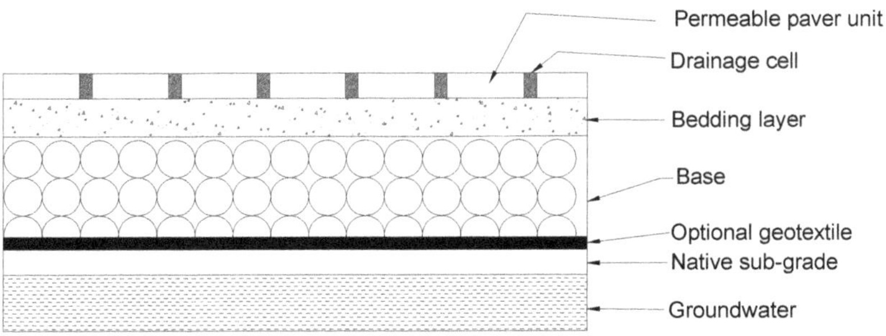

Environment agencies such as the Scottish Environment Protection Agency (SEPA) usually accept permeable paving surfaces as SuDS techniques. For example, SEPA's considerations for acceptance of surface drainage systems must be in line with the "General Binding Rules" contained within "The Water Environment (Controlled Activities) (Scotland) Regulation" [4]. For new developments, surface water must drain through a SuDS system if discharged into the environment and all "reasonable steps" should be taken to ensure that the discharge shall not result in pollution to the water environment. The use of proprietary permeable paving systems with a geotextile and a cellular (or modular attenuation system) meets this requirement where a single level of treatment is a requirement (e.g., small housing developments).

For situations such as commercial and retail sites, SEPA considers that two levels of treatment are required and as such a washed stone-filled sub-base below a proprietary paving system and in conjunction with a geotextile, preventing fines from entering the sub-base, would provide two levels of treatment. Such an arrangement would deliver the requirement for "reasonable steps" [4] to be taken to protect the water environment. This would assume that an adequate depth of sub-base is provided to allow filtration through a washed stone-filled sub-base.

With respect to the case study areas located in Scotland (Sections 4 and 5), SEPA works on the assumption that the presence of any geotextile within a standard permeable pavement system has a water quality improvement function [5]. However, no specific scientific evidence has been officially referenced by SEPA to avoid creating the impression that the agency favors a particular commercial product.

1.2. Rationale, Aim and Objectives

Very few ecological engineering research studies on permeable pavement systems produce directly comparable water quality results for paving constructions with and without an upper geotextile layer. Therefore, this paper aims to critically analyse research studies undertaken to determine the role of a geotextile layer in pollution control. The objectives are:

- To conduct a review of geotextiles within the SuDS context;
- To briefly assess recent permeable pavement system research;
- To critically review selected research projects on geotextiles within permeable pavement systems undertaken for the concrete and aggregate industry;
- To draw conclusions based on the critical literature review; and
- To recommend further research work.

International ecological engineering research has been reviewed. However, a specific focus is on case studies with relevance to areas experiencing temperate and oceanic climates. This includes most parts of Northern America and Europe. Such a restriction in focus is necessary because environmental boundary conditions vary greatly across the globe. Only a few recent studies directly concerned with the geotextile and water quality were identified in the literature review comprising more than 200 documents. Therefore, Sections 4 and 5 focus on these relevant research studies addressing the role of geotextiles with respect to pollution control.

2. Critical Review of Geotextiles in the Context of Permeable Pavements

2.1. Relevant Types of Geotextiles

Geotextiles can be characterised as being either woven or non-woven. Most woven geotextiles are formed by interlacing two or more sets of yarns, fibers or filaments where they pass each other at right angles [6]. Specific weaving methods create four main types of geotextiles: monofilament, slit film, multifilament and fibrillated. Monofilament geotextiles offer little resistance to through-flow of water and are generally made from polyethylene (HDPE) or polypropylene (PP). Standard geotextiles are semi-inert materials with predominantly physical properties [1], which are relevant in the context of this review paper.

A multifilament yarn consists of many fine continuous filaments that are held together by twisting of the strands. Fibrillated tapes are made by splitting and twisting extruded films. Woven slit films are produced with yarns formed by longitudinally splitting of a polymeric film to form a slit tape yarn. However, this type of woven geotextile is not suitable for most drainage and filtration applications [7].

Woven geotextiles are characterized by their excellent strength properties and are generally less expensive than non-woven types of the same strength [6]. Non-woven geotextiles are typically manufactured by putting small fibers together in the form of a sheet or web, and then binding them by mechanical, chemical and/or solvent means. They are usually grouped into three categories: needle punched, chemical bonded or heat bonded [6].

Non-woven geotextiles are generally not as strong as their equivalent woven geotextiles, but they exhibit better filtration and separation properties [8]. For this reason, nonwoven geotextiles are the preferred geotextile type for permeable paving applications.

The polymers used to construct both woven and non-woven geotextiles are synthetic polymers (polyester, polypropylene or a mixture of polyester and polypropylene). Polyester and polyolefins such as polypropylene are hydrophobic materials. Whilst this is advantageous in circumstances that require water and/or suspended solids to be trapped above the surface of the geotextile, it may lead to ponding within a permeable pavement structure, if geotextiles with the incorrect flow rate and permittivity are being used. Polyesters and polypropylene materials are highly resistant to chemical and biological degradation [6] and therefore suitable for application in the construction industry.

The majority of manufacturers use polypropylene in the construction of their geotextiles, because polyester deteriorates over time under both acidic and alkaline conditions. However, the degradation is more severe under alkaline conditions, which are rarely the case in urban runoff [2,9].

2.2. Geotextile Applications and Their Properties of Relevance for Permeable Pavements

Geotextiles can be used for the separation and strengthening layer under new roads and car parks, and as a filter in certain SuDS applications including permeable pavements and infiltration trenches. Geotextiles can also enhance organic matter (e.g., leaf litter and hydrocarbons) removal by trapping the contaminants on the surface cavities, then allowing microbial biodegradation to occur [10]. Moreover, geotextiles may support drainage but there are potential problems with frost in cold climatic regions such as Scotland and Canada [11].

Pavement engineers concerned with assessing geotextile properties may refer to Jersey and Tingle [12]. Behavioural trends were characterised for geotextile material types and manufacturing processes. The implications of the trends for design applications and product specification were noted. However, no specific reference to water quality improvement issues has been made.

The functions of geotextiles are usually divided into five main categories: separation, filtration, drainage, protection and reinforcement. With respect to the case studies discussed in Sections 4 and 5, British guidance on the properties of geotextiles for use in drainage systems and in trafficked areas is given in BS EN 13252:2001 [13] and BS EN 13249:2001 [14]. These standards have subsequently been interpreted by the concrete and aggregate industry operating in Britain (e.g., [2]).

The ability of a geotextile to retain fines (e.g., suspended solids) depends primarily on its opening size [15]. The Pore Size (or Characteristic Opening Size) Test is designed to assess the mean size of the holes in the fabric. The gap sizes for common geotextiles vary widely between 70 and 380 microns. The 85% size of soil is compared with the apparent opening size of geotextiles. The apparent opening size refers to the approximate largest opening dimension available for soil to pass through it. The findings indicate that for sand and silt size particles, a geotextile with apparent opening size (O-95) less than 85% size [d(85)] of retained soil would perform satisfactorily. However, for fine soils in suspension, the ratio of geotextile O-95 to soil d(85) should be restricted to 0.5 or less. This recommendation helps to select the most appropriate geotextile when designing for water quality improvement.

Permeability tests for geotextiles may differ between 36 and 120 L/(m^2s), and are generally a function of the weight and thickness of the geotextile [16]. This test is of great relevance when assessing the suitability of a geotextile for its suspended solids retention potential within a permeable pavement system. A further discussion on permeability test results as a function of opening sizes, materials and test standard conditions is beyond the scope of this paper, which focuses on water quality issues (see Sections 4 and 5).

The presence of a geotextile layer on top of the base of the permeable pavement parking lot structure (experimental case study example) is one key factor restricting vertical percolation to the deeper parts of the permeable pavement system [9]. Clogging of the permeable surface due to the accumulation of suspended solids was most pronounced in heavy traffic areas and below snow pile storage areas. Corroborated by high electric conductivity and chloride measurements, sand brought in by cars during winter was the principal cause for clogging. The study clearly highlighted the limitations of the geotextile properties during extreme conditions.

3. Assessment of Permeable Pavement Systems

3.1. Need for a Permeable Pavement Systems Review

A typical permeable pavement consists of a permeable paving layer, bedding layer, base and sub-base [17]. Building and environment geotextiles are generally placed at one or two levels within permeable paving structures; at the upper level separating the bedding layer and sub-base; and/or at the lower level separating the sub-base from the sub-grade. A geotextile layer is usually placed between the bedding layer and the base to increase the structural integrity (if the infiltrating runoff is relatively free from particles), pollutant retention capabilities and biodegradation processes for organic contamination within the pavement systems [18].

The geotextile layer also encourages microbial activity in this area, leading to an improved treatment of runoff due to biological degradation processes [10,18]. Furthermore, the geotextile also prevents fine particles (partly responsible for clogging) in the bedding layer from moving downwards into the aggregate, subsequently creating air pockets within the bedding layer, contributing to a potentially structurally unstable surface [17].

With direct relevance to the case studies discussed in Sections 4 and 5, various researchers in the UK (e.g., [17,19]) and SEPA [5] have made claims implicitly or explicitly that a geotextile is needed to achieve good environmental performance. However, there is a current debate particularly amongst civil engineers and representatives from the concrete and aggregate industry about the water quality benefits gained by incorporating an upper geotextile.

This review paper covers a wide range of assessed literature including more than 150 relevant ISI Web of Knowledge-listed journal papers contributing to this discussion. It is evident that a large number of international studies have been conducted on the pollution removal efficiency of permeable pavements, their hydraulic properties and the effect of clogging. However, the literature review indicates that only a relatively small number of these experiments included an upper geotextile layer (e.g., [20–22]). The removal processes of key contaminants within various permeable pavement systems are reviewed in the following sub-sections to clarify their role in terms of water quality improvement.

3.2. Removal of Heavy Metals

The quality of runoff waters from porous pavements has been studied by Legret *et al.* [23]. The filtration effect of runoff by the reservoir structure incorporated within the pavement system decreased the pollutant concentrations by about 64% for suspended solids (often associated with adsorbed metals) and 79% for lead. Most metallic micro-pollutants (lead, copper, cadmium and zinc) accumulated on the surface of the pervious asphalt. A smaller proportion of these pollutants also accumulates at the level of the geotextile layer separating the structure from the underlying soil.

A comparison between the runoff quality from asphalt, crushed stone and paver driveways has been undertaken in Connecticut, USA [24]. The study was, however, inconclusive regarding the potential impact of a geotextile. A further study [25] evaluated the pollution retention capacity of a paving area for lead, zinc, cadmium and copper in Germany. Five laboratory rigs, each containing different joint fillers, showed high retention abilities for all metals. It was found that the overall removal efficiencies for cadmium, lead, copper and zinc were 99%, 99%, 98% and 94%, respectively.

3.3. Removal of Oils

A study concerning two rigs was published by [26]; one rig had an upper geotextile and another "virtually identical" rig had no geotextile. The presence of an upper geotextile was found to be important during oil retention studies. Furthermore, both a laboratory and a field study to simulate crank case leakage have been conducted previously [27]. The apparatus contained both an upper and lower geotextile. It was observed from the experiment that only 2.4% of the oil applied is not retained within the system. A further study [28] by the same research group indicated that a permeable pavement structure's efficiency in degrading oil was a function of nutrient supply. The authors found that permeable paving systems were associated with high oil removal rates of 99.6%.

Geotextiles incorporating inorganic nutrients to enhance the growth of oil-degrading micro-organisms when geotextiles are used in pervious pavement applications have been shown to be effective in previous studies [28]. A relatively low-cost polypropylene random mat geotextile incorporating an alternative polymer additive as a source of phosphorus has been investigated as a potential self-fertilising geotextile. Initial findings regarding nutrient leach rates, biofilm formation and biodegradation activity were positive. Biofilm formation on the geotextile layer improves the water quality due to biodegradation of contaminants such as oils.

Bio-degradation by microbial communities in three differently sized permeable pavement structures, each with different concentrations of oil applied per week, was studied by [29]. All rigs were constructed with an upper geotextile. Some of the rigs were inoculated with Biothreat HD, an oil degrading microbial inoculum, and some of the rigs also had a slow release fertiliser added to them. Oil was applied using a dripper to simulate vehicle engine leakage. Both the large and the medium rigs (inoculated or not), retained 99% of the oil applied. For medium-sized rigs, the amount of oil on the geotextile was slightly less for non-inoculated rigs compared to inoculated rigs (8.9% to 9.9%). However, no reference has been made with respect to the proportions that were removed by biodegradation and evaporation.

3.4. Removal of Suspended Solids

Geotextiles with fine pores should be able to retain fines including suspended solids (see above). The accumulation of water on a permeable pavement layer, also called ponding, is often a result of a clogged system due to the presence of too many suspended solids. Researchers compared the ponding depths on different permeable paving surfaces [30,31]. The depth of ponding indicated the severity of clogging. Clogged geotextiles clearly limited infiltration. Furthermore, when comparing asphalt, block paving and crushed stone driveways with each other, the infiltration rates were 0.0, 11.2 and 9.0 cm/h, respectively [24]. Moreover, infiltration rates for both block paving and crushed stone driveways declined over the course of this study. The reason for this observation is pore clogging by suspended solids. It follows that it is important to select a pavement material type that would not lead to the clogging of the geotextile within the same system.

The processes and characteristics of solids removal in two types of permeable pavements were assessed in Canada [32]: UNI Eco-Stone and porous asphalt. Results from the study showed that both pavement types are capable of excellent suspended solids removal (90% to 96%). Laboratory results indicated that, although solids removal occurs throughout the entire structure, the sieving action occurs primarily at the geotextile interface, confirming findings from other reviewed studies.

Different types of pervious pavements were tested in Northern Spain [33–35]. Pervious surface materials had a greater effect than the geotextile layer in terms of water quality improvements. The treated water could be harvested and recycled. Nevertheless, the researchers state that the differences in terms of storm water management using the different pervious pavement types tested still need to be confirmed in further more specific studies regarding the impact of the geotextile on water quality [33].

3.5. Removal of Other Parameters

This section covers water quality parameter that are only of interest under specific circumstances. There is little direct focus on the removal of other parameters such as organic matter, nutrients and chloride (due to road salting), and the interactions between different contaminants such as herbicides and hydrocarbons. Particles containing organic matter and nutrients are being partly retained by the geotextile. However, the majority of the solids is dissolved, and they are therefore simply being washed through the geotextile [1,2].

Road gritting and salting has been identified as a major water quality problem in countries with cold regions such as Canada, UK, Scotland, Germany and Sweden (e.g., [36]). The application of grit mixed with salts usually contributes to elevated suspended solids concentrations, and high conductivity, salt and chloride values [1,36]. Road salts are usually washed through the permeable pavement system with a negative impact on the biomass growth [1]. Conductivity values are not affected significantly by the presence of a geotextile [9]. Therefore, very little chloride is retained by the geotextile layer [1,2,22].

Finally, a recent experimental investigation was carried out to determine the effect of glyphosate-containing herbicides on the hydrocarbon retention and biodegradation processes known to occur in permeable pavement systems [37]. Findings indicated that glyphosate-containing herbicides disrupted hydrocarbon retention by geotextiles.

4. Critical Review of the "Abertay Study"

4.1. Essential Background

This section is concerned with the critical review of a research study [38,39] on the role of a geotextile in permeable pavement systems undertaken by the University of Abertay. The study focused on assessing the impact of a geotextile on removing selected heavy metals, oil and suspended solids. The metal concentrations applied were twice the typical values for polluted highway runoff [40]. The oil contamination levels were based on a previous publication [19]. Moreover, suspended solids contamination levels followed those reported previously [41]. However, these data refer to Australian studies, which might not be representative for this Scottish case study.

4.2. Summary of Methodology

Researchers report on ten above-ground (not insulated) test rigs with dimensions of 1 m length × 1 m width × 0.5 m depth, which were constructed at a test site near Dundee in Scotland (Figure 2) [38,39]. The test rigs were designed in accordance with the standard specifications used by Marshalls for their Priora Paving system incorporating the non-woven geotextile Terram 1000 (produced by Terram, The Causeway, Maldon, Essex CM9 4GG, England, UK). The design methodology and base specifications were in accordance with BS EN 13242:2002 + A1:2007 [42] and BS 7533-13:2009 [43].

Rainfall was simulated using a branch sprinkler system. Three different categories of pollutants were applied: metals, oils and suspended solids obtained from street surfaces. Water samples were taken from sample pots every two minutes using Epic automatic samplers. Three composite samples were used for analysis.

Contaminant loads representing a total of 10 years were applied to the test rigs in batches of 1, 2 and 7 years [38,39]. An 'accelerated' timescale was applied for the tests. The estimated load of pollutants for each of the time periods (1, 2 and 7 years) was applied with one year of rainfall (1200 mm) over 100 min. In the case of street dust, a total of 20 years was applied in batches of 3, 3, 4, 5 and 5 years.

The metals were obtained from suppliers already in solution at the required concentrations. A concentrated solution containing a 'cocktail' of metals was added to the appropriate water tanks. The content of the water tank (Figure 2) was then mixed before the solution was applied to the paving area using the sprinkler system.

Figure 2. Main experimental set-up used in the "Abertay study" (picture provided by Marshalls).

Light motor oil (10W/40) was used to best represent oil drips from modern cars. Oil was dripped onto the paving area using a bucket with holes in the base. The equivalent of one year of oil load was applied before starting the rainfall simulation. In the case of the equivalent of two years of oil load, hydrocarbon was applied in two batches; the first batch before the test run began followed by the second one after 45 min into the test run. The water was turned off to allow the oil to be dripped onto the pavement. The remaining water volume was subsequently sprinkled onto the pavers. For the seven-year duration simulation run, the water was stopped every 15 min to allow the equivalent of one year of oil to be applied. Once the oil had been used, the rainfall simulator was placed back onto the paving unit and water was sprinkled for another 15 min, until the equivalent of seven years of oil load had been applied.

Street dust was spread onto the paving area evenly and washed into the gaps between the pavers using 15 L of water from a watering can. The annual rainfall volume was then applied using the rainfall simulator. For test runs using the corresponding five years of sediment load, street dust was applied in two batches at 90° angles to one another. The weight of each batch was 550 g.

4.3. Review of Key Findings

Results from the application of one year equivalent of metal loads showed varied metal removal rates [38,39]. After the application of the equivalent of three years of metals, the removal rates of cadmium, zinc and lead were higher (*i.e.*, between 2% and 5%) in rigs, which included a geotextile layer than those without. Copper elimination rates were generally low. Nickel removal rates were high in the test rig with a geotextile.

After the equivalent of ten years of metals had been applied, all metals (cadmium, copper, lead, zinc and nickel) showed higher removal (between 2% and 6%) rates for the rig, which contained an upper geotextile. However, the measurement error was estimated to be high and a statistical analysis was not undertaken [38,39].

Oil removal rates for all test rigs were above 90% at the end of the simulation for year one confirming related findings [28]. Test rigs with a geotextile removed slightly higher amounts of hydrocarbon. For the simulation of year two, the oil-only rig with a geotextile removed a greater proportion (approximately 10%) than the equivalent rig without a geotextile. The rig receiving metals and oil without a geotextile had slightly higher oil removal efficiencies (approximately 4%) than the comparable rig without the geotextile. After the equivalent of ten years of oil had been applied to the test rigs, the rig receiving metals and oil and containing a geotextile had removed 13% more oil than the other test rigs. In contrast, there was no difference in the removal of oil in the two oil-only rigs. The results indicate no clear evidence that the presence of a geotextile had an impact on the removal of oils.

The application of street dust to the paving units caused increased ponding and overflowing as the sediment mass applied increased. Findings confirmed those reported earlier [28]. Moreover, in the two runs representing the equivalent of three and six years of street dust, there was minimal interference with the flow of water through the paving system. After the equivalent of ten years of application, both test rigs showed significantly more ponding during the watering stage, and larger agglomerations of sediment were left in the gaps between the pavers after watering in comparison to previous runs. After simulating year 15, sediment agglomerations on the surfaces of the pavers were even greater than in previous test runs. This resulted in reduced flow rates indicating blockage. For year 20, the rigs failed due to complete clogging.

4.4. Summary of the Conclusions

The results for year three showed insignificantly higher metal removal rates for cadmium, lead and zinc when the geotextile was present. Test rigs with a geotextile performed best after the application of the equivalent of 10 years of metals.

Oil removal was greatest for the test rigs containing a geotextile after ten years of application. After three years of simulation concerning the oil-only experiments, the test rig containing a geotextile removed a greater proportion of oil. The rig receiving oil and metals with a geotextile removed slightly less than the corresponding non-geotextile test rig with results similar to that of the oil-only geotextile test rig. No statistical tests were performed. The presence of a geotextile had little impact on the removal of oil [38].

With respect to the street dust application, there was no evidence of any obvious impact on the water quality by including a geotextile. There was, however, great variability in the results for all rigs. There was insufficient information to conclude whether an upper geotextile is beneficial or not [38,39].

4.5. Critical Assessment of the 'Abertay Study'

The experimental set-up [38,39] is impressive due to the high number of rigs and their relatively large size. However, the overall study was undertaken subject to the following conditions and assumptions:

- The test rigs were located above the ground (Figure 2), which exposed them to unrealistic environmental conditions such as high temperature fluctuations and enhanced wind exposure impacting on removal processes. In terms of water quality, removal rates are over-estimated during warm periods and under-estimated during cold periods.
- The simulation of multiple years of pollution represents the application of a series of severe one-off shock loads. Most pollutants were simply being forced hydraulically through the system, and very little biodegradation activities took place. Moreover, total metal adsorption is lower than under long-term test conditions. Accelerating loading by increasing contaminant concentrations also affects the corresponding sorption isotherms, which were not determined in this study.
- The combination of different pollution loads simulates worst case scenarios in parallel and in series. The testing period of about two months is too short to represent different seasons and allow representative biomass to mature in the systems.
- The hydraulic flow rate and both the loads and concentrations of most pollutants selected were too high.

Considering the above circumstances, the study may be viewed as applied research covering extreme scenarios in the 'real' world. Therefore, a clear judgment on the purification capacity that could be contributed to the geotextile cannot be made.

5. Critical Review of the 'Edinburgh Study'

5.1. Essential Background

This section is concerned with the critical review of a long-term and well-reported research study [3,10,22] undertaken by the The University of Edinburgh for Hanson Formpave (Hanson UK, 14 Castle Hill, Maidenhead SL6 4JJ, England, UK). Several types of combined permeable pavement and ground source heating pump systems used to treat urban runoff were evaluated. The study was originally designed to assess the effectiveness of removing urban runoff containing dog faeces and not the potential benefits associated with a geotextile.

5.2. Summary of Methodology

Two permeable pavement system (Figure 3; Table 1) rigs were operated under controlled and uncontrolled environmental conditions for more than three full calendar years [22]. An example experimental permeable pavement system incorporating a geothermal heating or cooling system is shown in Figure 3. The increase or decrease in temperature of the sub-base will either enhance or reduce microbial activity impacting therefore on the biodegradation activity of species.

Typical polyethylene 240-l wheelie-bins have been used as basic construction devices. The bins mimicked impermeable tanked systems (*i.e.*, no ground infiltration) and provided suitable conditions for water collection.

Figure 3. Schematic outline of the main design principles of an experimental permeable pavement set-up without and with a geothermal system used in the "Edinburgh study" (after [10]).

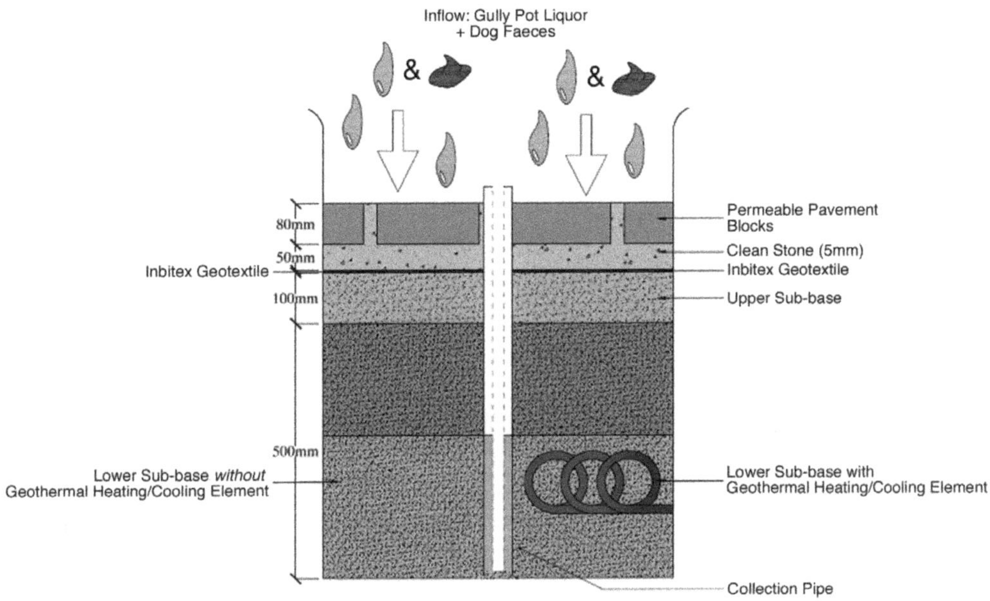

Table 1. Schematic layout of the experimental rigs of the Edinburgh study.

Feature	Bins of the inside rig						Bins of the outside rig					
	1	2	3	4	5	6	1	2	3	4	5	6
Inbitex composite	√	√	√				√	√	√			
Inbitex geotextile				√	√	√				√	√	√
Cooling or heating	√	√		√	√		√	√		√	√	
Animal feaces added	√			√			√			√		
Air thermometer	√				√	√	√				√	√
Vessel thermometer	√				√		√				√	
Carbon dioxide sampling point	√				√		√				√	

The indoor system was composed of six bins and placed in a temperature-controlled room with a mean ambient temperature of 16 °C. The outdoor rig was submerged within the ground and located outside the local laboratory building where atmospheric temperature conditions prevailed. All bins were partly filled with the inflow water, and operated in batch flow mode, which therefore simulates real car park and pavement runoff conditions better than a continuous flow mode.

Commercially available pre-washed aggregates were used for the construction of the sub-base. The porous Inbitex geotextile (Table 1), which is made of polyethylene and polypropylene fibres (see above) was placed in the top part of the upper-base, as this is the area where considerable microbial degradation of pollutants is expected to take place. Either Inbitex on its own or Inbitex together with an impermeable layer (Terram Drainage Composite), called composite, were used in the experiments

(Table 1). The impermeable layers were overlapped with each other to allow water to percolate through the system but to avoid evaporation.

Water was exchanged twice per week. The influent samples were prepared by collecting gully pot liquor and fresh dog faeces on the same day of analysis. Approximately 2.2 L of "outflow" sample water was slowly collected approximately 100 mm from the bottom of each bin by a hand lever pump. The temperature of the sample was immediately recorded at this stage. Finally, carbon dioxide samples were collected via collection tubes located at various depths within the bins.

5.3. Review of Key Findings

Because of the strong variability of the chosen pollutants, the standard deviation for suspended solids was 411 mg/L and 181 mg/L for the inflow water with and without additional pollutants, respectively. Similar observations were made for conductivity and ammonia-nitrogen. Road gritting and salting in winter leads to high fluctuations of suspended solids, conductivity and chloride concentrations [2,9].

Relatively stable and uniform values were only recorded for pH, DO and nitrate-nitrogen. The mean bin intakes for ortho-phosphate-phosphorus were 1.9 mg/L and 26.2 mg/L without and with dog faeces, respectively. The corresponding concentrations for ammonia-nitrogen were 14.7 mg/L and 39.3 mg/L, respectively.

The variability of pH was relatively low. In contrast, the maximum standard deviations for conductivity ranged between 25 and 80 μS for the inside and between 8 and 124 μS for the outside rig, respectively. Outdoor variability was usually greater than indoor (controlled environment) variability as expected. However, the most significant ($p < 0.002$) variability has been recorded for suspended solids with respect to the outside bin 5 and inside bin 2 (Table 1); corresponding standard deviations reached concentrations of 208 mg/L and 269 mg/L, respectively.

Mean dissolved oxygen concentrations were similar for both rigs: they were between 5 and 6 mg/L for the inside rig and between 5.5 and 7 mg/L for the outside set-up. Overall reductions in dissolved oxygen for both systems ranged between 22% and 46%. The BOD reductions ranged between 98% and 100%.

Concerning nutrients, high reductions in ortho-phosphate-phosphorus and ammonia-nitrogen were observed. For the inside system, ortho-phosphate-phosphorus concentrations were less than 1 mg/L (corresponding reduction of 95%). For the outside system, concentrations fluctuated between 0.2 mg/L and 0.6 mg/L with corresponding reduction rates of approximately 95%. Ammonia-nitrogen reductions were up to 100% for both systems and the corresponding concentrations ranged between 0.1 mg/L and 0.2 mg/L for the inside and between 0.03 mg/L and 0.14 mg/L for the outside system.

An increase in nitrate-nitrogen had been recorded. For the inside and outside bins, which received dog faeces, the highest releases of nitrate-nitrogen have been noted. This is due to the additional load of nitrogen. There is also a slight increase for the inside bin 6 and outside bin 6 (no faeces, and no heating or cooling; Table 1). For the outside rig, nitrate-nitrogen reductions were observed for bins 2, 4 and 5. For the outside bins 1, 3, 6 and all inside bins, removal efficiencies were negative (–440% to –62%). In general, systems comprising a geotextile had lower nitrate-nitrogen concentrations.

Microorganism counts varied considerably. For the outside system, total heterotrophic colony forming units (CFU) ranged between 39,000 and 121,000 for the outflow water, and with means of 101,000 and 7,605,000 for the inflow water without and with dog faeces, respectively. For the inside system, the corresponding numbers ranged between 52,000 and 180,000 for the outflow water, and had means of 172,000 and 378,000 for the inflow without and with faeces, respectively.

The microbial activities within the systems mirrored the corresponding carbon dioxide concentrations. The highest concentrations were recorded close to the first two (*i.e.*, the shallowest) sampling points for each bin. This indicates that the most intensive microbial activity takes place around the geotextile [28,29], which was responsible for lower microbial counts within the outflow of most systems during the majority of the monitoring period [3].

5.4. Summary of Conclusions

The data variability of the inside rig was reduced by applying controlled environmental conditions such as a relatively stable temperature. Suspended solids values for outside rigs were on average 100% higher than the corresponding concentrations for the inside rigs, indicating the importance of a relatively high temperature for biodegradation. Ortho-phosphate-phosphorus and ammonia-nitrogen removal rates were very high (up to 95%), and the corresponding absolute concentrations fulfilled European urban wastewater treatment standards.

The microbial activities during high temperature durations were high, which lead to better treatment performances. The elevated carbon dioxide concentrations and corresponding reductions in biochemical oxygen demand are evidence for the increased microbial activity within the sub-base, especially on the geotextile. The cell counts for most bacteria groups with respect to the outflows for systems were usually low.

5.5. Critical Assessment of the Edinburgh Study

The outside rig represents "real" environmental conditions (e.g., pavement systems are surrounded by soil except at their tops), and is therefore more appropriate than the rig operated in the 'Abertay study'. In comparison, the inside rig allows for modelling due to a reduced degree of freedom (*i.e.* more stable variables such as temperature and humidity) but temperature conditions are unrealistic.

The Edinburgh study was not conducted with the aim to assess the impact of the geotextile on water quality in a statistically sound experimental set-up. However, the findings can be used to assess the indirect influence of the geotextile on some key water quality parameters. During most periods, the presence of a geotextile was beneficial in keeping suspended solids and nitrate-nitrogen concentrations as well as bacteria colony counts relatively low in the outflow. However, the statistical set-up was not optimized to come to conclusive findings regarding the role of the geotextile. Moreover, other important pollutants such as metals and oils were not assessed.

6. Conclusions

Most relevant ecological engineering research on permeable pavement systems has been undertaken in Europe and Northern America. The review of permeable pavement system literature indicates that there are very few studies that directly research the impact of geotextiles within permeable pavement systems on improving the water quality. However, there is an indication that the presence of a suitable geotextile within a permeable pavement system reduces the breakthrough of suspended solids.

The studies covered in detail as part of this paper suggest only a minor statistically insignificant improvement of some water quality parameters (predominantly suspended solids and associated contaminants) when a geotextile is present. Most other parameters such as chloride are virtually unaffected.

A review of the 'Abertay study' on geotextiles within permeable pavement systems indicated that the chosen methodology had its clear limitations and that some findings were inconclusive. In comparison, a review of the 'Edinburgh study' on geotextiles within combined ground source heat and permeable pavement systems shows that the presence of geotextiles makes a minor contribution to improving the water quality.

7. Recommendations for Further Research

The author proposes to conduct a long-term (at least two full years) scientific study with large test rigs located belowground (*i.e.* simulating 'real' conditions). 'Real' runoff spiked with a realistic composition of key pollutants of reasonable concentrations and loads reported for road runoff in the scientific literature should be used within a statistical set-up of different experimental rigs.

There are a few innovations that should be considered at the same time for further research. For example, a heat-bonded geotextile could be used to slow down the release of small oil droplets, and their subsequent transport through the permeable pavement system. Furthermore, geotextiles incorporating trace elements to enhance the degradation of specific contaminants such as oils might be suitable in environments where runoff contains insufficient nutrients.

Considering that this review has identified relevant research predominantly in North America and Northern Europe, new research on geotextiles within permeable pavements should be conducted in areas experiencing warmer and dryer climate. This may include tropical regions in South America, Africa, Asia, Australia and New Zealand suffering from severe flooding during the rainy season. Alternatively, corresponding weather conditions could be simulated in a temperature- and humidity-controlled laboratory or greenhouse.

The overall image of concrete-based permeable pavements could be improved by addressing more ecosystem services variables as part of the new green infrastructure initiative in the UK. For example, more sustainable geotextiles could be selected and permeable pavements could be combined with other SuDS such as infiltration structures and filtration systems including planted filter strips to increase the sustainability rating, improve water quality, and enhance ecology and amenity at the same time.

Acknowledgments

The author acknowledges support received by block paving manufacturers and suppliers including Marshalls and Hanson Formpave in the past. However, the views expressed by the author are not necessarily shared by these companies. No conflict of interest has been identified. Piotr Grabowiecki and Kiran Tota-Maharaj provided technical assistance for the Edinburgh study.

References

1. Scholz, M. *Wetland Systems to Control Urban Runoff*; Elsevier: Amsterdam, The Netherlands, 2006.
2. Scholz, M. *Wetland Systems—Storm Water Management Control*; Springer Verlag: Berlin, Germany, 2010.
3. Scholz, M.; Grabowiecki, P. Combined permeable pavement and ground source heating pump systems to treat urban runoff. *J. Chem. Technol. Biotechnol.* **2009**, *84*, 405–413.
4. Scottish Government. *The Water Environment (Controlled Activities) (Scotland) Regulation*; Scottish Government, The National Archives: Edinburgh, Scotland, UK, 2011. Available online: http://www.legislation.gov.uk/ssi/2011/209/contents/made (accessed on 16 May 2012).
5. McLean, N.; Marshalls. SEPA. E-Mail Communication, 5 February 2008.
6. Holtz, R.D. Geosynthetics for soil reinforcement. In *Frontier Technologies for Infrastructures Engineering: Structures and Infrastructures*; Chen, S., Ang, A.H., Eds.; Taylor and Francis Group: London, UK, 2009.
7. John, N.W.M. *Geotextiles*; Blackie and Son: London, UK, 1987.
8. Cook, D.I. *Geosynthetics*; Rubber and Plastics Research Association Technology Limited: Shrewsbury, UK, 2003.
9. Boving, T.B.; Stolt, M.H.; Augenstern, J.; Brosnan, B. Potential for localized groundwater contamination in a porous pavement parking lot setting in Rhode Island. *Environ. Geol.* **2008**, *55*, 571–582.
10. Tota-Maharaj, K.; Scholz, M.; Ahmed, T.; French, C.; Pagaling, E. The synergy of permeable pavements and geothermal heat pumps for stormwater treatment and reuse. *Environ. Technol.* **2010**, *31*, 1517–1531.
11. Raymond, G.P.; Bathurst, R.J. Facilitating cold climate pavement drainage using geosynthetics. In *Testing and Performance of Geosynthetics in Subsurface Drainage*; Suits, L.D., Goddard, J.B., Baldwin, J.S., Eds.; American Society for Testing and Materials Special Technical Publication: West Conshohocken, PA, USA, 2000; Volume 1390, pp. 52–63.
12. Jersey, S.R.; Tingle, J.S. Geotextile response to common index property tests. *Transport. Res. Rec.* **2007**, *1989*, 102–112.
13. BSI. *Geotextiles and Geotextile-related Products. Characteristics Required for Use in Drainage Systems*; The British Standards Institution: London, UK, 2001; Standard BS EN 13252:2001. Available online: http://shop.bsigroup.com/ProductDetail/?pid=000000000030144789 (accessed on 10 May 2012).
14. The British Standards Institution (BSI). *Geotextiles and Geotextile-related Products. Characteristics Required for Use in the Construction of Roads and Other Trafficked Areas (Excluding Railways and Asphalt Inclusion)*; BSI: London, UK, 2001; Standard BS EN 13249:2001. Available online: http://shop.bsigroup.com/ProductDetail/?pid=000000000030144365 (accessed on 10 May 2012).
15. Narejo, D.B. Opening size recommendations for separation geotextiles used in pavements. *Geotext. Geomemb.* **2003**, *21*, 257–264.
16. Shukla, S.K. *Geosynthetics and Their Applications*; Thomas Telford Publishing: London, UK, 2002.

17. Scholz, M.; Grabowiecki, P. Review of permeable pavement systems. *Build. Environm.* **2007**, *42*, 3830–3836.
18. Coupe, S.J.; Smith, H.G.; Newman, A.P.; Pühmeier, T. Biodegradation and microbial diversity within permeable pavements. *Eur. J. Protistol.* **2003**, *39*, 495–498.
19. Pühmeier, T.; Newman, A.P. Oil retaining and treating geotextile for pavement application. In Proceedings of the 11th International Conference on Urban Drainage, Edinburgh, UK, 31 August–5 September 2008.
20. Newman, A.P.; Pühmeier, T.; Kwok, V.; Lam, M.; Coupe, S.J.; Shuttleworth, A.; Pratt, C.J. Protecting groundwater with oil-retaining pervious pavements: Historical perspectives, limitations and recent developments. *Quart. J. Eng. Geol. Hydrogeol.* **2004**, *37*, 283–291.
21. Pratt, C.J.; Mantle, D.G.; Schofield, P.A. UK research into the performance of permeable pavement, reservoir structures in controlling stormwater discharge quantity and quality. *Water Sci. Technol.* **1995**, *32*, 63–69.
22. Tota-Maharaj, K.; Scholz, M. Artificial neural network simulation of combined permeable pavement and earth energy systems treating storm water. *J. Environ. Eng. ASCE* **2012**, *138*, 499–509.
23. Legret, M.; Colandini, V.; LeMarc, C. Effects of a porous pavement with reservoir structure on the quality of runoff water and soil. *Sci. Total Environ.* **1996**, *190*, 335–340.
24. Gilbert, J.K.; Clausen, J.C. Stormwater runoff quality and quantity from asphalt, paver, and crushed stone driveways in Connecticut. *Water Res.* **2006**, *40*, 826–832.
25. Dierkes, C.; Lohmann, M.; Becker, M.; Rassch, U. Pollution retention of different permeable pavements with reservoir structure at high hydraulic loads. In Proceedings of the 10th International Conference on Urban Drainage, Copenhagen, Denmark, 21–26 August 2005.
26. Rowe, A.A.; Borst, M.; O'Connor, T.P. Pervious pavement system evaluation. In Proceedings of the World Environmental and Water Resources Congress 2009, Great Rivers, MI, USA, 17–21 May 2009; Starrett, S., Ed.; American Society of Civil Engineers: Reston, VA, USA, 2009; pp. 1–8.
27. Pratt, C.J.; Newman, A.P.; Bond, P.C. Mineral oil bio-degradation within a permeable pavement: long term observations. *Water Sci. Technol.* **1999**, *39*, 103–109.
28. Newman, A.P.; Coupe, S.J.; Henderson, J.; Morgan, J.A.; Pühmeier, T.; Pratt, C.J. Oil retention and microbial ecology in porous pavement structures. Presented at the European Forum of Environmental Research Laboratories, Campus Ker Lann, Rennes, France, 2001. Available online: http://perviousconsulting.com/resources/Microbial%2BEcology%2BIn%2BPorous%2BPavement.pdf (accessed on 3 May 2012).
29. Newman, A.P.; Pratt, C.J.; Coupe, S.J.; Cresswell, N. Oil bio-degradation in permeable pavements by microbial communities. *Water Sci. Technol.* **2002**, *45*, 51–56.
30. Yong, C.F.; Deletic, A.; Fletcher, T.D.; Grace, M.R. The clogging behavior and treatment efficiency of a range of porous pavements. In Proceedings of the 11th International Conference on Urban Drainage, Edinburgh, UK, 31 August–5 September 2008.
31. Fernández-Barrera, A.H.; Castro-Fresno, D.; Rodriguez-Hernandez, J.; Calzada-Pérez, M.A. Infiltration capacity assessment of urban pavements using the LCS permeameter and the CP infiltrometer. *J. Irrig. Drain. Eng.* **2008**, *134*, 659–665.

32. Brown, C.; Chu, A.; van Duin, B.; Valeo, C. Characteristics of sediment removal in two types of permeable pavement. *Water Qual. Res. J. Can.* **2009**, *44*, 59–70.
33. Gomez-Ullate, E.; Castillo-Lopez, E.; Castro-Fresno, D.; Bayon, J.R. Analysis and contrast of different pervious pavements for management of storm-water in a parking area in Northern Spain. *Water Resour. Manag.* **2011**, *25*, 1525–1535.
34. Gomez-Ullate, E.; Bayon, J.R.; Coupe, S.; Castro-Fresno, D. Performance of pervious pavements parking bays storing rainwater in the north of Spain. *Water Sci. Technol.* **2010,** *62*, 615–621.
35. Gomez-Ullate, E.; Novo, A.V.; Bayon, J.R.; Rodriguez-Hernandez, J.; Castro-Fresno, D. Design and construction of an experimental pervious paved parking area to harvest reusable rainwater. *Water Sci. Technol.* **2011**, *64*, 1942–1950.
36. Stotz, G.; Krauth, K. The pollution of effluents from pervious pavements of an experimental highway section: First results. *Sci. Total Environ.* **1994**, *146–147*, 465–470.
37. Mbanaso, F.U.; Coupe, S.J.; Charlesworth, S.M.; Nnadi, E.O. Laboratory-based experiments to investigate the impact of glyphosate-containing herbicide on pollution attenuation and biodegradation in a model pervious paving system. *Chemosphere* **2013**, *90*, 737–746.
38. Mullaney, J.; Jefferies, C.; Mackinnon, E. The performance of block paving with and without geotextile in the sub-base. In Proceedings of 12nd International Conference on Urban Drainage, Porto Alegre, Brazil, 11–15 September 2011.
39. Mullaney, J.; Rikalainen, P.; Jefferies, C. Pollution profiling and particle size distribution within permeable paving units—With and without a geotextile. *Manag. Environ. Qual. Int. J.* **2012**, *23*, 150–162.
40. Construction Industry Research and Information Association (CIRIA). *Control of Pollution from Highway Drainage Discharges*; Report 142; Luker, M., Monague, K., Eds.; CIRIA: London, UK, 1994.
41. Duncan, H.P. *Urban Stormwater Quality: A Statistical Overview*; Cooperative Research Centre for Catchment Hydrology: Melbourne, Australia, 1999.
42. The British Standards Institution (BSI). *Aggregates for Unbound and Hydraulically Bound Materials for Use in Civil Engineering Work and Road Construction*; BSI: London, UK, 2002; Standard BS EN 13242:2002+A1:2007. Available online: http://shop.bsigroup.com/en/ProductDetail/?pid=000000000030147952 (accessed on 10 May 2012).
43. The British Standards Institution (BSI). *Pavements Constructed with Clay, Natural Stone or Concrete Pavers. Guide for the Design of Permeable Pavements Constructed with Concrete Paving Blocks and Flags, Natural Stone Slabs and Sets and Clay Pavers*; BSI: London, UK, 2009; Standard BS 7533-13:2009. Available online: http://shop.bsigroup.com/ProductDetail/?pid=000000000030159352 (accessed on 10 May 2012).

MDPI
St. Alban-Anlage 66
4052 Basel
Switzerland
www.mdpi.com

MDPI Books Editorial Office
E-mail: books@mdpi.com
www.mdpi.com/books

www.ingramcontent.com/pod-product-compliance
Lightning Source LLC
Chambersburg PA
CBHW061503220926
51850CB00004B/161
* 9 7 8 3 0 3 9 2 8 6 0 9 6 *